THE ELIZABETHAN JOURNALS
1591–1603

G. B. HARRISON

Author of :—

Shakespeare at Work—1933—Routledge.
Shakespeare's Fellows—1923—Lane. (Out of print.)
Shakespeare—1927—Benn's Sixpenny Library, 9th edition, 1938.
John Bunyan : a study in personality—1928—Dent.
Elizabethan England—1930—Benn's Sixpenny Library.
The Life and Death of Robert Devereux, Earl of Essex—1937—Cassell.
The Day Before Yesterday : a Journal of 1936—1938—Cobden-Sanderson.
etc., etc.

Editor of :—

The Bodley Head Quartos, 15 vols., 1922–6—Lane.
The Pilgrim's Progress, 1928—Nonesuch Press.
The Church Book of Bunyan Meeting, 1928—Dent.
The Diary of Agnes Beaumont, 1928—Constable.
Breton's Melancholic Humours, 1929—Scholartis.
The Trial of the Lancaster Witches, 1929—Peter Davies.
De Maisse's Journal, 1931 (with R. A. Jones)—Nonesuch.
Guilpin's Skialethia, 1931—Shakespeare Association Facsimiles.
The Letters of Queen Elizabeth, 1935—Cassell.
Day's Isle of Dogs, 1936—Shakespeare Association Facsimiles.
The Penguin Shakespeares, 1937–8—Penguin Books.
etc., etc.

General Editor of :—

The Shakespeare Association Facsimiles, 1931-8.
A Companion to Shakespeare Studies, 1934 (with Harley Granville-Barker)—Cambridge.

THE ELIZABETHAN JOURNALS

BEING A RECORD
OF THOSE THINGS MOST TALKED OF
DURING THE YEARS
1591–1603

Comprising
An Elizabethan Journal 1591–4
A Second Elizabethan Journal 1595–8
A Last Elizabethan Journal 1599–1603

By
G. B. HARRISON

LONDON
GEORGE ROUTLEDGE AND SONS, LTD.
Broadway House, Carter Lane, E.C. 4

An Elizabethan Journal 1591–4; first published 1928
A Second Elizabethan Journal 1595–8; first published 1931
A Last Elizabethan Journal 1599–1609; first published 1933

Revised and Reprinted in one volume, 1938

"The hand of the Lord was upon me, and carried me out in the Spirit of the Lord, and set me down in the midst of the valley, which was full of bones, and caused me to pass by them round about: and, behold, there were very many in the open valley: and, lo, they were very dry.

"And He said unto me, 'Son of man, can these bones live?'
"And I answered, 'O Lord God, Thou knowest.'"

PRINTED IN GREAT BRITAIN BY LOWE AND BRYDONE PRINTERS LTD., LONDON, N.W. 10

CONTENTS OF AN ELIZABETHAN JOURNAL

CONTENTS OF A SECOND ELIZABETHAN JOURNAL

CONTENTS OF A LAST ELIZABETHAN JOURNAL

ADDENDA AND CORRIGENDA

AN ELIZABETHAN JOURNAL

3rd March, 1593. DR. UDALL'S PETITION. Udall died in prison a few days afterwards.

2nd February, 1594. THE ALCHEMIST'S BEQUEST. This note is wrong. From subsequent letters in *Salisbury Papers* it appears that the Queen was to be given first offer of the bodies for £500. Ultimately she decided not to buy.

24th December, 1594. 'A CONFERENCE ABOUT THE NEXT SUCCESSION.' This entry is premature. The book was not generally known in England until late September, 1595 (*Sidney Papers*, i, 350).

A SECOND ELIZABETHAN JOURNAL

26th July, 1595. THE SPANIARDS LAND IN CORNWALL. A long account of the raid is given in Richard Carew's *Survey of Cornwall*, 1603. See iii, *Eliz. Journal*, p. 262.

9th April, 1596. THE BISHOP OF ST. DAVID'S UNHAPPY SERMON. This entry is eleven days too late, for the sermon was preached on 28th March. It was published after the Queen's death in 1603 (S.T.C., 21432).

10th December, 1596. THE SCOTTISH PRINCESS BAPTIZED. The promise was handsomely honoured. In a letter to Dudley Carleton at the time of Princess Elizabeth's marriage in 1612 it is noted that Scotland has very unexpectedly sent her £20,000 for a wedding present (*Calendar of S.P. Dom.*, James I., 1611–18, No. 64, p. 161).

30th November, 1597. AN ACCIDENT AT THE SWAN. This entry should be deleted. The event is again recorded in its proper place in iii, *Eliz. Journal*, p. 315.

23rd August, 1598. THE LORD KEEPER'S LETTER TO THE EARL OF ESSEX. In John Speed's *History of Great Britain* both letters are printed, the first being dated 18th July, which is probably correct.

A LAST ELIZABETHAN JOURNAL

25th February, 1601. THE CHARACTER OF THE LATE EARL OF ESSEX. Since the *Elizabethan Journals* were published I have expanded these views on Essex's character in *The Life and Death of Robert Devereux, Ealr of Essex*, 1937.

25th June, 1601. A BOOK AGAINST TOBACCO. *Work for Chimney Sweepers* has now been reprinted in Shakespeare Association Facsimiles, No. 11, edited by S. H. Atkins, 1936.

4th August, 1601. THE QUEEN AND MR. LAMBARDE. The old gentleman's antiquarian enthusiasm proved fatal; he died on 19th August. In an anonymous letter on the proper preservation of the Tower records it is noted that "ye unholsome ayer of ye recordes, not well ayreed, and ye paines he tooke in that unholsome place brought him that sicknes and consumpcon wich was an end of him, and he take it principally through his nose into his head" (*Harleian MSS.*, 1877, f. 58).

3rd January, 1602. A DESPERATE ATTEMPT ON OSTEND. 'Francis the Gurmer' (p. 254), though thus described in the original source, should probably be 'Francis the Gunner'.

PREFACE

THIS work originated in the summer of 1921. I was preparing an edition of Will Kemp's *Nine Days' Wonder*, the record of his adventures during his famous dance to Norwich in the spring of 1600,[1] which caused great excitement at the time, and was discussed for years. In that summer Mr. Charles Chaplin had visited England, where he was received most royally. His triumphant progress was a prime item of news in every popular paper, though other events—the first implementing of the Versailles Treaty, for instance—were of greater historical importance. It was likely that though historians and politicians of the future would have much to say about the Versailles Treaty, they would not notice Mr. Chaplin's visit to England as one of the most-discussed events of the summer of 1921. Neither he nor Will Kemp came within their horizon; yet both had a larger place in the hearts of their contemporaries than those more august personages who are usually regarded as historic. It seemed, therefore, that to understand the interests of Englishmen during the age of Shakespeare a new kind of history book was necessary, a record of those things most talked of when Shakespeare, Marlowe, Jonson, Bacon, Donne, and the rest were writing and first being read.

It was not easy at first to decide the form of such a book It should be something more coherent and intimate than a Source Book, less personal and individual than a private diary. At the same time chronology, as exact as posible, was essential, for English literature developed so rapidly during the last decade of the sixteenth century and the first of the seventeenth that the difference of even a few weeks sometimes altered the whole conception of its growth. It seemed therefore that the

[1] See iii, *Eliz. Journal*, pp. 68–79.

book should be a Journal, and as far as possible a day by day record.

There were difficulties in this arrangement. Many records can only be dated approximately ; and even with those which bear a date there is abundant chance for mistakes, especially in the first quarter of each year, because in the 1590's there were three methods of reckoning the beginning of the year. The regnal year, dating from the completed years of the Queen's reign, began on 17th November ; the year of the Christian era began with the feast of the Annunciation—25th March ; but the reckoning of the Julian Calendar, which started the year on the 1st January, was coming into use. Hence a document dated 1st February, 1590, may belong either to 1590 or to 1591. This practice has caused much confusion, particularly in the dating of books, for unless there is some means of checking, either by an entry in the *Stationers' Register* or a dated preface, it is often impossible to tell in which of two years a book first appeared.

With a few exceptions each entry in the *Journals* was based on a contemporary source, which is recorded in the Notes ; but I used my sources freely, at one time borrowing phrases, sentences, and even whole pages, at another condensing or paraphrasing as suited my purpose. I did this deliberately, believing that if the book was to have any artistic unity all the events should be seen in the same perspective, for it was my hope that the *Elizabethan Journals* should be readable and not merely a work of reference.

To preserve the unity of tone, and especially as I was as often trying to convey a mood as to state a fact, it was necessary to preserve a contemporary style of writing. There was, as I well realized, a danger that the whole might smack of 'Ye Olde Village Inne' ; but the problem of how a historical work should be written is considerable, and especially when the author is trying to convey something more than information ; and I agree entirely with Anatole France's observations in his *Life of Joan of Arc* :—

"I believe that unless it possesses a certain unity of language a book is unreadable, and I want to be read. It is neither affectation of style nor artistic taste that has led me to adhere as far as possible to the tone of the period and to prefer archaic forms of language whenever I thought they would be intelligible, it is because ideas are changed when words are changed and because one cannot substitute modern for ancient expressions without altering sentiments and characters."[1]

Each entry was therefore recorded as it might have been noted down by a contemporary in his journal; and as gossip varies from place to place I imagined the diarist to be such a man as Edward Knowell, senior, before he began to take his family responsibilities too seriously; one who was more interested in events than in their historical significance, and who regarded authors, dramatists, and players as not less important members of the State than generals, politicians, and clergymen. It was essentially, and by intention, a Londoner's Journal.

At the same time I did not keep too rigidly to the idea of a personal diary. It would be a criticism too captious and pedantic that no single man could have known everything here recorded. Gossip at all times is elusive, and in attempting to chronicle the gossip of a past age the difficulty is not so much to find news as to discover how far any particular event was generally known or generally discussed, and in what mood. From the years 1591 to 1594 few private letters survive by which general news can be checked, but from 1595 onwards, when the letters of John Chamberlain and his friends, or of Rowland Whyte to Sir Robert Sidney, become available, and when the Satirists begin to comment on immediate events, it is possible to estimate how far news, confidential or otherwise, was generally circulated.

The Elizabethan gentleman had an excellent nose for news of any kind. Far more was discussed than was ever committed

[1] *Life of Joan of Arc* by Anatole France, translated by Winifred Stephens, 1925, vol. i, lxv.

directly to writing. Moreover, my own experience between the years 1914 and 1919 of conditions of life not wholly dissimilar, showed that those on foreign service in small forces, whether as political officers or soldiers, occupied about a fifth of their leisure time in jests of the kind that I afterwards found in *The C. Merry Tales*, another fifth in planning the agenda of their return to London, and the remainder in prying (and usually with some success) into the affairs of their superiors. More things were bandied about a mess tent than were ever recorded in an official *communiqué*. However, with much that is preserved in manuscript sources, one could only guess whether it was or was not a matter for talk. When there is no check, the chronicler must follow his own instinct whether any particular item was likely to be generally known or discussed. If I occasionally erred on the side of generosity, let it be forgiven.

Actually, however, I was at some pains to verify the publicity of my news items ; and in the *Second* and *Last Journals* I have from time to time noted evidence of confidential matters being publicly discussed. It is clear that even the private letters which passed between the Earl of Essex and his enemies at Court were widely known and discussed.

As the Journal progressed, the problems changed. In the *First Journal* there were months when it was difficult to find any news at all. I had therefore recorded, from Henslowe's *Diary*, the performance of plays at the Rose Theatre week by week. In the *Second Journal* there was no room for these weekly lists ; for, as the years went on, the records were multiplied fivefold. In the *Salisbury Papers*, to mention but one instance, the Calendar for the four years 1591–4 occupies 622 pages ; over 4,000 pages are required for the years 1595–1602. Moreover the Sidney papers, Chamberlain's letters, and the State Papers, Ireland, all began to yield new sources of information. So much material remains that for some months during the last eight years of Queen Elizabeth's reign it would be possible to compile a daily newspaper.

The method of compilation may interest students. First a detailed calendar of the years was constructed, either on cards or in notebooks. The main source for this calendar were such works as Stow's *Annals*, Camden's *Elizabeth*, the various Calendars of State Papers and Historical Manuscripts, the *Acts of the Privy Council*, Birch's *Memoirs*, Collins's *Sidney Papers*, Strype's *Annals of the Reformation*, Chamberlain's *Letters*, Dyson's *Proclamations*, and D'Ewes's *Journals*.

Stow and Camden were particularly valuable as general guides. John Stow's *Annals of England from the first inhabitation* was first published in 1592, re-issued and brought up to date in 1600, 1601, and 1605, and continued by others after his death. Stow kept some sort of diary, and as he had no sense of proportion but a curious interest in the unusual he was frequently more useful than a better historian. William Camden's *The True and Royal History of Elizabeth, Queen of England* (first published in Latin in 1615, in English in 1625–6) is a very different book, and an excellent piece of historical writing. Camden had a large understanding ; he knew how to use his sources, both contemporary pamphlets and original documents, and he had been an eye-witness of many of the events which he described. He was therefore a useful source and often gave some additional detail or valuable comment ; but he wrote when James of Scotland had succeeded Elizabeth, and in retrospect he saw the importance of events in Scotland in the history of England. He gave therefore about the same space to Scotland as to France in his history : if the *Stationers' Register* is any guide publishers sold twenty books on French affairs to one on Scottish.

Then the *Stationers' Register* and the *Short Title Catalogue* were consulted and a list of every book and pamphlet which seemed of any significance was compiled. As the *Journals* were originally intended to be a background to literature I paid particular attention to books printed, and those interested in the Elizabethan book trade will find details in two papers in the *Library*, 1591–4,[1] *Books and Readers*, 1591–4, and *Books and Readers*, 1599–1603, of which the first is summarized in Appendixes 1 and 2 of the *First Journal*. Of over 2,000 entries in the three *Journals*, about a fifth are concerned with books of various kinds. About one in five of contemporary books originally read yielded an entry. Particular attention was paid to news-pamphlets, and to private letters. When this structure had been erected, I began to write the *Journal*.

The first *Elizabethan Journal* appeared in 1928, the *Second* in 1931, and the *Last* in 1933, ending a work planned eleven and begun seven years before. In this volume I noted in the preface : " My purpose in the *Elizabethan Journals* was not to compile a book of reference but to write a journal of those things which most occupied the minds of Englishmen during the years 1591–1603. Such a book, collected from sources so diverse and considerable, cannot be made by any mechanic rule or rigid principle : it must be as much a work of art as of scholarship. Others, doubtless, might have shown themselves more learned scholars or better artists, had they but tried ; but, since no one had hitherto endeavoured to re-create this background to Shakespeare, and many have erred through ignorance of it, I undertook it myself. If the common reader, who is the ultimate judge of all books, has found that the *Elizabethan Journals* have brought a freshness and colour to his reading of Shakespeare and his contemporaries, the work has fulfilled its intention ; and if, further, he has taken some pleasure in the *Journals* themselves, the pains of the author have been well rewarded."

The present reprint of the three *Elizabethan Journals* in one volume has been reproduced photographically from the original text. A few misprints have been corrected and a list of addenda and corrigenda added. One new entry has been substituted for another on 15th March, 1596, which was wrongly dated. The original Appendix 1, SHAKESPEARE, has been omitted from the *First Journal* as it was afterwards

[1] 4th series, vol. viii, no. 3, vol. xiv. no. 1.

incorporated in *Shakespeare at Work*, 1933. The present Preface supersedes the original introductions to the *First* and *Second Journals*. A new Index to the whole work has been substituted for the original three indexes. Apart from these changes text and notes remain as they were.

I wish to repeat my grateful acknowledgment to those who in various ways helped me, by advice, guidance, criticism, or proof reading, and particularly to Dr. S. H. Atkins, Mr. R. L. Atkinson, the late Mr. A. L. Attwater (whose memory will not fade in those who knew him), Professor Geoffrey Callender Miss Molly Chamberlain, Dr. D. C. Collins, Professor J. E. Neale, Miss G. Puddifoot, Mr. S. C. Ratcliff, Miss Doris Rosling, Professor C. J. Sisson, the late Sir Emery Walker, Professor J. Dover Wilson. And, most of all, to Professor A. W. Pollard for encouragement when it was most needed and for allowing me access to material which saved me much labour ; and to the late Sir Israel Gollancz, who stimulated me to undertake this work and to whose interest and help many scholars, particularly of the younger generation, owed much, and I not least ; and to Miss Helen Waddell, whose inspiration, particularly in the earlier volumes, can now publicly yet inadequately be recorded.

G. B. Harrison.
24th August, 1938.

AN ELIZABETHAN JOURNAL

1590-1594

A BRIEF SURVEY OF THE YEAR 1590

In the beginning of spring, the Queen, lest she should be taken unawares by the Spaniard, made levies of men in England and the south part of Ireland, fortifying Duncannon in the mouth of the river and also Milford Haven in Wales; and for the safeguard of the Navy assigning £8970 yearly. She was at great charges in lending money for the Army in Germany; and for the pay of the garrisons in Flushing and Brille she paid every two months 125,000 florins, and to the 3000 horse and foot serving in the Netherlands 260,000 more. She was also at great charges against the attempts of the Pope and the Spaniard in Scotland.

Nevertheless she repaid beyond expectation the money borrowed not long since of her subjects, so that many wondered whence this money came, seeing she was in no man's debt. But the truth was that, being providently frugal, she scarcely spent anything but for the maintenance of her royal honour, the defence of the Kingdom or the relieving of her neighbours; and Burleigh, the Lord Treasurer, looked narrowly into those that had the charge of customs and imports, by whose avarice much was underhand embezzled, and through negligence much not exacted. Not long before this the Queen being informed by one Carmarden of the mysteries of her farmers of Customs had caused Sir Thomas Smith, the customer, as he was called, who farmed the Customs for £14,000 a year, to pay from thenceforth £42,000 and afterwards £50,000.

Abroad the Zealanders were reconciled with the Hollanders. The ships of the Venetians and Florentines taken by the English were restored and strict proclamation made that no violence should be offered to the Italians, Venetians, French, Danes, Netherlanders or those of the Hanse Towns. Yet the Spaniards were grievously afflicted, many prizes being taken near the Azores, and the castle in the isle of Faiall razed to the ground by the Earl of Cumberland.

Between the Turks and Moldavia peace was established and the Poles saved from the threat of a difficult war.

In Scotland, to confirm amity with the Scottish King, the Earl of Worcester was sent to congratulate him on his marriage and safe return from Denmark, and to signify to him that he and the French King had been chosen Knights of the Garter, and withal to put him in mind to suppress in time the Popish faction growing strong in Scotland. The King received him very graciously, and to show his amity to England sent Colonel Stewart into Germany that some course might be taken with the King of Denmark and the Ambassadors of the Princes for renewing the peace between England, Spain and France.

In France, the rebellion of the Leaguers aided by the Spaniards held many dangers, and in England there was much deliberation whether the old soldiers in the Low Countries should join with the Germans, or whether a strong army should be sent to the Netherlands to stay the Duke of Parma, who was now proposing to come through France, but especially to keep the coast of France from the Spaniard, who was said to be practising to reduce Newhaven by corruption, and send a fleet into lesser Brittany.

In the midst of these consultations, the Duke of Parma entered France with a strong army, after the French King had won a notable victory at Ivry, overran Picardy, victualled Paris, then miserably famished, won Carboil and Laigny, that victuals might be carried into Paris, and led back his forces. On the other side, in the autumn, other companies of Spaniards arrived at Blavet in Brittany under the conduct of Don John D'Aquila, besieged Henebon, a little town on the sea, and took it with the aid of Philip Emanuel, Duke of Mercure, of the House of Lorraine. Against these Spaniards, Henry Bourbon, Prince de Dombes, who was Governor of Brittany with La Noue, craved aid from England, which the Queen and the Council thought not fit to send on the request of a subject, as the King himself did not then request it. Yet the danger was well understood that the Spaniard might bring under subjection a country so convenient for annoying or invading England, Holland or Zealand.

Some urged that the Queen should spare her money and put no trust in the French, alleging that they had been lately treacherous to their own kings, murdering the one who had been a most devout Catholic, and another, professing the reformed religion, they now pursued with popish curses and arms; that within remembrance of their fathers they had unjustly withdrawn from the German Empire, Metz, Toul and Verdun; and that they had so often deceived the English in money matters that those creditors whom they meant to deceive they called by a by-word '*les anglais*.' But the Queen, much affecting the safety and honour of the French, rejected these counsels, and when others put her in mind of that saying of Charles of Burgundy, 'that the neighbouring nations would be in happy case when France should be subject not to one sceptre but to twenty petty kings,' she rejected it with much stomach, saying, 'whensoever the last day of the Kingdom of France cometh, it will undoubtedly be the eve of the destruction of England.'

During this year died Ambrose Dudley, Earl of Warwick, and not long after Sir Francis Walsingham, the Queen's secretary.

In Ireland, Hugh Gairlock had accused the Earl of Tyrone of having had secret conference with some Spaniards, shipwrecked in 1588. To prevent this charge the Earl took him and caused him to be strangled, then being summoned to England, upon submission obtained the pardon of the Queen; undertaking most religiously to keep the peace with his neighbours, not to put any man to death but by law, and to reduce Tyrone into more civility. Being sent back to Ireland, he confirmed these things before Sir William FitzWilliams, the Lord Deputy. Shortly before the Lord Deputy had taken Hugh Roe MacMahon, a great lord in the territory of Monaghan, and hanged him for that he had with banners displayed exacted contributions of his people. His lands were divided between the English and certain of the MacMahons, so that the family might be weakened, being strong and powerful through many tenants and adherents, and the tyranny of MacMahon blotted out together with the title.

Whereupon Brian O'Rourke, a great lord in the neighbouring County of Bren, fearing lest the same might happen to him, took arms against the Queen; but being hunted and put to flight by Sir Richard Brougham, Governor of Connaught, fled into Scotland, and was by the Scottish King delivered into the Queen's hands when she required it, he protesting that he accounted all the Queen's enemies as his own.

1591

1st January. THE PRIVY COUNCIL.

At the beginning of this year the Lords and others of the Queen's most Honourable Privy Council are Dr. John Whitgift, Lord Archbishop of Canterbury ; Sir Christopher Hatton, Lord Chancellor of England, Knight of the Garter ; Sir William Cecil, Lord Burleigh, Lord High Treasurer of England, Knight of the Garter ; Charles Howard, Baron of Effingham, Lord Admiral of England, Knight of the Garter ; Henry Carey, Lord of Hunsdon, Lord Chamberlain, Knight of the Garter ; Thomas, Lord Buckhurst, Lord High Butler of England, Knight of the Garter ; Sir Francis Knollys, Treasurer of the Queen's Household ; Sir Thomas Heneage, Vice Chamberlain to the Queen, Chancellor of the Duchy Lancaster ; Mr. John Wolley, Esquire, Secretary for the Latin Tongue, Chancellor of the most Honourable Order of the Garter ; Mr. John Fortescue, Esquire, Master of the Great Wardrobe, and Under Treasurer of the Exchequer.

DR. SUTCLIFFE'S 'TREATISE OF ECCLESIASTICAL DISCIPLINE.'

Dr. Matthew Sutcliffe dedicateth to the Earl of Bath his *Treatise of Ecclesiastical Discipline*, which is sent to the press, wherein is confuted article by article the doctrine and practice of those who attack the Church of England, either preferring the Presbyterial Government or disliking the disorders of the Church. Of these, some have consumed their own goods and devoured the late lands of Abbeys and are now so eager that they would digest not only tithes but also glebe and parish churches.

Others are moved by violent ambition, that although they talk much of equality, yet hope to be chosen presidents of the consistory, willing to hazard all and have a part in the government, for they disdain to be governed by others. Added thereunto are the stirring minds of men malcontent who however they fare always deem their present condition most burdensome, and so that they may see an innovation and change care not whether church or commonwealth be changed.

13th January. STEPNEY'S 'SPANISH SCHOOLMASTER.'

The Spanish Schoolmaster, by William Stepney, professor of the Spanish tongue in the city of London, is entered, containing seven dialogues, wherein is plainly shown the true and perfect pronounciation of the Spanish tongue, together with proverbs, sentences, the Lord's Prayer, the Articles of belief, the ten commandments and other necessary things. Mr. Stepney giveth many pithy and useful examples, meet for travellers on a great variety of occasions both at home and abroad. Noteth it as a new custom that divers dames in London do break their fast in their beds, and when they have broken it, they will lie down again, and sleep on it.

14th January. THE MURDER OF THE LORD BURKE.

Arnold Cosby, better known as Captain Cosby, a professional soldier, well known about the Court, hath stabbed to death the Lord Burke in a field near Wandsworth.

23rd January. WRIGHT'S 'PILGRIMAGE TO PARADISE.'

The Pilgrimage to Paradise, a book written by Leonard Wright, is entered, compiled for the direction, comfort and resolution of God's poor distressed children, in passing through this irksome wilderness of temptation and trial, and giving consolation to Christians in the warfare of their passage to Paradise.

25th January. THE TRIAL AND CONDEMNATION OF COSBY.

Arnold Cosby was this day brought from Newgate and taken over London Bridge to the Sessions on St. Margaret's Hill, where he was immediately put into the docket. He was wearing a yellow frieze doublet over which a loose nightgown had been thrown. A great pair of bolts was put on his feet and his arms were pinioned, though his hands were free.

Soon after there came to the Court, the Lord Chamberlain, the Earl of Wormwood, Sir George Carey, Knight Marshal of England, and Mr. Popham, the Queen's Attorney General.

For the Queen the chief witness was Mr. Powell of Wandsworth, who declared that the Lord Burke's footman coming to him had told him that his master and Cosby had gone out to fight. Thereon he had immediately taken horse and spurred as fast as he could until he came to a place where the Lord Burke lay wounded and on point of death. There he found a woman giving such help as she could; she had laid her frieze safeguard over him and was trying to stop the bleeding with cloths. The Lord Burke, being asked how he had come by his hurts, replied, 'Cosby hath villainously wounded me to death, I striking never a blow, nor giving thrust, but whilst I was striving to unbuckle one of my spurs, having unbuckled the other before through his persuasions, saying they would be some trouble, he most cowardly thrust me in at the top of the shoulder which ran far into the body; yet if I had striven but two blows with him, it would never have grieved me, had he manfully slain me in fight.' Then procuring a cart, Mr. Powell took the Lord Burke to his own house, where he died about two hours after, twenty-one wounds being found on his body.

In his defence, Cosby declared that the cause of the quarrel was that the Lord Burke had the night before pulled his nose. When they met in the field, having the Lord Burke at his mercy, he had offered him his life if he would break the point of his sword, return to the Court and acknowledge that he had wronged him, fought with him, and been spared by him.

While the jury were away, the Lord Chamberlain spoke to those present, showing how manifestly God had wrought in this case. When Cosby tried to escape on the Lord Burke's gelding, it had broken from him; even his own nag could scarcely be forced to take him to the wood at Wimbledon. Finally, when he passed behind the house where the body lay, the wounds began to bleed afresh.

The jury, after a short deliberation, gave in a verdict of guilty, and Cosby was condemned to be hanged.

27th January. Cosby Hanged.

Arnold Cosby was hanged at Wandsworth for the murder of the Lord Burke near to the place where his crime was committed.

30th January. Sir Edmund York sent to the French King.

Sir Edmund Yorke is to be sent to the French King to treat for the sending of English forces to Brittany. He is instructed when he shall have audience with the King to say her Majesty thinks it strange that in the four months since the Spaniards have invaded Brittany, she has not received any knowledge from him of what he means to do for the repelling of these forces, nor that he has sent any aid to the Prince de Dombes, who is unable with his present power to encounter the enemy though at this time reduced to 1800 men. But it appears from sundry sources that the King of Spain makes ready a greater number of ships, men and victuals to possess himself of all Brittany; whereof her Majesty is very mindful, first for the loss of so rich a dominion as Brittany, and by consequence of the evil neighbourhood of so mighty a Prince possessing so great enmity towards her.

Whilst she was in this doubtful state, there came a gentleman from the Prince de Dombes moving the French ambassador to be a means to her to help him with 2000 footmen to be sent into Brittany, whose charge should be answered by the King. To this she had answered the ambassador that it was a strange thing for her to be required of a subject to send forces into the King's country and more strange would it be for her to send them without the King's knowledge, or even request. Nevertheless having now heard that the succours which are coming in to the King are but few, and that the enemy prosper in possessing all the ports, saving Brest, where they have their galliasses and ships, and intend to fortify the mouths of the ports, the Queen hath told the French ambassador that she is content, if the King so wishes it, to prepare some 2000 or 3000 men or more to be sent into Brittany. For the ambassador's better information certain articles were delivered to him to be sent to the King, but no answer has been received. Sir Edmund Yorke is now to procure answer to every point in these articles and especially to procure for our shipping and people the use of the haven of Brest, the commodity of the roads for the ships, and the town and lodgings for the men; without this assurance neither ship nor men can be in any safety.

1st February. DRAYTON'S 'HARMONY OF THE CHURCH.'

The Harmony of the Church, containing The Spiritual Songs and Holy Hymns of Godly Men, patriarchs and prophecy; all sweetly sounding to the praise and glory of the highest, now newly reduced into sundry kinds of English metre; meet to be read or sung, for the solace and comfort of the godly, written by Michael Drayton, (a gentleman of the household of Sir Henry Goodere), is entered, being dedicated to the Lady Jane Devereux of Merivale. In this book are gathered nineteen songs and prayers from the Old Testament and Apocrypha rendered in English verse.

For an example, the Song of Deborah and Barach, from the fifth chapter of Judges, hath been thus reduced :

Praise ye the Lord, the which revenge on Israel's wrongs doth take,
Likewise for those which offered up themselves to Israel's sake,
Hear this, ye kings, ye princes all, give ear with an accord,
Smile, give thanks, yea sing the praise, of Israel's loving Lord.

And Sisera's death thus :

Jael the Kenit Heber's wife, most happy shall be blest,
Above all other women there, which in the tents do rest,
He asked water for to drink, she gave sweet milk to him,
Yea butter in a lordly dish, which was full trick and trim,
Her left hand to the nail she put, her right the hammer wrought,
Wherewith presumptuous Sisera unto his death she brought,
And from his corpse his head she cut, with mortal deadly wound,
When through the temples of his head, she nailed him to the ground.
He bowed then unto the earth, and at her feet gan fall,
And where he fell there still he lay, bereaved of senses all.

3rd February. FLESH PROHIBITED DURING LENT.

As in years past the killing and eating of flesh during the season of Lent is restrained. Six butchers only may be licensed to kill flesh for the City and liberties, to be bound by bonds of £200 to sell no flesh in Lent but to such sick persons as should show a special warrant from the Lord Mayor. Moreover they shall truly keep books of their daily sales and the names of those to whom they sell, with the quantities and the times.

The Lord Mayor will also cause to appear before him or his deputy before Lent all innkeepers, table keepers, victuallers, ale house keepers, and taverners and to take bonds of every one of them in good sums of money, not under £100 a piece to her

Majesty, not to dress any flesh in their houses this Lent time for any respect except for some person lying in their house that had licence through sickness or any other necessary cause.

As for the butchers and others that come out of the country, certain persons, of whom some shall be named by the Wardens of the Fishmongers' Company, are appointed to watch at the gates where flesh might be brought in to view, search, and intercept it. And if any flesh shall be found to be brought to a person not licensed to eat it, to be forfeited at the discretion of the Lord Mayor for the use of the poor in the Hospitals and prisons of the City, and the bringers imprisoned. If any of these watchmen be found negligent and corrupt in this charge, he is to be committed to prison, there to continue during the whole Lent.

A PROCLAMATION AGAINST PIRACY.

A proclamation is published to inhibit the offending on the seas of any persons in their ships or goods being subjects of any Prince, Potentate or State in amity with her Majesty. Certain complaints of late are made against some of the Queen's subjects, who have been this last summer under colour of recovering recompense on the Spaniard for the notable injuries by arrests and barbarous cruelties practised in Spain and Portugal, and have taken the ships and goods of the subjects of other princes and states. Lately one ship belonging to the Venetians and another claimed to belong to subjects of the Grand Duke of Tuscany were taken into some of the western ports but are certainly in safety.

Her Majesty doth now command that whosoever hereafter should break any bulk of the goods of any prize (though the prize be lawful) before the title thereto is allowed in the Court of the Admiralty shall be imprisoned, and his ship with the prize forfeited. Likewise any person whatsoever that shall knowingly take any ship belonging to any subjects of her friends and allies, and doth not forbear to keep them, or takes out of them any goods, shall be reputed and tried as a pirate, and receive the due punishment for piracy.

9th February. JOB HORTOP'S 'TRAVELS.'

A book written by Job Hortop is entered called *The Travels of an Englishman. Containing his sundry calamities endured by the space of twenty and odd years in his absence from his native country ; wherein is truly deciphered the sundry shapes of wild beasts, birds, fishes, fowls, roots, plants, etc.*

This Hortop being born at Bourne in Lincolnshire became servant to a gunpowder maker of Redriffe, in whose service he was pressed to serve in Sir John Hawkins' Guinea Voyage in 1567, and appointed to be gunner in the *Jesus of Lubec*. After many sufferings he returned to England in December last. Relateth many strange stories of things seen in his travels. In Guinea two of the company were slain by a sea horse who ate them ; this sea horse being a beast in form like a horse in all proportions, saving that his feet are very short, and his teeth very great, long, and crooked like to the tusks of a wild boar. In this place also be many elephants which the negroes take by policy, for in the day time they search out the haunt of the beast which is every night against a great tree. Then they sever the tree almost in sunder, whereby the elephant coming at night, leaneth against it and falleth on his belly, whereby he cannot rise, being of a huge bigness ; whereupon he roareth and the negroes come and kill him. The elephant hath a great trunk in his nose wherein he draws the negroes to him and kills them.

In the island of Corasa called the River de Latch, they took a monstrous aligarta ; a beast which hath a head like a hog, bodied like a serpent and full of scales on the back, every one as broad as a saucer, his tail long and full of knots, of which one was taken by seven men in the pinnace, using a dog as bait ; and as soon as the aligarta had swallowed the dog they rowed hard until it was choked. This beast was four and twenty feet long by the carpenter's rule ; and his skin after being flayed was stuffed with straw to have been brought to England, but the ship perished by the way.

The General and the other ships soon after came into the port of San Juan de Ullva through stress of weather, where hostages were exchanged with the Spaniards that no occasion for breach of the league might be given ; on our side six of the gentlemen, on the Spaniards' six arrayed in rich habits in the apparel of gentlemen but indeed the basest slaves in their company. But in a few days the Spaniards treacherously set upon the English ships and sunk four, Sir John Hawkins scarcely withdrawing with the Admiral, and Hortop himself escaping from the *Jesus of Lubec* to the General's ship. Hence in great distress through lack of victuals, they sought the river Pannico for water where the mariners mutinied, saying that they would rather be on shore to shift for themselves amongst their enemies than starve on ship board, so that ninety-six wishing to depart were set on shore, amongst whom was Hortop.

This company fell among the Indians and by them were robbed of all their goods, and many of them slain; but in the end Hortop and the remainder were carried to the city of Mexico, where they were examined by two friars and two priests, who willed them to cross themselves and say their prayers in Latin; this many of them did, so that the priest returned to the Viceroy and said they were all good Christians.

In Mexico they stayed two years until they were sent to Spain. On their voyage thither, they discovered a monster in the sea who showed himself three times from the middle upwards, in which part he was proportioned like a man, of the complexion of a mulatto or tawny Indian. When they came near the island called the Serres, Hortop and some others essayed to escape in the pinnace, but being discovered were like to have been hanged had not one of the Admirals of the Spanish ships declared that if he were a prisoner he would have done the like himself. When they came to Spain they were sent to the Contratation House at Seville. A year after Hortop and six others tried to escape but they were brought back, and condemned by the Inquisition. Two were burnt, but Hortop with one other was sent to the galleys, there to row at the oars for ten years, and then to be brought again to the Inquisition House, to have the coat with St. Andrew's cross put on their backs, and from thence to go to the everlasting prison remediless.

Thereafter Hortop served twelve years at the galleys, being thence returned to Seville where he wore the coat four years, but at great risk had it taken off for 50 ducats which Hornanda de Soria, treasurer of the King's mint, lent him; with whom he served as a drudge for seven years until in October 1590 he came away in a fly boat laden with Flemish goods, which was taken by an English ship, and Hortop set on shore the 2nd day of December 1590.

FRAUNCE'S 'COUNTESS OF PEMBROKE'S IVYCHURCH' AND 'EMANUEL.'

The Countess of Pembroke's Ivychurch, together with *The Countess of Pembroke's Emanuel*, by Abraham Fraunce, one of her gentlemen, is entered; *The Ivychurch* being a translation in English hexameters founded on Tasso's Italian and Mr. Thomas Watson's Latin. In his dedication to the Countess of Pembroke, Mr. Fraunce defendeth himself against those who mislike the reformed kind of verse, saying that as there is no penalty appointed for him that would not read, so if any begin to read, when he beginneth to take no delight, let him leave off and go no further. The first part of the *Ivychurch* is in form of a pastoral dialogue wherein Amyntas lamenting of the hardness of his Phillis is at last comforted by her love; the whole being written in such hexameters as these:

Once on a time when Nymphs and Pastors chanc'd to be sporting,
Standing all in a round, and each one whispered a secret,
Into another's ear, poor fool I began to be buzzing,
'Phillis, I burn with love. O take compassion on me;
Help, or I die, Phillis.' But Phillis straight with a lowring
Look and frowning face, and downcast eyes to the groundward,
Blush'd for spite and shame, and gave not a word for an answer,
But conveyed her away, and flew from the place in a fury.

Phillis having died after their betrothal, Amyntas laments her in twelve days of Eclogues.

In the *Countess of Pembroke's Emanuel* are related the Nativity, Passion, and Resurrection of Christ, together with certain psalms of David, all in rhymed hexameters.

13th February. A PETITION OF THE SKINNERS.

The handicraftsmen of the Mystery of Skinners presented a petition to the Queen, complaining of the decay of their trade, which is due in part to the lavish and unnecessary use of velvets and silks, partly to certain bad and ill-disposed persons that roam and range about the realm buying skins which they sell abroad. These men, not having the proper skill to choose or sort out skins, cause those at home, who would otherwise buy, to be put off with inferior skins so that foreign wares are come to be preferred to English.

20th February. THE SCOTTISH KING'S POOR ESTATE.

From Scotland it is reported that the King is in some peril of surprise by the Earls of Arroll, Moray and Athol which will not be prevented because the King is of such a disposition that he will not believe such matters until they are too evident; nor will he be restrained from the fields or in his pastime, for any respect. Such dangers might be avoided if the King had a guard, but this he is not by any means able to maintain, for his table and the Queen's are almost unserved through want. The Queen and her house are more costly to him than his own, all the servants of great place abuse him, serving one another's turn; and the King, being over frank and somewhat negligent, endureth this want and shame, for he hath nothing that he accounteth certain to come into his purse but what he receiveth from her Majesty.

26th February. HARINGTON'S 'ORLANDO FURIOSO.'

The English translation of *Orlando Furioso* upon which Mr. John Harington hath been long employed is this day entered for the press by Richard Field, the printer.

It is said that Mr. Harington first translated that story of Giacondo in the twenty-eighth book, in which are told the adventures of Jocundo and Faustus who discovered their wives to be false, and ranged over Europe to see if anywhere was to be found a faithful dame. But after their wanderings, having tried many ladies, and being at length beguiled even in their own bed by their maid Fiametta, they concluded that fidelity was no part of woman's nature.

> 'We had a thousand women prov'd before
> And none of them denied our request;
> Nor would and if we tried ten thousand more,
> But this one trial passeth all the rest.
> Let us not then condemn our wives so sore,
> That are as chaste and honest as the best;
> Sith they be as all other women be,
> Let us turn home and with them well agree.'

The translation of this story being handed about among the ladies of the Court at length reached the hands of the Queen, who thereupon sent for her godson and severely censured him for endangering the manners of her ladies with so bawdy a tale, laying on him a punishment to translate the whole of the work before he should again be allowed to come into the presence.

11th March. PURITAN DISCONTENTS.

There is much discontent at this time amongst those that favour the Puritan principles; for the labouring and striving to bring in a uniformity causes, and seems likely to cause, nothing but desolation. The best and faithfullest preachers, say they, are cast into prison, sometimes being closely shut up from the speech and company of their dearest friends, degraded and deprived of their livings, some even having six or seven children, who are sent begging, for all the pillars of the church would do for them. Mr. Cartwright has lain in the Fleet since September; Mr. Fenne of Coventry with many more is in the Clink; Udall, a profitable preacher of Kingston-on-Thames, lies sentenced to be hanged for a book called *Demonstration of Discipline*; and having been condemned before as its author, they now try to make him acknowledge it as his doing. His life is spared hitherto by the intercession of Sir Walter Ralegh. All these things seem but a way to bring in popery, for atheism is here already, and soon will overflow the land. It is rumoured that a general demand is proposed not only of the ministry but of all who bear public office throughout the land to subscribe that the authority of the bishops is lawful by God's Word. When the Lord Treasurer was asked to subscribe to it, he answered, 'It is lawfully the positive law; but to say it is lawful by the Word of God, that is another matter.' There the matter stayed for the time.

12th March. RUMOURS.

The loans that are being levied are to meet the triple charge for the companies in Brittany, the ships at sea, and the army coming from Germany. Men are willing to pay because they see the necessity for helping the King of Navarre, and are angry that the Council did not help him more roundly.

The not naming of a Secretary to succeed Sir Francis Walsingham proceedeth from quietness at home, and the Queen's slowness in bestowing places of importance; the great ones about her would each have his friend. The Earl of Essex labours for Mr. Davidson's restitution; the Lord Treasurer for his son, Robert Cecil, and is like to prevail, and the Chancellor concurs, but either there is secret opposition or else the Queen is unwilling. The Lord Treasurer meanwhile executeth the office, as almost all other places of the realm, to the discontent of many.

There is a jar between the Lord Treasurer and the Archbishop of Canterbury because the Treasurer said the Spiritual Courts would fall into the *praemunire* for taking oaths of men against law. The Archbishop answered stoutly, as if the other affected patronage of the Puritans. The Treasurer was sick for a few days upon it.

The Earl of Essex and Sir Walter Ralegh are still rivals, but the Earl of Essex is like enough, if he have a few more years, to carry Leicester's credit and sway.

22nd March. Town Gossip.

It is said that the Attorney and Solicitor General are busied with proofs against Sir John Perrot, the same who was Lord Deputy in Ireland in '88, and now a prisoner in the Tower. There is much diversity of opinion about him, according as men incline to the Chancellor or the Lord Treasurer, who was said to be sick when Perrot was committed to the Tower and has not since left his chamber.

The Vice-Chamberlain and the Earl of Essex (whose sister is married to Sir Thomas Perrot) favour him; but the Chancellor has a great dependence, and, if his proofs be as evident as his accusations odious, they will weigh all down. He is said to have dealt with the King of Spain to be received into the Church of Rome, and to have practised with the Northern Lords of Scotland; but all the proofs rest on one priest, and he defamed. Advantages are now being taken from his insolent government in Ireland and his irreverent speeches against the Queen, which now come to light, as is usual when men are called in question, and being better proved, make the rest more probable.

The Earl of Cumberland is expected daily to depart with his fleet, but is detained by the lack of money, as the most part of his preparation is at his own charges. His design is upon the King of Spain's treasure. Some of the Low Country's forces are arrived; the rest to make up 2000 were expected daily with Sir John Norris.

The pique between the Archbishop and Lord Treasurer about Ecclesiastical proceedings is thought likely to cause a great quarrel between them. The Puritans are the weaker party but they hope well of the Earl of Essex, who makes Ralegh join him as an instrument from them to the Queen.

25th March. COCKAINE'S 'TREATISE OF HUNTING.'

Sir Thomas Cockaine hath written *A Short Treatise of Hunting: compiled for the delight of noblemen and gentlemen.* Sir Tristram, saith he, one of King Arthur's knights, was the first writer of the exact knowledge of hunting, whose terms in hunting, hawking and measures of blowing he holds to be best and fittest to be used. These first principles of Sir Tristram, joined with his long experience of hunting these forty-two years past, have moved him to write more at large concerning the breeding and training of hounds, terriers, and whelps for hunting the fox, the hare, the roe, the stag, the buck and the otter; together with a note of Sir Tristram's rules for blowing the horn in hunting.

30th March. THE CAPTAINS' PAY.

The schedule of the pay of the forces to be sent to France:

	Per diem.	Per mensem.
The General Captain of the English Forces - - - - -	£5	£140
Lieutenant Colonel and for the regiment of one-third part of the forces - - - -	40s. and 10s.	£70
Two other Colonels of 2 regiments, besides the Captain of 2 bands at 10s. per diem, to each Colonel - - - -	20s.	£28
A Provost Marshall (6s. 8d.) to occupy the office of a Quarter-master - - - - -	10s.	£14
A Sergeant Major - - -	20s.	£28

	Per diem.	Per mensem.
A Commissary for Musters (6s. 8d.) and for munition (3s. 4d.) -	10s.	£14
Three Corporals at 6s. 8d. a piece -	20s.	£28
A Paymaster (6s. 8d.) with two clerks (3s. 4d.) - - -	10s.	£14

The two cannoneers sent with great ordnance to be paid 12d. per diem each, and two labourers 8d. each.

31st March. CAPTAIN GLEMHAM'S EXPLOITS.

News is come to London of the safety and exploits of Captain Edward Glemham who had been reported lost at sea in a fight with the Spaniards.

Edward Glemham, Esquire, of Benhall in Suffolk, set sail in August last in the *Edward and Constance* of the burden of 240 tons, and one pinnace, the *Falcon*, which alone at his own cost, he had equipped, furnished, and victualled in such sort and with such plenty as had seldom been known before. From Dover he shaped his course for the Islands of the Suryes and Canaries, leaving his pinnace at Dover for the repairing of some small fault which had appeared, but through the negligence of her master he never saw her again. Contrary winds drove them out of their course for two months, till, at the end of November, he returned to the Islands, having done little good, but being loath to return home without achieving some notable exploit for the honour of his country and the profit of his men, he resolved to land on St. George's Island.

Calling his company together and taking counsel with them he found them willing to follow him. So the long boat and the carvel were hauled up alongside, into which entered eighty-five men, sixty being musketeers, the rest armed with pikes or brown bills.

The watch of the island, seeing so large a company draw near, had given warning and the whole force of the island was ready to receive them when they should attempt a landing. But the gunner letting fly on them from the ship from a sacer charged with a chain, slew or dismembered ten or twelve of them, and continued to play upon them so that, after two hours' fight, the Spaniards sounded a retreat and fled with all speed into the high country, leaving our men to land with the loss of but two killed.

Thence they marched inland about a mile and made a camp, posting a strong watch for the night.

Day being come, the company divided into two parts, the General leading one, Mr. Edward Florecourt the other, at some distance so that their numbers might appear greater. So with colours displayed and drums and trumpets, they marched with easy pace, yelling terrible cries which might have terrified a great company.

When they had proceeded about half a league, the scouts brought word that a mounted man was approaching as if to speak with them; but the General sent forward a guard of musketeers to stay him from coming nearer to view his forces. He was a gentleman sent by the Governor to know what they were and what they required. The General answered that he was a gentleman of England, but would not say what he intended to any private man; but if the Governor himself should come, he promised, by the faith of an English gentleman, that he should pass and repass in safety.

After a time the Governor with twelve of his gentlemen approached the camp and halted about half a mile from the court of guard, where hostages were sent forward as pledges for his safety. The General having conferred for a while with the Governor declared that if the island should be surrendered to the Queen of England's use, the Spaniards might depart with their possessions; but if not, he would commit all to the hazard of the sword, for what advantage he had won and what spoil he could make he would keep or die for it. To this the Governor flat refused, but said that provided they neither spoiled the King of Spain's subjects nor their goods, he would give them what they wished from the island.

Hearing this the General went apart with his company and conferred with them, whether to accept the offer or to venture on force. They answered that they would ratify whatsoever he decided. But he, seeing the smallness of his own forces in the enemy's country, thought it best not to refuse what the Governor offered. So he returned to the Governor, and demanded victuals of all sorts for his ship and 1000 crowns as recompense for the loss of the two men slain at landing. To these conditions the Governor agreed and departed.

The next day the General feasted the Governor and his company in a brave manner to the honour of his country and his own worthy commendation, and, on the day following, wind and tide being favourable, they set sail and so ranged about the islands seeking their fortune.

The day after they had left St. George's Island two tall ships were discovered which they chased until the following noon when they came up with them, and commanded to strike for the Queen of England. Whereon as they showed the Leaguers' flag and refused to strike, the gunner shot one of them through, being the Admiral, so that she was forced to lie by the lee to stop her leak. Then the Vice-Admiral bare up to rescue her consort, whom the General commanded also to strike, but they answered despitefully they would not, but would sink in the seas ere they would yield or strike. So the company demanded who they were. They answered that they were the *Dolphins*, the *Great Dolphin* and the *Little Dolphin* of St. Malo, stout ships and well appointed, the least of them having two and twenty cast pieces.

'Well,' quoth the General, 'strike your flag, for never shall so base villains as you carry your flag where an English gentleman is.'

They said again that they would not.

Then the General bare with them and gave them his whole broadside and sheered close in to board, but by the negligence of the helmsman they fell off, to the General's great discontent. By this time the men in the Admiral had stopped her leak, and as they saw the General bearing upon them they made ready to fight, and first they gave a whole broadside which hit not the ship at all.

Then began a hot fight in which they suffered loss, for some of our men who entered the Admiral saw seven or eight men slain and hauled up in their forecastle. At the third encounter our men grappled with the Admiral so that she was not able to sheer away, and the General with twenty more boarded her ; but the Vice-Admiral coming up on the other side entered her men so that ours were forced to retire and break away, having given the enemy great damage but received little hurt themselves. For four hours longer the fight continued until night came on, when the General called his company together, first gave thanks to God for their preservation and then caroused with them, binding them all by their faith to fight it out with the enemy or die for it; but when day dawned, no Frenchmen were to be seen.

Their hurts being repaired, they made thence for the Northern Cape but were chased by six Spanish galligoes whom they shook off after a hot fight of three hours.

The General, having thus sustained great hurt and accomplished but small good for himself, being still unwilling to return to England, determined to make for the Straits of Gibraltar, whither they framed their course, but meeting with tempests by the way the main mast, which had been damaged by shot during the last fight, was lost. So they harboured in Algiers to repair the ship. Here they remained for nearly two months waiting for the company of the English Fleet; but then refusing to stay any longer, the General resolved to sail by himself with no other company than the *Flower de Luce*, a ship of Dieppe. But as they came near the mouth of the Straits, they met with four of the King of Spain's gallies which engaged the *Edward and Constance* alone, for the French ship was unwilling to put herself into any danger until the General had fought with all four and sunk one, when she came up and at her approach the rest of the Spaniards withdrew. The rigging was so much damaged by shot in this encounter that the General was forced to put back again to Algiers, leaving the *Flower de Luce* to go on to Dieppe alone.

3rd April. INSTRUCTIONS FOR SIR R. WILLIAMS.

On his leaving for Dieppe in command of 600 soldiers for service in Normandy, Sir Roger Williams is instructed to confer with the Governor of Dieppe in what sort his services shall be required, especially in defending the town, but unless some special and manifest cause for some good attempt against the enemy appears he may not hazard the Queen's people out of the town. If, however, other forces be joined to those of the Governor's, and opportunity of doing some good service should appear, he may join with him provided that he and his men be not further burdened with any action than the Governor himself should be.

A FRAY AT LIMEHOUSE.

A certain Edward Glasse made an attack on Mr. Thomas Andrews, who was appointed steward, overseer and paymaster of the workmen fitting out the ships for Mr. Thomas Cavendish. In the attack Andrews struck Glasse a blow in self-defence of which he died in a quarter of an hour.

14th April. A QUARREL IN THE PRESENCE CHAMBER.

The Earl of Essex and the Earl of Kildare, who had fallen out in the Presence chamber and used towards each other words very unfit to be uttered in that place and by persons of their quality, are summoned before the Council. Finding that the quarrel had arisen upon a very small matter the Council consider that the honour of the Queen may be greatly prejudiced by a fray begun so near her person and that great inconvenience would ensue if these noblemen pursue the cause in the heat of revenge. Therefore they enjoin them on their allegiance to keep the peace, binding each in securities of £10,000 not to assault, challenge or provoke the other.

16th April. SENTENCES AT THE SESSIONS.

At the Sessions Elizabeth Arnold, an unmarried woman, was found guilty of stealing an embossed ring worth 40s., a hollow ring with a whistle worth 40s., a turquoise ring worth 20s., a ring with a pearl worth 20s., a folding ring worth 13s. 4d., a black enamelled ring worth 6s. 8d., together with divers articles of wearing apparel from Thomas Collier of Turnhill Street. Also of stealing three silver whistles worth £5, seven silver spoons worth 40s., two gold rings worth £3, a gold ring with an emerald worth £5, with other articles of jewellery, and £7 in numbered money from John Smythe at Limehouse. At the same time Elizabeth Hawtrey, wife of John Hawtrey, was found guilty of feloniously receiving and comforting her after the first theft, and Elizabeth Johnson, spinster, after the second. Elizabeth Johnson pleaded guilty, and was sentenced to be hanged. The other two acknowledged the indictment but pleaded pregnancy; a jury of matrons being empanelled both were found not pregnant and sentenced to be hanged.

The same day Edmund Chapman was found guilty of having seized and raped a girl of nine years old, and sentenced to be hanged.

24th April. A PROCLAMATION AGAINST TRADING WITH THE FRENCH REBELS.

A Proclamation by the Queen is published declaring that Henry the Fourth, King of France and Navarre, is justly entitled the King of France, being recommended to the realm by the last king before his death, in presence of all the Princes of the blood and of the rest of the nobility, to be his most lawful successor. It now manifestly appears that this unnatural rebellion is favoured by none of the ancient nobility of France but by a very few of a strange blood, lately brought in and planted by marriages in France, and only branches depending of the House of Lorraine. Her Majesty therefore is moved to yield to the King, her brother and confederate, her favour, both in approbation of his right and wishing to him prosperity against his rebels, as she thinks there is no Monarch nor Sovereign Potentate in Christendom but does the like, save only one, who not contented with all the kingdoms and dominions which his noble father left him, by reason of his abundant riches brought out of the Indies, attempts to augment his estate by encroaching to himself the Dominions of his neighbours.

This rebellion against the French King is fed and maintained in sundry port towns of France and especially in Normandy and Brittany, where the people live by exchange of merchandise and by receiving succours of victuals and munitions of war from foreign countries, without which the rebels in their ports could neither continue their rebellions nor yet relieve their fellow rebels in the land. Her Majesty therefore expressly commands all her natural subjects and all other persons resorting to her realm to forbear to trade with any of the King's rebels, either in France or fraudulently here in England, upon pain of being punished as traitors, and relievers and succourers of the Queen's enemies.

Her Majesty is informed that many of her subjects, outwardly making their entries with the officers of the Custom houses as if to repair to the ports of France which obey the French King, or to other ports of the realm, or to Jersey or Guernsey, craftily and by stealth carry powder, shot, copper and other habiliments of war to the ports held by the enemy. For the repressing of which abuse the officers of the Custom houses are to have good regard to the conditions of all that lade any wares to be transported out of the realm by sea.

26th April. A PROCLAMATION AGAINST UNAUTHORISED POSTS.

A Proclamation is published forbidding any to carry packets or letters to the countries beyond the seas except such as are ordinarily nominated to this service by the Master of Posts or otherwise show good warrant for their voyages and despatches under the hands of one of the principal Secretaries, an Ambassador, or others sufficiently authorised. All in authority, and especially the searchers, customers and controllers of the ports, shall make diligent search of all mails, budgets, and other carriages of such disavowed carriers, messengers and suspected persons coming or going out of the realm with packets of letters; all such discovered to be apprehended and kept in custody until by the view of their writings, sent up to the Privy Council, it is seen and advised what further should be done with them.

29th April. 'THE SHEPHERD'S STAR.'

The Shepherd's Star being a paraphrase dialoguewise upon the third of the Canticles of Theocritus, in prose, part with songs interspersed, is entered. It is written by Mr. Thomas Bradshaw, lately a gentleman of the company and retinue of the Lord Burgh at Brille.

30th April. FLORIO'S 'SECOND FRUITS.'

Signor John Florio, that wrote the *First Fruits*, being an induction to the Italian tongue, thirteen years since, now perfecteth his *Second Fruits* in twelve chapters, both in the Italian tongue and the English. In these witty and familiar discourses many subjects are treated of, such as the set at tennis, games of cards or chess, fencing, the thirty bodily parts of beauty in a woman; ending with a pleasant discourse of love and women. To this book is added *The Gardine of Recreation*, yielding six thousand Italian proverbs.

2nd May. LODGE'S 'ROBERT, DUKE OF NORMANDY.'

The famous, true and historical life of Robert, second Duke of Normandy, surnamed for his monstrous birth and behaviour, Robert the Devil, is sent to the press, being dedicated to Mr. Thomas Smith, and penned by Mr. Thomas Lodge, that last year wrote *Rosalynde, Euphues' Golden Legacy*.

This Robert, being the son of Aubert, Duke of Normandy, and Editha, his wife, was from his birth of a monstrous and devilish disposition; for while yet a boy he poisoned the son of his schoolmaster, afterwards cutting the throat of the father with his penknife. Being come to manhood he was to be knighted by his father, but being set to watch the night in the Abbey of St. Peter at Rouen, there to perform his vigil, when all had departed, issued from the church and walked in the fields until at last he arrived at a nunnery. Calling the Lady Abbess before him he commanded all the young nuns to be brought before him; then immodestly stripping them naked he made choice of the fairest, and dragged her by the hair of her head into a shady wood near adjoining, where in spite of her incessant intreaties he deflowered and afterwards slew her. After many other crimes and horrible murders he was outlawed by his father and betook himself to the woods, until his band was overcome by his father's cavaliers and he forced to wander away sore travailed by his wounds; and meditating upon his sins he thought that a voice sounded in his ear, 'The reward of sin is death.' In this desperate state a hermit who had long lived from the world found him and took him to his hermitage, where he was so schooled, that of a bad young man he became reconciled to a staid and holy course of life. At length being enjoined by the hermit for a penance to go barefoot to Rome, he came thither after many travels and served the Emperor as his fool, and afterward when the Sultan of Babylon would by force have married the Emperor's daughter, in disguise of a knight he saved the city from destruction. Absolved thereby of his penance, he was married to the Lady Eunice and returned to Normandy, his father being dead, to find his mother charged with the murder of her husband by the Lord Villiers. The lists being set for a champion to defend her, he defeated her adversary and reconciled himself to her, so that her sorrow was at last paid home with great solace, and Robert of being an irreligious person became the only royal paragon of the world.

3rd May. BRETON'S 'BOWER OF DELIGHTS.'

A book of Mr. Nicholas Breton's poems called *The Bower of Delights* is to be printed, containing his *Amoris lachrimae*, a discourse of the life, death and funeral of Sir Philip Sidney, with other poems to his memory, and pastorals and sonnets.

A Poem on Sir P. S.

P Perfection peerless, Vertue without pride,
H Honour and Learning, linked with highest Love,
I Joy of the thought in true discretion tied,
L Love of the life that highest honours prove.
I In Angels' arms with heavenly hands embraced,
P Paradise pleased, and all the world disgraced.

S Seek all the world, oh seek and never find,
I In earthly mould, the mount of such a mind :
D Divinest gifts that God or man bestoweth,
N No glory such as of such glory groweth.
E End of the joys that hath all grief begun,
Y Yet let one weep when all the world is done.

8th May. The French King's Ordinances.

Certain ordinances, which had been set forth by the French King two months since in the camp at Chartres, are published in English. These were afterwards proclaimed at Caen, being in the form of a proclamation, signed by the King and Monsieur Potier, and sealed in yellow wax with his Majesty's broad seal upon a single label. The King meaneth to take order against the complaints commonly made to him concerning the infinite oppression of his people through sundry imposts levied upon them by men of war that without his commission force them to contribute money, meat, and munition, whereby his poor subjects will be forced to abandon their habitations and the tilling of the earth, whereof there must ensue a general famine with the curse of God against the whole state. If any man of war shall levy troops or seize upon any place without the King's commission, the Governor or Lieutenant General shall with all speed besiege and force him ; and all taken alive to be hanged up without other order of process.

Cartwright the Puritan before the High Commission.

Mr. Thomas Cartwright, formerly master of the Hospital at Warwick, one of the chiefest of the English Presbyterians who has lain in prison since October, was brought before the High

Commissioners in Causes Ecclesiastical, the Bishop of London, the Attorney General, and four doctors. As it is now become a custom with the Puritans to refuse to take the oath before examination, the Bishop began in a long speech by demanding that he should take it.

Mr. Cartwright opening his mouth to speak, Mr. Attorney took the speech from him and also showed at length how dangerous a thing it was that men should upon the conceits of their own heads and yet under colour of conscience refuse the things that had been received for laws of a long time. This oath that was tendered was according to the laws of the land, which he commended above the laws of all other lands, yet because they were the laws of men, they carried always some stain of imperfection.

After much controversy, Mr. Cartwright still resolutely refusing to take the oath, the Bishop commanded an act thereof to be entered. Then Mr. Cartwright put the Bishop in mind that he had promised him leave to answer the charge which had been given against him; the Bishop replied that he had no leisure to hear his answer, and if he would answer it should be by private letter.

12th May. Ripley's 'Compound of Alchemy.'

The Compound of Alchemy is entered, showing the ancient hidden art of Alchemy, the perfectest means to make the philosopher's stone, *aurum potabile*, and other excellent experiments. George Ripley, sometime Canon of Bridlington in Yorkshire, first wrote this book, which he dedicated to King Edward the Fourth; but Mr. Ralph Rabbards, student and expert in alchemical arts, now sets it forth for the first time for the press. It is penned in twelve gates or books, each in verse, showing severally the properties of calcination, dissolution, separation, conjunction, putrefaction, congelation, separation, cibation, sublimation, fermentation, exhalation, multiplication, and projection. There is added also an Epistle to King Edward briefly summarising the whole and ending:

> First calcine, and after that purify,
> Dissolve, distill, sublime, discend, and fix,
> With *Aqua Vitae* oft times both wash and dry,

And make a marriage the body and spirit betwixt,
Which thus together naturally if you can mix,
In loosing of the body the water congealed shall be,
Then shall the body die utterly of the flux,
Bleeding and changing colours as you shall see.

The third day again to life he shall arise,
And devour birds and beasts of the wilderness,
Crows, popinjays, pies, peacocks, and mavois,
The Phoenix, with Eagle, and the Griffin of fearfulness,
The Green Lion, with the Red Dragon he shall distress,
With the White Dragon, and the Antelope, Unicorn and Panther,
With other beasts also, which almost each one doth fear.

In *bus* and in *nibus* he shall arise and descend,
Up to the Moon, and sith up to the Sun,
Through the Ocean Sea, which round is withouten end,
Only shippen within a little glass tun ;
When he is there come, then is the mastery won,
About which journey, great goods you shall not spend,
And yet you shall be glad that ever it was begun,
Patiently if you list to your work attend.

For then both body and spirit with oil and water,
Soul and tincture, one thing both white and red,
After colours variable it containeth, whatsoever man clatter,
Which also is called after he hath once been dead,
And is revived, our Markaside, our Magnet, and our lead,
Our Sulphur, our Arsenic, and our true Calx vive,
Our Sun, our Moon, our ferment and our bread,
Our toad, our basilisk, our unknown body, our man, our wife.

Our body thus naturally by craft when he is renovate,
Of the first order, is medicine, called in our Philosophy ;
Which often times again must be propertualicate,
The round wheel turning of our Astronomy,
And so to the Elixir of spirits you must come : for why,
Till the son of the fixed by the son of the fixer, be overgone,
Elixir of bodies, named it is only,
And this sound secret point deceiveth many one.

This natural process by help of craft thus consummate,
Dissolveth Elixir spiritual in our unctuous humidity,
Then in balneo Mare together let them be circulate,
Like new honey or oil, till perfectly they be thickened,
Then will that medicine heal all infirmity,
And turn all metals to Sun and Moon perfectly,
Thus you shall make the great Elixir, and *Aurum potabile*,
By the grace and will of God, to whom all honour and glory.

Wishing by all means possible to profit the Kingdom and State, Mr. Rabbards hath dedicated this work to her Majesty.

15th May. THE 'CENTURION'S' FIGHT WITH FIVE SPANISH SHIPS.

There has returned to London the *Centurion*, commanded by Mr. Robert Bradshawe, a very tall ship of burden yet weakly manned, that in November took a cargo to Marseilles. Here the master waited for about five weeks, and being about to sail, some ships of smaller burden entreated him to stay a day or two longer so that for their better safety they might sail in company, vowing together that they would not fly from each other if they should happen to meet with the Spanish galleys, but rather than be taken by the Spaniards to endure their accustomed cruelty, would fight it out to the end.

These small ships sailing along the Straits of Gibraltar upon Easterday, were suddenly becalmed, and immediately five galleys made towards them in very valiant sort, the chief leaders and soldiers bravely apparelled in silk coats, with great plumes of feathers in their hats and silver whistles round their necks. By ten o'clock they came up alongside the *Centurion* and grappled with her, two on either side and the Admiral at the stern which with her shot so sorely galled and battered the *Centurion* that the mainmast was greatly weakened, the sails filled with many holes, and the mizzen and stern almost unserviceable. In each of the gallies were about five or six hundred Spaniards, on the *Centurion* but forty-eight in all, men and boys.

For five and a half hours the fight continued, during which the trumpet of the *Centurion* sounded forth the deadly points of war and encouraged them to fight against their adversaries, but on the Spaniards' gallies there was no music, only the sound of the silver whistles. Many a Spaniard was turned into the sea, as they came crawling in multitudes and hung upon the sides of the ship intending to have entered into the ship. Five times was the *Centurion* fired with wild fire which the Spaniards threw in, yet by the diligent foresight of the master no harm was done at all. Four of her men were slain, one being the master's mate, and ten others hurt by splinters which the Spaniards shot; until, when their shot was almost spent and they were now constrained to shoot at them with hammers and the chains from their staves, by spoiling and overwearying the Spaniards our men at last constrained them to ungrapple themselves and get going.

Whilst the two other small ships had fled away, the *Dolphin* lay aloof and durst not approach near, so that one of the gallies went from the *Centurion* and set upon the *Dolphin*, which immediately caught fire through her powder so that both ships and men perished. The next day six other gallies came and looked at the *Centurion* but durst not approach her.

16th May. AN INVASION EXPECTED.

The Lords-Lieutenant and others, charged with the defence of the places on the coasts, are warned to have all things prepared to resist any attempt that the enemy may make. Forces are to be put in readiness and reviewed, and immediate order taken to watch and guard the beacons as has been done before in time of danger.

19th May. A SEDITIOUS FELLOW.

At the sessions Nicholas Haselwood, yeoman, was found guilty of having spoken with malice and feloniously against the Queen, saying that he desired and wished her death; and further that he hoped to see his enemies burnt at Smithfield before Michaelmas. He pleaded not guilty of felony, but guilty of contempt and trespass and is sentenced to be put on the pillory, with a paper setting forth his offence over his head.

21st May. THE QUEEN AT THEOBALD'S.

On the 10th May the Queen came to Theobald's to stay with the Lord Treasurer, and there finding him very melancholy she caused to be delivered to him a charter addressed to 'the disconsolate and retired sprite, the eremite of Theobald's,' giving him leave to retire to his old cave, and abjuring desolations and mourning to the frozen seas and deserts of Arabia Petrosa. Amongst the shows there presented was a conference between a gentleman usher and a post, pretending to deliver letters from the Emperor of China. At her departure yesterday she knighted Mr Robert Cecil, the Treasurer's younger son, whom some expected to be advanced to the Secretaryship; but in the Court it is said that the knighthood must serve for both.

Rumours.

It is rumoured that Sir John Norris has entered Brittany, taking an island near St. Malo, and has joined with the Prince de Dombes' forces; and that 20 Spanish ships are off Cornwall. The Earl of Cumberland has sailed out from Plymouth to meet them with his ships. 1500 men are to go to Ireland, whither these ships are suspected of going, and 1500 more to be taken from Brittany; Sir Walter Ralegh posts down to Cornwall. The Queen is much moved with this news, and was very melancholy at the Lord Treasurer's. In Scotland witches are discovered that, with the privity of Bothwell, have practised the King's death.

24th May. Dr. Gervase Babington's Sermon.

Dr. Gervase Babington, Bishop of Llandaff, preached before the Court at Greenwich on the Second of Kings, the fifth chapter; he compared the Lords of Council to the servants of Naaman, advising him for the best though it were to their own hurt. And speaking of the present discontents in religion, 'Woe is me to speak it,' quoth he, 'some of us cry, and too many of us cry instead of this, "No church, no sacraments, no ministers, no discipline at all"; and therefore we must leave all open assemblies in this land, and combine ourselves together to erect a form according to our wills, in woods, in fields, in holes and corners where we can. Yea, with more woe I speak it, some fear not to write, "Pharaoh of Egypt gave the Israelites leave to worship God truly, but our magistrates, IF they should give us leave, yet could we not be suffered for such and such." Making an IF after these infinite mercies poured upon us by God, in the gracious government we live under, and casting the governors in merit towards us, beneath Pharaoh of Egypt. O sinful IF! O damnable and undutiful IF!'

26th May. SIR R. WILLIAMS COMMENDED.

The Council have sent a special letter to Sir Roger Williams, Colonel of the English companies at Dieppe, commending him for the good service performed by him and those who served with him in the late encounter with the forces of the Governor of Rouen.

THE GALLANT ACTION OF SIR R. WILLIAMS.

In the beginning of May provisions being scarce in Rouen, two regiments of the enemy had been despatched to the village of Cingcens, to secure such supplies as they could. This village, which is nine leagues from Dieppe, they fortified with trenches and barricades, and lest they should be molested from Dieppe a troop of horse was sent out to a wood, two leagues off, covering the highway, so that if any force should come out from Dieppe they might either retire back to give intelligence or by making resistance should give those at Cingcens time to prepare themselves and to procure help from Rouen.

When news of this force was brought to the Governor, the Lord Chartres, formerly governor for the King in Malta, and Sir Roger Williams, who had lately arrived, they resolved to set out from Dieppe in the evening of 19th May with 400 Frenchmen and 300 English. After marching all night they came to the wood early the next morning, where they found the troop of horse waiting to stop their passage. On these they made so fierce an assault that all were slain and not one escaped. Accordingly, leaving the bodies in the wood and taking some of their horses, the Lord Chartres and Sir Roger Williams marched on, reaching Cingcens somewhile before noon; and there they descried the enemy with their ensigns displayed within the fort.

The Lord Chartres, seeing that the fortification was so strong, declared that it was impossible to enter it, and tried to persuade Sir Roger to go back again, considering that the enemy was two to their one. But Sir Roger answered that it were a great dishonour to him to so do, and declared that he would set on them with his own three hundred, though it should cost him and them their lives. The Lord Chartres, being much encouraged with this bold resolution of Sir Roger, protested that he too would take part with his four hundred, whatever should chance. Thereupon he displayed his ensign, and together with Sir Roger, he vowed, with God's assistance, to enter the barricades and charge the enemy. So he spoke to his soldiers, exhorting them to fight for their lawful king whose right they were bound to defend.

Sir Roger likewise encouraged his men, showing them that though they were few and had to fight a great multitude, skilful, stout, hardy and trained in martial discipline, yet their enemy was but a multitude of traitors, opposing themselves to God's ordinance, and therefore condemned of God to a shameful death both here and in the world to come. He assured them that in putting their confidence in God not one of their hairs should fall, and finishing his speech, he prayed to the Lord with great confidence. Having ended his prayer, he made them promise to die every man rather than that they would fly one foot.

Then they marched forward with great courage, displayed their ensigns, struck up their drums and with their trumpets sounded defiance. In this spirit of resolution they assaulted the enemy as freshly as if they had not marched all night. The fight continued for two hours until at length they entered the barricades ; Sir Roger himself being one of the foremost fought hand to hand with the chief officers of the enemy ; and from the other side, the Lord Chartres also behaved valiantly. At length the enemy began to give back, and being enclosed in their barricades like a flock of sheep in a sheepcote they were all put to the sword, not one man being suffered to escape alive.

Having obtained this victory, on their knees they gave thanks to God, who had subdued their enemies under foot, and praised Him with psalms.

The losses of the Lord Chartres and Sir Roger are eleven men killed and a few slightly wounded. The Generals then immediately took order to return speedily to Dieppe lest some fresh force from Rouen should come upon them, or by casting about should meet them on the way. They gave order also that the soldiers should leave all spoil behind them, except that which could easily be carried. Thus they returned safely to Dieppe. The enemy, as was afterwards learned, did indeed come with a large force to meet them, but they had passed that place four hours before.

31st May. RUMOURS.

Six ships are being victualled to be sent to Lord Thomas Howard who has sailed for the islands with charge to do somewhat upon the coast of Spain as he goes. The talk of the slaughter of the men of Rouen by Sir Roger Williams is in everyone's mouth.

1st June. SIDNEY'S 'ASTROPHEL AND STELLA.'

Sir Philip Sidney's *Astrophel and Stella* that hitherto is known but in private copies is now printed and set forth before the world with a preface by young Nashe. 'Put out your rush candles,' quoth he, 'you poets and rimers, and bequeath your crazed quatorzains to the chandlers ; for lo, here he cometh that hath broken your legs. Apollo hath resigned his ivory harp unto Astrophel, and he, like Mercury, must lull you asleep with his music. Sleep Argus, sleep Ignorance, sleep Impudence, for Mercury hath Io, and only Io Paean belongeth to Astrophel. Dear Astrophel, that in the ashes of thy love livest again like the Phoenix ; O might thy body, as thy name, live again likewise here amongst us : but the earth, the mother of mortality, hath snatched thee too soon into her chilled, cold arms and will not let thee by any means be drawn from her deadly embrace ; and thy divine soul, carried on an angel's wings to heaven, is installed in Hermes' place, sole prolocutor to the Gods.'

THE FIRST SONNET OF ASTROPHEL

Loving in truth, and fain my love in verse to show,
That the dear *She*, might take some pleasure of my pain :
Pleasure might cause her read, reading might make her know,
Knowledge might pity win, and pity grace obtain.
I sought fit words to paint the blackest face of woe,
Studying inventions fine, her wits to entertain,
Oft turning others' leaves, to see if thence would flow,
Some fresh and fruitful shower, upon my sunburnt brain.
But words came halting out, wanting Invention's stay,
Invention, Nature's child, fled Stepdame Study's blows :
And others' feet still seemed but strangers in my way,

Thus great with child to speak, and helpless in my throes,
Biting my tongue and pen, beating myself for spite:
'Fool,' said my Muse to me, 'look in thy heart and write.'

Tempus adest plausus, aurea pompa venit, so ends the scene of idiots, and enter Astrophel in pomp.

5th June. THE TAKING OF GUINGCAMP.

From Brittany it is reported that Sir John Norris hath taken Guingcamp, a town very strongly fortified, with ditches and walls, and protected on one side with marshes.

The General having found that part of the town which was fittest for a breach, made a show on the contrary part, causing trenches to be dug at the south side, and passages to be made through the old houses, even up to the counterscarp itself. A long trench was likewise made on the east side of the town, with a platform of earth in the middle as if the cannon should have been placed there. In the meantime great labour was used in making a mine near to the intended breach, and in preparing passages and emplacements for the cannon. This was performed with such zeal that on the 20th May the artillery was brought down to the Jacopins' cloister, and there set up within less than a hundred paces of the wall. In this action the General exposed himself unceasingly.

On 21st May the battery began, and though it continued all day, yet by reason of the few pieces of artillery not able to make sufficient battery, the day's work brought no further effect than the crushing of two flankers and the beating down of the parapet so that but a very small breach was made, which was repaired continually by the soldiers and inhabitants within the town, who maintained the rampart with featherbeds, horse dung, and bags of earth almost to the lowest part of their parapet.

Very early the next day the battery began again, and continued until two or three in the afternoon, by which time the breach seemed very fair. Whereupon the French urged hotly to an assault and so importuned the Prince de Dombes that he consented. Sir John was not in favour of an immediate assault, as he learned from a sergeant, whom he had sent forward to examine the breach, that the approach was very steep, sliding, and difficult, but especially because his mine had not yet been pushed far enough forward. Nevertheless, seeing that if the Frenchmen offered to attempt the place themselves, it would be a disgrace to us, he instantly demanded the point and honour of the assault for the English. Such was the emulation of the English captains that to avoid contention the General caused the dice to be cast and it fell to Captain Jackson and Captain Heron to lead the first two hundred to the assault, which, after devout prayers recommending themselves to God, they performed very valiantly, scrambling up the slope, and standing for half an hour at the push of the pike in the face of a whole storm of small shot, but through the steepness of the place the soldiers were unable to get up, and in the end withdrew in as good order as they had assaulted. Captain Heron was killed by a shot in the throat, and about twelve others, Captain Jackson dangerously hurt, and some thirty were wounded.

The second attempt was made by the Baron de Molac, Colonel General of the French infantry in those parts, who attacked bravely with some few of the French gentlemen, the common soldiers advancing to the breach but coldly received greater hurt, and many were slain. Some others then presented themselves for a third assault, but it was considered best to stay until the next day when the battery should have made the breach larger. In these assaults, Captain Dennis, being sent to another part of the town with some forces to make a feint of scaling, advanced too near and received a musket shot in his stomach, whereof he died at midnight.

During the night those within the town demanded a parley, and when this was granted some deputies from the town came next morning to the Prince de Dombes. Terms of capitulation being agreed on, on Whitsunday the town was surrendered and on the 24th May the garrison marched out, being 120 horse, and about 260 foot. Great store of victuals was taken, 2000 weight of powder and some cannon.

The capture of this town of Guingcamp is of great import to the French king, for all lower Brittany depends on it, and the Courts of Parliament ordinarily held at Rennes have by the Leaguers been transferred thither.

6th June. UNLAWFUL GAMES TO BE PUT DOWN.

Unlawful games are again to be put down, since the Queen is informed that archery, though an exercise not only of good recreation but also of great use in the defence of the realm, is now greatly decayed; she knows that many at great charge furnish themselves with the muskets and harquebusses now come into use and that it will seem hard to lay on them the burden which the law imposes; yet, with very good reason, she requires those games and pastimes prohibited by law, that is, bowls, dicing, cards and such like, to be forthwith forbidden, and instead archery revived and practised; for by this ancient weapon hath our nation won great honour in times past. Moreover by this means those poor men whose living chiefly depends thereon, as bowyers, fletchers, stringers and arrowhead makers, will be maintained and set to work in their vocations.

23rd June. LEONARD DIGGES' 'TECTONICON.'

A new edition is entered of the book named *Tectonicon* by Leonard Digges, first published in 1556, briefly showing the exact measuring and speedy reckoning of all manner of land, squares, timber, stone, steeples, pillars and globes. The book further sets forth the use of the carpenter's rule, containing a quadrant geometrical, the use of the squire, and of the instrument called the staff.

25th June. TERMS OF AGREEMENT FOR THE DESPATCH OF FURTHER TROOPS TO NORMANDY.

At Greenwich this day articles of agreement were signed for the despatch of a further force of 3400 to be added to the 600 men under Sir Roger Williams at Dieppe in Normandy; by Monsieur de Beauvoir and Monsieur de Reau for the French King, and by the Lord Treasurer and the Lord Admiral for the Queen. The King to pay all the costs of the levying, furniture, transportation and wages of these soldiers, with a General Captain to govern them, and all accustomed officers; and to discharge this and the charges due for the men in Brittany with Sir John Norris, he grants the Queen all profit of the tolls, customs and taxes to be received from the towns of Rouen and Newhaven, which her Majesty shall begin to receive so soon as either town be restored in its obedience to the King.

There are in Brittany at this time 1675 men; with Sir John Norris 722, and with Sir Henry Norris 540, and Captain Anthony Shirley 413.

1st July. RUMOURS.

Sir John Norris was reported to have received a blow and his brother to be slain; but later letters show that there have been several skirmishes but no fight. The Earl of Essex is now to go to France, although the Queen was long unwilling, and his friends in England advised him to the contrary, wishing him rather to seek a domestical greatness like his father-in-law, but the Earl is impatient of the slow process he must needs have during the life and greatness of the Chancellor and the Lord Treasurer.

5th July. THE WAR IN BRITTANY.

After winning the town of Guingcamp, the purpose of the Prince de Dombes was to have assailed the town of Morlaix and to bring the rest of lower Brittany to the King's obedience; but, learning that the Duke Mercury, commanding the French rebels in those parts, had joined with 4000 Spanish, and was marching towards Morlaix by way of Corlay, he considered that it would be most dangerous to engage his army before the town until he had made himself master of the field, especially as the enemy were of greater strength, and he was in an unfriendly country where there were many peasants, armed and hostile. Accordingly he stayed at Guingcamp to repair the fortifications and the breach made by our artillery, and also to await the coming of two cannon and two culverin.

THE DUKE MERCURY BRAVES THE PRINCE DE DOMBES

On 7th June the Duke Mercury arrived at Corlay, within three leagues of Guingcamp, where the castle was treacherously yielded to him, and thence the Duke sent a trumpeter to the Prince de Dombes about some prisoners, who signified that he had in charge to entreat the Prince to appoint some day and place of battle. To this the Prince answered that it was the most acceptable news that could be brought, for it was a thing he had long sought and desired. He refused therefore to send an answer by word of mouth through the trumpeter lest it should afterwards be denied, but wrote a letter, signed with his own hand.

The next day the Duke removed from Corlay to St. Gilles, less than two leagues from Chateau Laudran, whither the Prince de Dombes moved with his army and encamped. There the trumpeter of the Duke met the trumpeter of the Prince and delivered the Duke's answer, signed with his own hand, which was that he would be ready with his army on the Thursday following at ten o'clock in the morning in the fittest place for action between Corlay and Guingcamp ; and if the Prince should refuse this offer, he should show the world that his actions were not answerable to his brags.

Whereupon the Prince sent this reply, couched in such terms as to give the Duke all provocation possible to force him to give battle.

'The Prince de Dombes, Governor of Dauphine, Lieutenant General for the King in his Army in Brittany,

Having seen the answer of Duke Mercoeur of the eighth of this month signed with his own hand, upon the offer made of the day and place of battle to be given, saith : He was sent into this province to chastise and punish those that have traitorously rebelled against the King, of whom the said Duke, being chief, doth manifest how he shameth and feareth the presence of the said Prince and the pain and punishment of his rebellion : and in regard of the lewd imputations given by his answer to the King, and to the said Prince, he saith he lieth, and shall lie as often as he shall say so.

At the Camp at Chateau Laudran, the ninth of June, 1591.'

The cartel was sent by a trumpeter and delivered to the Duke in the presence of many of the principal men of his army.

The Skirmish near Quenelac

The Duke, being greatly moved, openly vowed a solemn oath to offer battle to the Prince within three days. On the 9th June (which was Wednesday) he moved his camp to Quenelac, a village about a league and a half from Chateau Laudran, situated at the foot of a high hill which by deep hedges, ditches, and inclosures, confronted a little heath of two miles' compass. As soon as he heard of the enemy's approach the Prince mounted on horseback to make choice of a place for battle between the enemy and the hill, and found about three-quarters of a league off the village, a large plain or heath, skirted on the side of the enemy with a coppice and a little hill, and the ground crossed by ditches, of great advantage for the enemy, who without any difficulty could enter the heath by three large passages.

The next day the enemy within a quarter of a league of the heath showed his whole army in order of battle on the top of a hill, and the Prince also set his troops within the heath, disposing of them, by the advice of Sir John Norris, into three battalions, of which the English infantry made two, the lance-knights the third. The day was spent in slight skirmishes.

On 11th June the enemy drawing his army to the foot of the hill, placed his artillery upon the side of the heath where it commanded the whole place, and bordered all the hedges with shot. By this time our army was marched into the heath, and immediately 200 infantry were sent out to view the contenance of the enemy. These advanced and charged the enemy, and, driving them back to their main body, cleared the hedges and barricades, and slew several; but on our men withdrawing, the Duke sent out 500 French and 200 Spanish to repossess these places, following them with main body of his army.

When the Prince, who remained in the plain with the advanced guard, perceived this, order was given for 300 infantry, commanded by Captain Anthony Wingfield, Sergeant Major, and Captain Morton, and the English horse under Captain Anthony Shirley, to be sent forward. Meanwhile, under cover of the hedges the enemy despatched a number of musketeers, thinking to lodge them on our left and to take some two or three houses and a small wood on the edge of the heath. Against this the Prince sent 100 men, musketeers and pikemen, and 150 French musketeers, led by the Baron de Molac, and supported by 40 light horse, under Monsieur de Tremblay.

The action was so gallantly performed, especially by our English, that the enemy's horse and foot in the plain were forced to fly, many being slain and the rest driven to save themselves within the artillery, where the whole strength of the Spaniards and the rest of the army was placed. In this charge, Monsieur de Guebrian, Colonel of the foot, was taken by Monsieur de

Tremblay; Don Roderigo, chief Marshal of the Spaniards, was killed, together with a Spanish Captain, 200 French and 60 Spanish. The attack so amazed the enemy that our men were allowed within ten paces of the cannon to disarm the dead, and lead away the prisoners, none ever offering to follow. The rest of the day was spent in slight skirmishes and cannonades.

Next day, the enemy made a great show but at last sent out some shot to skirmish, whom Captain Anthony Shirley, with 15 horse and a few foot, speedily put to their heels, pursuing them to their barricades, where his horse was shot. In the skirmish, Mr. Kempe, a gentleman of the cornet, was killed, and Mr. Charles Blunt had his horse killed under him with a cannon shot.

On 13th June, the enemy made some light skirmishes but would not abide a charge either of horse or foot. The day following, being St. John's day with the Spaniards, it was expected that the enemy would give battle, but nothing was done. In the night the Duke prepared to remove, and withdrawing his cannon, the next day he repassed the hill on which he had first appeared, and retired to Quenelac.

The Prince, having now waited with his army on the heath from Friday the 11th June to the 15th, in readiness to give battle, also withdrew his artillery and returned his troops to quarters.

16th July. A Conspiracy for Pretended Reformation.

There is much disquiet in the City by reason of three fanatical preachers, Hacket, Arthington and Coppinger. About ten o'clock this morning, these men, having met in a house in Broken Wharf, set out, and began to proclaim to passers-by that Christ was come again from heaven. Thence Coppinger led the way by Watling Street and Old Change towards Cheapside, all the time crying out, 'Repent, England, repent.'

Moved by the unwonted sight of these new prophets arisen in London, the people soon crowded about them until by the time that the Cross in Cheapside was reached, the throng was so dense that they could go no further. Whereupon they got up into a cart from which Coppinger and Arthington spoke to the people, declaring that Hacket was Christ's representative on earth by partaking of His glorified Body, by His Spirit, and by the office, which had been conferred upon him, of separating the good from the bad. They themselves were two prophets, the one of Mercy, the other of Judgment, sent and extraordinarily called of God to assist Hacket in his great work. Then one pronounced mercy, comfort, and joy unspeakable to those that should repent; the other denounced terrible judgments on those who refused to hear them.

They went on to declare that Hacket was King of Europe and that all other kings must obey him. The Queen of England had forfeited her crown and was worthy to be deprived. Finally they prayed God, in very unmannerly and saucy terms, to confound especially the Archbishop of Canterbury and the Lord Chancellor, cursing them even to the pit of hell.

They had at first hoped to repeat this declaration at different parts of the City, but as the people still increased, they were forced to go into the Mermaid Tavern in Cheapside. Here they rested for some time and then returned to the place whence they had set out, Arthington all the way repeating his cry of 'Repent, England, repent.'

When rumours of these happenings reached the Queen at Greenwich, two of the Council, Mr. Wolley and Mr. Fortescue, were sent post haste to the City to find out the truth and to take action. About one o'clock in the afternoon, Hacket and Arthington were arrested and taken to the Lord Mayor's house, where they were examined by the two councillors. Here they refuse to show any signs of respect to those present, even remaining covered until their hats are plucked off, though all the time Arthington treateth Hacket with the utmost reverence, even kneeling before him.

They say that this Hacket, in former time an evil-liver, who was converted to Presbyterianism, hath wrought himself into the belief that he is Christ's representative on earth. He has been the servant of a gentleman at Oundle, where his loose life and violent temper are notorious. Once his master, a certain Mr. Hussey, had quarrelled with a certain Freckington, an artificer of the town, whose son was the schoolmaster. Hacket taking up the quarrel and one day meeting with this schoolmaster at an inn, pretended to be exceedingly sorry that there should be bitterness between him and his master. The schoolmaster deluded thus into thinking that he meant friendship, was taken unawares and thrown on the ground, where Hacket having him now at his mercy, with great savagery, bit off his nose. Yet though both Freckington and a surgeon who chanced to be present, begged him to restore the nose so that it might be stitched on again while the wound was still green, he not only refused to part with it, but showed it exultingly to all who cared to look; some even say that he ate it up.

19th July. RUMOURS.

The Queen herself is said to be going down to Portsmouth with the Earl of Essex, but his friends mislike the voyage, and wish that he had left it to some other in respect of the great charge it is to him to put himself forward according to his dignity; but he and his think the cost well bestowed, conceiving that the coming of the Duke of Parma maketh worthy the adventure. The Queen allows him only 100 lances and 50 harquebusiers; but there are 100 more of his own cost, and his friends have sent him bountifully, both horse and money. There are great expectations for him, and if he should return with honour from his voyage, he is like to be a great man in the state; both soldiers and Puritans wholly rely on him.

The ships to be set forth for the supply of Lord Thomas Howard are yet not ready, wanting mariners who refuse to go upon the uncertainty who should pay them, whether the Queen or the merchants.

Hacket's conspiracy is in everyone's mouths, some liking him to John of Leyden who took on himself the kingdom of the Anabaptists, and thinking that Hacket plotted some such kingdom as these prophets might have assembled; others take them to be mere fanatics; but the enemies to the Puritans take great advantage against them, as these prophets have been great followers of their preachers and have solicited with their books and letters all those that they knew affected to their sect, especially the Lord Treasurer, the Earl of Essex, the Countess of Warwick and Mr. Davidson. Meanwhile the Queen is more troubled with them than it is worth.

24th July. SIR HENRY UNTON MADE AMBASSADOR TO THE FRENCH KING.

Sir Henry Unton is appointed ambassador to the French King, being furnished with certain instructions signed by the Queen's own hand.

He is commanded in all his behaviour to preserve the reputation and royal dignity of her Majesty, and especially by observing the rites of religion and following the form of Daily Prayer both himself and his household according to the Church of England as established by law. To acquaint himself with the ambassadors of Venice and of the Duke of Florence, and through them to learn of the affairs of Italy, as well as of the Pope and the King of Spain ; and if any should come from the King of Scots or the King of Denmark or any other of the Protestant Princes of the Empire, to let them understand how friendly the Queen is to them. With regard to the money which is owing from the French King, not to press for it by any expostulation or to move any unkindness, but to put him in remembrance of the benefits he hath received.

He shall have especial regard to the actions of the Earl of Essex, giving him understanding from time to time what is thought of them, approving to him what are considered to be good, informing of such things as are to the contrary, and giving him good advice to reform them. He is charged on his allegiance not to fear to deal plainly with the Earl.

25th July. A RESTRAINT OF PLAYING.

Notwithstanding former orders to restrain the playing of interludes and plays on the Sabbath day, these orders are being neglected to the profanation of this day, and by reciting their plays on all other days of the week, the players cause great hurt to the game of bear baiting and like pastimes maintained for the Queen's pleasure. The Lord Mayor and the Justices of Middlesex and Surrey are required to take order that no plays be shown openly either on Sunday or on Thursday when the games are usually practised.

26th July. THE TRIAL AND CONDEMNATION OF WILLIAM HACKET.

This day Hacket was brought up from Bridewell to the Sessions house near Newgate for trial before the Commissioners, amongst them the Lord Mayor, Lord Wentworth, Sir Gilbert Garrard, Master of the Rolls, Sir Wolfstone Dixie, Sir Richard Martin, Mr. Sergeant Fleetwood (the Recorder), and Mr. Daniel.

He was arraigned on two indictments. Being asked to plead to the first, he answered, 'All must be as you will'; which was taken as a plea of guilty. To the second, he answered, 'You have wit enough to judge for me and yourselves too.' The question being put to him again, he replied, 'Few words are best; it is good to know much and say little.' It was shown that this answer would of itself condemn him of treason if he still refused to answer to the point, and being once more asked if he pleaded guilty or not guilty, he said, '*ambo*.' At last he was persuaded to plead not guilty to the second indictment.

He was next asked by whom he would be tried, but refused to give answer according to the form of the law, 'By God and my country.' Instead he replied, 'By the jury.' But realising that he now stood in very great danger, he began to blaspheme violently.

At last, seeing that Hacket obstinately refused to plead according to the form of the law, the Attorney General rose and demanded judgment.

As Hacket had pleaded guilty to one indictment and refused to plead to the second, there was no need to call witnesses or to enlarge on the case. Nevertheless for the better satisfaction of those present, both the Attorney General and the Solicitor General spoke at length. This done, the Recorder sentenced Hacket to death as a traitor, and he was taken away to Newgate.

28th July. THE EXECUTION OF HACKET.

In the morning William Hacket was brought from Newgate to execution for treason. All the way as he was dragged on the hurdle, he cried out continually, 'Jehovah Messias, Jehovah Messias,' and at another time, 'Look, look, how the heavens open wide and the Son of God cometh down to deliver me.'

The crowd was so vast that it was a long time before the officers could bring him to the gibbet which had been set up by the Cross in Cheapside. There, when silence had been called for, Hacket was exhorted to ask God and the Queen for pardon, and to fall to his prayers, but he began to rail and curse her Majesty. Being the more vehemently urged to remember his present state, he began to pray thus:

'O God of Heaven, mighty Jehovah, Alpha and Omega, Lord of Lords, King of Kings and God Everlasting, that knowest me to be the true Jehovah whom Thou has sent, send some miracle out of a cloud to convert these infidels and deliver me from mine enemies. If not, I will fire the heavens and tear Thee from Thy throne with my hands.' Then turning towards the executioner, he said, 'Ah, thou bastard's child, wilt thou hang William Hacket, thy king?'

The magistrates and people were much angered by these speeches and called out to the officers to have him despatched; so with much ado they got him up the ladder, where he struggled with his head, to and fro, to avoid the noose. Then he cried out very fearfully, 'O what do you, what do you? Have I this for my kingdom bestowed on me? I come to revenge thee, and plague thee——' and so was turned off.

But the people, unwilling in their fury that any mercy should be shown him, cried out that he should be cut down at once, being very angry with the officers for not showing more haste. As soon as he was taken down, almost in a trice, his heart was cut out and shown openly to the people.

29th July. COPPINGER DIES IN PRISON.

Coppinger, who had been Hacket's companion in the 'Conspiracy for pretended Reformation,' has died in Bridewell prison, having refused all food for more than a week.

Now that Hacket is dead there is much discontented murmuring. Some that seem moderate men, yet favour his opinions in Church government, think that he and his fellows intended good though they mislike the manner of the action. Others, extenuating the fault, believe that they were stark mad, and knew not what they said or did. Some even are heard to mutter that matters were made out to be worse and of greater peril and consequence than they were in fact, and that they were persecuted with greater sharpness than the offence deserved.

2nd August. SIR ROBERT CECIL A PRIVY COUNCILLOR.

Sir Robert Cecil, second son to the Lord Burleigh, Lord High Treasurer of England, was this day sworn of her Majesty's Privy Council.

3rd August. A SUSPECTED PORTUGUESE.

Mr. Mills, Signor Botello and Dr. Lopez, the Portuguese physician, are instructed to go to Rye to examine certain prisoners lately sent over from Dieppe. First, Emanuel Andrada, a gentleman of Don Antonio, who had previously offered to do the Queen some secret service but is suspected of designs against her. He is to be dealt with civilly at first, and then threatened with fear of his life to induce him to declare the truth; his papers are to be examined through Dr. Lopez. The second, John Semple, a Scot, to be examined about rebels and fugitives and his connexions in England and Scotland. The other two are Portuguese.

7th August. AN ASSAULT IN ST. PETER'S, WESTMINSTER.

At the special Session of Oyer and Terminer, William Dethick, Garter King of English Arms, was indicted for assaulting Henry Brown in the Church of St. Peter's at Westminster, drawing his dagger and striking him on the head. He pleaded not guilty and was acquitted.

A BUILDING ALLOWED IN BLACKFRIARS.

Harman Buckhold, goldsmith, is by the Council's special licence, allowed to build on the little piece of waste ground in Blackfriars, though by the proclamation of ten years ago new buildings were prohibited within the City or three miles of it. This is allowed, being supported by most of the inhabitants of Blackfriars, for that this plot is very noisome not only to those who pass by it but also to the neighbours because of the great heaps of soil and filth continually laid there. By giving this licence the nuisance will be abated.

13th August. ANDRADA'S DECLARATIONS.

Emanuel Andrada, the Portuguese prisoner, has declared to Mr. Mills that he is sent by King Philip to treat in his name with the Queen for a false peace, and to take her answer to the Duke of Parma who will write to the Council of Spain, the King replying by way of Italy. This is to while away time that by coming and going he may thoroughly understand what is happening in England. He was ordered by Don Christophoro Moro and Idiaques, the present rulers in Spain, to try by all means to kill Don Antonio, and there should be no lack of money or honour. To sound them he asked what should be done if any were willing to kill the Queen; they replied that King Philip had often been desired to do it, but he hoped before her death to see the ruin of her kingdom, and to have her in his hands, and would not therefore treat of her death.

Andrada further reporteth that in many ports of Spain and Portugal forty galleons are building, stronger than the King ever had. He has contracted with the Genoese at Madrid for forty Flemish ships, armed and victualled for six months, to be prepared at Antwerp and other free cities. From Germany and Biscay are coming this winter quantities of gunpowder, cordage, masts, munitions, and victuals to Brittany, where the King forms a magazine of ships, artillery and so forth; that province will furnish mariners, and then they will assault England. Don Juan, a captain of St. Malo, intends to assault Jersey in September.

20th August. A QUACK FIGURE CASTER.

Robert Henlack has petitioned the Council for redress against certain men who robbed him. He complains that while he was absent in the night a confederacy of certain evil disposed persons broke open his chamber door in the house of one Isabel Piggott in Thames Street and took away goods and money to the value of £400. Further, one Nathaniel Baxter hath since then robbed him of £12 more, pretending that by casting a figure he would help him to his goods and money again.

21st August. THE QUEEN ON PROGRESS.

On Saturday the 14th the Queen in her progress came from Farnham to Cowdray in Sussex, where she was royally entertained by the Lord Montague.

As the Queen and her train came into sight about eight o'clock in the evening, they were greeted with loud music which ceased suddenly as soon as she came to the bridge. Here a person in armour, standing between two porters carved out of wood, with a club in one hand and a golden key in the other, made a speech, after which he delivered the key to the Queen, who alighted from her horse and embraced the Lady Montague and her daughter, the Lady Dormir.

The next day being Sunday, the Queen rested and was most royally feasted, the portion for breakfast being three oxen and one hundred and forty geese.

On Monday, about eight o'clock in the morning, the Queen and her train rode out into the park to a delicate bower which had been prepared for her. Here while the musicians played, a nymph delivered her a cross-bow with which to shoot at the deer, some thirty in number, enclosed in a paddock. The Queen killed some three or four, and the Countess of Kildare one.

The rest of the week was spent in feasting and entertainment, and on Friday the 20th, the Queen moved from Cowdray to Chichester.

22nd August. THE BORDEAUX WINE FLEET TO BE STAYED.

An open placard is sent by the Council to all officers of the Port of London, the Cinque Ports and other ports on the south and west to stay all vessels about to trade with Bordeaux at the vintage time. It is credibly reported that certain merchants intend to set out in a very disorderly manner, and not in one or more fleets, forgetting that the state is interested in their private loss and that those ships which went unprotected last year have not yet returned.

28th August. MR. THOMAS CAVENDISH'S EXPEDITION.

Mr. Thomas Cavendish hath departed two days since from Plymouth with his fleet of three tall ships and two barks, *The Galleon*, wherein Mr. Cavendish himself sails, being the Admiral, *The Roebuck*, vice-admiral, whereof Mr. Corke is Captain, *The Desire*, with Mr. John Davis as Captain, *The Black Pinnace*, and a bark of Adrian Gilbert, commanded by Mr. Randolph Cotton.

31st August. RUMOURS.

The Queen is said to be at Portsmouth, having been at Chichester, whither she came from Lord Montague's at Cowdray, where she and the whole Court were magnificently entertained. Nothing is heard from Normandy from the Earl of Essex. From

Brittany it is reported that there hath been some quarrelling with the French, who laid in wait for the English and slew eight of Sir John Norris's horsemen ; whereupon he marched into the Prince de Dombes' camp, and slew a great number of his, and told the Prince that he would not serve under such rash heads. It is also said that 110 Spanish ships are at sea, to waft home the Indian fleet ; the Earl of Cumberland and the rest of the venturers are wished home again safe.

3rd September. ILLEGAL BUILDING IN LONDON.

The Justices of the Peace for Middlesex are sharply rebuked for allowing the Queen's express commandment to be broken, in that during this vacation when the Queen was on progress divers disobedient persons not only finish those buildings lately begun about the City of London but also begin new. The Council warn them how little the Queen will like this negligence, for not only did the magistrates refrain from removing the tenants of these cottages, according to the order given in the Star Chamber, but allow them still to be inhabited and others to be built.

4th September. THE EARL OF ESSEX IN FRANCE.

The news from France is that the Lord General (the Earl of Essex) leaving his army hath been to see the King and is at Pont de l'Arch, some three leagues from Rouen. On their way to the King not above ten people were seen ; the villages and houses were utterly abandoned, yet milk, cider, fresh water and bread were set ready to relieve our soldiers almost in every house, which the grooms and footboys brought their masters, for there was no straggling because the enemy followed from hill to hill, but only, as it seemed, to view and discover the size of the company.

At the gates of Noyon the Marshal Biron awaited him to conduct him to the King, who was in a garden attended by the Duc de Longueville, the Count St. Pol and many more. The King received my lord most kindly, and after a long discourse led him into the castle where he banqueted him. Afterwards, escorted by the Marquis Pisana and many other nobles, the Lord General was conducted out of the town and taken into a village a mile off ; but before the troops reached this place the King, accompanied by two or three, overtook them and said to all the train in English, 'You are welcome.' Having brought the Earl to his lodging, he remained half an hour and after was escorted back to his own quarters by the Earl and his company.

Next morning my Lord went to the King and attended a preaching in his house, being afterwards entertained to dinner. In the afternoon, the Earl accompanied only with a dozen gentlemen attended the King to Noyon (which he had recently besieged and taken), to consult with the Marshal Biron who lay there sick of the gout. Here the pitiful tokens of these lamentable wars were very manifest, the country being all spoiled, the bridges broken, all the suburbs of the town burned, orchards and gardens utterly destroyed, churches beaten down, the walls rent and the town within very filthy.

The Lord General came to the Pont de l'Arch on the 30th, where he held a council and determined to send for his army to Arques. He was advertised by letter that in his return from the King he was in great danger of being taken by Villiers, Governor of Rouen, who pursued him at the trot with at least 700 horses.

6th September. THE QUEEN DISCONTENTED AT THE ILL SUCCESS IN FRANCE.

The lack of all news from the ambassador in France breeds much disquietness, for though many rumours were noised abroad there hath been no certainty until the coming of Monsieur de Reauloc, which causeth the Queen to hold much offence both towards the King for not holding to his purpose to besiege Rouen, and the Earl of Essex for departing from his camp so long a journey without her licence. The Queen is therefore much discontented, saying that she wishes with all her heart, that she had never consented to it, though she had lost double the sum of money spent in the expedition.

10th September. NEWS FROM FRANCE.

It is reported that the Lord General sentenced a gentleman of his cornet to be disarmed for striking a woman. His army has now joined him at Pont de l'Arch.

12th September. MR. WALTER DEVEREUX SLAIN.

Mr. Walter Devereux, the only brother of the Earl of Essex, was slain with a small shot in the head four days since. The

Lord General being then at a village called Pavilly with his horse and foot marched, in a bravado, to see whether Villiers or any of his troops in Rouen durst come out and skirmish ; and in that skirmish Mr. Devereux was slain.

THE BORDEAUX WINE SHIPS TO SAIL IN CONSORT.

The Council order all who purpose to trade in wine or salt with Rochelle or Bordeaux to be ready with their ships, furnished with men and munitions, by the 25th of the month, either at the Downs or Dover, where there shall be a company of good ships with which they may pass safely. Those that cannot be ready by this time to forbear their voyage until they can go with a company of at least fourteen or fifteen good ships. Any disobeying this order of the Council shall be punished at their return for their contempt in putting in danger the Queen's people and the shipping of the realm, the owners of the ships, the masters and principal mariners ; and all the lading of the ships shall be arrested until full satisfaction has been made for the offence.

13th September. THE EARL OF ESSEX REBUKED.

The Council very sharply rebuke the Earl of Essex, for the Queen greatly dislikes that he left his army without any head except a Sergeant-Major and, not without danger, journeyed to the King, especially since she understands by letters from the French King that this journey was made voluntarily without any request from him. She therefore condemns him of rashness, reminding him that the purpose of his voyage was the recovery of Rouen and Newhaven. Moreover, she has contracted to pay the force but for two months from the time of their arrival, which was the 2nd August. She much misliketh that he came so near the town of Rouen to make a bravado upon the enemy in sight of the town, whereby to his own great loss and as a reward for his unadvisedness he hath lost his only brother.

Accordingly, considering how untowardly this action falls out under his government, the Queen is resolved that he shall return at the end of the two months. Moreover, she is determined to recall the force as well ; nevertheless if it appear probable that in one or two months more the King will retake either Rouen or Newhaven, and furnishes good assurance for the payment of the

English forces, then will she be content for some to stay, but not all.

16th September. A PROCLAMATION AGAINST SUPPLYING THE KING OF SPAIN WITH CORN.

'For as much as it is manifestly seen to all the world how it hath pleased Almighty God of His most singular favour to have taken this Our Realm into his special protection these many years, even from the beginning of Our reign, in the midst of the troubled estate of all other kingdoms next adjoining, with a special preservation of Our own person, as next under his Almightiness, supreme Governor of the same, against any malicious and violent attempts :—'

It is commanded that no corn or grain nor any ordnance of brass or iron be carried to any foreign countries without special licence upon pain that the owner and master of the vessel so offending be committed to close prison for a year and further until they have answered fines to the quadruple value of the goods carried. And because this year there is such plenty of corn it is likely that some of the people near the sea coasts will desire to vent some part of the corn of their own growing for lack of sale in the country. Principal persons of wealth are advised and earnestly required to buy in the markets near the sea coasts such quantities of grain as the owners should be constrained to sell for their necessity, and to keep it in store to serve the markets in the latter end of the year.

This proclamation is very necessary because though the King of Spain hath abundance of treasure by his Indian mines yet his own country is greatly wanting in victual, especially of corn and of munitions of war, and of mariners, and other furniture for his navy. He hath attempted to corrupt some of the Queen's subjects and some strangers inhabiting the realm to satisfy his wants either directly by stealth to his own country, or indirectly and colourably first to some other countries next adjacent to his.

21st September. A SECRET MARRIAGE.

The Queen hath for some time been highly displeased with Mr. Thomas Shirley, son of Sir Thomas Shirley, her Majesty's Treasurer for the wars in the Low Countries, for that he secretly married Mistress Frances Vavasour, one of the Ladies in Waiting. When this became known Mr. Shirley was committed to the Marshalsea. She hath now somewhat abated her wrath, but Sir Robert Cecil is to write to Sir Thomas that her pleasure is that he shall make it publicly known that he cannot digest such an act of contempt to her Court, as well as wilful perjury and disobedience to himself, nor do for a son that has so highly offended her who always furthers any honourable marriage or preferment for any of hers, when broken to her without infamy and scandal. Should Sir Thomas come to Court, she will tell him her mind.

24th September. THE QUEEN, ON PROGRESS, VISITS ELVETHAM.

On Monday, 20th September, the Queen came to Elvetham to stay with the Earl of Hertford, where great preparations had been made for her worthy reception. As the house is small and unable to accommodate so large a company, there were built especially the following:

A room of estate for the nobles, with a withdrawing place for her Majesty; the outsides all covered with boughs, and clusters of ripe hazel nuts, and inside with arras, the roof with works of ivy leaves, the floor with sweet herbs and green rushes. Near to this were the special offices: the spicery, lardery, chandery, wine-cellar, ewery, and pantry, all of which were tiled. There were also a large hall for the entertainment of knights, ladies and gentlemen of account; a separate place for the Queen's footmen and their friends; a long bower for the Queen's Guard; another for the Officers of the Household; another to entertain all comers, suitors and others; another for the Earl's steward; another for his gentlemen that waited on him.

There were also made a great common buttery; a pitcher house; a large pastery, with five new ovens, some of them fourteen feet deep; a great kitchen, with four ranges and a boiling place; another great kitchen for all comers; a boiling house for the great boiler; a room for the scullery; and another for the cooks' lodgings.

Between the house and the hill, where these buildings were set up, was made in the valley a pond, cut to the perfect figure of a half moon. In this pond were three isles; the first the Ship

Isle, a hundred feet long and forty broad, with three trees for masts ; the second the Fort, twenty feet square and overgrown with willows ; the third the Snail Mount, rising to four circles of green privy hedges, twenty feet high, and forty feet broad at the bottom. In the water were boats prepared for musicians and a pinnace fully furnished.

Everything being in readiness, the Lord Hertford, calling his retinue apart, in a few words put them in mind of the quietness and diligence they were to use so that their services might bring her Majesty content and thereby his honour and their credit, with the increase of his love and favour to them. This done, the Earl with his train, amounting to the number of three hundred, most of them with chains of gold about their necks, and in their hats yellow and black feathers, rode out to meet the Queen, who entered the park between five and six in the evening. Proceeding towards the house, a poet met them and saluted them with a Latin oration. This poet was clad in green to signify the joy of his thoughts at her entrance, a laurel wreath on his head to express that Apollo was the patron of his studies, an olive branch in his hand to declare what continual peace and plenty he wished her Majesty, and booted to betoken that he was *vates cothurnatus*, and not a loose and creeping poet. His speech being ended, the poet presented the scroll to the Queen, who graciously received it with her own hands, and all moved on toward the house, being preceded by six maidens who strewed flowers, singing this song :

With fragrant flowers we strew the way,
And make this our chief holiday :
For though this clime were blest of yore,
Yet it was never proud before.
O beauteous Queen of second Troy,
Accept of our unfeigned joy.

Now th' air is sweeter than sweet balm,
And satyrs dance about the palm ;
Now earth with verdure newly dight,
Gives perfect sign of her delight.
O beauteous Queen of second Troy,
Accept of our unfeigned joy.

Now birds record new harmony,
And trees do whistle melody;
Now everything that nature breeds,
Doth clad itself in pleasant weeds.
O beauteous Queen of second Troy,
Accept of our unfeigned joy.

After supper, a consort of six musicians was admitted to the presence and played before the Queen, who was so pleased with their music that she gave a new name to one of their pavans, made by Thomas Morley, formerly organist of St. Paul's.

The next day broke stormy and the rain continued until after dinner so that no devices could be shown in the morning. But the afternoon and evening were fine and the pageant was able to proceed. Immediately after dinner, a large canopy of estate was set up at the head of the pond for the Queen to sit under and view the sports. This canopy, which was held by four of Lord Hertford's chief gentlemen, was of green satin, lined with green taffeta sarcenet, every seam covered with broad silver lace; valanced about and fringed with green silk and silver, more than a hand's-breadth in depth; it was supported with four silver pillars, and decked above with four white plumes spangled with silver. All about the head of the pond was tapestry spread. The Queen came down to the pond about four o'clock and sat under the canopy, when a pageant of Nereus and the Tritons and Sylvanus was enacted in the water.

On Wednesday morning, as the Queen looked out of her casement window about nine in the morning, three musicians, disguised in the ancient country attire, greeted her with a country song of Coridon and Phillida:

In the merry month of May,
In a morn by break of day,
Forth I walked by the wood side,
When as May was in his pride.
There I spied, all alone,
Phillida and Coridon.
Much ado there was, God wot,
He would love, and she would not.
She said, never man was true!
He said, none was false to you.

He said, he had loved her long ;
She said, love should have no wrong.
Coridon would kiss her then ;
She said, maids must kiss no men,
Till they did for good and all.
Then she made the shepherd call
All the heavens to witness truth,
Never loved a truer youth.
Thus with many a pretty oath,
Yea and nay, and faith and troth,
Such as silly shepherds use,
When they will not love abuse ;
Love, which had been long deluded ;
Was with kisses sweet concluded :
And Phillida, with garlands gay,
Was made the Lady of the May.

This song was so acceptable to the Queen that she commanded it to be sung again.

The same day after dinner, about three o'clock, ten of the Lord Hertford's servants, all Somersetshire men, hung up lines in a green court in the form of a tennis court, making a cross line in the middle. In this square they played, five against five, with the hand ball at 'board and cord' to the great liking of her Majesty, who sat watching them for more than an hour and a half.

After supper, the two delights prepared were curious fireworks and a sumptuous banquet. During the time of these fireworks from the pond, two hundred of the Earl's gentlemen served the banquet, all in glass and silver, every one carrying so many dishes that the whole number amounted to a thousand ; and there were to light them in their way a hundred torches. The dishes in the banquet were :—The Queen's arms and the arms of all the Nobility in sugar work ; men, women, castles, forts, ordnance, drummers, trumpeters, soldiers of all sorts, lions, unicorns, bears, horses, camels, bulls, rams, dogs, tigers, elephants, antelopes, dromedaries, apes, and all other beasts ; eagles, falcons, cranes, bustards, heronshaws, bitterns, pheasants, partridges, quails, larks, sparrows, pigeons, cocks, owls and all birds; snakes, adders, vipers, frogs, toads, and all kinds of worms; mermaids, whales, dolphins, congers, sturgeons, pikes, carps, breams, and all sorts of fishes. All these were in sugar work, some in standing dishes, some in flat work. There were also in flat sugar work and marchpanes, grapes, oysters, mussels, cockles, periwinkles, crabs, lobsters, as well as apples, pears and plums of all kinds, preserves, suckets, jellies, leaches, marmalades, pastes, and comfits.

On Thursday the day began with a song by the Fairy Queen, dancing round a garland with her maids, which so pleased the Queen that she caused it to be repeated twice over, graciously dismissing the singers with largess.

An hour later, the Queen and her nobles took their departure from Elvetham. On all sides as they went, the actors in the entertainment were grouped in melancholy postures, wringing their hands in dumb show at her going away. Last of all, as the Queen passed under the park gate, a consort of musicians, hidden in a bower, played while two sang:

O come again, fair Nature's treasure,
Whose looks yield joys, exceeding measure.

O come again, heaven's chief delight,
Thine absence makes eternal night.

O come again, world's starbright eye,
Whose presence doth adorn the sky.

O come again, sweet beauty's sun,
When thou art gone, our joys are done.

So highly was the Queen pleased with her reception at Elvetham, that she declared to the Lord Hertford that the beginning, process and end of his entertainment was so honourable that hereafter he should find reward in her especial favour.

29th September. THE BEACON WATCHES.

To those asking that the watches at the beacons be discontinued, the Council answer that they would be very willing but that they have been advertised of the arrival of certain galleys of the King of Spain in the Narrow Seas, and some attempt may be made on the coast, especially on those parts that lay towards France. Nevertheless, that the charges may be diminished, the beacons need only be kept when there are land winds blowing and at spring tides, and at such times three or four only need be appointed to each beacon, provided they be vigilant.

30th September. DR. COSIN'S 'THE CONSPIRACY FOR PRETENDED REFORMATION.'

Dr. Richard Cosin hath written an account of the conspiracy and death of William Hacket that was executed on 28th July, called *Conspiracy for Pretended Reformation: viz. Presbyteriall Discipline. A Treatise discovering the late designments and courses held for advancement therefore, by William Hacket, yeoman, Edmund Coppinger, and Henry Arthington, Gent., out of others' depositions and their own letters, writings, and confessions upon examination. . . . Also, an answer to the caluminations of such as affirm they were mad men: and a remembrance of their action with the like, happened heretofore in Germany.* The book is now at the press to be printed by Christopher Barker, the Queen's printer.

2nd October. THE CAPTURE OF GOURNAY.

The town of Gournay having been besieged for some days by the troops of the Marshal and the Lord General is now taken. Those within had at first refused to yield, defending themselves in hope of relief until the cannon played and two fair breaches were made. When the English were ready to go to the assault, the town was yielded with very hard conditions; the composition being that the governor, captains, leaders, officers and gentlemen of quality should become prisoners, but not *de guerre*, for want of these words being at the King's mercy; the soldiers were to depart with white sticks only in their hands and the burgesses to be used as others of the King's subjects. It was agreed also that any of the Queen's subjects taken therein should be delivered, but only one was found, an Irishman who had run away from Sir Edward Norris.

4th October. THREE OF LYLY'S PLAYS TO BE PRINTED.

Three of Mr. John Lyly's plays are to be printed, being *Endimion*, *Galathea*, and *Midas*, that were formerly played before the Court at Greenwich by the Children of Paul's.

'So nice is the world,' saith he, 'that for apparel there is no fashion, for music no instrument, for diet no delicate, for plays no invention, but breedeth satiety before noon and contempt before night.

'Come to the tailor, he is gone to the painter's to learn how more cunning may lurk in the fashion than can be expressed in the making. Ask the musicians, they will say their heads ache with devising notes beyond Ela. Enquire at ordinaries, there must be sallets for the Italian; picktooths for the Spaniard; pots for the German; porridge for the Englishman. At our exercises soldiers call for tragedies, their object is blood; courtiers for comedies, their subject is love; countrymen for pastorals, shepherds are their saints. Traffic and travel hath woven the natures of all nations into ours, and made this land like arras, full of device, which was broadcloth, full of workmanship.

'Time hath confounded our minds, our minds the matter; but all cometh to this pass, that what heretofore hath been served in several dishes for a feast is now mingled in a charger for a gallimaufry. If we present a mingle-mangle, our fault is to be excused, because the whole world is become an hodge-podge.'

7th October. A CASE OF SORCERY.

Stephen Trefulack, gentleman, was indicted at the Sessions for having exercised certain wicked, detestable and diabolical arts called witchcrafts, enchantments, charms, and sorceries, with the intention of diabolically provoking George Southcott to the unlawful love of a certain Eleanor Thursbye. He pleaded guilty, but the judgment of the Court is deferred.

10th October. THE BORDEAUX WINE FLEET.

Sir John Hawkins, Sir George Barnes, Sir George Bond and William Burrows, Esquire, are to call in two of the Masters of the Trinity House and with them to view the fleet about to set sail for Bordeaux and to set down such orders for their strengthening as they thought necessary. Further to impress two suitable merchant ships of those lying in the Thames to be furnished in warlike manner at the charges of the merchants who trade for wines.

16th October. THE EARL OF ESSEX TAKES LEAVE OF HIS ARMY.

The gentlemen in the army in Normandy were much distressed on learning that they were to return to England.

It was hoped at this time to attempt some enterprise against Rouen, and on the 6th of the month every man was ordered to put himself in readiness to march by two o'clock in the morning. Very early next day, the Lord General with his voluntary gentlemen went to the Marshal Biron's quarters, where he found the Marshal ready and accompanied with many of the nobility.

The Lord General being very glistering with a great plume of feathers in his hat, the Marshal began to say to him merrily, 'What, you young gallant, are you come hither to brave me with your white feathers? I think I have white feathers too'; and with that called for a hat set with a mighty plume, and a horseman's coat of tawny velvet frill of silver lace; and thereupon put on the hat which caused him to look like an old cutting ruffian of Smithfield. This pleasant humour grew out of a confident hope he had of the good success of some intelligence received from Rouen, which was that one of the Colonels of the Governor of Rouen had promised, on account of some injury he had received from the Governor, to deliver a gate of the town to Monsieur Rollett, Governor of Pont de l'Arch.

An hour before day, Monsieur Rollett with the Lord General came to the rendezvous at Martinville. With him were about 2000 Gascons, harquebusiers on foot, two regiments of Swiss, Hallard Mountmorency with five troops of mounted cuirassiers; and the English under Sir Roger Williams, 2500 men with 140 horses. The troops that before were dull with sickness and discontent now grew into wonderful of hope of what the French promised, and after a short breakfast marched towards Rouen three leagues, but here, having reached a wood in sight of the town not half a league off, a messenger came from the Marshal to the Earl of Essex who was with the foremost troop that he should halt because there was treason in the intelligence; which much amated the soldiers.

After resting a while the Marshal came up and directed that they should march to a place called Direntoun, about as near as Mile End is to London from Rouen, which was reached so suddenly that many of the inhabitants were surprised in their homes. There much booty was taken, and in the morning great store of wine was found under the ground, of which the soldiers took as much as they could carry and let the rest run.

The next day (8th) the Earl of Essex took his horse very early and went to a hill near the town, not far from St. Katherine's Castle, bemoaning his fortune that he was recalled before he was master of the market place; and there on a fair green in sight of the town (where there were 3000 soldiers besides the inhabitants), commanding all the gentlemen to dismount, he told them he was very sorry that no opportunity was offered him to have led them into a place where they might have gained honour; but the fault was not his neither was it theirs, for he had received great good will in all, and thereof was determined to give notes of honour to some. And there he made twenty-four knights.

The Lord General then took his leave of the army and attended with all his gentlemen went to the Marshal's quarters, where he stayed an hour in consultation. Then the Marshal rode with him for a league on his way until they came to a windmill, where they halted for a while. They reached Dieppe about ten o'clock at night, and the Lord General scarcely stayed to eat, but went on board, leaving behind him a great many mourning but hoping for his return.

The next day Mr. Robert Carey came from England with good news, but the Earl was gone before him.

18th October. THE BORDEAUX WINE FLEET.

The Council having received Sir John Hawkins' report on the state and strength of the fleet about to sail for Bordeaux, order the ships to be stayed until further information is received of the disposition of Monsieur Lucon.

20th October. THE LOSS OF THE 'REVENGE.'

News is received in London of a great fight about the Azores, in which the Queen's ship, the *Revenge*, was lost. This report is confirmed by certain Spanish prisoners who fought in that action.

On 31st August, Lord Thomas Howard, with six of the Queen's ships (the *Defiance*, being the admiral, the *Revenge*, commanded by Sir Richard Grenville, vice-admiral, the *Bona-*

venture, commanded by Captain Cross, the *Lion* by George Fenner, the *Foresight* by Mr. Thomas Vavasour, and the *Crane* by Duffield, these two last being small ships), were riding at anchor near Flores, one of the westerly islands of the Azores, when news was brought of the approach of the Spanish fleet, and the report no sooner made than the enemy was in sight.

The English ships were all in confusion, many of the ships' companies being on shore, everything out of order, and in every ship half of the company sick and unserviceable. From the *Revenge* there were ninety men sick ashore ; in the *Bonaventure* not enough left to handle the mainsail, and, had not twenty men been taken out of a bark of Sir George Carey's, which was then burnt, she would never have reached England. In this plight the Spanish fleet, having shrouded its approach by the island, came upon them so swiftly that the English ships had scarcely time to weigh their anchors, some even being forced to slip their cables and set sail.

Sir Richard Grenville, having stayed to recover his sick men from the shore, was the last to weigh, and had by now delayed too long to recover the wind before the enemy was upon him. The master of the ship and others urged him to cut his mainsail and cast about, but Sir Richard refused to turn from the enemy and persuaded his company that he would pass through their two squadrons and force them to give way before him. This he did with the first ships, but the *San Philip*, a great ship of 1500 tons, coming towards him took the wind out of his sails so that the *Revenge* could neither keep way nor feel the helm. The *Revenge* being entangled with the *San Philip*, four other ships boarded her ; two on the starboard and two on her larboard.

The fight thus beginning at three o'clock of the afternoon continued very terrible all that evening. But the great *San Philip*, having received the lower tier of the *Revenge*, discharged with crossbar-shot, shifted herself with all diligence from her sides, utterly misliking her first entertainment. The Spanish ships were filled with companies of soldiers, in some two hundred, in some five, in others eight hundred, besides the mariners. In the *Revenge* there were none at all besides the mariners but the servants of the commander and some few voluntary gentlemen only. After many vollies had been interchanged from the great ordnance and small shot the Spaniards essayed to enter the *Revenge* by boarding, hoping to force her by the multitudes of their armed soldiers and musketeers, but were repulsed again and again, and at all times beaten back either into their own ships or into the sea.

In the beginning of the fight, the *George Noble* of London, having received some shot through her by the armados, fell under the lee of the *Revenge* and asked Sir Richard what he would command him; Sir Richard bad him save himself and leave him to his fortune.

After the fight had thus without intermission continued while day lasted and some hours of the night, many of our men were slain and hurt, and one of the great galleons of the armada, and the *Admiral of the Hulks* both sunk and in many other of the Spanish ships great slaughter was made.

The Spanish ships which attempted to board the *Revenge* as they were wounded and beaten off so always others came in their places, and having never less than two mighty galleons by her sides and aboard her. So that ere morning, from three of the clock the day before, there had been fifteen several armados assailed her; and all so ill approved their entertainment that they were by break of day far more willing to hearken to a composition than hastily to make any more assaults or entries. But as day increased, so our men decreased; and as light grew more and more, by so much the more grew our discomforts. For none appeared in sight but enemies, saving one small ship called the *Pilgrim* commanded by Jacob Whiddon, who hovered all night to see the success; but in the morning bearing with the *Revenge*, was hunted like a hare among many ravenous hounds.

All the powder of the *Revenge* to the last barrel was now spent, all her pikes broken, forty of her best men slain, and the most part of the rest hurt. In the beginning of the fight she had but one hundred free from sickness, and fourscore and ten sick, laid in hold upon the ballast; a small troop to man such a ship and a weak garrison to resist so mighty an army. By those hundred all was sustained; the volleys, boardings, and enterings of fifteen ships of war, besides those which beat her at large. On the contrary, the Spanish were always supplied with soldiers brought from every squadron; all manner of arms and powder at will. Unto ours there remained no comfort at all, no hope, no supply either of ships, men or weapons; the masts all beaten overboard, all her tackle cut asunder, her upper work altogether razed, and in effect evened she was with the water, but the very foundation or bottom of the ship nothing being left over either for flight or defence.

Sir Richard finding himself in this distress, and unable any longer to make resistance, having endured in this fifteen hours' fight the assault of fifteen several armados, all by turns aboard him, and by estimation 800 shot of great artillery, besides many assaults and entries; and seeing that he himself and his ship must needs be possessed by the enemy, who were now all cast in a ring about him, for the *Revenge* was not able to move one way or other but as she was moved with the waves and billows of the sea, commanded the master gunner, whom he knew to be a most resolute man, to split and sink the ship that thereby nothing might remain of glory or victory to the Spaniards, and persuaded the company, or as many of them as he could induce, to yield themselves unto God and to the mercy of none else; but as they had like valiant and resolute men repulsed so many enemies, they should not shorten the honour of their nation by prolonging their own lives for a few hours or a few days. The master gunner readily condescended and a divers few others; but the Captain and the Master were of another opinion and besought Sir Richard to have a care of them, alleging that the Spaniard would be as ready to entertain a composition as they were willing to offer the same; and that there being yet divers sufficient and valiant men still living, and whose wounds were not mortal, they might do their country and Prince acceptable service hereafter; and that where Sir Richard had alleged that the Spaniards should never glory to have taken one ship of Her Majesty's, seeing that they had so long and so notably defended themselves, they answered that the ship had six foot of water in hold, three shot under water which were so weakly stopped as with the first working of the sea she must needs sink, and was besides so crushed and bruised as she could never be removed out of place.

The matter being thus in dispute and Sir Richard refusing to hearken to any of those reasons, the master of the *Revenge* (while the Captain won unto him the greater party) was conveyed aboard to the General, Don Alfonso Bassan. Who finding none over hasty to enter the *Revenge* again, doubting lest Sir Richard would have blown them up and himself, and perceiving by the report of the master his dangerous disposition, yielded that all their lives should be saved, the company sent to England, and the better sort to pay such reasonable ransom as their estate would bear, and in the mean season to be free of the galley or imprisonment.

When this answer was returned and safety of life was promised, the common sort being now at the end of their peril, the most drew back from Sir Richard and the master gunner, it being no hard matter to dissuade men from death to life. The master gunner, finding himself and Sir Richard thus prevented and mastered by the great number, would have slain himself with a sword had he not been by force withheld and locked in his cabin. Then the General sent many boats aboard the *Revenge* and divers of our men fearing Sir Richard's disposition, stole away aboard the General and other ships. Sir Richard thus overmatched was sent unto by Don Alfonso Bassan to remove out of the *Revenge*, the ship being marvellous unsavoury, filled with blood and bodies of dead and wounded men, like a slaughter house. Sir Richard answered that he might do what he list, for he esteemed it not, and as he was carried out of the ship, he swooned, and reviving again desired the company to pray for him. The General used Sir Richard with all humanity and left nothing unattempted that tended to his recovery, highly commending his valour and worthiness.

The *Admiral of the Hulks* and the *Ascension of Seville* were both sunk by the side of the *Revenge*; one other recovered the road of St. Michael's and sunk there also; a fourth ran herself on the shore to save her men. Sir Richard died, as it was said, the second or third day aboard the General and was by them greatly bewailed; what became of his body, whether it were buried at sea or on land, is not known.

A few days after the fight was ended and the English prisoners dispersed into the Spanish and Indy ships, there arose so great a storm from the West and Northwest that all the fleet was dispersed, as well as the Indian fleet which were then come unto them as the rest of the Armada that attended their arrival, of which fourteen sail, together with the *Revenge*, were cast away upon the Isle of St. Michael. On the rest of the islands there were lost in this storm fifteen or sixteen more of the ships of war; and of a hundred and odd sail of the Indian fleet, expected this year in Spain, what in this tempest and what before in the Bay of Mexico and about the Bermudas there were seventy and odd consumed and lost with those taken by our ships of London, besides one very rich Indian ship which set herself on fire being boarded by the *Pilgrim*, and five other taken by Master Watts and his ships of London between the Havanna and Cape St. Antonio.

22nd October. AN AFFRAY AT WESTMINSTER.

This day one John Keckham, servant of Margaret Bray, a widow, was going on his mistress's business on the public way from Tuthall Street to the Gatehouse at Westminster when he met a certain Robert Crosyer, who crossed over to encounter him, and assaulting him with a cowlstaff, beat and struck him down, intending to slay him. Keckham seeing that he was in danger of his life, defended himself with his drawn rapier, and being unable to rise from the ground thrust at his adversary, giving him a mortal wound in the breast.

25th October. PRECAUTIONS AGAINST DISORDER AT THE PORTS.

News is received that the Lord Thomas Howard's ships have taken prizes from the Indian and Mexican fleet, laden with treasure and things of great value. Sir Thomas Gorges and Mr. Carmarden are to be sent down to take order in those ports where the ships shall arrive that no mariners be permitted to come on shore until the ships have been visited and the goods inventoried lest the sailors embezzle or take away short ends and such things as they may come by.

27th October. DISORDERS AT DARTMOUTH.

The mariners and other loose and dissolute persons have committed foul outrages and disorderly embezzlements of the goods brought in to Dartmouth by the two prizes newly arrived. Sir Francis Drake is required with all speed and circumspection to restrain these contempts and to recover from any party such parcels or portions as he can find by proof, suspicion or examination ; and to this end to use the assistance there of any gentleman of quality.

28th October. THE TRIAL OF BRIAN O'ROURKE.

Brian O'Rourke was brought to trial and arraigned at Westminster. As he spoke no English, Mr. John Ly of Rathbride, a gentleman from Ireland, interpreted between him and the Judge. He was charged on several counts of having sought the deprivation of her Majesty from her royal seat, the destruction of her person and the overthrow of her realm of Ireland.

Amongst other accusations it is declared :

That at Dromaher he caused a picture of a woman to be made, setting to it Her Majesty's name, and causing it to be tied to a horse's tail and drawn through the mud in derision ; and after he caused the galliglasses to hew it in pieces with their axes, uttering divers traitorous and rebellious words against Her Majesty ;

That after the Spanish fleet sent by the King of Spain and Pope Sixtus V. had been dispersed by the English fleet till they came round Scotland and so into Ireland, O'Rourke entertained and succoured divers of the Spaniards who had been employed in the invasion ; and that after proclamation was made by the Lord Deputy that upon pain of death no man should keep any of the Spaniards but send them to him by an appointed day, O'Rourke kept the prisoners and afterwards despatched them safe to Spain with a Spanish friar and an Irish friar ;

That he violently entered and burned Ballingaffe and other villages in Roscommon, and the town of Knockmallen, murdering Her Majesty's subjects, and continuing these outrages until he was forced by the Queen's forces to fly to Scotland ;

That at Glasgow he offered the King of Scots that if he would maintain him and suffer his subjects to join him he would bring the realm of Ireland to his subjection.

After many speeches had passed between O'Rourke and his judges, he declared that he would not consent to be tried by the jury unless he might have a week's respite to allow of papers from Ireland being sent to him, and a good man of law to be assigned to him who should swear to deal as truly for him as for the Queen's heir apparent if he were in his place ; and besides he would have the Queen herself to be one of the jury. Upon this it was shown through Mr. Ly, that the law was that if he refused to be tried by twelve men he should be judged guilty forthwith and so be guilty of his own death. Yet for all this as he still refused trial he was condemned to death as a traitor. When the sentence was explained to him, he said nothing but if that were their will, let it be so.

31st October. RUMOURS.

Now that the loss of the *Revenge* is generally known, some condemn the Lord Thomas Howard for a coward, saying that he is for the King of Spain. The Lord Admiral and Sir Walter Ralegh have quarrelled and offered combat. Seven prizes have recently been brought in by the merchants who went to second Lord Thomas Howard.

The war in Normandy and Brittany is greatly liked, and 1000 pioneers are to be sent over to the siege of Rouen and 1000 new soldiers to the Earl of Essex, who has obtained leave to remain there till he has done something to revenge his brother's death; but his making of twenty-four knights is greatly mocked. General musters were assembled on a rumour being received that the traitor Sir William Stanley would attempt an invasion. The Lord Chancellor is very sick with a strangury and not expected to recover. A proclamation against the Jesuits is being printed but is not yet published.

1st November. FATHER JENNINGS, A NOTABLE JESUIT, TAKEN.

Edmund Jennings, a Jesuit, hath been taken prisoner by Richard Topcliffe at the house of Mr. Swithin Wells in Holborn where he had been saying Mass. Topcliffe came on him while he was still in his vestments, and he, with some ten others who were present, was taken to prison. During the fray Topcliffe was thrown down the stairs by Mr. Brian Lacy's man.

3rd November. THE EARL OF ESSEX IN NORMANDY.

On 17th October the Earl of Essex, Lord General, returned to the army from England to the surprise and delight of most: that day he took counsel and resolved to send off to tell both the King and the Marshal of the success of his journey into England. The next morning Sir Roger Williams was sent to the King. News was now brought of the rendering up of Caudebec, by composition that all the men of war should depart to Rouen with a convoy for their security, the drums beating, ensigns flying, matches lighted and the horsemen with pistols in their hands.

On the 21st the Earl held a martial court where many grievances were heard and determined ; some being condemned to die for going without passport to England and for other offences. On the 24th the Earl and his gentlemen were invited to dine with Monsieur D'O, where they were most sumptuously entertained, and so far from meaner things that they feasted on musk and amber in tarts ; and the day following the Earl brought Monsieur D'O to see the army which was drawn up, over 2000 strong, besides 300 sick. On this day the English army began to draw their pay from the French King, but not to their content.

On the 28th the army marched towards Rouen and was well lodged in certain villages. That night Sir Roger Williams returned with letters from the King to the Earl showing his full determination to besiege Rouen with might and main and that he was marching thither with all expedition. Sir Roger was then despatched to England with the news, and the army moved to a village called Ophin, and the next evening marched towards Rouen which was about six miles off.

Next morning (29th) the point of the English army entered the village of Mount de Mallades about a quarter of a mile from the walls of Rouen, and looking down from thence they saw a great skirmish between the enemy from Rouen and the Marshal Biron's companies, the enemy holding on to a house and the hill until five in the evening when about 250 men issued out of the town to a place of advantage and assaulted the quarters of Hallard Mountmorency, which were next to the English, so sorely that he was forced to quit some part of them. The enemy so pursued him that they burned half his quarters, his troops offering no resistance, and would have burnt the rest if the Lord General had not sent certain harquebusiers to draw them into a skirmish, and offering to cut in between them and the town ; which was so well performed that they were forced by our horse to wheel about, and by some pikes led by Sir John Wingfield to give ground. In this skirmish Captain Barton's lieutenant was slain, and two knights and one captain besides others wounded.

Several horses were hurt and the Earl's was shot dead under him. Towards night the fight was broken off and our men returned to their lodging.

THE EXECUTION OF O'ROURKE.

Brian O'Rourke was to-day drawn to Tyburn for execution. As they came to the gallows, while he was still standing in the cart, Mr. John Ly, with many good exhortations, bade him to remember the many odious treasons he had committed, and to ask Her Majesty and the world for forgiveness. But he obstinately refused, saying that if she would have given him time, and the writings which had been sent from Ireland against him so that he might answer them, and also if she would give him his life, then he would ask her forgiveness and henceforth serve her truly ; adding further that he little thought the King of Scots would have sent him to the Queen without good assurance of his life and pardon for his offences.

Still Mr. Ly urged O'Rourke to repent and ask forgiveness, and likewise to forgive for that was the only way for him to come to the Heavenly Kingdom, and the standers by also urged him to repent. To all this he replied that they should make means for themselves to come to God, and he would look after himself ; and with that fell to his prayers. The standers by then asked Meylerns, Lord Archbishop of Cashell, who was present, to counsel O'Rourke to call to God ; but O'Rourke turning on him answered that he had more need to look to himself and that he was neither here nor there. So the cart went from him. His body was taken down, his members and bowels cut out and burned in the fire, and his heart taken out by the hangman, who showed it to the people as an archtraitor's heart ; then his head was cut off and his body quartered.

4th November. AN AFFRAY NEAR WHITEHALL.

Thomas Coxon and Daniel Carter, yeomen, were going together between the two gates at Whitehall, when Coxon violently assaulted Carter, giving him several wounds with his dagger on the face. To this Carter said, 'What meanest thou to strike me ? I have nothing to do with thee,' and did his utmost to withdraw from his adversary, who followed him with drawn sword until he reached the angle of a wall beyond which he could not go. After receiving divers wounds Carter drew his sword in self-defence, whereupon Coxon ran in on him and received a mortal wound in his body.

SPANISH DISASTERS.

News is received from the isle of the Tercera that there were three thousand men in the island saved from the Spanish ships which foundered in the great storm, and that by the Spaniards' own confession there were ten thousand cast away in that storm besides those that perished between the islands and the main.

'MEDIUS' PRINTED.

Medius, being the second book of sacred songs, some made for five, some for six voices, by William Byrd, the Queen's Organist, hath been printed with the music.

5th November. A PROCLAMATION AGAINST VAGRANT SOLDIERS.

A Proclamation is published against vagrant soldiers, declaring that there is a common wandering abroad of a great multitude, of whom the most part pretend that they have served in the wars on the other side of the seas, though it is known that very many of them neither served at all, or else ran away from their service and are justly to be punished and not relieved; some indeed have served, and, falling with sickness, are licensed to depart; these deserve relief.

Her Majesty therefore commands that discretion be used between unlawful vagrant persons and the soldiers now lawfully dismissed from their service. The vagrants, who have neither been brought to sickness or lameness in their service and are not able to show sufficient passport for their dismission, to be taken as vagabonds and so punished. And if any allege that they have been in the Queen's pay on the other side the seas and cannot show sufficient passport from the Lord General, he shall be indited and suffer as a felon, as a soldier that hath run away and left the service traitorously.

The Treasurer of Wars will make payment of sums of money to those who lawfully return to conduct them to the places where they were levied. Furthermore for the repressing of the great number of mighty and able vagrants now wandering abroad under pretence of begging as soldiers, by whom open robberies are committed, the Lieutenants of every county, who have sufficient warrant by their commissions to execute martial law upon such offenders, are charged to appoint Provost Marshals for the apprehension of such notable offenders, and to commit them to prison thereupon to be executed.

MEASURES OF RELIEF FOR RETURNED SOLDIERS.

Every soldier on landing, having the passport of the Lieutenant General or any special officer of commandment, to be paid five shillings for his conduct to the place where he was levied. Where there is no person of the Treasurer, the principal officer of the place to pay this sum immediately, which will be duly repaid by the Treasurer of Wars or the Council. On payment of the conduct money, the passports of the soldier shall be retained and a new passport given for his travel allowing sufficient time by convenient journeys from the place of landing to the place of his first levy. To be warned at the same time that if he lingers by the way in roguish manner or does not reach his former abode within the time limited, he shall be taken as a vagabond and punished according to the law.

8th November. SOUTHWELL'S 'MARY MAGDALEN'S FUNERAL TEARS.'

Mary Magdalen's Funeral Tears, written as it is said by Robert Southwell the Jesuit, though without his name inserted on the title-page, has been entered, wherein is expressed the sorrowful thoughts and lamentations of Mary Magdalen at the Sepulchre of Christ, in the manner of the writers of romantic tales. The author seeing how the finest wits are now given to write passionate discourses hopeth by his book to woo them to make choice of such passions as it were neither shame to utter nor sin to feel.

15th November. SPANISH LOSSES.

By examination of various Spaniards and Portuguese it appears that the King of Spain sustained very heavy losses this last summer. Of the Nova Spania fleet of 52 ships but 33 returned to Havannah, there being 2600 lost in 19 sail; of the Terra Firma fleet only 23 ships came to Havannah, having lost some 3000 men. As well as these 55, there met at Havannah 12 ships from S. Domingo and 9 from Funduras, 77 in all, and set sail on

17th July, keeping company till the 10th August, when they were scattered by tempests so that by the end of August all but 48 had been lost, 5000 men being thought to have perished in the ships cast away. The King of Spain's treasure is all landed at Havannah to be sent home in frigates in January.

20th November. THE DEATH OF SIR CHRISTOPHER HATTON.

This day Sir Christopher Hatton, the Lord Chancellor, died at Ely House in Holborn of a flux of his urine, aggravated with grief of mind because the Queen somewhat vigorously exacted of him a great sum of money collected of tenths and first fruits, whereof he had charge, and which he had hoped, in regard of the favour he was in with her, that she would have forgiven him. Neither could she once having cast him down with a harsh word raise him up again, though she visited and endeavoured to comfort him. He was reputed to be a man of pious nature, a great reliever of the poor, of singular bounty and munificence to students and learned men (for which reason those of Oxford chose him as their Chancellor of their University), and one who in the execution of the office of Lord Chancellor could satisfy his conscience in the constant integrity of his endeavours to do all with right and equity.

21st November. THE PROCLAMATION AGAINST JESUITS.

The Proclamation declaring the great troubles intended against the realm by seminary priests and Jesuits is now published though dated 18th October and printed some time since. The dangers and preparations made against the realm by the Pope and the King of Spain, and by English fugitives beyond the seas, are set forth and severer measures to be taken.

'And before all things, We do first require of the Ecclesiastical State, that the like diligence be used by the godly ministers of the Church, by their diligent teaching and example of life to retain Our People steadfastly in the profession of the Gospel and their duty to Almighty God and Us; as it is seen a few capital heads of treason are continually occupied within their Seminaries in withdrawing a multitude of ignorants to their inchantments.

'And secondly, for having sufficient forces in readiness by Sea, We hope by God's goodness and with the help of our subjects to have as great or greater strength on the seas as at any time we have had to withstand these puffed vaunts from Spain. And for Our forces by land, Our trust is that seeing We have distributed Our whole realm into several charges of Lieutenancies, that they by themselves when they may be personally present, and otherwise by their deputies and assistants of other Our ministers, will now after the general musters which have been by Our special order taken, consider of all things requisite to perform, and make perfect all defects that shall appear necessary, to make the bands both of horsemen and footmen fully furnished with armour, weapons and munition and with all other things requisite for their conduction to the place of service; and there also to continue as time shall require to defend their country. And so We do most earnestly require and charge all manner of Our subjects, with their hands, purses and advices; yea, all and every person of every estate, with their prayers to God, to move Him to assist this so natural, honourable and profitable a service, being only for the defence of their natural country, their wives, families, children, lands, goods, liberties and their posterities against ravening strangers, wilful destroyers of their native country, and monstrous traitors.

'And lastly, to withstand and provide speedy remedy against the other fraudulent attempts of the seminaries, jesuits, and traitors, without which as it appeareth his forces should not now be used, the same being only wrought by falsehood, by hypocrisy, and by undermining of Our good subjects under a false colour and face of holiness, to make breaches in men's and women's consciences, and to train them to their treasons: and that with such a secrecy, by the harbouring of the said treacherous messengers in obscure places, as without very diligent and continual search to be made, and severe orders executed, the same will remain and spread itself as a secret infection of treasons in the bowels of Our Realm; most dangerous, yea, most reproachful to be suffered in a well ordered Commonwealth.

'Therefore we have determined by advice of Our Council to have speedily certain commissioners, men of honesty, fidelity and good reputation, to be appointed in every shire, city, and port-town within Our realms to enquire by all good means what persons by their behaviours or otherwise worthy to be suspected to be any such persons, or have been sent, or that are employed in any such persuading of Our people, or of any residing within Our realm to treason, or to move any to relinquish their allegiance with Us, or to acknowledge any kind of obedience to the Pope or to the King of Spain ; and also of all other persons that have been thereto induced, and that have thereto yielded : And further to proceed in the execution of such their commission, as they shall be more particularly directed by instructions annexed to their commission.

'And furthermore, because it is known and proved by common experience upon the apprehension of sundry of the said traitorous persons sent into the realm, that they do come into the same by secret creeks, and landing places, disguised both in names and persons ; some in apparel as soldiers, mariners, or merchants, pretending that they have heretofore been taken prisoners, and put into galleys, and delivered. Some come in as gentlemen, with contrary names, in comely apparel, as though they had travelled into foreign countries for knowledge : and generally all, for the most part, are clothed like gentlemen in apparel, and many as gallants ; yea in all colours, and with feathers and such like, disguising themselves ; and many of them in their behaviours as ruffians, far off to be thought or suspected to be friars, priests, jesuits, or popish scholars. . . .

'And finally, We admonish and strictly charge and command all persons that have any intelligence with any such so sent, or come from beyond the seas to such purpose, to detect them to the commissioners, in that behalf to be assigned as aforesaid, within twenty days after the publication hereof, in the shire town, or city or port, within the precincts of the said commission : upon pain that the offenders herein shall be punished as abettors and maintainers of traitors : wherein We are resolutely determined to suffer no favour to be used for any respect of any persons, qualities or degrees : nor shall allow nor suffer to be allowed any excuse of negligence for not detection, or for not due examination of the qualities of such dangerous persons, according to the order hereafter prescribed, being no wise contrary, but agreeable to the most ancient laws and good usages of Our realm, devised for the good order of all manner of subjects in every precinct of every leet, to be forthcoming, to answer for their behaviours towards the Dignity of Our Crown, and the common peace of Our realm.

'Given at Our Manor of Richmond, the 18th of October, 1591, in the 33rd year of Our reign.'

Instructions set forth for the guidance of the commissioners show the form of questions to be put to those suspected of being recusants. The commissioners shall obtain from the *custos rotulorum*, the clerk of the peace, or the clerk of assizes, the names of those suspected, but their names not to be published unless some probable cause appear why they should be examined or apprehended. Nor shall suspected persons be pressed to answer any matter touching the conscience in religion, other than whether they usually come to Church or not; if they appear wilful recusants, then are they to be examined concerning their allegiance to the Queen, and of their devotion to the Pope or to the King of Spain, and whether they maintain any Jesuits, Seminaries, priests or other persons sent from beyond the seas to dissuade the Queen's subjects from their allegiance. In every town or large parish where the parsons or vicars are faithful and careful of their cures, they are to be urged to observe all such as refuse obstinately to come to Church. Those called before the commissioners, but not punished by the law, to be warned that their recusancy causeth them to be suspected of being disloyal in the duties towards the Queen and State or of favouring the common enemies.

25th November. THE SIEGE OF ROUEN.

The Earl of Essex hath returned from Rouen, which is now besieged. There have been skirmishes but nothing of great moment.

On the 4th November in the night there sallied out of the Castle against the quarter of Monsieur Flavencourt 400 soldiers, burnt it over his head and slew as many as stood the defence, took his baggage, his horses and mules; but were at last forced to retire by certain Gascons and a regiment of French, leaving on the ground 26 dead and 8 prisoners, of whom two were English and one Spanish.

The next day one of the enemy's horse issued forth, a brave fellow all in crimson velvet, and called out one of ours to the sword on horseback, which he bravely answered and wounded his enemy in two places, and would have brought him in prisoner, had he not been rescued by his fellows. The Lord General the same day invited the three Colonels of the Switzers and there was general drinking of healths till some of them were sick and asleep. After dinner the General's party went out and came near a gate of the town where Villiers, the Governor of Dieppe, was quartered, and it happened that he was there with some twenty horse. Seeing the General's party he drew out certain shot and so began to come up the hill; but the General knowing who he was called to him and said he would speak with him at a blow with a sword or pistol, but he answered nothing except the shot of four or five harquebus. On the 7th our horsemen brought in some sixty kine, as well as sheep and swine. There came too a soldier from the Governor of Dieppe, sent from his master to the General, who reported that they had great desire to force the English quarter. There was a hot skirmish both of horse and foot near the castle of St. Katherine, where the people of the town stood on the bulwarks of the town, beholding as if it had been a triumph or a sport.

The Governor's Challenge

On the 9th a trumpet of one Jerpenville being sent into the town, Villiers the Governor desired him to signify to the Lord General that whereas he had sent unto Chevalier Pickard to break a pike with him, he would the next day bring him into the field, either armed or in his doublet, to answer his challenge; and if he listed he would bring sixteen of his gentlemen against sixteen of the General's.

To this the Earl of Essex answered in writing, that at his first coming into France he was occasioned to send his drums thither, understanding that the Chevalier Pickard was in the town, to tell him that he was sorry for old acquaintance that he should persist in so bad an action and against so brave a King. But since it were so, he would be glad to find him at the head of his troop with a pike. And he was to know that he was a General of an army from an absolute Prince in which there were many chevaliers, Pickard's equal at least. Besides, that if he or any others had desire to find him, all those of his could justify that the first day of his sitting down here he was twice at the head of his troop and offered to charge ; and he refused and wheeled about. But for that he himself was in some respect of his government, he challenged him that he would make it good upon him either armed or in his doublet ; that the King's cause was more just and honest than that he upheld of the League, that he himself was a better man than he, and his mistress fairer than his. And if he would have help and parley, he would bring twenty of like quality to Chevalier Pickard, or sixty, that the meanest of them should be a Captain in Chief.

The answer of Villiers was received on the 11th to the effect that, in saying the cause of the King was juster cause than that of the League's and that the General was a better man than he was, he did lie ; and would fight thereon when the Duc de Mayne should come.

To this the Earl answered by trumpet that his lie was very frivolous and did no way concern him considering it was not given him upon a good ground ; yet eftsoons he did call him to the maintenance of that he had denied, and if he did not answer now, he had no excuse ; then shame and infamy must light upon him, which was generally spoken of him by all the French themselves.

The Governor also sent a challenge to any foot captain, man to man with shot and with rapier, which was accepted ; and Captain Acton, desirous of that combat, had his name sent to the Governor. But in the end they made excuses and nothing came of it.

On the 13th after breakfast, the General went to the Marshal's quarters accompanied by sundry gentlemen in their best attire to meet the King, when all dismounted to kiss his hand, and he alighted to embrace the Marshal and the General ; after which they brought him to his quarter and went to council.

The 16th it was rumoured, as it had been ever since he came, that the King was going to Dieppe to hasten provisions and necessaries ; but some of his servants said that his journey was to meet a Saint (for he owed devotion to more than one Gabriel only) to whom he had long been devout, whose body was transported thither from Caen, that his devotion and his vows might be performed with more ease.

On the 19th about twelve o'clock at night some of the King's nobility and eight gentlemen approached the castle of St. Katherine, and there the pioneers began to build a fort, and, because it could not be finished in one night, the King's nobles and twenty-five of the Lord General's principal gentlemen, armed with pikes, came thither to guard against any sally that should be made out of the town or castle; and about an hour after day, the King himself came to cheer the pioneers to work and the rest to a resolute defence. The King seemed very desirous of some sport, and turning to Mr. Thomas Coningsby asked him whether the enemy would sally or no; who answered that if they were honest men they should, but if they were Englishmen they would; to which the King replied, 'By my faith, I believe it.' In the evening came news that the Lord General was to return to England in the morning.

On the 20th the Lord General rose very early and went towards the King's quarters, having first despatched and ordered many things for the army, and so accompanied with Sir Henry Unton and many others he alighted on a fair plain, and there he knighted Sir Henry Killigrew. After despatching his business in the King's quarters he took his journey towards Dieppe.

26th November. THE QUEEN'S LETTERS TO THE EMPEROR OF RUSSIA.

Sir George Barnes, who tradeth much with Russia, understanding that the Queen, at the request of the King of Scotland, is about to write to the Emperor of Russia for the enlargement of a Scottish Captain, a prisoner in Moscow, writes to the Lord Treasurer that since the Queen hath sent several letters for particular men and causes of little moment, it is said in the Emperor's Court that the Queen of England's letters are very cheap.

ABUSES IN THE CLOTH TRADE.

The Council being desirous of repressing certain abuses in the cloth trade have written to the Queen's Attorney General and others asking them for their advice. In the reign of King Edward the Sixth and of King Philip and Queen Mary certain laws were made concerning the true and perfect making of the cloth called Devonshire kerseys or dozens whereby a certain length, breadth and weight was presented, the penalty being laid on the clothier ; but now slight and bad devices put in use by weavers prevent the good intended by that statute. These weavers escape because no provision was made in the statute for their punishment.

THE CHARGES OF THE BORDEAUX FLEET.

A charge of 3s. on the tun of all wines and other merchandise is to be levied on all wines and other merchandise arriving from the ports of Rochelle and Bordeaux at any port in England to cover the cost of waftage for the fleet. These charges fell formerly on the merchants of London, but as the ships of other ports take advantage of the convoy they shall be borne by all.

4th December. A PETITION OF THE PURITAN PRISONERS.

Thomas Cartwright and eight other Puritan prisoners have petitioned the Lord Treasurer praying that they may be allowed bail until the Council is pleased to call them for further trial of their innocency. His lordship, say they, will easily discern that over a year's imprisonment strikes deep into their healths. It is well known that divers papists, who not only deny the Queen's lawful authority but give it to a stranger, a sworn enemy of theirs and all other Christians, yet receive favour of freedom from their imprisonment. Never a one of them but has been sworn to the Queen's supremacy and is ready to take the oath again.

ORDERS FOR REFORMING THE ARMY IN NORMANDY.

Orders are sent by the Council for the better ordering and reforming of the army in Normandy under the Earl of Essex. He shall cause all captains of the foot bands to deliver on oath perfect rolls of all their officers and soldiers showing those now serviceable and any others remaining there sick and unable to serve ; and in another roll the names of all that first came over with them but are not now present, making a distinction of those sent away by passport, those dead, and those that have run away ; further they shall deliver in the roll a certain note of all the armour and weapons of those no longer in service, and where it is.

Having received these rolls the Lieutenant General shall consider how many bands of 150 (allowing 15 dead pays) or how many bands of 100 (allowing 10 dead pays) can be made of the whole number. And because this cannot be done without cassing some of the bands, he shall, for an example, cass his own band of 200, and also the bands of those receiving special allowance as officers of the army or colonels of regiments; also the bands which are weakest.

He shall take special care to preserve the ordnance and munition from water, and to recover, if he can, such as have fled away from the Queen's service. If they are apprehended in France they should be hanged as they deserve, and proclamation made that any who presume to come over to England will be hanged up whensoever he shall be apprehended.

5th December. AN UNSUCCESSFUL AMBUSCADE AT ROUEN.

From Rouen it is reported that the commanders taking at heart the ill success of a recent skirmish in which two brave soldiers had been killed and their bodies lost, planned to lay an ambuscade on the 30th November. Captain Barton with 24 shot hid in the cellar of a house pulled down near the ditch and town port; Captain Henry Power in another place with 16 pikes; and some shot of Monsieur Hallard Mountmorency on the other side of the port. This ambush being laid before day, about 8 o'clock the enemy opened the ports and came to the usual place of the court of guard, which was some six or eight score paces from the port.

After they had been there a while and set out their sentinels, Sir Roger Williams and the choicest of the gentlemen being in the trenches, caused some musketeers to shoot at their sentinels and sent other shot to beat them in. As the skirmish grew warm, our men according to directions retreated to bring the enemy more within danger of the ambuscade; then the sign was given, which was the throwing up of a hat with feathers of Sir Thomas Baskerville. But this was not observed by Captain Barton, who should first have discovered himself, so that our men were fain to call and cry, which caused the enemy to suspect and to retreat as fast as their legs could carry them to the port. Captain Barton, for want of better speed than they fell short of them, but some four or six were said to have fallen, and our men had the spoil of the court of guard, some cloaks and weapons.

As our men retreated some artillery were shot, one of which lighted upon Monsieur Hallard Mountmorency, slaying his horse and breaking his leg below the knee.

6th December. GREENE'S 'A MAIDEN'S DREAM.'

A Maiden's Dream; upon the death of the Right Honourable Sir Christopher Hatton, written by Robert Greene, is entered, being dedicated to the Lady Elizabeth Hatton, to whom he noteth that, having long wished to gratify the father with something worthy of himself, he now takes opportunity to show his duty to him in his daughter. In this funeral elegy is shown the complaint of Justice, of Prudence, of Fortitude, Temperance, Beauty, Hospitality, and Religion; and of primates, soldiers, and people for the loss of the Lord Chancellor, ending with the maiden's vision of the soul of Sir Christopher carried by Astraea among the hierarchies:

> 'With that methought within her golden lap,
> (This sunbright goddess smiling with her eye,)
> The soul of Hatton curiously did wrap,
> And in a cloud was taken up on high.
> Vain dreams are fond, but thus as then dreamt I,
> And more, methought I heard the angels sing
> An "Alleluia" for to welcome him.'

10th December. SEVEN CATHOLICS EXECUTED.

White, Plassden and Lacy, Jesuit priests, with two lay Catholics, taken by Topcliffe at the beginning of November, were executed at Tyburn. Edmund Jennings, the Jesuit, and Mr. Swithin Wells were dragged on hurdles to Holborn, over against Mr. Wells' house, where Jennings was discovered saying Mass. When Jennings arrived at the gallows he began to say, '*O Crux diu desiderata et iam concupiscenti animo praeparata*.' Being bade to confess his treason, for so the Queen would doubtless pardon him, he answered, 'I know not ever to have offended her. If to say Mass be treason, I confess I have done it and glory in it.' These words so enraged Topcliffe that he refused him leave to say any more, scarcely even to recite the *Pater noster*, but caused him to be turned off the ladder and the rope immediately cut. Jennings was thus thrown on his feet, but the hangman tripped up his heels, cut off his members and disembowelled him. In this agony Jennings began to call on St. Gregory to the great astonishment of the hangman, who cried out with a loud voice, 'God's wounds! his heart is in my hand and yet Gregory is in his mouth.'

13th December. GREENE'S 'NOTABLE DISCOVERY OF COSNAGE' AND 'THE SECOND PART OF CONNY-CATCHING.'

Robert Greene that was wont to write for the pleasure of our gentlemen and ladies hath penned a *Notable Discovery of Cosnage* and *The Second Part of Conny-Catching* now that riper days call him to repentance. These books are for the commodity of his countrymen, to warn them, and especially merchants, farmers, and honest-minded yeomen, against the practisers of the Art of Conny-Catching and the Art of Crossbiting.

For the Art of Conny-Catching, or cosening at card play, there be needed three parties, the setter to draw in the conny (that is to be cheated) familiarly to drink with him, the verser to join them in the tavern and to offer to play with them, and the barnacle appearing to be but a stranger that is invited to join them. The barnacle and the verser begin to cut the cards, and the verser, asking the conny secretly by signs if he will help him to cheat the barnacle, begins his game, and at the first winneth the stakes until the conny is also drawn in and venturing a high stake, by some sleight the cut falls against him and he is cheated of all.

The art of crossbiting is the practice of harlots and their mates that entice a young man into their houses and there either pick his pockets or else, on the woman sending for her husband or friend, the crossbiters fall upon him and threaten him with Bridewell and the law so that for fear he gives up his purse or makes them out a bill to pay a sum of money by a certain day.

In the *Second Part of Conny-Catching* are displayed the villainies of the nip and the foist, the priggar, the Vincent's law, the lifting law, the courber, and the black art.

The nip and the foist, though their subject, a well-lined purse, is the same, yet is their manner different; the nip using a knife to cut the purse, the foist his hand to draw the pocket. These foists holding themselves to be of the highest degree term themselves Gentlemen foists, and so much disdain to be called cutpurses that the foist refuseth even to wear a knife about him lest he be suspected to be a nip.

The priggar is the stealer of horses. The courber worketh with a hook or curb, made with joints (like an angle rod that he might hide it beneath his cloak), which he thrusteth through at a window to draw out what he shall find. The black art is the picking of locks, and Vincent's law the cheating at bowls.

It was objected by some that read the first book that Greene used no eloquent phrases as in his former works, and to this he answereth that it were an odious thing to apply a fine style to so base a subject.

15th December. THE DEFENCE OF PLYMOUTH.

The Council write to Sir John Gilbert, Sir Francis Drake and other gentlemen concerning the defence of the town of Plymouth against any sudden attempt that the enemy might make. As they are not resolved whether it is better to build a fort on the sea side within or near the town, or else to make a wall about the town, they instruct these gentlemen to seek the advice of some skilful engineer to view the circuit and to estimate the charge after a certain rate by the perch. Towards this charge besides the sums which the country might be induced to contribute the Queen will be pleased to grant an imposition to be laid upon each tun of pilchards taken out of Plymouth; and because the time is past for this season they deem it best that they should deal with the county to induce them to disburse by way of loan or otherwise such reasonable sums of money as may begin and maintain the work until the next season. But before they proceed with the work they should advertise the Council what they shall resolve and what hope they find of their endeavours with the county for beginning it.

A NEGLIGENT COMMISSARY DISMISSED.

Thomas Wyatt, commissary for the companies in the Low Countries dispersed under Sir Francis Vere, is dismissed from his post, having neglected to send over certificates or muster rolls of the companies whereby their strength might be discerned. By reason of his omission the strength of the companies lately sent into France was not known, so that instead of 1000 complete with the dead pays but 638 arrived, which numbers might have been redressed, if it had appeared before by his timely certificate.

16th December. SIR CHRISTOPHER HATTON'S FUNERAL.

Sir Christopher Hatton was this day honourably buried in St. Paul's; one hundred poor people having gowns and caps given them going before; of gentlemen, and yeomen, in gowns, cloaks and coats, more than three hundred, with the Lords of the Council and others, besides fourscore of the Guard which followed.

17th December. MASTERLESS MEN IN THE CITY TO BE TAKEN UP.

The Lord Mayor and Aldermen are required to take up within the City and liberties of London 100 loose and masterless men, there being at this time a great many, especially of those returned from service in France. These men are to be sent forthwith to Ostend in Flanders to complete the companies serving there under Sir Edward Norris. The men are to be bestowed in Leadenhall or some other fit place where they can be kept together and not allowed to slip away until the whole number is complete; and thence to be safely conveyed to their shipping near about St. Katherine's. The manner employed, either by privy search in the night or otherwise, is referred to their discretion. Orders have already been taken by Sir Edward for their victualling until they be embarked so that the City shall not be charged with them.

18th December. TWO SUSPECTED RECUSANTS.

The Attorney General and the Solicitor General are to examine two Englishmen, Anthony Skinner and Richard Acliffe, who were apprehended at Gravesend coming up the river in a small boat of Calais. These men are both recusants and had been absent from the realm for eight years, remaining for the most part at Rome, the one as servant to Cardinal Allen, the other with the Bishop of Cassano.

A NOTABLE INSTANCE OF THE CORRUPTION OF THESE WARS.

A gentleman that had a fair house in a village not far from Rouen was desirous to have protection from the Lord General, who promised to provide him with a certain quantity of oats and hay weekly. Two Englishmen were sent to guard his house, but certain of Monsieur Hallard Mountmorency's lackeys coming for forage to the village roughly intreated them and took away their horses. Whereupon, returning to their master, the following night at midnight, forty cuirassiers entered the house, with force took the two Englishmen prisoners, wounded the master to death, spoiled his house, took the Englishmen's horses and all his; and the next news heard was that the Englishmen were prisoners in Rouen, having been sold to the enemy.

19th December. Further Measures against Recusants.

The Commissioners specially chosen to inquire into the secret repair into the realm of Jesuits and seminary priests are warned that as the special commission will be renewed when necessary, they shall privately inform the Council whether any in the commission are suspected to be unsound in religion or have wives, children or any of their families known recusants or harbour persons suspected to be backward in religion. Moreover if they find the number not sufficient or not so placed for their habitations that they may divide the service, or that others meet to be employed in this service are omitted, they are likewise to certify their names and dwelling places, with their opinions of the men.

21st December. Masterless Men to be taken up in Kent.

The Lord Mayor hath not been able to find above eighty masterless men in the City for service in the Low Countries. The Lord Cobham is now to give order to his Deputy Lieutenants in the County of Kent to take up loose and vagrant persons to make up the total number to one hundred.

24th December. A Highhanded Arrest.

The Recorder of the City of London is summoned to appear before the Council on St. Stephen's Day to declare upon what foundation he subscribed a warrant whereby one Paine was taken out of his lodging in the night by a constable and a servant of his and a dozen persons, servants and friends of Sir Francis Willoughby, and conveyed to the Counter in Wood Street, there to be forthcoming to answer divers points touching high treason. They think it strange for him to be committed to prison upon treason that should hereafter be laid to his charge, as though a man should be made prisoner before his offence was known.

26th December. The Tripoli Merchants recommended to Charity.

There be six Turks lately arrived from France in an English vessel, of whom three are said to be of the guard of the Grand Signior. They allege that they have been retained more than twenty years as slaves in the galleys of the Spanish King before they found means to escape. These men have made humble suit to the merchants trading in Tripoli to be relieved by the loan of some hundred crowns, offering to be bound to repay the money when they come to the first place of Turkish dominion, before they set foot on shore. The Council recommend their request to the merchants, praying and requiring them to furnish this aid, which would be gratefully accepted by the Grand Signior and the other people in general of that country.

Beacon Watches.

Beacon watches are now to be discontinued until 15th March; but nevertheless the beacons to be kept in good order and furnished with sufficient fuel to be used if cause should require.

29th December. Goods rifled from Prizes in Cornwall and Devon to be restored.

The captains of the London ships in the Lord Thomas Howard's fleet are reported to have carried their prizes into remote ports and havens and there enriched themselves by rifling the prizes and selling divers parcels to persons dwelling in the port towns, to the great slander and prejudice of sea discipline and wrong to the merchant adventurers of London. Her Majesty not willing to suffer so great a disorder now causeth proclamation to be made in Cornwall, Devonshire, Dorsetshire and Hampshire straightly charging all that in any ways have received any foreign coin, bullion of gold or silver, jewels, pearls, stones, musk, wrought or raw silk, cochenilia, indigo or other merchandise, within ten days to bring in a note of it in writing showing the prices they paid and the names of those off whom they bought, declaring also the day, time, and place. Those not obeying this order shall be held and taken as felons and abettors to pirates, and proceeded against as in the case of felony is customary to be done by the law of the realm.

THE SIEGE OF ROUEN.

From Rouen there is news of a sally made by the enemy on the 6th of the month, who came on with such speed that the sentinels had no leisure to give the court of guard any warning but by coming away without resistance. They quitted three of Hallard Mountmorency's courts of guard, not without the loss of their lives. The fourth court of guard, where the greatest strength lay, was a large house without a roof, the walls being a pike length high, with many loopholes to shoot out at. The enemy, with men for the purpose excellently well armed, by the advantage of the walls got to the top and leaped in amongst them most resolutely, putting to the sword all within, and those that escaped there fell upon the horsemen who had the like mercy. The horsemen advanced so far that our sentinels and the rest quitted the trenches, but Sir Thomas Gerrard at the instant drew out the guard of the day into the field to make stand, and gave alarm to all our army which came out full fast.

When the enemy perceived the fast stand of our pikes, they had no will to come nearer, but after some discharge of pistols towards our forward gallants, when Captain Barton was dangerously hurt in the face, seeing 150 of our pioneers coming out with their pikes, they retired and our men repossessed the trenches. After the fight nearly fifty dead were counted in the court of guard. Two captains in chief were slain, and two gentlemen of especial mark, both whose bodies the enemy took away. Soon after there grew a new alarm, and our men began to run in panic but were stopped by Sir Roger Williams, Sir Thomas Baskerville, Sir Thomas Gerrard and other gentlemen.

On the 7th Sir Richard Acton died of the disease of the camp, a pestilent ague, now very prevalent.

On the 12th, a sergeant of the pioneers was discovered to be conspiring to lead away fifty or sixty of the principalest into Rouen. Whereupon a Council of War was held, and all brought to the tree but the sergeant only executed for example in presence of them all.

On the 14th the Lord General returned to the army from England, and notwithstanding his long and great journey, he would needs before alighting go down to the trenches, and, hearing of the great threatenings which were expected, must call to a sentinel of the enemy and bid him tell Monsieur Villiers that he was come with some twenty gentlemen with him ; and that if he would enterprise anything against the English quarter he must do it that night or never, for the next day we should be too strong for him, there being 2000 English of the old bands of the Low Countries coming this night.

On the 17th and 18th muster was taken, and it was found that there were less than 200 horse. The 25 old companies were reduced to 8, and those short of their number. On the 19th the bands of the Low Countries were mustered, and five of them sent to another quarter where they watched every third night, and the Lord General himself with many other principal gentlemen also watching every third night within three pikes length of the enemy's guard, where they had continual shooting. The Lord General had great speech with Monsieur Pickard, who asked for his mistress that he had in England, and promised to come and dine with him one day.

On the 24th the Lord General went to the trenches with many, where they forced the enemy from the counterscarp and slew many, taking cloaks, weapons and the like. Marshal Biron took upon him to defend the ground that was won, which was of great importance, but the enemy sallying out in great numbers the next day about eleven o'clock forced the guard there. Our men fought bravely for about half an hour, never seconded of the French ; the soldiers spending all their powder and shot, and the enemy with great fury driving down the barrels of earth. Sir Thomas Baskerville saw no remedy, but to sally out, and beat them with the pike and halbert, but he was slenderly followed, and forced to retire, abandoned of too many of our common soldiers ; but seventeen gentlemen and officers rallied and made a stand.

SOMEWHAT TO READ FOR THEM THAT LIST

1591

CLAPHAM'S 'NARCISSUS.'

Narcissus, siue Amoris iuvenilis et praecipue Philautiae breuis atque moralis descriptio, written in Latin hexameter verses, and dedicated to Henry, Earl of Southampton, by John Clapham. Herein Narcissus,

quem luminis orba
Prosperitas genuit, peperit Superbia vana,
Et tepido erroris nutriuit Opinio lacte,

being smitten by the arrow of love came to the fountain Philautia, and there falling in love with his own image, cried out to it; but was answered back in mockery by Echo. Night coming on, the image vanished, and the infatuate youth unable anywhere to find his love, fell from the bank into the river and so perished.

COSIN'S 'APOLOGY FOR SUNDRY PROCEEDINGS.'

An Apology: of and for sundry proceedings by jurisdiction Ecclesiastical, of later times by some challenged, and also diversly impugned by them, written by Dr. Richard Cosin, though without the name either of author or printer on its title. He noteth that of late certain disturbers of Her Majesty's happy reformation had rested themselves most in advancing a new-found discipline and in discrediting the present government Ecclesiastical by their speeches and writings, as well by impugning the callings and form of Ecclesiastical government as by defaming the persons of the governors with unchristian gibes, contumelies and other indignities. But when these had not succeeded according to their wish, they pursue a more politic course; for by themselves, and others more simple excited cunningly by them, they challenge divers received proceedings in Courts Ecclesiastical as not justifiable by law; and by their frequent clamours, some very grave, wise and learned (no way affected to their other fancies), either not being well informed of proceedings Ecclesiastical, or not weighing for want of leisure certain points doubtfully reported in the book of common law as their learning doth afford. In a kind of commiseration toward some of those who seem distressed and to be otherwise well meaning men divers proceedings Ecclesiastical have lately been called in question, both for matter and for circumstance and manner, that they are contrary to the laws of this realm.

Therefore he taketh in hand to show the reasons for the contrary based on the law and the Scriptures.

DIGGES' 'PANTOMETRIA.'

A new edition of *A Geometrical practical treatise named Pantometria*, revised by the author, Mr. Thomas Digges and his son, Mr. Leonard Digges. This book besides giving the theories of Geometry, addeth many engravings showing the practical use of measuring distances and heights with such instruments as the quadrant geometrical, the geometrical square, the theodolitus, the measuring of plane surfaces, the contents of solids, and so forth.

GARRARD'S 'ART OF WAR.'

The Art of War, written by William Garrard, gentleman, who had served the King of Spain in his wars of fourteen years and died in 1587, corrected and finished by Captain Hitchcock, dedicated to the Earl of Essex. Herein are five books, of which the first treateth of the behaviour of a good soldier, disnier or corporal, together with the martial laws of the field; the second, adorned with many figures, the office of a sergeant, ensign bearer, lieutenant, and gentlemen of a band; the third of the governing of bands, squadrons and battles, of captains, colonels, and sergeant-majors-general; the fourth of the general of horsemen, the scout-master, and the office of the marshal of the field; the fifth of the great master of the artillery, of the master gunner, and of general notes of fortification; of the besieging, expugning and defending of a fortress.

GIBBON'S 'WORK WORTH THE READING.'

A Work worth the Reading, by Charles Gibbon, of Bury St. Edmunds, dedicated to Sir Nicholas Bacon, wherein is contained five profitable and pithy questions, *videlicet*: 1st, whether the election of the parents is to be preferred before the affection of their children in marriages; 2nd, whether the father may lawfully disinherit his first born; 3rd, whether a reasonable allowance may be taken for lending of money; 4th, whether the rich or the poor are to be accounted most blessed; 5th, whether there be degrees of glory in Heaven or differences of pains in Hell. These questions are argued by Philogus and Tychicus, two lovers of learning, the latter supporting his arguments more from the Scriptures, the former rather from common experience.

Of the rights of parents in marriage Tychicus saith that if a man may bestow his goods to whom he will, he may as well bestow his children where he thinketh best, for children are the goods of the parents. To which Philogus answereth that if parents impose upon their children a match more to content their desire for more than their children's godly choice for love then they should not be obeyed, for what greater occasion of incontinency could be given than to match a young and lusty maid against her own mind with an infirm and decrepit person to satisfy another's pleasure? To this Tychicus replieth that to match a young maid and an old man is indeed most miserable.

GILES FLETCHER'S 'OF THE RUSSE COMMONWEALTH.'

The Book of the Russe Commonwealth, by Mr. Giles Fletcher (that was employed in the Queen's service to the Emperor of Russia in 1588), being dedicated to the Queen. Herein is described the cosmography of the country; the ordering of the state, with the condition of the commonality or vulgar sort; the judicial procedure; their warlike provisions and martial discipline; the ecclesiastical state; ending with a chapter upon the œconomy or private behaviour of the people of that nation.

The Emperor of the country is a person of mean stature, somewhat low and gross, of a sallow complexion, and inclining to the dropsy, hawk nosed, unsteady in his pace by reason of some weakness of his limbs, heavy and inactive, yet commonly smiling, almost to a laughter. For quality otherwise simple or slow witted, but very gentle and of an easy nature, quiet, merciful, of no martial disposition, nor greatly apt for matter of policy, very superstitious, and infinite that way.

The Russe because he is used to extremities both of heat and cold beareth both very patiently. They can be seen coming out of their bath stoves, all on a froth, and fuming as hot almost as a pig at a spit, and straightway to leap into the river stark naked, and that in the coldest of winter time. The women to mend the bad hue of their skins, use to paint their faces with white and red colours so visibly that any man can perceive it. But this is no matter, because it is common and liked well by their husbands, who make them an ordinary allowance to buy colours to paint their faces, delighting themselves much to see their foul women become fair images. This practice parcheth the skin, and helpeth to deform them when their painting is off.

Of the vulgar sort he noteth that they are much oppressed by the nobility so that though otherwise hardened to bear any toil, they give themselves to idleness and drinking, as passing no more than from hand to mouth.

Quercetanus' 'Spageric Preparation of Minerals, Animals, and Vegetables.'

The true and perfect spageric preparation of minerals, animals and vegetables, originally written by Dr. Josephus Quercetanus of Armenia, now set forth with divers rare secrets not heretofore known of many, by John Hester, a practitioner in the spagerical art; and dedicated to Sir Robert Carey.

Amongst those remedies especially recommended for the plague is a preparation of mummy (in former times prepared of bodies embalmed with pitch, frankincense, myrrh or aloes, but now made only of dried flesh), either in liquid, balm or tincture; also *balsamum urinae*, which Mr. Hester regardeth almost as *catholicum* in its uses.

This tincture to be made thus: 'Take the urine of young children about the age of twelve years, that hath drunk wine for certain months if it be possible; the same putrefy *in balneo* or dung a philosopher's year; then distil it with a gentle fire in sand, being also luted, the which ye shall note diligently. The flame ye shall put upon the feces four times; then the last water keep close shut, the which is white and stinking, and therefore ye may give it both taste and smell with cinnamon and sugar. The feces that remained in the bottom being black ye shall sublime by degrees of fire, and you shall have a most precious salt, the which some affirm will dissolve gold, silver and other metals; some philosophers call it their *menstrua*.'

'THE TROUBLESOME REIGN OF KING JOHN.'

The two parts of *The Troublesome Reign of King John*, a play that hath been sundry times acted by the Queen's players in the City of London. In the first part is shown the discovery of King Richard Cordelion's base son (commonly named the Bastard Faulconbridge), the wars in France and the supposed death of Arthur, being a play very fitting to the times, as the prologue proclaimeth:

> You that with friendly grace of smoothed brow
> Have entertained the Scythian Tamburlane
> And given applause unto an Infidel,
> Vouchsafe to welcome, with like courtesy,
> A warlike Christian and your countryman.
> For Christ's true faith indured he many a storm,
> And set himself against the Man of Rome,
> Until base treason (by a damned wight)
> Did all his former triumphs put to flight,
> Accept of it, sweet gentles, in good sort,
> And think it was prepared for your disport.

In the second part is portrayed the death of Arthur Plantagenet, the landing of Lewis, and the poisoning of King John at Swinstead Abbey.

WILMOT'S 'TANCRED AND GISMUND.'

The Tragedy of Tancred and Gismund, compiled and acted by Robert Wilmot and other gentlemen of the Inner Temple before the Queen more than twenty years before, being newly revised and polished according to the decorum of these days, on the importunity of some of Mr. Wilmot's friends. This tragedy, whereof the story is taken from Boccaccio, is written after the pattern of the ancients, the action being related and not shown upon the stage.

1592

1st January. SPENSER'S 'DAPHNAIDA.'

Mr. Edmund Spenser hath sent his *Daphnaida, an Elegy upon the death of the noble and virtuous Douglas Howard, daughter and heir of Henry Howard, Viscount Bindon, and wife of Arthur Gorges, Esquire,* to the Lady Helena, Marquess of Northampton, wherein in the form of a pastoral Alcyon complains of the death of his Daphne.

3rd January. ANOTHER PROCLAMATION AGAINST THE DISORDERS AT PORTS.

Information hath now been given that some of the Captains, Masters and Mariners besides those in the west broke bulk and made spoil of goods on the seas before their ships had come to port. Another proclamation in terms similar to that of the 29th December is now published, commanding all such offenders to declare themselves in writing within twenty days.

7th January. THE LEVANT COMPANY.

The Levant Company are granted a patent allowing them with other privileges the sole right of trading to the Levant Seas, Turkey and Venice, and of importing the small fruits called 'currants,' being the raisins of Corinth.

THE COMMISSION AGAINST JESUITS RENEWED.

The Commission for enquiry of Jesuits and Seminaries is renewed for the counties of Kent, Buckingham, Middlesex, Surrey and Durham.

MR. HENRY CAESAR RELEASED.

Mr. Henry Caesar that was committed to the charge and custody of Sir Richard Martin for his recusancy is now to be released, since the Council learn that through conference of learned preachers he now conforms himself in religion, professing that he is indeed resolved in his conscience according to the truth. They therefore let him understand that they see no cause but that he may be set at liberty to be at the disposition of his brother, Dr. Julius Caesar, who means to place him at the University for his better instruction and furtherance in learning.

9th January. A PROTEST ON BEHALF OF THE PURITANS.

Sir Francis Knollys hath written to the Lord Treasurer on behalf of the Puritans still in prison that he marvels how the Queen can be persuaded that she is in as much danger of the Puritans as of the Papists; for she cannot be ignorant that the Puritans are not able to change the government of the clergy but by petition; and even then the Queen could not do it but she must call a parliament for it, and no act could pass unless she give her royal assent thereto. As for their seditious conduct, if the bishops or the Lord Chancellor or any of them could have proved *de facto* that Cartwright and his fellow prisoners had gone about any such matter seditiously, then they had been hanged before this. But the Queen must keep a form of justice as well against Puritans as any other subjects, and they tried in convenient time, whether suspected for sedition or treason or Puritanism or by whatever name it is called.

AN ATTORNEY'S UNSEEMLY APPAREL.

One King, an attorney in the Court of Common Pleas, that was committed to prison for his misdemeanour in raising and laying the street for the assisting of an arrest with lewd words which were likely to have bred some tumult, was brought before the Council. And because he appears before their Lordships in apparel unfit for his calling, with a gilt rapier, extreme great ruffs, and like unseemly apparel, they certify the Lord Chief Justice of the Common Pleas of his behaviour that he shall be dismissed of his office and place in that Court.

16th January. A CASE OF CONTRABAND GOODS.

This day the Privy Council heard a cause between the Earl of Cumberland and one Harman Langerman, factor for certain merchants of the Stoad Towns, of whom some ships and goods appertaining were taken on the seas by the Earl. He claimed them as good prize going into Spain by the North Seas, being laden with prohibited goods of divers sorts for the use of the enemy. Amongst these was canvas of six sundry sorts which was claimed as prize being fit for use as sails for ships of war, for cartilages for powder and like use for the wars; but which Langerman said served only for merchandise.

The controversy had been referred to Sir John Hawkins and William Burrows, officers of the Admiralty, and to four men skilful in these matters, two chosen by each party. Whose report being heard and also what Langerman could say on his own behalf, the Council consider that the fourth and fifth sort of these canvases, called euphards or soutages, might be used for sails and other necessary purposes for the seas and for wars; yet, because Langerman shows that the merchants of the Steeds did not understand the sorts of canvases to be prohibited, they offer that either Langerman shall receive of the Earl the sum of £300 for all the two sorts of canvases, or shall give the Earl £300 and himself take the canvases, or else that they shall be sold to the uttermost value and one half to be given to Langerman. The sixth sort of canvas called guttings, which they judge to be of the nature of merchandise and not for any use in war, shall be delivered back to Langerman.

They also require Langerman to certify his countrymen that the kind of canvas called euphards as well as the other three kinds of canvas are reputed as wares prohibited, and may not be carried into Spain so long as the King of Spain should continue his hostility against the Queen's majesty and her dominions.

CERTAIN GOODS PROHIBITED TO BE CARRIED TO SPAIN.

Notwithstanding former warnings to the citizens of the Hanze Towns and Stade that they should forbear to send into Spain or Portugal any kind of provision fit for the wars upon pain of confiscation, the enemy is daily being furnished with corn, munition, and other things. The Council now add to the list of prohibited wares iron, steel, all sorts of weapons, planks, deal boards, wainscot, pipe staves, flax, tow, hemp and resin.

19th January. THE EARL OF ESSEX RETURNS TO COURT.

The Earl of Essex on his return from France hath come to the Court, and being received very graciously by the Queen is able to allay her anger with Sir Henry Unton, the ambassador, for that he had allowed the Earl to see a certain letter of hers. This letter was sent to Sir Henry by Sir Robert Cecil, written in Her Majesty's own hand, and to be shown to the Earl only if

he refused to return to England. When the packet of letters reached the ambassador, being brought by one of my Lord's servants and delivered in his presence, he required the packet to be opened forthwith, saying that he hoped there were letters for him. Upon Sir Henry opening the packet, my Lord seeing a letter addressed to himself, snatched it out of his hands before he had time to read that letter of Sir Robert Cecil's which accompanied it. The Queen hath hitherto been much displeased that her letter should have reached the Earl's hands thus, and by the hands of the Lord Treasurer had severely censured the ambassador. Moreover the Earl speaketh very highly of the ambassador's good services to the Queen, who is thus appeased. It is believed that his return to Court will make the Queen more favourable to helping the French King.

22nd January. A PROCLAMATION TO REFORM ABUSES IN THE CLOTH TRADE.

A proclamation is published for the reformation of sundry abuses about making of cloths, called Devonshire kersies or dozens, ordering that from the Feast of the Annunciation of Our Lady these cloths as they come raw from the weaver's beam shall weigh fifteen pounds at the least and contain between fifteen and sixteen yards in length.

8th January. A SPECIAL COMMISSION TO DEAL WITH IMPRISONED RECUSANTS.

Owing to matters of greater weight and importance, to which the members of the Council are bound to attend, some prisoners suspected of being Jesuits or Seminaries from over seas remain for a long time without being thoroughly heard or examined. A special commission of twelve gentlemen, amongst them Sir Richard Martin, Mr. Sergeant Fleetwood, the Recorder of London, Richard Topcliffe and Richard Young, is now appointed. On any special cause three or more of them shall summon such persons before them, and for their better proceeding the keepers of the prisons shall deliver weekly the names of such prisoners as they have received. They meet once a week in some convenient place, either at the prison or some place near, to examine them on such information as they receive. Moreover as some are prisoners at large, and some may be bestowed in prisons not fit for them to remain by reason of favour shown to them, the commissioners will take order, as they think fit, for their more straight keeping or removing to other prisons.

30th January. FLESH PROHIBITED DURING LENT.

The Lords-Lieutenant of the counties near London are charged that the orders restraining the use of flesh during the time of Lent shall be put in execution and not as in former years so neglected that at this time of the year wherein young cattle should most be spared for increase a greater quantity is killed than in any other season. The money received from the butchers for their licences is reserved for the use of poor soldiers, lame, impotent or maimed in the wars.

4th February. DANIEL'S 'DELIA.'

Delia, containing certain sonnets, by Samuel Daniel, is entered. In the Epistle Dedicatory to the Lady Mary, Countess of Pembroke, Mr. Daniel writeth that although he rather desired to keep in the private passions of his youth from the multitude, as things uttered to himself and consecrated to silence, yet seeing that he was betrayed by the indiscretion of a greedy printer and had some of his secrets betrayed to the world uncorrected, doubting the like of the rest, he is thus forced to publish that which he never meant.

6th February. NEWS FROM FRANCE.

The news from France is that the Duke of Parma is likely to give battle, and if he doth not besiege some town by the way will reach Rouen within a week. Sir Henry Unton, the ambassador, is not only out of favour with the Queen over the matter of her letter to Essex, but with the King, who is advertised that he hath done ill offices for him with the Queen.

SIR FRANCIS WILLOUGHBY BEFORE THE COUNCIL.

Sir Francis Willoughby was called before the Council at the suit of Robert Paine, a prisoner in the King's Bench, for certain hard and unconscionable dealings offered by his servants, which appeared to their Lordships to be rather of malice than of any good ground or proof. They move him to have a charitable consideration of the poor man's estate, to which he willingly consenteth, promising to write letters to his servants to cease their negotiations and to redeliver his writings, goods, and other things taken away, if they should be found wrongfully detained. Sir Francis is accordingly dismissed of his farther attendance, but Paine remitted to the prison of the King's Bench to follow his trial for the criminal matters alleged against him.

7th February. GREENE'S 'THIRD PART OF CONNY-CATCHING.'

Greene hath written a *Third and last part of Conny-Catching, with the newly devised knavish art of fool-taking.* Herein are set forth notes of the devices of the conny-catchers delivered to him by a certain justice of the peace, and showing how divers had been beguiled.

12th February. THE QUEEN REFUSES FURTHER AID TO THE FRENCH KING.

Notwithstanding the letters of the King, and the solicitations of the French ambassador to yield more succour, the Queen will in no wise be induced to consent, though no more than 1500 men are required, 3000 having been asked for at first. Some fourteen days since the Lord Treasurer made ready letters and warrants for the Queen to have sent over one or two thousand pikemen; but when they came to the signing, she changed her mind, and ever since denies it, putting forward these reasons:

Firstly, her former offence against the King for that the last summer he neglected the taking of Rouen which he might have done, and yet wasted his own people and her treasure to no purpose.

Secondly, she thinketh so hardly of the King's fortune and success that she is loath to adventure any more of her people with him.

Thirdly, she thinketh it impossible to levy and send any power out of the country to be able to join with the King's forces before the Duke of Parma should force the King to battle.

Lastly, she is loath to send 2000 of her men out of the Low Country, and to hazard and waste her disciplined soldiers; for if need be to have their service in England she will be greatly disappointed by the loss of them.

But in truth the Queen and her realm are become very weary with the great expense both in loans of money, and in waging of men both by land and sea.

14th February. NEWS FROM FRANCE.

From France it is reported by the ambassador that the Duke of Parma hath captured Neuchâtel upon honourable composition, a place of great advantage to the enemy.

On the 7th the King was engaged with the enemy, and in the fight the Count Challigny (the Duke Mercury's brother) who commanded them was taken prisoner by Chicott, the King's fool, and very sore hurt. Many were slain and some captured; the rest escaping gave the alarum to the Duke of Guise's quarter, who barricaded their lodgings, and armed themselves. Most of their horse and foot sallied out, but by this time many shot had come up to the Baron de Biron and the enemy were forced back into Bures, where the King's men entering pell-mell with them slew two hundred in the village and took divers prisoners. The rest were forced to retire to the other side of the river. All the Duke of Guise's baggage was taken, his plate and money, and all he had there.

In this engagement Sir William Sackville is either taken or slain, having been separated from the rest. For himself the ambassador declareth that he is in great straits; all his horses are dead or harried out, for they never rest, being on horseback almost day and night; his servants die daily, and many of them are very weak and sick and cannot live long.

The King meanwhile anxiously expects succour from England.

15th February. FLESH PROHIBITED IN LONDON DURING LENT.

As in former years, killing and eating flesh in London during Lent is restrained.

19th February. PLAYING RESUMED.

The Lord Strange's Players now begin to play at the Rose Theatre on the Bankside, and act this day *Friar Bacon*.

THE QUEEN RESOLVES TO SEND SOLDIERS TO FRANCE.

The Queen having now resolved that 1600 soldiers shall be sent with diligence to Dieppe to the aid of the French King, the Council have ordered 300 to be levied in Sussex, which in heads are to be only 270, deducting the dead pays after the usual rate of 10 in the hundred, to be coated and armed forthwith and embarked at Rye; similarly another 300 from Kent to be embarked at Dover on the 28th of the month.

20th February. NEWS OF ROUEN.

Two lackeys of Monsieur Villiers, Governor of Rouen, taken returning from the Duke of Parma, who has now advanced to Cinqsens, declare that he would succour Rouen or force the levying of the siege.

21st February. THOMAS PORMORT, A JESUIT, EXECUTED.

Thomas Pormort, a seminary priest, was executed for high treason. This Pormort, being lodged in the house of Topcliffe after his arrest in October 1591, had been pressed very straightly to give information. He declared that in the course of these examinations Topcliffe, hoping to persuade him to recant, used very lewd and familiar speeches to him to show his favour with the Queen. Topcliffe said that all the Stanleys in England were to be suspected as traitors; he himself was so familiar with Her Majesty that he hath very secret dealing with her, having not only seen her legs and knees but felt her belly, saying to her that it was the softest belly of any womankind. She had said unto him, 'Be not these the arms, legs and body of King Henry?' to which he answered 'Yea.' She gave him for a favour a white linen hose wrought with white silk. He said that he was so familiar with her that when he pleased to speak with her he might take her away from any company; and that she was as pleasant with anyone that she loved. The Archbishop of Canterbury, he declared, was a fitter councillor in the kitchen among wenches than in a Prince's Court; as for Justice Young, he would hang the Archbishop and three hundred more if they were in his hands.

At the execution Pormort was forced to stand in his shirt almost two hours on a very cold day while Topcliffe pressed him to deny these words; but he would not.

23rd February. A LITIGIOUS FELLOW.

The magistrates of Essex are directed to look into the case of one, John Feltwell, of Great Wendon. This man, a very contentious person, cited certain inhabitants of the parish into the

Ecclesiastical Courts of London for tithes which had been answered, and, purposely to undo them, put in long and tedious libels, the copies of which were for the most part eighty sheets of paper, so that the poor men were not able to take them out by reason of the charges, much less to follow the causes at law. As this Feltwell, to avoid arrests and processes to be served on himself at the suit of sundry persons whom he has wronged, often removes as a fugitive to unknown places, the magistrates are to examine the matter and to make such good end therein that the poor men shall have no further cause to trouble the Council.

Sir R. Williams in Command in Normandy.

On the return of the Lord General from Normandy Sir Robert Williams succeedeth to the command.

24th February. Victuals sent to Normandy.

It is said that some hard measure was offered to the Vice-Treasurer by the captains of bands in Normandy for refusing to satisfy them in their undue demands of pay for soldiers under them. Sir Roger Williams is instructed to cause this matter to be reformed and to require the captains to forbear to demand their pay till a muster can be made; and also to let them know that the matter is very offensively taken.

As there hath been so great waste and spoil made in Normandy that victual will be scant and dear, a supply to the value of £1000 is being sent over with the 1600 men under Sir Edmund Yorke, to remain in magazine at Dieppe for the relief of the forces when needful but not otherwise. The price of this victual is to be defalked accordingly from the captains' weekly payments.

The rates to be charged for victual:

Beer, 3 pints - -	2d.	Cheese, 1 lb. - - - -	3d.
Biscuit, 1 lb. - -	1½d.	Beef, 1 lb. - - - -	3d.
Butter, 1 lb. - -	5d.	Bacon and Pork, 1 lb. -	5d.

25th February. A Petition against Plays.

The Lord Mayor of London hath complained to the Archbishop of Canterbury of the daily and disorderly exercise of players and playing houses erected in the City whereby, saith he, the youth is greatly corrupted and their manners infected by the wanton and profane devices represented on the stages prentices and servants withdrawn from their work; and all sorts in general from their daily resort to sermons and other godly exercise, to the great hindrance of the trades and traders of the City and the profanation of religion. To the playing houses resort great numbers of light and lewd persons, harlots, cutpurses, coseners, pilferers, and such like. The Lord Mayor understandeth that the Queen must be served by this sort of people, and for this purpose did licence Mr. Tilney, the Master of the Revels, to reform, exercise and suppress all manner of players, by which he first licensed the playing houses within the City, for the Queen's service. But the Aldermen conclude that the Queen's players might as conveniently exercise in some private place, the City be freed from these continual disorders, and the great offence to the Church removed which would be to the contentment of all good Christians, especially the preachers and ministers who have long time made complaint for the redress of these abuses.

26th February. PLAYS OF THE WEEK.

The plays acted at the Rose Theatre this past week were *Muly Mullocco*, *Orlando Furioso*, *The Spanish Comedy*, *Sir John Maundeville*, *Harry of Cornwall*, *The Jew of Malta*.

THE DUKE OF PARMA RETREATS.

The ambassador now reporteth that on the 18th the King dislodged his whole army from Claire, fully resolved to give the Duke of Parma battle rather than to suffer his siege to be raised, for he had heard that the night before the Duke had marched from his camp near Cinqsens, with the greatest part of his vanguard to Cinqsens and Bellencombre with intent to raise the siege or thrust succours into Rouen. But the enemy, having received news of this intent, and being advertised of the effect of the last sally, retired with all possible diligence to Aumale, intending to go along the river to Abbeville. The next day the enemy lodged at Sinarpoint; and the next day still continued his way to Abbeville. This sudden retreat and the diligence used therein cannot be understood, neither is the siege raised nor the town succoured, except that a few men are sent in by stealth, 15 or 20 in a company at several times.

28th February. Maimed Soldiers to be Examined.

A proclamation signed by the Lords of the Privy Council is published ordering all soldiers who allege that they have served in the wars and still remain in London to be brought before those appointed at the Sessions Hall in the Old Bailey on Saturday next at one o'clock. They are to be examined and viewed so that some good order may be taken for the maimed in service, and for the punishment of the others, common beggars, rogues and able persons, counterfeiting the name of soldiers.

29th February. The Scottish Witches.

A pamphlet is printed called *News from Scotland* declaring the damnable life and death of Doctor Fian, a noted sorcerer who was executed at Edinburgh in January last, together with the examination of the witches, as they were uttered in the presence of the Scottish King.

The conspiracy of these witches was first brought to light by one David Seaton, deputy bailiff of the town of Trewent. This Seaton had a maid servant called Geillis Duncan that used secretly to be absent from her master's house every other night when she took in hand almost miraculously to help all that were troubled with any kind of sickness or infirmity, which caused such wonder that her master began to suspect these things to be done by some unnatural or extraordinary means. Whereupon he began to be very inquisitive, and when she gave him no answer, that he might the better learn the truth, with the help of others he tormented her with the torture of the pilliwinks upon her fingers and by binding a rope round her head. Still she would not confess anything, which made them suspect that she had been marked by the devil, and making diligent search about her they found the enemy's mark in her throat, whereon she confessed that all her doings were done by witchcraft through the wicked allurement of the devil.

After her confession she was committed to prison, where through her accusations she caused certain other notorious witches to be apprehended, notably Agnes Sampson of Haddington, and Dr. Fian, *alias* John Cunningham, master of the school at Saltpans in Lowthian. This Agnes Sampson was brought to Holyrood House before the King and others of the nobility of

Scotland, but stiffly denied all that was alleged against her, whereon they caused her to be taken back to prison, there to receive the tortures which had lately been provided for witches. Moreover it has been found by careful examination of witches and witchcraft, and by the confession of the witches themselves, that the devil marketh them with some secret mark; for when he receives them as his servants he licketh them with his tongue in some privy part of the body, which is commonly covered with hair, so this mark may not easily be seen, and so long as the devil's mark is not seen by the searchers the witch will not confess to anything.

For over an hour this Agnes Sampson was grievously tortured with a rope thrawen round her head, according to the Scottish custom, but would confess nothing until the devil's mark was found upon her privities, when immediately she confessed all that was demanded of her. And now being again brought before the King she confessed that on All Hallowe'en last she with a great company of other witches, to the number of two hundred, had gone to sea, each one in a riddle or sieve, drinking and making merry as they sailed until they came to the kirk of North Berwick in Lowthian, where they landed and danced a reel; Geillis Duncan going before them playing on a small trumpet, called a 'Jews' trump,' until they entered the kirk. This declaration so astonished the King that he sent for Geillis Duncan, who played this dance upon the trumpet before him, much delighted to be present at such strange examinations.

Agnes Sampson said further that the devil in likeness of a man had waited for their coming at North Berwick kirk, and being vexed that they tarried over long in the journey had enjoined on them a penance, which was to kiss his buttocks in sign of duty to him. Then he made an ungodly exhortation, greatly inveighing against the King of Scotland; and took their oaths for their good and true service. So they returned to sea and home again. At this time the witches asked the devil why he so hated the King of Scotland, and he replied that the King was his greatest enemy in all the world.

Sundry other things Agnes Sampson confessed before the King so strange and miraculous that he said they were all extreme liars. Whereupon she answered that she would discover a matter whereby he should not doubt. So taking him a little aside, she declared the very words which had passed between him and his Queen at Upslo in Norway the first night of their marriage, with their answers one to the other ; whereat the King wondered greatly and swore by the living God that he believed all the devils in hell could not have discovered the same, acknowledging that her words were most true. Thereafter he gave more credit to what she confessed.

The examination of Dr. Fian also showed the great subtlety of the devil ; for being apprehended at the accusation of Geillis Duncan, when he was tortured with the accustomed torments his tongue would not serve him to speak until the rest of the witches bad them search under his tongue, where two pins were found thrust up to the head. At this the witches cried, 'Now is the charm stinted.' Then he was immediately released and brought before the King ; his confession was taken, and he willingly set his hand to it. Amongst other things confessed, he declared that he had sought the love of a gentlewoman by witchcraft and sorcery. This gentlewoman being unmarried had a brother who went to his school. Calling the boy to him he asked if he slept with his sister ; he answered that he did. Therefore Dr. Fian secretly promised the boy that if he would bring three hairs of his sister's body he would teach him without stripes, giving him a piece of conjured paper to wrap them in.

The gentlewoman being asleep with the boy suddenly cried out to her mother that her brother would not let her sleep ; whereon her mother, having a quick understanding, for she was a witch herself, rose immediately and asked the boy very closely what he meant, and the better to extort the truth she beat him. The mother recognising the doctor's purpose thought it best to answer him in his own art, so she took the paper from the boy in which he should have wrapped his sister's hair and went to a young heifer which had never gone to the bull and clipping off three hairs from the udder she told the boy to deliver them to his master, which he immediately did.

As soon as the schoolmaster had received them, he wrought his art upon them, thinking that they were the maiden's hairs ; but no sooner had he conjured than the heifer whose hairs they indeed were came to the door of the church where he was, and made towards him, leaping and dancing upon him, and following him out of the church and wherever he went, to the great astonishment of all the townsmen of Saltpans.

Having signed this confession Dr. Fian was taken back to prison, where for a time he appeared very penitent, but in the night he found means to steal the key of the prison door, which he opened and fled away to Saltpans. Hot pursuit was made after him, and he was taken and brought back to prison. There being called before the King he was again examined concerning his flight and what had happened before. But notwithstanding his former confession, he utterly denied all. The King therefore thinking that he had made a fresh league with the devil, commanded a new and most strange torment to be applied to him. The nails on his fingers were split and pulled off with a pair of pincers and under every nail were thrust two needles up to the heads. But for all this, and for the torments of the boots which followed, he would not confess, but said that what he had said and done before was for fear of the pains which he had endured. After great consideration by the King and his Council, Dr. Fian was arraigned and condemned to be burned according to the law of the land. Whereupon he was put in a cart, and being first strangled was cast into a fire made ready and so burned on the Castlehill in Edinburgh on a Saturday at the end of January last past.

1st March. MEN TO BE IMPRESTED FOR SERVICE IN FRANCE.

As well as the 330 already impressed, the Lord Mayor is to cause 200 able and sufficient men to be taken up and delivered to Sir Matthew Morgan; and because there are but 400 men musketeers in the whole 1600 soldiers and it is thought that more shots in proportion to the number of the pikes are needful, so these 200 serve as shot.

SIR EDMUND YORKE'S INSTRUCTIONS.

Sir Edmund Yorke is required immediately on his arrival at Dieppe to muster all his companies and to deal very earnestly with the Governor of Dieppe in the Queen's name to take strict order that no bark or vessel whatever receive any English soldier that cannot show his licence to depart.

ANOTHER PETITION OF THE PURITAN PRISONERS.

Thomas Cartwright and the other Puritan prisoners have again written to the Lord Treasurer asking for release from imprisonment on bail. If, say they, they have transgressed some of the laws of the land, whereof their consciences set in the presence of God do not accuse them, yet seeing it plainly appears by their own answers on oath and by the depositions of witnesses that they have special care in their meetings to keep within obedience of the laws, their transgression, being of ignorance, may find the easier pardon.

Since their coming to prison, divers papists, known enemies of the state, of the Church and commonwealth, have been delivered without renovation of any error ; and it is universally granted to any, either papist or schismatic, that upon promise of coming into the Church, they enjoy the same freedom as other subjects. Their hope therefore is that they who not only come to church but labour to the utmost to entertain men in the fellowship of the Church and to reduce others estranged from it, should not be more hardly dealt with in being forced to any confessions or submissions against the testimony of their consciences. Moreover by reason of their long imprisonment and lack of convenient air some five or six of them are sore and dangerously sick.

2nd March. SIR WALTER RALEGH'S EXPEDITION.

A proclamation is published ordering all mariners, who are pressed to serve with Sir Walter Ralegh, Captain of her Majesty's Guard, to repair to their ships immediately, upon pain of death, so that the service be in no way delayed.

3rd March. MUSTER ROLLS IN THE COUNTIES.

The Lords-Lieutenant of the Counties of Somerset, Wiltshire, Monmouth, Pembroke, Anglesey, Cornwall, Chester, Devon, Huntingdon, Sussex, Rutland, Leicester and York, are rebuked for their slackness in rendering a certificate of the forces of their several counties and again required to certify how many able men there are, how many trained and received into bands, how many untrained, under what captains and officers, and how furnished with horse and weapon. The numbers of those taken out of the trained bands for foreign services, to be supplied by good and able men sorted with such arms and weapons as the others so that the trained and enrolled bands be whole and complete for the defence of the country.

At the same time the Council commend the zeal of the Lords-Lieutenant of Berkshire, Cambridge, the Isle of Ely, Suffolk, Norfolk, Surrey, Kent, Buckingham, Bedford, Dorset and Gloucester.

THE FISHMONGERS REBUKED FOR NEGLECTING TO SUPERVISE THE BUTCHERS.

The Wardens of the Fishmongers' Company are rebuked for their negligence in carrying out the restraint of the killing and uttering of flesh in Lent, for where they were authorised to appoint some trusty and discreet persons to search the houses and shops of victuallers, they did appoint but some mean men for that purpose who negligently execute it. Though but one butcher is licensed for the County of Middlesex and six for the City, there are twenty about the City and suburbs that licentiously and contemptuously kill and utter flesh. The Wardens are therefore to appoint at least six discreet persons of their company to repair at least twice a week to the houses of those butchers not licensed to sell flesh, and if any be found offending they shall not only lose the flesh found in their shops but be carried before the Mayor or some of the Justices and by them committed to prison, bonds being taken of them to answer the same at the next Sessions.

4th March. PLAYS OF THE WEEK.

The plays at the Rose Theatre this past week were *Cloris and Ergasto*, *Muly Mullocco*, *Pope Joan*, *Machiavel*, *Harry the Sixth* (for the first time), *Bindo and Richardo*.

5th March. RUMOURS OF PEACE.

The ambassador in France reporteth that the French King is resolved to conclude a peace with his subjects upon any reasonable conditions, to which they are now as much inclined as himself, being weary of the Spanish yoke, and that it is likely to take effect.

7th March. REPORT OF SIR JOHN NORRIS ON THE STATE OF FRANCE.

Sir John Norris, who has been called home from Brittany to report on the state of affairs in France, saith that the retreat of the Duke of Parma is not because he intendeth to desert those of his party besieged in Rouen but to join certain troops that come to him under conduct of the Duke of Brunswick and the Count Mansfield, nor is it because of some fear of confusion in the Low Countries, nor of dislike or disagreement with the French. Had this been so he would have hastened to his own Government, and not have taken care to fortify the Bridge of St. Remy where he passed. Seeing his obstinacy in continuing enterprises and his jealousy for reputation, it is likely that he will venture the extremity of his fortune rather than that Rouen be taken.

He doubteth whether the King's army can hope for any good event of the siege. His French disband very fast, all those of Normandy being already retired, his rutters are diminished and will shortly want pay, his lance-knights so decayed with want and sickness that not above 3000 are left, his Switzers ready every day to mutiny. The greatest ground of the siege lies upon the English and Dutch, and whether they are strong enough to take the town when the Duke of Parma shall seek to succour it must be advised on; or whether the King, leaving the siege if the Duke of Parma should approach, should be able to compel him to fight.

Brittany is in worse case, for the King of Spain has continual care to see his party strengthened; they are possessed of the best towns, and have but weak enemies; only the Queen's assistance kept them well the last year, and as that decayed, so they prevailed; and if it be not now increased, the whole province will be lost, for it is a vain hope to attend any succour from the King. Its maintenance must proceed from her Majesty, and the longer it is deferred, the more difficult will it be; and if much time passes before it is looked into it will be irrecoverable.

Orders against those who aided Deserters.

The Lord Mayor is required to cause verbal proclamation to be made throughout the City and suburbs that all victuallers, innkeepers, alehouse keepers and others having in their houses any soldier that has been levied shall upon severe penalties bring him forth to receive punishment according to the laws. Likewise if any soldier hath run away from his captain and sold or pawned his armour and furniture, it shall be seized and the party with whom it is found committed to prison.

8th March. UNDUTIFUL GENTLEMEN.

Some of the inhabitants of Middlesex, divers of them gentlemen of good calling, and some being her Majesty's servants, very wilfully refuse to bear their contribution in the levy of sums of money for the setting forth of soldiers and other public services, so that oftentimes for the expedition of the service the Justices are themselves constrained to disburse money for armour, weapons, and other provisions, whereof some are not yet satisfied for money disbursed three years since. The Council have instructed the Justices to will and require these persons, of what quality and sort soever, to contribute the sums demanded of them (excepting only the ordinary yeomen and grooms of her Majesty's Chambers). If by this gentle disposition they be not drawn to do that which in all duty and good respects they ought to do, their names to be sent to the Council that their perverse disposition may be made known to her Majesty.

9th March. A SPANISH PRISONER'S ACCOUNT OF THE STATE OF ENGLAND.

A certain Spanish prisoner that was released about a month since hath declared that many of all conditions, men and women, assured him of their good wishes for the success of the Spanish in England, and their zeal for the Catholic faith. If they do not openly avow their sympathy it is that they may not lose homes and possessions; others confess themselves Catholics, and, though they have suffered many punishments, yet openly say that they will remain firm and die in the faith. Many complaints, saith he, are made of the large number of declared Catholics, and the Queen is petitioned to have them punished, but she hath ordered that such complaints should not be made against them, and that they shall be allowed to live freely as they wished. There is great fear of the galleys and their commander. Sir Francis Drake is very unpopular, the people of quality saying that he is but of mean origin to have risen so high, the common people regarding him as the cause of the wars; but the Queen esteemeth him highly. They cannot bear the name of

Don Antonio, who is called 'The King of Portugal,' as he is considered the cause of all the wars in Portugal. They threaten to stone him, and it is said that the Queen keeps him in a castle which he does not leave. He is miserably poor, lacking both money and servants.

11th March. PLAYS OF THE WEEK.

The plays at the Rose Theatre this past week were *Four Plays in One*, *Harry the Sixth*, *A Looking Glass for London*, *Zenobia*, *The Jew of Malta*, *Harry the Sixth*.

12th March. THE EARL OF BOTHWELL AND THE SCOTTISH BORDER.

The Wardens of Border are bidden to keep watch for the Earl of Bothwell and his complices in the late treasonable attempt on the Scottish King at Holyrood House, since they are reported to have been received into the northern parts of the kingdom. Thus is the Queen's government maliciously slandered as though her realm by her permission or offer were a refuge to the rebels of the Scottish King, with whom she is in good amity. Special search is to be made at the races and running of horses in the wardenry of the Lord Scroop, and knowledge of this order to be given to the opposite Wardens or their deputies, requiring them to advertise if they know or suspect any of the rebels to be in this realm.

18th March. PLAYS OF THE WEEK.

The plays at the Rose Theatre this past week were *The Spanish Comedy*, *The Spanish Tragedy*, *Harry the Sixth*, *Muly Mullocco*, *The Jew of Malta*.

21st March. HOPEFUL NEWS FROM FRANCE.

The Ambassador in France reporteth that the King and his Council resolve to batter Rouen, though everything is done by the Catholics in his army to hinder that resolution. The King now awaiteth the coming of the English, and then will immediately begin his approaches. The Governor of Rouen hath lately much angered the burgesses by a stratagem to enrich himself by a trick. Some days since a part of the wall of the town fell down, leaving a breach of forty paces. Thereupon Monsieur Villiers assembled the people, using feigned persuasions to them to make a composition with the King and alleging that the late succours were not sufficient for their defence, the Duke of Parma had retired and that the King was resolved to batter the town. On this speech sixty of the burgesses, best inclined to the King's service, answered that they would very willingly agree to his motion; then these men, well noted by the Governor, were sent for from their houses, and made prisoners, being forced to pay great ransoms at his pleasure for their release.

The late offer of a peace is likely to come to nothing, for the first part of the Leaguers' demand will be for the King to become a Catholic. They have proffered it but to confuse the King, distaste his Catholics, and to better their condition with Spain.

24th March. Volunteers to be Levied in London.

The Lord Mayor and the Justices of Peace for the County of Middlesex now begin to impress and take up 200 voluntary men to fill up the companies of the bands remaining in Brittany under Sir John Norris.

25th March. Distress in Rouen.

The garrison of Rouen are reported to be daily thrusting out forty or fifty women and many prentices; they want wine and have forbidden the making of beer because they would spend no corn in drink. They cannot hold out longer than two months if the King do not force them otherwise to yield. Two thousand French that had disbanded have rejoined the army and more return daily in hope of spoil at Rouen. Sir Edmund Yorke with twelve companies arrived at Dieppe on the 18th.

Plays of the Week.

The plays at the Rose Theatre this past week were *The Spanish Tragedy*, *Constantine*, *Jerusalem*, *Harry of Cornwall*, *Friar Bacon*.

Complaints against the Governor of Ostend.

Complaints against Sir Edward Norris, Governor of Ostend, have been renewed by the Council of the States of the United Provinces. The Council now give orders that he shall repair to them when they should send for him to satisfy their demands and yield account of how the contributions of the country have been expended, and to clear himself of the imputations preferred against him ; but they in requiring his presence should make choice of a fit time so that the enemy may have no advantage by his absence. When they have viewed his accounts and heard what he can say in his own defence and excuse, they shall not give any sentence or decree against him until the Queen hath been duly informed. She hath given order in respect of the dislike which they conceive of him, that, if they be not satisfied with his answers, he shall be recalled home as soon as he is dismissed by them to be charged with those matters wherein they find fault with him.

RECUSANCY IN THE NORTH.

The Earl of Derby is much commended for his zeal in the reformation of his tenants from their sinfulness in not resorting to their parish churches. He hath also joined with the Commissioners to reduce the recusants throughout Lancashire, now almost overflown with a multitude of obstinate persons, offending publicly in the sight of the world, as it seemeth without any fear of punishment. Her Majesty greatly allows of their honourable, wise and politic proceedings ; and the Council pray him not to stay the good cause begun in restraining the principal obstinate recusants either by imprisonment or by committing them to the custody of such as be sound in religion.

This course is a most necessary to be taken in the present dangerous state of the country ; nor should the reformation be delayed by following a long course in answering strictly all the statutes, howsoever any of the Justices may have delivered their opinions upon the strict point of law, not respecting what is most necessary at this time and in that county. If any should repine against his former proceedings upon conceit that any Justice or learned man showeth opinions to the contrary, he is to be forthcoming and caused to declare the name of the Justice who shall be charged therewith, as a matter not any wise allowable.

27th March. THE CASE OF ROBERT PAINE.

Dr. Aubrey and Mr. Justice Peryam are to examine the controversies between the widow of Robert Paine, lately deceased, and Sir Francis Willoughby, and either to conclude a final end between them or to report their full proceedings and opinions to the Council.

CAPTAIN GLEMHAM'S SHIPS TO BE STAYED.

It appeareth that certain goods and merchandise have lately been taken out of a Venetian argosy at sea by Captain Glemham and his consorts. The Council order that any of his ships that be found shall be stayed and the goods in them sequestered, and six of his chiefest ships stayed.

31st March. THE PURITAN PRISONERS RELEASED.

The Puritan prisoners are now released from prison, the Council being pleased that the charges against them should no further be proceeded with.

1st April. PLAYS OF THE WEEK AT THE ROSE.

This past week were played *The Looking Glass for London*, *Harry the Sixth*, *Muly Mullocco*, *The Spanish Comedy*, *The Spanish Tragedy*, *Sir John Maundeville*.

2nd April. MERCY TO BE SHOWN TO DEBTORS.

Some time since Commissioners were appointed to inquire into the causes of poor prisoners detained a long time in prison for debt. They report that the adverse parties will not be reduced to conformity or commiseration. Now are the Council moved by the pitiful complaints of the prisoners, and by reports that of late very many of them are dead in prison, whereby their creditors lose all their debts, whereof in time they might have received a good part if not the whole sum.

But if no persuasion or intreaty shall move the creditors to compassion, then shall they be plainly let to understand, that, if at any time information be brought against them upon a penal statute, or other advantage taken against them in any matter by the strictness of the law, let them look for no favour but all extremity that may be used.

If they refuse still, the Commissioners shall advertise the Judges of the Queen's Bench and Common Pleas to send for the parties to see what they shall be able to prevail with these wilful and hard hearted persons ; and if they will still by no means be brought to reasonable order, the Judges to let them understand that they must look for like measure and to have no favour at their hands.

7th April. Two Prisoners' Ransom.

Some time since John Dipford and Walter Horsey, merchants of Exeter, sent their servants John Gupwell and Thomas Dipford to the town of Lanyon in Brittany with lawful merchandise. Not only did the Leaguers take their goods but committed the men to prison to the Castle of Callett near Morlaix, whence Thomas Dipford was released on ransom, but Gupwell is held to ransom by the first of May or else is threatened with execution. For the relief of their losses and the discharge of their servants' ransoms, the Council instruct the customers of Dartmouth and Opsam to permit these merchants to transport 20 packs of kerseys, 4 packs of broad cloths, 3 packs of bays, and 3 packs of coarse cloth stockings, after paying the customs due, in a bark of twenty or thirty tons.

Distress in Rouen.

It appeareth that Rouen is in some distress for victual by the disbanding of many soldiers of the garrison who daily leave the town and submit themselves to the King's mercy, whereby the King and his Council have great hope of the timely rendering of the town if it be not relieved by the return of the Duke of Parma.

8th April. Plays of the Week.

The plays at the Rose Theatre this week were *Machiavel*, *The Jew of Malta*, *Harry the Sixth*, *Brandimer*, *The Spanish Tragedy*, *Muly Mullocco*.

12th April. Breton's 'The Pilgrimage to Paradise' and 'The Countess of Pembroke's Love.'

The Pilgrimage to Paradise, joined with *The Countess of Pembroke's Love*, compiled in verse by Nicholas Breton, gentleman, is sent to the press. The first telleth of the journeyings of the Soul, with his five servants the senses, past the snaring temptations of the flesh until he reaches an angel by whom he is forewarned against the beast with seven heads which are ambition, avarice, gluttony, sloth, lechery, malice, and murder, and protected with seven books by which, after long debate, the monster is slain. At length the pilgrim comes to a fisherman with whom he sails and who tells him his story. And continuing their way they meet a world of people making piteous moan:

> The courtier, he complained of love's disgrace,
> The soldier, he cried out of lack of pay,
> The lawyer, lack of hearing of his case,
> The client, how his coin went to decay,
>   The merchant of the loss of his adventure,
>   The prentice of the bands of his indenture.
>
> The landlord, of his tenants' beggary,
> The passenger, of lack of amity,
> The tenant, of the landlord's misery,
> The beggar all of lack of charity,
>   The churchmen of their small possessions,
>   The laymen of the Church transgressions.

And past these to an army set out in the field, and to a city sacked till the pilgrims reached the true Church

> Where sacred Mercy first did solemnise
> The Spirit to the Flesh in marriage,
>   And here the heart did find his spirit blest
>   To bring the senses to eternal rest.

In *The Countess of Pembroke's Love* he likeneth her to a phœnix in rarity, aspiring to the Heavenly Love and despising all earthly gifts which men of all kinds and degrees brought in to her.

15th April. PLAYS OF THE WEEK.

At the Rose Theatre this week past *The Spanish Comedy*, *Titus and Vespasian* (for the first time), *Bindo and Richardo*, *Harry the Sixth*, *The Jew of Malta*, *Sir John Maundeville*.

16th April. A FRAY AT FULHAM.

William Arnold, yeoman, was journeying to his father's house at Fulham between six and seven in the evening when a certain Peter Jones came up to him, calling out, 'Sirrah, sirrah, you with the long sword, stay for I must talk with you.' To whom Arnold answered, 'I have nothing to say to thee'; whereon Jones assaulted Arnold, and in the ensuing affray received a blow in the breast of which he died then and there.

English Mariners Forbidden to Sail with a Stranger.

Information has been given that there is at Dartmouth a flyboat of Enghuizen called *The Dolphin* prepared to go to Flushing and the Newfound Land, that, for her better conduct, intends to be furnished with English mariners. The Council order that no English pilot, master or mariner, in any wise be permitted to go either in that ship or in any other strange bottom to the Newfound Land. If (notwithstanding the Queen's straight commandment) any person be hired for lucre by a stranger, he shall be committed to prison for his contempt.

17th April. The Siege of Rouen Raised.

It is reported from France that the siege of Rouen is raised, the King having been suddenly advertised that the Duke of Parma was marching towards his camp with 12,000 foot and 4000 horse. He was within four leagues of Rouen before the army rose, using all possible diligence in his march to surprise the King and defeat his army of rutters in their lodgings and the English troops in their quarters. This was only prevented by the discovery and advertisement of the Duke of Boullion, who made his retreat with the rutters in view of the Duke of Parma's army with great hazard and no loss. Thus the King's army was forced to march away with all haste, and at its rising had very hot skirmishes but without loss. Sir Roger Williams' horse was shot, and his hat in two places ; he served very honourably with great courage and discretion in the view of the King, greatly to his commendation, as did many of the English who were the last to retreat.

That night the army encamped within a league of Pont de L'Arch, expecting the coming of the Duke of Parma to give battle whereunto the Duke of Mayne and Villiers earnestly pressed him. Whereupon the King was immediately advertised and made choice of the place of battle, fortifying and trenching the place.

The Duke of Parma lodged at Croissett, and his army along the river. He sent to all castles and gentlemen's houses where was great store of corn to cause them to bring it to Rouen.

21st April. 'The Defence of Conny-Catching.'

The conny-catchers have one 'Cuthbert Connycatcher' that answers Greene in a book called *The Defence of Conny-Catching, or a Confession of those two injurious pamphlets published by R. G. against the practitioners of many nimble witted and mystical sciences.* Herein Greene is attacked for having touched small scapes but let gross faults pass without any reprehension, and himself accused of conny-catching; 'ask the Queen's players if you sold them not *Orlando Furioso* for 20 nobles, and when they were in the country sold the same play to the Lord Admiral's men for as much more?' And to show the nature of more gross abuses examples are given of the villainy of an usurer; a miller; a serving man, counterfeiting to be gentlemen to make a good match; a man that was married to sixteen wives but well cured by the last; and a tailor.

22nd April. Plays of the Week.

The plays at the Rose this past week were *Muly Mullocco*, *The Jew of Malta*, *The Looking Glass for London*, *Titus and Vespasian*, *Harry the Sixth*, *The Comedy of Jeronimo.*

The Enghuizen Ship Released.

Notwithstanding direction formerly given, the Council order that a ship called *The Lion of London*, with the master and mariners, may be allowed to pass to the fishing at the Newfound Land, and likewise the ship of Enghuizen now at Dartmouth to go on her intended voyage, provided that she hath in her no English masters or mariners soever.

27th April. The French King attacks Parma.

The Ambassador reporteth that on the 17th Caudebec surrendered by composition to the Duke of Parma, who had encamped his army within a league of Ivetot in open field where he was strongly entrenched; the Dukes of Mayne and Guise with 2000 horse and 1200 foot, lodging at Ivetot. Hereupon the King marched towards them with all his army in order of battle, and ten pieces of artillery, until he was within a mile and a half. There he made a stand, and himself with 500 horse advanced further to discover the enemy. The Duke of Mayne showed himself with 1000 horse, whom the King charged with two troops of horse and pursued to their quarter, in which charge Monsieur Coutenan, a special commander of horse, was taken prisoner, who assured the King that the Duke of Parma had but then taken the alarm of his coming and would not believe that the King durst look upon him ; if he did, he was resolved to give battle.

This news much contented the King, who retired in time to lodge his army in the villages, preparing the next day to give the Duke of Parma battle, if he would accept it, near Ivetot in a fair champaign field.

Early in the morning (18th) the King drew all his forces together waiting for the enemy ; but finding no likelihood of their preparation to fight, he resolved to force their lodging of Ivetot, and to lodge there himself in despite of them or else to force them to accept the battle. He therefore marched with his whole army, advancing certain cuirassiers and harquebusiers on horseback to observe the enemy's countenance who were now marching towards him with horse and foot. On perceiving the King with his forces to come on so resolutely, they retired most dishonourably, quitting their quarter and setting it on fire, and fled in disorder until they came to the Duke of Parma's camp. The King with his horse had them in chase, himself conducting them, killing many and taking some gentlemen prisoners, amongst them the Baron of Chastre, son of Monsieur Chastre. The Duke of Mayne hardly escaped, for he fled so fast that his horse was like to have failed him for want of breath.

That night the King lodged at Ivetot, and the rest of the army in the villages a league beyond it, within three-quarters of a mile of the Duke of Parma's intrenchment, who was much amated with this dishonour, imagining that he was betrayed by his French.

The 19th the King's army stayed at Ivetot, offering many skirmishes to the enemy, which they coldly entertained.

The 20th the King dislodged with his army and marched to Varqueville, a mile and a half from Ivetot towards Newhaven, which way the Duke of Parma's army most lodged, in order to cut off his victuals from Newhaven and for want thereof to force him to a battle.

After the King's army was quartered and lodged, the enemy's

horse made towards them; whereupon the King sent for Sir Roger Williams to come to him with 200 muskets and 150 pikes of his best, who were no sooner come to the King but five cornets of Spanish and Italian horse charged them before any horse could succour them. The English encountered them with so great resolution and courage that they took two or three cornets; whereof one the King sent to the Queen, another was torn by the soldiers. Divers of the chief leaders of the horse were slain, and many other of the enemy. 600 Spanish foot, with muskets and pikes, came to second their horse and entered a very hot skirmish with the English; in the meantime other English companies came to their succour. In the end they forced the enemy's horse and foot to retire into their quarters with very great dishonour and loss. Of the English, 40 were hurt and 8 slain; Captain Rush was hurt in the thigh, no other men of quality hurt or slain.

Sir Roger Williams unarmed served most honourably and unhorsed their best leader, and, encountering besides with George Basta, did, as it was thought, hurt him in the neck, giving him a very great blow with his sword. The King commended him highly and did more than wonder at the valour of our nation. Sir Matthew Morgan and his brother also served very valiantly, and Captain Henry Poore. This action greatly encouraged our men, who had very good spoils of the enemy and discouraged the enemy. The King gave great honour to Sir Roger Williams and his men, whom he had held as lost, and caused public thanks to be given to God.

A letter of the Duke of Parma to the King of Spain was intercepted wherein he represented his misery for want of sufficient forces to encounter the King, and his want of victuals and means to return. He complained greatly of the Duke of Mayne and the French, concluding that he must hazard the loss of his army, for without fighting he could not return.

The Duke of Parma had been wounded some days before, being shot in the arm between the bones; the hurt is not dangerous of itself, yet his sickly body and the accidents that usually follow such hurts give some cause of doubt to physicians. Many troops are now daily coming to the French King, and more daily expected.

THE TRIAL OF SIR JOHN PERROT.

Sir John Perrot, who hath lain a prisoner in the Tower for more than a year past, was brought to his trial before the King's Bench Bar, before the commissioners being the Lord Chamberlain, the Lord Buckhurst, Sir Robert Cecil, the Lord Chief Justice and other judges. He was charged on two indictments; the first that in 1587 he went about to depose and raise rebellion against the Queen, that he had promised help to the King of Spain, and that he had procured and moved Sir Brian O'Rourke to rebellion. The second indictment charged him with having conferred with Sir William Stanley in 1586 about his treasonable practices.

To these indictments he pleaded not guilty very vehemently. The jury was then sworn, and the indictments having been read, Sergeant Puckering for the Queen rehearsed the principal points of the indictment. But before he came to the particular offences, he told them that the origin of these treasons proceeded from the imagination of the heart; which imagination was of itself high treason, albeit the same proceeded not to any overt fact; and the heart being possessed with the abundance of his traitorous imagination and not being able so to contain itself, burst forth in vile and traitorous speeches and from thence to horrible and heinous actions.

At this Sir John prayed Sergeant Puckering to lay aside words and proceed to the matter of the indictment; to which he answered that he would proceed by degrees, but would first begin with his contemptuous words which in themselves contained the high treason.

Amongst other speeches, it was reported that when Sir Nicholas Bagnol, Marshal of Ireland, was with Sir John in his house, hot words had broken out and Sir John cried, 'If it were not for yonder pilled and paltry sword that lieth in the window I would not brook these comparisons,' meaning her Majesty's Sword of Justice which was carried before him.

Sir John answered that he had called the sword 'pilled and paltry' because the scabbard was old and worn; and within a week after he had caused a new scabbard to be made. Then falling into other idle discourse, the Lord Buckhurst begged him not to speak from the purpose for it would but hurt his cause.

Then it was shown that Sir John, having called a parliament in Dublin, moved, amongst other matters, to suppress the Cathedral Church of St. Patrick; and her Majesty then sending letters to the contrary he said, with a stern countenance, 'Nay, God's wounds, I think it strange she should use me thus.' With these words the Bishop of Meath was moved to find fault with his undutiful demeanour, for he spoke as though the kingdom were his own and not the Queen's.

Sir John answered that the Archbishop of Dublin was his mortal enemy, and the reason why he was moved to suppress the Cathedral was to have a University created thereon, but he was withstood by the Archbishop because he and his children received 800 marks a year from the Cathedral, and further the Archbishop bore him great malice because when the Queen had sent him letters to discharge idle and unnecessary pensioners he had discharged among the rest one of the Archbishop's sons.

Then it was shown that when the office of the Clerk of the Exchequer was empty and letters were sent from the Queen that Mr. Errington should be admitted to this office, Sir John said, 'This fiddling woman troubles me out of measure: God's wounds, he shall not have the office, I will give it to Sir Thomas Williams.' This was proved by the oath of Philip Williams.

Sir John declared that this Williams was his mortal enemy, a naughty, lewd man of no credit who had abused the Lord Treasurer in a letter, for which he had beaten him in his chambers.

It was also shown that when the Queen had written him a letter about the time that the Spaniards should come, to look well to his charge, he said, 'Ah, silly woman, now she shall not curb me, she shall not rule me; now, God's lady dear, I shall be her white boy now again: doth she think to rule me now?' Shortly after John Garland brought Sir John a letter, which so greatly displeased him that he broke forth into these terms: 'God's wounds, this it is to serve a base bastard pissing kitchen woman; if I had served any prince in Christendom, I had not been so dealt withal.'

All these speeches Sir John denied very vigorously with oaths.

Next Mr. Attorney proceeded to open the treasons which were alleged against Sir John. He declared that when Dr.

Craugh, a known traitor and papist, should have been arrested, Sir John sent out warrants that he should be sought in all places except the White Knight's country, where he knew Craugh to be. To this Sir John answered that there was a God above all, and he marvelled that he who had known religion these forty-six years should be charged with favouring of papists and mass-mongers.

But Mr. Attorney willed him not to stand upon religion; 'for then,' said he, 'we shall prove you irreligious. Will any men of religion seek to have men murdered? Will any men of religion stab a man in the cheek, and after bring him to the fire to be roasted, to make him confess that he knoweth not, and afterwards hang him by martial law?'

Mr. Attorney further to prove him of no religion showed that Sir John being once in his chamber in the Castle at Dublin had looked out at the window and espied Sir Dennis O'Roughan who knew all his secret treasons, and willed his chamberlain to call to him Stephen Seager. When he came, Sir John commanded away his chamberlain and locking the chamber door willed Seager to look out at the window, saying, 'Seest thou not one beneath in a black mantle?' Seager answered that he saw none. Sir John said, 'There is one there; you see how I am crossed by some of the Council here, and he is going to the North with letters from some of the Council to move them against me: I would have thee take those letters from him, kill him, cast him aside, and bring those letters to me.' Seager answered that he would take those letters from him, but he would not kill him; but if Sir John should give commandment to hang him by martial law he would see it done. Whereupon Sir John said, 'Go thy ways, thou art a paltry fellow; I did it but to prove thee.' This was proved by the oath of Seager.

Sir John then called for Seager to speak to him face to face, when he justified all he had said. Then the Lord Chamberlain said, 'Now you see you bad him kill one.' Sir John answered, 'Because he hath sworn I will not reprove him; it may be I spake such words, but I remember it not.'

Other witnesses showed that he had favoured traitors, amongst them Sir Brian O'Rourke, lately executed at Tyburn, whom he might have arrested had he wished.

Then Sir Dennis O'Roughan was called to testify against

Sir John, and the book being offered him to swear, Sir John said it was no matter whether he swore or not, for his word and his oath were all one ; for there was neither truth nor honesty in him. Sir Dennis testified amongst other things that Sir John had used extreme malice towards the Cavener, and the better to execute his purpose, he had found means that the Cavener should offend the law by making an escape out of prison, and, being afterwards taken, he was hanged for having escaped.

Sir John now began to discredit the evidence of Sir Dennis, declaring he had changed his religion five times in six years ; was a common drunkard, a common liar, and had been forsworn a thousand times. Sir Dennis, being again called, swore that Sir John Perrot and Sir Brian O'Rourke had been confederates together in the last Parliament and that each had sworn to the other to help the King of Spain. Here Sir John grew very angry with O'Roughan and declared that he was a lousy villain, a rogue, and had the pox on him.

Other witnesses declared that Sir John had exchanged letters with Sir William Stanley, and that when he came to England he went about to get a pardon, wherein he showed his guilty conscience.

After the Queen's Counsel and Sir John had addressed the jury, they departed from the bar and within three-quarters of an hour they returned with a verdict of guilty. Then Sergeant Puckering in the Queen's name began to pray judgment ; but Sir John desired most humbly that he might speak with some of their honours before sentence should be pronounced.

To this after some conference they agreed, and judgment was deferred until the Queen's pleasure should be known. Then the Court was adjourned until the 2nd May.

29th April. PLAYS OF THE WEEK.

The plays at the Rose Theatre this past week were *The Spanish Tragedy*, *Jerusalem*, *Friar Bacon*, *Muly Mullocco*, *The Second Part of Tamar Cam* (for the first time), *Harry of Cornwall*.

30th April. THE COUNCIL DECEIVED.

Some days since John Dipford and Walter Horsey, merchants of Exeter, were allowed to transport certain merchandise in a bark to Morlaix to recover their losses when their goods and servants were seized by the Leaguers. Now the Council are credibly informed that the suggestion is false, for that the parties came safely from Morlaix without ransom. The bark is to be stayed and no goods hereafter to be taken to Morlaix or St. Malo.

A Contemptuous Sea Captain.

On the 25th March, Mr. Leman, on behalf of certain merchants of Amsterdam, appeared before the Council in the matter of a Dutch ship called the *Jonas*, laden with sugars and other goods coming from Barbary, that was taken at sea by the *Prudence* of Barnstable, whose captain was Captain William Batten. Both parties had willed their case to be referred to Drs. Aubrey, Herbert and Caesar, who decided in favour of Mr. Leman. The Council ordered the *Jonas* to be delivered to him. It now appeareth that Captain Batten, to avoid the ship being given up, hath practised with certain lewd persons who violently seized her and took her to some places unknown, to the great offence of the Queen; and it is greatly to be suspected that they mean to carry the ship and the goods to some remote part of the realm or into Ireland and there to make sale of the goods. The ship is to be stayed and delivered to Mr. Leman if she shall arrive at any port; and Captain Batten to be apprehended and required to appear before the Council or the Judge of the Admiralty within fourteen days.

4th May. An Accident at Greenwich.

A tiltboat of Gravesend carrying some forty persons was run down by a hoy near Greenwich, where the Court now remains. Most of the passengers were drowned in sight of the Queen, who hath been much frightened.

6th May. Plays of the Week.

The plays at the Rose Theatre during this past week were *Muly Mullocco*, *The Spanish Tragedy*, *Titus and Vespasian*, *Harry the Sixth*, *The Jew of Malta*, *Friar Bacon*.

7th May. The Duke of Parma's Camp Pillaged.

From France the ambassador reporteth that the Duke of Parma, who intended by stealth to regain Rouen and to pass from thence to Neuchâtel, was pursued with such diligence by the King that he was forced to retire towards Caudebec, where for want of a bridge he resolved to cross over in boats, having gathered together all the boats of Rouen. But the weather is so tempestuous that they cannot as yet pass many over.

On 30th April, the King assembled early in the morning 1000 English, as many Scots and Netherlands, 800 lance-knights, 1500 Switzers, 2000 French shot, 1500 French cuirassiers and as many rutters, causing three small pieces of artillery to march with them. The rest were left at their quarter. The King gave the leading of 200 cuirassiers and as many rutters and 300 shot to the Baron of Biron, and 1500 French shot to Grilion. Sir Roger Williams was appointed to second him with 200 English and 400 Scottish and Netherlands; the Marshal D'Aumont with 300 cuirassiers; the rest of the force remained with the King for their retreat. The Baron Biron and the others were commanded to give in to the quarter where the Duke of Parma's horse were lodged, to defeat them, to take spoil of their baggage and burn their quarter; which they accordingly performed. But the Baron's overhastiness, entering the quarter with the troops before the rest could come to second him, and the greediness of the soldiers to spoil, hindered the performance of the enterprise and was the occasion that the enemy escaped and that few were killed; and had not Sir Roger Williams with his 200 English withstood the enemy better, the Baron with his companies and the Marshal D'Aumont had been overthrown. But God gave them very good success, for the enemy wanted courage, and our men, forcing the quarter, killed 150, taking the spoils of 500 waggons, and all the baggage, and brought away 1000 horse of all sorts, and as much spoil as is worth 50,000 crowns at least. The rest of the quarter and spoils our men set on fire and then retired without loss. The attempt was most desperate and resolved by the King to force the enemy to fight, which nothing could work.

The English soldiers in these days are much harried and many disband daily for want of money and victuals.

8th May. FURTHER REINFORCEMENTS FOR FRANCE.

The Queen upon the present great and urgent occasion determines to have 2000 footmen complete, and 100 horsemen from the troops in her pay in the Lowlands to be speedily transported by sea into France.

13th May. AN UNLUCKY GAOLER.

Richard Mudford, Keeper of the Counter in Southampton, had in his custody one Edmund Mellish, imprisoned for debt. This Mellish escaped some two years since, and, notwithstanding the Council's warrant for help and assistance in the speedy recovery and apprehension of the prisoner, and Mudford's diligent travail in search of him, yet is he still at large; and the keeper, unless some charitable course be taken, liable to pay his debt of two hundred crowns and £14 in costs, besides the loss of his great expenses and travail, amounting to no less sum. The Council therefore write to Mellish's mother, the Lady Allot, moving her charitably to consider the poor keeper's distress by discharging him of the whole payment of her son's debt.

DESERTERS FROM FRANCE AT DOVER.

It is credibly reported that, notwithstanding the Council's orders for the restraint of such soldiers as without passport draw themselves from the service of the French King in Normandy, above two hundred men of strong and able bodies are landed at Dover and the places near without passport, in the company of some few sick men, and without stay. These men are allowed to beg in the county with the passport of the Mayor, using most slanderous speeches of the Queen's service and entertainment, tending to the great discouragement of such as be willing to serve. Mr. Verney, Mr. Edward Boyes, and Mr. William Pertridge, Esquires, are to repair to Dover, and discover the truth of the matter; and in case they shall find the Council's orders have been neglected, good bonds are to be taken of the Mayor and such others who are found culpable for their personal appearance; and to cause all soldiers that of late are landed without passport to be stayed and punished.

PLAYS OF THE WEEK.

The plays at the Rose Theatre during this past week were *Brandimer*, *Harry the Sixth*, *Titus and Vespasian*, *The Spanish Tragedy*, *The Second Part of Tamar Cam*, *The Jew of Malta*.

17th May. A Claim against Captain Glemham.

In the Admiralty Court was heard the cause between John de Riviera, a merchant stranger residing in London, acting on behalf of certain Venetians, and Captain Edward Glemham of the *Edward and Constance*, touching sugars and other goods taken in the Levant Seas, which Riviera claims, though without proof, as belonging to Venetians. The judges order that the goods shall be appraised by six experienced men chosen by de Riviera and Glemham, and the inventory lodged in the Admiralty Court; Glemham to have possession and to dispose of them at his pleasure in a bond in double their value to pay their first value within two months after proof has been made or for so much as can be proved to belong to Venetians or others not the subjects of the King of Spain.

20th May. Plays of the Week.

The plays at the Rose Theatre this week past were *The Spanish Tragedy*, *Harry the Sixth*, *Titus and Vespasian*, *Sir John Maundeville*, *Muly Mullocco*, *Harry of Cornwall*.

21st May. The Weakness of the Normandy Companies.

It appears from the certificates sent by Sir Edmund Yorke before his death that on the first of the month the companies in Normandy are so decayed that there are not above 1500 men, and since then these are much more weakened by sickness, famine, escaping and other indirect means. By good estimation the numbers remaining there, though in the name of nineteen captains, will not make above eight companies, whereby her Majesty is much abused both in her opinion of the strength of the forces there and in the greatness of her charge, as much by weekly pays and lendings as if the companies were full and complete. Sir Roger Williams is now ordered to take a general muster and to reduce all unto eight companies or according to the numbers of able men, appointing 100 men to serve under such captains of the old bands from the Low Countries as by their valour and by careful preserving their companies together best deserve. The captains of every band to be caused to be paid and discharged without unnecessary delay.

25th May. A Rumour.

This morning it is said that the Queen is out of quiet with her foreign foes and home broils. It is expected that the new Lord Chancellor will be nominated to-day, and the choice believed to be between the Solicitor-General and Sergeant Puckering; but the Queen is not yet determined.

Puckering made Lord Keeper.

John Puckering, Esquire, one of her Majesty's Sergeants at Law, about three o'clock in the afternoon was by the Queen made a Knight in the Privy Chamber, and straightway going into the Council Chamber he took the oath of supremacy and of a privy councillor at the Council Board. Thereupon being placed in the lowest place of the Council according to his calling, and having signed a letter as Councillor, he returned to the Queen, in company with the rest of the Council, into the Privy Chamber, where, after some grave speeches and admonitions how to use such a great office to the pleasing of God and the content of all people having any causes afore him, her Highness delivered into his hands the Great Seal, to have and keep the same as Lord Keeper of the Great Seal of England. And so he came down again into the Council Chamber, took his place as Lord Keeper and signed letters accordingly.

27th May. Plays of the Week.

The plays at the Rose Theatre during this past week were *Harry the Sixth*, *The Jew of Malta*, *The Spanish Comedy*, *The Spanish Tragedy*, *The Tanner of Denmark*, *Titus and Vespasian*.

28th May. Seditious Books from Abroad.

There have recently been divers traitorous and seditious books brought into the country by most lewd persons, who the better to colour their vile doings wrap them up in merchandise and after disperse them to evil disposed persons, infecting them and others with their poisoned libels. All ships arriving in the realm are to be searched, as well as any houses or places where it is suspected that such slanderous books may be hidden.

31st May. A Disaster in Brittany Rumoured.

Sundry rumours are abroad of a great success of the enemy under the Duke Mercury against the Princes of Conde and

Dombes, who were besieging the town of Craon in Brittany. The Princes have been compelled by the Duke's Bretons and Spaniards to leave their siege and forced to fly with the loss of the most part of their footmen, amongst them many English, about whom there is no certain news how many be lost, taken or escaped. Sir Henry Norris, that is lieutenant to his brother, the General in that part, is to repair thither with all speed to understand the true estate of the Queen's people. To take with him a quantity of arms and powder, and order from Sir Thomas Shirley, the Treasurer for Wars, for a proportion of money so that the English who want weapons may be furnished, and those saved may have money to relieve them for their victualling and other necessaries. He carries a special letter from her Majesty to Monsieur Hallard Mountmorency, Governor of Caen, requesting his advice and assistance. Also he shall resort to both the Princes (if he finds it convenient), declaring to them how much her Majesty is discomfited with this great loss, and requiring them to show all favour to her people that be saved.

MR. JOHN HARINGTON AND THE PRINTER.

Mr. John Harington, High Sheriff of the County of Somerset, some time since did withdraw one Thomas Wells, a prentice, from his master Augustine Rither, printer and graver of London, to serve him in his profession. The man with much ado was restored to his master, but by indirect means Mr. Harington hath lately gotten him away from his master, to his utter impoverishing, whose living consisteth solely in his occupation, wherein with much travail and many charges he brought up his apprentice. The Council rebuke Mr. Harington for so uncharitable an action, not fitting a gentleman of his quality. He is strictly charged to redeliver Wells to his master or to make personal appearance without delay to answer his default.

1st June. SIR WALTER RALEGH DISGRACED.

It is rumoured that Sir Walter Ralegh hath been recalled from the fleet which is now at sea and hath been cast into the Tower. He hath offended with Mistress Elizabeth Throckmorton, one of her Majesty's Ladies-in-Waiting.

2nd June. FOREIGN ARTISANS IN ENGLAND.

Monsieur Caron, Agent for the States of the United Provinces of the Low Countries, hath lately made suit to the Queen and the Council on behalf of divers poor men of those countries living in London, some of them candlemakers or exercising like manual trades. He petitioned that certain proceedings under penal statutes made against them might be stayed, and these poor men permitted to continue their accustomed trades whereby they maintain themselves and their families. Hereupon those that laid the informations, being called before the Council, brought in their defence some requests from the Lord Mayor showing that of late years the numbers of handicraftsmen of strangers are so much increased within the City and suburbs that the freemen of the City are supplanted and their living taken from them. These strangers who came hither in these times of trouble abroad the better to enjoy the free exercise of their consciences are so extraordinarily favoured that some are grown to great wealth. Some of them convey beyond the seas the commodities of this realm, whereby the prices of divers things are increased and the Queen deceived in her custom.

The Council now instruct Sir Henry Killigrew and other gentlemen to make inquisition how many strangers of every nation use handicrafts that are not allowable in the City and suburbs, where they inhabit, what occupations they use, how many both men and women they keep in their houses, how long they have been in the realm, to what churches they resort, and whether they keep any English born in their houses.

This inquisition is to be made with as much secrecy as may be whereby neither the English artisans and apprentices take any comfort or boldness to contemn the strangers, or the poor strangers be made afraid to be hardly used.

3rd June. PLAYS OF THE WEEK.

The plays at the Rose Theatre during this past week were *Harry the Sixth*, *Tamar Cam*, *The Spanish Tragedy*, *Machiavel*, *The Jew of Malta*, *Muly Mullocco*.

5th June. THE DISASTER IN BRITTANY.

Sir Henry Unton, the ambassador in France, hath now reported at length upon the disaster in Brittany. It appeareth that on the 13th May, the Princes of Conde and Dombes raised their siege from Craon, understanding of the approach of the Duke Mercury towards them with all his forces ; and intending to retire (for they were too weak to encounter their enemies) they were suddenly surprised through want of advertisements, of counsel and good resistance, being charged by the enemy both before and behind, they having taken an unfit, straight passage to retire with their cannon and their forces. The English and lance-knights only came to blows who served with great courage and paid for it accordingly, being most of them slain. The rest of the French ran away at the first and saved themselves until the Duke Mercury coasted them, and then overtaking some of them in rout killed many but took the most part prisoners. Of the artillery they saved not one piece, having seven cannon and four demi-culverin, without ever making shot with them.

The Princes' forces were about 3500 foot and 400 horse, and the enemy between 5 and 6000 foot and 800 horse. The Duke Mercury hath since pursued his victory and taken Chateau Goutyer and Le Val, which surrendered voluntarily, both being passages of the Mayne and therefore of very great importance. He is now before Mayne, the chief town.

This unhappy accident hath struck a great fear and terror into all the hearts of the King's subjects in Brittany, and therefore will hazard the loss of the towns and places there if they be not relieved immediately and better assured. The King's designs of blocking Rouen and Newhaven and clearing Normandy are frustrated, he is diverted from following the Duke of Parma, as before he intended, and hath now been forced to return to Vernon to take counsel for his best course to succour Brittany. The Leaguers are animated and the Parisians receive 1200 Spaniards, Italians and Walloons into garrison, and in a manner become less willing for peace.

Immediately after the receipt of these news the King sent for Sir Henry Unton and imparted them to him at length with great passion and discontent, discoursing at large of his miserable estate, of the factions of his servants, and of their ill dispositions. Then he required the ambassador's opinions touching his course for Brittany, and also what further aid he might expect from the Queen, alleging that unless he were immediately strengthened from England, it was impossible for him to resist the greatness of Spain who assailed the country by Brittany, Languedoc, by the Low Countries, by the Duke of Savoy and the Duke of Lorraine.

The ambassador replied mildly, humbly craving pardon from the delivery of any opinion as a public minister, but not refusing as a private person to deliver his conceit by way of discourse, not of advice. On this being granted by the King he began to set out the importance of Brittany; the King's want of providence therein; his breach of promise in not sending forces thither; the King of Spain's great desire to have that country and how much his honour, profit, and safety might be specially impeached and endangered. He then delivered such reasons as might urge the necessity of his defence of that country; and lastly peremptorily pressed his going in person with an army into Brittany to resist the enemies' pursuit of victory, concluding by giving him neither any manner of comfort nor discomfort of the Queen's resolution.

To this the King gave a willing ear, and replied with many thanks, yielding many excuses of his want of means, not of disposition to provide a remedy. In the mean season, he said he would take counsel and then acquaint the ambassador with his resolution.

Soon after this, the Queen's letters for the ambassador's revocation (for which he hath long petitioned) came to hand; whereupon he took occasion to repair to the King and to crave his leave to depart, which the King very willingly granted, requesting him, partly for his better safety, but chiefly for the better understanding of his further resolution concerning his affairs, to attend him to Vernon, where within six days he should meet his Council.

6th June. LEWDNESS IN A CONDUIT.

A man and a woman, both aged persons, were set in the pillory in Cheapside towards Paul's upon a scaffold with papers on their heads, the man being keeper of the conduit there. These two lewd persons in the night entered the conduit, washed themselves, and evacuated their bowels therein.

10th June. PLAYS OF THE WEEK.

The plays at the Rose Theatre this past week were *Bindo and Richardo*, *Titus and Vespasian*, *The Looking Glass for London*, *Tamar Cam*, *The Spanish Tragedy*, *A Knack to Know a Knave* (for the first time).

12th June. RIOTS IN SOUTHWARK.

There was great disorder in Southwark last evening, until about 8 o'clock at night, when the Lord Mayor, taking with him one of the Sheriffs, came down upon the rioters, finding great multitudes of the people assembled, especially some apprentices of the feltmakers, out of Barmsey Street and the Blackfriars, together with a number of loose and masterless men. Whereupon proclamation was made and, the multitude having been dismissed, the Lord Mayor apprehended the doers of the disorder and committed them to prison. This morning, examinations being taken, it is found that the disorder began upon the serving of a warrant from the Lord Chamberlain by one of the Knight Marshal's men upon a feltmonger's servant who was committed to the Marshalsea without any cause of offence. Whereupon the apprentices, under pretence of meeting at a play, assembled themselves to make a rescue. The inhabitants of Southwark of best reputation complain that the Knight Marshal's men in serving their warrants use not themselves with good discretion and moderate usage, but by their most rough and violent manner provoke them whom they have to arrest by their rough and violent manner. In this case they entered a house where a warrant was to be served with a dagger drawn, affrighting the good wife of the house who sat by the fire with a young child in her arms; and afterwards taking the party and several others committed him to prison where they lay five days without making their answer. When therefore the apprentices' men assembled themselves before the Marshalsea, the Knight Marshal's men issued forth with their daggers drawn and bastinadoes in their hands, beating the people, of whom some came, as their manner was, merely to gaze; and afterwards drew their swords, whereby the tumult was incensed and they themselves endangered but that help came to prevent further mischief.

15*th June*. SOME ENGLISH SAILORS ILL-TREATED.

Sir Henry Unton, the ambassador in France, is to make complaint to the King of the hard treatment offered to certain English sailors. It seemeth that in August last a ship called the *Mary of Waterford*, laden with salt, pepper, suckats, marmalade, and other commodities, about 60 leagues from Cape Finisterre was taken by one Govant, Captain of the *Salamander* of Dieppe, and other subjects of the French King. This man spoiled them of all their goods, worth £800, beside the hindrance and damage to the extent of £200, and so left the company of the ship, being sixteen persons, only with a basket of broken bread and a small roundlet of cider mixed with water. In this state they continued at sea twenty-five days before they could recover any land, so that two died with hunger and the rest were brought in so weak that they were greatly endangered.

DISTRESS AT CANTERBURY.

After deliberate consideration of some good means to be used for the present relief of the decayed estate of the City of Canterbury and the great number of poor people there inhabiting, the Council think it best to put into execution an Act of Parliament, made for this purpose in 6th of Henry VIII. (1515) for the making of the river running from the City of Canterbury navigable for craiers, boats and lighters to pass to the town of Fordwich, as at present from Fordwich to Sandwich, whereby the inhabitants of the City might have more trade to employ them. But as this work far exceedeth the abilities of the inhabitants of the City, the magistrates of Kent are required at some speedy convenient time to assemble themselves and consider an estimate of the whole work; and first to set down a liberal contribution themselves, and afterwards to exhort also the gentlemen and wealthiest inhabitants to bestow rateably such convenient proportion of money as should be laid upon them.

17*th June*. SIR HENRY UNTON RETURNS.

Sir Henry Unton, ambassador to the King of France, hath come to London, having received his despatch on the 10th.

PLAYS OF THE WEEK AT THE ROSE.

This past week were played *Harry the Sixth*, *Muly Mullocco*, *The Jew of Malta*, *A Knack to Know a Knave*, *Sir John Maundeville*.

19th June. RECUSANCY IN WALES.

The Council write to the Earl of Pembroke praying him certify the names of those gentlemen in the Principality of Wales, that be sound in religion and well affected, to be appointed commissioners for the inquiry of Jesuits, Seminaries and other suspected persons. Since no commission is appointed for Wales numbers of recusants flee thither so that there is daily infection and falling away from religion in those parts.

In Carmarthen many, both men and women, in the night season and by day repair to certain places where in times past were pilgrimages, images or offerings ; they assemble sometimes in great numbers, a thing intolerable to be permitted after so long a time of the preaching of the Gospel. These superstitious and idolatrous monuments are to be pulled down, broken, and quite defaced so that no remnant, token or memory may remain. Should any hereafter repair to those places they shall be apprehended and severely punished for their lewd behaviour that others may be warned by their examples to take heed of such intolerable abuses.

21st June. A COZENER PILLORIED.

One Kirby, a gentleman in countenance, but a cozener by quality, was set in the pillory without Aldersgate and there lost one of his ears.

22nd June. FATHER SOUTHWELL THE JESUIT.

Topcliffe hath written to the Queen concerning Father Southwell the Jesuit that he took prisoner a few days since, saying that he keeps him very straitly in his strong chamber at Westminster ; and if her Majesty wishes to know anything in his heart, then shall he be made to stand against the wall, his feet standing upon the ground and his hands put as high as he can reach against the wall—like a trick at trenchmore—shall enforce him to tell all.

23rd June. PLAYING CEASES AT THE ROSE THEATRE.

The Lord Strange's men have ceased from playing at the Rose Theatre, their plays during the five days past being *The Spanish Tragedy*, *Harry the Sixth*, *The Comedy of Jeronimo*, *Tamar Cam*, *The Knack to Know a Knave*.

RUMOURS OF PEACE IN FRANCE.

It is reported that peace in France is expected and the King has sent M. de Saucy to acquaint her Majesty therewith or else to see how he may be helped at her hands to stand the war. The Duke de Mayne is at St. Denis with the King on safe conduct, the terms offered by the League being liberty of religion on both sides where it is, and, where it is not, no inquisition; the Protestants to have churches in the fauxbourgs, and the Leaguers to have in every province certain towns of caution for certain years.

ABUSES IN THE NORTH.

It is reported that in the north those evilly disposed towards religion hold May games, Morris dances, plays, bear baitings, ales and other pastimes on Sundays and holy days at the time of Divine Service and other godly exercises to draw away the people when men assemble together for the hearing of God's Word and to join in common prayers. The Council have prayed the Earl of Derby to give special direction to all Justices to forbid these and the like pastimes to be in any place whatsoever on Sunday or holy days at the time of Divine Service, sermons, or other godly exercises; and to cause the favourers, maintainers or chief offenders to be sent up to answer their contentious and lewd behaviour.

Small reformation has been made in those parts by the Ecclesiastical Commissioners as appeareth by the emptiness of churches on Sundays and holy days, and the multitude of bastards and drunkards; great sums have been levied under pretence of the commission, but the counties are in worse case than before and the number of those that do not resort to Divine Service greater. The people lack instruction, for the preachers are few, most of the parsons unlearned, many of those learned not resident, and divers unlearned daily admitted into very good benefices by the Bishop. The youth are for the most part being trained up by such as possess papistry; and no examination made of schools and schoolmasters. The proclamation for the apprehension of seminaries, Jesuits, and mass priests, and for calling home children from parts beyond the sea is not being executed. Some of the coroners and justices and their families do not frequent church, and many of them have not communicated at the Lord's Supper since the beginning of the Queen's reign. In many places the seminaries have lately offered disputations against the settled religion, but nothing is said to them.

They that resort to church are so few that preachers who were determined to preach on Sundays and holy days refrain from lack of auditors; the people so swarm in the streets and alehouses during service time, that open markets are kept and in many churches only the curate and the clerk are present.

Marriages and christenings are celebrated by seminary and other priests in corners, and in some parts children baptized according to law have afterwards been rebaptized by priests. Divers mass priests, being apprehended, refuse to be examined npon oath as to where they frequent. Alehouses are innumerable, and the law for suppressing and keeping them in order not executed, whereby toleration of drunkenness, unlawful games and other abuses follow. Small or no reformation has followed the letters of the Council. The recusants have spies about the Council to give intelligence when anything is intended against them so that they may shift out of the way and avoid being apprehended.

Rioting Expected in London.

The magistrates of the City of London and the suburbs are warned that certain apprentices and other idle people their adherents, the same that were the authors and partakers of the late disorder in Southwark, have a further purpose on Midsummer evening or night to renew their lewd assembly by colour of the time and to commit a breach of the peace or other foul outrage. To prevent this mischief, a strong and substantial watch, sufficient to suppress any tumult, is to be kept both on Midsummer evening, Midsummer night and Sunday night of householders and masters of families, to continue from the beginning of evening to the morning. All masters of servants to be straightly charged, as they shall answer to their perils, to keep their servants in their houses for these two nights, and not to let them have any weapons if they be disposed to execute any evil purpose. If, notwithstanding this strait charge, any servants, apprentices or suspected persons be found in the streets they shall immediately be committed to prison. Moreover for avoiding of these unlawful assemblies, no plays may be used at the Theatre, Curtain or other usual places, nor any other sort of unlawful or forbidden pastime that draws together the baser sort of people from henceforth until the Feast of St. Michael.

26th June. SIR JOHN PERROT CONDEMNED.

Sir John Perrot, that was found guilty of high treason on 27th April, appeared to-day before the Commissioners for judgment. He was brought in a coach from the Tower to the Old Swan, thence conveyed by water to Westminster Bridge where he landed and so into Westminster Hall between 8 and 9 in the morning. He was accompanied by Mr. Blunt and Mr. Cooke, son and son-in-law to the Lieutenant of the Tower, and strongly guarded by divers of the yeomen of the guard with halberds and the Lieutenant's men all round him. In this fashion he was brought to the Queen's Bench bar where he stood for a quarter of an hour waiting for the Commissioners. He was clothed in a doublet and hose of plain black satin and a gown of wrought velvet furred, with a plain white ruff and wearing a square, or flat crowned, black felt hat with a small band ; and he carried a carnation in his hand.

The Commissioners having taken their places, Sergeant Snagg for the Queen prayed that judgment might be given. Then the Clerk of the Court asked Sir John whether he had anything to say why judgment to die should not be given.

Sir John made protestation of his innocence in a speech of about a quarter of an hour in which he complained very bitterly of the hard and false dealings of the witnesses against him. He said that he knew of her Majesty's mercy which proceeded from the providence of God, who knew his innocence and so stayed him so long from judgment. Whereupon the Lord Chamberlain, conceiving his meaning to be that the Queen had deferred judgment being persuaded of his innocency, interrupted his speech and declared that he had received more favour than any traitor he ever saw. But Sir John prayed the Lord Chamberlain not to misconstrue his meaning.

Mr. Attorney Egerton now stood up, and directing his speech to the Commissioners urged that Sir John Perrot by protesting his innocency thought to deceive the audience into believing that he was not guilty of treason.

To this Sir John angrily replied, 'Mr. Attorney, you did me wrong now as you did me before.'

'I never did you wrong,' said Mr. Attorney.

'You did me wrong,' said Sir John.

'Instance where I did you wrong,' answered Mr. Attorney.

'You did me wrong,' again said Sir John.

'I never did you wrong,' replied Mr. Attorney.

Both the Lord Buckhurst and the Lord Chamberlain spoke to Sir John declaring that he had been most manifestly proved guilty of treason by a number of witnesses. Sir John answered that the matter had been set forward by his enemies in Ireland, and that he was condemned by Irish witnesses all; and further, that the Irish witnesses had no respect of an oath, and for a small value, a man might procure a number to swear anything.

After further talk with the Commissioners, Anderson, the Lord Chief Justice of the Common Pleas, asked him whether he had anything to say in arrest of judgment. Sir John answered that seeing it had pleased God and the Queen to bring him to that pass he had nothing to say, but humbly submitted himself to the law and their lordships.

Then the Lord Chief Justice began with a long discourse, showing how God from time to time had revealed the treasons that had been practised at home and abroad. He said that he agreed with the others that Sir John was justly condemned of treason, and so proceeded to judgment: that he should be carried by the Lieutenant of the Tower to the Tower which was the place from which he came, and thence to be drawn upon a hurdle through the City of London to the place of execution, and there to be hanged, and to be cut down alive, and his bowels and privy members to be cut off and cast into the fire in his sight, his head to be cut off and his body to be cut in four quarters, to be disposed at the Queen's pleasure, and God have mercy upon him.

Sir John then again declared his innocency very fervently and concluded by asking that certain petitions might be granted. He asked that, if it would please the Queen to grant him his life, he might have a better room, for his lodging was a small chamber, room only for his chair and table. To this the Lord Chamberlain answered that the room was fit for such a man as he was. He begged that if he should suffer death he might die a gentleman's death and be spared from drawing through the streets and the rest of the judgment. He also asked, amongst other petitions, that their Lordships would enlist the Queen to be good to his son and his wife, and, as he heard, to a little son which they had who might hereafter do her Majesty service.

Then Sir John was taken away from the bar in the same manner as he had been brought thither, and so back to the Tower. The Commissioners having sat a little longer after his departure caused proclamation to be made that the present commission of Oyer and Terminer was ended, and on the stroke of ten o'clock at night, the court broke up.

28th June. THE MURDER OF JOHN BREWEN.

This day Anne Brewen and John Parker were executed in Smithfield for the murder of John Brewen.

Two and a half years before Anne Welles (as she then was) by divers young men was beloved, but especially by John Brewen and John Parker, both goldsmiths, being bachelors and good friends. Brewen had the favour of her friends and kinsfolk, but notwithstanding his long suit and the gifts of gold and jewels that he gave her he was disdained in favour of Parker, who enjoyed her love in secret. At length seeing his suit despised and having no hope of her favour, Brewen determined to demand again his gold and jewels, and coming to her he requested that his gifts might be given back; to this she answered contemptuously that he should stay for it. Without more ado the young man had her arrested for the jewels.

The damsel was so astonished and dismayed that she promised if he would let his action fall nor ever think the worse of her, she would marry him and make him her husband by a certain day; and this before witnesses she vowed to perform. Brewen therefore was not a little joyful and made preparation for his marriage; but when Parker heard of it he was grievously vexed and taunted her so bitterly that she repented of the promise made to Brewen, and began to hate him; and after this Parker would never let her rest but continually urged her to make away with him.

She had not been married above three days to Brewen when she put in practice to poison him. Although her husband loved her dearly she would not stay with him after the first night of their wedding, saying she had vowed not to lie with him until he had got her a better house, and the more to cover her treachery and to show her discontent with him she provided a lodging near to the place where Parker lived, so that he had free access to her.

Two days after her marriage Parker brought her a deadly poison that would work speedily on the heart without any swelling on the body or outward sign of infection. This poison she carried secretly to her husband's house, and, coming in the next morning with a pleasant countenance, she asked him if he would have a mess of sugar sops that cold morning. 'Ay, marry, with all my heart,' said he, 'and I take it very kindly that you will do so much for me.' Then she prepared a mess for him with the poison, but in rising from setting the pot back on the fire her coat spilled the mess, and she began to lament that so good a mess of sugar sops should be wasted. But her husband said, 'What, woman, vex not at the matter, your ill luck go with them.' 'Marry, amen,' answered she. Then she asked him to fetch her a pennyworth of red herrings.

When he came back, he found that she had made ready a fresh mess of sugar sops for him, one for herself and another for a little boy that she brought with her.

In a little while Brewen began to wax very ill about the stomach, with a grievous inward griping; and immediately after to vomit exceedingly so that he requested her to help him to bed. When it grew somewhat late, she told her husband that she must return to her lodging, and though he begged her to stay with him, she said she could not and would not; and so left the poisoned man all alone for the whole night without comfort or company. All that night he was extremely sick, worse and worse, never ceasing to vomit until (as was afterwards supposed) his entrails were all shrunk and broken within him. The next morning she came to him again but made little show of sorrow. When he rebuked her for her unkindness, she asked him if he would have her forsworn. 'Well, Anne,' said he, 'stay with me now, for I am not long to continue in this world.' 'Now God forbid,' she replied, affecting a great show of sorrow. Then she made a caudle with sugar and spices which she gave him, and immediately after he had eaten it, he died. The next day he was buried, none of the neighbours suspecting that any evil had been done to him.

Parker now became very bold with the widow so that ere long she durst deny him nothing or he would threaten to stab her with his dagger. In this state he kept her unmarried for two years after her husband's death until at length she was with child. And now, to save her credit, she begged him to marry her, but he reviled her most shamefully, taunting her with Brewen's murder. While they were thus quarrelling very vehemently, some of the neighbours overheard their words and revealed them to the magistrate. Whereupon the woman was carried before Alderman Howard to be examined, and the man before Justice Young; but both denied the deed very stoutly until the woman was made to believe that Parker had confessed, when she revealed all. She was therefore taken into the country to be delivered of her child and then brought back to prison. Both were arraigned and condemned at Newgate; the woman to be burnt in Smithfield, the man to be hanged before her eyes.

10th July. Sir W. Ralegh's Complaints against the Deputy of Ireland.

Sir Walter Ralegh hath written from the Tower to Sir Robert Cecil complaining that when his disgrace was known in Ireland, the Deputy, Sir William Fitzwilliams, an enemy of his, dealt very despitefully with him. Pretending a debt to the Queen of £400, he sent a sheriff to take away all the cattle of Sir Walter's tenants in Munster and unless the money were paid the same day to sell them on the next. The debt was but for 50 marks, and paid; but the sheriff did as he was commanded, and took away five hundred milch kine from the poor people; of whom some had but two, and some three, to relieve their poor wives and children, and in a new country set down to milch and plant. He had forcibly thrust Sir Walter out of possession of a castle because it was in law between him and his cousin, and would not hear his attorney speak. He had admitted a ward (and given it to his man) of a castle which was the Queen's, which Sir Walter had built and planted with English these five years; and to profit his man with a wardship, lost the Queen's inheritance; and would plant the cousin of a rebel in the place of an Englishman, the castle standing in the most dangerous place in all Munster.

18th July. A PROGNOSTICATION.

In the *Calendar* for the next twelve months that James Carre, Master of Arts, hath penned, it is prognosticated that in the winter months sickness, engendered of cold humours and of phlegmatic matter, will this quarter afflict divers persons; and the trembling ague will cause many to tremble, not only those that have it, because they have it, but such also as have it not, lest they should have it. For the spring, the weather will be very seasonable and temperate, but notwithstanding there shall be some painful and perilous sicknesses, together with wars and rumours of wars. In the summer the drought less than in the two former summers: and yet greater store of drought in divers places to dry up the strong ale, than of strong ale to quench the drought: the winds at this season likely to be very variable. The harvest time will be inclined unto sundry wet and unexpected perries of rain, growing still from hot and dry exhalations to cold and moist vapours.

21st July. MILITARY EQUIPMENT IN THE COUNTIES.

The Lords Lieutenant of certain Counties are directed to enquire how much of the armour and furniture given to soldiers sent into foreign services has been returned; for it is reported to the Council that there is not such honest regard as there should be for the return of this armour, for which cause the country might be unfurnished. The armour that has not been returned shall be replaced as soon as possible by some general and reasonable contribution which the Queen earnestly desireth shall not be levied on the meaner sort but on those best able to bear it, such as farmers, landed men, and persons grown in wealth by any other trade.

It is also reported that some recusants have good quantity of armour in their houses. In 1585 special commissioners were chosen to receive the armour and weapons belonging to recusants until such time as they should conform to the laws; but since that time others have declared themselves recusants who are thought to have armour. The armour and weapons of all certified as recusants is to be collected into safe custody to be returned again to the owners when they shall conform. This is especially necessary at this time because the enemy make great brags of the assistance which they shall receive from those backward in religion.

21st July. GREENE'S 'QUIP FOR AN UPSTART COURTIER.'

Greene's *Quip for an Upstart Courtier*, or *A Quaint Dispute between Velvet Breeches and Cloth Breeches* is entered, being dedicated to Mr. Thomas Barnaby, Esquire, wherein in the form of a dream are set down the disorders in all estates and trades.

Velvet Breeches and Cloth Breeches coming upon each other began to dispute which was of the more ancient lineage. They agreed therefore to impanel a jury to try the title of Velvet Breeches, and as men of all occupations passed by so were they examined and accepted or challenged by both parties. The jury having at last been impanelled the case was put to them and in a short space they found that Cloth Breeches had the better title, being one that had been formerly a companion to Kings, an equal with the nobility, a friend to gentlemen and noblemen, a patron of the poor, a true subject, a good housekeeper and as honest as he was ancient, whereas Velvet Breeches was an upstart come out of Italy, begot of Pride, nursed by Self Love, and brought into this country by Newfangledness; that of late he was a raiser of rents and an enemy to the commonwealth, and not in any way to be preferred in equity before Cloth Breeches.

In some copies of this book is printed a very bitter satire on ropemakers, aimed at the father of Dr. Gabriel Harvey, who hath caused offence to Greene and his friends; but in others this leaf is cancelled either because Greene thinketh better of it or because he feareth lest that he bring himself within the law.

23rd July. A MONOPOLY IN STARCH.

The Council have granted to Mr. Richard Young an open letter preventing all persons from buying or bringing starch into the country contrary to the special grant giving him sole licence and authority for the making, bringing in and selling of starch in the realm.

28th July. ROBERT SOUTHWELL SENT TO THE TOWER.

Southwell, the Jesuit, is now committed to the Tower by order of the Council to be kept a close prisoner, and to see none but the keeper that Mr. Topcliffe shall appoint.

31st July. SIR WALTER RALEGH'S LAMENTABLE COMPLAINT.

Sir Walter Ralegh, writing to Sir Robert Cecil from the Tower, complaineth in very extravagant terms of the departure of the Court and of the Queen from London. 'My heart was never broken,' saith he, 'till this day that I hear the Queen goes so far off; whom I have followed so many years with so great love and desire, in so many journeys, and am now left behind her, in a dark prison all alone. While she was yet near at hand that I might hear of her once in two or three days my sorrows were the less; but even now my heart is cast into the depth of all misery. I that was wont to behold her riding like Alexander, hunting like Diana, walking like Venus, the gentle wind blowing her fair hair about her pure cheeks, like a nymph; sometimes sitting in the shade like a goddess; sometimes singing like an angel; sometimes playing like Orpheus.' He concludeth, 'Do with me now, therefore, what you list. I am more weary of life than they are desirous I should perish, which if it had been for her, as it is by her, I have been too happily born.'

6th August. DESERTERS IN HERTFORDSHIRE.

Many soldiers of a company levied in Hertfordshire have deserted their captain without leave, both before embarking and after landing. These men now lurk in very riotous and disordered sort in the remote places in the county, not only to the harm and prejudice of peaceful subjects but also showing a dangerous example. The magistrates from whose divisions the men come are ordered to apprehend the ringleaders and commit them to the common jail.

7th August. ABLE-BODIED IRISHMEN TO BE DEPORTED.

Certain able-bodied Irishmen, masterless men, that now for a long time frequent the City and the suburbs begging, are to be despatched to Ireland and set to work by Mr. William English, that complains that by reason of his long imprisonment in England his tenants and followers have left his lands and possessions waste and unpeopled.

8th August. NASHE'S 'PIERCE PENNILESS.'

Nashe hath written a book called *Pierce Penniless; his Supplication to the Devil*, being a satirical pamphlet on the abuses of the times.

Seeing that now gentle Sir Philip Sidney is dead and no one left to care for poor scholars, Pierce Penniless in despair pens his supplication to the devil, wherein he writeth invectively of usurers, the deadly sins of greediness, nigardize, and pride (attacking by the way the antiquaries for their rusty wits in so doting upon worm-eaten eld), envy, murder, wrath, and railery, and especially those that rail upon playing. For the policy of playing, saith he, is very necessary for a state, since those that are their own masters (as gentlemen of the Court, the Inns of Court, captains and soldiers) needs must spend their afternoons upon pleasure, either gaming, following of harlots, drinking, or seeing a play, of which the last is the least evil. Nor are plays evil, though some petitioners of the Council dislike them; for no play encourages any man to tumults or rebellion but lays before him the halter and the gallows; or praises or approves pride, lust, whoredom or prodigality but beats it down utterly; and besides they bring upon the stage our forefathers' valiant acts. Thence Pierce passeth to gluttony, drunkenness, sloth and lechery, and so to a discourse on the nature of Hell and the Devil. Amongst many others attacked in this book are Dr. Gabriel Harvey and his brother Richard.

11th August. THE COUNT MOMPELGARD IN LONDON.

This day Frederick, Count Mompelgard, is come to London, having set out from Mompelgard with his train of servants to travel and see the world. They reached Dover two days since, being much frightened at sea through their unfamiliarity with the waves, and distressed through their frequent horrible vomitings. Having landed, noting on the way the wrecks of the Spanish Armada still lying on the beach, they took post horses for Gravesend. The journey hath been very wearisome to them by reason of our English saddles, which being covered only with bare hide are painful to strangers and hard to ride upon, especially for the Count who is corpulent and heavy.

They are much amazed with the throngs of people in London,

and their magnificent apparel, but they complain that the inhabitants are extremely proud and overbearing; and because the greater part, especially the tradespeople, seldom journey into other countries but always remain in their houses in the City attending to their business, they care little for strangers, but scoff and laugh at them.

Moreover, say they, no one dare oppose our citizens else the street boys and apprentices collect together in great crowds, and strike right and left unmercifully without regard to person.

13th August. THE COUNT MOMPELGARD FEASTS WITH THE FRENCH AMBASSADOR.

Being Sunday the Count Mompelgard attended the French service and afterwards at midday partook of a magnificent banquet provided by the French Ambassador. The French wine did not agree with the Count, though he relished the beer exceedingly.

15th August. A SCURRILOUS JESUIT PAMPHLET.

Some copies have been found in England of a book written in Latin by Father Parsons, the Jesuit, under the name of 'Andreas Philopater,' answering the proclamation made against the Jesuits and seminary priests dated 18th October, 1591. There is also a digest in English, pretended to be put forth by an English Intelligencer in a letter to the Lord Treasurer's secretary. The Latin book hath been translated into French and circulated amongst the Queen's enemies. In this book the proclamation is answered point by point in a preface and six sections, and some of the Council and principal men of the state very slanderously described.

Of Sir Christopher Hatton, Philopater saith that he departed very unwillingly from this life on the very day before this edict was published, which he was said to have resisted so long as he lived and would never have assented to, partly because, being a more moderate man, he would not have approved such cruelty, partly because he differed so heartily from Cecil and the Puritans, to whom Cecil showed patronage, nor would he that they should be increased to oppressing of the Catholics. Hence arose that suspicion of poison for his removal which was written in divers letters from England. Being born of a family honest rather than famous, he had come to London to study the municipal laws of the kingdom ; but when the labours of study seemed to him too heavy to be borne of an equal mind he did, what now a great part of the youth of England are wont to do who come to London to study, but frequent the presence chamber rather than the school. It happened not long after the accession of Queen Elizabeth to the throne, when there was much rejoicing, with merriment, shows, mummings and other childish exercises, that on the very birthday of Our Lord a comedy with the utmost show was presented in the Queen's hall in the name of the University by the students themselves. On this occasion when many acquitted themselves very fairly, Christopher Hatton was thought to have excelled them all in beauty of person and grace of action, by which he so pleased the Queen that henceforward she always had him in the presence chamber, and promoted him through all the grades of honour to the very top, which is the Chancellorship ; for first he was Captain of the Queen's Body-guard, then of the Bed-chamber, finally Chancellor.

Of Cecil it is written that though he is Treasurer, guardian of the wards of nobles, and controls almost all things in England by his own judgment, yet he came of humble and obscure origin. For his father, whose name was David Cecil, served almost in the meanest rank in King's Wardrobe ; his grandfather was one of the Guard of the King's Person, and kept a public tavern in the town of Stamford. After spending some time in the study of letters at the University of Cambridge, where for a time he sought part of his living by tolling the bell in St. John's College, at the beginning of the reign of King Edward the Sixth Cecil insinuated himself into the household of the Duke of Somerset, the Protector.

After thus running through the Lord Treasurer's life from his youth, this Philopater declareth though he would not deny that the Queen assented to the Proclamation (for which she would render her account to God), yet it was not of her own accord, but extorted from her by the importunity of others and especially by the fraud and importunity of Cecil, who is believed to be not only the instigator and procurer of the proclamation but even the writer, because as well as other offices which he has ambitiously grasped, he alone has usurped the office of Secretary after the death of Walsingham. From him proceeded the framing of the whole affair; from him the odious names and phrases newly applied to the Catholics, and not taken over from previous proclamations; from him the insults and lies against Catholic Princes which in the eyes and judgments of all are manifestly false and impudent.

Of Sir Walter Ralegh it is written that he keeps a school of Atheism much frequented, with a certain necromantic astronomer as schoolmaster, where no small number of young men of noble birth learn to deride the Old Law of Moses as well as the New Law of Christ with ingenious quips and jests; and among other things to spell the name of God backwards.

He compareth the seminaries, which the proclamation denounced, with the colleges in the two Universities of England, declaring that the students come out of England neither for lack of living nor for crimes committed, for they are commonly gentlemen, or wealthy peoples' children, and might easily have had preferment if they would apply themselves to the protestants' proceedings. Moreover he showeth that a great multitude of gentlemen's sons leaving their inheritances and other hopes of worldly possibilities at home come over daily to study and to be made priests with infinite desire to return again quickly to England. He declareth that there are more gentlemen at this time in the English seminaries of France, Rome and Spain than in all the clergy of England twice told, to which no gentleman will afford his son to be a minister and much less his daughter to be a minister's wife.

With the order and studies observed in the seminaries are compared the loose proceedings of the English Universities and Colleges where Cecil, Leicester and such like, cancellers of virtue rather than Chancellors of Universities, have overthrown all. The porters are taken away from College gates which used to keep students in awe, whence come confusion and immodesty in apparel, every man wearing either as his pride or his fancy serve, or his purse and ability permit. To this is attributed the filling up and pestering all colleges with harlots to be baits for the young men, headships given to light and wanton companions, fencing and dancing schools crowded, taverns filled with scholars, statutes of founders condemned and broken, leases embezzled, the goods made away, and the places of fellows and scholars publicly sold.

17th August. THE COUNT MOMPELGARD SUMMONED TO COURT.

The Count Mompelgard being summoned to the Court which is now at Reading, arrived there about noon and lodged with the Mayor. Hardly had he changed his apparel when the Earl of Essex visited him in his lodging, welcoming him in the Queen's name and inviting him to take dinner in his apartments, whither the Count was conveyed in a coach. After being most sumptuously feasted, he was entertained with sweet and enchanting music. The repast being ended, he was again accompanied by the Earl of Essex to his lodging, but shortly afterwards he was summoned by the Queen and conducted to her own apartments.

18th August. THE COUNT MOMPELGARD AGAIN VISITS THE QUEEN.

In the afternoon the Count had another audience with the Queen, when she herself made and delivered an appropriate speech in the French language in the presence of Monsieur de Beauvoir, whom she holds in especial favour. After he had been conversing with her in a very lively and good-humoured manner he so far prevailed on her that she played very sweetly and skilfully on her instrument, the strings of which are of gold and silver.

20th August. THE COUNT MOMPELGARD AT WINDSOR.

The Count was conducted to Windsor, and the day being Sunday, he visited the Chapel where he listened for more than an hour to the music, the usual ceremonies and the English sermon. He noted especially the beauty of the playing of the organ and the singing of a little boy, finding the ceremonies very similar to the papists'. Dinner being ended the Count with the English and French deputies went to inspect the Castle of Windsor, and on the lead of the highest tower of all he hath cut his name. After this, he was shown the beautiful royal bed-hangings and tapestries of gold and fine silk, also a unicorn's horn and other costly things.

21st August. GREENE'S 'BLACK BOOK'S MESSENGER.'

Greene's *Black Book's Messenger* is entered, wherein is laid open the life and death of Ned Browne, one of the most notable cutpurses and crossbiters that ever lived in England. This is the messenger to that Black Book, giving a beadroll of all the notable conny-catchers about London which Greene promised in his *Disputation*. Telleth the merry tales of Ned Browne's villanies until he went over to France, where being condemned for robbing a church near Aix he was hanged at a window, in default of a gallows; and his body being buried without the town was in the night torn out of his grave by a company of wolves and devoured.

24th August. CONDEMNED CRIMINALS AS SOLDIERS.

Some of the prisoners remaining in the common jails in Oxford and Berkshire on criminal charges and in danger of capital sentences have promised that if they be sent abroad as soldiers they will not return without special leave. Since some of these men are able and strong, and may prove good subjects to the State, the Council have ordered that means be taken in the discretion of the Lord Chief Baron to deliver them to Sir John Norris after examination of their charges.

27th August. A PRIEST'S INFORMATIONS.

James Young, *alias* Dingley, an arrested priest, hath declared to the Lord Treasurer that he heard from Father Parsons that the King of Spain had promised Sir William Stanley to invade England, but not till 1593, because of the hindrances in France. By which time he hoped to have brought in Brittany and have thence 16 great ships and 10,000 men, and more commodity to come to the Irish kerns; thence Sir William Stanley could go to his own country, where the Earl of Derby would be ready to assist him. He hoped that the young Lord Strange would also help; but now he discloses every one that moved in the matter. The King of Spain said that he remembered the Earl very well, as he was one of the last noblemen married in his time, and that if Lord Strange had been unmarried, none would have been more fit to have been proclaimed King at their first arrival.

A certain Captain Cripps, that came to the Jesuits' College at Seville, spoke to Father Parsons on an embassy wherein Lord Derby was sent, and of a minister that came there from whom a soldier stole a portmanteau; whereupon Parsons replied, he would rather he had stolen my Lord's golden breeches with which he had been known these thirty years at least.

The assault of Stanley is to be attempted next April, and as soon as his arrival is reported, the whole Spanish fleet is to be ready; Parsons is to be present, and Cardinal Allen to come from Rome, but not to England until the event of the navy is seen.

ANXIETY FOR OSTEND.

Great anxiety is felt that the enemy will attempt to surprise the town of Ostend. The Council have ordered that the companies in Ostend which were to have proceeded to Brittany to reinforce Sir John Norris be retained. Further, that Sir Francis Vere and Sir Thomas Morgan who are in command of the companies in Holland shall have everything in readiness at Flushing by the 6th September to embark for Brittany.

29th August. SIR ROGER WILLIAMS' COMPLAINTS.

Sir Roger Williams writeth to the Lord Treasurer from France that the estate of the poor King is now very desperate and our own far from any hope of peace, for in time the greater purses will eat and consume the lesser. The Spaniard will not greatly feel the matter unless the war is made in his own country, or his Indian navy (the armadas and not the merchant ships) defeated, or the Duke of Parma defeated in battle. It seems strange to him to see how we entered into war for the Netherlanders' defence, who traffick freely with the Spanish, whilst we ourselves are barred; by which means Holland and Zealand grow rich, and England greatly impoverished, and will be far greater if it continue any time. Holland and Zealand are rich and invincible, France ruined and poor, ready to be conquered; wherefore the Queen's forces in the Low Countries, saving strong garrisons in Flushing and Brille, should be transported for service in France.

1st September. AN INVASION EXPECTED ON THE SOUTH COAST.

It is credibly reported that a large fleet of ships with a great store of men and munitions have been sent out by the King of Spain and the Leaguers and are now in the Sleeve, which forces are believed to be intended against the Isle of Wight or one of the seaports of Sussex. All armour, furniture, munitions and weapons in those parts are forthwith to be put in readiness, and upon the first notice or discovery of their arrival the forces shall immediately assemble to repulse the enemy; beacon watches also to be renewed and diligently kept.

3rd September. THE DEATH OF ROBERT GREENE.

Robert Greene, author of plays, poems and pamphlets, is dead, having lain sick for a month of a surfeit which he had taken with drinking, and though he continually scoured, yet his body continued to swell upward until it swelled him at the heart and in his face. All this time he hath continued most patient and penitent, with tears forsaking the world, renouncing oaths and desiring forgiveness of God and men for all his offences, so that throughout his sickness he was never heard to swear, rave or blaspheme the name of God as he was accustomed to do before, but he was continuously calling on God even until he gave up the ghost, to the great comfort of his well willers to see how mightily the grace of God worked in him. It is noted that his sickness did not so greatly weaken him, for he walked to his chair and back again the night before he died.

About nine o'clock last night as he lay in bed a friend of his told him that his wife sent her commendations, whereat he greatly rejoiced, and, confessing that he had mightily wronged her, wished that he could see her before he died. But, feeling that his time was short, he took pen and ink and wrote her this letter:

'SWEET WIFE,

As ever there was any good will or friendship between me and thee, see this bearer (my host) satisfied of his debt. I owe him ten pound, and but for him I had perished in the streets. Forget and forgive my wrongs done unto thee, and Almighty God have mercy on my soul. Farewell, till we meet in heaven, for on earth thou shalt never see me more. This 2nd of September, 1592.

Written by thy dying husband,

ROBERT GREENE.'

4th September. THE COUNT MOMPELGARD DEPARTS.

The Count Mompelgard after visiting the Universities of Oxford and Cambridge hath received his passports and is embarked at Gravesend for Flushing.

5th September. DR. HARVEY AND ROBERT GREENE.

Dr. Gabriel Harvey is at this time in London, intending to prosecute Greene at law for what he wrote of his father and brothers in *The Quip for an Upstart Courtier.* But learning that Greene was lying dangerously sick in a shoemaker's house in Dowgate he was speaking of the matter with some friends when he heard that Greene was dead.

Accordingly he went down yesterday to Dowgate to speak with Mrs. Isam, the shoemaker's wife, who told him of Greene's poverty and miserable end: how in his extremity he would beg a penny pot of malmsey, and how none of his old acquaintances came to comfort him except a certain Mistress Appleby and the mother of his bastard son, Fortunatus. Even Nashe, his fellow writer, that was his companion at the fatal banquet of rhenish and pickled herring never after came near him. Mrs. Isam also told Dr. Harvey, with tears in her eyes, how he was fain, poor soul, to borrow her husband's shirt whilst his own was a-washing; and how his doublet and hose and sword were sold for three shillings; and besides the charges of his winding sheet, which was four shillings; and the charge of his burial in the new churchyard near Bedlam, which was six shillings and fourpence; how deeply he was indebted to her poor husband as appeared by his bond for ten pounds, and how, for a tender farewell, she herself crowned his head with a garland of bays.

All these things Dr. Harvey spreads about to his friends.

Greene's lamentable end is much talked of, for he was notorious in London for his dissolute and licentious living, his unseemly apparel and his loose companions, his monstrous swearing and impious profanation of sacred texts, his outrageous surfeiting. He had in employment one 'cutting' Ball, till he was hanged at Tyburn, to levy a crew of his trusted companions to guard him from arresting, and kept this Ball's sister as his mistress, of whom was born his bastard son, Fortunatus Greene, having forsaken his own wife a few months after marriage.

6th September. GREAT WINDS.

To-day the wind blowing west and by south as it hath for two days past, very boisterous, the Thames is so void of water by forcing out the fresh and keeping back the salt, that in divers places men have gone over two hundred paces and then flung a stone to land. A certain collier on a mare rode from the north side to the south and back again on either side of London Bridge; but not without great danger of drowning. This unusual event causeth much wonder especially among the Dutch, who fear lest the sea by some violent inundation has broken the banks in some of the Low Countries.

THE RETURN OF SIR MARTIN FROBISHER'S FLEET EXPECTED.

Sir Martin Frobisher's fleet is expected to return soon, and it is likely that on news of his coming merchants from the city of London will resort to Plymouth and Portsmouth to buy up the goods, and thereby carry the plague from London to those parts still free from infection. No one may be allowed to go to these towns unless licensed by the Council or the Lord Admiral; and as some of them may come in disguise, sufficient guards are, by the Council's order, to be set at the gates to examine all who repair thither.

7th September. THE PLAGUE IN LONDON.

The soldiers levied in Nottinghamshire, Leicester and the neighbouring counties are not to enter the City because of the infection, but to march by land to Southampton.

10th September. THE TAKING OF THE GREAT CARRACK.

The *Madre de Dios*, the great carrack, that was taken at the Islands of the Azores, was brought into Dartmouth the 7th, and the manner of her taking reported.

The season being so far advanced before the expedition set sail, Sir Walter Ralegh abandoned his enterprise upon Panama, and before leaving the fleet, gave directions to Sir John Burgh and Sir Martin Frobisher to divide the ships into two parts; Sir Martin, with the *Garland*, Captain George Gifford, Captain Henry Thin, Captain Grenville and others to lie off the South Cape and thereby to amaze the Spaniards and keep them on their own coasts; while Sir John Burgh, Captain Robert Cross,

Captain Thompson and others should attend at the Islands for the carracks or other Spanish ships coming from Mexico or other parts of the West Indies. This direction took good effect; for the King of Spain's Admiral receiving intelligence that the English Fleet was come on the coast, attended to defend the south parts of Spain, and to keep himself as near Sir Martin Frobisher as he could to impeach him in all things that he might undertake, and thereby neglected the safe conduct of the carracks.

Before the fleet severed themselves, they met with a great Biscayan on the Spanish coast, called the *Santa Clara*, a ship of 600 tons, which after a reasonable hot fight was entered and mastered, being found to be freighted with all sorts of small iron work as horse shoes, nails, plough shares, iron bars, spikes and the like, valued by our men at £6000 or £7000 but worth to them treble the value. This ship, which was sailing towards St. Lucar, there to take in further provision for the West Indies, was first rummaged and after sent for England.

The fleet now coasted along towards the south cape of St. Vincent, and on the way about the Rock near Lisbon, Sir John Burgh in the *Roebuck* spying a sail afar off gave her chase, which being a flyboat and of good sail drew him far southwards before he could fetch her. Not long after, sailing back toward the rest of his company he discovered the Spanish fleet to seaward of him, and they also having espied him between them and the shore spread themselves before him; but trusting to God's help only he thrust out from among them; and knowing that it was but folly to expect a meeting there with Sir Martin Frobisher (who when he understood of this armada as well as himself would be sure not to come that way) he began to shape his course towards the Azores.

Arriving before Flores upon Thursday, the 21st of June, towards evening, accompanied only with Captain Caulfield and the master of his ship, for the rest were not yet arrived, he made towards the shore with his boat, finding all the people of Santa Cruz in arms to bar their landing and ready to defend their town from spoil. Sir John contrariwise made signs to them by advancing a white flag which was answered with the like. Whereupon ensued intercourses of friendship, and pledges were taken on both sides, the Captain of the town for them, Captain Caulfield for ours; so that whatsoever our men wanted which the place would supply either in fresh water, victuals or the like, was very willingly granted by the inhabitants; and good leave given to refresh themselves on shore as much and as oft as they would without restraint.

At this Santa Cruz Sir John was informed that there was indeed no expectation of any fleet to come from the west but from the east, three days before his arrival a carrack had passed by for Lisbon, and that there were four carracks behind of one consort. Sir John being very glad of this news, stayed no longer on shore but at once embarked himself and quickly discovered one of the carracks. Meanwhile, part of the rest of the English fleet drew also towards the Azores, so that the same evening Sir John descried two or three of the Earl of Cumberland's ships (whereof one Mr. Norton was captain), which having in like sort perceived the carrack pursued her by that course which they saw her run towards the Islands. But on no side was there any way made by reason of a great calm, so that to discover what she was Sir John took his boat and rowed the space of three miles to make her out more exactly: and being returned he consulted with the better sort of the company upon boarding her in the morning.

But a very mighty storm arose in the night, the extremity whereof forced them all to weigh anchors; yet their care not to lose the carrack in wrestling with the weather was such that in the morning the tempest being now qualified, and our men bearing in again with the shore, they perceived the carrack very near the land and the Portugals confusedly carrying on shore such things as they could in any manner convey out of her. Seeing the haste our men made to come upon them, they forsook her, but first set fire to that which they could not carry away, intending wholly to consume her that neither glory of victory nor benefit of ship might remain to our men, and, lest the English should extinguish the flames, they entrenched themselves on the land, being four hundred men, to protect the carrack and keep our men aloof so that the carrack might be utterly destroyed. When Sir John Burgh noted this, he landed one hundred of his men, whereof many did swim and wade more than breast high to shore easily scattering those that guarded the coast, and he no sooner drew towards their new trenches but they fled immediately, leaving as much as the fire had spared to be the reward of our men's pains.

Here was taken among others one Vincent Fouseen, a Portugal, purser of the carrack, with two others, one an Almain, the other a Low-Dutchman, both cannoneers, who refused to make any voluntary report of those things which were demanded of them till the torture was threatened ; the fear whereof at last wrested from them the intelligence that within fifteen days three other greater carracks would arrive at the same island. Five carracks had set out from Goa, being specially commanded by the King of Spain not to touch at the island of St. Helena, where the Portugal carracks were always wont to refresh themselves, because of the English men-of-war who (as he was informed) lay there in wait to intercept them. The last rendezvous for them all was the Island of Flores, where the King assured them not to miss his armada sent thither to waft them to Lisbon.

Upon this information Sir John drew to counsel, meeting there Captain Norton, Captain Bownton, Captain Abraham Cock, Captains of three ships of the Earl of Cumberland, Mr. Thompson of Harwich, the Captain of the *Dainty* of Sir John Hawkins, one of Sir Walter Ralegh's fleet, and Mr. Christopher Newport, Captain of the *Golden Dragon*, newly returned from the West Indies, and others. These being assembled, he communicated with them what he had learned and what great presumption of truth the relation did carry, wishing that forasmuch as God and good fortune had brought them together in so good a season, they would show the uttermost of their endeavours to bring these Easterlings under the lee of the English obedience. Hereupon a present accord on all sides followed not to part company or leave of those seas till time should present cause to put their consultations in execution. The next day, the Queen's good ship, the *Foresight*, commanded by Sir Robert Cross, came in to the rest, and he, being likewise informed of the matter, was soon drawn into the service.

Thus Sir John with all these ships departing thence six or seven leagues to the west of Flores, they spread themselves abroad from north to south, each ship two leagues at least distant from another, by which order of extension they were able to discover the space of two whole degrees at sea.

In this sort they lay from 29th June to 3rd August, what time Captain Thompson in the *Dainty* had first sight of the huge carrack called the *Madre de Dios*. The *Dainty* being of excellent sail got the start of the rest of the fleet, and began the conflict, somewhat to her cost, with slaughter and hurt of divers of her men. Within a while after Sir John Burgh in the *Roebuck* of Sir Walter Ralegh's was at hand to second her, who saluted her with shot of great ordnance and continued the fight within musket shot, assisted by Captain Thompson and Captain Newport, till Sir Robert Cross, Vice-Admiral of the fleet, came up, being to leeward. At his arrival Sir John demanded of him what was best to be done, who answered that if the carrack were not boarded she would recover the shore and fire herself as the other had done.

Whereupon Sir John concluded to entangle her and Sir Robert promised also to fasten himself at the same instant; which was accomplished. But after a while Sir John Burgh receiving a shot with a cannon perrier under water and being ready to sink desired Sir Robert to fall off that he might also clear himself and save his ship from sinking, which with much difficulty he did; for both the *Roebuck* and the *Foresight* were so entangled that they had much ado to clear themselves.

The same evening Sir Robert Cross finding the carrack then sure and drawing near the island persuaded his company to board her again, or else there was no hope to recover her. And they after many excuses and fears were by him encouraged and so fell athwart her foreships all alone and so hindered her sailing that the rest had time to come up to his succour. Toward the evening after he had fought with her for three hours alone, the Earl of Cumberland's two ships came up and with very little loss entered with Sir Robert Cross, who had in that time broken their courages and made the assault easy for the rest.

The General having disarmed the Portugals and stowed them for better security on all sides, now saw the true proportion of the great carrack which did then and may still justly provoke the admiration of all men; yet the sight of so many bodies slain and dismembered drew each man's eye to lament and hands to help.

No man could step but upon a dead carcase or a bloody floor, especially about the helm; for the greatness of the steerage required the labour of twelve or fourteen men at once, and some of our ships beating her in at the stern with their ordnance, oftentimes with one shot slew four or five labouring on either side the helm. Whereupon our General moved with singular commiseration of their misery sent them his own surgeons, denying them no possible help that he or any of his company could afford.

Sir John intending not to add too much affliction to the afflicted, at length resolved freely to dismiss the captain and most part of his followers to their own country, and bestowed them in certain vessels furnished with all kinds of necessary provisions. This business thus despatched, he had good leisure to take a more convenient view of the goods, having first, to prevent the pillage to which he saw many inclined, seized upon the whole to the Queen's use.

The carrack is in burden estimated at 1600 tons, of which 900 tons are stowed with merchandise. Her length from the beak head to the stern (whereon is erected a lantern) is 165 feet; her breadth at the widest in the second close deck (whereof she hath three) is 46 feet 10 inches. She drew in water 31 feet at her departure from Cochin in India but not above 26 at her arrival in Dartmouth. She carries in height seven several stories, one main orlop, three close decks, one forecastle, and a spar deck of two floors apiece. The length of the keel is about 100 feet, of the main mast 121 feet, and the circuit about at the partners 10 feet 7 inches; the main yard is 106 feet long. There were between 600 and 700 persons on board.

The Plague in London.

The plague is greatly increased, and it is feared that the infection may grow with the prisons pestered with the great numbers committed for debt or on small charges. The Lord Mayor is required in common charity to cause speedy inquiry to be made, and, having summoned debtors and creditors, to persuade them to come to some composition; for if the imprisoned die, the creditors will lose their whole debt.

TWO RICH SPANISH PRIZES BROUGHT IN.

Mr. Thomas White in the *Amity* is returned to London with two Spanish prizes which he reporteth to have taken on the 26th July off the coast of Barbary.

At four in the morning, having sighted two ships about three or four leagues distant, that proved to be a Biscayan and a flyboat, they came within gunshot by seven, supposing by their boldness in having the King of Spain's arms displayed that they were ships of war.

The enemy having placed themselves in warlike order, one a cable's length from the other, the *Amity* began the fight, in which our men continued as fast as they were able to charge and discharge for the space of five hours, being never a cable's length distant from either.

In this time they received divers shot both in the hull of the ship, masts and sails to the number of 32 great, besides 500 musket shot, and harquebuses a crock at least. And because they perceived the enemy to be stout, our men thought good to board the Biscayan which was head on to the other, where lying aboard about an hour and playing their ordnance, in the end they stowed all the enemy's men. Then the other in the flyboat, thinking our men had entered into their fellow, bare room with the *Amity* meaning to have laid her aboard and so entrapped her between them both. But the *Amity*, quitting herself of her enemy, hoisted top sails and weathered them both. Then coming hard aboard the flyboat with her ordnance prepared, gave her whole broadside and slew several so that our men saw the blood running out at the scupper holes. After that they cast about, new charged all the ordnance, and, coming upon them again, willed them to yield or else they would sink them : whereupon the one would have yielded, which was shot between and water, but the other called him traitor. To whom our men made answer that if he would not also yield immediately, they would sink him first. Thereupon, understanding their determination, he put out a white flag and yielded, yet they refused to strike their own sails because they were sworn never to strike to any Englishman. The captains and masters were then commanded to come aboard, which they did ; and after examination and stowing some, certain of our men were sent aboard who struck their sails and manned their ships, finding in them 126 persons living and 8 dead, besides those whom they themselves had cast overboard. Our men were but 42 and a boy. These two ships are rich prizes, laden with 1400 chests of quicksilver with the arms of Castile and Leon fastened upon them, and a great quantity of bulls or indulgences, and gilded missals or service books, besides a hundred tuns of excellent wines, so that what with his silver which should have delivered from the quicksilver and his taxes on the bulls at 2 reals the piece, the King of Spain's loss amounts to £707,700.

14th September. SPANISH HOPES.

The priest, George Dingley, is again examined before the Lord Keeper, Lord Buckhurst and Mr. John Fortescue about the things he had heard in Spain. He declareth that many of our nobility were believed to be discontented at not being advanced and would easily be moved to follow the Spaniard, who would promise to put them in places of authority if he should possess England. The Earls of Oxford and Cumberland, and the Lords Strange and Percy are much talked of as alienated by discontent. Their chief hope is the Queen's death ; wherefore the Spaniard lingers in his attempt at again assaulting England because time will call her away, when they have certain hope of a debate between the two houses of Hertford and Derby, who will seek the throne, each for himself ; during which contention the Spaniard thinketh entry into England would be without danger.

They greatly rejoiced in the mutterings of the Martinists, translating the book into Spanish and presenting it to the King, judging from its hot words that some uproar would shortly be moved by that faction which would find favour amongst the noblemen in hopes of enjoying the bishops' and other spiritual revenues.

They think Lancashire and the north will soonest favour them, and Sir William Stanley would have the Spanish navy come to Milford Haven rather than to the narrow seas.

Though there are many beyond sea who wish this new assault attempted, yet Father Parsons is the only man England need fear ; he by his travail and credit with the Spaniard, solicits the

King and his councillors by all means possible, and maintains Cardinal Allen and Stanley with accounts. There is not a man executed in England for religion who is not known there, and sermons openly preached in his praise, with bitter inveighing against the cruelty of our present governors.

16th September. The Great Carrack.

The sailors are making great pillagings of the spoil of the Great Carrack. Sir Robert Cecil and Mr. Thomas Middleton are sent down in haste to take charge of the matter, being instructed to inquire into the proceedings of Sir Ferdinand Gorges and the other Commissioners; to cause all lading to be viewed and entered in registers and especially to search out all precious things; and also to hire sufficient ships to bring the goods into the Thames. Sir Walter Ralegh, in the charge of Mr. Blunt, is also despatched from the Tower to join them on the Commission.

17th September. Thame Fair put off.

Thame fair that is usually held on Michaelmas day is postponed for 15 days lest the Londoners resorting thither should spread the plague, to the danger of the Queen who proposes at that time to visit Lord Norris at Ricott on her progress.

19th September. The Spread of the Plague.

The plague is now reported at East Greenwich. Sir John Hawkins is to take special measures to prevent it from spreading to Deptford and Lewisham, lest the Queen's service should be hindered; also to cause the making of starch at a house in Deptford Strand to cease because of the number of dogs used therein which, being a noisome kind of cattle, especially at this contagious time, are very apt to draw on the infection.

20th September. Greene's 'Groat's-worth of Wit.'

Chettle hath sent to the press *Greene's Groat's-worth of Wit, bought with a million of repentance*, collected out of certain papers that Greene left at his death. In the forepart of the book are displayed the adventures of one Roberto, a scholar, that despising the wealth heaped by his dying father, a miser and an usurer, was left but a groat. The money thus passing to his younger brother Lucanio, Roberto practised to fleece him with the help of Mistress Lamilia, a courtesan, and found small difficulty in bringing the two together. But no sooner hath Lamilia enticed Lucanio into her power than she betrayed Roberto to his brother, who cast him out of doors. Then Roberto, being in extremities, began to lament his woes in verse when a player, chancing to come, offered him employment, which, seeing no other remedy, he accepted; and thereafter falling into bad company, mingled with thieves and harlots, until by immeasurable drinking and the scourge of lust he now lay comfortlessly languishing. Here, noting that Roberto's story agreed in most parts with his own, Greene broke off his tale, adding certain rules for young gentlemen that are delighted with the like fantasies, warning them of God's judgment on those who follow their own lusts.

To his fellow scholars in the City that also made plays he wrote a very invective letter, especially warning two of them, the one termed a 'famous gracer of tragedians' to beware of atheism, the other, a 'young Juvenal that biting satirist,' that with him lately wrote a comedy, to avoid getting enemies by bitter words. To these is joined a third, that also dependeth on the making of plays, to shun the ingratitude of the players, for, saith he, 'there is an upstart crow, beautified with our feathers, that with his *Tiger's heart wrapped in a player's hide*, supposes he is as well able to bombast out a blank verse as the best of you; and being an absolute *Johannes factotum*, is in his own conceit the only Shake-scene in a country.'

These words are very offensively taken by those intended.

22nd September. THE GREAT CARRACK.

Sir Robert Cecil having now reached Exeter writeth that he has brought back everyone he met within seven miles of Exeter that had anything in a cloak, bag or mail, which did but smell of the prizes (for he could smell them almost, such had been the spoils of amber and musk). He stays anyone, who might carry news to Dartmouth or Plymouth, at the gates of the town; he compels them also to tell him where any trunks or mails are, and finding the people stubborn, has committed two innkeepers to prison; had this been done a week ago, it would have saved the Queen £20,000. In a Londoner's shop, he found a bag of seed pearls, pieces of damask, cypresses and calicos, a very great port of musk, and certain tassels of pearl.

He hath left an impression by his rough dealing with the Mayor and orders a search of every bag coming from the west. There never was such spoil; letters have been intercepted to friends in London to come down, all which he keeps to charge the parties at Dartmouth, and over two thousand buyers are assembling; them he will suppress.

In his search he hath found an armlet of gold, and a fork and spoon of crystal with rubies, which he reserves for the Queen. Sir Walter Ralegh came after him, but having outridden him will be at Dartmouth first.

THE QUEEN AT OXFORD.

The Queen, on her progress, leaving Woodstock is gone to Oxford.

She entered the bounds of the University at Godstow Bridge about three o'clock in the afternoon, where she was waited for by the Vice-Chancellor of the University, the Heads of Colleges in their scarlet gowns, and the proctors and beadles. As soon as the Queen learned that the Vice-Chancellor and the rest were ready to present their duties to her, she caused her coach to be stayed, notwithstanding the foulness of the weather, and signified her pleasure to hear a speech, provided it were not too long. Whereupon Mr. Saville, the Senior Proctor, being then on his knees with the rest of the company, entered into a short speech signifying the great joy of the University. This done, the Queen with the nobility and the rest of her royal train went towards the City, being met by the Mayor, with the Aldermen and Bailiffs, the Recorder and the townsmen, who received her in a short speech, offering in the name of the city a cup of silver gilt containing sixty angels. As she entered the City, she was received with great applause from the crowds of scholars that thronged the streets from the North Gate to Christchurch, signifying their joy by speeches and singing. Then as she passed by St. John's College she was presented with a private speech on behalf of the College and so to the Carfax, where the Reader in Greek offered a short speech in Greek, being thanked by her Majesty in the same tongue. Thence they moved to the great quadrangle of Christchurch where the Public Orator declared the abundant joy of the University. After a short time the Queen entered the Cathedral Church under a canopy borne by four doctors, where the *Te Deum* was sung and thanksgiving offered for her safe arrival.

CONSTABLE'S 'DIANA.'

Mr. Henry Constable hath sent to the press his *Diana*, eight decads of sonnets, dedicated in a sonnet by Mr. Richard Smyth to 'Her Sacred Majesty's honourable Maids.'

23rd September. THE QUEEN AT OXFORD.

Between two and three o'clock in the afternoon the Queen went to the Church of St. Mary, riding in a rich carriage and attended by the nobility on horseback with foot cloths. The Queen being placed under her cloth of estate upon a very fair stage, purposely erected for her in the east end of the church, a philosophy act was provided for her, which was begun on the word '*incipiatis*' being uttered by her. Whereupon the proctors called on the first replier, who after three conges to the Queen propounded the questions unto the answerer. Hereupon the answerer, Mr. Thomas Smith, Orator of the University, repeated the questions, which were:

i. '*An anima cuiusuis fit in se praestantior anima alterius?*' (Whether the soul of one man be more excellent than the soul of another.)

ii. '*An, ob mundi senectam, homines minus sunt heroici nunc quam olim?*' (Whether, on account of the age of the world, men be less heroic now than formerly.)

And so entered into his position, which continued for almost half an hour, which the Queen thought somewhat long, for when the Proctors said to the replier, in the accustomed words, '*procede magister*,' she supposing that they spoke to Mr. Smith said that he had been too long already.

Upon these words Mr. Gwynne first addressing himself to her Majesty to excuse his disability to speak in that honourable presence, spoke discreetly and wittily for about a quarter of an hour, and was then cut off by the Proctors. After the others had spoken the argument was ended by Mr. Saville, who determined the questions in a very good speech though somewhat long, ending with thanks to her Majesty for her great patience in hearing. This done the Queen returned to her lodging attended as she had come.

A PROCLAMATION ABOUT THE GREAT CARRACK.

A proclamation is published charging all who have taken or received goods of any value out of the Spanish carrack lately brought to Dartmouth, either while she was on the seas or since her coming into the haven, that within ten days they discover to the principal officer of the place where they reside what they have received or sold.

Likewise all innkeepers, householders, or owners of any vessels, where any person shall come with any carriage wherein they may suspect any portion of the commodities from the carrack to be bestowed, shall cause the same to be stayed.

Further, that if anyone who claims any portion of the goods by reason of his consort or adventure in the late service be proved to have taken or bought anything from the carrack without revealing it to the Commissioners, he shall lose all the benefit he might claim from the adventure.

24th September. THE QUEEN AT OXFORD.

Being Sunday the sermon was preached before the Queen by the Dean of Christchurch, Dr. James; and at night a comedy, called *Bellum Grammaticale*, was acted in the hall of the College which was most graciously and patiently heard by the Queen, though but meanly performed.

SIR ROBERT CECIL AT DARTMOUTH.

Sir Robert Cecil now writeth from Dartmouth of his dealings with the Great Carrack. As soon as he came on board the carrack with the rest of the Commissioners, Sir Walter Ralegh arrived with his keeper, Mr. Blunt. His poor servants to the number of 140, and all the mariners came to him with such shouts of joy that he was much troubled to quiet them. But his heart is broken, and he is extremely pensive unless he is busied, in which he can toil terribly. The meeting between him and Sir John Gilbert, his half-brother, was with tears on Sir John's part; but Ralegh finding that it is known that he hath a keeper, whenever he is saluted with congratulation for his liberty answers, 'No, I am still the Queen of England's poor captive.' Sir Robert wished him to conceal it, because it diminished his credit, which was greater among the mariners than he had thought; therefore he graces him as much as possible, finding Ralegh very greedy to anything to recover the conceit of his brutish offence.

They have found a thing worth looking on, rats, white and black, and a drink like smoke in taste.

25th September. THE COURT AT OXFORD.

At nine in the morning a divinity lecture was read by Mr. Holland, her Majesty's Reader in Divinity, at which many scholars were present but few of the nobility. The Lords of the Council dined with Mr. Saville at Martin College in the common hall, where, after dinner, they heard a disputation in philosophy which was determined by Mr. Saville, who because one of the questions had been '*An dissensiones ciuium sint respublicae utiles?*' (Whether the disagreements of citizens are useful for the state) took occasion to commend by name the Lord Treasurer, who was present, the Lord Chamberlain, the Lord Admiral and the Earl of Essex. This done the Lords went to sit in Council.

27th September. THE QUEEN AT OXFORD.

In the afternoon the Queen came again to St. Mary's and listened to questions in Law and Divinity, the last act being determined by the Bishop of Hereford, who argued against the question, '*An licet in Christiana respublica dissimulare in causa religionis?*' (Whether it be lawful in a Christian commonwealth to feign in the cause of religion). Upon which he made so copious and eloquent an oration that the Queen twice sent to him to cut short his words because she meant herself to make a speech that night. But he either would not, or else could not, put himself out of a set methodical speech for fear lest he should have marred it all and perhaps confounded his memory. The Queen was so tired that she forbore her speech that day.

28th September. THE QUEEN LEAVES OXFORD.

About ten in the forenoon the Queen sending for the Vice-Chancellor and the Heads of Houses made them a speech in Latin in which she thanked them for their entertainment; but in the middle of her oration casting her eye aside and seeing the Lord Treasurer standing for want of a stool, she called in all haste for a stool for him, and would not proceed in her speech till she saw he was provided with one. Then she fell to it again as if there had been no interruption, whereupon one, who might be so bold with her, afterwards told her that she did it of purpose to show that she could interrupt her speech and not be put out although the Bishop of Hereford durst not do so for a less matter the day before. Shortly afterward, about eleven in the forenoon, the Queen and her train left the University, and heard, lastly, a long tedious oration made by the Junior Proctor of the University, at the very edge of their boundaries near Shotover.

1st October. THE INCREASE OF THE PLAGUE.

The plague still grows in the City. The Lord Mayor and Aldermen are straightly warned that if the infection do not abate the Queen will remove the Term to some other place, to the great hindrance of the City. Moreover, by the Queen's special direction, the Council demand what means are being taken to keep the sick from the sound, and to relieve those whose houses were shut up; and why the Lord Mayor and Aldermen refuse to allow fires to be lit in the streets which has been found by good experience very effective in purging the air in places infected.

REINFORCEMENTS FOR BRITTANY.

A further reinforcement of 1000 men is to be enrolled for Sir John Norris in Brittany; of whom one-third to be armed with pikes and halberds, the remainder furnished with harquebusses and calivers, of which one-fourth were to be muskets. In choosing men especial care is to be taken that they be of able body and fit for service and not, as is too common, so light or so fearful that, after they have marched to the seaside or to their destination, they either run away from their captains, or offer them money to be discharged and suffered to return.

6th October. 'THE REPENTANCE OF ROBERT GREENE.'

The Repentance of Robert Greene is entered, being written by himself as he lay dying, in which he relates the story of his life and the misery of his end brought on himself by loose company, drunkenness, swearing, contempt of the Word, and other gross and grievous sins.

KYD'S 'SPANISH TRAGEDY.'

The Spanish Tragedy, written by Thomas Kyd some years before, that was lately played at the Rose Theatre, is to be printed.

11th October. CITY FEASTS TO BE FORBORNE.

Because of the infection the Lord Mayor sought directions for the keeping or omitting of the feasts and ceremonies usual at the taking of the oath. The Council now approve the omitting of the feasts at the Guildhall and in other Halls of Companies, and desire that the money so saved be given to relieve those whose houses are infected. For this end the preacher at Paul's Cross on the Sunday following shall notify to the people why the feasts are for this time to be forborne, and let them understand that it is not to spare charge but because of the inconvenience that might come from drawing together assemblies; and also that the money is being put to a use more acceptable to God and for the good of the City. Moreover those poor men who are thereby relieved will be more willing to keep within their houses.

12th October. PRECAUTIONS AGAINST THE PLAGUE.

That the Court may be the better preserved from the infection, it is proclaimed that no one, except those who have cause to come thither for their ordinary attendance on the Queen's person, repair to the Court or within two miles of it.

Nor shall anyone attending on the Queen repair to London or the suburbs or places within two miles of the city without special licence in writing, upon pain to be imprisoned by attachment of the Knight Marshal. He is to cause search to be made for all vagabonds, commonly called rogues, that haunt about the Court or within the verge.

18th October. PLAGUE DEATHS.

This last week 198 persons died of the plague in London.

19th October. SIR JOHN NORRIS DELAYED.

The weather at Southampton remains contrary so that the soldiers with Sir John Norris are unable to sail. Upwards of one hundred men have run away, and though Sir John has written to the justices thereabout to apprehend them, yet such is the slender care found in them and in the constables and other officers charged to follow the hue and cry that not a man has been returned. They are received into houses in the country, and helped to convey themselves and their furniture away. Sir John hath asked the Council that one hundred men may be pressed in Hampshire to fill up their places and to give the county better minds than to hinder the soldiers and assist them to escape.

Not finding sufficient shipping at Southampton, Sir John wrote to the Mayor of Poole, who showed himself very willing, charging the masters and owners of some suitable shipping in the road to put themselves in readiness; but they disobediently and contemptuously took down their masts and rigging, using very bad language and threatening revenge. For this the Mayor has committed them.

21st October. A PROCLAMATION CONCERNING THE PLAGUE.

A proclamation is published that, as the infection in London and Westminster is but little abated, the remainder of the term is adjourned to Hertford, and all with causes or suits in the Courts of Chancery, Starchamber, Exchequer, Wards and Liveries, the Duchy of Lancaster or Court of Requests to proceed thither.

Further if there should be any access at the Castle or Town of Hertford of those that have the plague in their houses or have been infected with it, there may ensue great evil and damage to the rest of the realm. It is commanded that no persons who have had the plague in their houses or have been infected themselves since the 1st of July shall repair to the town of Hertford unless summoned by special process for their personal appearance. Any one so summoned shall openly notify by some message his state to those appointed by the Lord Keeper of the Great Seal to keep the gates. If the party then be ordered to come into the town or castle, to bear in his hand, upright to be seen, one red rod of the length of a yard or more.

20th October. THE DEATH OF COUNT MONTAIGNE.

News is received in London of the death of Count Michael de Montaigne, which occurred on the 13th September from a quinsy.

THE GREAT CARRACK.

Certain persons from Antwerp and other towns of the Low Countries, subjects of the King of Spain, are lately arrived in London to buy part of the goods taken in the Carrack. As they have come without licence or safe conduct, the Lord Mayor is to make immediate search within the City that it may be known who they were; and, when any are found, their hosts to be made chargeable that they be forthcoming to obey such directions as shall be given them. Also they are to be searched for jewels, and if any be found in their possession these are to be taken away and kept in safe custody.

22nd October. EDWARD ALLEYN MARRIES.

Edward Alleyn, the tragedian, hath married Joan Woodward, step-daughter to Philip Henslowe that built the Rose Theatre.

23rd October. BEACON WATCHES TO BE DISCONTINUED.

Now that the nights grow very long and cold with the approach of winter, the watching of beacons is become very tedious and troublesome, and no longer necessary. The Council have ordered it to be discontinued until the spring.

27th October. THE NORMANDY FORCES TO BE SENT TO BRITTANY.

The companies in Normandy are ordered to be sent to Brittany in the conduct of Sir Roger Williams to serve under Sir John Norris in Brittany. On arrival Sir Roger shall be appointed a Marshal of the Field in place of Sir Henry Norris, and Colonel of one of the regiments of 400.

30th October. ABUSES AT HERTFORD.

Now that the Michaelmas Term is adjourned to Hertford excessive prices are being demanded by the inhabitants for chambers and lodgings. Her Majesty hath caused her Clerk of the Musket to repair thither and to set reasonable prices on all manner of victuals, as dear at least as in London, and likewise on the houses, lodging, stables, shops and other rooms; and for the convenience of those that repair thither, a harbinger of the Queen's to inform them of these prices. Moreover divers Londoners have already hired houses and lodgings, intending to offer victuals for sale, retail wares, and let out chambers for their own private gains. The magistrates shall suffer no one from the City of London, Westminster, the suburbs, or Southwark to hire any houses or chambers or other rooms that is not a professed Counsellor, Attorney or Solicitor of the law.

THE LORD MAYOR REBUFFED.

In answer to the suit of the Lord Mayor and Aldermen that the term might be held in London, the Council have written that they wish with all their hearts that the Lord Mayor had observed the orders prescribed for preventing the spread of infection, and then the Queen would have had no cause to remove the Term. Had their suit been made earlier it might have been considered, but her Majesty is now fully resolved on it and the preparations are too far forward for them to be recalled without great inconvenience.

4th November THE DEATH OF SIR JOHN PERROT.

Sir John Perrot died last night in the Tower, where he has remained under sentence of death since June.

THE CHARACTER OF SIR JOHN PERROT.

Sir John Perrot was exceedingly tall and big in stature, yet his body was very compact and well proportioned, and as he exceeded most men in stature so did he in strength of body. His countenance was full of majesty, his eye marvellously piercing and carrying a commanding aspect, insomuch that when he was angry he had a very terrible visage, but when he was pleased or willing to show kindness, he had then as amiable a countenance as any man. His mind was answerable to his body, for he was of an undaunted spirit, never regarding his adversaries were they never so many or so great. In time of danger he showed himself always resolute and valiant ; he had a very sharp wit and was naturally wise. But he had also some defects ; for he was by nature choleric and could not brook any crosses or dissemble the least injuries although offered by the greatest personages, and thereby he procured to himself many and mighty adversaries who in the end wrought his overthrow. In anger he would sometimes deal roughly, and so long as any man did oppose him he would contend with him by sword or by law: but if submission were offered by an inferior or reconciliation by his equal he would receive it readily. When moved by wrath he would swear excessively, partly from custom, partly from choler. He was also addicted to incontinence, leaving children by several ventures, as well as his lawful son, who succeeds him.

Many declare that his fall was brought about through the malice of Sir Christopher Hatton, the Lord Chancellor, whom Sir John had taunted because, as he said, he danced himself into favour. But the Chancellor hath a greater injury against Sir John, in that he seduced his daughter. On his return from his trial he cried with oaths and fury to Sir Owen Hopton, the Lieutenant of the Tower, 'What, will the Queen suffer her brother to be offered up as a sacrifice to the envy of my flattering adversaries?' These words being carried to the Queen, she refused to sign the order for his execution, and swore that he should not die, for he was an honest and faithful man. His mother was a lady of great honour in the Court of King Henry the Eighth who was married to Sir Thomas Perrot, a gentleman of the Privy Chamber, but Sir John in his person, qualities, gesture and voice so much resembled the late King that it is very generally believed that he was indeed a surreptitious child of the blood royal.

4th November. HARWARD'S 'SOLACE FOR THE SOLDIER AND THE SAILOR.'

The Solace for the Soldier and the Sailor, written by Simon Harward, that was a Chaplain in the Earl of Cumberland's fleet, is to be printed, being dedicated to the Archbishop of Canterbury. In the preface to the Christian Reader, Mr. Harward saith that he hath written this pamphlet for three causes; the first because he is thereunto requested by certain godly and valiant captains and shipmasters amongst whom he laboured on the Spanish seas; the second, to answer the obloquies and reproachful speeches of many that affirm that his voyages are a blot and discredit to the doctrine which he delivereth on land; and thirdly because of the many seditious malcontents who by their unthankful grudgings will not afford a good word to those that are willing to undergo so many dangers abroad to procure peace and quietness at home. In his book he justifieth from Scripture the lawfulness of the profession of arms, and especially of the war against the Spaniard.

13th November. MR. HERRICK'S GOODS.

Mr. Nicholas Herrick, a goldsmith, hath of late fallen from an upper window in his house in the City and is dead, whereupon some credibly think that he cast himself out wilfully, whereby his goods and chattels are forfeited to the Queen's Almoner, though by others the matter is endeavoured to be found casual. The coroners of the City of London are straightly charged that they receive no verdict until the evidence which the Almoner shall bring is thoroughly known and examined.

14th November. SIR JOHN NORRIS'S COMPLAINTS.

Sir John Norris writeth that fresh Spaniards to the number of 2500 have appeared in Brittany, but his own men run away infinitely, so that when all shall come together there will not be 3000, wherewith he will not spare himself, but he can make them no more worth than they are, for he never saw men more fearful. The King has sent for these troops to assist him to the recovery of the Castle of Pont de l'Arch, and Sir John awaiteth the Queen's instructions thereon.

17th November. CORONATION DAY.

Upon the Coronation Day, at night, there came into the Privy Chamber two armed knights (being the Earl of Essex and the Earl of Cumberland) and there made a challenge that upon the 26th February next they will run all comers to maintain that their mistress is the worthiest and fairest Amadis of Gaul.

20th November. A FAVOURITE LADY-IN-WAITING.

Her Majesty is so pleased with the behaviour of the Lady Bridget Manners, one of her Ladies-in-Waiting, and daughter of the Countess of Rutland, that she hath caused Sir Thomas Heneage, her Vice-Chamberlain, to write to the lady's mother to this effect:

'The exceeding good, modest and honourable behaviour of my Lady Bridget your daughter with her careful and diligent attendance of her Majesty is so contenting to her Highness and so commendable in this place where she lives (where vices will hardly receive vizards and virtues will most shine) as her Majesty acknowledgeth she hath cause to thank you for her, and you may take comfort of so virtuous a daughter, of whose being, love and attendance, her Majesty hath bidden me to tell your Ladyship that you shall have no cause to repent.'

'SOLIMAN AND PERSEDA.'

The Tragedy of Soliman and Perseda is entered for printing.

7th December. UNWILLING CAPTAINS TO BE PUNISHED.

Certain captains and soldiers of the forces ordered to pass from the Low Countries to Brittany excuse themselves for frivolous reasons. It is ordered that the Deputy-Treasurer in the place shall withhold the pay and imprest money of any who refused to embark, and also inform the Governor, requiring him to commit the offender to prison, not to be released until he hath certified the Council and received direction.

8th December. CHETTLE'S 'KINDHEART'S DREAM.'

Chettle hath entered his *Kindheart's Dream*, wherein he taketh occasion to clear himself of the charges made against him for having allowed the letter in Greene's *Groat's-worth of Wit* to be printed. 'With neither of them,' saith he, 'that take offence was I acquainted, and with one of them I care not if I never be. The other, whom at that time I did not so much spare as since I wish I had, for that as I have moderated the heat of living writers, and might have used my own discretion, especially in such a case (the author being dead); that I did not, I am as sorry as if the original fault had been my fault, because myself have seen his demeanour no less civil than he excellent in the quality he professes; besides, divers of worship have reported his uprightness of dealing, which argues his honesty and his facetious grace in writing that approves his art. For the first, whose learning I reverence, and at the perusing of Greene's book stroke out what then in conscience I thought he in some displeasure writ; him I would wish to use me no worse than I deserve. I had only in the copy this share: it was ill written, as sometimes Greene's hand was none of the best; licensed it must be, ere it could be printed, which could be never if it might not be read.

To be brief, I writ it over, and, as near as I could, followed the copy, only in that letter I put something out, but in the whole book not a word in; for I protest it was all Greene's; not mine nor Master Nashe's as some unjustly have affirmed.'

16th December. THE FUNERAL OF THE DUKE OF PARMA.

The Duke of Parma died of his wound on the 3rd of this month and on the 10th his body was brought with great pomp and solemnity from Arras to Brussels. The soldiers and fraternities, all the clergy, the Counts Von Mansfield, Arenburg, Barlaimont, and de Fuentes, with all the rest of the nobility, and the members of the Council came out to meet the corpse with lighted lanterns in their hands, and escorted it to the Castle Chapel.

18th December. 'ELIOT'S FRUITS FOR THE FRENCH.'

Mr. John Eliot hath written *Orthœpia Gallica or Eliot's Fruits for the French*, being penned for the practice, pleasure, and profit of all English gentlemen, who will endeavour by their own pain, study and diligence, to attain the natural accent, the true pronunciation, the swift and glib grace of this noble, famous and courtly language.

In the first part of the book are three dialogues, showing the words and sentences used by the scholar and traveller, followed by the two books of *The Parliament of Prattle* , giving the words and sentences needed by gentlemen on two and thirty kinds of occasion. In the former of these books the French words are shown in the first column; in the second the way of pronouncing them; and in the third the English.

30th December. PLAYING RESUMED.

Yesterday the Lord Strange's players began again to play at the Rose Theatre after their inhibition in the summer, and played *Muly Mullocco*; and to-day *The Spanish Tragedy*.

31st December. THE BILLS OF MORTALITY FOR THE YEAR.

This year first beginneth a custom of keeping weekly bills of mortality for the City of London and the parishes immediately adjoining. When anyone dies either the tolling and ringing of the bell or the bespeaking of a grave intimateth it to the searchers (who keep a strict correspondence with the sextons);

and thereupon the ancient matrons sworn to that office repair to the place where the corpse lies, and upon their own view and others' examination, make a judgment of what disease or casualty the corpse died, which judgment they report to the parish clerk. He on every Tuesday night bringeth to the clerk of the Hall an account of every christening and burial that week; whence on Wednesday the general account is made up, and printed. During this year 1592, there have died in London from March to December 25,886 persons, whereof of the plague 11,503.

SOMEWHAT TO READ FOR THEM THAT LIST

1592.

COLONNA'S 'HYPNEROTOMACHIA.'

Hypnerotomachia : the Strife of Love in a Dream. Written in Italian by Francisco Colonna, and translated into English by Richard Dallington, being dedicated to the thrice honourable and ever living virtues of Sir Philip Sidney, Knight, and to the right honourable and others whatsoever, who living loved him, and being dead gave him his due, and the epistle written to the Earl of Essex. The story telleth of the amorous visions of the monk Potiphilus, and the first Italian copy is much noted for the beauty of its cuts.

GREENE'S 'DISPUTATION.'

A Disputation between a He Conny-catcher and a She Conny-catcher, written by Robert Greene, in which Lawrence, a foist, and Nan, a traffic, dispute for a supper whether a thief or a whore is more prejudicial to a commonwealth, both alleging instances out of their experience until Lawrence confesseth that he is beaten.

Appended to the *Disputation* is the *Conversion of an English Courtesan*, relating how a certain young woman, the daughter of wealthy parents, became a strumpet. Being from childhood cockered by her parents, she flouted the warnings of her kinsmen, and refused the wealthy farmer whom her parents chose for her husband but fell in with the humour of the odd companion of a gentleman that dwelt hard by, a fellow of small reputation and no living, that had no excellent qualities save thrumming on the gittern, and the singing of quaint and ribald jigs. Having yielded herself to him, he carried her away to an Inn, when as his money ran short, he left her to see how her parents took their departure. The report of her beauty being spread abroad, many youthful gentlemen came to the Inn to seek her favour, with one of whom she went off to the Bath, where she lived as his wife ;

until growing tired of her new lover, she inveigled one of his friends to take her to London, and here after a time he left her, and she betook herself to a place of good hospitality as a common strumpet.

Hither came a sober young clothier with whom she fell violently in love, but he refused at first to have aught to do with her. Coming a second time he asked for a chamber, and she gladly took him apart into the fairest room where they fell to dalliance. But he complained that the room was too light; whereupon she took him to another room and drawing the curtain asked if that was too light. Still he asked for a darker room, so that she took him into a back loft, so dark that at noon it was impossible for a man to see his own hands.

'How now, sir,' quoth she, 'is not this dark enough?'

He, sitting on the bed, fetched a deep sigh and said, 'Indifferently, so, so; but there is a glimpse of light in at the tiles; somebody may see us.'

'In faith, no,' quoth she, 'none but God.'

'God,' said he, 'why, can God see us here?' and so entering into talk with her so wrought upon her that she was struck with remorse and fearful terror of her sins, and besought him that he would help her out of her misery. Hereupon, after further talk, they went down together and he provided her with another lodging, where she used herself so honestly that after a time he took her to his wife.

In writing these two discourses Greene declared that he was acting for the good of his countrymen at the peril of his own life, for the conny-catchers had protested his death, and one evening had beleaguered him being at supper in the Saint John's Head within Ludgate, and thought to have slain him, but that the citizens and apprentices took his part, so that two or three of them were carried to the Counter, although a gentleman in his company was sore hurt.

Greene also promiseth that he will print a bead-roll of all the foists and conny-catchers about the City.

'The Groundwork of Conny-catching.'

The Groundwork of Conny-catching, purporting to be a new book, but in fact Thomas Harman's *Caveat for Common Cursetors* (first printed in 1567).

JOHNSON'S 'NINE WORTHIES OF LONDON.'

The Nine Worthies of London: explaining the honourable exercise of arms, the virtues of the valiant, and the memorable attempts of magnanimous minds; pleasant for gentlemen, not unseemly for magistrates, and most profitable for prentices: compiled by Richard Johnson, being dedicated to Sir William Webb, Knight, Lord Mayor of the City of London. Herein Fame and Clio, meeting together, cause the ancient worthies of the city to rise from the ground and declare their own fortunes in verse. First Sir William Wallworth, fishmonger, who slew Wat Tyler; Sir Henry Pritchard, vintner; Sir William Sevenoake, grocer; Sir William White, merchant tailor; Sir John Bonham, mercer; Sir Christopher Croker, vintner; Sir John Hawkwood, merchant tailor; Sir Hugh Caverley, silk weaver; and Sir Henry Maleveret, grocer, surnamed Henry of Cornhill, which last having fought in the Holy Land, to rescue the oppressed Jews, was by envious tongues defamed, and maketh complaint:

The good that I had done was clean forgot,
  Ingratitude prevailed against my life,
And nothing then but exile was my lot,
  Or else abide the stroke of fatal knife;
    For so the ruler of the Jews concluded,
    His Grace by false reports was much deluded.

There was no striving in a foreign soil,
  I took it patient, though 'twere causeless done,
And to avoid the stain of such a foil,
  That slanderous tongues had wickedly begun,
    Where, to the holy well of Jacob's name,
    I found a cave to shroud me from their blame.

And though my body were within their power,
  Yet was my mind untouched by their hate,
The valiant faint not, though that Fortune lower,
  Nor are they fearful at controlling fate,
    For in that water none can quench their thirst,
    Except he meant to combat with me first.

By that occasion for my pleasure sake,
  I gave both knights and princes heavy strokes:

The proudest did presume a draught to take,
Was sure to have his passport sealed with knocks :
Thus lived I till my innocence was known,
And then return'd ; the King was pensive grown,

And for the wrong which he had offered me,
He vowed me greater friendship than before,
My false accusers lost their liberty,
And next their lives ; I could not challenge more :
And thus with love, with honour and with fame,
I did return to London whence I came.

1593

3rd January. RUMOURS.

There is great disagreement about the goods of the Great Carrack. The Earl of Cumberland would claim them, having taken her when she was like to have carried away the Queen's ship, and had beaten Sir John Burgh's; but for the Queen's part it is alleged that by her prerogative she may challenge the services of all her subjects' ships, that are bound to help her at sea, and recompense them according to her princely bounty, which she would do liberally enough to the Earl, but for some that would make a profit by buying it at her hands. All the others, that served the Queen, and Sir Walter Ralegh, receive only their pay, and are discontented at receiving so little out of so rich a prize, worth £150,000, though indeed much of the richest is purloined and embezzled.

The Lord Treasurer is much offended with the libels printed against him and lately brought over; it is thought that they will do no good to the Catholics, against whom a book is being written.

6th January. PLAYS OF THE WEEK.

The plays at the Rose Theatre this past week were *A Knack to Know a Knave* (twice), *The Jew of Malta*, *Sir John Maundeville*, *The Jealous Comedy* (for the first time), *Titus and Vespasian*.

8th January. THE WAR IN FRANCE.

Fresh levies are demanded of the Lord Mayor of London and the Lords Lieutenant of ten counties for Normandy to the number of 1200, of which 450 are from the City, to be ready to embark on the 12th February. It is commanded that special care be taken in the choice of the men and their appointments.

From Brittany it is reported that the English Captains are still prisoners, being held at extreme ransoms, especially the Sergeant-Major, for whom they demand 10,000 crowns. If they be not relieved, others will be discouraged from undergoing the like dangers.

12th January. NASHE'S 'STRANGE NEWS.'

Nashe hath replied to Dr. Gabriel Harvey in a book called *Strange News of the intercepting of certain letters and a convoy of verses as they were going privily to victual the Low Counties*, where, in the form of a commentary paragraph by paragraph upon the *Four Letters*, Dr. Gabriel Harvey is very abusively handled.

In Greene's defence Nashe noteth that he inherited more virtues than vices; a jolly long red peak like the spire of a steeple, he cherished continually without cutting, whereat a man might hang a jewel, it was so sharp and pendant. Why should art answer for infirmities of manners? 'He had his faults, and thou follies. Debt and deadly sin who is not subject to? With any notorious crime I never knew him tainted (and yet tainting is no infamous surgery for him that hath been in so many hot skirmishes). In a night and day would he have yarked up a pamphlet as well as in seven year, and glad was that printer that might be so blessed to pay him dear for the very dregs of his wit.'

To Dr. Harvey's praise of the English hexameter Nashe answereth that the hexameter verse is a gentleman of an ancient house (so is many an English beggar), yet this clime of ours he cannot thrive in: our speech is too craggy for him to set his plough in, he goes twitching and hopping in our language like a man running up quagmires, up the hill in one syllable and down the dale in another, retaining no part of that stately smooth gait which he vaunts himself with amongst the Greeks and Latins.

13th January. PLAYS OF THE WEEK.

The plays at the Rose Theatre this past week: *The Spanish Tragedy*, *Muly Mullocco*, *Friar Bacon*, *The Comedy of Cosmo*, *Sir John Maundeville*, *The Knack to Know a Knave*.

18th January. RUMOURS.

The Parliament that hath been summoned for 19th February is said to be only for money to maintain the troops in Brittany and elsewhere, the last payment of the last Parliament's subsidy being now due, and almost all spent already if the soldiers' debts were paid.

The mariners of the Earl of Cumberland are angry that the Great Carrack should have been awarded to the Queen, for were the prize the Earl's they would have their shares by the composition made with him before going out; whereas those who went with Sir John Burgh, on the Queen's adventure, Sir Walter Ralegh's, or the City of London's are to be paid wages. These mariners, being much discontented, have combined to seize upon the goods in London, and it is thought they will take occasion to be slack in some action hereafter, divers of them even threatening to go to the enemy. The whole prize is offered to the City of London, but they expect so great a pennyworth and the State affords them so little that nothing is likely to come of it.

Now that the Duke of Parma is dead, it is thought that the King of France will have the upper hand, and 3000 men under Sir Roger Williams are being sent to him.

The Lord Treasurer is now well recovered of his dangerous sickness, at which there is much satisfaction, for on him the whole state of the realm dependeth; and if he were to go there is no one about the Queen able to wield the State.

20th January. PLAYS OF THE WEEK.

The plays at the Rose Theatre this week past were *The Comedy of Cosmo, Titus and Vespasian, Harry the Sixth, Friar Bacon, The Jew of Malta, Tamer Cam, Muly Mullocco.*

21st January. THE PLAGUE AGAIN INCREASES.

The weekly returns of the plague which for some weeks past were diminishing now show an increase, so that the Lord Mayor and Aldermen of the City are sharply rebuked for their neglect, because either they do not observe good order for preventing the plague or else the orders themselves are insufficient. They are commanded by the Council at their utmost peril to cause immediate note to be taken of all houses infected or suspected to be infected and themselves to see them shut up either by locks hanging outwardly in the doors or by a special watch on every house. Thus the infected shall be prevented from resorting abroad to mix with the sound. Those so shut up shall be provided with sufficient food and other provision, to be paid for by those of ability; but the poorer sort, artificers or those who live by handiwork or by alms, to be relieved with the charity of the parish and of the City, especially to be collected for that purpose. The Lord Mayor and the Aldermen are further warned that if they continue to be careless, her Majesty, in addition to the punishment she meaneth to inflict on them, will remove the Parliament away from the City.

27th January. PLAYS OF THE WEEK.

The plays at the Rose Theatre this past week were *The Spanish Tragedy*, *Cosmo*, *The Knack to Know a Knave*, *Titus and Vespasian*, *The Massacre at Paris* (for the first time), *Sir John Maundeville*.

28th January. EVASION OF SERVICE IN PRIVILEGED PLACES.

Many of late resort to St. Martin's, Blackfriars, Whitefriars, and other places privileged and exempt from the authority of the Lord Mayor to avoid the imprest for service. The officers and principal inhabitants of these places are now required to assist the Lord Mayor and his deputies to imprest suitable men and to contribute towards their charges.

SIR HENRY KNIVETT'S SUBMISSION.

Sir Henry Knivett was this day called before the Council and after he had confessed his fault in showing contempt for the authority of the Lord Keeper was admonished to beware of such presumption hereafter and given leave to depart.

He had been committed to the Fleet by the Lord Keeper for having allowed his servants to commit an outrage upon a person coming to serve a process on a gentlewoman then residing in his house. Being released he wrote a letter to some of her Majesty's Privy Council in which he slandered the proceedings of the Lord Keeper, alleging them to have been unjust; which letter being read at the Council Board in his presence, the Lord Keeper, although not liable to render account for his sentences given in the Queen's Court to any but her Majesty, was nevertheless willing that their Lordships should hear the proofs of the accusation.

Accordingly Sir Henry was called to the Council Board and required to show proofs of his allegations; which being carefully heard, it appeared that he had unjustly, undutifully and indiscreetly slandered the Lord Keeper, and for this offence he was committed to the Fleet; whence after some days he wrote a letter of submission, acknowledging his offence, beseeching the pardon of their Lordships and their favourable mediation with the Lord Keeper.

PLAYS AND GAMES PROHIBITED BY REASON OF THE PLAGUE.

As the plague increaseth continually all manner of concourse and public meetings of the people (preaching and Divine service at churches excepted) at plays, bearbaiting, bowling and other assemblies for sport are inhibited.

2nd February. PLAYING CEASES.

At the Rose Theatre *The Jew of Malta* was played, and on the days before *Friar Bacon* and *Harry the Sixth.* Owing to the increase of plague the theatre is now shut up.

3rd February. 'GREENE'S NEWS FROM HEAVEN AND HELL.'

Greene's News both from Heaven and Hell, commended to the press by B. R., is to be printed, being dedicated to Gregory Coolle, chief burgomaster of the Castle of Clonars. In this collection of merry tales B. R. saith that he met the ghost of Robert Greene which popped into his hands his papers to be committed to the press. Herein, Greene, speaking in his own person, declareth that his ghost wandering breathless up a steep hill there found Velvet Breeches and Cloth Breeches fast together by the ears. Having parted them, all three made their way to Heaven Gate, where St. Peter demanded of Greene his name, but learning that he was Robert Greene, he rebuked him for describing the pilfering cosenages of petty varlets whilst looking with indifference on the corruption of great ones, refusing entrance to Heaven to a man that could look with one eye and wink with the other. Nor would he allow Velvet Breeches to enter, but seeing the simplicity of Cloth Breeches he was for letting him in. Whereupon, Cloth Breeches hastily demanded whether his wife had come to Heaven, and learning that she had, he replied that all Heaven would be too small for the two of them: so he turned away with the other two toward Purgatory. Nor would Lucifer allow Greene to remain in Hell, for as he entered there an infinite number of conny-catchers gathered together and exclaimed against him, so that Lucifer was fain thrust him out, charging him to remain a restless spirit, wandering through the world and never after to make any return again to that place.

7th February. LAWLESSNESS ON THE SCOTTISH BORDER.

The Bishop of Carlisle and others have sent to petition the Council by the gentlemen of the county chosen to sit in the Parliament complaining of the spoils and robberies made not only by the Scottish borderers but the English also, especially since Michaelmas. Divers gentlemen have been invaded in their dwelling-houses, their goods and chattels taken by violence and carried into Scotland, and themselves put to ransom. Most of the gentry dwelling within twenty miles of Carlisle go in fear of their lives and goods, so that not only they but justices of the peace even are forced to keep their cattle within their houses nightly, and dare not suffer them to pasture on their grounds. The justices and sheriffs are unable to give any relief, nor can the Warden help them.

8th February. AN INVASION EXPECTED.

Reliable information is received that the Spaniard will attempt an invasion of the realm by means of some dangerous conspiracy with some of the nobility of Scotland. As they will pass the seas between Ireland and England, it is thought likely that they will try to surprise the Isle of Man, and fortify it as a place very convenient for their victualling and watering. The Earl of Derby is therefore to send trustworthy persons straightway to put the island in a state of defence, but especially to take care of any trusted with the charge of any place because some be suspected. Good heed especially to be taken of one Mr. Dudley that hath of late been in Scotland to some evil purpose.

11th February. CONTRIBUTIONS EVADED.

Many persons of quality, having houses in the City, and especially most of the Doctors of the law, now refuse to contribute to the charges of the Lord Mayor in the present public services. The Council order that anyone refusing to contribute to the defence of the realm be informed of their wish ; and if he still refuse, bonds shall be taken of him to appear before them. Further, if he refuse to enter into a bond, it is necessary that her Majesty be acquainted with his unwillingness and to this end the Lord Mayor shall commit him to prison.

12*th February*. RUMOURS: THE GREAT CARRACK.

The goods taken in the Great Carrack are said to have amounted to £150,000, whereof the Earl of Cumberland receiveth £37,000 by way of reward, Sir Walter Ralegh for his adventure £24,000, the City of London £12,000, some others £7000 or £8000, and the rest to be the Queen's. £10,000 worth of goods are already sold at Dartmouth to pay the mariners' wages, besides other booty plundered at sea. The Queen's share is £80,000 with all the pepper.

14*th February*. INSUFFICIENT MEN IMPRESTED AS SOLDIERS.

Sir George Carew, Lieutenant of the Ordnance, Sir Thomas Baskerville and Sir Thomas Morgan, that were appointed to view the levies from the counties and to report the sufficiency of the men and their furniture, find that of 50 men sent by the County of Bedford 14 were unable and insufficient, and most of them very evilly apparelled, their coats of very bad cloth and unlined. Of the 50 men levied in the County of Cambridge but 49 had arrived in London, one having run away, and of the rest ten were insufficient; most of them are ill and nakedly apparelled, wanting doublets, hose, stockings, shirts and shoes, their cassocks also of very bad cloth and unlined. Yet from Buckinghamshire, Essex and Middlesex come men able and sufficient, well furnished with armour and weapons.

18*th February*. REGULATIONS FOR BUTCHERS DURING LENT.

The Lord Mayor is advised to take strict charge that the orders concerning the eating of flesh in Lent be duly enforced and the disorders of last year avoided, wherein over 12,000 lbs. of the meat of calves, sheep and lambs were sold in the space of five weeks to the great prejudice of the State by the spoil of the breed of young cattle. Every butcher having licence to sell meat at this time shall pay £10 for the relief of poor maimed and impotent soldiers. The Lord Mayor is also to join the Wardens and chief of the Butchers with those of the Fishmongers that are willing to travail and take pains in the reformation of these abuses more exactly than last year.

19*th February*. PARLIAMENT ASSEMBLES.

Parliament having been summoned for this day, in the morning the knights and burgesses came to Westminster, where each one, after declaring his name to the Clerk of the Crown who entered it in his book, went into the House.

The House being set, the Earl of Derby, Lord High Steward for this Parliament, came in to take their oaths, being instructed by Sir Thomas Heneage as to what order he should use. First, all removed into the Court of Requests where the Lord High Steward, sitting at the door, called the knights and burgesses of every county according to the letters of their names in the alphabet. Each one, having answered as he was called, went next to the Parliament House door and there took the Oath of Supremacy given to him by one of the Privy Councillors; this done he entered again and took his place as a member of the House.

There was no further proceeding until two o'clock in the afternoon, about which time the Queen, having come privately by water, entered the House of Lords, accompanied by Sir John Puckering, Lord Keeper of the Great Seal, and many of her lords spiritual and temporal. The members of the Lower House, having received intelligence that the Lords had taken their places, went to attend in the Upper House before the Bar, and, when as many had been admitted as conveniently could be, the door was shut, and the Lord Keeper, by command of the Queen, began to speak to the effect that the assembling of Parliament hath anciently been, and still was, for the enacting of laws and reforming of grievances and abuses of the subjects of the Realm; yet at this time the Queen was chiefly desirous to have the advice of her loving people concerning the defence and preservation of herself, her realms and subjects from the power and oppression of a foreign enemy.

At this point the Lord Keeper's speech was interrupted by the murmuring outside. It appeared that the place of the Lower House in the chamber had been filled by those who came in privately before the Commons had been summoned, so that when the rest came up they found the door shut, contrary to custom, and were so discontented that the noise reached the Queen's ears. When she understood the cause of the discontent, she immediately commanded the doors to be set open, and the Lord Keeper continued his speech.

This enemy, he said, was the King of Spain, and his malice

was increased by his loss and shame received in '88. That his resolution still was to invade this kingdom did plainly appear by his building and getting together many ships of less bulk, which would be fitter for service in our seas, than those greater galliasses and galleons had been in '88. He desired some nearer place from whence to invade England, and therefore at that time he was labouring to plant himself in Brittany, a part of France. He had also raised factions in Scotland and conspiracies against the King there, finding him an enemy to his ambitious designs.

'And therefore,' quoth the Lord Keeper, 'we, her Majesty's subjects, must with all dutiful consideration think what is fit for us to do; and with all willingness yield part of our own for the defence of others, and assistance of her Majesty in such an unsupportable charge. Were the cause between friend and friend, how much would we do for the relief of one another? But the cause is now between our Sovereign and ourselves; seeing there is so much difference in the parties, how much more forward ought we to be?

'The aid formerly granted to her Majesty in these like cases is so ill answered, and with such slackness performed, as that the third of that which was granted cometh not to her Majesty. A great show, a rich grant, and a long sum seems to be made; but little it is, hard to be gotten, and the sum not great which is paid. Her Majesty thinks this to be for that the wealthier sort of men turn this charge upon the weaker and upon those of worst ability; so that one dischargeth himself, and the other is not able to satisfy that he is charged withal. These things should be reformed by such as are commissioners in this service.

'Wherefore it is her Majesty's pleasure that the time be not spent in devising and enacting new laws, the number of which is so great already as it rather burdeneth than easeth the subject; but the principal cause of this Parliament is that her Majesty might consult with her subjects for the better withstanding those intended invasions, which are now greater than ever before were heard of. And where heretofore it hath been used that many have delighted themselves in long orations, full of verbosity and vain ostentations, more than in speaking things of substance; the time that is precious would not thus be spent. This session cannot be long; the spring time is fit that gentlemen should repair to their counties; the Justices of Assize also to go their circuits; so the good hours should not be lost in idle speeches, but the little time we have should be bestowed wholly on such business as is needful to be considered of; and Thursday next is appointed as the day to present the Speaker.'

As soon as the Lord Keeper's speech was ended, the Clerk of Parliament read the names of receivers of petitions, and, after the other business was ended, the Parliament was adjourned by the Lord Keeper in these words: '*Dominus Custos Magni Sigilli ex mandato Dominae Reginae continuat praesens Parliamentum usque in diem Jovis proximam futuram.*'

20th February. PRECAUTIONS AGAINST DESERTION.

The officers of ports on the south and east are ordered to search any ship from beyond seas in which deserters might be carried, and all suspected to have come from Normandy or Brittany without sufficient passport from Sir John Norris or Sir Roger Williams to be committed to prison.

21st February. THE FRENCH AMBASSADOR ALLOWED MEAT.

The French ambassador with his family is specially allowed by the Council to be served with meat by his own butcher during Lent, but bonds are put in that the butcher do not sell meat to others under colour of this order.

22nd February. THE SPEAKER PRESENTED.

The Queen herself came to Westminster about three o'clock this afternoon accompanied by the Lords spiritual and temporal; there being present the Archbishop of Canterbury, Sir John Puckering, Lord Keeper of the Great Seal, William, Lord Burleigh, Lord Treasurer of England, the Marquis of Winchester, twelve Earls, two Viscounts, fifteen bishops and twenty-three barons.

The Queen and the Lords having taken their places, the members of the House of Commons were summoned, and immediately came up with their Speaker, Edward Coke, Esquire, the Queen's Solicitor, into the Upper House. The Speaker being led up to the Bar at the lower end of the House between two of the most eminent personages of the Lower House, as soon as silence was made and the rest of the House of Commons had placed themselves below the bar, spake as follows:

'Your Majesty's most loving subjects, the knights and burgesses of the Lower House, have nominated me, your Grace's poor servant and subject, to be their Speaker. This their nomination hath hitherto proceeded that they present me to speak before your Majesty; yet this their nomination is only a nomination yet and no election until your Majesty giveth allowance and approbation; for, as in the Heavens a star is but *opacum corpus* until it hath received light from the sun, so stand I *corpus opacum*, a mute body, until your bright shining wisdom hath looked upon me and allowed me.

'How great a charge this is, to be the mouth of such a body, as your House of Commons represent, to utter that is spoken, *grandia regni*, my small experience, being a poor professor of the law, can tell. But how unable I am to undergo this office, my present speech doth tell that of a number of this House, I am most unfit: for amongst them are many grave, many learned, many deep wise men, and those of ripe judgments; but I am untimely fruit, not ripe, nay, but a bud not scarce fully blossomed, so as I fear your Majesty will say, *neglecta fruge, liguntur folia*; amongst so many fair fruits, you have plucked a shaking leaf.

'If I may be so bold to remember a speech used the last Parliament in your Majesty's own mouth, "many come hither *ad consulendum qui nesciunt quid sit consulendum*"; a just reprehension to many, as to myself also, an untimely fruit, my years and judgment ill befitting the gravity of this place. But howsoever I know myself the meanest and inferior unto all that ever were before me in this place, yet in faithfulness of service and dutifulness of love, I think not myself inferior to any that ever were before me: and amidst my many imperfections, yet this is my comfort; I never knew any in this place but if your Majesty gave him favour, God, Who also called them to this place, gave them also a blessing to discharge it.'

The Lord Keeper having received instructions from the Queen made answer:

'Mr. Solicitor, her Grace's most excellent Majesty hath willed me to signify unto you that she hath ever well conceived of you since she first heard of you, which will appear when her Highness selected you from others to serve herself: but of this your modest, wise and well composed speech, you give her Majesty further occasion to conceive of you above that she ever thought was in you: by endeavouring to deject and abase yourself and your desert, you have made known and discovered your worthiness and sufficiency to discharge the place you are called to. And whereas you account yourself *corpus opacum*, her Majesty by the influence of her virtue and wisdom doth enlighten you, and not only alloweth and approveth you, but much thanketh the Lower House and commendeth their discretions in making such a choice, and electing so fit a man.

'Wherefore, Mr. Speaker, proceed in your office and go forward to your commendation as you have begun.'

Then began the Speaker a new speech wherein, after expressing his loyalty to the Queen for the great and wonderful blessings which had been enjoyed under her rule, he related the great attempts of the Queen's enemies against us, especially the Pope and the King of Spain, from whom we were wonderfully delivered in '88. Then having touched on the supremacy which the Kings of England since Henry the Third's time had maintained, he went on to speak of the laws that are so many and great that they are fitly to be termed *elephantinae leges*; wherefore it might seem superfluous to make more laws, yet the malice of the devil, though it is always great, was never so great as now; and, *dolus* and *malum* being crept in so far amongst men, it was necessary that sharp ordinances should be provided to prevent them, and all care used for her Majesty's preservation.

'Now,' quoth he, 'am I to make unto your Majesty three petitions, in the names of your Commons. First, that liberty of speech and freedom from arrests, according to the ancient custom of Parliament, be granted to your subjects: that we may have access to your Royal Person to present those things which shall be considered of amongst us: and lastly, that your Majesty will give us your Royal Assent to the things that we agreed upon. And, for myself, I humbly beseech your Majesty, if any speech shall fall from me, or behaviour be found in me not decent and unfit, that it may not be imputed blame upon the House but laid upon me, and pardoned in me.'

To this speech the Lord Keeper, having received new instruction from the Queen, replied that he commended the Speaker greatly for his speech ; and he added some examples for the King's Supremacy in Henry the Second's time, and Kings before the Conquest. As for the deliverance we received from our enemies, and the peace we enjoyed, he said the Queen would have the praise of all those to be attributed to God only. To the commendations given to herself, she said well might they have a wiser Prince, but never should they have one that more regarded them, and in justice would carry an evener stroke without acceptation of persons ; and such a Princess she wished they might always have.

'To your three demands,' he concluded, 'the Queen answereth, liberty of speech is granted you, but how far, this is to be thought on. There be two things of most necessity, and those two do most harm ; which are, wit and speech : the one exercised in invention, the other in uttering things invented. Privilege of speech is granted, but you must know what privilege you have, not to speak everyone what he listeth, or what cometh in his brain to utter ; but your privilege is to say, "Yea or no."

'Wherefore, Mr. Speaker, her Majesty's pleasure is that if you perceive any idle heads which will not stick to hazard their own estates, which will meddle with reforming of the Church and transforming of the Commonwealth, and do exhibit any Bills to such purpose, that you receive them not until they be viewed and considered of by those whom it is fitter should consider of such things and can better judge of them.

'To your persons all privilege is granted with this *caveat*, that under colour of this privilege no man's ill doings or not performing of duties be covered and protected.

'The last, free access is also granted to her Majesty's person, so that it be upon urgent and weighty causes, and at times convenient, and when her Majesty may be at leisure from other important causes of the Realm.'

The Parliament was then adjourned to the Saturday following.

24th February. MR. WENTWORTH'S PETITION.

Mr. Peter Wentworth and Sir Henry Bromley delivered a petition to the Lord Keeper, desiring the Lords of the Upper House to join with the Lower House as suppliants to the Queen that she would entail the succession to the Crown ; and for this purpose they have a bill already drawn. When the Queen heard of it, she was so highly displeased, for this is a matter directly opposite to her commands, that she charged the Council to call the parties before them. Sir Thomas Heneage therefore hath sent for them, and they are commanded to forbear coming to Parliament and not to go out of their lodgings.

24th February. THE SPEAKER SICK.

This day the House being set and Mr. Speaker not coming to the House, some said that they had heard that he was sick, whereon it was moved that the Clerk should in the meantime proceed to the saying of the Litany and prayers. Which done, the Sergeant of the House brought word that the Speaker had been this last night and also the present forenoon extremely pained with a wind in his stomach and looseness of the body so that he could not as yet without great peril adventure into the air. Whereupon all the members of the House being very sorry for Mr. Speaker arose and departed away.

SIR ROGER WILLIAMS' COUNSEL.

Sir Roger Williams writeth his opinion that the greatest danger to England may proceed by the Scots or the Irish, especially by Ireland, where it stands her Majesty upon to make sure of those people by cutting off the principal instruments and persuading the rest of the faction by fair means; if not, immediately with good squadrons of horsemen and footmen, for there is such meanings in them that if 8000 strangers, with the treasure they would carry with them, join them, there will be great mischief. The state of France is not too desperate so long as the King keeps the field, and the Spanish do not possess the rest of the parts of Brittany and Normandy; if this were to happen, then will there be wars in England.

25th February. MR. WENTWORTH BEFORE THE COUNCIL.

Mr. Wentworth, Sir Henry Bromley and two others have been called before some of the Council, being the Lord Treasurer, the Lord Buckhurst and Sir Thomas Heneage, who treated them favourably and with good speeches. But so highly was the Queen offended that they said they had no choice but to commit them. Whereupon Mr. Wentworth is sent to the Tower, Sir Henry Bromley and the others to the Fleet.

THE EARL OF ESSEX ADMITTED TO THE COUNCIL.

This day the Earl of Essex, Master of the Horse, having taken the Oath of Supremacy, and of a Privy Councillor, took his place at the Council Board.

DESERTERS IN GLOUCESTERSHIRE.

It is reported from Gloucestershire that of 150 soldiers that were impressed in that county and await a favourable wind at Southampton, 40 have escaped or been released by the indirect means of the officers that have the conducting of them.

26th February. A COMMITTEE OF THE HOUSE APPOINTED.

In the House it was proposed that a grave Committee should be elected to consult about the provision of treasure in this present time of danger.

Sir Robert Cecil spoke first, showing that when the King of Spain sent his navy against us, it was almost upon our banks ere we were aware of it; yea, and we were so slack in provision that it was too late to make resistance, had not God preserved us. Now he hath gone about to win France, wherein he hath greatly prevailed, and specially in Brittany, having most part of the port towns in his possession, whither he sendeth supply daily, and reinforces them every four or five months. This province he specially desireth, for it lieth most fit to annoy us, whither he may send his forces continually and there have his Navy in readiness; and besides may keep us from traffic to Rochelle and Bordeaux; as he hath done in the Straits from Tripoli and St. Jean de Luce. And so he hindereth us from carrying forth and bringing into this land any commodities from those parts, where the realm might be inriched and her Majesty's impost ever eased, being one of the great revenues of the Crown. In Scotland also the King of Spain's malice daily increaseth against us, and at home the number of papists, or at leastwise becomes more manifest.

After him Sir John Wolley exhorted the House to a speedy agreeing of a subsidy, and then Sir John Fortescue spake showing the great charges that her Majesty had been at, insomuch that the burden of four Kingdoms rested upon her, which she maintained with her purse, England, France, Ireland and Scotland. She had assisted the French King with men and money which hath cost her about £100,000; and as for the Low Countries, they stood her in yearly, since she undertook the defence of them, £150,000.

'All which,' quoth he, 'her Majesty bestowed for the good of the Realm, to free us from war at home. Besides when her Majesty came to the Crown, she found it £4,000,000 indebted; her Navy, when she came to view it, greatly decayed: yet all this hath discharged, and (thanks be to God) is nothing indebted, and now she is able to match any Prince in Europe, which the Spaniards found when they came to invade us. Yea, she hath with her ships encompassed the whole world whereby this land is famous throughout all places. She did find in her Navy all iron pieces, but she hath furnished it with artillery of brass, so that one of her ships is not a subject's but a petty King's. As for her own private expenses, they have been little in building; she hath consumed little or nothing in her pleasures. As for her apparel it is royal and princely, beseeming her calling, but not sumptuous or excessive. The charges of her house small, yea, never less in any King's time.'

After Sir Edward Stafford and Mr. Francis Bacon had spoken, the whole House agreed to the committee.

27th February. UNREASONABLE DEMANDS FROM PRISONERS.

The Queen hath been credibly given to understand that some that receive grants for the keeping of gaols and others to whom the charge of gaols is assigned have leased them out at exceeding great rents or other profits. Thus their assigns are constrained to exact excessive prices for victual, bedding, fire, fees of irons and other things from poor prisoners, who for want of means to satisfy these unreasonable demands, so perish through famine: for they remain in prison a long time after they are discharged of the principal cause of their commitment only for lack of ability to defray the great sums exacted of them for such intolerable impositions.

The Justices of the Assizes at every place of gaol delivery in the next circuit shall inform themselves thereof; and because they will not have leisure themselves they shall appoint certain of the discreetest Justices of the Peace, and such as be not interested with the granters of the goods, to examine strictly the prisoners in every place and bolt out what hath been laid on them for their meat, drink, bedding and so forth. These being recorded in writing, a reasonable rate and prices shall be set down to be paid by the prisoners from time to time.

A Bill against the Bishops.

Mr. Morris, Attorney of the Court of Wards, delivered a Bill to the Speaker which touched on the abuses of the Bishops in the matter of lawless inquisition, injurious subscription and binding absolution, asking that, if the House thought well of it, they might petition the Queen to have it allowed. Thereupon Mr. Dalton and Sir John Wolley spoke against the Bill, but Sir Francis Knollys was for reading it. Sir Robert Cecil, putting the House in mind that her Majesty had strictly forbidden them to meddle in such cases, the Speaker, perusing the Bill, answered that it was so weighty and long that he needed time to consider it, and to this end asked the leave of the House to keep it for a while. It was therefore put to the House whether the Bill should be committed to the Speaker only, or to the Privy Council and to him ; but as it was held to be against the Order of the House that a Bill should be committed before it was read, it was agreed that the Speaker should keep it.

About two o'clock in the afternoon the Speaker was summoned to the Court, where the Queen herself gave him commandment what to deliver to the House.

27th February. The Subsidies.

The committee of the House yesterday appointed have agreed that, should the House assent thereto, the treasure to be provided for her Majesty be two entire subsidies and four fifteenths and tenths. After consultation the House agreed that the Bill to this effect should be drawn, with a preamble signifying that so great and extraordinary supply is at this time given for resisting the power and preventing the malice of the King of Spain.

Roger Rippon's Corpse.

Roger Rippon, a Barrowist, having died in Newgate, his body was taken by his friends and enclosed in a coffin which they laid at the door of Justice Young, bearing this inscription :

'This is the corpse of Roger Rippon, a servant of Christ and her Majesty's faithful subject, who is the last of sixteen or seventeen which that great enemy of God, the Archbishop of Canterbury, with his High Commissioners, have murthered in Newgate within these five years, manifestly for the testimony of Jesus Christ. His soul is now with the Lord; and his blood crieth for speedy vengeance against that great enemy of the saints and against Mr. Richard Young, who in this, and many the like points, hath abused his power, for the upholding of the Romish Antichrist, Prelacy and priesthood.'

Many copies of this libel are spread about the City.

28th February. THE BILL AGAINST THE BISHOPS.

Mr. Morris hath been sent for to Court and committed into Sir John Fortescue's keeping.

In the Lower House the Speaker showed that he had kept the Bills delivered him the day before by himself and no one else had seen them. A little after he had perused them, he was sent for by special messenger from her Majesty, who commanded him to deliver a message to the House.

'I protest,' he declared, 'a greater comfort never befell me than that this my integrity and faithful promise to this House is not violated; for her Majesty, in her gracious wisdom, before my coming determined not to press me in this, neither indeed did she require the Bill of me; for this only she required of me: what were the things spoken of by the House? Which points I only delivered as they that heard me can tell.

'The message delivered me from her Majesty consisteth of three things: First, the end for which Parliament was called. Secondly, the speech which her Majesty used by my Lord Keeper. Thirdly, what her pleasure and commandment now is.

'For the first it is in me and my power (I speak now in her Majesty's person) to call Parliaments, and it is in my power to end and determine the same; it is in my power to assent or dissent to anything done in Parliament.

'The calling of this Parliament was only that the Majesty of God might be more religiously served, and those that neglect this service might be compelled by some sharper means to a due obedience and more true service of God than there hath been hitherto used.

'And, further, that the safety of her Majesty's person, and of this realm, might be by all means provided for against our great enemies, the Pope and the King of Spain.

'Her Majesty's most excellent pleasure being then delivered unto us by the Lord Keeper, it was not meant that we should meddle with matters of State, or in causes ecclesiastical, for so her Majesty termed them. She wondered that any should be of so high commandment to attempt (I use her own words) a thing contrary to that which she had so expressly forbidden; wherefore with this she was highly displeased. And because the words then spoken by my Lord Keeper are not now perhaps well remembered, or some be now here that were not there, her Majesty's present charge and express commandment is *That no Bills touching matters of State, or Reformation in Causes Ecclesiastical, be exhibited.* And upon my allegiance, I am commanded if any such Bill be exhibited not to read it.'

FLESH IN LENT.

The Lord Mayor is rebuked for his forwardness in giving leave to certain butchers to kill and utter flesh during this season of Lent.

The Council have asked that a butcher may be admitted to provide flesh for the use of Don Antonio, who hath never used to eat fish.

A PLOT TO KILL THE QUEEN.

Gilbert Laton, a recusant, that was taken, hath voluntarily confessed that he was sent over to England by Father Parsons, Sir Francis Englefield, and Don Juan de Idiaques to kill the Queen. It was to be performed while she was still on progress, with a wire made with jemos or with a poniard.

1st March. ROGER RIPPON'S CORPSE.

Christopher Bowman, goldsmith, being examined before Justice Richard Young concerning the corpse of Roger Rippon, declareth that his whole congregation consented to the making of the coffin, for which they paid 4s. 8d. He will not disclose who the congregation are, nor their secrets, nor the place of meeting. He will not be persuaded to go to his parish church, nor to Paul's Cross to hear a sermon, seeing that any man, however wicked he might be, is admitted to receive the communion; and he would not join with the minister who gave holy things to dogs. Moreover, he refuseth to sign his examination.

Extreme Tenets of the Puritans.

Amongst the more extreme opinions of the Puritans, shown either in their writings or examinations, it appeareth that in Church matters they would take away all gifts of bishoprics and deaneries from the Queen by dissolving them, and all patronages; for they hold that all ecclesiastical functions should be elective by the people or their elders. When supremacy was restored to the crown, one chief supereminency was that the final appeal in all ecclesiastical causes should be made to the King in chancery; this they would take away, making the appeal from an Eldership Consistory to a Conference, thence to a Provincial Synod, lastly to a National Synod which should be final.

They would have the Queen, being a child of the Church, subject to the censures of examination by their elderships as well as any other person, and that all, great or small, must willingly be ruled and governed, and must obey those whom God had set over them. If the Prince without God's warrant intermeddle with the Church, he must think it none injury to be disobeyed; for we are not bound to obey the Prince's law for conscience' sake, because only God's laws bind men's consciences. The Prince must take heed that he pass no weighty matter of the Commonwealth without the assembly of all the estates of the realm, whereby he is debarred from treating or capitulating, either for war, peace or league with any other prince without the Parliament being privy to it. In all matters of the Church the highest ecclesiastical authority belongeth to the eldership.

They would administer baptism to no known papist's children, to none excommunicate person's children and to none but to their children that be within the Church, that is, to those who submit themselves to their order of discipline, all others being accounted out of God's covenant and so no true Christians.

They would have the judicial law of Moses for punishing divers sins with death to be in force, so that no prince nor law could save the lives of those who offend wilfully as blasphemers of God's Name, conjurers, soothsayers, persons possessed with an evil spirit, heretics, perjurers, breakers of the Sabbath day, neglecters of the sacraments without just reason, any that disobeys or curses his parents, incestuous persons, daughters who commit fornication in their fathers' houses, adulterers, and all incontinent persons, save single fornicators, and any who conspire against any man's life. The *lex talionis*, that is an eye for an eye, ought to be observed in every commonwealth.

They would cut off the state ecclesiastical, being one of the three in Parliament, and have all laws made by the lords temporal and the commons only. It is unlawful, say they, for any State to tolerate the present Government Ecclesiastical, for it is false, unlawful, bastardly and unchristian, and can be defended by no good or sound subject ; those that do so are traitors to God and His Word, enemies to the Queen and the land, and shall answer for the blood which the Spaniard or other enemies might spill, for they bring in hazard the Queen's life and the prosperity of the kingdom, being its greatest enemies.

The sect called the Barrowists holdeth all these positions and besides, that it is not lawful to use the Lord's Prayer publickly in church for a set form ; for all set prayers are a mere babbling in the sight of the Lord. The Church of England in its public prayers and worship is false and superstitious, and, as now established, antichristian and popish.

If the Prince or Magistrate should refuse or defer to reform the faults in the Church, the people may take the reforming of them into their own hands before or without his authority. The Presbytery and Eldership may for some causes, after admonition, excommunicate the Queen if there ensue no reformation. They will not communicate with those in the Church of England, neither in prayer nor in sacraments, nor come to church because they hold that the Church of England as by law established possesses neither a true Christ nor a true religion nor has it indeed ministers nor sacraments.

3rd March. DR. UDALL'S PETITION.

Dr. John Udall, the Puritan preacher, hath petitioned the Lord Treasurer for release from prison, where he hath lain these three years. He hath consented with the Turkey merchants to go to Syria and remain there two years with their factors if his liberty may be obtained.

The Archbishop hath consented and the Lord Keeper promised his furtherance; the Earl of Essex hath the draft of a pardon ready when the Queen would sign it; but unless he have liberty out of hand the ships will be gone.

3rd March. THE SUBSIDY.

This morning in the House of Commons was received a message from the Lords to the effect that they did look to have heard something from the Commons before this concerning the provision of treasure; and desiring that according to former usage a committee of some grave and settled members of the House be appointed to have conference with a committee of the Lords. It was agreed accordingly that a committee should be appointed to meet with the Lords at two in the afternoon.

A STRANGER IN THE HOUSE.

In the House of Commons it was found that a certain man, being no member, had sat there during the greater part of the forenoon. He was brought to the Bar and examined by Mr. Speaker of his name and place of abode. He answered that his name was John Legg, a servant to the Earl of Northumberland; and pleading simplicity and ignorance for his excuse, alleged that he had some business from his master to Mr. Dr. Herbert, the Master of Requests; and therefore he entered the House, not thinking any harm nor knowing the danger thereof. After humbly praying pardon he is committed to the custody of the Sergeant of the House till the House shall upon further examination take other order.

4th March. PENRY TO BE ARRESTED.

A warrant directed to all public officers is issued by the Council for the arrest of John Penry, that is said to have written *Martin Marprelate.*

THE SUBSIDY.

In the House of Commons Sir Robert Cecil showed that at the conference had yesterday between the committees of the two Houses their Lordships signified that they would by no means assent to pass any Act for less than for three entire subsidies to be paid in the next three years. Sir Robert urged therefore that further conference should be held with their Lordships. Whereupon arose a question on the matter of privilege, Mr. Francis Bacon showing that the custom and privilege of the House was to make offer of a subsidy or else to assent to a Bill presented to the House, but not to pair with them in this motion.

After much debate it was agreed that the committee should have further conference with their Lordships.

5th March. 'THE GARLAND OF GOODWILL.'

A collection of ballads and songs is to be printed, entitled *The Garland of Goodwill*, amongst them *A Mournful Ditty on the Death of Rosamond ; The Lamentation of Shore's wife ; How Coventry was made free by Godiva, Countess of Chester ; Locrine ; A Song of Queen Isabel, wife to King Edward the Second ; A Song of the Banishment of the two Dukes, Hereford and Norfolk ; Patient Grissel.* Also *A Dialogue between plain Truth and blind Ignorance*, wherein Ignorance lamenteth the passing of the old religion :

TRUTH

God speed you, aged Father,
And give you a good day :
What is the cause, I pray you,
So sadly here to stay ?
And that you keep such gazing
On this decayed place,
The which for superstition
Good Princes down did rase ?

IGNORANCE

Chile tell thee by my vazon
That sometime che have known
A vair and goodly Abbey
Stand here of brick and stone :
And many holy Friars,
As ich may say to thee,
Within these goodly cloisters
Che did full often zee.

TRUTH

Then I must tell thee, Father,
  In truth and verity:
A sort of greater hypocrites
  Thou couldst not likely see;
Deceiving of the simple
  With false and feigned lies:
But such an order truly
  Christ never did devise.

IGNORANCE

Ah, ah, che smell thee now, man,
  Che know well what thou art;
A fellow of new learning,
  Che wis not worth a vart:
Vor when we had the old Law
  A merry world was then:
And every thing was plenty,
  Among all zorts of men.

TRUTH

Thou givest me an answer,
  As did the Jews sometime
Unto the prophet Jeremy,
  When he accused their crime.
''Twas merry,' said the people,
  'And joyful in our realm,
Which did offer spice cakes
  Unto the Queen of Heaven.'

IGNORANCE

Chile tell thee what, good vellow;
  Bevore the vriers went hence,
A bushel of the best wheat
  Was sold for vorteen pence:
And vorty eggs a penny,
  That were both good and new:
And this che zay my self have seen
  And yet ich am no Jew.

But in the end Truth prevaileth over old Ignorance.

6th March. LEGG RELEASED.

John Legg, that has remained prisoner at the bar of the House these three days, after good exhortation given him by the Speaker, and the Oath of Supremacy pronounced by him, is upon his humble submission and craving of pardon, set at liberty by the order of the House, on paying his fees.

6th March. THE SUBSIDY.

After further debate yesterday, it was today agreed that the committee of the House of Commons should confer with the committee of the Lords, but not in anywise to conclude or resolve of anything in particular without the privity and consent of the House.

7th March. MUSTERS TO BE HELD IN THE NORTH.

The Earl of Huntingdon, Lieutenant in the North Part and President of the Council of the North, is to muster and view the strength of the counties towards Scotland as well for men and horses as for castles and houses of strength, and to cause all wants to be supplied.

7th March. THE SUBSIDY.

In the House of Commons to-day there was further debate concerning the subsidy and of the poverty of the country.

Sir Henry Knivett affirmed that the principal reason of our poverty was because we bring in more foreign wares than we vent commodities, and so by this means our money is carried out of the country. He made two motions; first, that the Queen should be helped by a survey taken of all men's lands and goods in England, and so much to be levied yearly as to serve the Queen to maintain wars, the proportion being set £100,000 yearly; secondly, if this were misliked, every man upon his word and power to deliver what were the profits of his lands and worth of his goods, and so a proportion to be had accordingly.

Sir Walter Ralegh, answering those who argued the poverty of the realm by the multitude of beggars, said that those who came back maimed from the wars in Normandy and the Low Countries never went back to the towns whence they came. For a multitude of clothiers now have their own looms and spin wool for themselves, and unless these men could spin for them cheaper than they could for themselves, they will never give them work to do. This engrossing of so many trades into their hands beggareth many that usually live by trade. He thought it inconvenient to have men's lands surveyed because many are now esteemed richer than they are, and if their land and goods were surveyed they would be found beggars; and so their credit, which is now their wealth, would be bound nothing. But he agreed to three subsidies, for the longer we defer aid, the less shall we be able to yield aid, and in the end the greater aid will be required of us.

Sir Francis Drake described the King of Spain's strength and cruelty where he came, and wished a frank aid to be yielded to withstand him; and he agreed to three subsidies.

In the afternoon the House considered of the subsidies in committee and after long debate it was agreed for three subsidies payable in four years.

9th March. BARROWISTS ARRESTED.

Many of the sect called Barrowists have been taken at one of their meetings at Islington. One, Daniel Buck, a scrivener, was to-day examined before Justice Young. Concerning the bishops he thinketh that they have no spiritual authority over the rest of the Church. Being demanded who was their pastor, he said one Mr. Francis Johnson; and about six months since this Johnson delivered the sacrament of baptism to seven persons; but they had neither godfathers nor godmothers. He took water and washed the faces of them that were baptised, saying only in the administration of the sacrament, 'I do baptise thee in the name of the Father, of the Son, and of the Holy Ghost,' without using any other ceremony therein, as is usually observed according to the Book of Common Prayer.

Being further demanded the manner of the Lord's Supper administered among them, he saith that five white loaves or more were set upon the table. The pastor did then break the bread, and delivered it to some of them, and the deacons delivered to the rest; some of the congregation sitting and some standing about the table. And the pastor delivered the cup unto one, and he to another, till all had drunken, using the words at the delivery thereof as it is set down in the eleventh of the Corinthians, the 24th verse.

10th March. THE SUBSIDY AGREED.

After further deliberations of the committee of the House of Commons, the articles which they have drawn up were read before the House. It was resolved that a triple subsidy and six fifteenths and tenths to be paid in four years should be yielded to her Majesty towards the provision against the great and imminent perils of this Realm.

11th March. THE BUTCHERS DEFIANT.

Many butchers, apart from those six specially licensed, do kill and make open sale of flesh. The Warden of the Fishmongers is ordered to call them before him and to examine them by what authority they do the same, certifying their names and dwelling-places, and from whence they received their licence. He shall also examine the six licensed upon their oath what money they have paid to the Lord Mayor for their licences.

12th March. A BILL AGAINST RECUSANTS.

A Bill against recusants was read in the Lower House for the first time. When this Bill had been presented to the committee of the House, divers hard penalties in goods and lands were set down; but many of these were altered before the Bill came before the House. Among the penalties proposed are these:

> A recusant shall be disenabled to be Justice of Peace, Mayor, Sheriff, etc.
>
> He shall forfeit for keeping a recusant in his house, either servant or stranger, £10 every month.
>
> His children being ten years old shall be taken from him till they be sixteen to be disposed of at the appointment of four Councillors, the Justices of Assize, the Bishop of the diocese or the Justices of the Peace.
>
> He shall be disenabled to make any bargain or sale of his goods or chattels.

MR. DARCY'S UNSEEMLY CONDUCT.

There have of late been complaints made of Mr. Edward Darcy's patent for sealing of leather. Yesterday he went to the house of the Lord Mayor to confer with him and with Sir George Barnes and Dr. Fletcher, who usually attend the Lord Mayor in such cases. They having said that in some things Mr. Darcy's fees were hard and excessive, he in a very unseemly and unreverent manner '*thou'd*' Sir George Barnes (who had used him with very moderate and friendly terms), preferring himself above the knight in birth and degree, which in good discretion and modesty he might have forborn. Not content withal he suddenly strake Sir George with his fist on the face in most violent manner, wherewith the blood gushing out and embruing his face, his eye also was in great danger by the force of the stroke.

Moreover Mr. Darcy would hardly have escaped without great hurt and peril of his life, especially if his abuse and outrage had been known to the apprentices and those dwelling thereabout; but the Lord Mayor thought good to dismiss him with all present speed and to be conducted part of his way before the fact was rumoured abroad.

To-day the Lord Mayor maketh complaint to the Council of this injury towards an ancient Alderman of the City of London, begging them to take notice of it, and showing what great mischiefs and tumults might have arisen, especially seeing the original cause of Mr. Darcy's negotiation was a thing not very grateful to the common sort of the City, nor, as he supposeth, to any other of her Majesty's subjects.

13th March. A Spanish Nobleman sent home.

Don Pedro Valdes, a Spanish nobleman, that was taken prisoner at sea by Mr. Richard Drake during the fighting in 1588, is given leave to depart. A few days ago he was taken to Court by orders of the Queen and treated very handsomely, being visited by the Council, the nobles and the captains of ships. All request, saith he, that when he shall reach the Spanish King's Court he will use his best offices in favour of peace. He was then taken to the City and entertained to a banquet by the Lord Mayor and the Aldermen. Next day he visited the Lord Treasurer, who also pressed him to use his influence for peace. The Lord Treasurer is now very ill, and the doctors give up hope of saving him.

16th March. Measures against the Butchers.

When the Wardens of the Fishmongers' Company called on the butchers to appear before them, they withdrew themselves and would not be found when they were sent for, to the contempt of the Council's orders. The butchers' shops are to be shut up.

19th March. BUNNY'S 'TRUTH AND FALSEHOOD.'

There is entered a book by Mr. Francis Bunny, Fellow of Magdalen College in Oxford, called *Truth and Falsehood, or A Comparison between the truth now taught in England, and the Doctrine of the Romish Church*, to which is added *A Short Answer* to reasons which commonly the popish recusants in the north parts allege why they will not come to our churches. At the head of each chapter is set the doctrine of the protestants and beside it the answer of the papists, upon which is argued the position, thus running through the chief points of variance between the reformed and the Catholic doctrine. The magistrates are exhorted not to show lenity to recusants, seeing that God commands idolaters to be stoned, nor to atheists, though nothing so dangerous as papists.

21st March. KELLWAY'S 'DEFENSATIVE AGAINST THE PLAGUE.'

Mr. Simon Kellway hath written *A Defensative against the Plague*, containing two parts, the first how to preserve from the plague, the second how to cure those that are infected, with a short treatise of the smallpox, is entered, being dedicated to the Earl of Essex.

The causes of the plague are great and unnatural heat and dry or great rain and inundations of waters; great store of rotten and stinking bodies lying unburied which corrupt the air so that corn, fruit, herbs and waters are infected; dunghills, filthy and standing pools of water; by thrusting a great number of people into a close room, as in ships, common gaols, and in narrow lanes and streets where many dwell together. But for the most part it cometh from clothes and such like that have been used about some infected body. It may also come by dogs, cats, pigs and weasels.

Certain signs foreshow the plague, as when the spring time is cold, cloudy and dry, the harvest stormy and tempestuous with mornings and evenings very cold, and at noon extreme heat; fiery impressions in the firmament, especially in the end of summer, such as comets; great store of little frogs in the beginning of harvest, or of toads creeping on the earth having long tails, or when there is abundance of gnats, caterpillars, spiders and moths, showing the air to be corrupt. Also when young children flock together in companies, and feigning one of their members to be dead, solemnise the burying in mournful sort.

Our magistrates are advised to observe certain rules:

To command that no stinking dunghills be allowed near the City.

Every evening and morning in hot weather to cause cold water to be cast in the streets, especially where there is infection, and every day to cause the streets to be kept clean and sweet, and cleansed from all filthy things.

Where the infection is entered to cause fires to be made in the streets every morning and evening, wherein should be burnt frankincense, pitch or some other sweet thing.

Not to suffer any dogs, cats or pigs to run about the streets.

To command that all excrements and filthy things voided from the infected places be not cast into streets or into sewers that are daily used to make drink or dress meat.

No surgeons or barbers that use to let blood should cast it into the streets or rivers. Nor should vaults or privies be emptied therein, for it is a most dangerous thing.

All innholders should make clean their stables every day and cause the filth and dung therein to be carried out of the City, for by suffering it in their houses as some use to do a whole week or a fortnight, it putrefies so that when it is removed there is such a stink as is able to infect the whole street.

To command that no hemp or flax be kept in water near the City or town, for that will cause a very dangerous and infectious savour.

To have special care that good and wholesome victuals and corn be sold in the markets, and to provide that no want thereof shall be in the City, for there is nothing that more increases the plague than want and scarcity of necessary food.

In the remainder of the book are given receipts for perfumes, pomanders, preservatives, purges, cataplasms, powders, unguents and so forth for the various occasions of the plague, with directions for its prevention and cure.

22nd March. BARROW, GREENWOOD AND OTHER PURITANS CONDEMNED.

Yesterday at the Session Hall without Newgate, Henry Barrow, John Greenwood and three others were indicted of felony before the Lord Mayor, the two Lord Chief Justices of both benches and others of the commission. To-day they are arraigned and condemned, Barrow and Greenwood for writing sundry seditious books, the others for publishing and setting them forth.

23rd March. A DISHONEST CAPTAIN.

Sir John Norris is to call before him one Captain Joshua Hilliard, and to command him to appear before the Council. This Hilliard, when the 150 men levied in Gloucestershire were sent to Southampton under their proper officers, taking upon himself to be their captain received £10 for the discharge of certain of the company.

24th March. GYER'S 'ENGLISH PHLEBOTOMY.'

The English Phlebotomy or method and way of healing by letting of blood, written by Nicholas Gyer, minister of the Word, is published, being dedicated to Mr. Reginald Scott that wrote the *Discovery of Witchcraft*. This book is directed against those that for want of skill in blood-letting either straightway kill or leastwise accelerate the immature deaths of divers faithful Christians. Giveth the reasons for phlebotomy; the method of practice; the proper astrological observation, showing what members and parts of the body are to be opened according to the several seasons of the year; the observation of the blood with the signs of the excess or deficiency shown therein.

25th March. ABUSES OVER IMPRESSMENTS IN GLOUCESTERSHIRE.

The Queen is greatly offended that certain soldiers, levied in Gloucestershire for service in France, were licensed to depart after their arrival at Southampton and on their way thither for certain sums of money. The Sheriffs shall cause the constables to bring before them those that dwell not far off, and examine them on their oaths by whom and where they were discharged, and what they gave to their conductors or to any other to purchase licence; and the Justices should do the same. The examinations to be sent up to the Council.

27th March. A RECUSANT EXECUTED AT WINCHESTER.

Two days since James Bird, a young layman, was executed at Winchester for recusancy, having been condemned some time before, after enduring ten years in prison. When he was arraigned at the General Assizes, the Lord Chief Justice Anderson addressing the jury said, 'Here you have James Bird, a recusant. You know what a recusant means. A recusant is one that refuseth to go to church; this no one refuseth unless he hath been reconciled to the Church of Rome. The man that hath been reconciled to the Church of Rome is a rebel and a traitor. Now you know your evident duty.' After a short retirement, they pronounced Bird to be a traitor.

The execution having been long delayed, at length the men arrived to lead Bird to the gallows, and he went down to meet them with joy and gaiety, when a messenger came to say that the execution was again put off; at which he showed evident signs of grief.

When at length the day arrived, as he was on the ladder, he said to the Sheriff, 'I beg you, Mr. Sheriff, seeing that I am a native of this city, that you would grant me one favour before I die.'

'What favour?' said he.

'Tell me what I die for,' answered Bird.

'I know not,' quoth the Sheriff; 'you received the sentence of death in the presence of the Judge; who can know better than you the reason for which you were condemned?'

'Nay,' said he, 'I do not understand it at all.'

Then said the Sheriff, 'Come now, confess your crime, promise to go to church, and the Queen's pardon will be begged for you.'

'Right heartily do I thank thee,' then answered Bird; 'if by going to church I can save my life, surely all the world will see this, that I am executed solely for faith and religion, and nothing else. It was just this that I wished to elicit from you. Now I gladly die.' And with these words he was thrown from the ladder.

31st March. BARROW AND GREENWOOD RESPITED.

Barrow and Greenwood, that were condemned on the 22nd March, were brought in a cart to Tyburn, but respited as they were about to be trussed up.

1st April. A Counterfeit Captain.

From Rutland it is reported that one calling himself Captain Bayton hath been in that county, and by colour of a counterfeit commission to levy men and horse for the Queen's service taken sums of money from sundry of the inhabitants.

2nd April. Maimed Soldiers to be Examined.

A Commission is appointed to meet in two days' time to view and examine a number of captains and soldiers that claim to have been maimed or sore hurt within the last four years' war in France, the Low Countries or on the seas. The names of the men are to be enrolled, showing their names and surnames, the counties where they were born, and where they were levied, with the times and places, and under what captain or leader they were hurt.

4th April. A Bill against the Brownists.

The question of the Brownists again arose in Parliament on the Bill for the explanation of a branch of a Statute made in the 23rd year of the Queen's reign, entitled '*An Act to retain Her Majesty's subjects in their due obedience.*' After divers members had spoken, Sir Walter Ralegh said that in his conceit the Brownists are worthy to be rooted out of a Commonwealth; but what danger may grow to ourselves, if this law passed, it were fit to be considered. 'For it is to be feared,' said he, 'that men not guilty will be included in it; and that law is hard that taketh life, or sendeth into banishment, where men's intentions shall be judged by a jury, and they shall be judges what another man meant. But that law that is against a fact is just, and punish the fact as severely as you will.

'If two or three thousand Brownists meet at the seaside at whose charge shall they be transported? or whither will you send them? I am sorry for it; I am afraid there is nearly twenty thousand of them in England; and when they are gone, who shall maintain their wives and children?'

5th April. Charitable Contributions for Maimed Soldiers.

It is agreed in the House of Lords that there shall be a charitable contribution made towards the relief and help of soldiers maimed and hurt in the wars of France, the Low Countries and on the seas. To this end every Archbishop,

Marquis, Earl and Viscount shall pay 40s., every Bishop 30s., and every Baron 20s. The Queen's Almoner, the Bishop of Worcester, is appointed to collect the money of the Bishops, and the Lord Norris of the Lords Temporal. These sums are willingly being paid by all who attend the Parliament. Further, it is agreed that those who have saved their charges by not attending the Parliament shall pay double, that is, the Archbishop of York and every Earl £4, Bishops £3, and Barons 40s.; and those who have been present but seldom shall pay a third part more than those who have attended regularly. And if any Lord Spiritual or Temporal should refuse or forbear to pay (which it is hoped in honour none will) the ordinary means to be used to levy the money.

PRECAUTIONS AGAINST PLAGUE.

The Lord Mayor is bidden take extraordinary care to prevent the increase of the infection in the City, and to keep the streets clean and sweet, especially because the Queen proposes to stay longer at St. James's, being near the City. All infected houses are to be shut up and watched, the other orders which have been devised to be obeyed.

The Justices of Middlesex shall do the like, giving strict charge that such as have grounds where there are laystalls have them removed at once; and that they allow no dung or filth to be laid in any of the highways, being a great annoyance both to breed infection and to her Majesty riding sometimes in the fields to take the air.

6th April. BARROW AND GREENWOOD HANGED.

Barrow and Greenwood, that were respited last week, were hanged early this morning. It is said that the execution proceeded through the malice of the Bishops towards the Lower House because the dislike shown yesterday to the Bishops' Bill against the Puritans. The reprieve was through a supplication to the Lord Treasurer that in a land where no papist was ever put to death for religion theirs should not be the first blood shed who concurred about faith with what was professed in the country and desired conference to be convinced of their errors. The Lord Treasurer spoke sharply to the Archbishop of Canterbury, who was very peremptory, also to the Bishop of Worcester, and wished to speak to the Queen, but none seconded him.

7th April. SPECIAL WATCH TO BE KEPT FOR TRAITORS.

Now that the King of Spain dischargeth many English, Irish and Scotch fugitives and rebels of the pensions given by him, many of them are likely to come into the realm in secret and covert manner. The officers of the Cinque Ports are ordered to make diligent search and enquiry upon the arrival of any shipping, causing all suspicious persons to be stayed and examined.

8th April. THE DISORDERLY BUTCHERS.

The Justices of the Peace of Middlesex are to call before them the butchers who have killed and uttered flesh contrary to the proclamation and to the wrong of those poor men that paid good sums of money for licences for the use of maimed soldiers. They shall be indicted by a jury and for their contempt fined in good round sums of money to be converted to the use of maimed soldiers.

The Lord Mayor is forthwith to send the sum of £90, being the balance of £120 collected for maimed soldiers from the butchers' licences to the Council, that it may be distributed; otherwise the Council will send a number of the maimed soldiers with tickets to receive money from him, and to be relieved until they be satisfied of the sum. Further, seeing that the Lords of the Upper House, and the Bishops and Clergy of the Convocation House have made a charitable contribution for this purpose, the Lord Mayor and the rest of the Aldermen are required to show the same forwardness amongst themselves and the City Companies. Hereby the poor men may have some reasonable relief, and the City be eased of the clamour and trouble of these lame, maimed and poor creatures, going up and down the streets begging.

9th April. 'CHURCHYARD'S CHALLENGE.'

Churchyard's Challenge, being a collection of twenty pieces of prose and verse written at divers times by Thomas Churchyard, and by him presented to different gentlemen and ladies at Court, is to be printed, the whole being dedicated to Sir John

Wolley, secretary of the Latin Tongue and one of her Majesty's privy councillors. Among these discourses are 'The Tragedy of Shore's Wife,' much augmented; 'A commendation to them that can make gold'; 'A warning to the wanderers abroad, that seek to sow dissension at home'; 'The man is but his mind,' a prose discourse of the different kinds of mind; 'A discourse of true manhood'; 'The honour of a soldier.'

THE WITCHES OF WARBOYS.

On the 7th April Alice Samuel and her husband, John, and her daughter, Agnes, were executed at Huntingdon for having bewitched to death the Lady Cromwell, wife of Sir Henry Cromwell, and for bewitching the daughters of Robert Throckmorton, Esquire.

It appears that for many months past, beginning at the end of the year 1589, the daughters of Mr. Throckmorton have been thrown repeatedly into strange fits, wherein they accused Mother Samuel of bewitching them, and of having a spirit in the form of a chicken which snatched at her chin. Soon after the beginning of this time, the Lady Cromwell, who then lay at Ramsey, a town two miles distant from Warboys, came with her daughter-in-law, Mrs. Cromwell, to visit the children and to comfort the parents. She had not been long in the house before the children all fell into their fits, to the great distress of the lady, who could not abstain from tears. She therefore caused the old woman Samuel to be sent for, who, because her husband was a tenant of Sir Henry Cromwell, durst not refuse; but so soon as she was come the children grew much worse. Then the Lady Cromwell took her aside and charged her deeply with the witchcraft, using hard speeches to her, which she stiffly denied, declaring that Mr. Throckmorton and his wife did her great wrong to blame her without cause.

The lady answered that neither Mr. Throckmorton nor his wife accused her, but the children in their fits did it, or rather the spirit of them. One of the children, by name Joan, being then in her fit, when she heard the old woman clearing herself (though by reason of her fit she heard neither the Lady nor any other), said that it was she who caused all this, 'and something there is,' said she, 'doth now tell me so,' asking if nobody heard it but she, affirming that it squealed very loud in her ears.

Mother Samuel still continuing in her denial, the Lady Cromwell would have taken her into a chamber where Dr. Hall, a doctor of Divinity, was present, to examine her more closely, but she refused to go with them. At length, when the Lady perceived that she could not prevail with her, she suddenly pulled off Mother Samuel's kercher and taking a pair of shears clipped off a lock of her hair and gave it privily to Mrs. Throckmorton together with her hairlace, willing her to burn them. Mother Samuel seeing herself thus dealt with spake to the Lady, 'Madam, why do you use me this? I never did you any harm as yet.'

Towards night the Lady departed, leaving the children much as she had found them. That night the Lady Cromwell suffered many things in her dreams concerning Mother Samuel and was very strangely tormented by a cat (as she imagined) which Mother Samuel had sent to her which offered to pluck off all the skin and flesh from her arms and body. Such was the struggling and striving of the Lady in her bed and the mournful noise which she made, speaking to the cat and to Mother Samuel, that she awakened her bedfellow, who was Mrs. Cromwell, wife of Mr. Oliver Cromwell. Not long after, the Lady fell strangely sick and so continued until her death which occurred in about a year and a quarter. The manner of her sickness, except that she always had her perfect senses, was much like the children's, the pains taking her sometime in one part of the body, sometime in another, but always the grieved part shook as if in a palsy. But the saying of Mother Samuel would never go out of her mind: 'Madam, I never hurt you *as yet*.'

Some time after Mother Samuel, who was then staying at Mr. Throckmorton's house, became very sick, and being very penitent in her sickness she confessed her witchcraft. Mr. Throckmorton sent to Dr. Dorrington, the minister of the town, relating the whole circumstance and desiring him to console her. The next day being Sunday, and Christmas Eve, Dr. Dorrington to comfort her chose his text of repentance out of the Psalms, and there declared in the whole assembly all the matter of Mother Samuel's confession, applying himself especially to the consolation of a penitent heart. All through this sermon Mother Samuel did nothing but weep and lament, and was so loud in her passion, that she caused all in church to look at her. That night she returned to her husband and daughter, who thereon set upon her for having confessed, so that the next day she denied all.

Then Dr. Dorrington and Mr. Throckmorton went to her house to learn the truth, and there found the husband and daughter talking of the matter. Being asked whether she had not confessed, she now answered, 'I confessed so indeed, but it is nothing so.' This so angered Mr. Throckmorton that the next morning early he went to Dr. Dorrington and told him he would not let the matter rest there lest the worser sort of people should imagine that it was some device of theirs against the old woman. Therefore they sent for the constables, and giving both mother and daughter in their charge ordered them to provide for the journey, for they should go before the Bishop of Lincoln at Buckden. They were therefore taken before him the same day (26th December) and there examined.

She was then asked whether a dun chicken did ever suck on her chin and whether it was a natural chicken. She answered that it had sucked twice, and no more, since Christmas Eve. She declared that it was a natural chicken, for when it came to her chin she scarce felt it, and when she wiped it off with her hand, her chin bled, and further she declared that all the trouble that had come to Mr. Throckmorton's children had come by means of this dun chicken.

Mother Samuel was again examined three days afterwards before the Bishop of Lincoln, and Francis Cromwell and Richard Fryce, Justices of the Peace. At this examination she declared that she knew the dun chicken had now gone from the children because it had returned to her with the rest and was now at the bottom of her belly with the others, which made her so full that she could scarce lace up her coat, and that the way as she came they weighed so heavy that the horse fell down. She said also that she had five spirits given her by an upright man in the shape of dun chickens, three she called to her by the names of Pluck, Catch and White; the others by smacking her lips. She was then committed, with her daughter, to the jail at Huntingdon till the Assizes; but Mr. Throckmorton, hoping to get something out of the daughter, persuaded the Justices to let her out on bail to come home with him.

The fits continued very grievous with the children all the while she was in prison. On Wednesday, 4th April, Mistress Joan Throckmorton went to Huntingdon, and was very well on her way, but half an hour after they had entered the Crown Inn, she fell again in her fit, and neither saw nor heeded any. In the evening after the Court had broken up, Mr. Justice Fenner, the Judge, who was lodging at the same inn, went into the garden to see the girl, still greviously tormented by her fit. Mr. Throckmorton told the Judge that if he would command Agnes Samuel, who was standing by, to say certain words his daughter would immediately be well. The words were these: 'As I am a witch and a worse witch than my mother, and did consent to the death of the Lady Cromwell, so I charge the devil to let Mistress Joan come out of her fit at present.' But first, the Judge himself and others to make trial of these words repeated them themselves without avail.

Then the Judge bade Agnes Samuel pray for the girl, and whenever she named God or Jesus Christ in her prayer, Mistress Joan was more troubled than before. Then she was commanded to say, 'As I am no witch, neither did consent to the death of the Lady Cromwell, so I charge the devil to let Mistress Joan come out of her fit at this present'; but all was to no purpose until Agnes Samuel repeated the first words, when Mistress Throckmorton immediately wiped her eyes and came out of her fit, and made a low reverence to the Judge. But a short while after she fell into another fit, first shaking one leg, then another, with many other extraordinary passions. When the Judge and others had prayed without avail, Agnes Samuel was ordered to speak these words: 'As I am a witch and would have bewitched to death Mistress Joan Throckmorton in her last week of her great sickness, so I charge the devil to let Mistress Joan to come out of her fit at this present.' This said, Mistress Joan was immediately well again.

The next day Mother Samuel, her husband, and her daughter were indicted with having bewitched to death the Lady Cromwell, and having bewitched Mistress Joan Throckmorton and others, contrary to God's Laws and the Statute made in the 15th year of the Queen's reign. These things and many others were sworn in testimony against them, and the jury brought in a verdict of guilty.

Then the Judge, passing sentence, asked old Father Samuel what he had to say for himself; he answered that he had nothing to say but the Lord have mercy on him. Then he asked Mother Samuel what she had to say to stay judgment; she answered that she was with child, which set all the company laughing, for she was nearly eighty years old, and she herself more than any, because she thought that for this reason no judgment should be given. The Judge moved her to leave that answer; but she would not be driven from it till at length a jury of women was empanelled, who gave up their verdict that she was not with child, unless, as some believed, by the devil.

All three were therefore condemned to be hanged and shortly executed in Huntingdon.

10th April. THE PARLIAMENT DISSOLVED.

Between five and six this afternoon, the Queen accompanied by her Officers came to the Upper House, and as soon as she was seated with the Lords Spiritual and Temporal, the knights, citizens and burgesses of the Lower House were summoned, and came up with their Speaker, bringing the Bill of Subsidy. The Speaker being placed at the Bar of the Upper House with as many of the Commons as could be admitted, after humble reverence to the Queen, spoke thus:

'The High Court of Parliament, most High and Mighty Prince, is the greatest and most ancient court within this your Realm; for before the Conquest in the high places of the West Saxons we read of a Parliament holden, and since the Conquest they have been holden by all your royal predecessors, Kings of England and Queens of England. In the times of the West Saxons, a Parliament was held by the noble Queen Ina by these words: "I, Ina, Queen of the West Saxons, have caused all my fatherhood, aldermen and wise commons, with the godly men of my kingdom to consult of weighty matters, etc.," which words do plainly show the parts of this Court still observed to this day. For in Queen Ina is your Majesty's most royal person represented; the fatherhood in ancient time were those whom we call Bishops, and still we call them reverend fathers, an ancient and free part of our State. By aldermen were meant your noblemen; for so honourable was the word alderman in ancient time that the nobility only were called aldermen. By wisest commons is signified your knights and burgesses, and so is your Majesty's writ *De discretioribus et magis sufficientibus*. By godliest men is meant your Convocation House, it consisteth of such as are devoted to religion and as godliest men consult of weightiest matters; so is your Highness writ at this day *Pro quibusdam arduis et urgentissinis negotiis nos, statum et defensionem regni nostri et ecclesiae tangentibus*. Your Highness's wisdom and exceeding judgment with all careful providence needeth not our counsels, yet so urgent causes there were of this Parliament, so importunate considerations as that we may say (for we cannot judge) if ever Parliament was so needful as now or ever so honourable as this.

'If I may be bold to say it, I must presume to say that which hath been often said, but what is well said cannot be too often spoken; this secret counsel of ours I would compare to that sweet Commonwealth of the little bees; *Sic enim paruis componere magna solebam*. The little bees have but one governor whom they all serve; he is their king. *Quia latrea habet latiora;* he is placed in the midst of their habitations *ut in tutissima turri;* they forage abroad sucking honey from every flower to bring to their king: *ignavum fucos pecus a principibus arcent*, the drones they drivé out of their hives *non habentes aculeos;* and whoso assails their king in him *immittunt aculeos et tamen rex ipse est sine aculeo*.

'Your Majesty is that Princely Governor and noble Queen whom we all serve; being protected under the shadow of your wings we live; and wish you may ever sit upon your throne over us; and whosoever shall not say Amen, for them we pray *ut convertantur ne pereant et ut confundantur ne noceant*. Under your happy government we live upon honey, we suck upon every sweet flower; but where the bee sucketh honey, there also the spider draweth poison. Some such there be; but such drones and door bees we will expel the hive and serve your Majesty, and withstand any enemy that shall assault your own lands or goods.

Our lives are prostrate at your feet to be commanded ; yea, and thanked be God and honour to your Majesty for it, such is the power and force of your subjects that of their own strengths they are able to encounter your greatest enemies ; and though we be such yet have we a Prince that is *sine aculeo*, so full of that clemency is your Majesty. I must now to your laws.

'The laws we have conferred upon this session of so honourable a Parliament are of two natures ; they are such as have life but are ready to die, except your Majesty breathe life into them again. The other are laws that never had life, but being void of life do come to your Majesty to seek life.

'The first sort are those laws that had continuance until this Parliament and are now to receive new life. The other that I term capable of life are those which are newly made but have no essence until your Majesty giveth them life.

'Two laws there are, but I must give the honour where it is due, for they come from the able, wise lords of the Upper House, the most honourable and beneficial laws that could be desired ; the one a confirmation of all Letters Patents from your Majesty's most noble father of all Ecclesiastical livings, which that King of most renowned memory took from those superstitious monasteries and priories, and translated them to the erecting of many foundations of Churches and Colleges, thereby greatly furthering the maintenance of learning and true religion. The other law to suppress the obstinate recusant and the dangerous sectary; both very pernicious to your Royal Government.

'Lastly, your most loving and obedient subjects, the Commons of the Lower House, most humbly and with dutiful thanks stand bound unto your gracious goodness for your general and large pardon granted unto them, wherein many great offences are pardoned, but it extendeth only to offences done before Parliament.

'I have many ways since the beginning of this Parliament by ignorance and insufficiency to perform that which I should have done offended your Majesty, I most humbly crave to be partaker of your most gracious pardon.'

The Lord Keeper then received instructions from the Queen and afterwards replied to the Speaker that her Majesty did most graciously accept of these services and devotions of this Parliament, commending them that they had employed their time so well, and spent it on necessary affairs ; save only that in some things they had spent more time than was needed ; but she perceived some men did it more for their own satisfaction than the necessity of the thing deserved.

She misliked also that such irreverence was shown towards Privy Councillors (who were not to be accounted as common knights and burgesses of the House that were but councillors during the Parliament) ; whereas the others were standing councillors, and for their wisdom and great service were called the Council of State.

Then he said that the Queen's Majesty had heard that some men in the case of great necessity and grant of aid had seemed not to regard their country and made their necessity more than it was, forgetting the urgent necessity of the time and dangers that were now eminent.

Her Majesty would not have the people feared with reports of great dangers but rather to be encouraged with boldness against the enemies of the State. And therefore she charged and commanded that the mustered companies in every county should be supplied if they were decayed and that their provisions of armour and ammunition should be better than heretofore it had been used.

For this offer of three subsidies her Majesty most graciously in all kindness thanketh her subjects ; but except it were freely and willingly given she did not accept it ; for her Majesty never accepteth anything that is not freely given.

If the coffers of her Majesty's treasure were not empty or if the revenues of the Crown and other Princely ornaments could suffice to supply her wants and the charges of the Realm, in the word of a Prince she did pronounce it, she would not now have charged her subjects nor accepted of this they gave her.

The Lord Keeper's Speech being ended, after some intermission, the Queen herself, sitting in her chair of State, spoke to the two Houses :

'This Kingdom hath had many wise, noble and victorious Princes : I will not compare with any of them in wisdom, fortitude or any other virtues, but saving the duty of a child that is not to compare with his father, in love, care, sincerity and justice, I will compare with any Prince that ever you had or should have.

'It may be thought simplicity in me, but all this time of my reign I have not sought to advance my territories and enlarge my dominions; for opportunity hath served me to do it. I acknowledge my womanhood and weakness in that respect, but though it had not been hard to obtain yet I doubted how to keep the things so obtained; that hath only held me from such attempts, and I must say my mind was never to invade my neighbours or to usurp over any.

'I am contented to reign over mine own and to rule as a just Prince.

'Yet the King of Spain doth challenge me to be the quarreller and the beginner of all these wars, in which he doth me the greatest wrong that can be; for my conscience doth not accuse my thoughts wherein I have done him the least injury; but I am persuaded in my conscience, if he knew what I know, he himself would be sorry for the wrong that he hath done me.

'I fear not all his threatenings; his great preparations and mighty forces do not stir me, for though he come against me with a greater power than ever was his *Invincible Navy*, I doubt not (God assisting me, upon Whom I always trust) but that I shall be able to defeat and overthrow him. I have great advantage against him; for my cause is just.

'I heard say, when he attempted his last invasion, some upon the sea coast forsook their towns and flew up higher into the country and left all naked and exposed to his entrance. But I swear unto you by God if I knew those persons, or of any that shall do so hereafter, I will make them know and feel what it is to be fearful in so urgent a cause.

'The subsidies you give me I accept thankfully, if you give me your goodwills with them; but if the necessity of the time and your preservations did not require it I would refuse them. But let me tell you that the sum is not so much but that it is needful for a Prince to have so much always lying in her coffers for your defence in time of need, and not be driven to get it when we should use it.

'You that be Lieutenants and gentlemen of command in your counties, I require you to take care that the people be well armed and in readiness in all occasions. You that be judges and justices of the peace, I command and straightly charge that you should see the laws to be duly executed and that you make them living laws when we have put life with them.'

And so with most gracious thanks to both Houses, her Majesty ended her speech.

Then the titles of all the Acts were read in order, beginning with the Bill of Subsidies, to which the Clerk of the Parliament, standing up, did read the Queen's answer : *La Royne remercie ses loyaule Subjects, accept leur benevolence, et ainsi le veult.*

Next the Clerk pronounced the thanks of the Lords and Commons in these words : *Les Prelates, Seigneurs et Communes en ce present Parliament assembles, au nomes de touts vous autres subjects, remercient tres humblement vostre Majesty, et prient Dieu que vout il done en sante bonne vie et longue.*

At each Public Act, to everyone allowed by the Queen the Clerk said, *Le Royne le veult* ; to every Private Act, he said, *Soit fait come il est desiré* ; and to such Acts as the Queen forebore to allow, *Le Royne se advisera.*

After which the Parliament was dissolved by the Lord Keeper of the Great Seal in Latin with these words : *Dominus Custos Magni Sigilli, ex mandato Dominae Reginae tunc praesentis dissoluit praesens Parliamentum.*

11th April. RELIEF FOR MAIMED SOLDIERS.

Until the Act of Parliament made for the relief of maimed soldiers can be put into execution the Lords Lieutenant of counties shall give every man weekly the sum of two shillings. For the convenience of those too impotent to come themselves to fetch the money from the Deputy Lieutenant, some trusty person residing near is to be appointed to receive and pay the money. All these maimed soldiers having received conduct money at the rate of 1d. a mile, and to the most lame 2d. a mile, are ordered to return to their own counties where they shall receive relief.

14th April. FALSE REPORTS CONCERNING THE QUEEN'S DEALINGS WITH THE TURKS.

There have of late been set forth in Germany many scandalous libels about her Majesty as if she had invited the Turk to make war against Christendom ; and the letters which she sent the Turk published, but falsified and corrupted many things being added. A letter is now sent to the Emperor very strongly denying these calumnies and showing how by the Turk's own confession her Majesty did make peace between him and the King of Poland. This letter also setteth forth the insatiable desire for conquest of the King of Spain, and the troubles which he stirreth up in France and in Scotland.

15th April. THE QUEEN'S DIRECTIONS TO SIR JOHN NORRIS.

Some days since Sir John Norris wrote showing what inconveniences would follow if his troops were withdrawn and to ask for absolute directions whether to stay or return. The Queen now answereth that his doubts appear strange, for she could not have written more plainly or directly to him than she had done ; for she had first assured him that not one man would be sent if the King had not in those parts such settled troops as might make head against the enemy ; she had also commanded him to take special care not to be so engaged by any siege as to be driven either dishonourably to quit the place, or else to plunge her into the necessity of relieving him ; being an action of more charge and hazard than for the town of Pempole or Brehat she meant to be put. Yet if he were not likely to be pressed by the forces of the enemy he might remain a short time ; but in referring anything to his judgment as General, it ought not to be used as a reason to complain of want of plain direction ; unless he preferred her either to judge certainly of things there which time and distance must make uncertain, or else to leave him no more reputation of his opinion than as a cipher that could judge of nothing.

However understanding his apprehension of the dangers the country will take from his sudden return, she is now content that he shall stay for a short time if he find the enemy retired from him, or can have such intelligence of his approach as not to be overtaken with a siege. If not, he is commanded to retreat to the Islands with the ships already provided.

16th April. THE LIBELS AGAINST STRANGERS.

A certain man hath been arrested on suspicion of being the author of a libel against strangers. He is to be very strictly examined by the Lord Mayor of his meaning and purpose in making that writing and who are in any way privy of that fact; if there be any pregnant matter to argue him to be guilty of writing the placard and he will not by fair means be brought to utter his knowledge, he shall be punished by torture and compelled to reveal it.

17th April. MEASURES AGAINST VAGABONDS.

An order is to be printed and set up in the City that all poor, aged and impotent persons repair to the place where they were born or where they were most conversant during the space of three years, there to be maintained; likewise all others wandering about as beggars, being whole and strong in body and able to get work, having no lands or other means to get their living, shall be taken as rogues and vagabonds. And if any impotent person so provided for wander abroad out of his parish without licence he shall be whipped and returned, but if eftsoons he offend again then to be punished as a rogue. To this end the officers of the City of London and of Westminster shall make inquisition of all beggars to compel them to depart to the places where they were born.

18th April. 'VENUS AND ADONIS' ENTERED.

Venus and Adonis, a poem written by William Shakespeare, is entered, being dedicated to Henry Wriothesley, Earl of Southampton. In this poem is described the hot love of Venus for the youth Adonis who scorneth her love, and leaving her to pursue the boar is by it slain. And she hearing his dismal cry:

> As falcon to the lure, away she flies;
> The grass stoops not, she treads on it so light;
> And in her haste unfortunately spies
> The foul boar's conquest on her fair delight;
> Which seen, her eyes, as murder'd with the view,
> Like stars asham'd of day, themselves withdrew:
>
> Or, as the snail, whose tender horns being hit,
> Shrinks backward in his shelly cave with pain,
> And there, all smother'd up, in shade doth sit,
> Long after fearing to creep forth again;
> So, at his bloody view, her eyes are fled
> Into the deep dark cabins of her head:

Where they resign their office and their light
To the disposing of her troubled brain;
Who bids them still consort with ugly night,
And never wound the heart with looks again;
  Who, like a king perplexed in his throne,
  By their suggestion gives a deadly groan,

Whereat each tributary subject quakes;
As when the wind, imprison'd in the ground,
Struggling for passage, earth's foundation shakes,
Which with cold terror doth men's minds confound.
  This mutiny each part doth so surprise
  That from their dark beds once more leap her eyes;

And, being open'd, threw unwilling light
Upon the wide wound that the boar had trench'd
In his soft flank; whose wonted lily white
With purple tears, that his wound wept, was drench'd:
  No flower was nigh, no grass, herb, leaf, or weed,
  But stole his blood and seem'd with him to bleed.

This solemn sympathy poor Venus noteth,
Over one shoulder doth she hang her head,
Dumbly she passions, franticly she doteth;
She thinks he could not die, he is not dead:
  Her voice is stopp'd, her joints forget to bow,
  Her eyes are mad that they have wept till now.

22nd April. THE LIBELS AGAINST STRANGERS.

Dr. Julius Caesar, one of the Masters of Requests, Sir Henry Killigrew, and others are appointed commissioners to examine by secret means the authors of the libels against the strangers, and their favourers and abettors, and to discover their intentions.

THE LIBEL

'Doth not the world see that you, beastly brutes, the Belgians or rather drunken drones, and faint-hearted Flemings; and you, fraudulent fathers, Frenchmen, by your cowardly flight from your own natural countries, have abandoned the same into the hands of your proud, cowardly enemies, and have by a feigned hypocrisy and counterfeit show of religion placed yourselves here in a most fertile soil under a most gracious and merciful Prince; who had been contented, to the great prejudice of her own natural subjects, to suffer you to live here in better case and more freedom than her own people?

'Be it known to all Flemings and Frenchmen, that it is best for them to depart out of the realm of England, between this and 9th of July next. If not, then to take what follows. For there shall be many a sore stripe. Apprentices will rise to the number of 2336. And all prentices and journeymen will down with Flemings and Strangers.'

23rd April. DRAYTON'S 'IDEA.'

The Shepherd's Garland, fashioned in nine Eclogues, Rowland's Sacrifice to the nine Muses, by Michael Drayton, being dedicated to Mr. Robert Dudley, is entered. In the first of these eclogues (founded after the pastoral mode of *The Shepherd's Kalendar*), Rowland malcontent bewaileth the winter of his grief; in the second old Wynken reproveth Motto's unbridled youth, giving him Rowland's example; in the third Perkin rouseth Rowland to song, who praises Beta the Queen of Virgins. Wynklyn in the fourth bewaileth the loss of Elphin (Sir Philip Sidney). In the fifth, Rowland singeth the praises of Idea, his lady; and of Pandora (the Countess of Pembroke) in the sixth, whom he calleth

> Arabian Phoenix, wonder of thy sex,
> Lovely, chaste, holy, miracle admired,
> With spirit from the highest heaven inspired,
> Oh thou alone, whom fame alone respects,
> Nature's chief glory, virtue's paradise;

declaring that

> Ages shall tell such wonders of thy name,
> And thou in death thy due desert shall have,
> And thou shalt be immortal in thy grave,
> Thy virtues adding force unto thy fame,
> So that virtue with thy fame's wings shall fly,
> And by thy fame shall virtue never die.

In the seventh eclogue Dorrill, an aged shepherd swain, rebukes Batto for falling in love.

In the eighth, Gorbo sings of the age of the golden world, ending with a tale of Dowsabel and her shepherd lover.

The book ends with the lament of Rowland that his Idea is unkind to him.

24th April. PLAGUE DEATHS.

The plague is not yet died out of London, 34 persons being reported dead of it during the past week.

29th April. A CHARITABLE GENTLEMAN.

Some years since Mr. Edward Cotton of his charity disbursed the sum of £444 for the redemption of four captives from the Turks, yet hath he hitherto received but £40, though letters were then sent to the Lord Mayor that his charges should be satisfied from the collections ordinarily made about Easter for this charitable purpose. The Council have again written to the Lord Mayor that the money specially collected for the redemption of captives since Maundy Thursday or before at Spittle sermons or other places be now paid to him, that others may be encouraged to the like good and charitable deed upon like occasions.

4th May. THE NUMBERS OF STRANGERS IN LONDON.

The certificates giving the numbers of strangers in London show the total of all strangers living in London with their children and servants born out of the realm to be 4300; 267 being denizens. This scrutiny hath been taken in every ward because of the complaints of English shopkeepers that the strangers are not content with manufactures and warehouses but would keep shops and retail all manner of goods.

5th May. LIBELS AGAINST STRANGERS.

Between eleven and twelve o'clock at night a rhyme was found set up on the walls of the Dutch Churchyard beginning:

> 'You strangers that inhabit in this land,
> Note this same writing, do it understand;
> Conceive it well for safeguard of your lives,
> Your goods, your children and your dearest wives.'

This was taken down and brought to the constable.

10*th May*. 'PARTHENOPHIL AND PARTHENOPHE.'

Parthenophil and Parthenophe, by Barnabe Barnes, is entered. In this book are contained sonnets, madrigals, elegies and odes setting forth the passion and desire of Parthenophil for Parthenophe, his mistress, his distress at her refusing, and at the last his enjoyment of her love; with sonnets to the Earl of Northumberland, the Earl of Essex, the Earl of Southampton, the Countess of Pembroke, the Lady Strange and the Lady Bridget Manners. The wantonness of some few of the verses in this book much to be noted, especially of that sonnet wherein the poet wisheth himself the wine that his lady drinketh.

11*th May*. MORE LIBELS AGAINST STRANGERS.

The malicious libels against strangers continuing to be set up and one especially upon the wall of the Dutch Churchyard that excels the rest in lewdness, the special Commissioners are ordered to take extraordinary pains to discover the author and publisher thereof; to make search and apprehend every person suspected, and for that purpose to enter into all houses where they may be staying; and upon their apprehension, to make search in chambers, studies, chests and the like for all manner of writings or papers that might give light for the discovery of the libellers. All that after due examination be suspected and refuse to confess the truth are to be put to the torture in Bridewell, that by its extremity (to be used as often as the Commissioners deem necessary) they shall be drawn to discover their knowledge.

12*th May*. THOMAS KYD ARRESTED.

Thomas Kyd, that wrote the *Spanish Tragedy* some years since, hath been arrested and carried to Bridewell by the officers of the Lord Mayor searching for the authors of the libels against strangers. When they examined his papers some fragments of a disputation denying the divinity of Jesus Christ were found; these papers Kyd declareth to have been left in his study by Marlowe when they wrote together two years ago.

15*th May*. CONTEMPT OF THE COUNCIL'S ORDER AT BRISTOL.

Some months since, on earnest complaint of the French Ambassador of the taking of sundry ships belonging to Bayonne and St. Jean de Lurg, by English men-of-wars, some being of Bristol, and the owners subjects of the King of France, the Council instructed the case to be referred to arbitrament. By the award the captors were condemned to restore the hulk in such state as she was at the taking, together with 100,000 fish and the sum of £60. This ought to have been performed in December; yet notwithstanding the Council's earnest letters nothing is yet effected. The Mayor and Council of Bristol are now required to see that the owner of the ship is satisfied; or in default the Council will be constrained to consent to letters of marque being granted to those of Bayonne and St. Jean de Lurg against the City of Bristol, which will turn to no small prejudice of their adventures.

20th May. MARLOWE BEFORE THE COUNCIL.

This day Christopher Marlowe, who was sent for by the Council two days since, hath entered his appearance and is commanded to give his daily attendance until licensed the contrary.

21st May. A PRIEST'S DECLARATION OF HIS MOTIVES.

William Harrington, a priest, that was taken, being charged with treason, and examined, hath set forth his reasons for coming to England in a letter to the Lord Keeper.

He saith that he is a gentleman by birth, a Catholic, and a priest of the Seminary of Rheims. He first left his country, desiring to imitate others of innocent lives and glorious deaths, especially Campion (the Jesuit that was executed in 1580), whom he believed guilty of no treason to the Queen nor the country. He hath always abhorred treachery but is not amazed at being accused as a traitor, nor troubled at the popular outcry, 'Hang him, hang him.' If his cause is good, he suffereth for Justice's sake, and that law is too severe that maketh his function treason; if his cause be bad, death itself is too merciful a punishment. He is compelled by his conscience to discharge his priestly office, but hath refrained from other practices, which he detests. Having so determined, he would make his life of no account. He hath never been made privy to any plot against the Queen or the country or he would have been forced by his oath of allegiance to give notice of it. Since he will not serve his Prince or country by betraying his friends, he hopeth to be excused for not wishing to live with such a spot of infamy. He therefore beggeth life and liberty on such conditions as he may conscientiously observe; if not, he resigns himself to God's disposal.

23rd May. THE PLAGUE IN THE SAVOY.

The Master of the Hospital of the Savoy is to forbear for the time to receive any into the hospital because of the danger that the poor people repairing there daily may be infected with the plague, to the great danger of the inhabitants in general and especially to some of the Council that dwell in those parts and are often occasioned to be at Court and near the Queen. This hospital was founded in former times for poor suitors from the country that are unable to defray the charge of lodging during their abode in the City on their necessary business, but the greater part of those now received are young boys, rogues and vagabonds.

24th May. PENRY CONDEMNED.

John Penry, the Puritan, was arraigned this day. At his trial many seditious and slanderous speeches were urged against him, collected from his papers and writings. He had said that the Queen stands against the Gospel and will not move a finger to help it, nor speak a word to reform it. The magistrates, ministers and people are conspirators against God, murder whole troops of souls, and are godless men. The Council are rebels against God and levy their force against the Gospel. Nor may the people serve God under the Queen but are bond slaves of the man of sin; nor would the Queen have embraced the Gospel if she could have received the crown without it, and only useth it to strengthen her sceptre. If Queen Mary had reigned to this day, the Gospel would have flourished more; without the Gospel, outward peace is nothing.

A REQUEST OF THE CITIZENS OF PARIS.

From Paris it is reported that 500 of the inhabitants went to the lodging of Monsieur de Blyn, and signified to him that they would live and die in the maintenance of the Catholic religion, but if the King would render himself a Catholic they would make a peace with him that would not be in the power either of the Governor or of Monsieur de Mayne to impeach. They prayed him signify so much to Monsieur de Mayne; and if he would have it better confirmed, they would within an hour bring ten thousand persons who would affirm their resolution.

25th May. ABUSES OF THE QUEEN'S SERVICE IN GLOUCESTERSHIRE.

The Justices of the Peace for the county of Gloucester are ordered to inquire into the complaints that the Queen's services are much hindered and neglected by the inferior officers that from time to time have the conducting of the soldiers pressed for service in Normandy and Brittany. These officers have sold, freed or exchanged the most part of those of any suffering and ability before they were delivered over to their captains to be embarked.

26th May. MARLOWE'S BLASPHEMIES.

Information hath been received by the Lord Keeper of the opinions of Christopher Marlowe, and by him laid before the Queen. This Marlowe is accused of many vile and horrible blasphemies concerning Christ and His Mother; affirmeth that Moses was but a juggler and that one Harriott, Sir Walter Ralegh's man, can do more than he. Into every company he cometh he would persuade men to atheism, willing them not to be afeared of bugbears and hobgoblins, and utterly scorning both God and His ministers.

28th May. PRECAUTIONS AGAINST PLAGUE.

Trinity Term is adjourned owing to the great increase of the plague in London, Westminster, and the parts adjoining. But seeing that great prejudice would grow to many in their causes and suits if the term be wholly adjourned, some few days at the beginning and ending of the term shall be held for the better expediting those causes that can be performed in the absence of the parties by their attorneys. No party, save in case of outlawry, is compelled to appear in person.

STRATFORD GOOSE FAIR FORBIDDEN.

At this time of the year there is usually held a 'Goose feast' at Stratford Bow, whither a disordered assembly of all the vagabond and idle persons come from the City; whereat through excess of drinking, divers quarrels and other great inconveniences have fallen out in that place. As an opportunity is offered thereby to the worst sort of apprentices and others ill disposed to resort thither to make their matches and appointments to sundry ill purposes, and also because the infection is more dispersed that way than towards any other villages, the Council have ordered the magistrates to take timely order to prevent this inconvenience. They shall charge the taverners, alehouse keepers and other victuallers to forbear to make extraordinary provision of victuals and to cause a straight watch to be set about the place for better intercepting all that pass to the town without good and lawful occasion.

Mr. Wentworth in the Tower.

Mr. Peter Wentworth, who is very old and subject to continual infirmities, is much impaired in health, by reason of his close imprisonment and especially owing to the great heat of the present season. The Council allow him the liberty of the Tower in company with some trusty servant and also to see his sons, friends, and physicians for his better comfort and recovery of health; but he shall not be permitted to have any conference with them except in the presence of the Governor or his servants.

30th May. Marlowe Slain.

Christopher Marlowe is slain by one Ingram Frizer at the Bull Inn at Deptford.

31st May. The Execution of John Penry.

John Penry, suspected of being the author of the Martinist pamphlets, that was condemned at the King's Bench on the 24th May, was hanged at St. Thomas Watering, with little warning and few spectators, lest he should have raised some tumult, either in going to the gallows or upon the ladder.

Three Suspected Soldiers.

Three soldiers that arrived at Poole without passports and were arrested, are now to be released and dismissed with passports to their homes. It is found on examination that they were abandoned by the rest of the troops at a place called St. Susan's, not far from Laval, and thereby constrained hazardously to adventure the saving of their lives by attempting to recover Caen, whence they have come to England.

1st June. THE INQUEST ON CHRISTOPHER MARLOWE.

At the inquest on the body of Christopher Marlowe, it was testified by those present at the time that Marlowe with three gentlemen, Ingram Frizer, Robert Poley and Nicholas Skeres, met in the house of a certain Eleanor Bull, and there dined. After dinner they walked in the garden until 6 o'clock in the evening, when they returned and supped. Thereafter malicious words passed between Marlowe and Frizer about the payment of the reckoning, until Marlowe, who was lying on a bed, sprang on Frizer, then sitting at the table, and taking Frizer's dagger from his back wounded him twice in the head. Frizer being then put in fear of his life strove to get back his dagger, and in the struggle gave Marlowe a mortal wound over the right eye of which he instantly died.

Frizer is found to have acted in defence of his own life. But though this is the Coroner's verdict, there want not other stories making his end more fearful. He is reported to have been an atheist, a blasphemer, given to the vice of sodomy; which offences with many others of a like nature had been charged against him in a paper sent to the Lord Keeper but three days before his death. It is much noted that he was smitten in the brain where he conceived his blasphemies and by his own hand wherewith he wrote them, and that together with his last breath an oath fled out of his mouth. Some say that the quarrel first arose over a lewd love. He is buried in the churchyard at Deptford.

5th June. PRECAUTIONS AGAINST PLAGUE AT WINDSOR.

Since the Queen will make her residence at Windsor for most part of the summer, the Mayor of Windsor is to order that no citizen of London or other person coming from any place where there is infection do resort to the town or make stay there. Those persons that are obstinately and undutifully refusing to obey the orders of the Mayor, shall be admonished to remove from thence with their families; and if any of them refuse, the Mayor to take bonds of them to appear before the Council to answer their contempt.

7th June. MR. COTTON'S CLAIMS TO BE SATISFIED.

Mr. Edward Cotton complaining that the Lord Mayor not only refuseth to pay him any money but will not so much as vouchsafe an answer to the Council's letters, the Council have required the Lord Mayor either to make some reasonable satisfaction or else to send a true and perfect account of the collection for the release of captives of every year from the beginning of 1589 until the end of April last, showing what captives have been released and for what sums of money.

8th June. RELIEF OF MAIMED SOLDIERS.

The Sheriffs and Justices of the Peace throughout the realm are ordered to confer together and consider of the Statute passed this last Parliament for the relief of those hurt or maimed in the service of the Queen. Officers shall be ordained for receipt of the collections, that such as should come with warrant to demand their allowances may receive the benefit without any further trouble to them or occasion ministered to the Queen to think any slack in the performances of their duties.

10th June. CHARITY FOR A PRISONER IN THE HANDS OF THE LEAGUERS.

The Lord Mayor and Aldermen are asked to bestow on Peter Brown, a captive, so much money as will satisfy his ransom from the collections that have been made for this purpose. This Brown, one of the ordinary posts, coming towards England in a voyage from Sir Roger Williams, has lately been taken by the garrison of Rouen. There he remains, and will not be delivered without paying so great a ransom as far exceedeth his ability to pay.

12th June. RUMOURS OF CHANGES IN FRANCE.

There is much talk at this time of the likelihood that the King of France has turned Catholic, and of a peace between the King and the League. This detaineth all resolution with the Vidame of Chartres, his ambassador. The Queen stormed at first but it is believed that nothing will come of the matter.

16th June. CHUTE'S 'BEAUTY DISHONOURED.'

Beauty Dishonoured: written under the title of Shore's Wife, by Mr. Anthony Chute, is entered, being dedicated to Sir Edward Wingfield.

> Even on her dying bed divinely sorry,
> Pensive in heart she weeps thus forth her story.

She complaineth that her great beauty caused her to be suspected of immodesty even when she was still bashful and chaste. Being then forced into marriage with an old man that she loathed, she was importuned by many lovers and at first despised them all, but in time, saith she,

> My speed from humble, decent, pure and true,
> That hid no secrets in a plainly meaning,
> To courtlike, wanton, pleasant did ensue;
> I left my nature to my follies meaning:
> And I by practice learn'd so well
> In wanton art the best I could excel.

Her fame was now carried to the King, whose mistress she became. But he dying soon after, she was accused by Richard, Duke of Gloucester, of witchcraft, shamed, and turned out to beg; and so died.

18th June. A PROCLAMATION TO RESTRAIN SUITORS AT COURT.

A Proclamation is published to restrain the access of so many suitors to the Court. No persons but such as have cause to come to the Court for their ordinary attendance on the Queen shall repair within two miles upon pain of contempt, and all that attend on the Queen, her Councillors and the Officers of her Chamber and Household, are straightly commanded to see these orders obeyed.

If for any extraordinary cause anyone do come to the Court with matter to be certified to the Queen or to any of the Privy Council, he may not enter within the gates until he be licensed by the Lord Chamberlain or some other of the Council. If he have only letters to deliver, then not to come within the gates but to send in the letters, and when answer is given not to tarry longer on pain of imprisonment.

20th June. CAPTAIN JOHN DAVIS RETURNS TO ENGLAND.

Captain John Davis hath returned with some few of his men to Cornwall on the 16th, being but the poor remainder of the company of seventy-six that had left Plymouth on 26th August, 1591, on board the *Desire* with Mr. Thomas Cavendish's fleet.

After losing sight of Mr. Cavendish, their General, on the night of the 20th May, 1592, they had returned to Port Desire, being now in very miserable case, the shrouds all rotten, without pitch, tar or nails, and living only upon seals and mussels. Here they remained hoping for sight of the General until 6th August, when they made for the Straits of Magellan, and there stayed, in the deep of winter, with but little victual and not enough clothing to defend the extremity of the winter's cold. In these seas they were lamentably driven by storms until on 25th October they came to an island named Penquin Island. There the boat was sent on shore, which returned laden with birds' eggs; and the men said that the penquins were so thick that the ships might be laden with them. The Captain therefore sent some of the men ashore whilst he sailed the ship up a river in the mainland, where she was run aground and made fast to the shore with running ropes moored to stakes. Here nine of their men were slain by savages, but the rest remained feeding on eggs, penquins, young seals, gulls, and other birds. In this place they found a herb called scurvy grass which so purged the blood that it took away all kinds of swelling, of which many had died, and restored them to perfect health of body.

In this harbour they stayed until 22nd December, in which time they had dried 20,000 penquins on the island, of which 14,000 were taken on board, but not being able to fetch the rest by reason of the dangerous tides, they shaped course for Brazil. On 30th January, 1593, they landed at the Isle of Placencia, hoping to surprise the Portugals, but when they came to the houses they were all burnt, so that they thought no man remained on the island. Then the Captain went to the gardens and brought thence fruits and roots for the company, and all laboured to put the water casks in order.

The 5th February at night many of the men dreamed of murder and slaughter, and the Captain likewise having dreamed very strangely himself, gave straight charge that those who went on shore should take weapons with them. All the forenoon they laboured in quietness, but when it was ten o'clock, the heat being now extreme, they came to a rock near the woods' side (for all this country was nothing but thick woods) and there they boiled some cazavi roots and dined. After dinner some slept, some washed themselves in the sea, all being stripped to their shirts, and no man keeping a watch. Suddenly as they were thus sleeping and sporting, having gotten themselves into a corner out of sight of the ship, there came a multitude of Indians and Portugals upon them, and slew them sleeping; only two escaped, one very sorely hurt, one unharmed, who ran to the ship.

With all speed the boat was manned and landed to succour the men, but they found them all slain, and laid naked in a rank, with their faces upward and a cross set by them. Moreover, they saw in the river two very great pinnaces full of men. So the next day, choosing rather to fall into the hands of the Lord than into the hands of men, they cast off in great distress, having only eight tuns of water in bad casks.

And now as they came near to the sun the dried penquins began to corrupt and there bred in them a most loathsome and ugly worm of an inch long, which so mightily increased and devoured the victuals that there was in reason no hope of avoiding famine; for there was nothing they did not devour, only iron, cloths, boots, shoes, hats, shirts, stockings, and for the ship they did so eat the timbers that there was great fear lest they should gnaw through her side. In this woeful case after passing the equinoctial toward the north, the men began to fall sick of a monstrous disease so that their ankles and whole bodies began to swell, and some to grow raging mad, and perished thus in most loathsome and furious pain, so that all but sixteen died, and of these but five were able to move, and upon them only stood the labour of the ship.

Thus as lost wanderers upon the sea, it pleased God that they arrived at Bearhaven in Ireland the 11th of June, and there ran the ship on shore, where the Captain left the master and three or four of the company, and within five days after he and certain others passed in an English fishing boat to Padstow in Cornwall.

25th June. THE COUNCIL'S LICENCE ABUSED.

A certain John Wilson hath been travelling about the realm with a counterfeit licence bearing the seal of the Court of Admiralty and the hands of the Lord Admiral and the Archbishop of Canterbury, pretending that he is a sailor that sustained great losses and captivity with the Spaniards, and thereby hath he collected divers sums of money. This man was imprisoned at York and his licence sent to the Lord Admiral, who declared it counterfeit. As this offence of late years had been very frequent, the man is to be set on the pillory at York with one of his ears nailed, and, if the Lord President sees cause, cut off, with a writing set over his head signifying the cause of his punishment.

26th June. 'A DISCOVERY OF THE CONSPIRACY OF THE SCOTTISH PAPISTS.'

A discovery of the unnatural and traitorous conspiracy of Scottish Papists against God, his Church, their native country, the King's Majesty's person and estate, is entered, being extracted from the confessions and letters of Mr. George Ker, that is still in prison, and David Graham of Fintry, justly executed for his treason the 15th February, 1593, with other letters intercepted. This book was first printed and published in Scotland at the special commandment of the King, and is now again to be printed in London.

29th June. CITY FEASTS TO BE CURTAILED.

Owing to the plague, the customary great feasts made by the City Companies at this time are to be curtailed, and the choice of officers made with as small an assembly as conveniently may be. The charges so saved are to be converted to the relief of those infected; and that this contribution may be made without fraud, the Lord Mayor is required to find out what is usually spent by the heads of companies at their feasts.

There is great negligence in the City in suffering houses and shops to remain open or only to be shut up a few days in places where the plague is well known to have been. The Queen is so greatly offended therewith that, except the Lord Mayor and Aldermen take better regard, she will be moved to seize their liberties and commit the government of her City to some others.

1st July. Mr. Cavendish's Voyage.

From letters received from Mr. Thomas Cavendish, who sailed from England nearly two years since, it appeareth that he hath passed through the Straits of Magellan into the South Sea, where prizes of great value are sometimes taken. Sir Francis Drake and others are ordered that, if God should bless these ships with any such purchase, and if the ships or prizes taken by them should enter any port, they should immediately go on board and see the hatches nailed down. A just inventory shall be taken of all goods found in the cabins or above hatches lest any disorder be committed by the ship's company to the loss of the owners and adventurers and the prejudice of the Queen's customs.

Fairs to be Abandoned.

Owing to the dangerous increase of the plague, her Majesty out of her princely care for the preserving of her living subjects, and preferring the same before private benefit, commandeth the fairs usually held in the months of July, August and September to be abandoned. In London, St. Bartholomew's Fair in Smithfield upon 24th August and the Fair in Southwark on 8th September; and near London in July, Uxbridge the 20th, St. James's the 25th, and Brainford the 27th; in September, St. Giles in the Bush the 1st, Ware the 7th, Waltham Abbey the 13th, Croydon and St. Catherine Hill near Guildford the 21st.

6th July. Marlowe's 'Edward the Second.'

The play of *The Troublesome Reign and Lamentable Death of Edward the Second, King of England, with the tragical fall of proud Mortimer*, written by Christopher Marlowe, and sundry times acted by the Earl of Pembroke's players, is entered for the printing.

9th July. The Plague.

The Lord Mayor hath written to the Council showing the discommodity which will arise, especially to the clothiers, if Bartholomew Fair be not held. The proclamation forbidding the Fair may now be stayed for a while until it is seen how by God's goodness and the Lord Mayor's careful endeavour the increase of sickness be allayed.

Since the white crosses painted on those houses visited with the plague are wiped away in a short space, red crosses are to be nailed upon the doors and a watch kept to prevent those within from going abroad.

THE COLLECTION OF THE SUBSIDY.

The High Sheriffs are appointed commissioners for the collections of the fifteenths and tenths voted for the Queen's use. They are urged to choose men of sufficient worth for this work. As for the Justices of the Peace, since by the statute none should be admitted unless they hold lands to the value of £20 per annum, so is it expected that none of these shall be assessed at under this rate. The commissioners themselves shall give a notable example in the taxation of themselves so that the rest which are able may be drawn the more willingly to assent to the larger taxation now laid on them.

SPANISH SHIPS OFF THE BRITTANY COAST.

From the Isle of Jersey it is reported that 30 ships of the enemy and 5 galleys have been seen on the coast of Brittany about Conquett. Letters are therefore sent to Sir John Gilbert and Sir Francis Drake to warn the forces of the counties on the sea coast to be ready against any sudden incursion that might be made, and especially to take care for the defence of Plymouth now being begun to be fortified.

BLUNDEVILLE'S 'EXERCISES.'

Master Blundeville, His Exercises, is to be printed, being six treatises; the first, of Arithmetic; the second, of the first principles of Cosmography; the third, a plain and full description of the globes, both celestial and terrestrial, with certain tables for the better finding out of the true place of the sun and moon and of all the rest of the planets on the celestial globe; the fourth, a plain description of the universal map of Petrus Plancius set forth in 1592; the fifth, a plain description of Mr. Blagrave's Astrolabe; the sixth, the first and chiefest principles of navigation, showing how the navigator should use his proper instruments and presage the movements of the celestial bodies.

14th July. SIR THOMAS WILKES SENT TO THE FRENCH KING.

Because of the continual rumours that the French King is turned Catholic, Sir Thomas Wilkes is urgently despatched as a special ambassador to the King. He is instructed, after delivering his letters of credence, to say to the King that her Majesty hath forborne hitherto to inquire what course he meaneth to hold in the present state of his affairs, but now she findeth occasion to delay no longer sending unto him. If either the King hath not fully yielded to his conversion to the Catholic religion, or hath not bound himself by promise to perform it, the ambassador shall say that her Majesty can in no wise allow or think it good before God that for any worldly respect or cunning persuasion he should yield to change his conscience and opinion in religion from the truth wherein he was brought up from his youth, and for the defence whereof he hath continued many years in arms. He shall require that the King not only hear a number of reasons conceived by her Majesty to stay his resolution, but also to permit them to be communicated to his principal Catholic estates.

But if in coming thither Sir Thomas Wilkes shall find that the King hath indeed been converted, nevertheless he shall show the reasons conceived by the Queen to stay his resolution, that he may understand her mind and good will towards him. And though she would be grieved with his conversion, being contrary to her opinion and conscience, and indeed by good policy to be misliked, because he would become thereby subject to the Pope, who is her mortal enemy, and who might enjoin him to keep no amity with her ; yet she requireth him to advertise her what she may expect thereof.

First she wisheth to know how and by what means he will be stronger in his estate by his conversion than he was before as well against his rebels, that will not be content with his conversion, as also against the King of Spain. Then shall the ambassador ask how the King meaneth to proceed to acquit Brittany of the Spaniards, telling him that her Majesty thinketh it the principal matter of weight that he hath to take in hand after he shall be established in his crown ; and is of such importance that she thinketh it more convenient for the King himself to take the same in hand, and in his own person, than to commit it to others, as hitherto.

Further, the King is to understand that until some port town in Brittany be allowed to her Majesty's forces whither they may repair when sent, or to which they may retire for their relief, she cannot with any honour or the good respect of her natural subjects send any more forces thither to be wasted and spoiled as the former have been for the lack of such a place of retire.

The ambassador is also to know of the King what assurance her Majesty may have of him that he will continue jointly with her in offence and defence against the King of Spain. She doubteth not that he will give her this assurance under his hand and the great seal of France; for without it she will think all her kindness, favours and expenses of her treasure and wasting of her people to be as lost and of no effect. Then the ambassador is to require the King to call to his memory how long she hath aided him both before his title to the crown of France, and since, with money (as yet never repaid according to his bonds), and with her subjects with their lives, and in such number as England never yielded in any age to serve in foreign countries.

16th July. The Plague Increases.

The Council have written to the Lord Mayor and Aldermen saying that the Queen is greatly grieved at the increase of sickness, and although these plagues proceed from the hands of God as a due punishment of our wickedness, yet ought we to use all possible means to prevent their increase. If as good care were used in keeping the orders as had been taken for their making, and especially in restraining the infected from the sound, it would, with the help of God, do great good. In the town of Kingston, upon the first infection, they caused a house to be made in the fields distant from the town where the infected might be kept apart and provided for all things convenient for their sustenance and care; and the same should be done in London.

There was also a little book set forth in the time of the great plague and the last year printed again which contained divers good precepts and orders; this might be recommended by the minister of every parish to all housekeepers.

The Council require the suppression of all those that sell old apparel, a trade greatly used of late, and in no wise to be suffered in time of infection.

17th July. PLAGUE DEATHS.

In London this last week 149 persons are dead of the plague. The crops promise well, but notwithstanding corn is risen in price from £9 to £11 10s. owing to the shortage of corn in Spain and Portugal.

19th July. THE ASSIZES HELD IN ST. GEORGE'S FIELD.

This day the Court of Assize for Surrey was held in St. George's field, a tent being set up for the purpose. Many prisoners were there arraigned, condemned, and had judgment, nineteen being burnt in the hand but none executed. This assize is ended in one day which was thought would have needed three days' work, for the Justices (all duties being paid) make haste away for fear of being infected with the pestilence by the repair of people thither.

PLAGUE DEATHS.

The infection is much increased this past week, for out of 666 deaths in the City of London, 454 are from the plague.

29th July. THE COUNCIL'S LETTERS TO THE UNIVERSITIES OF OXFORD AND CAMBRIDGE.

The Council have written to the Vice-Chancellor of the University of Cambridge showing how the Universities are nurseries to bring up youth in the knowledge of God and in all manner of good learning and virtuous living whereby they may serve their Prince and country in divers callings. For this respect a special care is to be had of these Universities that all means may be used to further the bringing up of the youths that are bestowed there in all good learning, education and honest manners; and like care used that all such things that may allure and entice them to lewdness, folly, and riotous manners, whereunto the nature of man is more inclined, in no wise be used. Understanding therefore that common players ordinarily resort to the University of Cambridge to recite interludes and plays, some of them being full of lewd example, and most of vanity, beside the gathering together of multitudes of people, the Council require the Vice-Chancellor to take special order that no plays or interludes of common players be set forth either in the University or any place within the compass of five miles, and especially in the town of Chesterton. Moreover, as Stourbridge Fair is at hand the Masters and Heads of the College should, because of the great infection, cause the gates of the College to be shut and no scholar permitted to repair thither.

A like letter is to be sent to the Vice-Chancellor of Oxford.

30th July. THE RECRUITS TO BE STAYED.

Upon the new advertisements that are come out of France those soldiers that were to be levied in Hertford and Essex are stayed for a season that the county may not be charged with them. The men nevertheless are to be in readiness upon any new warning, and the armour and furniture provided by the county kept for use as occasion may serve.

3rd August. DR. HARVEY'S 'PIERCE'S SUPEREROGATION.'

Dr. Gabriel Harvey hath answered Nashe's *Strange News* in a book entitled *Pierce's Supererogation or a new praise of the Old Ass.* He saith that if he is an ass, what asses are those courteous friends, excellent and learned men, worshipful and honourable personages that have written him letters of excellent commendation. As for Nashe, he is the son of a mule, a raw grammarian, a babbling sophister, a counterfeit crank, a stale rakehell, a piperly rhymer, a stump-worn railer, a dodkin author whose gayest flourishes are Gascoigne's weeds, or Tarleton's tricks, or Greene's cranks, or Marlowe's bravados; his jests but the dregs of common scurrility, the shreds of the theatre, or the off-scouring of new pamphlets; his freshest nippitaty but the froth of stale inventions, long since loathsome to quick tastes. His only art and the vengeable drift of his whole cunning is to mangle the sentences of the *Four Letters*, hack the arguments, chop and change the phrases, wrench the words, and hale every syllable most extremely, even to the disjoining and maiming of his whole meaning.

4th August. THE PLAGUE INCREASES.

The numbers of plague deaths are reported to be much increased, but the Lord Mayor is rebuked because no certificates of those dead or infected have been sent in these last two weeks.

5th August. A Book on Astronomy.

A translation of M. Auger Ferrier's *Learned Astronomical Discourse* (first printed in 1549) made by Thomas Kelway, gentleman, one of her Majesty's Trumpets in Ordinary, is to be printed, being dedicated to the Lord Henry, Earl of Northumberland. In the address to the courteous reader Mr. Kelway requesteth that those who find this work of the judgment of nativities harsh and unpleasant shall not wound it with injurious words, thereby charging themselves with folly; for he that readeth with derision, because he understandeth not, must blame his own insufficiency, and not the book. The *Discourse* is divided in three books, whereof the first treateth of the celestial figure of a nativity, showing the fortunes and infortunes of the planets; the second of the signification of the twelve signs and the twelve houses; the third of revolutions and eclipses.

Plague Deaths.

The plague is worse than ever this last week and whole households have died. Of 1603 deaths, 1130 are from the plague.

6th August. The Truce in France.

The terms for a truce general between the French King and the Leaguers were agreed and by sound of the trumpet proclaimed on the 31st July.

The truce is for three months, during which all persons may return to their houses and estates, and enjoy them, except where garrisons are employed. Every man may freely travel through the realm without constraint of taking of passport. Prisoners of war that have not compounded for their ransom shall be delivered fifteen days after the truce; the common soldiers without ransom; the other men of war, having pay of either side, on procuring one quarter of their pay, except the leaders and chief of horsemen, who together with other gentlemen bearing charge shall be acquitted for the half year's worth of their revenue. All other persons shall be used, as touching their ransom, as courteously as may be, respecting their faculties and calling. Any woman or maid a prisoner to be set at liberty immediately without paying ransom, also children under the age of sixteen and men from sixty and upward not bearing arms.

All men of war of either side are to be put in garrison, not being permitted to range and forage the country. No enterprises shall be made upon any foreign princes who hath assisted either side, but they shall withdraw their forces from the field and not make any re-enter of them during the truce. Those in Brittany to be sent back or separated, and put in garrison in such places as may not give matter of suspect.

BARTHOLOMEW FAIR.

In answer to the Lord Mayor's reasons against holding the fair on St. Bartholomew's Day in the fields towards Islington, her Majesty hath hardly consented, though she were otherwise disposed to have no manner of fair or assembly at this time, to allow leather, butter, cheese and such like to be sold by gross in Smithfield but not by retail; but to avoid any access of the people no booths may be erected for victuallers. A proclamation is now published for the restraining of Smithfield Fair on Bartholomew's Day.

12th August. UNLAWFUL SPOILS.

Complaints have been made to the Council by certain merchant strangers of Holland and Zealand that in November and December three ships were cast away on the Goodwins, laden with wax, linen cloth, sayes, grograms and other merchandise. These goods floated ashore at divers places on the coast, and were seized upon by the inhabitants as spoil, without regard to the misery and affliction of the owners and sailors. They are now ordered to make restitution.

14th August. PLAGUE DEATHS.

No exact figures of the mortality were given out for this past week because there is commandment to the contrary, but it is rumoured that within the City and without the number is between 1700 and 1800 in one week.

16th August. RUMOURS CONCERNING FRANCE.

This proceeding of the French King in changing his religion is much wondered at and was not at first believed, but the news being now confirmed, the 1500 men levied for France are stayed and determination taken to recall those in Normandy and Brittany. There is great expectation of the treaty of peace now in hand between the King and the Leaguers, being necessary and grateful to the towns, and their great hindrance being removed by the King's coming within the Catholic Church, so that it is likely that they will embrace the peace upon easier conditions.

19th August. SIR THOMAS WILKES' CONVERSATION WITH THE FRENCH KING.

From St. Denis near Paris, Sir Thomas Wilkes writeth that he arrived there on the 11th of the month, finding the King about to depart on the next morning for Fontainebleau; who granted him a brief audience. He presented the Queen's letters of credence, which the King opened but did not read at that time, alleging the difficulty of the hand. Then the King of his own accord fell into a slight discourse of the reasons of his conversion, promising at the next audience to detail it at large. To which Sir Thomas answered little more than to signify how strange it would appear to the Queen that of so resolute and long continued a Protestant he should so suddenly become a Catholic.

The ambassador saith that the King by his action hath assured his Catholics that were declining from him, and by breaking the neck of the third party hath doubtless gotten a strong party: the poverty of the Dukes of Mayne and Guise, the not performing of the promises of the Pope and the King of Spain, the uncertainty of the people of their faction, who all desire a peace, and the general misery of the country which is pitiful to behold, will drive them all to end their present dissensions.

22nd August. THE FORTIFICATIONS OF PLYMOUTH.

The fortification of Plymouth, which had been in good forwardness, is now slacked because very few of the gentlemen of Devon, except the Earl of Bath, who hath given £100, contribute anything at all.

DISBANDMENT OF THE SOLDIERS FROM FRANCE.

Sir John Hawkins prepareth seven hoys to bring 700 or 800 men from Dieppe. Sir Edward Brook and the muster master are to ascertain and record how many men there are in every company, how armed and weaponed, and from what counties they were sent. The treasurer's deputy shall give every soldier at his discharge some portion of what was due to him to discharge his debts. If any so desire they may be suffered to tarry and serve the French King, and be paid their wages then due, but their armour to be detained and brought into England. Every captain shall see that the armour and weapons of all that return is brought to England and delivered to the Mayor at Dover or Rye by indenture, and to give to each soldier of his band a billet of discharge and licence to pass to his county.

23rd August. Sir Thomas Wilkes' second conversation with the French King.

Sir Thomas Wilkes writeth that the French King hath given him a second private audience whereat he delivered at large the sum of his instructions, acquainting the King with her Majesty's care and desire to have prevented his conversion as tending the good of his soul, and giving a summary of the articles which he had received. These the King took in very grateful part, and did acknowledge that they were no small tokens of the Queen's love to him, but the necessity of his State was such that no verbal reasons could have prevented the mischief whereunto he had fallen if his conversion had not then been performed; which he confessed was precipitated by reason that the dangers came more suddenly on him than he expected, for that the day of his promised conversion was to have been two months after.

To the Ambassador's demand for a place of retreat in Brittany, he desired respite to confer with his Council, and promised that in case he might be so happy as to pacify his estate there, he would not fail with all the force he could make to repair in person to Brittany to remove the Spaniard.

26th August. Two Counterfeiters sent to the Galleys.

By order of the Lord Admiral, two men, Walter Pepper and George Ellis, very lewd and loose fellows that have beforetime been censured in the Star Chamber for counterfeiting the hands of some of the Lords of the Council and are now again apprehended and found culpable of the same offence, are committed to the new galleys to be employed as occasion should serve, and to be fast tied with chains that by no means they be allowed to escape.

8th September. NASHE'S 'CHRIST'S TEARS OVER JERUSALEM.'

Nashe hath written a godly book called *Christ's Tears over Jerusalem, whereunto is annexed a comparative admonition to London*, being dedicated to the Lady Elizabeth Carey, wife of the Knight Marshal. Herein is shown how the Jews after God's great mercies to them refused to listen to Christ when He pitifully reproached them ; and how forty years after our Lord's lifting up into Heaven, when the Jews pretended a weariness of the Roman regiment, Jerusalem was sacked and destroyed. So likewise is this London equally in danger of destruction by reason of the deadly sins committed within her walls, being ambition, avarice, vainglory, atheism, discontent, contention ; disdain between courtier and citizen, merchant and retailer, retailer and craftsman ; gorgeous attire, wherein England is become the ape of all nations' superfluities, the continual masquer in outlandish habitments ; delicacy, gluttony, lechery, and the great abundance of cunning bawds whose trade is such that a great office is not so gainful as the principalship of a College of Courtesans ; sloth and security ; the whole ending with a prayer against the plague.

In the Epistle to the reader Nashe saith that he hath bidden farewell to fantastical satirism, desiring reconciliation even with Dr. Harvey, whose fame and reputation he hath so rashly assailed.

10th September. PLAGUE DEATHS.

There is still no sign of an end to the mortality from plague. About a thousand deaths of plague weekly are now being reported in the City, and outside some five hundred.

15th September. A RESTRAINT OF SUITORS AT WINDSOR.

A Proclamation is published to reform the disorder in the great number of persons who attend the Court at Windsor. In many of the houses are lodged more than are allowed by the officers of the town and the Queen's harbingers, and many of these persons with their wives, children and servants. The Queen's Knight Harbinger is now commanded to make a new search with the assistance of the servants of the Knight Marshal and the Mayor of the town. All owners of houses in Windsor, Eton and the towns adjoining within five miles of the Court are warned that within two days of the publication of the Proclamation from Windsor Cross they exclude all persons not warranted by the harbingers' billets to have lodging, upon pain of fine and having their houses shut up.

17th September. NASHE'S 'UNFORTUNATE TRAVELLER.'

A book called *The Unfortunate Traveller*, or *The Life of Jack Wilton*, written by Nashe, is entered, being dedicated to the Earl of Southampton, wherein this Jack Wilton, that was a page at the Court of King Henry the Eighth, telleth his own tale of what he did at the siege of Tournay, and afterward in his travels how he fared at Rotterdam and Wittenberg, and in Venice, Florence and Rome.

28th September. PLAGUE DEATHS.

It is reported that the plague deaths have abated during these last two weeks by 430; the last week between 1100 and 1200 in all died.

1st October. DR. HARVEY'S NEW LETTER OF NOTABLE CONTENTS.

A New Letter of Notable Contents, together with a *Strange Sonnet entitled Gorgon or the Wonderful Year*, being a letter of Dr. Gabriel Harvey's to Mr. John Wolfe, the printer, is printed. He noteth the strange conversion of Nashe from the *Strange News* to *Christ's Tears*. As for Nashe's protestations of repentance, great penmen and pamphlet merchants play much upon the advantage of the time and care not who be the enemy so long as Term be the friend. He loveth *osculum pacis*, but hateth *osculum Judae*; reverenceth the tears of Christ, but feareth the tears of the crocodile.

8th October. HIGH-HANDED DEALINGS.

The Lady Elizabeth Russell hath petitioned the Council for the punishment of her neighbour, Mr. Lovelace, to whom, saith she, she hath shown every friendship these twenty-six years, but who is guilty of foul riots against her.

On Monday last he came to her house with sixteen or twenty men with halberds and long poles, broke open her porter's lodge and the lock of her stocks, and removed thence two of his men who had behaved very lewdly towards her. If she has offered him or his any wrong, the law is open, and it is not for him, a justice of the peace, to break his oath by so foul a riot.

On Thursday last, he sent a man for the key of the Tower at Windsor, where she had been all the year, having all her stuff there ; she refused to leave upon such sudden warning, unless by order of the Lord Admiral, and offered him as much rent as it was worth, but it was refused. Two days since, being Saturday last, he and his men changed the lock of her lodging and commanded that none should undo it.

Now she petitioneth that this spite and injury be punished, and Mr. Lovelace put out of the commission of the peace, otherwise it were better to be a mean justice of the peace than a noble woman that dependeth upon God and her Majesty.

19th October. DANIEL'S 'DELIA AND ROSAMOND' AND 'THE COMPLAINT OF ROSAMOND.'

Mr. Daniel hath augmented his *Delia and Rosamond*, and added thereto *Cleopatra*, some few new sonnets, and *The Complaint of Rosamond*, in which the Ghost of Rosamond complaineth that though Shore's wife is graced, her well-told tale finds no such compassion. She runneth through the story of her sin with King Henry the Second, and her death by poison at the hands of his wronged Queen.

The Tragedy of Cleopatra is dedicated to the Lady Mary, Countess of Pembroke, for that she

> 'Call'd up my spirits from out their low repose,
> To sing of State, and tragic notes to frame.'

He promiseth so to work that posterity may find how much he contendeth to honour her.

> 'Now when so many pens (like Spears) are charg'd,
> To chase away this tyrant of the North,
> Gross Barbarism, whose power grows far enlarged,
> Was lately by thy valiant brother's worth,
> First found, encountered and provoked forth :
> Whose onset made the rest audacious,
> Whereby they likewise so discharg'd,
> Upon that hideous beast incroaching thus.'

This *Tragedy of Cleopatra* is not written for the English stages, but after the manner of the ancients, preserving a unity of the time, though not of place, and between each act a chorus to point the moral of the action. The death of Cleopatra at the end of the play is related by a *Nuntius*, concluding thus:

'This said, she stays and makes a sudden pause
As were to feel whether the poison wrought;
Or rather else the working might be cause
That made her stay, as likewise may be thought,
For in that instant I might well perceive
The drowsy humour in her falling brow:
And how each power, each part oppressed did leave
Their former office, and did senseless grow.
Look how a new-plucked branch against the Sun
Declines his fading leaves in feeble sort,
To her disjoined jointures as undone
Let fall her weak dissolved limbs support.
Yet lo! that face, the wonder of her life,
Retains in death a grace that graceth death,
Colour so lively, cheer so lovely rife,
That none would think such beauty could want breath.'

22nd October. EDWARDS' 'CEPHALUS AND PROCRIS.'

Cephalus and Procris, a poem written by Mr. Thomas Edwards and dedicated to the Right Worshipful Master Thomas Argall, Esquire, together with *Narcissus*, is to be printed. Herein is described how Aurora wantonly loved the hunter Cephalus and would have kept him; but he disdained her, being wan with love for Procris. Aurora then taunting him, he went back to Procris and by force and intreaty won his desire on her. But Procris, thereafter overcome with shame at what she had allowed, fled away, and, hiding in a thicket, was by chance struck with an arrow that Cephalus shot. In *Narcissus* the boy betrayeth his effeminate love for his own reflection, supposing it to be a maiden until he seeks it in the stream.

'This done, amain unto the spring I made,
Where finding beauty culling nakedness,
Sweet love reviving all that heavens decayed,
And once more placing gentle maiden likeness,
Thus sought I favour of my shadowed mistress;
  Embracing sighs, and telling tales to stones,
  Amidst the spring I leapt to ease my moans.'

9th November. THE PLAGUE ABATING.

The plague deaths reported in London this past week amount to 420.

14th November. DICKENSON'S 'ARISBAS.'

Mr. John Dickenson hath written a book called *Arisbas, Euphues amidst his slumbers: or Cupid's journey to Hell. Deciphering a mirror of constancy, a touchstone of tried affection, begun in chaste desire, ended in choice delights. And emblazoning Beauty's Glory, adorned by Nature's bounty; with the triumph of true Love, in the foil of false Fortune.*

This Prince Arisbas, having lost his lady, wandered alone, distracted with moody passions, and coming to one Damon who seemed a shepherd, lamented his hard fate, and told how refusing to wed the lady chosen by the King, his father, he had fallen in love with Timoclea.

Pretending, therefore, that he was a poor man and that Timoclea was his sister, he hired a ship and sailed away but, landing alone on the coast of Arcadia to view the country, a tempest arose; and the next morning the ship was nowhere to be seen.

In reply to his laments Damon telleth him that in the autumn before a youth had been cast on their coasts, so beautiful that he was loved of all shepherds and liked by all lasses. Arisbas, hoping that this might indeed be his Timoclea, asked more, and in reply Damon narrateth the story of Hyalus, taken away from Arcadia by Zephyrus. After some days Damon taketh Arisbas to the festivals in memory of Hyalus at the city, where, as he had hoped, he findeth the beautiful youth that was leader of the choir of boys to be no other than his Timoclea.

Arisbas being now reunited to his beloved Timoclea returneth to Cyprus to his aged sire, where there is great change, for the old King, having despaired of Arisbas' safety, had married his second son to the daughter of the Prince of Lemnos. Now with great joy is celebrated Arisbas' wedding with Timoclea, and, his father having resigned the diadem, he reigneth in Cyprus.

17th November. CHURCHYARD'S VERSES.

The poet Thomas Churchyard, in resentment that the Lord Treasurer refused him what the Queen had granted, hath sent her these verses:

'Madam,

You bid your treasurer on a time,
To give me reason for my rhyme;
But since that time and that season,
He gave me neither rhyme nor reason.'

20th November. A CASE OF PLAGUE AT COURT.

There is much alarm in the Court because a page of the Lady Scroop, one of the ladies of the Queen's bedchamber, is dead of the plague in the keep at Windsor Castle. It is expected that the Queen will remove within a day or two.

28th November. THE ARRAIGNMENT OF RICHARD HESKETH.

This day Richard Hesketh, a Jesuit, was arraigned for having treasonably attempted to persuade Ferdinando Stanley, the new Earl of Derby, to revolt against the Queen.

This man had come from Sir William Stanley and the Catholics abroad, being authorised to offer the Crown of England to the Earl of Derby. He was instructed first to approach the Earl signifying to him in general that he had a message of importance to deliver from special friends of his, and to desire leave to utter it, and his promise of good security that he should incur no danger.

Having received this promise and given mutual promise of fidelity and secrecy, he should declare in general that the message concerned the common good of all Christendom, especially of England, and in particular of the Earl. If the Earl was content to hear, though drily and with small desire, he should name Sir William Stanley as having sent him, adding that there was another greater than he; and to know expressly whether the Earl would hear his message or no.

It he were willing, then Hesketh was to offer him all the endeavour, services and helps that the Catholics could employ if he would accept and agree to the Catholic faith; but to be capable he must be a Catholic, and bind himself to restore, advance and perpetually maintain the Catholic faith in England. Let the Earl signify what help he needed and when, and by God's help it would be provided: 4000 or 5000 men might be sent within seven or eight months. He was not to fear strangers; neither did the King of Spain now seek the Kingdom of England for himself; nor would the Pope or Cardinal Allen agree to it, if there was any other remedy; nor could the King of Spain hold it though he might invade and conquer the realm, for the people of England were most impatient of foreign government. The Pope himself held it better for Christendom to have many Christian Catholic kings than one too great and monarch of all, and the Cardinal was a true Englishman. It was better that he should obtain the crown now before the Queen's death, because he might prevent competition; besides, the Cardinal and Sir William Stanley were now able to assist, the Pope was willing (and perhaps another would not be); the state of France could not hinder but rather further, for now he could have some Spaniards, but not too many; it was like that some other was provided to challenge it after her death; and he had many enemies that were daily seeking his overthrow.

Hesketh delivered his message to the Earl, but was by him denounced and arrested. At his trial he acknowledged all his former confessions to be true so that there needed no further testimony against him. Nevertheless the Attorney General laid open all the plot and course of his treasons for the satisfaction of the standers-by, making collections from his confessions to note that the malice of those fugitive traitors and other enemies of the Queen proceeds from no other ground but that she preferreth the true worship of God and the peaceable government of her subjects above all other things. The Lord Chief Justice also, before passing judgment, used a very grave speech to the comfort of the Queen's subjects by these and the like graces which God hath showed.

29th *November*. A RECUSANT'S CONFESSION.

Edward Pemberton, a recusant, being examined by order of the Archbishop of Canterbury as to the coming and going of Catholic priests from overseas, declareth that those who leave England take shipping either at Portsmouth or Arundel, agree with the ship master to come at night and are away before morning. Those sent to England take shipping at Antwerp or any other place; if the ship is for London they take a boat between Gravesend and London and so escape examining. When they come, if they are caught privily, any justice of the peace will take £10 and let them go, and the tithing men 20s.

30th November. THE QUEEN'S LETTER TO SIR JOHN NORRIS.

The Queen having been earnestly sued to grant Sir John Norris leave to return on his own affairs giveth him licence to repair home at his convenience. But he is put in mind what disaster happened in his last absence. If he is not assured of the troops being in safety and well guided he should not take the benefit of this favour; but if things are in such terms that he dare adventure he may choose his brother to command, who will have due care of her Majesty's honour, of Sir John's, and of his own. In times past when the generals came away they brought with them captains and lieutenants, leaving the people without leaders. He is admonished not to commit any such error, as nothing can be more grievous to her Majesty than by negligence to suffer the poorest soldier in the company to perish.

7th December. GREENE'S 'ORLANDO FURIOSO.'

A play called *Orlando Furioso*, written by Robert Creene, is entered for printing, in which Alleyn played Orlando. This play was performed before the Queen.

11th December. HESTER'S 'PEARL OF PRACTISE.'

The Pearl of Practise, or practiser's pearl for physick and chirurgery, found out by John Hester (a spagerick or distiller), is entered, having since his death been gathered and brought into some method by James Fourestier. This book is dedicated to Sir George Carey and setteth out the methods, cures and prescriptions for many diseases, swellings, wounds, and injuries.

21st December. ANXIETY IN GUERNSEY.

From Sir Thomas Leighton, Governor of Guernsey, it is reported that five thousand or six thousand Spaniards are lately arrived at Blavet in Brittany. He beseecheth that the sum of £500, the remainder of the £1000 promised for the works to be done at the Castle, may be sent speedily.

22nd December. PEPPER FROM THE GREAT CARRACK.

The merchants that lately contracted with the Queen for the pepper taken in the Great Carrack are unable to vend any quantity of it except at very mean prices because of the great quantities still remaining in the realm and being brought in. As they are bound to pay her great sums of money at Christmas and other short periods, the Queen in answer to their petition hath caused restraint to be put on the bringing in of all pepper into the realm from 25th December.

26th December. PLAYING RESUMED.

As the plague is now abated, playing begins again at the Rose Theatre by the Earl of Sussex's men, who played *God Speed the Plough* this day.

29th December. PLAYS AT THE ROSE.

During these three days past the Earl of Sussex's men played *Huon of Bordeaux*, *George a Green*, *Buckingham*, and *Richard the Confessor*.

31st December. GENTLEMEN'S SONS OVERSEAS.

The Council issue a warrant for inquisition to be made in the counties of Lincoln, Hertford and Essex as to what gentlemen have sons relieved or maintained out of the realm that are sent over under colour to learn languages or for any other respects, and are not notoriously employed in the Queen's martial services or trade or merchandise as apprentices to known merchants. A catalogue is to be made as well of the parents as of the sons so sent over ; in what parts they be ; and how long they have been absent. Bonds are to be taken of the fathers if any are known recusants or have been evil affected or are but feignedly reformed ; and their houses to be searched for seminary priests, Jesuits and other suspected persons, books, letters and writings concerning matter against the State or established religion.

CHAPMAN'S Σκιὰ νυκτὸς.

Σκιὰ νυκτὸς, or *The Shadow of Night, containing two poetical hymns*, devised by Mr. George Chapman, is entered, being dedicated to Mr. Matthew Roydon, to whom he writeth that it is the exceeding rapture of delight in the deep search of knowledge that maketh men manfully endure the extremes incident to that Herculean labour. But what a supererogation in wit this is, to think Skill so mightily pierced with their loves who read but to curtail a tedious hour that she should prostitutely show them her secrets, when she will scarcely be looked upon by others but with invocation, fasting, watching, yea, not without having drops of their souls like a heavenly familiar. Yet are there those that most profitly entertain learning in themselves to the admirable lustre of their nobility, such as the most ingenious Derby, deep-searching Northumberland, and the skill embracing heir of Hunsdon.

Of the two hymns, the first is dedicated to Night, which the poet calleth the day of deep students,

> Rich taper'd sanctuary of the blest,
> Palace of ruth, made all of tears, and rest,
> To thy black shades and desolation,
> I consecrate my life.

The second hymn he dedicateth to Cynthia, under whom is figured the Queen, in whose sacred state

> The circles of our Hopes are compassed :
> All wisdom, beauty, majesty and dread,
> Wrought in the speaking portrait of thy face ;

yet fearing

> that sable day,
> When interposed earth takes thee away,
> (Our sacred chief and sovereign general),
> As crimson a retreat, and steep a fall,
> We fear to suffer from this peace and height,
> Whose thankless sweet now cloys us with receipt.

Plague Deaths.

There have died in London and the suburbs during this year 17,893 persons, whereof 10,675 were from the plague.

SOMEWHAT TO READ FOR THEM THAT LIST

Dr. Bancroft's 'Dangerous Positions and Proceedings.'

Dr. Richard Bancroft's *Dangerous positions and proceedings, published and practised within the Island of Britain, under pretence of a Reformation, and for the Presbyterial Discipline.* Herein is shown the history of the Consistorian Puritans from the first preaching of the Gospel by Farellus, Viretus and others at Geneva to the conspiracy of Hacket, Arthington and Coppinger in July 1591.

Giffard's 'Dialogue concerning Witches and Witchcraft.'

A Dialogue concerning Witches, penned by George Giffard, wherein in form of a dialogue between Samuel, and his wife, Daniel, M.B. a schoolmaster, and the goodwife, is shown how craftily the devil deceiveth not only the witches but many others.

In the Epistle Dedicatory to Mr. Robert Clarke, one of the Barons of the Court of Exchequer, Mr. Giffard declareth that the devils are now let loose, and prevail more than ever he hath heard before, so that Satan is now heard speak and believed, speaking through conjurors, sorcerers and witches. But the devils do this by God's special providence, seeking by this means to punish the world. Yet are the witches themselves deceived when they believe that at their request or pleasure their spirits lame and kill men and beasts; and then to spread the opinion among the people, these subtle spirits betray them, and would have the witches openly confess that they do such things, which all the devils at man's request could never do; for if they could, they would not stay to be intreated. The devil worketh by his other sort of witches, whom the people called cunning men and women, to confirm all his matters, by them teaching many remedies that so he may be sought and honoured as a God.

These positions are demonstrated in the dialogue; Daniel holding that Satan can do nothing without God's leave, so that the witches are of themselves powerless to do much harm ; and in the end convincing the others.

Their talk being finished, there cometh to them the good wife R., being one of those upbraided as herself a witch for having thrust a hot poker into her cream when the butter would not come, burning a hen or a hog alive and other such devices. To their speeches she answereth, 'Is that witchcraft ? Some Scripture men hath told you so. Did the devil teach it ? Nay, the good woman at R.H. taught it my husband and she doeth more good in one year than all these Scripture men will do as long as they live.'

LODGE'S 'PHILLIS.'

Mr. Thomas Lodge's *Phillis*, being a collection of Sonnets and Eclogues wherein Damon declareth his love for Phillis and lamenteth her neglect, being followed by an Ode, bitterly complaining of her falseness ; to which is annexed *The Complaint of Elstred*, who telleth the story of her life and death. Being widowed of Humber, her husband, who was slain by Locrine, she loved the conqueror. Locrine, by the consultations of his Lords, was betrothed to Gwendolen of Cornwall ; but continuing his love to Elstred he made her a labyrinth where they dallied in secret, until he tired of his betrothed wife, and drove her away to put his mistress in her place. Whereupon the Cornishmen rose to aid Gwendolen, and in the ensuing battle Locrine was slain. Elstred pitifully embracing the corpse of her paramour was by robbers taken and brought before Gwendolen, by whose command she and her daughter Sabrina were cast into the Severn and drowned.

LODGE'S 'LIFE AND DEATH OF WILLIAM LONGBEARD.'

Mr. Lodge's *The Life and Death of William Longbeard*, being dedicated to Sir William Webb, the Lord Mayor. This Longbeard was a man of great strength and parts that in the time of King Richard I. became an instigator of sedition and leader of the people. Being called in question by the Hubert, the Archbishop of Canterbury, he and his fellows took refuge in the church, whence, refusing submission, they were driven out by fire and forced to yield themselves. Being arraigned before his judges, Longbeard thus defendeth himself: 'You Lords and honourable Judges, though I know it a hard thing to strive against the obstinate or to extort pity there, where all compassion is extinguished, yet I will speak, using the office of nature to work you although I know I shall not win you. I am here called and indited before you for high treason ; a heinous crime, I confess it ; and worthy of punishment. I deny it not. But may it please you with patience to examine circumstances. I have emboldened the poorer sort to innovation, to fight for liberty to impugn the rich, a matter in the common weals of Greece highly commended ; but here accounted factious, and why ? There subjects made Kings ; here Kings master subjects. And why not, say you ; and why not, think I ? Yet am I faulty under a good precedent, and the ambition which hath intangled me, hath not been without his profit. To offend of obstinate will were brutish ; but under some limits of reason to default, can you, my Lords, but think it pardonable ? I have raised one or two assemblies ; and what of this ? Peace was not broken, only my safety was assured ; and were it not that the law had been injured, might not the righting of a hundred poor men's causes merit pardon for two unlawful assemblies ? But, you will say, I have animated subjects against their prince. I confess it, but under a milder title. I have counselled them to compass liberty, which, if nature might be equal judge between us, I know should not be heinously misconstered.' But the judges condemned him to die a traitor's death, and the next day he was executed.

There are also in this book divers pleasant histories of pirates and others.

NORDEN'S 'SPECULUM BRITANNIAE.'

The first part of Speculum Britanniae, a historical and chorographical description of Middlesex, compiled by the travel and view of John Norden, being consecrated to the Queen by the author, with an epistle of thanks to the Lord Treasurer. After a brief declaration of the titles, inhabitants, divisions and situation of England, the author describeth the history, the limits and bounds, the nature of the soil and fertility, the Ecclesiastical and Civil Government of the shire, its divisions, parks, and ancient highways ; which are followed by an alphabet of the cities, towns, hamlets and villages, including the City of London, and concluding with the principal highways and a list of noblemen and gentlemen having houses within the shire.

SUTCLIFFE'S 'LAWS OF ARMS.'

The Practice, Proceedings and Laws of Arms, described out of the doings of most valiant and expert Captains, and confirmed both by ancient and modern examples and precedents, written by Dr. Matthew Sutcliffe, being printed by the Queen's printer, and dedicated to the Earl of Essex. In the Epistle Dedicatory Dr. Sutcliffe saith that all men's eyes are fixed upon the Earl of Essex, who hath already made his name honourable by his experience in the service of the Low Countries, of Portugal and France, so that the general hope of soldiers is that he who so well understandeth the common disorders of the wars, will one day be a means to correct them. It is not the courage of the Spaniard, nor force of the Dutch, nor bravery of the French that frustrated our late attempts; neither doth force so often overthrow armies in field, as dalliance, irresolution and delay; then, through niggardize and good husbandry, want of pay and necessary furniture; thirdly, presumption and want of strength and sufficient force; and lastly, those abuses which through want have crept into the armies of late times and cannot be corrected; for what conscience could punish those that spoil and wander abroad when otherwise they would starve. For all these things and for the abuses of imprests, false musters and accounts the only remedy is the true discipline of arms.

In the Epistle to the Reader he saith that this discourse is framed because of the general lamentation that in those actions which have of late been attempted publicly the success hath been so slender, the loss of men so great, the charge so burdensome, and the proceedings and effects so contrary to antiquity.

MR. SMITH'S SERMON AGAINST ATHEISTS.

God's Arrow against Atheists, a sermon preached by Mr. Henry Smith, wherein in seven chapters he showeth the reasons for a belief in God; in the first touching on the absurdity of Atheism and irreligion; demanding who made the world, since it had a beginning and it must needs follow that it had an efficient cause or maker. In the second it is shown that the

Christian religion is the only true religion in the world, and wherewith only God is pleased; in the third the Christian religion is defended against the Gentiles and all the infidels of the world; in the fourth that the religion of Mahomet is false and wicked; in the fifth that the Church of Rome is not the true Church of God nor observeth the right religion; and in the last he toucheth on schism and schismatical synagogues.

1594

1st January. A Prognostication.

It is prognosticated in the Almanack for this year that the spring shall be moist and windy but not very cold, the summer indifferent but with many unkind storms, sudden lightnings and thunder-claps; sicknesses not many but passing dangerous, with hot and fervent agues, great distemperature of men's brains, and immoderate heat, whereby many will run frantick. In the autumn there are like to be mighty storms to the great hindrance of those that shall be late in harvest, especially in the north; together with a great pestilence.

4th January. A Mysterious Stranger.

Mr. Thomas Jeffreys, an English merchant at Calais, hath written to Lord Burleigh that a certain man is come to him with a private communication for the Council. He knoweth not the man but hath seen him divers times with Emanuel Andrada: he may do good, as he hath dealings with Count Fuentes and the King of Spain's principal secretary for war, whereby, as he saith, he hath discovered great matters pretended by the enemy which must be seen to with speed. This man's name is Emanuel Louis Tinoco.

5th January. Plays of the Week.

This past week the Earl of Sussex's men at the Rose played *Richard the Confessor*, *Buckingham*, *George a Green*, *Huon of Bordeaux*, *William the Conqueror* and *God Speed the Plough*.

6th January. Court Revels.

Twelfth Night was celebrated at Court by dancing which continued till one o'clock after midnight, the Queen being seated in a high throne, and next to her chair the Earl of Essex with whom she often devised in sweet and favourable manner.

7th January. CATHOLIC STORIES FROM SCOTLAND.

About a month since (7th December) James Maxwell, Earl of Morton, the Scottish King's Lieutenant General, was slain in pursuing the Lord Johnston to arrest him according to the King's warrant, and the Catholics make much note of his death.

Not many years since, the Earl of Morton, though he was a Catholic, had been persuaded to sign the articles expressing conformity and directed against the Catholic religion. But at 12 o'clock that day, being alone in his room, an angel appeared to him in the form of a youth who said, 'My Lord, do not as your kinsmen would persuade you; for if you do you shall lose the hand with which you sign, and your days shall end with shameful death.' Moved by this appeal, the Earl again put on the gold crucifix and an *agnus dei* which he used to wear round his neck, but had taken off when he abandoned his former professions. He then told the principal kinsmen who had persuaded him to sign how remorseful he was for his error, and what the angel had told him; and in order that God's mercy might for ever be remembered by his house, he added to his arms the figure of an angel. He refused also to sign the articles declaring himself an enemy of the ministers.

But after a time he was greatly moved by his kinsmen, and the King himself made him many offers, creating him his Lieutenant General, so that at last he gave way and signed the articles. But shortly afterwards going to arrest the Lord Johnston with 5000 soldiers he met with the end the angel foretold him.

For when he came up the Lord Johnston, taking advantage of the ground, had posted 600 horsemen in three squadrons in a triangle at some little distance from each other. The Earl of Morton's regiment entering into their midst, Lord Johnston and his men who were on one side threw themselves with such fury upon the Earl's men that they broke and fled; and the Lord Johnston, reaching the Earl, at the first blow smote off his right hand, and at the second cut off a leg. Then being thrown from his horse, the Earl was cut into a thousand pieces.

The Catholics also say that the Lord Claud Hamilton, against his conscience and at the persuasion of his wife and her brothers, had also subscribed to please the King and the ministers. At one time he was dining and, as was the custom in some Scottish houses, the gospel was being read at table during the repast. The reader came to the words, 'Whoso denieth me before men, him will I also deny before my Father'; and as he pronounced these words the Lord Claud rose from the table and attempted to cut his wife's throat, crying out that by her persuasion and that of her brothers, he had denied the faith and sacrificed his soul. For several days after this he remained in a state of frenzy so that it was necessary to bind him; nor is he yet entirely recovered.

12th January. PLAYS OF THE WEEK.

The Earl of Sussex's men played this past week *Friar Francis*, *George a Green*, *Abraham and Lot*, *Buckingham*, *Huon of Bordeaux* and *The Fair Maid of Italy*.

15th January. AN ALCHEMIST'S BEQUEST.

Mr. Robert Smith of Great Yarmouth hath brought a letter from one Roloff Peterson of Lubec to the effect that a certain Clement Ouldfield, born in Kent, came to lodge in his house at Lubec in 1587 and continued there until September 1593 when he died. He had studied alchemy night and day, and brought himself to such perfection that, if the Lord had spared his life but six months longer, he believed he would have reaped his heart's desire. The day before he died he secretly informed Peterson that he had at last found out and long kept a secret of such high value, and so far exceeding all other, that none but high and mighty Princes should participate in it; and then delivered to him three glass bodies, containing alchemical preparations, sol, luna, and mercury, explaining the use of these and of sundry others.

Moreover, he declared that he had a most wonderful secret, which in the hands of any man but meanly skilful in this art, would work wonderful things, wishing Peterson to make profit thereby in regard of his kindness; but insomuch as the great and infinite treasures that might be attained by these means rather appertained to the majesty of Kings and Princes than to men of his estate, he bound him by an oath to present the same to the Queen of England, and to await her answer six months before opening the matter to any other, or making profit thereof;

which he might then do, if she refused. After this he yielded up the ghost.

If the Queen will send any skilful man to be further advertised, and to see the things, Peterson promises that he is ready to discharge his trust; but if he shall have had no knowledge within six months, then will he esteem himself free of the covenant, and at liberty to dispose thereof.

ATTEMPTS AGAINST THE QUEEN.

The Portuguese that was sent over from Calais, by name Emanuel Louis Tinoco, being taken to the house of Sir Robert Cecil, hath delivered an advertisement of many things which should be made known to the Queen for the sake of her person. He declareth that he was the servant of Don Antonio from the day when he was proclaimed King until July last, serving him always with zeal, fidelity and love; but seeing him ungrateful, and poor of council and government, he consented with one Stephen Ferrara de Gama to seek liberty for their country, seeing that they had the Duke of Braganza, a young man and well beloved in the Kingdom. They therefore went to the Count Fuentes to seek the favour of the King of Spain, by means of Don Christofer de Moro, and to offer him service.

Upon this the King wrote to Count Fuentes that he should send Tinoco to England and that Stephen Ferrara should leave his wife there, feigning that he hath business in France, and thence go together to Don Antonio who would employ them. For less suspicion Ferrara was to go alone and bring Tinoco orders what to do; he was to try and win Dr. Lopez, the Portugal Jew that is her Majesty's physician, and endeavour to draw a letter from him, promising to do him service; he was to remind Lopez that he had daughters and that they should not want good marriages. They were to take knowledge of all affairs of England, especially of any secret preparations of an army, how many ships the Queen hath at home and abroad, the names of their captains, and to take a good view of the Isle of Wight and the Downs, and to note the forts and weak places.

16th January. ANOTHER DECLARATION BY TINOCO.

Tinoco having been very straightly examined by the Earl of Essex, and in some respects confused, hath again written to Sir

Robert Cecil to clear himself. He declareth that he will show the true intentions of his coming so as to clear all doubts, and that without reward ; which shall be reserved until it should be lawful for him to demand recompense. He saith that he has come voluntarily to Court, and gives his word as a gentleman to serve the Queen with all possible diligence and fidelity by giving secret advertisements of all things. He hath served Don Antonio for thirteen years and thereby lost all he had in Portugal, and the best part of his life ; for the remainder he would serve the Queen, but knew of nothing that would do her service.

18th January. PLAYS OF THE WEEK.

This last week the Earl of Sussex's men played *Friar Francis*, *George a Green*, *Richard the Confessor*, *Abraham and Lot*, *King Lud*.

23rd January. DR. LOPEZ DEEPLY IMPLICATED.

Emanuel Louis Tinoco the Portuguese hath made further declaration, saying that Andrada had offered him, on behalf of Dr. Lopez, service to the King of Spain, and brought a jewel of great value from the King of Spain to Lopez, which he now hath. Stephen Ferrara de Gama also wrote to Count Fuentes that Dr. Lopez would do the King great service.

24th January. PLAYS OF THE WEEK.

During this past week the Earl of Sussex's men played *Friar Francis*, *The Fair Maid of Italy*, *George a Greene*, and *Titus Andronicus* (for the first time).

DR. LOPEZ EXAMINED.

Dr. Lopez was called before the Lord Treasurer, Sir Robert Cecil, and the Earl of Essex, who are appointed by the Queen to this end. The Earl hath for a long time been sifting out matter against Dr. Lopez but the other two opposed him.

After the first hearing Sir Robert Cecil posted to the Court before the Earl, and related to the Queen that there was no matter of malice, for in the poor man's home were found no kind of writings of intelligences of which he was accused, or otherwise that hold might be taken of him. In the meantime he is committed to the custody of Mr. Gelly Meyrick, the Earl's Steward, at Essex House. Upon my lord coming to the Queen, she, being prepossessed of the matter by the others, took him up, calling him a rash and temerarious youth to enter into a matter against the poor man, which he could not prove and whose innocence she knew well enough ; but malice against Dr. Lopez, and no other, hatched all this matter, which displeaseth her much, and more for that her honour is interested therein.

These words of the Queen's so angered the Earl of Essex that he went back to his chamber, with great fury casting open the chamber door before him, and so passed into his cabinet where he kept himself shut in for an hour.

Essex and Lopez

This enmity between the Earl of Essex and Dr. Lopez is of old standing. Some time since, the Earl of Essex, having resolved to make use of intelligencers to do him service, to this end spoke to Dr. Lopez, telling that many did practise treason against her Majesty. The Spaniard hated her ; the Papists would do her what hurt they could ; she was ancient and childless ; and the good of the Kingdom wholly depended on her life. Now for preventing this design it would be best to find someone on whom the Spaniard might repose trust. After some talk with the Queen, Lopez undertook the business, and made offer of his service to some special friends in Spain or Portugal. They to whom he wrote gave him encouragement and promised a good reward.

Here began a mutual intercourse of letters between them ; and as soon as ever Lopez received any intelligence, he went instantly to the Queen to acquaint her therewith ; and afterwards he went to the Earl of Essex and acquainted him. Then did the Earl of Essex come to the Court and acquaint her with the same : and the Queen knowing it before did but laugh at the Earl of Essex. And so it fell out several times, whereby the Earl saw himself utterly disappointed, for though he had gotten an intelligencer yet he proved not to be his but went in immediately to the Queen. This hath bred very ill blood between the Earl and Lopez.

In the last vacation, Dr. Lopez went to visit Don Antonio and Antonio Perez ; and making merry with them, Lopez began to inveigh against the Earl of Essex, telling them some secrecies, how he had cured him, and of what diseases, with some other things that did disparage his honour. But as soon as Lopez was gone, they went instantly to the Earl and, to ingratiate themselves into his favour, acquainted him with all. Whereupon the Earl was so much incensed that he resolved to be revenged.

25th January. A Notable Jesuit taken in the North.

From York Topcliffe reporteth that Father Walpole, a very notable priest and Jesuit, was taken on landing at Flamborough, together with his younger brother and one Lingen, both soldiers of Sir William Stanley. After the Lord President of the Council, with the aid of his chaplain, had toiled day and night with the prisoners, he so prevailed with the young Walpole to see his offence, that all the truth, secrets, and matter, even against himself, flowed from him as fast as the questions could be put. He confessed that his brother gave him six small pieces of parchment and twelve letters. When all had been examined, the Lord President sent the Jesuit and Lingen to rest; but to prove young Walpole's honesty, he despatched him to the sea side, well guarded, to see if he could find the place where he said that the letters were buried. The bundle was found, but all wet with rain, and brought to his Lordship who leapt for joy, and after tenderly handling them before a fire twenty-two are unfolded without blemish.

31st January. Rumours at Court.

Since his rebuke by the Queen the Earl of Essex hath kept to his chamber these two days, opening it to none but the Lord Admiral, who passeth to and fro about atonement which at last is made, and they two go off to London. It is rumoured that on further examination Dr. Lopez is found to be deeply touched in the plot for working the Queen's destruction, and discovered to have been the King of Spain's pensioner these seven years, the ground of which treason is believed to have been discovered by Don Antonio before his recent going over to France. The Queen hath forbidden all access to her, except only of four persons, besides the Council and the ladies of nearest attendance, by which it appeareth that all is not yet discovered.

PLAYS OF THE WEEK.

At the Rose this week are played *Buckingham*, *Titus Andronicus* and *Abraham and Lot.*

1st February. BARNFIELD'S 'GREENE'S FUNERALS.'

Danter hath printed *Greene's Funerals*, by R. B., gentleman, contrary to the author's expectation and wish; wherein Greene's death and works are celebrated in fourteen sonnets of various metres. In the seventh, written in the English hexameter, R. B. protesteth against those

That inveigh against the dead, like deadly maligners,
What if he was a man, as bad or worse than a hell-hound?
As shall I think that he was as bad or worse than a hell-hound?
Yet it ill became sweet minds to haunt in Avernus,
Ill became such cutes, to bark at a poor silly carcase,
Some had cause to moan, and mourn, and murmur against him,
Others none at all, yet none at all so against him,
For myself I wish that none had written against him,
But such men which had just cause t'have written against him.

2nd February. THE ALCHEMIST'S BEQUEST.

In the matter of Roloff Peterson's letter concerning the three glasses or bodies in alchemy bequeathed to the Queen by Mr. Ouldfield, Mr. Robert Smith now promiseth Sir Thomas Wilkes, at peril of his head, to bring 40,000 dollars to the Queen's coffers for these glasses without one penny of expense, if it shall please her not to meddle with the receiving of them. Since doubts have been moved as to how the Queen might consider the virtues of these glasses as being without error or deceit, and whether she would accept them or the money, he confirmeth on his allegiance and life the first two particulars, offering to bring Peterson, if he be alive, and the glasses before the Queen to be examined: after which, if she shall refuse them, he will be bound to procure the money at his own charge.

3rd February. BURGLARY AT WINDSOR.

Yesterday four of the gentlemen pensioners of the Court were robbed at Windsor. In their absence at six o'clock at night their chamber door, which is in one of the five towers of the tiltyard, was broken open, and all their trunks likewise, out of which the thieves took in jewels and ready money to the value of £400.

Sir Robert Cecil is reported to be very busy coming and going very often between London and the Queen, so that he appeareth with his hands full of papers and his head full of matter, and so occupied passeth through the presence chamber like a blind man, not looking upon any.

PLAYING PROHIBITED.

Owing to the great multitudes of people who daily resort to the common plays, lately again set up in and about London, the Council fear that the sickness may gain very dangerous increase. The Lord Mayor is required to take straight order that no plays or interludes be exercised by any company within the compass of five miles of the City.

4th February. A PLOT TO KILL THE QUEEN.

A certain Polwhele that came over from Calais to give information to the Lord Treasurer hath declared that one Captain Jacques, a soldier from Sir William Stanley's company, hath a design to kill the Queen. This Jacques, saith he, several times urged him to come to England to murder the Queen, and on his refusing Jacques said that the end of a soldier was but beggary, to be killed with a bullet and thrown into a ditch, and to take such a matter in hand would be glorious before God, the Queen being a wicked creature, and likely to overthrow all Christendom. Jacques directed him how to get to England safely, and what speeches to use to the Lord Treasurer if intercepted, saying that if he himself could go to England, the killing of the Queen would be the first thing he would do. Polwhele also draweth in two men, John Annias and Patrick Collen, an Irish soldier, with having come to England to kill the Queen. Both are already taken and lodged separately in prison.

5th February. LOPEZ SENT TO THE TOWER.

Dr. Lopez for all those that favour him at noon is committed to the Tower, the Earl of Essex having so busied himself with the examinations for several days past that he scarce had leisure even to eat.

THE CARTER'S WORDS.

The remove of the Court from Windsor is still constantly put off. The carter that three times came to Windsor with his cart to carry away some of the stuff of the Queen's wardrobe, when he repaired there for the third time and was told by those of the wardrobe that the remove held not, clapping his hand on his thigh cried out, 'Now I see that the Queen is a woman as well as my wife.' These words being overheard by her Majesty, who then stood at the window, she said, 'What a villain is this!' and so sends him three angels to stop his mouth.

6th February. A PLOT TO BURN THE TOWER.

John Daniel, an Irishman, hath given Mr. Justice Young to understand of a plot that is pretended for the firing of the Tower. He declareth that there is a vault where brimstone lies and over it gunpowder, and near to it a trapdoor that stands much open. It is purposed that two men like labourers shall come in as though they were workmen in the Tower, and cast certain bales into the vault where the brimstone is so that in a short time it shall take fire and consume all. Further, that there is a device to set the ships at Billingsgate on fire, and the houses also; and then to set the inns and woodstacks on fire in London.

THE ROSE THEATRE CLOSED.

At the Rose this week the Earl of Sussex's men play *The Jew of Malta*, and *Titus Andronicus*, and now cease playing.

'TITUS ANDRONICUS' ENTERED.

The most lamentable Roman Tragedy of Titus Andronicus, sometime played by the servants of the Earl of Derby, the Earl of Pembroke and the Earl of Sussex, is to be printed.

A CONVERSATION BETWEEN SIR ROBERT CECIL AND THE EARL OF ESSEX.

At seven in the morning Dr. Lopez was again examined before the Earl of Essex and Sir Robert Cecil, and confesseth more than enough.

The office of Attorney-General is still vacant, and canvassed by the Earl of Essex for Mr. Francis Bacon, though the Lord Treasurer and Sir Robert Cecil favour Sir Edward Coke. As the Earl of Essex and Sir Robert returned back in a coach together, Sir Robert began to broach the matter of the Attorney-General, saying, ' My lord, the Queen has resolved e'er five days pass without any further delay to make an Attorney-General. I pray your lordship to let me know whom you will favour.'

The Earl answered that he wondered Sir Robert should ask him that question seeing that it could not be unknown to him that he favoured Francis Bacon.

' Good lord,' replied Sir Robert, ' I wonder your Lordship should go about to spend your strength in so unlikely or impossible a manner.'

After further talk passed between them, Sir Robert said, ' If at least your Lordship had spoken of the Solicitorship, that might be of easier digestion to her Majesty.'

Upon this the Earl answereth, ' Digest me no digestions ; for the Attorneyship for Francis is that I must have, and in that will I spend all my power, might, authority and annuity, and with tooth and nail defend and procure the same for him against whosoever ; and that whosoever getteth this office out of my hand for another, before he have it, it shall cost him the coming by, and of this be you assured of, Sir Robert, for now do I fully declare myself. And for your own part, Sir Robert, I think it strange both of my Lord Treasurer and you that can have the mind to seek the preference of a stranger before so near a kinsman. For if you weigh in a balance the parts every way of his competitor and him, only excepting five poor years of admitting to a house of court before Francis, you shall find in all other respects whatsoever, no comparison between them.'

THE CONFESSION OF PATRICK COLLEN.

Patrick Collen now declareth that Jacques had persuaded him to kill Antonio Perez, formerly the King of Spain's Secretary, which he undertook, whereupon Jacques gave him £30 in gold, for his voyage. He then departed immediately from Brussels for St. Omar, where he found an old priest to whom he confessed. The priest dissuaded him, saying that it was unlawful to commit murder ; but next day Jacques took him to Father Holt who said that he might lawfully enterprise anything for the King's service, and, advising him to prepare himself to God, gave him absolution.

8th February. A RUMOUR OF THE QUEEN'S DEATH.

There is a rumour in London that the Queen is dead and hath been carried to Greenwich, but it is being kept very secret in Court.

11th February. CLERKE'S 'TRIAL OF BASTARDY.'

William Clerke's *The Trial of Bastardy* is entered, wherein are shown the civil and ecclesiastical laws of matrimony and legitimate issue, together with the statutes in marriage from the 25th year of Henry VIII.

17th February. PRECAUTIONS AGAINST SUSPICIOUS PERSONS.

Because of the dangers threatened at this time to the Queen's person, these special directions are proposed by the Lord Treasurer. Officers are to be appointed in every port that shall not suffer any person to land until examined as to the cause of his coming, and if the cause do not appear clear, he shall be committed to prison, or kept on board until his examinations have been taken and sent to the Council. It is especially likely that such persons will land at Dover, Sandwich, Rye, Gravesend, Yarmouth and London. Every Irishman in London or about the Court that is neither a known householder, nor a resident in commons, in any house, court or chamber as a servant, nor in service with a householder for five years past, must present himself to one of the Council or to the Lord Mayor to be examined how he lives and why he remains in England.

To restrain the great resort of unnecessary persons lodging near or frequenting the Court, the Lord Chamberlain shall appoint an usher and a quarter-waiter, with one or two clerks of the household, to attend and daily view all persons that offer to come to Court; and the Knight Harbinger and Marshal, with some tipstaffs, and, if need be, with the aid of some of the Yeomen of the Guard, shall twice or thrice a week discover who are lodged within two miles of Court; and if any are found not allowed they shall be examined, and if they cannot give just cause be committed to prison.

18th February. FERRARA DE GAMA'S CONFESSION.

Stephen Ferrara de Gama, being examined before the Earl of Essex, Sir Thomas Wilkes, and Mr. William Waad, hath declared that ten months since he received two letters from Dr. Lopez, written in his house in London to be delivered to Don Christophero de Moro. He wrote the letters from Lopez's lips wherein, though obscurely worded, he promised to do all the King required. He thinks that the Doctor would have poisoned the Queen had he been required. Andrada had said that Lopez was willing to poison both the Queen and Don Antonio ; and afterwards Lopez said that Don Antonio should die the first illness that befel him.

20th February. THE ALCHEMIST'S BEQUEST.

Mr. Robert Smith hath received the Queen's reply to the letter from Roloff Peterson of Lubec and is to repair thither, deliver the letter, receive the glass bodies and bring them to the Queen ; also to ascertain whether the materials therein were considered by Ouldfield to be brought to full perfection and, if anything be lacking, what it is ; also to recover any books or papers of Ouldfield's relating thereto or others which treat of alchemy, also a secret *menstruum* without which the materials could hardly be brought to perfection. All these things are to be brought to the Queen.

21st February. A PROCLAMATION AGAINST VAGABONDS.

A proclamation is published for the suppressing of the multitude of idle vagabonds. On certain days in the week, monthly watchers and privy searchers shall be appointed to attach and imprison these idle vagabonds and to send the lamed into their counties according to the statute.

In the City of London, and about her Majesty, a great multitude repair, whereof some are men of Ireland that of late years have unnaturally served as rebels against her Majesty's forces beyond the seas, and cannot have any good meaning towards her, as is manifestly proved in some already taken. These men have secretly come into the realm, by procurement of the devil and his ministers, the Queen's enemies, to endanger her noble person. Such kind of persons are to be directly taken wheresoever they be found and proceeded withal as traitors. But as for the procurers and authors thereof, that are known to be of sundry conditions, some rebellious subjects, fugitives, some of the order of their priesthood yielding dispensation and shrifts to the intended mischiefs, some others more able by reward to hire the offenders, being persons of high degree in the world; the revenge thereof belonged to Almighty God in Whose hands the Queen had of long time reposed herself.

But seeing that the discovery of Irish traitors can hardly be made when so many other vagrants of that nation haunt about the Court, it is commanded that no person born in Ireland (except he be an householder known in some town, or a menial servant with some nobleman, gentleman or other honest householder, or resides, or is in commons, in any house of court or Chancery, as a student in the laws, or a student in any of the Universities, or sent out of Ireland by her Majesty's Deputy) do remain in this realm but repair without delay into the realm of Ireland to the place of his natural habitation, where he ought to live.

The Confession of Hugh Cahill.

Hugh Cahill, an Irishman, hath voluntarily confessed before Topcliffe that when at Brussels, Father Holt and others said it would be a most blessed thing to kill the Queen, as by it he would win Heaven, and become a saint if he should be killed; he that should do it would be chronicled for ever. He was advised to go to Court, and serve someone about the Queen's privy chamber, and then to waylay her in some progress and kill her with a sword and a dagger at a gate or narrow passage, or as she walked in one of her galleries. They promised him 100 crowns towards his charges, and 2000 more to be paid when he had killed her, and his pension augmented from 15 crowns a month to £30.

25th February. Dr. Lopez.

There hath been a great consultation at the Lord Treasurer's about the persons apprehended for Dr. Lopez's plot; at which all now appears manifest, as well by the confessions of those taken as by the letters found of the others beyond the seas, whereby it is evident that this practice hath long continued, and that Lopez is no new traitor. Great expedition is being made to bring the affair before the public, but it seemeth that this cannot be done so soon as the Court desire, since the indictment must have many branches and there are many Spanish and other foreign letters to be translated and abstracted.

28th February. Dr. Lopez Arraigned.

This day Dr. Lopez was arraigned at the Guildhall before the Commission on which sit the Lord Mayor, the Earl of Essex, Lord Charles Howard, the Lord Admiral, Lord Buckhurst, Robert, Lord Rich, Sir Thomas Heneage, Vice-Chamberlain, Sir John Popham, Chief Justice of the Queen's Bench, Sir Robert Cecil, Sir John Fortescue, Chancellor of the Exchequer, and other persons of worth.

The case against Lopez was conducted by the Solicitor-General, Sir Edward Coke, who opened by showing that the grounds of all the plots against the Queen and the realm are not for any offence on her part, but for her constant defence of Christ's cause and His Holy Word against the Pope, and for protecting her dominions against the ambitions of the King of Spain. These were the original causes of the cursed bull of Pius V., and from this root sprung all the rebellions, treasons and devilish practices since attempted. After the 'Invincible Navy,' as they termed it, had been defeated by God and her Majesty's princely care and providence, and by the valiantness of her nobles and true subjects, the King of Spain and his priests, despairing of prevailing by valour, turned to cowardly treachery, and what they could not do by cannon, they attempted by crowns. To achieve this, have they put in practice three devilish attempts: to burn the navy and ships with poisoned fireworks; to seduce some of the nobility to rebellion; and to take the blood of a virgin Queen. To this end many needy and desperate young men are seduced by Jesuits and seminary priests with great rewards and promises to kill the Queen, being persuaded that it is glorious and meritorious, and that if they die in the action, they will inherit Heaven and be canonised as saints.

This Lopez, a perjured murdering traitor and Jewish Doctor, worse than Judas himself, undertook the poisoning, which was a plot more wicked, dangerous, and detestable than all the former. He is her Majesty's sworn servant, graced and advanced with many princely favours, used in special places of credit, permitted often access to her person, and so not suspected, especially by her who never feareth her enemies nor suspecteth her servants. The bargain was made and the price agreed upon, and the fact only deferred until payment of the money was assured. The letters of credit for his assurance were sent, but before they came to his hands, God most wonderfully and miraculously revealed and prevented it. The manner of it is as follows:

Some followers of Don Antonio, hoping to raise themselves by his fortunes, and finding his success not answerable to their expectations, grew discontented, and so became instruments to betray their master to the King of Spain, and practise any treason that could be devised, either against Don Antonio's state or the Queen's person. Lopez, outwardly pretending to favour Don Antonio, was a secret instrument for the King of Spain, and carried his actions therein more covertly under pretext of service for Don Antonio. He continued his secret course of intelligence with the King of Spain for many years by means of Emanuel Andrada, Bernardino Mendoza and others. Andrada wrote to Mendoza that he had won Lopez, but the letter being intercepted, Andrada was apprehended and committed. Lopez practised to have secret speech with Andrada before he was examined, and directed him what answer he was to make, insomuch that Andrada was released. These services were so acceptable to the King of Spain that he sent Lopez a jewel.

After this Andrada dealt with Lopez for poisoning the Queen. They had many conferences when Lopez undertook to do it, and directed them to signify this to Count Fuentes and to Stephen de Ibarra, the King's secretary. Andrada then went to Calais to convey intelligence between Lopez and the King of Spain and his Ministers; he told Ferrara de Gama that he might commit all things to Lopez, who hoped to do one great service to the King, and a remedy for Christendom, which was to poison the Queen, the King paying for it. Lopez and Ferrara afterwards conferred together, and Lopez undertook the poisoning for 50,000 crowns, which Ferrara signified by letters to Count Fuentes and Stephen de Ibarra. Ferrara, with the privity of Lopez, wrote to Christofero de Moro, assuring him of Lopez's affection to the King of Spain. Lopez also sent two packets of letters to Count Fuentes, de Moro and de Ibarra, wherein he promised to do all the King of Spain should command, and, since the King knew the business, as he told Ferrara, he made him write in obscure and covert words.

Lopez often asked if the money and answer were come, and

said he was ready to do the service. The money he was to receive at Antwerp, where he meant to go after the treason had been committed, and to this end he gave directions for a house to be prepared for him, intending afterwards to go and live at Constantinople.

Tinoco, who acted as go-between, was apprehended with the letters from the Count Fuentes and Ibarra, letters of credit for the money being found upon him, and, although Ferrara de Gama was then in prison, and examined long before and Tinoco since, without any conference with each other, both agreed in all things concerning the plotting of the treason. It is also to be observed that in handling of these treasons Lopez was so careful that he never wrote anything himself nor treated directly with Tinoco, but used Ferrara de Gama as a means between them. Nor did he ever discover any part of their proceedings or pretences to her Majesty or to any of the Council.

Being often charged with these treasons by his examiners, Lopez, with blasphemous oaths and horrible execrations, denied that he had ever had speech with any person or any understanding at all of any such matter, but then confessed that he had indeed spoken of it and promised it, but all to cozen the King of Spain. But when he saw that his intent and overt fact were apparent, the vile Jew said he had confessed talking of it, but belied himself only to save himself from racking.

At the bar Lopez said little in his own defence, but cried out that Ferrara and Emanuel were made up of nothing but fraud and lying. He had intended no hurt against the Queen, but abhorred the gifts of a tyrant; he had presented the jewel to the Queen that was sent by the Spaniard; and he had no other design in what he did but to deceive the Spaniard and wipe him of his money.

All these charges being plainly and fully proved by witnesses, by the intercepted letters, and by the confession of Lopez himself to the great satisfaction of the judge, jury and hearers, he is found guilty in the highest degree and judgment passed on him with universal applause.

5th March. 'A Looking Glass for London.'

A Looking Glass for London, a play written by Thomas Lodge and Robert Greene some years since, and played by the Lord

Strange's players, is to be printed, wherein is shown the story of the prophet Jonas and the repentance of the Ninevites.

6th March. THE CORONATION OF THE FRENCH KING.

The account of the anointing and crowning of the French King is at hand. The King, having been advised by the Princes of his blood, the Lords of his Council and other notable persons to frame himself to his anointing as other Kings his predecessors always used, would have wished the ceremony to be performed at Rheims; but in as much as the city of Rheims was still in possession of the rebels it was determined to hold the Coronation at the Church of Our Lady at Chartres. From the 17th February when the King entered the town to the day of the Coronation all the preparations were being finished.

Upon the 19th the Holy Vial, preciously preserved in the Abbey of Marmonster, near Tours, was brought to the City of Chartres, being conducted by the Lord of Souure, the Governor and King's Lieutenant-General in the land and Duchy of Tourraine, accompanied by four friars of the Abbey. Being arrived at Chartres, the vial was carried with great ceremony to St. Peter's Abbey, attended on by the clergy and a great number of people, the streets being hanged all the way in honour and reverence of so precious a relic.

Thither was brought the Imperial Close Crown, the Middle Crown, the Royal Sceptre, the Hand of Justice, the Cloak Royal, the Shirt, the Sandals, the Spurs, the Sword, the Tunicle, and the Dalmatic, with all the other ornaments royal, as fair and rich as might be, but they had to be newly made because the rebels had molten and defaced the others which time out of mind had been preserved in the Church of St. Denis.

Upon Saturday the 26th, at eight o'clock at night, the King came to the Church of Our Lady there to do his devotions and to be shriven.

On the 27th, about six in the morning, the King sent four Barons to fetch the Holy Vial from the Abbey of St. Peter's. The King having been escorted to the Church, the different ceremonies of the anointing were performed, after which the Bishop of Chartres, then subrogated for the Archbishop Duke of Rheims, delivered to the King the garments he was to wear above his doublet, that is the tunicle, representing a subdeacon, the dalmatick representing a deacon, and the cloak royal a priest. The King being thus clothed, the Bishop took again the plate whereupon lay the Holy Ointment, and laid some upon the palm of the King's hands, which being thus hallowed he laid them close upon his breast. After this the Bishop put on the Ring wherewith the King married the realm ; and then delivered him the Sceptre Royal and the Hand of Justice.

These things ended, the Lord Chancellor, standing against the Altar, and turning to the King, with a loud voice called the twelve peers according to their dignities, beginning first with the six lay peers. Then the Bishop rose from his chair, and turned to the High Altar from which he took the Close Crown and held it over the King's head, without touching it, whereto immediately all the peers temporal and spiritual set their hands to support it, the Bishop saying '*Coronet te Deus corona gloriae*,' etc. This prayer ended the Bishop set the crown upon the King's head.

All the other ceremonies being ended, Mass was celebrated, after which the King came forth arrayed in his royal garments, being received by the people with great acclamation and signs of joy.

13th March. DR. LOPEZ'S HEALTH.

Dr. Lopez hath kept his bed for the most part since his trial, and it is suspected that he practises by slow poison to prevent his execution. The trial of the other conspirators is fixed for to-morrow but the Lord Chief Justice is ill. It is much feared that if the trial be longer deferred, Lopez may die before his execution, and great dishonour and scandal ensue thereby.

14th March. LOPEZ'S ACCOMPLICES ARRAIGNED.

This day Emanuel Louis Tinoco and Stephen Ferrara de Gama, the Portuguese conspirators with Dr. Lopez, were brought before the Commissioners at the Guildhall to their trial. Tinoco was arraigned upon an indictment from his own confession :

That he had sent secret messages and intelligences to the King of Spain and his ministers of things treated in this realm in order that they might prepare their forces and direct their actions against the Queen ;

That Christoforo de Moro, one of the King's most secret counsellors, wrote letters to de Gama touching his service to the King and that Tinoco brought them to him in London;

That he came from Brussels to London to deliver a message and an embrace from the Count Fuentes, as also a credence from Andrada to Lopez for himself;

That he wrote word to Lopez that Count Fuentes had sent him a message and an embrace, and was glad that he was such a good servant to the King of Spain and that he should be liberally rewarded, requiring Lopez to procure the treaty of peace between the Queen and the King to be renewed as the King desired it; meaning by 'peace' her destruction by poison; which letters he delivered to Lopez;

That under a false name he had written letters to de Gama in obscure words, such as 'the bearer will tell you the price in which your pearls are held,' by which was meant the poisoning of the Queen, and by 'musk and amber' the burning of the Queen's ships.

That Count Fuentes told him on oath of secrecy that he had received order from the King of Spain to give Lopez whatever he required for poisoning the Queen, and that he delivered to de Gama in London several letters written by him in obscure words in the Spanish tongue concerning it, knowing their interests, which letters were found upon him when apprehended.

These matters being declared to him through a Portuguese interpreter he affirmed them from point to point, acknowledged his faults and called for mercy.

Stephen Ferrara de Gama being also indicted pleaded not guilty; but his former confessions and other proofs being produced against him, confessed all to be true; whereupon he also was convicted by judgment of the Court for imagining and compassing the death of the Queen.

26th March. ATHEISTICAL SPEECHES OF SIR WALTER RALEGH.

At Cerne Abbas in Dorsetshire, on the 21st, was held an inquiry by the High Commissioners in Causes Ecclesiastical concerning blasphemous and atheistical speeches made by some in these parts. It is declared by several witnesses that Sir

Walter Ralegh, his brother, Mr. Carew Ralegh, and Mr. Harriott of their household, are much subjected to atheism, also one Allen, Lieutenant of Portland Castle. This Allen tore two leaves out of a Bible to dry tobacco on, and spoke as if he denied the immortality of the soul, saying, on an occasion when he was like to die and one persuaded him to make himself ready to God for his soul, that he would carry his soul up to the top of a hill, and 'Run God, run Devil, fetch it that will have it.'

Of Sir Walter and his brother, one witness, being the parson of Weeke Regis, declareth that some three years past on coming to Blandford his horse was stayed and taken for a post horse by Sir Walter and Mr. Carew Ralegh. When he entreated to have his horse released to ride home to his charge, from whence he had been some time absent, to preach there next day, being Sunday, Mr. Carew Ralegh replied that he might go home when he would but his horse should preach before him.

Some months before, at Sir George Trenchard's table, at which there were also present Sir Ralph Horsey, Lord Lieutenant of the County of Dorset, Sir Walter Ralegh, Mr. Carew Ralegh, Ralph Ironside, minister of Winterbottom, and others, Mr. Carew Ralegh uttered some loose speeches and was rebuked by Sir Ralph Horsey. Whereupon turning to the minister he demanded what danger he might incur by such speeches.

To which Mr. Ironside answered, 'The wages of sin is death.' Whereunto Mr. Ralegh making light of death as common to all, sinner and righteous, the minister inferred further that 'As life which is the gift of God through Jesus Christ is life eternal, so that death which is properly the wages of sin is death eternal, both of the body and of the soul also.'

'Soul,' quoth Mr. Ralegh, 'what is that ?'

'Better it were,' answered Mr. Ironside, 'that we should be careful how the soul might be saved than to be curious in finding out its essence.'

Sir Walter then requested that the minister would answer the question that had been proposed by his brother ; 'I have been,' quoth he, 'a scholar some time in Oxford, I have answered under a bachelor of art, and had talk with divines, yet hitherunto in this point (to wit, what the reasonable soul of man is) have I not by any been resolved.'

The dispute was then continued until Sir Walter wished that grace might be said; 'for that,' said he, 'is better than this disputation.'

30th March. GREAT STORMS.

This month there have been great storms of wind, that overturn trees, steeples, barns and houses; in Beaulieu forest in Worcestershire, many oaks are uprooted, and on the Thursday before Palm Sunday, more than fifteen hundred in Horton Wood. In the town of Stafford the steeple is thrown down, and a thousand pound's worth of damage done to the roof. In Cankewood more than three thousand trees overthrown, and some fifty other steeples in Staffordshire fallen.

31st March. DEATH OF SIR JOHN BURGH.

Sir John Burgh, that took the great carrack, hath been slain in a duel by Mr. John Gilbert, after various letters had passed between them. Sir John first challenged his adversary to meet him at five o'clock in the morning between Charing Cross and Hyde Park, with dagger and rapier, and accompanied only by one gentleman of good quality, or alone. No treachery would be used; let him not therefore use any boyish excuses or delays as he did the last time he sent to him, or else he would pick out a time to beat him like a boy.

To this Mr. Gilbert replied that he would fight, but that the time, place, and manner of the meeting, and the weapons belonged to the challenged.

4th April. THE QUEEN'S BOUNTY TO MR. WILLIAM CAMDEN.

The Queen, having used the services of Mr. William Camden, schoolmaster, in things wherein he has attained skill and intending to employ him again, desireth him to be settled somewhere near her, and eased of the charge of living. She hath required the Dean of Westminster to admit Mr. Camden to the table of the Dean and prebends, and allow him diet for one service; this to be granted for life. The grant she will have sent to her that she may herself present it to Mr. Camden as a token of her gratitude.

6th April. PLAYS AT THE ROSE THEATRE.

The Queen's men and the Earl of Sussex's men have begun to play together at the Rose Theatre and during this week play *Friar Bacon*, *The Rangers' Comedy*, *The Jew of Malta*, *The Fair Maid of Italy*, *Friar Bacon* and *King Leir*.

9th April. PLAYS AT THE ROSE THEATRE.

Yesterday *The Jew of Malta* and to-day *King Leir* are played at the Rose Theatre.

11th April. A GREAT RAINSTORM.

The rain hath continued very sore for more than twenty-four hours long and withal such a wind from the north as pierces the walls of houses be they never so thick.

16th April. DEATH OF THE EARL OF DERBY.

Ferdinando Stanley, the young Earl of Derby, that hath been sick of some strange sickness these eleven days, is dead at Latham. Outwardly his diseases were vomiting of sour or rusty matter with blood, the yellow jaundice, melting of his fat, swelling and hardness of his spleen, a vehement hiccough, and, for four days before he died, stopping of his water. All these were caused in the opinion of his physicians partly by surfeit, partly by the excessive exercise that he took for four days together in Easter week. In all the time of his sickness, which began on the 5th April and continued until he died, he often took Beza's stone and Unicorn's horn; his pulse was always good but his strength indifferent, the number of his vomits being fifty-two and of his stools twenty-nine. His death is so unaccountable that many begin to suspect that he was bewitched. In the beginning of his sickness he had strange dreams. On the 10th April, Mr. Halsall, one of his gentlemen, found in my lord's chamber about midnight an image of wax with hair in colour like his hair twisted round the belly. This image was spotted and soon after spots appeared also upon the Earl's sides and belly. Mr. Halsall hastily cast the image in the fire before it was viewed by others, thinking that by burning it he should relieve his lord of the witchcraft and burn the witch who so much tormented him; but unhappily it fell out the contrary for after the melting of the image the Earl declined.

A homely woman about the age of fifty years was found mumbling in a corner of his chamber. She seemed often to ease his lordship both of vomiting and hiccough, but it was noted that whenever he was so eased she herself was much troubled in the same way, and the matter which she vomited was like that which passed from him. But at the last, one of the doctors, spying her tempering and blessing the juice of certain herbs tumbled her pot down and rated her from the chamber. The Earl himself cried out in all his sickness that the doctors laboured in vain because he was certainly bewitched. During this last illness the Bishop of Chester and his chaplain, Mr. Lee, were with him.

18th April. LOPEZ EXECUTION POSTPONED.

The execution of Lopez, Ferrara, and Tinoco, that was fixed for to-morrow morning at 9 o'clock is by the Queen's orders stayed, to the great discontent of the commissioners and the people who much expect it.

23rd April. ST. GEORGE'S DAY. FOREIGN ORDERS.

There is great press of the people at Court, though very few Knights of the Garter ; the Lord Treasurer being unable to go in the procession because of his foot. The Queen is reported to be very angry with Sir Anthony Shirley and Sir Nicholas Clifford for having accepted the Order of St. Michael from the French King, first because they took it without her privity, and next for that they took the whole oath, one part whereof is to defend the Mass while they live.

GIBBON'S 'PRAISE OF A GOOD NAME.'

Mr. Charles Gibbon hath written *The Praise of a Good Name* in answer to certain slanders made against him, being a collection of apothegms, epigrams, and pithy sayings in praise of a good name, and of brief essays showing the reproach of an ill name.

29th April. LADY BRANCH BURIED.

The Lady Helen Branch, wife first of John Minors, citizen and grocer of London, secondly of Sir John Branch, was buried, having died on the 10th of the month in the ninetieth year of her life. Her funerals were very honourably furnished, and accompanied by the Lord Mayor, many mourners, doctors, gentlemen, and kinsfolk, honourable ladies, servants and poor men. In honour of these ceremonies, an *Epicedium* is printed, being a sequence of twelve sonnets describing her life, wherein the author invoketh our living poets :

You that to shew your wits have taken toil,
In registering the deeds of noble men,
And sought for matter in a foreign soil,
(As worthy subjects of your silver pen)
Whom you have raised from dark oblivion's den;
You that have writ of chaste Lucretia,
Whose death was witness of her spotless life,
Or penned the praise of fair Cornelia,
Whose blameless name hath made her name so rife,
As noble Pompey's most renowned wife,
Hither unto your home direct your eyes,
Whereas unthought on much more water lies.

For her obsequies Joshua Sylvester also hath written *Monodia*, an Elegy in commemoration of the virtuous life and godly death of the right worshipful and most religious lady, Dame Helen Branch.

THE GROWTH OF POPERY.

It is said by some that for all the dangers of Catholics and their narrow sifting, infinite numbers run daily into the Church and are reconciled to the Catholic faith. Good men, making no account of losing their lives, hazard themselves to save men's souls; and even in the Court there are as many Masses said daily as in any country abroad.

1st *May*. SIR JOHN SMYTHE'S 'INSTRUCTIONS, OBSERVATIONS AND ORDERS MILITARY.'

A book called *Instructions, Observations and Orders Military*, written in 1591 by Sir John Smythe, is now printed. Herein is shown the reducing of single bands of horsemen or footmen into their simple or single order of ranks from point to point, and how to draw out many troops into squadrons and battles formed, as well to march into the field as to give battle with most advantages. As for those that allege new or old fashions used by such or such nations in matters military without reasons or allowable experience to fortify and confirm them, these Sir John holdeth for vain and frivolous. To those that think a far greater number of archers are not able to encounter a smaller number of musketeers, he answereth that their opinion proceedeth of nothing else but from their lack of understanding and knowing the wonderful imperfections and failings that belong to muskets and musketeers in the field by reason of the heaviness of their pieces; nor are harquebusiers of greater advantage, being more uncertain of their aim so that if they discharge at ten, eleven, or twelve score paces distant at the archers, it will be found that in ten thousand of their shot they would not hit so many as ten archers.

2nd May. 'THE TAMING OF A SHREW.'

The play of *A Pleasant conceited History called the Taming of a Shrew*, is to be printed, a play that was sundry times acted by the Earl of Pembroke's players.

3rd May. GREAT FLOODS.

Yesterday in Sussex and Surrey there came down great water floods by reason of sudden showers of hail and rain that have fallen, which bare down houses, iron-mills, the provision of coals prepared for the mills, and carried away cattle.

SIR NICHOLAS CLIFFORD AND THE ORDER OF ST. MICHAEL.

Sir Nicholas Clifford, that was imprisoned in the Tower for receiving the order of St. Michael from the French King, finding that his former letters to the Queen are received with displeasure hath now sent her the order to be disposed as she considereth best, and petitioneth for enlargement.

9th May. SHAKESPEARE'S 'THE RAPE OF LUCRECE.'

The Rape of Lucrece, a poem written by William Shakespeare, is entered, and dedicated, as was his *Venus and Adonis*, to the Earl of Southampton. In the dedication the poet toucheth upon the favours which he hath received. 'The warrant I have of your honourable disposition, not the worth of my untutored lines makes it assured of acceptance. What I have done is yours; what I have to do is yours; being part in all I have devoted yours. Were my worth greater my duty would show greater.' This poem telleth of the ravishing of the chaste Lucrece by the tyrant Tarquin, and of his everlasting banishment therefor.

LUCRECE'S INVOCATION TO NIGHT.

'O comfort-killing Night, image of hell!
Dim register and notary of shame!
Black stage for tragedies and murders fell!
Vast sin-concealing chaos! nurse of blame!
Blind muffled bawd! dark harbour for defame!
  Grim cave of death! whispering conspirator
  With close-tongu'd treason and the ravisher!

'O hateful, vaporous, and foggy Night!
Since thou art guilty of my cureless crime,
Muster thy mists to meet the eastern light,
Make war against proportion'd course of time;
Or if thou wilt permit the sun to climb
  His wonted height, yet ere he go to bed,
  Knit poisonous clouds about his golden head.

'With rotten damps ravish the morning air;
Let their exhal'd unwholesome breaths make sick
The life of purity, the supreme fair,
Ere he arrive his weary noontide prick;
And let thy misty vapours march so thick,
  That in their smoky ranks his smother'd light
  May set at noon and make perpetual night.

'Were Tarquin Night, as he is but Night's child,
The silver-shining queen he would distain;
Her twinkling handmaids too, by him defil'd,
Through Night's black bosom should not peep again;
So should I have co-partners in my pain;
  And fellowship in woe doth woe assuage,
  As palmers' chat makes short their pilgrimage.

'Where now I have no one to blush with me,
To cross their arms and hang their heads with mine,
To mask their brows and hide their infamy;
But I alone alone must sit and pine,
Seasoning the earth with showers of silver brine,
  Mingling my talk with tears, my grief with groans,
  Poor wasting monuments of lasting moans.

'O Night! thou furnace of foul-reeking smoke,
Let not the jealous Day behold that face
Which underneath thy black all-hiding cloak
Immodestly lies martyr'd with disgrace:
Keep still possession of thy gloomy place,
That all the faults which in thy reign are made
May likewise be sepulchred in thy shade.'

14th May. GREENE'S 'FRIAR BACON.'

The play of *The Honourable History of Friar Bacon and Friar Bungay*, written some years before by Robert Greene and played by the Queen's players, is to be printed, containing the story of the wooing of Margaret, the keeper's daughter of Fressingfield, by Lacy, Earl of Lincoln, and of Friar Bacon's Brazen Head.

16th May. PLAYING RESUMED.

The Admiral's men that were forced to travel through the inhibition on playing during the plague are returned to the Rose where they play *The Jew of Malta*, *The Ranger's Comedy* and *Cutlack*.

17th May. MARLOWE'S 'JEW OF MALTA.'

There is entered for the printing the famous *Tragedy of the rich Jew of Malta*, written some years since by Christopher Marlowe and now being played at the Rose Theatre. To this play the ghost of Machiavel as prologue beginneth:

Albeit the world think Machiavel is dead,
Yet was his soul but flown beyond the Alps,
And now the Guise is dead is come from France
To view this land, and frolic with his friends.
To some perhaps my name is odious,
But such as love me guard me from their tongues,
And let them know that I am Machiavel,
And weigh not men, and therefore not men's words;
Admired I am of those that hate me most.
Though some speak openly against my books,
Yet will they read me and thereby attain
To Peter's chair; and when they cast me off,
Are poisoned by my climbing followers.
I count religion but a childish toy
And hold there is no sin but ignorance.

The Prologue endeth:

I come not, I,
To read a lecture here in Britain,
But to present the tragedy of a Jew,
Who smiles to see how full his bags are cram'd,
Which money was not got without my means.
I crave but this; grace him as he deserves,
And let him not be entertained the worse
Because he favours me.

30th May. DRAYTON'S 'IDEA'S MIRROR.'

Mr. Michael Drayton hath sent to the press his *Idea's Mirror*, containing fifty-one sonnets or amours, being dedicated to the dear child of the Muses, and his ever kind Mecenas, Mr. Anthony Cooke, Esquire.

3rd June. THE DEATH OF THE BISHOP OF LONDON.

This day John Aylmer, Bishop of London, died at Fulham.

THE PLAYERS OF THE LORD ADMIRAL AND THE LORD CHAMBERLAIN UNITE.

The Lord Chamberlain's players have also returned to London and join with the Admiral's men to play together at the little theatre in Newington Butts.

7th June. LOPEZ, TINOCO AND FERRARA EXECUTED.

This day Roderick Lopez, with the two other Portuguese, was executed. They were conveyed from the Tower of London by the Lieutenant to the Old Swan, and thence by water to Westminster, where being brought before the King's Bench Bar, the Lieutenant was called to bring in his prisoners, which he then delivered and was discharged of them.

Then it was declared to them by the Court how they had been charged with high treason against the Queen, had been tried, found guilty, and had received judgment; wherefore it was demanded of them what they could say for themselves that they should not suffer death accordingly. Whereunto one of the Portuguese began in his own language to tell a long tale, but was willed to be short, to which he answered that it could not be done without circumstances. Whereupon he was willed to hold his peace. The second answered by a writing in his own language, which being read by an interpreter, the Attorney General bade stay for it was not true. Lopez in English made his submission, affirming that he never thought harm to her Majesty.

Then the Marshal of the King's Bench was called and charged with the prisoners to convey them to the prison of the King's Bench and there to deliver them to the Sheriffs of London with a writ to see them executed. So they were conveyed by water from Westminster to the Bishop of Winchester's stairs in Southwark, from thence to the King's Bench, there laid upon hurdles and conveyed to the Sheriff of London over the bridge, up to Leadenhall, and so to Tyburn.

At the gallows Lopez declared that he loved the Queen as well as he loved Jesus Christ, which coming from a man of the Jewish profession moved no small laughter in the standers-by.

8th June. PLAYS OF THE WEEK.

The plays at Newington Butts this last week are *Hester and Assuerus*, *The Jew of Malta*, *Titus Andronicus*, *Cutlack*.

15th June. PLAYS OF THE WEEK.

The plays at Newington Butts this past week are *Bellendon* (for the first time), *Hamlet*, *Hester and Assuerus*, *The Taming of the Shrew*, *Titus Andronicus*, *The Jew of Malta*.

18th June. LYLY'S 'MOTHER BOMBY.'

Mother Bomby, a play formerly written by Mr. John Lyly, and sundry times played by the Children of Paul's, is entered for printing.

19th June. 'THE TRUE TRAGEDY OF RICHARD THE THIRD.'

The play of *The True Tragedy of Richard the Third*, that used to be played by the Queen's players, is to be printed; wherein is shown the death of Edward the Fourth, with the smothering of the two young Princes in the Tower; the lamentable end of Shore's wife, an example for all wicked women; and lastly the conjunction and joining of the two noble houses of Lancaster and York.

21st June. THE SPANIARDS AT BREST.

From the west Sir Walter Ralegh hath received trustworthy intelligence of the strength of the Spanish Fleet and its readiness to sail. It seemeth likely that some surprise is intended, for the carpenters and all others about the fleet work on the Sabbath Day, which is confirmed by the hugeness of the ships, that will carry many soldiers, since smaller vessels are far fitter for the coast of Brittany. At Brest, the Spaniards, having received no impediment, have finished the fortification of Old Croyzon, within the port, and, the better to command the haven, have also built a strong place at the very entrance. Now that Blavet and Belle Isle are theirs, there will be no entrance for the Queen's fleet. Their ships are huge, eight being between 800 and 1000 tons, two others of good burden, and divers galleys, full filled with soldiers.

22nd June. The Chamberlain's Break with the Admiral's.

The Chamberlain's men have broken with the Admiral's and go to play at James Burbage's house, the Theatre, in Shoreditch. Their chief players now are Richard Burbage, Will Kemp, the Clown, William Shakespeare, Thomas Pope, John Heminges, Augustine Phillips and George Bryan. The Admiral's, with Edward Alleyn, are returned to the Rose, where they played this week *Bellendon* (twice), *Cutlack*, *The Ranger's Comedy*, *The Massacre at Paris*; with Alleyn go John Singer, Richard Jones, Thomas Towne, Martin Slaughter, Edward Juby, Thomas Dutton and James Dunstan.

26th June. The Funeral of the Bishop of London.

This day John Aylmer, Bishop of London, was solemnly interred in his cathedral church of St. Paul before St. Thomas' Chapel.

The Character of Bishop Aylmer.

Bishop Aylmer was a man but mean of stature, yet in his youth very valiant, which he forgot not in his age. No bishop was more persecuted and taunted by the Puritans than he was by libels, by scoffs, by open railing and privy backbiting. The story is well known of what passed between him and one Mr. Madox, a Puritan; for when the bishop had reproved him about some matter and he answered somewhat untowardly and overthwartly, the bishop (as he was ingenious ever) said unto him, 'Thy very name expresseth thy nature, for *Madox* is thy name, and thou art as mad a beast as ever I talked with.' The other not long to seek of an answer, 'By your favour, sir,' said he, 'your deeds answer your name righter than mine; for your name is *Elmar*, and you have *marred* all the *elms* in Fulham by lopping them.'

He used for recreation to bowl in a garden; and Martin Marprelate thence takes this taunting scoff, that the bishop would cry, 'Rub, rub, rub,' to his bowl, and when it was gone too far, say, 'the devil go with it'; and then, saith Martin, the bishop would follow.

When there was talk of dangers and rumours of war and invasion, then he was commonly chosen to preach in the Court, and he would do it in so cheerful a fashion as not only showed he had courage, but would put courage in others. 'Here is much doubt,' saith he, 'of *malum sub Aquilone*, and our coal-prophets have prophesied that *in exaltatione Lunae Leo jungetur Leonae*. The astronomers tell of a watery trigon; that great inundations of water foreshow insurrections of people and downfall of princes; but as long as Virgo is the ascendant with us we need fear of nothing; *Deus nobiscum, quis contra nos?*' And for this the Queen would much commend him; yet would she not remove him. It is noted as an ill fortune of his to have died Bishop of London, which eight before him in one hundred have not done, but been either preferred or deprived.

27th June. PLAYS OF THE WEEK.

The plays at the Rose Theatre this past week are *The Ranger's Comedy*, *The Jew of Malta*, *Cutlack* (twice), *The Massacre at Paris*, *Galiaso*.

5th July. VIOLENCE IN WESTMINSTER.

To-day Mr. Edmund Wilton, was sitting in the parlour of Nicholas Nelson in Westminster, when Mr. George Barton, with a drawn dagger and a curtleaxe assaulted him, furiously throwing the dagger at him. Thereupon Mr. Wilton withdrew himself to a corner of the parlour, but Mr. Barton followed with drawn sword intending to have slain him. But his adversary coming between him and the door, Mr. Wilton turned and defended himself with his sword, and in self-defence gave Mr. Barton a mortal blow of which he instantly died.

6th July. PLAYS OF THE WEEK.

The plays this week at the Rose Theatre are *The Jew of Malta*, *Bellendon* (twice), *The Massacre at Paris*, *Cutlack*, *The Ranger's Comedy*.

12th July. SIDNEY SUSSEX COLLEGE IN CAMBRIDGE FOUNDED.

A licence is granted to the Earl of Kent and Sir John Harington, the executors of Frances, Countess of Sussex, to erect a college, to be called Sidney Sussex College in Cambridge University, to consist of a master, ten fellows, and twenty scholars.

13th July. PLAYS OF THE WEEK.

Plays at the Rose Theatre this week: *The Massacre at Paris*, *Philipo and Hippolito* (twice), *The Jew of Malta*, *Bellendon*, *Galiaso*.

15th July. CRUELTY IN PORTUGAL.

Certain merchants coming from Lisbon report that recently the chief Commander of the galleys invited three score and upwards of the chiefest of the city of Lisbon to a banquet aboard the galleys. After much feasting and triumph, having tricked them to sport down the river, he showed them a commandment he had received from the King to execute them all; which was immediately carried out. They were all beheaded; their bodies being taken back to Lisbon and their heads carried with speed to the King of Spain. The cause alleged for this murder is that letters were intercepted wherein they had intelligence with England.

16th July. SOLDIERS FOR BREST.

Three thousand soldiers and 50 pioneers are to be sent into Brittany to seize Brest, where the King of Spain is making fortifications. The pioneers are to be raised by Sir Walter Ralegh in Cornwall and ready to embark at Plymouth on 5th August.

20th July. THE SPANISH PREPARATIONS.

Sir Walter Ralegh reporteth that the recent news of the Spanish preparations seem to be confirmed, for within the last week three great Spanish men-of-war have given chase to an English ship and her two prizes, driving them even to the very mouth of Dartmouth. All the Newfoundland men are like to be taken by them if they be not speedily driven from the coast, for the Newfoundland fleet is expected at the beginning of August, above 100 sail. If these are lost it will be the greatest blow ever given to England.

PLAYS OF THE WEEK.

At the Rose this last week *Cutlack*, *The Massacre at Paris*, *The Ranger's Comedy*, *Philipo and Hippolito*, *The Second Part of Godfrey of Bulloigne*, *Belendon.*

21st July. CAPTAIN DAWTRY'S OFFER TO LEAD AN IRISH REGIMENT.

A certain Captain Dawtry, one on whom an Irish pension has been conferred, hath written to Sir Robert Cecil asking to be entrusted to fetch a regiment of 1500 or 2000 trained soldiers of Irish birth out of Ireland to serve the Queen in the expedition to Brittany, which will bring commodity to her and her whole dominions. She will leave at home, saith he, many of her people of England to reserve their lives until further necessity. She will disarm her ill disposed subjects of Ireland whose unnatural mutinies and rebellions are supported by these trained soldiers. They will win more spoil on the enemy than thrice as many soldiers of any other nation, for there are no better soldiers on earth than they, either for the use of their weapons or the strength of their bodies and minds, being such seasoned men of war that they can endure all fortunes, and keep their health when others with a little extremity will lie by the wall. Lastly, if they live, the Queen is like to be well served by them ; if they die, she will be better served, for it is a pity they should ever go back again into their own country so long as she hath any employment for soldiers. If he may have this charge and lay down his opinion of the Captains, he will answer for their true and faithful behaviour.

25th July. THE EARL OF ESSEX NOT ALLOWED TO GO TO BREST.

The expedition to Brest being finally resolved, the Earl of Essex is eager to go, but the Queen using very gentle words to him says that his desire to be in action and give further proof of his valour and prowess is to be liked and highly commended ;

but she loveth him and her realm too much to hazard his person in any lesser action than that which shall import her crown and state, and therefore willeth him to be content, giving him a warrant for £4000 and saying, 'Look to thyself, good Essex, and be wise to help thyself, without giving thy enemies advantage; and my hand shall be readier to help thee than any other.'

26th July. JOHN BOSTE, A JESUIT, EXECUTED.

John Boste, a Jesuit, was executed for high treason at Durham on the 24th. When he was taken from prison towards the place of execution, more than three hundred ladies and women of good position, all with black hoods, set out to follow him, and being asked where they were going, they answered, 'To accompany that gentleman, that servant of God, to his death, as the Maries did Christ.' A minister offered to dispute with them by the way, but a horseman came up and pushed him away, crying, 'Begone, knave, Mr. Boste has shown himself a true gentleman and a true man.'

Having come to the scaffold, he kissed the ladder and mounting the first step, said, '*Angelus ad Mariam dixit: Ave gratia plena: Dominus tecum Benedicta tu in mulieribus.*' On the second, '*Verbum caro factum est, et habitavit in nobis,*' at the third, '*Ecce ancilla Domini, fiat mihi secundum verbum tuum.*' Turning to the people, as he began to speak he was told that he came not to preach but to die.

'At least,' quoth he, 'you will allow me to thank these ladies and gentlemen who have done me the honour and kindness to accompany me to-day. Although I am now to be deprived of life, my blood withal and death and innocence shall preach in the hearts of those whom God will call and gather to His Holy Catholic Church. My head and quarters will preach every day on your gates and walls the truth of the Catholic Faith.'

Then he placed himself in prayer for a short while, and, as it were awakening, asked leave to recite the 114th Psalm, '*Dilexi quoniam,*' then returning thanks to God, he ended by saying that God had given him grace to die for the Catholic Roman Church, 'outside of which,' he declared, 'believe me, brethren (for this is not the time to dissemble nor to lie), it is impossible to enter unto the Kingdom of Heaven.'

27th July. DISORDERS AT THE PORT OF IPSWICH.

The officers of the port of Ipswich report that divers woodmongers buy up most of the wood and charcoal in Suffolk and Essex, and, under cover of loading it for London and elsewhere, convey it by themselves and in Flemish hoys into Flanders and Zealand ; and in their loading sometimes they cunningly lay under their wood, corn, butter and tallow. When the searcher found this out, they altogether refused to come to the Customs Houses to enter the same.

Divers of them, when the officers rode ten miles out to view their loading, falsely affirmed that they were loaden with her Majesty's wood, and such was their obstinacy that they refused to be brought into order. At Harwich of late the searcher's deputy was cast overboard in performance of his duty.

PLAYS OF THE WEEK.

The plays at the Rose this past week are *The Jew of Malta*, *Galiaso*, *Philipo and Hippolito*, *Godfrey of Bulloigne*, *The Massacre at Paris*.

1st August. A PROCLAMATION CONCERNING PRIZES.

A proclamation is issued against those that disorderly enter with ships brought as prizes into any haven, and secretly buy or convey away the goods before they can be customed and allowed as lawful prizes. For the reformation of this frequent abuse, all who go aboard any prizes, or buy, bargain, or receive any goods from the prizes, or from any of the company, shall not only forfeit his goods, but he and the seller be committed to prison, there to remain until order shall be given from the Lords of the Privy Council for their release. And for the better preventing of these disorders, it is commanded that immediately upon the coming in of any prizes from the seas, some of the officers of the Custom House of the port shall go aboard, and remain aboard quietly without any interruption or resistance of the captain, owner, master or mariners until the ship be discharged.

4th August. PLAYS OF THE WEEK.

The plays at the Rose Theatre this past week : *Cutlack*, *The Merchant of Emden*, *Bellendon*, *The Ranger's Comedy*, *Philipo and Hippolito*, *Galiaso*.

8th August. PLATT'S 'JEWEL HOUSE OF NATURE.'

There is entered for printing *The Jewel House of Art and Nature*, brought together by Mr. Hugh Platt, of Lincoln's Inn. In the first book are set down more than a hundred new and conceited experiments, such as to write a letter secretly, to walk safely upon a high scaffold without any danger of falling, to fetch out any stain, the art of memory, one candle to make as great a light as two or three, to close the chops of green timber, to speak by signs only, to refresh the colours of old oil pictures, and many others. To prevent drunkenness, he adviseth to drink a good large draught of salad oil, for that will float upon the wine which you shall drink and suppress the spirits from ascending into the brain.

The second book entreateth of sundry new sorts of soil or marl for the better manuring of pasture or arable ground; the third containeth divers chemical conclusions concerning the art of distillation; the fourth the art of casting and moulding; the last part is an offer of certain new inventions which the author will be ready to disclose upon reasonable consideration, being a new kind of fire in the form of balls made partly of seacoal; a vessel of wood to brew in; a bolting hutch; a portable pump; a wholesome, lasting and fresh victual for the navy; a speedy way for the inning of any breach; a light garment yet sufficient against all rainy weather; and a new conceit in peter works.

10th August. PLAYS OF THE WEEK.

The plays at the Rose Theatre this past week are *The Jew of Malta* (twice), *The Second Part of Godfrey of Bulloigne*, *Philipo and Hippolito*, *The Massacre at Paris*, *Cutlack*.

17th August. PLAYS OF THE WEEK.

This last week at the Rose the plays are *Bellendon*, *Tasso's Melancholy*, *Galiaso*, *Godfrey of Bulloigne*, *Mahomet*, *Philipo and Hippolito*.

19th August. CAPTAIN GLEMHAM'S EXPLOITS IN THE LEVANT SEAS.

News is published of all that befell Captain Edward Glemham since his departure from London in February 1593, whence he sailed with his ship the *Galleon Constance* to meet the rest of his company at Dartmouth. So many were the storms in the spring of last year that not until the 17th of April did he leave the English coast, being separated three days later from the others who believed him to have been cast away in the Gulf. Thence they made their way to Santa Cruz where, finding many other English ships, they refreshed themselves, and were joined by the *Tiger* and the *Elizabeth of Plymouth*, two of their company.

After meeting with several of the enemy it was concluded at length that they should make for Algiers. Here the King entertained them in the best manner, and to show the General what extraordinary favour he could, he came aboard to see the ship. Whereon the General prepared a sumptuous banquet, for which he would not stay, but taking a small repast of such confections as the General had brought for his store at sea he departed, being presented with a cup of silver, double gilt, a fair quilt of Damask with his arms embroidered and a purse, richly wrought, with fifty double pistolets. All of which the King thankfully received, and at the General's departure gave him under his hand and seal free liberty to sell, exchange, carry over and recarry at his pleasure all such goods as he or any of his should bring for his port, without any manner of let or disturbance.

The company then set sail from Algiers to attempt some prize, but though they fought very valiantly with several of the enemy all escaped them, and at length for lack of victual they were obliged to put back to Algiers where they found that the King had seized the ship *Examiner* of their consort, imprisoning the Captain and owner and the company. Whereupon the General immediately went to the King demanding the cause of this vile dealing with his company; but he subtlely smiling on the General gave him good speeches and mused on his choler, saying that he wondered to hear him speak so rashly and unadvisedly to him being in so great authority. After some further parley, the General seeing he could have no answer of his business to his content, departed in fury without bidding farewell but leaving him to the devil whom they served. The next day the King sent to have the General's sails taken ashore. Upon hearing thereof the General commanded his companies that were ashore to repair on board, caused his ship to be provided, his nettings laced, and his ordnance all out, resolutely determined to sink there. But at length a composition was offered and the Englishmen and Flemings that were in prison were released.

But soon afterward other misfortune befell them. While the men were still in prison one of the chiefest men of the French leaguer who was consul in that place entered the prison where they were and began to abuse in most opprobrious terms the name of the Queen. Thereafter two of the Englishmen chanced to meet this Frenchman, and remembering his words, for lack of a weapon began to beat him with their fists, and the quarrel was taken up by others.

When the French Consul heard of it, he went immediately to the King with his complaint, who sent for the General. But he being advertised of the truth by one of his followers made answer that if the quarrel were such as was reported, he would kill him with his own hands that should not offer with his life to maintain the honour of his Mistress, whose match the world afforded not. After further talk the Consul offered his handkerchief to the General's face who was so moved thereat that he struck him over the face with his fist, and craved of the King to grant him the combat against the Consul. But the King, who had received abundance of gold from the Frenchman would not allow it and dismissed them for that night.

About eight o'clock the next morning the King sent for the General and the men who had begun the brawl, and caused the men to receive the bastinado and the General to be committed prisoner, threatening that if he did not become friends with the Consul, he should lose his hand. The General dreading naught his threats refused, but his company came to him and on their knees besought him to tender both his own estate and theirs, for on his welfare depended all their goods. So likewise his especial friend Mr. Benedick Winter pleaded with him, to whom he yielded. Then being sent for by the King he made friends with the Consul who ever afterward showed wonderful great kindness and pleasure to the General and all his company. And so, after many troubles, on the first of February, 1594 they departed the road towards the bottom of the Straits to seek their better fortunes: and from that time they engaged many times with enemy but without success until the 8th of May, when they met with the London fleet by whom news was brought of Captain Glemham's actions.

20th August. THE LADY BRIDGET MANNERS.

The Queen is much incensed at hearing of the marriage of the Lady Bridget Manners, one of her favourite ladies-in-waiting, that took place in the country without her consent.

Two months since, the Countess of Rutland, the Lady's mother, concluded with the executors of Mr. Tyrwhitt for the wardship of his young son, and in July wrote asking that her Majesty would allow her daughter to visit her, whom she had not seen these five years. The Queen having given her consent, the Lady Bridget returned home to her mother and in a short while after is wedded to Mr. Tyrwhitt.

Now that the marriage is known, the Queen is especially enraged with the Countess, refusing to believe that she could be ignorant of it, for the marriage was in her own house, and by her own chaplain, nor will she believe that the Lady Bridget is so undutiful a daughter to have adventured so great a breach of duty without her mother's acquaintance and consent had first been obtained. Her Majesty has therefore ordered that Mr. Tyrwhitt and his wife be sent to London, the former to be committed to prison, the latter, by her favour, not imprisoned but put in custody of some lady.

A PLOT TO KILL THE QUEEN.

Captain Edmund Yorke, a prisoner, son of Sir Edmund Yorke, under examination hath confessed that he was persuaded by Father Holt to come over on the Queen's pardon, and to live in the Court, having the money due to his uncle sent for his maintenance and an assurance on oath of 40,000 crowns with present payment guaranteed by Stephen de Ibarra the Secretary of the King of Spain if he performed the required service of killing the Queen, by his own agents or by others. At the conference held thereon, Sir William Stanley and others were present; some spoke of a poisoned arrow or rapier, or a dagger as she walked in the garden. He was to serve the Earl of Essex; his fellows, Williams and Young, the Lord Chamberlain. They swore on the Sacrament to do it and were absolved by Father Holt.

He declares that one Moody has come, or soon will, to kill the Queen, when the crown will be offered to the Earl of Derby with the King of Spain's assistance. If their plot should fail they were to move some rebellion in the Earl of Derby's name, though he were not privy to it.

SUITORS AT COURT TO BE RESTRAINED.

A commandment is published by the Council to restrain the inordinate repair of multitudes of suitors coming to the Court with petitions and complaints to the Queen or the Privy Council, which for the most part are either private, unmeet to be preferred to her or for a Council of State to deal in, or such as may be decided in some of the Courts of Justice.

It is now ordered that any suitor, intending to exhibit complaint or petition, shall first acquaint one of the Masters of Requests, if any be in Court; who, with one of the Clerks of the Council, upon view and consideration, shall indorse the substance of the matter with their opinions subscribed with their hands. All suitors whose causes are neither meet to be preferred to the Queen nor heard by the Privy Council nor of any other ordinary Court of Justice or Equity shall depart and not remain about the Court upon pain of imprisonment.

The Master of Requests also to deliver the names of the parties that be rejected to the Porter that he may know whom to exclude.

21st August. A FURTHER CONFESSION OF CAPTAIN YORKE.

Captain Yorke adds to his former confession that when he was first moved to perform the service he was promised 40,000 crowns, and told that many at Court would be glad and were looking for it. Having agreed that if they would give him a resolute man to execute the part, he was promised Richard Williams, cousin to that Throckmorton who was executed in 1585. He had then asked time to consider; they replied that they made him the offer as an honour and bade him not undertake it unless he were resolved. Williams has sworn to kill the Queen, he to aid him. Moody and two others are also coming over to kill her; and, if the English should fail, a Walloon and a Burgundian are to be employed.

24th August. FURTHER CONFESSIONS OF THE PLOTTERS.

Captain Edmund Yorke adds to his former confessions that he and Williams had often wished the deed were done and they on their horses again, for they were to buy the best they could get. They resolved that when one drew sword, the other would do the same, to do the act if the other were hindered. It was plotted that Sir William Stanley should deny them a passport and that the governor of Burborow should stay them. Then Williams should seem to be in want and he would write for a pardon. Williams prevented his coming over without a passport lest he might damn himself, having taken the Sacrament to kill the Queen, by being taken and forced to confess it.

Henry Young, one of the conspirators, examined at the same time declared that at Calais Yorke said he wondered at any man's wronging his friends for a little torture, and that he was armed for any torture. He said if they were secret they might soon ride in London streets with foot-cloths of cloth of silver. Williams declared that he would die rather than betray his friends, and if he said anything when on the rack would deny all again when freed from it.

PLAYS OF THE WEEK.

The plays at the Rose Theatre this past week are *The Massacre at Paris*, *Tasso's Melancholy*, *Bellendon*, *The Ranger's Comedy*, *Galiaso*, *Cutlack*.

27th August. WILLIAMS' CONFESSION.

Richard Williams being examined hath confessed that he was sent by Father Holt and Sir William Stanley to kill the Queen, with promise of great reward, and that he received the Sacrament thereon. Later he acknowledged his confession before the Earl of Essex, declaring that he will avow it to his death, even before Yorke's face.

28th August. YORKE AND WILLIAMS CONFRONTED.

Yorke and Williams being confronted together before the Commissioners in the Tower, Yorke swears that they took the Sacrament to kill the Queen and that Williams had wished his sword in her belly. Williams denying this, Yorke tells him he denies it on account of his oath, but it was unlawfully taken and therefore may be broken.

An Order at Court.

A very special strait commandment from the Queen is given by the Lord Chamberlain that no man shall come into her presence or attend upon her Majesty wearing any long cloak beneath the knee : which order comes in a good hour for tailors, mercers, and drapers, when all men are now wearing long cloaks.

The Return of the Earl of Cumberland's Ships.

The three ships sent out at the charges of the Earl of Cumberland and his friends, the *Royal Exchange* as Admiral wherein Mr. George Cave was Captain, the *Mayflower* under conduct of William Anthony, and the *Sampson* under Nicholas Downton, have returned to Portsmouth, having set out from Plymouth at the latter end of last year.

They reported that on 13th June they met with a mighty carack of the East Indies called *Las Cinque Llagas*, or *The Five Wounds*. The *Mayflower* was in fight with her before night, and soon after the *Sampson*, never ceasing to ply her with their great ordnance until midnight when the Admiral came up and Captain Cave wished them to stay till morning, when both should give three bouts with their great ordnance and then clap her aboard.

At ten o'clock the next morning the Admiral laid her aboard in the mid-ship, the *Mayflower* coming up in the quarter, as it should seem, to be at the stern of the Admiral on the larboard side ; but her Captain was slain and the ship fell to the stern of the out-licar of the carack which, being a piece of timber, so wounded her foresail that her men said they could come no more to fight. The *Sampson* went aboard on the bow, but not having room enough her quarter lay on the *Exchange's* bow, her bow on the carack's bow. The *Exchange* also at her first coming up had her Captain shot through both legs, so that he was not able to do his office and in his absence had not any that would undertake to lead out her company to enter the carack's side. Captain Downton also had been wounded the night before, but his men were led by Captain Grant ; but his forces being small and not manfully backed by the *Exchange's* men, the enemy became bolder than he would have been, slew six and wounded many more, so that the rest returned on board and would not renew the assault.

The Portugals, thus encouraged by the slack working of our men, had barricades made where they might stand without any danger of our shot, and plied our men with fire so that most of them were burnt in some place or other, and while our men were putting out the fire, they kept on assailing them with small shot or darts. When the *Sampson's* men were not able to enter they plied their great ordnance, mounted as high as they could, and by shooting a piece out of the forecastle, they fired a mat on the carack's keal, which ran from thence to the mat on the bowsprit, and from the mat up to the wood of the bowsprit, and thence to the top sail yard, which made the Portugals to stagger and to make show of parle. But they that had the charge encouraged them that it might easily be put out, so they stood again stiffly to the defence.

Anon the fire grew so strong that Captain Downton seeing it was beyond all help, desired to be off, but had little hope of saving his ship unlit, until by the burning asunder of the sprit sail yard with the ropes and sail, whereby they were fast entangled to the carack, she fell apart. The *Exchange* also being further off from the fire was easier clear and fell off from abaft. Soon the fire crept into the forecastle of the carack where was store of Benjamin and other combustible matter which flamed and ran all over the ship so that the Portugals leapt over in great numbers. Then Captain Downton sent Captain Grant with the boat with leave to use his own discretion in saving of them. So he brought aboard two gentlemen, one an old man called Nuno Velis Pereira, who had been governor of Mocambique and Cefala in 1582; three of the inferior sort were also saved in the boat. The rest which were taken by the other boats were set ashore in the Isles of Flores.

The carack burnt all that day and the night, but next morning her powder which was lowest, being 60 barrels, blew her asunder. Some said she was bigger than the *Madre de Dios*, some that she was less; but though much undermasted and undersailed yet she went well.

On the 30th June after long traversing the seas another mighty carack was sighted which some of the company took to be the *San Philip*, the Admiral of Spain, but next day fetching up with her they found her indeed to be a carack, which after a few shot was summoned to yield, but they stood stoutly to their defence and utterly refused. Whereupon seeing that no good could be done without boarding her, Captain Downton consulted what course should be taken in her boarding, but partly because the chief captains had been slain or wounded in the former conflict, and because of the murmuring of some disordered and cowardly companions, his purpose was crossed, and the carack escaped.

After waiting about Corvo and Flores for some West Indian purchase, but being disappointed of their expectation, and victuals growing short, they returned for England.

29th August. SIR JOHN NORRIS DELAYED.

Sir John Norris who is not yet embarked for Brittany writeth from Portsmouth that his men are continuing to run away. He desires that those counties which have so little care for the furtherance of the Queen's service, as a punishment may be commanded to send as many others in the place of those missing, especially Norfolk and Suffolk. He feareth that the seamen do not well intend the service for the fort by Brest, and asketh that any pinnaces sent after them may have special charge to have greater regard to that service than to anything else, otherwise they will seek the liberty of the sea ; for he hath no authority but by bare advice to let them know what is fit for them to do, which is left to their discretion to follow.

31st August. PLAYS OF THE WEEK.

This past week the plays at the Rose were *Philipo and Hippolito*, *The Venetian Comedy*, *Godfrey of Bouloigne*, *Mahomet*, *The First Part of Tamburlane*, *Bellendon*.

3rd September. 'WILLOBIE HIS AVISA.'

A certain book entitled *Willobie His Avisa* is entered, setting out the triumphs of Avisa, a chaste British dame, over the many suitors who attempted her charity. It is believed that under guise of these suitors certain great ones are attacked, especially a young man, called 'Henrico Willobego,' with his familiar friend 'W. S.,' an old player.

DAVIS'S 'SEAMAN'S SECRETS.'

Captain John Davis hath written a book of navigation called *The Seaman's Secrets*, which he dedicates to the Lord Admiral, defending himself against the charges written by Mr. Richard Cavendish with his dying hand that he was the cause of his overthrow, and ran from him. He declares that his ship *The Desire*, separated by stress of weather and forced to seek a harbour to repair his most miserable wants, being without boats, oars, sails, cables, cordage, victuals, or health of the company sufficient for the attempt to find the North-West Passage, upon which he had set out.

In his searches for the North-West Passages where navigation must be executed in most exquisite sort, he has been enforced to search all possible means required in sailing which are here gathered in his treatise.

His book is divided into two parts ; in the first are displayed the terms of the art of navigation, the movement of the moon, the tides, the use of the compass, the cross-staff and the chart ; in the second are taught the nature and necessary use of the globe, with the circles, zones, climates and other distinctions, the perfect use of sailing, also the use of the cross-staff, the quadrant, and the astrolabe.

5th September. THE SCOTTISH KING'S SON BAPTISED.

The infant son of the King of Scotland was on 30th August baptised at Stirling, after some delays caused by the lateness of the English Ambassador in coming. The Earl of Cumberland was first chosen for this service, and had prepared himself very richly with an honourable convoy of noblemen and gentlemen of renown, but falling sick, the Earl of Sussex was sent in his place ; so it fell out that through the sickness of one nobleman and the hasty preparations of the other, the day for the baptism had constantly to be postponed.

During the time of their stay the King entertained the Ambassadors with banqueting and revelling, and, to make this occasion the more magnificent, he committed the charge of the revels to the Lord of Lendore and Mr. William Fowler, that by reason of their travels were much skilled in such things. Having consented together they concluded that the exercises should be divided into field pastimes, with martial and heroical exploits, and household with rare shows and singular inventions. At the first show, three Christians (presented by the King, the Earl of Mar, and Thomas Erskine, Esquire) were followed by three Turks and then by three Amazons, all having pages riding on their led horses, each bearing his master's *impresa* or device. The King's device was a lion's head with open eyes, which signified fortitude and vigilance. All having solemnly entered, they ran three courses at the ring and glove, and the prize was given to the Duke of Lennox.

When at last all the Ambassadors had reached Stirling the baptism was performed. The Chapel Royal had been richly hung with a royal seat of state for the King, and at his right hand a fair wide chair over which was set the arms of the King of France; next to him sat the Ambassador of England, and after him, and also on the King's left hand, the other Ambassadors. The King having taken his seat, the Ambassadors were led into the presence of the infant Prince who was carried with great ceremony into the Chapel. All being seated, Mr. Patrick Galloway, one of the King's preachers in ordinary, went up to the pulpit, and entreated upon the text of the 21st of Genesis. This done, the Bishop of Aberdeen stood up in his seat and explained the Sacrament of baptism, first in the vulgar tongue, next in Latin, that all might understand. Then the provost and the prebends of the Chapel sang the 21st Psalm. Next the Prince was baptised, being named 'Frederick Henry, Henry Frederick.' When all were again seated the Bishop went up into the pulpit where he delivered in verse a praise and commendation of the Prince, and then, turning the rest of his Latin oration into prose, he addressed the Ambassadors, beginning with the English Ambassador and so to the rest, making mention of the chronology of each of their princes, and reciting the proximity and nearness of blood they had with the King. In conclusion, when the blessing had been given, Lyon King of Arms cried with a loud voice, 'God save Frederick Henry, Henry Frederick, by the Grace of God, Prince of Scotland.'

The Prince was then carried into the King's Hall where he was dubbed Knight by his father, and proclaimed by Lyon King of Arms, Knight and Baron of Renfrew, Lord of the

Isles, Earl of Garrick, Duke of Rosay, Prince and Great Steward of Scotland.

That night was held a very magnificent banquet, at which, after the guests had refreshed themselves at the first service, there entered a blackamoor, very richly attired, drawing as it seemed, a triumphal chariot wherein stood Ceres, Fecundity, Faith, Concord, Liberality, and Perseverance, set round a table richly set out. This chariot should indeed have been drawn by a lion, but because his presence might have brought some fear to the nearest, or the sight of the lights and torches might have moved his tameness, it was thought best to supply the blackamoor in his place.

The chariot being withdrawn, a most sumptuous ship entered, her keel 18ft. long, in breadth 8 foot, and to the top of her highest flag 40 feet, and the motion so artificially devised that none could perceive what brought her in. Neptune sat in the forestern, with Thetis and Triton, and round about were all kinds of marine people, such as the sirens, and within, mariners and musicians, besides Arion with his harp. By this device was set forth the King's voyage into Norway to fetch his Queen when he was detained by the devices of witches; and as Neptune had then brought them safely home, so now he brought them such gifts as the sea affords to adorn this festival.

After these revels were ended the King and the Ambassadors went to another Hall where for the collation a most rare, sumptuous and prince-like dessert of sugar had been prepared, whence, after leave-taking and good-nights, the company departed about three o'clock in the morning.

7th September. PLAYS OF THE WEEK.

The plays this last week at the Rose were *The Jew of Malta*, *Tasso*, *Philipo and Hippolito*, *The Venetian Comedy*, *Cutlack*.

8th September. GILES FLETCHER'S 'LICIA.'

Licia or Poems of Love, in honour of the admirable and singular virtues of his Lady, to the imitation of the best Latin poets, and others, by Mr. Giles Fletcher, is sent to the press, being dedicated to the Lady Mollineux, wife of Sir Richard Mollineux. To her the author writeth in his Epistle Dedicatory that though his thoughts and some reasons draw him rather to deal in causes of greater weight, yet the present jar of this disagreeing age drives him into a fit so melancholy that he has leisure only to grow passionate.

There are some fifty-two sonnets in honour of Licia, and other poems, one being *The Rising to the Crown of Richard the Third*, spoken with his own mouth, and imitated from *Shore's Wife* and *Rosamond*.

9th September. THE COUNTESS OF RUTLAND AND THE LADY BRIDGET.

The Queen is not a little offended, thinking herself undutifully handled, because the Countess of Rutland neither answers nor obeys her command to send the Lady Bridget to London. The Lord Hunsdon hath therefore written in the Queen's name commanding the Lady to be sent up forthwith, and demanding why the order has not been obeyed hitherto.

10th September. NEWS FROM BREST.

Sir John Norris landed with new forces at Pempole on the first of the month, where he received letters from the Marshal D'Aumont and Sir Thomas Baskerville showing in what terms they lay outside Morlaix, expecting every day to be attacked by the Duke Mercury. But when the Duke Mercury heard of the coming of Sir John, he not only refrained from coming to the succour of Morlaix but withdrew his forces further away, so that those in the Castle yielded themselves when they heard of it.

11th September. SIR THOMAS WILKES TO BE SENT TO THE ARCHDUKE ERNEST.

The Queen wisheth to expostulate with the King of Spain for his barbarous action in contriving and furthering the foul and dangerous practices of Lopez and the others, and to force him either to avow it or else to cause him to correct those that were the instruments in these plots, such as Christofero de Moro, the Count Fuentes, and Ibarra. She hath resolved therefore to send Sir Thomas Wilkes, her Secretary, to the Archduke Ernest, Governor in the Low Countries for the King of Spain, to open the matter and the proofs. A special messenger is now sent requiring safe conduct for the Secretary's coming and going.

14th September. PLAYS OF THE WEEK.

The plays at the Rose this past week were *Godfrey of Bulloigne*, *Mahomet*, *Galiaso*, *Bellendon*, *Tamburlane*, *Philipo and Hippolito*.

18th September. THE WAR IN BRITTANY.

The news from Brittany is that after the taking of Morlaix Sir John Norris stayed ten days while the Marshal raised money to satisfy the men. Then Monsieur de Lyseot with some harquebusiers, aided by Sir Martin Frobisher and 400 men from the English ships, was sent forward to block up the fort of Croyzon by Brest.

The same night the Marshal with 400 French and Sir John with as many English marched to Quimpar-Corantin, and suddenly surprised the suburbs, entering them with small resistance. The town was willing to yield but the garrison would not allow them. So Sir John Norris, being still intent on some exploit against the Spaniards at the fort of Croyzon, left the town invested by the Marshal, and three English regiments; himself with one regiment and his own company of horse marched towards Croyzon and lodged there that night. He is now preparing approaches and platforms for the artillery, but much hindered by the badness of the weather.

A DUTCH MILL.

Two Dutchmen, Jacob Senoy and George Frise of Utrecht in Holland, have lately brought with them a certain mill which they have invented that will in very short time grind a greater quantity of corn than will be believed but by such as see the trial of it. These men are recommended to the Lord Mayor and Aldermen for albeit their mill most properly serveth for a camp or besieged city in time of distress yet it may serve the City of good purpose in times of frost when the mills go not. If the mill may be had at a reasonable rate it will be both a good monument to lay up in the Bridgehouse against time of need and also for use as a pattern whereby to frame others by it.

21st September. PLAYS OF THE WEEK.

The plays this past week at the Rose were *The Venetian Comedy*, *The Ranger's Comedy*, *Palamon and Arcite* (for the first time), *Tasso*, *Philipo and Hippolito*, *Godfrey of Bulloigne*.

28th September. PLAYS OF THE WEEK.

The plays this week at the Rose Theatre were *Mohamet*, *The Venetian Comedy* (twice), *Bellendon*, *The Love of an English Lady*, *The Massacre at Paris*, *Cutlack*.

30th September. THE ALCHEMIST'S BEQUEST.

Some months since one Clement Ouldfield made a bequest containing certain secrets of alchemy to Roloff Peterson of Lubec on condition of their being first offered on composition to her Majesty. The Queen now ordereth that the bequest shall be delivered unopened to the deputy of the Merchant Adventurers at Stade for Peterson; or if she is pleased to keep it, he shall receive £500 for it within six months.

THE BAD WEATHER AND THE PRICE OF GRAIN.

This summer, in May, there fell many great showers of rain, but much more in June and July; for it has commonly rained every day or night till St. James' Day. Notwithstanding there followed in August a fair harvest, but in September fell great rains, which raised high waters and bare down bridges at Cambridge, Ware, and other places. The price of grain grows to be such that a bushel of rye is sold for 5s., a bushel of wheat for six, seven and even eight shillings; this dearth according to common opinion, is caused more by means of overmuch transporting by the merchants for their private gain than through the unseasonableness of the weather.

3rd October. INMATES TO BE REMOVED.

Great inconveniences grow daily more and more by the number of inmates, and by the erecting of new tenements within the City of London, Westminster and the suburbs, which are a great cause of infection by reason of the multitude of poor people that inhabit them, many dwelling together in one small house. There was a statute made in the last Parliament for the reformation of these inconveniences and especially for the avoiding of inmates. Now, seeing that the greatest number of those dead of the late infection are out of those houses that were pestered with inmates, the Lord Mayor and the Aldermen are bidden to give order that no new persons shall be admitted to these tenements in the room of those that are deceased.

5th October. PLAYS OF THE WEEK.

The plays this past week at the Rose were *Tamburlane*, *Galiaso*, *Doctor Faustus*, *The Ranger's Comedy*, *The Venetian Comedy*, *The Love of a Grecian Lady*.

6th October. LE ROY'S 'OF THE INTERCHANGEABLE COURSE OF THINGS.'

Mr. Robert Ashley hath translated into English and dedicated to Sir John Puckering, the Lord Keeper, a book entitled *Of the Interchangeable Course or Variety of Things*, first written in French by Louis le Roy.

Herein are surveyed the variety of tongues and arts, the state of arms, and learning, of religion in former ages compared with the present, concluding in the last chapter that the truth has not yet been thoroughly discovered, neither all knowledge fore-stalled by our forerunners. The learned therefore should add by their own inventions what is wanting in the sciences, doing for posterity that which Antiquity did for us, to the end that learning be not lost, but day by day receive some increase.

12th October. PLAYS OF THE WEEK.

The plays at the Rose this week were *Godfrey of Bulloigne*, *Philipo and Hippolito*, *Tasso*, *Doctor Faustus*, *The Venetian Comedy*.

15th October. THE LADY BRIDGET AT COURT.

The Countess of Rutland is come to London with the Lady Bridget. Mr. Tyrwhitt, who has been sick in prison, now begins to sue for liberty and the Lord Chamberlain promises to move the Queen on his behalf.

18th October. CAPTAIN ANTHONY WINGFIELD SLAIN.

From Brittany the news is that on the 6th October the enemy assaulted the trenches before Croyzon but were beaten back with the loss of 7 or 8 men, but on our side was killed Captain Anthony Wingfield, the Sergeant-Major General, who was shot by a cannon shot from the garrison, as he stood with his rapier drawn, which was by the shot beaten through his bowels.

Captain Wingfield hath served the Queen with great reputation in the wars of the Low Countries, Portugal and France. It is noted at his last going into Brittany that he so disposed of his estate as if he were never to return, and on the day of his death he took such order for his debts as if he had a presage of his end.

The next day the Marshal D'Aumont and Sir Henry Norris with the rest of the English regiments came up from Quimpar that is now taken and were quartered at Croyzon. Four days were now spent in mounting the artillery and making platforms for them to play. On the 12th the enemy made a sally upon the trenches of the French who not having the leisure to arm themselves lost between 30 and 40 men, and as many wounded; from thence they advanced towards the English trenches but were repulsed with the loss of 10 or 12.

19th October. PLAYS OF THE WEEK.

The plays this past week at the Rose Theatre were *Bellendon*, *Mohamet*, *Tamburlane* (twice), *Palamon and Arcite*, *The French Doctor*.

20th October. THE DISRESPECT OF THE ARCHDUKE ERNEST.

The messenger that was despatched to the Archduke Ernest to require a safe conduct for Sir Thomas Wilkes is returned with a passport in ample style, and a letter from the Archduke that greatly displeaseth her Majesty, for on perusing it she found the style and form far inferior to that which she expected from the Duke, being barely addressed *Royne D'Angleterre*, and omitting all the honours formerly given her in all letters sent by Emperors and Kings. Moreover the Archduke expressed in his letter that he expected to have nothing propounded that might be to the disservice to the King of Spain. She hath determined to deal no more in this way, but in a more public manner to declare to the world how far the King was directly touched by these foul practices.

The messenger is now sent back with the passport and a bare and meagre letter to Monsieur Richardott, one of the Duke's Council, signed by the Lord Treasurer, the Earl of Essex, the Lord Buckhurst, the Vice-Chamberlain and Sir Robert Cecil.

In this letter it is written that at some other time the Queen might have overlooked the style and form but she is too tender of the greatness of her state, being by God an anointed Queen over Kingdoms and countries, to disregard so notorious an omission of her dignities whether made by error or of purpose.

As for the Archduke's expectation to have nothing propounded to him that might be to the disservice to the King of Spain, the matters are in very truth such as, without some extraordinary course taken by the King for his clearing, there will be left upon him a most notorious and foul imputation in the judgment of the whole world. The Queen is resolved to trouble the Duke neither with letter or with message any more, being now rather through his cold and unrespectful manner towards her (which she little expected at his hands) induced to look for small indifference at his hands. She hath reserved to herself a further consideration how the same may be made known, even according to the naked truth confessed and sealed with the blood of the conspirators, without any addition or colouring of anything therein.

25th October. PLAYS OF THE WEEK.

The plays this last week at the Rose were *The Jew of Malta*, *Doctor Faustus*, *A Knack to Know an Honest Man* (for the first time), *Tasso*, *The Love of an English Lady*, *Galiaso*.

NASHE'S 'TERRORS OF THE NIGHT.'

Nashe's book *The Terrors of the Night, or a Discourse of Apparitions*, wherein he describeth the nature of dreams, spirits, prophecies and omens, is entered, being dedicated to Mistress Elizabeth Carey, daughter to the Knight Marshal.

The spirits of fire are by nature ambitious, with a humour of monarchising that maketh them affect rare qualified studies; many atheists are with these spirits inhabited. The spirits of water be dull and phlegmatic; and all rheums, dropsies and gout of their engendering; seafaring men are their chief entertainers, and greedy vintners likewise, who having read no more Scripture than that miracle of Christ's turning water into wine at Canaan, think to do a far stranger miracle than ever He did by turning wine into water. Spirits of the earth do especially infect soldiers, for they delight in nothing but iron and gold. As for the spirits of the air, in truth they be all show and no substance, deluders of the imagination, and nothing else; carpet knights, politic statesmen, women and children they most converse with.

Of conjurors and cunning men, Nashe saith that they ascend by degrees, first raking a dunghill from which to temper up a few ointments and syrups, until as their fame grows, at last they set up a conjuring school, and all malcontents intending evasive violence against their prince and country run headlong to this oracle. As for the interpretation of dreams and the arts of physiognomy and palmistry, this is the sum of all; some subtle humorist to feed fantastic heads with innovations and novelties first invented this childish gloss upon dreams and physiognomy, wherein he strove only to boast himself of a pregnant, probable conceit beyond philosophy or truth.

31st October. SIR JOHN NORRIS'S ATTACK ON THE FORT AT CROYZON.

From Brittany it is reported that an assault on the fort of Croyzon was begun on 23rd October. This place is very strongly defended, defended by water on two parts, and the rest as strong as could be made by art or charge. On the south front of the fort are two exceedingly strong bastions, that on the west having frontage of 17 paces, that on the east 10 paces; the curtain between them 37 ft. thick at top, and within these they have a very large entrenchment. The bastions are well defended on the flanks by the water and great ordnance. Our trenches were within four paces of the counterscarp, the French being on the east side, the English on the west, with the battery between them.

On that day the artillery began to play and fired some 700 shot but did so little harm that scarcely any breach appeared; but as the cannon beat upon the parapet and some of the flankers, some 400 men, commanded by Captain Lister, were sent to view it, and to see if they could hold the counterscarp. Thereupon many of the men and the gallants, thirsty after honour and desirous to achieve something further, having possessed themselves of the enemy's counterscarp, undertook the breach as well, and, notwithstanding the inaccessibleness of the place and the great resistance of the enemy, most of them reached the very top and held it for a time, though afterwards they were repulsed, so that six of the officers were killed and some 16 or 18 soldiers, and twelve other officers were hurt or burned with powder.

This attempt was made by the Englishmen only on the bastion of the west side, for the Frenchmen never attempted anything against their bastion, alleging that it was not assailable.

The next day the Marshal and Sir John seeing the little effect that the artillery wrought, devised to make a mine against the east bastion towards the French trenches.

2nd November. PLAYS OF THE WEEK.

The plays at the Rose Theatre this last week were *Palamon and Arcite*, *The French Doctor*, *A Knack to Know an Honest Man* (twice), *Godfrey of Bulloigne*, *Bellendon*.

3rd November. THE SERMON AT PAUL'S CROSS.

The sermon at Paul's Cross was this day preached by Dr. John Dove, on the Second Coming of Christ, and the disclosing of Antichrist, taking as his text I. John ii., verse 18. He spoke very strictly of those that buy patronages of Church livings to give them to base, ignorant, and beggarly men, who would easily accept of benefices upon unlawful conditions. In concluding he demonstrated at length that the Bishop of Rome was that Antichrist spoken of in the Revelations.

A PETITION AGAINST A NEW THEATRE.

Learning that some intend to erect a new theatre on the Bankside the Lord Mayor hath written to the Lord Treasurer begging him rather to suppress all stages than to erect any more. Nor will he allow the defence of these plays alleged by some that the people must have some kind of recreation and that policy requires idle and ill-disposed heads to be directed from worse practise by this kind of exercise. These plays, saith he, are so corrupt, profane, containing nothing else but unchaste fables, lascivious devices, shifts, cozenage, and matter of like sort that only the base and refuse sort of people, or such young gentlemen as have but small regard for credit or conscience, are drawn thither. Hence plays are become the ordinary place of meeting for all vagrant persons and masterless men, that hang about the City, thieves, horse stealers, whoremongers, cozeners, conny-catching persons, practisers of treason and such like; there they consort and make their matches. Nor can the City be cleansed of this ungodly sort (the very sink and contagion not only of the City but of the whole realm) so long as plays of resort are by authority permitted.

4th November. THE STATE OF IRELAND.

From Ulster it is reported by Sir Richard Bingham that the great ones are of late more openly showing themselves in nature of a rebellion than at first; and it seems that it will be necessary for the Queen to take up the matter by correcting the offenders, for her subjects there have been promised peace, and by degrees much violence has been committed. But if the Queen and the Council wish the Lord Deputy to do anything against the Ulster men let him be given all due assistance and countenance that he might with less strength and time go through with it. The province of Connaught is generally first.

9th November. PLAYS OF THE WEEK.

The plays at the Rose this last week: *Tamburlane*, *Doctor Faustus*, *Mahomet*, *The Knack to Know an Honest Man*, *Caesar and Pompey* (for the first time), *Palamon and Arcite*.

15th November. THE ASSAULT ON THE FORT AT CROYZON.

It is reported from Brittany that Croyzon is taken. By the 7th November the mine being reasonably well perfected, it was determined to begin the battery again with the resolution that so soon as the mine (which was made against the bulwarks opposite the French trenches) should be blown up, the French should attack that part, the English their bastion; and others with scaling ladders should make attempts in every corner so that the defenders should be assailed on every part. But the Marshal being that day sick sent in the morning to our General, showing him that he had learned that Don John d'Aquila, General of the Spaniards, was marching with his Spaniards to rescue Croyzon and had already reached La-coman, a village within five leagues. He therefore advised our General to defloge to Croyzon, thinking it unfit to hazard any more men with so strong an enemy at hand ready to join battle.

But Sir John, nothing daunted, answered that it would be a dishonour to abandon the siege and that if the fort were taken the enemy would have little purpose in coming any nearer. He so importuned the Marshal that he gave him the ordering of that day's service. The General immediately commanded the cannoneers to begin the battery; and every man was assigned his charge, some to the assault, others with scaling ladders to attempt to make entry. By 12 o'clock he gave order for the mine to be fired which albeit it did not do so much as was expected, yet it gave easy access to the French. On the other bulwark our men led by Captain Lathom, Captain Smith, and Captain John Norris, with other gentlemen, assailed the bulwark and continued the assault until at half past four they made entry, and seized upon three ensigns that were there, putting every man they found to the sword, except a certain Alferez. Some of the Spaniards leapt from the rocks into the water, but the mariners in their small boats met them and slew them. Three or four were taken and their lives spared, for no man was slain in cold blood.

In this fight there were slain four officers, eight gentlemen of the General's own company, besides other gentlemen and some 20 or 30 private soldiers. There are wounded Sir Thomas Baskerville who by his bravery won the admiration of all men, Sir Martin Frobisher, and Captains Norris, Brett and Smith.

Throughout the siege the enemy were worthy of all praise, especially their commander; they never showed themselves daunted, and made sundry sallies, mostly on the French, with great resolution. In the last assault, fifty of them were slain by the cannon, but they never quailed until their commander was killed shortly before the entry of our men. By that time the greater part were slain, the rest, overtired and hurt, were forced to give way before our gallants. There were killed of the Spaniards in this fort nearly 400.

The next day the fort was destroyed and the force moved from Croyzon to join the rest of the army and to wait for what the enemy should attempt; but two days afterwards he withdrew five leagues further off. The day after the fight Don John d'Aquila sent a trumpet to redeem his prisoners, to whom our General answered that their ransoms were already paid and that he was now ready and at leisure to fight with him. The three Spanish ensigns he hath sent into England to be presented to the Queen.

16*th November.* PLAYS OF THE WEEK.

The plays at the Rose this last week were *The Venetian Comedy*, *Tasso*, *The Grecian Comedy*, *Caesar and Pompey*, *Bellendon*, *Dioclesian* (for the first time).

17*th November.* MEASURES AGAINST VAGRANTS AND BEGGING POOR.

The Lord Mayor hath written to the Council asking that the measures proposed against vagrants may be approved.

THE QUEEN'S ACCESSION DAY.

This day, on the anniversary of her accession thirty years before, the Queen gave a great banquet. The three flags captured from the Spaniards in Brittany have been presented to her.

19*th November.* SPENSER'S 'AMORETTI' AND 'EPITHALAMIUM.'

Mr. Edmund Spenser's *Amoretti* together with his *Epithalamium*, written in honour of his own wife that he married in July last, are sent to the press.

THE FIFTY-FOURTH SONNET.

Of this world's theatre in which we stay,
My love like the spectator idly sits
Beholding me that all the pageants play,
Disguising diversely my troubled wits.
Sometimes I joy when glad occasion fits,
And mask in mirth like to a comedy :
Soon after when my joy to sorrow flits,
I wail and make my woes a tragedy.
Yet she beholding me with constant eye,
Delights not in my mirth nor rues my smart :
But when I laugh she mocks, and when I cry
She laughs, and hardens evermore her heart.
What then can move her ? If not mirth nor moan,
She is no woman but a senseless stone.

20*th November.* THE USE OF THE CITY GARNERS REFUSED.

When of late Sir Francis Drake and Sir John Hawkins demanded the use of the garners and bakehouses in the Bridgehouse to bake bread for the fleet about to be set forth, the Lord

Mayor refused the same. He allegeth that these garners and bakehouses were built solely for the use of the poor in times of scarcity who would be utterly disappointed if they should be employed for any other use. At the same time he hath petitioned the Lord Treasurer that the corn for the fleet may be bought from Kent or other shires and not in the City. Sir Francis and Sir John purpose to make their provision out of the wheat brought from foreign parts for the benefit of the City, and have already bought some, enforcing the same to a lower price than is usual or can be well afforded; hereby the merchants shall be discouraged from bringing in any more.

23rd November. PLAYS OF THE WEEK.

At the Rose Theatre this past week: *The French Doctor*, *Doctor Faustus*, *The Knack to Know an Honest Man*, *Dioclesian*, *The Grecian Comedy*.

27th November. THE LADY BRIDGET MANNERS.

The Queen hath caused the Lady Bridget Manners to be set free; Mr. Tyrwhitt was released some days since on the mediation of his friends and in respect of his sickness. Her Majesty now bids the Lord Hunsdon to write to the Countess of Rutland in her name that she imputes the fault more to her than to the young couple, for though the Lady Bridget took the fault on herself to excuse her mother, yet the Queen is well assured that the Lady Bridget would never have married without her mother's consent. There now remains only that the Countess should send for the Lady Bridget from the Countess of Bedford, and the sooner the better, and her husband will come down with her.

30th November. PLAYS OF THE WEEK.

The plays at the Rose this last week were *Caesar and Pompey*, *The Venetian Comedy*, *Tamburlane*, *Warlamchester* (twice), *The Knack to Know an Honest Man*.

A CONFERENCE ABOUT THE SUPPRESSING OF ROGUES.

Since the Council approve the measures proposed against vagrants the Lord Mayor hath summoned the Justices of Middlesex and Surrey to meet with him and with the Lord Chief Justices touching the orders to be put in execution for the apprehending and suppressing of vagrant persons and the begging poor.

It is proposed that precise and strait charge shall be given to every several ward that watch and ward be continued from 9 or 10 of the clock at night till 6 in the morning, and the day watch to begin when the night watch giveth over, and to give over again when the night watch beginneth. For the better furnishing and executing of these watches the constable shall be compelled to execute his office not by deputy but in his own person, as the execution thereof by deputy constables is thought to be an occasion of great negligence and abuse in this service.

The watches shall make continual searches at times convenient in all victualling houses, tippling cellars and other places likely to entertain idle and suspicious persons, men, women and children. Those that shall be found not able to give an account of some dwelling-place and honest faculty to live by but shall appear to be vagabonds, rogues and idle beggars, having able bodies, them shall the watch commit to Bridewell, there to be kept till the morning following; what time the constables with other honest persons of the same watch shall resort thither, there to charge them before those who are farther authorized to proceed against them for their lawful punishment.

The Lord Mayor, sheriffs or justices of the peace shall come to Bridewell or other place appointed where the vagabonds shall be brought before them; for the law doth require the presence of some of them at the least at the convicting of such persons. There shall they determine for their enlargement or punishing or both; and that shall be done in as short a time as possibly may be for the easing of the place whither they shall be committed and of the charges that they shall otherwise be put to by the restraining of them.

For the better and more speedy avoiding of such vagabonds present consideration shall be had of some bodily labour to set them on work, as by beating of hemp, scouring the town ditches, abating the shelves in the river Thames, or such other, wherein no detriment can be done by them, in case they should demean themselves wilfully or negligently; which otherwise in matter of art they might and are likely to do. The young ones that can more easily be reclaimed and enforced shall be appointed to some occupation. Women walkers that be of the City or suburbs shall be forced to abide at their prescribed dwelling-places in some honest labour, making of flax, spinning, or such like.

2nd December. A PROCLAMATION AGAINST FIREARMS.

The great disorders in different parts of the realm, and especially in the City of London and the highways towards it, have caused much terror to all people professing to travel and live peaceably. A proclamation is now published reaffirming the former proclamations against the carrying of dags and longer pieces, such as calivers, in times and places not allowable for service, and against the carrying of small or pocket dags and the wearing of privy coats of armour. Yet is it to be allowed to those who come to the musters to serve as horsemen with dags, and also to any of the Queen's ministers or their servants for their more surety to carry her treasure or bring her revenue to places appointed, provided always that the dags be carried openly and manifestly seen.

DE LA MARCHE'S 'THE RESOLVED GENTLEMAN.'

The Resolved Gentleman, first written in French in 1483 by Oliver de la Marche who served Philip, and his son, Charles, Dukes of Burgundy; hence translated into Spanish verse by Don Hernando de Ancunia, and now with additions Englished by Mr. Lewis Lewkenor is entered, being dedicated to the Lady Hune, Countess of Warwick. In this allegorical fiction the author depicteth those qualities which sustain a man against the misfortunes of life, accident and old age; the evils of a courtly life; the blessings of memory, and the like, ending with a prophecy of the Destinies concerning Queen Elizabeth.

6th December. SIR W. RALEGH'S COMMISSION.

A commission is granted to Sir Walter Ralegh to prepare and arm two ships and two small pinnaces in which to do her Majesty service against the King of Spain and his subjects. As his own ability is not sufficient to furnish out such vessels, and he is driven to use the assistance of friends to adventure with him, the Queen for his satisfaction and their assurance further promises that he and they shall enjoy to their own use all goods and merchandise, treasure, gold, silver, and whatever else may be taken by him or his associates, either by sea or land, from the subjects of the King of Spain, after paying such customs and duties as appertain. He is given full power and authority over all captains, masters, mariners, and others, who are commanded to obey him. Whatever he shall do by virtue of his commission for the furtherance of the service and the enfeebling of the subjects and adherents of the King of Spain, he and all who serve under him shall be clearly acquitted and discharged.

7th December. PLAYS OF THE WEEK.

The plays at the Rose Theatre this last week were *The Grecian Comedy*, *The Wise Man of West Chester* (for the first time, twice) *Tasso*, *Mahommed*.

8th December. THE DEATH OF CARDINAL ALLEN.

It is reported that Cardinal Allen hath died at Rome, whereat the Catholics make great lamentation. He was in the sixty-third year of his age and is buried in the English Church of the Holy Trinity.

William Allen, commonly called the Cardinal of England, was born in the county of Lancashire of honest parents and allied by kindred to some noble families. He was brought up at Oriel College in Oxford, where in Queen Mary's time he was proctor of the University, and afterwards a Canon in the Church of York. When religion changed in England, he departed the land, and professed divinity at the University of Douay in Flanders that was founded two and thirty years since. He procured the seminary for the English to be founded at Douay, and the second seminary at Rheims, the third at Rome, and two others in Spain, for the conservation of the Romish religion in England, for the zeal whereof he cast off both his love for his country and his duty to his Prince, instigating both the King of Spain and the Pope of Rome to the conquest of England. Upon that account he engaged himself in dangerous counsels and designs for which Pope Sixtus V. honoured him with the title of Cardinal of St. Martin in the Mounts.

When the Invincible Armada threatened England he it was that brought into the Low Countries that Bull of Excommunication against the Queen, causing it to be printed in English;

and withal he wrote an admonition to the English to adhere to the Pope and the Spaniard. But being disappointed of his hopes he returned to Rome, there greatly wearied by the dissensions and animosities of English fugitives, as well students as gentlemen.

14th December. REVELS TO BE HELD AT GRAY'S INN.

The gentlemen at Gray's Inn, after many consultations, have now determined to hold revels this Christmastide, and more especially as these pastimes have been discontinued for three or four years. They make choice of Mr. Henry Helmes, a Norfolk gentleman, one accomplished with all good parts, a very proper man of personage, and very active in dancing and revelling, to be elected their 'Prince of Purpool' and to govern the state for the duration of the revels. Privy Councillors and all officers of state, of the Law and of the household are assigned to him, and an invitation in the form of a privy seal dispatched to the Gentlemen of the Inner Temple, bidding them appoint an Ambassador to be a minister of correspondence between the two houses or kingdoms.

PLAYS OF THE WEEK.

The plays this past week at the Rose were *Doctor Faustus*, *The Jew of Malta*, *Caesar and Pompey*, *Warlamchester*, *The Knack to Know an Honest Man*, *The Set at the Maw* (for the first time).

20th December. THE REVELS AT GRAY'S INN.

The revels were begun this night. The Prince of Purpool with all his train marched from his lodging to the great Hall and there was installed on his Throne, under a rich cloth of State, with his councillors and great lords about him and before, the rest of his officers taking their places as belonged to their condition. Then the trumpeters were commanded to sound thrice, which being done, the King at Arms, in a rich surcoat, stood forth before the Prince and proclaimed his style. After this entered the Prince's champion in complete armour, on horseback, and so came riding about the fire and in the midst of the Hall made his challenge and then departed.

King at Arms having next blazoned the Prince's Arms, the Attorney stood up and made a speech of gratulation, wherein he showed what happiness was like to ensue by the election of so noble and virtuous a Prince as then reigned over them. To whom the Prince answered that he did acknowledge himself to be deeply bound to their merits, and in that regard did promise that he would be a gracious and loving Prince to so well deserving subjects. Then the Solicitor, having certain great old books and records before him, made a speech to the Prince showing the names of such homagers or tributaries as held lordships, and the services belonging thereto.

Alfonso de Stapulia and Davillo de Bernardia held the Archdukedoms of Stapulia and Bernardia, being there to right and relieve all wants and wrongs of all ladies, matrons and maids within the said Archduchy.

Marotto Marquarillo de Holborn held the Manors of High and Nether Holborn by Cornage in *capite*, rendering on the day of the Prince's Coronation for every of the Prince's pensioners one milk-white doe.

Lucy Negro, Abbess de Clerkenwell, held the Nunnery of Clerkenwell by night service in *cauda*, and to find a choir of nuns with burning lamps to chant *placebo* to the gentlemen of the Prince's Privy Chamber on the Coronation day.

Cornelius Combaldus de Tottenham held the Grange of Tottenham in free and common soccage by the twenty-fourth part of a night's fee, and by rendering to the Master of the Wardrobe so much conny fur as would serve to line his nightcap and face a pair of mittens.

Bawdwine de Islington held the town of Islington by grand sergeantry, rendering at the Coronation, for every maid in Islington continuing a virgin after the age of fourteen years, one hundred thousand million sterling.

Then was a Parliament summoned, but certain necessary officers being absent, the purpose was frustrated, except that a subsidy was granted by the Commons, and the Prince gave his gracious and free pardon, which was read by the Solicitor, and after a further short speech the Prince called for his Master of Revels, and willed him to pass the time in dancing. So the gentlemen pensioners and attendants, very gallantly appointed, in thirty couples, danced the old measures, and their galliards and others kinds of dances, revelling until it was very late, when it pleased the Prince to take his way to his lodging, with the sound of trumpets and his attendants.

21st December. PLAYS OF THE WEEK.

The plays at the Rose Theatre this last week were *Tamburlane*, *The Second Part of Tamburlane*, *Doctor Faustus*.

24th December. 'A CONFERENCE ABOUT THE NEXT SUCCESSION.'

There are being circulated in England some copies of a book called *A Conference about the next Succession to the Crown of England*, dedicated to the Earl of Essex, which was published abroad and written by one N. Doleman, who is believed to be Parsons the Jesuit.

The alleged occasion of the treatise was a meeting in Amsterdam after the late Parliament of certain gentlemen of divers nations qualities and affections, who, hearing that the question of the succession had not been settled by the Parliament in England, began to debate the matter, and especially two lawyers, who agreed that each should deliver his opinion on the case, the one considering the principles of succession, the other the claims of those who pretend to the succession in England.

The first argueth that government by nearness of blood is not the law of nature nor is it divine law; and being only by human law, might upon just causes be altered, and the King deposed. The second, enumerating those who have claim by birth and family, noteth the King of Scots, whose favourers (of whom there are but few in England) believe him the first and chiefest pretender. In this line also is the Lady Arabella Stuart, whom the Lord Treasurer is supposed to favour.

The Puritans at home are thought to be the most vigorous of the parties in religion, having a great part of the best captains and soldiers on their side; but the Catholics by reason of the persecution of seminarists are also strong. The Earl of Beauchamp and the Earl of Derby have some voices, as also the Earl of Huntingdon.

But whoever shall succeed it is likely that the affair cannot be ended without war at the first. As for the future he conjectureth that if a foreign Prince be admitted, the Infanta of Spain is likest to bear away the prize; if, on the other side, one of the domestical competitors, the second son of the Earl of Hertford, or the issue of the Countess of Derby.

26th December. AN ATTEMPT TO MURDER THE FRENCH KING.

From France it is reported that on 17th December a young man, one John Chastel, seminary of the Jesuit College at Claremont, attempted to murder the French King, piercing his cheek with a poniard, and breaking some of his teeth. This Chastel has been tried and executed by the French Parliament, and their decree is now translated and published in English. He was condemned to go before the principal gate of the chief church in Paris, and there, naked to his shirt, with a burning torch of wax of the weight of two pounds, on his knees to acknowledge and confess that wretchedly and traitorously he had attempted the most inhuman and most abominable parricide, and that with a knife he wounded the King in the face. Also that being falsely instructed and persuaded he had affirmed that it was lawful to kill the King, and that King Henry the Fourth, now reigning, was not in the Church until he had received approbation of the Pope; whereof, and every part whereof, he repented and asked forgiveness of God.

This done he was to be conveyed in a tumbril to the place called the Greve; there to have his arms and his thighs rent with burning pincers, and his right hand holding the knife wherewith he had endeavoured to have committed the parricide to be cut off. Then his body to be drawn in sunder and dismembered by four horses, and his carcase and quarters cast into the fire, and so consumed into ashes; and the said ashes to be scattered in the wind. Before the execution of this sentence he was to be put to the torture ordinary and extraordinary thereby to find out the truth of his confederates.

It was also ordained that all priests and scholars of the College of Claremont, and all others that entitled themselves to the Society of Jesus, as corrupters of youth, disturbers of common quietness, and enemies to the King and the State, should within three days after notice of this decree depart out of all towns and places where their colleges were situate, and within fifteen days more out of the whole realm.

27th December. PLAYS OF THE WEEK.

The plays at the Rose this past week were *The Grecian Comedy*, *The Siege of London*, *Doctor Faustus*.

28th December. THE CHAMBERLAIN'S PLAYERS AT COURT.

The Lord Chamberlain's players acted before the Court at Greenwich on St. Stephen's Day, among them being Richard Burbage, William Kemp, and William Shakespeare.

GRAY'S INN REVELS: A NIGHT OF ERRORS.

This night there was a great presence of Lords, Ladies and Worshipful personages, expecting some notable performance, especially after the common report of that which had gone before, but the multitude of beholders was so great that the inventions and conceits could not be performed. Against these performances the Emperor of the Inner Temple sent his Ambassador who was very graciously welcomed by the Prince.

But when the shows were to begin there arose a disordered tumult and crowd upon the stage whither came so great a throng of worshipful personages that might not be displaced, and gentlewomen whose sex did privilege them from violence that when the Prince and his officers had in vain a good while endeavoured reformation at length there was no hope of redress. The Lord Ambassador and his train thought themselves not so kindly entertained as was before expected, and thereupon would not stay any longer but departed in a sort discontented and displeased.

After their departure the tumults somewhat ceased, though still so much as was able to confound any good inventions. In regard whereof, and especially since the sports were intended for the gracing of the Templarians, it was thought good not to offer anything of account saving dancing and revelling with the gentlewomen. After which a *Comedy of Errors* (much like to the *Menechmus of Plautus*) was played by the players. So the night was begun and continued to the end in nothing but confusion and errors, whereupon it was called 'The Night of Errors.'

30th December. DR. FLETCHER ELECTED BISHOP OF LONDON.

Dr. Richard Fletcher, Bishop of Worcester, hath been elected Bishop of London.

PLAYS AT THE ROSE.

Yesterday at the Rose they played *The Wise Man of West Chester*, and to-day *The First Part of Tamburlane*.

SOMEWHAT TO READ FOR THEM THAT LIST

'THE DISPLAY OF FOLLY.'

The Display of Folly, by one O. B., in which under the form of a dialogue, Huddle and Dunstable, two old men, the one a retired gentleman, the other a middling or new upstart franklin, discourse upon the follies and vices of the time, especially amongst the wanton gentlemen of the City. The dedication is to the Earl of Essex.

BARNFIELD'S 'AFFECTIONATE SHEPHERD.'

The Affectionate Shepherd, by Richard Barnfield, containing the very passionate complaints of Daphnis the shepherd for the boy Ganymede, that he would forsake Queen Gwendolen to be his love ; and followed by 'The Shepherd's Content,' or the happiness of a harmless life, written upon occasion of the former subject, which endeth :

Thus have I showed, in my country vein,
The sweet content that shepherds still enjoy,
The mickle pleasure and the little pain,
That ever doth await the shepherd's boy :
His heart is never troubled with annoy ;
He is a king for he commands his sheep ;
He knows no woe, for he doth seldom weep.

He is a courtier, for he courts his love ;
He is a scholar, for he sings sweet ditties ;
He is a soldier, for he wounds doth prove ;
He is the fame of towns, the shame of cities ;
He scorns false fortune, but true virtue pities ;
He is a gentleman, because his nature
Is kind and affable to every creature.

Who would not then a simple shepherd be,
Rather than be a mighty monarch made ?

Since he enjoys such perfect liberty
As never can decay, nor never fade :
He seldom sits in doleful cypress shade,
But lives in hope, in joy, in peace, in bliss,
Joying all joy with this content of his.

But now good fortune lands my little boat
Upon the shore of his desired rest :
Now must I leave awhile my rural note,
To think on him whom my soul loveth best ;
He that can make the most unhappy blest ;
In whose sweet lay I'll lay me down to sleep,
And never wake till marble stones shall weep.

BARWICK'S 'BRIEF DISCOURSE.'

A Brief Discourse concerning the force and effect of all manual weapons of fire, written by Humphrey Barwick, Gentleman, Soldier, Captain, in which he contesteth the opinions set forth by Sir John Smythe, and Sir Roger Williams; the former holding that the long bow of England was the only weapon in the world for the obtaining of battles and victories in these days, the latter accepting weapons of shot except the musket.

Captain Barwick showeth from his experiences of the wars (which began at the age of 18 in 1548) the greater worth of weapons of fire, being more certain and more deadly, and urging that there should be more men trained in their use. As for Sir John Smith's saying that harquebusiers could give their volleys but at eight, ten or twelve yards while archers could wound and sometimes kill at nine, ten or eleven score, he would stand at six score yards distant from the best archer, armed but in pistol proof, and let him shoot ten arrows one after another at him, and if he stirred from his place let him be punished.

As for those gentlemen and soldiers that reason from their knowledge and experience in the Low Countries and other Civil Wars, and who hold that the like discipline hath not been seen neither in this age nor in any before, and seem thereby to disgrace some more ancient and of greater experience in service than themselves, their knowledge, saith Captain Barwick, is not so worthy as that got in the greater armies of Princes whose subjects were both rich and loyal.

'The Death of Usury.'

The Death of Usury, wherein are shown reasons against usurers from the jurists, divine and civil, and the statutes now in force concerning usury, being printed at Cambridge.

Grassi's 'True Art of Defence.'

Giacomo de Grassi His True Art of Defence, being translated from the Italian by I. G., gentleman, and dedicated to the Lord Burgh, governor of the Brille, in an epistle by Thomas Churchyard. Herein is described the manner of single combat with the single rapier or single sword, the rapier and dagger, the sword and buckler, the sword and square target, the sword and round target, the case of rapiers ; the two-hand sword, and the weapons of the staff as the bill, the partisan, the halberd, and javelin ; together with a treatise of deceit or falsing ; and a mean how a man may practise himself to get strength, judgment and activity.

Hooker's 'Ecclesiastical Polity.'

Of the Laws of Ecclesiastical Polity, by Richard Hooker. Dr. Hooker saith that he undertook this book because of the wonderful zeal and fervour wherewith the Puritans withstand the received orders of the Church of England ; which led him to a consideration of their claiming that every Christian man standeth bound to enter in with them for the furtherance of the 'Lord's Discipline.' But after with travail and care he had examined the reasons he concludeth to set down this, as his final persuasion is that the present form of Church government which the laws of the land have established is such as no law of God nor reason of man hath hitherto been alleged of force sufficient to prove that they do ill who to the uttermost of their power withstand the alteration thereof. Contrariwise, the other which men are required to accept is only by error and misconceit named the ordinance of Jesus Christ ; no one proof is as yet brought forth whereby it might clearly appear so in very deed.

The work is four books, with a long preface to the Puritans wherein Dr. Hooker runneth through the history of the Puritan discipline from the time of Calvin, showing their doctrines which are based upon the Bible only (for they think no other writings in the world should be studied), and in rites and ceremonies professing their hatred of all conformity with Rome. The pretended end of their civil reformation is that Christ may have dominion over all, and the means whereby they allure and retain so great multitudes most effectual. They show a wonderful zeal towards God, a hatred of sin, and a singular love of integrity, which men think to be much more than ordinary in them by reason of the custom which they have to fill the ears of the people with invectives against their authorized guides. They bountifully relieve the broken estates of such needy creatures as are apt to be drawn away; and they show a tender compassion for the miseries of the poorer sort, over whose heads they use to pour down showers of tears in complaining that no respect is had unto them, that their goods are devoured by wicked cormorants, their persons had in contempt, all liberty both temporal and spiritual taken away from them, and that it is high time for God now to hear their groans and send them deliverance.

In the first of the four books that follow are considered laws and their several kinds in general; in the second is answered the position of those who urge reformation, in that Scripture is the only rule of all things which in this life may be done by men; in the third is answered the assertion of those who hold that in Scripture there must be of necessity contained a form of Church polity, the laws whereof may in no wise be altered. The fourth book answereth the assertion that the Church polity of the Established Church is corrupted with papist orders, rites and ceremonies.

LAMBARD'S 'EIRENARCHA.'

A new edition of *Eirenarcha, or of the office of the Justices of Peace*, by William Lambard of Lincoln's Inn, having been gathered in 1579, first published in 1581, and now revised according to the reformed Commission of the Peace.

Eirenarcha is written in four books; the first containing a theoric of the office of the Justices of the Peace; the second, the practique of one Justice of the Peace out of the Sessions; the third the practique of two or more Justices out of the Sessions; the fourth book intreating of the Sessions of the Peace and of things incident or belonging thereunto.

MARLOWE AND NASHE'S 'DIDO, QUEEN OF CARTHAGE.'

The Tragedy of Dido, Queen of Carthage, a play written by Christopher Marlowe and Thomas Nashe, and sometime played by the Children of Her Majesty's Chapel.

'THE ORCHARD AND THE GARDEN.'

The Orchard and the Garden, containing certain necessary, secret and ordinary knowledge in grafting and gardening. Herein the author giveth directions for the preparing of the soil and the divers fashions and ways of grafting. To make cherries grow without stones, pare a little cherry tree of one year old at the stump, and cleave it asunder from the top to the root, which do in May; and make an iron fit to draw the heart or marrow from both sides of the tree; then tie it fast together and anoint it with ox dung or loam; and within a year after, when it is grown and healed, another little tree of the same should be grafted upon it; so shall it bring forth fruit without stones.

'THE BATTLE OF ALCAZAR.'

The Battle of Alcazar, fought in Barbary, between Sebastian, King of Portugal and Abdelmelec, King of Morocco; with the death of Captain Stukeley, a play written by George Peele, and sundry times played by the Lord Admiral's men.

PERCY'S 'SONNETS TO THE FAIREST COELIA.'

Sonnets to the Fairest Coelia, by William Percy, containing twenty sonnets in which he vainly begs his mistress's favour; the last ending:

> Receive these writs, my sweet and dearest friend,
> The lively patterns of my liveless body,
> Where thou shalt find in hebon pictures penn'd,
> How I was meek, but thou extremely bloody.
> I'll walk forlorn along the willow shades,
> Alone complaining of a ruthless dame;
> Wherere I pass, the rocks, the hills, the glades,
> In piteous yells shall sound her cruel name.
> There will I wail the lot which fortune sent me,
> And make my moans unto the savage ears,

The remnant of the days which nature lent me,
I'll spend them all, conceal'd, in ceaseless tears.
Since unkind fates permit me not t'enjoy her,
No more, burst eyes, I mean for to annoy her.

PRESENT REMEDIES AGAINST THE PLAGUE.'

Present Remedies against the Plague. In this little book the people are advised to keep their houses, streets, yards, backsides, sinks and kennels sweet and clean from all standing puddles, dunghills, and corrupt moistures ; and not to let dogs, which be a most apt cattle to take infect of any sickness, to come running into the house. Rooms should be aired with charcoal fires, made in stone pans or chafing dishes, and not in chimneys. Of remedies against the plague a good preservative is to chew the root of angelica, setwall, gentian, valerian or cinnamon : to eat a toast of bread, sprinkled with red rose vinegar, buttered and powdered with cinnamon, and eat fasting ; to drink rue, wormwood, and scabias, steeped in ale a whole night and drunk fasting every morning, or the water of *carduus benedictus*, or *angelica*, mixed with *mithridatum*.

'A TRUE REPORT OF SUNDRY HORRIBLE CONSPIRACIES.'

A little book is published entitled *A True Report of sundry Horrible Conspiracies of late time detected to have* (*by barbarous murders*) *taken away the life of the Queen's most excellent Majesty*. It manifestly appeareth to the world how unjust and dishonourable the King of Spain and his ministers' actions are against the Queen of England ; for contrary to all warlike, princely, manlike and Christian examples in any wars or other contentions he has attempted to take her life not by arms or other warlike actions but by secret murder, hateful to God and man from the beginning of the world. Bernardine Mendoza and other of the King of Spain's ministers are shown participant in the conspiracies of Lopez and his fellows, and Ibarra with Yorke and Williams.

THE ENVOY

I HEAR new news every day, and those ordinary rumours of war, plagues, fires, inundations, thefts, murders, massacres, meteors, comets, spectrums, prodigies, apparitions, of towns taken, cities besieged in *France*, *Germany*, *Turkey*, *Persia*, *Poland*, *&c.* daily musters and preparations, and such like, which these tempestuous times afford, battles fought, so many men slain, monomachies, shipwrecks, piracies, and sea-fights, peace, leagues, stratagems, and fresh alarms. A vast confusion of vows, wishes, actions, edicts, petitions, lawsuits, pleas, laws, proclamations, complaints, grievances, are daily brought to our ears. New books every day, pamphlets, currantoes, stories, whole catalogues of volumes of all sorts, new paradoxes, opinions, schisms, heresies, controversies in philosophy, religion, &c. Now come tidings of weddings, maskings, mummeries, entertainments, jubilees, embassies, tilts and tournaments, trophies, triumphs, revels, sports, plays: then again, as in a new shifted scene, treasons, cheating tricks, robberies, enormous villanies in all kinds, funerals, burials, deaths of Princes, new discoveries, expeditions; now comical then tragical matters. To-day we hear of new Lords and officers created, to-morrow of some great men deposed, and then again of fresh honours conferred; one is let loose, another imprisoned; one purchaseth, another breaketh; he thrives, his neighbour turns bankrupt; now plenty, then again dearth and famine; one runs, another rides, wrangles, laughs, weeps, &c. Thus I daily hear, and such like, both private and publick news.

Democritus Junior. To the Reader.

ABBREVIATIONS

The following abbreviations have been used for authorities which are frequently cited :

A.P.C. *Acts of the Privy Council,* edited by J. R. Dasent, 1900, etc.

A.R. *A Transcript of the Registers of the Company of Stationers of London ;* 1554-1640 A.D. Edited by Edward Arber, 5 vols. 1875-1894.

CAMDEN'S ELIZABETH. *The History of the Most Renowned and Victorious Princess Elizabeth, late Queen of England . . . composed by way of annals.* By William Camden. Translated into English, 1630, etc.

BIRCH'S MEMOIRS. *Memoirs of the Reign of Queen Elizabeth from the year 1581 till her Death . . . from the original papers of his [the Earl of Essex's] intimate friend, Anthony Bacon, Esquire, and other manuscripts never before published.* By Thomas Birch, D.D. 2 vols. 1754.

D'EWES JOURNALS. *A Compleat Journal of the Votes, Speeches and Debates both of the House of Lords and House of Commons throughout the whole Reign of Queen Elizabeth.* Collected by . . . Sir Simonds D'Ewes, Baronet. Published by Paul Bowes, of the Middle Temple, Esq. 1693.

FUGGER NEWS LETTERS (2nd Series). *Fugger News Letters, being a further selection from the Fugger papers especially referring to Queen Elizabeth.* Edited by Victor von Klarwill. Translated by L. S. R. Byrne, 1926.

HAKLUYT. *The Principal Navigations, Voyages, Traffiques and Discoveries of the English Nation.* By Richard Hakluyt. References to the edition in 8 vols. in the Everyman Library, 1907, etc.

HENS. DIARY. *Henslowe's Diary.* Vol. i., The Text ; vol. ii., The Commentary. Edited by W. W. Greg, 1904-7.

MIDDLESEX SESSIONS ROLLS. *Middlesex County Records.* Vol i., *Indictments, Coroner's Inquests post mortem, and recognizances from 3 Edward VI. to the end of the reign of Queen Elizabeth.* Edited by John Cordy Jeaffreson, 1886.

PROCLAMATIONS. *A Book containing all such Proclamations as were published during the Reign of the late Queen Elizabeth. Collected together by the industry of Humphrey Dyson, of the City of London, Publique Notary,* 1618. This is an actual collection, not a printed book : references are to the manuscript pagination of the volume in the British Museum (G. 6463).

RYMER'S FŒDERA. *Fœdera, conventiones, literæ, et cuiuscumque generis Acta Publica inter Reges Angliæ et alios quosuis . . .* ex schedis Thomæ Rymer potissimum edidit Robertus Sanderson, 2nd edition, 1727.

S.P. DOM. *State Papers Domestic.* Abstracted in the *Calendar of State Papers Domestic.*

S.P. FOREIGN. *State Papers Foreign.* There is as yet no Calendar or abstract of this collection in the Record Office.

ABBREVIATIONS

SALISBURY PAPERS. *Historical Manuscripts Commission. Calendar of the Manuscripts of the Marquis of Salisbury preserved at Hatfield House*, 1892.

SIEGE OF ROUEN. *Journal of the Siege of Rouen*, 1591. *By Sir Thomas Coningsby.* Edited by J. G. Nichols. Camden Miscellany, vol. i. 1847.

STOW'S ANNALS. *Annales or a General Chronicle of England.* By John Stow, 1592, etc. As there are several editions both of Stow and Camden, and references are quite easy to find, I have not specified particular editions or pages.

STRYPE, ANNALS. *Annals of the Reformation . . . during Queen Elizabeth's happy reign.* By John Strype, 4 vols. 1731 and 7 vols. 1824. [The later edition marks the pagination of the earlier; my references are therefore to the earlier.]

TOWNSHEND. *Historical Collections, or, An exact account of the Four Last Parliaments of Queen Elizabeth* . . . Faithfully and laboriously collected by Heywood Townshend, Esq., a Member in those Parliaments, 1680.

Apart from a few details, there is nothing in Townshend which is not more fully reported in D'Ewes, but I have thought it best to give references to both.

UNTON CORRESPONDENCE. *Correspondence of Sir Henry Unton, Knt, Ambassador from Queen Elizabeth to Henry IV., King of France, in the years* 1591 and 1592. Edited by Rev. Joseph Stevenson, Roxburgh Club, 1847.

NOTES

1590

A Brief Survey of the Year 1590. Camden's *Elizabeth*. The Catholic League had been formed in 1589 when, on the death of the Duke of Anjou, Henry of Navarre (a Protestant) became heir to Henry III. Civil war followed between Henry III. and the League, whose leaders were the Dukes of Guise and Mayne. Shortly afterwards Henry III. was assassinated, leaving his throne to Henry of Navarre. With the aid of Queen Elizabeth (£22,000 in gold and 4,000 men) he defeated the Leaguers at Arques and invested Paris, but being unable to draw Du Mayne to a pitched battle, he withdrew. The English army having done notable service was disbanded, and a way thereby left open for the Spaniards.

1591

1st January. The Privy Council. *A.P.C.*, xxii. 3, under date 1st October, 1591, where the name of Sir Robert Cecil (sworn 2nd August) is added.

Dr. Sutcliffe's 'Treatise of Ecclesiastical Discipline.' Matthew Sutcliffe, *A Treatise of Ecclesiastical Discipline*, 1591, dated 1st January, 1590[-1], in the Epistle Dedicatory. Entered 3rd July. A good statement of the case of the Church of England against the Presbyterian Discipline.

13th January. Stepney's 'Spanish Schoolmaster.' *A.R.*, ii. 573. William Stepney, *The Spanish Schoolmaster*, 1591. A racy little book, giving the Spanish equivalent of those intimate inquiries which the provident traveller makes on arriving at his inn ; also the necessary dialogue for a brief wooing of the chambermaid.

14th January. The Murder of the Lord Burke. See 25th January.

23rd January. Wright's 'Pilgrimage to Paradise.' *A.R.*, ii. 573. Leonard Wright, *The Pilgrimage to Paradise*, 1591.

25th January. The Trial and Condemnation of Cosby. *The Arraignment, Examination, Confession and Judgment of Arnold Cosbye*, entered on 25th January, the day of the trial. This sensational case inspired two ballads, entered on 26th January, and 6th February, and three pamphlets.

27th January. Cosby Hanged. As for 25th January.

30th January. Sir Edmund Yorke sent to the French King. Rymer, xvi. 89.

1st February. Drayton's 'Harmony of the Church.' *A.R.*, ii. 574. M.D., *The Harmony of the Church*, 1591. The Epistle is dated 10th February. Drayton is a notable exception to the rule *poeta nascitur non fit*.

3rd February. Flesh Prohibited during Lent. *Proclamations*, 289. See Appendix I., p. 395.

A Proclamation against Piracy. *Proclamations*, 288.

9th February. JOB HORTOP'S 'TRAVELS.' Job Hortop, *The Travels of an Englishman*, 1591. Another version came out the same year under the title *The Rare Travels of Job Hortop an Englishman, who was not heard of in three and twenty years space.* Both books were printed for William Wright, but neither has the printer's device; the first book is a more polished effort than the second; the present entry is founded on both.

FRAUNCE'S 'COUNTESS OF PEMBROKE'S IVYCHURCH' AND 'EMANUEL.' *A.R.*, ii. 575. Abraham Fraunce, *The Countess of Pembroke's Ivychurch*, and *The Countess of Pembroke's Emanuel*, 1591. For an account of Fraunce see D.N.B. Jonson's comment to Drummond was 'that Abram Francis in his English Hexameters was a fool'; he was at least a very persevering enthusiast. The Countess of Pembroke was an admirable and justly famous lady, but she was partially responsible for the continuance of the attempt to foist classical metres on to the English tongue.

13th February. A PETITION OF THE SKINNERS. *Salisbury MSS.*, iv. 91.

20th February. THE SCOTTISH KING'S POOR ESTATE. Rymer xvi. 148. Approximate date.

26th February. HARINGTON'S 'ORLANDO FURIOSO.' *A.R.*, ii. 576. The editor of *Nugae Antiquae* received this well-known story from a Mr. Walker, who had it from the Earl of Charlemont. It is clear from some references in *Nugae*, and from the prefatory stanzas in Book xxviii. of the translation, that the story is not without foundation. 'That John Harington's *Ariosto* under all translations was the worst,' said Jonson to Drummond.

11th March. PURITAN DISCONTENTS. *Birch's Memoirs*, i. 62. From a letter written to Anthony Bacon, from London, dated 11th March, 1591.

12th March. RUMOURS. *S.P. Dom. Addenda*, xxxii. 7.

22nd March. TOWN GOSSIP. *S.P. Dom.*, ccxxxviii. 82. (Phellippes.) Thomas Phellippes held a post in the Customs, but was employed by Lord Burghleigh as an expert decipherer of captured papers. He used also to send news-letters to spies abroad. These news-letters are particularly valuable summaries of contemporary gossip, as Phellippes had special opportunities for obtaining information.

25th March. COCKAINE'S 'TREATISE OF HUNTING.' Sir Thomas Cockaine, *A Short Treatise of Hunting*; dated 1591 on title-page; 31st December, 1590, in the preface.

30th March. THE SOLDIER'S PAY. *A.P.C.*, xxi. 15.

31st March. CAPTAIN GLEMHAM'S EXPLOITS. The date is approximate. *The Honourable Actions of E. Glemham, Esquire, against the Spaniards*, 1591. Entered 29th April; a ballad on the same subject was entered on 12th May. After putting into Algiers to refit, Glemham returned to England in 1592, having captured a ship laden with spices on the way. The cargo on arrival in London was claimed by Philippo Corsini, representing the Venetian traders, and a lawsuit followed. I suspect that both pamphlet and ballad were inspired by commercial interests to cover a somewhat shady transaction. See 17th May, 1592, and 19th August, 1594.

3rd April. INSTRUCTIONS FOR SIR R. WILLIAMS. Rymer, xvi. 94.

A FRAY AT LIMEHOUSE. *Middlesex Sessions Rolls*, i. 193.

14th April. A QUARREL IN THE PRESENCE. *A.P.C.*, xxi. 53.

16th April. SENTENCES AT THE SESSIONS. *Middlesex Sessions Rolls*, i. 193. Several other cases of rape committed on children are recorded.

24th April. A PROCLAMATION AGAINST TRADING WITH THE FRENCH REBELS. *Proclamations*, 291.

26th April. A PROCLAMATION AGAINST UNAUTHORISED POSTS. *Proclamations*, 293.

29th April. 'THE SHEPHERD'S STAR.' *A.R.*, ii. 579. Thomas Bradshaw, *The Shepherd's Star*, 1591. A dull work.

30th April. FLORIO'S 'SECOND FRUITS.' John Florio, *Florio's Second Fruits*, 1591; so dated in the Epistle to the reader. Florio is more concerned with wit than utility in his phrases; still the book is a good example of the conversation of bright young men, such as Shakespeare heard at Southampton's house in '93-'94 and transmuted into the *Sonnets*, *Venus and Adonis* and *Love's Labours Lost*. Florio enters Southampton's service shortly afterwards.

2nd May. LODGE'S 'ROBERT, DUKE OF NORMANDY.' Thomas Lodge, *The History of Robert, Second Duke of Normandy*, 1591; dated 2nd May, 1591, in the Epistle Dedicatory. A gruesome yarn but well told.

3rd May. BRETON'S 'BOWER OF DELIGHTS.' *A.R.*, ii. 581. N.B., Gent., *Britton's Bower of Delights*. Modern edition by A. B. Grosart in *The Complete Works of Nicholas Breton*, 1876. See note on 12th April, 1592.

8th May. THE FRENCH KING'S ORDINANCES. *Ordinances set forth by the King, for the rule and government of his Majesty's men of war*, 1591. Entered *S.R.*, 8th May.

CARTWRIGHT THE PURITAN BEFORE THE HIGH COMMISSION. *Lansdowne MSS.*, lxviii.; printed in A. F. Scott Pearson, *Thomas Cartwright and Elizabethan Puritanism*, 1925, p. 458.

12th May. RIPLEY'S 'COMPOUND OF ALCHEMY.' *A.R.*, ii. 582. George Ripley, *The Compound of Alchemy*, 1591. Jonson makes effective play with all this apparatus in the *Alchemist*.

15th May. THE 'CENTURION'S' FIGHT WITH FIVE SPANISH SHIPS, *A.R.*, ii. 582. *The valiant and most laudable fight performed in the Straights, by the 'Centurion' of London against five Spanish Gallies. Who is safely returned this present month of May. Anno. D. 1591.* Entered 15th May; a ballad was entered at the same time.

16th May. AN INVASION EXPECTED. *A.P.C.*, xxi. 133.

19th May. A SEDITIOUS FELLOW. *Middlesex Session Rolls*, i. 195.

21st May. THE QUEEN at THEOBALD'S Nicholls' *Progresses*, vol. ii; Strype's, *Annals*, iv, 77.

RUMOURS. *S.P. Dom.*, ccxxxviii. 159. (Phellippes.) For an account of the trial of the witches see 29th February, 1592.

24th May. DR. GERVASE BABINGTON'S SERMON. Gervase Babington, *A Sermon preached at the Court at Greenwich the xxiiii of May, 1591.* On this occasion no virtue at all in IF!

26th May. SIR R. WILLIAMS COMMENDED. *A.P.C.*, xxi. 167.

THE GALLANT ACTION OF SIR R. WILLIAMS. Antony Colynet, *The True History of the Civil Wars of France*, 1591, p. 532.

31st May. RUMOURS. *S.P. Dom.*, ccxxxviii. 188. (Phellippes.)

1st June. SIDNEY'S 'ASTROPHEL AND STELLA.' Sir Philip Sidney, *Astrophel and Stella*, 1591. Modern editions by A. Feuillerat, 1922, etc. Nashe's preface is included in *The Works of Thomas Nashe*, edited by R. B.

M'Kerrow, 1905, vol. iii. The date here given for the publication of *Astrophel and Stella* is a guess; the evidence, such as it is, being (*a*) a sneer at alchemists in Nashe's preface, possibly a reference to Ripley (see 12th May); (*b*) the publication of Breton's *Bower of Delights* (see 3rd May), evidently written at the time of Sidney's death, suggests a particular revival of interest at this time; (*c*) a second edition of *Astrophel* was issued during 1591, but without Nashe's effusion; the first therefore was presumably issued some little time earlier. *Astrophel and Stella* is the most important volume of poetry published during this year; hereafter for the next five years all the pet poets litter sonnets in Paul's Churchyard.

5th June. THE TAKING OF GUINGCAMP. *The True Report of the service in Brittany. Performed lately by the Honourable Knight Sir John Norris and other Captains and Gentlemen soldiers before Guingcamp*, 1591. Entered 5th June.

6th June. UNLAWFUL GAMES TO BE PUT DOWN. *A.P.C.*, xxi. 174.

23rd June. LEONARD DIGGES' 'TECTONICON.' *A.R.*, ii. 585. *A Book named Tectonicon*, Leonard Digges, 1591.

25th June. THE TERMS OF AGREEMENT FOR THE DESPATCH OF FURTHER TROOPS TO NORMANDY. Rymer, xvi. 102, 127. Newhaven was the Elizabethan name for Le Havre.

1st July. RUMOURS. *S.P. Dom.*, ccxxxix. 70. (Phellippes.)

5th July. THE WAR IN BRITTANY. *A Journal, or brief report of the late service in Britaigne, by the Prince de Dombes, General of the French King's Army in those parts, assisted with Her Majesty's forces at present there under the conduct of Sir John Norris: advertised by letters from the said Prince to the King's ambassador here resident with Her Majesty and confirmed by like advertisements from others, imployed in that service. Published to answer the slanderous bruits raised of late by some evil affected to that and other good actions undertaken against the enemy of God's true Religion*. 1591. Entered 5th July. A piece of Privy Council propaganda; the book was entered in the *Stationers' Register* 'by order of the Council under Master Wilks his hand, one of the clerks to the Council.' The 'slanderous bruits' seem to have been caused by a feeling that the English casualties were not justified by the results obtained.

16th July. A CONSPIRACY FOR PRETENDED REFORMATION. Richard Cosin, *The Conspiracy for Pretended Reformation*, dated on the title-page 30th September, 1591, published 1592; a long and detailed account of the whole affair, from which Camden apparently draws. See also Stow's *Annals*, Camden's *Elizabeth*, *A.P.C.*, etc.

19th July. RUMOURS. *S.P. Dom.*, ccxxxix. 93. (Phellippes.)

24th July. SIR HENRY UNTON MADE AMBASSADOR TO THE FRENCH KING. *Unton Correspondence*, p. 1. It has been pointed out to me that ambassadors' letters and instructions were secret documents and therefore not general gossip; still, seven years later John Chamberlain had a wide knowledge of confidential news. Even during the Great War indiscreet revelations by Cabinet Ministers and political jackals were not unknown.

25th July. A RESTRAINT OF PLAYING. *A.P.C.*, xxi. 324.

26th July. THE TRIAL AND CONDEMNATION OF WILLIAM HACKET. Richard Cosin, *The Conspiracy for Pretended Reformation*, 1592.

28th July. THE EXECUTION OF HACKET. Authorities as for 16th July. There seems to have been a recognised etiquette in quartering. Prisoners who annoyed the crowd, or the authorities, were quartered living; but as a mark of favour those who behaved in a markedly courageous and seemly manner (*e.g.* by praying for the Queen or expressing genuine repentance) were allowed to hang until they were dead or at least insensible.

29th July. COPPINGER DIES IN PRISON. Authorities as for 16th July. For the connection of Hacket and his companions with the Puritan leaders see A. F. Scott Pearson, *Thomas Cartwright and Elizabethan Puritanism*, 1925.

2nd August. SIR ROBERT CECIL A PRIVY COUNCILLOR. *A.P.C.*, xxi. 358.

3rd August. A SUSPECTED PORTUGUESE. *S.P.D.*, ccxxiv. 123. See also 23rd January, 1594.

7th August. AN ASSAULT IN ST. PETER'S, WESTMINSTER. *Middlesex Sessions Rolls*, i. 194.

A BUILDING ALLOWED IN BLACKFRIARS. *A.P.C.*, xxi. 367.

13th August. ANDRADA'S DECLARATIONS. *S.P. Dom.*, ccxxxix. 135. See 24th January, 1594, the case of Dr. Lopez. Don Antonio was the pretender to the throne of Portugal. To carry the war into the enemy's country, Drake and Norris, joined by the Earl of Essex, led a great expedition in 1589 to Portugal. But though the English soldiers showed great valour, the voyage was a signal disaster. The Portuguese lacked enthusiasm; and out of 11,500 men 6000 died, mostly from disease. Since then Don Antonio had remained an unwelcome pensioner in England. See pages 115, 278, 280.

20th August. A QUACK FIGURE CASTER. *A.P.C.*, xxi. 409.

21st August. THE QUEEN ON PROGRESS. *The Honourable Entertainment given to the Queen's Majesty in Progress at Cowdray in Sussex by the Right Honourable the Lord Montacute*, 1591; modern editions in Nichols' *Progresses of Queen Elizabeth*, vol. ii.; and *The Works of John Lyly*, edited by R. W. Bond, 1902, who believes that these entertainments are of Lyly's devising; the evidence does not seem strong. Both this pamphlet and the account of the entertainment at Elvetham (see 24th September) went into further editions.

22nd August. THE BORDEAUX WINE FLEET TO BE STAYED. *A.P.C.*, xxi. 413.

28th August. MR. THOMAS CAVENDISH'S EXPEDITION. Hakluyt, viii. 289.

31st August. RUMOURS. *S.P. Dom.*, ccxxxix. 159.

3rd September. ILLEGAL BUILDING IN LONDON. *A.P.C.*, xxi. 422.

4th September. THE EARL OF ESSEX IN FRANCE. *Siege of Rouen*, p. 13 *et seq.*

6th September. THE QUEEN DISCONTENTED AT THE ILL SUCCESS IN FRANCE. *Unton Correspondence*, 59.

10th September. NEWS FROM FRANCE. *Siege of Rouen*, p. 21 *et seq.*

12th September. MR. WALTER DEVEREUX SLAIN. *Memoirs of Robert Cary*, King's Classics, 1905, p. 14.

12th September. THE BORDEAUX WINE SHIPS TO SAIL IN CONSORT. *A.P.C.*, xxi. 442.

13th September. THE EARL OF ESSEX REBUKED. *Unton Correspondence*, p. 72.

16th September. A PROCLAMATION AGAINST SUPPLYING THE KING OF SPAIN WITH CORN. *Proclamations*, 296. The opening words of this proclamation are a good example of the doctrine of 'God's own Englishmen.'

21st September. A SECRET MARRIAGE. *S.P. Dom.*, ccxl. 17. This Mr. Thomas Shirley was one of the three famous brothers, and father of the dramatist; Captain Anthony Shirley (see pages 41, 298), who distinguished himself in the French war, was another.

24th September. THE QUEEN, ON PROGRESS, VISITS ELVETHAM. *The Honourable Entertainment given to the Queen's Majesty at Elvetham in Hampshire, by the Right Honourable the Earl of Hertford*, 1591; modern editions in Nichols' *Progresses*, vol. ii., also in *The Complete Works of John Lyly*, edited by R. W. Bond, 1902, i. 421. From the tone of the pamphlet, it seems to have been written by one of the household. It was entered on 1st October, and went into three editions the same year. The song, 'With Fragrant Flowers,' is attributed to Thomas Watson in *England's Helicon*, and *Coridon and Phillida* to Breton.

29th September. THE BEACON WATCHES. *A.P.C.*, xxi. 470.

30th September. DR. COSIN'S 'THE CONSPIRACY FOR PRETENDED REFORMATION.' Richard Cosin, *The Conspiracy for Pretended Reformation*, 1592. 30th September is the date given on the title-page.

2nd October. THE CAPTURE OF GOURNAY. *Unton Correspondence*, p. 96. Gournay was captured on 26th September.

4th October. THREE OF LYLY'S PLAYS TO BE PRINTED. *A.R.*, ii. 596. John Lyly, *Endymion*, 1591; *Galathea*, 1592; *Midas*, 1592. Modern edition by R. W. Bond in *The Complete Works of John Lyly*, 1902, vols. ii. and iii. The importance of this publication has been generally overlooked. Lyly's plays were written for a courtly audience and not acted on the public stages, and might not therefore be expected to appeal to the usual play-going public. The printer realised that the publication was an experiment, and appealed for support—'I refer it [*Endymion*] to thy indifferent judgment to peruse, whom I would willingly please. And if this may pass with thy good liking, I will then go forward to publish the rest. In the meantime let this have thy good word for my better encouragement.' The printed drama, in short, now becomes literature, and not merely the book of words of a stage play.

7th October. A CASE OF SORCERY. *Middlesex Sessions Rolls*, i. 197.

10th October. THE BORDEAUX WINE FLEET. *A.P.C.*, xxii. 17.

16th October. THE EARL OF ESSEX TAKES LEAVE OF HIS ARMY. *Siege of Rouen*, p. 23.

17th October. THE BORDEAUX WINE FLEET. *A.P.C.*, xxii. 30.

20th October. THE LOSS OF THE 'REVENGE.' Sir Walter Ralegh, *The Report of the Truth of the Fight about the Azores*, 1591. Entered 23rd November; reprinted in *Hakluyt's Voyages*. This date is approximate, but Phellippes, writing on 31st October, says the news is now stale. Probably some of the survivors reached London before the main fleet came to Plymouth.

22nd October. An Affray at Westminster. *Middlesex Sessions Rolls*, i. 200.

25th October. Precautions against Disorder at the Ports. *A.P.C.*, xxii. 37.

27th October. Disorders at Dartmouth. *A.P.C.*, xxii. 44.

28th October. The Trial of Brian O'Rourke. Stow, *Annals*. See page 3 and 3rd November.

31st October. Rumours. *S.P. Dom.*, ccxl. 53. (Phellippes.) Sir William Stanley being governor of Deventer had betrayed it to the Spaniards in 1587. They pensioned him with the intention of using his services for the proposed invasion of England.

1st November. Father Jennings, a Notable Jesuit, taken. *Cath. Rec. Soc.*, v. 206. Topcliffe was in charge of the counter-recusant secret police; he greatly distinguished himself by his success in rounding up the Jesuits who came over with Fr. Campion in 1580, and since then had enjoyed considerable extra-legal power. He was expert in the methods of the 'third degree' and had certain special tortures of his own; see p. 140.

3rd November. The Earl of Essex in Normandy. *Siege of Rouen*, p. 29.

The Execution of O'Rourke. Stow, *Annals*.

4th November. An Affray near Whitehall. *Middlesex Sessions Rolls*, i. 200.

Spanish Disasters. Walter Ralegh, *The Report of the Truth of the Fight about the Azores*, 1591.

'Medius' Printed. William Byrd, *Liber Secundus Sacrarum Cantionum*, 1591.

5th November. A Proclamation against Vagrant Soldiers. *Proclamations*, 300. In this company are to be found such ex-soldiers as Ancient Pistol (after Agincourt), Brainworm, Peter Skirmish (of the *Puritan Widow*) and other stage worthies.

Measures of Relief for Returned Soldiers. *A.P.C.*, xxii. 58.

8th November. Southwell's 'Mary Magdalen's Funeral Tears.' *A.R.*, ii. 598. Robert Southwell, *Mary Magdalen's Funeral Tears*, 1591.

15th November. Spanish Losses. Strype, *Annals*, iv. 77.

20th November. The Death of Sir Christopher Hatton. Camden's *Elizabeth*, Stow's *Annals*. See page 152-3.

21st November. The Proclamation against Jesuits. *Proclamations*, pp. 298, 301. Strype's *Annals*, iv. 56, 62.

25th November. The Siege of Rouen. *Siege of Rouen*, pp. 33-47. Gabriel D'Estrée was Henry's mistress.

26th November. The Queen's Letters to the Emperor of Russia. *S.P. Dom.*, ccxl. 70.

Abuses in the Cloth Trade. *A.P.C.*, xxii. 89.

The Charges of the Bordeaux Fleet. *A.P.C.*, xxii. 86.

4th December. A Petition of the Puritan Prisoners. *Lansdowne MSS.*, lxviii., printed in A. F. Scott Pearson, *Thomas Cartwright and Elizabethan Puritanism*, 1925, p. 470.

Orders for Reforming the Army in Normandy. *A.P.C.*, xxii. 98.

5th December. An Unsuccessful Ambuscade at Rouen. *Siege of Rouen*, p. 52.

6th December. Greene's 'A Maiden's Dream.' *A.R.*, ii. 600. Robert Greene, *A Maiden's Dream*, 1591. This professional ululation in form parodies in anticipation some of the most notable English elegies, *Lycidas*, *Adonais*, and *The Vision of Judgement*—Southey's. Modern editions in A. B. Grosart, *The Complete Works of Robert Greene*, 1881 ; and J. C. Collins, *The Plays and Poems of Robert Greene*, 1905.

10th December. Seven Catholics Executed. *The Life and Death of Mr. Edmund Geninges . . .* at S. Omers, 1614. *Cath. Rec. Soc.*, v. 206. See 1st November.

13th December. Greene's 'Notable Discovery of Cosnage,' and 'The Second Part of Conny-Catching.' *A.R.*, ii. 600. Robert Greene, *A Notable Discovery of Cosnage*, 1591, and *The Second Part of Conny-Catching*, 1592. Modern editions by A. B. Grosart in *The Complete Works of Robert Greene*, 1881 ; and *The Bodley Head Quartos*, vol. i., 1923. Though entered together, the *Notable Discovery* was evidently published some little time before the *Second Part*. Both pamphlets went into second editions in 1592. There were two important results of Greene's conny-catching pamphlets ; they turned the attention of the gentleman reader, now beginning to grow weary of *Arcadia* and *Euphues*, to new interests, and they attracted a new kind of reader. Greene's previous works, *The Mourning Garment* and *Never Too Late*, were dedicated to the gentlemen scholars of both Universities ; now he successfully appeals to merchants, apprentices, farmers, and plain countrymen. The conny-catching pamphlets are a symptom of the reaction to realism which was the first stage towards the satires and the humour plays at the end of the century.

15th December. The Defence of Plymouth. *A.P.C.*, xxii. 121.

A Negligent Commissary Dismissed. *A.P.C.*, xxii. 125.

16th December. Sir Christopher Hatton's Funeral. Stow, *Annals*.

17th December. Masterless Men in the City to be taken up. *A.P.C.*, xxii. 129.

18th December. Two Suspected Recusants. *A.P.C.*, xxii. 131.

A Notable Instance of the Corruption of these Wars. *Siege of Rouen*, page 60.

19th December. Further Measures against Recusants. *A.P.C.*, xxii. 138.

21st December. Masterless Men to be taken up in Kent. *A.P.C.*, xxii. 150.

24th December. A High-handed Arrest. *A.P.C.*, xxii. 151.

26th December. The Tripoli Merchants recommended to Charity. *A.P.C.*, xxii. 158.

Beacon Watches. *A.P.C.*, xxii. 160.

29th December. GOODS RIFLED FROM PRIZES IN CORNWALL AND DEVON TO BE RESTORED. *Proclamations*, p. 302.

31st December. THE SIEGE OF ROUEN. *Siege of Rouen*, page 56.

SOMEWHAT TO READ FOR THEM THAT LIST

Under this heading are grouped some of the more interesting books that appeared during the year, which were not entered in the Stationers' Register *and cannot be more accurately dated.*

CLAPHAM'S 'NARCISSUS.' John Clapham, *Narcissus*, 1591. This is one of several poems, written during these years, wherein the physical attraction of male youth is unduly glorified. See also *Cephalus and Procris* (p. 263), *Arisbas* (p. 264), *The Affectionate Shepherd* (p. 344); Shakespeare's *Sonnets*; Marlowe's *Edward II.*, and *Hero and Leander*; and E. K.'s gloss on Hobbinol in the first month of *The Shepherd's Calendar*.

COSIN'S 'APOLOGY FOR SUNDRY PROCEEDINGS.' Richard Cosin, *An Apology: of and for sundry proceedings by Jurisdiction Ecclesiastical*, 1591. This was Whitgift's reply to Burleigh's criticism of his persecution of the Puritans; see page 16.

DIGGES' 'PANTOMETRIA.' Thomas Digges, *A Geometrical practical treatise named Pantometria*, 1591. A learned and finely printed folio.

GARRARD'S 'ART OF WAR.' William Garrard, *The Art of War*, 1591, so dated on title-page, dated 1590 in the Epistle to the reader. A complete and important military manual, with many diagrams. Anyone who had studied the elaborate numerical diagrams, illustrating the formation of troops in close order, in this and the other military manuals of the time would realise why Iago called Cassio a 'great arithmetician.'

GIBBON'S 'WORK WORTH THE READING.' *A Work worth the Reading*, 1591. The question of the right of parents to enforce a marriage on their children was much discussed at this time, especially after the sensational murder of old Mr. Page of Plymouth by his girl-wife Ulalia in 1590, recorded in ballads, a pamphlet, and afterwards in a play (now lost) by Jonson and Dekker. Deloney in writing a suitable dying speech for the murderer lays the ultimate responsibility for the murder on the girl's parents. See page 246.

GILES FLETCHER'S 'OF THE RUSSE COMMONWEALTH.' Giles Fletcher, *Of the Russe Commonwealth*, 1591. Reprinted in Hakluyt.

QUERCETANUS' 'SPAGERIC PREPARATION OF MINERALS, ANIMALS, AND VEGETABLES.' Joseph Du Chesne, *A Brief Answer*, etc., and *The True and Perfect Spageric*, 1591.

'THE TROUBLESOME REIGN OF KING JOHN.' *The first part* and *the second part of The Troublesome Reign of King John*, 1591. Modern edition in Farmer's Facsimile Reprints, 1911.

WILMOT'S 'TANCRED AND GISMUND.' Robert Wilmot, *The Tragedy of Tancred and Gismund*, 1591. Modern edition by W. W. Greg, The Malone Society, 1914.

1592

1st January. SPENSER'S 'DAPHNAIDA.' Edmund Spenser, *Daphnaida*, 1591. Modern edition by J. C. Smith and E. de Selincourt in *The Poetical Works of Edmund Spenser*, 1916 ; etc.

3rd January. ANOTHER PROCLAMATION AGAINST THE DISORDERS AT PORTS. *Proclamations*, p. 303.

7th January. THE LEVANT COMPANY. *S.P. Dom.*, ccxli. 11.

THE COMMISSION AGAINST JESUITS RENEWED. *A.P.C.*, xxii. 174.

MR. HENRY CAESAR RELEASED. *A.P.C.*, xxii. 174.

9th January. A PROTEST ON BEHALF OF THE PURITANS. Thomas Wright, *Queen Elizabeth and her Times*, ii. 417.

AN ATTORNEY'S UNSEEMLY APPAREL. *A.P.C.*, xxii. 175.

16th January. A CASE OF CONTRABAND GOODS. *A.P.C.*, xxii. 181.

CERTAIN GOODS PROHIBITED TO BE CARRIED TO SPAIN. *A.P.C.*, xxii. 183.

19th January. THE EARL OF ESSEX RETURNS TO COURT. *Unton Correspondence*, pp. 251, 265, 276, 294.

22nd January. A PROCLAMATION TO REFORM ABUSES IN THE CLOTH TRADE. *Proclamations*, p. 304.

28th January. A SPECIAL COMMISSION TO DEAL WITH IMPRISONED RECUSANTS. *A.P.C.*, xxii. 214.

30th January. FLESH PROHIBITED DURING LENT. *A.P.C.*, xxii. 217.

4th February. DANIEL'S 'DELIA.' *A.R.*, ii. 603. *Delia, containing certain sonnets*, by Samuel Daniel, 1592.

6th February. NEWS FROM FRANCE. *Unton Correspondence*, p. 301.

SIR FRANCIS WILLOUGHBY BEFORE THE COUNCIL. *A.P.C.*, xxii. 240. See 24th December, 1591.

7th February. GREENE'S 'THIRD PART OF CONNY-CATCHING.' *A.R.*, ii. 603. Robert Greene, *The third and last part of Conny-Catching*, 1592. Modern editions by A. B. Grosart in *The Complete Works of Robert Greene*, 1881-3 ; vol. iii. in *The Bodley Head Quartos*, 1923.

12th February. THE QUEEN REFUSES FURTHER AID TO THE FRENCH KING. *Unton Correspondence*, p. 319. The war weariness of the 1590's is sometimes forgotten by those critics who take the hearty patriotism of the history-plays as an expression of the general mood.

14th February. NEWS FROM FRANCE. *Unton Correspondence*, p. 303.

15th February. FLESH PROHIBITED IN LONDON DURING LENT. *Proclamations*, p. 306.

19th February. PLAYING RESUMED. *Hens. Diary*, i. 13 and ii. 151. *The Honourable History of Friar Bacon and Friar Bungay* was written by Robert Greene in 1588 or 1589. The record of plays acted from day to day at the Rose, and recorded in *Henslowe's Diary*, justifies, in my opinion, their inclusion as literary gossip. Unfortunately there is no similar record for the other London Theatres—The Theatre and The Curtain—where, presumably, as many plays were being acted.

THE QUEEN RESOLVES TO SEND SOLDIERS TO FRANCE. *A.P.C.*, xxii. 256.

20th February. NEWS OF ROUEN. *Unton Correspondence*, p. 331.

21st February. THOMAS PORMORT, A JESUIT, EXECUTED. *Catholic Record Society*, v. 209. Topcliffe was a lewd liar.

23rd February. A LITIGIOUS FELLOW. *A.P.C.*, xxii. 247.

SIR R. WILLIAMS IN COMMAND IN NORMANDY. *A.P.C.*, xxii. 248.

24th February. VICTUALS SENT TO NORMANDY. *A.P.C.*, xxii. 273, 279.

25th February. A PETITION AGAINST PLAYS. *Remembrancia*, i. 635, quoted in *Malone Society Collections*, i. 68.

26th February. PLAYS OF THE WEEK. *Hens. Diary*, i. 13 and ii. 152. *Muly Mullocco* is perhaps George Peele's *Battle of Alcazar*. *Orlando Furioso* was written by Greene about 1589. *The Jew of Malta* was written by Christopher Marlowe early in 1589. *The Spanish Comedy* (called also in the *Diary*, *Don Horatio* and *The Comedy of Jeronimo*) was apparently the first part of *The Spanish Tragedy*; it does not survive. *Sir John Maundeville* and *Harry of Cornwall* are also lost.

THE DUKE OF PARMA RETREATS. *Unton Correspondence*, p. 341.

28th February. MAIMED SOLDIERS TO BE EXAMINED. *Proclamations*, p. 307.

29th February. THE SCOTTISH WITCHES. *Newes from Scotland*, 1591[-2]. Modern edition in *The Bodley Head Quartos*, vol. IX. There was excuse for King James's excessive interest in witchcraft; some of the evidence brought out at these trials was afterwards incorporated in *Dæmonology*, first published in 1597.

1st March. MEN TO BE IMPRESTED FOR SERVICE IN FRANCE. *A.P.C.*, xxii. 297.

SIR EDMUND YORK'S INSTRUCTIONS. *A.P.C.*, xxii. 297.

ANOTHER PETITION OF THE PURITAN PRISONERS. *Lansdowne MSS.*, lxix. 45, printed in A. F. Scott Pearson, *Thomas Cartwright and Elizabethan Puritanism*, 1925, p. 477.

2nd March. SIR WALTER RALEGH'S EXPEDITION. *Proclamations*, p. 308.

3rd March. MUSTER ROLLS IN THE COUNTIES. *A.P.C.*, xxii. 301.

THE FISHMONGERS REBUKED FOR NEGLECTING TO SUPERVISE THE BUTCHERS. *A.P.C.*, xxii. 305. See Appendix I., p. 395.

4th March. PLAYS OF THE WEEK. *Hens. Diary*, i. 13, ii. 152. *Harry the Sixth* is probably the first part of the play included in the First Folio as Shakespeare's *Henry VI*. *Cloris and Ergasto*, *Pope Joan*, *Machiavel*, *Bindo and Richardo* have perished.

5th March. RUMOURS OF PEACE. *Unton Correspondence*, p. 352.

7th March. REPORT OF SIR JOHN NORRIS ON THE STATE OF FRANCE. Rymer's *Fœdera*, xvi. 174.

ORDERS AGAINST THOSE WHO AIDED DESERTERS. *A.P.C.*, xxii. 318.

8th March. UNDUTIFUL GENTLEMEN. *A.P.C.*, xxii. 312.

9th March. A SPANISH PRISONER'S ACCOUNT OF THE STATE OF ENGLAND. *Spanish State Papers*, iv. 593. It is not perhaps fair to include this entry; but as such accounts at first hand are rare and valuable, it may be excused. For Don Antonio see note on 13th August, 1591.

11th March. PLAYS OF THE WEEK. *Hens. Diary*, i. 13; ii. 153. *The Four Plays in One* was part of a play dealing with the Seven Deadly Sins; the theatre 'plat' survives in the Alleyn Collection but the text has perished. *A Looking Glass for London* was written by Lodge and Greene. *Zenobia* is lost.

12th March. THE EARL OF BOTHWELL AND THE SCOTTISH BORDER. *A P.C.*, xxii. 331.

18th March. PLAYS OF THE WEEK. *Hens. Diary*, i. 13, ii. 153. *The Spanish Tragedy* (better known at this time as *Jeronimo* or *Hieronimo*), written by Thomas Kyd between 1586 and 1588, was the most popular of all Elizabethan plays.

21st March. HOPEFUL NEWS FROM FRANCE. *Unton Correspondence*, pp. 361, 379, 384.

24th March. VOLUNTEERS TO BE LEVIED IN LONDON. *A.P.C.*, xxii. 361.

25th March. DISTRESS IN ROUEN. *Unton Correspondence*, p. 391.

PLAYS OF THE WEEK. *Hens. Diary*, i. 13, ii. 154. *Constantine* and *Jerusalem* have perished.

COMPLAINTS AGAINST THE GOVERNOR OF OSTEND. *A.P.C.*, xxii. 363.

RECUSANCY IN THE NORTH. *A.P.C.*, xxii. 369.

27th March. THE CASE OF ROBERT PAINE. *A.P.C.*, xxii. 372. See 6th February.

CAPTAIN GLEMHAM'S SHIPS TO BE STAYED. *A.P.C.*, xxii. 373. For other ventures of Captain Glemham see pages 18, 132, 311.

31st March. THE PURITAN PRISONERS RELEASED. Pearson, *Cartwright*, 357, 479. Approximate date.

1st April. PLAYS OF THE WEEK AT THE ROSE. *Hens. Diary*, i. 13.

2nd April. MERCY TO BE SHOWN TO DEBTORS. *A.P.C.*, xxii. 384.

7th April. TWO PRISONERS' RANSOM. *A.P.C.*, xxii. 392. See 30th April.

DISTRESS IN ROUEN. *Unton Correspondence*, p. 408.

8th April. PLAYS OF THE WEEK. *Hens. Diary*, i. 13.

12th April. BRETON'S 'THE PILGRIMAGE TO PARADISE' AND 'THE COUNTESS OF PEMBROKE'S LOVE.' Nicholas Breton, *The Pilgrimage to Paradise, joined with the Countess of Pembroke's Love*, 1592. Modern edition by A. B. Grosart in *The Complete Works of Nicholas Breton*, 1876. Nicholas Breton has not received his due because few of his works are available in any accessible reprint. *The Pilgrimage* is an interesting forecast of Bunyan's

Pilgrim's Progress, *The Countess of Pembroke's Love* an indication of the respect and admiration felt for this remarkable patroness of letters. Dated 12th April in the Epistle.

15th April. PLAYS OF THE WEEK. *Hens. Diary*, i. 14, ii. 155. *Titus and Vespasian* is perhaps an earlier version of *Titus Andronicus*.

16th April. A FRAY AT FULHAM. *Middlesex Sessions Rolls*, i. 206.

ENGLISH MARINERS FORBIDDEN TO SAIL WITH A STRANGER. *A.P.C.*, xxii. 399.

17th April. THE SIEGE OF ROUEN RAISED. *Unton Correspondence*, p. 413.

21st April. 'THE DEFENCE OF CONNY-CATCHING.' *A.R.*, ii. 609. Cuthbert Connycatcher, *The Defence of Conny-Catching*. Modern editions by A. B. Grosart in *The Complete Works of Robert Greene*, 1881-3; vol. x. of *The Bodley Head Quartos*, 1924.

22nd April. PLAYS OF THE WEEK. *Hens. Diary*, i. 14.

THE ENGHUIZEN SHIP RELEASED. *A.P.C.*, xxii. 402.

27th April. THE FRENCH KING ATTACKS PARMA. *Unton Correspondence*, p. 424.

THE TRIAL OF SIR JOHN PERROT. Cobbett's *State Trials*, vol. i., 1315.

29th April. PLAYS OF THE WEEK. *Hens. Diary*, i. 14.

30th April. THE COUNCIL DECEIVED. *A.P.C.*, xxii. 411. See 7th April.

A CONTEMPTUOUS SEA CAPTAIN. *A.P.C.*, xxii. 371, 396 and 417.

4th May. AN ACCIDENT AT GREENWICH. Stow, *Annals*.

6th May. PLAYS OF THE WEEK. *Hens. Diary*, i. 14. In recording these plays from *Henslowe's Diary* I have throughout followed Dr. Greg's corrections of Henslowe's entries (ii. 325).

7th May. THE DUKE OF PARMA'S CAMP PILLAGED. *Unton Correspondence*, p. 435.

8th May. FURTHER REINFORCEMENTS FOR FRANCE. *A.P.C.*, xxii. 431.

13th May. AN UNLUCKY GAOLER. *A.P.C.*, xxii. 443.

DESERTERS FROM FRANCE AT DOVER. *A.P.C.*, xxii. 448.

PLAYS OF THE WEEK. *Hens. Diary*, i. 14.

17th May. A CLAIM AGAINST CAPTAIN GLEMHAM. *S.P.D.*, ccxlii, 19. For Glemham's adventures see 31st March, 1591.

20th May. PLAYS OF THE WEEK. *Hens. Diary*, i. 14.

21st May. THE WEAKNESS OF THE NORMANDY COMPANIES. *A.P.C.*, xxii. 478.

25th May. A RUMOUR. *S.P. Dom.*, ccxlii. 25.

PUCKERING MADE LORD KEEPER. *A.P.C.*, xxii. 500.

27th May. PLAYS OF THE WEEK. *Hens. Diary*, i. 14.

28th May. SEDITIOUS BOOKS FROM ABROAD. *A.P.C.*, xxii. 486.

31st May. A DISASTER IN BRITTANY RUMOURED. *A.P.C.*, xxii. 502.

MR. JOHN HARINGTON AND THE PRINTER. *A.P.C.*, xxii. 504. This seems to be an interesting and early case of an amateur in letters attempting to run his private press.

1st June. SIR WALTER RALEGH DISGRACED. See W. Stebbing, *Sir Walter Ralegh*, 1899, p. 88. There is no direct contemporary evidence of Ralegh's offence, though Camden briefly records it. It must have caused considerable scandal.

2nd June. FOREIGN ARTISANS IN ENGLAND. *A.P.C.*, xxii. 506.

3rd June. PLAYS OF THE WEEK. *Hens. Diary*, i. 14.

5th June. THE DISASTER IN BRITTANY. *Unton Correspondence*, p. 460. News of the disaster in general terms had reached London by 29th May. Lord Burghleigh answered Unton's letter of the 24th on 6th June.

6th June. LEWDNESS IN A CONDUIT. Thomas Wright, *Court and Times of Queen Elizabeth*, ii. 418. Approximate date.

10th June. PLAYS OF THE WEEK. *Hens. Diary*, i. 15, ii. 156.

12th June. RIOTS IN SOUTHWARK. *Remembrancia*, i. 662. Printed in *Malone Society Collections*, i. 71.

15th June. SOME ENGLISH SAILORS ILL-TREATED. *A.P.C.*, xxii. 532.

DISTRESS AT CANTERBURY. *A.P.C.*, xxii. 534.

17th June. SIR HENRY UNTON RETURNS. *Unton Correspondence*, pp. 470, 471.

PLAYS OF THE WEEK AT THE ROSE. *Hens. Diary*, i. 15.

19th June. RECUSANCY IN WALES. *A.P.C.*, xxii. 543.

21st June. A COZENER PILLORIED. Stow, *Annals*.

22nd June. FATHER SOUTHWELL THE JESUIT. Strype's *Annals*, iv. 132.

23rd June. PLAYING CEASES AT THE ROSE THEATRE. *Hens. Diary*, i. 15.

RUMOURS OF PEACE IN FRANCE. *S.P. Dom.*, ccxlii. 58.

ABUSES IN THE NORTH. *A.P.C.*, xxii. 547; *S.P. Dom.*, ccxl. 138.

RIOTING EXPECTED IN LONDON. *A.P.C.*, xxii. 549. For an account of the Midsummer Watch see Stow's *Survey of London*, edited by C. L. Kingsford, i. 101-3.

26th June. SIR JOHN PERROT CONDEMNED. Cobbett's *State Trials*, i. 1327.

28th June. THE MURDER OF JOHN BREWEN. *The truth of the most wicked and secret murthering of John Brewen*, 1592; modern edition by F. S. Boas in *The Complete Works of Thomas Kyd*, 1904. The book was entered on 28th June (the day of the execution); four ballads were entered in July—a sure sign of the public excitement. Dr. Boas attributes the pamphlet to Kyd on the strength of a signature 'Tho. Kydde' written at the end of the only surviving copy, now in Lambeth Palace Library.

10th July. SIR W. RALEGH'S COMPLAINTS AGAINST THE DEPUTY OF IRELAND. E. Edwards, *Life of Sir Walter Ralegh*, 1868, ii. 48. Approximate date.

18th July. A PROGNOSTICATION. James Carre, *An Almanack and Prognostication for the year of our Redemption*, 1593.

21st July. MILITARY EQUIPMENT IN THE COUNTIES. *A.P.C*, xxiii. 39.

GREENE'S 'QUIP FOR AN UPSTART COURTIER.' *A.R.*, ii. 617. Robert Greene, *A Quip for an Upstart Courtier*, 1592. Modern edition by A. B. Grosart in *The Works of Robert Greene*, 1881-3. The suppressed passage is printed in my *Shakespeare's Fellows*, p. 58. This is the beginning of the famous quarrel between Gabriel Harvey and the Greene-Nashe set; for an excellent account see R. B. M'Kerrow, *The Works of Thomas Nashe*, v. 65. The book was very popular (three editions came out in 1592) and started a new vogue for allegory on social problems, well spiced with personal abuse.

23rd July. A MONOPOLY IN STARCH. *A.P.C.*, xxiii. 45. One of several grants of monopoly.

28th July. ROBERT SOUTHWELL SENT TO THE TOWER. *A.P.C.*, xxiii. 70.

31st July. SIR WALTER RALEGH'S LAMENTABLE COMPLAINT. Quoted in E. Edwards, *Life of Sir Walter Ralegh*, 1868, ii. 51. Approximate date.

6th August. DESERTERS IN HERTFORDSHIRE. *A.P.C.*, xxiii. 94.

7th August. ABLE-BODIED IRISHMEN TO BE DEPORTED. *A.P.C.*, xxiii. 99.

8th August. NASHE'S 'PIERCE PENNILESS.' *A.R.*, ii. 619. Thomas Nashe, *Pierce Penniless*, 1592. A most popular book, and an epitome of the gossip of these years. It went into three editions immediately and was again reprinted in 1595. Its popularity was due to the slashing vituperation of well-known personages. In answer to their protests, Nashe took refuge in the conventional defence of the satirist that he was not attacking individuals, and if antiquaries, for instance, took offence it was not his fault or intention. Still it can scarcely have been coincidence that Stow first produced his laboured *Annals of England* this same year. For an official answer to the defence of plays see page 330. Modern editions by R. B. M'Kerrow in *The Works of Thomas Nashe*, vol. i., 1904; and *The Bodley Head Quartos*, vol. xi., 1925.

11th August. THE COUNT MOMPELGARD IN LONDON. W. B. Rye, *England as seen by Foreigners in the days of Elizabeth and James the First*, 1865.

13th August. THE COUNT MOMPELGARD FEASTS WITH THE FRENCH AMBASSADOR. Rye, p. 9.

15th August. A SCURRILOUS JESUIT PAMPHLET. Andreas Philopater, *Responsio ad Edictum Reginae Angliae*, 1592, and John Philopatris, *An Advertisement written to a Secretarie of My L. Treasurers' of England*, 1592

17th August. THE COUNT MOMPELGARD SUMMONED TO COURT. Rye, p. 11.

18th August. THE COUNT MOMPELGARD AGAIN VISITS THE QUEEN. Rye, p. 12.

20th August. THE COUNT MOMPELGARD AT WINDSOR. Rye, p. 16.

21st August. GREENE'S 'BLACK BOOK'S MESSENGER.' *A.R.*, ii. 619. Robert Greene, *The Black Book's Messenger*, 1592. Modern editions by A. B. Grosart in *The Works of Robert Greene*, 1881-3; and *The Bodley Head Quartos*, vol. x., 1924.

29th August. SIR ROGER WILLIAMS' COMPLAINTS. *S.P. Foreign, France*, xxix. f. 55. Letter dated 23rd August.

24th August. CONDEMNED CRIMINALS AS SOLDIERS. *A.P.C.*, xxiii. 151.

27th August. A PRIEST'S INFORMATIONS. *S.P. Dom.*, ccxlii. 121.

ANXIETY FOR OSTEND. *A.P.C.*, xxiii. 137.

1st September. AN INVASION EXPECTED ON THE SOUTH COAST. *A.P.C.*, xxiii. 160.

3rd September. THE DEATH OF ROBERT GREENE. *The Repentance of Robert Greene, Master of Arts*, 1592. Modern editions in A. B. Grosart, *The Complete Works of Robert Greene*, 1881-3 ; and *The Bodley Head Quartos*, vol. vi. 1923.

4th September. THE COUNT MOMPELGARD DEPARTS. Rye, p. 47.

5th September. DR. HARVEY AND ROBERT GREENE. Gabriel Harvey, *Four Letters and Certain Sonnets*, 1592. Modern editions by A. B. Grosart, *The English Works of Gabriel Harvey*, 1884 ; and vol. ii. of *The Bodley Head Quartos*, 1923. I suspect (but without tangible evidence) that the 'fatal banquet' was held to celebrate the publication of *The Quip* and *Pierce Penniless*, and that Nashe and Greene loudly drank damnation to the Harveys thereat.

6th September. GREAT WINDS. Stow, *Annals*. Birch, *Memories*, i. 86.

THE RETURN OF SIR MARTIN FROBISHER'S FLEET EXPECTED. *A.P.C.*, xxiii. 177.

7th September. THE PLAGUE IN LONDON. *S.P. Dom.*, ccxliii. 5.

10th September. THE TAKING OF THE GREAT CARRACK. *Hakluyt's Voyages*, v. 57. The previous adventures of the company of the *Golden Dragon* before joining Sir John Burgh are recorded in *Hakluyt's Voyages*, vol. vii. p. 148.

THE PLAGUE IN LONDON. *A.P.C.*, xxiii. 183.

TWO RICH SPANISH PRIZES BROUGHT IN. *Hakluyt's Voyages*, v. 55.

14th September. SPANISH HOPES. *S.P. Dom.*, ccxliii. 11.

16th September. THE GREAT CARRACK. *S.P. Dom.*, ccxliii. 14.

17th September. THAME FAIR PUT OFF. *A.P.C.*, xxiii. 195.

19th September. THE SPREAD OF THE PLAGUE. *A.P.C.*, xxiii. 203.

20th September. 'GREENE'S GROAT'S-WORTH OF WIT.' *A.R.*, ii. 620. *Greene's Groat's-worth of Wit*. Modern editions by A. B. Grosart in *The Complete Works of Robert Greene*, 1881-3 ; and *The Bodley Head Quartos*, vol. vi. There can be little doubt that the 'famous gracer of tragedians' is Marlowe, 'young Juvenal' Nashe, and 'the only Shake-scene' Shakespeare.

22nd September. THE GREAT CARRACK. *S.P. Dom.*, ccxliii. 16. Letter dated 19th September.

THE QUEEN AT OXFORD. *Nicoll's Progresses*, vol. ii.

CONSTABLE'S 'DIANA.' *A.R.*, ii. 620. Henry Constable, *Diana*, 1592. Modern edition by M. F. Crow in *Elizabethan Sonnet Cycles*, 1896. The original edition of Constable's *Diana* is interesting as an example of the pretty pocket volume for ladies, and the vogue of the sonnet during the early 1590's ; as poetry fairly smooth, passionless and drowsy.

23rd September. THE QUEEN AT OXFORD. Nicoll's *Progresses*, vol. ii.

A PROCLAMATION ABOUT THE GREAT CARRACK. *Proclamations*, p. 311.

24th September. THE QUEEN AT OXFORD. Nicoll's *Progresses*, vol. ii.

SIR ROBERT CECIL AT DARTMOUTH. *S.P. Dom.*, ccxliii. 17. Letter dated 21st Sept.

25th September. THE COURT AT OXFORD. Nicoll's *Progresses*, vol. ii.

27th September. THE QUEEN AT OXFORD. Nicoll's *Progresses*, vol. ii.

28th September. THE QUEEN LEAVES OXFORD. Nicoll's *Progresses*, vol. ii.

1st October. THE INCREASE OF THE PLAGUE. *A.P.C.*, xxiii. 220.

REINFORCEMENTS FOR BRITTANY. *A.P.C.*, xxiii. 223.

6th October. 'THE REPENTANCE OF ROBERT GREENE.' *A.R.*, ii. 621. *The Repentance of Robert Greene*, 1592. Modern editions by A. B. Grosart, *Complete Works of Robert Greene*, 1881-3; and *The Bodley Head Quartos*, vol. vi., 1923.

KYD'S SPANISH TRAGEDY. *A.R.*, ii. 621. Thomas Kyd, *The Spanish Tragedy.* The earliest extant edition is not dated. Modern editions by F. S. Boas in *The Works of Thomas Kyd*, 1901; etc.

11th October. CITY FEASTS TO BE FORBORNE. *A.P.C.*, xxiii. 232.

12th October. PRECAUTIONS AGAINST THE PLAGUE. *Proclamations*, p. 312.

18th October. PLAGUE DEATHS. *Fugger News-Letters*, 2nd series, p. 243.

19th October. SIR JOHN NORRIS DELAYED. *S.P. Dom.*, ccxlii. 43.

21st October. A PROCLAMATION CONCERNING THE PLAGUE. *Proclamations*, p. 313.

20th October. THE DEATH OF COUNT MONTAIGNE. Birch's *Memoirs*, i. 87. Approximate date.

THE GREAT CARRACK. *A.P.C.*, xxiii. 246.

22nd October. EDWARD ALLEYN MARRIES. E. K. Chambers, *Elizabethan Stage*, ii. 296.

23rd October. BEACON WATCHES TO BE DISCONTINUED. *A.P.C.*, xxiii. 264.

27th October. THE NORMANDY FORCES TO BE SENT TO BRITTANY. *A.P.C.*, xxiii. 268.

30th October. ABUSES AT HERTFORD. *A.P.C.*, xxiii. 274.

THE LORD MAYOR REBUFFED. *A.P.C.*, xxiii. 276.

4th November. THE DEATH OF SIR JOHN PERROT. *The History of that most eminent statesman Sir John Perrot*, 1728, published from the original manuscript by Richard Rawlinson; Sir Robert Naunton, *Fragmenta Regalia*, 1649: reprinted in *The Harleian Miscellany*, vol. ii.; and *D.N.B.* See Appendix I., p. 393.

HARWARD'S 'SOLACE FOR THE SOLDIER AND SAILOR.' *A.R.*, ii. 622. Simon Harward, *The Solace of the Soldier and the Sailor*, 1592.

13th November. MR. HERRICK'S GOODS. *A.P.C.*, xxiii. 289; F. W. Moorman, *Robert Herrick*, 1910, p. 19. This is the father of Robert Herrick the poet, then aged 14 months.

14th November. SIR JOHN NORRIS'S COMPLAINTS. *S.P. Foreign*, xxix. f. 296. Letter dated 8th November.

17th November. CORONATION DAY. *Letters of Philip Gawdy*, p. 67. Roxburgh Club, 1906.

20th November. A FAVOURITE LADY-IN-WAITING. *Hist. MSS. Com., Rutland MSS.*, i. 305. See 20th August, 1594.

'SOLIMAN AND PERSEDA.' *A.R.*, ii. 622. *The Tragedy of Soliman and Perseda.* The earliest quarto is undated. Modern editions by F. S. Boas (who attributes the play to Kyd) in *The Works of Thomas Kyd*, 1901 ; J. S. Farmer, in *Students' Facsimile Texts.*

7th December. UNWILLING CAPTAINS TO BE PUNISHED. *A.P.C.*, xxiii. 348.

8th December. CHETTLE'S 'KINDHEART'S DREAM.' *A.R.*, ii. 623. Henry Chettle, *Kindheart's Dream*, n.d. Modern edition in *The Bodley Head Quartos*, vol. iii., 1923.

16th December. THE FUNERAL OF THE DUKE OF PARMA. *Fugger News-Letters*, 2nd series, p. 244.

18th December. 'ELIOT'S FRUITS FOR THE FRENCH.' *A.R.*, ii. 624. John Eliot, *Ortho-Epia Gallica*, 1593.

30th December. PLAYING RESUMED. *Hens. Diary*, i. 15.

31st December. THE BILLS OF MORTALITY FOR THE YEAR. John Graunt, *Reflections on the Weekly Bills of Mortality*, 1665, p. 3, and *Natural and Political Observations made upon the Bills of Mortality*, 1662, p. 33. I have assumed that the practice in 1592 was similar to that in later years.

COLONNA'S 'HYPNEROTOMACHIA.' Francisco Colonna, *Hypnerotomachia*, translated by R. D., 1592. Modern edition by Andrew Lang, with a short introduction, 1890. Lang draws attention to the many quaintnesses of vocabulary, reminiscent of Keat's *Endymion.* A good example of Renaissance 'lusciousness' but dull reading.

GREENE'S 'DISPUTATION.' Robert Greene, *A Disputation between a He Conny-catcher, and a She Conny-catcher*, 1592. Modern editions by A. B. Grosart in *The Complete Works of Robert Greene*, 1881-3 ; and in *The Bodley Head Quartos*, vol. iii., 1923.

'THE GROUNDWORK OF CONNY-CATCHING. Thomas Harman, *The Groundwork of Conny-catching*, 1592.

JOHNSON'S 'NINE WORTHIES OF LONDON.' Richard Johnson, *The Nine Worthies of London*, 1592. The book went into a second edition this year. Reprinted in *The Harleian Miscellany*, vol. viii., 1746. This is one of the books written for a citizen reader to glorify the tradesman.

1593.

3rd January. RUMOURS. *S.P. Dom.*, ccxliv. 1. The libels presumably were the books summarised under 15th August, 1592.

6th January. PLAYS OF THE WEEK. *Hens. Diary*, i. 15. Fleay, and more recently Dr. Dover Wilson (in *The New Shakespeare*), suggest that the *Jealous Comedy* was the basis of Shakespeare's *Merry Wives of Windsor*. See Appendix I., p. 401.

8th January. THE WAR IN FRANCE. *A.P.C.*, xxiv. 14. *S.P. Foreign*, xxx. f. 7. Letter dated 2nd January.

12th January. NASHE'S 'STRANGE NEWS.' *A.R.*, ii. 624. Thomas Nashe, *Strange News of the Intercepting of Certain Letters*, 1592[-3]. Modern edition by R. B. M'Kerrow in *The Works of Thomas Nashe*, 1904. This piece of abuse made good gossip: two editions are dated 1592, *i.e.* were printed before 25th March, 1593; three are dated 1593.

13th January. PLAYS OF THE WEEK. *Hens. Diary*, i. 15; ii. 156.

18th January. RUMOURS. *S.P. Dom.*, ccxliv. 18.

20th January. PLAYS OF THE WEEK. *Hens. Diary*, i. 15; ii. 157.

21st January. THE PLAGUE AGAIN INCREASES. *A.P.C.*, xxiv. 21.

27th January. PLAYS OF THE WEEK. *Hens. Diary*, i. 15; ii. 157. *The Massacre at Paris* (called in the *Diary* 'the tragedy of the gyves') was printed in an undated quarto with the title, *The Massacre at Paris; with the Death of the Duke of Guise. As it was played by the Right Honourable the Lord High Admiral, his servants. Written by Christopher Marlowe.*

28th January. EVASION OF SERVICE IN PRIVILEGED PLACES. *A.P.C.*, xxiv. 30.

SIR HENRY KNIVETT'S SUBMISSION. *A.P.C.*, xxiv. 33.

PLAYS AND GAMES PROHIBITED BY REASON OF THE PLAGUE. *A.P.C.*, xxiv. 31.

2nd February. PLAYING CEASES. *Hens. Diary*, i. 16.

3rd February. 'GREENE'S NEWS FROM HEAVEN AND HELL.' *A.R.*, ii. 626. B. R., *Green's News from Heaven and Hell*, 1593. Modern edition by R. B. M'Kerrow, 1922.

7th February. LAWLESSNESS ON THE SCOTTISH BORDER. *S.P. Dom. Addenda*, xxxii. 66.

8th February. AN INVASION EXPECTED. *A.P.C.*, xxiv. 53.

11th February. CONTRIBUTIONS EVADED. *A.P.C.*, xxiv. 44.

12th February. RUMOURS: THE GREAT CARRACK. *S.P. Dom.*, ccxliv. 35. The signed award of the Commissioners (*Lansdowne MSS.*, 73, f. 40) gives the following figures: The Earl of Cumberland, £18,000; Sir Walter Ralegh, £15,900; Sir John Hawkins, £2,400; the City of London, £12,000 in goods.

14th February. INSUFFICIENT MEN IMPRESTED AS SOLDIERS. *A.P.C.*, xxiv. 62, 65 and 66. See Appendix I., p. 397.

18th February. REGULATIONS FOR BUTCHERS DURING LENT. *A.P.C.*, xxiv. 71.

19th February. PARLIAMENT ASSEMBLES. D'Ewes' *Journals*, pp. 456, 468. Townshend, p. 32.

20th February. PRECAUTIONS AGAINST DESERTIONS. *A.P.C.*, xxiv. 72.

21st February. THE FRENCH AMBASSADOR ALLOWED MEAT. *A.P.C.*, xxiv. 75.

22nd February. THE SPEAKER PRESENTED. D'Ewes' *Journals*, p. 458. Townshend, p. 34.

PROFESSOR J. E. NEALE pointed out (*Eng. Hist. Rev.* xxxi. 129) that in another version of this speech a member might say 'yea or no' to any Bill 'with some short declaration of his reason therein,' but not to 'speak there of all causes as him listeth.'

24th February. MR. WENTWORTH'S PETITION. D'Ewes' *Journals*, p. 470. Townshend, p. 54.

THE SPEAKER SICK. D'Ewes' *Journals*, p. 470.

SIR ROGER WILLIAMS' COUNSEL. *S.P. Foreign*, xxx. f. 118. Letter dated 18th February.

25th February. MR. WENTWORTH BEFORE THE COUNCIL. D'Ewes' *Journals*, p. 470. Townshend, p. 54.

THE EARL OF ESSEX ADMITTED TO THE COUNCIL. *A.P.C.*, xxiv. 78.

DESERTERS IN GLOUCESTERSHIRE. *A.P.C.*, xxiv. 81.

26th February. A COMMITTEE OF THE HOUSE APPOINTED. D'Ewes' *Journals*, p. 471.

27th February. UNREASONABLE DEMANDS FROM PRISONERS. *A.P.C.*, xxiv. 82.

THE SUBSIDIES. D'Ewes' *Journals*, p. 477.

A BILL AGAINST THE BISHOPS. D'Ewes' *Journals*, p. 474. Townshend, p. 61.

ROGER RIPPON'S CORPSE. Strype, *Annals*, iv. 133.

28th February. THE BILL AGAINST THE BISHOPS. D'Ewes' *Journals*, p. 478. Townshend, p. 61.

FLESH IN LENT. *A.P.C.*, xxiv. 84, 87.

A PLOT TO KILL THE QUEEN. *S.P. Dom.*, ccxliv. 55.

1st March. ROGER RIPPON'S CORPSE. *S.P. Dom.*, ccxliv. 62.

EXTREME TENETS OF THE PURITANS. *Two kinds of schismatics, and the danger of their opinions, either directly or by necessary consequence gathered, to be holden by those who urge a new Church Government.* 'This paper seems to have been drawn up by the Lord Keeper Puckering, to be produced against them in the Star Chamber, after their examinations before him.' Strype, *Annals*, iv. 140.

3rd March. DR. UDALL'S PETITION. *S.P. Dom.*, ccxliv. 64.

THE SUBSIDY. D'Ewes' *Journals*, p. 480.

THE SUBSIDY. D'Ewes' *Journals*, p. 483.

A STRANGER IN THE HOUSE. D'Ewes' *Journals*, p. 486.

4th March. Penry to be Arrested. *A.P.C.*, xxiv. 94.

5th March. 'The Garland of Goodwill.' *A.R.*, ii. 627. Thomas Deloney, *The Garland of Goodwill*, earliest surviving edition, 1631. Modern edition by F. O. Mann in *The Works of Thomas Deloney*, 1912. It is perhaps doubtful whether the book was issued in 1593. The original entry to Wolfe, dated 5th March, 1593, is crossed out, and 'Edward White the xxvij of August 1596' substituted. As one of the ballads in the third part refers to the attack on Cadiz (1596), it is possible that two parts appeared in 1593, and a third was added in 1596. It is worth noting how the ballad-maker borrows the stories of the gentlemen writers and the dramatists.

6th March. Legg Released. D'Ewes, *Journals*, p. 491.

The Subsidy. D'Ewes' *Journals*, p. 489.

7th March. Musters to be held in the North. *A.P.C.*, xxiv. 105.

The Subsidy. D'Ewes' *Journals*, p. 491.

9th March. Barrowists Arrested. Strype, *Annals*, iv. 174.

10th March. The Subsidy Agreed. D'Ewes' *Journals*, p. 495.

11th March. The Butchers Defiant. *A.P.C.*, xxiv. 112.

12th March. A Bill against Recusants. D'Ewes' *Journals*, p. 498.

Mr. Darcy's Unseemly Conduct. *Remembrancia*, i. 651.

13th March. A Spanish Nobleman sent home. *Spanish State Papers*, iv. 596.

16th March. Measures against the Butchers. *A.P.C.*, xxiv. 118.

19th March. Bunny's 'Truth and Falsehood.' Francis Bunny, *Truth and Falsehood*, 1595. Entered 19th March, 1593, and 13th April, 1593. *The Short Answer* is bound with *Truth and Falsehood*, but has its own title-page.

21st March. Kellway's 'Defensative against the Plague.' *A.R.*, ii. 629. Simon Kellway, *A Defensative against the Plague*, 1593.

22nd March. Barrow, Greenwood and other Puritans condemned. Stow, *Annals*.

23rd March. A Dishonest Captain. *A.P.C.*, xxiv. 133. See Appendix I., p. 398.

24th March. Gyer's 'English Phlebotomy.' Nicholas Gyer, *The English Phlebotomy*, 1592. Approximate date of publication. From mention of 'this Spring time' on the title-page, and of Penry, Brown and Barrow, it seems likely that the book should be dated 1592-3 rather than 1591-2.

25th March. Abuses over Impressments in Gloucestershire. *A.P.C.*, xxiv. 136. See Appendix I., page 398.

27th March. A Recusant Executed at Winchester. *Catholic Record Society*, v. 228-232.

31st March. Barrow and Greenwood respited. Stow, *Annals*. See page 222.

1st April. A Counterfeit Captain. *A.P.C.*, xxiv. 149.

2nd April. Maimed Soldiers to be Examined. *A.P.C.*, xxiv. 159.

4th April. A Bill against the Brownists. D'Ewes' *Journals*, p. 516. Townshend, page 76

5th April. Charitable Contributions for Maimed Soldiers. D'Ewes' *Journals*, p. 463. Townshend, page 42.

Precautions against Plague. *A.P.C.*, xxiv. 163.

6th April. Barrow and Greenwood hanged. Stow, *Annals*. *S.P. Dom.*, ccxlv. 124 (Phellippes).

7th April. Special Watch to be kept for Traitors. *Hist. MSS. Com.* *Rye MSS.*, page 105.

8th April. The Disorderly Butchers. *A.P.C.*, xxiv. 166, 170.

9th April. 'Churchyard's Challenge.' *A.R.*, ii. 629. Thomas Churchyard, *Churchyard's Challenge*, 1593. A very tedious old man.

The Witches of Warboys. *The most strange and admirable discovery of the three Witches of Warboys*, 1593. A very long and detailed description of the whole affair written by an eye-witness (not improbably Dr. Dorrington). The Lady Cromwell was second wife of Oliver Cromwell's grandfather. The pamphlet seems to have caused some excitement when it was entered at Stationers' Hall, as the entry in the *Register* notes that it was 'recommended for matter of truthe by master Judge Ffenner vnder his handwrytinge shewed in a Court or assemblie holden this Daye according to the ordonnances of the company'; 'the note vnder master Justice Ffenners hand is Layd vp in the Wardens cupbord.' *A.R.*, ii. 633.

10th April. The Parliament Dissolved. D'Ewes' *Journals*, p. 465. Townshend, p. 45. See Appendix I., p. 394.

11th April. Relief for Maimed Soldiers. *A.P.C.*, xxxiv. 178.

14th April. False Reports concerning the Queen's dealings with the Turks. Strype, *Annals*, iv. 154.

15th April. The Queen's Directions to Sir John Norris. *S.P. Foreign*, xxx. f. 272.

16th April. The Libels against Strangers. *A.P.C.*, xxiv. 187.

17th April. Measures against Vagabonds. *A.P.C.*, xxxiv. 193. A copy of this order is included in the volume of *Proclamations* (317a).

18th April. 'Venus and Adonis' entered. *A.R.*, ii. 630. William Shakespeare, *Venus and Adonis*, 1593. Modern edition by C. Knox Pooler in the Arden Shakespeare, 1911: etc.

22nd April. The Libels against Strangers. *A.P.C.*, xxiv. 200; Strype, *Annals*, iv. 167.

23rd April. Drayton's 'Idea.' *A.R.*, ii. 630. Michael Drayton, *The Shepherd's Garland, fashioned into nine Eclogues*, 1593. An interesting imitation of Spenser, and for the philologist useful for its archaic and rare words. The ballad of Dowsabel is pleasing, otherwise the collection is second-rate, though a considerable advance on *The Harmony of the Church*. Modern edition in Arber's *English Garner*, vol. vi.

24th April. Plague Deaths. *Fugger News-Letters*, 2nd series, p. 248.

29th April. A Charitable Gentleman. *A.P.C.*, xxiv. 209.

4th May. The Numbers of Strangers in London. Strype, *Annals*, iv. 167.

5th May. Libels against Strangers. Strype, *Annals*, iv. 168.

10*th May*. 'PARTHENOPHIL AND PARTHENOPHE.' *A.R.*, ii. 631. Barnabe Barnes, *Parthenophil and Parthenophe*, 1593. Modern edition by A. B. Grosart, 1875; and in Arber's *English Garner*, vol. v. Barnes annoyed several of his contemporaries who made the most of the shortcomings of *Parthenophil*; for details see Grosart's Introduction. All the same, though not a Donne, he is trying to explore his own sensations and to get away from the tired conventions of the sonneteers.

11*th May*. MORE LIBELS AGAINST STRANGERS. *A.P.C.*, xxiv. 222.

12*th May*. THOMAS KYD ARRESTED. See F. S. Boas, *The Works of Thomas Kyd*, 1901; Introduction, pp. lxx-lxxiii.

15*th May*. CONTEMPT OF THE COUNCIL'S ORDER AT BRISTOL. *S.P. Dom.*, ccxlv. 25. Approximate date.

20*th May*. MARLOWE BEFORE THE COUNCIL. *A.P.C.*, xxiv. 244.

21*st May*. A PRIEST'S DECLARATION OF HIS MOTIVES. *S.P. Dom.*, ccxlv. 66. Approximate date.

23*rd May*. THE PLAGUE IN THE SAVOY. *A.P.C.*, xxiv. 252.

24*th May*. PENRY CONDEMNED. *S.P. Dom.*, ccxlv. 21.

A REQUEST OF THE CITIZENS OF PARIS. *S.P. Foreign*, xxxi. f. 60. Letter dated 18th May.

25*th May*. ABUSES OF THE QUEEN'S SERVICE IN GLOUCESTERSHIRE. *A.P.C.*, xxiv. 257. See Appendix I., p. 398.

26*th May*. MARLOWE'S BLASPHEMIES. The whole accusation is to be found in *Harleian MSS.*, 6848, f. 155; reprinted (with some omissions) in Dr. Boas' edition of *The Works of Thomas Kyd*, p. cxiv.

28*th May*. PRECAUTIONS AGAINST PLAGUE. *Proclamations*, 39.

29*th May*. STRATFORD GOOSE FAIR FORBIDDEN. *A.P.C.*, xxiv. 265.

MR. WENTWORTH IN THE TOWER. *A.P.C.*, xxiv. 269.

30*th May*. MARLOWE SLAIN. J. L. Hotson, *The Death of Christopher Marlowe*, 1926, p. 31.

31*st May*. THE EXECUTION OF JOHN PENRY. See W. Pierce, *John Penry*, 1923, p. 480.

THREE SUSPECTED SOLDIERS. *A.P.C.*, xxiv. 278.

1*st June*. THE INQUEST ON CHRISTOPHER MARLOWE. *The Death of Christopher Marlowe*, by J. Leslie Hotson. Dr. Hotson's discovery of the copy of the Coroner's verdict revealed the 'official' account of the murder; but it is to be noted that the survivor in these numerous fatal quarrels is always the innocent party. The stories are retailed by Thomas Beard in his *Theatre of God's Judgments* (1597), Francis Meres in *Palladis Tamia*, and others; relevant extracts are given in Dr. Hotson's book. The evidence that Marlowe was given to blasphemy and unnatural vice is convincing and, indeed, could be deduced from his writings.

5*th June*. PRECAUTIONS AGAINST PLAGUE AT WINDSOR. *A.P.C.*, xxiv. 284.

7*th June*. MR. COTTON'S CLAIMS TO BE SATISFIED. *A.P.C.*, xxiv. 295. See *ante*, 29th April.

8*th June*. RELIEF OF MAIMED SOLDIERS. *A.P.C.*, xxiv. 298.

10th June. CHARITY FOR A PRISONER IN THE HANDS OF THE LEAGUERS. *A.P.C.*, xxiv. 305.

12th June. RUMOURS OF CHANGES IN FRANCE. *S.P. Dom.*, ccxlv. 30.

16th June. CHUTE'S 'BEAUTY DISHONOURED.' *A.R.*, ii. 632. Anthony Chute, *Beauty Dishonoured*, 1593. The pleading of the lady against the miseries of enforced marriage seems to owe something to Deloney's ballad of *The Lamentation of Mr. Page's Wife*. See page 92. This lament was imitated by Daniel and Giles Fletcher (see pages 262 and 322). The interest in Mistress Shore at this time is worth noting.

18th June. A PROCLAMATION TO RESTRAIN SUITORS AT COURT. *Proclamations*, 318. See 12th October, 1592.

20th June. CAPTAIN JOHN DAVIS RETURNS TO ENGLAND. Hakluyt, viii. 295-312.

25th June. THE COUNCIL'S LICENCE ABUSED. *A.P.C.*, xxiv. 332.

26th June. 'A DISCOVERY OF THE CONSPIRACY OF THE SCOTTISH PAPISTS.' *A.R.*, ii. 633. *A Discovery of the unnatural and traitorous conspiracy of Scottish Papists*, 1593. One of the few pamphlets of news from Scotland.

29th June. CITY FEASTS TO BE CURTAILED. *A.P.C.*, xxiv. 342.

1st July. MR. CAVENDISH'S VOYAGE. *A.P.C.*, xxiv. 346.

FAIRS TO BE ABANDONED. *A.P.C.*, xxv. 347.

6th July. MARLOWE'S 'EDWARD THE SECOND.' *A.R.*, ii. 634. Christopher Marlowe, *Edward the Second*, 1594. Modern editions by C. Tucker Brooke in *The Works of Christopher Marlowe*, 1910 ; etc.

9th July. THE PLAGUE. *A.P.C.*, xxiv. 373.

THE COLLECTION OF THE SUBSIDY. *A.P.C.*, xxiv. 376.

SPANISH SHIPS OFF THE BRITTANY COAST. *A.P.C.*, xxiv. 406.

BLUNDEVILLE'S 'EXERCISES.' Thomas Blundeville, *His Exercises*, 1594.

14th July. SIR THOMAS WILKES SENT TO THE FRENCH KING. *S.P. Foreign*, xxxi. f. 248.

16th July. THE PLAGUE INCREASES. *A.P.C.*, xxiv. 400. The 'little book' is probably that summarised on page 349, though no copy earlier than 1594 now exists.

17th July. PLAGUE DEATHS. *Fugger News-Letters*, 2nd series, p. 249.

19th July. THE ASSIZES HELD IN ST. GEORGE'S FIELD. Stow, *Annals*.

PLAGUE DEATHS, *Fugger News-Letters*, 2nd series, p. 250.

29th July. THE COUNCIL'S LETTERS TO THE UNIVERSITIES OF OXFORD AND CAMBRIDGE. *A.P.C.*, xxiv. 427. This letter, written in the Council's best literary style, was in answer to a petition from the Vice-Chancellor and heads of Colleges in Cambridge asking for public plays and shows to to be restrained. See Strype's *Annals*, iv. 162.

30th July. THE RECRUITS TO BE STAYED. *Salisbury Papers*, iv. 341.

3rd August. DR. HARVEY'S 'PIERCE'S SUPEREROGATION.' Gabriel Harvey, *Pierce's Supererogation*, 1593. Modern edition by A. B. Grosart in *The Works of Gabriel Harvey*, 1884. Not entered in *S.R.*, but dated in several places varying from 27th April to 3rd August.

4th August. The Plague Increases. *A.P.C.*, xxiv. 443.

5th August. A Book on Astronomy. *A.R.*, ii. 635. Auger Ferrier, *A Learned Astronomical Discourse*, 1593. Kelway's protest is significant of the growth of incredulity in astronomy.

Plague Deaths. *Henslowe Papers*, edited by W. W. Greg, p. 37. The date is approximate, and as Henslowe's style is none of the clearest his figures are somewhat doubtful, though they agree in general with the other sources.

6th August. The Truce in France. *Articles accorded for the Truce General in France*, 1593. Entered 25th August.

Bartholomew Fair. *A.P.C.*, xxiv. 448. *Proclamations*, 319.

12th August. Unlawful Spoils. *A.P.C.*, xxiv. 456.

14th August. Plague Deaths. *Henslowe Papers*, p. 39.

16th August. Rumours concerning France. *S.P. Dom.*, ccxlv. 79.

19th August. Sir Thomas Wilkes' conversation with the French King. *S.P. Foreign*, xxxii. f. 34. Letter dated 13th August.

22nd August. The Fortifications of Plymouth. *A.P.C.*, xxiv. 477.

Disbandment of the Soldiers from France. *S.P. Dom.*, ccxlv. 86.

23rd August. Sir Thomas Wilkes' second conversation with the French King. *S.P. Foreign.*, xxxii. f. 51. Letter dated 17th August.

26th August. Two Counterfeiters sent to the Galleys. *A.P.C.*, xxiv. 486. The original volumes containing the Acts of the Privy Council from 26th August, 1593, to 1st October, 1595, are unfortunately missing.

8th September. Nashe's 'Christ's Tears over Jerusalem.' *A.R.*, ii. 635. Thomas Nashe, *Christ's Tears over Jerusalem*, 1593. Modern edition by R. B. M'Kerrow in *The Works of Thomas Nashe*, 1904. When Nashe found that Harvey was suspicious of his offers of friendship (see 1st October) he retracted his apology in a violently abusive preface to the 1594 edition of *Christ's Tears*.

10th September. Plague Deaths. *Fugger News-Letters*, 2nd series, p. 251.

15th September. A Restraint of Suitors at Windsor. *Proclamations*, 320.

17th September. Nashe's 'Unfortunate Traveller.' *A.R.*, ii. 636. Thomas Nashe, *The Unfortunate Traveller*, 1594. Modern editions by R. B. M'Kerrow in *The Works of Thomas Nashe*, 1904; H. F. Brett Smith in *The Percy Reprints*, 1920.

28th September. Plague Deaths. *Henslowe Papers*, p. 40.

1st October. Dr. Harvey's 'New Letter of Notable Contents.' *A.R.*, ii. 636. Gabriel Harvey, *A New Letter of Notable Contents*, 1593. Modern edition by A. B. Grosart in *The Works of Gabriel Harvey*, 1884.

8th October. High-handed Dealings. *S.P. Dom.*, ccxlv. 135. The Lady was sister-in-law to Lord Burghley; from the tone of an earlier letter in *S.P. Dom.* (ccxlv. 23) she appears to have been a grasping and cantankerous woman.

19th October. DANIEL'S 'DELIA AND ROSAMOND' AND 'THE COMPLAINT OF ROSAMOND.' *A.R.*, ii. 638. Samuel Daniel, *Delia and Rosamond, augmented with Cleopatra. Rosamond's Complaint*, as Daniel acknowledges in his reference to Shore's wife, is an imitation of Chute's *Beauty Dishonoured* (see 16th June). Daniel is by far the better writer, but Rosamond's pious moralisings savour of the ballad-monger. In his attack on barbarism he is joining forces with Sidney's *Apology for Poetry* (in circulation but not printed for another eighteen months) and Nashe's *Piers Pennilesse*. There can be little doubt that the barbarians at this time were raising the cry of 'Down with poetry, down with plays.' See Appendix I., p. 399.

22nd October. EDWARDS' 'CEPHALUS AND PROCRIS.' *A.R.*, ii. 638. Thomas Edwards, *Cephalus and Procris*, 1595. Only one perfect copy is known, not apparently a first edition. Modern edition by W. E. Buckley, Roxburghe Club, 1882. The envoy to *Narcissus* contains references to various contemporary poets, including the well-known lines beginning '*Adon* deafly masking through'; indeed the influence of *Venus and Adonis* is obvious throughout. See the note on Clapham's *Narcissus*, p. 91.

9th November. THE PLAGUE ABATING. *Fugger News-Letters*, 2nd series, p. 252.

14th November. 'ARISBAS.' *A.R.*, ii. 639. John Dickenson, *Arisbas, Euphues amidst his slumbers*, 1594. A very charming story in the best euphuistic vein; including some interesting and pleasing poems; among them 'The Strife of Love and Beauty'; an English Sapphic, 'Dorylus his Odes'; and an English Elegiac, 'Arisbas his Elegy.' There is an atmosphere of *Twelfth Night* about Timoclea's shipwreck, and strong likeness between Shakespeare's Adonis and Hyalus.

17th November. CHURCHYARD'S VERSES. Birch's *Memoirs*, i. 131.

20th November. A CASE OF PLAGUE AT COURT. Birch's *Memoirs*, i. 133.

28th November. THE ARRAIGNMENT OF RICHARD HESKETH. *Salisbury Papers*, iv. 423 and 461.

29th November. A RECUSANT'S CONFESSION. *S.P. Dom.*, ccxlvi. 18.

30th November. THE QUEEN'S LETTER TO SIR JOHN NORRIS. *S.P. Dom.*, ccxlvi. 22. Approximate date.

7th December. GREENE'S 'ORLANDO FURIOSO.' *A.R.*, ii. 640. Robert Greene, *Orlando Furioso*, 1594. Modern edition by J. Churton Collins in *The Plays and Poems of Robert Greene*, 1905.

11th December. HESTER'S 'PEARL OF PRACTISE.' *A.R.*, ii. 641. J. H., *The Pearl of Practise*, 1594.

21st December. ANXIETY IN GUERNSEY. *Salisbury Papers*, iv. 440.

22nd December. PEPPER FROM THE GREAT CARRACK. *S.P. Dom.*, ccxlvi. 40.

26th December. PLAYING RESUMED. *Hens. Diary*, i. 16; ii. 157. A play of this name was entered on 1st March, 1600, but does not survive.

29th December. PLAYS AT THE ROSE. *Hens. Diary*, i. 16; ii. 158. *Huon of Bordeaux* is lost. Commentators see a connection between Oberon of *A Midsummer Night's Dream* and Oberon of the medieval romance; if so, the link was probably this play. *George a Greene, the pinner of Wakefield*, was entered 1st April, 1595. It is reprinted in the *Malone Society Reprints*. *Buckingham* and *Richard the Confessor* are unknown.

31st December. GENTLEMEN'S SONS OVERSEAS. *Salisbury Papers*, iv. 448.

CHAPMAN'S *Σκιὰ νυκτὸς*. *A.R.*, ii. 642. George Chapman, *Σκιὰ νυκτὸς*, 1594. Modern edition by A. C. Swinburne, 1875.

PLAGUE DEATHS. Stow, *Annals*. J. Graunt (*Natural and Political Observations . . . upon the Bills of Mortality*, 1662) gives the figures as 17,844 and 10,662.

DR. BANCROFT'S 'DANGEROUS POSITIONS AND PROCEEDINGS.' Richard Bancroft, *Dangerous Positions and Proceedings*, 1593. An important contemporary account of the Puritan movement.

GIFFARD'S 'DIALOGUE CONCERNING WITCHES AND WITCHCRAFT.' George Giffard, *A Dialogue concerning Witches and Witchcraft*, 1593. There are some illuminating stories imbedded in this 'popular' treatise and good patches of dialogue, especially when the women talk; but like most of his Puritan brethren, Mr. Giffard allows his logic to be somewhat distorted by his intense respect for the devil.

LODGE'S 'PHILLIS.' Thomas Lodge, *Phillis: honoured with pastoral Sonnets, elegies and amorous delights. Whereto is annexed the tragical complaint of Elstred*, 1593. More than one of these sonnet collections contain a 'lament,' as do Shakespeare's. Modern edition by Edmund Gosse in *The Complete Works of Thomas Lodge*, Hunterian Club, 1880.

LODGE'S 'LIFE AND DEATH OF WILLIAM LONGBEARD.' Thomas Lodge, *The Life and Death of William Longbeard—with many other most pleasant and pretty histories*, 1593. Modern edition by Edmund Gosse in *The Complete Works of Thomas Lodge*, 1875.

NORDEN'S 'SPECULUM BRITANNIAE.' John Norden, *Speculum Britanniae*, 1593. Modern edition by W. B. Gerish, 1903.

SUTCLIFFE'S 'LAWS OF ARMS.' Matthew Sutcliffe, *The Practice, proceedings and laws of arms*, 1593. There is no entry, but the book was written after the peace.

MR. SMITH'S 'SERMON AGAINST ATHEISTS.' Henry Smith, *God's Arrow against Atheists*, 1593.

1594

1st January. A PROGNOSTICATION. Robert Westhawe, *An Almanack and Prognostication serving for the year of Our Lord MDXCIIII.*

4th January. A MYSTERIOUS STRANGER. *S.P. Dom.*, ccxlvi. 39. The letter is dated 31st December.

5th January. PLAYS OF THE WEEK. *Hens. Diary*, i. 16.

6th January. COURT REVELS. Birch's *Memoirs*, i. 146.

7th January. CATHOLIC STORIES FROM SCOTLAND. *Spanish State Papers*, iv. 591. Not dated. For further details of James Maxwell, see *D.N.B.*

12th January. PLAYS OF THE WEEK. *Hens. Diary*, i. 16 ; ii. 159, *Friar Francis* : 'We learn from Heywood's *Apology for Actors* (1612) that this play . . . contained the story of a woman who, for the sake of a lover. murdered her husband, and was haunted by his ghost.'—(Greg.) Nothing is known of *Abraham and Lot* or *The Fair Maid of Italy*.

15th January. AN ALCHEMIST'S BEQUEST. *S.P. Dom.*, ccxlv. 130. Approximate date. Peterson's letter is dated 20th October, 1593, but it seems not to have been received much earlier than this. See also 2nd February and 30th September, 1594.

ATTEMPTS AGAINST THE QUEEN. *S.P. Dom.*, ccxlvii. 12.

16th January. ANOTHER DECLARATION BY TINOCO. *S.P. Dom.*, ccxlvii. 13.

18th January. PLAYS OF THE WEEK. *Hens. Diary*, i. 16 ; ii. 159. Nothing is known of *King Lud*.

23rd January. DR. LOPEZ DEEPLY IMPLICATED. *S.P. Dom.*, ccxlvii. 19.

24th January. PLAYS OF THE WEEK. *Hens. Diary*, i. 16 ; ii. 16. For a long discussion of the origin and history of *Titus Andronicus*, see Dr. Greg's note and E. K. Chambers, *Elizabethan Stage*, ii. 129.

DR. LOPEZ EXAMINED. Birch's *Memoirs*, i. 149, 150. Bishop Godfrey Goodman, *The Court of James I.*, 1839, i. 149.

25th January. A NOTABLE JESUIT TAKEN IN THE NORTH. *S.P. Dom.*, ccxlvii. 21. For an account of Fr. Walpole, see A. Jessop, *One Generation of a Norfolk House*, 1878 ; and *Cath. Rec. Soc.*, vol. v.

31st January. RUMOURS AT COURT. Birch's *Memoirs*, i. 151.

PLAYS OF THE WEEK. *Hens. Diary*, 8, 16.

1st February. BARNFIELD'S 'GREENE'S FUNERALS.' *A.R.*, ii. 644. R[ichard] B[arnfield], *Greene's Funerals*, 1594. Modern edition by R. B. M'Kerrow, 1922.

2nd February. THE ALCHEMIST'S BEQUEST. *S.P. Dom.*, ccxlvii. 36. See 15th January and 30th September, 1594. There is no mention of the bequest of money in Peterson's letter. Apparently the Queen had the choice either of the glasses or a cash payment.

3rd February. BURGLARY AT WINDSOR. Birch's *Memoirs*, i. 155.

PLAYING PROHIBITED. *Remembrancia*, ii. 6. Quoted in *Malone Society Collections*, i. 73.

4th February. A PLOT TO KILL THE QUEEN. *S.P. Dom.*, ccxlvii. 39. For an account of these very complicated plots see Martin Hume, *Treason and Plot*, 1901.

5th February. LOPEZ SENT TO THE TOWER. Birch's *Memoirs*, i. 152.

THE CARTER'S WORDS. Birch's *Memoirs*, i. 155.

6th February. A PLOT TO BURN THE TOWER. *Salisbury Papers*, iv. 474.

THE ROSE THEATRE CLOSED. *Hens. Diary*, i. 16. The *Jew of Malta* reappears with the Lopez sensation.

SHAKESPEARE'S 'TITUS ANDRONICUS.' *A.R.*, ii. 644. William Shakespeare, *Titus Andronicus*, 1594. Modern edition by H. B. Baildon in the *Arden Shakespeare*, etc.

A CONVERSATION BETWEEN SIR ROBERT CECIL AND THE EARL OF ESSEX. Birch's *Memoirs*, i. 153.

THE CONFESSION OF PATRICK COLLEN. *S.P. Dom.*, ccxlvii. 45. See 4th February. The author of the *Troublesome Raigne of King John* makes heavy play with the anticipatory absolution given to the monk who is about to poison King John.

8th February. A RUMOUR OF THE QUEEN'S DEATH. *S.P. Dom.* ccxlvii. 50.

11th February. CLERKE'S 'TRIAL OF BASTARDY.' *A.R.*, ii. 645. William Clerke, *The Trial of Bastardy*, 1594. A book of some interest to anyone concerned with the marriage laws at this period.

17th February. PRECAUTIONS AGAINST SUSPICIOUS PERSONS. *S.P. Dom.* ccxlvii. 66.

18th February. FERRARA DE GAMA'S CONFESSION. *S.P. Dom.*, ccxlvii. 70.

20th February. THE ALCHEMIST'S BEQUEST. *S.P. Dom.*, ccxlvii. 72.

21st February. A PROCLAMATION AGAINST VAGABONDS. *Proclamations*, 324.

THE CONFESSION OF HUGH CAHILL. *S.P. Dom.*, ccxlvii. 78.

25th February. DR. LOPEZ. Birch's *Memoirs*, i. 158.

28th February. DR. LOPEZ ARRAIGNED. *S.P. Dom.*, ccxlvii. 97, 102, 103. Camden, *Elizabeth*.

5th March. 'A LOOKING GLASS FOR LONDON.' *A.R.*, ii. 645. Thomas Lodge and Robert Greene, *A Looking Glass for London*, 1594. Modern edition by J. Churton Collins in *The Plays and Poems of Robert Greene*, 1905.

6th March. THE CORONATION OF THE FRENCH KING. *The Order of Ceremonies observed in the anointing and Coronation of the most Christian French King, and of Navarre, Henry IV. of that name*, 1594. Entered 23rd April.

13th March. Dr. Lopez's Health. *S.P. Dom.*, ccxlviii. 26.

14th March. Lopez's Accomplices Arraigned. *S.P. Dom.*, ccxlviii. 26.

26th March. Atheistical Speeches of Sir Walter Ralegh. *Harleian MSS.*, 6849, ff. 183-9, printed as an appendix in my edition of *Willobie His Avisa*, Bodley Head Quartos, vol. xv.

30th March. Great Storms. Stow, *Annals.*

31st March. Death of Sir John Burgh. *S.P. Dom.*, ccxlviii. 54. Approximate date. For the inference that Sir John met his death at this time see the *D.N.B.* See Appendix I., page 395.

4th April. The Queen's Bounty to Mr. William Camden. *P.S. Dom.*, ccxlviii. 60.

6th April. Plays at the Rose Theatre. *Hens. Diary*, i. 17. *King Leir and his three daughters* was entered *S.R.* 14th May, 1594; beyond the general outline it bears little resemblance to Shakespeare's tragedy.

9th April. Plays at the Rose Theatre. *Hens. Diary*, i. 17.

11th April. A Great Rainstorm. Stow, *Annals.*

16th April. Death of the Earl of Derby. Stow, *Annals*, where further symptoms are detailed.

18th April. Lopez Execution Postponed. *Salisbury Papers*, iv. 512, 513.

23rd April. St. George's Day. Foreign Orders. *Letters of Philip Gawdy*, p. 81. Roxburghe Club, 1907.

Gibbon's 'Praise of a Good Name.' *A.R.*, ii. 647. C. G., *The Praise of a Good Name*, 1594. The essays at the end of the book in style are not unlike Bacon's, which they anticipate by four years. It is interesting to note that Gibbon's *Work worth the Reading*, was dedicated to Sir Nicholas Bacon, elder brother of Francis.

29th April. Lady Branch Buried. W. Har[?]. *Epicedium. A Funeral Song upon the death of Lady Helen Branch*, 1594. This is the first reference to Shakespeare's *Lucrece*, which was entered 9th May. Joshua Sylvester, *Monodia*, n.d.; it is quite as bad as the *Epicedium.*

The Growth of Popery. *S.P. Dom.*, ccxlviii. 83.

1st May. Sir John Smythe's 'Instructions, Observations and Orders Military.' Sir John Smythe, *Instructions, Observations and Orders Military*, composed in 1591, entered 12th April, 1594; dated 1st May in the preface. See page 345 and note thereon.

2nd May. 'The Taming of a Shrew.' *A.R.*, ii. 648. *The Taming of a Shrew*, 1594. Modern edition by F. S. Boas, 1908. The source play for Shakespeare's *Taming of the Shrew.*

3rd May. Great Floods. Stow, *Annals.*

Sir Nicholas Clifford and the Order of St. Michael. *Salisbury Papers*, iv. 523.

9th May. The Rape of Lucrece. *A.R.*, ii. 648. William Shakespeare, *The Rape of Lucrece*, 1594. Modern edition by C. Knox Pooler, in the *Arden Shakespeare*, 1911; etc.

14th May. GREENE'S 'FRIAR BACON.' *A.R.*, ii. 649. Robert Greene, *The Honourable History of Friar Bacon and Friar Bungay*, 1594. Modern edition by J. Churton Collins, *Plays and Poems of Robert Greene*, 1905; A. W. Ward, *Dr. Faustus* and *Friar Bacon*, 1878; etc.

16th May. PLAYING RESUMED. *Hens. Diary*, i. 17; ii. 163. *Cutlack* has not survived.

17th May. MARLOWE'S 'JEW OF MALTA.' *A.R.*, ii. 631. Christopher Marlowe, *The Jew of Malta*, first surviving edition, 1633; modern editions by C. Tucker Brooke, 1910, etc.

30th May. DRAYTON'S 'IDEA'S MIRROR.' *A.R.*, ii. 648. Michael Drayton, *Idea's Mirror*, 1594. Modern edition by Cyril Brett, 1907. The best of the Idea Sonnets are mostly to be found in the later editions.

3rd June. THE DEATH OF THE BISHOP OF LONDON. Stow, *Annals*.

THE PLAYERS OF THE LORD ADMIRAL AND THE LORD CHAMBERLAIN UNITE. *Hens. Diary*, i. 17.

7th June. LOPEZ, TINOCO AND FERRARA EXECUTED. Stow, *Annals*; Camden, *Elizabeth*.

8th June. PLAYS OF THE WEEK. *Hens. Diary*, i. 17; ii. 163. *Hester and Assuerus* is unknown.

15th June. PLAYS OF THE WEEK. *Hens. Diary*, i. 17; ii. 164. *Bellendon* is probably *Belin Dun*, entered on 24th November, 1595, as 'The time-tragical history of King Rufus the first with the life and death of Belin Dun the first thief that ever was hanged in England.' No copy is known, but the play was one of the Admiral's most successful.

18th June. LYLY'S 'MOTHER BOMBY.' *A.R.*, ii. 654. John Lyly, *Mother Bomby*, 1594. Modern edition by R. W. Bond in *The Complete Works of John Lyly*, 1902.

19th June. THE TRUE TRAGEDY OF RICHARD THE THIRD. *A.R.*, ii. 655. *The True Tragedy of Richard the Third*. Modern edition by W. C. Hazlitt, 1875.

21st June. THE SPANIARDS AT BREST. *Salisbury Papers*, iv. 552.

22nd June. THE CHAMBERLAIN'S BREAK WITH THE ADMIRAL'S. *Hens. Diary*, i. 17. J. Tucker Murray, *English Dramatic Companies*, i. 88 *et seq.* I assume that Shakespeare had now joined them; but see Appendix I. p. 392.

26th June. THE FUNERAL OF THE BISHOP OF LONDON. Stow, *Annals*.

THE CHARACTER OF BISHOP AYLMER. Sir John Harington, *Nugae Antiquae*.

27th June. PLAYS OF THE WEEK. *Hens. Diary*, i. 17; ii. 165. Nothing is known of *Galiaso*.

5th July. VIOLENCE IN WESTMINSTER. *Middlesex Sessions Rolls*, i. 215.

6th July. PLAYS OF THE WEEK. *Hens. Diary*, i. 18.

12th July. SIDNEY SUSSEX COLLEGE IN CAMBRIDGE FOUNDED. *S.P. Dom.*, ccxlix, 26.

13th July. PLAYS OF THE WEEK. *Hens. Diary*, i. 18; ii. 160. Nothing certain is known of *Philipo and Hippolito*.

15th July. CRUELTY IN PORTUGAL. *Salisbury Papers*, iv. 562.

16th July. Soldiers for Brest. *S.P. Dom.*, ccxlix. 29.

20th July. The Spanish Preparations. *Salisbury Papers*, iv. 566.

Plays of the Week. *Hens. Diary*, i. 18 ; ii. 166. *Godfrey of Bulloigne* probably dealt with the Siege of Jerusalem. See Dr. Greg's note.

21st July. Captain Dawtry's Offer to lead an Irish Regiment. *Salisbury Papers*, iv. 566.

Mr. J. Dawtrey (in *The Falstaff Saga*, 1927) claimed Captain Dawtry as the original of Falstaff. The gallant Captain certainly had many of Falstaff's characteristics; he was moreover 'very large and unwieldy,' and a difficult object to move when wounded.

26th July. John Boste, a Jesuit, Executed. *Cath. Rec. Soc.*, v. p. 286.

25th July. The Earl of Essex not allowed to go to Brest. Birch's *Memoirs*, i. 181.

27th July. Disorders at the Port of Ipswich. *Salisbury Papers*, iv. 570.

Plays of the Week. *Hens. Diary*, i. 18.

1st August. A Proclamation concerning Prizes. *Proclamations*, 326.

4th August. Plays of the Week. *Hens. Diary*, i. 18 ; ii. 166.

8th August. Platt's 'Jewel House of Nature.' *A.R.*, ii. 656. Hugh Platt, *The Jewel House of Art and Nature*, 1594. For details of Platt's life see *D.N.B.* A most interesting and entertaining book. Some of the receipts belong to the long order of untried experiments, but Platt is a genuine inventor who observed for himself and was not merely content to use the scissors on other men's books.

10th August. Plays of the Week. *Hens. Diary*, i. 18.

17th August. Plays of the Week. *Hens. Diary*, i. 18 ; ii. 167. *Tasso's Melancholy* is not known.

19th August. Captain Glemham's Exploits in the Levant Seas. *A.R.* ii. 657. Entered 19th August. R. H., *News from the Levant Seas*, 1594.

20th August. The Lady Bridget Manners. *Hist. MSS. Com.*, *Rutland MSS.*, i. 322. See 20th November, 1592.

A Plot to Kill the Queen. *S.P. Dom.*, ccxlix. 98. One of several confessions.

Suitors at Court to be Restrained. *Proclamations*, 327.

21st August. A Further Confession of Captain Yorke. *S.P. Dom.*, ccxlix. 103.

24th August. Further Confessions of the Plotters. *S.P. Dom.*, ccxlix. 114.

Plays of the Week. *Hens. Diary*, i. 18.

27th August. Williams' Confession. *S.P. Dom.*, ccxlix. 117.

28th August. Yorke and Williams Confronted. *S.P. Dom.*, ccxlix. 125.

An Order at Court. *Letters of Philip Gawdy*, p. 90. Roxburgh Club, 1906.

The Return of the Earl of Cumberland's Ships. Hakluyt, v. 69.

29th August. SIR JOHN NORRIS DELAYED. *S.P. Dom.*, ccxlix. 128.

31st August. PLAYS OF THE WEEK. *Hens. Diary*, i. 19; ii. 167. *Mahomet*, probably Greene's *Alphonsus of Aragon*. For the *Venetian Comedy* see Dr. Greg's note (ii. 170).

3rd September. 'WILLOBIE HIS AVISA.' *A.R.*, ii. 659. *Willobie His Avisa*, 1594. For a discussion and a tentative solution of the problem of *Willobie His Avisa* and its connection with Shakespeare, see my essay, appended to the reprint in vol. xv. of *The Bodley Head Quartos*, 1926.

DAVIS'S 'SEAMAN'S SECRETS.' *A.R.*, ii. 659. John Davis, *The Seaman's Secrets*, 1594.

5th September. THE SCOTTISH KING'S SON BAPTISED. *A True Reportarie of the most triumphant and Royal accomplishment of the Baptism of the most Excellent, right High and Mightie Prince, Frederick Henry: by the Grace of God, Prince of Scotland. Solemnized the 30th day of August, 1594. Printed by R. Waldegrave, Printer to his Royal Majesty.* Reprinted in London in 1603 on the accession of King James. See Appendix I., p. 401.

7th September. PLAYS OF THE WEEK. *Hens. Diary*, i. 19.

8th September. GILES FLETCHER'S 'LICIA.' Giles Fletcher, *Licia, or Poems of Love*: dated in the Epistle Dedicatory 4th September, 1594; in the Epistle to the reader 8th September. The sonnets are not above the average, but the reference to the 'jar of this disagreeing age' is an interesting sign of the growth of the melancholic humour which was so prevalent five years later. Modern edition in Arber's *English Garner*, vol. viii.

9th September. THE COUNTESS OF RUTLAND AND THE LADY BRIDGET. *Hist. MSS. Com., Rutland MSS.*, i. 323. See 20th August.

10th September. NEWS FROM BREST. *News from Brest. A diurnal of all that Sir John Norris hath done since his last arrival in Brest*, 1594.

11th September. SIR THOMAS WILKES TO BE SENT TO THE ARCHDUKE ERNEST. *Salisbury Papers*, v. 12, 13.

14th September. PLAYS OF THE WEEK. *Hens. Diary*, i. 19.

18th September. THE WAR IN BRITTANY. *News from Brest.*

A DUTCH MILL. *Remembrancia*, ii. 15.

21st September. PLAYS OF THE WEEK. *Hens. Diary*, i. 19; ii. 168. Nothing is known of *Palamon and Arcite*, but presumably it was founded on Chaucer's *Knight's Tale*.

28th September. PLAYS OF THE WEEK. *Hens. Diary*, i. 19; ii. 160. *The Love of an English Lady* is unknown.

30th September. THE ALCHEMIST'S BEQUEST. *S.P. Dom.*, ccl. 9. See 19th January and 2nd February.

THE BAD WEATHER AND THE PRICE OF GRAIN. Stow, *Annals*. See Appendix I., p. 400.

3rd October. INMATES TO BE REMOVED. *Remembrancia*, ii. No. 17. Inmates are lodgers; in the spacious days men lived as close as in a modern Oriental bazaar, and as squalidly. The original is dated 1593, but as (*a*) it occurs in the middle of a number of letters written in 1594, and (*b*) the infection in the beginning of October 1593 was far from 'late,' I venture to correct what seems an obvious error.

5th October. PLAYS OF THE WEEK. *Hens. Diary*, i. 19 ; ii. 169. Nothing is certainly known of *The Love of a Grecian Lady.*

6th October. LE ROY'S 'OF THE INTERCHANGEABLE COURSE OF THINGS.' Louis Le Roy, *Of the Interchangeable Course of Things*, 1594. Dated in the Epistle ; no entry in *S.R.* The author is very vaguely probing after scientific methods of inquiry.

12th October. PLAYS OF THE WEEK. *Hens. Diary*, i. 19.

15th October. THE LADY BRIDGET AT COURT. *Hist. MSS., Rutland MS.*, i. 324. See 9th September.

18th October. CAPTAIN ANTHONY WINGFIELD SLAIN. *News from Brest.*

19th October. PLAYS OF THE WEEK. *Hens. Diary*, i. 19 ; ii. 170. For a discussion of *The French Doctor* see Dr. Greg's note.

20th October. THE DISRESPECT OF THE ARCHDUKE ERNEST. *Salisbury Papers*, v. 12, 13. See page 349 and note.

25th October. PLAYS OF THE WEEK. *Hens. Diary*, i. 20 ; ii. 171. *A Knack to Know an Honest Man.*

NASHE'S 'TERRORS OF THE NIGHT.' Thomas Nashe, *The Terrors of the Night*, 1594. Modern edition by R. B. M'Kerrow in *The Works of Thomas Nashe*, vol. ii. 1904. The book, for some reason, was entered twice, on 30th June, 1593, and again on 25th October, 1594 ; but the earliest edition is dated 1594, and on internal evidence (for which see Dr. M'Kerrow's notes) was not written before that date. An amusing skit, and, as are all Nashe's books, an admirable gloss on contemporary gossip.

31st October. SIR JOHN NORRIS'S ATTACK ON THE FORT AT CROYZON. *News from Brest*, 1594.

2nd November. PLAYS OF THE WEEK. *Hens. Diary*, i. 20.

3rd November. THE SERMON AT PAUL'S CROSS. John Dove, *A Sermon preached at Paul's Cross the 3rd November*, 1594.

A PETITION AGAINST A NEW THEATRE. *Remembrancia*, ii. 73. Quoted in *Malone Society Collections*, i. 74. It is no small tribute to Nashe that the Lord Mayor should officially condemn the arguments in favour of plays made by Pierce Penilesse (see p. 151).

4th November. THE STATE OF IRELAND. MSS. Harl, 6996, f. ii. 6. Quoted in Thomas Wright, *Queen Elizabeth and her Times*, 1838, ii. 438.

9th November. PLAYS OF THE WEEK. *Hens. Diary*, i. 20 ; ii. 171. Nothing is known of *Caesar and Pompey.*

15th November. THE ASSAULT ON THE FORT AT CROYZON. *News from Brest*, 1594.

16th November. PLAYS OF THE WEEK. *Hens. Diary*, i. 20 ; ii. 171. For *Dioclesian*, see Dr. Greg's note.

17th November. MEASURES AGAINST VAGRANTS AND BEGGING POOR. *Remembrancia*, ii. No. 74.

THE QUEEN'S ACCESSION DAY. *Fugger News-letters*, 2nd series, p. 262.

19th November. SPENSER'S 'AMORETTI' AND 'EPITHALAMIUM.' Edmund Spenser, *Amoretti* and *Epithalamium*, 1595. *A.R.*, ii. 655. Modern edition by J. C. Smith and E. de Selincourt, 1912, etc.

20th November. THE USE OF THE CITY GARNERS REFUSED. *Remembrancia*, ii. No. 79.

23rd November. PLAYS OF THE WEEK. *Hens. Diary*, i. 20.

27th November. THE LADY BRIDGET MANNERS. *Hist. MSS. Com. Rutland MSS.*, i. 324. See 15th Oct.

30th November. PLAYS OF THE WEEK. *Hens. Diary*, i. 20 ; ii. 172. Nothing is known of *Warlamchester*.

A CONFERENCE ABOUT THE SUPPRESSING OF ROGUES. *Remembrancia*, ii. Nos. 75, 76.

2nd December. A PROCLAMATION AGAINST FIREARMS. *Proclamations*, 328.

DE LA MARCHE'S 'THE RESOLVED GENTLEMAN.' Oliver de la Marche, *The Resolved Gentleman*, translated by L. Lewkenor, 1594.

6th December. SIR W. RALEGH'S COMMISSION. *S.P. Dom.*, ccl. 46.

7th December. PLAYS OF THE WEEK. *Hens. Diary*, i. 20 ; ii. 172. *The Wise Man of West Chester* is Anthony Munday's *John a Kent and John a Cumber* which exists in manuscript. It has been reprinted by the Malone Society.

8th December. THE DEATH OF CARDINAL ALLEN. Camden's *Elizabeth ; Salisbury Papers*, v. 27. A racy account of Allen's English college at Rome, and the various squabbles, is given in Anthony Munday's *English Roman Life*, 1582 ; printed in vol. xii. of *The Bodley Head Quartos*.

14th December. REVELS TO BE HELD AT GRAY'S INN. *Gesta Grayorum*, first printed in 1688. Modern editions in Nichol's *Progresses of Queen Elizabeth*, and the Malone Society's Reprints, 1914.

PLAYS OF THE WEEK. *Hens. Diary*, i. 20 ; ii. 172. For the *Set at Maw*, see Dr. Greg's note.

20th December. THE REVELS AT GRAY'S INN. *Gesta Grayorum*. See Appendix I., p. 402-3.

21st December. PLAYS OF THE WEEK. *Hens. Diary*, i. 21.

24th December. 'A CONFERENCE ABOUT THE NEXT SUCCESSION.' N. Doleman, *A Conference about the next Succession*, 1594. The date is approximate and possibly too soon.

THE ORCHARD AND THE GARDEN. *The Orchard and the Garden*, 1594.

26th December. AN ATTEMPT TO MURDER THE FRENCH KING. *The Decree of the Court of Parliament against John Chastel*, 1595. Entered 28th December, 1594.

27th December. PLAYS OF THE WEEK. *Hens. Diary*, i. 21.

28th December. THE CHAMBERLAIN'S PLAYERS AT COURT. E. K. Chambers, *Elizabethan Stage*, iv. 164.

GRAY'S INN REVELS : A NIGHT OF ERRORS. *Gesta Grayorum*. For discussions of the Shakespearean allusions, see the commentators and Mrs. C. C. Stopes' *The Third Earl of Southampton*, pp. 71-6.

30th December. DR. FLETCHER ELECTED BISHOP OF LONDON. Stow, *Annals*. He was the father of the dramatist, at this time aged 15.

PLAYS AT THE ROSE. *Hens. Diary*, i. 21.

'THE DISPLAY OF FOLLY.' O. B., *The Display of Folly*, 1594. The book is catalogued thus in the Short Title Catalogue, and in the Catalogue of the British Museum, but its title page reads *Questions of Profitable and Pleasant concernings*; the sub-title of the text is 'The display of Folly' and the running title 'The Display of vain Life.'

BARNFIELD'S 'AFFECTIONATE SHEPHERD.' Richard Barnfield, *The Affectionate Shepherd*, 1594. Modern edition by J. O. Halliwell, Percy Society, 1847.

BARWICK'S 'BRIEF DISCOURSE.' Humphrey Barwick, *A Brief Discourse Concerning the force and effect of all manual weapons of fire*, n.d. See page 299. Sir Roger Williams in *A Brief Discourse of War*, 1590, had claimed that 'a hundred muskets are to be valued unto two hundred calivers or more: the calivers may say they will discharge two shot for one, but cannot deny but one musket shot doth more hurt than two calivers, shot far or near, and better cheap, although the musket spend a pound of powder in eight or twelve shots, and the other smaller shoots twenty and thirty of a pound.'

'THE DEATH OF USURY.' *The Death of Usury*, 1594. An anonymous work, apparently a young law student's notebook.

GRASSI'S 'TRUE ART OF DEFENCE.' *Giacomo di Grassi his true Art of Defence*, translated by I. G., 1594.

HOOKER'S 'ECCLESIASTICAL POLITY.' Richard Hooker, *Of the Laws of Ecclesiastical Polity*, 1594. Entered 29th January, 1593. Modern edition by Ronald Bayne in the *Everyman Library*, 1907, etc.

LAMBARD'S 'EIRENARCHA.' William Lambard, *Eirenarcha*, 1594.

MARLOWE AND NASHE'S 'DIDO, QUEEN OF CARTHAGE.' Christopher Marlowe and Thomas Nashe, *Dido, Queen of Carthage*, 1594. Modern edition by C. F. Tucker Brooke, in *The Works of Christopher Marlowe*, 1910.

'THE BATTLE OF ALCAZAR.' *The Battle of Alcazar*, 1594. Modern edition by W. W. Greg, Malone Society Reprints, 1907. See also Dr. Greg's *Orlando and Alcazar*, in the same series.

PERCY'S 'SONNETS TO THE FAIREST COELIA.' William Percy, *Sonnets to the Fairest Coelia*, 1594. Modern edition by A. B. Grosart, 1877.

'PRESENT REMEDIES AGAINST THE PLAGUE.' *Present Remedies against the Plague*, 1594.

'A TRUE REPORT OF SUNDRY HORRIBLE CONSPIRACIES.' *A True Report of Sundry Horrible Conspiracies*, 1594; propaganda for neutrals, possibly prepared for the edification of the Archduke Ernest's subjects, or else issued after his rebuff (see p. 327). The pamphlet was translated into French.

APPENDIX I

THE STATIONERS' REGISTER

In theory every book ought to have been entered in the *Stationers' Register* before printing; in practice the Elizabethan printer was as casual over his entries in the *Register* as in his obedience to any other kind of regulation. Many books were never entered at all, some after printing but before publication, some after publication. A few of the entries in the *Register* were intended to establish copyright and thereby to block publication; some were made before the books were even written.

For the four years the total number of new books entered was roughly 138 in 1591, 136 in 1592, 110 in 1593 (the plague year), rising to 162 in 1594. These figures are approximate, as it is not always possible to tell whether a book is new or old, though entered for the first time. In 1591, for instance, the total includes 14 foreign works entered to Wolfe, and 9 classics, all entered together. In 1592, 5 ballads, included in the total, may be old ballads, entered to maintain copyright. A margin of error of at least 10 per cent. should therefore be allowed in all totals.

(1) *Books not entered*. Many books (probably not less than one-fifth) were never entered; but there seems to be no principle governing either entry or omission. Of a total of 36 books written by Greene, 29 were entered. Of his five Conny-catching pamphlets written in 1591 and 1592, the *Notable discouery of Coosenage*, the *Second part of conny-catching* and the *Third part* were entered; *A disputation betweene a hee conny-catcher and a shee conny-catcher* was omitted; *The blacke bookes messenger* was entered. Only 6 out of 16 works by Lodge were entered; whilst of 11 by Nashe, only 3 were left out—two anti-Martinist pamphlets, and *Haue with you to Saffron-walden*, whose omission is not surprising. Hence, of these three authors, 20 books out of a total of 63 were not entered, or rather less than a third.

(2) *Normal entry*. It is rare for the biography of a book to survive. One instance is Simon Forman's *Grounds of Longitude*. Forman noted in his Diary that he sent the book to the press on 6th July, 1591; it was entered on 12th July, and published before the end of the year. Another instance is *The most strange discouerie of the three witches of Warboys*, who were executed on 7th April, 1593 (p. 224 and note). The book was submitted for entry on 30th June, and probably published at the end of November, as a ballad, *The Lamentable Song of the*

Three Witches of Warboys, was entered on 4th December, being presumably founded on the printed book.

Ballads were often published when a sensational book or play came out, and publishers sometimes entered both book and ballad together to secure their double right. Thus on 29th August, 1594, Gosson, Millington, and Dawson entered a pamphlet describing the execution of Thomas Merry for murdering Robert Beeche and his servant, and at the same time a ballad of 'Beche his ghoste, complayninge on ye wofull murder committed on him and Thomas Winchester his Servaunt.' There are several other instances.

(3) *Books entered after printing*. Two instances may be noted. The first is Greene's *Notable discouery of Coosenage*, which was entered as *The Arte of Connye katchinge*, together with the *Second parte of Connye katchinge*, on 13th December, 1591. Greene in his preface to the *Second part* answered certain objections to the style of the *Notable discovery*, which had therefore been published and criticized before the preface to the *Second part* was written.

A second instance is Simon Kellwaye's *Defensative against the plague* (p. 217), which is worth following in detail because the evidence is unusually full. The book was entered on 21st March, 1593. An epistle dedicatory to the Earl of Essex is dated 25th March, 1592 (*i.e.* 1593); the Epistle to the Reader is dated 25th March, 1593; next comes a commendation of the author by George Baker, dated 'from my chamber in Court this 7 of Aprill 1593'; finally, the preliminary matter ends with the 'Author to the Reader,' noting the faults escaped, and dated 8th April, 1593. The text of the book begins with signature B 1, as is usual with first editions, and contains 100 pages of matter, set up mainly in black letter, with many medical prescriptions tabulated in roman and italic, and an index.

The history of the book's publication seems to be that as soon as the text had been set up, Windet took a copy to Stationers' Hall and entered it from the printed title-page, which reads: *A defensative against the Plague: contayning two partes or treatises: the first, showing the meanes how to preserve vs from the dangerous contagion thereof: the Second, how to cure those that are infected therewith*. The entry, except for the words 'showing the meanes,' is word for word the same. Next, a few advance copies were assembled, without the preliminary matter, one of which the author sent to the Earl of Essex, others to his friends. Meanwhile the text was checked by Kellwaye, who on 8th April sent in the preliminary matter, corrections, and index.

If, on the other hand, this interpretation of the dates is wrong and *A defensative against the Plague* was entered before printing, it follows that the whole of the text was set up, proofs read, and an index prepared between 21st March and 8th April, which is quick work.

The title of a book as entered in the *Stationers' Register* sometimes varies considerably from that printed on the title-page, but that at other times quite a long title is quoted word for word, or else the beginning is quoted and the rest cut off by '&c.' The probable explanation (though it cannot be proved definitely) is that when a 'long-tailed title' is accurately transcribed in the *Register*, then the entry was made from a *printed copy*. Thus, on the one hand, Shakespeare's *Merchant of Venice* was entered on 17th July, 1598, as 'a booke ot the Marchaunt of Venyce or otherwise called the Jewe of Venyce,' but on the title-page reads 'The most excellent Historie of the Merchant of Venice. With the extreame cruelties of Shylocke the Iewe towards the sayd Merchant, in cutting a iust pound of his flesh: and the obtayning of Portia by the choyse of three chests. As it hath beene diuers times acted by the Lord Chamberlaine his Seruants. Written by William Shakespeare.' On the other hand the *Firste part of the Contention* is entered as 'the firste parte of the Contention of the twoo famous houses of York and Lancaster with the deathe of the good Duke Humfrey and the banishement and Deathe of the Duke of Suffolk and the tragicall ende of the prowd Cardinall of Winchester with the notable rebellion of Iack Cade and the Duke of Yorkes ffirste clayme vnto the Crowne,' which is word for word the same as the title-page except that the *Register* reads 'of the twoo' for 'betwixt the twoo.'

(4) *Blocking entry*. Blocking entries used to prevent the publication of a manuscript against the owner's wishes are usually difficult to establish, because when there is a wide interval between the date of entry and of the first known edition it may be due to the fact that no copy of an earlier issue has survived.

A probable instance of a blocking entry is Thomas Campion's *Observations in the arte of Englishe poesie*, entered on 12th October, 1591. The earliest known edition is that of 1602, which evoked a reply in Daniel's *Defence of Ryme* (1603). On internal evidence the *Observations* was more likely to have been written in 1591, when the use of classical metres in English verse was being widely discussed, but the 1602 edition bears every sign of being the first: it is, moreover, dedicated to the Lord Buckhurst as Lord High Treasurer, an office which in 1591 was held by Lord Burleigh.

Another instance is Sir Philip Sidney's *The defence of poesie*, which was entered on 29th November, 1594. *Astrophel and Stella* had been published without the consent of the family in 1591, and it was apparently to prevent another unauthorized publication that Ponsonby (who was the authorized printer of Sidney's works) entered *The defence*. Some months later (12th April, 1595) Olney entered and printed another version, *An apologie for poetry*, but Ponsonby naturally complained, the entry was cancelled, and the note added, 'This belongeth to master ponsonby by a former entrance And an agrement is made between them whereby Master Ponsonby is to enioy the copie according to the former entrance.' Ponsonby's edition is dated 1595.

(5) *Books entered before they were written*. The evidence for this practice is simply cold chronology. On 25th January, 1591, Captain

Arnold Cosbye was executed forty-eight hours after trial for the murder of the Lord Burke (p. 7); the same day was entered to Edward White *The arraynement and Condemnacon of Arnalt Cosbye for murderinge the lord Burghe*. It is a long semi-official account of the trial and gives a short note of the execution. On the other hand the 'mournful Dyttye' which White produced on the same subject was not entered till 6th February, being forestalled by R. Robinson, who entered the 'sorowfull sighes of a sadd soule' for the untimely loss of Lord Burke on 26th January.

Similarly, on 28th July, 1591, was entered to Robert Bourne *The Life, araynement, Iudgement and Execution of William Hacket*, who was quartered that morning in Cheapside (p. 45). This book, not to be confused with Cosin's *Conspiracy for Pretended Reformation* (p. 59), has perished.

On 28th June, 1592, John Parker and Anne Bruen were executed for poisoning John Bruen, goldsmith (p. 145). The same day was entered to John Kyd, 'the Iudgment and execucon of John Parker, goldsmithe, and Anne Bruen for poysoninge her late husband John Bruen goldsmithe.' John Kyd was an enterprising publisher, who tried to forestall competitors by entering his book early; but the officials of the Company were not entirely satisfied, for there was added a note in the Register, 'Prouided that this booke before yt be printed shalbe drawen into good forme and order and then laufullie allowed to be printed.' The title of the printed book is:

> 'The trueth of the most wicked and secret murthering of Iohn Brewen, Goldsmith of London, committed by his owne wife, through the prouocation of one Iohn Parker whom she loued: for which fact she was burned, and he hanged in Smithfield, on wednesday, the 28 of Iune, 1592, two yeares after the murther was committed.'

The Bruen case inspired several ballads. Jeffs got in with 'The Lamentation of Agnes Bruen' on 1st July: Wolfe followed with 'A ballad of the Burnynge of Anne Bruen' on 10th July, and 'John Parker's lamentacon' on the 11th: finally Jeffs provided another 'lamentacion' for John Parker on the 15th. This last entry from its fullness suggests that the ballad was already in print; it reads: 'The Lamentacion of John Parker whoe for consentinge to the murder of John Bruen was hanged in Smithfeild the 28 of June 2 yeres after the fact was committed to the tune of fortune.' The similarity between this title and the title of the pamphlet is worth noting.

On 22nd August, 1592, occurs an entry, again to John Kyd, which is conclusive: 'Entred for his copie by warrant from master Watkins, a booke, of the true reporte of the poysoninge of Thomas Elliott Tailor of London. Prouided that this booke must be perused by master Watkins before yt be printed.' Clearly Master Watkins had not seen the book.

Finally, on 15th November, 1594, was entered 'a ballad of the triumphes at the tilte and thanksgyvinge the xvii of November 1594 for their maiesties xxxvii yeares Reigne,' that is, two days *before* the event happened.

In all five entries the circumstances are similar; they show that entry in the *Register* was used to stake a claim in a piece of startling news, as well as to prevent an unlawful publication. Unfortunately for the *Elizabethan Journal* most of these pamphlets and ballads have perished.

APPENDIX II

NEWS PAMPHLETS

Of the total of some 546 new books entered in the *Stationers' Register* during the period 1591-4, 129 items are concerned with current news, of which 79 are prose and 46 verse, mostly ballads. These figures again are approximate: it is not always possible to tell whether an entry refers to a prose or a verse work, or whether it is news or fiction. Greene's *Black bookes messenger*, for instance, is entered as 'The Repentance of a Cony catcher with the life and death of Mourton and Ned Browne, twoo notable cony catchers The one latelie executed at Tyborne the other at Aix in ffraunce' (p. 155). At first sight it appears to be a news pamphlet; actually the book, as published, contained only the life and death of Ned Browne, and that a manifest fiction.

The issue of news pamphlets was very erratic, and the list is more remarkable for what it omits than what it includes. Nothing was entered which bears on the Lopez conspiracy,[1] and Hacket's execution was unsung in any ballad; as, however, he died blaspheming, a doleful repentance would have been out of place. The figures for 1591-4 are as follows:

	1591. Prose.	1591. Verse.	1592. P.	1592. V.	1593. P.	1593. V.	1594. P.	1594. V.
Foreign News.								
(*a*) The War in France.	24	2	12	–	3	–	10	2
(*b*) General.	4	–	1	–	2	1	4	3
Naval.	4	2	–	1	–	–	1	–
Home News.	4	4	6	6	2	9	2	17
	36	8	19	7	7	10	17	22

The wars in France account for most of the news pamphlets. Twenty-six publications (including two ballads) were entered between 23rd January and 21st November, 1591, after which there was a break for three months, until 28th February, when their issue began again, and twelve were entered in four and a half months. Then there is a considerable gap, for from 19th July, 1592, to 14th April, 1594, only three entries are recorded. The reason for this is that the war was fluctuating and uncertain. The output of pamphlets rose in 1594 to ten in prose, with two ballads.

[1] There were, however, a number of news pamphlets and ballads which were not entered, e.g. *A true report of sundry horrible conspiracies* (p. 349).

Of these 49 French war pamphlets John Wolfe printed no less than 36. Most of them are founded on official or semi-official sources, such as proclamations or orders issued by the French King, the printed terms of truce with the Leaguers, information supplied by the French ambassador in England, and so forth. Those which describe the actions of the English troops are most interesting. Reverses and disasters, needless to say, were not recorded, nor was there much glorification of the army under the Earl of Essex, which accomplished very little.

Other foreign news takes up some fifteen entries, if indeed one may include under the heading of news certain strange birds seen in Flanders, or a monstrous child born in the Dukedom of Brabant, or such items as 'a booke of newes of Twoo angels that came before the Cytie of Droppa in Slesia' with 'a ballad of the same Twoo angelles.'

Naval events occupy two ballads and four prose works in 1591, one of them being Sir Walter Ralegh's account of the loss of the *Revenge*.

There are 50 entries of home news, of which 36 are ballads, mostly of murders, executions, and marvels, with half a dozen laments and epitaphs. Of the fourteen prose pamphlets, six are accounts of criminal trials and executions, and one is a description of Queen Elizabeth's progress to Elvetham.

These figures are taken from the *Register*; a number of books in each class survive which were never entered. It is worth noting that there is no attempt to record home news of any real importance, nor do affairs in Scotland occupy much space. Two semi-official Scotch pamphlets were entered between 1591 and 1594, the first dealing with the conspiracy of the papists in 1593 (p. 249), the second describing the baptism of Prince Henry in August 1594 (p. 320), which also gave birth to a ballad. No Irish pamphlet was entered.[1]

[1] The conclusions summarised in Appendices II and III are worked out at some length in my paper 'Books and Readers, 1591-4,' printed in the *Library*, vol. viii. p. 273.

A SECOND ELIZABETHAN JOURNAL

1595-1598

1595

3rd January. The Revels at Gray's Inn.

The revels at Gray's Inn were this night continued and because of the tumults on the 'Night of Errors' good watch was kept with whifflers, so that all had good places to their liking and contentment. There were present many great and noble personages, as the Lord Keeper, the Earls of Shrewsbury, Cumberland, Northumberland, Southampton and Essex, the Lords Buckhurst, Windsor, Mountjoy, Burleigh, Mounteagle, Thomas Howard; Sir Thomas Heneage, Sir Robert Cecil; and a great number of Knights, Ladies and very worshipful persons.

When all were placed, the Prince of Purpool came into the Hall with his wonted state and ascended his throne at the high end of the Hall, and after him the Ambassador of Templaria with his train; who, after variety of music, were presented with this device. At the side of the Hall within a curtain was erected an altar to the Goddess of Amity, her arch-flamen ready to attend the sacrifice that should be offered, and round about nymphs and fairies with instruments of music. Then issued forth of another room, the first pair of friends, being Theseus and Perithous. They came arm in arm, and offered incense upon the altar, which shined and burned very clear without blemish, and so departed; and in like manner came Achilles and Patroclus, Pilades and Orestes, then Scipio and Lelius. But when Graius and Templarius came lovingly to the altar and offered their incense, the Goddess did not accept of their service, for the flame was choked by a troubled smoke and dark vapour. Hereat the arch-flamen, willing to pacify the angry goddess, preferred certain mystical ceremonies and commanded the nymphs to sing some hymns of pacification, so that when the friends again proffered their devotion the flame burnt more clear than at any time before: and so they departed. Whereupon the arch-flamen pronounced Graius and Templarius to be friends, and denounced a heavy curse upon them that in any way go about to break the bond and league of sincere amity.

Then the Prince, in token of their amity, offered the Ambassador of the Templarians and some of his retinue the Knighthood of the Helmet, an order of his own institution. So the King at Arms placed the Ambassador and some of his followers, and also some of the Templarians, that they might receive the dignity at his hands; which done, the Prince came down from his chair of state, and put a Collar about the Ambassador's neck, he kneeling on his left knee, and said to him, '*Sois Chevalier*'; and so was done to the rest, to the number of twenty-four. Then the King at Arms stood forth, and after a speech read out the Articles of the Order, being of this nature:

Item, No knight shall be inquisitive towards any lady or gentleman, whether her beauty be English or Italian, or whether with care taking she have added half a foot to her stature, but take all to the best. Neither shall any knight presume to affirm that faces were better twenty years ago than they are at this present time, except such knight have passed three climacterical years.

Item, No knight shall put out any money upon strange returns or performances to be made by his own person, as to hop up the stairs to the top of St. Paul's without intermission, or any such like agilities or endurances, except it may appear that the same practices do enable him to some service or employment; as if he do undertake to go a journey backward, the same shall be thought to enable him to be an Ambassador unto Turkey.

Item, No knight, that hath licence to travel, be it by map, card, sea or land, and hath returned, shall presume upon the warrant of a traveller to report any extraordinary varieties; as that he hath ridden through Venice on horseback post, or travelled over the most part of the countries of Geneva.

Item, Every knight shall endeavour to be much in the books of the worshipful citizens next adjoining to the territories of Purpool; and none shall unlearnedly, or without looking, pay ready money for any wares, to the ill example of others, and utter suppression of credit betwixt man and man.

Item, Every knight shall endeavour to add conference and experience by reading; and therefore shall not only read and peruse Guizo, *The French Academy*, Galiatho, *The Courtier*, Plutarch, the *Arcadia*, and the Neoterical writers from time to time; but also frequent the Theatre, and such like places of experience; and resort to the better sort of ordinaries for conference, whereby they may not only become accomplished with civil conversations, and able to govern a table with discourse; but also sufficient, if need be, to make epigrams, emblems, and other devices appertaining to his Honour's learned revels.

Item, No knight that weareth fustian, cloth, or such statute stuff for necessity shall pretend to wear the same for the new fashion's sake.

Item, No knight in walking the streets or other places of resort shall bear his hands in the pockets of his great rolled hose with the Spanish wheel, if it be not either to defend his hands from the cold or else to guard forty shillings sterling, being in the same pockets.

Item, That no knight shall take upon him the person of a Malcontent, in going with a more private retinue than appertaineth to his degree, and using but certain special, obscure company, and commending none but men disgraced and out of office; and smiling at good news, as if he knew something that were not true, and making odd notes of his Highness's reign, and former governments, and the like.

When all these Articles of Knighthood had been read and the ceremonies finished, there was variety of consort music; and in the meanwhile the Knights of the Order, which were not strangers, brought into the Hall a running banquet in very good order, and gave it to the Prince, the Lords and other strangers. This done the Prince held a Council of six of his Privy Councillors, to whom he gave charge that they should advise him in general of the scope and end whereunto the government of the State might best be directed.

Then the first Councillor made a speech advising the exercise of war whereby in later years he should find a sweet respect into the adventures of youth, enjoy his reputation, eternize his name, and leave deep footsteps of his power in the world.

The second Councillor would have him study philosophy, commending four principal works to the Prince. The first was the collecting of a most perfect and general library, wherein whatsoever the wit of man hath heretofore committed to books of worth, be they ancient or modern, printed or manuscript,

European or of other parts, of one or other language, might be made contributory to his wisdom. Next a spacious wonderful garden wherein whatsoever plant the earth bringeth forth may be set and cherished : this garden to be built about with rooms to stake in all rare beasts, and to cage in all rare birds, with two lakes adjoining, the one of fresh water, the other of salt, for like variety of fishes ; and so he might have in small compass a model of Universal Nature made private. The third, a goodly huge cabinet wherein shall be stored whatsoever the hand of man by exquisite art or engine hath made rare in stuff, form, or motion. The fourth, such a still house so furnished with mills, instruments, furnaces and vessels as may be a palace fit for a philosopher's stone.

The third Councillor, confuting those that had gone before, would have the Prince's fame eternized by the magnificence of goodly and royal buildings and foundations, and the new institutions of orders, ordinances and societies.

The fourth Councillor advised absoluteness of state and treasure, for he had needs conquer at home the overgrowing of his grandees in factions and too great liberties of the people, the great reverence given to laws and customs in derogation of his absolute prerogatives.

The fifth Councillor advised virtue and gracious government, but the sixth would have him take counsel only of his five senses and follow his pleasures.

To all of which the Prince said he must take his time to consider. Then rising from his seat, he made choice of a lady to dance withal, and so likewise did the Ambassador and the courtiers attending on the Prince. So the rest of the night is spent in these pastimes, being so carefully and orderly handled that the former disgrace is now quite taken away.

4th January. GRAY'S INN REVELS.

To-day the Prince of Purpool, accompanied with the Ambassador of Templaria and attended by both trains, took a progress from Gray's Inn to Crosby's Place, the Lord Mayor's house in Bishopsgate Street, having before been invited to dine with him. This show was very stately and orderly performed, and everyone had his feather in his cap to distinguish of what state he was, the

Grayans using white and the Templarians ash-coloured. Thus they rode very gallantly from Gray's Inn, through Chancery Lane, Fleet Street, so through Cheapside, Cornhill and to Crosby's Place, where was a very sumptuous and costly dinner. Dinner being ended, the Prince and his company having revelled awhile returned the same way, the streets being thronged with people to see the gentlemen as they passed by, who thought there had been some great prince in very deed passing through the City.

10th January. A NOTABLE CASE OF COSENAGE.

A certain widow, by name Mrs. Mascall, hath been notably cosened by one Judith Phillips, otherwise known as Doll Pope. Two men, the one called Peters, the other Vaughan, dealt with this Judith to be a means to procure Peters' favour with the widow. Thereupon Vaughan devised a letter in the name of one Mr. Grace, a near friend of the widow's, to the effect that she should make much of Judith, for she was one that could do her great good. Peters and Vaughan also told Judith what suitors the widow had and where they dwelt, also of many accidents which they knew to be true, to the intent that she might seem to be a wise woman.

Whereupon Judith going to the widow was well entertained and had into her chamber. After some speeches past Judith looked into her hand, and then began to tell her what suitors she had. Also she asked of the widow whether she was not troubled in the night with sights and noises in her house; to which the widow answered yea.

'Yea,' said Judith, 'hath there not been lights seen in your house?'

'How know you that?' said the widow.

'I know it well,' quoth Judith, 'and the cause too; for there is money hid in your house.'

The widow therefore being more persuaded of Judith's great skill began to speak of her suitors and prayed that she would get the money hid in the house. Judith then told her that first she must have such gold as the widow had, which she would not carry away but leave in the house; and within two days the gold hid in the house should be found in the place which she appointed for this gold to be. So the widow brought forth certain gold, a chain of gold, seven rings and a whistle, all of which were put in a purse and delivered to Judith. Judith wrapped this purse up in yarn, and having before wound two stones in other yarn, closely conveyed the yarn with the two stones to the widow, which she took and laid up in the appointed place with charge from Judith not to look at it until three days were past. She also told the widow that she must have a turkey and a capon to give to the Queen of the Fairy, which the widow provided. Also she made the widow say certain prayers in sundry places of the house, and then departed. Judith then departed with the gold and the chain, which she divided with Peters and Vaughan, but the rings she took out secretly and kept them to herself.

The next morning, intending to cosen the widow of her plate also, Judith brought the head and legs of the turkey in a basket to the window, and began to tell the widow that she must lay one leg under the bed and the rest in other places ; but the widow having by this discovered the stones in the yarn knew herself to be cosened and caused Judith to be apprehended.

This Judith hath long used her trade of cosenage, wandering about the country in company with divers persons that call themselves Egyptians. For that kind of life she was condemned to die at Salisbury, but afterwards had her pardon.

13th January. GOSSON'S 'PLEASANT QUIPS.'

Mr. Stephen Gosson, parson of Great Wigborough in Essex, hath written very invectively against the fantastical foreign toys daily used in our women's apparel, which he entitleth *Pleasant Quips for Upstart New fangled Gentlewomen.*

Complaineth that masks were once to hide the face from wantons bold :

But on each wight now are they seen,
The tallow-pale, the browning-bay,
The swarthy-black, the grassy-green,
The pudding-red, the dapple-grey,
So might we judge them toys aright
To keep sweet beauty still in plight.

What else do masks but masquers show,
And masquers can both dance and play:
Our masking dames can sport, you know,
Sometime by night, sometime by day:
'Can you hit it' is oft their dance,
Deuce-ace falls still to be their chance.

17th January. BARNFIELD'S 'CYNTHIA' AND 'CASSANDRA.'

Mr. Richard Barnfield hath written two poems, the one in praise of Cynthia, the other of the life and death of Cassandra. Of Cynthia, he saith that the gods and goddesses all promised her wealth, wisdom and beauty, but that between the goddess and her Gracious Majesty there is this difference:

She shines by night; but thou by day dost shine;
She monthly changes; thou dost ne'er decline.
And as the sun to her doth lend his light,
So he by thee is only made so bright:
Yet neither sun, nor moon, thou canst be named,
Because thy lights have both their beauties shamed.
Then since an heavenly name doth thee befall,
Thou Virgo art, if any sign at all.

Of Cassandra, telleth the story of her lamentable life; how the god Apollo loved her so that, encouraging his love, she caused him solemnly to promise her the gift of prophecy, which promise being made she chastely counterchecked his approaches. Hereat the god, being greatly enraged, cursed her that she should indeed foretell truly of things to come, but for her falsehood no man should believe her; and moreover, for a penance on that sex, a constant woman should be hard to find; which prophecy (saith the author) hath proved true for that their 'sex are subject to inconstancy as other creatures are to destiny.'

23rd January. COMPLAINTS AGAINST PATENTS.

The leather sellers in the City send a petition to her Majesty concerning the enormities of Mr. Darcy's patent for stamping of leather which the Lord Mayor upholdeth; for, saith he, the exactions and other inconveniences of Mr. Darcy's patent cause great grief and murmur of the people throughout the land, and Mr. Darcy's violent manner of proceeding is very unmeet in this time of dearth when great numbers of poor people are grieved already and exasperate enough by their own misery and great want of food. There are at this present time seven such patents, being, for leather to Mr. Darcy; for brushes, bottles and stone pots; for soap and barrel butter; for cards; for vinegar, alliger, *aqua vitae*, *aqua composita*; and for steel to a stranger.

'THE ESTATE OF THE ENGLISH FUGITIVES.'

There is entered a work entitled *The Estate of the English fugitives*, being the true copy of that book which, contrary to the author's intention, was lately printed in Paul's Churchyard, but corruptly and ignorantly intermixed with fictions of the publisher. Herein our unexperienced gentlemen and credulous Catholics are warned by many examples of the monstrous cruelty and treacheries of the Spaniard towards those who have entered into his service.

Of the Jesuits it is written that there is not any man's business but they must have an oar in it; they never plant themselves in any places but in the midst of goodly cities where they wring themselves into the fairest palaces. Their churches are rich and sumptuous, their movables and household stuff magnificent rather than decent, their gardens fine and comely, their fare plentiful and of the best; nor are they tied to any risings in the night, or any the like hardness to which other religious houses are subjected. Their first mass doth never at any time begin before 8 of the clock. They are accounted the greatest intelligences and statesmen of the world. They may not receive any higher office or dignity, but they take the name of a Jesuit not to be any whit inferior to the title of a bishop; nor are they subject to any controlment but only the Provincial of their order. But the best is to see how busy and diligent they are when they hear of a wealthy man that lieth sick and in danger of death.

As a proof of the affection of the subjects for the Queen in England, note the behaviour of the people when a traitor is carried to his arraignment or execution; which though it should move the minds of men to commiserate the calamitous estate of those unfortunate wretches, yet are the people, in jealousy of her Majesty's safety and hatred of her enemies, many times hardly restrained by the officers from doing violence to the prisoners on the way. Then do they curse, ban and revile them with the most opprobrious speeches they can invent; and commonly applaud the instant of their deaths with a general shout of joy, and cries of 'God save the Queen and confound all traitors'; whereas they do usually accompany all other kinds to their deaths with a kind of feeling of sorrow and compassion.

24th January. THE SCOTTISH AMBASSADOR GIVEN AUDIENCE.

To-day the Lord Wemyss was given audience by the Queen who taxed the King of Scots with unkindness in that he goes about to make a new league with the French King, to which he answereth that it is but the renewing of the old. When he had drawn to an end the Queen willed him to assure the King, his master, that when he had tried all his new friends, he should find that her kindness overweighted all theirs; to which he replied, 'As you have, madam, proved his love and fidelity to have been above that which you can expect at the rest of your kind friends' hands.' Coming forth from the Privy Chamber he asked the Lord Chamberlain for Sir Robert Cecil. 'Why, sir,' said he, 'he was within.'

'By my soul,' said Lord Wemyss, 'I could not see him.'

'No marvel,' said Sir George Carey, 'being so little.' Whereat the Lord Wemyss burst out of laughing.

25th January. THE IRISH REBELLION.

Rebellion is now broken out in Ireland and if forces be not sent both Enniskillen and all the North will be lost. Such is the strong combination of the Earl of Tyrone that there is not any dare show himself a dutiful subject.

THE VACANT SOLICITORSHIP.

Mr. Francis Bacon's friends at Court now deal with the Queen for his advancement to the Solicitorship; for if he get not promotion, he declareth that he will travel. But my Lord of Essex carrying the matter somewhat too far, her Majesty sweareth that if Mr. Bacon continue in this manner, she will seek all England for a Solicitor rather than take him. She hath never, saith she, dealt so with any as with him; she hath pulled him over the Bar and used him in her greatest causes.

27th January. HURAULT'S DISCOURSES.

Mr. Arthur Golding hath translated into English the politic moral and martial discourses written in French by M. Jaques Hurault, one of the French King's Council, wherein in three parts he treateth firstly of the office, duties, and necessary qualities of a king; in the second, of wisdom and discretion, fortitude, prowess, diligence, continence and other virtues; in the third, of leagues, and governors, of the leading of an army, of divers policies and sleights necessary in war.

28th January. GRAY'S INN REVELS.

The revels at Gray's Inn have been discontinued these three weeks past by reason that the Prince of Purpool made a pretended voyage to Russia; and at his return it was intended to have performed certain good inventions wherewith his reign should have been very conceitedly determined. But the purpose of the gentlemen was frustrated by the Readers and Governors who caused the scaffolds to be taken away from the Hall and would not have them built again by reason of the term. This night there came into the Hall the King at Arms to announce the Prince's return from Russia and summon his subjects to meet him on the 1st February.

31st January. THE JESUITS AT WISBEACH CASTLE.

The state of the seminary priests and Jesuits that are confined in Wisbeach Castle is reported to be grown as dangerous as a seminary college by liberty and favour of their keeper. There are about twenty-eight of them who have compounded with their keeper for their diet, provision and servants as if they were in a free college. They send abroad their servants into the town to the market where they buy up the best victuals. Great resort is daily made there of gentlemen and gentlewomen and others who dine and sup with them, walk with them in the castle yard, and confer in their chambers, whereby they receive and send intelligence. They want no money, and by giving alms and devotions at the gate the poor esteem them for godly men. They keep eight poor townsborn children and two strangers of good wit and choice, beside their cooks, and those recusants. They are all young and lusty people, disposed to mirth and viciousness with women, and attempt them, as the keeper's maid and two daughters have been, in whorish manner. Most of these men were banished and have returned, some were men condemned for treason. Hereby scholars of the Universities and priests beyond the sea hold that if they be taken and so entertained the worst is but good cheer, and great hopes of bishoprics and preferments hereafter.

1st February. THE GRAY'S INN REVELS.

This day the Prince of Purpool with his train came up the Thames in fifteen barges, bravely furnished with flags and streamers from Blackwall, and so to Greenwich where a letter is despatched to Sir Thomas Heneage, praying that the Prince may pay his homage on Shrove Tuesday. To which the Queen returned answer that she liked well his shows that were made at his triumphant return, and that if he come at Shrovetide, he and his followers shall have entertainment according to his dignity. Then the Prince and his company continued their course until they came to the Tower where, by the Queen's commandment, he was welcomed with a volley of great ordnance by the Lieutenant of the Tower. At Tower Hill there waited for the Prince's landing men with horses, very bravely furnished, to the number of a hundred, whereon they rode very gallantly through Tower Street, Fenchurch Street, Grace Church Street, Cornhill, Cheapside, and so through St. Paul's Churchyard where at St. Paul's School his Highness was entertained with an oration made by one of the scholars, whom the Prince rewarded very bountifully before continuing on his way by Ludgate and Fleet Street to Gray's Inn.

3rd February. GRAY'S INN REVELS AT COURT.

This night the Prince of Purpool and some of his followers performed a masque of Proteus before the Queen at Court, who is much pleased by the good performance of all that was done and wished the sports might continue longer, which might well appear by her answer to the courtier who danced a measure immediately after the masque was ended. 'What,' said she, 'shall we have bread and cheese after a banquet?' Her

Majesty willeth the Lord Chamberlain that the gentlemen shall be invited to-morrow, and presented unto her.

4th February. SIR JOHN NORRIS'S RETURN.

Sir John Norris is now returned from Brittany having been delayed for want of shipping, and by ill weather. The soldiers that were employed in those parts are at Paimpol, waiting for their return.

THE GRAY'S INN REVELS ENDED.

The gentlemen of Gray's Inn were presented to her Majesty this evening, and she gave them her hand to kiss with most gracious words of commendation, and particularly of Gray's Inn, as an House she was much beholding unto for it doth always study for some sports to present unto her. And afterwards there was fighting at the barriers, the Earl of Essex and others challengers, and the Earl of Cumberland and his company defenders; into which number the Prince of Purpool was taken and behaved so valiantly and skilfully that he had the prize adjudged due unto him, which it pleased the Queen to deliver with her own hands, telling him that it was not her gift, for if it had been it should have been better. The prize is a jewel set with seventeen diamonds and four rubies, in value accounted worth 100 marks.

Thus are these sports and revels ended at the Court, and the principality of Purpool determined in the greater brightness of the royal presence of her Majesty.

7th February. AN ALARM AT OSTEND.

There is new alarm of an attack at Ostend for that a prisoner from the garrison, to save his life, is reported to have promised to show some places in the defences which would be easily battered and entered by reason of the new fortifications not half perfected. Wherefore the enemy sent men to discover the places, but nothing is yet come of it.

8th February. SIR WALTER RALEGH'S VOYAGE.

Sir Walter Ralegh set out with his fleet from Plymouth two days ago.

9th February. THE QUEEN'S LETTER TO THE GRAND SIGNIOR.

The Queen writeth to the Emperor of Turkey at the importunity of Sigismund, the Vayrod of Transylvania, that she should intercede on his behalf. Wherefore the Queen, by reason of her old friendship with Sigismund, and for that he followeth the same form of Christianity as we, (having rejected the superstition of the Pope of Rome and the worshipping of images), now urgeth the Grand Signor that the Vayrod's complaints may be heard and remedied according to law.

11th February. BISHOP FLETCHER'S MARRIAGE.

Dr. Fletcher that was made Bishop of London at the end of last year hath of late married a gallant lady and widow, sister to Sir George Gifford the pensioner, (the Bishop himself also being a widower), who if she be virtuous is the more unhappy in that the world believeth it not. Hereat the Queen is so greatly displeased that she sendeth the Lord Buckhurst to confer with the Archbishop about sequestrating him from his function of Bishop.

15th February. FLESH PROHIBITED DURING LENT.

As in former years orders are published for the restraint of killing and eating of flesh during this coming season of Lent. Six butchers are to be licensed for the City and the sums so paid to be for the relief of maimed soldiers and mariners.

18th February. MOSSE'S 'ARRAIGNMENT AND CONVICTION OF USURY.'

There is a book of sermons called *The Arraignment and conviction of usury*, by Miles Mosse, Minister of the Word, dedicated to the Archbishop of Canterbury, wherein are handled four principal points, namely: usury, what it is and what are the kinds and branches thereof; proof that it is manifestly forbidden by the Word of God, and sundry reasons alleged why it is justly and worthily condemned; the objections answered which are usually made out of the Scriptures for the defence of some kind of usury and towards some kind of persons; divers causes why usury should not be practised of a Christian, especially not of an Englishman, though it could be proved that it is not simply forbidden in the Scriptures.

20th February. THE TRIAL OF FR. SOUTHWELL.

Robert Southwell, the Jesuit, was arraigned at the King's Bench before Lord Chief Justice Popham, having been removed from the Tower to Newgate some days since. Being brought along with halberts and bills, and his arms tied with a cord, at length he came through the press to the bar, and there, having his hands loosed, he put off his hat and made obeisance. The Chief Justice, casting his eyes upon him, asked him his age, who answered that he was about the age of Christ when he was brought before Pilate. 'Why then,' quoth he, 'you make yourself Christ, his companion?' 'No,' saith Southwell, 'but a poor worm created for to serve him.'

Then was the indictment read, to which Southwell after some pause answered, 'I confess I am a Catholic priest and, I thank God for it, no traitor: neither can any law make it treason to be a priest.' The Chief Justice importuned him to answer according to form of law, and his answer was 'Not guilty of treason.'

Then Mr. Coke, the Attorney-General, began to open the indictment. 'I had not thought,' quoth he, 'to have spoken anything this day; but that the prisoner let fall a word, *videlicet*, that no law could make his case treason. I have occupied this room but three years, and there have been divers high points of treason practised by Jebusites, I should say Jesuits'; and drawing upon recent examples, concluded that the statute upon which the prisoner was arraigned was not made but upon some urgent cause. 'They pretend conscience,' saith he, 'but you shall see how far they are from it.'

One Bellamy's daughter was then brought in that had betrayed Southwell to Topcliffe. Her deposition was that Southwell told them that if any should inquire for him and propose to them an oath whether they had seen him, they might deny it by oath though they had seen him that same day, reserving this intention—'not with a purpose to tell you.'

Hereupon the Attorney exclaimed that the rotten Chair would down which maintained a doctrine by which all judgments, all giving of testimonies, should be perverted.

Southwell answered that his words were not altogether as she reported; 'but I told them,' said he, 'that to an oath were required justice, judgment and truth.' Some few words he spake more; but his utterance was somewhat unready, and they always cut him off when he began to speak.

And now Topcliffe began to question him, and as he answered, he was often interrupted so that he could seldom or never end one sentence when he did begin. Then said he, 'I am decayed in memory with long and close imprisonment, and I have been tortured ten times. I had rather have endured ten executions. I speak not this for myself but for others; that they may not be handled so inhumanely, to drive men to desperation if it were possible.'

To this Topcliffe answered, 'If he were racked, let me die for it.'

'No,' quoth Southwell, 'but it was as evil a torture, of late device.'

'I did but set him against a wall,' quoth Topcliffe.

To which Southwell answered, 'Thou art a bad man.'

'I would blow you all to dust, if I could,' said Topcliffe.

'What, all?' asked Southwell.

'Ay, all,' said Topcliffe.

'What, soul and body too?' said Southwell.

Hereupon Topcliffe exclaimed that he found him in a corner treading upon books, and also having letters directed to him from Parsons the Jesuit; which letters Topcliffe showed, but nothing was read of them, nor of other papers nor books which he poured out of a bag.

The jury staying not above a quarter of an hour, returned saying 'Guilty'; so he is condemned to death.

21st February. New Plays at the Rose.

New plays by the Lord Admiral's men this month at the Rose are *The French Comedy* and *The Mack*.

22nd February. The Execution of Fr. Southwell.

This day Southwell was haled upon a draw from Newgate, laid upon straw, to the place of execution by Tyburn, having a cord fastened about his wrists. All the way he prayed, with his countenance and eyes lifted towards Heaven, and used not any speech.

When he was come to the place, as they were taking him off the draw, the minister of the Tower came to him and used these words: 'You hold the decrees of the Council of Trent for authentical?'

'I do,' said Southwell.

'Therein,' said he, 'is decreed that no man shall presume to believe that he is sure to be saved, but is to doubt. If you believe to be saved, you contradict the Council; if you doubt, being about to die, your case is hard; and you doubting, we must needs doubt.'

Southwell replied, 'I hope to be saved by the merits of my Saviour; but I pray you trouble me not.'

So he was lifted into the cart, at which time his countenance appeared very modest, yet cheerful, like the sun when it breaketh out after that it hath dispersed the clouds. The minister began to speak to him again, to whom he answered, 'I pray you Master Minister, give me leave.' So turning himself to the under-sheriff, he asked him whether he might speak; who answered that he might, so that he would confess his fault. 'I will,' said he, 'speak nothing against the State.'

His beginning to pray had entrance with this place of the apostle, '*Siue viuimus Domino viuimus, siue morimur Domino morimur; siue viuimus siue morimur, Domini sumus*'; at which words the sheriff interrupted him, so where it seemed he would have made some speech, being cut off, he desired all Catholics to join with him in prayer to Almighty God, that it would please Him to forgive him all his sins which he had committed in this miserable life; miserable not for that he died a reproachful death, ignominious in the sight of the world, but honourable before God, for that it was for the testimony of His cause; but miserable for that he had sinned so often against so merciful and gracious a God. He then prayed for the Queen, that she might enjoy all gifts of nature and grace, all helps of friends and faithful councillors, whereby she might reign to God's glory, and after this life be inheritor of the Kingdom of Heaven, and wished that she would pardon him for that he had come into her kingdom without licence. He prayed that God would be merciful to the whole land and vouchsafe to convert them which were out of the way of truth.

And so protesting that he died a Catholic priest and in the Roman faith, standing in his shirt, often repeating these words, '*In manus tuas, Domine*,' the cart was removed. When he had hanged a while, the sheriff made a sign to the sergeants to cut the rope, at which there was a great confused cry in the company that he prayed for the Queen; 'And therefore let him hang till he be dead,' said they. So he was not cut down till he was senseless as far as could be perceived. A man might perceive by the countenances of the beholders that there was almost a general commiseration; none railed against him. The Lord Mountjoy was present, who is said, having beheld the mild and godly end of this man, to have uttered these words: 'I cannot judge of his religion; but pray God, whensoever I die, that my soul may be in no worse case than his.'

26th February. THE FORT AT BLACKWATER TAKEN.

Ten days ago the rebels in Ireland assaulted and took the fort and castle of Blackwater. Some forty or fifty of Tyrone's men, having passed through the town and within the stone castle, made sudden assault against the door of the inner castle which was made of wood; there being within only Henry Marche, the warder, and four others, whereof two were straightway sore wounded. These killed and galled thirteen of the rebels. When the assault had continued for a quarter of an hour, the warder and three others came out of the castle and drave them away with their swords. But afterward learning from the other Englishmen in the place that their munition was gone, and that the rebels would burn the castle, they were forced to yield.

4th March. A FATAL MISCHANCE.

Yesterday evening two youths called Goldstone and Carpenter were playing together in the house of one William Harrison when they found in the hall a dag and a fowling piece, and not knowing them to be loaded Carpenter by mischance shot Goldstone in the face, whereof he died instantly.

5th March. A NEW PLAY.

There is a new play at the Rose entitled *Selio and Olimpo.*

6th March. THE WIDOW OF DR. LOPEZ.

The Queen hath granted to the widow and children of Lopez, that was executed for his treasonable practices in June last year, the leases that he held in London, and of his goods, forfeit by his attainder, not exceeding £100, but excepting a jewel set with a diamond and a ruby that was sent to Lopez by some minister of the King of Spain.

15th March. THE EARL OF CUMBERLAND'S SHIP.

My Lord of Cumberland, not liking his ill partage with the Great Carrack in '92 nor the unhappier loss of two carracks last year for want of sufficient strength to take them, now buildeth a ship of his own of 900 tons at Deptford; which the Queen at her launching named the *Scourge of Malice*, the best ship that hath ever been built by any subject.

26th March. MR. CHAMPERNOUN'S CHOIRBOYS.

It hath been reported about the Court that Mr. Richard Champernoun, the music master, to satisfy his own humour doth use boys otherwise than were fit for one that professeth Christianity, gelding them to preserve their voices; which report he vehemently denieth.

1st April. NEWS OF SIR WALTER RALEGH.

A ship of Portugal is lately come into Plymouth, of 80 tons burden, laden with fish, a prize that was taken near Cape St. Vincent. The Portugals of this ship declare that they with five others were taken by Sir Walter Ralegh on the 28th February; and that he had some of the principal men aboard him for two days, and finding their lading to be but fish, took some small quantity out of every ship, also a pipe of wine and a pipe of water, and thus let them pass. They say that he was merry and in good health.

2nd April. THE LEWDNESS OF DOLL PHILLIPS.

There is a pamphlet written by one calling himself 'Oliver Oatmeal' concerning the knaveries of Judith or Doll Phillips and the beguiling of Mrs. Mascall, the tripe-wife. This old woman, being much sought after in marriage for her goods, was at last beguiled to the house of one of her sisters, where the wine walking lustily about and many merry matters familiarly disputed on, it was set down that the tripe-wife must dine next day at her suitor's house. Next day thither she comes, where the time being wasted in conference, home he would not let her go that night, and then they so whittled her with wine that he drew a promise of marriage from her. Shortly after, the widow sitting asleep by the fire, he valiantly coming behind her pulled the stool from her, when down fell she, and he by (or upon) her, with that learned and witty adverb in his mouth, 'Keep the widow waking.' Small rest had she that night, for before it was daylight, they made her pass through his cellar, enter a boat lying ready for her, and to sail so far as Pepper Alley and thence to St. George's Church, where she is married at two o'clock in the morning. But now the wooer, being a grocer by trade, made such a brag of his tricking the tripe-wife, and she such lamentations and complaints, that the matter is not only come to the law but also is sung abroad by the ballad makers.

4th April. A STRANGE MANNER OF DEATH.

Last night one William Saxton slew his wife in strange manner. The woman was in her bedroom preparing herself to go to bed with her husband, but he, having a quarrel with her and not wishing her to lie with him, threw a metal chamberpot at her, striking her so violently in the belly that her breath was taken away and she died instantly.

5th April. SOUTHWELL'S 'ST. PETER'S COMPLAINT.'

A poetical book by Southwell, the Jesuit, is entered for the press, entitled *St. Peter's Complaint*, wherein the author saith, 'Poets by abusing their talent, and making the follies and feignings of love the customary subject of their base endeavours, have so discredited this faculty, that a poet, a lover and a liar are by many reckoned but three words of one signification.' In his complaint Saint Peter mourneth his betraying of Christ, and the griefs arising therefrom, together with loss of sleep:

> Sleep, Death's ally, oblivion of tears,
> Silence of passions, balm of angry sore,
> Suspense of loves, security of fears,
> Wrath's lenitive, heart's ease, storm's calmest shore,
> Senses and souls, reprival from all cumbers,
> Benumbing sense of ill, with quiet slumbers.

There is added *Mary Magdalene's Blush* with her *Complaint at Christ's death*, '*Look home*,' *Fortune's Falsehood*, *At home in Heaven*, *Lewd Love is loss*, and other short poems.

12th April. DRAYTON'S 'ENDIMION AND PHOEBE.'

Mr. Michael Drayton hath written a poem of *Endimion and Phoebe: Idea's Latmus*, wherein is told that fable of the love of the goddess Phoebe for the shepherd Endimion whom she found upon Latmus; and when he had declared his love for her she revealed herself to him, and transported him from earth to heaven.

THE DESCRIPTION OF ENDIMION.

Endimion, the lovely Shepherd's boy,
Endimion, great Phoebus' only joy,
Endimion, in whose pure-shining eyes
The naked fairies danced the hey-de-geys.
The shag-haired satyrs, mountain climbing race,
Have been made tame by gazing in his face.
For this boy's love, the water Nymphs have wept,
Stealing ofttimes to kiss him whilst he slept:
And tasting once the nectar of his breath,
Surfeit with love and languish unto death;
And Jove ofttimes bent to lascivious sport,
And coming where Endimion did resort,
Hath courted him, inflamed with desire,
Thinking some nymph was clok'd in boy's attire.
And often-times the simple rural swains,
Beholding him in crossing o'er the plains,
Imagined Apollo from above
Put on this shape to win some maiden's love.

SIR PHILIP SIDNEY'S 'DEFENCE OF POESY.'

Last November Mr. Ponsonby entered his copy of that treatise of poetry written by Sir Philip Sidney, but without printing it; now Mr. Olney, ignorant of the former entry, hath entered another copy and published the same. Hereupon Mr. Ponsonby claimeth his prior entry, and agreement is made between them that Mr. Ponsonby shall have it.

In this treatise, entitled *The Defence of Poesy*, Sir Philip went about to defend poetry against those that speak against it, saying that it is not only a divine art, but greater than either history or philosophy. 'The poet,' quoth he, 'beginneth not with obscure definitions, which must blur the margent with interpretations and load the memory with doubtfulness; but he cometh to you with words set in delightful proportion, either accompanied with, or prepared for, the well inchanting skill of music; and with a tale forsooth he cometh unto you, with a tale which holdeth children from play and old men from the chimney corner.'

THE BENEFITS OF FISH DAYS.

There is set forth in print by the Lord Mayor a brief note of the benefits that grow by fish days, very necessary to be placed in the houses of all men and especially common victuallers. Firstly, forasmuch as our country is for the most part compassed with the seas, so by a certain expense of fish fishermen are the better maintained and men at all times held in readiness for her Majesty's navy. Secondly, because of the decay of many towns and villages upon the sea coast that in times past were not only replenished with fishermen, but also with shipwrights, ropemakers, sailmakers and divers other trades. Furthermore the trade of grazing cattle, through unlawful expense of flesh, is so much increased that many farm houses and villages are entirely decayed. Showeth also that by one day's abstinence in a week 13,500 beeves might be saved yearly in this City of London.

15th April. DR. FLETCHER'S DISGRACE.

The Bishop of London that was to have had the place of the Queen's Almoner at the Maundy is now commanded not to deal it. It is said that both he himself and his wife have used insolent speeches and words to be wondered at concerning her Majesty.

16th April. 'THE OLD WIVES' TALE.'

There is entered for printing that play written by George Peele entitled *The Old Wives' Tale* which was played by the Queen's Players about five years since.

17th April. SPANISH PREPARATIONS IN BRITTANY.

It is reported that there are many men of war of the Spaniards come to the coast of Brittany. Of late the Spaniards took a bark of Guernsey, and sent all the men home saving four ancient men and good pilots for that coast, which putteth the people of that place in great fear of some attempt of the Spaniard. At Blavet are seventeen flyboats and three galleys.

23rd April. THE FEAST OF ST. GEORGE.

This year at the feast there were present thirteen of the Knights of the Garter. The Communion in the Chapel being ended, the Knights of the Order proceeded into the castle yard before her Majesty, who walked beneath a canopy of cloth of gold, lined with red, and held up by four. There were present many noblemen and ladies and gentlemen of the Court; who passed three times round the yard that all might take a good view of them. At the feast my Lord Cobham represented her Majesty, being honoured as if she herself had been present, the guards serving him on the knee, and the Earls (who handed the water to him before and after) on both knees. The feast began at one o'clock and continued for over three hours, many foreign gentlemen being present, among them the envoy of the Duke of Wirtenberg who would remind her Majesty of her pretended promise to bestow the Order on his master.

26th April. THE DUKE OF WIRTENBERG'S ENVOY.

To-day the Queen gave audience to the envoy of the Duke of Wirtenberg that would importune her of a promise that he should be admitted to the Order of St. George; to whom the Queen returned answer that no such promise had been made nor could be, seeing that the Garter is not yet despatched to certain Kings that were a long time past elected by the Order. She added that the Duke should suffer our merchants to carry on their trade in his realms with all security, and put down those that slander her person.

30th April. TROOPS IN THE LOW COUNTRIES.

Her Majesty hath now in her pay in the Low Countries 50 foot companies, being 4 of 200 men, 44 of 150, and 2 of 100 each, making in all 7,600, which men with their winter and summer apparel, victuals, pay and other expenses cost annually £109,600.

6th May. LODGE'S 'FIG FOR MOMUS.'

There is a new book of Mr. Thomas Lodge entitled *A Fig for Momus*, dedicated to my Lord of Derby, being sundry satires, eclogues, and epistles. Of these, the satires are here published to prepare the ear of the reader; because if they pass well, the whole *centon* of them, already written, shall suddenly be published. Treateth in this book of the necessity for parents to set good examples in their lives before their children; of dreams; of covetousness and the folly of ambition; of saving and spending. Concludeth with an Anatomy of Alchemy, very invectively condemning the professors of that science, yet, saith he, unto artists there is a certain quality that can be perceived:

> It feeds the ear, it amplifies the thought,
> Except to those that know it, it is nought.

There is also an epistle to a lady that wrote to him asking both the cause and the remedy of pursiness and fat. Giveth this remedy:

> Much sitting, and long abstinence from care,
> Drinking of oily wines our fat prepare;
> Eggs, white meat, pottage, do increase the same
> And bring the waxing body out of frame.
> Let therefore men grown fat by gluttony
> (For to the rest no medicine I apply)
> Open a vein; or if that seem too sore,
> Use cuppings, and oft rubbings evermore,
> Live in that air which is both hot and dry,
> Watch much, and sleeping little, hardly lie.
> Walk much, and toss, and tumble in the sun,
> Delight to ride, to hawk, to hunt, to run;
> Drink little, gargarize, fly grosser food,
> Or if some deem a hare or partridge good,
> Feed modestly thereon, and if he hath
> Some crowns to spend, go often to the Bath.

Nevertheless he is of an opinion that fatness is no deformity, for

> fat, slick, fair and full
> Is better lik'd than lean, lank, spare and dull.

8th May. A CATALOGUE OF ENGLISH PRINTED BOOKS.

A catalogue of English printed books is to be printed by Mr. Andrew Maunsell, bookseller, whereof the first part treateth of such matters of divinity as have been either written in our own tongue or translated out of other languages; the second of books concerning the sciences mathematical, arithmetic, geometry, astronomy, astrology, music, the art of war, navigation, physic, and surgery.

9th May. THE EARL OF CUMBERLAND'S COMMISSION.

The Earl of Cumberland is granted special commission to attack the powers of the King of Spain or any of his subjects and adherents with his ships, which shall not exceed the number of six. He shall also have full power to distribute all merchandises and prizes taken as he will, saving the usual customs and duties due upon all goods brought into the realm.

15th May. BANKS' HORSE.

There is one Banks hath a bay gelding, called Morocco, of wondrous quality, that can fight, and dance and lie; and find your purse and tell you what money you have.

22nd May. 'CERTAIN VERY PROPER SIMILES.'

Mr. Anthony Fletcher, a minister, hath collected more than two hundred and thirty godly similes and set them forth in a book with this title: *Certain very proper and most profitable similes, wherein sundry, and very many, most foul vices, and dangerous sins of all sorts are so plainly laid open, and displayed in their kinds, and so pointed at with the finger of God, in his sacred and holy Scriptures, to signify his wrath and indignation belonging unto them, that the Christian Reader, being seasoned with the spirit of grace, and having God before his eyes, will be very fearful, even in love that he beareth to God, to pollute and to defile his heart, his mind, his mouth or hands, with any such forbidden things. And also many very notable virtues, with their due commendations, so lively and truly expressed, according to the holy word, that the godly Reader, being of a Christian inclination, will be mightily inflamed with a love unto them.* Addeth thereto the cut of an idle tree.

23rd May. NEW PLAYS.

At the Rose this month the Admiral's men played a new play called *The first and second part of Hercules.*

25th May. THE NEGOTIATIONS WITH THE STATES.

These past weeks Mr. Thomas Bodley, her Majesty's Agent in those parts, hath urged her demands to the States that they should ease her of the great charge of maintaining garrisons and repay some part of her expenses, appointing commissioners to settle a course how the whole sum disbursed upon their account and due to Sir Horatio Palavicino, to whom she payeth great sums in interest. Mr. Bodley is now come over with the answer of the States, which is that they acknowledge themselves infinitely bound to the Queen, and would pay according to their ability as may be brought to pass with liking of the inhabitants; but as for the demand made by the Lord Treasurer for £100,000 they are destitute of means to satisfy it, or even a far lesser sum. These proposals have greatly moved the Queen, who was even heard to say in Court that she wished Mr. Bodley had been hanged; whereat he stirs not abroad these ten days.

27th May. DR. JOHN DEE PROMOTED.

The Queen hath granted to Dr. John Dee the wardenship of Christ's College in Manchester.

'THE WORLD'S HYDROGRAPHICAL DESCRIPTION.'

To-day is published a little book entitled *The World's Hydrographical Description*, written by Captain John Davis, wherein is shown, not only by authority of writers, but also by late experience of travellers, and reasons of substantial probability, that the world in all his zones, climates and places is habitable and inhabited; and the seas likewise universally navigable, whereby it appears that from England there is a short and speedy passage by northerly navigation into the South Seas to China, Molucca, Philippine and India. In his book Captain Davis writeth much of his own travels into the frozen parts of the north. Noteth that, being deserted of his consort, in one small bark of thirty tons without further comfort or consort he proceeded northward until he came to a great strait which he followed for eighty leagues until he came to many islands, whence he concludeth the north part of America to be all islands.

28th May. THE IRISH REBELLION.

The rebels, being led in those parts by a notable traitor called Feogh MacHugh, have taken the fort at Enniskillen, that was held by some thirteen or fourteen with the constable. The rebels allowed them to come out of the castle with bag and baggage and promise of life, and then put them to the sword. Thirty-six heads of MacHugh's men have been brought to Dublin where Tyrone shall shortly be proclaimed traitor.

THE CRUELTY OF THE TURKISH EMPEROR.

The Turk hath lately caused to be executed his brother-in-law for having discovered some matter of state. He caused a butcher to be quartered on his own stool, and a baker to be burnt in his own oven for false weights.

30th May. MR. ROBERT DUDLEY'S RETURN.

Mr. Robert Dudley is returned to England, having set out last November in the *Bear* as admiral, with the *Bear's Whelp*, vice-admiral, and two small pinnaces, the *Frisking* and the *Earwig*. The vice-admiral and one of the pinnaces being separated from him in a storm at their starting, he went on alone with the other, sailing along the coast of Spain, and thence to the Canaries. Thereafter shaping his course to Trinidad in the West Indies, he came at length to Waliame, the first kingdom of the Empire of Guiana.

Here he was told by an Indian, his interpreter, of a golden mine in a town called Orocoa in the river of Owrinoicke, but his men being utterly unwilling that he should go himself, Mr. Dudley sent forward a company of his discreetest men. These went forward up the river, and there they were met by the Captain of the town of Orocoa and of the mine, who told them that by force they should have nothing but blows, yet if they would bring him hatchets, knives and jews-harps he would trade in gold with Mr. Dudley. Also he told them of another rich nation that sprinkle their bodies with powder of gold and seem to be gilt, and far beyond them a great town called El Dorado.

The men being satisfied returned, having been absent sixteen days, but in pitiful case, almost dead with thirst, for they had not drunk in three days before they recovered the ship, so long were they out of the fresh rivers. Hereupon Mr. Dudley attempted his company to go with them again but they flat refused.

On his return he came to the Isles of Flores and Cuervo, hoping to meet with some great fleet from England, but finding none and his victuals being almost spent, he directed his course alone for England. Soon after he met with a great armada of 600 tons (the *Bear* being but of 200 tons), and fought with her for two days, till his powder being all spent, he left her 300 leagues from land and in miserable state so that in short space she sank.

In this voyage have been taken, sunk or burnt nine Spanish ships, which is a great loss to the enemy, though Mr. Dudley himself hath gained nothing.

3rd June. A NEW PLAY.

There is a new play at the Rose called *The Seven days of the week.*

5th June. A RIOT IN LONDON.

To-day a certain citizen, being a silkweaver, came to the Lord Mayor's house, using some hard speeches concerning him and in dispraise of his government. The Lord Mayor said he was mad and so committed him to Bedlam as a madman, but not having his officers about him sent him thither by some of his own servants; but without Bishopsgate he was rescued by prentices and divers other to the number of two or three hundred persons.

9th June. NEWS FROM LISBON.

One lately come from Lisbon reporteth that eight ships of the Indian fleet have come in, bringing two English Captains, Captain John Middleton, and Captain Goddard, the Earl of Cumberland's man, and nine or ten mariners, who report that in the South Seas the *Dainty* is captured with Captain Hawkins who had taken great treasure. In March and April on a report that Sir Francis Drake was coming with a fleet of English, French and Hollanders' ships, about 8,000 fled; and now the coast is replenished with soldiers. The Canaries and the Azores are also being fortified.

0th June. A SKIRMISH WITH TYRONE.

On 27th May it was determined to revictual the garrison in Monaghan, our soldiers set out from Newry, under Sir Henry Bagnal, being 1500 foot and 250 horse. On the way 1500 horse of the enemy appeared on a hill and would have drawn our horse after them, but the General would not. Next morning Tyrone brought all his forces to a straight which our men were to pass and turned off seven or eight companies to skirmish which annoyed them much, the passage being between a bog and a wood. They passed through this straight and reached Monaghan, having lost twelve slain and thirty hurt, the enemy's loss being 100 slain and many hurt. Having put victual into Monaghan and changed the ward, our men dislodged and marched back, being harassed by the rebels in the straights and passages, but at length they reached Newry, where our losses were found to be thirty-one slain, 109 hurt, but none hurt of account except Sir Henry Duke, Captain Cunye, five lieutenants, an ensign and a sergeant.

In this fight Tyrone had 14,000 foot, and 300 shot in red coats, like our English soldiers.

MacHugh is reported to be shot in the thigh and hurt with a skeyne in the body, flying from our men so fast that he threw away his helmet, target and sword, which are brought in.

13th June. Disorders in the City.

Divers prentices this day being pinched in their victuals took butter from the market people in Southwark, paying them but 3d. the pound, though they demanded 5d. Certain of these prentices are apprehended.

15th June. Further Rioting in the City.

Some prentices being to-day committed to the Counter by the constable for certain misdemeanours, others congregating themselves came to the Counter, and said they would have them forth again, using very hard speeches against the Lord Mayor; but the gates being shut against them, they tarried not long but departed away.

Not long after a serving man, whose brother, being a prentice, had complained of his master's hard dealing, came to the master, and quarrelled with him; and in the multiplying of words the master's head was broken. By this brawl the people gathered together and much hurly-burly followed so that Sir Richard Martin hearing thereof came into the street, apprehended the serving man and sent him to the Counter by the constable. As they were going, the prentices that had already resorted to the Counter met them, rescued the serving man from the Counter, and brought him back to Cheapside. Whereupon Sir Richard Martin came forth suddenly with such company as he had of his own servants and forthwith he apprehended the serving man again, reprehended the prentices for their so great disorder, took six of the principal offenders, and so by the constable sent them all to the Counter, causing irons to be laid upon them.

About an hour afterwards, when all was quiet, the Lord Mayor cometh into Cheapside and commandeth Sir Richard Martin and Sir John Hart to take order for the safe keeping of these prentices. On his return, about London Wall, a prentice meeting him will not put off his cap ; whereupon he also is sent to the Counter, which is done quietly and without opposition of any.

16th June. The Riotous Prentices.

Certain prentices and soldiers or masterless men are said to have met together in Paul's, and there had conferences, wherein the soldiers said to the prentices, 'You know not your strength.' Then the prentices asked the soldiers if they would assist them ; and the soldiers answered that they would within an hour after be ready to aid them and be their leader ; and that they would play an Irish trick with the Lord Mayor, who should not have his head upon his shoulders within an hour after.

The causes of these present inconveniences are said to be the great number of loose and masterless men about the City, pretending to be soldiers ; the great dearth of victual ; and the remiss care of the magistrates in time to have remedied the same. The Lord Mayor also is blamed for his insatiable avarice ; for his selling and converting of offices to his own gain and then suffering those officers to be negligent ; and for his refusing to bear or join with his brethren.

17th June. Sligo taken by the Rebels.

From Ireland comes news that as Captain George Bingham sat writing in his chamber in Sligo Castle, his ensign, one Burke, and twenty of his men, all Clanricarde men, fell upon him suddenly and slew him.

20th June. 'THE TRUMPET OF FAME.'

There is published by one H. R. a poem of encouragement to all sailors and soldiers that are minded to go with Sir Francis Drake and Sir John Hawkins, wherein are related the names of the ships and their former actions against the enemy, ending thus:

Thus valiant hearts, which now to seas are bound
To cheer you on, that erst hath been renown'd,
I have explain'd the names of your brave fleet,
That careth not with what foes they shall meet.
What other ships of foreign sail there go,
I do omit, because I do not know.
Nor what they be, you need not much to care,
God and your generals doth for you prepare.
Then frolic hearts! and to your healths one can,
Let love united be firm with every man:
And love and duty in each one so abound,
That faithful subjects you may still be found.
'Tis England's honour that you have in hand;
Then think thereof if you do love your land.
The gain is yours, if millions home you bring;
Then courage take to gain so sweet a thing.
The time calls on, which causeth me to end;
Wherefore to God I do you all commend.
For whom all subjects that do love our Queen,
Shall truly pray to send you safe again.
And, for my part, I wish you always health
With quick return; and so much store of wealth
That Philip's regions may not more be stor'd
With pearl and jewels, and the purest gold.

23rd June. DISORDERS IN SOUTHWARK.

About 4 o'clock this afternoon certain prentices and other servants, being sent to Billingsgate by their masters to buy mackerels and finding none there, were informed that divers fishwives a little before had gone on board the fisherboats and bought up the whole share and carried it with them to Southwark. Hereupon the prentices, in number sixty or eighty, pursued after them without any weapons, having only baskets under their arms; and coming to the fishwives they took their mackerels from some of them, giving them money 4 for the groat (which is the rate formerly set by the Lord Mayor). Then one of the fishwives began to lay about her, and offered to strike some of the prentices with her fish basket; but when the constable, seeing the disorder, commanded these rude and unruly persons to surcease their strife then without any further unkindness or breach of the peace they departed.

27th June. Riotous Prentices Whipped.

The riotous prentices that took from the market people at Southwark their butter were this day punished with whipping, setting in the pillory, and long imprisonment.

29th June. Unruly Youths on Tower Hill.

This Sunday afternoon a number of unruly youths on Tower Hill being blamed by the warders of Tower Street ward, drave them back with stones, being heartened thereunto by the sound of a trumpet. The trumpeter, one that formerly was a soldier, and many of the company are taken by the Sheriffs and in prison. About 7 o'clock this evening, Sir John Spencer, the Lord Mayor, with his officers rode to Tower Hill to see the hill cleared of tumultuous persons; and here some warders of the Tower and men of the Lieutenant told the Lord Mayor that the Sword ought not to be borne up in that place; and thereupon two or three of them catching hold of the Sword, there was some bickering and the sword-bearer hurt. But the Lord Mayor by his discretion and by proclamation in the Queen's name in short time cleared the hill of all trouble and rode back, the sword-bearer bearing up the Sword before him.

Sir John Hawkins' Agreement with the Queen.

It is agreed between the Queen and Sir John Hawkins concerning the voyage that he purposeth to the southward, that she shall at her own charges put in order and furnish six ships, for which she shall have a third part of any booty taken from the enemy; and Sir John at his own charge shall victual the same ships for four months, for which he shall have another third; the remaining third shall be to the sailors and servitors in those ships. If her Majesty shall stay the journey, the charges disbursed by Sir John shall be refunded.

A Seditious Pamphlet.

The Lord Mayor, being required to advertise the Council concerning the printing of a certain pamphlet by the Company of Weavers, hath discovered that fifteen of them were privy to it. The pamphlet was printed by one Gabriel Simpson, and the proof of the first print was then read in the house of a certain Muggins in the hearing of the whole number. Twelve of them showed their dislike to have the pamphlet proceed into print, but the other three continued in their purpose and required the printer to print for them some 40 copies, which they would have delivered to the French Church, the Dutch Church, and one apiece to the Lord Mayor and Aldermen; but only 22 were printed, whereof 19 are taken. The principal doers in this business are one Millington, Muggins and Deloney, who with the printer are committed to Newgate.

2nd July. A Case in the Star Chamber.

This day was begun the hearing of the suit for slander brought against one Wood by Mr. Edward Talbot, brother to my Lord of Shrewsbury. This Wood had charged Mr. Talbot that he secretly intended the poisoning of the Earl by means of himself, and to this end had given him an annuity of £100 per annum. Mr. Talbot's counsel enforced the impeachment of Wood's credit by sundry deceitful practices in physic (he practising physic, being neither licensed nor graduate in any University), of ministering oil of stag's blood to the Countess of Shrewsbury for the gout, and divers other sophisticated oils, receipts and compositions, as oil of wax, butter, antimony, liquor of pearl and such like. Moreover he would show that this Wood had treacherously concealed this practice from my Lord for two years and a half, and had manifestly forged the deed of annuity. For the credit of the defendant, it was argued that things done in his youth should not be brought forward; gentlemen of Inns of Court and others have done many worse practices, and as for sophisticated drugs, many apothecaries in the town are in like fault. But the case is left unfinished.

4th July. A Proclamation against Unlawful Assemblies.

Because of the great disorders lately committed in and about the City there is now issued a proclamation straitly charging all her Majesty's officers, that have authority to preserve the peace, more diligently to punish offenders, and especially to suppress all unlawful assemblies, upon pain to be not only removed from their offices but to be also punished as persons maintaining or rather comforting the offenders. And because the late unlawful assemblies and riots are compounded of sundry sorts of base people, some known prentices, such as are of base manual occupation, some others, wandering idle persons of condition of rogues and vagabonds, and some colouring their wandering by the name of soldiers returned from the wars, therefore certain special orders are to be prescribed and published in and about the City. These her Majesty will have strictly observed, and for that purpose meaneth to have a Provost Marshal, with sufficient authority to apprehend all such as shall not readily be reformed and corrected by the ordinary Officers of Justice, and without delay to execute them upon the gallows by order of martial law.

Orders prescribed by the Council in this time of tumult.

The Council have prescribed and caused to be published these and other orders for the preservation of peace.

No persons but such as be officers for preservation of peace or such as be of known honest conversation shall walk up and down the streets or fields after sunset or nine o'clock at night; nor assemble themselves in a company at any time or in any place, other than in churches for prayers or sermons, or for appearances before Officers of Justice or by their commandment, or in common Halls of Companies.

That no householder nor any that keepeth inns or lodging for strangers do suffer his servants or guests (not being gentlemen) to go out into the streets in the evening; and if they cannot be restrained then to inform the officers speedily.

That no person do write or be privy to any seditious bills to be dispersed or set up, upon pain to be executed by martial law. And any person who shall reveal an offender, the information being found true and the party taken, the revealer shall have £20 or a better reward.

All persons arrested by any officer shall obey him, and if any make resistance, every other person there present if required by the Officers shall assist to the best of his power. If any shall attempt to aid the party that should be arrested to be rescued, he and all those accompanying him shall be apprehended and executed by the Provost Marshal by martial law.

THE CASE OF MR. EDWARD TALBOT CONCLUDED.

Mr. Talbot's case against Wood is concluded, the Lords condemning Wood for a most palpable machiavellian, but deferring their sentence till they had heard the next suit, of the Earl of Shrewsbury against his brother, Mr. Edward Talbot, for that by practice of Wood he should have poisoned the Earl, first by gloves, and then by potion or plaster. This charge my Lord essayed to prove by no direct witnesses save Wood (who was not allowed but taken as infamous), and by circumstances that at the first seemed somewhat probable. My Lord's Counsel endeavoured to discredit the defendant for his haughtiness of mind, his prodigality and the like, showing that he had spent 10,000 marks in three years since the death of his father: and for his religion, for defending one John Baldwin who questioned whether there was a God; if there were, how He should be known; if by His Word, who wrote the same; and if the prophets and the apostles, they were but men, and *humanum est errare*; and such like most damnable doubts, which were not suffered to be read in the hearing of the court. Then the plaintiff argued that Mr. Talbot practised and agreed with Sir Edward Stapleton for effecting of the poisoning, and Sir Edward had suborned a man of his, of his own name, to buy the gloves.

At this the Court seemed dubious for a long time. The milliner therefore was summoned, and his man that sold the gloves, who denied upon the sight of Stapleton that he could be the man. So after long hearing (for this day the Lords sat from 9 in the morning until 6), Wood is herein condemned as a palpable ass, a very villain, and of Satan's brood, being called *Diabolos* for that he is an accuser.

After the Counsel had argued very learnedly, the Queen's Attorney craved that his silence might not prejudice the defendant's cause, for whom he spake in the former action wherein he was plaintiff, but could not now speak for him seeing that he was defendant. Whereupon he proved Wood to be no scholar for he used false orthography, for 'process' writing '*prossus*,' whereas every scholar knoweth 'process' to come of *procedendo*.

The sentence of the whole court, excepting only my Lord of Essex and the Archbishop of Canterbury, is that Wood shall ride from the Fleet to Westminster with his face to the horse's tail, and there stand upon the pillory, and so ride to the Fleet again; and another day from thence to Cheapside to the pillory there; and be fined to the Queen £500 and to be imprisoned at her pleasure. But the Lord Treasurer moved that if Wood should confess his fault and submit himself to Mr. Talbot at the next assizes, then the £500 should be released.

16th July. THE EXPEDITION FROM PLYMOUTH.

Sir Thomas Gorges that hath been sent down to Plymouth to join with Sir John Hawkins and Sir Francis Drake reporteth that the ships are in very good sort, for that Sir John is an excellent man in those things and sees all things done properly. Sir Thomas's coming at first greatly amazed them, they fearing that he had been sent to stay them; but when they knew the contrary they were very joyful that her Majesty had sent down someone to see their bravery. Their expedition cannot depart for fourteen days at least as some pinnaces are not yet ready.

17th July. THREE NOTABLE OUTRAGES.

This past month there have been three notable crimes committed, whereof two of the doers are already hanged and the other shortly shall be.

The first, in the parish of Upmaster in Essex, where dwelt one Thomas Chambers with his mother and his step-father, a certain John Wright. This Chambers, being a young man of great towardness, was by his father left heir to £30 a year and a portion of £200 and upwards in money, which money and land were to come to him at Christmas next; but if he should die under age, then a great part of it to fall into the hands of his sister, that was married to one John Graygoose. For this cause Graygoose and Wright plotted to murder him in the Whitsun holidays.

On 6th June therefore between the hours of 10 and 12 Wright

waited for him at a place called Rushy Green near Barrow Hill in the parish of Hornchurch ; and there, with a stake taken out of a stile, he assaulted the unmistrusting young man and at one blow given on the right side of the head struck out his brains. Which done he dragged him into a bush and there hid the murdered body ; then with a bold face he returned home. The youth being well beloved was in sundry places sought for, and at length on Whitsun Monday (being the 9th June) a grey-hound found the murdered body and never left baying until it was drawn forth.

When Chambers' body was thus found a rueful sight it was to look upon ; his fair countenance was discoloured, worms crawled in his mouth, nose and ears, and his whole body was putrefied. The missing of Wright that evening the deed was done, some suspicious words, but chief God's will, made Wright suspected ; and albeit at the first he sought to face it out, yet before a Justice he confessed it, for which he worthily suffered death last Monday (14th) at Romford in Essex. Graygoose abideth his trial in Chelmsford.

The second felony was acted at Ruislip in Middlesex, in which parish dwelt two neighbours, Murdox, the one, an honest wealthy farmer, Pets, the other, a carpenter, though not rich yet of honest reputation. Murdox had among divers children a young man to his youngest son, of body well proportioned, of face lovely, a great company keeper, given over to much riot. This youth, being persuaded Pets was very rich, on Sunday, 22nd June, after his own father was rid to Hounslow, entered the house (Pets and his wife being at church), and there found a son of Pets, about ten years old. The child knowing young Murdox had no fear, albeit Murdox in his sight did rifle the house, but missed £4 that was tied in the corner of a sheet, taking only a little purse wherein 14d. was. Finding no more, he called the boy : 'Jack,' saith he, 'wilt thou not tell ?' 'No, indeed,' saith the child. 'Then come and bring a knife,' quoth Murdox, 'and we will into the grove to cut whip-stocks.'

The simple child took a knife and followed him ; and being come through a close into the grove, he, with the knife the child brought, gashed him about the throat but missed the weazand ;

and so thinking the child to be dead left him. But hearing the boy cry, he returned and stabbed him into the right breast. Then listening a second time he returned and stabbed him again: and the third time coming back, stopping the child's mouth with moss, and thinking him to be surely dead, he went toward the church. By which time, morning prayer being done, he with his mother returned home, where being but newly entered they heard an outcry at their neighbour Pets'. Thither the mother and her eldest son came to see the cause; the young son would not go.

When Murdox's wife came there, they saw the house rifled, but the woeful mother cried only for her son, her son. Some neighbours spied a footing towards the grove, followed it, and found the boy all-to-beweltered in gore; and perceiving life to be in him, two laid him on a cloak and between them brought him home, where, when he had recovered speech, Murdox's mother most of any other sought to have him tell who did the deed. At last with great fear he told, and forthwith young Murdox was apprehended, but found bail, denying the deed with many bitter curses. That day he carelessly followed his pleasures; but the child's constancy in his accusation made the parents to bring him before Sir Edmund Anderson, Lord Chief Justice, who so sifted him that he confessed the fact; for which he was condemned at the Sessions at Newgate and executed on the 14th July. The moan he made, the grief he had of his misspent life, too late, too helpless, was lamentable. The child (by God's power) is recovered and at the bar gave evidence against him.

The third is the murder of one William Randolph, a grazier dwelling about Cardiff and having much dealing about London. This Randolph being very open with one Dernley, a man of the same profession, told him that he was to ride through Aylesbury to Wales with above £300. Hereupon Dernley acquainted two men, called Parry and Richardson, of the matter, who fell in company with Randolph and very courteously bare him company to Aylesbury. By the way one Tayler of Aylesbury chanced among them, and noting by Randolph's talk that he concealed not his charge of money, besides observing how Parry and Richardson were horsed and weaponed, warned Randolph against them ; but the good old man refused to believe him. These speeches came to the ears of Parry and Richardson. Whereupon making show of displeasure, in the morning they went before him out of town. Randolph hearing they were gone greatly blamed the chamberlain of the inn, and posted after, overtaking them near a wood side where the way was hollow.

Then these hollow hearted companions, under colour of kind salutation, turned their horses' heads to bid him welcome, and Parry first with a Judas-like welcome discharged his pistol in his bosom, while Richardson with the second bullet shot him through hand and belly. So he fell down and they doubling in his death wound upon wound mangled his face with inhuman cruelty. Then drew they him into a thicket and rifled his dead body, where Richardson yet unsatisfied with cruelty stabbed him into the neck with such violence that in pulling back his hand, the pummel and handle of his dagger came off, but the blade he left sticking in his neck ; which blade was one witness against him.

This done they turned his horse into the wood and hovered about the country some two days and more after, for it was the second day before the body was found by a fellow that sought cattle. When the hue-and-cry came to Aylesbury, Tayler among others went to see the body, and by the apparel better than the face knew it was the wretched man that had refused his counsel at Aylesbury. He described the murderers' apparel, proportions, horses and all such marks as he advisedly had taken while he rid in their company. To London, toward Wales, and every way the hue-and-cry went. Parry was taken in Wales, and confessed the fact ; Richardson at his own house in London. A while he denied the deed, but long he stood not on it, both of them accused Dernley ; and to Aylesbury are they all gone to suffer deserved death.

18*th July*. THE PROVOST MARSHAL APPOINTED.

Sir Thomas Wyllford is appointed a provost marshal for these times of tumult, with power to attach notable and incorrigible offenders upon signification of the justices of peace and by justice of martial law to execute them openly. Likewise he shall repair with a convenient company to all common highways near London to apprehend all vagrant and suspected persons.

23rd July. AN ENGLISHMAN BURNT IN ROME.

About five weeks ago during a procession in Rome a young Englishman smote the Sacrament out of the hands of an archbishop that was carrying it in procession with such force that it fell to the ground, the crystal of the monstrance being broken and his hand cut withal. Whereon a crowd collected and thrusting burning torches in his face would have killed him had not the archbishop restrained them. The Englishman was then thrown into prison and tried by the Inquisition. A week afterwards he was handed over to magistrates; and the next day he was bound to a cart and his right hand cut off. Then he was taken through the City, being frequently smitten by the executioner with burning brands, and at last burnt alive in the Piazza del Capitolio.

24th July. THE UNRULY YOUTHS CONDEMNED.

Five of the unruly youths apprehended for the disorder on Tower Hill on 29th June were arraigned in the Guildhall and condemned of high treason two days since, and to-day were drawn from Newgate to Tower Hill, where they were hanged and bowelled as traitors.

25th July. EXCESSIVE PRICES.

This year by reason of the transportation of grain into foreign countries, the same is grown into an excessive price, as in some places from 14s. to 4 marks the quarter, and more. In London, such is the scarcity of victual, that an hen's egg is sold for a penny, or three eggs at the most for 2d., a pound of sweet butter for 7d., and the like of flesh and fish, exceeding measure in price, such are our sins in deserving it.

26th July. THE SPANIARDS LAND IN CORNWALL.

From Cornwall it is reported that four hundred Spanish soldiers were landed from four galleys who have burnt Moldsey, a small village, and Newlin, with Penzance, a very good town. The town of Penzance had been saved if the people had stood with Sir Francis Godolphin, but the common sort utterly forsook him, saving for some four or five gentlemen.

This landing of the Spaniards hath bred in the Court diversity of passions; but the most part take courage against them in such sort as they that have heretofore seemed abated in spirit do now lift up the crest. This night Sir Roger Williams hath, in presence of all the Court, received of her Majesty a friendly public welcome. This afternoon the Lord Admiral rode to Chatham to put order to the navy; and in effect it is a stirring world.

27th July. THE IRISH REBELLION.

This past month the army in Ireland under Sir William Russell, the Lord Deputy, and Sir John Norris, have made a journey through the rebels' country, setting forth from Dundalk on the 18th June and returning on the 17th July.

28th July. THE SPANISH LANDING.

Certain Englishmen that were landed by the Spaniards in Mount Bay say that after they had burned Penzance and other villages they had mass the next day on the Western Hill by a friar, and there they vow to build a friary when they shall have conquered England.

7th August. A NEW SPANISH ARMADA.

It is reported that a new armada is preparing by the King of Spain at Lisbon. There are ten Biscayan ships and thirty others, and some not yet come in; and enough biscuit prepared for 10,000 men.

11th August. THE SPANISH SHIPS.

From Portsmouth it is reported that fifteen or sixteen Spanish sail, whereof six are very great ships, were sighted off Scilly, and as many ride the other side of the Scillys.

13th August. IRISH NEWS.

The Council in Ireland meeting to consider the measures to be taken to bring the rebels into obedience, it was concluded to send 1600 men under Sir John Norris through the Pale, and to this end pioneers, masons, carpenters, boats and carriages are being prepared. From the borders daily come the complaints of the soldiers, who have neither money, victuals, nor clothes, so that they grow into desperate terms and spare not to say to their officers that they will run away and steal rather than famish. There is considerable sickness, as much as twenty in every band, amongst the men from Brittany who, though they made no good impression on the Lord Deputy when they first came, are in proof found very good, though they like so ill of the country that they run away as fast as they can by any means escape; which to prevent some have been hanged for an example to the rest. Sir John Norris himself declareth that if there were good order and good provision made, not only these rebels might be in short time extirpated, but the country reduced into such terms as they should never be able to lift up their heads; but no other success than an unprofitable expense and a lasting rebellion can be looked for so long as those that have the chiefest disposition of things there care not how long the war last so they may make their profit, whilst in England the chiefest hope of the good event is reposed upon accidents, whereby timely provisions are neglected and time lost. In Ardes 4000 Scots are landed to succour Tyrone, who offereth to give in marriage to the bachelors of them the daughters of his gentlemen and freeholders, every one a wife of degree proportionable to the man that is to marry her.

17th August. THE DEATH OF DON ANTONIO.

Don Antonio, that is called King of Portugal, is dead in Paris five days since. He died in great poverty, and frequent collections were made for him at the French Court. The King appointed for him certain revenues yet these were not paid regularly, wherefore Don Antonio had to throw himself on the charity of others.

22nd August. RUMOURS.

There is a most certain expectation of the enemy attempting us next year, either directly here at home or by the way of Scotland; and these fears are grounded not on apprehension only but upon the sure knowledge that the preparations in Spain be far greater than in '88. Whereupon there is great diversity of opinions of the proceeding of this sea voyage; some would have it stayed, alleging the impossibility of their return in small time, should need require; the hazard of loss of so many mariners going into hot countries; the absence of ships and ordnance. The other party alleging the loss of the Queen and the adventurers if it break off; the dishonour, and the probability that the return might be timely enough, besides the hope of treasure, which is our greatest desire and want. Some there be that propose to convert this fleet to an offensive course upon the ports of Spain; but this is checked above, or crossed under hand, not without great distemperature of humours on both sides for a few days; yet in most men's judgments this is likeliest to succeed.

23rd August. THE LANDING IN CORNWALL.

From Fowey in Cornwall comes news that the four Spanish galleys which made spoil of the west parts about four weeks ago encountered a fleet of hulks of seventy sail and gave chase to fourteen of them that were severed from the company. In that fight they lost 140 of their men and had one of the galleys so torn that they could not carry her to Blavet; one of the hulks laden with salt was sunk.

26th August. 'ORPHEUS HIS JOURNEY TO HELL.'

There is entered a poem of *Orpheus his journey to Hell* written by one R. B., telling the story of Orpheus, how his bride Eurydice being slain by a serpent on her wedding day, he went down to Hades with his harp to charm Pluto into giving her back again; but on his return looking back on his beloved, she was snatched away from him, and thereafter Orpheus would sit complaining in invective ditties of the uncertain pleasures of unconstant love, until the women fell upon him in their rage and slew him.

A BOOK OF MERRY TALES.

A book of merry tales from the Spanish entitled *Wits, Fits and Fancies*, by Antony Copley, being a general collection of sententious speeches, answers, jests and behaviours of all sorts of estates, from the throne to the cottage, is to be printed.

MR. BARNES' 'DIVINE CENTURY OF SPIRITUAL SONNETS.'

Mr. Barnabe Barnes hath published *A Divine Century of Spiritual Sonnets*, which he dedicateth to Dr. Toby Matthew, Bishop of Durham.

THE LXIX SONNET.

Who to the golden Sun's long restless race
Can limits set ? What vessel can comprise
The swelling winds ? What cunning can devise,
With quaint arithmetic, in steadfast place
To number all the stars in heaven's palace ?
What cunning artist ever was so wise
Who by the stars and planets could advise
Of all adventures the just course and case ?
Who measur'd hath the waters of the seas ?
Who ever, in just balance, pois'd the air ?
As no man ever could the least of these
Perform with human labour, strength and care :
So who shall strive in volumes to contain
God's praise ineffable contends in vain.

TWO TALES OF MR. BARNABE BARNES.

Of this Mr. Barnabe Barnes Nashe hath these two tales. The first of his French service four years ago, when, having followed the camp for a week or two, and seeing there was no care had of keeping the Queen's peace, but a man might have his brains knocked out, and no justice or constable near at hand to make hue-and-cry after the murderers, he went to the General and told him he did not like of this quarrelling kind of life and common occupation of murdering, wherein, without any jury or trial or giving them so much leave as to say their prayers, men were run through and had their throats cut, both against God's laws, her Majesty's laws, and the laws of all nations; wherefore he desired leave to depart, for he stood every hour in fear and dread of his person. Upon this motion there were divers warlike knights and principal captains who offered to pick out a strong guard amongst them for the safe engarrisoning and better shielding him from peril. Two stepped forth and presented themselves as musketeers before him, a third and fourth as targeteers behind him, a fifth and sixth vowed to try it out at the push of the pike before the malicious foe should invade him. But home he would and nothing could stay him.

The second of how he got him a strange pair of Babylonian breeches, with a codpiece as large as a Bolognian sausage, and so went up and down town and showed himself in the Presence at Court where he was generally laughed out by the noblemen and ladies.

29th August. A New Play.

Since the end of June till five days ago there was no playing at the Rose, but now they begin afresh and to-day they play a new play called *Long Shanks*.

31st August. Drake and Hawkins Sail.

The fleet of Sir Francis Drake and Sir John Hawkins are sailed from Plymouth, being the *Defiance*, *Garland*, *Hope*, *Bonaventure*, *Foresight* and *Adventure*, the Queen's ships, together with twenty other ships and barks, and containing 2500 men and boys. With them is gone Sir Thomas Baskerville as commander by land.

5th September. The Earl of Essex's Advice on Travel.

Now that the Earl of Rutland hath a purpose to travel, my Lord of Essex hath composed for him sundry letters of advice for his guidance. In the first, setteth down the purposes of travel; to see the beauty of many cities, to know the manners of the people of many countries, and to learn the language of many nations. Some of these may serve for ornaments and all of them for delights. By travel men reach of study, conference, and observation which is knowledge; and the true end of knowledge is clearness and strength of judgment, and not ostentation or ability to discourse. The second letter giveth more exact particularities for the traveller. He shall restrain his affection and participation of his own countrymen and seek the acquaintance of the best sort of strangers, who will instruct him in their abilities, dispositions and humours. Nor should his aim be, like an intelligencer, to fish after the present news, humours, graces or disgraces of the Court, which may haply change before he come home, but to know the consanguinities and alliance of Princes, the proportion between the nobility and the magistracy, the constitution of the courts of justice, the state of their laws; how the sovereignty of the King infuseth itself into all acts and ordinances; how many ways they lay down impositions and taxes, and gather revenues to the Crown; what be the liberties and servitudes of all degrees; what discipline and preparation for wars; what inventions for increase of traffic at home, for multiplying their commodities, encouraging arts or manufactures of worth of any kind: also what good establishments to prevent the necessities and discontents of the people, to cut off suits at law and quarrels, to suppress thieves and all disorders. In the last letter noteth other matters worthy of observation, concluding that if they be too many to remember then should he rather trust his notebook than his memory.

13th September. A PETITION AGAINST PLAYS.

Since the commission of the provost marshal was revoked the masterless and vagabond persons that had retired out of his precinct are returning to their old haunt and frequent the plays at the Theatre and Bankside. Wherefore the Lord Mayor petitioneth the Council for the suppressing of stage plays, declaring that they contain nothing but profane fables, lascivious matters, cozening devices, and other unseemly and scurrilous behaviours which are so set forth that they move wholly to imitation. Moreover he verily thinketh them to be the chief cause of the late stir and mutinous attempt of those few apprentices and other servants, who no doubt drew their infection from these and like places, and also of many other disorders and lewd demeanours which appear of late in young people of all degrees.

14th September. ABUSES IN THE CITY.

Mr. Richard Carmarden that was lately appointed to be Surveyor of the port of London seeketh to reform the abuses caused through the blindness and impotency of the late surveyor. Whereupon the better sort of the merchants yield, but some four or five most frowardly resist him. When by his command some packs belonging to one Leveson were stayed, this man on Wednesday last, with wild words despising the Queen's authority, beat Mr. Carmarden's substitutes and arrested one of them in an action of £200. The sheriffs' sergeants carried Leveson violently to prison, and the Clerks of the Court refused bail, Leveson saying that the Queen's letters patents, the order of the Exchequer and the Lord Treasurer's letters were all without the law.

CAPTAIN AMYAS PRESTON'S VOYAGE.

Captain Amyas Preston that set forth in the *Ascension* six months since is returned, being arrived in safety at Milford Haven in Wales. On his outward passage he surprised the Isle of Porto Santo to the northward of Madeira which is inhabited by old soldiers of the Kings of Portugal. Here after some skirmishes, our men possessed themselves of the town, though the inhabitants had conveyed their wives and children and the rest of their goods into a high hill. Nor would Captain Preston allow them to redeem their town, because of their cruelty and treachery offered beforetime to some of ours, but caused the town and villages to be utterly burned.

Thence having joined with Captain Somers and his ship the *Gift* and three other ships they sailed westward to the Island of Dominica and from there to Margarita where the Indians fish for pearls. In the end of May they took the city of S. Iago de Leon, a very strong place, surrounded by high mountains, which they reached by a path used by the Indians. And here they had conference with the Spaniards for the ransoming of the town, Captain Preston demanding 30,000 ducats but the Spaniard refusing more than 4000, so the town was set on fire and consumed.

In July, off Cape St. Anthony, they met with Sir Walter Ralegh returning from his discovery of Guiana, with his fleet of three ships, but lost them in the night.

15th September. A GREAT FIRE AT WOBURN.

Last Saturday (13th) there was a great fire at Woburn in the County of Bedford, whereby houses and buildings to the number of one hundred and thirty are consumed, as well as barns, stables and the rest, with the goods and provisions therein, besides what was carried out into the streets and there purloined and embezzled. This fire started in a poor cottage at the further end of the town towards Brookhill where dwelt a single old woman, slow in speech, deaf in hearing, and very dull of understanding. She had shifted her bed straw and put new therein, laying the old in the chimney, supposing that there had been no fire therein, and afterwards going abroad upon her business. In the meanwhile the cinders in the chimney took hold of the straw and so set on fire this thatched house and others adjoining, which by the wind was soon driven from place to place. And so fierce did it wax that it made as it were a glade from the end of the town to the church; where by the violence of the wind a flake of burning thatch, as broad as it were a sheet, was carried clean over the chancel of the church, the school house and other buildings, and fell on the east side of the town. Moreover the confusion was much increased by those that came in to help from the country, many of them leaving their own labours, and freeing their hired workmen from their tasks (and paying them notwithstanding their day's wages), who in their hurly-burly increased rather than lessened the desolation and waste.

19th September. NEWS FROM IRELAND.

This morning there comes from Ireland advertisement that Tyrone hath drawn our force to fight of necessity; that Sir John Norris is shot in the belly, Sir Thomas Norris shot in the thigh, and Capt. Richard Wingfield in the elbow with a musket and likely to lose life or arm, but the others not in danger of life. The hope of a peace is now turned to an assured war for 'twere much dishonour to dally longer.

BEGGING IN THE CITY.

There continue to be erected great numbers of poor tenements, which they call 'pennyrents,' in Southwark and Kentish Street, wherein are placed a great company of very poor people. These having no trade nor honest endeavour to maintain themselves, nor to pay their rent (which must usually be done at the week's end), make it their daily occupation to beg in the streets of the City. At this time one Mr. Sawyer hath given leave to a bricklayer to build a great number of tenements upon his ground within Kentish Street whereby he hath encroached three feet upon the common street.

20th September. FRENCH NEWS.

Because of the constant rumours concerning affairs in France, Sir Roger Williams was sent over to the French King some days since and arrived at Paris, all unexpected, on the 9th. The next day the King himself came to Paris, preparing to depart immediately to the succour of Cambray; but on the 14th he received advertisement that the enemy were in the town, and the soldiers forced to retire to the Castle. At Paris news is received that the Pope in public, with great solemnity, hath given absolution to the King in the person of the Bishop of Evreux, and that the greatest ceremony of joy was performed there in applause of it.

BRETON'S 'SOLEMN PASSION.'

Mr. Nicholas Breton hath written a poem called *A Solemn Passion of the Soul's Love*, setting forth the great love of God for man in this high strain:

Confess thyself unworthy of the sense
To learn the least of the supernal Will;
Beseech the heavens in strength of their defence,
To save and keep thee from infernal ill:
Then fall to work, that all the world may see
The joyful love betwixt thy God and thee.

Tell of His goodness how He did create thee,
And in His justice how He doth correct thee,
And in His love how He will never hate thee,
And that His mercy never will reject thee,
And how He helped thee when the world distressed thee,
And with His graces how He sweetly blessed thee.

MARKHAM'S 'MOST HONOURABLE TRAGEDY OF SIR RICHARD GRENVILLE.'

There is also Mr. Gervase Markham's poem of *The Tragedy of Sir Richard Grenville* that was slain in her Majesty's ship *Revenge* off the Azores in '91.

THE DEATH OF GRENVILLE.

They took him up, and to their General brought
His mangled carcase, but unmaimed mind.
Three days he breathed, yet never spake he ought,
Albe his foes were humble, sad, and kind;
The fourth came down the Lamb that all souls bought,
And his pure part, from worser parts refin'd;
Bearing his spirit up to the lofty skies,
Leaving his body, wonder to wonder's eyes.

22nd September. LYLY'S 'WOMAN IN THE MOON.'

Mr. John Lyly's comedy of *The Woman in the Moon*, that was formerly presented before the Queen, is to be printed.

23rd September. THE EARL OF SOUTHAMPTON.

It is said at Court that my Lord of Southampton doth with too much familiarity court the fair Mistress Vernon, while his friends observing the Queen's humours to my Lord of Essex do what they can to bring her to favour him, but it is yet in vain.

27th September. THE FIGHT IN IRELAND.

The conflict between Sir John Norris and the Earl of Tyrone happened on the return of Sir John to Newry from victualling the fort by Blackwater, wherein he was assailed by 500 horse and 2000 foot of the enemy, Sir John having only 1000 foot and 120 horse. In this encounter Sir John was hurt with two musket shots, the one through the left arm, the other athwart the belly, but neither of them dangerous. Few of ours were slain but 400 of the enemy left dead in the field.

Notwithstanding there is an expectation of the Earl of Tyrone coming in upon pardon for himself, O'Donnell and Macguire; and to that end authority is given to the Lord Deputy.

SIR WALTER RALEGH'S RETURN.

Now that Sir Walter Ralegh is come back to England from his voyage to Guiana there are not wanting many to traduce him, saying that his going to sea was but a bravado or even that he went not to sea but lay hidden in Cornwall or elsewhere. Others, at his setting out, prejudged that he would rather become a servant of the King of Spain than return to England, and that he was too easeful and sensual to undertake a journey of so great travail. Nor hath he returned with riches, for, saith he, it became not his former fortune to go journeys of picory, to run from cape to cape and place to place for pillage of ordinary prizes.

But Sir Walter's friends do tell her Majesty what great service he hath done unto her in discovering the way to bring home the wealth of India and in making known to that nation her virtues and her justice. He hath brought hither a supposed prince and left hostages in his place. The Queen gives good ear unto them.

30th September. NEW PLAYS.

There were two new plays by the Lord Admiral's men this month, the one called *Crack me this Nut*, and the other *The World's Tragedy*.

2nd October. THE HIGH PRICE OF CORN.

In the county of Leicester is great complaint of the high price of all corn and grain, to the grief of the poor people whose want is increased by the evil custom of the farmers and graziers in those parts that feed their sheep with pease, which in time of scarcity is the best relief that the poor find for their bread.

6th October. THE SOLDIERS FURNISHED BY THE CLERGY.

Her Majesty being desirous to be truly informed of the state of the whole forces of the realm, the Lords Lieutenant have been directed to have the enrolled soldiers viewed, mustered, and trained. The clergy also who in '88 found certain able men as well of horse as of foot are now to review and supply the like number; and where there is defect in their armour, horse or furniture, to cause the same to be amended or supplied, and perfect rolls to be made of the names and surnames of the soldiers and of those that set them forth which shall be sent to the Council.

TROUBLE OVER THE STARCH MONOPOLY.

Of late certain apprentices of London violently took away a 1000 lbs. weight of starch that had been seized on for her Majesty's use by Mr. James Anton, her patentee, and not only carried the same to a warehouse but did grievously beat and wound Mr. Anton's deputies. The Lord Mayor shall examine this foul outrage and not only commit the offenders to prison, but certify the manner of the outrage to the Council.

9th October. M. LOMENIE'S STOUT SPEECHES.

Sir Roger Williams is returned from the French King, and with him one Monsieur de Lomenie, a secretary of the King's Chamber, who both by the King's letters and his own speech hath dealt so roundly with the Queen and the Council that there is great offence at Court; for, not concealing that Cambray is lost to the Spaniard, yet he would urge that some auxiliary forces might forthwith be sent over into Picardy; and that afterwards commissioners appointed to treat about the managing of the war. These things appearing preposterous to the Queen and the Council, he grew impatient, imputing the loss of Cambray to the Queen, saying that she rejoiceth in the King's misery. Moreover the King declareth that he hath his absolution from the Pope and that there are deputed four cardinals to give him the solemnity thereof; but that their chief errand is to draw him to a peace with Spain and to unite against all that are divided from the Church. He saith that the King is assured to receive for himself honourable conditions, but knowing that he shall be sought to be divided from the Queen and the Low Countries, desireth by her to be enabled by a common concurrency of both their forces that he be not compelled to such a peace as willingly he would not make, but such as may comprehend them all in such terms, as holding always together, they might be a balance against Spanish greatness. That if she refuse him in it, he must provide for himself as he may. These letters delivered with very stout speeches have greatly offended the Queen who loveth not to be terrified, so the gentleman is despatched without any hope of obtaining relief from hence.

14th October. WHEAT SPENT WEEKLY.

The Lord Mayor complaineth to the Lord Treasurer how hard is this restraint on the City from buying wheat from Kent and Essex, for great quantities of wheat are required in the City, and by reason of the restraint the prices are enhanced in more remote counties. There is consumed weekly in the City, brown bread, 535 qrs.; white bread, 1317 qrs.; in markets, 600 qrs.; in houses providing for themselves, 40 qrs.; in all 2492 qrs.; besides Hackney and Stepney.

15th October. MR. HUGH PLATT'S INVENTIONS.

Mr. Hugh Platt that last year put forth a book of inventions called the *Jewel House of Art and Nature* hath caused to be printed a little pamphlet, being *A Discovery of certain English wants*, wherein he complaineth that in his own experience it is an easier matter to devise many and very profitable inventions than to dispose of one of them to the good of the author himself; and because there are many gentlemen that be always ready and willing to entertain good suits, he giveth them to understand that he is still well furnished with inventions for them if they come in time, and whilst his small store lasteth, *videlicet* ;—a means to prepare flesh without any salt, and fit to be laid up in storehouses for many years or to furnish ships withal ; a defensative in the highest kind of all armour and artillery whatsoever from rusting in seven years after one preparation ; some English secrets whereby we may be less beholding either unto France or Spain in some of their best commodities ; an excellent oily composition defending all iron works from rust wherewith Sir Francis Drake is furnished in this last voyage ; a pump not weighing 20 pounds in weight and yet sufficient to deliver five tuns of water in one hour, being an excellent engine to water all houses that are near the river Thames or any river, also for ships of war ; a liquor to keep either boot, shoe or buskin made of dry leather both black in wearing and defensible against all rain, dew or moisture, to be had of the author in several kinds.

All those that are desirous to have any conference with the author may be advertised of his abode by William Ponsonby, stationer in Paul's Churchyard.

SIR WALTER RALEGH.

Sir Walter Ralegh is now in London and goes daily to hear sermons, because he hath seen the wonders of the Lord in the deep ; 'tis much commended and spoken of.

27th October. HIGH PRICES.

Notwithstanding the seasonable harvest this summer, the price of corn and of white meat is of late greatly risen in many counties, which is thought due to the want of care of the Justices to seek reformation, and to the covetous dispositions of farmers that, not acknowledging God's goodness, seek immoderate gain by enhancing the price of corn to the great oppression of the poor. The Council recommend that the Justices should bestow their pains that the orders set down and published last year with certain new additions be carefully looked unto for the relief of the poor. The Justices moreover should contribute amongst themselves and by their good example induce others of the richer sort to do the like, whereby a good sum of money might be collected to make a stock to be employed in corn, out of which a proportion might be sent weekly to the markets to be uttered to the poor at reasonable rates.

Likewise in London the price of sea coals standeth at a very high rate to the great oppression of the poor that are not able to furnish themselves with wood; the occasion whereof is that some of the richer sort of the town of Newcastle, having a lease of the Bishop of Durham of twelve coal pits, forbear to work the same but work in certain coal pits of their own which yield a worse sort of coal and less quantity. Moreover these owners outbid and hire from the rest all the coal wains that bring coals to the waterside. Another reason of raising the price of coals is that great quantities are transported to Rouen and other places beyond the seas. The Mayor of Newcastle is ordered to cause one or two of the chief coalmasters to be sent before the Council who shall bring with them the covenant wherein they are bound not to exceed a certain limit imposed on them: and in the mean season to take order that less quantity be transported out of the realm.

29th October. An Attack on Ireland Feared.

A Spanish pilot, taken by a captain of the Earl of Cumberland's upon the south coast of Spain, confesseth that there are a number of Levant ships of war of great burden come to Lisbon this month, where there are also eight or nine great ships of war and others expected: of these the Adelantado is to take charge and to come with them upon some parts in the West of Ireland. If the Lord Deputy shall find the Spaniard to attempt any landing in any place of the South as Waterford or Cork, he shall leave the prosecution of the rebellion in Ireland and march against them, leaving the forts of Armagh and Monaghan well guarded; and to encourage the great towns to stand fast, 1000 footmen are to be put in readiness to be sent thither from Chester upon a day's warning.

30th October. New Plays at the Rose.

At the Rose this month were three new plays, being *The Disguises*, *The Wonder of a Woman* and *Barnardo and Fiametta*.

1st November. The Account of Sir Walter Ralegh's Voyage.

Sir Walter Ralegh hath now brought to completion and sent the account of his voyage to Guiana to the Lord Admiral.

After leaving Plymouth last February, he reached the island of Trinidad on 22nd March, where there is an abundance of stone pitch at a point called Tierra de Brea or Piche, wherewith he made trial in trimming the ships, for this pitch melteth not with the heat of the sun as the pitch of Norway. Thence by night he attacked a Spanish city called St. Joseph which they took, together with a Spanish gentleman called Berreo who was the governor there and hath travelled in Guiana, whom Sir Walter used very courteously as his prisoner. When this Berreo learned that Sir Walter would make his way up the river to see Guiana he was stricken with great melancholy and sadness, using all the arguments he could to dissuade him, and saying that they could not enter any of the rivers with their barks or pinnaces, it was so low and sandy. Further, none of the country would come to speak with them, but would all fly, and if followed would burn their dwellings; and besides, that winter was at hand when the rivers begin to swell, and that the kings and lords of all the borders of Guiana had decreed that none of them should trade with any Christians for gold, because the same would be their overthrow, and that for love of gold the Christians meant to conquer and dispossess them of all together.

When Sir Walter had by experiment found Berreo's words to be true he resolved to go on with the boats, and a galego boat, cut down and fitted with banks to row on. Into the galego were thrust sixty men, in three other boats and in Sir Walter's own barge ten a piece, making 100 in all. With this company, having passed over some twenty miles of rough sea, they entered one of the rivers which their guide declared would take them into the great river of Orenoque; and there might they have been lost in the labyrinth of rivers but by chance they met with a canoa with three Indians, one of them an old man; and him they took for guide. Up these rivers they sailed westward for many days often in great distress for lack of victuals.

At length they reached a port called Morequito where they were visited by the old King of that place called Topiawari, to whom Sir Walter made known the cause of his coming thither, of her Majesty's greatness, her justice, her charity to all oppressed nations, with many other of her beauties and virtues, and that her pleasure was to deliver them from the tyranny of the Spaniards; all which being with great admiration attentively heard and marvellously admired, he began to sound the old man concerning Guiana.

The next day they sailed westward up to the river called Caroli, as well because it was marvellous of itself as also because it led to the strongest nations of all the frontiers; these are enemies of the Epuremi, that abound in gold, being subjects to Inga, Emperor of Guiana and Manoa. But when they came to this river, they could not row one stone's cast in an hour by reason of the force of the stream. Sir Walter therefore sent his guide to the people of those parts and there came down a lord or casique called Wanuretona, with many people and much store of provision. Of them he learnt that all who were either against the Spaniards or the Epuremi would join with him, and that if he entered the land over the mountains of Curaa he should satisfy himself with gold and all other good things.

Here they landed to go by foot to view the great river, and to see if they could find any mineral stone alongst the river side; and when they came to the tops of the hills adjoining to the rivers they beheld that wonderful breach of waters which ran down Caroli, and might from that mountain see the river how it ran in three parts over twenty miles off; and there appeared some ten or twelve overfalls in sight, every one as high over the other as a church tower. For his own part Sir Walter would have returned from thence, but the rest were all so desirous to go near the strange thunder of waters that they drew him on by little and little, till they came into the next valley where they might better discern it. 'I never saw,' saith he, 'a more beautiful country, nor more lively prospects, hills so raised here and there over the valleys, the river winding into divers branches, the plain adjoining without bush or stubble, all fair green grass, the ground hard sand, easy to march on either for horse or foot, the deer crossing in every path, the birds towards the evening singing on every tree with a thousand several tunes, cranes and herons of white, crimson, and carnation, perching in the river's side, the air fresh with a gentle easterly wind, and every stone that we stooped to take up promised either gold or silver by his complexion.'

But now the fury of the river Orenoque began daily to threaten them with dangers on their return, for no half day passed but the river began to rage and overflow very fearfully, and the rains came down in terrible showers, and gusts in great abundance. Having for well near a month passed westward farther and farther from their ships, at length they turned eastward. Returning therefore to the country of Topiawari, Sir Walter again had conference with the old man, who told him that four days' journey from his town was Macureguarai, and that those were the next and nearest subjects of Inga and of the Epuremi, and the first town of apparelled and rich people, and that all those plates of gold which were carried to other nations came from the Macureguarai and were there made; but that those of the land within were far finer, and fashioned after the images of men, beasts, birds and fishes. The old King would indeed have had Sir Walter stay and attempt this people, but he, knowing that Berreo did daily expect a succour out of Spain and from Granada, was unwilling to attempt the enterprise at that season but promised to return next year.

Of marvels in those parts, noteth that in the parts south of the river there be a race of Amazons, and they accompany with men but for one month in the year, and at that time all the Kings of the borders assemble and the Queens of the Amazons, and, after the Queens have chosen, the rest cast lots for their valentines. If they conceive and be delivered of a son, they return him to the father; if of a daughter, they nourish it and retain it; and as many as have daughters send a present to the begetters. At the port of Morequito one gave him a beast called by the Spaniards 'armadilla,' which seemeth to be barred all over with small plates somewhat like to a rhinoceros, with a white horn growing in his hinder parts as big as a great hunting horn, which they use to wind instead of a trumpet. In those parts there be a people called Ewaipanoma; they are reported to have their eyes in their shoulders, and their mouths in the middle of their breasts, and a long train of hair groweth backward between their shoulders: these Sir Walter saw not, but so many of the inhabitants declare the truth of the matter that he is fain to believe. Moreover such a relation was written of by Mandeville whose reports were many years holden for fables, and yet since the Indes were discovered we find his relations true of such things as heretofore were held incredible. A Spaniard also, a man in all things else esteemed a man of his word, declareth that he hath seen many of them.

Sir Walter urgeth very vehemently the advantages of this country of Guiana, being a country that hath yet her maidenhead, never sacked, turned nor wrought, the face of the earth not torn, nor the virtue and salt of the soil spent by manurance, the graves not opened for gold, the mines not broken with sledges, nor the images pulled down out of the temples. It is besides so defensible that it could be held by two forts built on a channel by which all ships must pass; nor is there other way of entry.

5th November. COURT NEWS.

On Monday last the Queen showed the Earl of Essex a printed book, which was that *Conference about the Succession to the Crown of England*, written two years since (as is supposed) by Parsons the Jesuit and dedicated to my Lord; than whom, he saith, no man is in more high and eminent place at this day in the realm, whether we respect his nobility, or calling, or favour with the Queen, or high liking of the people; and consequently no man like to have a greater part or sway in deciding of this great affair, when the time shall come for determination.

At his coming from Court the Earl was observed to look wan and pale, being exceedingly troubled at this great piece of villainy done unto him. He is sick and continues very ill. Yesterday in the afternoon the Queen visited him; but the Earl is mightily crossed in all things, for Mr. Bacon is gone without the place of Solicitor. The Lord Treasurer is come to London and lies in bed so ill of the gout in his hands, arms, knees and toes that his pains make him pitifully groan.

6th November. MR. BACON DISAPPOINTED OF THE SOLICITORSHIP.

Mr. Sergeant Fleming was yesterday made Solicitor, so my Lord of Essex and Mr. Bacon are finally disappointed. When the matter was concluded, my Lord came over from Richmond to Twickenham Park, where Mr. Bacon was, to break it with him, in these words: 'Master Bacon, the Queen hath denied me yon place for you, and hath placed another. I know you are the least part of your own matter, but you fare ill because you have chosen me for your mean and dependence. You have spent your time and your thoughts in my matters; I die if I do not somewhat towards your fortune; you shall not deny to accept a piece of land which I will bestow upon you.'

At first Mr. Bacon was somewhat unwilling to accept of the gift lest he should be too much bound to my Lord by this obligation. But my Lord bade him take no care for that, and pressed it. Whereupon Mr. Bacon saith, 'My Lord, I see I must be your homager and hold land of your gift: but do you know the manner of doing homage in law? Always it is with a saving of his faith to the King and his other Lords. And therefore, my Lord,' quoth he, 'I can be no more yours than I was, and it must be with the ancient savings, and if I grow to be a rich man, you will give me leave to give it back to some of your unrewarded followers.'

MR. DARCY'S PATENT.

Mr. Darcy in pursuit of his patent hath caused divers of the leather sellers to be committed to prison, notwithstanding they gave attendance in the cause three times at the Star Chamber and once at the Court at Richmond; whereat the Lord Mayor petitioneth the Council for a trial at law touching the validity of this and other patents made by her Majesty.

9th November. A TRUCE WITH TYRONE.

The Earl of Tyrone hath now made submission, complaining he was led into these courses chiefly from the bad usage of him by Sir John Perrot. Now he would have pardon and declares that he will not join with any foreign prince. A truce is therefore made until the 1st January.

12th November. THE EARL OF HERTFORD COMMITTED.

The Earl of Hertford was committed to the Tower six days ago. The cause is said to be a record secretly put into the Court of Arches to prove his first marriage lawful and his children legitimate. 'Tis said he is one of the wealthiest subjects of England. It is since given out that by commandment his son shall no more be called Lord Beauchamp but Seymour; and it is credibly said that my Lady Hertford is become stark mad. Note that my Lord is the son of the Duke of Somerset that was Lord Protector to King Edward the Sixth; his first wife was the Lady Catherine Grey (sister to the Lady Jane), whom he married after she had been divorced by the Earl of Pembroke; and for whose sake he was nine years in the Tower. This lady died in 1567.

My Lord of Essex hath put off the melancholy he fell unto by reason of the printed book delivered to the Queen, wherein by her Majesty's gracious favour and wisdom the harm meant to him is turned to his good and strengthens her love towards him. Within these last days many letters sent to her from foreign countries are delivered to my Lord, and he to answer them.

EXTRAORDINARY MEASURES AGAINST INVASION.

The Lords Lieutenant of counties on the sea coast are specially warned to have all men that are apt for the wars in readiness to withstand any invasion of the enemy. These men shall be put into bands under principal leaders, and held in readiness with all necessary furniture to be sent to such landing places where the enemy hath a purpose to land. To every thousand men are appointed one hundred pioneers, with their necessary instruments, and provision made of carts and carriages with some small nags for the more speedy conveyance of the men, who shall take with them a convenient proportion of victual and some overplus of powder, lead and match to supply any want. It is further ordained by the Council that the Lords Lieutenant shall succour each other should the enemy land in other counties than their own. They shall also warn all persons having habitations near the sea coast to attend with all their forces for the defence of the coast and of their land and habitations, as by the law of nature and of the land they are bound to do upon pain of forfeiture of their livelihoods and further punishment. The sum total of men to be put in readiness by fifteen counties and the towns of Southampton and London is 61,800.

An Impudent Cook.

One Owen Saintpire, a cook in the City, a very perverse and obstinate fellow, was lately committed to prison by the Lord Mayor for refusing to pay such contribution as by his own company was proportioned upon him for the Queen's service, and for other misdemeanours and parts of disobedience. Hereupon he hath entered an action of wrong imprisonment against the Chamberlain and other officers of the City.

17th November. The Queen's Accession Day.

This day was held as a day of great triumph at London for her Majesty's long and prosperous reign. The pulpit cross in Paul's Churchyard is now newly repaired, painted and partly inclosed with a wall of brick; here Dr. Richard Fletcher, the Bishop of London, preached in praise of the Queen before the Lord Mayor, Aldermen, and citizens in their best liveries, and the sermon being ended, upon the church leads the trumpets sounded, the cornets winded, and the choristers sang an anthem. On the steeple many lights were burned, the Tower shot off her ordnance, and bonfires were made.

At the Tilt there was a device of my Lord of Essex which is much commended. Some pretty while before he came in himself, he sent his page with some speed to the Queen, who returned with her Majesty's glove. When my Lord himself came in, he was met with an old hermit, a secretary of state, a brave soldier, and an esquire. The first presented him with a book of meditations, the second with political discourses, the third with orations of brave fought battles, the fourth was but his own follower, to whom the other three imparted much of their purpose before his coming in. Each devised with him, persuading him to this and that course of life, according to their inclinations. Then comes there into the Tiltyard unthought on the ordinary post boy of London, a ragged villain all bemired, upon a poor lean jade, galloping and blowing for life, and delivered the secretary a packet of letters which he straightway offered to my Lord of Essex.

In the after-supper before the Queen they first delivered a well-penned speech to move this worthy Knight to leave his vain following of Love and to betake him to heavenly meditation; the secretary's speech tending to have him follow matters of state; the soldier's persuading him to the war; but the esquire answered them all, and concluded with an excellent, but too plain English speech that his Knight would never forsake his Mistress's love, whose virtue made all his thoughts divine, whose wisdom taught him all true policy, whose beauty and worth were at all times able to make him fit to command armies. He showed all the defects and imperfections of all their times, and therefore thought his course of life to be best in serving his Mistress. Hereupon many constructions are made of these speeches, comparing the hermit and the secretary to two of the Lords, and the soldier to Sir Roger Williams; but the Queen said that if she had thought there would have been so much said of her, she would not have been there that night; and so went to bed.

20th November. SOUTHWELL'S 'TRIUMPH OVER DEATH.'

Mr. John Trussell hath sent to the press that consolatory epistle written by Southwell the Jesuit on the death of the Lady Margaret Sackville, Countess of Dorset. 'Our life,' saith he, 'is but lent, a good to make thereof during the loan our best commodity. It is a due debt to a more certain owner than ourselves, and therefore so long as we have it, we receive a benefit. When we are deprived of it, we have no wrong; we are tenants at will of this clayey farm, not for term of years. When we are warned out we must be ready to remove, having no other title but the owner's pleasure. It is but an inn, not a home; we came but to bait, not to dwell, and the condition of our entrance was in fine to depart.'

'Nature's debt is sooner exacted of some than of others, yet is there no fault in the creditor that exacteth but his own, but in the greediness of our eager hopes, either repining that their wishes fail, or willingly forgetting their mortality whom they are unwilling by experience to see mortal. Yet the general tide washeth all passengers to the same shore, some sooner, some later, but all at the last: and we must settle our minds to take our course as it cometh, never fearing a thing so necessary, yet ever expecting a thing so uncertain.'

22nd November. COURT NEWS.

We wait to hear what the French King's countenance will be on the return of Monsieur Lomenie, who went hence discontented and speaks lewdly of us wherever he goes. The King has not yet seen him, but the answers thence to our excuses of our usage of Monsieur Lomenie are sour and savouring of an alienate mind. Sir Henry Unton is named as the man to be sent over but would stand upon terms. Then Sir Arthur Gorges had vogue one week; now it is Sir Henry again, who is warned on his allegiance and let to understand that Princes will not be capitulated with by their servants.

23rd November. IRISH NEWS.

Letters are come from Ireland with good news of Tyrone's submission which brought the Lord Treasurer to Court from his sick bed. The Council have been three days about this Irish peace, and a formal pardon, according to our Law, is now a drawing. Sir George Carew is presently to be sent over to take his oath and to be Commissioner in the business with the Lord Deputy, to whom small countenance or trust is committed in this or anything else; and the credit of all things given to Sir John Norris.

26th November. AN INQUISITION CONCERNING RECUSANTS.

Because of the increase of recusants at this time which may infect others and also cause a diminution of the forces for the defence of the realm, in the present dangers extraordinary care must be taken for their reformation. The Archbishops shall now cause the Bishops and ordinaries to make exact and diligent inquisition into the number of recusants, their state, degree and value, and how many be vagrants and fugitives, and what means are used to reform them by instruction and teaching, and how many are indicted by form of law.

30th November. NEW PLAYS.

This month there were two new plays at the Rose, *A Toy to please chaste ladies* and *Harry the Fifth.*

1st December. FRENCH OPINIONS.

Mr. Edmondes who is the English Resident in France reporteth that Monsieur de Lomenie (that came over with Sir Roger Williams about three weeks since) is returned to the King who is now besieging La Fere. The King by Monsieur de Lomenie's relation is reduced from ill satisfaction and weak hope into strange despair of the English Court, so that he is resolved not to send Monsieur de Sancy here as he had intended, being persuaded that it would serve no other purpose than to give him more discontent, and to heap more indignity on him. The French say that they see clearly into our dispositions toward them by our demand for Calais, which, they allege, doth much touch the heart of France: by our refusing to join in treaty with them; and this last proceeding with Monsieur de Lomenie. They declare that they are in so hard a condition that they know not how to subsist against the great forces wherewith the enemy doth threaten them; but that they see their apparent ruin before their eyes if, seeing they are abandoned by those who are interested in common fortune with them, they do not otherwise provide for themselves. These be their discourses; and to anything we can allege of former merit and future hope, they answer that past remedies do not cure present diseases; and that we pay them with words, and not with deeds, seeking nothing more than to keep them still miserable. The Spaniard so constantly seeking a truce in Brittany giveth great suspicion of further consequence, either of some attempt elsewhere, or else to extend it to a further treaty.

Mr. Edmondes much lamenteth his own miserable estate and inability to serve longer by reason of his great debts, and earnestly petitioneth that her Majesty would have compassion on him and grant his revocation.

5th December. THE LIEUTENANT OF THE TOWER COMMITTED.

Sir Michael Blount, the Lieutenant of the Tower, is put out of his place. It is said that he grew very familiar with Mr. Neville, *alias* Latimer, and Captain Wainman, and in discourse with them, they began to talk of the dangers of the time; from that to argue of the town, how it might be made defensible, what provision, what men would serve the turn, what a brave command it was in a change. Then they grew madder as to talk of titles, and it is reported that the Lieutenant delivered his mind how he was affected; that he and his friends would keep the place till he saw great reason to yield it. But when they had waded so far, 'Masters,' said he, 'these matters we speak of are perilous, and therefore I will have nothing to do with them.' But the other two found means to discover it first to the Queen, whereupon the Lieutenant was examined by the Lords and is now committed to the Tower. Sir Drue Drury is sworn in his place.

6th December. WOOD IN THE PILLORY.

Wood that was condemned in the Star Chamber last July hath now confessed. To-day on a pillory in Cheapside he had an ear cut off, and three letters burned in his forehead. He made an oration, declaring his confession is voluntary: in his examination he charges Lady Shrewsbury very deeply with the matter; but she denies it.

7th December. THE QUEEN'S LETTER TO THE KING.

On the 30th November Mr. Edmondes read before the French King a letter from her Majesty answering those complaints of Monsieur de Lomenie, and his demand for succours. Mr. Edmondes reminded the King of the great services which her Majesty had rendered him for a long space of time, and lastly at Brest when the Queen, though she had in hand several other designs both of honour and advantage, had consented for the King's service to employ her forces by land and sea to drive the enemy from thence. As for the declaration that the King might be obliged to agree with the common enemy without comprehending her Majesty in the treaty, she would not suffer herself to be disturbed with the thought that the King's honour and so many vows on his part and so many services on hers could admit so odious and dangerous a resolution.

After the letter had been read, the King answered that he was not alone able to sustain the burden of the war for such reasons as are too true and too well known to all men; and that he would consult with the princes and officers of his crown, what he was to resolve on ; wherein if necessity shall force him to change course, as the fault thereof shall not be his, so her Majesty on her part, instead of excuses and justifications, shall have only cause afterwards of sorrow.

12th December. THE QUEEN DINES WITH THE LORD KEEPER.

Her Majesty in these days cometh much abroad. Yesterday she dined at Kew, at the Lord Keeper's house, where her entertainment was great and exceeding costly. At her first alighting she had a fine fan, with a handle garnished with diamonds. When she was in the middle way, between the garden gate and the house, there came one running towards her with a nosegay in his hand, and delivered it to her with a short, well-penned speech ; it had in it a very rich jewel, with many pendants of diamonds, valued at £400 at least. After dinner in her privy chamber, the Lord Keeper gave her a fine gown and juppin, which things were pleasing to her Highness ; and to grace his Lordship the more, she of herself took from him a salt, a spoon, and a fork of fine agate.

13th December. THE NAVY TO BE SET OUT.

The Queen hath now given order for the speedy setting forth of the Navy to the seas and hath appointed the same to be victualled for five months for 12,000 men ; the victuals to be delivered aboard the ships by the last of March next.

THE DEATH OF SIR ROGER WILLIAMS.

Sir Roger Williams died of a surfeit in Baynard's Castle yesterday at 3 o'clock after midnight. He gave all he had to my Lord of Essex, who indeed saved his soul, for none but he could make him take a feeling of his end ; but he died well, and very repentant. His jewels are valued at £1,000 ; 'tis said he had £1,200 out at interest ; in ready gold £200 ; and £60 in silver. His plate is worth £60, his garments £30, his horses £60, and this is his end. He desired to be buried in Paul's, and my Lord of Essex means to have it done in very martial sort.

14th December. MR. DARCY'S GRANT.

Some days since three of the Company of the Leathersellers, having disobeyed her Majesty's grant made to Mr. Edward Darcy for viewing and sealing of leather, were committed to the

Marshalsea. To-day being at their own request admitted to make their excuse before the Council, there was relation made of the whole proceedings since the grant was first made ; but their Lordships, finding their obstinacy to proceed without due regard, return them to prison, there to remain until they shall submit themselves and permit Mr. Darcy to enjoy the benefit of his grant. Moreover the Lord Mayor shall inhibit the rest of the Leathersellers from putting on sale any leather until they have submitted themselves.

17th December. 'MAROCCUS EXTATICUS.'

There is a pamphlet called *Maroccus Extaticus*, or *Banks' Bay Horse in a trance*, set down in the form of a dialogue between Banks and his beast and anatomising some abuses and bad tricks of this age, and especially of those landlords who for raising of their rents will turn their houses into brothels.

19th December. THE LORD PRESIDENT OF THE NORTH DEAD.

The Lord Huntingdon, Lord President of the North, died on Sunday last past, the 14th of this month, having been sick for nine days. The Archbishop of York being with him desired two things of his hands ; to prepare himself to die, which he did, not using many words but such as did give good assurance he died a good Christian ; the second, to dispose of his estate, which by no means he would hearken unto, and said little to that, only that it was a wild world, which he would not think upon. This was at first kept from my Lady Huntingdon, but the Queen came to Whitehall very suddenly of purpose to break it to her herself.

When the news was brought on Wednesday morning, the Lord Keeper was sent to her from the Queen that my Lord was sick. In the afternoon he came again unto her to let her know the Queen was advertised he was in some danger and therefore besought her to consider what should be done about his estate. This morning my Lady Puckering came to see her, and finding her so disquieted, she told her by circumstances that his danger was great, and small hope of recovery. Being desired by my Lady to tell her the very truth, she then told her that indeed assured word was come he was dead. This evening, at 4 o'clock, the Queen herself came in a litter to visit her.

21st December. PRIVATE SHIPS FOR THE NAVY.

Letters are being sent to the mayors and principal officers of sundry port towns to the effect that upon advertisement made of some attempt against this kingdom by way of invasion this next spring, the Queen hath given order to put the Navy Royal in readiness and to have the same assisted with some reasonable number of good ships of her subjects. Wherefore ships of good burden shall be prepared, manned and furnished, provided with munition and victual for five months, by the same that did contribute in '88; these ships to be ready by the end of March.

SIR HENRY UNTON SENT TO THE FRENCH KING.

Sir Henry Unton is sent ambassador to France to discover how the French King standeth affected, and hoping to divert him from a course with Spain which by his own answers and Mr. Edmondes and other conjectures, it seemeth he is like to enter into, the Pope working earnestly to bring it to pass, and almost all his Council discovering no good conceit of our amity.

THE INVASION IN CORNWALL.

After the sudden incursion of the enemy in Cornwall last summer, a collection was made both in Cornwall and some other counties for the relief of the inhabitants of those villages that suffered spoil. Now it appeareth that this money was neither well ordered nor distributed, for the licence to gather was sold by the parties that undertook the collection, and the villages most spoiled like to be defrauded of it.

25th December. NEWS OF SIR FRANCIS DRAKE.

At Plymouth an Irish captain new come from Lisbon declareth that Sir Francis Drake and Sir John Hawkins have taken great treasure at St. John de Porto Rico, besides other pillage of great value, and that the fleet will speedily return to England.

28th December. SMUGGLING OF CORN.

From the Isle of Ely it is reported that divers boats come up in the night time and convey much grain by water from the inland counties to Lynne whence it is transported overseas.

'CHURCHYARD'S CHARITY' AND 'A PRAISE OF POETRY.'

A musical consort of heavenly harmony called *Churchyard's Charity*, by Mr. Thomas Churchyard, which he dedicateth to the Earl of Essex, noting that now, by reason of great age, his wits and inventions are almost wearied with writing of books, this being one of the last. In this poem, he lamenteth that great lack of charity in our days. Machievel, saith he, is now made an Englishman :

> Fine Machievel, is now from Florence flown
> To England where, his welcome is too great ;
> His busy books, are here so read and known
> That charity, thereby hath lost her meat.
> Who doth for debt, in danger long remain
> Must fall down flat, and seldom rise again.

Also, he hath written *A Praise of Poetry*, some notes whereof are drawn out of the *Apology* made by Sir Philip Sidney that was published this last spring.

HUNNIS' 'RECREATIONS.'

A book of godly verses entitled *Hunnis' Recreations*, written by Mr. William Hunnis, the Master of the Children of the Queen's Chapel, being Adam's Banishment, Christ his Crib, The Lost Sheep, The Complaint of Old Age, published together with The Life and Death of Joseph. Noteth in the Complaint of Old Age that he will speak the best of the dead :

> The common custom is,
> to flatter them that live ;
> And of the dead reproachful words
> and ill reports to give.
> But sure the fault is great,
> to speak ill of the dead,
> Who harm them not, but quietly
> do rest within their bed.

'POLIMANTEIA.'

From Cambridge a book called *Polimanteia* showing the means lawful and unlawful to judge of the fall of a commonwealth by signs astronomical and the like, being put forward against frivolous and foolish conjectures. To this is added a letter of England to her three daughters, being the two Universities and the Inns of Court, exhorting their children to write of the worthies of our time; England to all her inhabitants exhorting them to stand together for that England cannot perish but by Englishmen; Religion's speech to England's children; and lastly Loyalty's speech.

PLUTARCH'S LIVES.

A new edition of that translation which Sir Thomas North published in 1579, made from the French of James Amyot out of the original Greek of *The Lives of the Noble Grecians and Romans, compared together* by that grave, learned philosopher and historiographer Plutarch of Chaeronea.

1596

3rd January. THE LADY HUNTINGDON.

My Lady of Huntingdon continues so ill of grief that many doubt she cannot live. She is so much weakened by sorrow that no officers of hers dare go to her sight to know her pleasure, either in her own private fortune or to know what shall be done with the dead body of my Lord.

8th January. 'THE BLACK DOG OF NEWGATE.'

There is entered a book called *The Black Dog of Newgate* by one Luke Hutton, dedicated to Sir John Popham, the Lord Chief Justice, and containing a poem of the Black Dog, being the jailor of Newgate, whom for his cruelty he likeneth to a dog; also a discourse between the author and one Zawny, a prisoner, discovering the ways of certain connycatchers, E. N. or N. S., that prey especially upon their fellows.

THE CONDEMNED.

The sermon ended, the men condemned to die,
  Taking their leaves of their acquainted friends,
With sorry looks paysing their steps they ply,
  Down to a hall where for them there attends
A man of office, who to daunt life's hopes,
  Doth cord their hands and scarf their necks with ropes.

Thus roped and corded they descend the stairs;
  Newgate's Black Dog bestirs to play his part,
And doth not cease for to augment their cares,
  Willing the carman to set near his cart;
Which done, these men with fear of death o'erpanged,
  Bound in the cart are carried to be hanged.

Noteth that the rats be so many that they will take a candle from a man's hand, and when one dieth in the common ward they will prey upon his face ere he be fully dead.

18th January. VICTUALS FOR THE NAVY.

The Council having ordained the proportion of victuals of wheat, malt, pease, oxen, porks, bacon and cheese to be rendered by the several counties for the service of the navy, complaints are now being made by most of them that the charge is too heavy; so that in some cases the demand is abated.

The cities of New Sarum and Winchester, being cities near to the port of Southampton and taking special benefit from it, are required to consider of some contribution from such as exercise merchandize towards the setting forth of ships.

19th January. 'A WATCHWORD FOR WAR.'

There is from Cambridge a godly book called *A Watchword for War*, by one C. G., published by reason of the dispersed rumours amongst us and the suspected coming of the Spaniard. Noteth and confuteth these fearful objections which make against us; as that the power of the enemy is great, and it may be he shall have the aid of the Indians, the assistance of the Pope, and perhaps the help of such as have greater cause to gratify us than be against us. Or some sinister civil practice; yet this is the common saying: 'If we be true within ourselves, we need not care or fear the enemy.' Many suspect the papists, yet, albeit they jar about matters of religion, when they see the Spaniard, they will join with us against him, if it were but to save their lives.

20th January. 'THE SECOND PART OF THE FAERY QUEEN.'

The second part of Mr. Edmund Spenser's *Faery Queen* is now entered for the press, containing the fourth, fifth and sixth books, being the Legend of Cambel and Telamond, or of Friendship; the Legend of Artegal, or of Justice; and the Legend of S. Calidore, or of Courtesy.

23rd January. COPLEY'S 'FIG FOR FORTUNE.'

There is a poem entered by Mr. Anthony Copley, dedicated to the Lord Viscount Montague and entitled *A Fig for Fortune*, whereof the author giveth this argument:

An Elizian outcast of Fortune, ranging on his jade Melancholy through the desert of his affliction, in hope to find out somewhere either ease or end of the same, hapneth first upon Cato's ghost, a spirit of despair and self-misdoom, which would persuade him to kill himself. But for that she endeth her oratory with a sulphur vanish from his sight, he misdoubted both her and her tale. Then posting onward through the residue of the night, he chanceth next on the spirit of Revenge ; she persuadeth him blood and treachery against all his enemies as the only means to remount to pristine bliss in despite of Fortune. But she likewise manifesting in the end the treason of her tale by a sudden whip away from his eye at the sight of break of day in the east, left him also conceited of her danger. Thirdly, rapt from off his Melancholy, which now began to faint under him at the light of a new day of Grace, he was suddenly mounted upon the steed of Good Desire, and by him brought to Mount Sion, the Temple of Peace ; where by Catechrysius, an hermit (who greatly wondered to see a distressed Elizian in those parts under so happy days of Eliza), he was by him in the house of Devotion catechized, and there also celestially armed by an angel, and within a while after in-denized by the high Sacrificator a Champion of that Temple against the insults of Fortune, who is titled by the name of Doblessa in respect of the double danger both of her luring and lowering inconstancy. She, whiles the Sionites were all in peaceful adoration of Almighty God in the Temple, came with her Babellonian rout to assault the place, but was eftsoons by the nature of those Templars shamefully repulsed. Feast and thanks was made to God therefor throughout all the region ; in which solemnity the Grace of God, hovering over the multitude in the procession time (like a virgin attended upon with all the Court of heaven), showered down roses amongst them, leaving them there a scrambling for the same. The Elizian was one that scrambled his lapful among the rest ; and for he thought it was his sovereign Lady Eliza, and those roses hers, he was suddenly in joy thereof rapt home again to Elizium.

24th January. SIR HENRY UNTON AND THE FRENCH KING.

Sir Henry Unton reached La Fere, which the French King besiegeth, on the 7th, the King then being absent. On the 9th the King returned, and the next day gave audience to Sir Henry, who after due compliments delivered unto him the

Queen's salutations and her letters; next he declared that he was come over according to the Queen's promise given to Monsieur Lomenie to send one by whom she could more particularly express herself than by letters. Then, entering into particularities, he related why her Majesty was forced to withdraw her forces out of Brittany; why she could not assent to Monsieur Lomenie's demands for succour for Picardy, and therewithal Monsieur Lomenie's insolent carriage towards her Majesty; and lastly acquainted him with an Italian pamphlet wherein it was pretended that the King would make peace with Spain.

The King gave patient hearing, and after the ambassador's speech was ended asked whether that was all the satisfaction he brought; for he was little favoured and the ambassador little honoured to be employed in so fruitless a message of words. Time no longer permitted him to trust words, for he looked daily to be assailed by a mighty enemy, which he had sufficiently and often made known to the Queen; which seeing it will nothing prevail, he must, saith he, otherwise provide for his safety by such means as he may.

MR. DARCY'S PATENT IS ANNULLED.

The patent for searching and sealing of leather granted to Mr. Darcy is now revoked upon the leather sellers paying unto him the sum of £4,000.

25th January. CONDEMNED PRISONERS TO BE PARDONED.

Her Majesty hath resolved that those prisoners condemned to death at the late gaol delivery and meet to be favoured of their lives shall be pardoned and bestowed in the service of the wars with hope of their good demeanour hereafter.

26th January. NEWS FROM FRANCE.

Sir Henry Unton the ambassador is much cast down at his ill success, which had been much worse but for the King's special favour, who took some pity on him for his former merit; the French term his message '*un discours du foin*' among themselves, and both the King and his Council take great scorn thereat. The King gave him private audience in his cabinet, saying that it was for Sir Henry's particular satisfaction, being loath to discontent one who had so well deserved of him, reputing him his soldier after the old manner howsoever he was now qualified with the title of the Queen's ambassador.

It is believed that this general truce between France and Spain is likely to ensue, whereof the grounds are these: the King's reconciliation with Rome; his being given to pleasures and desire of repose; the necessity of his estate, wanting treasure and forces to maintain the wars; his subjects being harried and wearied out with the former wars, which cry out for peace; the zeal of all his Catholics in their religion; the forwardness of his choice Councillors to sway the King to the amity of Spain; the threats of the King of Spain's intended invasion of Picardy upon the arrival of the Cardinal of Austria in the Low Countries, who bringeth war and peace with him; and lastly the small comfort which the King expecteth from his confederates' association and aid.

30th January. A SECOND VOYAGE TO GUIANA.

Four days since Mr. Laurence Keymis set forth from Portland in the *Darling* of London to make a further voyage of discovery at the charges of Sir Walter Ralegh.

31st January. NEW PLAYS BY THE LORD ADMIRAL'S MEN.

The Lord Admiral's men have played three new plays this month, *Chinon of England*, *Pythagoras*, and *The Second Week*.

THE MILD WEATHER.

This month there hath been notable mild weather, and so like the spring time that the sparrows have been seen to build their nests.

1st February. FLESH PROHIBITED DURING LENT.

The customary orders against killing and eating of flesh during Lent are published. This year eight butchers are to be licensed within the City without paying anything for their licence, but being bound in reasonable sums of money to observe the orders prescribed to them.

2nd February. PROCEEDINGS WITH TYRONE.

Sir Henry Wallop and Sir Robert Gardiner, appointed commissioners to treat with Tyrone under the Great Seal of Ireland, have met with the Earl, O'Donnell, and others. The commissioners at first would have him come to Dundalk but he refused, and on the 20th January they with three others met Tyrone and O'Donnell a mile out of the town, none of either side having any other weapons than swords. The forces of either side stood a quarter of a mile distant from them, and whilst they parleyed (which was on horseback) two horsemen of the commissioners stood firm in the midway between Tyrone's troops and them, likewise two horsemen of Tyrone's were placed between them and the English forces; which were to give warning if any treacherous attempt were made on either side. This treaty continued for three hours but without conclusion. The next day they met again, at which time the Irish behaved as men exceeding fearful, continually gazing about, their spies riding near, and themselves less attentive than at first. At the conclusion of this parley it was agreed that they should set down dividedly all the causes of their grievances, their demands and offers, and thereupon the commissioners would answer them so reasonably as they hoped would be to their satisfaction.

3rd February. Contributions to the Fleet.

The inhabitants of certain ports and coast towns in Essex having made complaint that the setting forth of three hoys laid upon them is too great, the Council give order that the inhabitants of the county in general being as much interested as the parts maritime shall confer and resolve of some good proportion to be given in this behalf.

4th February. French News.

It is said in the French King's camp that the Cardinal of Austria hath power from the King of Spain to conclude a peace between France and Spain for certain years; but the Spanish King doth rather affect a long truce than a peace, whereby he might retain what he now possesseth in France. The Cardinal is now at Namur; he intendeth (as appeareth from certain letters taken) to draw out all the old soldiers into the field, being resolved to besiege Calais or Boulogne to divert thereby the siege of La Fere.

5th February. News of Drake.

A carvel from Havannah bringeth news that Sir Francis Drake has taken the castle there and landed 4000 men.

7th February. MR. THOMAS ARUNDEL'S RETURN.

Mr. Thomas Arundel that some months since went to take service under the Emperor against the Turk is now returned, having gotten an extreme cold by tumbling into the sea for safety of his life, when his ship was wrecked, and thereby his apparel, linen, horses, money, and whatsoever else all lost. So honourably hath he carried himself in the wars that the Emperor made him an Earl of the Empire. But when it was carried to the Queen that he hath presumed to a dignity from the Emperor without her privity he is to be committed to his lodging or to the Fleet until her pleasure be known.

11th February. FORGERS SENTENCED.

Five men called Nixen, Pepper, Ellis, Johnson and Anglesey, that had counterfeited the hands of the Lord Treasurer and others of the Council, were sentenced to-day in the Star Chamber. The first three are condemned to stand on the pillory and lose their ears, and be branded on the forehead with an F, and condemned perpetually to the galleys. Johnson suffereth the same ; but Anglesey, inasmuch as he wrote the names fearing lest Johnson would stab him, to the pillory and imprisonment only. The Lord Treasurer moved that since such burnings die out in a short time, they should be scarified on the cheeks with the letter F by a surgeon, and that some powder be put there to colour so it would never vanish ; but the others made no reply to this.

12th February. 'THE BLIND BEGGAR OF ALEXANDRIA.'

To-day there is a new play at the Rose by Chapman called *The Blind Beggar of Alexandria.* Herein one Irus, supposed a blind beggar, disguising himself as an humorous Count (one that maketh much of his pistol), an usurer, and a nobleman, marrieth several ladies to enjoy their love, and in the end, pretending that the Count and the usurer are suddenly slain, becometh King.

THE HUMOURS OF COUNT HERMES.

Come, gird this pistol closely to my side,
By which I make men fear my humour still,
And have slain two or three as 'twere my mood,

When I have done it most advisedly
To rid them as they were my heavy foes.
Now am I known to be the mad-brain Count,
Whose humours twice five summers I have held,
And said at first I came from stately Rome,
Calling myself Count Hermes, and assuming
The humour of a wild and frantic man,
Careless of what I say or what I do;
And so such faults as I of purpose do
Is buried in my humour and this gown I wear
In rain or snow, or in the hottest summer,
And never go nor ride without a gown,
Which humour does not fit my frenzy well,
But hides my person's form from being known.

13th February. FRENCH NEWS.

The Governors in Picardy take such alarm of the preparations of the Cardinal of Austria that upon the fear thereof they come to the French King to solicit his care of their preservation and to furnish them with money and means, and especially the Governor of Calais; but they are all returned home only with good words. It is feared that Calais is not very well furnished with means to endure a siege, and that the town is not so well fortified nor so strong for defence as it is in opinion.

COLSE'S 'PENELOPE'S COMPLAINT.'

There is entered a book called *Penelope's Complaint* or a mirror for wanton minions, by Peter Colse, dedicated to the Lady Edith, wife of Sir Ralph Horsey, Lord Lieutenant of the County of Dorset; which poem is committed to her Ladyship because an unknown author hath of late published a pamphlet called *Avisa*, overslipping so many praiseworthy matrons to praise the meanest. The book telleth of the complaint of Penelope at the departure of Ulysses, of the wooers' misrule, and of their slaughter at Ulysses' return.

14th February. THE FRENCH KING AND HER MAJESTY'S PICTURE.

The French King of late gave audience to Sir Henry Unton on the presenting to him of certain letters from the Queen.

After which the King sent for Madame Gabrielle, and at her coming he drew near to her with great reverence, holding his hat at first in his hand, and declaring that the ambassador was so well known unto them both as he doubted not that she would welcome him ; which she did, unmasking herself, and gracing the ambassador with her best favours. The King after these ceremonies passed took her on his left hand and the ambassador on his right hand, and so continued almost an hour walking together in the Park. Afterwards the King asked whether Sir Henry found his mistress anything changed, who answered sparingly in her praise and told him that, if without offence he might speak it, he had the picture of a far more excellent mistress and yet did her picture come far short of her perfection of beauty. 'As you love me,' said the King, 'show it me if you have it about you.' Sir Henry made some difficulties ; yet upon his importunity offered it to his view very secretly, holding it in his hand. The King beheld it with passion and admiration, saying 'You are right ; *je me rends*' ; protesting he had never seen the like ; so with great reverence he kissed it twice or thrice, the ambassador still retaining it in his hand. In the end, after some kind of contention, he took it away vowing that the ambassador might take leave of it, for he would not forgo it for any treasure ; and that to possess the favour of the lively picture, he would forsake all the world and hold himself most happy, with many other most passionate words.

23rd February. THE SUBURBS.

Great abuses continue to grow by the multitude of base tenements and disorderly houses erected in the suburbs of London, and though the Council from time to time have given direction to stay or suppress such buildings, yet they have found not such success and effect of their directions as was expected. For there is an increase of dissolute, loose and insolent people harboured in noisome and disorderly houses, such as be poor cottages and habitations of beggars and people without trade, stables, inns, alehouses, taverns, garden houses, bowling alleys and brothels ; all pestering these parts of the City with disorder and uncleanness, apt to breed contagion and sickness and serve for the resort of masterless men, and the cause of cosenages, thefts and other dishonest conversations; and which may also be used to cover dangerous practices. The magistrates in the County of Middlesex are now ordered to suppress such places and the unlawful games or exercises used therein.

25th February. The Condemned Prisoners.

The Lord Mayor, Recorder and Sheriff having now prepared a certificate of those condemned prisoners meet to be pardoned for service in the wars, the rest are to be executed, lest by overmuch toleration and evil example others be encouraged to like offences.

28th February. Masterless Men to be taken up.

For the defence of the new fort at Plymouth the Council require the Lord Mayor of London to take up fifty able men of such as are masterless and can best be spared, and to despatch them to Sir Ferdinando Gorges.

Reluctant Seamen.

Sundry mariners, carried with the desire of gain above the duty they owe to Her Highness and the love each man ought to have unto his country, have conveyed themselves into remote parts of the shires away from the port towns and seaside, to the end that they may absent themselves from the press and stay at home till her Majesty's Navy be at sea, and then to go on merchant voyages. Proclamation is to be made in market towns that all mariners shall, on pain of death, repair to the port towns and there remain until the commissioners and presters shall take view of them and choose such as be fit for the service.

1st March. A Horrible Murder.

Two days since there was one executed at Grinsted in Sussex for the murder of his wife at Mayfield. This man, by name Raph Meaphon, whose trade was to dig in the iron mines and to make coals, coming home, his wife with her son of 5 years of age being abed, he knocked and was let in, whereon he fell to railing and chiding with her; and in the end, whether it were a matter pretended or otherwise, he drew out his knife and cut her throat, and so leaving her weltering in her own gore went again to his work. Soon after, the house was seen to be on fire, which the neighbours and the whole town came to quench, marvelling where the good man and his wife was. The child was recovered from the fire and the body found, but they could not save the goods. Then was the child examined and required to tell when his father came home, and without any blushing fear (as commonly is seen in children) told them his father came home when his mother was in bed and first used some churlish speech unto her, then he drew out his knife, cut her throat and so left her ; describing in good order the bigness of the knife and the colour of the haft, but wherefore his father did this wicked deed he could not say anything.

Hereupon they sent for the father from his work and strictly examined him of the same, who stoutly and most audaciously denied the fact. But his tale not agreeing with the words of his fellow workmen, he was for that night committed to the stocks. The next day being more thoroughly again examined in the cause, though the evidences were found too apparent, yet he still denied it. The coroner therefore committed him to the jail at Lewes, whence on the 24th February he was arraigned at Grinsted ; where on the evidence of his son he was found guilty and on the 27th executed.

4th March. Soldiers for Ireland.

The Council have given order that 300 horsemen and 1500 footmen shall be sent over into Ireland at the beginning of next month, with another thousand to be held in readiness. Of these one half shall be shot, whereof a fourth part to be muskets, the other half to be armed with corselets and pikes saving some few halberts ; all to be furnished with coats of good cloth well lined and of blue colour.

8th March. The Soldiers' Coats.

The men levied in the County of Kent for Ireland having been already provided with coats of marble colour, the Council allow the coats to serve at this time.

11th March. Tyrone's Grievances.

Sir Robert Gardiner, Lord Chief Justice of Ireland, is come over from Ireland with the grievances and demands of Tyrone and the rest, which were laid before the Queen, whereof for some part she findeth great cause of mislike that the commissioners should receive or give ear to any such presumptuous and disloyal petitions and answers. As for their petition for free liberty of conscience, this request is deemed disloyal, for her Majesty will never grant to any subject of any degree the liberty to break laws, though heretofore she has acted mercifully. Nevertheless, rather than that the purpose of pacification should fail upon some private demands, not being dishonourable, nor not much disprofitable to her Majesty, it shall be lawful to yield thereto.

ABUSES IN PLAY.

There is of late great abuse in play arising especially by people of base quality dwelling in the City of London and the suburbs who make false dice and dice of advantage to the undoing of many, and against whom there is no statute law. The Lord Mayor is required to assist Mr. Cornwallis, her Majesty's Groom Porter, in his travail to suppress these abuses by providing some remedy for the stopping of such lewd people from uttering false dice, and that neither haberdashers nor any other shall sell any but such as are square and good.

13*th March*. THE QUEEN AND LORD BURLEIGH.

'Tis said in Court that the Queen purposeth to make a progress of some fifteen days to consume the Lent, and to return to Greenwich eight days before the solemn feast which she will keep there; for she seemeth weary of Surrey and would go over into Middlesex, from thence to Osterley, Highgate and Hackney. The old Lord Treasurer, upon some pet, would needs away against her will on Thursday last, saying that her business was ended; and that he would for ten days go take physic. When the Queen saw it booted not to stay him, she said he was a froward old fool.

15*th March*. THE LATE EARL OF HUNTINGDON.

By order of the Council the corpse of the late Lord President was embowelled, embalmed and closed in cerecloth and lead, but still lies unburied, attended nightly by four servants, for the Countess will neither accept administration nor give order for the funeral, to the great inconvenience of the Council in those parts.

17th March. A SPANISH RAID NEAR PLYMOUTH.

Three nights since a Spanish pinnace came into Cawsand Bay with twenty-five men in her, who landed armed with muskets, and fixed barrels of powder and brimstone to the doors of five several houses and to two boats, and set them on fire, whereby the whole village would have been burned had not force arrived. A man having fired one shot at them, they all fled to their pinnace and put to sea.

20th March. MR. THOMAS ARUNDEL.

Mr. Arundel being still restrained because of his Earldom from the Emperor complaineth that he is more straitly treated than was Sir Anthony Shirley. Moreover, saith he, this will be a slender satisfaction to the Emperor and a certain breaking off of all well-hoped-for proceedings of amity with the Queen, for the princes of Germany cannot but take it very ill when they shall see the Queen attempt to infringe their privileges by taking on her the unmaking of an Earl Imperial; all Italy and Germany will think her not willing to offend the Turk. Besides, though a King can make an Earl, yet cannot an Earl be unmade but being tried and convicted by his peers.

21st March. EVASION OF COMMON CHARGES.

Sundry persons of good ability in the county of Middlesex are refusing to contribute the reasonable taxation at which they are assessed by their neighbours, some alleging that they are merchants and have their habitations in London, others pretending that they are mint men, moneyers, or have their living in other counties, or privileged by reason of her Majesty's service. The Council require that all manner of persons, under the degree of Lord of Parliament or of the Privy Council, that inhabit or hold any houses or land in the county shall henceforth pay these sums; wherein, if any refuse to contribute, then shall the commissioners for musters require them friendly to contribute as good and dutiful subjects ought to do with their neighbours in this public service. And if any of them persist, then to inform the Council, who will take such further order with them as may be convenient.

To the like effect complaints are being made by inhabitants of the liberties of Salisbury Court and Ely Rents, alleging that it may in after times be drawn in argument against their liberties; to the avoiding of which the Council have commanded an order to be entered in the register of Council, and also enregistered as an Act by the Lord Mayor of London.

In the counties also many are unwilling to contribute to the charges of the Navy.

25th March. Sir Henry Unton Sick.

Sir Henry Unton is reported to be very sick, being visited for several days with a violent burning fever so that he hath no benefit of sleep, which redoubleth oftentimes with so extraordinary accidents (being as the physicians declare a malignant fever and accompanied with the purples) that he is in all opinion abandoned by them. The King hath visited him, although his own physicians would have dissuaded him, to whom he answered that he had not hitherto feared the harquebus shot and did not now apprehend the purples.

27th March. The Death of Sir John Hawkins reported.

A certain mariner, one of the company of Sir Francis Drake and Sir John Hawkins, that was taken by the Spanish and hath escaped to Plymouth, reporteth that his ship having lost company was taken by the Spaniards and the crew imprisoned in the Isle of St. John de Porto Rico. The Spaniards sunk ships in the harbour to hinder the entrance, but Sir Francis summoned the town, and when they refused to yield sent fifteen vessels to burn the frigates. Two were fired, but by the light thus made the Spaniards fired on the English ships and drove them away. The English attacked the fort and Sir John Hawkins was killed. Sir Francis then went to the south of the island to get provisions and thence sailed to Carthagena, but meanwhile the treasure ships in Porto Rico sailed and are come safe to St. Lucar.

28th March. Counterfeiting of Passports.

Certain vagrants, that have been taken with counterfeit licences and passports, being strictly examined have confessed the names of divers lewd persons about the City of London that not only counterfeit the names of the Generals of her Majesty's forces beyond the seas but affix seals of arms to the same. These persons are now to be apprehended and very straitly examined what passports and licences they have made.

A SCARCITY OF GAME.

The purveyors of poultry for her Majesty's household complain of the scarcity of rabbits and conies, also of partridges and pheasants wherewith the Queen is served daily throughout the year; wherefore it is required by the Council that bonds shall be taken of all victuallers and poulterers that no rabbits be bought or uttered before the first of June or any partridges or pheasants sold hereafter.

29th March. CALVIN'S 'APHORISMS.'

Mr. Henry Holland hath translated Calvin's *Aphorisms of Christian Religion*, a very compendious abridgment of his *Institutions* that were set forth in short sentences methodically by M. Piscator. Herein are handled twenty-eight commonplaces, as, Of knowledge of God, Of Faith, Of Christian liberty, Of Predestination, Of the Civil Magistrate, and the like. Noteth of predestination that it is the eternal decree of God, wherein He determined with Himself what He would have done with every man, as concerning their eternal salvation or damnation. Which doctrine hath two notable fruits; the one, that we may with humble adoration acknowledge how much we are bound unto God that hath vouchsafed to choose us, so unworthy, out of the company of the damned and to advance us to the state of heavenly glory; the other, that we may with good assurance rest ourselves on the unchangeable purpose of God touching our salvation, and therefore be fully persuaded and assured thereof in Jesus Christ.

30th March. A BOOK OF SURGERY.

Mr. William Clowes, one of the Queen's surgeons, hath written a profitable and necessary *Book of Observations*, for all those that are burned with the flame of gunpowder or wounded by musket or caliver shot, and such like accidents, relating the cases and cures of many of his own patients; also added thereto a treatise of *lues venerea*.

2nd April. CALAIS ASSAULTED.

Sudden news is come that the Cardinal Albert of Austria that was threatening the French King's siege of La Fere hath suddenly turned his course and is seated round Calais.

4th April. THE ATTACK ON CALAIS.

The Earl of Essex is now at Dover, whence he hath sent Sir Conyers Clifford to see whether he can get into Calais and view the state of the town, but the wind was so scant that he could not stem the tide; and another gentleman to Boulogne to find out what is become of the King and his army, and what means they propose on that side to succour Calais.

5th April. CALAIS.

My Lord of Essex, on his way from Dover yesterday to Court, met the Lord Admiral's packet between Canterbury and Sittingbourne, and seeing that the Queen had resolved to save Calais, he is returned to Dover to have all things ready. The enemy is now battering a ravelin to the east of the haven, which if taken will impede the succours; but the garrison promise to hold out two days.

SIR HENRY UNTON DEAD.

Sir Henry Unton is dead in the French camp, having been ill more than three weeks, although tended by the King's physicians. When the purple spots appeared above his heart they gave him *Confectio Alcarmas* compounded of musk, amber, gold, pearl, and unicorn's horn, with pigeons applied to his side, and all other means that art could devise to expel the strongest poison if he were not bewitched withal; notwithstanding he died shortly afterwards.

MR. NORDEN'S 'CHRISTIAN COMFORT.'

Mr. John Norden hath written *A Christian familiar comfort and encouragement unto all English subjects* not to dismay at the Spanish threats; to which is added an admonition to all English papists who openly or covertly desire a change, also to all inferior magistrates and loyal subjects to show themselves watchful in these dangers which may move sudden and indiscreet hurly burlies. Noteth especially the policy of the enemy that by sudden reports, dangerous bruits and open hoobubs would move indiscreet tumult, that factious people might draw the rest to violate their sworn obedience and under colour of some public good for them or of some imminent danger, working their own confusion, may yield the more ease to the enemies' purpose.

6th April. CALAIS.

My Lord of Essex makes all preparation for transport of the troops at Dover, hoping to embark them to-day, and to-morrow to send word that they are entered. All yesterday forenoon the enemy's battery played.

7th April. A MUTINY AT CHESTER.

From Chester is reported the lewd and mutinous carriage of the soldiers sent from North Wales for the Irish service, some of them running away from their conductors; and the conductors appointed by the counties themselves refusing to see the soldiers conducted beyond Chester to the ports.

9th April THE BISHOP OF ST. DAVID'S UNHAPPY SERMON BEFORE THE QUEEN.

The Bishop of St. David's lately preached before the Court at Richmond, taking his text out of Psalm xc., verse 12, 'O teach us to number our days, that we incline our hearts unto wisdom,' and therein began to speak of some sacred and mystical numbers as 3 for the Trinity, 3 times 3 for the Heavenly Hierarchy, 7 for the Sabbath, 7 times 7 for a Jubilee, and lastly 7 times 9 for the Grand Climacterical. The Queen perceiving whereto it tended began to be troubled with it. The Bishop discovering all was not well (for the pulpit standeth *vis-à-vis* to her closet), he fell to treat of some more plausible numbers as of the number 666, making 'Latinus,' with which, said he, he could prove the Pope to be Antichrist; also of that fatal number 88, which being so long before spoken of for a dangerous year, yet it had pleased God not only to preserve her but to give her a famous victory against the united forces of Rome and Spain. He ended with an excellent prayer, as if in her Majesty's person, in which there occurred these words:

'Oh Lord, I am now entered a good way into the climacterical year of mine age, which mine enemies wish and hope to be fatal unto me. But thou, Lord, which by Thy prophet Jeremy commanded the House of Israel not to learn the way of the heathen, nor to be afraid of the signs of heaven, and who by Thy Almighty hand and outstretched arm, madest the year of the greatest expectation, even '88, marvellous by the overthrow of Thine and mine enemies, now, for Thy Gospel's sake, which hath long had sanctuary in this land, make likewise '96 as prosperous unto me and my loyal subjects.' And again: 'Lord, I have now put foot within the doors of that age in the which the almond tree flourisheth, wherein men begin to carry a calendar in their bones, the senses begin to fail, the strength to diminish, yea all the powers of the body daily to decay. Now therefore grant me grace that though mine outward man thus perish, yet my inner man may be renewed daily. So direct me with Thy Holy Spirit that I may daily wax elder in godliness, wisdom being my grey hairs and undefiled life mine old age.'

The sermon being ended, the Queen, as is her manner, opened the window of her closet, but she was so far from giving him thanks or good countenance that she said plainly he should have kept his arithmetic for himself; 'but I see,' said she, 'the greatest clerks are not the wisest men.' With that the Queen went away discontented, and since by the Lord Keeper's command he has kept to his house.

Sudden Levies called for.

Because of the news from Calais, the commissioners of musters are ordered with all speed to levy out of the trained bands 6,000 men furnished with their armour to be sent to Dover with their captains, and to be at the port of Dover by Sunday night at the farthest. This afternoon the Lord Mayor and Aldermen being in Paul's Churchyard hearing the sermon at the Cross were suddenly called from thence and forthwith by a precept from her Majesty and Council are ordered to press 1,000. By eight of the clock the men are ready and their furnishing will be complete ere morning.

10th April. The Levies dismissed.

Further news having been received that the forces cannot reach Calais in time, those already impressed are now to be dismissed.

THE QUEEN AND THE BISHOP OF ST. DAVID'S.

The Queen being displeased at the restraint of the Bishop of St. David's hath now caused him to be released. Moreover she rebuked one of her ladies that spake scornfully of him and his sermon. And to show that the Bishop is deceived in supposing her to be so decayed in her limbs and senses as he, perhaps, and others are wont to be, she said she thanked God that neither her stomach nor strength, nor her voice for singing, nor fingering for instruments, nor lastly her sight was any whit decayed. And to prove the last before the courtiers, she produced a little jewel that hath an inscription of very small letters. She offered it first to my Lord of Worcester and then to Sir James Crofts to read, and both protested *bona fide* they could not. Yet the Queen herself did find out the posy and made herself merry with the standers-by upon it.

11*th April* (*Easter Sunday*). THE LEVIES AGAIN REQUIRED.

Fresh advertisement now being received from the French King that the citadel of Calais will hold out longer than was before reported, the soldiers are required with all speed to be sent to Dover by to-morrow night. Wherefore this morning, being Easter Sunday, about ten of the clock, comes there a new charge from the Council that the soldiers shall again be levied, so that, all men being in their parish churches ready to have received the Communion, the aldermen, their deputies and the constables are fain to close up the church doors till they have pressed so many men to be soldiers. By noon they have in the City 1,000 men and these, being furnished forthwith of armour, weapons, and all things necessary, are for the most part sent towards Dover to-night; and the rest follow in the morning.

THE SERVICE OF POSTS.

All mayors, sheriffs and other officers are commanded at their uttermost peril by the Council to assist in the service of posts, providing ten or twenty able and sufficient horses with furniture convenient to be ready at the town or stage where the post abideth. The owners to have such rates as the post from time to time payeth for his own horses.

13th April. THE EARL OF ESSEX'S COMMISSION FOR CALAIS.

The commission for my Lord of Essex is now drawn, making him Lieutenant-General of an army of 6,000 men for the relief of the citadel of Calais. But withal he is instructed not to carry over the forces unless the King signify his compliance with the condition of delivering the town to her Majesty until she is assured of her great expenses, and he better able to defend it without driving her still to these unsupportable burdens; not to take over more than the 6,000, and not to embark them unless he is likely to arrive in time to save the town; not to employ them unless the French King has such strength of horse and foot that the burden may not fall upon the Queen's subjects, but they be used as auxiliaries; not to attempt anything of importance without consulting the principal officers, and especially Sir George Carew and Sir Thomas Wilkes; to take with him only such nobles as have leave to go, namely, my Lords Sussex, Rich, Herbert and Burgh, but not Derby, Southampton, Mountjoy, Compton, Windsor, nor Sheffield, who shall return.

14th April. THE QUEEN'S LETTER TO THE EARL OF ESSEX.

This day the Queen went on board the ship *Due Repulse* and there with her own hand she wrote these words to the Earl of Essex. 'As distant as I am from your abode, yet my ears serve me too well to hear that terrible battery that methinks sounds for relief at my hands; wherefore, rather than for lack of timely aid it should be wholly lost, go you, in God's Blessed Name, as far as that place where you may soonest relieve it, with as much caution as so great a trust requires. But I charge you, without the mere loss of it, do in no wise peril so fair an army for another Prince's town. God cover you under His safest wings, and let all peril go without your compass."

CALAIS.

Yesterday hard shooting was heard about Calais, so the truce is broken. The French think that Monsieur Vidazon will hold out to the uttermost, and the King has sent him word that he shall hang him if he gives it up by composition.

15th April. Mr. Arundel released.

Mr. Thomas Arundel is now released. To-day he was with the Lord Treasurer, from whom he received his discharge and leave to go into the country or anywhere else, the Court excepted. The Lord Treasurer said that it was the Queen's pleasure to forbid his honour, and gave two reasons why he should satisfy himself that he had no wrong; the one, *nemo potest duobus dominis inservire*; the other, that stranger Earls have by courtesy a place above the Earls of this land, which to be granted to one that was but a squire were a great inconvenience.

A Murder at Oxford.

Of late Robert Lingard, servant to Dr. Colepepper, Warden of New College, was murdered by one Winckle (or Wrincle), a townsman. Whereupon the Mayor and Recorder of Oxford, by virtue of their commission of Oyer and Terminer, purposed to have brought the man before them for his trial; but the Council, knowing that partiality is not unknown to be used in such cases concerning a townsman, advise that this Winckle receive his trial before the Justices of Assize for the avoiding of suspicion and other inconveniences.

16th April. Calais taken.

My Lord of Essex and the Lord Admiral were very passionate at the delays in setting forth, but yesterday the whole afternoon was spent in embarking the army troop by troop with all their necessaries. In the evening as my Lord and the other noblemen were at supper on board the *Rainbow* with Captain Monson news was brought that the citadel of Calais was fallen.

17th April. The Troops for Calais Dismissed.

Now that the intended expedition for Calais is countermanded, the soldiers are to be returned under their captains to their own counties, and strict charge taken that the armour, weapons and furniture be well and truly delivered back. Notice also is to be given to the counties that her Majesty levied this force upon very special advertisement from the French King, which afterwards proving very variable and not agreeable to her intent hath been the cause of the alteration of her purpose. Howbeit the readiness of the country to do her service her Majesty very graciously accepteth and commandeth that knowledge be given thereof.

18th April. THE FRENCH TREACHERY.

Shortly before the Spaniards took the citadel of Calais the States sent 400 resolute old soldiers, who in despite of the Cardinal's forces attained the walls and parleyed with the French within to give them entertainment, but though these soldiers had come only to their aid they would not receive them within the walls, so that, not being able to make long resistance without the walls, they were all slain by the Spaniards. For the French were all in one mind, being willinger that the Spaniards shall possess Calais than to permit either the English or other their friends to relieve it, saying, 'If the Spaniards win it, yet there is good hope by mediation of the Church to regain it; but if the English repossess it, they will never restore it.'

20th April. ANOTHER ORDER CONCERNING POST-HORSES.

The Council have again very straitly required that their former order concerning the service of horses for the posts shall be obeyed.

22nd April. A DECLARATION OF THE CAUSES OF THE PRESENT NAVY.

There is published a *Declaration* showing the causes why the Queen's Majesty of England is moved to send a navy to the seas. Herein is shown how the Spanish King hath purpose to invade Ireland, and this last winter having amassed a great number of ships and men many of these same were destroyed. Nevertheless, not being warned by this just punishment by God's ordinance, and forgetting how by the favour of Almighty God his proud navy in the year '88 was overthrown, and his loss at Cadiz, yet still he pursueth his former purpose to animate the rebels in Ireland. Wherefore her Majesty doth appeal to all the world whether she be not necessarily enforced to send out this army to the seas. This declaration is printed also in the Latin, French, Dutch, Italian, Spanish and German tongues.

24th April. INSTRUCTIONS FOR THE FLEET.

It is ordained by the two generals that certain articles for the discipline of the fleet shall be read openly at service twice a week. Prayers are to be had twice a day, except urgent cause enforce the contrary, and no man shall dispute of matters of religion, unless to be resolved of some doubts, when he shall confer with the minister of the army; as it is not fit that unlearned men should openly argue of such high and mystical matters. Swearing, brawling and dicing are forbidden as they breed contentions and discords; picking and stealing shall be severely punished. Great care to be taken to preserve victuals, and every captain shall receive an account once a week how his victuals are spent, and what remains. Special charges shall be given for the avoiding danger by fire, and no candle to be carried without a lantern. The powder to be carefully preserved from spoil and waste, as without it there cannot be any great service; and care also taken not to bear too high a sail when going by the wind, and especially in a high sea, lest the spoil of masts endanger the enterprise. No spoil is to be made of any prizes, and whoever goes on board one to give an account for anything taken. No person shall land in any country without orders until his return to England upon pain of death. No person to strike any superior officer upon pain of death, nor any inferior under other severe punishment, and no report to be made which touches the reputation of any officer without producing the author, who will also be severely punished.

25th April. SIR ANTHONY SHIRLEY'S VOYAGE.

Sir Antony Shirley departed from Southampton two days since with nine ships and a galley, being the *Bevice*, admiral, 300 tons; the *Galleon*, vice-admiral, 240 tons; the *George*, rear-admiral, 160 tons; the *Archangel*, 250 tons; the *Swan*, 200 tons; the *George Noble*, 140 tons; the *Wolf*, 70 tons; the *Mermaid*, 120 tons; the *Little John*, 40 tons; together with the galley and a pinnace; all of which ships are furnished for ten months, and manned with soldiers and sailors, exceedingly well appointed, to the full number of 900 men.

26th April. THE RETURN OF DRAKE'S FLEET.

It is daily expected that the fleet of Sir Francis Drake and Sir John Hawkins will return to Plymouth, which may cause confusion since the place is appointed as the *rendezvous* of the army about to set out. The Council have ordered that a pinnace shall continually lie out to command any ships to forbear to come into Plymouth except in case of necessity, but to come directly to Portsmouth. A messenger of the Chamber is also to be despatched to the Mayors and Customers of all ports from Portsmouth to Penzance, St. Ives and Padstow that they suffer none to come to land until he has been diligently searched for Spanish money, pearls, jewels or any other thing of value, lest her Majesty or any of the adventurers in the voyage be defrauded of the benefit that ought to come to them. The messenger shall leave a copy of his warrant with every Mayor and receive from him a certificate.

27th April. THE DEATH OF DRAKE AND HAWKINS.

Several of Sir Francis Drake's fleet have now come in to Falmouth, but he and Sir John Hawkins, and many men of worth are dead. They have brought back some things but not enough to countervail the charge of the journey. They bring news that a very great fleet is preparing at Ferrol, by the Groyne.

29th April. ONE CONDEMNED FOR SPREADING FALSE RUMOURS.

One Smith, being a base fellow, a peasant and a boy, was this day sentenced in the Star Chamber to lose one of his ears upon the pillory at Westminster, the other at Windsor, to be whipped, and to have a paper on his head containing his slanderous words, to be imprisoned during pleasure, and fined £20. This fellow being recently one of the pressed men at Dover reported when he was dismissed that the news throughout the soldiers was that the Lord Admiral's ship being searched by the Earl of Essex, and he, opening divers barrels wherein he supposed to have been gunpowder, found ashes, dust and sand; and thereupon he called the Lord Admiral traitor. And so they came both to Court, and there the Earl of Essex and the Earl of Cumberland before the Queen took the Lord Admiral by the beard, saying, 'Ah, thou traitor.'

A New Play.

To-day the Admiral's men play for the first time *Julian the Apostate*.

1st May. Recusants in Sussex.

At the outside of Battle Park, Mr. Edmund Pelham, the chiefest justice of peace in that part and chief of Lord Montague's Council, is reported to be a man very backward in religion, and his wife a professed recusant. Many recusants resort to his house.

At the time of the siege of Calais one Mr. Dorel, a notable recusant, lay there hovering about toward the sea coast; and when the men were to be shipped from Rye and Dover to Calais, a servant of his, mounted upon a gelding and well appointed with a case of pistols, rid to Sussex and a great part of the Weald of Kent with an alarm that the Spaniards were landed at three places in Sussex and had burnt Bourne and Pevensey. He could not be stayed but fled, leaving his cloak in the constable's hand. Upon that false alarm there was the greatest hurly burly and woeful outcries of the people; the soldiers at Rye ready to march out of the town, and the Calais service greatly hindered.

At the same time the Lady Montague's people seeing the town of Battle in that uproar and miserable state, rejoiced and showed signs of joy; insomuch that the people fell into great exclamation and cursings of them openly in the streets. When news was brought that Calais was lost, they gave out these speeches: 'God be thanked, we shall have better neighbours.'

Drake's Fleet Return.

The remainder of the fleet that set sail with Sir Francis Drake and Sir John Hawkins are returned to Plymouth, the last to come in being the *Defiance*, the *Garland*, the *Adventure*, and the *Phoenix*.

The Last Voyage of Drake and Hawkins.

The first intent of this voyage was to land at Nombre de Dios and thence to march to Panama to possess the treasure that comes from Pene, and, if they saw reason, to inhabit and keep it; but a few days before they left Plymouth they received letters from her Majesty of an advertisement had out of Spain that the Indian fleet was arrived and that one of them with loss of her mast was put into Porto Rico. She commanded them therefore, seeing the weakness of Porto Rico, to possess themselves of that treasure and the rather for that it was not much out of the way to Nombre de Dios.

On 27th September of last year by break of day the fleet reached the chief town of Grand Canaria and by nine were at anchor before the fort to the eastward of the town. At one o'clock they offered to land 1,400 men in the sandy bay betwixt the fort and the town, but by this time the Spaniards had made a bulwark and planted ordnance so that our men could not land without endangering the whole force, which the General would not do. Then they went to the west end of the island and there watered; and here Captain Grimston going up the hill with six or seven in his company was set upon by the herdsmen, who with their dogs and staves killed him and most of his company. Moreover the *Solomon's* surgeon was taken prisoner, who also disclosed the purpose of the voyage so that the Viceroy sent a carvel into the Indies to all places where our fleet had intended to go. Howbeit they had previously received intelligence from the King of all our voyages the 8th August, which was three weeks before the fleet set forth from England; as also by a Fleming that had seen all their provision in London.

Thence the fleet stood away S.W. and S.S.W. some two hundred leagues until they came in the height of the islands of Cape Verde and so to Dominica and Guadalupe, where Sir John Hawkins who had been separated came up to them again. Here they watered, washed the ships, set up the pinnaces and refreshed the soldiers on shore. On 30th October Captain Wignol in the *Francis*, a bark of 35 tons, was chased by five of the King of Spain's frigates or zabras, ships of 200 tons apiece, which came of purpose with three other zabras for the treasure of St. John de Porto Rico. The *Francis* going room with them, supposing they had been our own fleet, was taken; but they left her driving with four or five sick men in her, taking the rest into their ships, as was afterwards learnt of prisoners.

In November they reached certain broken islands called Las Virgines but could find no fresh water there, though much fish was to be taken with nets and hooks, and fowls on shore. Here Sir John Hawkins grew extreme sick, which began upon news of the taking of the *Francis*. The 12th they set sail in the morning and that night came up to the easternmost end of St. John de Porto Rico, where Sir John Hawkins departed this life; whereupon Sir Thomas Baskerville went into the *Garland*.

Thence in the following afternoon they came to anchor in a sandy bay at the easternmost end of the chief town called Porto Rico, where they received twenty-eight shot from the forts and ordnance, of the which the last struck the admiral's mizzen, and the last but one, passing through her quarter into the steerage, struck the stool from under the General who was at supper; the shot hurt him not but wounded several who were at the same table, of whom Sir Nicholas Clifford and Mr. Browne died. Next day, shifting their anchorage to the west, they rode till night, when twenty-five pinnaces and small boats, manned and furnished with fireworks and small shot, went into the road within the great castles, and in despite of them fired the five zabras, quite burning the rear-admiral to the water, which was the greatest ship of them all, and also mightily spoiling the admiral and vice-admiral. But the treasure which the zabras had come to fetch had been conveyed into the strongest and surest castle of defence, being, as one of the prisoners confessed, 3,000,000 ducats or thirty-five tons of silver. The fight on our side was resolute, hot and dangerous, wherein 40 or 50 men were lost and as many hurt. There was also great death of the Spaniards aboard the frigates with burning, drowning and killing, besides some taken prisoners.

Some days being spent there, the fleet weighed anchor and came to Cape de la Vela, and in the morning of 1st December all the soldiers were embarked for Rio de la Hacha, which town our men took by ten o'clock at night. The 6th December the Spaniards came in to talk about the ransom, but not to the General's liking; and that night Sir Thomas Baskerville marched up into the country to overrun those parts, and the General the same night with some hundred and fifty men went by water six leagues to the eastward and took the Rancheria, a fisher town where they drag for pearl. The people all fled except some sixteen or twenty soldiers which fought a little but were taken prisoners, besides many negroes, with some pearls and other pillage. Next day Mr. York, captain of the *Hope*, died, and then Mr. Thomas Drake, the General's brother, was made captain. On the 10th the Spaniards concluded for the ransom of the town for 24,000 ducats, and one prisoner promised to pay for his ransom 4,000 ducats, and four days afterward they brought in the town's ransom in pearls, but rated so dear that the General misliking it sent it back again, giving them four hours to clear. The 16th December the Governor came into the town about dinner and after conference with the General told him plainly that he cared not for the town, neither would he ransom it; that the pearl was brought in without his consent; and that his detracting of time so long was only to send the other towns word that they were not of force to withstand our men that they might convey all their goods, cattle, and wealth into the woods out of danger. So the General gave him leave to depart according to promise, having two hours to withdraw himself in safety.

On the next day Sir Thomas Baskerville with the *Elizabeth and Constance*, the *Phoenix*, the carvel and four or five pinnaces went some five leagues to the westward, and landing, marched four leagues up into the country to a place called Tapia, which he took, and burned certain villages and farm houses about it. The 18th the General caused the Rancheria and the town of Rio de la Hacha to be burnt clean down to the ground, the churches and the house of a lady, who had written to the General, only excepted. On the day following they weighed and took the town of Santa Martha, the people all being fled except a few Spaniards, negroes and Indians which in a bravado gave them forty shot at their landing and so ran away. This town was burnt two days later, but that night the *Phoenix*, Captain Austin, Mr. Peter Lemond, and the *Garland's* pinnace which stood along the shore were chased by galleys out of Carthagena, and Mr. Lemond and nine men taken; the rest came back safe.

They took Nombre de Dios on the 27th, all the people being fled except some hundred Spaniards which kept the fort and played upon them, but seeing the resolution of our men in running upon them, they all fled and took to the woods. The town was big but nothing left of value, though there was a show in their shops of a great store of merchandise that had been there. There was a mill above the town, and upon the top of another hill in the woods stood a little watch house where was taken twenty sows of silver, two bars of gold, some money in coin and other pillage. The soil in this place is subject to much rain and very unhealthy, having great store of oranges, plaintains, cassavy roots and other such fruits, but very dangerous to be eaten for breeding of diseases.

On the 29th Sir Thomas Baskerville with 750 armed men, besides surgeons and provand-boys, went for Panama, but returned four days later, with his soldiers weary and hungry, having marched more than half way to the South Sea. This march was so sore as never Englishman marched before, the way being cut out of the woods and rocks, both very narrow and full of mire and water; and the Spaniards played upon them divers times from the woods. Having marched ten leagues, upon the top of a hill they came on a fort which the Spaniards had set up and kept with 80 or 90 men who played upon our men as they came up before they were aware of it, and so killed more than twenty, amongst them, Captain Marchant, Quartermaster-General, Ensign Sampson, Maurice Williams, one of her Majesty's guard, besides divers others hurt. When Sir Thomas learnt that he must pass two such forts more, if he got that, and besides that Panama was very strong, the enemy knowing of their coming, also that the soldiers had no victuals left nor any means to get more, these considerations caused him to return and give over his attempt.

In the meanwhile the General had burned Nombre de Dios, half on the 31st December and the rest on 1st January, with all the frigates, barks and galliots which were in the harbour and on the beach. On the 5th they again set sail, and on the 15th, the fleet being anchored at an island called Esendo, Captain Platt died of sickness, and then the General began to keep his cabin and to complain of a scouring or flux. The 23rd they set sail for Puerto Bello.

On 28th January at 4 o'clock of the morning the General, Sir Francis Drake, departed this life, having been extremely sick of the flux which began the night before to stop on him. He used some speeches at or a little before his death, rising and apparelling himself, but being brought to bed again within an hour died. He made his brother, Mr. Thomas Drake, and Captain Jonas Bodenham executors, and Mr. Thomas Drake's son his heir to all his lands, except one manor which he gave to Captain Bodenham.

That same day they anchored at Puerto Bello, where after the solemn burial of Sir Francis Drake in the sea, Sir Thomas Baskerville being aboard the *Defiance*, Mr. Bride made a sermon, having to his audience all the captains in the fleet. Then Sir Thomas commanded all aboard the *Garland* where he held a council, and there, showing his commission, he was accepted as General, and Captain Bodenham made Captain of the *Defiance* and Mr. Saville Captain of the *Adventure*. At that time also died Captain Josias of the *Delight*, Captain Egerton, a gentleman of the *Foresight*, James Wood, chief surgeon out of the *Garland*, and Abraham Kendall out of the *Saker*. Here they watered, washed the ships and made new sails, it being by the General and all the Captains agreed that if they could by any means turn up again for Santa Martha, they should; but if not, to go directly for England. Then the *Elizabeth* of Mr. Watts, the *Delight* and Captain Eden's frigate were discharged and sunk; and being mustered, there were left, sick and whole, 2,000. Thence they set sail on the 8th February.

On the 26th being off Cuba they espied twenty sail about one in the afternoon. This was a third part of the fleet which the King sent for Carthagena, the rest being gone for Honduras; they were in all sixty sails sent only to meet the fleet, being commanded wheresoever they heard our fleet to be that they should come upon them with all their forces. As soon as they descried our fleet they kept close upon a tack, thinking to get the wind; and when the admiral with all the rest of our fleet were right in the wind's eye of them, Sir Thomas Baskerville, putting out the Queen's arms, and all the rest of the fleet their bravery, bare room with them, and commanded the *Defiance* not to shoot but to keep close by to second him. The vice-admiral of the Spaniards being a greater ship than any of ours and the best sailor in all their fleet luffed by and gave the *Concord* the two first great shot, which she repaid again, and thus the fight began. The *Bonaventure* bare full with her, ringing her such a peal of ordnance and small shot that he left her with torn sides. The admiral also made no spare of powder and shot. But the *Defiance* in the midst of the Spanish fleet, thundering of her ordnance and small shot continued the fight to the end, so that the vice-admiral with three or four of her consorts were forced to tack to the eastward, leaving their admiral and the rest of the fleet who came not so hotly into the fight as they did. The fight continued two hours and better. At sunset all their fleet tacked about to eastward, but ours continued the course to lie westward for Cape de los Corrientes. In this conflict in the *Defiance* were slain five men, three Englishmen, a Greek and a negro. That night, some half hour after, their fleet keeping upon their weather quarter, our men saw a mighty smoke rise out of one of their great ships which stayed behind, and presently after she was all on a light fire, and so was consumed and all burnt.

The next day the Spanish fleet kept still upon the weather quarter but dared not come room with ours, although the admiral stayed for them, and not long afterward began to fall away astern. Thereafter they met with none of the enemy and on 9th April came to anchor on the south side of Flores in the Azores, where the *Defiance* was watered. Here they bartered with the Portugals for some fresh victuals and set on shore their two Portugal pilots which Sir Francis Drake had carried out of England with him. And so are they come back to Plymouth.

2nd May. SIR ANTHONY SHIRLEY'S VOYAGE.

The fleet which sailed from Southampton with Sir Anthony Shirley some days since is anchored at Plymouth. Three ships and 500 soldiers now go with the Earl of Essex.

3rd May. A PROCLAMATION AGAINST COUNTERFEIT MESSENGERS.

There have of late been divers dissolute and audacious persons that falsely take upon themselves to be messengers of her Majesty's chamber, and for that purpose undutifully wear boxes or escutcheons of arms as messengers are wont to do. These men go up and down the country with warrants wherein are counterfeited the names of the Lords of the Council or of the Ecclesiastical Commissioners, and by colour thereof they warn gentlemen, ministers of the church, women, yeomen and others to appear before the Council, and exact fees of them for their labour and travel. By this slanderous practice divers gentlemen and other honest persons have, to their further charge and hindrance, been caused to repair from counties far distant from the court. And although divers of these shameless counterfeit persons have been apprehended and brought into the Star Chamber, where some of them have been condemned and set on the pillory, lost their ears, and some also marked in the face, yet these notable abuses continue more and more.

Proclamation is now made that if any person so warned shall have any suspicion of the messenger or of the warrant to be counterfeit, he may cause the constable or the officer of the place to bring the supposed messenger before the next Justice of Peace, where the warrant may be viewed and the party thoroughly examined.

Moreover there are another sort of vagabond persons that bear counterfeit licences to beg and gather alms, pretending that they have been maimed in her Majesty's service or received some great loss or hindrance by casualty. All parsons and vicars, churchwardens, and other officers are ordered to consider well such licences, and those men that are suspected shall be strictly examined, and upon further cause of suspicion committed to prison till more certain information be known. The Justices of the Peace are likewise ordered to use all possible means to apprehend such vagabonds, for that they often assemble in great numbers together and commit robberies, spoils and other outrages.

11th May. SIR THOMAS EGERTON MADE LORD KEEPER.

Five days since Sir Thomas Egerton, Master of the Rolls, was made Lord Keeper and had delivered unto him the Great Seal. To-day accompanied of the nobility and great numbers, he rode to Westminster and there took his place.

16th May. THE DISPUTE BETWEEN YARMOUTH AND LOWESTOFT.

There hath of long time been dispute between the towns of Yarmouth and Lowestoft concerning the trade of buying and selling herrings, the town of Yarmouth claiming by virtue of their charter which giveth to the inhabitants privilege within the space of seven miles during the time of the fair. This dispute ariseth particularly touching the measuring of the seven miles, the one party saying that it should begin at the haven's mouth, the other at the quay where the fair useth to be kept. By the agreement of the parties before the Council there are now to be appointed commissioners to undertake the measuring and at the end of the seven miles to set down apparent marks.

18th May. A MISCHANCE AT LONDON BRIDGE.

Monsieur de la Fontaine that is to be the Duke de Bouillon's agent in London hath suffered a mischance like to have been very dangerous, being carried by the violence of the stream into the water mill at London Bridge through the negligence of a young waterman. To save himself the better he leapt out of the boat before he came to the fall of the water, and was carried through under the wheel and divers lighters as far as Billingsgate before he was recovered; and here he was miraculously preserved. He is very sorely bruised upon the forehead, but without any danger of loss of life, the skull being sound.

19th May. A NEW PLAY.

A new play of the *Tragedy of Phocas* was played at the Rose.

23rd May. SIR ANTHONY SHIRLEY'S VOYAGE.

Sir Anthony Shirley hath again put to sea from Plymouth with five ships, a galley and a pinnace.

31st May. CERTAIN MAYORS COMMENDED.

The Council have written letters commending and thanking the Mayors of Chester, Beaumaris and Liverpool, and the Sheriffs of Chester, for their care and diligence shown in her Majesty's service, and especially in their well ordering of the passage of the horse and foot lately sent over to Ireland.

1st June. THE ARMY AT PLYMOUTH.

Matters at Plymouth now grow to a ripeness, and the Generals have begun to embark their regiments, and will be gone when the wind is favourable. There are three hundred green headed youths, covered with feathers, gold and silver lace, and at least 10,000 soldiers, as tall handsome men as can ever be seen; in the navy, at least 150 ships, besides hoys and flyboats, whereof 18 of her Majesty's own, and since her reign never so many before. The States have sent 18 large ships of war and six others for the carrying of munition, but to be subject to our generals; they land 1000 men.

There have been some differences among the principal leaders at Plymouth, for it hath pleased my Lord of Essex to give Sir Francis Vere much countenance and to have him always near at hand, which draweth upon him no small envy; insomuch as open jars have fallen out betwixt Sir Francis and Sir Walter Ralegh and Sir Conyers Clifford. These my Lord hath qualified for this time, ordering that at all meetings at land Sir Francis shall have the precedence of Sir Walter, and he to have precedence at sea. Wherefore by Sir Francis' proposition are set down in writing the several duties that properly belong to every office in the field.

3rd June. THE FLEET SAILS.

The great fleet sailed from Plymouth on the 1st. All the soldiers and mariners being embarked, and the wind coming round to the N.W. and by N., the Lord Admiral being aboard the *Ark* commanded his master-gunner to shoot off a piece to give warning to all the fleet, which they did incontinently.

While they lay at Plymouth the Lords Generals governed their charge with very good justice and martial discipline. Two soldiers were hanged upon the Hoe with papers upon them showing their offences: upon the one was written, 'For drawing his sword and raising mutiny against his commander'; upon the other, 'For running away from his colours.' A lieutenant that had taken £60 to discharge men pressed in Wales was disarmed by proclamation, adjudged to repay the money, and banished the army. A soldier also in a Dutch regiment that had killed one of his companions was, by order of martial law, tied to the party murdered and so thrown both into the sea.

THE STATE OF THE MIDDLE MARCHES.

The state of the Middle Marches towards Scotland of late years is so negligently ordered that the Council have commanded the Lord Evre, the Lord Warden in those parts, to take a view of all the serviceable horses, armour and furniture of those chargeable before the end of the present month or some short time after. They shall supply all defects and wants, and a certificate of the musters shall be sent up ; which done the Lord Warden shall enjoin everyone to keep their tenants so furnished upon pain of forfeiture.

5th June. THE FLEET.

After setting sail on the 1st, the fleet reached Dodman's Point in Cornwall, but the wind scanting they were fain return again, the greater ships into the Sound of Plymouth, and the lesser into Cawsand Bay, lest any of the mariners should return again into Plymouth ; but on the 3rd they set sail again and are gone with a favourable wind.

6th June. SUPERFLUOUS ALEHOUSES.

Many of the alehouses in London and the county of Middlesex that were suppressed some months since are again restored so that the rogues and vagabonds, which the Provost Marshals do by day drive from about the City, keep the fields and commit pilferies in the country in the night season, and then stealthily return to the alehouses. The Council again require the alehouses to be suppressed, and no strong drink to be used or made in them.

DEFENCE OF THE REALM.

Seeing that the army and ships under the Earl of Essex and the Lord Admiral are to pass out of the Narrow Seas from the coasts of England to the Spanish Seas, it may be doubted that the enemy may make some particular attempts upon the coasts. The Lords Lieutenant of the counties by the sea are commanded to warn the inhabitants to put themselves in readiness, with continuance of watchings of beacons. Certain bands both of horsemen and footmen under meet conductors are to be ready upon convenient warning to repair to places subject to the danger of sudden landings. Furthermore, because there are reports that in divers places near the sea coast some have shown a disposition to withdraw inland, they shall be straitly warned in no wise to depart or to diminish their families that may serve for defence. If any shall attempt to do so they shall be warned on their allegiance to return, otherwise they shall be not only severely punished but have their houses and lands seized. All captains and constables in forts shall be resident with their retinues upon pain of forfeiture of their places.

In Kent where there are many foreigners, especially in Canterbury, Sandwich and Maidstone, the Lord Cobham is to take order that the exact number may be known, and that as they are partakers of the benefits of the realm in like sort as her Majesty's natural subjects, so they shall be contributory to the charges of the places where they remain. Furthermore, that the enemy may find less booty if any attempt be made perchance for spoil, the inhabitants by the coasts shall be warned that upon any probable alarum the herdsmen and shepherds shall withdraw their cattle to the more inward parts.

7th June. A Scottish Lord's Inventions.

One Lord Neper (or Napier), a Scottish lord, hath made some secret and profitable inventions for the defence of this island, being a burning mirror that receiveth the dispersed beams of the sun and doth reflect them, united and concurring, in one mathematical point where it must necessarily engender fire; a piece of artillery which being shot passeth not lineally through an army but rangeth abroad superficially within an appointed place. There is also a round chariot of metal made of proof of double musket, which motion shall be by those that be within more easy, light and speedy than so many armed men would otherwise be, and of use in moving to break the array of the enemy's battle and to making passage. By staying and abiding within the enemy's battle, it serveth to destroy the environed enemy by continual shot of harquebus through small holes, the enemy being thereby abased and altogether uncertain what defence or pursuit to use against a moving mouth of metal. Besides these inventions, divers of sailing under water and the like.

11th June. Sir John Smythe's Misdemeanour.

Very traitorous words are reported of Sir John Smythe that he uttered at a mustering of the train bands in the Windmill Field at Colchester. He rode on horseback with Mr. Seymour, the second son to my Lord of Hertford, and two other gentlemen into the field where Sir Thomas Lucas was training his band; and, coming in front of the pikemen as they stood in square with two wings of bowmen standing in flank, he said, 'My masters, if you will go with me, you shall not go out of the land, but I will spend my life with you.' The pikemen asked if they should go with him then, to which Sir John replied, 'You shall go with a better man than myself or Sir Thomas Lucas; here is a nobleman of the blood royal, brother to the Earl of Beauchamp, to whom I am assistant.' He said also that there was a press out for 1,000 men, but those who followed him should go no further than he went, that there were traitors about the Court, and that the Lord Treasurer was a traitor of traitors; the common people had been a long time oppressed and should have redress if they would go with him.

The two gentlemen held up their hands and said they would go with him; and some of the soldiers stepping out of their ranks would have followed him, but through the persuasion of those standing by, being gentlemen, constables and men of the wiser sort, who asked them if they would be hanged, they returned to their ranks and made a condition that if their captains would go, they would; whereupon Sir John and his company went away greatly discontented.

13th June. SIR JOHN SMYTHE.

The Council, being informed of the matter concerning Sir John Smythe, upon this offensive and unexpected accident send Sir Henry Gray to command him upon his allegiance to appear before them at Court forthwith; and if he shall make any extraordinary delay or attempt to escape, Sir Henry hath full authority to call unto him any forces which he may think necessary.

15th June. THE DEATH OF DR. FLETCHER.

Dr. Fletcher, the Bishop of London, is dead upon the sudden. He was taking tobacco in his chair (wherewith since his unfortunate marriage he hath sought to smother his cares), when he cried out to his man that stood by him, 'Oh boy, I die.' Hereat one hath written this epitaph upon him:

'Here lies the first prelate made Christendom see
A bishop a husband unto a lady;
The cause of his death was secret and hid,
He cried out, "I die"; and e'en so he did.'

Before he was made Bishop of London (coming hither by way of Bristol and Worcester) he was Dean of Peterborough when Mary, Queen of Scots, was beheaded at Fotheringhay; to whom he made a wordy oration of her past, present and future condition, wherein he took more pains than he received thanks from her who therein was most concerned.

Once when there were two Councillors sworn within compass of one year, and neither of them had a grey hair, he glanced at it in his sermon with a sentence of Seneca against *iuvenile consilium, priuatum commodum, inuestum odium.* The Queen found no fault with this liberal speech, but the friends of the Councillors taxing him for it, he had the pretty shift to tell the friends of either that he meant it by the other.

Sir John Smythe before the Council.

To-day Sir John Smythe made his appearance before the Council, and, being charged to answer what he did and said to the company of pikemen to follow him, he answered very unwillingly and uncertainly. Whereupon the Council charged him with his manner of coming to the field where his pikemen were standing in order and his lewd speeches then uttered. To these charges he answered very uncertainly, confessing part of the words, alleging that he meant no harm towards her Majesty; and in some parts he sought to excuse himself by forgetfulness of what he said, colouring also certain words that he used of the Lord Treasurer with oversight by reason of his drinking in the morning of a great deal of white wine and sack. And yet in the end, finding himself charged with a multitude of witnesses, he began to defend his speeches, pretending that by the laws of the realm no subject ought to be commanded to go out of the realm in her Majesty's service, and concluding that he might lawfully advise the people not to go in service out of the realm at this time, and therefore he had just cause to use those kind of speeches. Moreover, saith he, he had been so informed by two lawyers, named Ridgeley and Wiseman.

The Council now require further examinations and in the meanwhile Sir John is committed to the Tower.

16th June. The Treatment of Spanish Prisoners.

Divers of our Englishmen that have been taken prisoners and

carried into Spain are used there with great rigour and cruelty, some in Seville and other places condemned to death, others put into the galleys or afflicted with great extremities which is far otherwise than any of the Spanish prisoners are used here in England. Her Majesty, lest her favourable usage to her enemies may be taken for a neglect of her own subjects or a kind of awe of the King of Spain, now commandeth that such Spanish prisoners as yet remain in England shall be restrained from their gentle usage. Mr. Nicholas Owsley that hath heretofore brought prisoners from Spain and carried Spanish prisoners back is now appointed to search out all Spaniards that yet remain here and to carry them to Bridewell or some such prison of severe punishment; and all that have in their keeping any Spaniards shall deliver them to Mr. Owsley. Nevertheless any man that holdeth any prisoners for ransom is assured that no prisoner shall be sent out of the realm without the knowledge and satisfaction of the party whose lawful prisoner he is.

20th June. AN ALIEN BANISHED.

There is one Cornelius Waters, a stranger of the County of Brabant, that is now a prisoner in the King's Bench for certain unlawful and seditious books that he brought into the realm. This man, albeit deserving more punishment, having lived so many years in the realm that he could not be ignorant of his offence, is not to be further proceeded with than to be sent away out of the country in the vessel of some Fleming or Low Countryman and straitly charged not to return again.

22nd June. A NEW PLAY.

There is a new play at the Rose called *Troy*.

27th June. THE CASE OF SIR JOHN SMYTHE.

The Council suspecting Sir John Smythe's late misdemeanour to proceed not from mere rashness but some farther ground of practice and conspiracy have directed the High Sheriff of Essex to repair to all houses of Sir John and to make diligent search for all letters, writings, books and any other things appertaining to any disloyal purpose and to have the same sealed and kept in a place of safe custody. The Attorney General and Solicitor General are now to examine Sir John and the charges made against him with a view to his speedy trial.

4th July. SERVICE WITHOUT THE REALM.

Mr. Nicholas Ridgeley of the Inner Temple that was committed to the Fleet for his opinions to Sir John Smythe is now to be released on his humble submission to the Council. He protesteth that he had no evil intent but doth indeed hold that her Majesty both by the common law and statute laws of the realm may lawfully compel her subjects to serve her beyond the seas in any parts wheresoever it shall please her Highness, and that the experience of all time hath been so.

5th July. SIR ROBERT CECIL MADE SECRETARY.

This day is Sir Robert Cecil, second son to the Lord Treasurer, sworn Principal Secretary to her Majesty; which being done in the absence of my Lord of Essex is like to cause him much discontent. Before his going he recommended Mr. Thomas Bodley with extraordinary praise of him as the fittest man, detracting at the same time from Sir Robert Cecil with such odious comparisons that neither is the Queen pleased to admit Mr. Bodley for Secretary (for now she showeth less favour to those whom my Lord most commendeth); nor doth the Lord Treasurer think good to join as colleague and partner to his son (which they had determined to do) one that they now suspect to be drawn to my Lord of Essex's party by reason of the immoderate praises given him by my Lord.

11th July. BLACKAMOORS IN LONDON.

Divers blackamoors have lately been brought into the realm, of which kind of people there are already here too many, considering how God hath blessed this land with as great increase of people of our own nation as any country in the world; whereof many for want of service and means to set them on to work fall to idleness and great extremity. By order of the Council the ten blackamoors that were brought in by Sir Thomas Baskerville in his last voyage shall be transported out of the realm.

15th July. THE EARL OF NORTHUMBERLAND NAMED AS AMBASSADOR.

My Lord of Northumberland being named as ambassador to the French King hath craved her Highness's dispensation from the embassage, alleging two reasons in especial; the imperfection of his hearing and the poorness of his estate. Imperfection of hearing, saith he, must of necessity beget absurdities, as of trouble to the King who shall be forced to speak with often repetitions and to strain his voice above the ordinary. Further, my Lord protesteth that seeing the scoffing and scornful humours of the French to all of other nations in whom they discover the least imperfections they will lay upon him the reputation of a fool and grace him with some such disgrace which would nothing fit with her Majesty's honour or his contentment. As for his state, his debts are so great and for want of payments his credit for money matters so shaken that he knoweth not which way or by what means he may satisfy his desire to do her Majesty service.

17th July. IRISH NEWS.

The rebels led by O'Donnell now overrun the whole of Connaught; in Roscommon more than forty strong castles, besides forts, are lost without striking one blow, whereat Sir Richard Bingham the governor (whom some name *Improvido*) is greatly blamed. Nor is it yet concluded whether there should be a continuance of war or a pacification. A great occasion of the continuance of these troubles is the difference between Sir William Russell and Sir John Norris, Sir John blaming the Lord Deputy for hindering the service, for he provideth insufficiency of victual and carriage.

18th July. NEW PLAYS.

The two new plays this month at the Rose are *The Paradox* and *The Tinker of Totnes*.

ROGUES IN MIDDLESEX.

The Provost Marshals having lately ceased to go abroad, the rogues and vagabonds that for a time were driven out of the City and suburbs are again returned in greater numbers than heretofore. The justices of peace for Middlesex are requested to take present order that the Provost Marshals may be continued; and likewise the petty constables strictly charged in the several parishes to apprehend all masterless men, vagabonds, and suspected persons that beg or wander abroad, and bring them to the justices.

BLACKAMOORS IN ENGLAND.

Mr. Casper van Sanden, a merchant of Lubec, that at his own charges brought back eighty-nine of the Queen's subjects that were detained as prisoners in Spain and Portugal, hath desired licence to take up so many blackamoors and to transport them into Spain and Portugal; which her Majesty thinketh a very good exchange and that those kind of people may well be spared in the realm. The Lord Mayor of London and other mayors and public officers are required to aid Mr. Sanden to take up the blackamoors with the consent of their masters.

19th July. GREAT GOOD NEWS FROM SPAIN.

News is come that on 19th June, 8 of the Queen's ships entered the bay of Cadiz and fought with 22 galleys and 8 armadoes, whereof they took 18 galleys, sunk 4 and burnt the *St. Philip*, a great ship of war, with 4 others; that the next day the army arrived and took 40 sail richly laden; the 21st they took the town of Cadiz, and it is thought that they have taken St. Mary Port as the Flemings that bring the news saw a great fire which burnt all night.

22nd July. PLAYING INHIBITED.

The players are forbidden to use any plays about the City of London for that by drawing of much people together increase of sickness is to be feared.

25th July. THE SECOND VOYAGE TO GUIANA.

Captain Lawrence Keymis is returned from his voyage of discovery to Guiana and reporteth much of the rivers, nations, towns and casiques (or captains) of those parts. Of Berreo, that Spaniard whom Sir Walter Ralegh took in his voyage, he reporteth that after Sir Walter's departure he returned to Trinidad with but fifteen men, but being attacked by the natives and two or three of his men killed, fled away towards the River Caroli, where the Spaniards have made a fort to defend the passage of the river. Captain Keymis was told that the old King Topiawari is dead, and the boy Hugh Goldwin, that was left behind, eaten by a tiger. They returned therefore from Topiarimacko, that was Topiawari's port, by another branch of the main river to the port of Carapana. He himself came not, but sent one of his aged followers to say that he was sick, old and weak. This old man declared that Carapana had repented him of his ambition ever to have sought by the Spaniard's means to have enlarged his countries and people, for now that the plenty of gold in that country is known, there can be no greater misery than if the Spaniards prevail; who perforce do take all things from them, using them as their slaves, and (that which is worst of all) they must be content to leave their women if a Spaniard chance but set his eye on any of them to fancy her. On the other side they could hope for no better state and usage than her Majesty's gracious government; 'for,' said the old man, 'the other year when we fled into the mountains, and measured your doings by the Spaniards in like case, we made no other account but that your commander being able, as he was, would doubtless have persecuted us to the uttermost. We found it far otherwise, and that none of your well governed company durst offer any of us wrong and violence; no, not by stealth, when unknown they might have done it.' Wherefore Carapana doth crave of her Majesty for himself and his people that they may enjoy her protection.

Hereby Captain Keymis would give this caveat to our English (who to steal the first blessing of an untraded place will perhaps secretly hasten thither) that they may be assured that these people, as they no way sought to harm but rather used our men with all kindness, so are they impatient of such a wrong as to have any of their people perforce taken from them, and will doubtless seek revenge. He concludeth that it will be blindness and deafness in those that spend their days in serving the commonwealth to seek either to forslow so fit an occasion or to forsake so general a blessing. This country of Guiana doth not only propose some hope of gold mines, and certain pieces of made gold, but also in the trade of these rivers brasil-wood, honey, cotton, balsamum, and drugs to help to defray the charges. 'The case then so standing,' saith he, 'is it not mere wretchedness in us to spend our time, break our sleep, and waste our brains, in contriving a cavilling false title to defraud a neighbour of half an acre of ground; whereas here whole shires of fruitful rich grounds, lying now waste for want of people, do prostitute themselves unto us like a fair and beautiful woman, in the pride and flower of desired years.'

26th July. THE DUNKIRK PIRATES.

Of late divers Newcastle men have been taken on the coasts of Norfolk and Suffolk by the Dunkirkers for that those hoys of Newcastle go so slenderly armed that they give occasion to the enemy to set upon them. The Mayor and others of Newcastle are now to require these ships to be furnished with iron ordnance, powder and some calivers or muskets, and to see them properly manned. Moreover, they shall go together in consort.

A PRESUMPTUOUS BALLAD.

There is a certain ballad published, written by Deloney, containing a complaint of the great want and scarcity of corn within the realm; and because it containeth vain and presumptuous matter that thereby the poor may aggravate their grief and take occasion of some discontent, the Lord Mayor hath called before him the printer and the party by whom it was put to print, who pretended a licence; but finding it untrue the Lord Mayor hath committed him. In the matter complained of, the Queen is brought in to speak with her people in very fond and undecent sort, and prescribeth orders for the remedying of the dearth of corn, extracted (as it seemeth) out of the book published last year.

27th July. THE POSSESSION OF THOMAS DARLING.

At the late assizes held at Derby by Sir Edmund Anderson, the Lord Chief Justice, there is condemned a certain witch called Alse Gooderidge that very grievously bewitched a boy, one Thomas Darling.

This Darling at the end of February last went hunting the hare with his uncle, one Robert Toone, dwelling in Burton upon Trent; but his uncle being earnest in following his game was parted from the boy, who returned home alone, and afterward waxing heavy, and growing very sick, was got to bed. The next morning he had some fits with extreme vomitings, and would many times point with his hands, saying, 'Look where green angels stand in the window,' and complaining of a green cat that would trouble him. Moreover the use of his legs was taken from him. Many and strange fits he had, which being ended, he would fall upon his knees suddenly to prayer and that so pithily that the standers-by wondered thereat; and between the fits he requested them to read the scriptures. Wherefore they sent for one Jesse Bee, who read the 9th chapter according to St. John till he came to the 4th verse, at which time the boy was overthrown into a fit like the former, which fits lasted commonly about a quarter of an hour. Jesse continued reading the 11th, 12th and 13th of St. John's Gospel, and the 1st and 2nd of Revelations; during which time the fits continued one in the neck of another; and ending with a vomit he used to say, 'The Lord's name be praised.' When Jesse either ceased to speak of any comfortable matter, or to read the scriptures, the boy was quiet; but when he was so religiously occupied the fits came thick upon him, which Jesse Bee observing told the boy's aunt that he suspected the boy was bewitched.

The next morning the boy said unto the maid that made him ready, 'I heard my aunt tell Jesse Bee that I was bewitched: the same Saturday that my sickness took me, I lost my uncle in the wood, and in a coppice I met a little old woman; she had a grey gown with a black fringe about the cape, a broad thrummed hat, and three warts on her face. I have seen her begging at our door; as for her name I know it not, but by sight I can know her again. As I passed by her in the coppice, I chanced against my will to let fall a scape; which she taking in anger said, "Gyp with a mischief, and fart with a bell: I will go to heaven and thou shalt go to hell"; and forthwith she stooped to the ground.' Hereupon a more vehement suspicion arising, some judged it to be the witch of Stapenhill; others, because she was old and went little abroad, rather thought it to be Alse Gooderidge, her daughter, who was had in great suspicion of many as a doer of devilish practices.

The fits continuing thus by the space of five weeks, at length the boy's grandmother sent for Alse Gooderidge, and when, with much ado, she was brought into the chamber where the boy was, he fell suddenly into a marvellous sore fit.

Some days later Alse Gooderidge, together with her mother, was again brought into the boy's presence by order of Sir Humphrey Ferrers, and seeing that the boy straightway had fits at their presence, Sir Humphrey ordered them to be searched for those marks which are usually found upon witches. Whereupon behind the right shoulder of the old woman they found a thing like the udder of an ewe that giveth suck with two teats. So they bade her say the Lord's Prayer, which she huddled up after her manner, always leaving out the words 'Lead us not into temptation.' Then they searched Alse Gooderidge and found upon her belly a hole of the bigness of two pence, fresh and bloody, as though some great wart had been cut out of the place, which she declared to have been caused by a knife recently on a time when her foot slipped; but a surgeon judged it to be an old wound, for it was not festered and seemed to be sucken.

Sir Humphrey charged her with witchcraft about one Michael's cow, which brake all things that they tied her in and ran to Alse Gooderidge's house, scraping at the walls and windows to have come in: whereat her old mother Elizabeth Wright took upon her to help, upon condition that she might have a penny to bestow on her god. So she came to the man's house, kneeled down before the cow, crossed her with a stick in the forehead, and prayed to her god, since which time the cow continued well. Wherefore after further examination Alse Gooderidge was committed to Derby gaol, but her mother dismissed.

Next day the boy had very grievous fits, his eyes closed up, his legs lifted up as stiff as stakes, and all his senses taken from him, at which times he uttered very strange sayings. In the mean season others wishing to be eye witnesses of these strange reports, Jesse Bee would read the Bible, and when he came to the 4th verse of 1st chapter of St. John's Gospel, 'In it was life, and the life was the light of the world,' the boy was overthrown into a fit. Many and grievous torments did the boy suffer in the days following, and when the fits ended, Jesse Bee would say, 'Thomas, shall we take the sword with two edges and bid Satan the battle?' To whom the child answered, 'Yes, very willingly'; but as Jesse would read in the 1st chapter of St. John's Gospel, so the fits would come upon him again.

At length a cunning man declared that he would make the witch confess and within a sennight after cure the boy. So he sent for her from the Town Hall to the house of Mr. Robert Toone, where many worshipful persons were ready to see proof of his skill. Being brought, they laboured to make her confess;

to which she answered that it was the first that ever she committed and if they would give her liberty she would confess all the truth freely; whereat her speech was interrupted so that she could not speak, but she prayed them to forgive her. The cunning man seeing this would not prevail fell to trial of his conclusion. He put a pair of new shoes on her feet, setting her close to the fire till the shoes being extreme hot might constrain her through pain to confess. She, being thoroughly heated, desired a release and she would disclose all; which granted she confessed nothing. Being therefore threatened more sharply, she confessed to reveal all privately to Mistress Dethick, but when she began to speak her breath was stopped, so that she could say nothing but 'I pray you forgive me.' The company continued threatening and persuading her but she would say nothing to the purpose, and so she was sent again to the Town Hall, and the company departed; after which the boy had eight fits.

These torments having endured for nearly ten weeks, very grievously, on the 6th May the boy had twelve fits in the forenoon and ten in the afternoon. After one of them taking the chamberpot, he started suddenly saying, 'Look, where a man cometh out of the chamberpot'; in another fit he cried out, 'Flames of fire, flames of fire'; in another he said, 'I see the heavens open.' In most of these fits he bleared out his tongue, having his face wry turned towards his back, groaning and shrieking lamentably.

At length, the fits having in the meanwhile increased, there came one Mr. John Darrell, a preacher, who seeing the boy in divers of his fits, assured his friends that he was possessed with an unclean spirit, and exhorted both the boy and his parents and friends to resist Satan and to prepare themselves against the next day to that holy exercise of prayer and fasting.

The next day therefore the family with some others being assembled, the holy exercise of prayer and fasting was taken in hand, in the midst whereof the boy was taken with his fits but after a while fell into a trance, and there came from him a small voice saying, 'Brother Glassap, we cannot prevail; his faith is so strong, and they fast and pray, and a preacher prayeth as fast as they'; and, 'Brother Radulphus, I will go unto my master

Belzebub and he shall double their tongues'; and later, 'Radulphus, Belzebub can do no good, his head is stroken off with a word; but I will go fetch the flying eagle and his flock.' At this time the boy declared that he saw an angel in the window, like a milk white dove, sent from the Lord to be with him and assist him. Then the voice said, 'We cannot prevail, let us go out of him, and enter into some of these here.' This voice came twice, and it made the standers-by afraid. And after other sayings, 'We cannot prevail, we cannot prevail, their Church increaseth'; at which time there came in two to join in prayer with the company. Then the voice said, 'Here cometh one of my people'; with that they looked back, and were ware of a man of bad life coming into the parlour, and albeit the boy was in one of his trances, yet he made signs to the company to get him away, which one of them perceiving did so.

About two in the afternoon he had a marvellous strange fit, at which time, if he were possessed with two spirits (as it is probable he was), one of them went out of him. All day the fits continued, but decreasing in strength; and at last, being laid upon his bed, he began to heave and lift vehemently at his stomach; and getting up some phlegm and choler, pointing with his finger and following with his eyes, he said, 'Look, look, see you not the mouse that is gone out of my mouth?' Then he fell into a quiet trance; which ended, he was well until 7 o'clock, when he with two or three others went to supper. And as he sat at the table he fell into a trance and was thence carried to bed. As he lay there a voice was heard, saying, 'My son, arise up and walk, the evil spirit is gone from thee; arise and walk.' Upon this his keeper said, 'Let us see if he can go betwixt us'; for indeed he had lost the use of his legs since the beginning of his sickness. But he answered, 'No, I can go of myself, I thank God,' and so standing on his feet straightway he went forward without any difficulty.

The next day Mr. Darrell came again to him, and counselled him to be now most heedful, lest the unclean spirit returning, and his heart empty of faith, bring seven worse than himself with him. He did indeed again fall into his trances, but the Lord being with him, he was soon well both in mind and body, and so hath remained ever since.

28th July. THE SPANISH PRISONERS.

The Spanish prisoners that are in the City having had notice of the late order keep themselves close in secret places so that they may not be taken going abroad. The Lord Mayor is now to make diligent inquiry where any Spaniards or professed subjects of the King of Spain are harboured and to cause them to be apprehended and carried to Bridewell to receive at least some part of that usage whereof our countrymen do taste in more extremity in the King's dominions.

30th July. THE QUEEN'S PICTURE.

All public officers shall yield their assistance to the Queen's Sergeant Painter touching the abuse committed by divers unskilled artisans in unseemly and improper painting, graving and printing of her Majesty's person and visage, to her great offence and disgrace of that beautiful and magnanimous Majesty wherewith God hath blessed her. All such to be defaced and none allowed but such as the Sergeant Painter shall first have sight of.

31st July. A PROCLAMATION FOR THE DEARTH OF CORN.

In divers counties rich farmers and ingrossers pretending the unseasonableness of this summer are increasing the price of the old corn, of mere covetousness. The Justices are forthwith to peruse diligently the orders made last year and to consider such points as may tend to the reformation of those that by their disorder and covetousness cause the prices of grain to be increased in this lamentable sort beyond reason. Moreover the Sheriffs, Justices and principal officers shall certify monthly to the Council the names of those Justices of Peace who dutifully towards her Majesty and charitably towards their neighbours perform the charge committed to them that her Majesty may be informed, and contrariwise to mislike those that shall neglect the execution of this commandant.

It is also forbidden at this time of scarcity that starch be made of corn of the realm.

1st August. NEWS FROM THE FLEET.

To-day, being Sunday, Sir Anthony Ashley came to Court from the Fleet and made relation of all the action first at the Council table, and after dinner to the Queen.

2nd August. PREPARATIONS FOR THE RETURN OF THE FLEET.

Sir Ferdinando Gorges, Mr. William Killigrew, and Mr. Richard Carmarden, the surveyor of the custom-house in London, are appointed commissioners to Plymouth to view the prizes as the ships return from Spain. As formerly merchants of London or residents in the ports have bought from the soldiers and mariners goods of great value but small bulk and carried them away secretly, inquisition is to be made, and merchants suspected of any such intentions to be ordered to depart on pain of imprisonment.

4th August. 'THE METAMORPHOSIS OF AJAX.'

Mr. John Harington, that hath lain almost buried in the country these three or four years, thinking to give some occasion to be talked of hath written and caused to be printed a very foul book entitled *A New Discourse of a Stale Subject called the Metamorphosis of Ajax*, treating of a new way to make a jakes that shall be rid of stink; but intermixed with many other unsavoury matters. The device is this: You shall make a false bottom to that privy that you are annoyed with, either of lead or stone, the which bottom shall have a sluice of brass to let out all the filth, which if it be close plastered all about it and rinsed with water as oft as occasion serves, but especially at noon and at night, will keep your privy as sweet as your parlour.

MR. HARINGTON'S MERRY JEST OF MR. JAQUES WINGFIELD.

Mr. Jaques Wingfield coming one day either of business or kindness to visit a great Lady in the Court, the Lady bade her gentlewoman ask which of the Wingfields it was. He told her 'Jaques Wingfield.' The modest gentlewoman, that was not so well seen in the French to know that 'Jaques' was but 'James' in English, was so bashful that to mend the matter, as she thought, she brought her lady word, not without blushing, that it was 'Mr. Privy Wingfield.'

5th August. CHURCHYARD'S POEM ON SIR F. KNOLLYS.

Mr. Churchyard hath written *A sad and solemn funeral* of Sir Francis Knollys that died a few days since. Quoth he:

> The lords and knights that at thy table fed,
> And all good guests that thither did repair,

Shall honour thee and thine, though thou be dead;
Make of thy praise an echo in the air.
Yea, drum and fife, and all the martial crew
In warlike guise shall wait upon thy hearse;
Fine writers too, and laureate poets new,
On thy farewell shall pen out many a verse;
And garlands gay shall vestal virgins fling
On thy cold grave, whiles clampering bells do ring.

8th August. A DAY OF TRIUMPH.

To-day, being Sunday, great triumph is made at London for the good success of the two Generals and their company in Spain, the winning, sacking, and burning of the famous town of Cadiz, and the overthrow and burning of the Spanish Navy.

THE TAKING OF CADIZ.

On the 20th June, being Sunday, early in the morning the fleet came to anchor within half a league of St. Sebastian, a friary at the west end of Cadiz; and here the Generals attempted to land straightway. They filled many boats and barges with soldiers, but the weather was very foul and the water went so high that two boats with some eighty soldiers armed sank, whereof some were drowned, the others saved by the other boats and set on board their own ships. This mischance did not happen as any token that God was angry with the enterprise, but that they had mischosen the day for attempting so great a work upon the Day of Rest. It was also a mercy of Almighty God, for they could not have landed there without great difficulty and much loss.

The next day, early in the morning, the Spanish fleet, which had ridden before the town under the forts and bulwarks, shot with the tide within the point of the mainland, and immediately after the English fleet weighed and came to anchor near the place where the Spanish fleet rode before; and there the fort St. Philip and the rest played upon our ships with their great ordnance, and the galleys were very busy. But, by the Generals' commandment Sir John Wingfield in the *Vauntguard*, having some lesser ships, took them to task, and so lamed them that they were glad to seek to save themselves. These crept by the shore, first to the Puntal, and from thence into the Bay, and so to a bridge called Puente de Suazo, where striking their masts and by help of certain engines upon the bridge, they went round about the Isle of Leon and came to Rota.

But the eye and care of the two Generals was chiefly fixed upon the galleons and other great ships. Whereupon they resolved to send the Lord Thomas Howard to encounter with them in the *Nonpareil*, adjoining with him some few ships of the Queen's, for the place was so narrow that hardly ten ships could come to fight. With the Lord Thomas went Sir Walter Ralegh, Sir Francis Vere, Captain Robert Cross (with whom was the Earl of Sussex) and others. And although it had been agreed in council that the Generals should not hazard their ships of greatest burden in those shoals, yet the Earl of Essex could not endure to be only a looker-on in so honourable an action, but he put in amongst the thickest of them and fought very gallantly; which the Lord Admiral seeing, and not being able to bring in his own ship, took his long boat and went aboard the *Miranore*. With him into the fight went his young son Lord William, being at these young years very desirous to seek and share honour with the oldest captains.

This fight lasted till noon, by which time the galleons were cruelly rent and torn, and so much slaughter in them that the blood gushed out at the scuppet holes. Whereupon some of the Spaniards resolved to fly to Porto Real, some to burn their ships, some to run them aground; and divers of them leapt into the water, whereof some swam ashore, some were drowned, some taken, some slain. The Lord Admiral, beholding this miserable spectacle, had compassion of them, and took his boat and rowed up and down amongst them, forbidding these cruelties and preventing the firing of the Spanish ships so much as was possible; but they first fired and burnt the *St. Philip*, a ship of 1,500 tons, the *St. Thomas*, and the *S. Juan*. The other two apostles, *St. Matthew* and *St. Andrew*, ships of 1,200 tons apiece, were saved and are now brought back to England.

The battle by sea being thus happily fought and victory obtained, the Lords Generals straightway set in hand the landing of the soldiers, and in very little space there was such diligence shown that the Earl of Essex was on land near Puntal, about a league from Cadiz, with 8,000 shot and pikes; with him was the Earl of Sussex, the Earl Lodowick of Nassau, the Lord Burke of Ireland, and divers other gentlemen adventurers. So soon as he was landed, the Earl of Essex despatched the Sergeant Major, Sir Christopher Blount, and Sir Thomas Gerrard with their regiments to the Puente de Suazo, with charge to impeach the passage so that no succours might come to the Spaniards into the Isle of Leon; to break down that engine by help whereof the galleys might pass; and to surprise or force the castle at the head of the bridge, called by the Dutch 'Herod's house.'

Meanwhile the Earl of Essex, having for his guide Captain William Morgan, marched apace with his army toward the town, although in no hope to lodge therein that night. Upon the way he was encountered with 400 or 500 cavalleros of Xeres and 600 or 700 footmen, but without any great difficulty they were beaten back and ran into the town, offering to shut the gates. But my Lord made such haste that he entered with his troops pell-mell with them; and some made such shift to get into the town that they climbed over the walls.

By this time the Lord Admiral had landed his battle of some 1,200 or 1,500 men and followed the Earl with a very round march, being accompanied with all the chief commanders of sea and captains of ships with their retinue, among them the Lord Thomas Howard and Sir Walter Ralegh, who was not able to march so fast as the rest by reason that he was hurt in the leg with a splinter in the fight with the galleons. When the Lord Admiral came into the town, he found the Earl of Essex skirmishing and fighting with the Spaniards, who fought and fled still before him. Others threw down stones from the battlements of houses which annoyed much our soldiers. But after the forces of both the Generals were joined together, the fight and resistance of the Spaniards continued not long, for they fled into the Castle and into the Town-house in the market place, and other strong places. And here Sir John Wingfield riding upon a nag unarmed, having been hurt before in the thigh, was shot in the head from a loop in the Castle, whereof he instantly died. Before night the Town-house was taken, and therein the Generals lodged, being now masters of the whole town, except for the Castle and the fort St. Philip, both which were rendered in the morning.

The Corrigidor and the rest of the town yielded on condition that they should have their lives saved and only their wearing clothes permitted them ; all the rest of their goods and wealth should be spoil and pillage to the soldiers, and besides for their ransom they should pay to the Generals 120,000 ducats, and for payment thereof forty of the chief men are to be held in England as pledges till the money be paid.

And now proclamation was made that no Englishman should offer violence to any religious person, to any woman or child, or any other of the Spanish nation ; and the Generals sent away boats, barges and pinnaces first with the ladies and religious, and then the men and all other of the inhabitants of Cadiz (except the pledges and certain prisoners of the captains) to Porto Santa Maria. The women were suffered by the Generals to wear so much apparel as they were able to bear upon them and all their jewels, and because none of them should be spoiled by our ruder soldiers and mariners, the Lords Generals themselves stood at the water gates and saw to their embarking.

In this interim the Lord Admiral appointed the Rear-admiral to take some of the lesser Queen's ships and merchant ships that drew but little water to go after the Spanish ships which were fled to Porto Real, and there either to take them or to sink or fire them if they would not yield. While this was determined, offer was made of two millions to the Earl of Essex for the ransoming of the ships and their merchandise. The Lord Admiral would by no means agree to the ransoming of the ships but only of the merchandise. But the Duke of Medina Sidonia, the Admiral of Spain, decided this controversy ; for he, being at Porto Santa Maria and always ill affected to them of Cadiz, gave order that the next morning before day the whole fleet at Porto Real should be fired. This was put in execution ; nevertheless our men made such haste thither that they recovered much merchandise and divers pieces of ordnance, but none of the ships could be saved.

Thus is the whole fleet of the Spaniards, valued by some of them at ten or twelve million ducats, all either taken, sunk or burned in a short space ; together with much rich merchandise in Cadiz, and that which pincheth the King of Spain most (his ships excepted) are the 1,200 pieces of ordnance taken or sunk in his ships. The Spaniards' losses in all are reckoned to be worth 20,000,000 ducats at the least.

These things being happily achieved, Sir John Wingfield was very honourably buried in Santa Cruz, the chief church of Cadiz, with all the funeral solemnities of war; the drums and trumpets sounding dolefully, the shot bearing the noses of their pieces downward, the pikes trailed. His body was borne by six knights, and the Generals threw their handkerchiefs wet from their eyes into the grave; and at that instant the most part of all the shot, great and small, aboard and ashore, were discharged.

The 27th June being Sunday the Lords Generals, with all the chiefs and gentlemen of the army, heard a sermon at S. Francisco, where after dinner they made a great many knights, even all almost that did deserve it, or affect it, or not neglect it and refuse it, as some did. In this prodigality of honour fifty-seven Englishmen are knighted, and as with the Count Lodowick of Nassau, Don Christopher (son to Don Antonio that was called King of Portugal) and four Dutch gentlemen are knighted; but Sir Samuel Bagnal and Sir Arthur Savage had been knighted before the town was taken for their bravery in the field.

The next day being Monday the 28th the Lord Admiral went aboard to set things in order in the fleet and to make ready for a new enterprise; and by his example also to draw the seamen and mariners to their ships that were loath to come out of the town.

About this time the Lord Admiral received from the Duke of Medina Sidonia, his old acquaintance since '88, two very honourable answers to two letters which he had written about the exchange of prisoners, Spanish for English, in the galleys. The Duke's answer was that he liked well of the motion and would do it so much as lay in him, but the charge was more particularly in the Adelantado of the galleys. To whom he wrote so effectually that within a day the Adelantado sent a principal captain to the Lord Admiral, who made full agreement for the exchange.

Upon the 1st July about forty of our English prisoners were

delivered aboard the *Ark* by the galley called *La Fama*, and promise made for the rest, which was afterwards performed. This galley *La Fama*, whereof Don Julian Hurtado was captain, came from Rota to the English Fleet with a white flag of safe conduct according to the order of war, but an ignorant sea captain made a shot at her as she passed by him and hurt and killed three men in her. Whereat the Lord Admiral was much grieved, and greatly offended with the captain and threatened to have hanged him, but the Captain of the galley and Don Pavo Patin, one of the pledges, made earnest suit to the Lord Admiral, which they obtained.

The Earl of Essex stayed all this while in the town with the rest of the commanders and captains, and companies of the army by land, which he suffered not to be idle. On the 28th June the ordnance was taken from the walls, castles and forts. Upon the 30th he made a road into the Isle and burned, razed, and spoiled all that might serve the enemy to any strength or relief. The next day he set pioneers a work, to raze and deface the forts and castle in the town. The 1st July the tower of the Town-house was battered down, and lastly upon the 4th July, he set the whole town on fire (the churches excepted) and saw all his men embarked, himself coming on board last. The next day the whole fleet set sail.

THE TAKING OF FERROL.

After sailing from Cadiz the fleet sailed along the coasts of Spain until they came before Ferrol where the Generals resolved to land. First Sir Amyas Preston and Sir William Monson and Captain William Morgan were sent in the evening to discover the passage in their pinnaces, and to view the place, to espy the forces, and to seek for fresh water and victuals. They brought answer next morning that the people were fled and had carried away their goods, and that they could not yet find any fresh water or victuals. For all this in the afternoon the Lords Generals landed with all their forces ; but the Lord Admiral being not well, and having little hope of any relief there for their wants, at the earnest desire of the Earl of Essex, returned aboard his ship taking Sir Edward Wingfield with him, who was lame of a hurt which he had received at Cadiz.

The Earl of Essex being landed marched some two leagues with his army that night to Ferrol. He took the town with ease for the inhabitants had abandoned it and carried away most of their goods, but there was in the Nunnery some stuff, and in the palace of Bishop Ossorius a library of books, valued at 1,000 marks. There was also in the town some fruits and wines and a few hens; and in the Fort four pieces of great ordnance whereof one was the fairest and longest culverin which the King of Spain hath. Here the Earl appointed Captain Brett to march into the country with 800 soldiers of the strongest, chosen out of divers bands. He marched some two or three leagues to a town called Lotha, which he took and burnt, without any resistance; but if any of his troops straggled or were left sick upon the way, as many were, he found them at his return pitifully mangled, some with their hands chopped off, some their nostrils slit, and others killed. In this journey he got above a hundred cows and oxen and some swine for victual, and so returned to the Lord General who, after he had sacked and fired the town, the third day returned to the fleet.

All being now come on board again the Generals with their council held a new consultation on what was else to be done and how victuals and fresh water might be supplied. Some had great desire to go for Lagos; but ere anything was done the fleet was past the Cape St. Vincent, where a strong northerly wind took them and forced them to haul off into the sea and towards the Isles of the Azores. Here they called a council again and resolved to go for those islands, assuring themselves to have plenty of fresh water and victuals, and there to lie for the carracks and West Indian fleet and to encounter with the twenty-five Spanish men-of-war which lay at the Islands, as the Generals were advertised. But neither did this purpose hold, for the winds coming contrary, they held a new consultation and that was to bear with the coast of Spain and Portugal, and to search what shipping was in the harbours as they passed. This course was thought best, and kept for the most part until they came before the Groin on the 1st August.

Now lastly the Lords Generals resolved to come for England, and the rather by reason of the general wants of victuals and fresh water, and for that there were many sick men in the

Warspite and divers others of the fleet, and for a great leak that was sprung in the *Vauntguard*, and principally for her Majesty's straight command that they should stay forth but five months in this voyage. Whereupon the Lords Generals shaped their course for England.

8th August. THE SCARCITY OF CORN.

In spite of the orders formerly made the price of grain is still increased, and it is most evident that the ingrossing of corn and forestalling of markets by covetous men in buying great quantities of corn out of the market at farmers' houses hath been the cause of the dearth lately grown. The high sheriffs and justices of peace are required, even for conscience' sake, to have regard hereunto and speedily to deal severely with owners of corn that have any plenty thereof; and not only by assessment to compel them upon pain of imprisonment to bring weekly to the markets some proportions, but to overrule them in their prices so as the same may not be sold at any dearer rates than, at the least, these last two months. And if any shall murmur and repine against these orders in such a time of necessity, he shall be committed to prison until he conform.

Moreover the Council think it not amiss that the Archbishop of Canterbury should take order for the preachers generally in their sermons and exhortations to admonish farmers and owners of corn of this unchristian kind of seeking gain, recommending to the richer sort keeping of hospitality for relief of the poor and avoiding of excess. And therefore that housekeepers of wealth would be contented with a more sober diet and fewer dishes of meat in this time of dearth, and to forbear to have suppers in their houses on Wednesdays, Fridays and fasting days. Gentlemen and others of meaner sort might forbear the keeping of hounds. These and other charitable deeds would be earnestly commended by the preachers and ministers; and special order taken that beneficed clergy should reside upon their benefices to give good example to others in using hospitality.

To the like effect the Lord Mayor of London is advised to use all care to provide corn for the relief of the City, and that the citizens and especially the City Companies should use a more moderate and spare diet, leaving great feastings and superfluous fare. Moreover the order taken for inmates should be more carefully executed whereby many that have their dwellings in the country might be sent to their places of usual abode and the City disburdened of a great number.

LADY UNTON.

It is reported that Lady Unton abideth at Broad Histon, there beautifying her sorrow with all the ornaments of an honourable widow, her voice tuned with a mournful accent and her cupboard, instead of casting bottles, adorned with prayer books and epitaphs.

9th August. THE CADIZ FORCES.

The Council have written to the Generals that it is greatly to her Majesty's misliking that she should now be solicited to be put to further expense to defray the wages of the soldiers and mariners, remembering their earnest protestations that she should not only be eased of that burden but assured of great profit to defray these and all other incident charges and precedent expenses, whereby she was by their persuasions drawn, very hardly, to disburse aforehand the sum of above £50,000, apart from the great burden of charges to which the port towns and City of London were put unto in setting forth the ships.

As for the disposing of the soldiers, those drawn from the Low Countries to the number of 2,200 are to be sent back thither, as was promised through Sir Francis Vere. Of the rest, being about 3,000, 1,500 or 1,000 at the least are speedily to be sent to Ireland with their captains. All these soldiers shall be searched before they depart.

11th August. THE CADIZ VOYAGE.

Commissioners are appointed for the City of London to search the ships which are come up the Thames for all goods, money, jewels or other commodities taken in the spoil of Cadiz to be reserved towards defraying the charge of voyage; notwithstanding there may be allowed to the soldiers and mariners that which is fit for them.

12th August. THE EARL OF ESSEX AT COURT.

The Earl of Essex came to Court to-day about twelve, being a little lame by reason of a fall in his posting journey. My Lord hath now a beard which he began to grow on this voyage. The fleet is at the Downs and the greatest part of the army dispersed, many with leave, the rest without license, moreover there is infection among them.

When Sir Anthony Ashley brought the account of the action to the Court it was the Earl's intention to have it printed, but when his friends made a motion to the printers to have it published, they answered that they had received an inhibition from the Council by the Archbishop of Canterbury not to print any discourse of that kind without their special allowance. Moreover, the next day Mr. Fulke Greville was charged by the Queen to command Mr. Cuffe, my Lord's Secretary, upon pain of death not to set forth any discourse of this service without her privity. Hereupon Mr. Anthony Bacon resolved to send copies of it abroad, and his Lordship's friends would do the like.

The Queen these last few days hath been wholly possessed with discontented humours, which my Lord's backward friends nourish by all means possible. One great man being asked news of the expedition answered that there were many knights made; and that the Queen should not hereafter be troubled with beggars, all were become so rich; but where is the £50,000 she hath bestowed in the setting forth her navy and army to perform that service?

14th August. AN ITALIAN GENTLEMAN PRESENTED AT COURT.

One Signor Francesco Gradenigo, the son of a great man in Venice, was of late presented to her Majesty at Court with letters of commendation from the French King. No sooner had he kissed hands than she said to him in Italian: 'My brother, the King of France, writes to me that I am to show you the most beautiful things in this Kingdom, and the first thing you see is myself, the ugliest.' To which Signor Gradenigo replied that the splendour of her virtues was so great that the whole universe knew how excellent she must be, being their source; and now that he had satisfied his eyes and fed his soul with the sight of her person, he cared to see naught else, being right well aware that the rest could not compare with her. Whereat the Queen smiled and said, 'Once on a time when I was a princess, I was more esteemed by your Lords than now that I am a Queen; but you are afraid of that old fellow'—meaning the Pope.

16th August. THE FALL OF A HOUSE.

Last night between the hours of eight and nine o'clock at night, near to St. Bride's Church in Fleet Street, a house of timber, lately set up very high and not fully finished, suddenly fell down and with it an old house adjoining; by the fall the goodman, his servant, and a child are killed.

18th August. THE QUEEN'S TOUCH.

This year at the touching the Queen touched ten, and then washed her hands, being served by the Lord Treasurer, the Lord Chancellor and my Lord of Essex, all three on their knees; the Treasurer in the middle, opposite the Queen holding a basin, the Chancellor on his right with a ewer of water, and on the left the Earl of Essex with a napkin which the Queen used to wipe her hands.

19th August. THE CADIZ PLUNDER.

It is reported that certain ships followed the fleet not to do service but only to make private gain by buying from captains and soldiers commodities which they had got by spoils. By this means a great quantity of merchandise was taken into these ships and great store bought at an undervalue. Moreover, notwithstanding the order to the contrary, there hath been sale of goods both in Plymouth and other places. Gentlemen of those parts are appointed to take strict examination of such as can give any notice of commodity thus brought to land by these ships, and upon view of the nature and quality of the goods, the parties, if they shall be thought things fit to be sold, may have them again paying half so much again as they first gave. If any persons shall refuse to deliver up such goods, they shall break open their warehouses or chests, and commit the parties to prison.

THE ADVANTAGES OF THE CADIZ EXPEDITION.

By these late voyages much honour and profit has accrued to her Majesty. Being threatened with an invasion, she like a mighty and magnanimous prince, sent her army and navy to offer her enemies battle at their own doors, defeated and destroyed the best fleet the King of Spain had, and carried home in triumph two of his principal galleons, whereof one called the *St. Matthew* is thought to be equal with the *St. Philip* which was burnt. She hath defeated his fleet of galleys with so few of her ships, and when his galleys had such advantage, that their captain confessed on board the *Due Repulse* that forty galleys were not able to encounter one of her ships. She hath forced the Spaniards to deliver her poor subjects who were captives in the galleys, and in mercy has given up thousands of Spaniards who were captives under her. She has taken the fairest and strongest town the King of Spain had in those parts, and carried it as soon as her army was brought to look upon it. Her army was thirteen days on land, and no army of the King's dared look upon it.

She hath got two good ships to strengthen her navy, which were never built for £14,000 or £15,000, and her soldiers and mariners are made rich, and fit to go into any action or service, as well with more ability as greater courage.

As for the enemy, he hath lost thirteen of his best ships of war, two of which may serve to fight against himself. Of his Indian fleet he has lost forty merchantmen, all well appointed ships, as also four others that were in his harbour and bound for the Levant Seas. He has lost a town of greater importance than any especially for traffic with the West Indies; and therein his infinite sea provisions, the which will not be got together again for many years. His merchants have lost in the fleet that was burned twelve millions, and so much in the town that almost all the great traders in the Indies will be bankrupt. Above all, he has lost most in now being half disarmed at sea, and in being discovered so weak at home.

20th August. DISORDER ON THE BORDERS.

Proclamation is made straitly charging the Wardens and those that live within the Marches towards Scotland in no wise to make any incursion into Scotland publicly or privately. Great disorders have been committed by Scottishmen on the Borders, sundry murders, taking of prisoners, burning of houses, and taking of goods and cattle. Wherefore for the maintenance of the common peace between the Queen and the King of Scots, commissioners of both sides are appointed, amicably and peaceably to hear the complaints both of our nation and of the Scots, and to give speedy redress and satisfaction according to the laws and customs of the Borders.

22nd August. CAPTIVES IN ALGIERS.

There are yet eight Englishmen captives in Algiers that were left there by Captain Glemham three or four years since, still detained in very miserable sort until their ransoms be paid, for which a great sum is demanded for some piracy committed by Captain Glemham, who is since dead with very poor estate. The Archbishop of Canterbury is now moved to recommend a collection for these men, not only to relieve them out of thraldom, but lest they follow the example of others and turn Turk.

23rd August. MR. PLATT'S SUNDRY REMEDIES AGAINST THE FAMINE.

Mr. Hugh Platt hath written a little book of remedies against famine upon the occasion of this present dearth, compiled partly from his reading and partly from observation. Saith that an excellent bread can be made of the roots of aaron, called cuckoopit, or starch roots, also of pompions. If parsnip roots be sliced into thin slices, dried and beaten into a thin powder, of which one part be kneaded with two parts of fine flour and made into cakes, then you shall find them to taste very daintily. Travellers may make a speedy or present drink for themselves when they are distressed for want of beer or ale at their inn if they take a quart of fair water and put thereto five or six spoonfuls of good *aqua composita*, which is strong of annis seeds, and one ounce of sugar and a branch of rosemary, and brew them a pretty while out of one pot into another ; and then is your drink prepared.

29th August. THE TREATY WITH FRANCE SWORN.

The league offensive and defensive against the Spaniards between her Majesty and the French King was this day solemnly sworn by the Queen in the Chapel at Greenwich, before the Duke of Bouillon, and Viscount Turenne, Marshal of France, the Bishop of Chichester holding to her the book of the Gospel, and a great multitude of noblemen standing round about.

The principal terms of this treaty are that an army shall be raised as soon as may be to invade the Spaniard. Neither the King nor the Queen shall treat of either peace or truce separately without the consent of the other. Because the Spaniard at present infesteth the dominions of France that lie next to the Netherlands the Queen shall send 4,000 foot to serve for six months, and likewise for the same space in the years following if the state of England permit it; touching which the King shall stand to the Queen's affirmation and conscience. If the Queen be invaded and shall demand the King's assistance, he shall within two months raise 4,000 foot, which shall be sent into England at the King's charges. Each shall supply the other with all sort of munition and provision for war so far as may be done without prejudice to their own state. They shall reciprocally defend the merchants that are subjects of either prince in both their Kingdoms.

30th August. TWO NEW PRIVY COUNCILLORS.

This day, Sir Roger North, Lord North, was by the Queen's express commandment sworn of the Privy Council as Treasurer of her Majesty's Household; and at the same time Sir William Knollys as Controller of the Household.

THE QUEEN'S EXPENSES ON BEHALF OF THE FRENCH KING.

For 8 ships employed 3 months in the succour of Brest - - - - - - -	£14,173
Bonds of the Duke of Bouillon to M. Sancy for £6,000 payable in 12 months - - -	6,000
Bonds, Sept. 1589 to Sept. 1590 - - -	50,233
Before he was King of France - -	50,000
In Normandy, 1589 and 1591 - - -	48,502
In Brittany, 1591 and 1594 - - -	195,404
	£364,312

Since the year '89 there have been sent out of England to foreign parts 17,800 pressed men, and to Ireland nearly 3,300.

1st September. SPENSER'S 'FOUR HYMNS.'

Mr. Spenser hath written four hymns, of love and beauty, and of heavenly love and heavenly beauty, which he dedicateth to the Countess of Cumberland and the Countess of Warwick.

Noteth that he composed the two former hymns in the praise of love and beauty in the greener times of his youth, and finding that they too much pleased those of like age and disposition, he was persuaded by one of these Ladies to call in the same; but being unable so to do by reason that many copies were scattered abroad, he resolved at least to amend and by way of retractation to reform them, making instead of those two hymns of earthly or natural love and beauty, two others of heavenly and celestial.

5th September. VOLUNTEERS FOR THE LOW COUNTRIES.

There are needed 400 or 500 men to fill up the companies in the Low Countries under Sir Francis Vere. The Lord Mayor is therefore required to take up and impress such soldiers or other voluntary men as shall be willing to serve, but not to take any man by force.

10th September. SOLDIERS FOR IRELAND.

For Ireland a force of 1,000 men is to be levied out of eighteen counties, and special choice to be made of able men of good behaviour, and not vagrant nor of the baser sort, which commonly run away from their captains as soon as they can find the means. They shall be assembled at Chester by the last of the month.

12th September. COMPLAINTS AGAINST LORD CHIEF JUSTICE ANDERSON.

Many complaints are made of the Lord Chief Justice Anderson this last circuit that he carrieth himself with so much wrath, so many oaths and reproachful words, that there is offence taken at it by persons of principal credit and note.

At Lincoln, Mr. Allen, sometime the preacher at Louth, a man well accepted, by occasion of a variance with a justice of the peace concerning a lease was indicted by this justice for not reading all the prayers at once. Mr. Allen was caused to go to the bar and commanded to hold up his hand there: and my Lord Anderson standing up, bent himself towards him with strange fierceness of countenance. After he had insinuated some grievous faults (but not named) against Mr. Allen, he called him 'one of the great distempers,' putting him out of countenance, and not suffering him to speak for himself. He called him 'knave' oftentimes, and 'rebellious knave' with manifold reproaches besides. The simple people rejoiced in their return homeward saying that a minister's cause could not be so much as heard at the assizes and gathered that all preaching was now cried down.

At Northampton he showed himself greatly grieved at the preacher at the assizes; and at Leicester likewise, where he also fell out with the high sheriff and showed himself displeased with the grand jury. At Nottingham there was offensive variance between him and one of the justices about such matters.

16th September. THE DEPARTURE OF THE EARL OF SHREWSBURY.

The Earl of Shrewsbury and his company, together with Sir Anthony Mildmay that is the new ambassador to the French King, is departed on his way to France to take the oath of the King for the confirmation of this new league, and also to invest him with the Order of the Garter.

22nd September. THE QUEEN DISPLEASED WITH THE LORD TREASURER.

The Queen is highly displeased with the Lord Treasurer, with words of indignity, reproach, and rejecting of him as a miscreant and a coward for that he would not assent to her opinion that the Earl of Essex should not have the profit of the Spanish prisoners. The Treasurer wished that the Earl should first be heard that, upon the conditions with which the Earl received them, so her Majesty should direct the compt. But herewith the Queen increased her ireful speeches that the Treasurer either for fear or favour regarded the Earl more than herself. Coming from the presence the Lord Treasurer received a letter from the Earl of Essex, misliking him for the contrary reason that he would offend my Lord for pleasing of the Queen. The Lord Treasurer is now gone to Theobalds.

MONSIEUR DE REAULX'S UNFORTUNATE BREATH.

Monsieur de Reaulx that was about the Court on the French King's business is returned into France, and, as he gave out, to be married: but he was much troubled with a speech her Majesty did use of him which came to his ears. 'Good God,' said she, 'what shall I do if this man stay here? for I smell him an hour after he is gone from me.' It is indeed confirmed by divers at Court that the gentleman hath a loathsome breath.

Sir Walter Ralegh is not pleased that the Queen doth not esteem his services worth thanks, and protests that he will go to the plough and never hearken after employments any more.

23rd September. AN AID TO THE FRENCH KING.

A force of 2,000, chosen from thirteen counties or towns, is to be sent to France to the port of St. Valery in Picardy for the defence of Boulogne and to be ready by the 8th October. The men chosen shall be able and sufficient who are not to be taken out of the select or trained companies. Of these soldiers half shall be pikes and of the remainder half muskets, and provided with good strong cloth of a russet colour and lined. Sir Thomas Baskerville is to be their commander.

25th September. ROGUES IN SOMERSETSHIRE.

The rapines and thefts by rogues and vagabonds in the county of Somerset are greatly increased, yet through slackness of the magistrates many when brought for trial escape because no evidence is offered against them. In the two assizes this year in all 40 were executed, 35 burnt in the hand, 37 whipped and 112 were acquitted. These persons have their sinews so benumbed and stiff through idleness that they will rather hazard their lives than work, insomuch that they confess felony to the magistrate that they may not be sent to a house of correction where they should be forced to work. Nor will the parties robbed willingly give evidence to the jury, for the simple country man or woman looking no further than to the loss of their own goods are of opinion that they would not procure any man's death for all the goods in the world.

Hence are arisen infinite numbers of wandering idle people. This year there assembled sixty in a company and took a whole cartload of cheese from one driving it to a fair, and dispersed it among themselves. Which things may grow dangerous by the means of such numbers as are abroad, especially at this time of dearth, who animate them to all contempt of noblemen and gentlemen, continually buzzing their ears that the rich have gotten all into their hands and will starve the poor. Of late a thief confessed that he with two others lay in an alehouse three weeks, in which time they eat twenty fat sheep, whereof every night they had one.

The Egyptians that had been cut off by the law again spring up; but they are never so dangerous as these wandering soldiers, for the Egyptians went visibly in one company, and never above thirty or forty of them in one shire. But of these wandering idle people there are 300 or 400 in a shire, and grown so strong that the constables dare not apprehend them. At a late sessions a tall man, a sturdy and an ancient traveller, was committed, and being brought to the sessions had judgment to be whipped; but he in the face and hearing of the whole bench swore a great oath that if he were whipped, it would be the dearest whipping to some that ever was. It strake such a fear into the justice that had committed him as he prayed the man might be deferred until the assizes, when he was delivered without any whipping or other harm, and the justice glad to have so pacified his wrath.

28th September. SIR RICHARD BINGHAM'S FLIGHT.

Sir Richard Bingham, the Governor of Connaught, that was commanded to Athlone to stand his trial because of the many complaints against him, is fled away secretly to England; whereat his enemies in Ireland say that he hath sought to shun this trial, being either overcarried by the greatness of his stomach to answer before the commissioners or stricken with the guiltiness of his conscience that he could not justify. But Sir Richard himself declareth that he is constrained to avoid the hard measure of his adversaries against him who work to the utmost his overthrow by indirect proceedings contrary to the rules of law and justice. He complaineth also that Sir John Norris put his brother Sir Thomas in his charge before the Queen's pleasure that he should be sequestrated was known; and moreover when he was summoned to Athlone, Sir John gave orders that he should not come through to Athlone but be stayed some five miles short, and have none of his friends near him, being used as a man utterly disgraced in the eyes of those base traitors which he had governed twelve years, and be at the mercy of the Irish to be murdered; none of his own horsemen or footmen to be permitted to come to meet him for his safety in passing through the country or himself suffered to lodge in the castle.

29th September. THE SCHEDULE OF DAILY PAY FOR THE SOLDIERS IN FRANCE.

The first and chief colonel for his ordinary wages 10s., and 30s. more for his diet and extraordinary charges. The second colonel at 10s., with an augmentation of 10s.

The paymaster at 10s.

To his clerks, 3s. 4d.

The commissary for musters at 6s. 8d.

	Daily pay.	Weekly imprest for victuals.
In a band of 200 men—		
The captain - - -	8s.	56s.
The lieutenant - - -	4s.	28s.
The ensign - - - -	2s.	14s.
The sergeants - - -	2s.	14s.
Two drums - - -	2s.	14s.
One chirugeon - - -	12d.	7s.
180 men, with 20 dead pays at 8d. each man		3s. 4d.
In a band of 150 men—		
The captain hath - -	6s.	42s.
The lieutenant - - -	3s.	21s.
The ensign - - - -	18d.	10s. 6d.

30th September. 'ULYSSES UPON AJAX.'

There is one calling himself Misodiaboles hath written against *The Metamorphosis of Ajax* (that Mr John Harington wrote) a libel called *Ulysses upon Ajax*, roundly rebuking the author for his immodesty therein. 'It is an affectation of singularity,' saith he, 'a fruit of discontent, a superfluity of wanton wit, a madding with reason, a diligence without judgment, a work fit for Volumnius the jester not Misacmos the courtier. In form contrary to all rules of science; in matter undecent, filthy and immodest: and touching the authorities, they are so weak and so wrested, as no chaste or Christian ear may in reason endure them.' He declareth that Misacmos hath no judgment to find a law of reason against the law of reverence, for many necessities, of nature to be done, are not plainly to be talked of; a circumlocution and a blush is sufficient to interpret a filthy necessity.

3rd October. HIGHWAY ROBBERS.

At the Sessions Richard Weekes, alias Hartrow, gentleman, and Thomas Simpson, a yeoman, were found guilty of assaulting one Kidwell in the highway, when they robbed him of £46 9s. 9d. in money. Simpson is found guilty and to hang; but Weekes stood silent and is committed to the *peine dure*. On the same day at Hampstead in company with one Hurford, known also as Marvyn or Browne, Simpson shot a labourer in the head with a dag. Hurford also is condemned for being present and encouraging Simpson to shoot the man.

4th October. ADVICE FOR MY LORD OF ESSEX.

There is one of his followers that hath written to my Lord of Essex very familiarly warning him of the danger of his present courses and advising him how he should carry himself for the future. The Queen, saith he, will see in my Lord a man of a nature not to be ruled; that hath the advantage of her affection and knoweth it; of an estate not grounded to his greatness; of a popular reputation; of a military dependence; nor can there be presented a more dangerous image than this to any monarch living, much more to a lady, and of her Majesty's apprehension. So long as this impression continueth in her breast, my Lord will find no other condition than inventions to keep his estate bare and low; crossing and disgracing his actions; carping at his nature and fashions; repulses and scorns of his friends and dependants; thrusting him into odious employments and offices to supplant his reputation. As for my Lord's particular disposition, when he happeneth to speak with compliment to her Majesty, he doth it with formality and not as if he feeleth it, whereas he should do it familiarly.

To win her Majesty's favour he ought never to be without some particulars afoot which he should seem to pursue with earnestness and affection, and then let them fall upon taking knowledge of her Majesty's opposition and dislike; such as to favour for void places some whom the Queen is likely to oppose unto; or to pretend a journey to see his living and estate in Wales. Nor should he neglect, as he doth, the lightest particularities in his habits, apparel, wearings, gestures and the like.

But that which breedeth to my Lord greatest prejudice is

that of a military dependence; he should keep his greatness in substance, yet abolish it in shows to the Queen; for she loveth peace; she loveth not charge; and that kind of dependence maketh a suspected greatness. He should not therefore at this time seek the Earl Marshal's place, or the place of Master of the Ordnance, because of their affinity with a martial greatness; but rather that of Lord Privy Seal, for it is the third person of the great officers of the Crown; hath a kind of superintendence over the Secretary; and it is a fine honour, quiet place, and with its fees worth £1,000 by year. And if my Lord shall pretend to be as bookish and contemplative as ever he was, it should serve his purposes also.

Another impression is of a popular reputation. It is a good thing being obtained as my Lord obtaineth it, that is, *bonis artibus*; but would be handled tenderly. Therefore he should take all occasions to the Queen to speak against popularity and popular courses vehemently; to tax it in others; but nevertheless to go on his commonwealth courses. There is also the inequality of his estate of means and his greatness of respects; for till the Queen find him careful of his estate, she will not only think him more like to continue chargeable to her but also to have a conceit that he hath higher imaginations; and nothing can make the Queen or the world think so much that he is come to a provident care of his estate as the altering of some of his officers; who though they may be as true to him as one hand to the other, yet *opinio veritate maior*.

6th October. RYE FROM THE EAST COUNTRIES.

There is a ship of the East Countries come to Harwich having on board 800 quarters of rye for use in the present great scarcity of grain. This ship has been stayed, but the Council order it to be transported to London without any delay lest by keeping the rye on shipboard it become corrupt and unserviceable.

7th October. MY LORD OF LINCOLN'S RETURN.

My Lord of Lincoln is returned from his embassage to the Landgrave of Hessen that he undertook to present her Majesty's gift for the baptizing of the Princess Elizabeth, where he was most princely entertained both at the time of the solemnity and in going and coming. Upon his parting, the Landgrave presented my Lord with princely gifts, as cups of ivory, amber and crystal, and to fit his humour with Turks and jennets. But 'tis said that my Lord hath left behind him dishonours, clamours, and curses for his base miserliness and insupportable fancies or rather furies.

9th October. MR. MORLEY'S INTRODUCTION TO PRACTICAL MUSIC.

Mr. Thomas Morley hath written *A plain and easy introduction to practical music* (which he dedicateth to Mr. William Byrd, another of the gentlemen of her Majesty's Chapel), set down in form of a dialogue; whereof the first part teacheth to sing, with all things necessary for the knowledge of pricksong; the second treateth of descant and to sing two parts in one upon a plainsong or ground, with other things necessary for a descanter; the third of composition of three, four, five or more parts, with many profitable rules to that effect. To the reader Mr. Morley writeth of the great travail and difficulty of this book, and if any in friendship shall make him acquainted with ought they mislike or understand not, he will think himself highly beholding to them. 'But,' saith he, 'if any man, either upon malice or for ostentation of his own knowledge, or for ignorance (as which is more bold than blind Bayerd) do either in huggermugger or openly calumniate that which either he understandeth not, or then maliciously wresteth to his own sense, he (as Augustus said by one who had spoken evil of him) shall find that I have a tongue also: and that *me remorsurum petit*, he snarleth at one who will bite again, because I have said nothing without reason, or at least confirmed by the authorities of the best, both scholars and practitioners.'

10th October. THE FRENCH KING'S ENTRY INTO ROUEN.

From Rouen comes news of the French King's royal entry on the 5th of this month, which was on this manner.

In the suburbs of the town on the further side of the river was erected a most stately room of plaster of Paris where the King stood to behold the companies, and to receive the townsmen's submissions as they passed. First the order of the Friars Capuchins followed their cross, their habit russet, all be-patched, girt with hempen cords, shirted with haircloth, wearing sandals only. This order may have but one habit for a man during his life; they feed standing and sleep sitting, they live by alms and are much esteemed of the people. Secondly came the Grey Friars; which order hath a library in their house containing six and fifty paces in length with three rows of desks all along, replenished with many excellent books both of philosophy and of the Fathers, the most part manuscript. Thirdly followed the Carmelites and Celestins, the Jacobins, the Augustines. Then proceeded the priests and chantries of the town in their surplices, singing, bearing forty-two crosses of silver, and every cross with the great banner of a Saint.

Then followed the mint-masters of Normandy, the merchants, receivers, customers, treasurers, advocates, procurators, and other officers of the palace. Then came Bachelors and Masters of Art, Doctors of Physic, Civil Law and Divinity, clothed in very fair and reverent garments of damask, satin and black velvet, and for the most part riding upon mules.

Then followed the officers and chancellors of the Chamber of Normandy; Judges and officers of estate in scarlet, to the number of forty; and the four Presidents of Normandy in robes of scarlet furred, wearing on their heads great caps of maintenance.

Then proceeded the several bands of the town, containing four regiments of foot and three cornets of horse, suited in green, russet and carnation satin and velvet, garnished with silver lace; their hats, plumes, scarfs and shoes white. After upon great coursers rode forty *enfants d'honneur* or henchmen, the properest and choicest young men of the town. Then came all the gallants and young gentlemen of the French Court, corvetting and fetching up their great horse, accompanied with divers of the nobility, Barons, Viscounts, Earls; the Knights of the Holy Ghost, being known by their blue ribbons and white crosses hanging thereat.

Then marched the King's three guards after their drums and fifes; the Swissers with shot and pikes, the Scots and French with halberds, the King's trumpets in horsemen's coats of green velvet and very well mounted.

At last came the King himself, mounted on a white courser, his own apparel, plumes and horses white, wearing the order of the Holy Ghost at a broad blue ribbon about his neck.

Sundry gates of triumph had been erected, whereof one at the bridge; where as the King passed, from over his head certain clouds opened and a voice was heard as from God, declaring His love for the King. Then there descended upon him the similitude of the Holy Ghost, and an angel presented unto him a sword called 'the Sword of Peace'; and the angel ascending declared that peace was returned again. Having passed over the bridge, he went up the street called *Rue du Pont*, where was set up a very stately pyramid, about a hundred feet high, and painted with the labours of Hercules, and inscribed with French verses, thus to be Englished:

'Hercules and Henry are semblable,
In virtues, words and acts;
But that Hercules is in the fable;
And Henry in the facts.'

Having passed by these and several others the King entered the Cathedral Church of Notre Dame with all the ecclesiastical pomp that might be, whence after certain ceremonies he returned more privately to his Court by coach.

13th October. SIR THOMAS BASKERVILLE'S INSTRUCTIONS.

Sir Thomas Baskerville, being appointed to command the two thousand English soldiers sent to France, hath received instructions to this effect:

Of the 2,000 soldiers, 1,000 shall be under his rule, and 1,000 under Sir Arthur Savage who shall be at his commandment when he shall have cause to require their service. The English soldiers are to join with a like number of French, sufficiently armed, in the towns of Boulogne and Muttrell and no otherwhere, except when the King shall be personally in Picardy. Further it is covenanted that the English soldiers shall enter into wages from the time they arrive at St. Valery until their return, which shall be at farthest at the end of six months; in which time they shall make their musters every month and give their oaths to the King's commissioners faithfully to serve the French King, saving all fidelity and allegiance due to her Majesty.

The soldiers shall for all faults against the order of their own colonels and their discipline be corrected by their own chief

Colonel, and if any other offences shall be committed against the King's orders general then the offenders to be ordered by the King's army, so as the colonels and captains of the Englishmen be called thereto for the assistance of the King's officers in their judgments.

The Captain General shall take care that the soldiers be preserved in good estate and provided of victual, lodging and other furniture whereby they may be continued without danger, and specially to have great care how to avoid the repair of any soldiers to any houses infected with the plague. And if he shall be required to serve in places where he knoweth the plague to reign, he shall in all dutiful manner protest against the same, and shall utterly refuse to put her Majesty's people in such evident danger, affirming that her Majesty hath sent her people to aid the French King against their common enemies but not to endanger their lives wilfully by infection of the plague.

He shall take care not to be drawn to hazard himself farther than the French are ready to accompany him, neither shall he put the people in any manifest hazard nor direct them to assault where the places are not likely to be recovered without danger of life and expense of blood. Moreover he shall use the best means he may that the whole forces of 2,000 may serve together.

Also, considering that they are in a strange country, the captains and officers of bands shall be charged to keep their people severely in good order without suffering them to quarrel with the French, or to spoil any houses or persons of the French, or to take any goods without payment; and especially that none of her Majesty's subjects enter disorderedly into any church or religious house, or use violence to any monuments. In both regiments the usual prayers shall be made, as near as may be, according to the use of this realm of England.

For the martial discipline of the forces there shall be used the same orders as were established for the army in Spain, which shall be published by proclamation immediately upon landing.

14th October. A THIRD VOYAGE TO GUIANA.

Sir Walter Ralegh hath set out his pinnace called the *Wat* under Mr. William Dowle to make further exploration of Guiana; and to-day the company sail from Limehouse.

15th October THE LEAGUE WITH FRANCE.

On the 9th of this month the oath of confederation between the King and the Queen's Majesty was very solemnly taken in the Church of St. Owen in Rouen, in the presence of the French nobility, who that day took the right of the choir.

On the next day the Order of the Garter was most royally performed in the same Church, where both Princes had their estates and arms erected. The Queen's Majesty being Sovereign of the Order had that day the right hand of the choir and so had the Earl of Shrewsbury (the Lord Ambassador) with his arms, style and stall accordingly. Before the Queen's estate sat Mr. William Dethick, Garter, Principal King of Arms, in his robe of the Order. Before the Earl stood Mr. William Segar, Somerset Herald. Next to the Earl, the Lord Ambassador Lieger; then the Lord Cromwell, the Lord Rich, and all other knights and gentlemen according to their quality. On the left side sat the King between the Bishops of Anjou and Evreux, and attended by his nobility.

All things being accomplished with much honour, the King's Majesty invested and sworn, the vespers ended, and the benediction given by a bishop in his *pontificalibus*, the King took the Earl by the hand and they returned as they came, attended upon by the nobility, who two and two preceded before them. That night the King and the Earl supped together under one estate in the house of the Duke of Montpensier, where also was a general feast for all the English.

17th October. THE FORCES FOR FRANCE STAYED.

The forces to be sent for France that await passage are to be stayed, the Queen having thought good to enter into deliberation again touching the sending or staying of them.

18th October. THE FORCES TO BE SENT TO FRANCE.

The Queen being again resolved that the forces for France shall be despatched and sent away with speed, the officers at London, Harwich, Gravesend and Southampton are forthwith to proceed to their embarking with as much expedition as may be.

20th October. THE CONTRIBUTIONS TOWARDS SHIPPING.

Although the Council have written several letters concerning the contributions to the charge of shipping in the voyage to Cadiz in some counties the money is still unpaid. In Somerset it is alleged that there is dearth of corn and victual and loss of cattle. Likewise in Dorset, Poole and Lyme Regis the contribution is unpaid.

23rd October. NASHE'S 'HAVE WITH YOU TO SAFFRON WALDEN.'

Nashe hath now published an answer to that book of Dr. Harvey written three years since and called *Pierce's Supererogation*, to which he giveth this title: *Have with you to Saffron Walden, or Gabriel Harvey's Hunt is up; Containing a full answer to the eldest son of the haltermaker: Or, Nashe his confutation of the sinful Doctor.* He speaketh very invectively of Dr. Harvey and of his family, saying that it is bruited up and down that Harvey pissed ink as soon as he was born, and haply some would conclude that he was begotten of an incubus in the shape of an ink bottle that had carnal intercourse with his mother. Dr. Harvey he declareth to be so enamoured of his own beauty, that he useth every night to walk on the Market Hill in Cambridge, holding his gown up to his middle to show himself, that the wenches may see what a fine leg and a dainty foot he hath in pump and pantofles; and if they give him never so little an amorous regard, he boards them with a set speech of the first gathering together of societies, and the distinction of *amor* and *amicitia* out of Tully's *Offices*. During the late plague the doctor lived upon Wolfe the printer, and thence passed into the country with Wolfe's boy as his servant, still owing £36; till at last Mr. Wolfe, perceiving himself to be palpably flouted, went and fee'd bailiffs who arrested him in the Queen's name, and without more pause hurried him away, making believe that they were taking him into the City. But when they came to Newgate, they thrust him in there, bidding the keeper take charge of him. Here after fuming for some time, at length the keeper's wife (the keeper himself being absent) came up to him. Whereupon he runs and swaps to the door, and draws his dagger upon her, with 'O, I will kill thee too: what could I do to thee now?' and so extremely terrified her that she screeched out to her servants, who burst in in heaps thinking he would have ravished her. From this Castle Dolorous he was at length relieved by the charity of the minister of St. Alban's, then living in Wood Street, who entered bond for him : and many like stories.

To Dr. Harvey's objecting to his beardless state, answereth that the doctor hath a beard like a crow with two or three dirty straws in her mouth, going to build her nest. In the latter part of the book refuteth some of Dr. Harvey's former sayings.

28th October. A GREAT ALARM FROM SPAIN.

Three pinnaces or carvels are to be despatched with all speed from Plymouth to discover the intentions of the Spaniard, for there is some very credible intelligence that there are great and speedy preparations making in Spain.

31st October. GREAT PREPARATIONS FOR DEFENCE.

Because of this news out of Spain many preparations are being made for the defence of the realm. Certain knights and gentlemen residing about London are by the Queen's special command to return for the defence of their counties. Three or four ships with all diligence to be put in readiness and sent towards Tilbury hope to give intelligence. From Hampshire and Wiltshire 900 men are to be sent to the Isle of Wight. At Plymouth and other ports along the south coasts the fireworks to be in readiness. In the counties the men formerly held in readiness are to be mustered in bands, and for every 100 footmen shall be provided 10 pioneers with instruments to entrench and fortify, and carts and small nags to carry their armour and weapons, with good supply of powder, lead and match, weapons for store and victuals. The watching of beacons to be continued or renewed with all diligence. The numbers to be put in readiness are 69,000; from the maritime counties 41,000 men and from the inland 28,000.

CORN SHIPS IN LONDON.

There are come into the Thames twenty sail of ships laden with corn from the East Countries. The Lord Mayor is required to take special order that this corn may be sold in such sort as the poor may be relieved thereby, and not ingrossed by such as use to buy great quantities to sell the same after at excessive prices.

2nd November. THE EARL OF SHREWSBURY RETURNS.

My Lord of Shrewsbury and those that accompanied him to Rouen are returned.

A PROCLAMATION CONCERNING THE DEARTH.

Because of the great dearth of corn this year proclamation is made against those ingrossers, forestallers and ingraters of corn that increase the price of corn by spreading a false report that much quantity of corn is being carried out of the realm by sea and thereby occasion given of want. Likewise it is straitly forbidden to carry any corn by sea out of the realm. Moreover sundry persons of ability that had intended to save their charges by living privately in London or towns corporate, thereby leaving their hospitality and the relief of their poor neighbours, are charged not to break up their households; and all others that have of late time broken up their households to return to their houses again without delay. Likewise those that have charge of any castle or forts upon the sea coasts shall presently repair to their charges and there reside in their own person during all this winter season, and to have care how the forts are furnished, and to make petition for their defects.

4th November. VARIOUS OPINIONS CONCERNING THE SPANISH DANGER.

There are many advertisements from Spain of these great preparations and a purpose to come for England. It is said that every fifth man in Spain is taken for service, and that 40,000 soldiers are appointed, but most of them simple ill-apparelled boys. Mariners of all nations are constrained to serve, but there are great stirs among them for want of pay and victuals, and a great dearth both in Portugal and Spain. Wherefor some hold that an invasion is meant, others only some spoiling on the sea coast in revenge for Cadiz. Many think that they will invade the Isle of Wight, Portsmouth and Southampton or attack London from the Thames; but all that this attack will be in winter when unlooked for and the Queen's navy not ready.

5th November. Lodge's 'Wits' Misery.'

Mr. Thomas Lodge hath written a book called *Wits' Misery, and the World's Madness, discovering the devils incarnate of this age.* As of Vain-glory: he walketh in Paul's like a gallant courtier, where if he meet some rich choughs worth the gulling, at every word he speaketh, he makes a mouse of an elephant; he telleth them of wonders done in Spain by his ancestors, where if the matter were well examined, his father was but a swabber in the ship where Seville oranges were the best merchandise.

Or of Superfluous Invention, who infecteth all kinds so that the ploughman who in times past was content in russet must nowadays have his doublet of the fashion with wide cuts, his garters of fine silk of Granado to meet his Sis on Sunday: the farmer that was contented in times past with his russet frock and mockado sleeves now sells a cow against Easter to buy him silken gear for his credit.

Or of Scandal and Detraction; that is a right malcontent devil. He weareth his hat without a band, his hose ungartered, his rapier *punto reverso*, his looks suspicious and heavy, his left hand continually on his dagger; if he walk in Paul's, he skulks in the back aisles. Well spoken he is, and hath some languages, and hath read over the conjuration of Machiavel; in belief he is an Atheist or a counterfeit Catholic; hath been long a traveller and seen many countries, but bringeth home nothing but corruptions to disturb the peace of his own country.

Another devil is Adulation, who generally goes jetting in noblemen's cast apparel: he hath all the sonnets and wanton rhymes the world of our wanton wit can afford him; he can dance, leap, sing, drink upsee freeze, attend his friend to a bawdy house, court a harlot for him, take him up commodities, feed him in humours. If he meet with a wealthy young heir worth the clawing, 'Oh rare,' cries he, do he never so filthily. He pulls feathers from his cloak if he walk in the street, kisseth his hand with a courtesy at every nod of the younker. If he be with a martial man, or employed in some courtly tilt or tourney, 'Mark my Lord,' quoth he, 'with how good a grace he sat his horse, how bravely he brake his lance.'

The devil Arrogancy is one that never speaks but he first wags his head twice or thrice like a wanton mare over her bit, and after he hath twinkled with his eyes, and chewed the words between his lips, to his servant he saith, 'My deminitive and defective slave, give me the coverture of my corpse to ensconce my person from frigidity'; and all this while he calls but for his cloak.

There is also Lying, that hath long been a traveller. If you talk with him of strange countries, he will hold you in prattle from morningsberry to candlelight. He will tell you of monsters that have faces in their breasts, and men that cover their bodies with their feet instead of a penthouse, and of many more incredible wonders.

And Sedition, the trouble-world: this devil, detected for some notable villainy in his country, or flying under colour of Religion beyond seas, is lately come over with seditious books, false intelligences, and defamatory libels to disgrace his Prince, detract her honourable Council, and seduce the common sort. This fellow in Paul's takes up all the malcontents, telling them wonders of the entertainment of good wits in other countries. In the country he storms and rails against inclosures, telling the husbandmen that the pleasure of their Lords eats the fat from their fingers, and these racked rents (which in good sooth authority might wisely look into) are the utter ruin of the yeomanry of England.

7th November. THE PREPARATIONS FOR DEFENCE.

Musters of the horse and foot are now commanded in all counties, so that there may be a view of the whole forces of the realm; armour and horses shall be taken from recusants and put into the hands of those of better trust. Such as spread false rumours of malicious purpose to stir up the minds of the people, which oftentimes happeneth in these troublous times, are to be committed to the common gaol. In the City 10,000 are to be furnished and had in readiness.

8th November. MR. SPENSER'S 'PROTHALAMION.'

To-day there was celebrated at Essex House the double marriage of the Lady Elizabeth and the Lady Katherine Somerset, the daughters of my Lord of Worcester, to Mr. Henry

Gifford and Mr. William Petre; in honour whereof Mr. Spenser hath written a sponsal verse entitled *Prothalamion.*

9th November. THE DEATH OF GEORGE PEELE.

George Peele that wrote *The Arraignment of Paris* after long illness is dead, 'tis said by the pox; and this day is buried in Clerkenwell.

14th November. A LAMENTATION FOR DRAKE.

There is a long poem called *Sir Francis Drake; His honourable life's commendation and his tragical death's lamentation*, published at Oxford, and written by Mr. Charles Fitzgeffrey. Herein is the fame of Drake extolled and commended to gods and men, his exploits related, and the great loss of his countrymen set forth.

Spain clap thy hands, while we our hands do wring,
And while we weep, laugh then at our distress,
While we do sob and sigh, sit thou and sing,
Smile then, while we lament with heaviness,
While we our grief, do thou thy joy express:
  Since he who made us triumph and thee quake,
  Hath ceased to live; O, most victorious Drake.

Proud Spain, although our dragon be bereft us,
We rampant lions have enow for thee:
Magnanimous Essex (heaven's delight) is left us,
And O long may the heavens let him be!
Great Cumberland and Howard yet have we;
  And O long may we have them and enjoy
  These worthies to our wealth, and thine annoy.

These yet survive (O may they so for ever!)
To make eternal thunder in thine ears
With their heart-daunting names, and, like a fever,
To make thee tremble all distraught with fears,
When thou th' alarum of their trumpet hears:
  Eliza lives and while Eliza reigns
  Our England need not fear an hundred Spains.

18th November. A SPANISH STRATAGEM IN SCOTLAND.

The Spaniards in Scotland have a stratagem to make the Queen odious there. They have made a great number of ensigns with the picture of a headless lady, with an axe all bloody, and a shamble likewise bloody, with an inscription that the horror of this fact requireth a revenge from heaven and earth.

21st November. RECUSANTS TO BE COMMITTED.

About two years since divers recusant gentlemen of good hability and livelihood were restrained and committed, some to the palace of Ely, some to Banbury; but after bonds had been taken they were released. Now that the King of Spain is encouraged by the English fugitives beyond the sea that in his intended purposes he shall have the assistance of those that are backward in religion, it is thought meet that such recusants should again be restrained.

MR. DAVIES' 'ORCHESTRA.'

There is in the press that poem of dancing by Mr. John Davies entitled *Orchestra*, wherein Antinous wooeth Penelope, Ulysses' Queen, with a discourse of dancing, which, saith he, is a wondrous miracle devised by Love, and his proper exercise. Love shaped the world and the planets to dance, and the Moon to make her thirteen pavins in the year; and the winds also and the sea; only the Earth doth stand still for ever, for her rocks remove not. All things are ordered in dancing, as speech with grammar, rhetoric and poetry. To this the Queen maketh answer that Love's child must therefore be evil, but Antinous declareth that true Love danceth in all human actions.

DRAYTON'S POEMS.

There are entered three poetical fables by Mr. Michael Drayton, being the *Tragical Legend of Robert, Duke of Normandy*, the *Legend of Matilda the Chaste*, and the *Legend of Piers Gaveston*; of these the first being in the form of a dream seen by the poet, the last two related of themselves by the ghosts of the dead. Matilda, being approached by the messenger of King John, he tempteth her in these words:

> Wrong not thyself, nor yet the world deprive,
> Of that rare good which Nature freely lent,
> Think'st thou by such base nigardise to thrive,
> In sparing that which never will be spent?

And that is worst in age shall thee repent :
  Playing the churl, to hoard up beauty's pelf,
  And live, and die, and all unto thyself.

Fie on this lippish, lisping fond 'forsooth,'
This childish niceness, and these pettish 'noes,'
A graceful smile the wrinkling brow doth smooth,
Penance and Pleasure still are mortal foes,
Let springing youth rejourn old age's woes,
  Away with fasting, beggarly devotion,
  This is no way to climb unto promotion.

25th November. A THEATRE IN BLACKFRIARS.

James Burbage hath lately bought some rooms in the precinct of Blackfriars, near to the dwelling house of the Lord Chamberlain and the Lord Hunsdon, which he now altereth and would convert into a common playhouse. But the noblemen and gentlemen petition the Council that the rooms be converted to some other use, showing the annoyance and trouble that will be caused by the great resort of all manner of vagrant and lewd persons that under colour of resorting to the plays will come thither and work all manner of mischief ; also to the pestering of the precinct, if it should please God to send any visitation of sickness, for the precinct is already grown very populous. Besides, the playhouse is so near the church that the noise of the drums and trumpets will greatly disturb and hinder the ministers and parishioners in time of divine service and sermons. It is alleged moreover that the players think now to plant themselves in the liberties because the Lord Mayor hath banished them from playing in the City because of the great inconveniences and ill rule that followeth them.

27th November. BEARD'S 'THEATRE OF GOD'S JUDGMENTS.'

Mr. Thomas Beard hath compiled a collection of histories out of sacred, ecclesiastical and profane authors concerning the admirable judgments of God upon the transgressors of His commandments, translated out of the French and augmented with more than three hundred examples. This book is dedicated to Sir Edward Wingfield and named *A Theatre of God's Judgments*, being composed in two books, the first of thirty-five chapters, the second of fifty-one.

Of Atheists giveth notable examples.

There was a certain blasphemous wretch that on a time being with his companions in a common inn carousing and making merry, asked them if they thought a man was possessed with a soul or no. Whereunto, when some replied that the souls of men were immortal, and that some of them after release from the body lived in Heaven, others in Hell, he answered and swore that he thought it nothing so, but rather that there was no soul in man to survive the body, but that Heaven and Hell were mere fables, and for himself he was ready to sell his soul to any that would buy it. Then one of his companions took up a cup of wine and said, 'Sell me thy soul for this cup of wine'; which he receiving bad him take his soul and drank up the wine. Now Satan himself was there in man's shape and bought it again of the other at the same price, and by and by bad him give him his soul; the whole company affirming it was meet he should have it, since he bought it, not perceiving the Devil. But the Devil thereupon laying hold of this foul seller carried him into the air before them all towards his own habitation, to the great astonishment and amazement of all beholders; and from that day to this he was never heard of, but tried to his own pain that men had souls; and that Hell was no fable according to his godless and profane opinion.

Holdeth that for the same sin our poet Marlowe was notably punished, his death being not only a manifest sign of God's judgment but also a horrible and fearful terror to all that beheld him.

Concludeth (as St. Augustine saith) that many sins are punished in this world that the providence of God might be more apparent; and many, yea most, reserved to be punished in the world to come that we might know that there is yet judgment behind.

28th November. THE FORCE SENT TO THE ISLE OF WIGHT.

In the late alarm the 900 men sent to the Isle of Wight were very ill chosen, being unable in their persons, apparelled very raggedly, and the furniture unmeet for service; which is a great marvel that so small regard should be used in the choice of men in a manner naked and without any provision at all for the defence of a place of that importance. Moreover the men arrived not at the Isle of Wight within nineteen days after the Council had given order for them to be sent.

1st December. THE EARL OF ESSEX DEFAMED.

It is noted of many that since his safe return the Earl of Essex, that was beforetimes given to carnal dalliance, hath sithence changed his former ways. But of late there are bruits that he infameth a nobleman's wife, and one near to her Majesty; whereat his friends marvel at a course so dishonourable and dangerous to himself. Being taxed therewith the Earl protesteth that the charge is false and unjust.

8th December. A DREADFUL SUDDEN TEMPEST AT WELLS.

At Wells last Sunday Dr. Rogers, being newly made priest by the Bishop of Wells, preached his first sermon in the Cathedral Church there before a very goodly auditory. In his sermon, according to a text which he had chosen, and having made no prayer, he began to discourse of spirits and their properties; and within a while after there entered in at the west window of the church a dark and unproportionable thing of the bigness of a football, and went along the wall on the pulpit side; and suddenly it seemed to break but with no less sound and terror than if an hundred cannons had been discharged at once; and therewithal came a most violent storm and tempest of lightning and thunder as if the church had been full of fire.

In this strange tempest all the people were sore amazed, many of them being stricken down to the ground, and the preacher himself being struck down in his pulpit. Many in the body of the church were marked in their garments, arms and bodies with the figures of stars and crosses, but there was no manner of mark upon any that was in the choir. This tempest brought with it a most terrible stench, and suddenly as it ceased, it brake down some stone work, melted the wires and irons of the clock but burned no timber. The storm being ended and the people beginning to come to themselves, the Bishop, being in the choir, spake cheerfully to them, inviting them to a sermon there in the afternoon, wherewith he recomforted them all.

10th December. THE SCOTTISH PRINCESS BAPTISED.

On Sunday, 28th November, the infant daughter of the Scottish King was baptised at Holyrood House, being carried and presented to the baptism by Mr. Robert Bowes, the English ambassador, supplying that office for her Majesty the only godmother. The child is named Elizabeth, the whole honour in the solemnisation of all the ceremonies being given alone to her Majesty, with good observation of all due compliments. It was very generally thought that the child should have been presented with some gift from her Majesty, but as Mr. Bowes had neither gift to deliver nor knowledge of the Queen's pleasure, he thought good to pass it over in the fairest and most indifferent terms he could for the best satisfaction of the King and Queen.

The Bailiffs and chief of Edinburgh have in the name of the whole town given to the Princess 10,000 marks; to be paid at her marriage. The grant and assurance for payment is written in golden letters, enclosed in a golden coffer, and delivered to the Queen for her daughter.

14th December. SEDITION IN OXFORDSHIRE.

In Oxfordshire there was lately a rising planned at Enslow Hill of 200 or 300 seditious people from various towns of the shire that met with design of raising a rebellion when most of the gentlemen of the shire were to appear in a law suit at the King's Bench. They would spoil the gentlemen's houses of arms and horses and go towards London where they expected that they should be joined by the apprentices. These men are chiefly young and unmarried, and not poor; three are now in safe keeping.

18th December. COOTE'S 'ENGLISH SCHOOLMASTER.'

There is entered a book called *The English Schoolmaster*, written by Mr. Edward Coote, schoolmaster, of teaching the reading of the English tongue by syllables; setteth down an order how the teacher shall direct the scholars to oppose one another, a short catechism, with sundry prayers and psalms in verse, concluding with a table of words difficult to be understood. Hath also a poem of the schoolmaster to his scholars, beginning:

My child and scholar, take good heed
  Unto the words which here are set;
And see you do accordingly,
  Or else be sure you shall be beat.

19th December. A Loyal Recusant.

Sir Thomas Cornwallis, who notwithstanding his difference of religion hath never been touched with any suspicion of disloyalty or ill affection towards her Majesty, is dispensed from the measures taken against recusants at this time.

A Strange Earth Moving.

In East Kent, at a place called Oakham Hill, there have been strange movings of the earth in divers places; the ground of two water pits, the one six foot deep, the other twelve at least, having sundry tusses of alders and ashes growing in the bottoms with a great rock of stone under them, was not only removed out of its place, but withal is mounted aloft and become hills, with the sedge, flags and black mud upon the tops of them, higher than the face of the water by nine foot. There were sundry other movings of the earth, the whole measure of the breaking ground being at least nine acres.

23rd December. Tyrone's Treachery.

Tyrone now giveth many apparent proofs of his bad meaning; he hath made public restraint of all victuals to be carried to Armagh, stopping the convoy and cutting off some of the soldiers that went with the victuals. Of late an attempt was made to surprise the place, wherein thirty-five of the garrison were slain, himself countenancing the matter in person. His kinsmen and followers make violent incursions into the Pale with open force up to the River of Boyne. He hath treacherously attempted to surprise the castle at Carlingford, where, missing his main purpose, there were carried away as prisoners in lamentable manner two gentlewomen.

25th December. The Dearth.

The Council have written to the Lord Mayor putting him in mind of their orders last summer that all excess of fare might be avoided in public and private diet. And now because the greatest disorders are kept in tabling houses, taverns and inns, most strict order shall be taken that no persons have meat dressed in their houses at night on Wednesdays, Fridays or fast days; any that offend therein shall be committed to prison and their names certified to the Council. Moreover, in spite of her Majesty's proclamation, there are more gentlemen come out of the country and at this present about the City than in other years, for they come hither in this time of dearth to avoid housekeeping.

The Queen hath also caused the Archbishops to notify the Bishops to give strait order to all preachers that they exhort men especially at this time to abstinence and prayer, using all charitable devotion towards the relief of their poor neighbours, setting them on work, giving of alms and other charitable works. Further that especially at this time all persons be admonished not to give over housekeeping as many do, to live in good fellowship and discharge their servants to shift for themselves. Also the people shall be taught to endure this scarcity with patience and to beware how they give ear to any persuasions or practices of discontented and idle brains to move them to repine or swerve from the humble duties of good subjects, to the offence of God and displeasing of the Queen that hath so tender a care of their welfare.

26th December. CORN SHIPS TO BE STOPPED.

Owing to the great scarcity of corn, especially in Ireland, Sir Henry Palmer, Vice-admiral of the Narrow Seas, is expressly commanded to stay all shipping from the East Countries that shall pass by the Narrow Seas freighted with corn. This corn is to be sent to Waterford and Dublin, and for corn so seized Sir Henry shall give his bill and bind himself that, upon certificate from the place where the corn shall be unladen, there shall be good payment made to the owners or their assigns in London according to such prices as be thought reasonably worth, considering the place where it should be delivered. But if it manifestly appear that the corn was provided for Spain, it shall be seized as lawful prize. And for more assurance that these vessels with their corn sail immediately, to each of the ships shall be appointed one special man of trust and sufficient number of men to overcome the strangers if they should bend themselves to go to any other place. To waft these ships over to Ireland, the *Crane* is being sent out; and if the Vice-admiral think fit, the masters, factors and merchants of the strangers' ships shall be kept on board the *Crane* to prevent any practice against the Englishmen put on board, either of violence or carrying them to Spain against their wills.

OTHER BOOKS SET FORTH ANNO 1596.

THE BROWNISTS' CONFESSIONS.

The Brownists that are in exile beyond the seas have caused to be printed a little book called a 'true confession' of the faith that they hold; being led, as they declare, to publish this testimony by the 'rueful estate of our poor countrymen who remain yet fast locked in Egypt, that house of servants, in slavish subjection to strange Lords and laws, enforced to bear the burdens and intolerable yoke of their popish canons and decrees, being subject every day they rise to thirty-eight antichristian ecclesiastical offices, and many more Romish statutes and traditions almost without number: besides their high transgression daily in their vain will-worship of God by reading over a few prescribed prayers and collects which they have translated verbatim out of the Mass-book and which are yet tainted with many popish heretical errors and superstitions instead of true spiritual invocation upon the name of the Lord.' In this book are set down forty-five articles concerning the faith and duties of Christians, and very bitterly inveighing against the present state civil and ecclesiastical; as that Antichrist corrupted the offices and administrations of the Church and erected a strange, new forged ministry whereby all nations of the earth were forced to receive the Beast's mark and be brought into confusion and Babylonish bondage; that the Archbishops, deans, prebendaries and all others with the whole rabble of ecclesiastical courts are a strange and antichristian ministry and offices, and are not the ministry instituted in Christ's Testament, or allowed in or over his Church; that by God's commandment all that will be saved must with speed come forth of this Anti-Christian estate, leaving the suppression of it unto the magistrate to whom it belongeth.

A BOOK CONCERNING THE SPANISH SICKNESS.

A book by Dr. Peter Lowe, chirurgeon in ordinary to the French King, entitled *An easy, certain and perfect method to cure and prevent the Spanish sickness*, being dedicated to the Earl of

Essex, and treating of the causes, signs and cures of this disease. This disease was brought among Christians in the year 1492 by a Spaniard called Christopher Columbus with many Spaniards and some women who came from the new found Isles Occidental; afterward in 1493 when King Charles VIII. of France was besieging Naples with a puissant army, some of the Spaniards came to him, of which Columbus was chief, and spread this pernicious seed, terming it the 'Indian sickness,' which since hath its course not only among the Spaniards, who call it the 'Italian sickness,' but also among the Italians, who call it the 'malady of Naples,' for it began first to flourish in Naples. Amongst Frenchmen it is called the 'Spanish sickness'; in England the 'great pox'; in Scotland the 'Spanish fleas'; some call it the 'underfoot' because the infection often cometh by treading with the bare foot upon the spittle of the diseased. Some ignorant malicious people, saith he, call it the 'French disease,' without any cause or reason.

LAMBARD'S 'PERAMBULATION OF KENT.'

A new edition of the *Perambulation of Kent*, containing the description, history, and customs of that county. This book was first written in 1570 by Mr. William Lambarde, published in 1576, and now increased and altered after the author's own copy. There is added a new card of the beacons in Kent that was made by the direction of the late Lord Cobham, Lieutenant of the Shire, so that upon firing of the beacons a man with little labour might learn from the directory lines where the danger lies, and so confusions be avoided.

1597

1st January. BAD WEATHER.

There has been such great rain day and night that no one can travel on the roads either by coach or on horseback.

8th January. THE LATE INTENDED RISING.

Some of those charged with the late intended rising in Oxford being examined reveal that the matter arose concerning enclosures, for many in those parts have enclosed the common fields. One of them having complained to his fellow how hardly he maintained his wife and seven children with bread and water this hard year, the other made answer, 'Care not for work, for we shall have a merrier world shortly: there be lusty fellows abroad and I will get more, and I will work one day and play the other.' Saying also that there was once a rising at Enslow Hill when they were entreated to go down, and after hanged like dogs, but now would they never yield but go through with it. Servants were so held in and kept like dogs that they would be ready to cut their masters' throats. There was a mason in those parts who could make balls of wildfire and had a sling to fling the same whereby he could fire houses as occasion served. When they had risen they would go to my Lord Norris's in Ricott and get wine and beer, and take two of his brass ordnance and set them upon coach wheels and so proceed.

11th January. THE VICTUALS OF THE SOLDIERS IN IRELAND.

The soldier in Ireland when he is victualled from her Majesty's store hath in each week four flesh days and three fish days. On the former receiveth *per diem* loaf bread, 1½ lb.; beer, one pottle; beef, salt, 2 lb., or if it be fresh, 2½ lb., being without legs and necks. On fish days, loaf bread, 1½ lb.; beer, one pottle; butter, ½ lb., or instead thereof cheese, 1 lb., or 8 herrings *per diem*.

17th January. MR. NORDEN'S 'MIRROR OF HONOUR.'

Mr. Norden hath written a godly book entitled *The Mirror of Honour*, dedicated to the Earl of Essex; wherein every professor of arms, from the general, chieftains and high commanders to the private officer and inferior soldier, may see the necessity of the fear of God, and the use of all divine virtues, both in commanding and obeying, practising and proceeding in the most honourable affairs of war; a treatise most necessary, comfortable and expedient for all English subjects, whereby their duties to God, their Prince and their country, their assurance and safety, is lively set forth as in a glass before them.

Noteth the wicked assertion of a military man who affirmed that it is enough for the ministry to be masters of sin, and that it beseemeth soldiers to live like soldiers, to swear like soldiers, and to sin like soldiers.

23rd January. AN ITALIAN ARGOSY STAYED.

An Italian argosy of great burden, laden with grain and other provisions, that put into Portsmouth, is there stayed by the Lord Mountjoy. The Council order the grain to be unladen out of the ship and put in safe custody in the store houses at Portsmouth, and a perfect certificate made out of the quantity taken; and that the master and others of the ship may not conceive amiss, as though any wrong was intended unto them, they shall be assured that the corn, being taken only for her Majesty's service, will be paid for in good sort at reasonable prices.

24th January. A GREAT VICTORY AT TURNHOUT.

From Sir Francis Vere is come news of a great victory of the Count Maurice over the Spaniards at Turnhout in Brabant on the 14th. The *rendezvous* being appointed for the 12th of the month at Gertrudenberg there arrived from all parts to the number of 5,000 foot and 800 horse. Next morning, by break of day, they began to march, drawing with them two demi-cannon and two large field pieces, and by the evening reached Ravel, one league from Turnhout. That night was spent in consultation, and in the end it was resolved to show themselves on the passage to Herentaulx, being the way of the enemy's retreat, with purpose if they left their quarter to be in the head of them ; if they abode it to plant the cannon and dislodge them.

At dawn they marched, and the vanguard hastened to get the passage of a narrow bridge half way betwixt the quarters ; which being gotten, and the troops put in order, some horse were sent into the enemy's quarter to know what they did ; who presently returned word that the enemy was marched to Herentaulx and that his rearguard was in sight. Hereupon all the horse advanced and they followed with the most speed they could. A musket shot from their quarter their rearguard stood to countenance some few of their men appointed to break down a bridge by which they had passed, and by which only they could be followed. With some few shot these were beaten back and the bridge taken, there remaining no more than to carry a man abreast.

When one hundred musqueteers were passed the bridge, our horse began to follow the enemy, and continued for near three hours with a very small number, the speed of the enemy and the badness of the passage making it impossible for our troops of foot to overtake the horse.

During all this time by many messengers the Count Maurice was advertised that, if he would send forward his horse, he might have a fair victory ; if not, the enemy would soon be in safety. At length he gave a good part of the horse to the Count Hollocke to go before, and himself followed with the rest. The enemy by this time were gotten into a heath and making great haste towards the entry of a strait at the end of it, which gotten they would be safe, being now not far from Herentaulx ; but now our horse began to appear on the heath. The enemy kept near the edge of the heath with their horse on the outside, marching in their battalions, not ranged in one front but in length, the Almains marching in front of the column, in the middle the Walloons, and last the Neapolitans who were the rearguard.

The Count Hollocke made the flank of them, and charged towards their horse, which fled. He pursued them not far but turned towards the flank of the Almains, at which time Sir Robert Sidney and Sir Francis Vere charging the Neopolitans, at one instant their vanguard and rearward were assailed and put in rout, and the mid battle kept them company. The Neapolitans keeping together were in a manner all slain on the place.

Of the rest there are escaped very few, for of 4,000 foot, by their own confession they acknowledge that 2,400 were left dead in the field, and 600 taken prisoners, amongst which are sixteen captains. Their commander, the Count of Varras (or La Verall), was killed in the charge, and all their ensigns taken to the number of thirty-nine. On our side twenty men were slain and less hurt.

That same night the troops returned to Turnhout, and the next day, after some few cannon shot, the castle was yielded by composition. From thence the army returned to Gertrudenberg, and every troop was sent to its garrison.

This blow will touch the Cardinal shrewdly, and, he being disappointed of those forces he kept of purpose in Brabant to make incursions, our men will be the safer, even though it should chance to freeze.

26th January. THE DEATH OF LADY CECIL.

On the death of Sir Robert Cecil's Lady many do write to console him in his great grief, and among them Sir Walter Ralegh to this effect:

'There is no man sorry for death itself but only for the time of death; everyone knowing that it is a bond ever forfeited to God. If then we know the same to be certain and inevitable, we ought withal to take the time of his arrival in as good part as the knowledge; and not to lament at the instant of every seeming adversity, which, we are assured, have been on their way towards us from the beginning. It appertaineth to every man of a wise and worthy spirit to draw together into suffrance the unknown future to the known present; looking no less with the eyes of the mind than those of the body (the one beholding afar off, the other at hand) that those things of this world in which we live be not strange unto us when they approach, as to feebleness which is moved with novelties. But that like true men participating immortality and knowing our destinies to be of God, we do then make our estates and our wishes, our fortunes and our desires, all one.'

'I believe that sorrows are dangerous companions, converting bad into evil, and evil into worse, and do no other service than multiply harms. They are the treasons of weak hearts and of the foolish. The mind that entertaineth them is as the earth and dust whereon sorrows and adversities of the world do, as the beasts of the field, tread, trample and defile. The mind of man is that part of God which is in us, which, by how much it is subject to passion, by so much it is farther from Him that gave it us. Sorrows draw not the dead to life, but the living to death. And, if I were myself to advise myself in the like, I would never forget my patience till I saw all and the worst of evils, and so grieve for all at once; lest, lamenting for some one, another might not remain in the power of Destiny of greater discomfort.'

30th January. MR. BACON'S 'ESSAYS.'

Mr. Francis Bacon hath written a little book of *Essays*, being ten in number, *viz.*: of study; of discourse; of ceremonies and respects; of followers and friends; suitors; of expense; of regiment of health; of honour and reputation; of faction; of negotiating. There are added twelve Sacred Meditations in Latin, and a fragment 'Of the Colours of good and evil.'

MR. BACON'S ESSAY OF STUDIES.

'Studies serve for pastimes, for ornaments and abilities. Their chief use for pastimes, is in privateness and retiring; for ornament is in discourse, and for ability is in judgment. For expert men can execute, but learned ones are fittest to judge or censure.

¶ To spend too much time in them is sloth; to use them too much for ornament is affectation: to make judgment wholly by their rules is the humour of a scholar. ¶ They perfect Nature, and are perfected by experience. ¶ Crafty men contemn them, simple men admire them, wise men use them; for they teach not their own use, but that is a wisdom without them: and above them won by observation. ¶ Read not to contradict, nor to believe, but to weigh and consider. Some books are to be tasted, others to be swallowed, and some few to be chewed and digested: That is, some books are to be read only in parts; others to be read, but cursorily; and some few to be read wholly and with diligence and attention. ¶ Reading maketh a full man, conference a ready man, and writing an exact man. And therefore if a man write little, he had need have a great memory; if he confer little, he had need have a present wit; and if he read little, he had need have much cunning, to seem to know that he doth not. ¶ Histories make men wise, Poets witty: the Mathematics subtle, natural Philosophy deep: Moral grave, Logic and Rhetoric able to contend.'

31st January. New Plays.

This month the Admiral's men have played two new plays, being *Alexander and Lodovick* and *Woman hard to please.*

2nd February. A Dangerous Person taken.

There is lately apprehended one William Tomson, a very lewd and dangerous person, that is charged to have a purpose to burn her Majesty's ships or do some notable villainy. This man is to be examined concerning his devilish intents, and earnestly dealt with to declare by whom he hath been moved thereunto; wherein if by fair means and persuasions he be not moved to reveal the truth, then to be put to the manacles or the torture of the rack as in like cases is used.

5th February. A Quarrel at Court.

The Earl of Northumberland hath had a quarrel with the Earl of Southampton that was like to have proceeded to a combat, insomuch that my Lord of Southampton sent a gentleman with his rapier. Whereupon my Lord of Northumberland asked whether he brought a challenge; if so, he accepted it beforehand. The gentleman answered that he did not, only he brought his rapier. My Lord of Northumberland answered that he had not a novice in hand; he knew well when he was before or behind in points of honour, and therefore had nothing to say further unless he were challenged. But the affair came to nought, for by order of the Queen they were summoned to Court on bond of their allegiance and called before the Lords of the Council, who assured him, on their honours, that my Lord of Southampton had not spoken the words complained of, which afterward he affirmed himself. My Lord of Northumberland answered that he would rather believe their Lordships than any other; and the lie he had given was nothing. So my Lord Southampton hath revoked his challenge and they are made friends.

6th February. IRISH TRADE WITH SPAIN.

The Council have commanded that no ships either of traffic or of war from the ports of Waterford or Wexford in Ireland be permitted to go forth to the sea for the next six months unless very good bonds be given that they will not pass to any of the coasts of Spain or unto any of the King of Spain's dominions. This order is made because of the extraordinary preparations of the King of Spain, that in all likelihood are intended for Ireland, for which cause he stayeth and engageth in his service such serviceable mariners of other nations as do arrive there.

8th February. SPANISH DISASTERS.

An English pilot lately come from Ferrol declareth that he was pilot in the fleet of 90 ships, whereof 20 were men-of-war, that went out of Lisbon. Of these 45 were cast away between Lisbon and the Groin, one a great ship of 1,400 tons called the *Santiago*, with all the battery for the army; another the Admiral of the Levantiscos, with 1,200 men; 3 ships of 300 tons each, built by an Englishman called Lambart, with divers others all full of soldiers and provisions. In an Irish ship there were also cast away 14 Irishmen of name, capital rebels, and 200 common Irish soldiers. There now remain 70 ships of all sorts. They have great famine and sickness and daily look for provisions by sea from other parts of Spain. Their purpose was to go for Ireland, and they pretend so still.

THE BATTLE AT TURNHOUT.

In the late victory at Turnhout there were found about divers of the Spaniards which were slain certain inchantments and prayers in Latin, Englished thus:

'Whosoever shall carry about him this prayer hereunder written, let him not fear any enemy, neither can any weapon annoy him, neither darts nor other warlike instruments: neither the weapons of the inchanters, nor poisons, neither can the wicked spirit annoy him: he shall be safe at all times, and in all places. ✠✠✠

'*Barmasa* ✠ *leuitas* ✠ *buccella* ✠ *buicella* ✠ *agla* ✠ *agla* ✠ *tetra grammaton* ✠ *Adonai* ✠. Lord, great and admirable God, help Thy unworthy servant, N., from all danger of death of the body and soul, and from all the assaults of enemies, visible and invisible. ✠ There be ten names with which God is named, in whom ✠ they name God ✠ *Crux* ✠ *Ely* ✠ *Eloy* ✠ *Ela* ✠ *Adonai* ✠ *Corpus Christi cogi* ✠ *Sabaot* ✠ *Nomina Crux* ✠ the things are profitable to the servant of God, N., *hoc est enim corpus* ✠ *meum* ✠ *vt diligat me, Amen.*'

These and sundry others conjuring the weapons of the enemy not to hurt the bearer were found.

Since the battle little hath been done on either side. The Count Maurice sent the corpse of the Count of Varras to the Cardinal, who accepted it well, and yet was he buried without ceremony as one unworthy of any honour in that he had not better looked to his charge.

9th February. A NEW LOAN FOR THE QUEEN.

Her Majesty finding the charges sustained for preservation of the realm and subjects against their enemies so to increase thinketh it a reasonable purpose to require some present loan for the space of one year. The Lords Lieutenant are required to send for the collector of the last loan in their counties and by him and his books to understand the numbe and names of those that did lend sums of money to her Majesty in these later years; and if any be dead or departed out of the country to inquire who hath his lands and goods.

13th February. SUPERFLUOUS DIET AT THE ASSIZES.

The Justices, being about to go on their several circuits, are urged to make earnest admonishment to the Sheriffs to restrain their diets and entertainments at the Assizes, considering that these meetings were not ordained for feastings and prodigal expenses but for the administration of justice, and especially at this time of scarcity and dearth. They are reminded touching the abstinence from eating of flesh this time of Lent, that offenders against the orders should be punished; and also touching enclosures, whereby any highway is stopped, or villages or houses destroyed and dispeopled, or tillage greatly decayed; hereof they shall certify the Council.

COMPLAINTS FROM WILTSHIRE.

In Wiltshire it is declared that the soldiers despatched to the defence of the Isle of Wight last November were not sent back orderly so that their arms might be restored to the inhabitants that did set them forth; but very many of the soldiers being loosely dispersed ran away, and a great quantity of their arms and furniture (even to the number of 200) is either utterly lost or so broken and mangled as to be unserviceable. Moreover great abuses have been committed in the discharge of divers soldiers for sums of money. The Lord Chief Justice shall examine this matter very diligently, especially because, when like abuses have been committed before, the matter hath been so shifted from the county to those that had the government of the soldiers and from these again to the county, that it could hardly be found where the fault lay.

TROUBLES IN OXFORD.

The new Dean of Christchurch is much misliked of the students there who complain that like a new lord he maketh new laws, endeavouring an innovation that will enrich himself and undo the society. The cause of their complaint is that he seeketh to take away the allowance of commons enjoyed since the foundation of the college and to exchange for it an allowance of 2s. a week.

17th February. TROUBLES OF THE KEEPER AT WISBEACH.

The Keeper of the Jesuits at Wisbeach very earnestly craveth favour of Mr. Secretary because that two of his prisoners, both priests, are escaped from the castle by beating out the iron bars of their windows and letting themselves down by the bed cord. He would therefore have favour for three reasons; firstly, the prisoners escaped during his absence in London on a *subpoena*, wherefore his servants are to blame; secondly, because it was done in the night, when quiet rest is due to every man; thirdly, for that he is about to be married to a lady of sufficient ability, and if she should hear that he is in trouble, it might procure in her such an aversion that all his friends would hardly settle her again in any good affection.

21st February. COURT NEWS.

My Lord of Essex still keepeth his chamber, yet is he not believed to be sick. There is not a day passes that the Queen sends not often to see him, and himself goeth privately unto her. He giveth out very confidently that he will go into Wales, where his own land lies, to view it and see his friends. Sir Robert Cecil is now in greatest credit, the Queen passing the most part of the day in private and secret conference with him.

24th February. SIR THOMAS BASKERVILLE'S SOLDIERS.

The soldiers with Sir Thomas Baskerville are now at St. Valeries, their bands being weakened with the number fallen sick so that of late at a mustering there were found to be sick 300 and odd, but only fifty-seven missing. All their apparel is worn out, the bareness whereof in this wild, cold, and wasted country being a principal cause of their sickness.

25th February. THE LORD MAYOR REBUKED.

The Lord Mayor is rebuked for the great slackness in the execution of the orders for the restraint of killing and eating of flesh in Lent, and especially during this dearth; which abuse is made known to the Council not only by the information of some few but almost every man in the City is an eyewitness to it.

4th March. COURT NEWS.

The Lord Treasurer is not well, and in this sharp weather keeps in. Sir Walter Ralegh hath been very often private with the Earl of Essex and is said to be a mediator of peace between him and Sir Robert Cecil, who likewise hath been private with him. Sir Walter allegeth that much good may grow by it; her Majesty's continual unquietness will turn to contentment; despatches for all matters of war and peace for the safety of the land will go forward to the hurt of the common enemies.

The Earl, wearied with not knowing how to please, is not unwilling to hearken to these motions made to him for the public good. He purposeth in three days' time, by her Majesty's leave, for some twenty days to go towards Wigmore Castle and so to Raglan.

9th March. A Notable Stratagem at the Capture of Amiens.

The Spaniards suddenly took Amiens by a stratagem on the 1st of the month, which is a shrewd loss to the King, for whole magazines of provisions for war are there with forty pieces of battery.

The capture was on this wise. The whole affair was under the conduct of the Governor of Dorlans, who had often been inside Amiens disguised, as the Bishop of Amiens confesseth. Hereby he perceived that the gate of the city which lieth on the further side of the Somme towards Dorlans was very carelessly guarded, especially at the hour of the sermon, to which all the good citizens went, leaving the gate in charge of mercenaries and common troops. He therefore chose out 700 picked men, sending on ahead fifteen or twenty of them, armed and with cuirasses, and carrying pistols and daggers, but disguised as peasants. Behind them came a waggon covered with straw, and conducted by the Governor himself, also disguised. The rest of the troops marched through the night and in such excellent order that by the hour appointed they were within a very short distance of the city.

About 8 o'clock in the morning, five or six of those in advance entered the gate, carrying sacks of nuts and apples as though they were peasants from the neighbouring villages going to market. These sat down within the gate, feigning to be weary, and waited until the waggon and the other men came up. Then the waggon, having come on to the bridge, stopped in such a way that half was under the arch of the gate where the portcullis would fall, and the other half still upon the bridge. Hereupon the men with the sacks, as though by mischance, spilt their nuts and apples, and the guard rushed after them; whereat the Governor cut the traces of the horses in the waggon so that it could not be moved, whilst his men with their harquebusses fired upon the guard and slew them. The men behind the waggon sprang in, and though the portcullis was lowered, it came down upon the waggon, leaving space enough for the soldiers to pass in and out. By this the main body came up, and having raised the portcullis and drawn out the waggon, they made themselves masters of the gate, and (which is more to be wondered at) they marched right through the city with their drums beating and flags flying.

At first they were in doubt what to do, as these few men had intended only to seize the gate, but seeing that no opposition was offered, they placed guards at the cross streets and in the square without anyone raising a finger. Then the commander sent the Spanish by companies of fifteen and twenty to traverse the streets, and when they saw any of the townsfolk on the roads or at the windows they fired on them so that not a man had the courage to stir.

And in this wise a great city of 50,000 persons, amongst whom were 10,000 soldiers, is taken by 700, with the loss of less than ten on both sides.

10th March. THE WARDENSHIP OF THE CINQUE PORTS.

Owing to the death of Lord Cobham, there is competition for the post of the Cinque Ports, the Earl of Essex very earnestly moving the Queen for Sir Robert Sidney, that is governor of Flushing. But she said he was too young for the office and Mr. Harry Brooke, the now Lord Cobham, should have it. Whereupon the Earl was resolved to leave the Court, and this morning, himself, his followers and horse being ready, about ten o'clock he went to speak with my Lord Treasurer; and being by Somerset House, Mr. Killigrew met him and willed him to come to the Queen. After some speech had privately with her, she hath made him Master of the Ordnance, which place he accepteth and is contented thereby.

11th March. THE OFFICE OF LORD PRESIDENT.

There is still no one appointed as Lord President in the north, and again the Archbishop of York hath written to the Lord Treasurer that someone be appointed. The cause of this delay is said to be the want of fit men, but is rather that the race of nobles whom the Queen found at the beginning of the reign having passed away, she by her wisdom and experience knoweth all the defects and infirmities of the nobility now growing up. Yet if the Queen could resolve on a man, her commission and instructions and the ordinary proceedings of the Court would sufficiently enable him. My Lord Huntingdon was very raw when he first came down, but having a resolute will to serve God and her Majesty grew to great experience.

12th March. THE LORD TREASURER'S GRIEF.

This morning died Sir William Hatton in Holborn, and the Lady Kildare, it is said, hath begged the wardenship of his daughters. The Lord Treasurer takes it very heavily and weeps pitifully, calling to remembrance the many late crosses he hath been afflicted withal by the death of his friends. Sir John Fortescue, going to Court, lighted at his house, but word was brought that his Lordship was not to be spoken with, and all are turned back that have any business with him by this accident of Sir William Hatton's death.

14th March. A WITCH HANGED AT LANCASTER.

At the Assizes holden at Lancaster on the 6th there was condemned and afterwards hanged one Edmond Hartley that had bewitched seven persons in the house of Mr. Nicholas Starkie, a gentleman dwelling at Cleworth.

About three years since the two children of this gentleman being taken ill very strangely he was at great charges of £200 for their cures; seeking remedy without due regard, first of a seminary priest, and then of this Hartley, that at first wrought some cure on the children, who remained well for almost a year and a half. During this time he would come to visit them; but at length feigned that he would go away into another county. Mr. Starkie therefore besought him to stay, and offered him a pension of 40s. a year; but after a time he would have more.

After this Mr. Starkie on a time going to his father's house, Hartley went with him. And being tormented all night long in bed, next morning he went into a little wood, not far off the house, where he made a circle, the compass of a yard and a half, with many crosses and partitions; which being finished he came back to call Mr. Starkie desiring him to tread it out, for he said he might not do it himself. This also being despatched, 'Well,' quoth he, 'now I shall trouble him that troubled me, and be meet with him that sought my death.'

When he perceived this and other bad qualities in him, Mr. Starkie began to be weary of the fellow, especially as his children grew no better but rather worse. He then sought, though secretly, for help of the physicians; after that to Dr. John Dee at Manchester, who wished him to crave the help and assistance of some godly preachers, with whom he should join in prayer and fasting for the help of his children. He procured also this Hartley to come before him, whom he so sharply reproved that the children had better rest for some three weeks after. But then they began to have their accustomed fits; first John Starkie, Mr. Starkie's son, then his daughter, and five other women of his household, three being children of 14, 12 and 10 years, and two women of 30 years and more.

It was noticed that when this Hartley meant them a mischief he would kiss them if he could, and therewith breathe the Devil into their bodies.

Amongst those afflicted was one Margaret Byrom, a kinswoman of Mistress Starkie, who would fall into fits when this Hartley came to see her. Hereupon some preachers, finding Hartley with her, asked him what he did with the maid. He said that he came to pray with her. 'Pray,' quoth one, 'why, man, thou canst not pray.' 'Yes, but I can,' quoth he. 'Say then the Lord's Prayer,' said the preacher; and he began to fumble about it very ill favouredly, but could not for his life say it to the end. They then thought him to be a witch, and caused him to be apprehended and brought before two Justices of the peace, by whom he was further examined and sent to Lancaster gaol.

When the assizes came, he was brought up, arraigned and convicted, Mr. Starkie having charged him with bewitching his children, which he proved sufficiently and made evident to the whole Bench. Howbeit for that they could find no law to hang him; whereupon Mr. Starkie called to mind the making of the circle, which being delivered on oath was received. Nevertheless Hartley stiffly denied it and stood out against him, and told him to his face that he should not hang him (for the Devil had promised him no halter should hang him); yet the jury cast him and the judge condemned him. When Hartley was hanged, the halter brake; whereupon he penitently confessed that he had deserved that punishment, and that all which Mr. Starkie had charged him with was true. And so he was hanged out the second time.

16th March. THE PRICE OF BEER.

These few days past divers brewers have appeared before the Council, some of them committed to prison and the rest bound to answer their contempt next term for selling beer at 10s. to 16s. the barrel, whereas no beer should be sold above 5s. the barrel for small beer, and 8s. the better sort. Nevertheless in answer to their petition that the price of malt is excessive, the Council will allow beer to be sold at 5s. for small beer and 10s. for the strongest.

THE EARL OF ESSEX'S PATENT.

The Earl of Essex cannot yet get his patent signed as Master of the Ordnance. Sir John Fortescue offered it twice to the Queen but she found some exceptions, and this afternoon the Earl took his Bill and presented it himself; but for all that it is not done, which moveth him greatly, especially as it is believed that the Lord Cobham's patent will be signed before or as soon as his. The Lord Cobham who, it is said, shall marry my Lord of Oxford's daughter, hearing how disdainfully my Lord of Essex speaks of him in public, doth likewise protest to hate the Earl as much.

19th March. A NEW PLAY.

There is a new play at the Rose called *Guido*.

20th March. FRENCH PIRATES.

Some short time since the *Bonham* of Poole being driven into Dartmouth by contrary winds met there with two ships of Dieppe, which continued in the port the space of two months; and they making forth to the seas a few days before the English ship and meeting with her shortly after, these two ships of Dieppe set upon the Englishmen, robbed and spoiled them of all their lading, goods and merchandise, with apparel, victuals, and other furniture, in most treacherous and barbarous sort, leaving them so destitute that they were like to perish.

25th March. SECTARIES TO GO TO CANYDA.

There are two merchant strangers, Abraham and Stephen van Harwick, and Charles Leigh, a merchant of London, that would undertake a voyage of discovery and fishing into the Bay of Canyda, and will plant themselves in an island called Ramea whence they hope to transport commodities of special use for the realm, and to establish a trade of fishing. These men have made suit to transport with them divers artificers and others noted to be sectaries, whereof four would go in this present voyage. This is allowed by the Council, provided that they shall not repair again into the realm unless they be contented to reform themselves and live in obedience to the laws established for matters of religion. Before their departure they shall swear oaths of true faith and obedience to her Majesty.

27th March. AN EXPLOSION IN DUBLIN.

From Dublin Sir John Norris reporteth a lamentable accident of the burning of six lasts of powder on the quay. The ruin of the town is exceeding great and by estimation twenty houses near adjoining are thrown to the ground, nor any house or church within the walls but is marvellously damaged in the tilings, glass and small timbers. Six score persons of all ages and sexes are known to be slain, but few English, besides sundry headless bodies and heads without bodies that were found. There is little appearance of this having happened by treachery, but it is guessed that some nail in the bark struck fire.

28th March. THE POSSESSED PERSONS IN LANCASHIRE.

The children of Mr. Starkie having still continued in their fits since the execution of the witch Edmond Hartley, the gentleman sent for Mr. Darrell, that wrought with the boy of Burton. At first Mr. Darrell was unwilling to come, but at the third sending he came on the 16th March to Cleworth, with Mr. George More, another preacher, and soon after their coming the children were thrown into their fits, and scorned the two preachers. For when they called for a Bible, the children fell a laughing at it and said, 'Reach them the bibble babble, bibble babble,' and continued with many other scornings and filthy speeches. The preachers determined therefore to fast and pray with the family. Having therefore the whole family together, and divers honest neighbours for the holding and tending of the possessed, they made entrance into the preparation, which was by way of exhortation, intreating the Lord to put the Devil to silence and that He would charge and command the spirits to hold their peace so that they might have good audience in praying and speaking the Word; which indeed came to pass at that time.

Morning being come, great preparation was made in the family to set all things in good order, and having a fair large parlour already trimmed, they brought in thither beds upon which they laid the seven sick possessed persons, all of them greatly vexed by their torments. It being now 7 o'clock they began the exercise of humbling their souls unto God, and continued with the exercise till 3 o'clock in the afternoon without much interruption; but then, as if Satan was much heated by fasting and prayer, they all brake out into exceeding loud cries, all seven roaring and belling in extreme and fearful manner. Then was there such struggling and striving between those praying and the devils, crying out so loud with such violence and extension of voice, labouring who should be loudest, till the preachers' voices were spent and no strength almost left in them. This battle continued very near the space of two hours, till they were exceedingly weakened; but at last it pleased God to weaken Satan's power, for the possessed were cast down suddenly and lay all along, stretched out as they had been dead; and every one of them afterwards declared that the spirit had passed out in the likeness of some ugly creature, as a crow's head, or an urchin (or hedgehog), or a foul ugly man with a bunch on his back.

In these possessions the children of Mr. Starkie have been very strangely afflicted, one of them, a girl of the age of thirteen years, being possessed, as it seemeth, with a spirit of pride that did most lively express both by words and gestures the proud women of our times, that cannot content themselves with any sober or modest attire. Whereupon she said, 'Come on, my lad,' (for so she called the spirit), 'come on and set my partlet on the one side as I do on the other.' And as she was setting of it, she said unto him, 'Thus, my lad, I will have a fine smock of silk, it shall be finer than thine. I will have a petticoat of silk, not red, but of the best silk that is; it shall be guarded and a foot high: it shall be laid on with gold lace; it shall have a French body, not of whalebone for that is not stiff enough, but of horn for that will hold it out; it shall come low before to keep in my belly. My lad, I will have a French fardingale, it shall be finer than thine; I will have it low before and high behind, and broad on either side, that I may lay my arms upon it. My lad, thy gown is crimson satin, but mine shall be of black wrought velvet, it shall be finer than thine. I will have my sleeves set out with wire, for sticks will break and are not stiff enough. I will have my periwinkle so fine, finer than thine. I will have my cap of black velvet with a feather in it, with flews of gold, and my hairs shall be set with pearls, finer than thine. I will have my partlet set with a rebater, and starched with blue starch; and pinned with a row or two of pins. My lad, I will have a busk of whalebone, it shall be tied with two silk points, and I will have a drawn wrought stomacher embossed with gold, finer than thine. I will have my hose of orange colour, this is in request, and my cork shoes of red Spanish leather, finer than thine. I will have a scarf of red silk, with a gold lace about the edge. I will have a fan with a silver steel and a glass set in it, finer than thine. My lad, thou must bring me a pair of gloves of the finest leather that may be, with two gold laces about the thumb, and a fringe on the top with flews and red silk underneath, that I may draw them through a gold ring, or else I will none of them.'

29th March. ENGLISH PRISONERS IN SPAIN.

A poor mariner is lately returned to England escaped from St. Lucar. This man was one of the company of the *Little Exchange* whereof Captain John Cross was captain, that was taken by the Spaniards. Captain Cross and others were brought to Seville, where they had no allowances in their imprisonment but lived by the good help of the under-jailor who is an Englishman. There the English priests, Parsons, Thorne, and Walpole, that is head of the English college, came daily to persuade them to change their religion, and in the end so prevailed with the Cardinal of Seville that Captain Cross, Duffield, and Boyser, and eleven others were released and brought to the College, where all means were used to reconcile them to the Church of Rome, insomuch that they all reformed and received the sacrament; all but Captain Cross who was sent back to prison. While he was at Seville, seven persons were sent to England to be dispersed.

31st March. MENDOZA'S 'THEORIQUE AND PRACTISE OF WAR.'

The book of the *Theorique and practise of War*, written by Don Bernardino de Mendoza (that was Spanish ambassador here before '88) and published at Antwerp last year is now translated into English by Sir Edward Hoby. He counselleth that provisions or levies of men which are to be made for any manner of war, by sea or land, should be coloured with some different motive whereby no time may be given to the enemy to perceive it by preventing designs with the contrary. By no better means may this be effected than in sending upon such occasions ambassadors to those Kings who are most suspected would oppose, plotting with them treaties of new friendships and good correspondency according to the humour and disposition in which they shall find them, lulling them asleep with such offers as may hold in suspense and at the gaze the more part of the potentates.

'VIRGIDEMIARUM.'

There is entered a book called *Virgidemiarum*, to be in six books; the first three books being toothless satires of matters poetical, academical and moral; the other three not yet ready. Quoth the author:

> 'I first adventure with foolhardy might,
> To tread the steps of perilous despite:
> I first adventure; follow me who list,
> And be the second English Satirist.'

2nd April. THE SOLDIERS IN FRANCE.

The great extremity that our troops endure by reason of the want of money hath caused Sir Thomas Baskerville to lay in pawn all his plate and all the other means that he hath to relieve them. Of late an enterprise was made to surprise Arras upon a vain hope and an uncertain French plot to blow open a port with a petard, assuring themselves by that to have entrance. But at their arrival there the strength of the place with little assistance from the town did frustrate their expectation. Our men had no loss but their toilsome march, though the French lost some few. In the camp the King is taxed for lechery, and Madame Gabrielle accounted cause of all ill-fortune, although every man seeth many nearer causes which cannot be remedied in that broken commonwealth.

5th April. 'CLITOPHON AND LEUCIPPE.'

A book called *The most delectable and pleasant history of Clitophon and Leucippe* is entered, written in Greek by Achilles Stacius an Alexandrian, and now newly translated into English by Mr. William Burton, being dedicated to the Earl of Southampton. Herein is related how Clitophon fell in love with Leucippe of Tyre, and how they fled from Tyre towards Alexandria, but being shipwrecked and separated both lovers endured many chances until they were strangely united in the Temple of Diana at Ephesus.

7th April. SEMINARIES TO BE BANISHED.

Her Majesty hath an intention to banish the seminary priests that are in divers prisons in the realm, and to this end the Attorney and Solicitor General and Mr. Francis Bacon are required to inform themselves what priests are in the prisons within and about the city of London and how far they are to be charged with any matter against the Queen or the State.

8th April. FORCES FOR IRELAND.

The forces that were levied for service in Ireland last October but afterward dismissed to their several counties are again to be viewed and mustered, and sent to the ports of embarkation by the last of this month, being in all 1,900 men, and in addition 560 men levied from the Midland Counties.

10th April. AN ENGLISH PIRACY.

One William Holliday hath behaved in very contemptuous manner towards Mr. Michael Leeman and certain merchant strangers of Holland and Zealand. Some four years since great spoil was made on the seas by a ship called the *Tiger*, whereof this Holliday was owner, and two or three others upon certain ships belonging to merchants of Holland. These spoilers going to the seas without commission carried the goods to Barbary and then sold them; they sank one of the ships, and threw divers of the mariners overboard. Upon complaint whereof to the States of the United Provinces there had arisen some tumult in such sort that, if special care had not been taken, the English merchants there had been in danger of the loss of their goods and lives. Whereupon for satisfaction of the merchants, order was given that such other prize goods as should be brought in by the malefactors and their ships should be stayed and the monies made thereof converted to the satisfaction of the damnified merchants. After this the *Tiger* brought into Plymouth a Spanish carvel laden with ginger, sugar, hides, and some pearl, which by order of the Lord Admiral was seized and Mr. Leeman appointed to repair to Plymouth with a sergeant-at-arms and letters of assistance from the Council. This was done, but the merchants that were spoiled received not above 2s. in the pound towards their losses. Since which time Holliday, in contempt of these proceedings, hath commenced an action of *trouver* against Mr. Leeman for the same goods, and by the deposition of some of the mariners, that then stood indicted for piracy and since are condemned to die, a verdict was passed against Leeman for most part of the goods. The Council have now written to the Lord Chief Justice to take order in this matter.

A Fray in St. Martin's.

This afternoon in the parish of St. Martin's-in-the-Fields two men, called Langton and Pinkney, exchanged insulting words and began to fight, Langton with a staff, and Pinkney with a rapier until Langton received a mortal wound in the upper part of his right arm and died of it a quarter of an hour after.

13th April. Two Ladies-in-Waiting punished.

The Queen hath of late used the fair Mistress Bridges with words and blows of anger, and she with Mistress Russell were put out of the Coffer Chambers. They lay three nights at the Lady Stafford's, but are now returned again to their wonted waiting. The cause of their displeasure is said to be their taking of physic, and one day going privately through the Privy Galleries to see the playing at *ballon*. Some days since the Earl of Essex kept his chamber three days with a great heat in the mouth which happened by overmuch exercise at *ballon*.

THE MARINERS TO BE STAYED.

The mariners that were appointed to be at Chatham by the 25th of this month are now to be stayed till the midst of May.

HOUNDS FOR THE FRENCH KING.

The servants of the Earl of Shrewsbury carry over to France fourteen or fifteen couple of hounds and certain greyhounds that are sent to the French King.

16th April. COURT NEWS.

There is news come out of Ireland that Tyrone hath yet put off the parley for fifteen days more. The two thousand foot are gone, and the Lord Burgh follows. This day he met Sir Oliver Lambart by the garden door within the Court; and asked him if he did not know him, and bid him put off his hat. The other said he owed him not that duty in respect of his usage of him. My Lord offered to pluck off his hat, which the other resisted and willed him to call to mind the place where he was. 'I do,' said my Lord, 'else would I have thrust a rapier through thee ere this'; and so they parted. About dinner time they met again at my Lord of Essex's, where my Lord Burgh secretly told him that he saw he braved him and bid him look to himself, for he would disgrace him. 'So I will,' said the other.

17th April. THE CLOTH TRADE.

The Merchants Adventurers complain that divers disordered persons, not free of the Company of Merchants Adventurers, trade with English cloths and other woollen goods to Hamburgh in Germany as well as to Flushing and Amsterdam in the Low Countries, contrary to the special privilege. Hereby in the markets of Stade and Middleburgh, being the established mart towns, there is great loss to the Merchants Adventurers and the abating and pulling down of price of cloths, a thing much prejudicial to the woolgrowers and clothmakers of the realm. The customers are now required to take bonds of every person shipping woollen commodity in other than the Adventurers' ships that they shall land the same at Stade or Middleburgh and not elsewhere.

THE NEW LORD CHAMBERLAIN.

This afternoon the Lord Hunsdon had the White Staff given him and thereby made Lord Chamberlain; and the Lords being in Council, her Majesty sent him to them, where he was sworn Councillor and signed many letters thereupon.

A DECEITFUL PRACTICE.

One Ross, pretending himself to be servant to the Earl of Essex, with a counterfeit warrant in the names of the Council apprehended a certain Francis Barker in the county of Kent and brought him up to London, where he kept him certain days, shifting him up and down from place to place, and taking from him £47 in money and a gelding.

18th April. THE LORD BURGH TO BE DEPUTY IN IRELAND.

The Lord Burgh, that was Governor in the Brille, is now to be Lord Deputy in Ireland to reform the many great abuses in that country. He shall inquire of the state of religion, for notorious negligence is reported, and even in the English Pale multitudes of parishes are destitute of incumbents and teachers, and in the great towns of assembly numbers not only forbear to come to the church but are willingly winked at to use all manner of Popish ceremonies. Many captains in remote parts have untruly informed the Muster Master of their full numbers. To reform this abuse he shall consult with such of the Council as have no interest in these abuses, and appoint commissioners to take monthly musters in all remote places; which will be a hard matter seeing the great corruption used herein.

19th April. THE EARL OF ESSEX AND SIR R. CECIL.

Yesterday Sir Robert Cecil went in a coach with the Earl of Essex to his house, where Sir Walter Ralegh came and they dined together. After dinner they were very private, all three for two hours, where a treaty of peace was confirmed. Sir Walter hath taken upon him to provide victuals for three months for 6,000 men at an allowance of 9d. a man per diem. There is impressed unto him £3,000 a week for six weeks; he shall have Bridewell, Winchester House, and Durham House to be magazines for the victuals. He protesteth that he shall be loser by it, but few are of that opinion besides himself.

21st April. ALL SHIPS STAYED.

There is an order going forth for a general restraint throughout all the ports that no ship, hulk, or other vessel of what burden soever shall be suffered to depart until further notice.

23rd April. ST. GEORGE'S DAY.

This day, the Court being at Whitehall, great solemnity for the Order of the Garter was observed. First, morning service in the chapel, with solemn music and voices, Dr. Bull playing; the Lords of the Order were present, who both in coming and retiring made three congées to the seat royal and so departed. Some hour after, they came again before her Majesty with all the officers of arms; and then came the Queen, with three ladies carrying her train, which were the Countess of Warwick, the Countess of Northumberland, and the Countess of Shrewsbury; the Earl of Bedford carrying the Sword before her, six pensioners carrying a rich canopy over her head. Then, after several congées there was short service, the clergy all being in their rich copes, with princely music of voices, organs, cornets, and sackbuts, with other ceremonies and music. Five new knights of the Order are made, being the Duke of Wirtenberg (that was formerly the Count Mompelgard), the Lord Hunsdon, the Lord Mountjoy, the Lord Thomas Howard and Sir Henry Lee. The Earl of Essex was exceeding earnest with his companions for Sir Henry, which he obtained. Then had he much ado to bring the Queen to give her consent to him.

28th April. THE STAYED SHIPS.

The Merchant Adventurers have made humble suit that the ten ships ready laden might be permitted to go on their voyage, and will enter bond for their return by the end of May, unless hindered by contrariety of wind. This is allowed, seeing that there are ten ships with corn daily expected; also the five ships for Middleburg.

DESERTERS FROM THE IRISH FORCES.

Of 47 men that were levied in Staffordshire for service in Ireland 10 are run away, and of the 47 men of Derbyshire 18, who are returned to their counties.

29th April. DANGERS FROM FRANCE.

The Cardinal of Austria is now reported to have drawn great numbers of the forces out of the Low Countries towards the seaside and coast of Boulogne, a matter greatly to be regarded, which may breed great danger to the realm because it is uncertain what attempt he may make with this great preparation.

In Essex, therefore, Kent and Sussex, 600 are being mustered and trained to be ready on any occasion.

30th April. NEW PLAYS.

The new plays at the Rose Theatre this month are *Five Plays in One*, *A French Comedy* and *Uther Pendragon.*

1st May. A NOTABLE OUTRAGE ON A CORPSE.

In April last there died at Tonnerre in Burgundy one Monsieur de Lanne, a Doctor of Medicine, of the reformed religion, one that all right-minded men respected. Whereupon his widow asked of the Administrator of the Hospital that he might be buried in the burial ground there where several Protestants had already been buried. This was granted, but the Dean of the parish of Notre Dame protested, and for avoiding occasion of complaint the widow determined that the body should be buried by night. But when in the evening the friends of the dead man came together, news was brought that the monks of the Hospital would resist the burial by force, and that the Dean had assembled many lewd persons about the town to prevent it. It was agreed therefore by the widow that the body should be buried elsewhere, and so her friends departed, leaving only two women with the corpse in the house.

Being disappointed thereby, about midnight the Dean and his mob broke into the house, dragged the corpse into the market-place up to the pillory, broke open the coffin, wounded the body with pointed sticks, put cards in one hand and dice in the other, and would have set the body in the pillory had they not been prevented by some standers-by. They then took to insulting the body, threatening to throw it into the river.

In the morning the officers of the town, that had for the most part been of the faction of the League, had the body taken up by some peasants and buried without more ado in a dunghill, nor would they even allow it to be first returned into the coffin. Then they went back to the widow and demanded payment for their trouble, threatening that otherwise they would dig it up again and throw it to the dogs to eat. Nor would they allow any justice to be done to this woman without appealing to the King.

6th May. DISCONTENTS IN THE COUNTIES.

In the counties are many discontents by reason of this present scarcity. In the confines of Kent and Sussex divers have carried themselves in very tumultuous sort, inciting others with lewd words to commit outrage; wherefore it is purposed to renew the office of Marshal in the counties. In Norfolk, under pretence of need, some have entered into conspiracy to raise tumults and have begun with taking grain from the right owners by force and violence. In Sussex, Sir Thomas Palmer that was commanded a short while since to put in readiness 600 men was so slack and backward that the service was not executed, and is very sternly rebuked by the Council. At Hadley in Suffolk the Council have caused the Sheriffs to prohibit the officers of the town from making stage plays at the Whitsun holidays, for they doubt what inconveniences may follow thereon, especially at this time of scarcity when disordered people of the common sort are apt to misdemean themselves. Moreover the stage prepared is to be plucked down, and the officers informed that they are to obey this order as they will answer it at their perils.

9th May. MR. THOMAS ARUNDEL.

Mr. Thomas Arundel (that was made Count of the Empire) is again in close imprisonment for that of late he would have sent one Smallman, a soldier, to the Emperor's court that he might show his pedigree, whereby the Emperor should see that he had not bestowed that title of honour upon any base man. This Smallman is reported to be a dangerous man, one that hath been in Rome.

MUSTERS AGAINST INVASION.

The Commissioners for musters are ordered to have in readiness from the counties able men to the number of 6,000 to have special training to defend the realm and withstand the enemy that are now prepared to attempt some dangerous enterprise on the realm.

11th May. THE MAYOR OF CHESTER COMMENDED.

The Mayor of Chester is very highly commended by the Council for his diligence and discretion used in the transporting of soldiers to Ireland, for he so governed the matter of payment that he not only gave good satisfaction to all parties but yet saved some good part of her Majesty's charge. If others upon such occasions would use the like care, the Council would be less troubled in giving directions, and the Queen's service much better ordered than it is.

A Play of Humours.

To-day there is a new play of humours at the Rose, called *An Humorous Day's Mirth*, and written by Chapman. This play is of an old Count that hath a young Puritan to wife, who by a certain gallant is tempted to the Court and there mocked, so that she goeth back to her husband who would have hanged himself in jealous humour. There is a young gull who hath this humour in his manner of taking acquaintance, that he will speak to the very word of compliment after him of whom he takes acquaintance.

16th May. English Pirates.

There is a warrant for the arrest of a certain Captain Thomas Venables and his complices that in the ship *Dolphin* took by violence from the *John of Waterford* sundry parcels of goods and merchandises of good value belonging to the Earl of Ormond.

20th May. The Queen angry.

There hath been much ado between the Queen and the Lords of the Council about the preparation for sea; some of them urging the necessity of setting it forward for her safety, but she opposing it by no danger appearing towards her anywhere, and that she will not make wars but arm for defence, understanding how much of her treasure is spent already in victual only for ships and soldiers at land. She is extremely angry with them that make such haste in it, and at the Lord Treasurer for suffering it, seeing no greater occasion. Nor reason nor persuasion by some of the Lords could prevail but that she hath commanded order to be given to stay all proceeding, and sent Lord Thomas word that he should not go to sea.

23rd May. MacHugh slain.

News is come from Ireland that the traitor Feogh MacHugh is slain at Glynnes on the 8th, for our foot falling into that quarter where he lay, and coming several ways on him, he was so hardly followed that he was run out of breath and forced to take a cave where a sergeant to Captain Lee first lighted on him; and the fury of the soldiers was so great that he could not be brought away alive. Thereupon the sergeant cut off MacHugh's head with his sword and presented it to the Deputy. His head and carcase are now brought in to Dublin, to the great comfort and joy of all that are in that province. Many of his followers have been slain. If this blow be as well followed as it is well given, the storm in Leinster will be calmed for a long time and the Ulster rebels, having lost so capital a confederate, will grow to better feeling of their own condition. Sir Calisthenes Brooke, Sir Thomas Maria Wingfield and Sir Richard Trevor are knighted for their services in this action.

THE QUEEN AND THE LADY MARY HOWARD.

The Queen hath of late much annoyance from the Lady Mary Howard, one of her ladies-in-waiting, for as much as she refused to bear her mantle at the hour when her Highness is wont to air in the garden, and on small rebuke did vent such unseemly answer as bred much choler in her Mistress. On other occasion she was not ready to carry the cup of grace during dinner in the Privy Chamber, nor was she attending at the hour of her Majesty's going to prayer. All which doth so much disquiet her Highness that she swore she would no more show her any countenance but out with all such ungracious, flouting wenches; because forsooth she hath much favour and marks of love from the Earl of Essex, which is not so pleasing to the Queen, who doth still much exhort all her women to remain in virgin state, as much as may be. Moreover since the Irish affairs she seemeth more froward toward her women, nor doth she hold them in discourse with such familiar matter, but often chides for small neglects in such wise as to make these fair maids often cry and bewail in piteous sort.

The Lady Howard hath offended also in attiring her own person overfinely, which is rather to win my Lord of Essex than of good will to her Mistress. The lady is possessed with a rich border powdered with gold and pearl, and a velvet suit belonging thereto which hath moved many to envy; nor hath it pleased the Queen who thought it exceeded her own. Wherefore the Queen sent privately and got the lady's rich vesture, which she put on herself and came among the ladies. The kirtle and border were far too short for her Majesty's height and she asked everyone how they liked her new fancied suit. At length she asked the Lady Mary herself if it was not made too short, and ill-becoming; to which the poor lady did consent. 'Why then,' quoth the Queen, 'if it become not me as being too short, I am minded it shall never become thee as being too fine; so it fitteth neither well.' By this sharp rebuke the Lady Howard is abashed and hath not adorned her herewith sithence.

26th May. A New Play.

The Admiral's men to-day played a new play called *The Life and Death of Henry the First.*

27th May. A Debtor's Case.

The Council have written to the Commissioners for such causes on behalf of one Francis Metcalfe, a prisoner in the Fleet. This man for a debt of £7 hath been detained in prison for the space of five years.

30th May. Preparation for an Expedition.

Of those men ordered to be specially trained for the Queen's service 4,000 are now to be set in readiness and shortly to be despatched to London, there being discovered a very urgent cause and fit opportunity to employ them.

2nd June. Mr. Arundel released.

Mr. Arundel is now released, since upon exact and careful examination he is not found guilty of any disloyalty, though this practising to contrive the justification of his vain title, contrary to his duty, is an act of great contempt. Nevertheless, the Queen, out of favour to Sir Matthew his father, hath remitted his punishment; but since his own house is haunted by massing priests he is committed to the care of Sir Matthew. It is not without cause for the State to be jealous of him, seeing by how strait an obligation he hath bound himself to a Prince so nearly allied to the Queen's chiefest enemy, and his own precious valuation of his title, which all other men do hold to be of little worth, doth give cause to believe that his own heart's love must be divided between the Queen and the Emperor.

SIR WALTER RALEGH RESTORED TO HIS PLACE.

Yesterday, the Earl of Essex being absent, Sir Walter Ralegh was brought to the Queen by Sir Robert Cecil. She used him very graciously and gave him authority to execute his place as Captain of the Guard, which he immediately undertook, and swore many men into the places void. In the evening he rode abroad with the Queen and had private conference with her; and now he comes boldly to the Privy Chamber as he was wont. Though this is done in the absence of the Earl yet is it known to be with his liking and furtherance. There is now love and kindness in all things between the Earl and the Lord Treasurer, and all furtherance given to his desires. About twelve days since the Lord Treasurer allowed the passing of a lease that by him was delayed these three years.

3rd June. LANGHAM'S 'GARDEN OF HEALTH.'

Mr. William Langham, practitioner in physic, hath by his long experience gathered together the sundry rare and hidden virtues of all kinds of herbs and plants into a book entitled *The Garden of Health*; all which simples, being plainly described in the book, can be gotten without any cost or labour, the most of them being such as grow in most places and are common among us. And for the better direction of the reader, the simples are set down in the order of the alphabet, with two general tables added, the one containing all the simples in order, the other setting down the names of the diseases and other operations needing these simples for any remedy for the same.

Noteth among many others, these remedies. A fig tied to a bull will make him tame though he be never so wild. The flowers of the bugloss comfort the brain, heart, memory and wit, ingender good blood, and void melancholy, madness and frenzy, and purge also the choler that cometh from heat. For chastity, commendeth *agnus castus*, docks, hemlocks, vervine, woodbine; but to provoke lust, anise, artichoke, carrots, garlick, ginger, mints, mustard, parsnips, radish and others. Briony is good for the rising or suffocating mother. For the hair; black and white helebore is good for worms in the head and falling hair, as also aloes, garlic, leeks, mustard, nettle, oak, walnuts, and others; milsoil maketh it to curl;

box, ivy, marigold, walnuts will cause it to be yellow. Barley, hemp and nettle cause hens to lay. These and many hundreds of others hath Mr. Langham set down.

4th June. ABUSES IN SOMERSET.

Great abuses have been committed in Somerset in the impresting of soldiers to be sent for the defence of Jersey and Guernsey, by the chopping and changing of the soldiers either by bribes or other partial respects, by the loss of arms and furniture, and by the loose dispersal and running away of men that after their imployment should have been returned to their orderly trade and occupations.

8th June. MACHUGH'S HEAD.

The Council have written to the Lord Deputy of Ireland commending the service of Captain Lee in taking away that rebel Feogh MacHugh; but as for the sending over hither of the rebel's head (to make, as it is supposed, the fact of greater note or more acceptable to her Majesty), it would have pleased the Queen better that it should have been kept over there and bestowed among the fragments of heads and carcases of like rebels, for she would not have such ragged Robin Hoods to be regarded so honourably. Nevertheless because the meaning was good the error was less, and therefore the Council will send the head back again by the same messenger.

THE EARL OF ESSEX'S CLEMENCY.

One Chapman of Cunstall in Stafford was this day brought before the Council touching certain unreverend, lewd, scandalous speeches uttered of the Earl of Essex. Which words being proved, it was their Lordships' intention to have ordered him to be punished and to have appointed him to the pillory and to open whipping with loss of his ears had not the Earl prevented their resolution, who would not willingly have suffered the man to have been brought up had he known him to be so base and contemptible as he is. The Earl also signified his desire that the offence might pass for this time without the deserved punishment; and to this the Council assented seeing that Chapman made very humble submission, protesting that he uttered the speeches in great weakness and distemperature of mind after long sickness.

10th June. CALAIS.

A certain man newly come from Calais reporteth the place to be much fortified, a wall of earth and faggots made outside the ditch to the height of fifteen feet, but the old wall allowed to decay. There are 12,000 soldiers of all nations in twelve companies, but scarcity of victuals and mariners. The soldiers having only received a third of a month's pay since October are like to mutiny.

11th June. SIR THOMAS BASKERVILLE DEAD.

Sir Thomas Baskerville is dead in France. He lay sick not past five or six days and died raving; a man that loved not many to show them any extraordinary kindness, and is much taxed for covetousness; he is said to have detained a groat a week from every soldier upon pretence to have money to relieve them when they were sick.

Our troops are now before Amiens which the King besiegeth and in as great a lack of treasure as ever, some captains being five weeks unpaid, all four. The King hearing of their wants hath lent the companies now in the field 2,000 crowns and makes show to esteem better of them than at any time since their coming.

RUMOURS.

There is now great talk of these preparations for a sea voyage but it is not known where or how it shall be employed. The common sort talk of Calais, others of the Isles of the Azores, others that it is to set upon the King of Spain's navy wheresoever they can find it, or to meet with the Indian fleet. The whole number consists of fifteen of the Queen's ships, besides the two Spanish ships taken last year and now new fashioned after the English manner, twenty-two men-of-war of Holland, and twenty-four fly boats and hoys that serve for carriage of men and victuals. They have with them 4,000 pressed men, and 1,200 musketeers that come with Sir Francis Vere out of the Low Countries. The Earl of Essex is General both at sea and land, the Lord Thomas Howard Vice-Admiral and Sir Walter Ralegh Rear-Admiral. The Earl of Southampton, the Lord Mountjoy, and the Lord Rich go as adventurers; other noblemen pretend to go but it is thought they shall not get leave.

12th June. SIR ARTHUR SAVAGE TO COMMAND IN FRANCE.

Now that Sir Thomas Baskerville is dead, Sir Arthur Savage hath the principal charge of the 2,000 soldiers sent into France to aid the French King. He is to take order that as few Irish as possible be retained in his company, and those cassed as soon as may be, though those officers and others that have deserved well may be continued. The sick men shall be sent back forthwith, for it is a mere abuse that her Majesty should pay so many and have the service of so few. He shall not allow strangers to be passed in the musters, except it be two Frenchmen in a company that may be necessary to make any provision or otherwise to be employed on messages.

14th June. TIMOROUS GENTLEMEN.

Three gentlemen of the Isle of Wight recently left their livings there to dwell elsewhere; and, being rebuked for this desertion, they replied that they could dispose of their possessions as they pleased and make choice of their habitations where they listed. They are now very severely warned by the Council that if in a common danger they refuse to stand to the defence of their own and withdraw themselves for their private safety, her Majesty will enter into possession of it. Their ingratitude to her Majesty doth herein notably appear that it pleased her for their defence to send others thither that had no benefit by the Isle, yet they that have part of their possessions and living there would abandon the place and expose it to hazard: whereby they showed the weakness of their minds, unworthy of men fit to dwell in a commonwealth.

ABUSES OVER MUSTERS.

From the counties of Devon, Norfolk, Suffolk, Sussex, Somerset and Oxfordshire complaints of great abuses are reported, as of exacting or taking sums of money or other compositions of divers persons to keep them from being imprested, and in changing or dismissing others for bribes that were levied, also in defrauding the county of arms and furniture.

25th June. THE STATE OF IRELAND.

Ulster is now universally revolted; no part of it is free from hostility against her Majesty and adherence to the capital traitors of Tyrone. In Connaught not one of the six shires is free from revolt; Sir Conyers Clifford with 21½ companies of foot is not strong enough to reduce the rebels to obedience, for his companies are weak and O'Donnell tyrannizeth over most of the people at his pleasure. In Munster two rebels followed by a rabble of loose people stand out, and several murders of English undertakers have been committed, but many of the murderers are cut off. Leinster by the late cutting off of Feogh MacHugh will grow to better terms of settling and conformity, though many of his followers remain.

30th June. NEW PLAYS.

At the Rose this month there are two new plays of *Frederick and Basilia* and *The life and death of Martin Swart.*

2nd July. THE 'WAT' RETURNS.

Sir Walter Ralegh's pinnace the *Wat* is come back safe to the Lizard. The company report well of the climate of Guiana, for though it standeth within the Tropic yet is it temperate enough, insomuch that they lost not a man upon the coast, and one that was sick before he came there was nothing sicker for being there but is come home safe. Of commodities there is great store; whereof they bring examples, as a kind of long hemp, fine cotton wool wherewith the women make a fine thread that will make excellent good fustians or stockings; great store of pitch, sweet gums, West Indian pepper, balsamum, parrots and monkeys. On their return divers whales playing about the pinnace, one of them crossed the stern and going under rubbed her back against the keel, but they sustained no loss thereby.

5th July. SIR ANTHONY SHIRLEY'S RETURN.

Sir Anthony Shirley, that left Plymouth at the end of May 1596 with five ships, is returned.

Not long after starting, being off Cape Verde, the General fell exceeding sick, and being hopeless of life and his company all dismayed and comfortless, he called his captains, masters and officers to him, and having his memory perfect made a very pithy and brief speech to them. He said that as they were Christians and all baptized and bred up under one and the true faith, so they should live together like Christians in the fear and service of God; and as they were subjects of our most excellent

Sovereign and had vowed obedience unto her, so they should tend all their courses to the advancement of her dignity and the good of their country, and not to enter into any base or unfit actions. And because they came for his love into this action that for his sake they would so love together, as if he himself were still living with them, and that they would follow as their chief commander him whom under his own hand he would give commission to succeed him. All which with solemn protestation they granted to obey.

From this contagious filthy place they directed their course for S. Tome, but being by no means able to double the shoals of Madrabomba they were enforced to bear up and chose another course, for the men fell sick, and the water falling from heaven did stink and in six hours turned to maggots where it fell, either among their clothes or in wads of oakum. They departed therefore for the Isles of Cape Verde and landed upon the Isle of St. Iago, and here the General happily began to recover. And there they entered upon and captured the city of St. Iago, a very strong place, but being within they were so powerfully assaulted by the Portugals that they lost in the first assault eighty men; so that after two days they were forced to depart the town and make for the ships, having lost many men.

Thence they sailed to an isle called Fuego where there is a very high hill which continually burneth. Arriving at Dominica the 17th October with all the men sick and feeble they found two hot baths wherein the weak were greatly comforted, and in a month all made well again. From here they coasted until they came to the town of St. Martha where the Spaniards yielded to them, but could afford no ransom, only they took thence their ordnance and a prisoner lost there by Sir Francis Drake. Thence to Jamaica, a marvellous fertile island.

After other ill chances and in want of victuals, at last they shaped their course for Newfoundland, arriving there the 15th June, not having one hour's victuals to spare; and so after nine days they returned to England.

Mr. William Parker's Voyage.

With Sir Anthony is also come in Mr. William Parker, who at his own charges sailed from England in November last in the

Prudence, a tall ship of 120 tons, and a bark called the *Adventure*, with Captain Henn, having one hundred men in his company. In March he met with Sir Anthony Shirley at the Isle of Jamaica and went in his company till they reached Truxillo where they parted.

Mr. Parker then set his course for Cape de Cotoche on the East part of Yucatan, until he came to Cape Desconoscido. Here he put fifty-six of his men into a *periago* or Indian canoe, and leaving his ship six leagues from the town of Campeche, at 3 o'clock in the morning he landed hard by the monastery of San Francisco and took the town of Campeche, with the Captain and the *alcade*, finding therein 500 Spaniards; and in two towns close adjoining 8,000 Indians. The multitude of the Spaniards which had fled in the first assault by ten o'clock in the morning assembling together, renewed their strength and set furiously upon Mr. Parker and his men, insomuch that six were slain, and Mr. Parker himself was shot under the left breast with a bullet that yet lieth in the chine of his back.

Being thus put into shifts, they devised on a sudden a new stratagem; for having divers of the townsmen prisoners, they tied them arm in arm together and placed them instead of a barricado to defend them from the fury of the enemies' shot. And so with ensign displayed, taking with them their six dead men, they retired with more safety to the haven, where they took a frigate which rode ready fraught with the King's tribute in silver and other commodities, and brought it and the cannon to the *Prudence*. They took also a town of 300 or 400 Indians called Sebo, where they found champeche wood (good to dye withal), wax and honey. This done they left the coast and turned up to Cape de Cotoche again, but the *Adventure* with Captain Henn and thirteen of the men was taken by two frigates of war, whom the Spaniards afterward executed. After they had stayed five weeks upon that coast they shaped course for Havannah, and returning by the Isle of Bermuda, crossed over to the bank near Cape Race, and thence sailing for England fell in with Sir Anthony and reached Plymouth on the 3rd of this month.

6th July. A PROCLAMATION AGAINST INORDINATE APPAREL.

The great inconveniences that grow and daily increase in the realm by the ordinate excess in apparel have again caused her Majesty to make strait proclamation that the laws be duly executed. In this present time of difficulty the decay and lack of hospitality appears in the better sort in all counties, principally occasioned by the immeasurable charges and expenses which they are put to in superfluous apparelling their wives, children, and families; the confusion also of degrees in all places being great where the meanest are as richly apparelled as their betters, and the pride such inferior persons take in their garments, driving many for their maintenance to robbing and stealing by the highway. It is now laid down very exactly what stuffs may be worn by gentlemen and ladies in their several degrees.

SOLDIERS FOR PICARDY.

Seven hundred soldiers are to be sent as a supply for the forces in Picardy, to be gathered from the soldiers that were levied to serve in the voyage of the Earl of Essex but are now to be returned because that so many offer themselves voluntarily. The Lord Mayor is to make a privy search and to prest so many of the soldiers as he shall find new returned and such like vagrant persons of able body.

7th July. DELONEY'S 'JACK OF NEWBURY.'

There is a book called *The pleasant history of John Winchcomb in his younger years called Jack of Newbury*, the famous and worthy clothier of England that lived in the days of King Henry the Eighth, written by Deloney and dedicated to all famous cloth-workers of England. Herein is shown how Jack of Newbury was married to the widow of his master, and how she served him; how having become a man of great wealth after his dame's death he married one of his own servants; how he served King Henry; and how a draper in London that owed him money became bankrout, whom Jack found carrying a porter's basket, and set him up again so that he afterwards became an alderman of London.

8th July. THE COMPLAINTS OF THE COUNCIL OF WAR.

The Council of War of the fleet make great complaint that the ships are ill manned because of the monstrous abuse of the press-masters, who have furnished men of all occupations, of whom some did not know a rope and were never out at sea, while they let all the good men go at 20s. a piece. When they looked for a supply in the west, those of Dorsetshire sent not a man but all were either discharged underhand by the press-master or made a jest of the press.

10th July. THE FLEET ENTER PLYMOUTH.

The fleet are all come together safe to Plymouth, though as they were athwart the Bolt, three leagues short of Plymouth, a sudden storm overtook them with infinite lightning and thunder, and great wind, with the night exceeding dark save when the flashes of lightning came. Nevertheless God so blessed them that not so much as a boat miscarried.

12th July. THE FLEET SAILS.

The fleet sailed from Plymouth two days since with a fair wind.

VAGRANTS TO BE IMPRESTED.

The sheriffs and justices of Middlesex, Surrey and Kent are now bidden to aid the Lord Mayor to levy the 700 men for Picardy of the masterless men and such as have served in the wars, which will be a great ease and good to the country to be rid of those kind of people. And because they are more narrowly looked into by the provost marshals within the City than in the suburbs, the justices shall confer with the Lord Mayor that search may be made in the City, the suburbs and the counties at one time. Moreover standing watches shall be kept for the apprehending of masterless men, soldiers and vagrant persons, and as many as shall be taken shall be bestowed in Bridewell.

16th July. THE VAGRANTS.

Up to this time the Lord Mayor hath taken but eighty men, for the most part base persons and without apparel. It is not the intention of the Council that the City should be at charge to apparel them, but since the Lord Mayor may think it very unmeet to send men over to serve in the wars in such naked sort, they pray him to take order that the men may be furnished with such apparel as is necessary both in regard of the men and the honour of the realm, seeing they are to be sent over into a foreign country.

18th July. THE LORD MAYOR REBUKED.

The Lord Mayor is rebuked by the Council because, when he received direction to take up masterless men, he, as it seems, would only apportion to the City to the number of 100, and so that there might be fewer of this kind of people found in the City, he published abroad the directions given him by the Council in order to drive them out of the City into the counties adjoining. These proceedings are misliked, and the Council again require him to make up the number of 250 or else he shall be required to answer his backwardness before them.

20th July. THE FLEET DRIVEN BACK.

News is come that the fleet having been buffeted for four days continuously is driven back to port by the great and contrary tempests, but safe. My Lord of Essex is at Falmouth, Sir Walter Ralegh at Plymouth. So great was the storm that the beams, knees and stanching of Sir Walter's ship were shaken well nigh asunder, and on Saturday night they thought to yield themselves up to God, having no way to work that offered any hope, the men wasted with labour and watching, and the ship so open, her bulkhead rent, and her brick cook-room shaken to powder. Many of the gentlemen and the knights are returned extreme weak and dangerously sick, among them being Sir Ferdinando Gorges, the Sergeant Major, and Sir Carew Reynolds, captain of the *Foresight*. The ships are now repairing, but much of the victual is spoiled, and water lost by leaking of the casks; moreover the beer carried aboard the victual ships is found to be very unsavoury by the great abuse of the victuallers and London brewers, as well for their careless brewing as for the unseasonable stinking casks.

22nd July. THE EARL OF ESSEX AT PLYMOUTH.

The Lord General with his ships is now come to Plymouth and joined with Sir Walter Ralegh, being dismayed even to death by their mischances. My Lord was much aided in these distresses by the Admiral of the Low Countries.

23rd July. THE POLISH AMBASSADOR.

There lately arrived an ambassador from Poland, a gentleman of excellent fashion, wit, discourse, language and person, and the Queen was possessed that his negotiation tended to a proposition of peace. Her Majesty in respect that his father, the Duke of Finland, had so much honoured her, besides the liking she had of the gentleman's comeliness and qualities brought to her by report, resolved to receive him publicly in the Presence Chamber, where most of the Earls and noblemen about the Court attended, and made it a great day. He was brought in attired in a long robe of black velvet, well jewelled, and came to kiss her Majesty's hands where she stood under the state, whence he straight retired ten yards off her, and then with a strange countenance began his oration aloud in Latin.

The effect of his speech was that the King had sent him to put her Majesty in mind of the ancient confederacies between the Kings of Poland and England; that never a monarch in Europe did willingly neglect their friendship; that he had ever friendly received her merchants and subjects of all quality; that she had suffered his to be spoiled without restitution, not for lack of knowledge of the violence but out of mere injustice, not caring to minister remedy, notwithstanding many particular petitions and letters received. To confirm her disposition to avow these courses (violating both the law of nature and nations), because there were quarrels between her and the King of Spain, she took upon her by mandate to prohibit him and his countries, assuming to herself thereby a superiority not tolerable over other princes; which he was determined not to endure, but rather wished her to know that, if there were no more than the ancient amity between Spain and him, it was no reason why his subjects should be impeded, much less now when straight obligations of blood had so conjoined him with the illustrious house of Austria; and concluding that if her Majesty would not reform it, he would.

The Queen being much moved to be so challenged in public, especially so much against her expectation, after a short pause, answered him extempore in Latin. The words of her beginning were these: '*Expectavi Legationem, mihi vero querelam adduxisti*'; and continuing to this effect: 'Is this the business the King has sent you about? Surely I can hardly believe that if the King himself were present, he would have used such language; for if he should, I must have thought that being a King not of many years, and that *non de iure sanguinis sed iure electionis, immo noviter electus*, he may haply be uninformed of that course which his father and ancestors have taken with us, and which peradventure shall be observed by those that shall live to come after us. And as for you, although I perceive you have read many books to fortify your arguments in this case, yet I am apt to believe that you have not lighted upon the chapter that prescribes the form to be used between kings and princes; but were it not for the place you hold, to have so publicly an imputation thrown upon our justice, which as yet never failed, we would answer this audacity of yours in another style. And for the particulars of your negotiations, we will appoint some of our Council to confer with you, to see upon what ground this clamour of yours hath his foundation.'

24th July. THE POLISH AMBASSADOR.

The merchants that trade to Danzic or other parts in the East Countries forbear all offices of ceremony towards the Polish ambassador, as of visitation, sending presents or whatsoever of the like gratification, until it is resolved on the answer to be given him.

28th July. THE PLAYHOUSES ORDERED TO BE PLUCKED DOWN.

The Lord Mayor and Aldermen have again petitioned the Council for the present stay and final suppression of stage plays at the Theatre, Curtain, Bankside and all other places, alleging four reasons in particular.

Firstly, they corrupt youth, containing nothing but unchaste matters and ungodly practices which impress the very quality and corruption of manners which they represent, contrary to the rules and art prescribed for them even among the heathen, who used them seldom and at set times and not all the year long.

Secondly, they are the ordinary places for vagrant persons, masterless men, thieves, horse-stealers, whoremongers, coseners, connycatchers, contrivers of treason and other dangerous persons to meet together and to make their matches, which cannot be prevented when discovered by the governors of the City, for that they are out of the City's jurisdiction.

Thirdly, they maintain idleness in persons with no vocation and draw prentices and other servants from their ordinary work, and all sorts from resort to sermons and other Christian exercises, to the great hindrance of trades and profanation of religion.

Fourthly, in time of sickness many having sores and yet not heartsick take occasion to walk abroad and hear a play, whereby others are infected and themselves also many times miscarry.

In answer to this petition the Council direct that not only shall no plays be used in London during this summer, but that the Curtain and Theatre in Shoreditch and the playhouses on the Bankside shall be plucked down, and present order taken that no plays be used in any public place within three miles of the City till Allhallow tide. Likewise the magistrates shall send for the owners of the playhouses and enjoin them to pluck down quite the stages, galleries and rooms and so to deface them that they may not again be employed to such use.

A LEWD PLAY.

Much offence also is caused by a play called *The Isle of Dogs*, full of seditious and slanderous matter, written by Nashe and Jonson, and played by my Lord of Pembroke's men at the Swan. Nashe is fled away, but Spencer, Shaa and Jonson (who also acted in the play) are apprehended and committed to prison. Playing is now stayed.

29th July. TROUBLES ON THE BORDER AND IN IRELAND.

There is almost hourly complaint of devastation upon the Scottish Border, wherefore the Queen hath commanded that those principal gentlemen of the Border, as the Witheringtons, the Selbys and others, that are with the fleet at Plymouth shall be sent back.

In Ireland my Lord Burgh hath taken the fort at Blackwater on the 14th in a skirmish between some of the traitors' horse and foot; but his horse, led by Captain Turner, the Sergeant Major, engaged themselves too far into a wood so that he and nine others were slain. My Lord recovered the bodies, made good the place and killed 200 hard upon Tyrone's own camp, who hath 5,000 men near Duncannon. The place was well defended, as they had cast up sundry trenches and laid pikes in the ford, but my Lord led the vanguard himself and was the second man inside the fort.

2nd August. LORD HOWARD'S SHIPS RETURN.

The ships of Lord Thomas Howard are now returned safe to Plymouth, having been separated in the storm that drove back my Lord of Essex.

7th August. THE PICARDY FORCES DELAYED.

The two hoys that were to transport 400 men under command of Captain Henry Poore have for some days been delayed by contrariety of winds.

13th August. A PROCLAMATION CONCERNING THE SCOTTISH BORDER.

A proclamation is published commanding those that live on the Border to live in peace and quietness and to offer no manner of incursion, stealth or injury, since the King of Scots is desirous to yield satisfaction for the injuries committed by his subjects. Nevertheless if any offence shall be offered by the opposites which shall not presently be satisfied according to the laws of the frontier, the Queen will not only leave her subjects to their liberty of just revenge, but will further enable them with extraordinary powers. The King of Scots proposeth likewise to inform his subjects of this determination of the Queen.

17th August. A MALICIOUS MAYOR.

Of late the Mayor of Wareham, under colour of a warrant from the Deputy Lieutenant for the impresting of certain soldiers, to serve a private grudge did imprest one Richard Berd, a man of 60 years old and one that hath borne office of Mayor in that town, and reputed a subsidy man.

19th August. THE FLEET AGAIN SAILS.

Two days since the fleet again set forth from Plymouth, but much abated from the first assembly; for the former violent tempests much cooled and battered the courage of many of our young gentlemen, who, seeing that the winds and sea have affinity neither with London delicacy nor Court bravery, secretly retire themselves home, forgetting either to bid their friends farewell or to take leave of their General.

20th August. THE ALMSHOUSE AT STAMFORD.

The Lord Treasurer hath caused to be published the articles drawn up for the order and government of the hospital for a warden and twelve poor men that he hath founded at Stamford in Northampton; amongst which articles be these:

None to be named except those that have dwelt for seven years within seven miles of the Borough of Stamford, nor that is under 30 years of age, or hath a certainty of living of 53s. 4d. by the year, or is known to be diseased of any leprosy, or of the pox known as the French pox, or of any lunacy, or be a common drunkard, barretor, or infamous for theft, adultery, or the like. And any that after their choice shall fall into such infirmities of infectious diseases, or be infamed and convinced of such notable vices, shall be displaced. Nor shall any of these twelve poor men in alehouses or other places play at cards, dice or any unlawful game.

Everyone of them shall resort in their livery gowns to Common Prayer every Sunday, Wednesday, Friday and holy day to St. Martin's Church at morning and evening prayer; neither shall any be absent without just cause notified to the Vicar, and allowed by him; and for every default not excusable, the Parish Clerk shall have 6d. out of the wages allowed to the poor man.

There shall be paid to them every Sunday after evening prayer, to the Warden of the Hospital 3s., and to every other of the poor men 2s. 4d.

Upon the first Sunday of every quarter of the year, the Vicar shall assemble them together in the church before evening prayer, and severing them asunder shall hear them say the Lord's Prayer, and the Creed, and to answer to the Commandments. And he that shall not be able to say the same, after fourteen days' space given him to learn them, shall be avoided from his room. For this labour the Vicar to have 5s. every such Sunday, and the Parish Clerk 12d. for attending on the Vicar.

Upon this same Sunday, if the Lord of Burleigh or his lady keep house there, the poor men shall dine together at one table in the hall, and there receive two messes of meat, every mess being of two dishes, one with pottage and boiled meat, the other of roast; but if it be a fasting day then shall the messes be of white meat and fish. And if the Lord of Burleigh be absent, then each shall receive 4d.

For the maintenance of this almshouse, the Lord Burleigh giveth an annuity of £100 out of his lands called Cliff Park.

21st August. INGROSSERS.

Although Almighty God hath mercifully withdrawn His heavy hand wherewith we were deservedly punished by an universal scarcity through the unseasonable weather and now yieldeth us a change to the great comfort of all sorts of people, yet are there seen a number of wicked people, more like to wolves and cormorants than natural men, that most covetously seek to hold up the late great prices of corn and all other victuals by ingrossing the same into their private hands, bargaining beforehand for corn and in some part for grain growing, and for butter and cheese before it be brought to ordinary markets. The sheriffs shall therefore send up to the Council the names of all such; and for that in certain counties men of good livelihood and in estimation of worship enrich themselves by such ingrossings, the sheriffs shall seek to reform them, not only with sharp reprehensions but also certify their names, and thereby avoid the just offence of the inferior sort which cannot but be grieved to see such corruption of the better sort suffered without restraint.

22nd August. A BOOK ON CHEATING.

There is a book called *Mihil Mumchance, His discovery of the art of Cheating in false dice play and other unlawful games*, showing also divers new devices of cosenage practised at fairs and markets, with many deceitful practices used by bad and lewd women. At fairs and markets there are some who, attiring themselves in mean attire, will buy a piece of very fine lawn or holland, worth £5 or £6, bound up very handsomely, with another bundle bound up after the same manner but within stuffed with nothing but old rags and such trash. These bundles the cheater will carry till he meeteth with some simple countryman that seemeth to have store of crowns, to whom very secretly, as if he had gotten the lawn by stealth, he will proffer it at half its worth. The simple countryman being covetous of a good pennyworth bargains with him, and gives all the money in his purse, which is not above 40s. or 50s. Then the cheater having got the money pockets it up and bobs the poor man with the counterfeit bundle of rags, reserving the other bundle still to himself.

These cheaters have a treasurer, a very trusty secret friend, that whensoever there cometh any jewels or treasure to their share the present sale whereof might discover the matter, then he will take it in pawn and make out a bill of sale as if things were done in good order and dealing ; so that whensoever the cheater shall seek to make money of the pawn, if any question arise, he showeth a fair bill of sale for his discharge. Another help they have that of every purse which is cleanly conveyed, a rateable portion is duly delivered to the treasurer's hands, that whensoever by some misadventure any of them happen to be laid in prison this common stock may serve to satisfy the party grieved, thereby to save them from the gallows.

29th August. SHAKESPEARE'S 'RICHARD THE SECOND.'

Mr. William Shakespeare's play of *The Tragedy of Richard the Second* that was publicly acted by the Lord Chamberlain's men is being printed, but without that scene of the deposing of King Richard.

6th September. AN AMBASSADOR RECEIVED FROM DENMARK.

To-day Mr. Arnold Whitfield, Chancellor of the realm of Denmark, with his assistant, the Court being at Theobalds, had audience before the Queen, to whom they made certain requests which her Majesty answered without pause. The first, that the league and amity between the Queen and the late King should be continued to the new King, now newly adopted and crowned. The second was that it would please the Queen that the King his master might make a motion of peace between her Majesty and the King of Spain, and if he found the parties thereto addicted, to proceed further for the effecting thereof. To which her Majesty replied that she thought the King his master was too young to know the cause of the breach of the league between her and Spain, and as it was not broken by her consent, so it should not be sued nor sought by her, nor any in her behalf. 'For,' said she, 'know now, and be it known to the King your master, and all Kings, Christian or heathen, that the Queen of England hath no need to crave peace, for I assure you that I never endured one hour of fear since my first coming to my Kingdom and subjects.'

This being her Majesty's birthday the ambassador took occasion to say that sith it had pleased God on this day to glorify the world with so gracious a creature, he doubted not that the King should have an happy answer of his requests. 'I blame you not,' answered her Majesty, 'to expect a reasonable answer, and a sufficient; but you may think it a great miracle that a child born at four o'clock this morning should be able to answer so wise and learned a man as you are, sent from so great a Prince as you be, about so great and weighty affairs you speak of, and in an unknown tongue, by three o'clock in the afternoon.'

15th September. SLANDERS AGAINST THE LORD MAYOR.

A slanderous report is of late raised that the Lord Mayor hath caused the price of corn, that began to fall, to be enhanced to a higher rate, and that having brought into the Thames certain corn he kept up the market that he might sell his corn at a higher rate. The Queen being much offended at these reports now causeth a proclamation to be published, not only clearing the good name of the Lord Mayor, but showing that the grain was brought hither by his providence, whereof great numbers of poor people have been sustained in this time of dearth. Moreover, if any shall hereafter be found to disperse this or any other like untrue report, some severe punishment shall be inflicted on the offender, to the example of all others that for private malice and without just cause shall presume to defame any public person who shall be appointed under her Majesty for the good government of her people.

16th September. NEWS OF THE FLEET.

There is a gentleman come from my Lord of Essex with news that meeting with a stormy northerly wind as soon as they had doubled the South Cape, they were put off sixty or eighty leagues towards the Azores, and the wind so continuing, and fresh water lacking, they go for the Islands, to lie for the carracks and West Indian ships.

20th September. SIR JOHN NORRIS DEAD.

News is come that Sir John Norris is dead in Ireland, to the Queen's grief. He is succeeded as President of Munster by his brother Sir Thomas.

CONDEMNED PRISONERS.

There are at this time 28 persons lying in prisons condemned to be executed, 19 being men and 9 women; of these the Queen is pleased to pardon 8 men and 8 women.

22nd September. THE QUEEN'S LETTER TO THE LADY NORRIS.

Upon the news of Sir John Norris's death, the Queen wrote to the Lady Norris, his mother, in these terms: 'If it be true that society in sorrow works diminution, we do assure you, by this true messenger of our mind, that nature can have stirred no more dolorous affection in you as a mother for a dear son, than gratefulness and memory of his services past hath wrought in us his Sovereign apprehension of our miss of so worthy a servant. But now that nature's common work is done, and he that was born to die hath paid his tribute, let that Christian discretion stay the flux of your immoderate grieving, which hath instructed you both by example and knowledge that nothing of this kind hath happened but by God's divine Providence.' And at the top of the letter her Majesty wrote these words: 'Mine own Crow, harm not thyself for bootless help; but show a good example to comfort your dolorous yokefellow.'

23rd September. THE GOVERNOR OF DUNKIRK TAKEN.

Some of the garrison of Ostend have taken the Governor of Dunkirk and brought him prisoner to Sir Edward Norris. Sir Henry Palmer is now sent in person to bring the Governor over to England in all haste and to lodge him in Dover Castle.

24th September. MACHUGH'S HEAD.

Some days since two boys going to fetch their cattle from Enfield Chase found there a man's head. Hereupon, enquiry being made, Mr. John Dewrance, whose field it was, declareth that about a month since one John Lane brought this head to his house in Enfield, saying that it was the head of MacHugh, that arch traitor of Ireland, who was slain by Captain Thomas Lee and his company. Lane brought the head into England to the Earl of Essex, who referred him to Mr. Secretary for payment, but seeing that the head money had already been paid in Ireland Lane was told that he might bestow the head where he would; and having it with him he made proffer to leave it with Mr. Dewrance, who would no wise permit it nor suffer it be buried in his garden. Lane therefore gave the head to his boy to bury in Enfield Chase, but the boy set it upon a tree.

27th September. A PROCLAMATION AGAINST PROVIDING THE SPANISH KING WITH MUNITION.

There is issued a proclamation warning those foreigners that send or carry with Spain or Portugal any manner of grain, or victuals, or any provisions for building of ships of war, or any kind of munitions, that her Majesty will not only authorise her own Admirals and Captains of her ships of war, but will also approve her subjects to impeach and arrest such ships.

29th September. THE SPANISH DANGER CEASES.

Now that the season is so far advanced there would appear to be no danger of an attempt of the enemy against the realm; wherefore to save the charges the soldiers entertained for the defence of Guernsey and Jersey are to be withdrawn.

8th October. THE PLAYERS RELEASED.

Spencer, Shaa and Jonson, the players that were committed because of the play of *The Isle of Dogs*, are now to be released, from the Marshalsea.

9th October. A DISORDERLY ELECTION.

There hath been no small disorder in the election of those to serve in this forthcoming Parliament as Knights of the Shire for the county of York. On the 3rd October, about 8 o'clock, at the Castle at York the writ of summons for the election was duly read, also a letter sent from the Privy Council for the better direction of the election; proclamation was also made by order of the Archbishop and the Council that no person thither assembled, except he were a freeholder of 40s. per annum above all charges and reprises, should presume to give voice in the election. Which things being done, first were nominated Sir John Stanhope, Sir Thomas Hoby, and Sir John Savile; whereat Sir John Savile caused the sheriff to read out to the freeholders certain statutes to the effect that none should be chosen to that place but such as were resident in the county at the head of the writ. Then Sir John cried out to the people, 'Will you have a Maleverer or a Fairfax?' meaning, as some said, to make knights at his own will or otherwise to distract the voices of the freeholders from the other two nominated.

Hereupon for the space of two hours and more the cries and voices of the people continued confused and diverse for Sir John Stanhope, Sir Thomas Hoby, Sir John Savile and Sir William Fairfax; but for some good space after the first cries, the number for Sir John Stanhope and Sir Thomas Hoby seemed to be more in show by some 600. Afterwards the greater number seemed doubtful, and it was agreed that some indifferent gentleman should be assigned to discern the companies and voices of each part, first by view, and then by trial of the polls for their freehold or residency. Whereupon the companies on each part being severed and divided, the undersheriff with the gentlemen went up into a chamber where they might see the companies and reasonably esteem of the great number of persons; with result that they did esteem those that stood on the hillside for Sir William Fairfax and Sir John Savile (being next the gate) to be more in number than the side for Sir John Stanhope and Sir Thomas Hoby by about 200 persons. But then some of the gentlemen did think that there were on that side citizens and inhabitants of York, women and children and other strangers, not having lawful voices, to the number of 500 or 600. It was therefore agreed that the companies should be further examined by pools upon their corporal oaths.

The undersheriff and the gentlemen triers then proceeded to the gate, whither the sheriff went also and took paper with him, the gentlemen having sticks to take the number of them by scotches or marks. It was further concluded that the company of Sir John Savile, being nearest the gate, should first be tried. The gentlemen and the undersheriff being thus come to the gate, it was agreed to shut the gate and no more to let any in on any side; then that two of the gentlemen triers on either side should nick every score, and that all should be sworn and examined against whom any exceptions should be taken, and that the undersheriff and his man were there for the purpose. So Mr. Wortley (who was of the part of Sir John Stanhope and Sir Thomas Hoby) took a knife and a stick to nick on the scores on his side.

Thereupon the undersheriff commanded the people back from out of the gatestead. Whereat came Sir John Savile on horseback, and called the undersheriff and demanded what he was about; who answered, to proceed to trial by poll according to agreement and law.

Sir John replied, 'Though they would make you an ass, they shall not make me a fool.' He would have no such trial; he would hold what he had; and, after other words, commanded the gate to be opened. The undersheriff replied that it might not be so, for he must do as the law required; to which Sir John answered, 'Open the door or break it open,' and himself pressed forward, so that the gentlemen triers shifted themselves away as well as they could, and two were in danger of their lives. Then also the undersheriff went out with Sir John without staying to proceed, whereby those who stayed behind knew not whether any election had been made or not.

After this, by the space of two hours or more, the knights, gentlemen and freeholders on the part of Sir John Stanhope continued in the castle hall and yard expecting the return of the sheriff; but he would not be found, being with Sir John Savile at dinner. Then Sir John Savile and Sir William Fairfax returned together with the undersheriff, who, first making proclamation of silence, immediately and without any further proceeding did pronounce Sir John Savile and Sir William Fairfax to be the knights lawfully elected; which thing was denied by the other part of Sir John Stanhope and Sir Thomas Hoby.

10th October. THE ART OF BRACHYGRAPHY.

There is a new edition published of *The Art of Brachygraphy*, that is to write as fast as a man speaketh treatably, writing but one letter for a word, including also the order of orthography, for the speedy writing of true English, and the key of caligraphy opening the ready way to write fair, invented by Mr. Peter Bales. This art serveth for an infinite number of uses; the memory is strengthened and as much can be written in one day as in a whole week by other writing; by it you may with speed write out any excellent written book or copy, never yet imprinted, to your private use and benefit; moreover the sermons, lectures and orations of excellent learned men shall hereby be kept, recorded and registered. The method of this brachygraphy is to denote words by single letters, to each letter being added a prick or tittle.

11th October. 'THE TRIMMING OF THOMAS NASHE.'

There is an answer to Nashe's Epistle to Richard Lichfield, the barber of Trinity College in Cambridge (that he wrote in *Have with you to Saffron Walden*), entitled *The Trimming of Thomas Nashe.* Herein Nashe is very straitly trimmed for his many ribaldries and lewd courses of life. Saith that there was a time when Nashe and his fellow Lusher lay in Coldharbour together when they had but one pair of breeches between them both, but not one penny to bless them with; so that by course Lusher wore the breeches one day and went conny-catching for victuals whilst Nashe lay in bed; and the next day Nashe wore the breeches to go and beg, for all the world like two buckets in one well. Taunteth him also with his *Isle of Dogs* for which he was proclaimed by the crier, and deserved the cropping of his ears. Saith that Nashe hath been cast into many prisons and hath polluted them all.

PLAYING RESUMED.

To-day began my Lord Admiral's and my Lord Pembroke's men to play at the Rose after the restraint, the play being *The Spanish Tragedy.*

THE ELECTION AT YORK.

The Council being informed of the contemptuous behaviour of Sir John Savile have required the Archbishop of York to commit him to prison, thereby to notify to the world, not that her Majesty's meaning nor the Council's is to mislike any man to use that freedom for his election which the law doth warrant and discretion requireth, yet, where authority is established as in such a nature the Archbishop and his Council hath, she will not suffer any precedency of contempt to go unpunished for warning to others.

12th October. A PROCLAMATION AGAINST ENGLISH MERCHANTS.

News is come out of Germany that the Emperor by proclamation hath commanded all English merchants to depart the Empire within three months, they and their goods, on pain of confiscation and imprisonment, so that the Merchant Adventurers must needs leave Stade.

14th October. 'POLITEUPHUIA, WIT'S COMMONWEALTH.'

Mr. N. Ling hath completed the book called *Politeuphuia : Wit's Commonwealth* which was compiled by Mr. John Bodenham. Herein are to be found many definitions beginning with that 'Of God' and ending 'Of Hell' and beneath each certain pithy sentences expanding the same ; as 'Of Generals in War,' defined thus : 'Generals are the heads and leaders of armies, and they ought to be great, magnanimous and constant in all their doings ; free from the defects of rashness and cowardice.' Which definition is followed by such sentences as these :

'Unless wise and valiant men be chosen Generals, the old chaos will return and virtue die at the feet of confusion.'

'He that will be a commander in armies, first let him be commanded in the same, for an ambitious soldier will never make a temperate conductor.'

'A General after a battle ended must have a circumspect care how he praiseth one captain more than another.'

There are eight conditions that a general ought to have; to avoid unjust wrongs, to correct blasphemers, to succour innocents, to chastise quarrellers, to pay his soldiers, to defend his people, to provide things necessary, and to observe faith with his enemies.

16th October. HERRINGS TO BE STAYED.

The fishmongers of London making complaint of the dearth of white herrings by reason of the great quantity sent out of the realm to foreign parts, the Mayor of Yarmouth is bidden to stay those ships in the port which are now laden with herrings.

19th October. INGROSSERS AND BUILDERS PUNISHED.

To-day in the Star Chamber, one Francis Parker that hath been an ingrosser these sixteen years and every year carried corn to London in a boat without a licence is fined £500 to the Queen, imprisonment, £20 to the poor, to go to Westminster Hall with papers and to confess his fault. Others are fined £40 with imprisonment.

At the same time one Negoose and others for building cottages in London contrary to the proclamation are fined; one £100, one £40 and another £20; the houses to be destroyed for their base condition and the timber sold for the poor. If any be brothel houses, to burn them standing if it can be done without peril, otherwise to burn them in the fields; and those that are beautiful and spacious edifices to be converted into garners and storehouses.

DELONEY'S 'GENTLE CRAFT.'

Deloney hath written a book in praise of shoemakers called *The Gentle Craft*, showing what famous men have been shoemakers in time past in this land, with their worthy deeds and great hospitality. Relateth the pleasant history of St. Hugh (from whom cometh it that the shoemakers' tools are called St. Hugh's bones); the tale of Crispin and Crispianus; and lastly how Sir Simon Eyre, being first a shoemaker, became in the end Lord Mayor of London through the counsel of his wife, and how he builded Leadenhall.

20th October. 'RICHARD THE THIRD.'

There is to be printed that play acted by the Lord Chamberlain's men called *The Tragedy of King Richard the Third*, being written by Shakespeare, wherein Burbage played the King with great applause.

22nd October. THE LORD ADMIRAL TO BE ADVANCED.

It is said in Court that to-morrow the Lord Admiral shall be created Earl of Nottingham. The heralds have been with him; he hath borrowed my Lord of Pembroke's robes; his coronet is made and his patent is a drawing.

23rd October. THE LORD ADMIRAL ADVANCED.

As the Queen came from the Chapel this day, being Sunday, she created the Lord Admiral Earl of Nottingham. The Earl of Cumberland carried his sword, the Earl of Sussex his cap and coronet. He was brought in by the Earls of Shrewsbury and Worcester. Her Majesty made a speech unto him in acknowledgment of his services, and Mr. Secretary read the Letters Patent aloud, which are very honourable; all his great services *anno* '88 recited, and those lately at Cadiz. He is to take his place *vt Comes de Nottingham*, for so are the words in the patent. Hereby shall he take precedence over the Earl of Essex.

OSTEND THREATENED.

News is lately come of the approach of the enemy unto the town of Ostend, whereby it is supposed that some enterprise is intended. Four companies with Sir Arthur Savage are now to be sent from Picardy for the better security of the town.

24th October. THE PARLIAMENT ASSEMBLES.

This day the Parliament, being her Majesty's ninth Parliament, assembled at Westminster, where many of the knights of the shires, citizens of cities, burgesses of boroughs, and Barons of ports, having made their appearance before the Earl of Nottingham, Lord Steward of the Household, took the Oath of Supremacy seven or eight at a time before him and Sir William Knollys, Sir John Fortescue and Sir Robert Cecil. This done they passed into their own House to await her Majesty's pleasure.

The Queen being then come into the Upper House and set in her chair of estate, the Commons were summoned, and as many as conveniently could admitted. Then Sir Thomas Egerton, the Lord Keeper, by her Majesty's command, declared the cause of the summoning of this present Parliament, and having expressed his insufficiency for that task, spake to this effect:

'You are to enter into a due consideration of the laws, and where you find superfluity to prune and cut off; where defect to supply, and where ambiguity to explain; that they be not burdensome but profitable to the commonwealth. Yet as nothing is to be regarded if due mean be not taken to withstand the professed enemies which seek the destruction of the whole State, this before and above all is to be thought of; for in vain are laws if such prevail as go about to make a conquest of the

Kingdom. Wars heretofore were wont to be made either of ambition to enlarge dominions or of revenge to quit injuries; but this against us is not so. In this the Holy Religion of God is sought to be rooted out, the whole realm to be subdued, and the precious life of her Majesty to be taken away, which hitherto hath been preserved, maugre the Devil, the Pope and the Spanish Tyrant. Her Majesty hath not spared to disburse a mass of treasure and to sell her land for maintenance of her armies by sea and land, whereby, with such small helps as her subjects have yielded, she hath defended and kept safe her dominions from all such forcible attempts as have been made. Which though performed at infinite charge, her Majesty doth notwithstanding hear of nothing more unwillingly than of aids and subsidies from her people. The taxations at this day, howsoever they seem, are nothing so great as heretofore. In the time of Edward the Third, and of those before and after him, the payments of the Commons did far exceed any that have been made since her Majesty's reign; but never cause so great to employ great sums of money as now. To spare now is to spare for those which seek to devour all; and to give is to give to ourselves, her Majesty's part only being carefully to bestow what is delivered into her hands. This war is just; it is in defence of the Religion of God, of our most Gracious Sovereign, and of our natural country, of our wives, our children, our liberties, lands, lives, and whatsoever we have.'

Whereupon the Commons were dismissed to choose the Speaker, who shall be presented on Thursday next. The Commons therefore straightway repaired to their own House, and there being assembled and sitting some space of time very silent, at last Sir William Knollys, the Controller, stood up and spake:

'Necessity constraineth me to break off this silence and to give others cause for speech. According to the usual custom we are to choose our Speaker, and though I am least able and therefore unfit to speak in this place, yet better I deem it to discover my own imperfections than that her most Sacred Majesty's commandment to me delivered should not be fulfilled, or your expectation of this day's work by all our silences be frustrate.'

Having then spoken a little on the necessity for a Speaker, he saith, 'Now because that knowledge doth rest in certainty, I will with the more speed set afoot this motion, deliver my opinion unto you who is most fit for this place, being a member of this House, and those good abilities which I know to be in him '—here he made a little pause, and the House hawked and spat, and after silence made, he proceeded—' unto this place of dignity and calling in my opinion '—here he stayed a little—' Mr. Sergeant Yelverton '—looking upon him—' is the fittest man to be preferred '—at which words Mr. Yelverton blushed, put off his hat and sat bareheaded—' for I am assured that he is, yea, and I dare avow it, I know him to be, a man wise and learned, secret and circumspect, religious and faithful, no way disable but in every way able to supply this place. Wherefore in my judgment I deem him, though I will not say best worthy among us, yet sufficient enough to supply this place; and herein if any man think I err, I wish him to deliver his mind as freely as I have done; if not, that we all join together in giving general consent and approbation to this motion.'

So the whole House cried, 'Ay, ay, ay, let him be.' Then Sir William made a low reverence and sat down. After a little pause and silence Mr. Sergeant Yelverton rose up, and, after very humble reverence made , thus spake :

'Whence your unexpected choice of me to be your mouth or Speaker should proceed, I am utterly ignorant. If from my merits, strange it were that so few deserts should purchase suddenly so great an honour. Nor from my ability doth this your choice proceed; for well known is it to a great number in this place that my estate is nothing correspondent for the maintenance of this dignity; for my father dying left me a younger brother and nothing to me but my bare annuity. Then growing to man's estate and some small practice of the law, I took a wife by whom I have had many children, the keeping of us all being a great impoverishing to my estate, and the daily living of us all nothing but my daily industry. Neither from my person or nature doth this choice arise; for he that supplieth this place ought to be a man big and comely, stately and well spoken, his voice great, his carriage majestical, his nature haughty, and his purse plentiful and heavy; but contrarily, the stature of my body is small, myself not so well spoken, my voice low, my carriage lawyer-like and of the common fashion, my nature soft and bashful, my purse thin, light, and never plentiful. Where I now see the only cause of this choice is a gracious and favourable censure of your good and undeserved opinions of me. But I most humbly beseech you recall this your sudden election; and therefore, because the more sudden, the sooner to be recalled. But if this cannot move your sudden choice yet let this one thing persuade you, that myself not being gracious in the eye of her Majesty, neither ever yet in account with great personages, shall deceive your expectation in those weighty matters and great affairs which should be committed unto me. For if Demosthenes being so learned and eloquent as he was, one whom none surpassed, trembled to speak before Phocion at Athens, how much more shall I, being unlearned and unskilful, supply this place of dignity, charge, and trouble to speak before so many Phocions as here be? Yea, which is the greatest, before the unspeakable Majesty and Sacred Person of our dread and dear Sovereign, the terror of whose countenance will appal and abase even the stoutest heart; yea, whose very name will pull down the greatest courage? For how mightily doth the estate and name of a Prince deject the haughtiest stomach even of their greatest subjects? I beseech you therefore again and again to proceed unto a new election, here being many better able and more sufficient and far more worthy than myself, both for the honour of this assembly and general good of the public state.'

After this speech, Sir John Fortescue, the Chancellor of the Exchequer, stood up, affirming all the former commendations of Sir William Knollys, and inferring further that he well perceived by Mr. Yelverton's speech, tending to the disabling of himself to this place, that he was thereby so much the more meet and sufficient; and so for his part he also nominated Mr. Yelverton to be their Speaker, and moved the House for their liking and resolution therein, who all with one accord and consent yield unto this election.

Whereupon Mr. Controller and Mr. Chancellor rose up and placed Mr. Sergeant Yelverton in the Chair. Which done, Mr. Yelverton after some small pause stood up, and giving the whole House most hearty thanks for their good opinions and conceit of him, signified unto them nevertheless that by their good favours he will endeavour when he shall come before her Majesty, to be a humble suitor unto her Highness to be discharged of this place, if so he can.

After this the House immediately rose.

Divers people to-day pressing between Whitehall and the College Church to see the Queen and the nobility riding to the Parliament, Sir Thomas Gerrard the Knight Marshal and his men making way before them, were smothered and crushed to death.

26th October. A Sudden Very Great Alarm.

To-day is come to Court a gentleman with news that he discovered the Spanish fleet, and finding one ship lagging took prisoner her captain, master and purser. The ship was rescued, but some letters taken in her show that they will make their rendezvous at Falmouth. Mayors and chief officers in the ports on the south shall now, as they regard the Queen's service and upon peril of their lives, send out as espials some of the best fisher boats to gain early intelligence of the designs of the enemy. The Picardy soldiers are to be landed in England with all possible expedition. Victuals and all kinds of provision are being collected in the West parts to replenish the fleet of the Earl of Essex which is looked for within a few days.

27th October. The Forces Mustering.

In Devon, Cornwall, Dorset, Hampshire, Berkshire, Kent, Sussex, Surrey, Wiltshire and Somerset the whole forces, both horsemen and footmen, are being put in readiness. All men that dwell anywhere near the sea are forbidden to leave their houses; and gentlemen of every county for the most part are commanded to go home for the defence of the sea coast. The Lord Chamberlain departeth at once for the western coast to command such forces as shall be fit for the resistance of the enemy if they land, and captains are appointed to attend him.

The Lord Burgh dead.

The Lord Deputy, Lord Burgh, is dead in Ireland. Being on a journey to revictual the fort of Blackwater, he fell dangerously sick of an Irish ague at Armagh on the 6th, and being taken back in a litter to Newry died there on the 13th. His death comes very untimely, for there is not another fit man able to second the course already begun, all the money spent is lost, and besides there hangeth an imminent danger of a present and general revolt throughout that Kingdom.

THE SPEAKER PRESENTED.

To-day in Parliament, the House being set, Mr. Chancellor of the Exchequer moved and admonished that none of the House shall hereafter enter into the House with their spurs on for offending of others, and that none shall come in before they have paid the Sergeant's fees due to him according to the accustomed usage of the House.

This afternoon the Queen going by water repaired to the Upper House, accompanied with divers Lords spiritual and temporal, and the Commons having notice, Mr. Sergeant Yelverton was brought into the Upper House, and by the hands of Sir William Knollys and Sir John Fortescue, Chancellor of the Exchequer, presented.

Mr. Speaker in a speech full of gravity and moderation signified the election of the House of Commons, but, excusing himself by pretence of many disabilities and imperfections, and wishing earnestly he were of sufficiency to perform the duty of that place, made humble suit to her Majesty that he might be discharged and that the House of Commons might proceed to a new election. This excuse was not allowed by her Majesty, as the Lord Keeper delivered answer, who very well approved the choice of Mr. Yelverton and commended his sufficiency.

Mr. Speaker then proceeded in another speech, according to custom, to undertake this charge and to present her Majesty, in the behalf of the Commons, certain humble petitions, for access upon needful occasions, and for the using and enjoying of such liberties and privileges as in former times have been granted by her Majesty and her progenitors. Whereunto her Majesty, by the mouth of the Lord Keeper, yielded gracious assent, with admonition that these liberties should be discreetly and wisely used, as is meet.

The Parliament is adjourned until the 5th November.

PLAYING RESUMED.

To-day the Lord Admiral's players that have been absent for the last three months are now returned from the country and again begin to play at the Rose.

28th October. THE EARL OF ESSEX RETURNS.

This morning came letters to Court of the Earl of Essex's safe landing in Plymouth, that he hath unfortunately missed the King's own fleet with the treasure but fell upon the merchants' fleet. Four of them he hath taken and brought home safe, and sunk many more. The Earl of Southampton fought with one of the King's great men-of-war and sunk her. The Spanish fleet commanded by the Adelantado still hovers up and down upon the coast but as yet is not landed. The Earl of Essex put in to victual and to have fresh men, and with all possible speed to go to sea again ; my Lord Mountjoy sailing to Plymouth was by three of the Spanish fleet chased in.

The King of Spain is said to be dead, who made his son swear by the Sacrament that he should never make peace with England till he revenged these disgraces. The Adelantado, by the young Prince's threatening to hang him if he put not to sea, is upon our coast and vows to land though he never return.

A mass of money is being sent down to the Earl of Essex for all wants and supplies needed to refurnish the fleet. My Lord's offers and ready disposition to adventure his life in this service are very graciously accepted by the Queen. The Earl of Pembroke also is bidden to furnish such further aid as shall be required of him both in men and supplies.

30th October. PREPARATIONS IN THE WEST.

A sum of £3,000 has been sent into the West for provisions to revictual the fleet, of which sum the Lord Thomas Howard, Lord Mountjoy and Sir Walter Ralegh may draw up to £2,000, and more will be sent if need require. The loans of money hitherto respited are to be brought in with all speed for the service.

31st October. OSTEND BESIEGED.

The Cardinal hath now besieged Ostend, lying on the west side of it, but 'tis not yet known whether for a bravado or whether he will remain there for some design. Meanwhile the

Lord Cobham stayeth all the hoys at Dover and Sandwich so that, if there be cause, they may carry over men and victuals. The forces of the shire are mustered and the castles being viewed.

A New Play.

To-day there was a new play at the Rose called *Friar Spendleton.*

2nd November. The Islands Voyage.

The accounts of the late voyage are now to hand. Soon after the fleet had set sail, it was again caught by another great tempest on St. Bartholomew's Day, and many of the ships scattered, thirty ships with Sir Walter Ralegh the Vice-admiral being separated from the rest; but most of the remainder staying with the Earl of Essex. It had been ordained that if any separation should happen, there should be three places of rendezvous, the first at the North Cape, the second at the Rock, and the third at the South Cape. To the Rock therefore came Sir Walter Ralegh, who had been delayed by the breaking of his main mast, and there joined him some thirty sail; and here they met with a small bark of England by whom they were told that the Adelantado was gone to the Islands to waft home the Indian fleet; which news was afterwards found to be false. Sir Walter therefore thinking it very requisite that the Admiral should be informed of this advertisement, sent one of his small ships to seek the fleet, which by good hap it found the next day, so that within two days after Sir Walter received two letters from the Earl of Essex requiring him to follow him to the Islands forthwith. Which was accordingly done and the Isle of Tercera reached on the 8th September; and on the 14th they met with the rest of the fleet at Flores to the great joy of the General, especially as many had buzzed doubts and jealousies in his ear concerning Sir Walter. Then a council was held whereat it was determined to take in some of the islands and an orderly course was set down, which was for the Admiral and Rear-admiral to undertake Fayal; the Lord Thomas Howard and Sir Francis Vere to undertake Gratiosa; the Lord Mountjoy and Sir Christopher Blount to St. Michael's; and the Netherland squadron was quartered to Pyke where is the greatest store of wines, and therefore, it was presumed, would not be taken in ill part of them.

Here the ships of Sir Walter purposed to water whilst the rest of the fleet plied up and down, looking for the Adelantado. But whilst the casks were being prepared, about midnight, being the 16th September, a message was brought that my Lord General was borne up for Fayal, and meant to take it straightway, and therefore willed Sir Walter to follow with all speed instantly; further that all wants of water and fresh victuals should be supplied at Fayal. The ships with Sir Walter accordingly weighed anchor and next morning making Fayal entered the road but found not the Lord General; whereat they greatly marvelled, because when he had sent for them, he was six leagues nearer to it than they. As soon as the fleet was seen, the inhabitants of the town began to pack away with bag and baggage all they could. The town, which is some four miles from the place were they were, was defended by two forts, one at the end, the other on the top of a high mountain near adjoining, very inaccessible by nature, and artificially fenced with flankers, rampiers, and a ditch, and with six pieces of great artillery, and 200 Spaniards for a garrison. There were also sent six companies to intrench themselves on the shore side to impeach the landing of our men.

Hereupon Sir Walter in his barge rode close aboard the high fort and all along the shore side towards the town to see what fit place there was to make a descent against the Lord General's coming. So Sir Walter held a council of many captains and officers to consult of taking the town if still the Lord General came not. Moreover the soldiers and mariners began to mutiny and rail on the Rear-admiral and all the commanders as not daring the taking of the town; and besides they were more eagerly set upon the spoil because they saw no great likelihood of any other benefit to be gotten from this voyage. At this council, some would by no means consent to the landing without the Lord General's knowledge, and especially Sir Gelly Merrick, but those of Sir Walter's own squadron were of the contrary opinion. They stayed therefore two days, and then a third, but on the fourth Sir Walter determined to land.

They made ready therefore a barge, a long boat, and a pinnace with sixty muskets and forty pike rather to guard the landing than to attempt any encounter. But no sooner were the men in the boats, than many companies of foot began to hasten down to possess themselves of the trenches where our men were to land. Sir Walter therefore rowed to Sir William Brooke's ship and Sir William Harvey's, and desired them to accompany him ; to which they willingly assented, and there were made ready in addition with shot and pike 160 more men in the boats. Then the men from the Low Countries that belonged to my Lord of Essex's squadron cried out to be taken too, but Sir Walter durst not, not knowing for what service my Lord had intended them : but promised to send back his boats for them.

So the pinnaces hasted forward toward the landing place, but as the shot began to play thick upon them, the mariners would scarce come forwards, having the lesser liking to the business the nearer they came to it ; and some of the leaders themselves stood blank so that Sir Walter did not spare to call upon them openly and rebuke aloud with disgraceful words. Sir Walter, seeing that it was both more disgrace and more dangerous for the mariners to make stay, with a loud voice commanded his watermen to row in full upon the rocks and bad as many as were not afraid to follow him. Hereupon some boats ran in, and so clambering over the rocks, and wading through the water they passed pell-mell with swords, shot and pikes upon the narrow entrance. Whereupon those that were at the defence, after some little resistance, began to shrink, and then suddenly retiring cast down their weapons, and fled away to the hills. The landing being thus gained with some few men lost, the boats were sent back for the men from the Low Countries, who, when they were come ashore, made up a force of 460 men, well armed and appointed, and of these thirty or forty were captains and gentlemen.

They therefore resolved to pass by the two forts and enter the town, and the next morning to attack these forts ; which could not then be done, the day being far spent and the men overwearied with the last work, together with a long march and extreme hot weather, besides lack of victuals. So they set forward, the Rear-admiral with divers of the gentlemen going before the rest some twelve score paces in the manner of a vauntguard in a slow steady march, being shrewdly pelted by the muskets and great ordnance of the fort; but the main body that for a while marched in good order so soon as they began to find themselves within the mercy of the musket shot began to break their ranks, and from marching fell to flat running in straggling manner so that they were upon the heels of the vauntguard. Whereupon Sir Walter cried out on them for this shameful disorder and asked their captains if this was the manner of their old Low Country troops to show such base cowardice at the first sight of the enemy. To which they answered that these companies were men taken out of Flushing and Brille, and raw soldiers that ever lived in a safe garrison and seldom or never had seen the enemy. And indeed such as only serve to take pay, to walk rounds and guard ports in garrison towns, in the field will commonly be missing, or, if present, do little hurt for conscience' sake.

Then Sir Walter called for some to go out to survey the passage by the high fort, but the lieutenants and sergeants were very unwilling, so he said that he would go himself; 'notwithstanding,' quoth he, 'though I could enforce others to do it, they shall well perceive that I myself will do that which they dare not perform.' So with some few with him he went to discover the passage and to search out the strengths and ascents of the hill, being shrewdly troubled by the great artillery which beat upon the old walls as they passed, insomuch that two had their heads stricken clean from their bodies and divers others were hurt, and the Rear-admiral himself was shot through breeches and doublet. The passage being discovered, the rest of the troops were summoned to come on towards the town. But as they drew near the town, those in the other fort withdrew and fled up into the country; so that they entered the town peaceably, having lost some seven or eight slain and twenty-five hurt. Barricadoes were immediately made, good guards placed in divers places and a strong court of guard in the market place, and straggling forbidden on pain of death. That night they rested without further trouble than two false alarms.

Next morning, being 22nd September, the Lord General himself with his fleet bore into the road of Fayal, having all this while been looking about for the Adelantado and other adventures; and hereupon the intent to attempt the high fort was frustrated. Meanwhile the proceedings in Fayal were by Sir Gelly Merrick related at large to the Lord General, and so aggravated and wrested into an evil sense by him, Sir Christopher Blount, Sir Anthony Shirley and others, by putting into my Lord of Essex's head that these parts were played by Sir Walter Ralegh only to steal honour and reputation from him, and to set his own frowardness to the view of the world. Which intimation of theirs was an exception that they knew my Lord of Essex is very apt of his own dispósition to take hold of, being a man that affecteth nothing in the world so much as fame, and to be reputed matchless for magnanimity and undertaking, and can hardly endure any that shall obscure his glory in this kind, though otherwise he favour them never so much. It was besides alleged that the presumption and scorn to land such forces without my Lord's leave was not to be passed over without severe punishment, and a martial court fit to be called, to censure the offence and breach of order and discipline. These and such other bitter arguments were used to aggravate the General's wrath against all that were in this action, and especially against the Rear-admiral; against whom they spared not so far to inveigh as that he was well worthy to lose his head for his labour. So well did they persuade the General that all the forenoon was spent in reprehending and displacing the land officers that went in the action.

Sir Walter was then sent for to answer before the Lord General in his ship, but before the messenger came for him was already gone in his barge to see my Lord, looking for great thanks at the General's hands. But when he was entered my Lord's cabin, after a faint welcome, my Lord began to challenge him of breach of order and articles, in that he had landed troops without the General's presence or his order. To which Sir Walter answered that there was an article that no captain should land anywhere without direction of the General or other principal commander; but that he himself was a principal commander and therefore not subject to that article, nor under the power of the law martial, because a successive commander of the fleet under her Majesty's letters patent.

This dispute lasted some half hour and then the Lord General went ashore and rested himself in the Rear-admiral's lodging, being well enough satisfied at that time, this dispute having been brought to a quiet conclusion by the friendly mediation of Lord Thomas Howard. Thus the whole day was spent in reprehending and disciplining those with the Rear-admiral for their pains. That night the Spaniards in the high fort abandoned the place with all their baggage and fled into the country; and next morning, when it was too late, direction was given to guard the high fort. So when news was brought that they had abandoned the fort and carried all away, there was much murmuring, for if there had not been bestowed more labour in disciplining pretended faults than discretion in prosecuting the enemy who was at a disadvantage, then had not been lost the benefit of the prisoners' ransoms and the spoil which they had carried out of the town to that place for safety.

On the 26th September the whole fleet made towards Gratiosa, where the chief men of the Island submitted themselves to the Lord General, being required to yield some provisions of wine, fruits, and fresh victuals. Here the Lord General and some of the commanders would have stayed, but the Master of his ship, one Grove, was against that counsel, protesting that it would be dangerous for the whole fleet to anchor there. Wherefore they weighed anchor and made for St. Michael's Island, but as they came near two of the sternmost of the fleet shot off twice or thrice and bare up with all the sails they could pack on to the General's ship. These brought news of the Indian fleet, coming directly from the road of Gratiosa.

Upon this intelligence they cast about, and, within some three hours afterwards, they encountered and took three Spanish ships coming from Havannah, the greatest being of about 400 tons, and esteemed to be a very rich ship. To this Spaniard the *Wastspite*, being nearest, gave chase and caused her to strike and yield; but the Lord General, hasting after, would suffer none but his own boat to go aboard her, being full of good prisoners and pillage besides her lading, which was cochinella and other rich wares. This ship made relation of forty sail of Indiamen, whereof eight were freighted with the King's treasure, bound for Spain. Of these ships, some of ours fell in with sixteen, whereof they foundered one, and whilst they were busy seeking to take the spoil off her, the rest escaped and recovered Tercera. With all speed therefore our fleet followed them to Tercera, where they had entered some six hours before and had moored their ships under the town and fort.

Now there was a general council called aboard the Admiral what course to take herein, some of the colonels and captains offering with 1,500 men to take both island and forts but the sea commanders utterly against it, so that in the end it was deemed inconvenient and impossible to be effected as the forces then stood, and the time of year so far spent, with the winds and seas grown so tempestuous for landing in boats. The fleet therefore returned to St. Michael's and there anchored.

There it was consulted about landing and the taking of this good town, promising so many rewards to the victors. The General appointed that all companies should be made ready to land forthwith, but the Rear-admiral asked that he might first be permitted to view the place and to find out where the army might best make a descent. To this the Lord General at first yielded, but as Sir Walter was putting off, and scarce gone from the ship's side, my Lord, standing in his gallery with Sir Charles Blount, called him back again in great haste, and said that he would go himself and view it. Whereupon the Rear-admiral returned again, and my Lord went out of the ship into his barge, unarmed altogether but with his collar and sword, and without either shot or pike to wait on him. Sir Walter therefore called aloud to him, desiring him to take his casque and targetproof with him if he purposed to go near the shore, seeing there lay so many muskets on the rest there to receive him. Whereunto my Lord answered that he would none, because he disdained to take any advantage of the watermen that rowed with him.

The landing places being viewed afar off were not so well liked, so that upon another consultation being held it was agreed that the Rear-admiral, with all the strength of the fleet, should lie as near before the town of St. Michael as conveniently they could to hold them in expectation whilst my

Lord and the rest with 2,000 men should embark into the small barks and pinnaces and secretly in the night convey themselves about the point to land at a town called Villa Franca.

So the troops were shipped, and the Lord General also, and made haste to Villa Franca, where they arrived safe and were all landed by the next morning without any manner of resistance, while the ships under the command of the Rear-admiral all the night gave the enemy perpetual alarums with shot, drums and trumpets in such boats as were left, sometimes in one place, sometimes in another alongst the shore.

Next morning those with the Rear-admiral looked to see our troops marching over the hills and plains; but this good town of Villa Franca had so welcomed and entertained our men that the army was content there to ingarrison without any further pursuit of St. Michael's town; and there for six days they lay feasting, and carrying on board of oade, wheat, salt and other merchandise into certain private men's ships that followed the fleet for such a purpose.

While the fleet lay gaping for the coming of the army, which in all this time never sent word of their determination, there came a little Brazil man and let fall his anchor in the midst of our fleet, and a little after him a mighty huge carrack was discerned which made towards our fleet supposing it to be the Spanish armada, for indeed the King of Spain's men-of-war, when he makes fleets, are compounded of the shipping of divers nations, and besides with ours were not only Hollanders but the great Spanish galleon, the *St. Andrew.* Then by general commandment of the Rear-admiral, our ships took in all their flags, and directions were given that no man should weigh an anchor or shoot off a piece or put off a boat, but with leave and order. All this while she still bare in with all sails to the boat's end, when suddenly one of the Holland squadron weighed his anchors, hoisted his top sail and made towards the carrack. Whereupon discovering our ships to be enemy, she changed her course, and with the gale changing ran herself aground hard under the town and fort. Immediately there came out multitudes of boats, fetching away their men and best wares, and, that done, she was instantly set on fire in many places at once, so that though our men hasted all they could in all the boats that were left, they came all too late, for the broth was too hot for their supping. This vessel was judged to be of 1,800 tons, of infinite wealth, fraughted with the riches and wares both of the East and West, which was a loss as lamentable as inexcusable, for if the General and his troops had not lingered in Villa Franca, she had either fallen in their hands on shore or been taken at sea by the fleet.

After some days the fleet was summoned to Villa Franca, to the great joy of the inhabitants of St. Michael's. The wind and seas now beginning to rise and the opportunity being past of doing any damage to the enemy, preparations were now made for a return, and with all haste the soldiers were conveyed back to the boats with the help of the small pinnaces and boats, wherein my Lord twice was in very great danger of tumbling into the sea in overcharging his own boat with soldiers, amongst whom at such times it is very hard to keep any order or moderation. At this embarking the Spaniards and Portuguese made a brave skirmish, which being thoroughly answered, the General did make certain knights. At length on 9th October the fleet set sail for England.

5th November. OSTEND.

News is come from Sir Edward Norris, governor of Ostend, that there is no present danger. The enemy lie about the town and have divers times presented themselves before it; forces from the Low Countries have now been sent there.

THE QUEEN'S LETTER TO THE EMPEROR OF ETHIOPIA.

One Mr. Lawrence Aldersey, after many travels in foreign countries, being yet inflamed with a desire more thoroughly to survey and contemplate the world, now undertaketh a long and dangerous journey into the kingdom of the Emperor of Ethiopia. He beareth with him a letter from the Queen that he may enter that kingdom under the safeguard and protection of the Emperor's favour, and there remain safe and free from danger.

A MOTION IN PARLIAMENT AGAINST INCLOSURES.

To-day in the Parliament a Bill was read for the first time against forestallers, regrators and ingrossers. Whereupon

Mr. Francis Bacon spake first and made a motion against inclosures and depopulation of towns and houses of husbandry. He had perused, said he, the preambles of former statutes and by them did see the inconveniences of the matter, being then scarce out of the shell, to be now full ripened. It might be thought ill and very prejudicial to Lords that have inclosed great grounds, and pulled down even whole towns, and converted them to sheep pastures; yet considering the increase of people and benefit of the commonwealth, every man would deem the revival of former moth-eaten laws in this point a praiseworthy thing. 'I would be sorry,' quoth he, 'to see within this Kingdom that piece of Ovid's verse prove true, *iam seges ubi Troia fuit*, so in England, instead of a town full of people, nought but green fields, but a shepherd and a dog.'

After Mr. Bacon, Sir John Fortescue, the Chancellor of the Exchequer, in like manner showed his opinion, and so moving for a committee to consider of this motion, the House nominate all members of the Privy Council, being members of this House, all knights of the counties and all citizens of the cities returned to this present Parliament, together with Sir Edward Hoby, Mr. Francis Bacon, Mr. Nathaniel Bacon, Mr. Finch, Mr. Solicitor and divers others.

This concluded, Mr. Finch showing sundry great and horrible abuses of idle and vagrant persons, greatly offensive both to God and the world, and further the extreme and miserable estate of the godly and honest sort of the poor subjects of this realm, the matter is also referred to the same committee.

THE EARL OF ESSEX DISQUIETED.

The Earl of Essex is now returned to Court but is already disquieted, keeps in, and goes not to the Parliament. It is said that the Queen is not well pleased with him for his service at sea, wherein he might have done more than he did. Moreover his proceedings towards Sir Walter Ralegh in calling his actions to public question before a council of war where by a full court he was found guilty of death is greatly misliked. It is feared that the peace between the Earl of Essex and Sir Robert Cecil will burst out to terms of unkindness.

6th November. SPANISH PRISONERS AT LARGE.

Divers Spaniards that have of late been taken on the seas are allowed ordinarily to go up and down at their own liberty: but now the Lord Mayor shall inform himself of those that are within and without the City and see them committed to Bridewell, there to be safely kept with the diet of the house and set to work if they be not able to pay for their diet, and especially those lately taken by Newport; for it is against reason that any of the King of Spain's subjects should be suffered to enjoy their liberty here seeing the hard usage that is offered to our countrymen.

7th November. BARRET'S 'THEORICK AND PRACTICK OF MODERN WARS.'

Mr. Robert Barret hath written a book called *The Theorick and practick of modern wars*, discoursed dialogue-wise. Herein is declared the neglect of martial discipline and the inconvenience thereof; the imperfection of many training companies and its redress; the fittest weapons for our modern war, and their use; the part of a perfect soldier in general and in particular; the officers in degrees with their several duties; the embattling of men in forms now most in use, with figures and tables to the same; with sundry other martial points, comprehended in six books. Yet he would have captains trained by experience and not by book; for your reading captain when he is come into the field with an hundred men will rank them three and three, but at every third rank he must call to his boy, 'Holla sirrha, where is my book?' And having them all ranked, then marcheth he on fair, and far wider from his soldiers. Then cometh he to cast them into a ring, about, about, about, till he hath inclosed himself in the centre; now there is he puzzled—'Holla master, stand still until I have looked in my book.' Addeth to his book a table of the foreign words used by soldiers.

9th November. THE EARL OF ESSEX ABSENT FROM COURT.

To-day the Queen told my Lord Hunsdon that she much wondered at the absence of the Earl of Essex. He pleaded my Lord's want of health, the shooting in his temples upon cold or long speech, and yet his readiness to attend if she should be pleased to command his service. She accounted his duty and place sufficient to command him, and said that a prince was not to be contested withal by a subject. Nevertheless there is nothing but kindness and comfort to my Lord, if he will but turn about and take it.

The Privileges of the House.

Two days since Sir Thomas Knivett showing that since being a member of this Parliament he had been served with a *subpoena* to attend in the Chancery, the matter was referred to the committee for examination of such matters. Yesterday Mr. Brograve, Attorney of the Duchy, declared that the committee had met together and are of opinion that the serving of a *subpoena* is a manifest contempt committed against the whole House; for by reason of such process, a member so served must needs be withdrawn from the service of the House, both in his mind and person, by the mere necessity of following his own private business elsewhere. It was resolved therefore that two members should be sent to the Lord Keeper in the name of the whole House to require him to revoke the *subpoena*. Whereupon Sir Edward Hoby and Mr. Brograve went to the Lord Keeper and delivered the message of the House, to which the Lord Keeper asked whether they were appointed by any advised consideration of the House to deliver their message unto him with the word 'require.' They answered his Lordship, 'Yea.' Then his Lordship said that as he thought very reverently and honourably of the House and the liberties and privileges of the same, but so to revoke the *subpoena* in that sort is to restrain her Majesty in her greatest power, which is justice in the place wherein he serveth her. He saith that he will be advised further before giving his answer to the House.

Abuses in Bristol.

When Captain Docura, upon the recent alarm of the Spanish fleet, was sent into Bristol to see the trained bands which should have been in readiness and to train them to serve, the men were presented to him after many delays and altogether unarmed. Moreover he found very small care or feeling in the Mayor in these occasions, for he trusted to the situation of his town, being a great indraught in the land. This slender regard in these times of danger deserveth much to be blamed.

10th November. THE PARLIAMENT.

This day in the Parliament a Bill for taking away clergy from certain offenders was sent up to the Lords; committees were appointed touching the sundry enormities growing by patents of privilege and monopolies and the abuses of them; and a motion was made touching the abuses of licences for marriages granted by ecclesiastical persons.

14th November. THE KNIGHTS OF THE POST.

There is a book entered called *The discovery of the Knights of the Post*, written by one E. S. The knights of the post are those who will pretend themselves to be citizens of substance and so bail a man out of arrest for a reward. In term time they are most commonly to be found in Fleet Street, about St. John, or about Chancery Lane or in some of the pudding-pie houses in Westminster; but out of the term, then in Duke Humphrey's alley in Paul's, or at the Lion on the backside of St. Nicholas Shambles, or at the Rose in Pannier Alley, or the Dolphin at the end of Carter Lane, or the Woolsack.

INCESTUOUS MARRIAGES.

In the Parliament Sir John Fortescue declared that yesterday her Majesty called Mr. Secretary and himself unto her, and telling them that she had been informed of the horrible and great incestuous marriages discovered in the House, commanded them to take information of the grievances in particular of the members of the House that she might have certain notice thereof and thereupon give order for their due punishment and redress.

15th November. THE SUBSIDIES.

Mr. Chancellor, putting the House in remembrance of the Lord Keeper's speech on the first day of the Parliament touching the causes of the summoning of this Parliament, declared how great and excessive have been her Majesty's charges for the defence of her realm, amounting to more than treble the value of the last three subsidies and six fifteenths and tenths granted by the last Parliament. Then Mr. Secretary Cecil showed at large the purposes, practices and attempts of the King of Spain against her Majesty at sundry times, together with his great overthrows in the same by the mighty hand of God and of her Highness's forces, to his perpetual ignominy and great dishonour throughout the world. And so, after a large discourse most excellently delivered by him, concluded with a motion for proceeding to a committee; which is agreed by the House.

16th November. MY LORD OF ESSEX'S ABSENCE.

There are many different censures about my Lord of Essex's absence from the Parliament, some earnestly expecting his advancement, others that daily make use of his absence confess his worth but wish him well only in words. Yet is my Lord for all his good parts least perfect in working his own good, for his patience continually giveth way to his crosses, and upon every discontentment he will absent himself from Court. Some there be that would say to him 'Let nothing draw thee from the Court; sit in every Council, yet so that there may be nothing concluded but with thy good liking and privity. Thou hast 100,000 true hearts in this small isle that daily expect and wish thy settled content, and the fall of them that love thee not. What dignity is done to them, or indignity to thee, but in thy absence? Thy enemies are thereby made strong and thou weak. And whereas thou retainest many in thy favour as true and secret friends, remember that Christ had but twelve and one proved a devil.'

18th November. THE EARL OF ESSEX ABSENT FROM PARLIAMENT.

Report was made by the Lord Keeper in the House of Lords that the Earl of Essex received not the writ of his summons till yesterday, through the negligence of the messenger, and now wanting health to give his attendance desireth to be excused of his absence, the Earls of Worcester and Southampton testifying his sickness.

19th November. THE SUBSIDIES.

Sir John Fortescue, Chancellor of the Exchequer, showed that at the committee of Parliament yesterday it was agreed to grant unto her Majesty three entire subsidies and six fifteenths and tenths. Whereupon, some members of the House being for delay in the payments of these subsidies, Sir Robert Cecil gave very many forcible reasons and causes of great importance for the speedy performance of the subsidies; which done, it was upon question resolved that the last payment of the subsidies shall be made in one year and at one entire payment in like sort as the two first of the same three subsidies are to be paid.

Then Mr. Davies, showing many corruptions in the Masters of Colleges in the Universities of Oxford and Cambridge in their abusing the possessions of Colleges contrary to the intents of founders, converting the same to their own private commodities, prayed the advice and assistance of the House for the better digesting of a Bill which he had drawn to the purpose. Herein Mr. Speaker referreth him to such members of the House as are of the Temple. Whereupon Sir Edward Hoby, liking very well of Mr. Davies' motion, moveth that the like consideration be had of Deans and Chapters.

Yesterday one Mr. Thomas Layton, one of the knights for the county of Salop, having been much visited with sickness since his coming up to this session of Parliament, is for better recovery of his health licensed by Mr. Speaker to depart home.

20th November. DISORDERS IN WALES.

During the late attempt of the Spaniards two of their ships were driven ashore in Wales; whereof one was forced into a creek in a place called Galtop. Hereupon Mr. Hugh Butler, that was in command of the trained bands in those parts, prepared six fisher boats to board the ship; but the Spaniards set out a play of truce and offered to send their cockboat ashore. This being perceived by one John Wogan, a gentleman of those parts, he with his brother and other associates to the number of twenty entered the ship before Mr. Butler, and not only withstood him by force but wounded him in three places, while his company rifled the ship of all her goods, money and things of value. At Caldey, the other Spanish ship in which there was treasure for Dunkirk is escaped through the disorderly behaviour of others.

THE SPANISH LOSSES.

There is news from Spain that forty-nine ships are arrived back on the coast, whereof twenty nine are the King's galleons; fifty of the fleet are missing. The *St. Peter* is leaky, the *St. Lucas* ran aground; they had to cast most of their horses and mules overboard. The fleet was within two days' sail of Land's End. One of the galleons with Don Pedro de Guevara, General of artillery, in her took fire and hath not since been seen; another ship, wherein were the materials for fortification and for firing our ships in harbour, attempting to aid her, took fire and was blown up, and a French ship with her, full of soldiers. There is now nothing but confusion, stories of misfortunes, yet brags of what they will do next spring; yet the defeat of an army so long in preparing hath been very sudden. Their plan was to have landed 8,000 in long-boats westward of Plymouth by peep of day while the ships occupied our forces west of Falmouth till the whole army was landed.

The Spanish King hath been very sick, and there are bonfires and processions for his recovery. He had a palsy and for two days was fed with liquor blown into his throat by the Infanta.

21st November. PRIVILEGE OF THE HOUSE.

Sir Edward Hoby moved the House for privilege for Sir John Tracy, being a member of the House and at that time at the Common Pleas to be put on a jury. Whereupon the Sergeant of the House was sent straightway with the Mace to call Sir John to his attendance in the House, and Sir John then returned to his place.

22nd November. A PETITION OF THE UNIVERSITIES.

Because of the speeches lately uttered by Mr. Davies in the Lower House of Parliament greatly tending to the utter discredit of the Governors and Heads of Colleges generally, the Vice-Chancellors both of Cambridge and Oxford have petitioned their Chancellors that Mr. Davies may be compelled to make such proof as he can of those scandalous matters, lest by colour of these scandalous defamations uttered in so public a place some new statute may pass to the general prejudice of both Universities.

23rd November. THE PARLIAMENT.

Mr. Walgrave delivering a Bill to the Speaker declareth that the transportation of a great number of herrings to Leghorn both occasioneth a very great scarcity of herrings in the realm, and is, saith he, a great means of spending much butter and cheese to the enhancing of the price thereof.

Mr. Attorney General and Mr. Doctor Stanhop having brought from the Lords an Act passed with their Lordships concerning the deprivation of divers bishops at the beginning of the reign, after their departure it was shortly found by Sir Edward Hoby that the Act was not duly and rightly endorsed by their Lordships; the endorsement being made above the Contents of the Act which ought to have been made under it. Whereupon the House being made privy thereto by the Speaker, Mr. Comptroller, with divers members, was sent to the Lords with the Act to signify the error and to pray amendment. Later Mr. Attorney and Dr. Stanhop came from the Lords with the Act endorsed according to the ancient former usage of Parliament, signifying to the House that the faulty endorsement of the Act in such manner before did grow only by an error in the Clerk of the Upper House, who had never exercised the place before the present Parliament; moreover their Lordships, liking very well of what the House had done touching this error, withal wish the House to continue all former good order and courses in all Parliament proceedings.

28th November. THE FRENCH AMBASSADOR RECEIVED.

To-day M. de Maisse, who is sent over by the French King, was received in audience by her Majesty. When he was conducted to the door of the Privy Chamber he made reverence to the Queen who was sitting by herself, and at some distance from the Lords and Ladies. As he entered she rose and came forward to the middle of the Chamber. M. de Maisse kissed the border of her garment, and she raised him with both hands and with a favourable countenance began to excuse herself that she had not given him audience sooner, saying that the day before she had been sick of an affliction on the right side of her face, and he would believe it if he looked at her eyes and countenance, for she did not remember when she had been so ill before. At this meeting the Ambassador spoke but in general terms, noting that as he spoke the Queen ofttimes raised herself from her chair and seemed to be impatient at his words. She complained of the fire that it hurt her eyes, although there was a great screen before it, and called for water to put it out.

30th November. A Prisoner released.

One Gilbert Layton that hath lain a prisoner in the Tower these six years is now to be released with condition that he shall at all times be forthcoming upon warning given him to be at a certain place in London, and also to behave himself as a good subject, and when her Majesty shall be at any of her houses in London not to repair to the Court. This man formerly confessed that he would kill the Queen.

An Accident at the Swan.

There was a prize played at the Swan on the Bankside where Turner and one Dunn playing the prizes, Turner thrust Dunn into the eye and so into the brains that he fell down dead without speaking any word.

1st December. Gerard's 'Herbal.'

Mr. John Gerard, Master in Chirurgery, hath written a great work called *The Herbal or general history of plants*, being dedicated to the Lord Burleigh. This work is in three books, whereof the first treateth of grasses, rushes, corn, bulbous or onion-rooted plants in 106 chapters. The second containeth the description, place, time, names, nature, and virtues of all sorts of herbs for meat, medicine or sweet smelling use, etc., and hath 511 chapters. The third of trees, shrubs, bushes, fruit-bearing plants, rosins, gums, roses, heath, mosses, some Indian and other rare plants, also mushrooms, coral and their several kinds, which book hath 167 chapters; and to all the chapters are there one or more cuts of the things described therein. Concludeth with a description of the goose-tree or barnacle, found in the north parts of Scotland.

On this tree do grow certain shellfishes of a white colour tending to russet wherein are contained little living creatures; which shells in time of maturity do open and of them grow those little living things, which falling into the water become the fowls which we call 'barnacles,' in the north of England brant geese, and in Lancashire tree geese. Mr. Gerard hath himself found similar between Dover and Romney, for causing the trunk of an old rotten tree to be drawn out of the water, there were growing on it many thousands of long crimson bladders, in shape like unto puddings newly filled before they be sodden, very clear and shining. At the nether end did grow a shellfish, fashioned somewhat like a small mussel, but whiter. In these shells were found living things without form or shape; in others things that were very naked in shape like a bird; in others the birds covered with soft down, the shell half open and the bird ready to fall out.

3rd December. THE VENETIAN CORN SHIP.

There is still dispute concerning that Venetian ship the *St. Agatha Morisini* which was driven into Portsmouth last January laden with corn that was sold because of the then scarcity. Martin Frederico, a merchant of Venice, hath procuration from the Signiory to follow a cause, complaining that the corn was undervalued, sold at low prices, and a great part missing. Dr. Julius Caesar and others are appointed to examine the matter and to certify to the Council what fault they find in the dealing of the Commissioners, for her Majesty hath care that the Signiory should have all the satisfaction in these causes which in equity ought to be afforded them.

4th December. THE SERMON AT PAUL'S CROSS.

Mr. John Howson to-day preached the sermon at Paul's Cross on Matthew xxi., 12 and 13, showing how unlawful is the buying and selling of spiritual promotion. Saith that this buying and selling in the Church will make barren the two Universities; for those that be bred up in learning having in childhood suffered great and grievous affliction in the grammar schools, when they be come to the Universities live either of the College's allowance, needy of all things but hunger and fear, or being maintained by their own or their parents' cost, do expend in necessary maintenance, books, and degrees £500 or 1,000 marks before they be come to perfection. If they then cannot purchase a poor parsonage or vicarage of £40 or £50 a year unless they pay to the patron for the lease of their life either in annual pension or above the rate of a copyhold, what father will be so improvident to bring his son up at great charge? Concludeth that this buying and selling is indeed the sin of simony, an heresy intolerable, and one that will cause the Universities to be decayed, the Church supplied with ignorant pastors, hospitality removed from the clergy and the sign and forerunner of some evil to ensue to the Commonwealth.

8th December. A Boy possessed at Nottingham.

Some weeks since a boy called William Sommers of Nottingham began to be strangely tormented in body and gave great tokens that he was possessed by a wicked spirit; whereupon the Mayor and some of the Aldermen of Nottingham sent instantly for Mr. Darrell (who by prayer and fasting hath already restored eight or nine persons that have been vexed in like sort). At first Mr. Darrell was unwilling to come, but by their importunate letters and messengers at length he condescended to their desires, and came to Nottingham on the 5th November. The 7th was appointed for the exercise of prayer and fasting to the end that Sommers might be dispossessed; which at the prayers of Mr. Darrell and others to the number of a hundred and fifty is brought to pass. Hereupon Mr. Darrell is retained as preacher in Nottingham.

Sommers being dispossessed discovered certain witches, one whereof was called Doll Freeman, allied to one Freeman an Alderman of Nottingham. This Freeman offended that his kinswoman should be called in question threatened Sommers that he was himself a witch, and caused him to be committed to prison, where the Devil appeared unto him in the likeness of a mouse, threatening that if he would not let him re-enter and would not say that all he had done concerning his tormenting during his possession was but counterfeit, then he should be hanged; but if he would yield, the Devil would save him.

Thus a new stipulation being made between them, the Devil entered; and afterwards Sommers constantly declared that all which he had done before was only counterfeit. A general opinion being now conceived that Sommers hath counterfeited all his former proceeding, Mr. Darrell preacheth very bitterly against that conceit, persuading his auditory that

Satan will lurk sometimes about one out of whom he hath been cast, suffering the party to be well for a good space, but will not give him over until in the end he have repossessed him.

11th December. THE SUBSIDY.

The Bill for the granting of six fifteenths and tenths and three entire subsidies had a second reading to-day and was ordered to be ingrossed.

14th December. THE LORDS' PRIVILEGE ABUSED.

Six days since one William Cole, one of the Knight Marshal's men, that had arrested John York, the Archbishop's servant, was brought before the Lords by the Sergeant at Arms; and being found upon examination to have wilfully offended therein against the privilege of the House was committed to the Fleet; but to-day he is enlarged on paying only his fees.

THE ABUSE OF MONOPOLIES.

Mr. Francis Moore, one of the committees for consideration of the method and substance of the humble thanks to be yielded by Mr. Speaker unto her Majesty on behalf of the House for her care and favour in repressing sundry inconveniences and abuses practised by monopolies and patents of privilege, delivered a note of the meeting and travail of the committee therein. This being read by the Clerk was well liked of. Whereupon the Speaker moved the House that, albeit he was ready to perform their commandment according to the substance and effect of the note, yet they would not tie him to the strict and precise form of the words and terms; which is yielded unto accordingly.

14th December. MONSIEUR DE MAISSE.

M. de Maisse was again received by the Queen to-day, and saith that when he entered the Chamber one was playing the virginals, and she seemed to be so attentive to the music and as it were surprised by his entrance that he excused himself for interrupting her pastime. The Queen replied that she loveth music and every day playeth a pavan. She spoke several times of the King of Spain, his wishing to kill her. Whilst they conversed she would ofttimes make digression, as if she would gain time and not appear to be pressed by the ambassador's demands; which she would excuse saying, 'You will say, Master Ambassador, the tale I told you is mere trifling; see what it is to conduct affairs with old women such as I am.' She said also to him that she had long hands, both by nature and by power, for, quoth she, '*anne fas longas regibus esse manus?*' whereat she took off her gloves, showing her hands, longer than the ambassador's by three thick fingers.

17th December. Two London Crimes.

The body of Mr. Richard Anger, a double reader of Gray's Inn, that hath been missed almost a month, was lately found floating in the Thames; and being viewed by certain skilful surgeons it is thought he was not drowned in the water but stifled or murthered, and after thrown into the Thames, which by other conjectures is greatly to be suspected. There are great presumptions against one of his sons, Richard Anger, and Edward Ingram, the porter of Gray's Inn. Forasmuch as the fact is so horrible that an ancient gentleman should be murdered in his chamber, these two are to be examined very strictly, and if they cannot be brought to confess the truth, then shall they be put to the manacles in Bridewell.

There is also one Richard Remchin, a gentleman, that hath long used the clipping of coin, and upon search there is found in a house of his in Fetter Lane a great quantity of clippings and coin clipped, to the sum of £20 in gold. This man's goods are to be seized and kept in the Tower until he hath been convicted, when they shall be converted to the Queen's use.

20th December. A Dispute concerning Procedure.

The Parliament stands adjourned over Christmas until the 11th January at 8 o'clock in the morning.

Some days since a Bill was sent up to the Lords and by them passed with amendment of one word and so sent down to the Lower House, where it was found that the amendment had been affiled to the Bill and ingrossed in parchment with the words '*soit baille aux Communes*' contrary to precedent. Wherefore the House caused the Bill to be returned to the Lords for amendment, saying that they had no warrant to take notice of that amendment because it was in parchment and not in paper. To-day the Lords answer that they do not expect an exception of such levity from the gravity of the House, taking it to be immaterial whether such amendments be written in parchment or in paper, either white paper, black paper or brown paper. Thereupon some members of the House charged the Clerk that by his default and error the House was charged with levity; to which he himself prayed that some of the ancient Parliament men of the House might examine the matter. After the Clerk had been heard and the matter blamed on the inexperience of the Clerk of the Upper House, it is determined by these ancientest Parliament men that all the members of the House, being Privy Councillors, together with the best sort of the rest of the members, accompanied with the Sergeants of the Law, shall straightway be sent to the Lords to signify in the name of the whole House that the House has not in any manner of sort erred in returning that Bill and amendments in parchment to have the same done in paper according to the ancient order of Parliament; and that the House doth take itself to be very hardly dealt with to be taxed by their Lordships with imputation of levity, and reproached by other unusual and unnecessary terms.

21st December. THE EARL OF ESSEX'S INDIGNATION.

'Tis said in Court that the Queen hath advanced the Earl of Essex to be Lord Marshal, whereby his precedency over the Lord Admiral is restored. My lord doth now show himself in more public sort and is purposed to have the patent of the new Earl of Nottingham altered. But he will have none of it, and yesterday in the afternoon he gave over his White Staff as Lord Steward, and to-day is gone to Chelsea where he purposeth, as 'tis said, to be sick, for the Queen by this long patience and suffering of his is grown to consider the wrong done unto him, which now she lays upon the Lord Treasurer and Sir Robert Cecil, though with infinite protestations they deny it. The Earl of Essex desires right to be done him, either by a commission to examine it, or by combat, either against the Earl of Nottingham himself or any of his sons or name that shall defend it; or that it will please her Majesty to see the wrongs done to him, and so will suffer himself to be commanded by her. There is such ado about it as troubles the place and all proceedings. Sir Walter Ralegh is employed to end this quarrel and make atonement between them. But the resolution of Lord Essex is not to yield but with altering the patent, which cannot be done by persuasion to bring the Earl of Nottingham to it.

THE QUEEN AND M. DE MAISSE.

The Queen gave audience to M. de Maisse to-day, and in their conference together she declared that she would do naught without her Council, for there is naught so dangerous in affairs of State as self-opinion; but no longer hath she such a Council as formerly, for she hath lost twenty or twenty-two of them. The Ambassador replied that she could always make others; but the Queen answered that they were young and not yet experienced in matters of state. The Queen spake also of the love of her people, saying that it is incredible, and she loveth them no less for it, and would die rather than lose any of it, to which the Ambassador answered that they are indeed happy to live under so good a Princess. The Queen said also that she was now come almost to the edge of her grave, and ought to bethink her of death; whereat suddenly she checked herself in her speech saying, 'I think not to die so soon, Master Ambassador; nor am I so old as they think.'

Nevertheless Monsieur de Maisse complaineth that nothing is resolved, for the Queen cannot assemble the Council because of the discontents of my Lord of Essex who will not sit with the rest, and she will resolve nothing without him. Twice my Lord hath left the Court not to return again, but each time he has been sent for the same day and come back again. Since the ambassador's coming there has been nothing spoken of in Court but this brabble.

24th December. THE PRICE OF PEPPER.

This Christmastide pepper is being sold in London at 8s. the pound, which is much noted because of the former restraint of the bringing in of pepper till all that captured in the Great Carrack, four years since, should be sold. Raisins this year are being sold at 6d. the pound, Gascon wines at 2s. 8d. the gallon, and sweet wines at 4s.

31st December. NEW PLAYS.

The Admiral's men have played four new plays this month, being *Valteger*, *Stukeley*, *Nabuchodonozor*, and *That will be shall be*.

OTHER BOOKS SET FORTH ANNO 1597.

MERES' 'GOD'S ARITHMETIC.'

A little book called *God's Arithmetic* by Mr. Francis Meres, Master of Arts of both Universities, and student of Divinity. 'There be four parts of Arithmetic,' saith he, 'Addition, Multiplication, Substraction and Division, whereof the first two take their beginning from the right hand, and do multiply and increase: and these be God's numbers. The other two begin from the left and do substract and divide, and these be the Devil's.' Treateth of the advantage of marriage, and especially of ministers of religion. Saith that in old time Jacob served seven years for Rachel and bought his wife by his service, but now men must be hired to take wives, as if to take a wife were to take up a cross, and hence it ofttimes comes to pass that marriage is not good because the end of it is for goods and not for love.

BRETON'S 'WITS' TRENCHMOUR.'

A witty book by Mr. Nicholas Breton entitled *Wits' Trenchmour* in form of a pleasant conference between an angler and a scholar.

SHAKESPEARE'S 'ROMEO AND JULIET.'

The tragedy of *Romeo and Juliet*, written by William Shakespeare, that hath been often played publicly with great applause by the servants of the Lord Hunsdon.

1598

1st January. TYRONE AGAIN SUBMITS.

The Earl of Tyrone again submitted in his own person to my Lord of Ormond, on the 22nd December. Hereby Tyrone hath promised upon his honour and credit to keep the peace for eight weeks during the truce. He will not upon any supposed wrong committed upon him enter into any revenge, but will cause the same to be informed, with proofs, to the Lord Justice or the Lieutenant General. He will not entertain any practice or intelligence with the King of Spain; and if he receive any letters he will acquaint the State withal. He will also deliver cattle into the fort at Blackwater, and send a safe conduct with the victuals and munitions now to be sent there.

2nd January. REFLECTIONS ON A PEACE WITH SPAIN.

Now that the French King proposeth a peace with the King of Spain there are divers considerations whether it be more profitable to continue the war or not. A peace assuredly obtained is better than any war. It shall be profitable, in that by making peace with Spain we shall have commodity to reduce Ireland to quietness, and thereby be spared the excessive charges of treasures, victuals, munition and men to be sent out of England; trade will be open for our merchants to all countries of Spain, Portugal, Barbary and the Levant, as also to the countries in the East, as Poland and Denmark, and the maritime towns of Germany. Hereby also shall the shipping and mariners increase, and decayed port towns be succoured, as Newcastle, Hull, Boston and Lynn northwards; Southampton, Poole, Weymouth, Bristol and Chester west and southwards. By peace also shall the insolency of the King of Scots be avoided, the borders strengthened and, by increase of trade, the customs increased.

Yet are there discommodities upon dissolving of soldiers. The soldiers spared out of Ireland will, if left there, make waste or be ready to provoke the Irish to new rebellion; such as return to England will live disorderly if they be not forced to return to their native counties and former trade: and the like discommodities from those that return from the Low Countries. Moreover the Queen shall lose all hope of Calais and be unassured of the great sums lent to the French King. In France also the restitution of the Catholic religion, though liberty be promised to Protestants, will breed division and civil war, whereby the Catholics getting the upper hand, will be ready to please the King by depriving all Protestants of their states and liberties.

3rd January. SIR JOHN SMYTHE RELEASED.

Sir John Smythe, who was committed to the Tower for his seditions in the summer of '96, having made submission to her Majesty in writing before the Council, is now to be set at liberty, to repair to his own house in Essex and not to depart thence within the compass of a mile.

4th January. THE FRENCH AMBASSADOR.

M. de Maisse hath now taken his leave and will set out for France to-morrow. The Queen hath resolved to send Mr. Secretary Cecil to France. Hereat in Court they say that this will be in good earnest, but others take it for a sign that peace is toward.

5th January. TYRONE AGAIN SUBMITS.

Three days before Christmas Tyrone again submitted himself, making a very humble and penitent submission, declaring upon the knees of his heart that he is most sorry for his late relapse and defection, promising also that if he be granted a truce for two months there shall be no impediment to the victualling of the fort at Blackwater.

10th January. COMPLAINTS CONCERNING THE FRENCH COURTS.

The Queen having resolved to send Sir Robert Cecil into France together with some other Commissioners for special affairs, some order will be taken for the continued complaints of the spoils committed by the French in the Narrow Seas; and to this end Dr. Compton goeth with the Secretary with remembrances and informations that appertain to these matters.

11th January. THE PARLIAMENT RENEWED.

To-day on the meeting of the House of Lords the Earl of Essex, being now created Earl Marshal, taketh his place next after the Earl of Oxford, Lord Chamberlain of England, and before the Earl of Nottingham, Lord Steward and Lord High Admiral.

13th January. THE STILLYARD TO BE SUPPRESSED.

The Queen hath commanded the Lord Mayor and Sheriffs to repair to the Stillyard and give those that reside there notice to depart out of the realm by the 28th of this month, and to all others of the Hanse Towns residing in the realm. This is done because of that mandate of the Emperor forbidding our English merchants of the company of Merchant Adventurers any traffic within the Empire, and commanding them to depart upon great pains, and to forbear all havens and landing places or any commerce. The Stillyard shall remain in the custody of the Lord Mayor until some more favourable course shall be heard of the Emperor for restitution of our merchants to their former lawful trade within the Empire.

14th January. THE MERCHANTS TO DEPART.

This afternoon the Lord Mayor entered the Stillyard and commanded the merchants to depart the realm by the 28th of this month; their number was about sixteen. They stood much upon the privileges of the Stillyard but they see that it serves small purpose.

THE COMMONS OFFENDED.

This morning Sir Walter Ralegh, with a number of members of the Lower House, having been sent to repair to the Upper House to move for a joint conference in the Bill for the erection of houses of correction, on their return declared that their Lordships, in giving answer to these members at the Bar, did not use their former and wonted courtesy of coming down towards the Bar, but all of them sitting still in their great estates very solemnly and all covered, the Lord Keeper also in like manner delivered the answer, to the great indignity of the House and contrary to all former usage. Whereupon this innovation being very much misliked of by sundry members, Mr. Controller,

Sir Walter Ralegh, Mr. Chancellor of the Exchequer, Sir Anthony Mildmay with many others are appointed to meet this afternoon at two o'clock in Sergeants-Inn in Chancery Lane for further resolution herein.

19th January. THE COMMONS' OFFENCE.

The persons selected by the House of Commons to receive satisfaction for the innovation disputed five days ago, being Sir William Knollys, Sir Edward Hoby, and others, to-day came before the Lords who considered their answer. Which being resolved, they signified to the Lower House that if they should send any of the House up to the Lords to receive an answer to their demands, answer should be given them. Whereupon the same members as before came into the Upper House and having placed themselves at the lower end of the room, the Lord Keeper moved them to come nearer to receive their answer; but when they perceived that the Lords were resolved not to come from their places to the Bar, they protested by Sir William Knollys that they had no commission to receive answer in that form and so departed.

20th January. A QUARREL AT COURT.

The Earl of Southampton is full of discontentments. Some days since he with Sir Walter Ralegh and Mr. Parker being at primero in the Presence Chamber, and the Queen being gone to bed, Mr. Ambrose Willoughby as Squire for the Body desired them to give over. Soon after he spake to them again that if they would not leave he would call in the guard to pull down the board, which Sir Walter seeing put up his money and went his ways. But my Lord Southampton took exceptions at him and told him he would remember it; and so finding him between the Tennis Court wall and the garden struck him, and Mr. Willoughby pulled off some of his locks. The Queen gave Mr. Willoughby thanks for what he did in the Presence, and told him he had done better if he had sent my Lord to the Porter's lodge to see who durst fetch him out.

THE COMMONS SATISFIED.

After conference held between the members of both Houses, it was shown by those that had been present in many Parliaments, and especially by the Lord Treasurer, the most ancient Parliament man, that the order and custom of the House is this: When any Bills or messages are brought from the House of Commons to be presented to the Upper House, then the Lord Keeper and the rest of the Lords are to arise from their places and to go down to the Bar, there to meet such as come from the Commons and to receive their messages; but, contrariwise, when any answer is to be delivered by the Lord Keeper in the name and on behalf of the Upper House, the knights and burgesses are to receive the same standing towards the lower end of the Upper House without the Bar, and the Lord Keeper is to deliver the same sitting in his place with his head covered, and all the Lords keeping their places. Their Lordships' answer to the Commons is therefore that in the delivery of their message to Sir Walter Ralegh and the others, they have not given them any just distaste or therein offered the House of Commons any indignity whatever. And herein the House of Commons is satisfied accordingly.

A Bawd Carted.

To-day at the Sessions Prudence Crisp, otherwise known as Drury or Wingfield, is condemned to be carted. This woman hath a common brothel at Pickthatch where there have been many unlawful assemblies and atrocious riots.

26th January. The Stillyard.

News being received that our merchants at Stade have received longer time for their departure, the merchants of the Hanse Towns are now given until the end of February, or farther as our own merchants shall be used; they are charged on their peril not to depart in the mean season without satisfying their debts.

28th January. Cases of Piracy.

A certain Walter Artson, a Dutch merchant, hath complained and made proof in the High Court of the Admiralty that one Captain Elliot and his consorts in piratical manner took a ship called the *Neptune* with her lading of 120,000 of fish and two dry fats of linen cloth which they have disposed of in Dorsetshire and elsewhere.

On the coast of Cardigan a ship called the *Sea Cock* of Flushing, laden with goods to the value of £20,000, was by default of the pilot wrecked in her course from St. Lucar towards Middleburgh in Zealand. Whereupon the inhabitants of that county make an unconscionable spoil upon the utensils, apparel, munition, and furniture of the ship, together with a great part of the goods thrown upon the shore.

From Jersey also complaint is made that English pirates committed a spoil upon a ship named the *Judith*, laden with 20,000 of Newfoundland fish.

29th January. ABUSES IN THE NORTH.

A short while since the Council gave orders that those recusants in Lancashire who refused to pay the sums charged against them for the service in Ireland should be arrested, but though both the Bishop of Chester and the Sheriff used their best endeavours they missed of good success, because the recusants withdrew themselves from their abodes. The chiefest of them have now come to London to make friends to procure their release. There are still many disorders in the north. The prison at Lancaster is so ill kept that the recusants there have liberty to go when and whither they list, to hunt, hawk and go to horse races at their pleasure.

THE SPANISH PRISONERS.

The Spanish prisoners taken of late at sea are to be sent down to Plymouth and thence transported at her Majesty's great charges to Spain under the conveyance of Mr. Nicholas Owsley.

1st February. COURT NEWS.

The Earl of Southampton is now at Court again, having for a while absented himself by her Majesty's command. He is much troubled by her usage of him, for some have played unfriendly parts with him. Mr. Secretary hath procured him licence to travel, but his fair mistress doth wash her fairest face with too many tears; it is secretly said that he shall be married to her. The Lord Compton, Lord Cobham, Sir Walter Ralegh and my Lord Southampton severally feast Mr. Secretary before his departure, and have plays and banquets.

4th February. A Restraint on Cochineal.

There is such quantity of cochineal and indigo brought into the realm from prizes lately taken by the Earl of Essex that will serve this country for many years. The officers of the customs are now to forbear to receive any entry of cochineal for two years. If any be brought and the merchant be not content to carry it into some foreign port, it shall be laid up in the Custom-house till the two years be expired.

9th February. The Parliament Dissolved.

The Parliament, having sat since 24th October and considered of many Bills almost daily, is this afternoon dissolved.

Her Majesty came to the Upper House somewhat after 3 o'clock, and being set with divers Lords spiritual and temporal, the members of the Lower House with the Speaker having waited a good while at the door were at length admitted to the Upper House, as many of them as could conveniently get in.

Then the Speaker having made three reverences to her Majesty began to speak. First he showed the happiness of a Commonwealth governed by laws by which subjects are held in due obedience ; which her Majesty observing had now called a Parliament for the preservation of some laws, amending of others, cutting off of unnecessary statutes, and the making of new. And that her subjects in this Parliament, considering the strength of the realm to consist in the strength of the Prince and subjects, and their strength to stand first in the hands of God, and next in the provision of treasure, 'and therefore,' said he, 'your Majesty's most humble, dutiful and obedient subjects have by me their mouth and Speaker presented here a free gift of their free and loving hearts'—and so with that he kneeled down and delivered the Bill of Subsidy, which the Clerk of the Crown received and laid on a little table standing before the Speaker, betwixt two great wax candles on a plain green carpet—'the which I hope and think was granted without thought of "No," sure I am without word of "No."'

The second part of his speech showed a commandment laid on him by the House of Commons touching monopolies or patents of privilege, the which was a set and penned speech made at a committee. The third showed the thankfulness of the House of Commons for the pardon. The fourth and last showed the Speaker's own petition that if any faults had been committed in the House they might not now be revived; and if either he himself had spoken too much or not so much as in duty he ought to have done, he besought her Majesty's pardon.

This speech being ended, the Queen called Sir Thomas Egerton, the Lord Keeper, to whom, kneeling down before her, she spake in private; after which he went unto a place like a desk, made even with the cloth of estate on the right side, and there made answer to the Speaker's speech:

'Our most dread Sovereign, her Excellent Majesty, hath given me in charge to say unto you and the rest of her loving subjects that she doth thankfully accept of their free gift of subsidy, which she would not have required had not the puissance of the enemy required her thereunto. Secondly, touching the monopolies, her Majesty hopeth that her dutiful and loving subjects would not take away her prerogative, which is the chiefest flower in her garden, and the principal and head pearl in her crown and diadem; but they will rather leave that to her disposition. And as her Majesty hath proceeded to trial of them already, so she promiseth to continue that they shall all be examined to abide the trial and touchstone of the Law. Thirdly, touching her pardon, her Majesty's pleasure is that I show unto you that you do not so willingly accept it as she giveth it. Fourthly, for your pardon, Mr. Speaker, her Majesty saith that you have so learnedly and so eloquently defended yourself now, and painfully behaved yourself hitherto, as that your labour deserveth double her thanks. But in your petition I must also join with you in beseeching her most Excellent Majesty that if anything through want of experience or through mine own imperfections and ignorance have overslipped me it may be pardoned.'

These speeches being ended, the titles of all the Acts were read by Mr. Smith, the Clerk of the Upper House; of which her Majesty gave her royal assent to twenty-four public Acts or Statutes and nineteen private, but did refuse or quash forty-eight several Bills that have passed both Houses. Which done the Lord Keeper dissolved the Parliament in these words,

'*Dominus Custos Magni Sigilli ex mandato Dominæ Reginæ tunc dissoluit præsens Parliamentum.*'

An Outrage in the Middle Temple.

To-day a very notable outrage and great contempt was committed in the Hall of the Middle Temple by Mr. John Davies. While the Benchers and others of the Society were dining together in the Hall, Mr. Davies (who is himself a Bencher) came in wearing his cloak, his hat upon his head, and girt with his dagger; and accompanied with his servant and some stranger, both armed with swords. These two stayed at the lower end of the Hall, but Mr. Davies went up to the Benchers' table by the hearth and there drawing out a bastinado from under his cloak he struck Mr. Richard Martin over the head three or four times with such force that the cudgel was broken into pieces. This done he rushed through the Hall, and snatched a sword from his servant which he shook in the face of Mr. Martin. Then retiring out of the Hall, he drew his sword from the scabbard and repeatedly brandished it naked; after which he hastened to the Temple steps and betook himself off in a boat.

10th February. Sir Robert Cecil's Departure.

Mr. Secretary set off to-day for France, and Lord Thomas Howard, Sir Walter Ralegh and divers others go with him to Dover. Before his going Sir Robert moved the Queen to fix a privy seal for my Lord of Essex for £7,000 to be paid to him out of the cochinella as her Majesty's free gift.

A Note of the Chief Statutes enacted by the late Parliament.

An Act concerning the decay of towns and houses of husbandry because of late years more than in times past many towns, parishes, and houses of husbandry have been destroyed and become desolate. Hereby all houses that have been suffered to decay these seven years shall be repaired or again erected.

An Act for the maintenance of tillage and husbandry; for that the strength and flourishing estate of this kingdom hath always been and is upheld by the maintenance of the plough and tillage, being the occasion of the increase and multiplying of the people both for service in wars and in times of peace, being also a principal mean that they are set on work and thereby withdrawn from idleness, drunkenness, unlawful games and other lewd practices; and by the same means the greater part of the subjects are preserved from extreme poverty in a competent state of maintenance, and the wealth of the realm kept and dispersed in many hands where it is more ready to answer all necessary charges for the service of the realm. In the Parliament of 1593, partly by reason of the great plenty of grain at that time, the law ordaining a certain proportion of land to be kept in tillage was suffered to lapse; but since that time there have grown many more depopulations by turning tillage into pasture than ever before.

An Act for the relief of the poor, whereby the churchwardens of every parish and four substantial householders shall be made overseers of the poor, with power to set to work the children of all parents unable to maintain them; to gather a convenient stock of flax, hemp, wool, thread, iron and other necessary ware to set the poor that have no means to maintain themselves on work; to gather sums of money towards the necessary relief of the lame, impotent, old and blind; and also for putting out of children to be apprentices.

An Act for repressing of rogues, vagabonds and sturdy beggars, repealing all other Acts. Hereby shall be deemed as rogues and beggars all persons, calling themselves scholars, begging for money; seafaring men, pretending losses of their ships or goods; all idle persons, begging or using any subtle craft or unlawful games or plays; or feigning themselves to have knowledge in physiognomy, palmistry, or like crafty sciences, or pretending that they can tell destinies or fortunes, or such other like fantastical imaginations; proctors, procurers, patent gatherers; collectors for gaols, prisons, or hospitals; all fencers, bearwards, common players of interludes and minstrels wandering abroad (other than players belonging to any Baron of the realm or other honourable person of greater note, to be authorised under the hand and seal of arms of such Baron); jugglers, tinkers, pedlars and petty chapmen; labourers, able in body, loitering and refusing to work for such reasonable wages as are offered. And when such an one shall be taken, he shall be stripped naked from his middle upwards and shall be openly whipped until his or her body be bloody; and forthwith to be sent from parish to parish the next straight way to the parish where he was born, or, if that be not known, the parish where he last dwelt by the space of one year. Moreover, if a rogue shall appear to be dangerous to the inferior sort of people and will not be reformed, it shall be lawful for the Justices to commit him to a house of correction till the next Quarter Sessions, and thereafter to be banished out of the realm; and if any rogue so banished shall return without licence the punishment shall be death.

An Act for erecting hospitals or abiding and working houses for the poor by those charitably disposed, which may for the next twenty years be done by deed inrolled in the High Court of Chancery without necessity, as aforetime, of her Majesty's special licence.

Two Acts taking away of benefit of clergy; the one from those who shall force women with substance against their will, the other from those that rob houses in the day time.

An Act concerning labourers, whereby is amplified that Act passed in '63 which giveth to the Sheriffs, Justices of peace, Mayors and other officers the authority to rate the wages of labourers, weavers, spinsters, workmen or workwomen of every sort.

An Act against lewd and wandering persons pretending themselves to be soldiers or mariners; because that divers licentious persons, contemning both laws, magistrates and religion, of late days wander up and down in all parts of the realm, under the name of soldiers and mariners, abusing the title of that honourable profession to countenance their wicked ways, and do continually assemble themselves weaponed in the highways and elsewhere in troops to the great terror and astonishment of all true subjects, committing daily many heinous outrages, robberies, and horrible murders. It is enacted that all soldiers and mariners shall return to the place of their dwelling or birth and betake themselves to some lawful trade, on pain of being condemned as felons without benefit of clergy. But if, having so returned, no work can be found, then shall such soldier make complaint to two Justices of the peace, who shall take order for some honest work to be provided for him or else tax the whole hundred for his relief until sufficient work may be had.

The Act for the necessary relief of soldiers and mariners passed in '93 renewed, and greater penalties fixed for those that are remiss in their duty of making such provision.

12th February. THE MUSTERS.

Orders are again given this spring that all the forces within the counties shall be viewed and sufficient persons supplied in places of those found wanting by death or otherwise insufficient. They shall moreover be instructed in the discipline of war by the officers sent down as their trainers. The total number of men required at this time amounts to 45,800.

15th February. COURT NEWS.

It is said that before his departure Sir Robert Cecil was resolved not to stir a foot till the Earl of Essex assured him that nothing should pass here in his absence that might be a prejudice or offensive to him. The Earl of Essex is again fallen in love with his fairest B.; it cannot choose but come to the Queen's ears, and then he is undone and all they that depend on his favour. Yesternight Sir Gelly Merrick made a very great supper at Essex House; there were at it my Ladies Leicester, Northumberland, Bedford, Essex and Rich, and my Lords of Essex, Rutland, Mountjoy and others. They had two plays which kept them up till one o'clock after midnight.

16th February. A BAWD CARTED.

Elizabeth Holland being found guilty at the Sessions of keeping a brothel at Pickthatch, the Court adjudge that she shall be put into a cart at Newgate and be carted with a paper on her head showing her offence, and from thence to Smithfield, from thence to her house, thence to the Standard in Cheapside, and thence to Bridewell where she shall be punished; and all the way basins to be rung before her. Thence she shall be taken to Newgate, and there to remain until she have paid a fine of £40.

19th February. A COMPANY OF PLAYERS TO BE SUPPRESSED.

The third company of players now showing plays is to be suppressed, for only the companies of the Lord Admiral and the Lord Chamberlain are by licence allowed.

23rd February. MR. BODLEY'S MUNIFICENCE TO THE UNIVERSITY OF OXFORD.

Mr. Thomas Bodley hath written to the Vice-Chancellor of the University of Oxford that he will take upon himself the charge and cost to reduce the Public Library again to its former use, and to make it fit and handsome with seats and shelves and desks and all that may be needful, to stir up other men's benevolence, to help to furnish it with books; all which he purposeth to begin as soon as timber can be gotten. Moreover, because the Library never had any lasting allowance for the augmentation of the number or supply of books decayed (whereby when those that were in being were either wasted or embezzled the whole foundation was brought to ruin), now shall the University be assured of a standing annual rent to be disbursed every year in buying of books, in officers' stipends and other pertinent occasions. Thus, perhaps in time to come it may prove a notable treasure for the multitude of volumes, an excellent benefit for the use and ease of students, and a singular ornament in the University.

25th February. THE LORD TREASURER DANGEROUSLY SICK.

Yesternight upon a sudden the Lord Treasurer grew ill of a cough which put him to very great pain. The Queen sent very graciously to visit him; the Lord Cobham came to him, and so did the Lady Derby. He took his leave of her, charging her to be good and careful of her two sisters, and as his pain increased so did he think upon his end, calling upon God to receive his soul, and with little rest he passed over a tedious night. But this morning it pleased God for the good of this poor country to ease him of his pain and to give him some rest.

26th February. SHAKESPEARE'S 'HENRY THE FOURTH.'

There is entered for printing the play of *The History of Henry the Fourth* that is played by the Lord Chamberlain's men and written by Mr. William Shakespeare. Herein is shown the battle of Shrewsbury, with Harry Hotspur of the North, together with the humorous conceits of the fat knight, Sir John Falstaffe. When the actors first played this play, they called the fat knight Sir John Oldcastle, which caused offence to a certain nobleman whose wife is descended from that Oldcastle who was executed as a Lollard in the time of King Henry the Fifth. Wherefore the name is now changed.

FLESH IN LENT.

The customary orders concerning the killing of flesh in Lent are issued. The prices also to be charged for meat are this year laid down, namely, for carcases of the best sort of mutton, at 15s. or under, for the second sort at 13s. 4d., for the third sort at 10s.; for lamb, at 4s. 8d., 4s., 3s. 4d.; for veal, at 15s., 13s., or 11s.; and of each by joints or pieces at the same rates.

MARLOWE'S 'HERO AND LEANDER.'

Mr. Edward Blunt hath printed that unfinished poem of *Hero and Leander* left by Christopher Marlowe, dedicating it to Sir Thomas Walsingham. 'We think not ourselves discharged,' saith Mr. Blunt, 'of the duty we owe to our friend when we have brought the breathless body for the earth; for albeit the eye there taketh his ever farewell of that beloved object, yet the impression of the man that hath been dear to us, living an after life in our memory then putteth us in mind of further obsequies due unto the deceased.' In this poem is set forth how that Leander, having espied Hero at the feast of Adonis, swam over the Hellespont to her tower in Sestos and then enjoyed her love; but the rest of the fable is wanting.

THE CAPRICIOUS NATURE OF LOVE.

It lies not in our power to love, or hate,
For will in us is overruled by Fate.
When two are stripped, long ere the course begin,
We wish that one should lose, the other win;
And one especially do we affect
Of two gold ingots, like in each respect.
The reason no man knows, let it suffice,
What we behold is censur'd by our eyes.
Where both deliberate, the love is slight;
Who ever lov'd, that lov'd not at first sight?

1st March. THE DISORDERS IN GOVERNMENT IN IRELAND.

Notwithstanding the great mass of treasure which is often sent to Ireland with special direction to be converted only to the defraying of the army, the companies still cry out for pay, and the counties and towns that have strained themselves above their powers to diet the soldiers and furnish beeves are not satisfied but continually complain. Out of this want of pay to the army and the towns groweth all the disorders among the soldiers, who break loose upon the country and havoc the inhabitants, and is a great mean to estrange and alter the hearts of the people.

At Newry was a mutiny of the soldiers, for when the money for their pay was sent according to the certificate of the Marshal, it was found that he had made no mention of the absent and sick soldiers, which in some bands were ten, in some sixteen more than had been certified. These, finding themselves left out of all reckoning for money, victuals and clothes, fell with the rest of the garrison into so extreme a mutiny, that the Marshal and all the captains were in great doubt what would become either of the town or themselves. In the end when the paymaster entered the town the soldiers so battered him with a fury of snowballs that he fell off his horse, and with such tempest and rage did they prosecute him that if the captains and officers had not come speedily to his rescue, he had died in that place. The next day when every soldier was to have his part of his captain, and no band there but presenting ten more at least than there was money allowed for, they fell again into fury against the Marshal; but at the last he, by his friends, pawned all the credit he had that if by a certain date they were not satisfied by the State they should have all he had amongst themselves.

2nd March. THE LADY LEICESTER RECONCILED TO THE QUEEN.

The Earl of Essex hath many times laboured to have his mother brought into the Presence, for since her marriage to the late Earl of Leicester she hath been out of her Majesty's favour. Leave was often granted, and she brought to the privy galleries, but the Queen found some occasion not to come. Last Monday (27th) she was persuaded to go to Mr. Controller's at the Tilt End and there was my Lady Leicester waiting with a fair jewel of £300. A great dinner was prepared by my Lady Shandos; the Queen's coach ready; and all the world expecting her Majesty's coming, when upon a sudden she resolved not to go and so sent word. The Earl of Essex, that kept his chamber the day before, in his nightgown went up to the Queen by the privy way, but all would not prevail. But yesterday my Lady Leicester was at Court, kissed the Queen's hand and her breast, and embraced her, and the Queen kissed her. The Earl of Essex is in exceeding great favour. He doth carefully attend her Majesty and her service, and very honourably takes the pains to see all matters dispatched as if the Secretary were here.

5th March. A NOTABLE FRAUD.

Dr. Stephen Laks, doctor in civil laws, hath been most notoriously abused by one John Dean, a scrivener of London. Dr. Laks entrusted the sum of £3,000 to this Dean to put out to use for him, whereupon Dean counterfeited the hands and seals of divers credible persons to thirty or forty bonds and assurances, and brought the counterfeit obligations to Dr. Laks, making him believe them to be good. Having thus cozened him of above £3,000 he hideth himself in secret and privileged places.

6th March. MR. BODLEY'S GIFT TO OXFORD.

Mr. Bodley's liberality to the University of Oxford has received very good acceptance and thanks by public letters. The matter is very generally approved of and many think how by some good book or other they may be written in the scroll of benefactors.

'THE COUNSELLOR.'

There is newly translated into English that work called *The Counsellor*, written in Latin by Laurentius Grimaldus, and consecrated to the honour of the Polonian Emperor. Herein is pleasantly and pithily discoursed the office of magistrates, the happy life of subjects, and the felicity of commonwealths.

8th March. THE EARL OF CUMBERLAND SAILS.

The Earl of Cumberland set sail from Portsmouth two days ago in his ship the *Scourge of Malice*, and a fleet of seventeen other ships and two barges. He hath with him many mariners, and soldiers of whom Sir John Berkeley is made Colonel General. This is the twelfth voyage that my Lord hath undertaken.

10*th March*. 'LOVE'S LABOURS LOST.'

Love's Labours Lost, a play by Mr. Shakespeare that he wrote some time since, and being newly corrected and augmented was presented before her Majesty this last Christmas, is being printed.

12*th March*. INSTRUCTIONS FOR THE MUSTERS.

Certain instructions have been drawn up for the training of the musters at this time that all may be trained alike.

A company shall be equally compounded of armed men and shot; the armed men to be pikes, except the officers; the shot to be half muskets and the rest with harquebuses. Of the men, the strongest and best to be pikes; the strongest and squarest fellows will be fit to carry muskets; and the least and nimblest shall be put to the harquebus.

Every company shall be divided into three corporalships or squadrons; and every squadron into as many files as the number will bear; and every file into fellowships or camaradoes. The corporal of every squadron shall be the chiefest file of that squadron; the lanspesado shall lead the others.

The company being thus divided, in training they shall be taught, firstly, carriage and use of arms; secondly, march and motions; thirdly, understanding of all sounds of the drum and words of direction. The carriage of arms must be comely and readiest for use. The use of pike is either in receiving or giving a charge, and is most in knowing how and when every man, and so every rank, shall give his push.

In teaching the use of shot the soldier must first learn to present his piece, and to take his level, and how and when to give his volley with those of his rank; which is the proper office of the sergeant. But in teaching to give volleys the ancient and vulgar manner of discipline is utterly to be condemned, which is that the whole volleys shall be given of all the shot in one battalion at one instant as well behind as before; for either the hindermost must venture to shoot their fellows before through the head, or will overshoot and so spend their shot unprofitably. Besides, the volley once given the enemy comes on without impeachment or annoyance. Instead, let the first rank only give their volley, and if the battalion march then that rank that hath given is to stand, and the second pass through and give their volley and so stand, and the third is to come up, and consequently all the ranks. But if the battalion stand, then the first rank having given their volley shall fall back and the second come in their room, and so the third and fourth, till the first rank become last, and the last first; all which is easily performed if you do but make all the shot to open their ranks.

In teaching the soldier to know the sound of the drum, he must not only observe what the drummer doth beat, but what time he keeps, for according unto that the soldier is to march slower or faster. All other motions are taught him by the voice; wherefore, to make them perfect in these motions, it is good to use them to certain words which being once learned shall serve always for direction. The words used in training at Plymouth were such as these:

'Leaders stand forward with your files. Ranks open forward paces 5. Faces to the right hand, to the left hand. Faces about. Open your files, feet 3. Close your files. Open your files to the right hand paces. Double your files to the right hand. Double your rank to the right hand. Close your files to the left hand. As you were. Ranks from behind close. Ranks open backward paces 5. Files to the right hand turn. Ranks to the right hand turn. Front pass through. Followers pass through. Front as you were. Files as you were.'

16th March. THE ENVOYS OF THE STATES.

The envoys from the States General of the United Provinces being received by her Majesty declared that they were confident she would, in the interests of the realm, her allies and the Protestant world prefer a war of righteousness to a peace of peril; for this pretended peace in France would lead to a civil war, there being many in France to force the King into war with those of the Reformed Religion. They beseech the Queen to support them, declaring that still less than with France would treaties be observed with her, a schismatic, with whom by the papists' law no faith should be kept. The King of Spain and the Pope bear perpetual hatred to her, and the King's chief aim is to break up our league, divide its forces, and crush them separately. Though the States are already overburdened by ordinary charges for their armies, the help given to the King of France, and for ships which had joined her Majesty, yet they will oblige themselves, even beyond their proper ability, till both are contented.

17th March. THE SCOTTISH KING'S 'DAEMONOLOGY.'

The Scottish King hath written a treatise of *Daemonology*, in form of a dialogue, and divided into three books, whereof the first treateth in general of magic and necromancy, the second of sorcery and witchcraft, and the third of those kinds of spirits that trouble men. The Devil, saith he, enticeth men and women on to witchcraft by three passions which are within ourselves, curiosity in ingenious minds, thirst of revenge, or greedy appetite of gear caused through great poverty. The first is the only enticement of magicians and necromancers, the other two of the sorcerers and witches.

Declareth that they meet oftest in churches where they convene for adoring the Devil, their master; at which time, every one of them proposeth unto him what wicked turn they have done, either for obtaining of riches or for avenging them upon any whom they have malice at. At such times the Devil teacheth them how to make pictures of wax or clay, that by roasting thereof the persons represented may be dried or melted away by continual sickness; to others he giveth such stones or powders as will help to cure or cast on diseases; to others he teacheth kinds of uncouth poisons which mediciners understand not. These witches can make folks to become mad or frantic, or spirits to follow or trouble persons or haunt houses. Noteth that in the time of papistry these unlawful arts were far rarer, and never so much heard of nor so rife as they are now; but more ghosts and spirits were seen nor tongue can tell, where now a man shall scarcely all his time hear once of these things.

His Majesty wrote this book because of the fearful abounding of witches in his country, to prove that such assaults of Satan are most commonly practised, and that the instruments thereof ought most severely to be punished, contrary to the opinions of Mr. Reginald Scot, put forth in his *Discovery of Witchcraft* some years since.

24th March. KEEPING OF DAIRIES.

From Nantwich in the county of Chester come complaints that certain gentlemen not only convert tillage to keeping of dairies but sell beforehand their butter and cheese to Londoners. Hereby there is both decay of tillage and that provision ingrossed that is often needed for victualling the forces in Ireland.

29th March. PARLEYS WITH TYRONE.

The Earl of Ormond, Lord Lieutenant of Ireland, hath again met Tyrone and held parley with him on the 15th of this month and the three following days; yet although some agreement was made between them there is still no certainty or assurance of Tyrone's conformity. He still continueth the sending of messengers into Spain, and now that he is grown strong by reason of his combinations in several parts is it to be doubted that he will not stoop until he have received some blow.

30th March. 'VIRGIDEMIARUM,' THE LAST PART.

The second part of *Virgidemiarum*, being three books of biting satires, is now entered, whereto is added a postscript, wherein the author maketh his defence against the censures of his former satires. To those who wrest the matter to their own spite, answereth he; 'Art thou guilty? Complain not, thou art not wronged. Art thou guiltless? Complain not, thou art not touched.' As for the style, he declareth that the English is not altogether so natural to a satire as the Latin; nevertheless he thinketh that his first satire doth somewhat resemble the sour and crabbed face of Juvenal, which endeavouring in that one, he did determinately omit in the rest.

Of satires thus, in the fifth book:

'The satire should be like the porcupine,
That shoots sharp quills out in each angry line,
And wounds the blushing cheek and fiery eye
Of him that hears and readeth guiltily.
Ye antique satires, how I bless your days,
That brook'd your bolder style, their own dispraise,
And well-near wish, yet joy my wish is vain,
I had been then, nor were they now again:

For now our ears been of more brittle mould,
Than those dull earthen ears that were of old;
Sith those, like anvils, bore the hammer's head,
Our glass can never touch unshivered.'

1st April. THE BOY POSSESSED AT NOTTINGHAM.

The boy Sommers, from whom was cast an evil spirit last autumn, having again fallen into his fits, a commission was of late appointed from the Archbishop of York to search into the truth thereof.

Mr. Darrell having taken the names of threescore persons who were ready to be deposed touching the extraordinary handling of the boy, seventeen of them were sworn and examined before the commissioners. Then Sommers himself was called to be examined, whether he had counterfeited or not. He told them that all that he did was counterfeit. The high sheriff therefore exhorted him in the Name of God to tell the truth; whereat Sommers was violently cast into one of his fits before them all, wallowing up and down the chamber where they sat in a fearful manner. Pins were thrust deep into his hand and leg to try if he did counterfeit; but he was senseless, and no blood followed. At length being recovered as out of sleep, they asked what he had done. He said he could not tell. Being asked whether he had not been pricked with pins, he said yes; they asked where, and he showed the wrong hand. After some further questions he was conveyed away, and being absent he was worse tormented than before. They brought him back again to know if he would confess who had persuaded him to say he had counterfeited, and as he was coming up a pair of stairs through a gallery, he had cast himself over headlong to have broken his neck, if he had not been hindered.

When he was the second time brought before the commissioners he was more terribly handled than before, insomuch that the commissioners and all that were present were fully satisfied that he was corporally possessed and surceased to examine any more witnesses; even Mr. Walton, Archdeacon of Derby, being present and a principal enemy to Mr. Darrell, acknowledged that it was the finger of God upon this rare accident.

Herewith all that favoured Mr. Darrell began to rejoice and to run abroad into the town, telling their friends with great joy that Sommers was now found to be no dissembler. The rest that had held a contrary opinion were greatly checked, so that when some of them came out of the house where the commission sat they were rated at exceedingly, and at one of them a stone was cast. Thus for ten days Mr. Darrell and his friends triumphed.

But by direction of the Lord Chief Justice, Sommers is once again taken out of the hands of Mr. Darrell and his friends and confesseth, as before, the whole course of his dissimulation and why he had affirmed to the commissioners that his fits were counterfeit. With this alteration Mr. Darrell is greatly troubled; the parts taken on both sides begin to be more violent and the town is extraordinarily divided, one railing upon another at their meeting in the streets. The pulpits also ring of nothing but devils and witches, wherewith men, women and children are so frighted as many of them durst not stir in the night, nor so much as a servant go into his master's cellar about his business without company. Few grow to be sick or evil at ease but straightway they are deemed to be possessed. Such indeed are the stirs in Nottingham about this matter that it is feared the people will grow to further quarrels and mutinies or some greater inconvenience.

3rd April. BASTARD'S 'CHRESTOLEROS.'

Mr. Thomas Bastard hath written seven books of epigrams under the title of *Chrestoleros*, which are dedicated to Sir Charles Blount, Lord Mountjoy. Of my Lord of Essex, thus:

Essex, the ends which men so fain would find,
Riches, for which most are industrious,
Honour, for which most men are virtuous,
Are but beginnings to thy noble mind:
Which thou as means doth frankly spend upon
Thy country's good, by thy true honour won.

5th April. SEIZED BOOKS.

Of late there was a bark driven into Falmouth by tempest of weather and belonging to certain merchants of Wexford; herein were found papistical books, beads and other relics, not fit to be transported and brought into her Majesty's dominions.

All these are to be burnt in the market place of Perin, and he that first gave intelligence satisfied for his charges.

6th April. THE TOWN OF TWYFORD BURNT.

Twyford a town in Devon is consumed by fire. This fire began about one o'clock in the afternoon in a poor cottage where a woman was frying pancakes with straw for lack of other fuel; and in one hour and a half such was the rage of the fire that it consumed 409 houses, £150,000 in money, plate, merchandise, household stuff, and houses. Fifty persons are consumed, but an almshouse preserved with the poor men therein though in the midst of the flames. Nine thousand people were there maintained by the making of cloth. It is thought of many that this is a just punishment of God upon the town for the unmercifulness of the rich and small regard of the poor, which were daily seen to perish in the streets for lack of relief.

7th April. SIR ROBERT CECIL RECEIVED BY THE FRENCH KING.

Sir Robert Cecil did not reach the French King who was at Angers until the 17th March, having travelled more than 300 miles. Four days later he was received in audience of the King, and many nobles of great quality, when he delivered the Queen's letters, declaring further that it had pleased her Majesty to make election of him to communicate her secret and princely thoughts when it should please the King to discover his own disposition and judgment of this project of a general treaty. Mr. Secretary's intention was that this first audience should be but complimental where the King might make public acknowledgment of his obligation and respect towards her Majesty. Then he requested that the King would yield him some other access, beseeching him for this time only to permit him to present the Earl of Southampton who was come with deliberation to serve him. The King promised access the next day, and then very favourably embraced the Earl and the others presented to him. Then he suddenly took Sir Robert by the hand, saying that he would walk with him down into his garden *en qualité d'ami*, where for an hour and a half he entertained him with many pleasant and familiar discourses of his opinion of divers of his subjects and other particulars. The Commissioners from the States are now arrived.

9th April. CERTAIN LETTERS CAPTURED.

It is said that some days since certain fishermen fished up in the sea a packet of letters from the Cardinal of Austria to the King of Spain, wherein it appeareth that the French King will conclude peace without regard to her Majesty or to the States. Moreover the King of Spain requireth that if the French will have the English comprehended in the peace then shall the Catholic religion be free in England, and likewise with the Low Countries. Copies of these letters have been sent to Sir Robert Cecil.

10th April. MR. CHAPMAN TRANSLATETH HOMER'S 'ILIADES.'

Mr. George Chapman hath entered for the press *Seven Books of the Iliades of Homer*, *Prince of Poets*, translated according to the Greek, and dedicated 'To the most Honoured now living instance of the Achilleian virtues, eternized by divine Homer, the Earl of Essex, Earl Marshal, etc.' Writeth of my Lord in these terms: 'Most true Achilles (whom by sacred prophecy Homer did but prefigure in his admiral object) and in whose unmatched virtues shine the dignities of the soul, and the whole excellence of royal humanity, let not the peasant-common polities of the world that count all things servile and simple, that pamper not their own private sensualities, burying quick in their filthy sepulchres of earth the whole bodies and souls of honour, virtue and piety, stir your divine temper from perseverance in godlike pursuit of Eternity.'

APOLLO SENDETH THE PLAGUE.

Thus prayed he, and Apollo heard, who at the heart offended
Down from the topless brows of heaven, into the host descended,
His bow and quiver covered round, his golden shoulders wore,
His angry arrows, as he moved, did thunder on the shore;
So, like the lowring night he walked, and took his wreakful stand
Athwart the fleet: his silver bow, with his hard losing hand,

A dreadful sound did make; and first the mules and dogs he wounds,
And after with the breasts of men his mortal shafts confounds:
The funeral pyres did ever burn with heaps of men he slew;
Nine days together through the host his poisoned arrows flew;
The tenth a council through the camp Æcides designed,
Which Juno with the silver arms did put into his mind.

12th April. AN ATTEMPT TO POISON.

A very lewd fact is reported from the north where Mr. Barnabe Barnes, son to the late Bishop of Durham, attempted to poison John Brown, the Recorder of Berwick; but upon discovery he is fled and thought to have gone into Durham where the Bishop shall cause him to be apprehended and sent up to the Council in charge of some trusty person.

14th April. A SECOND PART TO 'HERO AND LEANDER.'

One Mr. Henry Petowe hath written *The Second Part of Hero and Leander*, containing their further fortunes, for that the history of *Hero and Leander*, penned by that admired poet Marlowe, but not finished, and resting like a head separated from the body with this harsh sentence '*Desunt nonnulla.*' Herein is shown how Leander was banished for his love to Hero, and she imprisoned for that the Duke Euristippus would have had her love; but that after long exile Leander came back and slew the Duke and was at length restored to Hero; and they living together in perfect love were at last transformed into two pine trees,

Whose nature's such, the female pine will die
Unless the male be ever planted by.

MR. PETOWE'S PRAISE OF MARLOWE.

Oh had that King of poets breathed longer,
Then had fair beauty's fort been much more stronger:
His golden pen had clos'd her so about
No bastard Æglet's quill the world throughout,
Had been of force to mar what he had made,
For why they were not expert in that trade:

What mortal soul with Marlowe might contend,
That could 'gainst reason force him stoop or bend?
Whose silver charming tongue moved such delight,
That men would shun their sleep in still dark night,
To meditate upon his golden lines,
His rare conceits and sweet according rimes.
But Marlowe, still admired Marlowe's gone,
To live with beauty in Elizium;
Immortal beauty, who desires to hear,
His sacred poesies sweet in every ear.
Marlowe must frame to Orpheus' melody,
Hymns all divine to make heaven harmony.
There ever live the Prince of Poetry
Live with the living in eternity.

16th April. THE NEGOTIATIONS WITH THE FRENCH KING BROKEN.

The negotiations between the French King are now broken, and Sir Robert Cecil and Dr. Herbert take their way homeward, for the King hath privately made agreement with the Spaniards which awaiteth only a commission sent out of Spain to conclude it. He excuseth himself by the delay which the Queen made, by the urgent necessity, and by the opportunity that was offered, referring Sir Robert Cecil and Monsieur Oldenbarnevelt, the ambassador from the States, to his Council.

To the Council Monsieur Oldenbarnevelt declared that the States, by God's mercy and the Queen's favour and assistance, are brought to that pass that they have not only been able to defend themselves, but also to assist France in her extremities, nor are they so to be neglected and slighted with whom the Kings both of France and England have thought fit to make strict leagues and alliances. After many other weighty reasons why they could not embrace peace with the Spaniard he concluded that some Kings to attain power and greatness have neglected and disregarded their leagues; but for the most part sad hath been the consequence, for the state of Kings, unless it stand upon faith and fidelity, cannot stand upon power. He propounded therefore that if the King would listen no longer after peace but besiege Calais, they would at their own charges beleaguer at the same time some other place that the enemy's forces might be divided; and besides, towards the besieging of Calais, they would allow pay for 7,000 men and set forth 25 men-of-war, provided that he for the siege would find 3,000 horse, 6,000 foot and 6 pieces of ordnance.

To these things the Chancellor of France answered that all kindness should be showed to the States, but that the opportunity of peace offered to France, now languishing with long wars, was not only to be accepted of but also of urgent necessity to be catched at.

The States therefore utterly refusing peace, Sir Robert Cecil can proceed no further towards the general peace. Nevertheless he replied to the Chancellor, denying that the Queen had used any delay, but had with all speed sent into France to treat of peace, and declared that they made the necessity greater than could be believed. Moreover he desired them to put the King in mind with what vows he had bound and engaged himself before the Earl of Shrewsbury after the ratification of the league, and before by many letters signed with his own hand. The Queen, said he, hath not at all receded from the conditions of the league, yea, she hath performed more than she was obliged; but the King hath stuck to nothing; and with that he produced the draft of the league. He asked also that some course may be taken whereof those great sums formerly lent by the Queen may be repaid; for being now forsaken and left in the lurch, she hath learned too late to provide for her own state more carefully in time to come, and not to confer her benefits on those who so ill deserve them.

And so with fair and gentle answers the ambassadors are dismissed, in great discontent.

18th April. The Spital Sermons.

It hath long been accustomed at the sermons at the Spital in the Easter holidays to have a gathering for the redemption of such as are prisoners of the Turk or other heathens; but as there are few of late years taken by the Turk, and at this present divers poor mariners come hither out of Spain where they have been cruelly racked and endured great misery, it is proposed that a collection shall be made to relieve their present necessities and send them home into their counties.

21st April. ARISTOTLE'S 'POLITIQUES.'

Aristotle's *Politiques or Discourses of Government* are now for the first time Englished by one J. D. from the French of Loys le Roy, called Regius, being set forth with expositions taken out of the best authors, conferred together, illustrated by innumerable examples both new and old concerning the beginning, proceeding and excellency of civil government. As there is no philosopher can in depth of knowledge equal Aristotle, whose works may be justly termed 'The Treasury of human wisdom,' so these his discourses of Government have not the meanest relish thereof; especially where he handleth the changes and destructions of every commonwealth, with their causes, setting down several precepts for the upholding and preserving of each.

24th April. TYRONE RENEWETH THE TRUCE.

On the 10th of the month the Earl of Ormond again met Tyrone in parley, which continued four days, when peace was further agreed upon for six weeks, for due observation whereof he took his oath and subscribed with his own hand. Yet there is little likelihood the peace will be kept, for albeit Tyrone took a solemn oath at this conference that he had not combined with any in Leinster since the Lord Lieutenant had this charge delivered to him, yet by interception of some letters it appeared plainly that he had made a combination but last month with two in Leinster and had authorised others to draw confederates into his faction.

25th April. LORD BURLEIGH'S REBUKE.

My Lord of Essex stiffly maintaining that no peace could be made with the Spaniards but such as would be dishonourable and fraudulent on their side, the Lord Treasurer answered that he breathed forth nothing but war, slaughter and blood; and after a hot dispute in this matter, he drew forth a psalm book, and saying nothing, pointed him to this verse, 'Men of blood shall not live out half their days.'

30th April. ABUSES IN TENEMENT HOUSE.

There are complaints of abuses in Shoreditch, St. Giles-without-Cripplegate, Clerkenwell and other places in the suburbs that divers owners of small tenements, most of them erected within these few years, do let the same out by the week to base people and harbour thieves, rogues and vagabonds, whereby great mischiefs and lewd disorders are committed. Moreover by often removing of those persons from place to place, there can no certain knowledge be taken of them what they are and how they live and maintain themselves, an abuse most intolerable, and in no wise to be permitted in a Christian commonwealth. The justices are now charged to take the view of these cottages and base tenements, and those that inhabit in them, taking true notes of those that dwell in them, their names, out of what part they come, how long they have dwelt there, what trade they use, for what time they hire their lodgings, and what rent they pay, and in what sort. Of the owners also bonds shall be taken hereafter to let no houses by the week or month or any less time than a year, nor to let out (as many do) their chambers alone or some few rooms to poor persons that keep whole families in the same; nor to admit hereafter any that shall not bring a true certificate whence they come and of their good behaviour allowed by two justices of the peace at least.

There is also another abuse in these parishes when certain persons of wealth convert fair dwelling houses into tenements with raising of great rent for the same. Hereby, in place of those of good ability that used to live in these houses and pay all other charges with the rest of the parishioners, in their rooms are placed many poor persons that need relief from the parish where the landlords reap great rents and are subject to no charge.

1st May. Sir Robert Cecil's return.

Sir Robert Cecil and Dr. Herbert to-day reached London and came to Court, having left the French King on the 15th April and landed in England on the 29th.

3rd May. 'Greene in Conceipt.'

A book of the tragic history of fair Valeria of London called *Greene in conceipt* written by J. D., is entered, purporting to have been set down before him by the ghost of Greene. This Valeria, being by nature and the liberality of her parents a wanton, was wooed and wedded by an old man called Giraldo. But after some short time growing tired of her husband, she was led into wantonness by some of her light companions, and soon came so to like the game that henceforth she could never leave it. For a long while Giraldo knew nothing of his wife's faithlessness till he was brought to a sight of it by his boy Jockey, and pining thereat, he died of a broken heart. And thereafter Valeria was married by Arthemio, that loved her for her old husband's wealth, who soon began to treat her despitefully, consuming her goods and even entertaining his trulls before her face; so that within a brief space their movables were sold and they turned out into the streets penniless. And now Valeria having nowhere to go at length betook herself to Jockey, that had married a widow and kept a simple victualling house; thither she went and was received with all kindness. But at length, whether hoping for some better place or loath to trouble him continually, she fondly left him and thereby replunged into her former miseries, falling in the end to little better than open beggary, from which abject state she never recovered till death gave truce to her distresses.

6th May. THE CURES OF THE DISEASED IN REMOTE REGIONS.

There is a little book by G. W. of *The Cures of the Diseased in remote regions* to prevent mortality incident in foreign attempts of the English nation; which diseases are especially the *calenture* (or burning fever), the *tabardilla*, the *espinlas* (a pricking disease), the *cameras de sangre* (that is laxativeness or bloody flux), the *erizipila* and the *tinoso* (which we call the scurvy).

7th May. MR. GOSSON'S SERMON AT PAUL'S CROSS.

To-day Mr. Stephen Gosson, parson of Great Wigborough in Essex, preached at Paul's Cross from 2 Chronicles, chap. xx, verse 20, on the action of war. War, said he, was just in reason, in religion and in practice of the Church, and man himself provided for it by reason and hands instead of the horns, hoofs, teeth and talons given to brute beasts. Just and lawful wars are of several sorts; when one prince withholds that which is another's; or when the laws of nations are denied; or the fame and honour of a Prince be hurt; or disgrace or indignity offered to his ambassadors; or in defence of a Prince's friend; the last injury of all being invasion. Thence he passed to the war with the Spaniard.

9th May. AN ABUSE IN DARTMOUTH.

The magistrates in Emden make great complaint of an abuse committed last winter at Dartmouth. At that time a ship of Emden, called the *Fortune*, laden with corn and bound for Rochelle, was driven by contrary winds into Dartmouth. Wherefore because of the great dearth in the county, the Council gave direction that the same should be sold with the consent of the master. Hereupon the Mayor of Dartmouth sold the whole lading to certain rich men of the county by great quantities at far lower prices than corn of like goodness did then bear, and kept a good part thereof himself, so that the poor had no relief, the buyers made an unlawful gain, and the proprietaries thereof were damnified to the sum of £400.

10th May. THE QUEEN'S LETTERS TO THE FRENCH KING.

Since the return of the ambassadors the Queen hath by Sir Thomas Edmonds, Secretary for the French tongue, lovingly and freely admonished him to remember his faith given, and to have a regard to his conscience towards God and his reputation amongst men, lest he insnare himself by the counsels of corrupt and wicked men; but amongst her grave admonitions are intermixed these nipping checks: 'If there be any sin in the world against the Holy Ghost it is ingratitude. If you get any reasonable terms at the Spaniard's hands, you may thank the English succours for it. Forsake not an old friend, for a new one will not be like him. The conscience and religion of a league and the faith of contracts are not used as nets to entrap, but only by wicked men. A bundle of rods bound together is not easily broken. There is no easier way to overthrow us both than by parting and disjoining us one from the other.'

14th May. THE VENETIAN ARGOSY.

The matter of the Venetian argosy, named the *St. Agatha Morisini* (that was stayed in January '97), is still in question, whereby the Council are greatly displeased to find themselves continually importuned with the complaints of the Venetian merchants and the business delayed, and charge those concerned to protract the time no longer but to make present satisfaction.

15th May. 'THE SERVINGMAN'S COMFORT.'

One J. M. hath written a book called *A health to the gentlemanly profession of servingmen or the Servingman's comfort*, wherein is set out the decay of good housekeeping from former days when the younger sons of gentlemen would be honest serving men; and the abuse of these times when to escape the service of the wars yeomen will send their sons to be gentlemen's servants, and maintain them at their own charges. Then must the country courtier be attired in the latest fashion with his venetians of the largest size (that will hold a bushel a breech at least), and his gait and gesture no longer of the plough but direct and upright, treading in time as though he would tell what paces are in a furlong. No longer can be seen the great chines of stalled beef, the great black-jack of noble beer, the long hall tables fully furnished with good victuals; these now be all changed into cates of less cost though dishes of rarer device, such as goose giblets, pigs' pettitoes, and other made dishes. Lamenteth how many misfortunes come by the decay of liberality, for when servingmen are turned away by their masters, then by necessity they be forced to rob passengers at Gadshill, Shootershill, Salisbury Plain or Newmarket Heath.

20th May. THE MONOPOLY IN STARCH.

The monopoly for importing starch that was formerly granted to Mr. Richard Young is now assigned to Sir John Pakington for eight years.

RUMOURS.

The talk in the City is now of Barnevelt, the agent and advocate of the States who is here and hath had audience these two days together, but no music will please us unless it be to the tune of peace. One of the chiefest reasons for it is a kind of disdain and envy at our neighbours' well doing, in that we, for their sake and defence entering into the war, and being barred from all commerce and intercourse of merchandise, they in the meantime thrust us out of all traffic to our utter undoing and their own advancement. Another motive to the peace is the troubles in Ireland which are like to put the Queen to exceeding charge, and withal there appears a black cloud in Scotland that threatens a storm.

21st May. MR. BARNABE BARNES.

A week ago Mr. Barnabe Barnes was brought before the Council and commanded to give attendance before their lordships from time to time and not to depart until he shall be dismissed. The charge that Mr. Barnes attempted and put in practice to poison the Recorder of Berwick is to be examined by the Attorney-General, Mr. Francis Bacon, and Mr. William Waad; and if by the testimony of witnesses and other good means there appear proof or pregnant supposition that Mr. Barnes is any way culpable therein, then shall they take advice with the Lord Chief Justice what course is fit to be followed for the punishing of so foul and odious an offence.

THE SERMON AT PAUL'S CROSS.

Mr. John Howson preached to-day at Paul's Cross, concluding that sermon upon the xxi. of Matthew, the 12 and 13 verses, which he began in December last. Concludeth that the sin of the Jews in making the Temple a den of thieves is committed by ourselves, who have added as great increases and strength to these sins as time hath added years and increase to the world.

25th May. SLANDERS AGAINST THE SCOTTISH KING.

Some weeks since one Valentine Thomas (or Anderson), an Englishman, a lewd caitiff, being taken on the Border and brought to London, thereupon made certain declarations greatly to the dishonour of the Scottish King. He delivered without torture or menace divers informations of practices contrived between the King of Scots and himself for taking away the Queen's life, for which he was promised great reward by the King. Hereat the King taketh it hardly that the Queen should not have discovered the accusations, either to his ambassador or to himself to clear her mind and his honour. It is reported that the King will be quit by sound of trumpet and by challenge in what numbers soever, yea of a King to a King in case of need, if he is not cleared of the slander of the murder, protesting that for all the crowns in the world he would not be guilty even in thought.

27th May. THE 'METAMORPHOSIS OF PYGMALION'S IMAGE; AND CERTAIN SATIRES.'

There is a poem called *The Metamorphosis of Pygmalion's Image*, telling that story of Pygmalion who wrought an image of a woman in ivory, and he hotly wooing it she was suddenly transformed into a woman and returned his love. Hereto are adjoined five satires of the men of these times. This book is written by one calling himself W. K. and dedicated 'To the World's Mighty Monarch, Good Opinion.'

HIS DESCRIPTION OF A PURITAN.

Who would imagine yonder sober man,
That same devout meal-mouth'd precisian,
That cries 'Good brother,' 'Kind sister,' makes a duck
After the antique grace, can always pluck
A sacred book out of his civil hose,
And at th' op'ning and at our stomach's close,
Says with a turn'd-up eye a solemn grace
Of half an hour; then with silken face
Smiles on the holy crew, and then doth cry,
'O manners! O times of impurity!—'
Who thinks that this good man
Is a vile, sober, damned politician?
Not I, till with his bait of purity
He bit me sore in deepest usury.
No Jew, no Turk, would use a Christian
So inhumanely as this Puritan.
Dromedes' jades were not so bestial
As this same seeming saint—vile cannibal!
Take heed, O world! take heed avisedly
Of these same damned anthropophagi.
I had rather been within a harpy's claws
Than trust myself in their devouring jaws,
Who all confusion to the world would bring
Under the form of their new discipline.

30th May. A FRAY AT OXFORD.

Last Sunday at Oxford the Mayor suffered a company of 150 trained soldiers and other young men to go early in the morning to try their pieces, and to return into the city in battle array; but in returning they were stayed by Mr. Daniel, the proproctor, and some scholars, who took from them their drum and divers weapons, striking and beating some, and committing others to prison; insomuch that there was a great uproar and concourse, both of scholars and citizens, and if the citizens had not given way there would have been a bloody day and much slaughter. The Mayor complaineth to the Council that the scholars have not been punished and moreover they keep that which they took away. But the Vice-Chancellor declareth that the townsmen, with drum and shot and other weapons, and men attired in women's garments, brought into the town a woman bedecked with garlands and flowers, and named by them Queen of May. Moreover they had morrice-dances and other unseemly sports, and intended next Sunday to continue the same abuses; in which riotous proceedings seditious speeches were used. When the Vice-Chancellor sent to entreat the Mayor to meet him, the Mayor made a frivolous and dilatory answer, and in the meantime preferred an unjust and scandalous complaint against the University.

1st June. THE APOLOGY OF THE EARL OF ESSEX.

My Lord of Essex, being of so many taxed as the hinderer of the peace and quiet of his country at this time, hath written an apology of his present opinions in the form of a letter to Mr. Anthony Bacon. That generally he is affected to the men-of-war should not seem strange to any reasonable man; for every man doth love them of his own profession, and since the Queen hath used him yearly in her late actions he must reckon himself among the men of war. He would not now dissent from peace, if those who propose it would build upon any one true principle; but if they will promise themselves that they may have peace without ground, or think that peace shall be good for us without reason, or to leap blindfold into a Treaty without undue circumstance, then doth he not suspect too much, but they too little.

No peace can be had for the United Provinces, without a Spanish sovereign be acknowledged, and then will the Popish religion be either universally established or at least freely exercised in towns and provinces whence it is now banished.

Allow the first, and they banish God's true service to bring in idolatry; allow the second (a plurality of religions) which is less, and it is against the policy of all States; because where there is no unity in the Church there can be no unity or order in the State, yea, it is the manifest ruin of that State.

We can have no advantage of this peace; yet some will say it is better to have a patched peace than an unsupportable war, and yet at this time never hath this realm been stronger. 'We,' quoth he, 'thanks be to God, have a Queen who hath never been wasteful in her private expense, yet will she sell her plate and jewels in the Tower ere her people shall be undefended. We are a people that will turn our silk coats into iron jacks, and our silver plate into coats of plate, rather than our Sovereign shall be unserved.' Moreover, now that the King of Spain is weakest is the unfittest time to make peace; for if we make peace now, then, when his coffers are full of treasure and his fleet supplied with ships, he will be able not only to trouble kingdoms by war but to purchase them with money. Then will our men of war either be driven to seek new countries and new fortunes or consumed in a beggarly and miserable Irish war, and our nation be grown unwarlike, in love with the name and bewitched with the delights of peace.'

Being charged with publishing this *Apology*, my Lord protesteth that so far from giving copies of it, he ordered his man that kept his papers not to let any of his friends see it, but in his hand or at least in his presence. He suspecteth that it is come abroad by corruption of some of his servants that had access to his chamber, who might take and copy out his loose papers which lay ever sheet by sheet under the bed's head till he had leisure to finish the whole. He hath never sent any papers to the press or to a scrivener's shop.

2nd June. A LEWD SHOW AT BRUSSELS.

At Brussels of late was a dumb show representing the French King and the Cardinal, who after long wars fell to a treaty. While they are conferring, in cometh a lady and conveys herself behind the French King and prieth what they say, expressing much perturbation at it, sometimes fawning and sometimes flattering and plucking the French King by the sleeve. In the meantime one of the minions begins to chafe, enquiring what she is that presumes so near; where it is gestured she is the Queen of England. So they whisper and laugh at the conceipt. With that there come in four or five fellows dressed like boors, and begin to press to the place and interrupt the treaty. Whereupon the Cardinal enquires who they are, and they are described to be boors of Holland. Whereat the King laughs at the rudeness of the poor; but the Cardinal gestures that he will hang them all up so soon as he hath done with his great business. So are we mocked by them while we treat of peace.

5th June. A Case of Piracy.

Mr. Nicholas Owsley, that lately transported the Spanish prisoners out of the realm to Lisbon in the *Unicorn* of Dansk and returned with such English prisoners as remained there, complaineth that in his course outward, he was set upon by a ship called the *Flying Dragon* of Bristol, and robbed of merchandise of good value.

7th June. Troubles at Plymouth.

During the last months there have been great differences between the Mayor of Plymouth and Sir Ferdinando Gorges commanding the fort in that place. The Council have therefore drawn up certain articles to be observed by both parties. The commander of the fort shall not meddle with the borough in matters of justice, nor shall he have anything to do with the Castle except at the time of some approach of the enemy. He shall not command any inhabitant to watch out of the town; nor shall he or his servants go on board to search any vessel except for her Majesty's special service, and then he shall acquaint the Mayor and take one of the Mayor's brethren and the searcher with him.

On the part of the town, it is commanded that if any townsman shall give occasion of offence unto any soldier, the officers of the town shall take order for just satisfaction unto the party grieved. At all times of approach of the enemy, the inhabitants shall be ready to obey the directions of Sir Ferdinando Gorges. No foreign prisoners shall be brought into the town but that notice shall be given to the commander of the Fort, and straight order taken that the prisoners be kept in safe custody and not suffered as heretofore to run up and down at their pleasure, whereby many inconveniences may ensue. If any passengers shall arrive from any foreign part, notice to be given to the commander that they may be examined upon points necessary to the furtherance of her Majesty's service.

In these troubles the two most blameworthy are the Town Clerk of Plymouth and Jennings, Sir Ferdinando Gorges' lieutenant. Both are to be put forth from their offices.

8th June. THE PEACE AT VERVINS.

Perpetual peace between the French King and the Spaniards was publicly proclaimed on the 26th May both at Paris and at Amiens in the presence of the Legate and the King's deputies. This peace was concluded and subscribed upon the 22nd April, but upon express condition that it should not be published till a month after, for the King of France wished the ambassadors of England and the States first to be gone from his Court. In this conference at Vervins the Spaniards have agreed to restore those towns which they hold in Picardy, Blavet in Brittany, and Calais. At first they would have kept Calais so long as the war lasteth with the States, giving the French an exchange in the meantime. The French stood to have Calais restored freely, and likewise Cambray; but they agreed, without much difficulty, that Calais shall be restored while the Spaniard keeps Cambray.

10th June. MURDERS IN IRELAND.

During this last truce, as at other times of cessation of arms, the rebels have taken great advantage and are grown to an exceeding great strength. The rebels in Leinster, by the granting of privileges to them, are grown to such strength and insolence that they have laid waste a great part of the county. Thence passing into the Queen's county they have so spoiled and utterly wasted it that the poor English gentlemen of the shire do scarcely dare to manure one foot of their land, or almost to look out of their castles; their tenants have joined the rebels, and this county which cost so much English blood and treasure to gain is almost lost.

After these murders and villainies this vile rabble of rebels drew into Wexford where, after many spoils and outrages committed upon the poor inhabitants of the county, they have lately slain the lieutenant, sergeant and six soldiers of Sir Henry Wallop's company; also 80 of two bands of Picardy soldiers, and besides these many of the gentlemen and inhabitants.

11th June. COMPLAINTS AGAINST THE EARL OF LINCOLN.

So many complaints have been made against the Earl of Lincoln by poor men's petitions and complaints that the Council have earnestly desired him to have some regard to satisfy them and prevent the occasion of any more. Now one Robert Blower declareth that, contrary to all law and conscience, certain disordered persons, by his Lordship's own appointment, have dispossessed him of a house and land in Oxfordshire. Whereupon the Council pray my Lord either to restore the poor man to the possession of his house or, if his complaint is unjust, to make it so sufficiently to appear that he shall be punished for false information or slander. Otherwise, if Blower receive no remedy, the Council must take some order for his relief.

15th June. JESUIT DEVICES.

Some priests in Lancashire have recently prevailed over divers persons to incline to papistry. They have a certain woman who pretendeth to be possessed with unclean spirits upon whom they have practised at some private places where for the novelty thereof sometimes as many as 500 persons would be drawn together, promising not to betray them. The party possessed being set in a chair maketh show to be most wonderfully writhen, and with very strange illusions; and thus daily they win many unto them. Now at least twenty persons are taken and sent to the Bishop of Chester for examination.

17th June. A CASE OF MANSLAUGHTER.

At the Sessions to-day Mr. Edward Harwood, a gentleman late of London, was arraigned for the murder of Mr. Adam Crosby whom he had slain in Bastian's Close in St. Giles-without-Cripplegate. Mr. Harwood put himself not guilty of murder but guilty of manslaughter, and asking for the book is branded with the letter T and released accordingly.

18*th June.* SOLDIERS FOR IRELAND.

For the service in Ireland there are now to be levied 2,000 men from the Principality of Wales and the counties near adjoining. Good and serviceable men are to be chosen, not admitting any rogues or vagabonds, and of them half shall be pikes, and half shot.

23*rd June.* NEWS FROM PARIS.

In the French Court it is declared that the towns will be given up under this treaty at the end of the month. A certain Dutchman, Sir Melchior Leven, that was knighted by my Lord of Essex at Cadiz, hath refused to fight Sir Charles Blount in Paris on the ground that the King hath forbidden duels, whereat all do mock him. Sir Charles who went with the Secretary on his embassage stayed behind on purpose to effect this challenge.

24*th June.* DISTRESS IN LINCOLNSHIRE.

The evil disposition of those who seek immoderate profit by ingrossing grain and transporting it out of the county is such that in the county of Lincoln there is great discontent of the people; insomuch that they were ready to break forth into great disorder but for the pains of the Bishop of Lincoln, Sir Henry Cromwell and Mr. Oliver Cromwell, who have committed to prison one notorious offender, by name William Baxter of Calcott. This Baxter is sent for by the Council.

28*th June.* THE TRUCE ENDED IN IRELAND.

The last truce with Tyrone expired on the 7th of the month, and within two days afterwards he made a division of his forces into three, whereof one part he sent to the Blackwater, which he now holdeth environed, swearing by his barbarous hand that he will not depart till he carry the fort; with another part he assaulteth the castle of the Cavan; the third part he hath laid ready to send into Leinster to strengthen his faction there. Such is the weakness of the forces in Ireland that nothing can be done to relieve the Blackwater; for the rest there is a strength of but 1,500 or 1,600 men until more troops arrive from England. Nevertheless the Lord Lieutenant hath not been idle. On the 13th of the month, hearing that some of the rebels were in the mountains near Dublin, he went after them stealthily with two companies, and would have slain many but for the rash overforwardness of certain gentlemen that galloped ahead and were engaged among the enemy ere they were aware, whereof four were slain. In these last weeks 434 of the rebels have been slain or executed by martial law.

2nd July. THE EARL OF ESSEX'S GREAT CONTEMPT.

The Earl of Essex is suddenly withdrawn from the Court, and it is said that yesterday there grew a smart debate between the Queen and my Lord, there being also present the Lord Admiral, Sir Robert Cecil and Mr. Windebank, Clerk of the Signet. Her Majesty thought Sir William Knollys the fittest man of any to be sent to Ireland; but the Earl of Essex obstinately insisted that Sir George Carew was fitter than he, and quite forgetting himself and neglecting his duty, he uncivilly turned his back upon the Queen as it were in contempt, and gave her a scornful look. She not enduring such contempt returned him a box on the ear and bade him get him gone and be hanged. Thereupon the Earl laid his hand on his sword, and the Lord Admiral stepping between, he swore a great oath that he neither would nor could put up with so great an affront and indignity, neither would he have taken it at King Henry the Eighth his hands, and in great passion withdrew himself forthwith from the Court.

6th July. THE GOVERNOR OF DUNKIRK.

Don Francisco D'Aquilla Alverado, the Governor of Dunkirk, that was taken in September last, and brought to England, is now to be sent back to Ostend where he will be nearer to his friends that speedier means may be wrought for the payment of his ransom.

7th July. STOW'S 'SURVEY OF LONDON.'

Mr. John Stow hath finished his *Survey of London*, containing the original, antiquity, increase, modern estate and description of the City, dedicating it to the Lord Mayor, the commonalty and citizens.

THE ANTIQUITY OF LONDON.

As Rome, the chief city of the world to glorify itself, drew her originals from the gods, goddesses and demy gods by the Trojan progeny, so this famous City of London for greater glory and in emulation of Rome deriveth itself from the very same original; for Brute, descended from the demy god Aeneas, the son of Venus, daughter of Juppiter, about the year of the world 2855 (the year before Christ's nativity 1108) builded a city near unto a river now called Thames, and named it Troynovant, or Trenovant, or Trinovantum as have some written copies. This afterwards being repaired by King Lud, he called it Caire-Lud or 'Lud's town,' and the strong gate which he builded in the west of the City, 'Ludgate.' Caesar in his *Commentaries* speaketh also of the City of the Trinobantes, which hath resemblance with Troynova or Trinobantum by no greater difference in the orthography than changing b into v.

MR. STOW'S COMMENDATION OF THE CITY OF LONDON.

'Besides the commodities of the furtherance of religion and justice; the propagation of learning; the maintenance of arts; the increase of riches; and the defence of countries (all which are before showed to grow generally by cities, and be common to London with them), London bringeth singularly these things following.

'By advantage of the situation it disperseth foreign wares (as the stomach doth meat) to all the members most commodiously.

'By the benefit of the river of Thames, and great trade of merchandise, it is the chief maker of mariners, and nurse of our navy; and ships (as men know) be the wooden walls for defence of our Realm.

'It maintaineth in flourishing estate the counties of Norfolk, Suffolk, Essex, Kent and Sussex, which as they lie in the face of our most puissant neighbour, so ought they (above others) to be conserved in the greatest strength and riches; and these, as it is well known, stand not so much by the benefit of their own soil as by the neighbourhood and nearness which they have to London.

'It relieveth plentifully and with good policy not only her own poor people (a thing which scarcely any other town or shire doth) but also the poor that from each quarter of the realm do flock unto it, and it imparteth liberally to the necessity of the Universities besides. It is an ornament to the realm by the beauty thereof, and a terror to other countries by reason of the great wealth and frequency. It spreadeth the honour of our Country far abroad by her long navigations and maketh our power feared, even of barbarous Princes. It only is stowed with rich merchants, which sort only is tolerable; for beggarly merchants do bite too near, and will do more harm than good to the Realm.

'It only of any place in the realm is able to furnish the sudden necessity with a strong army. It availeth the Prince in tonnage, poundage, and other customs, much more than all the rest of the Realm.

'It yieldeth a greater subsidy than any one part of the realm, I mean not for the proportion of the value of the goods only therein, but also for the faithful service there used, in making the assess; for nowhere else be men taxed so near to their just value as in London; yea, many are found there that for their countenance and credit sake refuse not to be rated above their ability, which thing never happened abroad in the country. I omit that in ancient time the inhabitants of London and other cities were accustomably taxed after the tenth of their goods when the country was assessed at the fifteenth, and rated at the eighth when the country was set at the twelfth, for that were to awake a sleeping dog, and I should be thought *dicenda tacenda locutus*, as the poet said.

'It only doth and is able to make the Prince a ready prest or loan of money.

'It only is found fit and able to entertain strangers honourably and to receive the Prince of the realm worthily.

'Almighty God (*qui nisi custodiat civitatem, frustra vigilat custos*) grant, that her Majesty evermore rightly esteem and rule this City, and He give grace that the citizens may answer duty as well towards God and her Majesty as towards this whole Realm and Country.'

10th July. A FENCER HANGED.

Nineteen persons were to-day hanged for felony at Tyburn and one pressed to death at Newgate. Also John Barrose, a Burgonian by nation and a fencer by profession, that lately came over and challenged all the fencers of England, was hanged all day long without Ludgate for killing an officer of the City which had arrested him for debt; such was his desperateness and bringeth such reward as may be example for others the like.

11th July. MR. BARNABE BARNES.

Mr. Barnabe Barnes that was committed to the Marshalsea is broken out of prison to avoid his trial and, as is supposed, fled away into the north.

12th July. DISORDERS IN IRELAND.

There is great disorder in Ireland since so many English soldiers disband themselves and run away, so that the country is at great charges both to fill up the decayed bands and further to strengthen the army. This abuse ariseth partly by the seducement of some lewd soldiers that convey themselves away so soon as they arrive, but chiefly through the negligence and lewd behaviour of some of the captains who for their own private gain dismiss the English and entertain the Irish. The Queen commandeth the captain shall be charged to take order for the apprehension of any that run away, and if he do not his duty for their apprehension then to be charged with the escape as consenting thereto. Likewise masters of ships shall be charged that they take no English soldiers into their ships if they be not maimed, hurt, or weakened with sickness and have sufficient passports.

16th July. THE QUEEN AND THE EARL OF ESSEX.

Yesterday the Queen was minded to have sent Mr. William Killigrew to the Earl of Essex as if of his own accord, but instructed by her; but being jealous that one of her chamber coming to the Earl might be thought by him to be commanded by her, she bad him stay.

A SAYING CONCERNING MY LORD OF ESSEX.

A certain great officer at Court when there was much talk of my Lord of Essex, his friends, and his enemies answered thus: 'I will tell you; I know but one friend and one enemy my Lord hath; and that one friend is the Queen, and that one enemy is himself.'

HORSE AND MEN REQUIRED FOR IRELAND.

Now that it is determined to subdue the rebels of Ireland to obedience by force, certain additional horse are required for the service. Of these the Bishops and clergy are required to furnish thirty; but because the last time like service was required of them the horse were so bad by reason of the long journey they made to the sea side, the negligence of the riders, and in part badly chosen, there shall now be sent in lieu £30 for the furnishing of each horseman with his horse. In like manner from the shires are required sixty-four horses. Recusant gentlemen also, to the number of twenty-six, each shall supply the cost of one horse apiece.

To Lough Foyle there is shortly to be sent a garrison of 2,000 men and 100 horse under the charge and conduct of Sir Samuel Bagnal: and for their furnishing and victuals is issued the sum of £8,000.

19th July. THE TROUBLES AT PLYMOUTH.

There are still disagreements at Plymouth, where the Mayor had a purpose to indict one John Hales, the sergeant of the band of Sir Ferdinando Gorges, for taking away the stocks in the town and some few deal boards, upon refusal of the Mayor to find firewood as he had indeed promised. Forasmuch as the matter was brought before the Council, who took order to compound the differences between the Mayor and Sir Ferdinando, this indictment is followed only upon spleen and stomach, and the Justices of Assize are ordered that, if the indictment is preferred against Hales at the Assize, it shall be forborne.

21st July. THE EARL OF ESSEX AND THE LORD GREY.

Of late the Earl of Essex, in doubt why the Lord Grey should be so well favoured at Court and especially by the Queen, forced him to declare himself either his only, or friend to the Secretary and so his enemy, protesting that there could be no neutrality. The Lord Grey answered that no base dependency should ever fashion his love or hate to the Earl's passions; and as for the Secretary he had diversely tasted of his favour and would never be dishonest or ungrateful. Whereupon the Earl of Essex answered that though he affected some parts in the Lord Grey, he loved not his person, neither should he be welcome to him, nor expect any advancement under him. Thereupon the Lord Grey complaineth greatly that the Queen will suffer one man to engross thus servilely all men of sword and derive the advancement of war only from his partial favour; for needs must the sovereignty of her princely authority be diminished, if not extinguished, if any save herself exercise these princely properties.

23rd July. ABUSES IN THE IRISH SERVICE.

It is said by those who have experience of this Irish service that it hath long been a general custom in Ireland for all sorts of people in all offices to make their most gain and private commodity, every man for himself, never regarding how wastefully or wilfully her Majesty's treasure was spent, how the poor subjects were spoiled, how the rebels increased, how well or ill her Majesty's service succeeded; but generally all men providing and caring only how to enrich themselves by their offices. Of the captains, most are so unconscionable that without pity or compassion they have kept from men of their own nation, even of their own blood, not only their imprest and diet money whiles they remained in garrison in extreme hunger and cold, but also have suffered them to make such havoc of the poor inhabitants of the land that the poor souls have nothing else to feed upon but roots, grass and boiled nettles. Yet will these captains swear most execrable oaths, stare and protest, as though heaven and earth came together, that their companies stood them in so many score pounds for so long a time to their utter undoing. Their abuse of her Majesty is such that it hath been usual in the time of musters for Irish soldiers to come from the rebels to make show at the musters with the English captains, and be passed away again without any further doings.

25th July. THE STILLYARD.

After these many delays to-day the Council desired the Lord Mayor to proceed to the seizing of the Stillyard, nevertheless to allow ten days wherein the goods may be removed.

25th July. MR. DARRELL BEFORE THE ECCLESIASTICAL COMMISSIONERS.

A few days since Mr. Darrell was called before the Commissioners for Causes Ecclesiastical at Lambeth, and from thence committed to prison by reason of his absurd and untrue, but yet very confident, assertions, giving just occasion thereby to suspect that he was but a counterfeit.

Moreover the boy Darling that was dispossessed at Burton two years ago was also brought to London, and he being closely examined also hath confessed that his possession was counterfeit, and wrote out a confession accordingly, which he signed. But being set at liberty he had conference with Mr. Darrell in the Gatehouse and thereupon wrote a letter to the Bishop of London affirming that he had been drawn on by subtleties to make this confession.

Hereafter he was called before the Archbishop of Canterbury, the Bishop of London, the Lord Chief Justices, and others, and the deposition against him heard in open court. Whereupon Mr. Darrell was by the full agreement of the whole court condemned for a counterfeit, and together with Mr. More, is committed to close prison till other order be taken for their further punishment.

At this Mr. Darrell's friends make great complaints on his behalf, as one whom God hath honoured to suffer for the testimony of His Holy Truth ; also that he was convicted before the Archbishop without hearing or examining. They say that his judges before any conviction exceedingly reviled him, becoming parties, pleaders and accusers ; and that there hath been running to court to forestall the Lords and Ladies of honour and others that would present a petition on his behalf. As for the boy Darling, he was kept in the Bishop of London's house, none of his friends suffered to come unto him. He was allured by promises, terrified by threatenings, as that he should be hanged as the Burgonian was, whom they showed unto him.

26th July. LORD BURLEIGH SICK.

The Lord Treasurer aileth greatly these last days. On the 24th he had no rest all the night, and yesterday attempting to rise out of his bed he was so weak that he could not sit up. To-day he would have one of the Queen's surgeons sent to him, and is much worse than he was after a very evil night, being still weaker and unable to read letters or sit up to do any business.

WANT OF ZEAL AT PLYMOUTH.

To the late demand for shipping to transport the soldiers for Ireland, the Mayor of Plymouth maketh answer that the quantity of shipping cannot be found there, and that the charge is too great for the town to furnish. Hereat the Council are displeased, noting the backwardness and indisposition of the Mayor, which is the more notable seeing the favour the town hath lately tasted in the cases brought before the Council. Bristol and Chester have performed the like service with great willingness and at very reasonable rates, and had present order for repayment of those sums that they laid out, as her Majesty always in most princely manner doth not delay the payment of any money disbursed for public service and promised by the Council's letters. Moreover the Mayor complaineth that the money disbursed for the charges of the Spaniards is not yet paid. To this the Council answer that the disbursement was of another nature and hath been very negligently solicited.

27th July. A WITCH CONDEMNED.

Josia Poley, a widow, was this day found guilty of practising witchcraft upon one Herbert Apshawe so that he languished for a space of thirty hours and then died. This was two and a half years since. About a fortnight since she practised witchcraft on a certain Margaret Burroughes who languished, but is still alive though in danger of her life.

29th July. GENERAL NEWS.

My Lord of Essex is not yet returned to the Court.

From Italy news is come of Sir Anthony Shirley, that went out of England the last winter giving out that he would serve the Emperor against the Turk, but now it appeareth that he doth serve the Turk against the Emperor; and so is he turned from a Christian to a Turk, which is most monstrous. No doubt if it be so the Lord will punish the same.

1st August. THE BLACKWATER FORT.

The fort of Blackwater is still held with great honour and resolution by Captain Williams who commandeth it, and although Tyrone lately bent his whole forces to surprise it, and hath left many men still who block them in on all sides of the fort, yet the worthy Captain doth still defend himself and the place;

and lately by some stratagem issued forth, and besides the killing of two or three of Tyrone's principal men hath gotten divers horses and mares of theirs into the fort.

4th August. The Death of Lord Burleigh.

This morning at 8 o'clock died Sir William Cecil, Lord Burleigh, Lord High Treasurer of England.

At 6 o'clock last night the physicians finding no distemper in his pulse or body affirmed that it was impossible he could be heart sick that had so good temper and so perfect pulse and senses, yet at 7 o'clock he fell into a convulsion like to the shaking of a cold ague. 'Now,' quoth he, 'the Lord be praised the time is come'; and calling for his children, blessed them and took his leave, commanding them to serve and fear God, and love one another. He prayed also for the Queen that she might live long and die in peace. Then he called for Thomas Bellot, his steward, one of his executors, and delivered him his will, saying, 'I have ever found thee true to me, and I now trust thee with all'; who like a godly honest man prayed his Lordship as he had lived religiously so now to remember his Saviour Christ, by Whose blood he was to have forgiveness of sins; with many the like speeches used by his chaplains; to whom he answered that it was done already, for he was assured God had forgiven his sins and would save his soul. Then he called his chaplains with all the company to say prayers for him, himself saying them after them all the time they prayed.

He continued languishing thus most patiently, still having memory perfect till 12 of the clock, lying praying to himself, saying the Lord's prayer in Latin; whereupon some inferred that he was papist, but it was not strange for him to pray in Latin because he never read any books or prayers but in Latin, French or Italian, very seldom in English. Now his speech began to fail him, and so languishing till 4 o'clock, sometimes wanting, sometimes having speech, he often said, 'O what a heart is this that will not let me die! Come Lord Jesus, one drop of death, Lord Jesus!' So he lay praying to himself softly; and at this time there were twenty in the chamber of his children, friends and servants, everyone praying and devising what to give him to hold the life in him if it were possible.

But when they strove to give him anything, he came to himself, saying, 'O ye torment me; for God's sake let me die quietly.' Then lying still the standers-by might hear him say softly to himself, 'Lord receive my spirit, Lord have mercy upon me'; which were the last words he was heard to speak.

So he continued speechless and senseless till 8 o'clock and then died; wherein one thing is observed most strange, that though many watched to see when he should die, he lay looking so sweetly and went away so mildly as in a sleep, that it could scarce be perceived when the breath went out of his body. Had he lived till the 15th September he should have been 77 years old.

The Character of Lord Burleigh.

He was rather meanly statured and well proportioned than tall, very straight and upright of body and legs, and, until age and his infirmity of the gout surprised him, very active and nimble of body, notably enduring travail and labour whereunto he used his body. Of visage very well favoured and of an excellent complexion, insomuch as even in his later days, when he was well and warm or had new dined or supped, he had as good colour in his face as most fair women; and altogether he was one of the sweetest and most well favoured, well mannered old men that hath been seen.

His natural disposition was ever gentle, temperate, merry, courteous, affable, slow to anger, ever shunning revenge, and never doing anything in fury or choler, neither yielding to passion, but always tempering his affections; insomuch as most part of his time he was noted to be most patient in hearing, so mild and ready in answering, as no man went away discontented, save that these last two or three years he was a little sharp in words sometimes. He was naturally merry and seldom sad, never moved with joyful or ill news. He could better cover his griefs than help it, and whatsoever was in his mind would never appear in his countenance or speech; he would of all things make great account of a little kindness. He was neither pompous nor proud, and yet loved to live honourably; being ever most charitable to the poor, whom he would better relieve in their parishes than in high ways or streets. He loved many times to be retired, to take air and recreation, and would then be as merry with his men as among his equals. In his business, most painful, careful, and watchful, never well till it was done.

THE LORD BURLEIGH'S PRECEPTS FOR HIS SON.

When Sir Robert Cecil was a young man the Lord Burleigh wrote out ten rules for the forming of his life, to this effect following:

1. Use great providence and circumspection in the choice of a wife, for from thence shall spring all thy future good or evil; and it is like a stratagem of war wherein a man can err but once. If thy estate be good, match near at home, and at leisure; if weak, far off, and quickly. Inquire diligently of her disposition, and how her parents were inclined in their youth. Let her not be poor how well born soever; for a man can buy nothing in the market with gentility. Neither choose a base and uncomely creature, nor a dwarf and fool; for by the one thou shalt beget a race of pigmies, and the other it will irk thee to hear her talk.

2. Bring up children in learning and obedience, yet without austerity; the foolish cockering of some parents and the over-stern carriage of others causeth more men and women to take ill courses than their own natural inclinations. Marry daughters in time, lest they marry themselves. Suffer not thy sons to pass the Alps: for they shall learn nothing there but pride, blasphemy and atheism. Neither train them up for the wars; for a soldier can hardly be an honest man or a good Christian; for every war is of itself unjust unless the cause make it just. Besides it is a science no longer in request than in use; soldiers in peace are like chimneys in summer.

3. Live not in the country without corn and cattle about thee; for he that puts his hand to purse for every household expense is like him that thinks to keep water in a sieve. Feed servants well and pay them with the most; and then thou mayest boldly require service and duty at their hands.

4. Let kindred and allies be welcome to thy table, but shake off parasites and sycophants that will fawn on thee in the summer of thy prosperity but in adverse storms will shelter thee no more than an arbour in winter.

5. Beware of suretiship for the best friends; for he that payeth another man's debts seeks his own decay. Neither borrow money of a friend, but of a stranger, where paying for it thou shalt hear of it no more; otherwise thou shalt eclipse thy credit, lose thy friend, and get pay as dear as to another. But in borrowing money be precious of thy word; for he that hath a care to keep days of payment is lord of other men's goods.

6. Attempt not law against a man before thou be thoroughly resolved that thou hast right on thy side; and then spare neither for money nor pains; for a cause or two so followed, and obtained, will free thee from suits a great part of thy life.

7. Be sure to keep some great man thy friend; but trouble him not for trifles. Present him with many yet small gifts and of little charge. And if thou have cause to bestow any great gratuity, let it be some such thing as may be daily in his sight. Otherwise in this ambitious age thou shalt remain as a hop without a pole living in obscurity, and be made a football for every insulting companion.

8. Towards thy superiors be humble yet generous; with thy equals familiar, yet respective; towards thy inferiors show much humility, and some familiarity; as to bow thy body, stretch forth thy hand, and uncover thy head, and such like compliments. The first prepares the way for thy advancement; the second makes thee known as a man well bred; the third gains a good report which once gotten is easily kept.

9. Trust not any with thy life, credit or estate; for it is mere folly for a man to entail himself to his friend.

10. Be not scurrilous in thy conversation nor satirical in thy jests; the one will make thee unwelcome in all company; and the other will pull on quarrels, and get thee hatred of thy best friends.

The Queen's Grief.

The Queen was certified of the Lord Treasurer's death this afternoon, which she seemed to take very grievously, shedding of tears and separating herself from all company. She hath sent my Lord of Buckhurst and Mr. Chancellor for the Seal and such things as concern her Majesty.

The absence of the Earl of Essex at this time is very unseasonable both for the common good and his own private; for the longer he persisteth in this careless humour towards her Majesty the more her heart will be hardened. If he should persist in contending with her in this manner it may breed such hatred in her as will never be reclaimed, so that though she may be forced to use his service, yet not having her Majesty's love therein he shall be subject to their tongues who will practise against him.

12th August. INSUFFICIENT SOLDIERS FROM RADNORSHIRE.

The men impressed in Radnorshire for the Irish service are said to have been very unserviceable, being taken out of the jails, rogues, and vagrant persons, evil armed and sent forth so naked and bare, without shoes or hose, as to be unfit for any service or to appear amongst men, besides of that lewd behaviour as they had like to have mutinied and made an uproar. The force for Lough Foyle is now in part embarked for Dublin.

14th August. VICTUALS FOR THE SOLDIERS.

The victuals appointed for the men to be sent to Lough Foyle:

Biscuit or wheat meal to make biscuit.	for each man per diem	1 lb.	Butter	to four men per diem	½ lb.
			Cheese		1¼ lb.
Sack		½ pint	Pease		1 quart
Aqua vitae		¼ pint			
Beer		1 quart	Oatmeal		1½ pint

Besides there is appointed for the men 4,000 lbs. of liquorice and 1,000 lbs. of aniseed to make beverage for those that be sick, or will drink it.

16th August. THE QUEEN AND THE EARL OF ESSEX.

The Queen sent Mr. William Killigrew with a message to the Earl of Essex that she looketh for a better answer from him of submission or else not to admit him again to her presence, but Sir William Knollys meeting him took him back to Court that he might let the Queen know that my Lord had a fit the night before and was ill with a cold and not yet freed from it. She blamed him for not going, to which he replied that my Lord's fit would have been imputed to her message; which she confessed, and concluded that he might stay until she heard from my Lord's physician. Her Majesty is now variable and distracted in herself.

22nd August. A GREAT DISASTER IN IRELAND.

The fort at Blackwater being reduced to great straits, it was resolved by Sir Henry Bagnal, the Marshal, to relieve it, alleging how greatly this service concerned her Majesty's honour. On the 14th August therefore the army, being by computation 3,500 foot and 300 horse, marched out of Armagh, leaving there all the victuals and some munition. Their form was in six regiments, marching severally at six or seven score paces between each regiment, the way being hard and the ground hilly, within caliver shot of wood and bog on both sides which was wholly possessed by the enemy, who played on them continually.

After marching thus for a mile, they approached a trench which the enemy had cast in front of their passage, a mile long, five foot deep, and four foot over, with a thorny hedge on the top, and in the middle of a bog. Over this ditch the vanguard passed, but the main battle stood for bringing up the saker, which stuck fast in a ford, and also for the rear which being hard set, had retired to Armagh. In the meantime the vanguard having passed were so distressed that they fell to run and were all in effect put to the sword. The Marshal, being chief commander, then came up to relieve them, but was shot dead in the head by a bullet; notwithstanding two other regiments passed over the trench. But as the battle came up two barrels of powder took fire amongst them, by which the men were disranked and routed, and in this confusion the two regiments that had passed the trench were for the most part put to the sword. Hereupon Sir Thomas Maria Wingfield, being now chief commander, commanded the retreat to Armagh, the battle being all in rout, but, with great resolution of the vanguard of horse, and the enemy's munition being well spent, recovered Armagh. Here the captains resolved to refresh their men with victuals and munition, and so to march directly to Newry. But in the meantime the enemy approached and fell round them on all sides with their force. Then the captains, finding the insufficiency both in mind and means of their men, concluded that the horse should venture to break forth through the enemy's quarter and so advertise the State, that present succour might be sent to fetch them off. This was done by the horsemen but with some loss. In this disaster are lost Sir Henry Bagnal and most of his regiment of 1, 000 slain; Captain Percy hurt, Captain Cosby slain and most of their regiment; Sir Calisthenes Brooke that led the horse was shot in the belly and is thought to be slain. In all about 2,000 footmen and fifteen captains.

23rd August. A PROCLAMATION AGAINST FORESTALLERS.

A proclamation is published straitly charging the justices and other officers that the orders against forestallers, ingrossers and regraters be strictly enforced, for that the price of grain is so increased by their unmerciful covetousness that many people are like to die of the dearth. Moreover it is forbidden from the 20th September next coming to employ upon the feeding of dogs any grain fit for the sustenance of men, or to make any starch.

THE LORD KEEPER'S LETTER TO THE EARL OF ESSEX.

It is said that the Lord Keeper hath written to the Earl of Essex (who came yesterday to the Council but the second time since June) warning him of the dangers of his present courses. He is not yet so far gone but that he may well return. The return is safe, but the progress dangerous and desperate. For his enemies he doth that which they could never do for themselves, whilst his friends are left to open shame and contempt, his own fortune overthrown, and his honour and reputation ruinated. His best remedy is not to contend and strive but humbly to submit; even if cause of scandal be given him, yet policy, duty and religion enforce him to his sovereign, for God Himself requireth it as a principal bond of service to Himself.

THE IRISH FORCES.

Upon the accident lately happened in Ireland the soldiers intended for Lough Foyle are now to be sent to Carlingford.

25th August. MY LORD OF ESSEX'S LETTER TO THE UNIVERSITY OF CAMBRIDGE.

On the death of the Lord Treasurer the University of Cambridge have chosen my Lord of Essex to be their Chancellor, which he accepting in a Latin letter declareth '*nec meditationem armorum strepitus, nec lectionem negotiantium frequentia permisere; ideoque acuendum esset ingenium iam obtusum; excolendus stilus iam plane barbarus; rediscenda mihi omnia Artium rudimenta iam essent, antequam uel Matri Academiae conceptus offerre, uel coram doctissimo uestro senatu uerba proferre satis confiderem.*' Nothing, quoth he, shall be more forward in his life than his love and care and watch in guarding their privileges and forwarding their affairs by his industry and constancy.

26th August. ESSEX'S REPLY TO THE LORD KEEPER.

The Earl of Essex hath answered the letter of the Lord Keeper, very vehemently protesting that the highest judge on earth hath imposed upon him, without trial or hearing, the most heavy judgment that ever hath been known. There is no tempest, saith he, to the passionate indignation of a prince; nor any time so unseasonable as when it lighteth upon those who might expect a harvest of their careful and painful labours. The indissoluble duty he oweth her Majesty is only the duty of allegiance; the duty of attendance is no indissoluble duty. He oweth her Majesty the duty of an Earl and of Lord Marshal of England; he hath been content to do her Majesty the service of a clerk, but can never serve her as a slave or a lackey. 'When,' saith he, 'the vilest of all indignities are done unto me, doth religion force me to sue? Or doth God require it? Is it impiety not to do it? What, cannot princes err? Cannot subjects receive wrong? Is an earthly power or authority infinite?' He saith further, 'As for me I have received wrong, and feel it. My cause is good, I know it; and whatsoever come, all the powers on earth can never show more strength and constancy in oppressing, than I can show in suffering whatsoever can or shall be imposed upon me.'

THE NEW MARSHAL IN IRELAND.

Sir Richard Bingham is appointed Marshal in Ireland in place of Sir Henry Bagnal that was slain.

27th August. NEW FORCES FOR IRELAND.

Soldiers to the number of 1,700 are required to strengthen the forces in Ireland. And because there hath been neglect used in choosing idle and loose people, so that it seemed the counties sought rather to disburden themselves of unprofitable people than to advance the Queen's service, the justices themselves shall repair to the villages and see good choice made of sufficient men, or cause them to be brought before them by the constables to be by them first viewed and allowed before they be presented to the general musters.

Two Patents.

The Council have directed warrants to all public officers on behalf of two that hold monopolies which have been repunged; the one being Sir Jerome Bowes that hath sole licence to make drinking glasses and to prevent the bringing in of glasses from any parts beyond seas. The other is Mr. John Spilman, the Queen's jeweller, that hath letters patent to gather rags for the making of writing paper, and forbidding the erection of any mill for making of paper without Mr. Spilman's consent.

29th August. The Defeat at the Blackwater.

The rebel Tyrone hath offered composition to the remnants of the army that were shut up in Armagh. First that they should surrender the Blackwater fort, leaving there the colours, drums and munition, the captains having left them only their rapiers and hackneys; the fort being delivered, the whole army with the men of the Blackwater to march away from Armagh with all their carriage and hurt men to Newry or Dundalk. These terms were accepted and the soldiers are now at Newry. Tyrone gave as his reason for this composition that he was at £500 charge by the day in keeping his forces together to attend our army, which he supposed had a month or six months' victual, in which time he knew that forces would land in Lough Foyle; and therefore he thought it better to save that charge, to gain the fort of the Blackwater, and to bend himself to hinder the landing of forces in Lough Foyle.

The Funeral of the Lord Treasurer.

To-day the Lord Treasurer's funeral was performed with all the rites belonging to so great a personage. First came two conductors in cloaks, then nigh on a hundred poor men; then the servants (a great company) of gentlemen, judges, knights, and noblemen ; then those of my Lord's own household ; the clerks and other officers of the offices of State ; the Bishop of London, the preacher ; the Heralds, the helm and crest borne by Rouge Dragon, the sword by Chester, the targe by Lancaster, the coat of arms by Norroy. Then came the body borne by eight gentlemen, with four assistants to carry the pall at each corner ; next the chief mourner, and after the Great Seal. Then followed the Earl of Essex, Earl Marshal, the Lord Keeper, the Lord Admiral, the Earl of Shrewsbury, the Earl of Worcester, and the Lord Chamberlain, all being on horseback with their footclothes of black cloth, in their mourning weeds according to their state. Then followed the Ancients of Gray's Inn, and all the rest after them, two and two ; then all yeomen in black coats ; and then all the people. The number of mourners, one and other, were above 500.

The funeral being honourably solemnised in the Abbey of Westminster, the corpse is now taken to Stamford to be interred.

It was noted that the Earl of Essex, whether it were upon consideration of the present occasion, or for his own disfavours, carried the heaviest countenance of the company. Presently after dinner he retired to Wanstead where they say he means to settle, seeing he cannot be received in Court, though he have relented much, and sought by divers means to recover his hold. But the Queen says he hath played long enough upon her, and that she means to play awhile upon him, and to stand as much upon her greatness as he doth upon stomach.

Upon Bartholemew day the Lord Cobham was installed Warden of the Cinque Ports at Canterbury at which solemnity were assembled almost 4000 horse. He kept the feast very magnificently, and spent 26 oxen with all other provision suitable.

Mistress Vernon, one of the ladies-in-waiting, hath been sent from Court and is at Essex House. Some say that she is with child, yet she complaineth not of foul play but says that the Earl of Southampton will justify it. It is bruited underhand that the Earl was in London four days in great secret of purpose to marry her and effected it accordingly.

31st August. RECUSANTS TO SUPPLY HORSES.

Certain recusants to the number of forty-six are required to provide £15 each towards the charges of furnishing light horse for Ireland.

5th September. LIGHTNING IN LONDON.

This afternoon there were two great cracks of lightning and thunder, whereby some men were smitten at the postern by the Tower, and one man slain at the bridgehouse in Southwark.

7th September. COURT NEWS.

The Earl of Southampton of late came over very secretly from France and married his Mistress Vernon. Yesterday the Queen was informed of the new Lady Southampton and her adventures, whereat her patience was so moved that she came not to the Chapel. The Queen has commanded that there shall be provided for her the sweetest and best appointed lodging in the Fleet; and the Earl is commanded, on his allegiance, to return with all speed to London, to advertise his arrival, but not to come to Court in person.

The Earl of Essex who was sick at Essex House is now gone in his litter towards Wanstead. The Queen hath sent her physician to attend him, and to-day he was visited by Mr. Killigrew, Mr. Greville and Lord Henry Howard from her.

MERES' 'PALLADIS TAMIA.'

There is a new book called *Palladis Tamia* by Mr. Francis Meres, being a collection of similitudes gathered from more than one hundred and fifty authors and set out under some two hundred and fifty diverse heads, whereof one is 'A Comparative discourse of our English poets with the Greek, Latin and Italian poets.' Saith that the English tongue is mightily enriched and gorgeously invested in rare ornaments by Sir Philip Sidney, Spenser, Daniel, Drayton, Warner, Shakespeare, Marlowe, and Chapman. Of lyric poets the best be Spenser (who excelleth in all kinds), Daniel, Drayton, Shakespeare, Breton. For the most passionate to bewail the perplexities of love, Henry Howard, Earl of Surrey, Sir Thomas Wyatt, Sir Francis Brian, Sir Philip Sidney, Sir Walter Ralegh, Sir Edward Dyer, Spenser, Daniel, Drayton, Shakespeare, Wheatstone, Gascoigne, Samuel Page, Churchyard, Breton.

The best for comedy be Edward, Earl of Oxford, Dr. Gager of Oxford, Mr. Rowley, Mr. Edwards, eloquent and witty John Lyly, Lodge, Gascoigne, Greene, Shakespeare, Thomas Nashe, Thomas Heywood, Anthony Munday (our best plotter), Chapman, Porter, Wilson, Hathaway and Henry Chettle. As tragic poets, the Lord Buckhurst, Dr. Legg, Dr. Edes, Mr. Edward Ferris, the author of the *Mirror for Magistrates*, Marlowe, Peele, Watson, Kyd, Shakespeare, Drayton, Chapman, Dekker, and Benjamin Jonson.

Moreover, saith he, 'as Plautus and Seneca are accounted the best for comedy and tragedy among the Latins, so Shakespeare among the English is the most excellent in both kinds for the stage: for comedy, witness his *Gentlemen of Verona*, his *Errors*, his *Love's Labours Lost*, his *Love's Labours Won*, his *Midsummer Night's Dream*, and his *Merchant of Venice*; for tragedy, his *Richard the Second*, *Richard the Third*, *Henry the Fourth*, *King John*, *Titus Andronicus* and his *Romeo and Juliet*.'

8th September. MARSTON'S 'SCOURGE OF VILLAINY.'

There is a book of ten Satires called the *Scourge of Villainy*, very invectively whipping the vices of these times, which the author dedicateth 'To his most esteemed and best beloved Self,' and beginning the first with this *proemium*—

I bear the scourge of just Rhamnusia,
Lashing the lewdness of Britannia.
Let others sing as their good Genius moves,
Of deep designs or else of clipping loves.
Fair fall them all that with wit's industry
Do clothe good subjects in true poesy.
But as for me, my vexed thoughtful soul,
Takes pleasure in displeasing sharp control.
Thou nursing Mother of fair wisdom's lore,
Ingenuous Melancholy, I implore
Thy grave assistance; take thy gloomy seat,
Inthrone thee in my blood. Let me intreat
Stay his quick jocund skips, and force him run
A sad pac'd course until my whips be done.
Daphne, unclip thine arms from my sad brow,
Black Cypress crown me whilst I do up plough

The hidden entrails of rank villainy;
Quake guzzle dogs, that live on putrid slime,
Scud from the lashes of my yerking rime.

Concludeth with a satire of the Humours of our City gallants.

9th September. LAWLESSNESS NEAR LONDON.

Many grievous and extraordinary outrages are in these days committed by rogues, vagabonds and other licentious persons in places not far distant from London, who have taken such boldness that they assemble themselves together, armed even with petronels and pistols. These men do such mischief as the ordinary course of justice sufficeth not to keep them in awe. Moreover the officers appointed for conservation of the peace are terrified with their violence, and some of late slain and murdered. The Lord Mayor and justices of Middlesex, Surrey and Kent are required to make privy search in inns, alehouses, houses of victualling and lodging, stables, outhouses and the like, and all persons found to lurk suspiciously to be committed forthwith to strait prison to await trial at a special Sessions. A proclamation is now issued that a Provost Marshal shall be appointed, with authority to apprehend such as will not be corrected by the ordinary officers of justice and without delay to execute them upon the gallows by order of martial law.

10th September. SOME LEVIES DISCHARGED.

Of the levies, to the number of 1,700, that were to be ready at this time for service in Ireland many are now to be discharged, but in such wise that they may be assembled again and sent forth at ten days' warning; but the rest, being 1,000, are to be set forth at once.

12th September. THE QUEEN'S LETTER TO THE COUNCIL OF IRELAND.

The Queen hath caused a letter to be written to the Council of Ireland informing them that Sir Richard Bingham is appointed Marshal, and showing her displeasure of the notorious errors in that government, but especially that she will not pass over their foul error to her dishonour when, after the late defeat, the Council framed such a letter to the traitor as was never the like read, either in form or substance for such baseness. This letter was not received by Tyrone, being stayed by accident. In it the Council had begged him to let the men in Armagh depart without doing them any further hurt, and especially, seeing his enemy the late Marshal was among the slain, they hoped that he would cease all further revenge against the rest.

15th September. THE EARL OF ESSEX RESTORED TO FAVOUR.

In the Court my Lord of Essex took his place in the Council five days ago and is now restored to the Queen's favour.

'SKIALETHEIA.'

There is a book entered called *Skialetheia, or a Shadow of Truth*, being a collection of certain epigrams and six satires on the follies of these times.

OF A LORD'S LIFE.

My Lord most court-like lies in bed till noon,
Then, all high-stomached, riseth to his dinner,
Falls straight to dice, before his meat be down,
Or to digest, walks to some female sinner.
Perhaps fore-tired he gets him to a play,
Comes home to supper, and then falls to dice,
There his devotion wakes till it be day,
And so to bed, where until noon he lies.
'This is a lord's life,' simple folk will sing.
A Lord's life? What, to trot so foul a ring?
Yet thus he lives, and what's the greatest grief,
Gnatho still swears he leads true virtue's life.

OF ONE THAT WOULD CRY 'OH RARE.'

As Caius walks the streets, if he but hear
A blackman grunt his note, he cries, 'Oh rare!'
He cries 'Oh rare' to hear the Irishmen
Cry 'Pip, fine pip,' with a shrill accent, when
He comes at Mercers' chapel; and 'Oh rare,'
At Ludgate at the prisoners' plainsong there:
'Oh rare' sings he, to hear a cobbler sing,
Or a wassail on Twelfth Night, or the ring
At cold St. Pancras Church; or anything:
He'll cry 'Oh rare,' and scratch the elbow too
To see two butchers' curs fight; the cuckoo

Will cry 'Oh rare' to see the champion bull;
Or the victorious mastiff with crown'd skull,
And garlanded with flowers, passing along
From Paris Garden; he renews his song,
To see my Lord Mayor's henchmen; or to see
(At an old Alderman's blest obsequy)
The Hospital boys in their blue equipage;
Or at a carted bawd, or whore in a cage.
He'll cry 'Oh rare' at a gong-farmer's cart;
'Oh rare,' to hear a ballad or a fart:
Briefly, so long he hath used to cry, 'Oh rare,'
That now that phrase is grown thin and threadbare,
But sure his wit will be more rare and thin,
If he continue as he doth begin.

16th September. JONSON'S 'EVERY MAN IN HIS HUMOUR.'

At the Curtain the Lord Chamberlain's men have a new play called *Every Man in his Humour*, written by Jonson, that displayeth the humours of our City gentlemen. A practice in it is to make a braggart captain, by name Bobadilla, boast much, but when it cometh to the proof to endure the bastinado, excusing himself that he was bound to the peace. Another is to make two gulls, one from the country and the other of the town, practise to each other this humour of melancholy, holding that 'tis the only best humour, for 'your true melancholy breeds your perfect fine wit.'

20th September. GENERAL NEWS.

In Ireland the Lord Ormond is hurt and since the great overthrow 400 more throats cut. Sir Francis Vere is coming towards the Low Countries, and Sir Alexander Ratcliffe and Sir Robert Drury with him. Honour pricks them on, and the world thinks that honour will quickly prick them off again. Sir Thomas Shirley has taken four hulks, Easterlings of Lubec, but it is hoped that the freight is Spanish. They are stayed and a commission granted to examine whether they are prize. The Court is now at Nonsuch, and last Sunday my Lord Chief Justice's expectation of being made a Councillor was disappointed. There was a French gentleman, a master of requests and resident of Lyons, brother to M. de Vicq, governor of Calais, a man honourably entertained by the Earl of Essex and greatly commended by the Queen for his speech and other carriage. There were divers Almains with him, whereof one lost 300 crowns at this new play of *Every Man in his Humour*.

22nd September. A PLAYER SLAIN.

Benjamin Jonson, the player that wrote the new play of Humours, whom they call the 'bricklayer,' to-day fought with Gabriel Spencer, one of the Admiral's players, in Shoreditch fields; Jonson is hurt in the arm, but Spencer being wounded in the right side is dead of it.

30th September. MR. SPENSER TO BE THE SHERIFF OF CORK.

The Council recommend Mr. Edmund Spenser to the Lords Justices of Ireland to be appointed Sheriff of Cork, he being well known for his good commendable parts, a man endowed with good knowledge in learning, and not without experience in the service of the wars.

2nd October. THE EARL OF CUMBERLAND'S RETURN.

My Lord of Cumberland is returned from his voyage, his losses in ships being two barges, the *Pegasus* and the old frigate; of the men, 600 died of the bloody flux and calenture at Porto Rico, 60 were slain in fight and 40 drowned in the two wrecks.

His first intention after leaving England was to go to Lisbon and there wait for five carracks and twenty-five ships that were laden for Brazil, but unluckily his fleet was espied by a carvel that gave the alarum and so the carracks came not forth. From thence therefore they went towards the Canaries to Lancerota, being informed that there dwelt a rich Marquis, worth £100,000 if he could be taken suddenly, but in this he was disappointed. Nevertheless my Lord thought it best to set his men on shore, for till this time he had never given them any training and many of them were very raw and unpractised to the service on land. Here they captured the town (which was most beggarly) and castle, but found nothing save a few pieces of ordnance and some little wine; which little was indeed too much, for the meaner sort were overthrown by it, and of the commanders, some were distempered with wine, some with pride of themselves or scorn of others, so that there were very few but that fell to most disorderly outrage one with another.

Thence they sailed on to Dominica and here my Lord made a speech to them all, rebuking them for the many gross faults committed amongst them since their coming to sea and warning them that his overpatient and forced sluggish humour was now shaken off, and that he would not for the future suffer to pass unpunished ill-deservers. At Dominica they stayed six days, watering the fleet and refreshing the sick men in a hot bath which was found near the sea as hot as either the Cross Bath or King's Bath in the City of Bath.

His Lordship now determined to attack the town of Porto Rico, and on the 6th June the soldiers were landed about three leagues from the town, towards which they marched along the sea shore till they met with a blackamoor whom they took to be their guide, and towards evening with much ado they came to the causeway that led out to the island. Wherefore the soldiers were led to a great lawn and there rested while a continual watch was kept to give immediate information of the ebb of the tide from the causeway. Early next morning the alarum was given very quietly and the companies quickly ranged; and after my Lord and Sir John Berkeley had somewhat disputed for the honour of leading the point, our men began the assault, which lasted for two hours, yet though they left noway unattempted they could not enter the gate. This causeway was so rugged that our men to keep on their feet made choice to wade in the water beside it. Here his Lordship was, by the stumbling of him that bore his target, overthrown even to the danger of drowning; for his armour so overburdened him that the Sergeant Major, that by chance was next him, had much ado at the first and second time to get him from under the water. When he was up he had received so much salt water that it drove him to so great extremity of present sickness that he was forced to lie down in that place upon the causeway.

In the fort the enemy had six pieces of great ordnance which were bent upon the causeway, and many musketeers, and at a port by the gate lay a fowler, which some call a murdering piece. For all this our soldiers came to the very gate, and began to hew at it with some two or three bills that they had; at the ports and loopholes they were at push of the pike, and having broken their own, with their naked hands took their enemies' pikes and perforce brake them. But the end was it could not then be taken; for the tide came in so fast that what was at their knees before was now come up to their middles. So the companies were withdrawn to the place where they had rested for the night.

Meanwhile my Lord went aboard, so sick that in truth he was to be feared for, with purpose to repose himself, but within a few hours he came ashore again and straightway put into execution a purpose which he had meantime digested. Wherefore he gave direction that one of the ships should bear close in, whatsoever it might cost, meanwhile musketeers should lie in the rocks and beat the enemy from his ordnance, so that 200 pike and shot might land between the fort and the town. This plot took such good effect that within a short space the enemy quitted the place. This fort having been made good, our men next marched towards a second fort, called the 'red fort'; but the enemy quitted that too. Next morning they began to march towards the town, which they found quitted of all able to make resistance, for besides women and men disabled for the wars the rest had taken themselves to their last hope, a fort called Mora.

When the town had been secured, his Lordship sent a drum to summon the fort to be delivered to him, which was refused by the Governor from within. After this summons his Lordship took exceeding great care for the taking of the fort with the least loss of men that possibly might be. He therefore took order to cut off all possible means of relief of victuals, and withal set up two platforms and several gabions that the wall might be beaten from two several places at once. For this purpose were brought from the *Scourge* two whole culverins, two demi-culverins, and four other pieces found about the town, whereof one was that very same which had slain Sir Nicholas Clifford. These were ready to batter on 17th June, being a Saturday, but my Lord would not have them begin on the Sabbath day, so that it was deferred till Monday.

In the meanwhile a martial court was called whereat two were condemned to death; the one, a soldier that had done violence to a Spaniard's wife, who was hanged in the market place; the other a sailor that for defacing some things in a church was thrice brought to the gallows, but at length his Lordship was intreated to grant him mercy.

On the Monday the battery began, and by evening it was seen that the *cavalero* flanking the gate being made of sandy earth was ready to fall at the next rain. Next day therefore they sent forth a drum from the fort to demand parley, the sum of their demands being that with colours flying, match in their cocks and bullets in their mouth, they should be set beyond the point at the Bridge to go whither they would; further that all the prisoners be delivered without ransom. My Lord utterly refused any such composition, but instead he offered them these articles written with his own hand:

'A resolution which you may trust to. I am content to give yourself and all your people their lives, yourself with your captains and officers to pass with your arms; all the rest of your soldiers with their rapiers and daggers only.

'You shall all stay here with me till I give you passage from the Island, which shall be within thirty days.

'Any one of you, which I shall choose, shall go with me into England, but shall not stay longer there than one month, but being well fitted for the purpose shall be safely sent home into Spain without ransom.'

It was doubted whether there were any in the fort that spake English, and therefore some were wishing the articles were translated into Spanish; but his Lordship peremptorily refused to seek their language but would have them find out his. Next morning the Spaniards accepted of these conditions, so that day the Governor and his company dined with my Lord, and after dinner the Governor went and brought out his companies (which of all sorts were near 400) and delivered the keys. The fort being occupied by our men, the fleet was commanded to come into the harbour, which all this time had rid without, for it is impossible that any ship should pass that point without sinking unless the fort grant her passage.

My Lord's intention now was to hold Porto Rico, for this is the very key of the West Indies which locketh and shutteth all the gold and silver in the continent of America and Brazilia.

But God otherwise disposed, for within a while many of our men fell sick. This sickness was an extreme looseness of the body which within a few days would grow into a flux of blood, sometimes in the beginning accompanied with hot agues, but always in the end attended by an extreme debility and waste of spirits. Towards the beginning of July there were not much above 200 dead, but by their departure on 13th August above 400, and as many so sick that most of them could not bring themselves on board. On their return to the Azores they were much distressed by grievous storms; and there they learnt that twenty-nine of the Spanish King's men-of-war, with five of them carracks, had passed that way a few days before. They set forth from Flores on 16th September. On Michaelmas day they sounded and the ground on the tallow assured them of being in the Sleeve, and the scollop shells confirmed their opinion that they were on the coast of France, though the Master judged otherwise; by whose judgment, if his Lordship had not contradicted out of his authority causing them to take a more northerly course, all had perished in all likelihood on the Ushant. Next morning they saw Normandy and are now come to shore.

3rd October. General News.

The Earl of Essex is now at Court on as good terms as ever he was, but there be no offices bestowed, nor no more show of bestowing them than the first day the Lord Treasurer died. One Stanley that came in sixteen days overland with letters out of Spain is lately committed to the Tower. He was very earnest to have private conference with her Majesty, pretending matters of great importance which he would by no means utter to anybody else. He affirms that the King of Spain was not dead at his coming away, but that he had retired himself and was coming on.

My Lord of Cumberland himself saith that he hath made a saving journey, but they that understand it better say that all he hath brought (whereof the greatest part is sugar and ginger) will not amount to above £15,000 or £16,000, which is not half the charge of setting out, besides the adventure and waste of his shipping and the loss of 600 men. Some find great fault and say his own wilfulness and want of direction overthrew the voyage, and that if he would have been advised, he might have done them all good, but he neglected present profit in hope of greater matters, and so forsook the substance for the shadow. By this and the rest the heat of our sea voyages is well allayed, which being no better conducted serve rather to fortify and confirm than hinder the enemy.

4th October. A MUTINY AMONGST THE LONDON SOLDIERS.

The soldiers that lately marched from London to the number of 300 have committed a notable outrage; for when they came to Towchester and should have marched further the same day by the order of their conductor Captain Garrett Dillon, well near 200 of them fell into mutiny, refused to march, threatened their captain to kill him, and wounded some of his officers so grievously as it is doubtful whether they are living or dead. The chief movers of this mutiny are one Willoughby, whom the mutineers make their captain calling him 'Lord Willoughby,' a footman of the Earl of Derby, and a footman of the Lord Compton.

7th October. MR. HAKLUYT'S 'PRINCIPAL NAVIGATIONS.'

Mr. Richard Hakluyt hath now completed the first volume of a new edition of *The Principal navigations, voyages, traffics and discoveries of the English nation*, treating of the discoveries towards the north and north-east, also an account of the defeat of the Spanish huge armada in 1588 and the famous victory achieved at the city of Cadiz, 1596; and this he dedicateth to Lord Charles Howard, Lord High Admiral, whom Mr. Hakluyt would to settle and establish a Lecture of Navigation to be read in this City of London, for the banishing of our former gross ignorance in marine causes, and for the increase and multiplying of the sea-knowledge in this age, wherein God hath raised so general a desire in the youth of this Realm to discover all parts of the face of the earth.

9th October. SIR THOMAS SHIRLEY'S PRIZES.

The Mayor of Portsmouth, being commissioned to search any one of the Lubecers' ships that Sir Thomas Shirley should nominate, has performed the same, not forbearing to rip up the very ceiling of the ship; nevertheless they have found neither treasure nor Spanish goods, but only salt and cork. The Lubec ships are therefore discharged and suffered to proceed on their voyage.

10th October. A TRAITOR TO BE SENT AWAY.

There is one Richard Zouch that hath served the King of Spain for many years who came over last summer and was committed to the Counter in Wood Street, where he hath remained these four months. Since none of his friends will relieve him and there is no reason her Majesty should be charged to maintain a fugitive and suspected person, the Council order that he shall be sent back again in some vessel bound for the Low Countries.

15th October. YARMOUTH HERRINGS.

It is allowed to the inhabitants of Great Yarmouth for one year to transport 600 lasts of herrings in strangers' bottoms to foreign parts, being in amity with her Majesty, in regard that in this troublesome time they cannot safely traffic in English ships.

28th October. FURTHER SOLDIERS FOR IRELAND.

Because of the spread of the rebellion to Munster there are now required a further levy of 2,000 soldiers to be sent to Ireland, these men being taken from Cornwall, Devon, Dorset, Southampton, Oxfordshire, Somerset and Wiltshire. They shall be ready by the 15th of next month.

4th November. THE DEATH OF THE SPANISH KING.

News is come that the King of Spain is dead, having been sick for many days of the gout, and numerous sores all over his body, so foul that one of his physicians fell ill of the very stench of them. In this last illness, he made himself very familiar not only with the thought of death but with the discussion thereof and all that should be done when he was gone, arranging each article of his funeral, and ordering the purchase of much black cloth to drape the Church of the Escurial. Also he caused them to bring to his bedside a shirt of lead wherewith, being dead, he should be wrapped, and the leaden coffin for his corpse. He examined them both, and, causing himself to be measured, gave order for their perfecting.

Some days before he died he summoned the Prince and the Infanta to his presence and gave them his blessing in words of affection, exhorting them to govern their subjects with love, to administer justice impartially, and to support and defend religion and the Catholic faith with all their might. He gave the Prince two sealed packets, instructing him to open them only after his death, and charging him to read, study and observe what was written therein as they would prove of the highest value to him. Also, that his wishes might be the more surely observed, the King placed in the Prince's service all his favourite ministers, causing the Prince himself to nominate them, thereby pledging himself not to dismiss them without necessary and good reason. During his illness he is said to have spent more than 700,000 crowns in gifts and in discharge of his conscience.

A few days later, in changing his bed, the King had such a sinking that for a while they thought him dead, but he recovered somewhat and they administered extreme unction. Though very feeble he had his memory perfect and asked for the cross which his father held when he was dying. Moreover he sent for the Prince and told him to remain that he might contemplate this example of earthly misery, exhorting him never to forget, when he had entered on his Kingdom, that he too must come to a like pass and must die. The Prince brake forth into weeping, but the King continued to speak calmly in most Christian spirit.

He died on 13th September at daybreak, having received all the sacraments of the Church with every sign of devoutness, piety, and religion, and to the apparent grief of all people, rich and poor. His death was announced that night, and thereupon began the funeral ceremonies, which were for nine days with continuous prayer and the tolling of bells that never ceased day nor night. He was buried the next day without any of the usual ceremonies and by his own orders without embalming. When the corpse had been laid in the leaden coffin the whole Council of State was summoned to witness; then the coffin was locked and the key taken to the King.

The Character of King Philip II.

The King was seventy-one years old, having reigned forty-two years. He was a Prince that fought with gold rather than with steel, by his brain rather than by his arms, acquiring more by sitting still, by negotiation, by policy than his father did by armies and by war, so that he was one of the richest Princes that the world has ever seen, yet hath he left the revenues of his Kingdom and of the Crown burdened with about a million of debts. He was profoundly religious, displaying great calmness and professing himself unmoved alike in good or evil fortune. On great occasions, in the conduct of wars, or in the magnificence of his buildings he never counted the cost. He was no close reckoner, but lavished his gold without a thought, yet in small matters, in the government of his household, in his presents and rewards, more parsimonious than became his station. He held his desires in absolute control, showing an immutable and unalterable temper; feigning injuries, and feigning not to feel injuries, but never losing an opportunity to avenge them. No one ever saw him in a rage, being always patient, phlegmatic, temperate, melancholy.

The Prince that succeedeth is the King's only son, twenty years of age. He was educated by his father in great obedience and piety, but it cannot yet be said what his opinions may be, for he hath always kept them concealed out of respect for his father. Yet is he thought to be peacefully disposed, and hath shown himself satisfied with the new peace; if he hath an intention of taking up arms it is against infidels.

5th November. Great Floods.

In the counties of Lincoln, Northampton, Huntingdon, the Isle of Ely, Sussex, Surrey and elsewhere great hurt hath been sustained this autumn by reason of the waters that have of late overrun most part of their grounds, whereby these counties are reduced to great distress.

6th November. Rebellion spreading in Ireland.

There is now most barbarous and fearful rebellion raging in Munster. Most of the followers of noblemen and gentlemen of Munster have gone over to the enemy so that Sir Thomas Norris, the Governor, was unable either to encounter the rebels or to defend himself and so was forced to withdraw from his own house. These combinations and revolts have effected many execrable murders and cruelties upon the English in the counties of Limerick, Cork and Kerry and elsewhere; infants being taken from the nurses' breasts and dashed against the walls; the heart plucked out of the body of the husband in the view of the wife, who was forced to yield the use of her apron to wipe the blood from the murderers' fingers; an English gentleman in a town at midday cruelly murdered and his head cleft in divers pieces; divers sent into Youghal amongst the English, some with their throats cut but not killed, some with their tongues cut out of their heads, others with their noses cut off; by view whereof the English might the more bitterly lament the misery of their countrymen, and fear the like to befall themselves. And these execrable parts are performed by the Irish tenants and servants of the English; and those that but the last day were fed and nourished by the English are now the thieves that violently before their faces take from them their corn, cattle and other goods; and the party spoiled thinketh himself happy if he escape without loss of life or other shameful villainy to himself, his wife or children.

8th November. RUMOURS.

It is generally held that the Earl of Essex will go to Ireland towards the spring as Lieutenant-General, and the Lord Mountjoy as his Lord Deputy, with divers other young lords and noblemen, and that he shall be accompanied with the most part of those knights that be his creatures, for it is thought fit they should not come too easily by their honours but that in this case, as well as in many others, it should be granted for service done and to be done.

The new Countess of Southampton is brought abed of a daughter, and to mend her portion the Earl, her father, hath lately lost 1,800 crowns at tennis in Paris.

A JEST ON THE KING OF SPAIN.

It is reported about the Court that the King of Spain for all his striving to enlarge his possessions in his last days was eaten by lice while still living. Hereat one of the courtiers said to the Queen, 'God grant me no further ambition than to be eaten by worms when I am dead.'

9th November. THE CONSPIRACY OF EDWARD SQUIRE.

Edward Squire was arraigned this day in Westminster for his high treason in compassing the Queen's death, and being found guilty is condemned to be quartered.

This Squire dwelt in Greenwich divers years, and took upon him the practice of a scrivener and for some two years held an employment about the Queen's stable, as deputy to one Kaies, a purveyor of provisions. But being of a wit above his vocation, he disliked that condition of life and went to sea in the late voyage of Sir Francis Drake into the Indies; in which voyage sailing in the *Francis*, it was his hap to be taken by five Spanish frigates. Squire was thus brought prisoner into Spain, where soon after he was set at liberty.

Not long after his enlargement, he became known to Richard Walpole, the Jesuit, that is a kind of Vicar-General there to Parsons in his absence. This Walpole observed Squire, and finding him a man of more than ordinary sense and capacity for his quality and education, well advised and yet resolved, and not apprehensive at all of danger, perceived in him two conditions of especial advantage; the one that, coming into Spain a prisoner and not a fugitive, his return into England would be subject to less suspicion; the other that he understood Squire had some attendance about the Queen's stable.

Whereupon to prepare him for his purpose and to give colour that when Squire should return into England he was a man that had suffered in Spain for his conscience, Walpole subtlely compassed that upon a quarrel picked Squire was put into the Inquisition. By this means he got Squire's heart into his hands, mollified by distress, and became sure of him that he was a fixed and resolved Papist. After sufficient preparation, Walpole began to discourse of the miseries of the Catholics in England, and of the slanders of the government and upon how few persons' lives the State did stand. And Squire on the other side, wanting no wit to perceive which way he was led, after some time made vehement protestation of his mind and devotion to do service to the cause. Whereupon, Walpole saith: 'It were no doubt an action very meritorious to kill the Earl of Essex; but one thing is necessary.' And having kept him in suspense awhile, brake with him plainly and told him that he would put a service into his hands that he might accomplish without any evident peril of his life. And it was the empoisonment of the pommel of the Queen's saddle at such time as she should ride abroad, her Majesty being like to rest her hand thereupon for a good time together, and not unlike for her hand to come often about her face, mouth, and nostrils. Unto which accursed propositions, after that Squire had assented, then did the Friar use all diligence to confirm and bind him to resolution and performance, at sundry confessions taking his vow to be constant, and causing him to receive the sacrament upon it. And for a conclusion and final benediction of this most execrable plot, Squire kneeling before Walpole at confession, he lifted him up, hugged him about the neck with his left arm (such were Squire's own words) and crossing him with the other hand, after some words mumbled in Latin, said distinctly to him in English, 'God bless thee and give thee strength, my son; be of good courage: I pawn my soul for thine, and thou shalt have my prayers dead and alive.'

Then Walpole gave him full direction for the disposing of the poison, showing him that he should receive it in a double bladder, and when it should be used, he was to prick the bladder full of holes upon the upper part, and so carry it within the palm of his hand with a thick glove for safeguard of the hand. Then he should turn it in his hand upside down and so press it hard upon the pommel of the saddle.

Squire, therefore, being arrived in England about a fortnight before the Earl of Essex's setting forth towards the Islands, addressed himself to a Councillor of estate, both to avoid suspicion and to advise a means to go with the Earl in his ship; which indeed he did.

Now a se'nnight after he came out of Spain he understood that the horses were being made ready for the Queen's riding abroad. So he came into the stable yard where her Majesty's horse stood ready and in a familiar and cheerful manner, in the hearing of divers that stood by, he laid his hand upon the pommel of the saddle and said, 'God save the Queen'; and therewith bruised the poison as he was directed. But so it was that her Majesty's going abroad was stayed.

Within five or six days after this fact was committed, Squire went to sea in my Lord of Essex's own ship, taking the remainder of the same poison with him in a little pot in his portmantua, and when the Earl was at sea between Fayal and St. Michael, he bestowed it upon the pommels of a chair of wood, where the Earl used to dine and sup; but nothing came of it neither.

Squire now slept in security, for, although he had failed of success, yet he took himself to be out of danger, thinking that because it was carried between his confessor and him, it could never be revealed. But his confessor imparted it to some principal fugitives there which raised a great expectation of some effect to ensue. One of the more passionate of them began to inveigh bitterly against Squire and how he had undone the cause, and the better to be revenged on him, was content that one should give information against Squire by means of a letter which he pretended to have stolen out of one of their studies. Hereupon it was collected that this was but an engine against Squire, and that he was an honest man. Yet because it was a tender matter, Squire was sent for and examined. For a time he denied, but after gave it to be understood that there was somewhat true. Hold was taken of that; and thereupon Squire, not knowing how far his confessor had broken trust with him, by good persuasion and God's good working disclosed all without any rigour to the world.

10th November. AN ATTEMPT IN DUBLIN.

Ireland is now universally shaken with rebellion, and even the cities and port towns of the English Pale are not free from Tyrone's treasonable practices, who did very lately employ some of his instruments to surprise the Castle of Dublin, and to subvert the city, and consequently to commit to massacre all the English and their goods. This conspiracy was far advanced and very near the time of execution. It should have been performed by thirty resolute men set on by twenty-nine priests lying in Dublin and should have been assisted with 1,000 men of Tyrone's forces, beside the help of 1,000 more from the mountain rebels; but it was happily discovered by one of the conspirators.

14th November. The Queen Royally Received.

This evening the Queen came to Westminster by torchlight and was received most royally, by the commandment of the Council, by the Lord Mayor, the Aldermen and Sheriffs in scarlet, and a great number of the wealthy citizens in velvet coats and chains of gold, and all on horseback.

15th November. The Soldiers in Ireland.

Sir Richard Bingham is now in Dublin and much complaineth of the new English soldiers; for it is strange to see how suddenly they decay. Of the last thousand the fourth part are run away and many of the rest so poor and simple as to be utterly unserviceable; which fault the Captains allege to be in the justices of the peace and their inferior magistrates rather than in the Lieutenants of the Shires.

16th November. Beacon Watches Discontinued.

The beacon watches are now to be discontinued for the winter, except upon places where a descent of the enemy is likely, and to be renewed in the spring.

17th November. Determinations for Ireland.

The Queen, taking to heart that with the charge of nine or ten thousand men she is no place able to defend herself in her Kingdom of Ireland, is now pleased to bethink her of sending some great person whereunto the Earl of Essex is named as a nobleman that will be greatly followed and feared; but there is not as yet any perfect conclusion of the matter.

20th November. The Execution of Luke Hutton.

Luke Hutton, that notable highway robber, committing a robbery on St. Luke's Day (for his name's sake) was taken and is hanged at York of late, being charged and condemned on ninescore and seventeen indictments. This Hutton was formerly a scholar of Cambridge and, some say, son to the Archbishop of York, though others more certainly declare his father to be a prebendary of Durham.

28th November. More Soldiers required.

Further levies to the number of 1,000 are now required for service in Ireland.

3rd December. THE DESPERATE STATE OF IRELAND.

The revolt and defection of the Irishry doth daily increase in every part, and of those who still seem to stand firm most are in effect gone in heart, so that there is no hope either to stay these dangers or preserve the Kingdom from losing unless new forces be immediately sent over. Rarely any week now passeth wherein there are not received advertisements either of the surprising of castles, burning of towns, or massacring the subjects and havocking their goods. Sir Thomas More, an Englishman by birth, was lately betrayed in his own house by the treachery of his watch, himself slain, and his wife and two daughters carried away by the traitors, who leaving his wife stripped in a bog she is dead since with the cold. Captain Gifford is slain in his own house, and his wife seeking to save her husband by prostrating herself upon him was in many places sore wounded.

Moreover, such is the nakedness of the soldiers for want of clothes, and their poverty for lack of lendings to buy them food, that many of them show like prisoners, half starved for want of cherishing, and like at any time to disband or break into some great mutiny; and if any of the companies should break and either run to the enemy or steal into England there would be small hope of the Kingdom.

PLAYS AT COURT.

Of late the Lord Chamberlain's players played four times at Court and the Earl of Nottingham's men twice, who played *The Downfall of Robin Hood*, and for this they are rewarded at the rate of £10 a play.

5th December. A LOAN IN THE CITY.

Because of the great charges of providing this army in Ireland her Majesty now seeketh a loan from the City, and lest it should be denied upon any just colour she is pleased to bind her own lands or give assignations of all customs. This loan is to be for six months at the rate of 10 in the 100. The strangers likewise that dwell in this country are required to lend 200,000 French crowns upon the same security.

11th December. AN ATTEMPT IN THE NORTH.

Six ships of Dunkirk were lately discovered on the coast of the North parts that did attempt to set some hundred men on land, but so good watch was kept that the beacons were fired, and, the country being ready to withstand them, they withdrew. Nevertheless it is thought likely that on their return they may make some attempt on the coast, either to surprise some gentlemen in their houses or set on fire some village or town near the coast, especially about Yarmouth.

15th December. SOLDIERS FOR IRELAND.

Orders are now given for 2,000 men from the garrisons in the Low Countries to be sent to Ireland, being better trained and hardened than any that can be levied at home; their places to be taken by others newly levied from London, Middlesex, Surrey, Essex, Kent and Sussex.

18th December. THE THAMES FROZEN.

These last days by reason of the great frosts the Thames hath been well-nigh frozen over at London Bridge, but now it beginneth to thaw.

20th December. A DECLARATION CONCERNING THE KING OF SCOTS.

Notwithstanding the satisfaction given to the King of Scots by the Queen's private letters, he remaineth still much grieved with the scandals imputed to him by Valentine Thomas, and hath earnestly moved the Queen to deliver some public testimony of her good opinion. Hereupon though in no way bound to yield account to any person on earth of her actions, more than in love and kindness, yet for further confirmation of her goodwill towards the King, she hath declared that she considereth him to be a Christian Prince of honour and religion, and that she giveth no credit to such things as Thomas hath affirmed against him.

24th December. THE LOAN IN THE CITY.

The money from the City comes in but slowly, so that the Queen's service is hampered. The Lord Mayor is required to use all expedition that the sum of £20,000 demanded be paid into the Receipt before the holidays. Some citizens of good ability have withdrawn themselves into the country, and they shall be sent for to appear before the Council to answer their careless behaviour.

THE REBELLION IN MUNSTER.

Mr. Edmund Spenser is come from Cork to the Court with letters from Sir Thomas Norris. There are 1,000 new soldiers arrived at Cork, 600 at Kinsale, and 400 at Waterford, men reasonably well chosen and furnished but very raw and inexpert, not having had any training before their arrival.

27th December. A SKIRMISH IN MUNSTER.

From Cork Sir Thomas Norris writeth that about a fortnight since he took in hand with thirteen of the new companies and four of the old to march to the relief of Kilmallock; but the traitors having notice of his setting forward, dislodged from the siege, burned their ladders and encountered him with skirmish. Nevertheless he entered Kilmallock and returned the next day, though the rebels began a new fight as soon as they were out of their quarters, and continued whilst they marched nine miles; in which time they gave many hot onsets, being so confident of the victory that they had in conceit divided the coats and arms of these new soldiers amongst themselves. But herein it pleased God so to assist our men that they only received in both fights the loss but of four men slain and some thirty hurt, and gave the enemy many repulses to their great loss and shame. Hereby hath grown to these new men such courage and boldness (being so far overmatched by the enemy in numbers) that they will be able to do her Majesty good service, if some speedy help may be sent to maintain them in their strength before they fall to weakness.

28th December. THE THAMES AGAIN FROZEN.

To-day there is a great fall of snow and the Thames again frozen over.

THE THEATRE PULLED DOWN.

There hath long been disputes between Mr. Giles Allen that owneth the land whereon the Theatre standeth and the Burbages concerning the renewing of the lease insomuch that the players these last months have left the Theatre and gone to the

Curtain. To-day Richard Burbage with one Peter Street, a carpenter, and some ten others, arming themselves with swords and other weapons, repair to the Theatre; and though Mr. Allen's people would prevent them, they break down the Theatre and take away the wood and timber to a place on the Bankside where, 'tis said, they would erect a new playhouse.

A Lewd Fellow.

Of late a certain Edward Francis of Melbury Osmond in Dorsetshire made very foul speeches of her Majesty. Wishing to persuade one Mistress Elizabeth Baylie to lead an incontinent life with him, and upon her refusing, he said that the best in England (meaning her Majesty) had done so, and had three bastards by noblemen of the Court, two sons and a daughter, and was herself base born; and that the land had been happy if she had been cut off twenty years since so that some noble prince might have reigned in her stead. When those who heard these words charged him with them he offered great gifts to stay his accusers, £40 each to four several men and £20 to the women; but they would not. But now seeing that he has to answer before the Council, he is stricken dead in conceit and is probably fled as he has forfeited £500 on a bond for not putting in a security.

29th December. Privileged Places in London.

During the late burdens and charges laid upon the City, the places privileged within the City have not only refused to furnish soldiers and to contribute themselves but retain those that have recourse thither to avoid the imprest. Moreover divers Doctors of Physic and others professing the law, besides many gentlemen, pretend themselves to be privileged and exempt from this charge because they are not free of the City. The Council order that the sums collected from the Liberties shall be proportionable to those levied in the City, and that any who have abode, house or dwelling in the City must contribute for the same.

30th December. A Play at Cambridge.

This last Christmas they have at Cambridge a play called *The Pilgrimage to Parnassus* wherein is shown the journey of two students, Philomusus and Studioso, to reach Helicon, and the temptations which they met in the way, as of Madido the drunkard, or Stupido the Puritan, or Amoretto by whom they are persuaded to lechery. At the last there meeteth them one Ingenioso who would turn them back from their journey, for, quoth he, 'come not there, seek for poverty no further; its too far to go to Parnassus to fetch repentance.'

31*st December*. NEW PLAYS THIS PAST YEAR AT THE ROSE.

During this past year my Lord of Nottingham's men have played these new plays at the Rose, namely, *Mother Redcap* (by Drayton and Munday), *Phaeton* (by Dekker), *The Downfall* and *The Death of Robert Earl of Huntingdon, called Robin Hood* (by Munday and Chettle), *A woman will have her will*, *The triplicity of Cuckolds* (by Dekker), *The famous wars of Henry the first and the Prince of Wales* (by Chettle, Dekker and Drayton), *Earl Godwin and his three sons*, in two parts (by Chettle, Dekker and Drayton), *King Arthur* (by Hathaway), *Black Bateman of the North*, in two parts (by Chettle, Dekker, Drayton and Wilson), *The Funeral of Richard Cordelion* (by Chettle, Drayton, Munday and Wilson), *The Isle of Women* (by Chapman), *The Madman's Morrice* (by Dekker, Drayton and Wilson), *Hannibal and Hermes or worse afeared than hurt* (by Dekker, Drayton and Wilson), *Valentine and Orson* (by Hathaway and Munday), *Pierce of Winchester* (by Dekker, Drayton and Wilson), *Brute* (by Day and Chettle), *Hot Anger soon cold* (by Porter), *Chance medley* (by Chettle, Dekker, Munday, Wilson and Drayton), *Catiline's Conspiracy* (by Chettle and Wilson), *Vayrode* (an old play remade by Chettle), *The Civil Wars of France*, in three parts (by Dekker and Drayton), *The fount of new fashions* (by Chapman), *Connan of Cornwall* (by Dekker and Drayton).

THESE BOOKS ALSO SET FORTH ANNO 1598.

MR. RICHARD BARNFIELD'S POEMS.

Mr. Richard Barnfield hath written these poems: *The Encomion of Lady Pecunia, or the praise of Money; The Complaint of Poetry for the death of Liberality; The Combat between Conscience and Covetousness in the mind of man*, and sundry short poems in divers humours; among these last being an epitaph upon the death of Sir Philip Sidney, an epitaph upon the death of his aunt, Mistress Elizabeth Skrymsher, together with a remembrance of some English poets:

Live Spenser ever, in thy *Faery Queen*:
Whose like, for deep conceit, was never seen.
Crown'd mayest thou be, unto thy more renown,
As King of Poets, with a laurel crown.

And Daniel, praised for thy sweet chaste verse:
Whose fame is grav'd on *Rosamond's* black herse.
Still may'st thou live, and still be honoured
For that rare work, *The White Rose and the Red.*

And Drayton, whose well-written tragedies,
And sweet epistles, soar thy fame to skies.
Thy learned name is equal with the rest;
Whose stately numbers are so well addressed.

And Shakespeare thou, whose honey-flowing vein,
Pleasing the world, thy praises doth obtain.
Whose *Venus* and whose *Lucrece* (sweet and chaste)
Thy name in fame's immortal book have plac'd.
Live ever you, at least in fame live ever:
Well may the body die, but fame dies never.

CHAPMAN'S ADDITIONS TO 'HERO AND LEANDER.'

A new edition of *Hero and Leander* wherein Mr. George Chapman concludeth the fable with three further sestiads of his own making, telling how Leander again swimming the Hellespont to visit his Hero was drowned and his body flung ashore; whereat Hero died straightway with the grief of it.

ACHILLES' SHIELD.

Mr. Chapman hath also translated into rimed decasyllabon verses that description of the Shield of Achilles from the 18th Book of Homer's *Iliades*; which work he undertook suddenly because, since the publication of the other books, comparison hath been made between Virgil and Homer, who, saith he, 'can be compared in nothing with more decisal and cutting of all arguments than in these two shields; and whosoever shall read Homer throughly and worthily will know the question comes from a superficial and too unripe a reader; for Homer's Poems were writ from a free fury, an absolute and full soul; Virgil's out of a courtly, laborious, and altogether imitatory spirit; not a simile he hath but what is Homer's; not an invention, person, or disposition but is wholly or originally builded upon Homerical foundations, and in many places hath the very words Homer useth.'

FLORIO'S 'WORLD OF WORDS.'

Signor John Florio hath compiled a most copious and exact dictionary in Italian and English, entitled *A world of words*, dedicated to the Earl of Rutland, the Earl of Southampton and the Countess of Bedford.

A BOOK OF PAINTING.

From Oxford *A tract containing the art of curious Painting, carving and building*, written first in Italian by John Paul Lomatius (or Lomazzo) and Englished by Richard Haydock, being dedicated to Mr. Thomas Bodley; which work is in seven books; the first of the Proportions of all things; the second of Actions and Gestures; the third of Colour; the fourth of Light; the fifth of perspectives; the sixth of practise; the seventh of history. To the third book addeth a discourse of the painting of women, which this author termeth 'painting upon the life,' noting the evil effects of those substances used by our dames, as of sublimate which the surgeons call corrosive; whereof such women as use it about their face have always black teeth, standing far out of their gums like a Spanish mule, an offensive breath, with a face half scorched, and an unclean complexion, whereby they hasten old age before time and give occasions to their husbands to seek strangers instead of their wives, with divers other inconveniences. Likewise much harm is wrought by all paintings and colourings made of iron, brass, lead, tin, ceruse (or white lead), camphire, juice of lemons, plume-alum, saltpeter, vitriol, and all manner of salts. Wherefore if there be no remedy but women will be meddling with this art of polishing, let them instead use such safe helps of beauty as these: cheerfulness and contentment, health, honesty, and wisdom, for even a hard favoured and brown woman being merry, pleasant and jocund will seem sufficient beautiful.

'The Comedy of Mucedorus.'

A play called *A most pleasant comedy of Mucedorus, the King's son of Valentia, and Amadine, the King's daughter of Aragon, with the merry conceits of Mouse.* Herein is shown how Mucedorus being in disguise saved Amadine both from a bear and a wild man and in the end wedded her.

Norden's 'Speculum Britanniæ.'

Mr. John Norden continueth his Survey of England and hath now a further part of *Speculum Britanniæ* in the description of Hertfordshire, noting as in the former books the fairs, markets and great houses, and also an alphabetical table of the towns, parishes and hamlets, together with a map of the county. Mr. Norden much complaineth that he was drawn unto this work by honourable Councillors and promised sufficient allowance, and herein he hath spent above a thousand marks and five years' time.

A Book of Riddles.

A book called *The Riddles of Heraclitus and Democritus*, whereof this is the 47th:

The Miller and the Miller's wife,
  That they might merry make,
Were set down with a dish of fruit,
  A cake and half a cake,
The parson of the town with them,
  His sister and no more:

Now have you heard of all the guests
  And of their bread the store;

Yet did they use the matter with
Such cunning, skill and art,
That everyone eat half a cake,
Before they did depart.

The answer: The miller's wife was the parson's sister, and so the division is not hard to make.

Mr. Tofte's 'Alba.'

Alba: the mouth's mind of a melancholy lover, divided into three parts and written by Mr. Robert Tofte, wherein the lover unsatisfied lamenteth his hard case.

'Tyro's Roaring Meg.'

An idle book called *Tyro's Roaring Meg, planted against the walls of melancholy*, containing sundry epigrams in verse; also *Tyronis Epistolae siue mus rampant in agro aureo*; and *The mean in spending*.

Tyro's Epistle of Love.

Tyro by chance did read 'that Generation
Was the sole final cause of Augmentation.'
Eftsoons he shook the hand with single life,
And set his wit on tenters for a wife.
He took his quill and penn'd this dainty plaint,
Unto a mincing minion, fine and daint.
'O thou Eliptic line, wherein the sun
Of my felicity doth daily run;
Eye-pleasing object, honeysuckle sweet,
Tyro thy vassal tumbles at thy feet:
He a Leander, ready for thy sake,
To pass an Hellespont of pain and ache.
Be thou a Hero standing on the shore
With open arms and clasp him more and more.
Thou shalt perceive, 'so by thy love be won,
I am no snow to melt against the sun.
My bleared eyes shall steep themselves in tears,
Till some mild answer ventilate my fears.
Ah, dearest Nymph, some lightfoot lackey send
With white and black to give me life or end.

Roses are in thy lips, O hellish smart,
If angry nettles grow upon thy heart.
Farewell thou pretty Mop, and me remember;
Written in haste the twentieth of December
About the dinner hour of eleven

1597

Tyro thy Delphic sword till crows be old,
Till Ister be lukewarm, and Ganges cold.'

MR. WENTWORTH'S 'PITHY EXHORTATION.'

Mr. Peter Wentworth (that was sent to the Tower at the time of the Parliament in '93 for pressing upon her Majesty, contrary to her strict command, to name the successor to the Crown), left behind him two treatises which are now printed in Scotland, a year after his death. In the first, entitled *A pithy exhortation*, urgeth upon her Majesty to establish her successor to the Crown, showing the conveniences and answering the inconveniences that would come of it; declareth that this would be the surest means to kill the hearts of all her enemies both here and in foreign countries, who are persuaded that if they could bereave the Queen of her life, then would her subjects have no one head to cleave and resort unto for succour, but should grow to civil war and unnatural division and be ready, every one of us, to cut each other's throats; and then were we easily all overrun by our enemies. In the second treatise answereth that *Conference* of Doleman and holdeth that the King of Scots is the true successor.

ABBREVIATIONS

The following abbreviations have been used for sources frequently cited :

A.P.C. *Acts of the Privy Council*, edited by J. R. Dasent, 1900, etc.

A.R. *A Transcript of the Register of the Company of Stationers of London* ; 1554-1640. Edited by E. Arber, 5 vols., 1875-1894.

BIRCH'S HISTORICAL VIEW. *An Historical View of the Negotiations between the Courts of England, France and Brussels*, 1592-1617. By Thomas Birch, 1749.

BIRCH'S MEMOIRS. *Memoirs of the Reign of Queen Elizabeth . . . from the original papers of . . . Anthony Bacon and other manuscripts*. By Thomas Birch, 2 vols., 1754.

CAMDEN'S ELIZABETH. *The History of . . . Elizabeth, late Queen of England*. By William Camden. Translated into English, 1630, etc.

CAREW MSS. *Calendar of the Carew Manuscripts in the Archiepiscopal Library at Lambeth*, edited by J. S. Bullen and W. Bullen, 1869.

CHAMBERLAIN'S LETTERS. *Letters written by John Chamberlain during the reign of Queen Elizabeth*. Edited by Sarah Williams. Camden Society, 1861.

DEVEREUX. *Lives and Letters of the Devereux, Earls of Essex* . . . 1540-1646. By the Hon. W. B. Devereux, 2 vols., 1853.

D'EWES' JOURNALS. *A Compleat Journal of the Votes, Speeches and Debates both of the House of Lords and House of Commons throughout the whole Reign of Queen Elizabeth*. Collected by . . . Sir Simonds D'Ewes, 1693.

ELIZ. JOURNAL. *An Elizabethan Journal, being a record of those things most talked of during the years* 1591-1594. By G. B. Harrison, 1928.

ELIZABETHAN STAGE. *The Elizabethan Stage*. By E. K. Chambers. 4 vols. 1923.

HAKLUYT'S VOYAGES. *The Principal Navigations, Voyages, Traffiques and Discoveries of the English Nation*. By Richard Hakluyt. References to the edition in 8 vols. in The Everyman Library, 1907, etc.

HAWARDE. *Les Reportes del Cases in Camera Stellata*, 1593-1609. By William Hawarde. Edited by W. P. Baildon, 1894.

HENS. DIARY. *Henslowe's Diary*. Vol. i., The Text ; vol. ii., The Commentary. Edited by W. W. Greg, 1904-7.

m.e. Modern edition.

M.S.R. Malone Society Reprint.

ABBREVIATIONS

MIDDLESEX SESSIONS ROLLS. *Middlesex County Records.* Vol. i., *Indictments, Coroner's Inquests post mortem, and recognizances from 3 Edward VI. to the end of the reign of Queen Elizabeth.* Edited by J. C. Jeaffreson, 1886.

MURDIN'S STATE PAPERS. *A Collection of State Papers relating to foreign affairs . . . 1571 to 1596.* By William Murdin, 1759.

NUGAE ANTIQUAE. *Nugae Antiquae : being a miscellaneous collection of original papers . . .* by Sir John Harington, etc. Edited by T. Park, 2 vols., 1804.

PENSHURST PAPERS. *Papers of Lord D'Isle and Dudley at Penshurst Place.* Historical Manuscripts Commission. [In course of printing.]

PROCLAMATIONS. *A Book containing all such Proclamations as were published during the Reign of the late Queen Elizabeth. Collected together by the industry of Humphrey Dyson, of the City of London, Publique Notary,* 1618. This is an actual collection ; references are to the manuscript pagination of the volume in the British Museum (G. 6463).

PURCHAS. *Hakluytus Posthumus, or Purchas his pilgrims,* 1625. References to the edition published by MacLehose and Co., 1907.

RYMER'S FŒDERA. *Fœdera, conventiones, literæ, et cuiuscumque generis Acta Publica inter Reges Angliæ et alios quosuis . . .* ex schedis Thomæ Rymer. Edited by Robert Sanderson, 2nd edition, 1727.

S.P. DOM. *State Papers Domestic* preserved in the Public Record Office Abstracted in the *Calendars of State Papers Domestic.*

S.P. IRELAND. *State Papers Ireland* preserved in the Public Record Office. Abstracted in the *Calendars of State Papers relating to Ireland in the reign of Queen Elizabeth.* Edited by E. G. Atkinson, 1893.

S.T.C. *A Short Title Catalogue of Books printed in England, Scotland and Ireland, and of English Books printed abroad.* Compiled by A. W. Pollard and G. R. Redgrave, 1926.

SALISBURY PAPERS. *Historical Manuscripts Commission.—Calendar of the Manuscripts of the Marquis of Salisbury, preserved at Hatfield House,* 1892, etc.

SIDNEY PAPERS. *Letters and Memorials of State . . . from the originals at Penshurst Place,* etc. By Arthur Collins. 2 vols. 1746.

SPEDDING. *The Life and Letters of Francis Bacon.* By James Spedding. 7 vols., 1861 ; [numbered vols. viii.-xiv. in the Spedding-Ellis edition of Bacon's Works].

STOW'S ANNALS. *Annales or a General Chronicle of England.* By John Stow ; first printed in 1592. As there are several editions both of Stow and Camden and references are quite easy to find, particular editions or pages are not specified.

STRYPE, ANNALS. *Annals of the Reformation . . . during Queen Elizabeth's happy reign.* By John Strype, 4 vols., 1731, and 7 vols., 1824. [The later edition marks the pagination of the earlier ; references are to the earlier.]

NOTES

1595

3rd January. THE REVELS AT GRAY'S INN. *Gesta Grayorum*, first printed 1688; m.e. in J. Nichols' *Progresses of Queen Elizabeth*, and *M.S.R.* Spedding claims that the speeches of the Councillors were written by Bacon, that on philosophy foreshadowing 'Solomon's House' in the *New Atlantis.* For the beginnings of the revels see *Eliz. Journal*, pp. 338-9, 342; also note on 4th February.

4th January. GRAY'S INN REVELS. *Gesta Grayorum.*

10th January. A NOTABLE CASE OF COSENAGE. *Salisbury Papers*, v. 82; see 2nd April.

13th January. GOSSON'S 'PLEASANT QUIPS.' *A.R.*, ii., 669; *S.T.C.*, 12096. This piece of Puritanical muck-raking is anonymous, but Gosson's name is written in a contemporary hand in the only surviving copy of the 1596 edition; m.e. privately 1847. Compare *Love's Labours Lost*, IV. ii. 128.

17th January. BARNFIELD'S 'CYNTHIA' AND 'CASSANDRA.' *A.R.*, ii. 669; *S.T.C.*, 1483; m.e. Roxburghe Club, 1816.

23rd January. COMPLAINTS AGAINST PATENTS. *Remembrancia*, ii. 82, 83, 84.

THE ESTATE OF THE ENGLISH FUGITIVES. *A.R.*, ii. 670; *S.T.C.*, 15562-5.

24th January. THE SCOTTISH AMBASSADOR GIVEN AUDIENCE. *Salisbury Papers*, v. 37.

25th January. THE IRISH REBELLION. *S.P. Ireland*, 178 : 10; letter from the Lord Deputy to Burleigh dated 15th January.

THE VACANT SOLICITORSHIP. Spedding's *Bacon*, i. 347-8.

27th January. HURAULT'S DISCOURSES. *S.T.C.*, 14000; dated in Epistle Dedicatory to Lord Cobham.

28th January. GRAY'S INN REVELS. *Gesta Grayorum*; see also pp. 1, 4, 11, 12.

31st January. THE JESUITS AT WISBEACH CASTLE. Strype, *Annals*, iv. 195. Wisbeach Castle was used as a place of internment for seminaries and recusants at this time.

1st February. THE GRAY'S INN REVELS. *Gesta Grayorum.*

3rd February. GRAY'S INN REVELS AT COURT. *Gesta Grayorum.*

4th February. SIR JOHN NORRIS'S RETURN. *S.P. Dom.*, 251 : 16. These were the troops who had been employed in the capture of Croyzon; see *Eliz. Journal*, pp. 329, 331.

THE GRAY'S INN REVELS ENDED. *Gesta Grayorum.* The Revels at Gray's Inn provide a most interesting revelation of the mentality of the bright young men of aristocratic and upper middle-class England. It seems extraordinary that this elaborate, and at times impudent, parody of State should not only have been tolerated but actively encouraged by the Council, the nobility, the City, and even by the Queen herself. *Gesta Grayorum* is a mirror of the mind of the younger generation—as brilliant as there has ever been in England—its wit, its tastes, amusements and aspirations. See also note on Chapman's *Humorous Day's Mirth*, 11th May, 1597.

7th February. AN ALARM AT OSTEND. *Salisbury Papers*, v. 104.

8th February. SIR WALTER RALEGH'S VOYAGE. Hakluyt's *Voyages*, vii. 280. See 27th September.

9th February. THE QUEEN'S LETTER TO THE GRAND SIGNIOR. *Salisbury Papers*, v. 105.

11th February. BISHOP FLETCHER'S MARRIAGE. *Salisbury Papers*, v. 106; *Nugae Antiquae*, ii. 46; Thomas Fuller's *Worthies* [Kent].

15th February. FLESH PROHIBITED IN LENT. *Proclamations*, 329. The regular opening formula of this annual order of the Council, repeated in 1595, 1596, 1597, 1598, reads a little hopelessly: 'First her Majesty's pleasure is, upon her understanding of the great disorders heretofore and *especially the last Lent* committed in killing and eating flesh in time of Lent . . .'

18th February. MOSSE'S 'ARRAIGNMENT AND CONVICTION OF USURY.' *A.R.*, ii. 671; *S.T.C.*, 18207. The Epistle Dedicatory is dated 1st January, 1595, the Epistle to the Reader 6th February, 1594[-5]; the book was entered 18th February (*i.e.* after printing).

20th February. THE TRIAL OF FR. SOUTHWELL. *Catholic Record Society*, v. 333; from an account by Thomas Leake, an eyewitness; see *Eliz. Journal*, pp. 140, 150.

21st February. NEW PLAYS AT THE ROSE. *Hens. Diary*, i. 21; ii. 174; neither play is known.

22nd February. THE EXECUTION OF FR. SOUTHWELL. See 20th February.

26th February. THE FORT AT BLACKWATER TAKEN. *S.P. Ireland*, 178 : 53.

4th March. A FATAL MISCHANCE. *Middlesex Sessions Rolls*, i. 220.

5th March. A NEW PLAY. *Hens. Diary*, i. 22; ii. 175. Dr. Greg suggests that the play may be Heywood's *Golden Age*.

6th March. THE WIDOW OF DR. LOPEZ. *S.P. Dom.*, 251 : 50. For the trial and execution of Dr. Lopez see *Eliz. Journal*, 289, 303, etc.

15th March. THE EARL OF CUMBERLAND'S SHIP. *Purchas*, xvi. 25. Approximate date. See *Eliz. Journal*, pp. 160, 317.

26th March. MR. CHAMPERNOUN'S CHOIRBOYS. *Salisbury Papers*, v. 155, 436.

1st April. NEWS OF SIR WALTER RALEGH. *Salisbury Papers*, v. 161; also *S.P. Dom.*, 256 : 100 (misdated 1596).

2nd April. THE LEWDNESS OF DOLL PHILLIPS. *A Quest of Enquiry by women to know, whether the Tripe-wife were trimmed by Doll yea or no*, by Oliver Oatmeal. This scandal is a continuation of 'A Notable Case of Cosenage' (10th January). Oliver's style is none of the clearest, but the case is here set down as near as may be; for a note on 'Keep the Widow Waking' see the *Library* for June 1930. *S.T.C.*, 18758; m.e. in A. B. Grosart's *Elizabethan England in Gentle and Simple Life*, 1881.

4th April. A STRANGE MANNER OF DEATH. *Middlesex Sessions Rolls*, i. 221.

5th April. SOUTHWELL'S 'ST. PETER'S COMPLAINT.' *A.R.*, ii. 295; *S.T.C.*, 22956; published anonymously; m.e. in *The Complete Poems of Robert Southwell*, by A. B. Grosart, 1872. Compare *A Midsummer Night's Dream*, v. i. 2-23; *Astrophel and Stella*, xxxix.; *Macbeth*, II. ii. 36.

12th April. DRAYTON'S 'ENDYMION AND PHOEBE.' *A.R.*, ii. 296; *S.T.C.*, 7192; m.e. by J. W. Hebel, 1925. A work of some interest and importance, not only from its place in the *Venus and Adonis*, *Hero and Leander* group, but also because of the mythological, philosophical and metaphysical ideas which Drayton weaves into the poem, especially in the later pages.

SIR PHILIP SIDNEY'S 'DEFENCE OF POESY.' *A.R.*, ii. 666, and ii. 295; *S.T.C.*, 22534-5. The *Defence* was first entered on 29th November, 1594, by Ponsonby, presumably as a blocking entry; *Astrophel and Stella* had been published in 1591, apparently against the wishes of the Sidney family, with a preface by Nashe. Olney entered a copy (called *The Apology for Poetry*) on 12th April and proceeded to print, but Ponsonby complained. Olney's entry was therefore cancelled, and it was agreed that Ponsonby should enjoy the copy. Olney's copy is usually preferred by editors, but Ponsonby's is the authorised edition; *The Defence of Poesy* would therefore appear to be the true title; m.e. by J. C. Collins, 1907, facsimile by Noel Douglas, 1927.

THE BENEFITS OF FAST DAYS. *A.R.*, ii. 296. *S.T.C.*, 9977. A reprint of a proclamation that had been issued in 1593.

15th April. DR. FLETCHER'S DISGRACE. *Salisbury Papers*, v. 171.

16th April. 'THE OLD WIVES' TALE.' *A.R.*, ii. 296; *S.T.C.*, 19545; m.e. by W. W. Greg, *M.S.R.*, 1908, etc.

17th April. SPANISH PREPARATIONS IN BRITTANY. *Salisbury Papers*, v. 171.

23rd April. THE FEAST OF ST. GEORGE. From a long and detailed account, given in the envoy's journal, printed in *Queen Elizabeth and some foreigners*, by V. von Klarwill, 1928, p. 375.

26th April. THE DUKE OF WIRTENBERG'S ENVOY. As for 23rd April; p. 385.

30th April. TROOPS IN THE LOW COUNTRIES. *S.P. Dom.*, 251 : 126.

6th May. LODGE'S 'FIG FOR MOMUS.' *A.R.*, ii. 297; *S.T.C.*, 16658; m.e. in *The Complete Works of Thomas Lodge*, vol. iii., Hunterian Club, 1883. Entered 2nd April; dated 6th May in the Epistle to the Gentlemen Readers. This collection is of some general interest. In the first Satire Lodge anticipates the manner of Hall and Marston, and can claim priority over both (see pp. 179, 266, and notes). The attack on alchemy is significant, but it concludes with a very obscure passage which is apparently an attempt to express that alchemy which occurs in the artist's mind as he turns to shapes the forms of things unknown.

8th May. A CATALOGUE OF ENGLISH PRINTED BOOKS. *A.R.*, ii. 297; *S.T.C.*, 17669.

9th May. THE EARL OF CUMBERLAND'S COMMISSION. Rymer's *Fœdera*, xvi. 274.

15th May. BANKS' HORSE. This date of the first appearance of Banks and Morocco is a guess, but the horse was certainly known before the end of the year (p. 66). There are several references to the performance, *e.g.*, *Love's Labours Lost*, I. ii. 58; Bastard's *Chrestoleros*, bk. 3, epig. 17; *Every Man in his Humour*, IV. iv. The completest Collection is by S. H. Atkins in *Notes and Queries*, 21st July, 1934.

22nd May. 'CERTAIN VERY PROPER SIMILES.' *A.R.*, ii. 296; *S.T.C.*, 11053; entered 12th April, dated 22nd May in Epistle Dedicatory to the Earl of Shrewsbury. See note on Bacon's *Essays*, 30th January, 1597.

23rd May. NEW PLAYS. *Hens. Diary*, i. 22; ii. 175. Dr. Greg identifies the first and second parts of this play as Heywood's *Silver* and *Bronze Age*.

25th May. THE NEGOTIATIONS WITH THE STATES. *Salisbury Papers*, v. 179; Camden's *Elizabeth*; Birch's *Memoirs*, i. 244.

27th May. DR. DEE PROMOTED. *S.P. Dom.*, 252 : 35. This is Dee the celebrated alchemist; see also p. 174.

'THE WORLD'S HYDROGRAPHICAL DESCRIPTION.' *A.R.*, ii. 299; *S.T.C.*, 6372. On the title-page is the uncommon inscription 'Published by I. Dauis of Sandrug by Dartmouth in the *Countie of Deuon. Gentleman.* Anno 1595. May 27.' The Epistle Dedicatory to the Lords of the Council bears the same date. It was entered on 1st June, 1595.

28th May. THE IRISH REBELLION. *S.P. Ireland*, 279 : 82; from a letter of the Lord Deputy to the Council.

THE CRUELTY OF THE TURKISH EMPEROR. *Salisbury Papers*, v. 189. This is the Emperor Amurath. Compare 'Not Amurath an Amurath succeeds, But Harry Harry.' *II. Henry IV.*, V. ii. 48-9.

30th May. MR. ROBERT DUDLEY'S RETURN. Hakluyt's *Voyages*, vi. 164.

3rd June. A NEW PLAY. *Hens. Diary*, i. 24; ii. 175. The play is lost.

5th June. A RIOT IN LONDON. *Salisbury Papers*, v. 249.

9th June. NEWS FROM LISBON. *S.P. Dom.*, 252 : 58. Captain Richard Hawkins was son of Sir John Hawkins.

10th June. A SKIRMISH WITH TYRONE. *Carew MSS.*, 154; *S.P. Ireland*, 179 : 95, 180 : 5, 6.

13th June. DISORDERS IN THE CITY. Stow's *Annals*. The exact date is given in *Salisbury Papers*, v. 249.

15th June. FURTHER RIOTING IN THE CITY. *Salisbury Papers*, v. 249.

16th June. THE RIOTOUS APPRENTICES. *Salisbury Papers*, v. 249, 250.

17th June. SLIGO TAKEN BY THE REBELS. *S.P. Ireland*, 180 : 16. Dated 7th June.

20th June. 'THE TRUMPET OF FAME.' *S.T.C.* 21088, where the poem is attributed to Henry Roberts ; m.e. by T. Park, 1818. Approximate date.

23rd June. DISORDERS IN SOUTHWARK. *Remembrancia*, ii. 97.

27th June. RIOTOUS PRENTICES WHIPPED. Stow's *Annals* ; see 13th June.

29th June. UNRULY YOUTHS ON TOWER HILL. Stow's *Annals.*

SIR JOHN HAWKINS' AGREEMENT WITH THE QUEEN. *S.P. Dom.*, 252 : 107.

A SEDITIOUS PAMPHLET. *Remembrancia*, ii. 98. This entry has a two-fold interest ; the incident in Deloney's career is apparently unrecorded ; it is moreover almost the earliest instance on record of a printer's proof.

2nd July. A CASE IN THE STAR CHAMBER. Hawarde, p. 13.

4th July. A PROCLAMATION AGAINST UNLAWFUL ASSEMBLIES. *Proclamations*, 330.

ORDERS PRESCRIBED BY THE COUNCIL. *Proclamations*, 331.

THE CASE OF MR. EDWARD TALBOT CONCLUDED. Hawarde, p. 16. Hawarde notes that Essex and the Archbishop were afterwards checked by the Queen. Wood after long imprisonment confessed that he was 'the only deviser, procurer, acter & plotter in all this action, for the which he loste both his eares in the pillorye, was slitte in the nose, sealled in the foreheade, and censured to perpetual imprisonment.' Hawarde's own spelling of 'process' is 'proces.' See p. 64.

16th July. THE EXPEDITION FROM PLYMOUTH. *S.P. Dom.*, 253 : 19.

17th July. THREE NOTABLE OUTRAGES. *A.R.*, iii. 45 ; *S.T.C.*, 18289.

18th July. THE PROVOST-MARSHAL APPOINTED. Rymer's *Fœdera*, xvi. 279.

23rd July. AN ENGLISHMAN BURNT IN ROME. *Fugger News Letters*, edited by V. von Klarwill ; translated by L. S. R. Byrne, 1926; pp. 527, 529, dated 17th, 24th June.

24th July. THE UNRULY YOUTHS CONDEMNED. Stow's *Annals.*

25th July. EXCESSIVE PRICES. Stow's *Annals.*

26th July. THE SPANIARDS LAND IN CORNWALL. *Salisbury Papers*, v. 290 ; Birch's *Memoirs*, i. 269 ; *S.P. Dom.*, 253 : 30.

27th July. THE IRISH REBELLION. *Carew MSS.*, 158 ; a long detailed account.

28th July. THE SPANISH LANDING. *S.P. Dom.*, 253 : 33.

7th August. A NEW SPANISH ARMADA. *Salisbury Papers*, v. 306.

11th August. THE SPANISH SHIPS. *Salisbury Papers*, v. 310.

13th August. IRISH NEWS. *S.P. Ireland*, 182 : 2, 5, 7 ; dated 1st-3rd August.

17th August. THE DEATH OF DON ANTONIO. *Calendar of State Papers Venetian*, ix. 365, 373.

22nd August. RUMOURS. *Sidney Papers*, i. 343.

23rd August. THE LANDING IN CORNWALL. *Salisbury Papers*, v. 322.

26th August. 'ORPHEUS HIS JOURNEY TO HELL.' *A.R.*, iii. 48 ; *S.T.C.*, 1060. Only one imperfect copy, in the British Museum, remains.

A BOOK OF MERRY TALES. *A.R.*, iii. 47 ; *S.T.C.*, 5738. Unlike most contemporary jest books this provides anecdotes which are quite witty, and some of them innocent enough for *Punch*.

MR. BARNES' 'DIVINE CENTURY.' *A.R.*, iii. 47 ; *S.T.C.*, 1467 ; m.e. by A. B. Grosart, 1875, and in Arber's *English Garner*. Barnes, though his work is not well known, is one of the best of the sonneteers, and some of the sonnets in this collection are noticeably full of feeling.

TWO TALES OF MR. BARNES. Nashe's *Have with you to Saffron Walden* (ed. by R. B. McKerrow, iii. 104, 109) ; see p. 146. Nashe, especially when malicious, is quite unreliable, but Barnes was certainly a notable character. See pp. 271, 279, 290.

29th August. A NEW PLAY. *Hens. Diary*, i. 24 ; ii. 176. This play, unless a revised version of Peele's *Edward the First* printed in 1593, is lost.

31st August. DRAKE AND HAWKINS SAIL. Hakluyt's *Voyages*, viii. 183.

5th September. THE EARL OF ESSEX'S ADVICE ON TRAVEL. Spedding's *Bacon*, ii. 1-20. Approximate date. Spedding points out that Bacon had a considerable share in the compilation of these letters, which were intended rather to display the wisdom of Essex than to benefit Rutland. They were well circulated ; there are three copies in the Harleian Collection alone. The letters are dated January 1596, but they were presumably earlier, as Rutland set out at the end of September 1595 (*Sidney Papers*, i. 353), and was at the Hague on 5th November (Murdin, p. 697).

13th September. A PETITION AGAINST PLAYS. *Remembrancia*, ii. 103 ; reprinted in *Elizabethan Stage*, iv. 318.

14th September. ABUSES IN THE CITY. *Salisbury Papers*, v. 376.

CAPTAIN AMYAS PRESTON'S VOYAGE. Hakluyt's *Voyages*, vii. 172.

15th September. A GREAT FIRE AT WOBURN. T. Wilcocks, *A short narration of the fearful fire that fell in the town of Woburn*, etc., 1595. *S.T.C.*, 25629 ; entered 28th November. *A.R.*, iii. 54.

19th September. NEWS FROM IRELAND. *Sidney Papers*, i. 347.

BEGGING IN THE CITY. *Remembrancia*, ii. 102.

20th September. FRENCH NEWS. Birch's *Memoirs*, i. 296, 298, 300.

BRETON'S 'SOLEMN PASSION.' *S.T.C.*, 3696 ; m.e. in A. B. Grosart's edition of *The Complete Works of Nicholas Breton*, vol. i., 1879. Breton, though seldom great, is always interesting, and his religious poetry is sometimes inspired by an ecstasy which is rare at this time. To Breton the love of God is symbolised rather by a kiss than a rod.

MARKHAM'S 'MOST HONOURABLE TRAGEDY OF SIR RICHARD GRENVILLE.' *S.T.C.*, 17385 ; m.e. by E. Arber, 1869. For the last fight of the *Revenge* see *Eliz. Journal*, pp. 62-7.

22nd September. LYLY'S 'WOMAN IN THE MOON.' *S.T.C.*, 17090 ; m.e. by R. W. Bond in *The Complete Works of John Lyly*, vol. iii., 1902.

23rd September. THE EARL OF SOUTHAMPTON. *Sidney Papers*, i. 348.

27th September. THE FIGHT IN IRELAND. *Sidney Papers*, i. 351.

SIR WALTER RALEGH'S RETURN. Hakluyt's *Voyages*, vii. 183. The date of Ralegh's return is fixed by a letter of Rowland Whyte to Sir Robert Sidney in *Penshurst Papers*, ii. 160.

30th September. NEW PLAYS. *Hens. Diary*, i. 24, 25; ii. 176. Neither play is known.

2nd October. THE HIGH PRICE OF CORN. *A.P.C.*, xxv. 7. The original volume of *A.P.C.* covering the period 26th August, 1593, to October, 1595, is missing, but the record is complete for the rest of the period covered by the *Second Elizabethan Journal*.

6th October. THE SOLDIERS FURNISHED BY THE CLERGY. *A.P.C.*, xxv. 15.

TROUBLE OVER THE STARCH MONOPOLY. *A.P.C.*, xxv. 16.

9th October. M. LOMENIE'S STOUT SPEECHES. *Sidney Papers*, i. 354; Camden's *Elizabeth*.

14th October. WHEAT SPENT WEEKLY. *Remembrancia*, ii. 109.

15th October. MR. HUGH PLATT'S INVENTIONS. *S.T.C.*, 19988; approximate date; reprinted in the *Harleian Miscellany*. For Platt's book of inventions see *Eliz. Journal*, p. 311. This is a very early example of the publicity pamphlet, or puff plausible.

SIR WALTER RALEGH. *Penshurst Papers*, ii. 173.

27th October. HIGH PRICES. *A.P.C.*, xxv. 25, 31.

29th October. AN ATTACK ON IRELAND FEARED. *A.P.C.*, xxv. 37, 47.

30th October. NEW PLAYS AT THE ROSE. *Hens. Diary*, i. 25; ii. 177.

1st November. THE ACCOUNT OF SIR WALTER RALEGH'S VOYAGE. *S.T.C.*, 20634-6, reprinted in Hakluyt's *Voyages*, vii. 272. Ralegh's admiration of the scenery is noteworthy, as genuine appreciation of natural beauties is not very commonly expressed in Elizabethan literature.

5th November. COURT NEWS. *Sidney Papers*, i. 357. The book is summarised, I fear prematurely, in *Eliz. Journal*, p. 340. Essex's sicknesses were not entirely politic. He was apparently 'a bundle of nerves,' and when thwarted or rebuked he would quickly worry himself into a state of acute melancholy or actual illness; his nervous energy was another symptom of this lack of balance.

6th November. MR. BACON DISAPPOINTED OF THE SOLICITORSHIP. Spedding's *Bacon*, i. 370-3. The details are taken from Bacon's *Apology*, which is naturally biassed; but it is apparent from a letter to Essex (*ibid.* i. 373) that he was careful not to commit himself. The obligation was not all on Bacon's side in the relationship between Bacon and Essex; and the notion of Bacon as the subtle viper who bit the hand that fed it, though picturesque, is somewhat fantastic. See also pp. 60 and 139 and notes.

MR. DARCY'S PATENT. *Remembrancia*, ii. 119.

9th November. A TRUCE WITH TYRONE. *Carew MSS.*, 172, 173, 174.

12th November. THE EARL OF HERTFORD COMMITTED. *Sidney Papers*, i. 356, 358, 360. Collins' *Peerage*, ed. E. Brydges, 1812, vol. i. 172.

EXTRAORDINARY MEASURES AGAINST INVASION. *A.P.C.*, xxv. 64. The orders to the counties are detailed and elaborate. Numbers are laid down (*a*) that each county should provide for its own safety, (*b*) that it should despatch to aid its neighbour. The total of 61,800 is reached by adding up the maxima of the county quotas, which are taken from Cornwall, Devon, Dorset, Wiltshire, Southampton, Berkshire, Sussex, Surrey, Kent, London, Essex, Hertford, Suffolk, Cambridge, Huntingdon, Lincoln and Norfolk.

AN IMPUDENT COOK. *Remembrancia*, ii. 122.

17th November. THE QUEEN'S ACCESSION DAY. Stow's *Annals*; *Sidney Papers*, i. 362. Spedding (*Bacon*, i. 377-92) showed that Bacon was responsible for the devices for which Essex received credit. The speeches in full are printed by Spedding and in Nicoll's *Progresses of Queen Elizabeth*. The festivals this year were particularly brilliant; they evoked three ballads.

20th November. SOUTHWELL'S 'TRIUMPHS OVER DEATH.' *A.R.*, iii. 53; *S.T.C.*, 22971; m.e. in E. Brydge's *Archaica*, 1815, vol. i. It is a sign of the great respect felt for Southwell that, so soon after his death, the printer should acknowledge the author's name and justify the publication in a poem 'To the Reader.' Compare *Hamlet*, III. i. 80.

22nd November. COURT NEWS. *Penshurst Papers*, ii. 189.

23rd November. IRISH NEWS. *Sidney Papers*, i. 362, 363.

26th November. AN INQUISITION CONCERNING RECUSANTS. *A.P.C.*, xxv. 85.

30th November. NEW PLAYS. *Hens. Diary*, i. 27; ii. 177. *Harry the Fifth* is presumably *The Famous Victories of Henry V*.

1st December. FRENCH OPINIONS. Birch's *Memoirs*, i. 328; from a letter of Edmondes to Essex dated 24th November.

5th December. THE LIEUTENANT OF THE TOWER COMMITTED. *Sidney Papers*, i. 372. For other papers in the case see Strype's *Annals*, iv. 238.

6th December. WOOD IN THE PILLORY. *Penshurst Papers*, ii. 195. See pp. 32, 34.

7th December. THE QUEEN'S LETTER TO THE KING. Birch's *Historical View*, p. 28. Camden's *Elizabeth*.

12th December. THE QUEEN DINES WITH THE LORD KEEPER. *Sidney Papers*, i. 376.

13th December. THE NAVY TO BE SET OUT. *A.P.C.*, xxv. 98.

THE DEATH OF SIR ROGER WILLIAMS. *Sidney Papers*, i. 377. This genuinely religious strain in Essex is notable; it explains the respect which the Puritans felt for him. The later exploits in Sir Roger Williams' career will be found in many places in *Eliz. Journal* (*e.g.*, p. 33).

14th December. MR. DARCY'S GRANT. *A.P.C.*, xxv. 106. For previous trouble over Mr. Darcy's patent, see *Eliz. Journal*, p. 215; also pp. 7, 58, 65 herein.

17th December. 'MAROCCUS EXTATICUS.' *A.R.*, iii. 55; *S.T.C.*, 6225.

19th December. THE LORD PRESIDENT OF THE NORTH DEAD. *Sidney Papers*, i. 380, 382.

21st December. PRIVATE SHIPS FOR THE NAVY. *A.P.C.*, xxv. 122.

SIR HENRY UNTON SENT TO THE FRENCH KING. *Sidney Papers*, i. 378, 396. With Unton Essex sent a secret memorandum on the way in which he should be received in France in order that the Queen might be forced to send reinforcements (Birch's *Memoirs*, i. 353-4). Essex was not over-scrupulous in furthering his own schemes.

The Invasion in Cornwall. *A.P.C.*, xxv. 129.

25th December. News of Sir Francis Drake. *S.P. Dom.*, 255 : 17. Letter from the Mayor of Plymouth to Lord Burleigh dated 23rd. For Drake's last voyage, see p. 94.

28th December. Smuggling of Corn. *A.P.C.*, xxv. 137.

OTHER BOOKS ALSO SET FORTH ANNO 1595.

Under this heading are grouped some of the more interesting books that appeared during the year which cannot be more accurately dated.

Churchyard's 'Charity' and 'A Praise of Poetry.' *S.T.C.*, 5245 ; m.e. in A. Boswell's *Frondes Caducae*, 1817. Churchyard was now aged about 75 ; he continued to write until his death in 1604. He comments in the margin of the stanza quoted : 'Want of charitie hath made me loose my pattent. My pattent shows that.'

Hunnis' 'Recreations.' *S.T.C.*, 13973 ; entered 4th December, 1587 ; *A.R.*, ii. 481.

'Polimanteia.' *S.T.C.*, 5883. It was written by W. Covell, and perhaps dates from the first quarter of 1596 ; m.e. in A. B. Grosart's *Elizabethan England in Gentle and Simple Life*, 1881. The book is apparently inspired by the genuine anxiety felt because on 5th September, 1595, the Queen had entered on her Grand Climacteric (*i.e.*, the ninth of the fatal astrological periods of seven years). It is an important revelation of the anxious thoughts of intelligent minds in this year of alarm. See also pp. 71, 85, 86.

'Plutarch's Lives.' *S.T.C.*, 20067 ; m.e. in *The Temple Classics* edited by H. D. Rouse.

1596

3rd January. THE LADY HUNTINGDON. *Sidney Papers*, i. 386.

8th January. 'THE BLACK DOG OF NEWGATE.' *S.T.C.*, 14029; for Hutton see p. 323; m.e. by A. V. Judges in *The Elizabethan Underworld*, 1930, p. 266.

18th January. VICTUALS FOR THE NAVY. *A.P.C.*, xxv. 108, 138, 161, 164, etc.

19th January. 'A WATCHWORD FOR WAR.' *A.R.*, iii. 57; *S.T.C.*, 11492. A valuable comment on the general alarm at the beginning of the year. Thomas Nun, in *A Comfort against the Spaniard*, 1596, begins his preface, 'Is it true that the Spaniards will come this spring? And is it not true that we are ready to receive them? Hath this land at any time had either better provision or more soldiers? Braver captains to lead them, or sounder divines to encourage them?' See also *Polimanteia* (p. 69 and note); and compare the closing words of Shakespeare's *King John*, written, I believe, a few months later.

20th January. 'THE SECOND PART OF THE FAERY QUEEN.' *S.T.C.*, 23082; m.e. by J. C. Smith and E. de Selincourt, 1912, etc. *A.R.*, iii. 57.

23rd January. COPLEY'S 'FIG FOR FORTUNE.' *A.R.*, iii. 57; *S.T.C.*, 5737; m.e. for the Spenser Society, 1883.

24th January. SIR HENRY UNTON AND THE FRENCH KING. Murdin's *State Papers*, p. 701. Murdin prints in full Unton's own interesting accounts of this and the subsequent negotiations.

MR. DARCY'S PATENT IS ANNULLED. *Remembrancia*, ii. 142.

25th January. CONDEMNED PRISONERS TO BE PARDONED. *A.P.C.*, xxv. 182.

26th January. NEWS FROM FRANCE. Murdin's *State Papers*, pp. 706, 707, 710.

30th January. A SECOND VOYAGE TO GUIANA. Hakluyt's *Voyages*, vii. 362. See p. 111.

31st January. NEW PLAYS BY THE LORD ADMIRAL'S MEN. *Hens. Diary*, i. 27, 28; ii. 178.

THE MILD WEATHER. T. Bastard, *Chrestoleros*, bk. ii., epig. 6.

1st February. FLESH PROHIBITED DURING LENT. *Proclamations*, 332.

2nd February. PROCEEDINGS WITH TYRONE. *Carew MSS.*, 184, 204.

3rd February. CONTRIBUTIONS TO THE FLEET. *A.P.C.*, xxv. 198. The collection of ship money caused the Council to dictate many letters at this time.

4th February. FRENCH NEWS. Murdin's *State Papers*, pp. 712, 715.

5th February. NEWS OF DRAKE. *S.P. Dom.*, 256 : 37.

7th February. MR. THOMAS ARUNDEL'S RETURN. *Salisbury Papers*, vi. 43, 49. See pp. 82, 90, 186, 189. Acceptance of honours from foreign

Princes was regarded by the Queen as an act of disloyalty. A few months before Sir Anthony Shirley and Sir Nicholas Clifford were punished for a similar offence; see *Eliz. Journal*, pp. 298, 300.

11th February. FORGERS SENTENCED. Hawarde, p. 37.

12th February. 'THE BLIND BEGGAR OF ALEXANDRIA.' *Hens. Diary*, i. 28; ii. 179; *S.T.C.*, 4965; entered 15th August, 1598; m.e. by W. W. Greg, *M.S.R.*, 1928, and in *The Comedies of George Chapman*, ed. by T. M. Parrott, 1913. Count Hermes is the first of the important 'humorous' characters and a good deal of play is made with his black patch and pistol. *The Blind Beggar* was the most fantastic of all the Rose plays, the chief part presumably being written for Alleyn, who had a fine opportunity of showing the range of his skill as a quick-change artist in a succession of very different parts.

13th February. FRENCH NEWS. Murdin's *State Papers*, p. 723.

COLSE'S 'PENELOPE'S COMPLAINT.' *A.R.*, iii. 59; *S.T.C.*, 5582; m.e. by A. B. Grosart, 1880. For *Willobie His Avisa* and its connection with *Penelope's Complaint* see *Eliz. Journal*, p. 319, and my edition in the *Bodley Head Quartos*, vol. xv., pp. 184, 234-5.

14th February. THE FRENCH KING AND HER MAJESTY'S PICTURE. Murdin's *State Papers*, p. 717. From a letter of Unton to the Queen dated 3rd February. Unton tactfully makes unfavourable comment on the King's mistress as 'attyred in a playne Sattayne Gowne, with a Velvet Hood all over her Head (to keape away the Weather from her) which became her verie ill; and, in my Opinion, she is altered verie much for the worse in her Complection and Favor, yeat verie grosselye painted.'

23rd February. THE SUBURBS. *A.P.C.*, xxv. 230. This problem was perennial; see for instance *Eliz. Journal*, p. 334.

25th February. THE CONDEMNED PRISONERS. *A.P.C.*, xxv. 233; see p. 73.

28th *February*. MASTERLESS MEN TO BE TAKEN UP. *A.P.C.*, xxv., 250.

RELUCTANT SEAMEN. *A.P.C.*, xxv. 253.

1st March. A HORRIBLE MURDER. *S.T.C.*, 17748.

4th March. SOLDIERS FOR IRELAND. *A.P.C.*, xxv. 262, 264, 281.

8th March. THE SOLDIERS' COATS. *A.P.C.*, xxv. 278.

11th March. TYRONE'S GRIEVANCES. *Carew MSS.*, 233, 234.

ABUSES IN PLAY. *A.P.C.*, xxv. 289.

13th March. THE QUEEN AND LORD BURLEIGH. Birch's *Memoirs*, i. 448.

THE LATE EARL OF HUNTINGDON *Salisbury Papers*, vi. 93. From letters from the Council of the North and the Archbishop of York dated 10th March, The Earl had now been dead three months; See pp. 66 and 70.

17th March. A SPANISH RAID NEAR PLYMOUTH. *S.P. Dom.*, 256 : 89.

20th March. MR. THOMAS ARUNDEL. *Salisbury Papers*, vi. 105.

21st March. Evasion of Common Charges. *A.P.C.*, xxv. 293, 296-301.

25th March. Sir Henry Unton sick. Murdin's *State Papers*, p. 730.

27th March. The Death of Sir John Hawkins reported. *S.P. Dom.*, 256 : 111 ; see p. 94 for the account of the voyage.

28th March. Counterfeiting of Passports. *A.P.C.*, xxv. 320.

A Scarcity of Game. *A.P.C.*, xxv. 322.

29th March. Calvin's 'Aphorisms.' *A.R.*, iii. 62 ; *S.T.C.*, 4374 ; entered 29th March, Epistle Dedicatory dated 18th May.

30th March. A Book of Surgery. *A.R.*, iii. 62 ; *S.T.C.*, 5442 ; an interesting work. In Chapter 27 is given the contents of the chest which the young surgeon should take with him to the wars by land or sea. The surgeon's tools are also illustrated.

2nd April. Calais assaulted. Stow's *Annals*.

4th April. The Attack on Calais. Devereux, i. 355. *S.P. Dom.*, 257 : 4. In the preparations made at Dover, Essex showed the utmost energy, never sparing himself, and writing sometimes three letters a day to the Court to expedite succours from London.

5th April. Calais. *S.P. Dom.*, 257 : 10.

Sir Henry Unton dead. *Salisbury Papers*, vi. 122.

Mr. Norden's 'Christian Comfort.' *A.R.*, iii. 62 ; *S.T.C.*, 18604. Another example of the general alarm in this year ; compare *King John*, IV. ii. 141 and 185.

6th April. Calais. *S.P. Dom.*, 257 : 12.

7th April. A Mutiny at Chester. *A.P.C.*, xxv. 331.

9th April. The Bishop of St. David's unhappy Sermon. *Nugae Antiquae*, ii. 215 ; *Salisbury Papers*, vi. 139. According to Fuller (*Church History*, book x.) the Bishop had previously made so favourable an impression on the Queen by honest plain speaking in his sermons that she promised him the reversion of the Archbishopric of Canterbury ; hereafter the offer was withdrawn. See Corrigenda, p. vi.

Sudden Levies called for. *A.P.C.*, xxv. 338 ; Stow's *Annals*.

10th April. The Levies dismissed. *A.P.C.*, xxv. 338.

The Queen and the Bishop of St. David's. *Nugae Antiquae*, ii. 218.

11th April. The Levies again required. *A.P.C.*, xxv. 340 ; Stow's *Annals*.

The Service of Posts. *Proclamations*, 333.

13th April. The Earl of Essex's Commission for Calais. *S.P. Dom.*, 257 : 22, 24.

14th April. The Queen's Letter to the Earl of Essex. *S.P. Dom.*, 257 : 32.

Calais. *S.P. Dom.*, 257 : 27.

15th April. Mr. Arundel released. *Salisbury Papers*, vi. 145.

A Murder at Oxford. *A.P.C.*, xxv. 350.

16th April. Calais taken. *S.P. Dom.*, 257 : 30, 35.

17th April. The Troops for Calais dismissed. *A.P.C.*, xxv. 353.

18th April. The French Treachery. Stow's *Annals*.

20th April. Another Order concerning Post-horses. *Proclamations*, 333.

22nd April. A Declaration of the Causes of the Present Navy. *S.T.C.*, 9203. According to Stow the *Declaration* was printed at this time.

24th April. Instructions for the Fleet. *S.P. Dom.*, 257 : 45.

25th April. Sir Anthony Shirley's Voyage. Hakluyt's *Voyages*, vii. 213 ; see also pp. 100, 102, 194.

26th April. The Return of Drake's Fleet. *A.P.C.*, xxv. 365, 367.

27th April. The Death of Drake and Hawkins. *S.P. Dom.*, 257 : 48, 50.

29th April. One condemned for spreading False Rumours. Hawarde, p. 39.

A New Play. *Hens. Diary*, i. 30 ; ii. 180. Nothing is known of the play.

1st May. Recusants in Sussex. Strype, *Annals*, iv. 289 ; approximate date.

Drake's Fleet return. Hakluyt's *Voyages*, vii. 183. The expedition had sailed on 31st August, 1595.

2nd May. Sir Anthony Shirley's Voyage. Hakluyt's *Voyages*, vii. 213.

3rd May. A Proclamation against Counterfeit Messengers. *Proclamations*, 334.

11th May. Sir Thomas Egerton made Lord Keeper. Stow's *Annals*.

16th May. The Dispute between Yarmouth and Lowestoft. *A.P.C.*, xxv. 401.

18th May. A Mischance at London Bridge. Birch's *Memoirs*, ii. 6.

19th May. A New Play. *Hens. Diary*, i. 30 ; ii. 180. Nothing is known of the play.

23rd May. Sir Anthony Shirley's Voyage. Hakluyt's *Voyages*, vii. 213. See p. 194.

31st May. Certain Mayors commended. *A.P.C.*, xxv. 421-4.

1st June. The Army at Plymouth. Birch's *Memoirs*, ii. 14, 15, 17 ; *The Commentaries of Sir Francis Vere* (m.e. in *Stuart Tracts*, 1603-1693, ed. Sir Charles Firth, 1903). Vere's minute of the duties of the several officers in an army survives in the *Harleian MSS.* (168, f. 119).

3rd June. The Fleet sails. Stow's *Annals*.

The State of the Middle Marches. *A.P.C.*, xxv. 430.

5th June. THE FLEET. Stow's *Annals*.

6th June. SUPERFLUOUS ALEHOUSES. *A.P.C.*, xxv. 438.

DEFENCE OF THE REALM. *A.P.C.*, xxv. 439, 442.

7th June. A SCOTTISH LORD'S INVENTIONS. Birch's *Memoirs*, ii. 28. This paper (dated 7th June) occurring among the *Bacon Papers* was presumably sent to the Earl of Essex. Lord Napier was thus one of the early projectors both of the submarine and the tank. Poison gas was among the inventions of the ingenious Mr. Platt; in Thomas Arundel's chamber was found a note of various military devices, including the words, 'Learn of Mr. Platt his way to poison air and so to infect a whole camp' (*Salisbury Papers*, vii. 167). Lord Napier was also the inventor of logarithms; see *D.N.B.*

11th June. SIR JOHN SMYTHE'S MISDEMEANOUR. *S.P. Dom.*, 259 : 16, 21.

13th June. SIR JOHN SMYTHE. *A.P.C.*, xxv. 450.

15th June. THE DEATH OF DR. FLETCHER. *Nugae Antiquae*, ii. 45; Fuller's *Worthies of Kent*; Camden's *Elizabeth*. The two councillors were presumably Sir Robert Cecil and the Earl of Essex. The Bishop left several children, of whom the eldest was John Fletcher, afterwards the dramatist, at this time aged 17. A slightly different version of the epitaph is preserved in the *Farmer Chetham MS.* (Chetham Society, 1873, part ii., p. 183).

SIR JOHN SMYTHE BEFORE THE COUNCIL. *A.P.C.*, xxv. 459. See also pp. 107, 108, 109, 248. The lawyer's name appears variously 'Ridgeley,' 'Ridley' and 'Ruggeley.'

16th June. THE TREATMENT OF SPANISH PRISONERS. *A.P.C.*, xxv. 468.

20th June. AN ALIEN BANISHED. *A.P.C.*, xxv. 479. Another instance of seditious books brought from overseas is reported in *A.P.C.*, xxvi. 10.

22nd June. A NEW PLAY. *Hens. Diary*, i. 42; ii. 180. Nothing is known of the play.

27th June. THE CASE OF SIR JOHN SMYTHE. *A.P.C.*, xxv. 501, 506. In the letter to the Attorney-General, Burleigh added this postscript: 'I praie you to forbeare to examine him of anie part of his false reportes of me.'

4th July. SERVICE WITHOUT THE REALM. *A.P.C.*, xxvi. 3.

5th July. SIR ROBERT CECIL MADE SECRETARY. *A.P.C.*, xxvi. 7; Camden's *Elizabeth*.

11th July. BLACKAMOORS IN LONDON. *A.P.C.*, xxvi. 16.

15th July. THE EARL OF NORTHUMBERLAND NAMED AS AMBASSADOR. *Salisbury Papers*, vi. 260.

17th July. IRISH NEWS. *S.P. Ireland*, 191 : 6 (xix.), 9, 10.

18th July. NEW PLAYS. *Hens. Diary*, i. 42; ii. 180-1. Neither play is known.

ROGUES IN MIDDLESEX. *A.P.C.*, xxvi. 23.

BLACKAMOORS IN ENGLAND. *A.P.C.*, xxvi., 20.

19th July. Great Good News from Spain. *S.P. Dom.*, 259 : 71.

22nd July. Playing inhibited. *A.P.C.*, xxvi. 38.

25th July. The Second Voyage to Guiana. Hakluyt's *Voyages*, vii. 358. The pamphlet was entered 11th October. This date of Keymis's return is approximate.

26th July. The Dunkirk Pirates. *A.P.C.*, xxvi. 61.

A Presumptuous Ballad. From a letter of Sir Stephen Slany, Lord Mayor, to Burleigh, printed in Thomas Wright's *Queen Elizabeth and her Times*, 1838, ii. 462. The ballad has not survived. See also p. 32.

27th July. The Possession of Thomas Darling. *The most wonderful and true storie of a certain witch named Alse Gooderidge of Stapenhill*, 1597; entered 6th June, 1597. The pamphlet gives a long and detailed account of the boy's sufferings, compiled from the notes of Jesse Bee. Both in this narrative, and that of the Warboys case (see *Eliz. Journal*, p. 224 and note), the significant details are most carefully recorded : the Elizabethan eye-witness receives too little credit for the skill and accuracy of his reports of observed phenomena. Samuel Harsnett notes (in *A Discovery of the Fraudelent practises of John Darrel*, 1599, p. 2) that the book ' being penned by one *Iesse Bee* a Sadler in *Burton*, the same was first contracted by one *M. Denison* a minister in that countrey : and then after it had beene seene and allowed by *M. Darrell*, & *M. Hildersham*, it was published in print : and was commonly sold and called for, by this title, vz. *The booke of the dispossessing of the boy of Burton*.' The date of the Derby Assizes is fixed by a letter of Sir Edmund Anderson written from Derby on 25th July (*Rutland MSS. Hist. MSS. Com.*, xii., Ap. iv., p. 332). Sir Humphrey Ferrers was a man of some importance in the neighbourhood. Darling subsequently admitted that the whole affair was a fraud. For further adventures of Mr. Darell, see pp. 176, 241, 267, 292. Falstaffe, hastily disguised as the old woman of Brainford, also wore a broad thrummed hat (*Merry Wives*, iv. ii. 82).

28th July. The Spanish Prisoners. *A.P.C.*, xxvi. 64. See 14th June.

30th July. The Queen's Picture. *A.P.C.*, xxvi. 69.

31st July. A Proclamation for the Dearth of Corn. *Proclamations*, p. 338.

1st August. News from the Fleet. Birch's *Memoirs*, ii. 95.

2nd August. Preparations for the Return of the Fleet. *S.P. Dom.*, 259 : 88.

4th August. ' The Metamorphosis of Ajax.' *S.T.C.*, 12779 ; m.e. by P. Warlock and J. Lindsay, 1927, wherein are printed a number of the epigrams called forth by this famous Rabelaisian tract. I have suggested (in a note on Jaques in the edition of *The Scourge of Villainy*, Bodley Head Quartos, vol. xiii.) that Shakespeare's melancholy philosopher may owe his name to this book ; on which unsavoury subject it may be noted that 'jakes' in the First Quarto of *Lear* is spelt ' jaques.' See also E. I. Fripp's *Shakespeare Studies*, 1930, p. 154.

5th August. Churchyard's Poem on Sir F. Knollys. *S.T.C.*, 5254 ; m.e. by T. Parks in *Heliconia*, vol. ii., 1815. Approximate date.

8th August. A Day of Triumph and The Taking of Cadiz. Stow's *Annals*. There are a number of different accounts of the taking of Cadiz apart from incidental details in various Collections of State Papers ; see, for instance, Sir Francis Vere's *Commentaries*, and especially the *Monson Tracts*, edited by M. Oppenheim for the Navy Records Society, 1902, which should be consulted for the more important naval events of these years.

THE SCARCITY OF CORN. *A.P.C.*, xxvi. 81, 95-8.

LADY UNTON. *S.P. Dom.*, 259 : 93.

9th August. THE CADIZ FORCES. *A.P.C.*, xxvi. 102.

11th August. THE CADIZ VOYAGE. *A.P.C.*, xxvi. 109.

12th August. THE EARL OF ESSEX AT COURT. Birch's *Memoirs*, ii. 103, 95, 96 ; *Calendar of State Papers Venetian*, ix. 505.

14th August. AN ITALIAN GENTLEMAN PRESENTED AT COURT. *Calendar of State Papers Venetian*, ix. 505. Approximate date. From Signor Gradenigo's letter to the Venetian Ambassador in France ; a short but interesting description of England, which impressed the writer as 'so opulent, fat, and abounding with all things that it may with truth be said that poverty hath no place there.'

16th August. THE FALL OF A HOUSE. Stow's *Annals*.

18th August. THE QUEEN'S TOUCH. *Calendar of State Papers Venetian*, ix. 505. From Signor Gradenigo's letter ; approximate date.

19th August. THE CADIZ PLUNDER. *A.P.C.*, xxvi. 120.

THE ADVANTAGES OF THE CADIZ EXPEDITION. *S.P. Dom.*, 260 : 46.

20th August. DISORDER ON THE BORDERS. *Proclamations*, 339.

22nd August. CAPTIVES IN ALGIERS. *A.P.C.*, xxvi. 126 ; for the adventures of Captain Glemham, see *Eliz. Journal*, pp. 18, 118, 132, 311.

23rd August. MR. PLATT'S SUNDRY REMEDIES AGAINST THE FAMINE. *A.R.*, iii. 69 ; *S.T.C.*, 19996. The book gives a number of nauseous substitutes (of the kind familiar during the later months of the Great War) for common food and drink.

29th August. THE TREATY WITH FRANCE SWORN. Camden's *Elizabeth*.

30th August. TWO NEW PRIVY COUNCILLORS. *A.P.C.*, xxvi. 135.

THE QUEEN'S EXPENSES ON BEHALF OF THE FRENCH KING. *S.P. Dom.*, 257 : 76 (dated 6th May) and 259 : 127.

1st September. SPENSER'S 'FOUR HYMNS.' *S.T.C.*, 23086 ; m.e. by W. L. Renwick, 1929, etc. The book was not entered, but is dated in the Epistle Dedicatory 'Greenwich this first of September, 1596.'

5th September. VOLUNTEERS FOR THE LOW COUNTRIES. *A.P.C.*, xvi. 140.

10th September. SOLDIERS FOR IRELAND. *A.P.C.*, xxvi. 161.

12th September. COMPLAINTS AGAINST LORD CHIEF JUSTICE ANDERSON. Strype, *Annals*, iv. 264 ; approximate date. For the portrait of Anderson and further harsh proceedings see *Eliz. Journal*, pp. 144, 220.

13th September. A PETITION AGAINST PLAYS. *Remembrancia*, ii. 103 ; quoted in *Elizabethan Stage*, iv. 318.

16th September. THE DEPARTURE OF THE EARL OF SHREWSBURY. Stow's *Annals*.

19th September. NEWS FROM IRELAND. *Sidney Papers*, i. 347.

22nd September. THE QUEEN DISPLEASED WITH THE LORD TREASURER. Devereux, i. 389; from a somewhat humble letter written by Burleigh to Essex, who answered politely next day. This letter evidently gave great elation to Essex's own circle. Anthony Bacon, writing to Dr. Hawkins, commented that the renewed favour of the Earl 'hath made the old fox to crouch and whine, and to insinuate himself by a very submiss letter to my Lord of Essex, subscribed in these terms, *Your lordship's, if you will, at commandment*'—an indication that neither Essex nor his followers were discreet in dealing with confidential matters. See Birch's *Memoirs*, ii. 153. Compare *I. Henry IV.*, I. iii. 29.

MONSIEUR DE REAULX'S UNFORTUNATE BREATH. *Penshurst Papers*, ii. 217.

23rd September. AN AID TO THE FRENCH KING. *A.P.C.*, xxvi. 192.

25th September. ROGUES IN SOMERSETSHIRE. Strype, *Annals*, iv. 290, 291.

28th September. SIR RICHARD BINGHAM'S FLIGHT. *S.P. Ireland*, 193: 28, 46, 51. Sir Richard's chief offence seems to have been honesty. See 26th August, 1598.

29th September. THE SCHEDULE OF DAILY PAY FOR THE SOLDIERS IN FRANCE. *A.P.C.*, xxvi. 216. These rates of pay were extremely generous compared with the incomes of some professional men; parsons and schoolmasters for instance.

30th September. 'ULYSSES UPON AJAX.' *S.T.C.*, 12782; approximate date. The answer lacks the wit, but none of the scurrility, of the *Metamorphosis*; it entirely misses the serious purpose behind Harington's book. It does, however, illuminate Elizabethan sanitary arrangements.

3rd October. HIGHWAY ROBBERIES. *Middlesex Sessions Rolls*, i. 229. Cases where the accused refused to plead and were sentenced to *peine forte et dure* are not uncommon. Of this penalty William Harrison in his *Description of England* says, 'Such felons as stand mute and speak not at their arraignment, are pressed to death by huge weights laid upon a board, that lieth over their breast, and a sharp stone under their backs; these commonly held their peace, thereby to save their goods unto their wives and children, which, if they were condemned, should be confiscated to the Prince.'

4th October. ADVICE FOR MY LORD ESSEX. Spedding's *Bacon*, ii. 40-45. This entry is based on Bacon's famous letter of advice to Essex. It is not likely that the letter was circulated, but most probable that his faults were discussed by his true friends, who realised as clearly as Bacon what should be done, and avoided. This letter shows Bacon's immense practical wisdom; it explains, and justifies, his desertion of Essex. But Essex would never listen to sober advice; as De Maisse observed, '*Il est tout son conseil luy mesmes.*' Compare *Richard II.*, I. iv. 25, for Bolingbroke's 'popular courses'; also *I. Henry IV.*, III. i. 176.

6th October. RYE FROM THE EAST COUNTRIES. *A.P.C.*, xxvi. 223.

7th October. MY LORD OF LINCOLN'S RETURN. *A.R.*, iii. 73. E. Monings, *The Landgrave of Hessen, his princely receiving of Her Majesty's ambassador*, 1596; *S.T.C.*, 18013; Birch's *Memoirs*, ii. 178. 'Turks' are horses.

9th October. MR. MORLEY'S 'INTRODUCTION TO PRACTICAL MUSIC.' *A.R.*, iii. 72 ; *S.T.C.*, 18133.

10th October. THE FRENCH KING'S ENTRY INTO ROUEN. Stow's *Annals* ; from the account by William Seager, Somerset Herald, who was present.

13th October. SIR THOMAS BASKERVILLE'S INSTRUCTIONS. *A.P.C.*, xxvi. 244.

14th October. A THIRD VOYAGE TO GUIANA. Hakluyt's *Voyages*, viii. 1 ; see also p. 194.

15th October. THE LEAGUE WITH FRANCE. Stow's *Annals*.

17th October. THE FORCES FOR FRANCE STAYED. *A.P.C.*, xxvi. 255.

18th October. THE FORCES TO BE SENT TO FRANCE. *A.P.C.*, xxvi. 257.

20th October. THE CONTRIBUTIONS TOWARDS SHIPPING. *A.P.C.*, xxvi. 260, 265, 266. As is shown by many entries in *A.P.C.*, the Council found great difficulty in persuading neighbouring towns to contribute to the expenses of the port towns in the Cadiz expedition.

23rd October. NASHE'S 'HAVE WITH YOU TO SAFFRON WALDEN.' Approximate date. *S.T.C.*, 18369 ; m.e. in *The Complete Works of Thomas Nashe*, by R. B. McKerrow, vol. iii., 1910 ; for an excellent account of the Harvey-Nashe quarrel see vol. v. p. 65. After a somewhat slow start, Nashe produced one of the best pieces of abuse in the language. The book is full of scurrilous and amusing gossip about Harvey's friends, such as Barnes (for which see p. 43).

28th October. A GREAT ALARM FROM SPAIN. *A.P.C.*, xxvi. 279.

31st October. GREAT PREPARATIONS FOR DEFENCE. *A.P.C.*, xxvi. 262-290.

CORN SHIPS IN LONDON. *A.P.C.*, xxvi. 281.

2nd November. THE EARL OF SHREWSBURY RETURNS. Stow's *Annals*.

A PROCLAMATION CONCERNING THE DEARTH. *Proclamations*, 340.

4th November. VARIOUS OPINIONS CONCERNING THE SPANISH DANGER. *S.P. Dom.*, 260 : 82, 87, 93.

5th November. LODGE'S 'WITS' MISERY.' Dated 5th November in the Epistle. *S.T.C.*, 16677 ; m.e. in *The Complete Works of Thomas Lodge*, Hunterian Club, 1883. Lodge owes the pattern of the work to *Piers Penniless*, as in part he acknowledges. The book is a mixture of rather heavy allegorical satire and odd book learning, with a foretaste both of the 'Humours' and the 'Character.' The devil Adulation is an acknowledged borrowing from 'The Flatterer' of Theophrastus—this being apparently the first instance of an English writer using the 'Characters' of Theophrastus—but instead of isolating his characters in separate essays, he blends them into the general scheme. *Wits' Misery* is best known for the oft-quoted allusion to 'the Visard of ye ghost, which cried so miserably at ye Theater like an oister wife, *Hamlet, revenge*.'

7th November. THE PREPARATIONS FOR DEFENCE. *A.P.C.*, xxvi. 292-302.

8th November. MR. SPENSER'S 'PROTHALAMION.' *S.T.C.*, 23088 ; m.e. by W. L. Renwick, 1929, etc.

9th November. The Death of George Peele. *Elizabethan Stage*, iii. 459.

14th November. A Lamentation for Drake. *S.T.C.*, 10943 ; a most interesting poem. The author's theology is classical throughout and he writes with catching enthusiasm ; to many of the poets (as to Milton later) the gods of Rome were quite as real as the persons of Christian theology.

18th November. A Spanish Stratagem in Scotland. Birch's *Memoirs*, ii. 196.

21st November. Recusants to be committed. *A.P.C.*, xxvi. 322.

Mr. Davies' 'Orchestra.' *A.R.*, iii. 74 ; *S.T.C.*, 6360 ; m.e. in *The Complete Poems of Sir John Davies*, edited by A. B. Grosart, 1876, vol. i. *Orchestra* was entered first on 5th June, 1594, and again on 21st November, 1596 ; the first was probably a 'blocking entry.' Several of the works of gentlemen authors were thus entered some time before an edition appeared ; *e.g.*, Sidney's *Defence of Poesy* (p. 20 and note) and Florio's translation of Montaigne's *Essays*, entered 20th October, 1595, and 4th June, 1600, but not published till 1603 (*A.R.*, iii. 50 and iii. 162).

Drayton's Poems. *A.R.*, iii. 74 ; *S.T.C.*, 7232. This is another specimen of the autobiographical lament, fashionable at this time, being admittedly a rival to *Shore's Wife*, *Rosamond*, *Lucrece* and *Elstred* (see *Eliz. Journal*, pp. 246, 262, 271, 330, 322).

25th November. A Theatre in Blackfriars. *S.P. Dom.*, 260 : 116 ; printed in *Elizabethan Stage*, iv. 319, 320 : approximate date. This enterprise, though unfortunate, was another of James Burbage's strokes of genius. As he had been the first to realise the possibilities of the permanent theatre twenty years before, so now he first saw that the gentleman spectator was taking a serious interest in the drama of the professional companies, and would pay a high price for the privacy and comfort of the indoor theatre : but it was nearly twelve years before his son's company were able to occupy the Blackfriars building ; see also note on Chapman's *Humorous Day's Mirth*, 11th May, 1597.

27th November. Beard's 'Theatre of God's Judgments.' *A.R.*, iii. 75 ; *S.T.C.*, 1659. A magnificent repertory of scandalous tales of the wicked, compiled with the highest of motives. As Beard prints very few contemporary examples, it is clear that Marlowe's death was notorious ; see *Eliz. Journal*, p. 244, and authorities therein quoted.

28th November. The Force sent to the Isle of Wight. *A.P.C.*, xxvi. 336, 337.

1st December. The Earl of Essex defamed. Birch's *Memoirs*, ii 218, 220.

8th December. A dreadful sudden Tempest at Wales. Stow's *Annals*. A similar phenomenon at Manchester was thus reported in the *Times* of 30th July, 1930 : '"I saw a ball of fire coming through the air. It was about the size of a football," said an eye-witness. "There was a terrific roar when the bolt struck the spire of the church. It appeared to rip it all the way down. Slates fell in every direction."'

10th December. The Scottish Princess baptised. Rymer's *Fœdera*, xvi. 304. This is the romantic Princess Elizabeth who married the Elector

Palatine in 1612. I have not discovered whether the post-dated cheque was ever honoured.

14th December. SEDITION IN OXFORDSHIRE. *S.P. Dom.*, 261 : 10.

18th December. COOTE'S 'ENGLISH SCHOOLMASTER.' *A.R.*, iii. 77; *S.T.C.*, 5711. This book reached a 42nd edition in 1684, and a copy printed in 1692 survives.

19th December. A LOYAL RECUSANT. *A.P.C.*, xxvi. 375.

A STRANGE EARTH MOVING. Stow's *Annals*.

23rd December. TYRONE'S TREACHERY. *Carew MSS.*, 257.

25th December. THE DEARTH. *A.P.C.*, xxvi. 380, 383 : see p. 127.

26th December. CORN SHIPS TO BE STOPPED. *A.P.C.*, xxvi. 393-7.

OTHER BOOKS SET FORTH ANNO 1596.

THE BROWNISTS' CONFESSIONS. *S.T.C.*, 237. This pamphlet largely confirms the opinions held by the authorities of the seditious nature of Brownism (see *Eliz. Journal*, p. 208); it appears to have been printed in Amsterdam.

A BOOK CONCERNING THE SPANISH SICKNESS. *S.T.C.*, 16872.

LAMBARD'S 'PERAMBULATION OF KENT.' *S.T.C.*, 15176.

1597

1st January. BAD WEATHER. *Fugger News Letters*, 585.

8th January. THE LATE INTENDED RISING. *S.P. Dom.*, 262 : 4.

11th January. THE VICTUALS OF THE SOLDIERS IN IRELAND. *Carew MSS.*, 259.

17th January. MR. NORDEN'S 'MIRROR OF HONOUR.' *A.R.*, iii. 78 ; *S.T.C.*, 18614. A conventional, pious book, but readable in parts.

23rd January. AN ITALIAN ARGOSY STAYED. *A.P.C.*, xxvi. 445.

24th January. A GREAT VICTORY AT TURNHOUT. *Salisbury Papers*, vii. 24-5, 26, 30. This account is taken chiefly from Vere's letter to Essex, dated 17*th*.

26th January. THE DEATH OF LADY CECIL. Letter printed in E. Edwards' *The Life of Sir Walter Ralegh*, 1868, ii. 161. Compare *Hamlet*, v. ii. 236 : 'Since no man has aught of what he leaves, what is't to leave betimes' ; also *All's Well*, I. i. 65 : 'Moderate lamentation is the right of the dead, excessive grief the enemy to the living.'

30th January. MR. BACON'S 'ESSAYS.' *A.R.*, iii. 79 ; *S.T.C.*, 1137 ; m.e. in the Hazlewood Books, edited by F. E. Etchells and H. Macdonald, 1924. Dated 30th January, 1597, in the Epistle Dedicatory to Anthony Bacon ; entered 5th February. This is the first edition of the *Essays* which reached their final form in 1624 ; other editions were published in 1598, 1606, 1612 (2), 1613 (3), 1614, 1624, 1625 (2), 1629, 1632, 1639. The essay 'Of Studies' is here reproduced complete in its original form ; at this time the essay is rather a collection of *sententiae* than a formal composition ; see also *Politeuphia*, p. 213 and note. Note also that Bacon dates his preface 1597 and *not* 1596 ; the method of beginning the new year on 1st January was coming to be the practice with certain authors and publishers.

31st January. NEW PLAYS. *Hens. Diary*, i. 50-1 ; ii. 182.

2nd February. A DANGEROUS PERSON TAKEN. *A.P.C.*, xxvi. 457.

5th February. A QUARREL AT COURT. Birch's *Memoirs*, ii. 274.

6th February. IRISH TRADE WITH SPAIN. *A.P.C.*, xxvi. 467.

8th February. SPANISH DISASTER. *S.P. Dom.*, 262 : 37.

THE BATTLE AT TURNHOUT. *A discourse of the late overthrow given to the King of Spain's army at Turnhout, etc., translated from the French*, 1597. *Salisbury Papers*, vii. 43.

9th February. A NEW LOAN FOR THE QUEEN. *A.P.C.*, xxvi. 468.

13th February. SUPERFLUOUS DIET AT THE ASSIZES. *A.P.C.*, xxvi. 481.

COMPLAINTS FROM WILTSHIRE. *A.P.C.*, xxvi. 487.

TROUBLES IN OXFORD. *S.P. Dom.*, 262 : 40. From a letter of Dudley Carleton to John Chamberlain.

17th February. TROUBLES OF THE KEEPER AT WISBEACH. *S.P. Dom.*, 262 : 42.

21st February. COURT NEWS. *Sidney Papers*, ii. 16, 17, 18.

24th February. SIR THOMAS BASKERVILLE'S SOLDIERS. *Salisbury Papers*, vii. 69.

25th February. THE LORD MAYOR REBUKED. *A.P.C.*, xxvi. 520.

4th March. COURT NEWS. *Sidney Papers*, ii. 24.

9th March. A NOTABLE STRATAGEM AT THE CAPTURE OF AMIENS. *Salisbury Papers*, vii., 88 ; *Calendar of State Papers Venetian*, ix. 558.

10th March. THE WARDENSHIP OF THE CINQUE PORTS. *Sidney Papers*, ii. 27.

11th March. THE OFFICE OF LORD PRESIDENT. *S.P. Dom.*, 262 : 64. The Earl of Huntingdon died on 14th December, 1595 (p. 66).

12th March. THE LORD TREASURER'S GRIEF. *Sidney Papers*, ii. 27.

14th March. A WITCH HANGED AT LANCASTER. George More, *A True Discourse concerning the certain possession and dispossession of 7 persons in one family in Lancashire*, etc., 1600. In 1598 Darrell and More were committed to the Clink, where this book was written to confute the Jesuits who declared that the Lancashire exorcisms were frauds perpetrated by the preachers ; though the Jesuits themselves made capital out of one of the possessed women (see p. 285). The assizes, according to More, were held on 6th March ; Hartley was probably executed about two days later ; he was dead some days before the 16th. The law did not condemn a man to death for witchcraft but for murder by witchcraft ; conjuration of evil spirits was however a capital offence; see C. L'Estrange Ewen, *Witch Hunting and Witch Trials*, 1929, and E. W. Notestein, *History of Witchcraft in England from 1558-1718* ; my edition of *The Trial of the Lancashire Witches* in 1612, and authorities therein quoted. Lancashire was a hotbed of witchcraft at this time.

16th March. THE PRICE OF BEER. *A.P.C.*, xxvi. 543.

THE EARL OF ESSEX'S PATENT. *Sidney Papers*, ii. 30.

19th March. A NEW PLAY. *Hens. Diary*, i. 51 ; ii. 183.

20th March. FRENCH PIRATES. *A.P.C.*, xxvi. 561.

25th March. SECTARIES TO GO TO CANYDA. *A.P.C.*, xxvii. 6.

27th March. AN EXPLOSION IN DUBLIN. *S.P. Ireland*, 198 : 21.

28th March. THE POSSESSED PERSONS IN LANCASHIRE. For authorities, see 14th March. The 'madness' and 'exorcism' of the Puritan Malvolio would be highly appreciated in 1600-1 when the pamphlet war, engendered by the efforts of Messrs. Darrell and More, was at its hottest. Malvolio's 'vain bibble-babble' and his fashionable yellow stockings show that he too was suffering from possession by the evil spirit of pride.

29th March. ENGLISH PRISONERS IN SPAIN. *S.P. Dom.*, 262 : 86.

31st March. MENDOZA'S 'THEORIQUE AND PRACTISE OF WAR.' *S.T.C.*, 17819 ; the book is commended at the end by a 'Censure' written by Don Francisco Arias de Bobadilla, who is apparently immortalised in Jonson's *Every Man in his Humour* (p. 309) ; Bobadil in the First Quarto of the play appears as Bobadilla.

'VIRGIDEMIARUM.' *A.R.*, iii. 82; *S.T.C.*, 12716. There is some difficulty about the issues of the 1st and 2nd parts. The book was entered on 31st March, 1597, and three satires were published in 1597, though the title-page of this edition reads, 'Virgidemiarum, Sixe Bookes.' The second part—'Virgidemiarum. The three last bookes *of byting Satyres*'—is dated 1598; it is a separate issue and was entered on 30th March, 1598. Presumably the title 'Virgidemiarum, Sixe Bookes' was printed for use with copies of the first series which were bound with copies of the last three books. The first publication was anonymous.

2nd April. THE SOLDIERS IN FRANCE. *Salisbury Papers*, vii. 125, 129, 130.

5th April. 'CLITOPHON AND LEUCIPPE.' *A.R.*, iii. 82; *S.T.C.*, 90; m.e. by S. Gaselee and H. F. B. Brett Smith, 1923. The translator was elder brother of Burton the Melancholick. The Earl of Southampton had a taste for this kind of book.

7th April. SEMINARIES TO BE BANISHED. *A.P.C.*, xxvii., 21.

8th April. FORCES FOR IRELAND. *A.P.C.*, xxvii. 21-6, 26-8.

10th April. AN ENGLISH PIRACY. *A.P.C.*, xxvii. 31. There are several instances of piracy committed by English mariners during this year.

A FRAY IN ST. MARTIN'S. *Middlesex Sessions Rolls*, i. 227. One of several fatal frays. At his trial Pinkney escaped by benefit of clergy.

13th April. TWO LADIES-IN-WAITING PUNISHED. *Sidney Papers*, ii. 38, 34.

THE MARINERS TO BE STAYED. *A.P.C.*, xxvii. 37.

HOUNDS FOR THE FRENCH KING. *A.P.C.*, xxvii. 38.

16th April. COURT NEWS. *Sidney Papers*, ii. 40.

17th April. THE CLOTH TRADE. *A.P.C.*, xxvii. 5.

THE NEW LORD CHAMBERLAIN. *Sidney Papers*, ii. 41.

A DECEITFUL PRACTICE. *A.P.C.*, xxvii. 54.

18th April. THE LORD BURGH TO BE DEPUTY IN IRELAND. *Carew MSS.*, 267.

19th April. THE EARL OF ESSEX AND SIR R. CECIL. *Sidney Papers*, ii. 42.

21st April. ALL SHIPS STAYED. *A.P.C.*, xxvii. 60.

23rd April. ST. GEORGE'S DAY. Hawarde, p. 74; *Sidney Papers*, ii. 45

28th April. THE STAYED SHIPS. *A.P.C.*, xxvii. 74.

DESERTERS FROM THE IRISH FORCES. *A.P.C.*, xxvii. 75; and xxvi. 164.

29th April. DANGERS FROM FRANCE. *A.P.C.*, xxvii. 80, 93.

30th April. NEW PLAYS. *Hens. Diary*, i. 52; ii. 183. On the identity of these plays see Dr. Greg's notes.

1st May. A NOTABLE OUTRAGE ON A CORPSE. *Salisbury Papers*, vii. 165; undated, but the doctor died on 19th April.

6th May. DISCONTENTS IN THE COUNTIES. *A.P.C.*, xxvii. 56, 88, 92, 96, 97.

9th May. MR. THOMAS ARUNDEL. *Salisbury Papers*, vii. 193, 195. See pp. 76, 82, 90.

MUSTERS AGAINST INVASION. *A.P.C.*, xxvii. 101-7.

11th May. THE MAYOR OF CHESTER COMMENDED. *A.P.C.*, xxvii. 115.

A PLAY OF HUMOURS. *Hens. Diary*, i. 52; ii. 184. *S.T.C.*, 4987; m.e. in *The Comedies of George Chapman*, edited by T. M. Parrott, 1914. This is the first surviving play in the new mode, of which Jonson's *Every Man in his Humour* is the most successful and famous example. The play is significant of several changes in the playgoing public: it is a society comedy, of special interest to the gentleman spectator who was now beginning to invade the theatre; it substitutes society wit for the usual clowning and romance which had hitherto been served up as comedy; and, in an elementary form, it presents a problem proper to comedy—whether Florilla is more Puritan than woman. Although the 'humours' of the characters are not labelled in big letters, the *Humorous Day's Mirth* certainly belongs to the type, for the essential of a Humour play is a practical joke (usually in bad taste), designed to place the 'humorous' person in a ridiculous situation where his particular humour can be displayed at its most foolish. Jonson was notably skilful in managing such plots because he could balance so many of these situations in one play. From this time onward the younger generation begins to be noticeable. Young people of independent means who belonged neither to immediate Court circles nor to the professions had not been much in evidence for some years; henceforward actors depend for support more on gentlemen of leisure and culture than on the old-fashioned patron or the crowd. Moreover, the gentlemen themselves not only write poetry, but a few months later begin to write plays, to produce them in private theatres, and to print them.

16th May. ENGLISH PIRATES. *A.P.C.*, xxvii. 116. Another case of piracy; see p. 180.

20th May. THE QUEEN ANGRY. *Sidney Papers*, ii. 52.

23rd May. MACHUGH SLAIN. *Carew MSS.*, *Russell's Journal*, p. 259; *S.P. Ireland*, 199: 25, 28.

THE QUEEN AND THE LADY MARY HOWARD. *Nugae Antiquae*, i. 232-4, 361.

26th May. A NEW PLAY. *Hens. Diary*, i. 52; ii. 185. Nothing is known of the play.

27th May. A DEBTOR'S CASE. *A.P.C.*, xxvii. 143.

30th May. PREPARATIONS FOR AN EXPEDITION. *A.P.C.*, xxvii. 160-164.

2nd June. MR. ARUNDEL RELEASED. *Salisbury Papers*, vii. 229; see 9th May.

SIR WALTER RALEGH RESTORED TO HIS PLACE. *Sidney Papers*, ii. 54. It was now five years since Ralegh had been thrown into the Tower for the scandal of his marriage; see *Eliz. Journal*, p. 134.

3rd June. LANGHAM'S 'GARDEN OF HEALTH.' *A.R.*, iii. 85; *S.T.C.*, 15195. The title-page is misdated 1579. This is a most important book for the understanding of Elizabethan homely medicine, and well worth the attention of Shakespearean students.

4th June. ABUSES IN SOMERSET. *A.P.C.*, xxvii. 167.

8th June. MacHugh's Head. *A.P.C.*, xxvii. 185; *S.P. Ireland*, 199 : 86. For further adventures of MacHugh's head see 24th September.

The Earl of Essex's Clemency. *A.P.C.*, xxvii. 181.

10th June. Calais. *S.P. Dom.*, 263 : 97.

11th June. Sir Thomas Baskerville dead. *Salisbury Papers*, vii. 232, 242, 256, 200, 286.

Rumours. Chamberlain's *Letters*, p. 4.

12th June. Sir Arthur Savage to command in France. *A.P.C.*, xxvii. 203.

14th June. Timorous Gentlemen. *A.P.C.*, xxvii. 193.

Abuses over Musters. A.P.C., xxvii. 197.

25th June. The State of Ireland. *Carew MSS.*, 268. This 'Summary Collection' of the state of Ireland is calendared 'April 1597' but must be later than the death of MacHugh.

30th June. New Plays. *Hens. Diary*, i. 53; ii. 185. Neither play survives but the 'plot' of *Frederick and Basilia* is reprinted by Dr. Greg in *Henslowe Papers*, p. 135, from the original in the British Museum.

2nd July. The 'Wat' Returns. Hakluyt's *Voyages*, viii. 1. See 14th October, 1596.

5th July. Sir Anthony Shirley's return. Hakluyt's *Voyages*, vii. 213. See 25th April, 2nd and 23rd May, 1596.

Mr. William Parker's Voyage. Hakluyt's *Voyages*, vii. 222.

6th July. A Proclamation against inordinate apparel. *Proclamations*, 343. The detailed list of the stuffs permitted to the several ranks occupies 3½ pages.

Soldiers for Picardy. *A.P.C.*, xxvii. 283.

7th July. Deloney's 'Jack of Newbury.' *A.R.*, iii. 87; *S.T.C.*, 6559—the earliest extant copy 'now the tenth time imprinted,' dated 1626; m.e. in *The Works of Thomas Deloney*, edited by F. O. Mann, 1912. The book was first entered to Millington on 7th March, who assigned it to Lowndes on 25th May; both entries include the condition that it be lawfully authorised—a reasonable precaution after the previous association of Deloney and Millington (see p. 32). A ballad on the subject, entered 8th July, probably gives the date of publication.

8th July. The Complaints of the Council of War. *S.P. Dom.*, 264 : 12.

10th July. The Fleet enter Plymouth. Devereux, i. 421.

12th July. The Fleet sails. *S.P. Dom.*, 264 : 21.

Vagrants to be impressed. *A.P.C.*, xxvii. 290. Dogberry, mindful of a similar order, charges his watch, 'You shall comprehend all vagrom men' (*Much Ado*, III. iii. 25).

16th July. The Vagrants. *A.P.C.*, xxvii. 292.

18th July. The Lord Mayor rebuked. *A.P.C.*, xxvii. 298.

20th July. The Fleet driven back. Purchas, xx. 41; *S.P. Dom.*, 264 : 32, 34.

22nd July. THE EARL OF ESSEX AT PLYMOUTH. *S.P. Dom.*, 264 : 40, 41.

23rd July. THE POLISH AMBASSADOR. *S.P. Dom.*, 264 : 57. This account is taken from a letter written by Sir R. Cecil to Essex on the 26th ; the full text of both speeches is given in Stow's *Annals*.

24th July. THE POLISH AMBASSADOR. *A.P.C.*, xxvii. 307.

28th July. THE PLAYHOUSES ORDERED TO BE PLUCKED DOWN and A LEWD PLAY. *Remembrancia*, ii. 171; *A.P.C.*, xxvii. 313 (both reprinted in *Elizabethan Stage*, iv. 321), 338 ; *Hens. Diary*, i. 54 ; *Elizabethan Stage*, iii. 454 ; McKerrow's *Nashe*, v. 29. Apparently the Lord Mayor had been reading Sidney's *Defence of Poesy*, but his immediate desire to reform the stage was more probably due to the quite real danger that the players might incite the mob at this uneasy time. Playing ceased until October (see pp. 209, 212), but the playhouses, as usual, survived intact.

29th July. TROUBLES ON THE BORDER AND IN IRELAND. *S.P. Ireland*, 200 : 24, 25, 27 ; and *S.P. Dom.*, 264 : 61—from a letter of Cecil to Essex.

2nd August. LORD HOWARD'S SHIPS RETURN. *S.P. Dom.*, 264 : 64.

7th August. THE PICARDY FORCES DELAYED. *A.P.C.*, xxvii. 324.

13th August. A PROCLAMATION CONCERNING THE SCOTTISH BORDER. *Proclamations*, 349.

17th August. A MALICIOUS MAYOR. *A.P.C.*, xxvii. 346.

19th August. THE FLEET AGAIN SAILS. Purchas, xx. 44.

20th August. THE ALMSHOUSE AT STAMFORD. *Proclamations*, 349b.

21st August. INGROSSERS. *A.P.C.*, xxvii. 359.

22nd August. A BOOK ON CHEATING. *A.R.*, iii. 89 ; *S.T.C.*, 17916.

29th August. SHAKESPEARE'S 'RICHARD THE SECOND.' *A.R.*, iii. 89 ; *S.T.C.*, 22307 ; facsimile edited by W. Griggs and P. A. Daniel, 1890. This was a most popular book and went quickly into three editions ; the first is anonymous, but Shakespeare's name appears on both editions of 1598. There was no further edition until 1608 which first included the Deposition Scene ; presumably after the troubles of Sir John Hayward (who was imprisoned in 1599 for injudiciously dedicating *The first part of the reign of King Henry IIII.* to Essex) it was thought inadvisable to continue publication.

6th September. AN AMBASSADOR RECEIVED FROM DENMARK. Stow's *Annals*.

15th September. SLANDERS AGAINST THE LORD MAYOR. *Proclamations*, 350.

16th September. NEWS OF THE FLEET. *S.P. Dom.*, 264 : 110.

20th September. SIR JOHN NORRIS DEAD. *S.P. Ireland*, 200 : 130.

CONDEMNED PRISONERS, *A.P.C.*, xxviii. 8.

22nd September. THE QUEEN'S LETTER TO THE LADY NORRIS. Printed in full in J. Nichols' *Progresses of Queen Elizabeth*, 1805, vol. iii.

23rd September. THE GOVERNOR OF DUNKIRK TAKEN. *A.P.C.*, xxviii. 10.

24th September. MacHugh's Head. *Salisbury Papers*, vii. 395. See 8th June.

27th September. A Proclamation against providing the Spanish King with Munition. *Proclamations*, 351.

29th September. The Spanish Danger ceases. *A.P.C.*, xxviii. 27.

8th October. The Players released. *A.P.C.*, xxviii. 33. See 28th July.

9th October. A Disorderly Election. *Salisbury Papers*, vii. 411-415. The matter was reported to the Council by the Archbishop of York, who blamed Sir John Savile.

10th October. The Art of Brachygraphy. *S.T.C.*, 1311 ; dated on title-page. The book was the work of an Oxford man and is sponsored by a number of dedicatory verses. Bales' system is very general and could not be used for anything more elaborate than note taking. Entered 10th November, 1599 (*A.R.*, iii. 150).

11th October. 'The Trimming of Thomas Nashe.' *A.R.*, iii. 92 ; *S.T.C.*, 12906 ; m.e. in *The Works of Gabriel Harvey*, edited by A. B. Grosart, 1885, vol. iii. Dr. McKerrow points out (*Nashe*, v. 107) that as the *Trimming* is concerned only with Nashe's Epistle to the barber and not with his quarrel with Harvey, it is not likely to be Harvey's work, nor does it resemble Harvey's style. I suspect that it was written by some Cambridge man, possibly with the approval of the barber, who may well have resented Nashe's unsolicited advertisement. With this book the Harvey-Nashe 'flyting' ceased.

Playing resumed. *Hens. Diary*, i. 54 ; ii. 186.

The Election at York. *Salisbury Papers*, vii. 426.

12th October. A Proclamation against English Merchants. *S.P. Dom.*, 264 : 143 ; *Salisbury Papers*, vii. 429 ; F. Peck's *Desideria Curiosa*, bk. v., p. 21.

14th October. 'Politeuphia, Wit's Commonwealth.' *A.R.*, iii. 93 ; *S.T.C.*, 15685. This was a most popular book ; the 17th edition appeared in 1655 and copies exist dated 1663, 1669, 1671, 1674, 1688, 1699. *Wit's Commonwealth* in design is not dissimilar to the first version of Bacon's *Essays* (see 30th January), being a large collection of apt remarks and quotations, and one of the many commonplace books so much in favour at this time ; compare also Meres' *Paladis Tamia*, p. 305.

16th October. Herrings to be stayed. *A.P.C.*, xxviii. 40.

19th October. Ingrossers and Builders punished. Hawarde, p. 78.

Deloney's 'Gentle Craft.' *A.R.*, iii. 93 ; *S.T.C.*, 6555. This is the 1st part, the 2nd being published some months later ; m.e. in *The Works of Deloney* by F. O. Mann, 1912. The earliest extant edition is dated 1648. Dekker in 1599 dramatised the last section in *The Shoemakers' Holiday*.

20th October. 'Richard the Third.' *A.R.*, iii. 93 ; *S.T.C.*, 22314 ; facsimile by W. Griggs and P. A. Daniel. The play was very popular, being reprinted in 1598, 1602, 1605, 1612, 1622, 1629, 1634.

22nd October. The Lord Admiral to be advanced. *Sidney Papers*, ii. 69.

23rd October. The Lord Admiral advanced. *Sidney Papers*, ii. 70.

Ostend threatened. *A.P.C.*, xxviii. 48.

24th October. The Parliament assembles. D'Ewes' *Journals*, pp. 548, 524. Stow's *Annals*. For the opening of the Parliament of 1593 see *Eliz. Journal*, 195, etc.

26th October. A Sudden very Great Alarm. *Sidney Papers*, ii. 71; *A.P.C.*, xxviii. 50-56.

27th October. The Forces mustering. *A.P.C.*, xxviii. 57-61; *Sidney Papers*, ii. 72.

The Lord Burgh dead. *S.P. Ireland*, 201 : 17, 14.

The Speaker presented. D'Ewes' *Journals*, pp. 550, 526.

Playing resumed. *Hens. Diary*, i. 49; *Elizabethan Stage*, ii. 141.

28th October. The Earl of Essex returns. *Sidney Papers*, ii. 72; *A.P.C.*, xxviii. 62, 63. The report of King Philip's death was premature, though expected.

30th October. Preparations in the West. *A.P.C.*, xxviii. 67.

31st October. Ostend besieged. *S.P. Dom.*, 264 : 163, 164.

A New Play. *Hens. Diary*, i. 54; ii. 187. After 5th November the daily record of performances in the *Diary* ceases, and in its place Henslowe notes payments made on behalf of the companies.

2nd November. The Islands Voyage. Purchas, vol. xx. This account is based on the narrative of Sir Arthur Gorges, who was an enemy of the Essex faction and therefore not impartial, but other writers are even more condemnatory; Monson, who was Essex's own captain, wrote: 'No man can receive blame hereby; all is to be attributed to the want of experience in my Lord, and his flexible nature to be overruled.' With the return of the expedition Essex's reputation amongst the intelligent observers began to wane as it was more generally realised that he was not only an incompetent commander but acutely jealous of other and abler leaders than himself; he was, moreover, attracting the devotion of the more desperate and reckless adventurers. From this time onward Essex begins to be a definite menace to the commonwealth. For the best modern commentary on the expedition see *The Naval Tracts of Sir William Monson*, edited by M. Oppenheim, 1902, for *The Navy Records Society* (vols. xxii.-xxiii.).

5th November. Ostend. *S.P. Dom.*, 265 : 3.

The Queen's Letter to the Emperor of Ethiopia. Hakluyt's *Voyages*, v. 77.

A Motion in Parliament against Inclosures. D'Ewes' *Journals*, p. 551.

6th November. Spanish Prisoners at large. *A.P.C.*, xxviii. 102.

7th November. Barret's 'Theorick and Practick of Modern Wars.' *A.R.*, iii. 95; *S.T.C.*, 1500; one of the most interesting and best written of the military text-books of the period. Michael Cassio, in Iago's estimation, was another of your reading captains, a bookish theoric.

9th November. The Earl of Essex absent from Court. *S.P. Dom.*, 265 : 7. From a letter of Hunsdon to Essex.

THE PRIVILEGES OF THE HOUSE. D'Ewes' *Journals*, p. 553. The answer is not recorded.

ABUSES IN BRISTOL. *A.P.C.*, xxviii. 111.

10th November. THE PARLIAMENT. D'Ewes' *Journals*, p. 555.

14th November. THE KNIGHTS OF THE POST. *A.R.*, iii. 96 ; *S.T.C.*, 214 : 89. A lively little book written in the form of conversations on the Plymouth road.

INCESTUOUS MARRIAGES. D'Ewes' *Journals*, p. 556.

15th November. THE SUBSIDIES. D'Ewes' *Journals*, p. 557. For the subsidies granted by the previous Parliament, see *Eliz. Journal*, pp. 203-4, 205, 210, 213-4, 228.

16th November. MY LORD OF ESSEX'S ABSENCE. *S.P. Dom.*, 265 : 10. From a long letter to Essex from 'thy true servant not daring to subscribe.' Compare Bacon's advice noted on p. 139. The register of attendances in *A.P.C.* shows that Essex was absent from Council meetings from 3rd November to 22nd December.

18th November. THE EARL OF ESSEX ABSENT FROM PARLIAMENT. D'Ewes' *Journals*, p. 529.

19th November. THE SUBSIDIES. D'Ewes' *Journals*, p. 559.

20th November. DISORDERS IN WALES. *A.P.C.*, xxviii. 119, 121.

THE SPANISH LOSSES. *S.P. Dom.*, 264 : 148 ; letter from a spy dated 19th October.

21st November. PRIVILEGE OF THE HOUSE. D'Ewes' *Journal*, p. 560.

22nd November. A PETITION OF THE UNIVERSITIES. *MSS. Addit.*, 5843, f. 449.

23rd November. THE PARLIAMENT. D'Ewes' *Journals*, pp. 562-3.

28th November. THE FRENCH AMBASSADOR RECEIVED. *Baschet Transcripts*, 30, f. 205. This and the other entries concerning De Maisse are taken from his Journal, of which a transcript is kept in the Public Record Office. A translation is in preparation to be published by the Nonesuch Press.

30th November. A PRISONER RELEASED. *A.P.C.*, xxviii. 156. See *Eliz. Journal*, p. 207.

AN ACCIDENT AT THE SWAN. *Letters of Philip Gawdy*, edited by I. H. Jeayes, Roxburghe Club, 1906, p. 93 ; approximate date.

1st December. GERARD'S 'HERBAL.' *A.R.*, iii. 85 ; *S.T.C.*, 11750 ; entered 6th June ; Epistle to the Reader dated 1st December.

3rd December. THE VENETIAN CORN SHIP. *A.P.C.*, xxviii. 167 ; see pp. 162, 277.

4th December. THE SERMON AT PAUL'S CROSS. Entered 9th January, 1598. *A.R.*, iii. 100 ; *S.T.C.*, 13881 ; there were two editions. The sermon was concluded on 28th May, 1598. Mr. Howson's estimate of £500-£666 in Elizabethan money seems excessive ; his argument, expressed in different terms, is that parents pay for a University career because it ensures for their children an income of £40-£50 per annum for life ; it is not surprising that so many parsons in the Church of England were second-rate men.

8th December. A Boy possessed at Nottingham. Approximate date; for authorities see note on 28th July, 1598.

11th December. The Subsidy. D'Ewes' *Journals*, p. 571.

14th December. The Lords' Privilege abused. D'Ewes' *Journals*, pp. 532, 533.

The Abuse of Monopolies. D'Ewes' *Journals*, p. 573.

Monsieur de Maisse. *Baschet Transcripts*, 30, ff. 218-220.

17th December. Two London Crimes. *A.P.C.*, xxviii. 187, 188, 219.

20th December. A Dispute concerning Procedure. D'Ewes' *Journals*, pp. 573-4, 575-7.

21st December. The Earl of Essex's indignation. *Sidney Papers*, ii. 77.

The Queen and M. de Maisse. *Baschet Transcripts*, 30, ff. 227 v.-231; 29, f. 161.

24th December. The Price of Pepper. Stow's *Annals*. For the Great Carrack and the pepper, see *Eliz. Journal*, pp. 195, 267.

31st December. New Plays. *Hens. Diary*, i. 50; ii. 181. Dr. Greg notes that *The famous history of the life and death of Captain Thomas Stukeley* was entered on 11th August, 1600, and printed in 1605; the printed version, however, has probably been cut down and altered. It is reprinted in R. Simpson's *School of Shakspere*, 1878.

OTHER BOOKS SET FORTH ANNO 1597

Meres' 'God's Arithmetic.' *S.T.C.*, 17833; except for occasional gems of phrasing this is a dull little book. For *Palladis Tamia* see p. 305.

Breton's 'Wit's Trenchmour.' *S.T.C.*, 3713; m.e. in *The Works of Nicholas Breton*, edited by A. B. Grosart. This is the kind of book which Beatrice and Benedick read; in style it is somewhat between *Euphues* and a 'metaphysical' poem.

Shakespeare's 'Romeo and Juliet.' *S.T.C.*, 22322. This is the pirated First Quarto; facsimile by C. Praetorius, 1886; a parallel text of the two quartos was edited by P. A. Daniel for the New Shakespere Society in 1874.

1598

1st January. TYRONE AGAIN SUBMITS. *Carew MSS.*, 278-281.

2nd January. REFLECTIONS ON A PEACE WITH SPAIN. *S.P. Dom.*, 266 : 3 ; from Burleigh's manuscript, 'Reflections upon the proposal of the French King to her Majesty.'

3rd January. SIR JOHN SMYTHE RELEASED. *S.P. Dom.*, 266 : 4. See pp. 105-6, etc.

4th January. THE FRENCH AMBASSADOR. *Baschet Transcripts,* 30, ff. 244 v-245.

5th January. TYRONE AGAIN SUBMITS. *Carew MSS.*, 278.

10th January. COMPLAINTS CONCERNING THE FRENCH COURTS. *A.P.C.*, xxviii. 234.

11th January. THE PARLIAMENT RENEWED. D'Ewes' *Journals*, p. 535.

13th January. THE STILLYARD TO BE SUPPRESSED. *S.P. Dom.*, 266 : 14.

14th January. THE MERCHANTS TO DEPART. *Sidney Papers*, ii. 81.

THE COMMONS OFFENDED. D'Ewes' *Journals*, p. 580.

19th January. THE COMMONS' OFFENCE. D'Ewes' *Journals*, p. 540.

20th January. A QUARREL AT COURT. *Sidney Papers*, ii. 82, 83.

THE COMMONS SATISFIED. D'Ewes' *Journals*, pp. 539-40, 584-5.

A BAWD CARTED. *Middlesex Sessions Rolls*, i. 235. Her sentence was the same as that of Elizabeth Holland (see p. 258).

26th January. THE STILLYARD. *S.P. Dom.*, 266 : 29.

28th January. CASES OF PIRACY. *A.P.C.*, xxviii., 283, 284, 285.

29th January. ABUSES IN THE NORTH. *S.P. Dom.*, 266 : 18, 32. Religion in the North was perpetually in a parlous state, hence the prevalence of witchcraft : see also *Eliz. Journal*, pp. 117, 141.

THE SPANISH PRISONERS. *A.P.C.*, xxviii. 287.

1st February. COURT NEWS. *Sidney Papers*, ii. 86, 87, 88.

4th February. A RESTRAINT ON COCHINEAL. *S.P. Dom.*, 266 : 43.

9th February. THE PARLIAMENT DISSOLVED. D'Ewes' *Journals*, pp. 546-7, 595-6.

AN OUTRAGE IN THE MIDDLE TEMPLE. *Archaeologia*, xxi. 107. For this display of temper Davies was ejected from the Middle Temple '*nunquam in posterum restituendus*' ; he was restored in October 1601.

10th February. SIR ROBERT CECIL'S DEPARTURE. *Sidney Papers*, ii. 89.

A NOTE OF THE CHIEF STATUTES ENACTED BY THE LATE PARLIAMENT. *S.T.C.*, 9493, etc.

12th February. THE MUSTERS. *A.P.C.*, xxviii. 303-307.

15th February. COURT NEWS. *Sidney Papers*, ii. 89, 90, 91.

16th February. A BAWD CARTED. *Middlesex Sessions Rolls,* i. 235. I met with a survival of this custom of ringing basins in a Lincolnshire village in the summer of 1919. The sergeant in charge of some German prisoners working for farmers in those parts was discovered one night in another's bed; whereupon all the village youth turned out armed with cans which they beat to the refrain of 'Ran, tan; he's a very bad man,' until dispersed by the village policeman.

19th February. A COMPANY OF PLAYERS TO BE SUPPRESSED. *A.P.C.,* xxviii. 327.

23rd February. MR. BODLEY'S MUNIFICENCE TO THE UNIVERSITY OF OXFORD. From *Letters of Thomas Bodley to the University of Oxford,* 1598-1611, edited by G. W. Wheeler, 1927, p. 4.

25th February. THE LORD TREASURER DANGEROUSLY ILL. *Sidney Papers,* ii. 92.

26th February. SHAKESPEARE'S 'HENRY THE FOURTH.' *A.R.,* iii. 105; *S.T.C.,* 22280; facsimile by W. Griggs and H. Evans, 1881. There is no direct contemporary evidence for the change of name, but the indirect evidence (for which see the introduction to this play in the Arden Shakespeare), together with the passages in Fuller's *Worthies* [Warwickshire] and Rowe's *Life of Shakespeare,* seems to be ample. Falstaffe, to judge by the number of references in the *Shakspere Allusion Book,* was the most popular of all Shakespeare's characters; he is the supreme comic figure of the Great War of 1588-1604. The Quarto of *I. Henry IV.* was reprinted in 1599, 1604, 1608, 1613, 1622, 1632, 1639.

FLESH IN LENT. *Proclamations,* 353.

MARLOWE'S 'HERO AND LEANDER.' *S.T.C.,* 17413; m.e. in *The Works of Christopher Marlowe,* edited by C. F. Tucker Brooke, 1910. The date is approximate, but Blunt's edition of the first part of *Hero and Leander* must have been issued early in 1598, for Henry Petowe had finished his sequel by 14th April (p. 271). On 2nd March Blunt assigned his rights to Linley, who published a second edition with Chapman's sequel later in the year (p. 329). Presumably Linley, possessing the rights in Chapman's addition, bought the copyright from Blunt to enable him to issue the whole poem. *Hero and Leander* was first entered to Wolfe on 28th September, 1593, but there is no trace of an edition earlier than 1598.

1st March. THE DISORDERS IN GOVERNMENT IN IRELAND. *S.P. Ireland,* 202: part i., 53, 54; letters dated 19th February.

2nd March. THE LADY LEICESTER RECONCILED TO THE QUEEN. *Sidney Papers,* ii. 92, 93. The Lady at this time was the wife of Sir Christopher Blount.

5th March. A NOTABLE FRAUD. *A.P.C.,* xxviii. 351.

6th March. MR. BODLEY'S GIFT TO OXFORD. *S.P. Dom.,* 266: 87.

'THE COUNSELLOR.' *A.R.,* iii. 106; *S.T.C.,* 12372. The late Sir Israel Gollancz (in *A Book of Homage to Shakespeare,* 1916, p. 173) maintained that Shakespeare took the name of Polonius, which in the First Quarto of *Hamlet* is Corambis, from this treatise.

8th March. THE EARL OF CUMBERLAND SAILS. Purchas, xvi. 28.

10th March. 'LOVE'S LABOURS LOST.' *S.T.C.,* 22294; facsimile by W. Griggs and F. J. Furnivall; m.e. by Sir A. T. Quiller Couch and J.

Dover Wilson, 1923. The play was probably first performed in 1593; see *Eliz. Journal*, p. 398.

12th March. INSTRUCTIONS FOR THE MUSTERS. *S.P. Dom.*, 266 : 100, endorsed 'March 1595'; see 12th February.

16th March. THE ENVOYS OF THE STATES. *Salisbury MSS.*, viii. 84.

17th March. THE SCOTTISH KING'S 'DAEMONOLOGY.' *A.R.*, iii. 106; *S.T.C.*, 14364; m.e. in *The Bodley Head Quartos*, vol. ix., 1924. The book was entered on this date, but no English edition is known earlier than 1603. Contrary to the opinion held by those who have not read it, *Daemonology* is concise, well written, and the best contemporary account of the full belief in witchcraft.

24th March. KEEPING OF DAIRIES. *A.P.C.*, xxviii. 372.

29th March. PARLEYS WITH TYRONE. *S.P. Ireland*, 202 : pt. i., 89.

30th March. 'VIRGIDEMIARUM,' THE LAST PART. *A.R.*, iii. 109; *S.T.C.*, 12716; see note on 31st March, 1597. The satires in the second book are more obscure and general than in the first; but at times Hall achieves some perfect eighteenth-century couplets, which was presumably the reason why Warton praised him so highly. Compare Jaques' similar apology for the satirist (*As You Like It*, II. vii. 70).

1st April. THE BOY POSSESSED AT NOTTINGHAM. For authorities see note on 28th July.

3rd April. BASTARD'S 'CHRESTOLEROS.' *A.R.*, iii. 110; *S.T.C.*, 1559; m.e. by E. V. Otterson, 1842.

5th April. SEIZED BOOKS. *A.P.C.*, xxviii. 387.

6th April. THE TOWN OF TWYFORD BURNT. Stow's *Annals*.

7th April. SIR ROBERT CECIL RECEIVED BY THE FRENCH KING. Birch's *Historical View*, p. 105; *Salisbury Papers*, viii. 90.

9th April. CERTAIN LETTERS INTERCEPTED. Birch's *Historical View*, p. 140; *Sidney Papers*, ii. 100.

10th April. MR. CHAPMAN TRANSLATETH HOMER'S 'ILIADES.' *A.R.*, iii. 110; *S.T.C.*, 13632. Contemporaries could hardly have failed to see an intentional likeness between Achilles in Shakespeare's *Troilus and Cressida* and the 'now living instance of the Achilleian virtues.' It should be noted that Shakespeare founded the Achilles episodes on this translation, his play presumably being privately staged either in the late summer of 1598 or during Essex's retirement in 1600.

12th April. AN ATTEMPT TO POISON. *A.P.C.*, xxviii. 393; see also pp. 42-3, 279, 290.

14th April. A SECOND PART TO 'HERO AND LEANDER.' *A.R.*, iii. 111; *S.T.C.*, 19807. This continuation of Marlowe's narrative is of no literary importance, though the praise of Marlowe is significant; about half is here quoted.

16th April. THE NEGOTIATIONS WITH THE FRENCH KING BROKEN. Camden's *Elizabeth*. Cecil's full and detailed account of the negotiations is given in Birch's *Historical Memoirs*.

18th April. THE SPITAL SERMONS. *A.P.C.*, xxviii. 408.

21st *April*. ARISTOTLE'S 'POLITIQUES.' *A.R.*, iii. 112; *S.T.C.*, 760; an important and beautifully printed volume.

24th *April*. TYRONE RENEWETH THE TRUCE. *S.P. Ireland*, 202: pt. ii., 9.

25th *April*. LORD BURLEIGH'S REBUKE. Camden's *Elizabeth*. Approximate date.

30th *April*. ABUSES IN TENEMENT HOUSES. *A.P.C.*, xxviii. 427, 435.

1st *May*. SIR ROBERT CECIL'S RETURN. Stow's *Annals*; Birch's *Historical View*, p. 161.

3rd *May*. 'GREENE IN CONCEIPT.' *A.R.*, iii. 114; *S.T.C.*, 6819; m.e. by A. B. Grosart, 1878. J. D[ickenson] imitates Greene's earlier euphuistic manner, as he acknowledges in the title; his story of Valeria reads as if it were true with but a minimum of transmutation. More of the Euphuistic novels may be founded on fact than would at first sight appear.

6th *May*. THE CURES OF THE DISEASED IN REMOTE REGIONS. *A.R.*, iii. 114; *S.T.C.*, 25106; m.e. in facsimile by Charles Singer, 1915, who identifies *calenture* as heatstroke or sunstroke, *tabardilla* as yellow fever or typhus, *espinlas* as 'prickly heat,' *cameras de sangre* as dysentery.

7th *May*. MR. GOSSON'S SERMON AT PAUL'S CROSS. *A.R.*, iii. 116; *S.T.C.*, 12099. This Gosson was the author of *The School of Abuse*, 1579, which Sidney answered in *The Defence of Poesy*; see p. 6.

9th *May*. AN ABUSE IN DARTMOUTH. *A.P.C.*, xxviii. 438.

10th *May*. THE QUEEN'S LETTERS TO THE FRENCH KING. Camden's *Elizabeth*. Approximate date.

14th *May*. THE VENETIAN ARGOSY. *A.P.C.*, xxviii. 440; see also pp. 162, 240.

15th *May*. 'THE SERVINGMAN'S COMFORT.' *A.R.*, iii. 115; *S.T.C.*, 17140. For the social student this is a most important book, of which Shakespeare probably owned a marked copy. This work and the mockery of the country 'gentleman' (such as Mr. Stephen, Sogliardo, Sir Andrew Aguecheek) on the stage seem to reflect a prevalent discussion on the 'new gentry' to which Hamlet refers (? autumn 1601) in "By the Lord, Horatio, these three years I have taken note of it; the age is grown so picked that the toe of the peasant comes so near the heel of the courtier, he galls his kibe'; see especially *Every Man out of His Humour*, Fungoso's letter to his father Sordido (III. ii.). Similarly the 'new rich,' or war profiteers, were especially a topic of comment at the end of the Great War; for which see *Punch*, 1918-22, *passim*.

20th *May*. THE MONOPOLY IN STARCH. *Proclamations*, 3546.

RUMOURS. Chamberlain's *Letters*, p. 11. Over a century later Swift makes a similar complaint of the Dutch in *The Conduct of the Allies*.

21st *May*. MR. BARNABE BARNES. *A.P.C.*, xxviii. 441, 456; see also pp. 279, 290.

THE SERMON AT PAUL'S CROSS. *S.T.C.*, 12099; see p. 240.

25th *May*. SLANDERS AGAINST THE SCOTTISH KING. *Calendar of Border Papers*, ii. 537; *S.P. Dom.*, 269: 20.

27th May. 'THE METAMORPHOSIS OF PYGMALION'S IMAGE; AND CERTAIN SATIRES.' *A.R.*, iii. 116; *S.T.C.*, 17482; m.e. in *The Works of John Marston*, by A. H. Bullen, 1887, vol. 3.

30th May. A FRAY AT OXFORD. *Salisbury Papers*, viii. 191, 201, 202.

1st June. THE APOLOGY OF THE EARL OF ESSEX. *S.T.C.*, 6788; *Salisbury Papers*, viii. 545. Essex's *Apology* (said to have been written by Anthony Bacon) was published in 1603, after the Queen's death, though in manuscript circulation at this time.

2nd June. A LEWD SHOW AT BRUSSELS. *Salisbury Papers*, viii. 190.

5th June. A CASE OF PIRACY. *A.P.C.*, xxviii. 456.

7th June. TROUBLES AT PLYMOUTH. *A.P.C.*, xxviii. 500, 517.

8th June. THE PEACE AT VERVINS. *Salisbury Papers*, viii. 193; *The History of the Civil Wars of France*, by H. C. D'Avila, 1678, p. 732.

10th June. MURDERS IN IRELAND. *S.P. Ireland*, 202: pt. ii., 56.

11th June. COMPLAINTS AGAINST THE EARL OF LINCOLN. *A.P.C.*, xxviii. 506.

15th June. JESUIT DEVICES. *Salisbury Papers*, viii. 213, 293. This affair is a sequel to the efforts of Mr. Darrell at Cleworth in March 1597, the woman being one of the seven possessed in the Starkie household (p. 173).

17th June. A CASE OF MANSLAUGHTER. *Middlesex Sessions Rolls*, i. 237.

18th June. SOLDIERS FOR IRELAND. *A.P.C.*, xxviii. 524, 527.

23rd June. NEWS FROM PARIS. *Salisbury Papers*, viii. 219 (where the story is that 'the German whom the Earl knighted refuses to fight a Frenchman'), and pp. 224-31 where a long account of the challenge is given; see also Chamberlain's *Letters*, pp. 10 and 14, where he says 'the news I wrote of Sir Charles Blount must be recalled, for it was a mistaking of a combat between a Frenchman and a Dutch baron.' All the same, Sir Melchior did refuse Sir Charles' challenge on the grounds stated. It is perhaps more than a coincidence that Jonson, who was finishing off *Every Man in His Humour* at this time, should cause Captain Bobadilla to offer a similar excuse to the blunt squire Giulliano (*alias* Downright).

24th June. DISTRESS IN LINCOLNSHIRE. *A.P.C.*, xxviii. 537.

28th June. THE TRUCE ENDED IN IRELAND. *S.P. Ireland*, 200: pt. ii., 62, 74; dated 10th and 18th June.

2nd July. THE EARL OF ESSEX'S GREAT CONTEMPT. The only direct authority for this famous incident is Camden's *Elizabeth*, which gives no date; but the date can be deduced from *A.P.C.*, wherein attendances at the Council Board are recorded. Essex had been present on 25th, 26th, 29th, 30th June; he next attended on 8th August; he was then absent until 22nd August, when he sat in the morning but was absent in the afternoon; his next appearance was on 10th September, and thereafter he attended regularly. The great offence therefore was committed on 30th June or 1st July. On 22nd August he attended the Council by request to advise on the Irish situation; his behaviour on this occasion—sulky, curious and defiant—probably provoked Egerton's letter (see pp. 301, 302). In early copies the letter is dated 15th October, but this seems too late; it might however have been written on the 9th or 10th August. See Corrigenda, p. vi.

6th July. The Governor of Dunkirk. *A.P.C.*, xxviii. 563; see p. 208.

7th July. Stow's 'Survey of London.' *A.R.*, iii. 121; *S.T.C.*, 23341; other editions appeared in 1599 and 1603, and, after Stow's death in 1605, in 1608 and 1633; m.e. by C. L. Kingsford in 1908.

10th July. A Fencer hanged. Stow's *Annals*.

11th July. Mr. Barnabe Barnes. *A.P.C.*, xxviii. 568.

12th July. Disorders in Ireland. *A.P.C.*, xxviii. 572.

16th July. The Queen and the Earl of Essex. Birch's *Memoirs*, ii. 389.

A Saying concerning my Lord of Essex. Quoted from Bacon's *Apothegms* in Spedding's *Bacon*, ii. 91.

Horse and Men required for Ireland. *A.P.C.*, xxviii. 567, 586, 588, 590, 591.

19th July. The Troubles at Plymouth. *A.P.C.*, xxviii. 598.

21st July. The Earl of Essex and the Lord Grey. *Salisbury Papers*, viii. 269.

23rd July. Abuses in the Irish Service. *S.P. Ireland*, 202 : pt. ii., 108.

25th July. The Stillyard. *A.P.C.*, xxviii. 613.

Mr. Darrell before the Ecclesiastical Commissioners. The affairs of John Darrell gave rise to a small pamphlet war between 1598 and 1603. In 1598 there was printed abroad the pro-Darrell *Brief narration of the possession, dispossession, and repossession of William Somers*, etc.; this was answered in 1599 by Samuel Harsnet, chaplain to the Bishop of London, in *A discovery of the fraudulent practises of John Darrell*, etc., which gives a long and detailed commentary on the whole series of exorcisms. The present account (pp. 241, 267) is based on both sources. For other books connected with the case and a general account of the controversy, see *A History of Witchcraft in England from 1558 to 1718*, by Wallace Notestein, 1911, chap. iv.

26th July. Lord Burleigh sick. *Salisbury Papers*, viii. 276, 277.

Want of Zeal at Plymouth. *A.P.C.*, xxviii. 622.

27th July. A Witch condemned. *Middlesex Sessions Rolls*, i. 225.

29th July. General News. *Stowe MSS.*, 55, f. 114. From a letter of Sir Thomas Ferrers to Sir Humphrey Ferrers.

1st August. The Blackwater Fort. *S.P.* Ireland, 202 : pt. ii., 105.

4th August. The Death of Lord Burleigh. *The Life of that great statesman William Cecil, Lord Burghley. . . . Published from the original manuscript wrote soon after his Lordship's death; now in the Library of the right honourable Brownlow, Earl of Exeter*, etc., edited by Arthur Collis, 1732.

The Lord Burleigh's Precepts for his Son. *S.T.C.*, 4897; reprinted in Strype's *Annals*, iv. 340. These observations were not printed until 1617, but such gifts were not meant to lie hid, and it is reasonably probable that they would be discussed at this time. Moreover, there is a 'damnable iteration' about Polonius' 'few precepts.'

THE QUEEN'S GRIEF. Birch's *Memoirs*, ii. 390; from a letter to Essex from Sir William Knollys.

12*th August*. INSUFFICIENT SOLDIERS FROM RADNORSHIRE. *A.P.C.*, xxix. 43.

14*th August*. VICTUALS FOR THE SOLDIERS. *A.P.C.*, xxix. 49.

16*th August*. THE QUEEN AND THE EARL OF ESSEX. Birch's *Memoirs*, ii. 390; approximate date.

22*nd August*. A GREAT DISASTER IN IRELAND. *S.P. Ireland*, 202: pt. iii., 3, 19, 20, 20 (i), 28 (ii). This was the greatest defeat suffered by English troops during the reign.

23*rd August*. A PROCLAMATION AGAINST FORESTALLERS. *Proclamations*, 355.

THE LORD KEEPER'S LETTER TO THE EARL OF ESSEX. Printed in Birch's *Memoirs*, ii. 385, where it is dated 15th October; see note on 2nd July.

THE IRISH FORCES. *A.P.C.*, xxix. 79.

25*th August*. MY LORD OF ESSEX'S LETTER TO THE UNIVERSITY OF CAMBRIDGE. *MSS. Addit.*, 5843, f. 450.

26*th August*. ESSEX'S REPLY TO THE LORD KEEPER. Printed in Birch's *Memoirs*, ii. 386, with the date 18th October. There are several copies in various collections, *e.g.*, *S.P. Dom.*, 268: 43. According to Fynes Moryson (*Itinerary*, MacLehose edition, ii. 316), Bacon, in detailing the charges against Essex at his appearance before the Commissioners on 5th June, 1600, made a special point of this letter, 'which letter he also said was published by the Earles own friends.' From this it would appear likely that both letters were much discussed by the friends—and enemies—of Essex.

THE NEW MARSHAL IN IRELAND. *A.P.C.*, xxix. 104.

27*th August*. NEW FORCES FOR IRELAND. *A.P.C.*, xxix. 94. On a similar occasion Justice Shallow at least tried to do his duty.

TWO PATENTS. *A.P.C.*, xxix. 101, 106.

29*th August*. THE DEFEAT AT THE BLACKWATER. *S.P. Ireland*, 202: pt. iii., 34.

THE FUNERAL OF THE LORD TREASURER. *S.P. Dom.*, 268: 32; Chamberlain's *Letters*, p. 18.

31*st August*. RECUSANTS TO SUPPLY HORSES. *A.P.C.*, xxix. 116.

5*th September*. LIGHTNING IN LONDON. Stow's *Annals*. In Richard Smith's little Diary—*Rerum vulgatorum notae* (Sloane MSS., 414)—the thunder is recorded on 4th and 5th of November.

7*th September*. COURT NEWS. *S.P.Dom.*, 268: 47, 50.

MERES' 'PALLADIS TAMIA.' *A.R.*, iii. 125; *S.T.C.*, 17834; a good specimen of literary ragbag which shows the range of Meres' reading. The English authorities quoted are *The Chronicles of England*, Dr. Playfair, Hugh Broughton, Fox, Lyly, Harington, Capgrave, Pettie, Hakluyt, Greene, Sidney and Warner.

8*th September*. MARSTON'S 'SCOURGE OF VILLAINY.' *A.R.*, iii. 125; *S.T.C.*, 17485. It was reissued in 1599 with an additional satire (*Stultorum plena sunt omnia*), and included in the bonfire of disreputable books on 4th June, 1599; m.e. in *The Bodley Head Quartos*, vol. xiii. 1925. I have tried to suggest the importance of Marston as a melancholic in an *Essay on Elizabethan Melancholy* appended to my edition of Breton's *Melancholic Humours*, 1929.

9th September. LAWLESSNESS NEAR LONDON. *A.P.C.*, xxix. 128, 140; *Proclamations*, 386.

10th September. SOME LEVIES DISCHARGED. *A.P.C.*, xxix. 155, 157.

12th September. THE QUEEN'S LETTER TO THE COUNCIL OF IRELAND. *S.P. Ireland*, 202 : pt. iii., 20 (ii) and 64.

15th September. THE EARL OF ESSEX RESTORED TO FAVOUR. *A.P.C.*, xxix. 154-7; *S.P. Dom.*, 268 : 56; from a letter to Dudley Carleton from Toby Matthew.

'SKIALETHEIA.' *A.R.*, iii. 126; *S.T.C.*, 12504; m.e. by J. P. Collins, 1870, and A. B. Grosart, 1878. The author is identified as E. Guilpin (of whom nothing is known) by passages quoted in *England's Parnassus*. It is an important book for the student, being full of personalities and intimate details, including several references to the theatres.

16th September. JONSON'S 'EVERY MAN IN HIS HUMOUR.' *S.P. Dom.*, 268 : 61; approximate date, fixed by Toby Matthews' letter (see 20th September). First published in Quarto in 1601 (*S.T.C.*, 14756); this edition is of the play as first presented in 1598; m.e. in *The Oxford Ben Jonson*, edited by C. H. Herford and P. Simpson, 1927, vol. iii. The version of the play usually printed is that revised by Jonson for his Folio of 1616. See note on Chapman's *Humorous Day's Mirth*, 11th May, 1597.

20th September. GENERAL NEWS. *S.P. Dom.*, 268 : 61; from Toby Matthews' letter (above). Compare 'Honour pricks me on. Yea, but how if honour prick me off when I come on, how then?' (*I. Henry IV.*, v. i. 131). Shakespeare may have invented this jest, but it is as likely that he was making use of a current phrase (as 'If you knows of a better 'ole, go to it'); after the Islands Voyage military glory began to grow somewhat fusty.

22nd September. A PLAYER SLAIN. A translation of the indictment is given in F. G. Fleay's *Chronicle of the English Drama*, i. 343; the original is reproduced in *The Oxford Ben Jonson*, by C. H. Herford and P. Simpson, 1925, i. 219. In the *Conversations*, Jonson's version of the affair is that 'since his coming to England being appealed to the fields he had killed his adversarie, which hurt him jn the arme & whose sword was 10 Inches longer than his, for the which he was Emprisoned and almost at the Gallowes. Then took he his Religion by trust of a priest who Visited him jn Prison' (*ibid.* i. 139). For the 'bricklayer' see *Henslowe Papers*, edited by W. W. Greg, p. 48.

30th September. MR. SPENSER TO BE SHERIFF OF CORK. *A.P.C.*, xxix. 204.

2nd October. THE EARL OF CUMBERLAND'S RETURN. Purchas, xvi. 29.

8th October. GENERAL NEWS. Chamberlain's *Letters*, p. 20.

4th October. A MUTINY AMONGST THE LONDON SOLDIERS. *A.P.C.*, xxix. 214.

7th October. MR. HAKLUYT'S 'PRINCIPAL NAVIGATIONS.' *S.T.C.*, 12626; dated in Epistle Dedicatory; m.e. published MacLehose, 1903, reprinted in *The Everyman Library*, 8 vols., 1907, etc.

9th October. Sir Thomas Shirley's Prizes. *Salisbury Papers*, viii. 385.

10th October. A Traitor to be sent away. *A.P.C.*, xxix. 224.

15th October. Yarmouth Herrings. *A.P.C.*, xxix. 230, 245.

28th October. Further Soldiers for Ireland. *A.P.C.*, xxix. 239.

4th November. The Death of the Spanish King. *Calendar of State Papers Venetian*, ix. 727, 731, 732, 737, 738, from the despatches of the Venetian Ambassador in Spain to the Doge. In Richard Smith's Diary (Sloan MSS., 414) the death of the King of Spain is noted between 4th and 12th November ; the news apparently did not reach London before this time.

5th November. Great Floods. *A.P.C.*, xxix. 264.

6th November. Rebellion spreading in Ireland. *S.P. Ireland*, 202 : pt. iii., 3, 127. From a letter to Cecil from the Lord Chief Justice of Munster, dated 26th October.

8th November. Rumours. Chamberlain's *Letters*, p. 26.

A Jest on the King of Spain. *Nugae Antiquae*, i. 175, 244.

9th November. The Conspiracy of Edward Squire. Stow's *Annals* and *A letter written out of England to a gentleman at Padua*, 1599 ; reprinted in Spedding's *Bacon*, ii. 110. Spedding on good grounds attributes the 'letter' to Bacon, who took part in the examinations. The original depositions are preserved in *S.P. Dom.*, 268 : 83, 86, 89 ; of which the official account is a fair summary.

10th November. An Attempt in Dublin. *S.P. Ireland*, 202 : pt. iii., 135. From a letter from the Council of Ireland dated 31st October.

14th November. The Queen royally received. Stow's *Annals*.

15th November. The Soldiers in Ireland. *S.P. Ireland*, 202 : pt. iii., 149.

16th November. Beacon Watches discontinued. *A.P.C.*, xxix. 288.

17th November. Determinations for Ireland. *S.P. Ireland*, 202 : pt. iii., 162.

20th November. The Execution of Luke Hutton. Approximate date, from the ballad *Luke Hutton's Lamentation* (m.e. by A. V. Judges in *The Elizabethan Underworld*, 1930, p. 292) ; *Nugae Antiquae*, ii. 253, and Fuller's *Church History* therein cited. See also p. 70.

28th November. More Soldiers required. *A.P.C.*, xxix. 312.

3rd December. The Desperate State of Ireland. *S.P. Ireland*, 202 : pt. iii., 168, 167.

Plays at Court. *A.P.C.*, xxix. 324 ; *Hens. Diary*, i. 98 ; ii. 190.

5th December. A Loan in the City. *A.P.C.*, xxix. 336, 339.

11th December. An Attempt in the North. *A.P.C.*, xxix. 356.

15th December. Soldiers for Ireland. *S.P. Dom.*, 269 : 12, 16 ; *A.P.C.*, xxix. 358, 388.

18th December. The Thames Frozen. Stow's *Annals*. The brick piles of Old London Bridge were so thick that the flow of the water was considerably retarded. Hence the freezing of the Thames was not infrequent in severe winters, and liable to be an embarrassment, as the force of flow was used to give power to the City corn mills. See *Eliz. Journal*, p. 324.

20*th December*. A DECLARATION CONCERNING THE KING OF SCOTS. *S.P. Dom.*, 269 : 20.

24*th December*. THE LOAN IN THE CITY. *A.P.C.*, xxix. 382, 401.

THE REBELLION IN MUNSTER. *S.P. Ireland*, 202 : pt. iv., 15.

27*th December*. A SKIRMISH IN MUNSTER. *S.P. Ireland*, 202 : pt. iv., 36.

28*th December*. THE THAMES AGAIN FROZEN. Stow's *Annals*.

THE THEATRE PULLED DOWN. The original complaint is quoted in J. O. Halliwell Phillipps' *Outlines of the Life of Shakespeare*, i. 360 ; see also *Elizabethan Stage*, ii. 398. There is some difference of opinion whether the Burbages removed all the timber on this occasion or completed the work on 20th January, 1599.

A LEWD FELLOW. *S.P. Dom.*, 269 : 22.

29*th December*. PRIVILEGED PLACES IN LONDON. *A.P.C.*, xxix. 414.

30*th December*. A PLAY AT CAMBRIDGE. *The Pilgrimage to Parnassus*, etc., edited from MSS. by W. D. Macray, 1886. This play, and more especially the two sequels—*The Return from Parnassus*, parts i. and ii.—are important expressions of the general discontent of university men that their studies neither satisfied the intellect nor led to preferment. Macray misdated the play 1597 ; references to Marston's *Satires* and Bastard's *Chrestoleros* show it to belong to 1598.

31*st December*. NEW PLAYS THIS PAST YEAR AT THE ROSE. This list is taken from Dr. Greg's catalogue of the plays mentioned in *Henslowe's Diary* (ii. 187-199), and is roughly chronological. As it is not possible to deduce from the entries of payments to dramatists and others the date of the first performance of a new play, I thought it best to group the list together. Of the plays mentioned, there only survive in print the two parts of *Robert, Earl of Huntingdon*, *Two angry women of Abingdon*, and *A woman will have her will*.

THESE BOOKS ALSO SET FORTH ANNO 1598.

MR. RICHARD BARNFIELD'S POEMS. *S.T.C.*, 1488 ; m.e. by the Roxburghe Club, 1816.

CHAPMAN'S ADDITIONS TO 'HERO AND LEANDER.' *S.T.C.*, 17414 ; m.e. in *The Works of Christopher Marlowe*, edited by C. F. Tucker Brooke 1910.

ACHILLES' SHIELD. *S.T.C.*, 13632.

FLORIO'S 'WORLD OF WORDS.' *S.T.C.*, 11098.

A BOOK OF PAINTING. *S.T.C.*, 16698. This is an important book for the study of the Elizabethan mind with its adherence to symmetrical systems of thought ; it is a good example of the 'Idols of the Theatre.' It details also the theory and practice of sensual appeal—a subject on which much curious observation was made.

'The Comedy of Mucedorus. *S.T.C.*, 18230. This ridiculous (though quite serious) romantic play is almost a burlesque in anticipation of tragi-comedy of the Beaumont and Fletcher kind. It was most popular with the citizens of London, 17 different editions in Quarto printed before 1670 survive; m.e. in *The Shakespeare Apocrypha*, edited by C. F. Tucker Brooke, 1908.

Norden's 'Speculum Britanniæ.' *S.T.C.*, 18637.

A Book of Riddles. *S.T.C.*, 13174. This is not apparently a first edition, though no earlier is known. It may have been Master Slender's aid to social accomplishment. (*Merry Wives*, I. i. 209)

Mr. Tofte's 'Alba.' *S.T.C.*, 24096. This very long lament is chiefly notable for the well-known reference to *Love's Labours Lost*; m.e. by A. B. Grosart, 1880.

Tyro's Roaring Meg. *S.T.C.*, 24477. A piece of undergraduate exuberance which owes something to Marston.

Mr. Wentworth's 'Pithy Exhortation.' *S.T.C.*, 25245. For Wentworth's offence see *Eliz. Journal*, pp. 201, 202, 243.

APPENDIX

A TABLE OF AGES

It may be an aid to the reader's imagination in visualising the Elizabethan age to note the ages of some of the more interesting men at the date when the *Second Elizabethan Journal* begins. The dates of birth are taken for the most part from the *Dictionary of National Biography*; dates in *italic numerals* are approximate.

OVER SEVENTY

William Cecil, Lord Burleigh, Lord High Treasurer (1520); Thomas Churchyard (*1520*); John Stow (*1525*).

OVER SIXTY

John Whitgift, Archbishop of Canterbury (*1530*); Sir John Hawkins (1532); QUEEN ELIZABETH (1533); Mr. Sergeant Yelverton, Speaker of the House in 1597-8 (*1535*).

OVER FIFTY

Lord Charles Howard, Lord High Admiral (1536); William Byrd (*1538*); Sir Thomas Egerton, Lord Keeper in 1596 (*1540*); Sir Francis Drake (*1540*); The Earl of Tyrone (*1540*); Thomas Deloney (*1543*); Nicholas Breton (*1545*); Thomas Bodley (*1545*).

OVER FORTY

George Carey, Lord Hunsdon, Lord Chamberlain in 1597 (1547); Sir John Norris (*1547*); Sir Walter Ralegh (*1552*); Richard Hakluyt (*1552*); Edmund Spenser (*1552*); Sir Edward Coke, Attorney-General (1552); John Lyly (*1554*); Richard Hooker (1554); Lancelot Andrews (1555).

IN THE THIRTIES

George Clifford, Earl of Cumberland (1558); Thomas Lodge (*1558*); George Peele (*1558*); George Chapman (*1559*); Sir Francis Vere (1560); Francis Bacon (1561); Lord Thomas Howard (1561); John Harington (1561); Robert Southwell (*1561*); Samuel Daniel (1562); Michael Drayton (1563); Charles Blount, Lord Mountjoy (1563); Sir Robert Cecil, Principal Secretary (*1563*); Henry Percy, Earl of Northumberland (1564); William Shakespeare (1564); Sir Anthony Shirley (1565).

IN THE TWENTIES

King James VI. (1566); Robert Devereux, Earl of Essex (*1566*); Edward Alleyne (1566); Thomas Nashe (1567); Richard Burbage

(*1567*); Barnabe Barnes (*1569*); John Davies (1569); Thomas Dekker (*1570*); Henry Wriothesley, Earl of Southampton (1573); John Donne (1573); Benjamin Jonson (*1573*); Joseph Hall (1574); John Marston (1574).

UNDER TWENTY

Roger Manners, Earl of Rutland (1576); Robert Burton (1577); John Fletcher (1579); John Webster (1580); Francis Beaumont (1584); George Wither (1588); Robert Herrick (1591); Prince Henry, afterwards Prince of Wales (1594).

A LAST
ELIZABETHAN JOURNAL

1599-1603

1599

3rd January. COURT NEWS.

The Earl of Essex now prepares with all diligence for Ireland, and it were more than time he were there, for the rebels are grown so bold that not long since they fetched away the Archbishop of Dublin's cattle out of his yard close by St. Patrick's Church in the suburbs of Dublin.

One Peter Browne, a French post, is clapt up in the Gatehouse for juggling with the French ambassador's letters, who complains that his master's letters and his are usually opened before they come at them.

It was expected that the Lord Treasurership should have been bestowed on the Lord Buckhurst for a New Year's gift, but it succeeded not; so that he must tarry the time, and it may light on him on the sudden when he doth least look for it, according to the custom of the Court that commonly knows not overnight what shall be done in the morning.

4th January. OPINIONS CONCERNING THE IRISH EXPEDITION.

Opinions upon the Irish expedition are diversely given. There are some who would urgently dissuade my Lord of Essex from this Irish expedition, declaring that his absence would exulcerate the Queen's mind whereby it would not be possible for him to carry himself so as to give her sufficient contentment; nor for her to carry herself so as to give him sufficient countenance. The Irish are such an enemy as the ancient Gauls or Britons or Germans were, yet the Romans (who had such discipline to govern their soldiers and the whole world in a manner to levy them), when they came to deal with enemies which placed their natural felicity only in liberty and the sharpness of the sword and had the natural elemental advantages of woods and bogs and hardness of bodies, they ever found they had their hands full of them. They conclude therefore that his going over with such expectation as he hath, and through the churlishness of the enterprise not able to answer it, will mightily diminish his reputation, foreseeing his overthrow, chained as it were by destiny to this journey.

Others say that my Lord of Essex goeth not forth to serve the Queen's realm but to humour his own revenge. Two or three of the Lord Mountjoy's kindred are being sent out in the army; they are to report all his conduct at home. If my Lord perform in the field what he hath promised in the Council, all will be well; but though the Queen hath granted him forgiveness for his demeanour in her presence, we know not what to think hereof. She hath in all outward semblance placed confidence in the man who so lately sought other treatment at her hands: yet some sore fear what may happen hereafter. If the old Lord Treasurer had lived longer, matters would go on surer. He was our great pilot on whom all cast their eyes and sought their safety. The Queen doth often speak of him in tears and turn aside when he is discoursed of; nay, even forbiddeth any mention to be made of his name in the Council.

5th January. ENGLISH PRISONERS RELEASED.

Of late there came to Dartmouth a hulk of 400 tons burden, laden with salt from Lisbon, bringing in her 90 English prisoners lately discharged from prison there.

6th January. BACKWARDNESS IN THE CITY.

There is much backwardness amongst the citizens that have been nominated to furnish the money required at this time by her Majesty, and amongst them divers of good and sufficient ability which by their example of undutifulness do make others the more perverse. These are now summoned to make their appearance before the Council.

7th January. SOLDIERS FROM THE LOW COUNTRIES FOR IRELAND.

Sir William Knollys is despatched to the Low Countries with 2,000 men levied in England in exchange for 2,000 old soldiers that shall be conducted to Ireland by Sir Henry Docwra; they shall be taken, 1,400 from the companies of Sir Francis Vere that are in the field, and 600 from Sir Edward Norris and the garrison of Ostend; and if there be any want in the numbers they shall be supplied out of Sir Robert Sidney's garrison at Flushing.

9th January. HINDRANCES TO TRADE WITH FRANCE.

Master Edmonds, the ambassador in France, reporteth that the French have a mind, now that they have made peace with Spain, to restrain the import of foreign manufactures to raise better their own. At first it was intended only to exclude silk as being rather an expense than a necessity, but since some would have all manufactures excluded to set their people to work and to keep their money in the country, and that a revenue might be had from tolerations granted to particular persons. To the ambassador's complaint, it was answered that seeing the afflicted state of the French people it is needful to restore their manufacturers by the same measures used by other countries and ourselves. It appears also that they are incensed by the continual complaints made by their merchants which are not satisfied.

10th January. HORSE FOR IRELAND.

One hundred horsemen with their horses are now required for Ireland, to be taken from the counties of Norfolk, Kent, Suffolk and Essex. They shall be armed with curats, open head-pieces or casques, and long pistols, and apparelled with long horsemen's coats of good strong cloth of orange tawny colour, trimmed with white lace.

11th January. NASHE'S 'LENTEN STUFF.'

There is a book of Nashe to be printed called *Nashe's Lenten Stuff*, written in praise of the red herring and of Yarmouth where he set up his staff after the troubles of the *Isle of Dogs*. Amongst many other things, complaineth that the lawyers wrested his words to a wrong meaning ; for, quoth he, 'He that shall have his lines bandied by our usual plodders in Fitzherbert, let him not care whether they be right or wrong ; for they will writhe and turn them as they list, and make the author believe he meant that which he never did mean ; and, for a knitting up conclusion, his credit is unreprievably lost that on bare suspicion in such cases shall but have his name controverted amongst them ; and if I should fall into their hands I would be pressed to death for obstinate silence and never seek to clear myself, for it is in vain, since both they will confound a man's memory with their tedious babbling, and in the first three words of his Apology with impudent exclamations interrupt him, whereas their mercenary tongues (lie they never so loudly) without check or control must have their free passage for five hours together.'

17th January. Court News.

The Earl of Essex's journey for Ireland is somewhat prolonged, for his victuallers that had order to make their provisions for February are now put over till March. He shall carry a great troup of gallants with him, if all go that are spoken of, as the Earls of Derby, Rutland and Southampton; the Lords Windsor, Grey, Audley and Cromwell, besides Knights sans number. Many that wish well to the journey have no great conceit of it, seeing so many raw youths press for the greatest charge. The Duke of Florence hath barred our nation from traffic in his territories, and it is feared the Venetians and French King will serve us in the same sort. The Queen is very angry with Sir Thomas Gerrard for the escape of one Blackwell, an archpriest, out of the Marshalsea.

The news now comes very hot that Sebastian King of Portugal, that was said to be slain in the battle in Barbary in 1578, is now at Venice and hath made so good trial of himself that the Venetians allow him, and maintain almost fourscore persons about him at their charge. They say he tells very strange stories, how he with fourteen more escaped from the battle and got up into the mountains, and so by many adventures, he went and he went until he came into Ethiopia, or Prester John's land, meaning from thence to have gone into the East Indies; but understanding that they were yielded and sworn to the King of Spain, durst not proceed, but turned back again, and *per tot discrimina* in this long pilgrimage (wherein he hath been taken, bought and sold twelve or fourteen times) got at last to Venice, where he tells them all that was negotiated betwixt him and them by letters or ambassadors, since he was of any good remembrance, and that with so many particulars as are thought infallible testimonies. Besides it is said that his confessor is come out of Portugal, and upon conference with him avoweth all to be true that he saith, touching what passed between them in confession, both at other times, and specially the day before the battle.

20th January. The Death of Edmund Spenser.

Master Edmund Spenser is dead at Westminster on the 16th of this month and is interred in the Collegiate Church near to Chaucer at the charge of the Earl of Essex, his hearse being attended by poets, and mournful elegies and poems with the pens that wrote them thrown into his tomb. Mr. Spenser was by birth a Londoner, and a scholar also of the University of Cambridge, born under so favourable an aspect of the Muses that he surpassed all the English poets of former times, not excepting Chaucer himself, his fellow citizen; but by a fate which still followeth poets, he wrested always with poverty, though he had been Secretary to the Lord Grey, Lord Deputy of Ireland. For scarce had he there settled in a retired privacy and got leisure to write, when he is by the rebels thrown out of his dwelling, plundered of his goods, and returned into England a poor man, less than a month since.

21st January. Deserters at Bristol.

Great distress is reported amongst the companies at Bristol that remain waiting for a favourable passage to Ireland by reason that they have caused a great scarcity of victuals there. Moreover many of them have deserted, so that the Mayor of Bristol is commanded to supply their defective numbers from among the very many loose and idle persons in and about that city.

26th January. 'A Woman's Worth.'

Mr. Anthony Gibson hath sent to the press a book by one of his friends translated from the French, written by a Lord of great reckoning, and by him given to a very honourable Duchess. This work is entitled *A woman's worth*, defended against all the men in the world, proving them to be more perfect, excellent and absolute in all virtuous actions than any man of what quality soever; written by one that hath heard much, seen much, but knows a great deal more. The book is dedicated to the Countess of Southampton, Mistress Anne Russell, Mistress Margaret Ratcliffe and Mistress Mary Fitton and the rest of her Majesty's Maids of Honour.

28th January. Irish News.

From Ireland the Earl of Ormond complaineth of the cold disposition of the Lords Justices to second him, always protracting the service upon excuses. Of late in the victualling of the fort of Maryborough my Lord took with him 700 foot and 140 horse, which the rebels would have hindered in their passage, presenting a battle of 1,200 foot besides many wings of shot and 30 horse, of whom not less than 200 were killed or hurt, with some of the chiefest men.

29th January. SIR RICHARD BINGHAM DEAD.

Sir Richard Bingham is dead in Dublin, having been very sickly since his arrival but two months ago, to the great loss of her Majesty's service, for his life and presence would have been a great daunt to the traitors. In Leinster the rebels grow daily in number. Great disorder groweth amongst the captains and soldiers, for the apparel which was delivered proved insufficient. Hereupon the Lords Justices would have issued 60 suits to each company for the furnishing of such soldiers that were in most want. But the captains and soldiers would none of it, whereof the soldiers are in great nakedness and like to mutiny.

30th January. SILVER'S 'PARADOXES OF DEFENCE.'

There is a treatise written by Mr. George Silver, which he dedicateth to my Lord of Essex, entitled *Paradoxes of Defence*, to prove our English weapons altogether fitter than the Italian, for if we will have true defence, we must seek it where it is, in short swords, short staves, the half pike, partisans, gleves, or such like weapons of perfect length, but not in long swords, long rapiers, nor frog pricking poniards. Hath many merry tales of those Italians that have set up as Masters of Fence in our time. As of Signor Rocco, that was challenged to fight with his long sword against one Austin Bagger, an Englishman, with sword and buckler; and the said Bagger, having closed with him, stroke up his heels and cut him over the breech, and trod upon him, and most grievously hurt him under his feet. There was also Signior Vincentio whom Mr. Silver and his brother challenged to play with them on a scaffold at the Bell Savage, but he would not. This same Vincentio being challenged by an English Master of Defence at Wells, he answered him 'By God, me scorn to play with thee.' With that word of scorn the Master of Defence was very much moved, and up with his great English fist, and stroke Signior Vincentio such a box on the ear that he fell over and over, his legs just against a buttery hatch whereon stood a great blackjack. The Master of Defence, fearing the worst against Vincentio's rising, catched the blackjack into his hand: but Vincentio, laying his hand on his dagger, with the other pointed with his finger, saying, 'Very well: I will cause to lie in the jail for this gear, one, two, three, four years.' Next day meeting this Master of Defence, Vincentio said, 'You remember how misused-a me yesterday; you were to blame, me be an excellent man, me teach you how to thrust two foot further than any Englishman,' and with that took him to a mercer's shop where he bought two dozen of best silken points.

31st January. SIR FRANCIS VERE REBUKED.

The Council have rebuked Sir Francis Vere because that of those 2,000 men sent from the Low Countries for Ireland not one was from his own regiment, but rather from the cautionary towns of Flushing and Brille. Moreover instead of sending entire companies with their officers he hath drawn away parcels of companies and given the preferment to others, especially to some of his own regiment; and besides there was no good choice made of serviceable men, as if Sir Francis would serve his own turn.

9th February. 'A NEW BOOK OF GOOD HUSBANDRY.'

Mr. George Churchey, fellow of Lion's Inn, hath caused to be translated and printed in English that treatise of James Dubravius called *A New book of good husbandry*, containing the order and manner of making of fishponds, with the breeding, preserving and multiplying of the carp, tench, pike and trout, and divers other kinds of fresh fish.

10th February. SCANDALS CONCERNING LADY COKE.

There are rumours that Master Edward Coke, the Attorney General, hath been notoriously cozened by the Lady Hatton, whom he married in November last. A servant of the Countess of Warwick declareth openly that he was lately sent with a message to Lady Hatton from his lady; and knocking upon the chamber door a gentlewoman came and told him that he could not speak with Lady Hatton as she was newly brought to bed with a son. Further that she was forward with child when she was married, and no marvel that Master Attorney wept sitting with the Judges, for he has gone up and down ever since his marriage like a dead man; that the child was by one of her servants who was sent away with a piece of money.

15th February. COURT RUMOURS.

Our provisions for Ireland go forward with leaden feet, and the Earl of Essex's commission is still not signed. The jars between my Lord and the Lord Admiral continue as they did, if not worse, by daily renewing, and our music runs so much upon discords that small harmony is like to be made in the end.

18th February. MORE MEN FOR IRELAND.

Notwithstanding that 3,000 men were of late demanded from the counties for service in Ireland, there are now to be levied a further 2,000. The choice is to be made of sufficient and serviceable men, not admitting any rogues or other idle and loose persons, wherein extraordinary pains are to be taken by the Justices to attend the service in person, and not to commit the charge (as the usual manner is) to the constables and other meaner officers. Of those men in each 100, there shall be 30 pikes armed with gorgets, curats and murrions, 30 muskets, 30 calivers and the rest short weapons. Moreover the men shall be provided of good lined coats of some strong cloth and sufficiently furnished of other apparel, and not sent out so naked that many times they are constrained to abandon their service, being more consumed by want than by the enemy.

19th February. A STRANGE AND MIRACULOUS ACCIDENT.

A very strange and miraculous accident is reported from Purmerend in the Netherlands, one which may indeed be taken as one of those signs and tokens in the Sun and Moon, monstrous births and strange marvellous things that betoken the coming of the latter day. In this city of Purmerend a certain virtuous woman, the wife of one John Martinson, being big with child and within eight days of her delivery, the child was heard to cry in her womb so loudly that the father, looking about thought it to be one of their other children. On New Year's Even the woman was delivered of her child, not monstrous or misshapen, but a well shaped man child and of a right human figure with all his limbs ; but being a week old and above it began to grow grievous sick and at last lay with such faintness that the father, thinking it had been dead, said, 'Alas, it is done.' But being returned to itself again, at night about seven of the clock the 13th of January, and casting up his eyes to heaven and thrusting out his arms and fists through anguish, it spake these words three times : 'O my God ; O my God ; O my God' ; which words were spoken with such distinction that between each time one might have spoken two or three words. This was done in the presence of the father and the mother and two other women.

The child growing sicker about two in the morning mumbled certain other words, amongst which were understood that he said, 'Aye me. Aye me. Aye me' ; but how often it is not remembered.

21st February. A History of Henry The Fourth.

There is newly come forth a book called *The First part of the life and reign of King Henry the IIII*, extending to the end of the first year of his reign, written by Dr. John Hayward, treating principally of the deposition and death of King Richard the Second. The dedication is to my Lord of Essex, with an Epistle in Latin in these terms : Ἀρίστῳ και γενναιοτάτῳ, optimo & Nobilissimo (inquit *Euripides*) ex qua sententia tu primus ac solus fere occurrebas (illustrissime comes) cuius nomen si Henrici nostri fronti radiaret, ipse & lætior & tutior in vulgus prodiret. Magnus siquidem es, & presenti iudicio, & futuri temporis expectatione : in quo, veluti recuperasse nunc oculos, cæca prius fortuna videri potest : Dum cumulare honoribus eum gestit, qui omnibus virtutibus est insignitus. Hunc igitur si læta fronte excipere digneris, sub nominis tui vmbra (tanquam sub *Aiacis* clipio *Teucer* ille *Homericus*) tutissime latebit. Deus opt. max. celsitudinem tuam nobis, reique publicæ diu seruet incolumem : quo nos vz. tam fide quam armis potenti tua dextra defensi, vltique, diutina, cum securitate tum gloria perfruamur.' To which there is added an epistle of 'A. P. to the Reader' concerning the profitable nature of the faithful records of history.

1st March. General News.

The Earl of Essex is crazed at the delays, but whether more in body or mind is doubtful. Things do not succeed as he would wish them but new difficulties arise daily about his commission as touching the time of his abode, his entertainment, the disposing of places and offices, upon which points and some others he is so little satisfied that many times he makes it a question whether he go or not.

On Saturday last Sir William Woodhouse, accompanied with four hacksters, understanding that Sir Robert Drury was to come from Tottenham towards London, waited for him in the way, and set upon him as he was coming out of his coach, wounding him in three or four places; and thinking they had dispatched him, left him for dead. But it falls out better with him, for he is like to recover; his man that offered himself in his master's defence was slain outright in the place. Upon the first alarm at Court there was commandment from the Council for a privy search to apprehend them, but within two hours it was countermanded.

We are still fed with rumours of Don Sebastian that he is *ipsissimus*, and that the Venetians have sent ambassadors to the King of Spain to signify so much to him; and that there have been some great men executed of late in Portugal about this business.

This new treatise of *Henry the Fourth* is the work of a young man of Cambridge, toward the Civil Law. There hath been much descanting about it, why such a story should come out at this time, and many exceptions taken, especially to the Epistle; commandment is now made that it shall be cut out of the book.

6th March. A Discourse of Marriage and Wiving.

One R. T. hath done into English two discourses *Of Marriage and Wiving*, the first by Hercules Tasso, the philosopher, declaiming against it; the second by that famous poet and orator Torquato Tasso answering the first and declaring that it is good to take a wife and that marriage is both honourable and necessary.

A verse upon wiving from the first:

Friend, marry when thou please, yet shalt thou find
Thy wife bad always ; and but use her ill
And she is worse ; but use her well and kind
She is worser then, and so continue will.
Yet is she good if she but once would die ;
But better if she packed before thyself ;
But best of all if she went speedily
Leaving behind to thee her hoarded wealth.

pit rem nam pit rem
Qui ca vxo poe ca atque dolo
ret re na ret re

8th March. A Spanish Ship Burnt.

From Plymouth comes news that a ship of Sir Ferdinando Gorges encountered a Spanish ship of 500 tons at the Rock, which had been discharged of the greater part of her ordnance and was to be made ready to go to St. John de Porto Rico. She had in her some 60 small shot, who by reason of the greatness of the ship, lying so high above, beat back our men with loss of seven upon their first entry. After this the mariners could not by any means be drawn to enter her afresh ; wherefore the captain was enforced to lay his sides unto hers, and so battered her until at last she was ready to sink. The enemy perceiving this cried for mercy, and so after expense of 164 shot of the demiculverin and saker, they took her. All the Spaniards that were left alive were set on shore and the ship burnt before their faces.

13th March. A Petition of the Merchants Trading in Italy.

The merchants trading in Italy have petitioned Sir Robert Cecil that the demands of the messenger come from Italy may be kindly and acceptably answered, and restitution made of the Venetians' goods, otherwise the Venetians will fall to seizing our ships and goods, and their example will draw on the Duke of Florence to oppress all the English ships in his ports. Hereby shall our traffic in all the Straits be brought to an end, and no employment left for English ships of any burden.

15th March. GENERAL NEWS.

The Earl of Essex's great commission for Ireland was despatched on the 12th and he hath all his demands, the Queen showing herself very gracious and willing to content him ; only the clause of liberty to return at pleasure is not inserted in the patent but must pass under the Broad Seal itself. He gives out that he will be gone the 19th of this month and all things are hasted accordingly. There be fourscore horse laid at every post twixt London and Chester, and so to Holyhead for him and his followers, and as many by way of Bristol. The Earls of Southampton and Rutland (who hath lately married the Countess of Essex's daughter by Sir Philip Sidney), and the Lords Grey, Audley and Cromwell do accompany him and Sir Christopher Blount is named Marshal of Ireland, though the Queen had a good meaning to Sir Harry Brounker. The whole force is said to be 16,000 foot and 1,400 horse, yet when they come to the poll they may fall far short.

18th March. THE PRISONERS IN THE TOWER.

Of late the liberty of access unto such persons as are not close prisoners in the Tower hath been abused insomuch that some repair thither at undue seasons and sometimes stay after the gates be shut. Hereafter none shall be permitted to stay with any prisoner in the Tower either in his chamber or in any retired place there at the time of dinner, or supper, or divine services unless it be in the presence of the Governor. Nor shall any other than a preacher, physician, apothecary or chirurgeon be permitted to repair to the prisoners save between the hours of 8 and 11 of the clock in the forenoon, and between 1 and 4 of the clock in the afternoon.

20th March. THE SCOTTISH PLEDGES' DESPERATION.

Those Scots that are kept as pledges in the castle at York of late made a very desperate attempt to escape, but one of the Council having some foreknowledge conferred with the gaoler and set one Canby (that was in prison about the killing of a man) to spy upon the Scots. Hereby their plot was laid open so that when they brake forth from a window at nine o'clock at night and leapt to the ground, the gaoler with his men was ready for them and pursued them, some into the water at the Castle dyke.

All were taken without hurt, save that the Laird of Whitto brake his leg.

25th March. Spanish Preparations.

There is arrived at Plymouth a small bark from St. John de Luce, the master whereof reporteth that at the passage and thereabouts in Biscay there are twelve great ships making ready to go to Ferrol. There is proclamation also that no ships of any port in Biscay shall go this year for the Newfoundland for that the King shall have cause to employ all mariners.

27th March. The Earl of Essex's Instructions.

My Lord of Essex at his departure is instructed upon his arrival in Ireland to assemble the Council and require to be informed of the state of that kingdom and the strength of the rebels. The army and people shall be instructed and contained in the exercise and service of God, and the bishops and ministers called to account. He shall check the abuse of false certificates whereby the bands have been continually filled up with Irishry in such sort as commonly the third person in one band hath not been English, and the Irish have run away with their arms to the traitor. Great care also is to be taken that ordnance and powder be not wasted, nor extraordinary sums of money paid away. My Lord shall not confer the honour of knighthood upon any that do not deserve it by some notorious service or who have not in possession or reversion sufficient living. Moreover if Tyrone shall make means to be received into the Queen's mercy, he shall not be received except upon simple and single submission.

To-day the Queen granted licence to my Lord to return to her Majesty's presence at such times as he shall find cause.

The Departure of the Earl of Essex for Ireland.

This day about 2 o'clock in the afternoon the Earl of Essex, Vicegerent of Ireland, took horse at his house in Seeding Lane, and from thence accompanied with divers noblemen and many others, himself very plainly attired, rode through Grace Street, Cornhill, Cheapside and other high streets, in all which places and in the fields the people pressed exceedingly to behold him, especially in the high ways, for more than four miles' space, crying out, 'God save your Lordship, God preserve your honour'; and some followed him until the evening only to behold him. When he and his company came forth from London, the sky was very calm and clear, but before he could get past Islington, there arose a great black cloud in the north-east, and suddenly came lightning and thunder with a great shower of hail and rain, which some do hold as an ominous prodigy.

28th March. A PRAYER FOR MY LORD OF ESSEX'S GOOD SUCCESS.

Mr. John Norden hath composed *A prayer for the prosperous proceedings and good success of the Earl of Essex and his companies*, moving us to prayer for that it concerneth every man to pray for the good of such as the Prince hath appointed for the restoration of the peace of God's Church and quiet of our realm by the suppressing of the violence and quenching of the fury of that bloody Tyrone and his rebellious adherents in Ireland: for God is a jealous God and holdeth no man guiltless that maketh no conscience of his brother's dangers.

CHURCHYARD'S 'FORTUNATE FAREWELL.'

At the departing of my Lord of Essex Mr. Thomas Churchyard hath written a poem called *The Fortunate Farewell to the most forward and noble Earl of Essex*, which is dedicated to Lord Harry Seymour. Saith he:

A traitor must, be taught to know his king,
When Mars shall march, with shining sword in hand,
A craven cock, cries creak and hangs down wing,
Will run about, the shrape and dare not stand,
When cocks of game, comes in to give a blow;
So false Tyrone, may faint when he would fight,
Though now aloud, on dunghill doth he crow,
Traitors want heart, and often takes the flight:
When rebels see, they are surprised by troth,
Pack hence in haste, away the rebels goeth.

31st March. A PROCLAMATION CONCERNING THE ARMY FOR IRELAND.

The Queen at this sending over her army into Ireland hath made proclamation denying that apprehension put into the rebels by their leaders that their nation shall be utterly extirpated and rooted out, and conquest made of their country. Herein it is declared, 'We do profess hereby to the world, that we are so far from any such purpose as the very name of conquest in this case seemeth so absurd to us, as we cannot imagine upon what ground it could enter into any man's conceit that our actions tending only to reduce a number of unnatural and barbarous rebels, and to root out the capital heads of the most notorious traitors, should need any such title of conquest when we have in that kingdom (to our great content) the best part of our nobility, the people of all our good towns, and divers of our subjects so assured in their loyalty to us as they give us no suspicion of falling from their duties.' Whereupon all subjects that are revolted from their duty are required to bethink themselves betimes of the extreme misery whereinto they shall throw themselves if by persisting in this rebellion they give cause to use against them the last, but worst of all remedies, the sword. Wherefore choice has been made of such a person to be in the Realm as minister of justice and mercy, whose wisdom, valour and success in other public actions may be a just terror to the wicked in making them see before their eyes the short and desperate end of their barbarous and unnatural courses and may sufficiently assure dutiful subjects there of the abundance of her Majesty's clemency and gracious disposition to those that shall deserve mercy, and of her resolution to make the obstinate enemies to God and traitors to her Crown and dignity to feel her powerful arm.

2nd April. 'THE FOUNTAIN OF ANCIENT FICTION.'

There hath been translated out of the Italian by Mr. Richard Linche a book entitled *The fountain of ancient fiction* wherein is lively depictured the images and statues of the gods of the Ancients, with their proper and particular expositions. Noteth also what is related of their gods by ancient writers.

3rd April. MR. BODLEY'S LIBRARY.

From Oxford it is said that Mr. Bodley's Library costs him more money than he expected because the timber works of the house were rotten and had to be new made.

5th April. A Skirmish in Ireland.

In Ireland Captain Marshall that had the command of the fort of Maryborough was by some of his own company trained forth, himself with four others slain, and the traitors ready to seize the fort. The Earl of Ormond thereupon set forth to its relieving, and though the rebels had made trenches and sconces to stop his passage he made his way through with no more loss than 10 slain and 13 hurt but of the traitors 160. In these last nine weeks more than 800 of the rebels have been slain or executed.

8th April. Hill's 'School of Skill.'

Mr. Thomas Hill at his death left behind a mathematical treatise called *The School of Skill* in two books, the first of the sphere, of the stars, of their orbs, and of the earth; the second of the spherical elements. Showeth that the heaven hath a round form and is carried circularly, and that the earth abideth fixed and unmovable in the centre about the ex-tree of the world, which by several reasons is manifest. For every grave or heavy matter is by nature carried after a most straight line unto the centre and there resteth upon the upper face of the earth, and were it not for the fastness of the earth they should so long be carried downwards until they came unto the centre itself. Moreover it is evident that if the earth should be moved or carried it would by necessity be drawn in right or circular motion, when (by reason that it is the heaviest of all things) it should by its swiftness move before all other things, and then should the living creatures and other things fastened to it be left hanging behind in the air.

14th April. 'Nosce Teipsum.'

Mr. John Davies hath written a long poem entitled *Nosce Teipsum* which oracle is expounded in two elegies, the first of human knowledge; the second of the soul of man and the immortality thereof.

Of the Difficulty of Knowledge.

And yet alas, when all our lamps are burn'd,
Our bodies wasted, and our spirits spent;
When we have all the learned volumes turn'd,
Which yield men's wits both help and ornament,

What can we know? or what can we discern?
When *Error* chokes the windows of the mind,
The divers forms of things, how can we learn,
That have been ever from our birthday blind?

15th April. NEWS FROM SPAIN.

There is news of great preparations of the galleys in Spain; the twelve new galleons in Biscay are almost finished, and at the Groin great quantities of wheat have come in French and Scottish ships, also great treasure from the Indians.

20th April. A PLAY OF KING HENRY THE FIFTH.

Shakespeare hath written a play of *The Life of King Henry the Fifth*, which the Lord Chamberlain's men play at the Curtain, showing the siege of Harfleur and the battle of Agincourt, together with King Harry's wooing of Katharine of France; but Sir John Falstaffe is seen no more for he is sick and dieth of a broken heart because that the King had rejected him. Yet Ancient Pistol liveth, to be well cudgelled in France, where one Captain Fluellen enforceth him to consume a Welsh leek.

26th April. THE EARL OF ESSEX IN DUBLIN.

My Lord of Essex landed in Dublin on the 14th of the month, having had a rough and dangerous passage. Upon their landing the Admiral and the Vice-Admiral (which were the *Popinjay* and the *Charell*) wherein all the Queen's treasure was, having all their sails up and full were like to stem each other but with much ado and by God's goodness escaped.

30th April. THE SPANIARDS OUTSIDE PLYMOUTH.

Four days since some fisher boats at the mouth of the harbour at Plymouth were chased by two Spanish galleys and one taken and sunk. Whereby it appeareth that they lie there for intelligence. They of Plymouth complain that the fort is ill furnished with men, and if they must needs themselves defend the fort their town will be too weak, especially in the summer time when their ships are at Newfoundland.

1st May. AN APOLOGY FOR DARRELL.

There is published, but without his knowledge, a little treatise entitled *A brief apology concerning the possession of William*

Somers, written by Master Darrell, with a dedication to the Lord Keeper, Sir John Popham, Lord Chief Justice, Sir William Periam, and other judges. The main point of the controversy is whether Somers was possessed and dispossessed, yea or no; and, whether when he confessed that he had but counterfeited possession, his confession was not wrought by the threats of Satan and his instruments in the shape of a black dog, a mouse and an ass. This writer complaineth that it hath been given out for this year past that all is counterfeit and Darrell a cosener as if he had been deliberately heard, the witnesses on both sides indifferently heard, and sentence in fine judicially and solemnly pronounced; yet in very truth the matter dependeth undecided. Endeth the epistle with this note: 'Enquire whether this royal law doth not bind a Bishop: *Nullus liber homo capiatur vel imprisonetur etc. Nulli vendemus, nulli negabimus, aut differemus iustitiam aut rectum.* Magna Carta Cap. 29.'

12th May. THE DUNKIRK PIRATES.

From Hull there are great complaints of the Dunkirkers. Four or five ships that have come home have been ransacked of all that they had and the like has been used to Flemings and Englishmen. These pirates put the whole country in fear about the Spurn Head and Flamborough, and chase the ships of Hull going to Newcastle for coals or to Berwick with corn into the Humber's mouth and upon the shore. They have done more mischief and are like to do much more for they take out of the ships such masters as they think good and force them to be pilots along these Northern coasts.

16th May. THE NEW LORD TREASURER.

Sir Thomas Sackville, Lord Buckhurst, is advanced to be Lord Treasurer, and Sir John Popham is made of the Privy Council.

19th May. CATHOLIC TROUBLES.

Of late years, ever since the death of Cardinal Allen in '94, there have been continual stirs amongst our English Catholics, not only in the English College at Rome but also at Wisbeach, among the prisoners there, which arose by reason that the secular priests opposed the domination of the Jesuits. Certain of the leading priests in England thereupon wrote to Rome petitioning that some order might be made amongst them, which matter the Pope referred to the Cardinal Cajetan, protector of the English seminary, one with whom Parsons the Jesuit had especial friendship and familiarity. So one Blackwell is made Archpriest of England, a man not a Jesuit himself, but wholly under the Jesuits. When the secular priests heard of it, they conferred together and resisted Blackwell, for seeing that his appointment was not warranted by any brief of the Pope but only by the Cardinal, they feared some false practise by Parsons. So two of their number contrary to the wish of Blackwell were sent to Rome about the end of last year, where by Parsons' practises they were cast into prison, and after a time banished into divers provinces. Then was a brief sent from Rome, which is now received, confirming the appointment of Blackwell, with whom the secular priests are now reconciled.

25th May. The French King and his Queen.

In Paris there is much talk that the French King goeth about to divorce his Queen that he may marry the Duke of Florence's niece, but that the Duke hath made a cold answer, saying that once before the King made the same motion, but afterwards falling in liking with Madame Gabrielle he left it, having drawn some loan of money from the Duke upon that pretence. In the mean time not to be utterly destitute the King causeth Mademoiselle D'Entragues his new favourite to follow his progress, to whom he assigneth 500 crowns a month for her charges.

26th May. The Trial of Mr. Darrell.

This day Mr. John Darrell was again examined at Lambeth before the Ecclesiastical Commissioners concerning the casting out of devils that he was said to have wrought, when it was alleged that he had taught the possessed persons to counterfeit, which he very vehemently denied. Whereupon it was shown that some of the persons had confessed that they had counterfeited possession at Darrell's persuasion. Darrell answered that in the case of the boy Darling his confession was forced from him by hard usage and threatenings, and the counterfeiting of sundry letters; nor could the things that he did have been counterfeited. Mr. Darrell's friends complain greatly that the

Lord Bishop of London refuseth him fair hearing, denying him copies of the depositions, and neglecting to call Darling, though present, that he might accuse Mr. Darrell to his face.

28*th May*. SPANISH PREPARATIONS.

One lately come prisoner from Spain declareth that there are great preparations at the Groin, the men working day and night, Sundays and holidays; and likewise at other ports ships are preparing to the number of 200. There are soldiers billeted at every farmer's house for 30 leagues round the Groin, and 10,000 Romans are come to man the fleet, and 300 pieces of ordnance from Italy. They expect to come to Brest and there have 10,000 Frenchmen, and stay there till they have opportunity to come for England. They speak with great joy in those parts of the Earl of Essex being in Ireland with the best soldiers that England yields.

31*st May*. SIR WALTER RALEGH MADE WARDEN OF THE STANNARIES.

Sir Walter Ralegh being newly made Warden of the Stannaries is requested to give favourable usage to the tinners, he having divers times represented their grievances. Of late years merchants and dealers in tin have used the poor tinners hardly by driving them to borrow money on deep interest and under great forfeiture. The Queen is now resolved by virtue of her prerogative reserved in the tinners' charters, to take into her hands as much tin of Cornwall as has usually been exported and sell it, but giving better conditions to the poor tinners. Sir Walter shall therefore call to him six able tinners out of each of the four courts and let them know that the merchants crossed her purpose to establish reasonable payments for tin. Now therefore he shall agree with the tinners to take the tin at a reasonable price, never to be brought lower whatever the selling price of tin may be, and thus to free them from usury, pay for the tin and advance them money without interest before they bring their tin to the coinage.

4*th June*. CERTAIN BOOKS BURNT.

This day in the Hall of the Company of Stationers certain lewd and satirical books were by order of his Grace of Canterbury publicly burnt, being *Pygmalion*, *The Scourge of Villainy*,

Skialetheia, the *Snarling Satires*, Davies' *Epigrams* with Marlowe's *Elegies*, the book against women called *Of Marriage and Wiving*, *The XV Joys of Marriage*. There are also to be stayed *Caltha Poetarum*, Hall's *Satires* and *Willobie his Avisa*. Nor hereafter shall any *Satires* or *Epigrams* be printed, nor English Histories except they be allowed by some of the Council, nor any plays except they be allowed by such as have authority. All Nashe's books and Dr. Harvey's are to be taken wherever they may be found, and none of their books ever printed hereafter.

7th June. A Defeat in Ireland.

On the 28th May Sir Henry Harington being commander at Wicklow, drew out his garrison and marched towards Ranelagh where he camped that night. Next morning, having intelligence that the rebels were drawing to a head against him, he determined to move and lodge nearer to Wicklow, and the baggage being loaded, the battle marched from camp about a mile, the enemy following but making no skirmish. Then they came to a little wood on a high hill by a ford. Across this ford the battle passed in good order, but somewhat fast; but those who should have stayed behind to guard the rear would not stand. The musketeers ran away leaving the pikes without protection so that the enemy came upon them and slew them, they making no resistance. Some of the captains with a few horsemen charged very valiantly upon the enemy and brought away the colours, but by reason that the battle could not be drawn to turn back, a great part of the forces were slain, at least half being said to have miscarried.

10th June. The Earl of Southampton.

News is come from Ireland that the Earl of Essex hath made my Lord of Southampton General of the Horse, which the Queen taketh very offensively, seeing that she did not only deny it when she was moved thereto by my Lord but gave express prohibition to the contrary that he should not be appointed thereunto. The Queen hath expressly commanded that my Lord of Southampton shall not longer continue in his charge, which shall be disposed to some other, esteeming it a very unseasonable time to confer so great a place upon one that so lately gave her cause of offence.

21st June. AN ASSAULT UPON SIR CHARLES CAVENDISH.

Three days since, Sir Charles Cavendish, being accompanied only by two men and his page was set upon by Mr. John Stanhope with about twenty men on horseback, near to his new house in Derbyshire. His horse fell and he was wounded by pistol shots in divers places. Nevertheless they four unhorsed six of their assailants, killed two in the place and sore wounded two others. Upon this some of the workmen came towards them and Mr. Stanhope with the rest of his party fled.

25th June. CATHOLIC TROUBLES.

Troubles are again broken out amongst the Catholics at Wisbeach, for Blackwell, their archpriest, declared to the secular priests that in Rome they were adjudged to be schismatics, and that he would receive none of them to his favour or absolve them which would not acknowledge that they had sinned and given a great scandal by their prolonging to acknowledge his authority; nor would he hearken to any composition.

28th June. GENERAL NEWS.

In Ireland Sir Samuel Bagnal had done some small service, if that may be called a service to defend himself when assaulted by the enemy. But the case is so altered there and we come to such an afterdeal that we are glad of anything and take all in good part. Yet Sir Thomas Norris hath gone further and given the rebels a blow wherein he hath slain above 200 and killed their leader (which was a Burke) with his own hands; which service is much magnified by her Majesty herself to the old Lord and Lady Norris with so many good and gracious words to them in particular as were able to revive them if they were in swoon or half dead. The Earl of Rutland is returned out of Ireland upon commandment, and they say the Earl of Southampton is either come or coming, having his place of General of the Horse taken from him by order from Court. The Queen is nothing satisfied with the Earl of Essex's manner of proceeding, nor likes anything that is done, but says she allows him £1,000 a day to go in progress. He is said to be returned to Dublin and tarries for more men to go toward the North.

30th June. RUMOURS.

The Secretary and many of the Council are said to be inclined for peace with Spain, but have not of late had any conference on the matter. A messenger is come from the agents who were here for the Archduke bringing letters for her Majesty and Mr. Secretary about further parley, but their forwardness seems to make us more backward than we should otherwise be. Our resolution is supposed to depend much on the success of the Irish wars and the Hollanders' navy, concerning which are many reports, as that they have had ill-success both by tempest and encounter with the Spanish armada; then to have taken the spoil of Lisbon and then Cadiz.

As for Irish affairs, it is forbidden to speak or write of them; what is brought by the post is known only to the Council; but it is very sure that Tyrone's party hath prevailed most. My Lord of Essex is thought to be much discontented, and it is muttered at Court that he and the Queen have threatened the other's head: without doubt all kindness is forgotten between them. My Lord of Southampton is not commanded to return but only to leave his office of General of the horsemen by reason of a quarrel between him and Lord Grey. This Lord having the command of a company of horse adventured on a piece of service against the will of his General, who complained to the Earl of Essex. My Lord, for example's sake, committed Lord Grey to the Marshal's ward for some few hours, and hence a great quarrel arose, and some say that they have fought and one is killed, but it is not known which or either. It is doubted whether the Earl of Southampton will leave his place, though commanded upon his allegiance; and if he would, whether my Lord of Essex would suffer it, as being contrary to his patent. All the money is gone for Ireland and yet does not suffice: all diligence is used to get more in time to prevent mutiny among the soldiers to which they have already shown themselves prone.

There is much private talk in Court and City about a Scottish accident. An Englishman named Ashfield or Ashton, having been employed by the Scottish King, as is thought, secretly in Spain, Rome and other places, some here in authority, wishing to understand the particulars and finding no other means, plotted with the Governor of Berwick and Sir William Bowes, the ambassador, to bring him into England ; which was lately performed. For on a day the King with many of his nobles was going to a horse-race, and this Ashfield, preparing to go also, was invited by the ambassador's secretary to go with him in a coach, which he accepted, but they soon turned the coach another way and came to a place where some eight horsemen met them and took the man back with them where he is committed to prison. When the King heard of it, he took it so ill that he commanded our ambassador to keep his house and has placed a guard about him, vowing he shall have the same treatment as the other has here. It is thought that we shall pacify the King by money or else by fair means win the man to reveal what he knows and then dismiss him as though nothing had been done.

At Court Sir Walter Ralegh and Sir John Stanhope strive to be of the Council, the one as Vice-Chamberlain, the other as Chancellor of the Duchy ; they have not as yet their suits but it is thought that they will. The Earl of Derby is busy penning comedies for the common players.

30th June. PLAYS AT THE ROSE.

During these six months past the Lord Admiral's players have played at the Rose these new plays following : *War Without Blows and Love Without Strife* (by Heywood) ; *Two Angry Women of Abingdon*, the 2nd part, (by Porter) ; *William Longbeard* (by Drayton) ; *The World Runs on Wheels* (by Chapman) ; *Joan as Good as My Lady* (by Heywood) ; *Friar Fox and Gillan of Brentford* ; *Troy's Revenge with the Tragedy of Polyphemus* (by Chettle) ; *Two Merry Women of Abingdon* (by Porter) ; *The Spencers* (by Chettle and Porter) ; *The Four Kings* ; *Troilus and Cressida* (by Chettle and Dekker) ; *Agamemnon* (by Chettle and Dekker).

5th July. DISSENSIONS AMONG OUR ENGLISH PAPISTS.

Great dissensions have grown amongst our English papists abroad who are now divided into two factions ; the one depending upon the Jesuits whereof Parsons is now the head, whose courses have been violent to seek the overthrow of the present estate by conquest or other means ; the other consisting chiefly of the laymen and gentlemen which are abroad, whereof Charles Paget hath been chief, who cannot be brought to consent to the invasion and conquest of our country by a foreign prince. This division began amongst them soon after the death of the Queen of Scots upon whom they did all concur whilst she lived; but since her death could never agree upon any one course either of conquest or proposed title. This contention hath proceeded unto great heat between them, but especially of late since the title of the Infanta of Spain hath been set on foot according to the books written by Parsons, under one Doleman's name. They are so divided thereupon as there is an extreme hatred grown between them, insomuch as Paget's side do openly inveigh against Parsons and his adherents as men seditious and factious, full of treachery and without conscience.

7th July. A Popish Trick.

In spite of the French King's edict of toleration for those of the reformed Religion there is great passion and malice yet remaining in the popish side against the protestants. At Limoges last Corpus Christi Day certain priests went into the church in the night and brake down some images, and (as some say) cast the Sacrament about the Church. In the morning, the people assembling, a great exclamation was made by the priests of this outrage, and some principal men of the Religion in that town were charged by name to be the doers of it. The people by and by grew in fury, and would have proceeded to their present execution, taking arms for the purpose, and the other side arming themselves likewise for their defence. Hereupon the Governor arriving and examining the matter found that one of the Religion, charged by name to have been an actor in it, had been in his company all that night. So he caused the accusers to be severely examined, and drew by threat of torture confession of the whole practice, and that they had done it to the intent to have moved the people to a sedition and to have cut the throats of them of the Religion.

10th July. 'As You Like It.'

My Lord Chamberlain's men have a new comedy called *As You Like It*, by Shakespeare, the argument whereof is like to that pastoral romance of *Rosalynde* that Lodge wrote, showing how

Rosalind, the daughter of the banished Duke, was by the usurping Duke her uncle forced to flee into the forest in disguise as a forester, and there caused Orlando her lover to woo her, supposing her to be a boy. At the court of the banished Duke there is a courtier, one Jaques, much afflicted with this humour of melancholy, but of a nature proper only to himself. Quoth he, 'I have neither the scholar's melancholy, which is emulation; nor the musician's, which is fantastical; nor the courtier's, which is proud; nor the soldier's, which is ambitious; nor the lawyer's, which is politic; nor the lady's which is nice; nor the lover's which is all these: but it is a melancholy of mine own, compounded of many simples, extracted from many objects, and indeed the sundry contemplation of my travels, which by often rumination wraps me in a most humorous sadness.'

THE ARCHBISHOP'S CHARITABLE FOUNDATION.

This day at Croydon was dedicated the chapel or oratory of the Hospital of the Holy Trinity, of the foundation of John Whitgift, Archbishop of Canterbury, which is appointed for the abiding place of such as be maimed, poor, needy or impotent, for a number not exceeding forty, together with a school house for the increase of literature.

14th July. A WITCH HANGED.

Two days since one Doll Barthram was hanged at St. Edmondsbury in Suffolk for her devilish witcheries upon a certain Joan Jordan, servant of Simon Fox of Stradbrook. First this Doll sent three toads to plague the woman in bed, and afterwards in the perceiving of many of good account (amongst them Anthony Aldam, gentleman, Will Godbolde, chief constable of Hoxham, Mr. Randall the vicar and others) she sent a spirit that came about 11 o'clock at night, first scraping on the walls, then knocking, after that shuffling in the rushes, and then (as his usual manner was) he clapped the maid on the cheeks as to awake her, and kissed her three or four times and slavered on her; and lying on her breast he pressed her so sore that she could not stir nor speak. The shape which they saw the spirit then to have was a thick dark substance about a foot high, like to a sugar loaf, white on top. This spirit had also a voice, for it spake divers times, saying 'Joan, Joan, I come for thy life'; and that his name was Giles and that Doll Barthram had sent him. Whereupon when one John Sheereman replied that he should not have her life, the spirit said, ' I will have thine then ; I come to thee ; I come ' ; and with that offered towards him to the great astonishment and fear of him and the rest present. But for that time he vanished away.

This maid was again and again tormented by the spirit, and thrown so violently against the wall as if it would have driven out the side of the chamber, and cast into a strange fit ; her head and body were bent backwards almost to her hips. She lay as it were dead. Her teeth were so fast closed that a man could not open them though with all his strength he assayed it with his dagger and a key. Nor would she move though a stiff dry rush was thrust into her nostrils, neither at the bending of her fingers, nor yet at a great quantity of *aqua vitae* which was poured into her mouth. At last she opened one of her eyes, gazing therewith very strangely, then the other, crying, ' O Barthram, thou hast killed me.'

21st July. COURT RUMOURS.

There is no news of the Irish wars, all advertisements thence being prohibited, and such news as comes to the Council carefully concealed ; yet is it feared that our part hath little success, having lost many captains and whole companies. My Lord of Essex is now preparing to go against Tyrone ; 3,000 are to go from Chester this week and 2,000 more are levying. My Lord hath little grace at Court. The Queen is quite averted from him and is wholly directed by Mr. Secretary, who now rules all as his father did ; though he pretends friendship to my Lord, he is thought at heart to be his greatest enemy, envying his former greatness with the Queen and intending his utter overthrow if the Irish affairs take no better effect. My Lord dissembles his discontent and shows so dejected a mind as to attempt nothing without direction, and labours to soothe and flatter Mr. Secretary. The common people still favour my Lord, hoping by his means to be freed from their intolerable exactions ; but if they saw him in adversity, they would respect him no more than they did the late Duke of Norfolk. They would follow any who would be more likely to procure them some immunities, for never were they more oppressed and subject to all servile conditions.

A messenger came from Brussels sixteen days ago with letters about peace ; he had speedy audience and quick return, and one of the Queen's ships conveyed him to Calais. It is thought that Mr. Secretary is labouring a peace as the best means of establishing his posterity. He has got for his brother, Lord Burleigh, who is of a mild temper and will govern by his instructions, a large commission to be Lord President of the North. He has altered his crest from a sheaf of wheat between two lions to two sheaves of arrows crossed and covered with a helmet to distinguish his retinue from his brother's.

The Queen has appointed a progress into Surrey, Hampshire, Wiltshire, Gloucestershire and Berkshire ; but her departure from Greenwich has often been deferred. Some think it is on account of this fleet ; others that her years make her unable to travel so that when she rideth a mile or two in the park, which now she seldom doth, she always complaineth of the uneasy going of her horse ; and when she is taken down, her legs are so benumbed that she is unable to stand, till the footmen falling down have a long time by earnest rubbing brought them to a better temper.

The King of Denmark hath confiscated five of our ships fishing as usual near his coast, sending some of the mariners home with charge that none come there without licence ; the rest he keeps prisoners, and would cast them into the sea but for the entreaty of his Council. He beat many violently with his own hand, so that both merchants and men fear his fury, and the hindrance of our trade into Muscovy unless some ambassador be sent speedily to pacify him.

26th July. A Stern Punishment in Ireland.

On 9th July the Lord General held a martial Court upon the captains who were under Sir Henry Harington and put to rout near Wicklow. In this court Peter Walshe, lieutenant to Captain Loftus, for giving the first example of cowardice and dismay to the troops was condemned to die and afterwards accordingly executed. The other captains, though they forsook not their place, but were deserted by their soldiers, yet because they did nothing extraordinary in such an extremity were all cashiered. The soldiers, being condemned all to die, were most of them pardoned by my Lord, yet for example's sake every tenth man executed. Sir Henry Harrington, because he is a Councillor in Ireland, my Lord forbore to bring to trial till the Queen's pleasure should be known.

30th July. THE QUEEN'S OFFENCE WITH THE EARL OF ESSEX.

The Queen is much offended that my Lord of Essex hath not yet made his journey into Ulster, seeing that this excessive charge was expressly to the end that the Northern traitor should be assailed and garrisons planted in his county, for it was ever my Lord's opinion in Council that all that was done in other kind in Ireland was but waste and consumption. This journey into Munster is held to be very unreasonable, and by the small effects thereof my Lord hath broken the heart of the best troops, weakened his strength upon inferior rebels and run out the glass of time that can hardly be recovered. The Queen hath therefore commanded that the Lord Deputy shall pass without delay into the North for the accomplishment of those counsels which were resolved at his departure to the intent that all these charges prove not fruitless, especially when these base rebels shall see their golden calf preserve himself without faint or loss as safe as in his sanctuary, while the Queen's treasure, time and honour are spent engaged in other enterprises.

Moreover the Lord Deputy is now straitly charged that, notwithstanding his former license to return and constitute some temporary Governor he shall not adventure to leave Ireland without her Majesty's warrant.

1st August. A GREAT ALARM.

There is great alarm in London, and all in a hurly as if the enemy were at our doors, which ariseth upon a report that the Adelantado hath an armada ready at the Groin of 30 galleys and 70 ships, though some say more. The Queen's ships are all making ready and the City is commanded to furnish 16 of their best ships to defend the Thames, and 10,000 men, whereof 6,000 are to be trained straightway, and every man else to have his arms ready. Letters are likewise going out to the bishops and their clergy, and all noblemen and gentlemen hereabout to prepare horses and all other furniture as if the enemy were expected within fifteen days. There is likewise speech of a camp to be raised at Tilbury, the Lord Admiral to be General, and the Lord Thomas Howard to have charge of the navy.

Irish News.

We have almost nothing out of Ireland; and many men marvel that my Lord of Essex hath spent so much time and done so little. He is now at Dublin, but yet hath one fortnight's journey more about those parts before he draw toward the North. There is a meaning that Sir Conyers Clifford should go to Lough Foyle with 3,000 men and Sir Thomas Norris with as many to Ballyshannon, and so to hedge Tyrone on all sides, who fortifies himself altogether in his places, and they say hath quit the Blackwater. My Lord hath lately made 16 knights, for what service is unknown, but belike it is *de bene esse*, in hope they will deserve it hereafter. My Lord's decimating Sir Harry Harington's companies is much descanted of, and not greatly liked, though in some opinions never men deserved it better, for first they were more than double the number of the rebels; then the enemy left his strength and assaulted them in the plain, which in all reason was our advantage; lastly we had horse and they had none. Sir Harry himself is referred over to be censured here.

3rd August. Instructions for the Lord Burleigh.

Upon his appointment as Lord President at York the Lord Burleigh is instructed to have an extraordinary care to remedy the disobedience and abuses that have crept into those parts. He shall examine the state of the forces and see that they are not left in the hands of persons of small ability who might be bribed to neglect their charges, nor of those notoriously affected to popery; and also that Captains and muster-masters do not make unlawful gain of the country. He must reform and correct that abundant falling away from religion, and stir up the Ecclesiastical Commissioners, who dispense with faults as though the laws were instituted not for punishment but for their enriching; for within the last five or six years whole parishes have grown recusant, and through toleration and negligence wilful papists are unpunished and authority abused.

THE SPANISH ALARM.

There is newly come to Plymouth a sea captain with news that the King of Spain hath a mind to be here in a few days with 70 galleys and 100 ships, in which come 30,000 soldiers. This Captain is but lately come from Brest, where it was reported that the Spanish fleet would be there in three or four days, and that it was openly rumoured at the Groin that the King himself will lead the fleet. Of late he has cut off the heads of two of his noblemen because they counselled him not to attempt this enterprise, and he says that he will make his finger heavier to England than was his father's whole body.

It is likely that if this design of the enemy be for the Thames or Kent they will come with their ships and galleys so close aboard the coast of France that neither her Majesty's ships, being to the westward, nor those in the Narrow Seas may discover them till they come too near. The fishermen of Dover and Rye are ordered continually to ply over as near the coast of France as they may, and upon discovery of the enemy to return with true and speedy advertisement.

4th August. MASTER EDWARD COKE'S LADY.

The Lady Hatton is recently brought to bed of a daughter, which stops the mouth of the old slander. It was christened with great solemnity, the Queen, by her deputy the Lady of Oxford, and the Countess Dowager of Derby being godmothers, and the Lord Treasurer godfather.

5th August. THE FORCES MUSTERING.

Order is now given for a camp to be raised whereof the Lord Admiral to be General, the Lord Mountjoy Lieutenant, Sir Francis Vere Marshal, and the Earl of Northumberland General of the Horse. Twelve of the Queen's ships are preparing in all haste, whereof the Lord Thomas Howard to be Admiral, Sir Walter Ralegh Vice-Admiral, Mr. Fulke Greville Rear Admiral. Sir Thomas Gerrard was appointed Colonel of the Londoners, but for an old grudge since the last Parliament they would none of him, whereupon the Earl of Cumberland was given them to have charge of them and the river, which he undertakes with great confidence, meaning to make a bridge somewhat on this side of Gravesend after an apish imitation to that of Antwerp, and to that end gets together all the lighters, boats, Western barges, cables and anchors that are to be found, giving out that with 1,500 musketeers he will defend the bridge or lose his life. All the noblemen about Court have rated themselves at round proportions to provide horse, as being the best advantage we are like to have if the enemy come, as the Lord Admiral 100, the Earl of Shrewsbury 100, the Earl of Pembroke 200, the Earl of Northumberland 100, Mr. Secretary 100, the Archbishop 100 and all the rest, both court and country according to their ability.

7th August. FRESH ALARMS.

Towards evening yesterday came news that the Spaniards are landed in the Isle of Wight and Southampton, which bred unwonted fear and consternation in London, with such a cry of women, chaining of streets and shutting of the gates as though the enemy had been at Blackwall; insomuch that many are ashamed that our weakness and nakedness on all sides showed itself so apparently as to be carried far and near to our disgrace both with friends and foes. Everywhere are to be met strange rumours and abundance of news spread abroad in the City and flying into the country; as that the Spaniards' fleet is 150 sail of ships and 70 galleys; that they bring 30,000 soldiers with them, and shall have 20,000 from the Cardinal; that the King of Denmark sends to aid him 100 sail of ships; that the King of Scots is in arms with 40,000 men, and the Spaniard comes to settle the King of Scots in this realm, which is so creditably bruited that a preacher, in his prayer before his sermon, prayed to be delivered from the mighty forces of the Spaniard, the Scots and the Dane; that my Lord Scroop was slain with 200 men more, by the Scots; that Sir William Bowes was turned out of Scotland by the King with great disclaim; that the Adelantado has taken the sacrament to come to London Bridge, and brings his wife and two daughters with him.

8th August. THE PREPARATIONS IN THE CITY.

The intention of making a bridge of boats near Gravesend is now, after much turmoil and great charge, quite given over, either upon trial because they find it not feasible, or as bearing another manner of breadth and billow than the river of

Antwerp. Now they have an imagination of sinking certain hulks in the channel if need should be, to which great objection is made. For after sounding the channel at that place called Barking Shelf, it is found that 83 ships will be necessary of which the cost will grow towards £25,000. Moreover the drowning of so many ships in that place will be the cause of the drowning of the marsh lands there adjoining, the loss whereof is esteemed at £40,000. Furthermore there is an impossibility to weigh and recover the ships, which must be half laden with ballast, and not being recoverable the river of Thames will be choked and spoiled, and the trade of the City wholly overthrown.

The Lord Mayor hath now put in readiness 3,000 men, well sorted and armed, and delivered them to be trained; besides these 3,000 more are enjoined to be ready at an hour's warning. These last, especially appointed for the defence of the City, are chosen of such householders and others as have their houses and states within the City, and so more sure and fit to be employed in the defence thereof. As for the conjecture made some days since that the City could afford and furnish 50,000 persons, the Lord Mayor hath remembered the Council that in 1588, when like occasion did enforce the choice and levy of men, at what time (being then the Term) there were conversing within the City divers gentlemen, lawyers and others with their attendants, there was in all of able men fit to bear arms betwixt the age of 16 and 60 not above the number of 22,000, and the City at that time more populous and better replenished with inhabitants than it is at this present.

10*th August*. 'THE SHOEMAKER'S HOLIDAY.'

The Earl of Nottingham's men have a new play that Dekker wrote, called *The Shoemaker's holiday, or a pleasant comedy of the Gentle Craft*, whereof the argument is this: Sir Hugh Lacy, Earl of Lincoln, had a young gentleman of his own name, his near kinsman, that loved the Lord Mayor's daughter of London; to prevent and cross which love the Earl caused his kinsman to be sent Colonel of a company into France; who resigned his place to another gentleman his friend, and came disguised like a Dutch shoemaker to the house of Simon Eyre in Tower Street, who served the Lord Mayor and his household with shoes: the merriments that passed in Eyre's house, his coming to be Lord Mayor of London, Lacy's getting his love, and other accidents, with two merry three-men's-songs.

12th August. THE DEFENCE FORCE.

To-day, being Sunday, the Lord Admiral and the other great officers of the field came in great bravery to Paul's Cross and dined with the Lord Mayor. The alarm is now very hot that the Spaniards are at Brest.

Of many rumours at this time one is that the cause of all this mustering is not because of Spaniards but that the Queen is dangerous sick or dead.

18th August. A LAMENTABLE DEFEAT IN IRELAND.

News is come from Ireland of a lamentable defeat at Carlow and of the death of Sir Conyers Clifford and Sir Alexander Ratcliffe. Mistress Ratcliffe as yet hears nothing of her brother's death; by the Queen's command it is kept from her, for the Queen is determined to break it unto her herself. It is said at Court that Sir Conyers was a brave executioner of orders but no good director; also that my Lord of Essex hath done little or nothing.

22nd August. THE MUSTERS.

Seeing the trouble that it would be to them of the City, the most of the soldiers being artificers, to muster them to-morrow, which is St. Bartholemew Eve, the mustering is forborne. Horse and foot are now being despatched away with as much speed as is possible to save her Majesty's pay, but with charge to be always ready at one hour's warning.

AN ORDER CONCERNING PRICES.

The Earl of Nottingham, being Captain General of all forces at this time, hath set out an order concerning the prices to be charged during the abode of the forces in and about London; and warning also all victuallers or others not to withhold or hide grain or other victuals from the markets on pain of imprisonment and fine. Certain of the prices ordained be these:

A full quart of the best ale or beer - - - - 1d.
A quarter of best wheat - - - - - - 30s.

A full quart of single ale or beer - - - -	ob.
A pound of butter sweet and new - - -	4d.
A pound of good Essex cheese - - - -	1d. ob.
A pound of good Suffolk cheese - - - -	2d.
Seven eggs, the best in the market - - -	2d.
A stone of best beef at the butchers weighing 8 lbs.	14d.
A fat pig the best in the market - - - -	16d.
A couple of good capons - - - - -	20d.
A pound of tallow candles made of wick or cotton -	4d.
Hay and litter day and night for one horse within every inn - - - - - - - -	3d. ob.
Good grass for one horse day and night and so depart	2d.
Every soldier receiving her Majesty's pay by 8d. the day having to dinner or supper good wheaten bread and drink, beef, mutton or veal boiled, and pig, beef, mutton, veal or lamb roasted, or otherwise upon the fish days to have good wheaten bread and good drink, salt fish or ling, eggs, butter, pease or beans buttered, and so having sufficient for the sustentation of his body to pay for his meal - - - -	3d. ob.

23rd August. THE FORCES DISPERSING.

The storm that looked so black is almost quite blown over; yet our navy is gone to sea prettily strong and in good plight for so short a warning, containing 23 ships and pinnaces of the Queen's, 12 good merchant ships provided by the City and 6 more hired by her Majesty, with 14 hoys well furnished with ordnance and made for fight. Our land forces are discharged little by little. The Hertfordshire men were sent home first, and so by degrees one after another; yet they all received pay more and less, some for four, some for five days, and some for a whole week. If occasion had arisen to draw forces to a head or into camp, it is thought the first proportion would have risen to 27,000 and 3,000 horse.

The vulgar sort cannot be persuaded but that there was some great mystery in the assembling of these forces, and because they cannot find the reason of it make many wild conjectures and cast beyond the moon; as sometimes, that the Queen was dangerously sick, otherwhile that it was to show to some that are absent that others can be followed as well as they, and, that if occasion be, military services can be as well and readily ordered and directed as if they were present ; with many other as vain and frivolous imaginations.

IRISH NEWS.

The Earl of Essex hath made many new knights, English and Irish, to the number of 59 in the whole since his first arrival. It is much marvelled that this humour should so possess him, that not content with his first dozens and scores, he should thus fall to huddle them up by half hundreds ; and it is noted as a strange thing that a subject in the space of seven or eight years (not having been six months together in any one action) should upon so little service and small desert make more knights than are in all the realm besides ; and it is doubted that if he continue this course he will shortly bring in tag and rag, cut and long tail, and so draw the order in contempt.

25th August. THE FORCES TO BE MUSTERED AGAIN.

Late this night news is come that the Spanish fleet is discovered upon the coast of France, wherefore the Lord Mayor is commanded again to put in readiness all the armed force of the City ; and for the defence of the river to have such vessels as are in the Thames ready to impeach the coming up of the galleys. Moreover he is bidden to proceed with all expedition and without such disputation and backwardness as hath been used heretofore. Posts are now being despatched to recall the horsemen to London with all speed possible.

26th August. THE MUSTERS.

Before six of the clock this morning (being Sunday) the 3,000 soldiers trained by the citizens were all in armour in the streets, attending on their captains till past seven ; at which time being thoroughly wet by a great shower of rain they are sent home again for the day.

27th August. THE MUSTERS.

This morning 30,000 citizens, householders and subsidy men, showed themselves at the Mile's End, where they have trained all day, and are commanded to continue so daily.

30th August. THE SCOTTISH AMBASSADOR.

To-day the King of Scotland's Ambassador had audience when he made known to her Majesty the dislike his master conceived at Sir William Bowes' manner of taking Ashfield away. The Queen was very loud and sharp in her answer, avowing Sir William's proceedings, and saying that his departure was not forcible but voluntary, as it should appear under his own hand.

31st August. ABUSES OF THE MUSTER.

There is much talk of the abuses shown in this mustering, like to have lost the realm had it been put to the proof. In the ships of Lord Thomas Howard and Sir Walter Ralegh the drink, fish and beef was so corrupt that it would have destroyed all the men if they had fed on it but a few days, so that they could not have kept the seas without new provision. In Dorsetshire the ignorant justices with their harrying up and down of the people, chargeable and untimely musters, together with their dismayed looks and speeches, struck such fear into the honester sort and gave such hope of novelties to the beggarly and rascally sort that great disorder was like to have come of it. In Sussex where the count was of 4,000 trained men there were found but 2,000. There was never Prince so deceived as her Majesty, insomuch that the Lord Admiral declared that there was not a thousand trained men in the shires nominated for the service that could so much as march in good and just order. He had rather 2,000 of Sir Francis Vere's men of the Low Countries, than 8,000 of these called 'trained' men. At Fowey in Cornwall there have been found hidden in a hogshead of salt a barrel of Papistical books, as well in English as Latin, composed by sundry English seminaries and others.

1st September. GENERAL NEWS.

The *Arcadia* that Sir Philip Sidney wrote is newly printed in Scotland, according to the best edition, which will make them good cheap, but is very hurtful to Mr. Ponsonby that hath the right of imprint, for he held them at a very high rate, and now must he sell as others do or they will lie upon his hands.

It is reported that the Adelantado is gone with 50 or 60 sail towards the Islands to meet the Hollanders and to secure the Indian treasure. Her Majesty's fleet is discharged this day;

and the victual that remains the merchants are to take as it cost her Majesty.

Mr. Secretary, almost tired with continual labour and pains, desires leave to go to Theobalds for 6 or 7 days; but it can hardly be granted for he cannot be spared.

2nd September. THE ADVICE OF THE CAPTAINS IN IRELAND.

On the 21st August the Lord Deputy held a Council of war at Dublin Castle, and there propounded his purpose of invading Ulster and bade the captains to deliver their opinions. After long debating, every one having spoken in order, at last by common consent all concluded that the service offered little or no hope and advised against it. They alleged two reasons in particular; that the army is so unwilling to be carried thither that some secretly run into England, others revolt to the rebels, a third sort partly hide themselves in the country and partly feign themselves sick. Moreover the army which passeth not the number of 3,500 or 4,000 of serviceable men would be far overmatched. This opinion being delivered, all the commanders and captains subscribed their names thereto. Nevertheless my Lord proposeth to take the field against the arch-traitor.

4th September. TRAINING CEASED.

To-day the training of the citizens under their captains is ordered to cease, the alarm of danger having passed away.

12th September. COURT NEWS.

Mr. Cuffe, my Lord of Essex's Secretary, is come over with letters of importance. He hath had access to the Queen, and being marvellous well instructed to answer such objections as her Majesty could lay to his charge he hath behaved himself very wisely to her better satisfaction. The unkindness between my Lord and Mr. Secretary is grown to extremity; my Lord is said to be infinitely discontented and in his discontentment uses speeches that may be dangerous and hurtful to his safety.

Sir Francis Vere of late came to Court, and Master Secretary took him to the Queen, with whom he was long and very graciously used. Only my Lord Mountjoy refrains speaking to him. My Lord of Sussex being in a corner of the Presence, my

Lord Admiral showed him to Sir Francis, but he never stirred foot to go towards him, but over his shoulder looked upon him, which the Earl took very ill and began to chafe at it.

THE STATE OF THE NORTH.

Since his coming to York the Lord Burleigh hath been busied with the examination of notorious recusants, both men and women, who have long been left asleep, and among them a priest who has been there 28 years but never taken. My Lord hath now filled a little study with copes and mass books and is like soon to return an army of recusants.

15th September. MR. BACON'S SAYING CONCERNING THE EARL OF ESSEX.

The Queen of late showing a passionate distaste of my Lord of Essex's proceedings in Ireland hath spoken of it to many, among them Mr. Bacon, who answered that he knew not particulars of State but otherwise, quoth he, 'if you had my Lord of Essex here with a white staff in his hand, as my Lord of Leicester had, and continued him still about for society to yourself, and for an honour and ornament to your attendance and Court in the eyes of your people, and in the eyes of foreign ambassadors, then were he in his right element, for to discontent him as you do and yet put arms and power into his hands, may be a kind of temptation to make him prove cumbersome and unruly.'

17th September. IRISH NEWS.

Yesterday Captain Lawson came to the Court with a letter from my Lord of Essex to her Majesty only. The news was that being in the Bronny with 2,500 foot and 300 horse Tyrone sent the Constable of Duncannon, a man highly favoured and trusted by him, to the Earl of Essex to signify his desire to parley. My Lord's answer was that he would not speak with him but the next day he should find him in the head of his troops. The 6th of September therefore my Lord with 2,000 foot and 150 horse went to the top of a little hill near to Lough Mill where runs a ford, having left behind him 500 foot and 150 horse to guard the baggage. Thence my Lord did descry six horse near the ford on the other side. Tyrone sent his base son to desire he might speak with my Lord, who then advancing his horse towards the ford, Tyrone alone came and thrust his horse into the water to the skirts of his saddle and with his hat in hand, full of reverence and respect craved her Majesty's mercy, and that his Lordship would be a mean to it; that the grievances of the country might be heard; that he bore no arms but for his own defence against the oppression of her ministers. When the parley was ended, my Lord returned back and that night made choice of six commissioners to conclude some treaty of peace. The next day the commissioners from both sides met and it was concluded between them that a cessation of arms should continue from six weeks to six weeks till May, which upon 14 days' warning might be broken: that if any of his confederates did not agree to the same truce, it might be lawful to my Lord General to make war against them, nor should they receive protection from Tyrone; that if any spoils were committed on either side, restitution should be made within 20 days and the offenders severely punished. For the performance of these covenants the Lord General's word was taken and Tyrone's oath. On the 8th the armies were dismissed and the Lord General went to Dredagh to take physic, his body being greatly out of temper.

Her Majesty despatched Captain Lawson back again with all speed to-day with her letter under her signature and a private letter from herself. This business seemeth not to be well liked.

21st September. A PLAY OF 'JULIUS CAESAR.'

At the new Globe Theatre the Lord Chamberlain's players have a play of *Julius Caesar* by Shakespeare, showing how that Brutus and Cassius conspired to kill him in the Senate house, but thereafter when Antony had inflamed the people of Rome against them at Caesar's funeral they were compelled to flee, and at last slain at the battle of Philippi.

25th September. THE HOLLANDERS' VOYAGE TO THE WEST INDIES.

This past summer the States of the United Provinces have set forth a fleet of 73 sail of ships which sailed to the West Indies and there wrought much damage upon the Spaniard, taking the town of Grand Canaria and destroying it by fire, and likewise the Island Gomera. This fleet set sail the 25th May and returned home the 10th of this month.

28th September. THE EARL OF ESSEX RETURNS.

The Earl of Essex is suddenly returned to London. This morning, about 10 o'clock, he lighted at the court gate at Nonsuch in post and made all haste up to the presence, and so to the privy chamber, and stayed not till he came to the Queen's bedchamber, where he found the Queen newly up, her hair about her face. He kneeled unto her, kissed her hands and her neck, and had some private speech with her, which seemed to give him great contentment, for coming from her Majesty to go shift himself in his chamber, he was very pleasant and thanked God that though he had suffered much trouble and storms abroad he found a sweet calm at home. 'Tis much wondered at that he went so boldly to her Majesty's presence, she not being ready, and he so full of dirt and mire, that his very face was full of it.

About 11 he was ready and went up again to the Queen and conferred with her till half an hour after 12. As yet all was well, and her usage very gracious towards him. He went to dinner and during all that time discoursed merely of his travels and journeys in Ireland, of the goodness of the country, the civilities of the nobility that are true subjects, of the great entertainment he had in their houses, of the good orders he found there. He was visited frankly by all sorts, of Lords, ladies and gentlemen; only a strangeness was observed between him and Mr. Secretary and that party.

Then he went up to the Queen but found her much changed in that small time, for she began to call him to question for his return, and was not satisfied in the manner of his coming away, and leaving all things at so great hazard. She appointed the Lords to hear him, and so they went to Council in the afternoon, the Lord Chamberlain, Lord North, Mr. Secretary and Mr. Controller; and my Lord went with them, where they sat an hour. But nothing is determined or yet known; yet all the Lords are sent for to be at Court to-morrow.

The manner of his departure was thus. An hour before he came away, he called the Council at Dublin before him and acquainted them with his resolution. He committed the Sword to the Lord Chancellor and the Treasurer, and the command of the army to the Earl of Ormond. There are come over with him the most part of his household, and a great number of captains and gentlemen. My Lord Southampton, Lord Donkelly and others are in London, but not yet gone to Court.

One thing is much spoken of. My Lord of Essex coming in to Westminster Bridge, he took oars and went to Lambeth, and there took such horses as he found staying for their masters. Sir Thomas Gerrard's horses were in the ferry boat coming over, ready to land. But my Lord went away, and Sir Thomas overtook him, and understanding that my Lord Grey was a little before rid somewhat hard till he overtook him also, and told him my Lord of Essex was a little behind if he would speak with him. 'No,' said the Lord Grey, 'I have some business at Court.' 'Then I pray you,' said Sir Thomas Gerrard, 'let my Lord of Essex ride before that he may bring first news of his return himself.' 'Doth he desire it ?' said my Lord Grey. 'No,' said Sir Thomas, 'nor I think will desire nothing at your hands.' 'Then,' said he, 'I have business'; and made greater haste than before. And indeed came to the Court a quarter of an hour before the Earl and went up to the Secretary; but the Earl was come ere any tidings was brought upstairs.

It is a very dangerous time for courtiers, for the head of both factions being at Court a man cannot tell how to govern himself towards them. There is such observing and prying into men's actions that they are to be holden happy and blessed that are away.

29th September. My Lord of Essex.

Late last night, between 10 and 11 o'clock, a commandment came from the Queen to my Lord of Essex that he should keep his chamber. To-day the Lords sat in Council but the Earl was not there till 2 in the afternoon, when he was sent for. When he came in all the Lords rose and saluted him; but they sat again. My Lord stood at the upper of the board, his head bare, to answer all that objected against him. Mr. Secretary at the other end in divers articles delivered the offence her Majesty conceived he had done against her. From 2 until 5 they remained in council, very private, for the clerks were commanded out. It is said that never man answered with more temper, gravity or discretion to those matters laid to his charge; his contemptuous disobedience of her Majesty's letters and will in returning; his presumptuous letters written from time to time; his proceedings in Ireland contrary to the points resolved upon ere he went; his rash manner of coming away from Ireland; his overbold going yesterday to her Majesty's presence to her bedchamber; his making of so many idle knights. After the Earl's coming from the Lords, he went again to his chamber where as yet he continues captive. The Lords sat a quarter of an hour after and then went all to the Queen and delivered unto her what had passed. But her answer was that she would pause and consider of her answers.

Afterwards my Lord of Essex was commanded from Court and committed to my Lord Keeper's; he is now come to London to York House in my Lord of Worcester's coach. At his going from Court few or none of his friends accompanied him.

My Lord's sudden return brings all sorts of knights, captains, officers and soldiers from thence that the City is full of them, to the great discontent of her Majesty that they are suffered to leave their charge. But the most part of the gallants have quitted their commands, places and companies, not willing to stay there after him, so that the disorder seems to be greater there than stands with the safety of that service.

To-day the two factions show themselves in Court, for Master Secretary went to dinner accompanied with the Earl of Shrewsbury and the Lord Admiral, the Lords Thomas Howard and Cobham, the Lord Grey, Sir Walter Ralegh and Sir George Carew. And with the Earl of Essex went the Earls of Worcester and Rutland, the Lords Mountjoy and Rich, Lord Lumley, the Controller and many knights.

It is a world to see the humours of the time, which is now so full of danger that a man must take good heed of what he say or write.

1st October. THE SABBATARIAN DOCTRINE.

These last years the Disciplinarians have made but little stir; but now they go about to preach the doctrine of Jewish Sabbath keeping, which was first put forth by one Bound in

1595, that the Christians are bound to rest upon the Sabbath day and to keep it as the Jews did. This doctrine is preached in divers places, the preachers alleging that to do any work on the Sabbath, or to throw a bowl, or make a wedding dinner, or to ring more bells than one is as great a sin as to commit murder or adultery. This severe doctrine taketh such hold upon the people that the Bishops in sundry courts have rebuked ministers for preaching of it.

5th October. My Lord of Essex.

All men's eyes and ears are open to what it will please her Majesty to determine with the Earl of Essex who still remains close prisoner at my Lord Keeper's. Her displeasure and indignation towards him is very great, the time at Court for the most part being spent about his affairs. Yesterday Mr. Attorney General was at Court, and it is said that the Queen conferred with him. This morning the Lord Keeper, the Lord Treasurer and Mr. Secretary were with my Lord of Essex from 8 in the morning till near 11 o'clock. What articles were brought against him is not publicly known, only in imagination, as of his contempt by returning, that he followed not his instructions; that his parle with Tyrone was dishonourable for the State; that he cashiered old soldiers, and made new, his own creatures; these and such like fancies men dream of, but what is truly handled is not truly known save to those who gravely govern under her Majesty. She knows what by the laws of her Realm and by her own Prerogative she may do with my Lord of Essex; what she will do, Time will make known.

5th October. A Book for Ladies.

Hugh Platt that formerly wrote of many and divers inventions hath compiled a book called *Delights for Ladies*, to adorn their persons, tables, closets, and distillatories with beauties, banquets, perfumes and waters, the whole being in four parts and treating of the art of preserving and candying, secrets in distillation, cookery and huswifery, together with sweet powders, ointments and beauties.

7th October. Foreign Rumours.

From Brussels it is reported that there is much talk of the groundless alarm taken in England about the six galleys. Men wonder that so wise a Council was not more provident than to put the Queen and realm to excessive charge in time of peace upon a false alarm, drawing ships together and assembling men in great numbers, and costing the realm more than a subsidy, besides the damage to private men, especially at harvest time. Some foolish fellow made a mad piece of work of it. It is disputed among statesmen whether it is wise to put arms in the people's hand, and most concur that they should not be brought together armed except on urgent occasions. The estimation of the English Council for prudence is hereby much diminished, and they say that there have been either malice and treachery, or great negligence and simplicity; that the Queen has been very ill served and her subjects no less troubled.

10th October. TYRONE'S TREACHERIES.

From Ireland it was first reported that Tyrone hath no intention to continue the present cessation long but of the sudden to take his best opportunity with his confederates to do all the mischief they can. Sir William Warren, that was appointed by my Lord of Essex to go to Tyrone, returned with no resolution but with an appointment for a further day to meet again. But now comes news that Tyrone hath agreed to a further cessation for six weeks more until the 2nd December.

12th October. THE FRENCH KING'S DIVORCE.

The Cardinal Joyeuse is now come to Paris and dealeth in the matter of the French King's divorce, who seeks to have his marriage pronounced *esse nullum*, for a simple divorce (which the Church of Rome doth peremptorily defend to be *a thoro non a vinculo*) will not give place to a second marriage. The Queen hath been often solicited to acknowledge that the marriage was enforced by fear and never consummated between them, to which she protesteth never to condescend, but fear of worse will in the end persuade her.

13th October. MY LORD OF ESSEX.

My Lord of Essex continues very close at the Lord Keeper's, very humble and submissive, wonderfully grieved at her Majesty's displeasure towards him.

The world speaks diversely of his imprisonment. 'Tis said that pamphlets have been cast out, but suppressed. The Ladies

Southampton and Rich were at Essex House but are gone to the country to shun the company that daily were wont to visit them in town because it gave offence to the Court. His very servants are afraid to meet in any place to make merry lest it might be ill taken. My Lord Southampton and Lord Rutland come not to Court; the one doth but very seldom; they pass away the time in London merely in going to plays every day.

It is given out that if he would desire his liberty and go to Ireland again, he should have it, but he seems resolved never to go thither again, nor to meddle with any matters of war or state, and only lead a quiet country life. The Lords are said to like very well of his reasons and that the Queen by them is reasonably satisfied of his proceedings in Ireland. What her Majesty will please to resolve shall shortly be seen; but he stands to have his liberty by the like warrant that he was committed. It is said that Sir Robert Cecil at his last being with him said that the Queen was well pleased with his courses and would do anything to further his good and contentment, which my Lord thanked him for.

18th October. LORD MOUNTJOY FOR IRELAND.

This day her Majesty made known to Lord Mountjoy her intention to send him to Ireland. He is said to have excused it, for he found himself unable to abide the climate of Ireland. Wherein he shows his love to the Earl, for it is thought that if anything procure his liberty, it will be the necessity of sending him over again. But it may be her Majesty would not have the world think she is so bare of commanders. If Lord Mountjoy can put it off, it will surely be laid on a meaner man, or Sir Robert Sidney if he were in England. But whose lot soever it is to go, shall find it a weary burden.

21st October. MY LORD OF ESSEX.

The Queen's anger towards my Lord of Essex seems to be appeased in nothing. To-day the Lords were at Court and with her in Council about my Lord's matters. The Lords were all desirous that her Majesty would enlarge him, commending his reasons for his proceedings in Ireland, and his manner of submission for his offence in returning. But she angerly told them that such a contempt ought to be publicly punished.

Answer was made by them that her Majesty by her sovereign power and the severeness of her laws might do it, but it stood not with her honour and clemency to do it. All the Lords are in this matter his friends, for all speak for him, and a great hope is conceived that he shall be pardoned and set at liberty. But in regard of the world, whose eyes are open to see what will become of him, it is thought he shall be removed to his own house for a while, and thence be called before four of the Lords and judges to the Treasury Chamber and there some punishment be laid upon him in private, which her Majesty may remit at her pleasure.

Much has been done to mediate a peace between the Earl and Mr. Secretary; but Sir Robert will not, saying that there is no constancy in my Lord's love, he is so violent in his passions. Moreover, his estate being broken, my Lord may peradventure be forced to be a suitor to her Majesty for better means, wherein if he should be denied, then my Lord would be jealous of him. Yet thus far is it brought that Mr. Secretary can be content to show no malice towards him though he hath good cause to do it, having heard what unfriendly speeches my Lord used of him, and hath seen the letters he sent to her Majesty, full of malice towards him.

My Lord is now grown very ill and weak by grief and craves nothing more than that he may quickly know what her Majesty will do with him. He eats little, sleeps less, and only sustains life by continual drinking, which increases the rheum.

24th October. A New Play.

To-day the overthrow of Turnholt was acted upon a stage, and all the names used of those that were at it: especially Sir Francis Vere; and he that played that part got a beard resembling his, and a watchet satin doublet with hose trimmed with silver. Sir Robert Sidney also was introduced killing, slaying and overthrowing the Spaniards in his seconding Sir Francis Vere. The play was full of quips.

26th October. Court News.

The voice continues that my Lord Mountjoy shall go to Ireland. Sir Melchior Leven is at Court, and came of purpose to save his reputation best here. Sir Charles Blount on his way coming to London died, and there is an end of the quarrel. Sir John Gilbert came to Sir Christopher St. Lawrence to know if, because he did not pledge my Lord of Essex, he would stab him; for so it was given out that Sir Christopher should say. Sir Christopher said it was a lie; but what he said he would maintain with his sword. Sir John replied he pledged it not because he was allied to a contrary faction.

28th October. A RASH CAPTAIN.

All captains that have charge in Ireland are commanded to be gone. To-day Sir Christopher St. Lawrence was at the Council table before the Lords. He was in question some days since because at an ordinary he took a cup and drank to the health of my Lord of Essex and the confusion of his enemies. Mr. Secretary told him that he had used undecent speeches of him and took him to be his professed enemy. Sir Christopher answered that he knew both how to govern himself and his speech towards him; that whosoever told him of it was a villain, and if he would name him, he would make him deny it, ay, by God, that he would; saying all this with very great reverence towards the place but passionate as a soldier moved with the speech of so great a Councillor. It was told him that he was an Irishman; to which he replied, 'I am sorry that when I am in England I should be esteemed an Irishman, and in Ireland an Englishman; I have spent my blood, engaged and endangered my life often to do her Majesty service, and do beseech to have it so regarded.'

1st November. A PLAY OF SIR JOHN OLDCASTLE.

This day at the Rose my Lord of Nottingham's men have a new play called *The first part of the life of Sir John Oldcastle the good Lord Cobham*, wherein is shown how Oldcastle was pursued and falsely accused to King Harry the Fifth by the malice of the Bishop of Rochester, and how he escaped from those dangers; also the lewdness of the parson of Wrotham, one Sir John, that kept a lusty wench called Doll as his quean for whom he would rob passengers. This play, saith the players, presenteth no pampered glutton, nor aged councillor to youthful sin, but one whose virtue shone as a valiant martyr, and a loyal peer to his sovereign. The poets that wrote it are Munday, Drayton,

Wilson and Hathaway, to whom Henslowe giveth 10s. as a gift, over and above their just payment.

4th November. THE EARL OF ESSEX.

A speech of my Lord Admiral that with such an army as the Earl of Essex had, the French King might be driven out of France, occasioned the French ambassador to come to Court, and he is said to have complained. It seems also that he had instructions to deal for my Lord of Essex's liberty but found the Queen very short and bitter in that point. Yesterday the Earl being in great extremity, her Majesty hearing of it, gave Mr. Controller and Dr. Brown leave to go unto him, and this day Sir John Fortescue. It is said that he is about to make his will, and to order a broken and a ruinous estate; he is infinitely troubled with the Irish looseness. Some lightening of grace and pity appears in her Majesty towards him, for she is pleased he shall have the liberty of the garden, but Sir Walter Ralegh is fallen sick upon it and her Majesty very graciously sent to see him. All the Earl's friends do constantly believe that he shall be removed to his own house, and in time shall come to Court but shall no more be employed.

7th November. A DICTIONARY OF THE SPANISH.

There is newly published *A dictionary in Spanish and English*, first published by Master Richard Percival, and now much enlarged by Mr. John Minsheu, to which is added a Spanish Grammar and sundry dialogues in Spanish and English.

10th November. TYRONE DENOUNCETH THE CESSATION.

On the 30th October Tyrone wrote to Sir William Warren, alleging that some soldiers that came from the Earl of Desmond were halted by the Earls of Thomond and Clanrickard, and therefore after 14 days he would renew the war. To my Lord of Ormond he wrote to the like effect, declaring that if the Earl of Essex had been there he would have had right done him. The traitor now giveth out that he and his fight for the Catholic religion and the liberty of their county.

12th November. THE DEATH OF MISTRESS RATCLIFFE.

There is much talk of the tragical death of Mistress Ratcliffe, the Maid of Honour, who ever since the death of Sir Alexander her brother hath pined in such strange manner as voluntarily she hath gone about to starve herself, and by the two days together hath received no sustenance, which meeting with extreme grief hath made an end of her maiden modest days at Richmond yesterday. Her Majesty commanded her body to be opened, and it was found well and sound, saving certain strings striped all over her heart. All the Maids go in black for her.

13th November. THE QUEEN ROYALLY RECEIVED.

This night the Lord Mayor, Aldermen and Sheriffs of London in scarlet and the commons, a great number in velvet coats and chains of gold, all well mounted on horseback, as of late times hath been used for honour of the Queen, by commandment received her at Westminster by torchlight.

THE CHILDREN OF PAUL'S.

My Lord of Derby hath put up the plays of the Children in Paul's to his great pains and charge. The Children play *Histriomastix or the player whipt*, written against the men players.

14th November. SIR CALISTHENES BROOKE HURT.

To-day my Lord Burgh fought in the field with Sir Calisthenes Brooke, and had only one thrust at him, and so the fray ended, for my Lord thrust him quite through the hand up into the arm. The cause was that Sir Calisthenes had promised his sister marriage and got her with child, and then refusing her, my Lord her brother undertook her just quarrel, which God justly revenged.

15th November. SIR JOHN HARINGTON AT COURT.

Of late Sir John Harington (who came back with my Lord of Essex) was at Court, and had been there but an hour when he was threatened with the Fleet, to which he answered poetically that coming so soon from the land-service, he hoped that he should not be pressed to serve in her Majesty's fleet in Fleet Street. Moreover when at length he came into the Presence, the Queen frowned upon him saying, 'What, did the fool bring you too? Go back to your business.' She chafed much, walking fast to and fro, and when Sir John kneeled before her, she caught him by the girdle and swore, saying, 'By God's Son,

I am no Queen ; that man is above me. Who gave him command to come here so soon ? I did send him on other business.' But after some days she sent for Sir John and gave him more gracious hearing, and learning that he had a Journal of the Earl of Essex's journeys in Ireland she demanded to see it. Then it was reported to him that on the perusing of it the Queen swore that they were all idle knaves, and the Lord Deputy worse, for wasting their time and her commands in such wise as the Journal wrote of. So she sent the Knight word that he should go home. He did not need to be bidden twice but is gone as if all the Irish rebels were at his heels.

A Discovery of Darrell's Practices.

Mr. Samuel Harsnett hath written a large treatise entitled *A discovery of the fraudulent practices of John Darrell*, showing the occasion that his practices were called in question by the Commissioners for causes ecclesiastical at Lambeth, the endeavours of Mr. Darrell's friends to extoll both him and his doings, the great uncertainty of the grounds whereupon he and all other casters out of devils do in these days build their skill, and of the shifts they have to maintain their credit when their juggling is called in question. Thence he proceedeth to intreat of Darrell's particular courses held with Somers ; of Somers' public confession that all he had done or pretended was counterfeited and devised ; and that there was no impossibility at all in the boy's fits.

17th November. The Sermon at Paul's.

This day, being the anniversary of her Majesty's accession, the sermon at Paul's Cross was preached by Dr. Thomas Holland, the Regius Professor of Divinity in Oxford, on Matthew xii. 42, wherein he took occasion to answer those both abroad and at home that uncharitably traduced the honour of the realm for observing this day in the form of an holy-day, and for the joyful exercise and Courtly triumphs exhibited in the honour of her Majesty.

'Hymns to Astræa.'

In honour of the Queen Mr. John Davies hath written twenty hymns, in all of which the first letters of each line spell out ELISA BETHA REGINA, which he termeth *Hymns to Astræa*.

THE FOURTH HYMN: TO THE MONTH OF MAY.

Each day of thine, sweet month of May,
Love makes a solemn holy-day.
I will perform like duty,
Sith thou resemblest every way
Astræa Queen of beauty,

Both you fresh beauties do partake,
Either's aspect doth Summer make,
Thoughts of young Love awaking;
Hearts you both do cause to ache,
And yet be pleased with aching.

Right dear art thou, and so is she,
Even like attractive sympathy,
Gains unto both like dearness;
I ween this made Antiquity
Name thee, sweet May of Majesty,
As being both like in clearness.

'A WARNING FOR FAIR WOMEN.'

There is printing that play of my Lord Chamberlain's men entitled *A warning for fair women*, containing a most tragical and lamentable murder of Master George Sanders, consented unto by his own wife; together with the induction where History and Comedy would hinder Tragedy, and Comedy declareth that 'tis the office of Tragedy to tell

How some damn'd tyrant, to obtain a crown,
Straps, hangs, imprisons, smothers, cutteth throats,
And then a Chorus too comes howling in,
And tells us of the worrying of a cat,
Then of a filthy whining ghost,
Lapt in some foul sheet or a leather pitch,
Comes screaming like a pig half sticked,
And cries '*Vindicta*, revenge, revenge';
With that a little rosin flasheth forth,
Like smoke out of a tobacco pipe, or a boy's squib.
Then comes in two or three like to drovers,
With tailors' bodkins, stabbing one another.

20th November. AN ENGLISH NUNNERY IN BRUSSELS.

There are sixteen English gentlewomen that wish to set up a nunnery in Brussels, to whom the Archduke gave £2,000, wherewith they bought a house. On the 4th of this month a daughter of Sir John Berkeley and sister of Sir Nicholas Pointz was solemnly created abbess by the Archbishop of Malines, and the next Sunday the Lady Mary Percy, Mistress Dorothy Arundel and six other English ladies took the habit. The ceremonies were very solemn and lasted till two in the afternoon, the Infanta, who was their godmother, the Archduke, and all the Court, and the Pope's nuncio being present. These eight ladies most bravely apparelled (borrowed ware) and adorned with rich jewels like brides were led into the Church by the Infanta and other great ladies; the ceremony over, they returned in pairs apparelled as nuns, the abbess following. The Infanta embraced them all, and assured them she would be a mother to them; then she made a banquet for a hundred persons, the great ladies, abbess and nuns dining at one of the tables. It was one of the solemnest things seen this hundred years; many ladies and others could not forbear weeping.

21st November. THE AMBASSADOR'S TART ANSWER.

Not long since complaint was made to Sir Henry Neville, her Majesty's ambassador in Paris, that the people murmured because he had a sermon in his house and some foreigners resorted to it, which might breed some danger of mutiny. The ambassador answered that he did nothing but what was warranted by the liberty and privilege of his place; and as for the people, he would not subject himself to their passions, but looked to be protected by the King as belonged to his place, and as he would look that his ambassador should be in England, where his mass was equally distasteful to the people.

22nd November. 'GODFREY OF BULLOIGNE' TRANSLATED.

Mr. Edward Fairfax hath translated into English heroical verse that allegorical poem of Torquato Tasso, entitled *Godfrey of Bulloigne or the Recovery of Jerusalem*, being twenty books with a preface upon the allegory of the poem.

THE DESCRIPTION OF JERUSALEM.

Hierusalem is seated on two hills,
Of height unlike, and turned side to side,
The space between a gentle valley fills,
From mount to mount expansed fair and wide.
Three sides are sure imbar'd, with crags and hills,
The rest is easy, scant to rise espi'd :
But mighty bulwarks fence that plainer part,
So art helps nature, nature strength'neth art.
The town is stor'd of troughs and cisterns, made
To keep fresh water, but the country seems
Devoid of grass, unfit for ploughman's trade
Not fertile, moist with rivers, wells and streams.
There grow few trees, to make the summer's shade,
To shield the parched land from scorching beams,
Save that a wood stands six mile from the town,
With aged cedars dark, and shadows brown.

23rd November. COURT NEWS.

Mistress Ratcliffe is buried this day at Westminster, all the Maids mourning but Mistress Anne Russell was chief ; she was buried as a nobleman's daughter by the Queen's command. Many of the nobility were at it ; and 24 poor women had cloaks, for so old it is said she was. My Lady Essex is a most sorrowful creature for her husband's captivity ; she wears all black of the meanest price and receives no comfort in anything. She is most desirous to see her Lord, but he is resolved, as they say, to see no creature, but as come from the Queen. Some or other told her of a warrant to send him to the Tower which infinitely grieves her. Her Majesty's anger continues, and an opinion is held that he shall have no liberty in haste. Mr. Secretary is unwell ; it is said that he hath done all good and honest offices for my Lord of Essex.

24th November. TYRONE'S DEMANDS.

Tyrone hath now set out his demands in the form of articles, as that the Catholic religion shall be openly taught throughout all Ireland, and the Church of Ireland wholly governed by the Pope ; that all cathedrals and churches and tithes be restored to the Catholics ; that an university be erected upon the

Crown rents of Ireland; that the Governor of Ireland be at least an Earl and of the Privy Council of England, bearing the name of Viceroy, but that all officers appertaining to the Council and law of Ireland be Irishmen; that the Queen nor her successor press an Irishman to serve them against his will; that an Irishman may as freely travel and traffic all merchandise in England as Englishmen; and all who will may learn and use all occupations and arts whatsoever; or that all Irishmen may freely build ships of what burden they will, furnishing the same with artillery and all munitions at their pleasure. When a copy of these articles was given to Sir Robert Cecil, he wrote upon it 'Utopia.'

25th November. THE PLAY OF ANTONIO'S REVENGE.

Mr. Marston hath written a play for the Children of Paul's called *The history of Antonio and Mellida*, the first part. This Antonio was the son of Duke Andrugio and loved Mellida the daughter of Piero, Duke of Venice. The two Dukes having gone to war, Piero was victorious and set a reward of 20,000 double pistolets upon the head of Andrugio and his son, which reward Andrugio himself claimed in person upon his own head, and at the end after many traverses the two Dukes were seemingly reconciled, and Antonio betrothed to Mellida. Note also the courtier Feliche, one that despiseth the Court and speaketh plainly at all occasions.

In the second part, entitled *Antonio's Revenge*, Duke Piero by night causeth Andrugio to be poisoned and Feliche stabbed and hung in the chamber of Mellida, whereby her chastity is called into question. Then beginneth he to woo Andrugio's widow to be his wife, to which she consenteth, until by the ghost of Andrugio and her son Antonio, she learns of the truth. Pandupho, the father of Feliche, and Antonio now begin to plot vengeance on Piero. Mellida being brought to trial for her supposed inchastity is cleared of that charge, but being falsely told that Antonio is dead swooneth and dieth. Antonio to appease the ghost of his dead father slayeth Piero's little son Julio and sprinkleth the gore upon Andrugio's tomb. At the last they seize upon Piero, bind him in his chair and pluck out his tongue. Then they show him the body of his own son and stab him, whereat the ghost of Andrugio is satisfied.

27th November. THE EARL OF ESSEX.

Two days since, being Sunday, my Lady Essex came to the Court all in black, and all she wore was not valued at £5. She came to the Countess of Huntingdon's, who came not to her, but by a second means her desire was made known that it would please her to move her Majesty to give her leave to go see my Lord who she had heard had been the night before in great extremity. This was all she desired ; and answer was returned that she must attend her Majesty's pleasure by the Lords of her Council, and come no more to Court. Yesterday at night it was verily believed that the Earl should have been sent to the Tower ; 12 of the Guard were appointed to be in readiness, and it was imagined for that purpose ; but it fell out otherwise, and one of the Guard that gave it out hath had his coat taken from him, and is committed to prison. My Lord is now extreme ill of the stone, strangulation, and grinding of the kidneys, which takes from him his stomach and rest.

28th November. PROCEEDINGS IN THE STAR CHAMBER.

To-day, being Thursday, was a Star Chamber day when a public declaration was made by the Lords for the satisfaction of the world of the Earl of Essex's imprisonment. The ground of it was that certain slanderous libels have been cast abroad that touch her Sacred Majesty and her Council's proceedings. All the Lords of the Council spoke, much blaming the Earl's courses, and a commandment was added that none shall busy themselves in matters of state that concern them not ; and for the libels if any hereafter do know the authors and will not reveal them they shall incur the like punishment and danger as the author himself, whosoever he is.

1st December. COURT NEWS.

The declaration of the Lords in Star Chamber in open court of the Earl's misgovernment in Ireland, where all the errors and faults he committed were plainly set down by them, hath given all the world satisfaction of the just cause her Majesty had to proceed against him. To-morrow the Earl's household, being 160, are dispersed, and every man to seek a new fortune ; some few are retained to attend him where it will be her Majesty's will to send him. This is the greatest downfall we have seen in our days, making us to see the vanity of the world.

My Lord Mountjoy must go into Ireland, but as yet it is not known in what sort. With him goes Sir George Carew to be Lord President of Munster, a worthy valiant gentleman that knows the country and is able to do her Majesty good service. He hath very good friends in Court.

My Lady of Northumberland and her lord are not yet come together. He once offered her £1,000 a year to live apart. She desired as much as she brought, which was £1,500, and now 'tis bruited he will give her but £500. Men lay most fault in her for this separation. The Earl himself and Sir Walter Ralegh are very great and inward friends.

4th December. A Witch Executed.

To-day a witch called Anne Kerke, that was arraigned before the Lord Anderson and other justices and then condemned, was executed at Tyburn. She was charged with many witcheries. At one time taking displeasure with a woman for not bidding her to her child's christening, she tormented the child twice or thrice a day in strange manner until the father with others went to Mother Gillams (that dwelleth on the Bankside), who told them that the child was forespoken, and that the witch had been (as indeed she was) twice with the mother of the child before they came home, and that for the child's recovery they should cut off a piece of the witch's coat with a pair of shears, and burn it together with the child's undercloth : which they did and the child accordingly was healed.

At another time this witch fell out with an innkeeper, and in revengement bewitched his only child so strangely as that by no means of physic which he could get it could be recovered ; but still it was from time to time tormented until it died. But before the death the father (finding no help by physic) went to a cunning man who told him that the cause of his child's death was one that was conversant in his house ; and (after promise made of not revealing the party) he showed him in a glass this witch Anne Kerke. After this he told his neighbourhood that she was a witch and had bewitched his child to death. Whereupon he going home fell sick and died.

Afterwards being brought before Sir Richard Martin, he having heard that a witch's hair could not be cut, commanded a sergeant to pull from her head ten or twelve of her hairs and try if he could cut them. The sergeant did so, and offering to cut them with a pair of barber's scissors, they turned round in his hand; and the edges were so battered, turned, and quite spoiled as that they would not cut anything. Then the sergeant took the hair and did put it into the fire to burn it; but the fire flew from it, and the hair lay in the midst thereof unburnt.

10th December. A TRUCE WITH TYRONE.

On the 1st of the month the Earl of Ormond and Sir Geoffrey Fenton met with Tyrone and there acquainted him with a letter that they received from her Majesty concerning his receiving again into mercy. After some parleying, upon the next day, a cessation is concluded until the end of this present month.

13th December. THE EARL OF ESSEX'S SICKNESS.

It is noted that the Earl of Essex received the Communion last Sunday; afterwards he sent unto her Majesty his two patents as Master of the Horse and of the Ordnance, which she sent back again; that of Earl Marshal he keeps and will during his life. My Lady Essex had leave yesterday to go to him, and so she did; but found him so weak that there is little hope of his recovery.

14th December. THE STATE OF IRELAND.

The state of Ireland is now grown very perilous, for the arch-traitor affirmates publicly that his conscience and the Catholic religion were the causes that carried him into this rebellion in which he will live and die. It is much feared therefore that if new forces be not speedily sent, the main blow to be struck for that kingdom is not far off. The companies are grown so weak that of the number of 2,800 assigned for the army at Navan there remains but 1,330 and of that number 200 or 300 might have been culled out for unserviceable. There are everywhere great deficiencies, partly by reason of the frauds of the commissaries of musters, partly also because great numbers are sick by their own disorder and the hardness of the climate and the ill-condition of a great portion of the victuals sent from England.

15th December. The Earl of Essex's Illness.

Yesterday, hearing the Earl of Essex was desperately sick, by her Majesty's command eight physicians of the best experience assembled and consulted what might speedily recover him to health; who sent in writing their opinion to her Majesty subscribed by them, which was that *salus magis optanda quam speranda.* That these three things were required; to have his mind quieted, that he might take rest; that he might have recreation; that he might change the air, for they found his liver stopped and perished, and his entrails and guts exulcerated so that they could not tell what now to minister but general glisters to keep him clean within.

The Queen, understanding the state he was in, was very pensive and grieved, and sent Dr. James unto him with some broth. Her message was that he should comfort himself, and that she would, if she might with her honour, go to visit him; and it was noted that she had water in her eyes when she spoke it. Some comfort it brought to the Earl, but it is thought and feared that it comes very late, for nature is decayed and he so feeble that to make his bed he is removed upon sheets and blankets. The Queen commanded he should be removed from that chamber he was in to my Lord Keeper's own chamber. This afternoon a general opinion is held that he cannot live many days, for he begins to swell, and he scours all black matter, as if the strength of nature were quite gone.

15th December. A New Play.

My Lord of Nottingham's men have a new play by Dekker called *The pleasant comedy of Old Fortunatus*, being the fable of Fortunatus, who was offered six gifts by Fortune, and choosing wealth, she gave a purse that should never be empty; and how grievously he and his sons misused that gift.

24th December. Boisterous Winds.

Yesterday the wind blew west and by south, boisterous and great, where through the tops of many chimneys are overthrown, lead blown off churches, trees and barns blown down. A tilt boat from London going towards Gravesend was lost against Woolwich by wilfulness of the watermen rowing against an anchor: and of 30 persons, men and women, but 11 are saved.

28th December. Court News.

This Christmas the Chamberlain's men played at Court on the 26th and the Admiral's yesterday. The Queen hath graced the dancing and plays with her own presence, and played at cards in the Presence at primero with the Lord Treasurer, Mr. Secretary and the Lord North. The Court was great and full of Lords and Ladies, and her Majesty came to the Chapel. At Court upon the very white walls much villainy hath been written against Master Secretary.

29th December. A Cambridge Christmas Play.

At St. John's College in Cambridge they have a Christmas play called *The Return from Parnassus*, being a second part to that play which they had last year. In this play is shown the hard hap of needy scholars when they leave the University that are forced to spend their wits as sextons, or tutors to young gentlemen, or in the service of gulls. They conclude therefore to go to Rome or Rheims and there mend their state.

30th December. A Defence of Darrell.

Some friend of Darrell hath published a little book called *The trial of Master Darrell*, or a collection of defences against allegations not yet suffered to receive convenient answer, which are intended to clear him from the imputation of teaching Somers and others to counterfeit possession of devils. Addeth thereto an epistle concerning Mr. Harsnett's treatise.

31st December. New Plays at the Rose.

The Lord Admiral's players have played these new plays at the Rose since Midsummer: *All Fools but the Fool* (by Chapman); *The Gentle Craft* (by Dekker); *The Stepmother's Tragedy* (by Chettle and Dekker); *Bear a Brain* (by Dekker); *Page of Plymouth* (by Dekker and Jonson); *The Poor Man's Paradise* (by Haughton); *Robert the Second, King of Scots* (by Chettle, Dekker and Jonson); *Tristram of Lionesse*; *Sir John Oldcastle* (by Drayton, Hathaway, Munday and Wilson); *Patient Grissel* (by Chettle, Dekker and Haughton); *Cox of Cullumpton* (by Day and Haughton); *Henry Richmond*, the 2nd part (by Wilson); *Thomas Merry, or Beech's Tragedy* (by Day and Haughton); *Fortunatus* (by Dekker).

THESE BOOKS ALSO SET FORTH ANNO 1599.

WIT'S THEATRE OF THE LITTLE WORLD.'

Mr. Robert Allott hath compiled from the ancient writers a book entitled, *The Theatre of the Little World*, wherein we may behold the inward and outward parts of man lively figured in his actions and behaviours, which he dedicateth to Mr. Bodenham that wrote *Politeuphuia* two years ago. Noteth that if any shall think his work perfunctory and idle because it is but a collection of the flowers of antiquities and histories, yet doth it comprehend those seven persons which have ever been thought most worthy subjects to be written of, as Kings, Knights, Bishops, Judges, Magistrates, Husbands in their houses and Religious men in their churches.

'DIET'S DRY DINNER.'

A book by Mr. Henry Buttes, Fellow of Corpus Christi College in Cambridge, entitled *Diet's dry dinner*, wherein are set forth the properties of things commonly used for food, giving on the one page their qualities, use and harm, seasons, and for whom most suitable to be used, and on the other page a story of the same for use at table talk. Noteth of garlic that it is of special use for seamen as an excellent preservative against all infection proceeding from the pump and the tainted meats which mariners are forced to eat: it pacifieth also the disposition to vomit, caused by the roughness of the sea. Of hares' flesh, it is a received opinion that it procureth beauty, fresh colour, and cheerful countenance for a sevenight space, insomuch as the Italians have a byword, which speaketh thus of a fair man; 'He hath eaten a hare.' The partridge, saith he, is so venerious that the cock opposed to the hen on the windy side, she conceiveth through the wind that blows from him. The oyster though a headless fish is yet passing toothsome; it is engendered of mere mire, or mud inclining to corruption, of the sea froth or spume which cleaveth upon fish: it is unseasonable in all months that have not the letter R in their name, because it is then venerious. For tobacco, noteth that we are not beholden to the Spaniards, for that our English Ulysses, renowned Sir Walter Ralegh, a man admirably excellent in Navigation, of Nature's privy council, and infinitely read in the wide book of the world, hath both far fetched it and dear bought it, and since it came in request there hath been *magnus fumi questus* and *fumivendulus* is the best epithet for an apothecary.

'The Mansion of Magnanimity.'

There is published by Mr. Richard Crompton a book entitled *The Mansion of Magnanimity*, dedicated to my Lord of Essex. Herein is shown the strength of this realm both by nature, and situation, by her Majesty's happy government and honourable Councillors; with the examples of divers noblemen who have adventured their lives in defence of their country; and how we ought to beware of sedition amongst ourselves. Addeth a note of divers laws that concern disloyal subjects. Noteth in an oration to be made by the General before battle what great miseries and calamities happened to this nation by the hard dealings of William, Duke of Normandy, when he conquered this land; how that there was no cruelty, no misery, no servitude or bondage which could be devised but he afflicted them therewith; and shall we look for any other if our enemies should prevail?

A Book Against Plays.

Dr. Rainolds that was made Master of Corpus Christi College in Oxford put forth a book called *The overthrow of stage plays*, being by way of controversy with Dr. Gager, wherein he goes to prove that it is not only unlawful to be an actor but also a beholder of those vanities.

'The Passionate Pilgrim.'

A little book of songs and sonnets by Mr. Shakespeare entitled *The Passionate Pilgrim*.

Weever's 'Epigrams.'

A book of *Epigrams in the oldest cut and newest Fashion* by John Weever, divided into seven weeks.

1600

2nd January. NEW YEAR'S GIFTS.

At the New Year many of the Court have given her Majesty gifts of divers sorts, jewels, kirtles, mantles, petticoats, ruffs, and other garments, pots of green ginger, marchpanes, perfumed gloves, and all kinds of devices; and some also offer money in gold to the sum of more than £750. And to her courtiers and servants the Queen hath given presents in gilt plate, 4,200 ozs. and more.

5th January. COURT NEWS.

The Queen is in very good health and comes much abroad these holidays, for almost every night she is in the Presence to see the Ladies dance the old and new country dances with the tabor and pipe. There was an exceedingly rich New Year's gift presented, which as it were in a cloud no man knowing how; it is neither received nor rejected. It comes from the poor Earl. His friends do hope that he shall be removed to his own house or to Mr. Controller's. He begins now to recover, for he is able to sit up and to eat at a table. His Lady comes every morning unto him by 7, and stays till 6, which is said to be the full time limited for her abode there. The Ladies, his sisters, my Lady Walsingham, nor his son, have no liberty to go to him as yet. Many of the ministers that made public prayers for him are commanded to silence; some indeed foolishly forgot themselves, their doubtful speeches tending to sedition.

Mr. Secretary hath disposed great and many New Year's gifts this year in Court. The Queen's favour increases towards him, so careful is he of her business and service; and indeed the whole weight of the State lies upon him. Some say he doth all good offices towards the Earl, but her Majesty's indignation cannot yet be removed.

7th January. PLAYERS AT COURT.

These Christmas holidays at Court the Lord Chamberlain's men played twice, as also the Lord Admiral's, who showed *Old*

Fortunatus and *The Shoemaker's holiday*; and for the former Dekker wrote a new beginning and ending in praise of the Queen. 'Are you then travelling to the temple of Eliza?' quoth one. To which the other answereth, 'Even to her temple are my feeble limbs travelling. Some call her Pandora; some Gloriana, some Cynthia: some Delphœbe, some Astræa: all by several names to express several loves; yet all those names make but one celestial body, as all those loves meet to create but one soul.'

11th January. A Fencer Hanged.

Henry Adlington, a fencer, was hanged without the bars of Aldgate for killing a man there, and after hanged in chains on the Mile's End.

12th January. Alleyn's New Playhouse.

Alleyn now prepareth to build a new playhouse in Redcross Street, with the favour of her Majesty, who was well content with his playing this last Chris mas, and of my Lord Admiral.

'The Preservation of King Henry the Seventh.'

A certain unknown author hath a poetical work called, *The first book of the Preservation of King Henry the Seventh*, compiled in English rhythmical hexameters chiefly from Mr. Grafton's *Chronicle*, being dedicated to the Queen's Majesty. This book is prefaced with an Epistle to the right honourable, worshipful, gentle and learned readers in commendation of hexameters, because that these hexameters and pentameters in English are misliked of many, even of some accounted learned doctors and linguists: as for the plain rhythmer, his books are stuffed with lines of prose with a rhythm in the end, which every fiddler or piper can make upon a theme given. This true kind of verse, declareth the author, will bring unto us four commodities; it will enrich our speech with good and significant words; it will bring delight and pleasure to the skilful reader when he sees them formally compiled; it will encourage and learn the good and godly students that affect poetry and are naturally inclined thereunto to make the like; it will direct a true *idioma*, and will teach true orthography. For as gold surpasseth lead, so the hexameters surpass rhythm prose.

THE AUTHOR TO HIS PRINTER.

Print with a good letter, this book, and carefully Printer :
Print each word legibil, not a word nor a syllable alter :
Keep points, and commas, periods, the parenthesis observe ;
My credit and thy report to defend, both safely to conserve.

COURT NEWS.

The Earl of Essex recovers ; his gift is not accepted in Court for the Queen is still very angry with him ; 'tis said that he shall be removed either to the Lord Archbishop's or to the Tower. The Lady Rich earnestly follows her desire to have leave to go see him ; she writes to her Majesty many letters, sends many jewels and presents. Her letters are read, her presents received, but no leave granted. The Lady Leicester sent the Queen a rich New Year's gift which was very well taken. The Lady Northumberland is in Court ; there hath been unkindness between her and the Earl, her husband. She spoke with the Queen, complained of the little means she had to live, and besought her Majesty's favour. The Earl of Northumberland is a perpetual courtier, and familiar with Sir Walter Ralegh at cards.

14th January. TWO PROCLAMATIONS MADE.

Two proclamations were to-day made. The first is for publication of the Commission under the Great Seal of England for avoiding of the trouble and charges that grow by concealment and that subjects may compound for security of their estates from her Majesty for a perpetual quiet to them and their posterities.

The second is for the due observation of fish days, suppressing of unnecessary number of alehouses, and for the better execution of the late act for punishment of rogues, vagabonds and beggars. Herein it is noted that after the late statutes for the suppressing and punishing rogues and vagabonds they were for a time greatly diminished, and idleness, thefts, and other insolencies and disorders much avoided ; but as soon as through the negligence and remissness of justices and other offices the laws were not put in due execution, many great enormities and disorders began forthwith to incumber the happy, quiet and good government of the Realm, which are likely daily more and more to grow if some speedy remedy be not employed in time. Wherefore high constables and other head officers are straitly commanded once in every month to call before them the inferior officers, to inquire how the laws and statutes have been observed and to admonish those in whom any default or negligence hath been found. Moreover those justices through whose negligence or connivancy these offences shall be continued, shall receive such condign punishment as to the quality of their offences and contempt shall appear most fit and convenient. It is further commanded that an abstract of the statutes shall be read publicly at every Quarter Sessions and once every quarter at least in every parish church by the parson.

16th January. CONTRIBUTIONS FROM THE LAWYERS.

Because of her Majesty's great need in these Irish affairs, letters have been severally addressed to many of the lawyers requiring contributions from them for the service whereby her Majesty shall make a judgment of their affection, and declaring that the lawyers especially, to whom God hath given more than ordinary understanding, will see how necessary it is that this wicked rebellion should be by all due courses suppressed. These letters have been sent to one hundred and thirty eight of them demanding in all more than £2,000.

19th January. RECUSANTS IN LONDON.

This day 16 priests and 4 laymen were removed out of divers prisons in and about London and despatched towards Wisbeach, whereof one is a Bishop of Ireland and another a Franciscan Friar of the Order of the Capuchins. This man wore his friar's weed all the way he went, a thing not seen in England these many years.

20th January. THE AMBASSADOR'S COMPLAINT FROM PARIS.

Sir Henry Neville, the ambassador in Paris, reporteth that these late alterations in England are much talked of throughout Christendom. As for himself he would be glad to return, for the burden is too heavy for his purse by repair of Englishmen to whom he cannot shut his gate, so that sometimes he hath 12 or 16 of them at his table. Noteth what idols we make of ambassadors here in England when scant courtesy is shown them over there.

22nd January. A Book concerning Fish and Fruit.

There is come forth a book called *Certain experiments concerning fish and fruit*, practised by Mr. John Taverner. Showeth the proper ways of making a pond of fish together with a discourse of their several kinds and natures; also the manner of planting and growing fruit trees.

24th January. Court News.

My Lady Egerton died three days since; and the Lord Keeper doth sorrow more than the wisdom of so great a man ought to do. He keeps private, and it is thought he will not come abroad this term. The Queen sent to comfort him, and to remind him that the public service must be preferred before private. Besides he is greatly discontented that his house is made a prison of so long continuance, for the Earl of Essex hath remained there now 17 weeks. My Lord is well recovered; and the world now attend what shall become of him.

2nd February. The Cross in Cheapside.

Of late the ancient cross that stands in the midst of Cheapside was taken down and the Lord Mayor had an intention to set up some other device there; which when the Queen heard of it, she was greatly displeased that so ancient a monument should be so defaced, and hath expressly ordered that since the monument has been repaired the cross shall be set up again as it formerly stood.

The Earl's Picture.

Some foolish idle-headed ballad maker of late hath caused many of the Earl of Essex's pictures to be printed on horseback, with all his titles of honour, all his service, and two verses underneath that gives him exceeding praise for wisdom, honour and worth; that heaven and earth approve it, God's elected; with such words as hath occasioned the calling of them in.

4th February. Delays in the Court of Admiralty.

Many complaints have been made both by Englishmen and by the ambassadors and subjects of other Princes of the great and intolerable delays in suits depending in the Court of Admiralty, which happeneth by reason of the prohibitions granted forth from the Courts of the Queen's Bench and the Common

Pleas. Hereby the honour of her Majesty, the justice of the realm, and the safety of merchants using traffic with those countries is in question; for by the often granting of such prohibitions the pursuit of causes is so tedious and chargeable to the complainants that either they are enforced to give over their suits or else to spend far more in charges than their principal amounts unto, oftentimes to their utter undoing and to the great slander of justice. Mr. Sergeant Yelverton, Mr. Attorney, Mr. Solicitor and Mr. Francis Bacon are therefore instructed to meet and consider how such prohibitions ought to be awarded.

DESERTERS FROM IRELAND.

The Mayor and officers of the ports adjoining to Ireland are straitly ordered that if any soldiers come in ships from Ireland without passports, they are to be committed to gaol. And for such as show passports, if they be sick or maimed they shall be suffered to pass, but if they be able men their passports shall be sent to the Council, for there is a new and more straight charge given to the Lord Deputy that no private captain ought to give a passport to any soldier but such as are appointed by the State or the Provincial Governors. Such able soldiers shall be imprested anew and sent back with the next shipping. Especial care also shall be taken that such of these soldiers as give forth slanderous speeches to discourage others and cover their lewdness in shifting away shall be committed to prison.

10*th February*. WILL KEMP'S WAGER.

Will Kemp the clown hath wagered that he will dance from London to Norwich, and this morning before 7 of the clock is set forward from the Lord Mayor's towards the Mayor of Norwich, accompanied by Thomas Sly his taborer and George Sprat that is appointed for his overseer. At his departure many gave him bowed sixpences and groats, blessing him with hearty prayers and God-speeds. Through Whitechapel, Mile End and Stratford Bow he passed with great throngs of people accompanying him; and here he rested for a while from dancing but had small rest from those that would have urged him to drinking. Thence they went on to Stratford Langton and so to Ilford where the people would have had him drink carouses in the great spoon. From Ilford he set forward by moonshine, dancing to within a quarter of a mile of Romford, where a gentleman of London alighting from his horse would have no nay but that he should leap into his saddle and so to his inn, where he resteth from his first day's morrice.

THE LORD. MOUNTJOY.

A few days since the Lord Mountjoy, her Majesty's Lord Deputy in Ireland, set forth from London. Amongst many matters delivered him in his instructions, he is enjoined to plant garrisons in the heart of the countries of the capital rebels which shall be of such condition as they shall not only serve for diversion by making good the places of their residence, but also be able to sally out and make continual incursions. It is to be feared that my Lord will be much delayed in his journeys by reason of the present great frosts which make the ways exceeding dangerous.

14th February. THE EARL OF ESSEX.

Yesterday it was expected that the Earl of Essex should have been called to the Star Chamber, and preparation was made for it in the Star Chamber, both for his diet and a place to stand in. Multitudes of people assembled to have seen or heard his trial; but by Mr. Secretary's care it was hindered, for he took a very submissive letter to the Queen and did all the good offices he could to remove her Majesty's resolution of having him called to the Star Chamber. Mr. Secretary hath won much honour and love by it, for he manifestly hath not been so adverse to the Earl as it is supposed; it is her Majesty who was wounded by the Earl's contemptuous courses and is not easily to be satisfied.

KEMP'S DANCE.

After resting two days at Romford, being much thronged by the townsmen and Londoners that came hourly to visit him, Kemp set forward again and reached Burntwood, whence he was fain to steal away by moonlight from those that would follow him. Yet do what he could there were above fifty that would needs trudge after him through thick and thin when they heard his tabor.

17th February. THE ARCHDUKE'S SECRETARY.

There is newly landed at Dover out of Flanders the Secretary of the Archduke and the Infanta, sent hither unto her Majesty.

The Queen hath signified both in regard of the quality of the gentleman and the good entertainment shown to her servant that was lately sent thither, that he shall be well used and lodged in the house of Mr. Alderman Banning, who shall have a care to see him accommodated of bedding, napery, household stuff, and other things necessary for him and his train, and to cause also a good and sufficient diet to be provided for him, the charge whereof shall be defrayed by her Majesty. At his landing on the Tower Wharf he shall be attended by Sir John Peyton, Governor of the Tower.

21st February. THE EARL OF ESSEX.

My Lord of Essex continues still at York House, all his friends awaiting his liberty, which is not yet granted ; for her Majesty's displeasure, though it was somewhat appeased, yet now and then it appears as bitter as it was ; for some or other hath told her that the world thinks my Lord's not coming to the Star Chamber was only for want of matter to proceed against him. Beside the libellers cease not from writing. No man can yet set down the time of the Earl's removing from the place where he is, but he is very well and merry.

23rd February. KEMP'S DANCE.

Kemp and his fellows are now come to Bury, which they reached yesterday in the afternoon at what time the Lord Chief Justice entered at another gate of the town, when the wondering multitude left the streets where he passed to gape at Kemp. The throng of them was so great that Kemp was seven times stayed ere he could recover his inn.

25th February. A PREACHING FRIAR.

This day one Campbell a friar that is imprisoned in the Marshalsea preached a sermon whereat 22 men and 26 women were present, who were all taken, but some afterwards released on bail. This man is now committed to close prison, and the keeper is commanded to take away his friar-like weeds.

THE EARL OF ESSEX.

The Earl of Essex is little spoken of at Court, only a mislike taken that my Lady Leicester (his mother), the Earl of Southampton, and many others of his friends have been in a house that looks into York Garden where he uses to walk, and they have saluted each other out of a window. The Lady Rich is commanded to keep her house, because, 'tis said, that by her means certain copies of a letter she writ to her Majesty are published abroad.

26th February. A SAYING CONCERNING THE QUEEN.

A certain Walloon that is employed about the affairs of the Infanta with her Highness has sent such a despatch of the person, riches, greatness and majesty of the Queen of England as is like to make him for very anger eat one meal a day the faster. This man declared that he was shrewdly amazed when he saw the Queen's fashion; 'for,' says he, 'the Infanta is *bontif* (which is as much to say of a good mild nature), but *par Dieu, cette Reine est extrêmement sage, et a des yeux terribles. Oh, che grandezza!'*

3rd March. AN AMBASSADOR FROM THE ARCHDUKE.

Verreyken, the Secretary of the Archduke, is come to London to consider of some proposal of peace. It is believed that his speeches have tended to show the desire of the Archduke, as Duke of Burgundy, to have her Majesty's amity, and to revive the ancient league between England and Burgundy. He has no full authority to conclude, but only by way of discourse to declare what by the Spaniards may be propounded and to hear what her Majesty will propound. He had audience a week ago when compliments passed between her Majesty and him. To-day Sir Walter Ralegh is appointed to accompany him to Westminster to see the tombs and singularities of that place.

Yesterday the Queen did that which usually she doth not. Being Sunday, and a very fair morning, she went privately abroad in my Lord Chamberlain's coach, none with her but my Lady Warwick, Sir John Stanhope, Sir Edward Carey and Mr. Greville. The weather hath been so foul this past month that she could not go abroad before; but ere she could return back it was commonly known.

KEMP'S DANCE.

Kemp is now come to Hingham, having been delayed for some days at Bury by reason of the great fall of snow last week.

At Rockland, when he desired to see the host of his inn, he would in no wise be spoken with till he had shifted himself from his working day's suit. Then being armed at all points, from cap to codpiece, his black shoes shining and made straight with copper buckles of the best, his garters in the fashion and every garment fitting correm-squandam (which was his own word), he enters the hall with his bonnet in his hand and began to cry out, 'O Kemp, dear Master Kemp, you are even as welcome as, as, as—thou art even as welcome as the Queen's best greyhound.'

Having rested him well, Kemp began to take his course for Hingham whither mine honest host of Rockland must needs be his guide, but he had not followed two fields but he lies all along and cries after Kemp to come back and speak with him. So Kemp coming to him, 'Dancer,' quoth he, 'if thou dance a' God's name, God speed thee: I cannot follow thee afoot farther, but adieu good dancer, God speed thee if thou dance a' God's name.'

8th March. SIR THOMAS WINGFIELD'S COMPLAINTS.

Sir Thomas Wingfield that saved the remnants of the army after the mischance at Armagh in August '98 is now in London. He complaineth in bitter terms that his pay, amounting to over a thousand pounds, is withheld from him, and because that a mighty one distasted of that service he hath long been put off the Queen's pay, and his reputation brought in question in every alehouse.

9th March. THE NEW PLAYHOUSE PROHIBITED.

Upon complaint from my Lord Willoughby and other gentlemen in the parish of St. Giles without Cripplegate the Council have required the Justices of Middlesex to take order that Alleyn's new playhouse be stayed.

THE LORD MOUNTJOY AT DUBLIN.

From Ireland it is reported that the Lord Mountjoy arrived at Dublin on the 27th of last month, and next day took the Sword. Tyrone continueth still in Munster passing from one county to another without impediment. Since the middle of the month he and the Earl of Desmond have burned 220 towns and villages in the county belonging to the Lord Barry in revenge that he will not sort himself with the traitors.

COURT NEWS.

All this week the Lords have been in London, and pass away the time in feasting and plays: for Verreyken dined upon Wednesday with my Lord Treasurer who made him a royal dinner. Upon Thursday my Lord Chamberlain feasted him, and there in the afternoon his players acted *Sir John Oldcastle* to his great contentment. To-day he was received at Court, and all places where he passed through full of people; the Presence Chamber full and brave, especially of ladies. In the Privy Chamber he had audience and took his leave of her Majesty who was exceeding brave and rich. He returned to the Council Chamber accompanied with my Lord Harry Seymour, where he had a collation. To him came all the Lords, one by one in degree, to bid him farewell and had some private speech with him; and so he departed, Sir Walter Ralegh bringing him to his coach.

There was expectation all the week that my Lord of Essex should have come to his own house, but it is not known why it is stayed. This reason is conjectured; that the great Ladies Leicester, Southampton, Northumberland and Rich, assembled themselves at Essex House to receive him, which hindered it at that time. He hath his health well again, and is much troubled at the indiscretion of his friends and servants, which makes him by their tattle to suffer the more.

KEMP REACHETH NORWICH.

Kemp hath now come to Norwich where he abideth, in great good cheer. He reached the city five days ago, but stayed his morris a little before St. Giles' gate, procrastinating his dance through the city until Saturday last (7th), when he returned without the city and began afresh. He entered in at St. Stephen's gate where one Thomas Gilbert, in name of all the rest of the citizens, gave him a friendly welcome. Passing the gates, whifflers made him way through the throng of the people, and with great labour he got through the narrow press into the market place, where on the cross, ready prepared, stood the city waits which with wind instruments, viol and violin and voice not a little refreshed him. Passing by the market place on he went towards the Mayor's, leaping over the churchyard wall at

St. John's and getting so into Master Mayor's gates a nearer way. And here is he plentifully entertained with good cheer by Mr. Mayor and his bountiful brethren, and many knights and ladies and gentlemen. The Mayor gave him £5 in Elizabeth angels, and besides 40s. yearly during his life, making him also a freeman of the merchant venturers. The measure of his jump is to be seen in the Guildhall at Norwich, where his buskins that he then wore and danced in from London thither stand equally divided nailed on the wall.

10th March. DISORDERLY SOLDIERS FROM WALES.

Great disorders are reported amongst the soldiers from Wales, who have been ready not only ofttimes to mutiny, but divers of them are run away, and some have taken their apparel with them; and generally the choice of the men out of the Welsh counties is so bad as it should seem they were picked out to disburden the counties of so many idle, vagrant and loose persons, rather than for their ability and aptness to do service.

12th March. DEFIANT SEAMEN.

The Mayor of Dartmouth being instructed by the Council to deliver to the master a Dutch ship called the *Jonas* of Hamburg, which was taken by Captain Anthony Crocker of the *Refusal*, went aboard her with certain officers of the town and the Council's officer. Hereupon 30 of the company of the *Refusal*, armed with rapiers and poniards, declared that they would keep possession by force and kill any officer who set hands on them to remove them, and although they were required in her Majesty's name to lay aside their weapons and depart peacefully, yet they refused.

15th March. COURT NEWS.

Sir Walter Ralegh, ill pleased to see nothing done for him, within two or three days goes out of town with his wife and family to the West country. My Lord Chamberlain is very sick at Drayton, being seized with an apoplexy. My Lord Southampton is in very good hope to kiss the Queen's hand before his going back into Ireland, Mr. Secretary is his good friend and attends it; his horses and stuff are gone before. By her Majesty's express command, my Lady Leicester, Lord and Lady

Southampton, Mr. Greville, Mr. Antony Bacon are all removed from Essex House, and this day my Lord is looked for there to remain with two keepers, Sir Dru Drury and Sir Richard Berkeley, and none to come and speak with him, but with her Majesty's leave.

18th March. A Proclamation concerning Gold and Silver.

The Queen hath caused proclamation to be made that because of late years coin, plate and bullion of silver and gold have been more abundantly conveyed out of this realm than in any former times by reason that the laws formerly made are not observed. It is now commanded that the mayor and bailiffs in seaports shall take oath of the merchants and masters of ships accordingly.

20th March. A History of the Turks.

Mr. Robert Carr of the Middle Temple hath translated from the French and Italian tongues *The Mahumetan or Turkish History*, wherein in three books he treateth of the origin of the Turks and of the four Empires that issued out of the superstitious sect of Mahumet; of their conquests and the succession of the house of Ottoman; of the wars and siege of Malta which Saliman the Great made; to which is added a discourse of the wars of Cyprus, what time Selimus the Second took from the Venetians the possession of that Island, and a small discourse of the causes of the greatness of the Turkish Empire.

21st March. The Earl of Essex.

About 8 o'clock last night my Lord of Essex came to his own house, where he is very private. Sir Richard Berkeley only is appointed to be his guardian who hath all the keys of the house in his custody and his servant is porter. He lies in the next chamber to the Earl and none is to be admitted to speak with him but with the Queen's leave. Her Ladyship doth come in the day time unto him but not otherwise, and all are removed out of the house but such as ordinarily must attend the Earl for his diet and chamber.

22nd March. A Petition for the New Playhouse.

The inhabitants of Finsbury in the parish of St. Giles Cripplegate have petitioned the Council that the building of Alleyn's playhouse may proceed, seeing that the place appointed standeth very tolerable, near the fields and so far distant from any place of account that none can be annoyed thereby; and besides he is contented to give a very liberal portion of money weekly towards the relief of the poor.

23rd March. SNOW.

To-day, being Easter day, it snowed and was extreme cold.

25th March. AN OUTRAGE IN THE CITY.

Of late Sir Edward Baynham and other disordered persons and captains in his company committed a foul outrage, enterprising to beat the watches in the City, for which they are committed to prison by the Lord Mayor. By the direction of the Council they shall answer this misdemeanour in the Star Chamber.

28th March. A PROCLAMATION AGAINST WOAD.

There is a proclamation issued forbidding the breaking and tilling of very fertile ground for the sowing of woad, for private and inordinate gain.

1st April. A PLAYHOUSE PREVENTED.

This day Mr. John Wolfe the stationer was called before the justices of the peace because that he hath begun to erect a playhouse in Nightingale Lane near East Smithfield contrary to the proclamation and orders set down in the Court of Star Chamber. He is bound in recognizance in the sum of £40 not to proceed any further in the same unless he shall procure sufficient warrant from the Lords of the Council.

3rd April. COURT NEWS.

My Lord Chamberlain came to Court but is removed to London; he is still not very well. Meanwhile at Court they begin to dispose of his places and to make suit for them. Upon Sunday last Dr. Andrews made a strange sermon at Court; his text was the 20th chapter of St. John, the 23rd verse, touching the forgiveness of sins upon earth. He said that contrition, without confession and absolution, was not sufficient; that the ministers had the two keys of power and knowledge delivered unto them, that whose sins soever they remitted upon earth should be remitted in Heaven. The Court is full of it, for such doctrine is not usually taught here. My Lord of Essex is very private at his own house, and little speech of him in Court. The Lords now meet at my Lord Treasurer's about the despatch of the Commissioners to Emden, who are to be there by the 15th; the Lord Bishop of London, Mr. Herbert and Dr. Parkins attend.

4th April. THE BISHOP OF LONDON.

The Bishop of London takes 40 men with him, whereof 20 shall wear chains. He takes 20 or 30 tun of beer, 6 tun of wine for his provisions, and great store of plate, some out of the Jewel House by her Majesty's command. It is likely that he will furnish himself very pontifically of all things for his journey, for her Majesty told him he must keep a bountiful house.

MORE SNOW.

Since the snow on Easter Sunday, it hath remained extreme cold and to-day there was more snow.

8th April. LEVIES FROM THE CITY.

The Lord Mayor is required to take up men for the Irish service to the number of 200 to take the place of those that are deficient at the port of embarking, partly by the choice of insufficient men, partly by sickness, but especially by the evil disposition of many lewd and dissolute persons that are run away. No new charge shall be imposed upon the City hereby, the charges of conduct, arming and apparel being defrayed by her Majesty. These men shall be taken from those that may well be spared from the City and the Liberties by reason of their idle and disorderly life, but nevertheless they shall be able and fit men to be employed in the service, being known not to be common rogues and vagabonds or mutinous persons.

ALLEYN'S PLAYHOUSE.

The Council now permit the building of Alleyn's new playhouse to go forward without further let.

10th April. The SELLING OF GAME.

The Council have written to the Lord Mayor, as at sundry times in the past, concerning the preservation of pheasants and partridges, provisions not meet for common persons nor to be openly sold by poulters by reason of the great scarcity of them. Now again they are so ordinarily uttered to the poulters in the City and suburbs by those that are poachers (as they are termed) and stealers that the game is exceedingly destroyed about her Majesty's houses, and so great scarcity that she can neither have pleasure abroad by hawking nor sufficient provision for her diet, nor any noblemen nor gentlemen be well served of them. Likewise the orders prescribed for the preserving of field rabbits, that none should be sold till they are of bigness to be taken in a hay, have been utterly neglected. The Lord Mayor shall therefore call before him all buyers and sellers of poultry and take bonds of them not to sell or buy pheasants or partridges at any time, nor rabbits until they be of meet bigness, which is usually about the 6th of June.

11th April. A Suicide.

One Dorrington, a rich man, to-day went up to St. Sepulchre's steeple and threw himself over the battlement, and broke his neck. There was found a paper sealed about him with this superscription; 'Lord save my soul and I will praise Thy Name.'

12th April. Court News.

My Lord of Essex hath a little more liberty in his own house, for Sir Richard Berkeley lies underneath him, but the gates are closed and nobody hath access unto him. My Lady, his wife, is a humble suitor to her Majesty by the Lords that she will be pleased to let her live in the house with her husband because my Lady Walsingham, her mother, is going to Barn Elms. My Lord often walks upon his open leads and in his garden with his wife, now he, now she, reading the one to the other.

15th April. 'The Strange Fortunes of Two Excellent Princes.'

Breton hath written a prose tale called *The Strange fortunes of two excellent princes*, in their lives and loves to their equal ladies in all the titles of true honour.

17th April. News from Ireland.

From Ireland comes news that the Lord Deputy hath a purpose to draw in person to the Newry and so higher to Armagh, thereby to entangle Tyrone by diversion whilst the forces that are now to be sent to Lough Foyle do make good their landing there. The headstrong humours of some of the rebels now seem to be somewhat abated, and in Leinster some capital men seek for pardon who before were obstinate traitors. There is great scarcity of victuals and munition, but since the coming of the Lord Deputy the army is drawn to hope for better measure hereafter so that their minds are better fashioned to follow the service with cheerfulness and resolution.

19th April. THE EARL OF ORMOND TREACHEROUSLY TAKEN.

The Earl of Ormond hath been treacherously captured by the rebels in Ireland. It is reported that he with the Earl of Thomond and Sir George Carew, President of Munster, had appointed to parley with a notorious rebel by name Onie McRory. When they came to the parley the Earl had but 17 with him unarmed except for swords, but the rebel had 500 foot and 20 horse. For an hour they spake together idly and nothing was concluded, but in the meantime the rebels left their standing and so mingled themselves with my Lord of Ormond's party that they stood environed as men in a fair. Hereupon the Earl of Thomond advertised his Lordship and willed him to be gone. Wherewith as he was turning his horse they seized upon him and pulled him down, but Sir George and the Earl of Thomond being strongly mounted brake from them without any other hurt save that the Earl of Thomond received a pike in the back. The Earl's horsemen were far dispersed and talking with particular rebels, but as soon as the alarm was raised every man ran away without looking behind him.

22nd April. KEMP'S DANCE.

Kemp hath written a book of his dance to Norwich called *Kemp's Nine Days' Wonder*, in answer to the lying ballad-mongers. Acknowledgeth that he put out some money to have threefold gain at his return, whereof some respected their promise and sent the treble worth, others at first sight have paid him, but the greater number he cannot see nor will they willingly be found.

23rd April. THE GARTER FEAST.

The Feast of St. George was solemnised with more than wonted care in regard of Monsieur Le Chatre being here, and other gallant French that accompanied him. There were 13 Knights of the Order present, a very great number of Ladies, and a great show of noblemen's servants. No new knights are chosen at this time. The entertainment of the French in Court is very great and magnificent. Shortly Monsieur Le Chatre will be gone to Windsor to be for the French King installed; he keeps a great house at Alderman Banning's upon his own charge. My Lord of Essex having asked the Queen's pleasure whether, because of the statutes of the Order, he should wear his robes on St. George's day in his dining chamber, or else privately in his bed chamber, or have dispensation not to wear them at all, was given leave to celebrate the Feast by himself. His Lady hath yet no leave to live with him for altogether.

A TOWN BURNT.

Two days since a most lamentable accident hath happened in the county of Cambridge, where the most part of the town of Gamlingay is burnt, seventy-six houses with divers barns and stacks of corn being suddenly consumed to the great extremity of the poor inhabitants there.

A BOOK OF STRANGE MIRACLES.

There is come forth a book called, *The Spanish Mandeville of miracles*, translated from the Spanish of Anthonio de Torquemada, collected from many authors and full of strange and pleasant histories. Herein in six treatises are contained many things worthy of admiration. In the first containeth that which Nature hath wrought contrary to her common and ordinary course: in the second are certain properties and virtues of springs, rivers and lakes, with some opinions touching terrestrial Paradise, and the four rivers that issue from thence: the third entreateth of visions, fancies, spirits, ghosts, hags, enchanters, witches and familiars: the fourth discourseth what fortune and chance is, and wherein they differ, what luck, felicity, happiness and destiny is, and what the influence of the heavenly bodies: the fifth is a description of the septentrional countries which are near and under the North Pole and of the lengthening and shortening of the days and nights until they come to be six months: the sixth containeth sundry wonderful things that are in the septentrional regions worthy of admiration.

24th April. A MISHAP AT HAMPTON.

To-day one Richard Chips was indicted for that whilst he was steering a barge drawn by three horses at Hampton, he had wilfully handled his barge to overset a boat in which Mr. Richard Nightingale, his wife and her servant were being rowed, and they cast into the water.

30th April. GENERAL NEWS.

It is said that Mr. Secretary affects the peace because he likes not the profession of war which keeps the Queen poor, and also because he will keep up his father's reputation who, long before his death, sang no other song than peace. Divers of the Council are doubtful lest the common people grow weary of impositions and fall into disorder, because the best sort murmur underhand that a good peace might be got, if the Queen were well advised. Some say that many journeys have been made in vain and that they would be glad to have peace or open war; besides this noise of the Flemings' prosperity in the Indies has set our nation so in a flame as rather than be barred from going to sea for spoil (to which the youth of this country is given) they would care not what subsidies they gave or promised. If peace may be had upon good conditions, all will be glad of it; if not the Queen will make this benefit of it that her people will see that she is not obstinate and will now provide for the contrary; which pretext shall save the Council at the next Parliament which will be about Michaelmas.

2nd May. THE FRENCH KING'S MISTRESS.

From Paris it is reported that the French King hath been much troubled to retrieve a promise that he made in writing under his hand unto Mademoiselle D'Entragues, his mistress, to marry her if she proved with child within six months after he enjoyed her. For a while she was very resolute to keep it for justification of her honour, that she yielded not to him upon any base consideration; likewise for a time she refused him her company, pretending that she was so enjoined by her confessor. But since both honour and conscience have yielded to profit;

she hath delivered up the writing and the King must give her a pension of 6,000 crowns a year, and to each of her parents 4,000 crowns, and besides in ready money 100,000 to marry her. Upon this accord they met again at Fontainbleau notwithstanding the confessor's inhibition. Nevertheless in this mean time of unkindness the King was not unprovided for but had sundry haunts in Paris.

4th May. A SKIRMISH IN IRELAND.

Of late Sir Oliver Lambert, having the command of 700 men, went to lay provisions in a certain fort, where the enemy would have impeded their passage but our men assailed them in their trenches and forced them to fly. On the way back the rebels took advantage of a small wood and there lay close with 400 shot and the rest of their forces with a great show stood on a hill fast by. Sir Oliver might have gone two musket shots inside of this wood, knowing the enemy to be there, but the day being St. George's day, our men forced the ambuscade and slew many of the enemy. More than three score were slain in the place and carried away on pikes, of ours 10 killed and 17 hurt. Hereby it may be seen that our men in Ireland begin to forget to run away.

5th May. A FEAST FOR M. LE CHATRE.

Last night my Lord of Shrewsbury made for M. Le Chatre so great a dinner as is much for his honour. All the Lords and Ladies that would come were invited; and to-day M. Le Chatre went away. At the dinner a Frenchman showed such strange wonders upon a rope that many thousands admired it.

7th May. BETTER NEWS OF IRELAND.

The army in Ireland is reported to be in good heart, desiring nothing better than to fight; the list was never more full nor never so many good men in Ireland. The rebels also, as with a little they are puffed up, so with less they are thrown down and begin to abandon their hopes. There is a great famine growing upon them.

9th May. IRISH NEWS.

The garrisons of Knockfergus and Newry have laid all waste about them for twenty miles, taken great preys, and done fine service; and it is generally believed that if the Spaniards do not come Tyrone will very shortly offer as humble conditions as ever he did.

10*th May*. THE EARL OF ESSEX'S 'APOLOGY' PRINTED.

Yesterday Mr. Cuffe, the Earl of Essex's man, came to the Archbishop to signify that his Lord had intelligence of the printing of that *Apology* which he wrote two years ago. Hereupon the Archbishop sent to the Master and Wardens of the Stationers to make inquiry, who found out both the press and the printers; the press being in one Dawson's house, and his two servants the printers. These are now committed to close custody in several prisons. They confess to have printed 292 copies, whereof 210 or thereabouts are already recovered. My Lord of Essex continues where he did and in the same manner; he plays now and then at tennis, and walks upon his leads and garden.

MR. HERBERT OF THE PRIVY COUNCIL.

This day Master John Herbert, esquire, one of the Masters of Requests was by her Majesty's special commandment sworn of the Privy Council and Second Secretary to her Majesty. Hereupon some malapert fellows do call him 'Secondary Herbert,' because in his patent he is not termed *principalis secretarius* but *secundus*.

11*th May*. THE CATHOLIC QUARRELS AND THE UNIVERSITY OF PARIS.

The quarrels between Blackwell the archpriest and the secular priests that oppose themselves against the Jesuits have continued very bitter these past months, insomuch that the seculars, despairing of any hearing of their cause, of late made appeal to the Divines of the University of Paris, to whom this question was propounded on the 3rd of May.

> 'The Archpriest and those who are of his side accuse the other priests of schism in that they deferred to obey the Cardinal's letters, which moreover he said were written according to his Holiness' mind and pleasure.
>
> The Question then is, *whether these priests be schismatics*, and if not, *whether they did commit at the least some grievous sin*.'

The head and chief men of the faculty of Divinity in Paris therefore assembled together and after full consideration gave this answer :

> 'First, that those priests who upon the above named causes deferred to obey were no schismatics.
>
> 'Secondly, that they committed no sin at all in that fact in itself considered.'

12th May. THE EARL OF ESSEX'S LETTER TO THE QUEEN.

My Lord of Essex hath lately written to her Majesty, beseeching the return of her favour ; for, saith he, 'as if I were thrown into a corner like a dead carcase, I am gnawed on and torn by the basest creatures upon earth. The prating tavern haunter speaks of me what he lists ; the frantic libeller writes of me what he lists ; they print me and make me speak to the world, and shortly they will play me upon the stage.' Wherefore he would beseech her to conclude his punishment, his misery and his life altogether, that he may go to his Saviour, 'Who,' quoth he, 'has paid Himself a ransom for me, and Whom methinks I still hear calling me out of this unkind world, in which I have lived too long and once thought myself too happy.' Upon the receipt whereof the Queen used good and gracious speeches of him, saying that her purpose was to make him know himself and his duty unto her and that she would again use his service.

16th May. A FRENCH TUMBLER.

One Peter Bromville is come to London, being specially recommended to the Queen by the French King, and hath showed feats of great activity before her. By her special favour and the instruction of the Council this man is allowed to show his feats of activity at the Swan in Old Paris Garden, Mr. Francis Langley's house. The Queen hath graced this Frenchman with being present at his feats upon his rope, which were many and admirable. It was in the Conduit Court, and 4,000 people at least were at it.

18th May. MR. RICHARD HAKLUYT.

Seeing that the benefice of Great All Hallow's in Thames Street is void by the decease of the incumbent, the Council specially recommend to the Archbishop of Canterbury that it be bestowed upon Mr. Richard Hakluyt, a learned preacher, and one that hath not only taken great pains in his calling and served a long time Sir Edward Stafford when he was her Majesty's ambassador in France in a very dangerous time, but hath bestowed his time and taken very great pains in matter of navigation and discovery, a labour of great desert and use.

22nd May. THE TREATY FOR PEACE.

The commissioners for the treaty of peace (being, for her Majesty, Sir Henry Neville, the ambassador in France, Mr. Robert Beale, Dr. John Herbert and Sir Thomas Edmonds) have met with the commissioners of the Spaniards at Boulogne and now exchange their commissions, each party finding some exceptions in the terms of the other's commission. The commissioners for the Spanish King are Balthazar Lord of Zuniga, Fonseca one of the Privy Council and ambassador in the Low Countries, Ferdinando Carillo, the King's Councillor in Castile; and for the Archduke, Ricardot, President of the Council of the Low Countries and Lodowick Verreyken, audiencer and principal Secretary.

25th May. A COLLECTION FOR GAMLINGAY.

Her Majesty hath granted a commission under the Great Seal of England, that a collection may be made within the Dioceses of London, Norwich, Lincoln and the Isle of Ely by way of benevolence towards the comfort of the poor inhabitants of Gamlingay, that they may have means to re-edify their houses and relieve themselves, their wives and children in their distressed estate caused by the late fire.

27th May. BLACKWELL'S CENSURE.

When the opinion of the University of Paris concerning the secular priests was carried to Blackwell the archpriest, he issued a decree to all Catholics, upon pain of suspension, that neither directly nor indirectly they maintain or defend in word or in writing the censure of the University of Paris (whether it be truly given or forged) as being prejudicial to the dignity of the See Apostolical, and expressly contrary to the Pope's brief.

29th May. BRETON'S POEMS OF PASQUIL.

Breton of late hath put forth sundry poems of Pasquil, namely *Pasquil's Madcap thrown at the corruptions of these times*, being an Invective against the wicked of the world, together with his Message; *Pasquil's Fool's Cap* sent to such as are not able to conceive aright of his *Madcap*, with a Passion for the world's waywardness; *Pasquil's Pass and passeth not*, set down in three parts, his pass, procession and prognostication.

HIS PROGNOSTICATION.

When that a churl doth grow so prodigal,
He cares not how he throw away his coin,
And a wise man grows so fantastical
As with a fool will for his counsel join,
And that a fencer lays away his foin
And a young spendthrift falls to purchase land:
I fear that Doomsday will be hard at hand.

31st May. UNSEASONABLE WEATHER.

Both last month and this it hath been cold and dry, with frosts every morning, except some three days little rain; which coldness of the spring and dryness of the ground maketh men doubtful of any good harvest to succeed; so that of a sudden the price of wheat is risen from 3s. to 6s., 7s., and 8s. the bushel.

1st June. COURT NEWS.

To-day being Sunday Mr. Richard Lee was knighted, who is her Majesty's ambassador for Russia. He was very extraordinarily brave attired and had 30 men in brave liveries, carnation and white, and the same collar, hats and feathers. The Queen and the Lords were very long together in the afternoon about the Earl of Essex, and it is said that upon Thursday next he shall be called before certain Lords of the Council and others in commission, when his faults shall be laid open to him and my Lord Keeper to give sentence.

2nd June. A PROCLAMATION AGAINST THOSE SPREADING RUMOURS.

Some time since divers justices of the peace and other officers in the counties petitioned that there might be some licence for the vent of corn, the lack whereof did keep the same at so low a price that the farmers were discouraged from tillage and disable to pay their rents or set poor labouring men on work. Hereupon the Lord Treasurer granted licence that some portion should be transported out of the realm to be sold. But now some malicious spirits have not only raised bruits in the country, but especially in the City, that by immoderate transportation great dearth is made among the people but have falsely taxed the Lord Treasurer with malicious accusations. It is therefore declared that there hath been no immoderate transportation and that this show of dearth hath appeared in certain places by practice of some unconscionable farmers that go about to hoard up their corn, hoping that an apprehension of an unseasonable year to come would raise the prices. Moreover all mayors, justices of peace, bailiffs, constables, headboroughs and other public officers are commanded to be diligent to find out and apprehend such unnatural vipers which do engross grain to the prejudice of poor people, and also to be very careful and vigilant to apprehend those that offend by railing speech or writing ; and also to make known that all who hear such speeches and reveal them not to the next officer shall be held partakers of these heinous offences. And likewise of those that make like false reports of leather to be transported out of the realm.

4th June. THE TREATY OF BOULOGNE.

Nothing is yet begun for the treaty of peace between the commissioners at Boulogne, for they can come to no agreement concerning precedency, the Archduke's commissioners being stiff to refuse her Majesty not only precedency but even equality, and ours likewise unwilling to give away any jot of her Majesty's honour. They allege many reasons for this precedency, as that the King of Spain holdeth his Kingdom by ancient descent from the Kings of the Goths who were saluted with great and universal reverence at a time when there were no dukes of Britain born nor created, nor for long after ; that the cosmographers do resemble Spain to the head of a body ; and many other idle stories. But it is to be feared that this *punctilio* without just reason is rather to serve some present turn than otherwise.

6th June. THE EARL OF ESSEX BEFORE THE COUNCIL.

Yesterday from 9 in the morning till 8 at night the Lords sat about my Lord of Essex's matter. The Attorney-General, Sergeant Yelverton, the Solicitor-General and Mr. Bacon, all of her Majesty's learned Counsel, laid open his offences and contempts. The effect of their speeches contained his making of my Lord Southampton General of the Horse, contrary to her Majesty's pleasure; his making of knights; his going into Munster contrary to his instructions; his return, being expressly commanded by her Majesty's own letter to stay; all which points were very gravely and sharply touched and propounded against him. At one point Mr. Coke in his speech would have proved wilful and malicious contempts to have been disloyalty in him, saying '*Regina uidit, consul uidit, senatus uidit, hic tamen uiuit.*' To this my Lord answered that, though he had come not to justify himself but to acknowledge his transgressions, now that his honour and loyalty was touched he should do God great wrong and his own conscience, and, taking his George and putting it with his hands towards his heart, quoth he, 'if I do not justify myself an honest man, this hand shall pull out this heart when any disloyal thought shall enter into it.' But the Lords interrupted this speech, clearing him generally of that, and proceeded to the other matters. Something he said to all, but no way to justify himself, and with all submissiveness besought her Majesty's mercy.

The Lords did all admire his discretion and carriage, for he was never moved at any speech that was spoken against him, but with patience heard all that was said. At first my Lord kneeled at the board's end, and had a bundle of papers in his hand, which sometimes he laid in his hat that was on the ground beside him. He never offered to leave kneeling, till the Lord Archbishop desired he might stand, and then that he might lean; and lastly that he might sit.

At length the Lord Keeper proceeded to deliver his opinion that his contempts deserved to be imprisoned in the Tower, to be fined as deeply as ever subject was, to have his offices of Councillor, Earl Marshal and Master of the Ordnance sequestered from him. The Lord Treasurer left out the fine; and the Lord Admiral the Tower. Mr. Secretary made a wise grave speech. All the rest spoke condemning him greatly for contemptuously offending so gracious a Sovereign. It was concluded that he should return to the place whence he came until her Majesty's further pleasure was known.

The poor Earl then besought their honours to be a mean unto her Majesty for grace and mercy, seeing there appeared in his offences no disloyalty towards her Majesty, but ignorance and indiscretion in himself. It was a most pitiful and lamentable sight to see him that was the minion of Fortune now unworthy of the least honour he had of many. Many that were present burst out in tears at his fall to such misery.

7th June. THE ALMSMEN'S COMPLAINT.

Those poor men that have reversions of the alms-room of the Collegiate church in Westminster have complained to the Council that there is great disorder committed in the buying and selling of the alms-rooms for money to the wrongful prejudice of those poor men that have reversions and to the abuse of her Majesty's grants for their relief.

10th June. 'A TREASURY OF SIMILES.'

Mr. Robert Cowdray hath newly set forth *A Treasury or Storehouse of Similes*, collected into heads and commonplaces alphabetically, and dedicated to Sir John Harington and his brother. Saith the author of his book: 'This work, in my simple opinion, for the choice of the argument, rarity of the matter and profit of the circumstance deserveth to be advisedly read, attentively considered, effectually ruminated and perfectly digested, because that it will breed and increase in all degrees no small skill in knowledge, wisdom and virtue. For I know no estate of man for whom this book is not necessary; for princes it is pretty, for preachers profitable, for sage councillors it is singular, meat for magistrates, laudable for lawyers, a jewel for gentlemen, a staff to lean on for students, good to further godliness, and therefore apt and profitable for all men.'

12th June. A FOUL CASE OF BAWDRY.

Judgment is now delivered in the Star Chamber in the case of Mr. Fowler that was so grievously abused by his wife. This Mistress Fowler, some time since, being as infamous as Mall

Newberry, parted from her husband, who is a most honest gentleman, and lived at her own pleasure and consorted herself with every companion, misusing of her husband every way and railing of him to the uttermost. At last she encountered with one William Haynes, that not long since was Sir George Gifford's boy, but now lives under the style of Captain, who insinuated so far into her familiarity as at every inn and alehouse they grew bed fellows. And not content with this liberty, but plotted a matter together to bring Mr. Fowler within compass of high treason, and dealt so cunningly as he lay innocent in the Tower half a year and was fain to work his own purgation by the discovery of their villainy. They were both brought into the Star Chamber and her brother Henry Boughton with her and one Gascoigne. Her censure is to be carried to Bridewell and there to be often well whipped and afterward to have perpetual imprisonment.

Haynes' judgment in regard of his incontinent life with her and complotting the death of her husband was fined at £200, to have perpetual imprisonment and to stand nailed on the pillory; and some gave judgment to have both his ears cut off. Most of the Lords spake very bitterly against him, that such base companions as he that often crept into familiarity of honest and virtuous gentlewomen, and seduced their mind not only to incontinency, but to all other mischief whatsoever.

Henry Boughton's judgment is a £100 fine, and imprisonment during their Honours' pleasure, for because that he hath been bawd to his own sister all of them rate him most extremely, calling him bawd and pandar, and to much the greater fault to his own sister, and that it is admirable in any man to have so base a mind as to be a bawd.

Gascoigne's judgment is to ride upon an ass with his face to the tail from Westminster to Cheapside and at each place to lose an ear; to have perpetual imprisonment, and a great fine.

13th June. NEWS FROM IRELAND.

During May the Lord Deputy to ease the safe planting of the garrison at Lough Foyle himself in person went to Newry, attended with most of the companies of the Pale, leaving the Earl of Southampton to follow him accompanied with the

Serjeant-Major and two companies of foot. Tyrone who before had a settled resolution to impeach the landing of the forces for Lough Foyle now withdrew himself and a good part of his force to attend the Lord Deputy, whereby our forces are landed without striking one blow. Tyrone's forces at that time not being comparable to my Lord's, he durst offer nothing upon him; yet hearing of my Lord of Southampton's being to come to my Lord and to pass one of his great fastnesses, he drew himself thither to intercept him. The Lord Deputy sent therefore a convoy of 500 men and himself seconded with the rest, so that my Lord of Southampton having behaved in this action with much valour, beat off the rebels and joined the Lord Deputy. They are now all returned to Dublin.

15th June. THE COUNCIL AND THE EARL OF LINCOLN.

Three days since one Mr. Henry Ascough was awarded damages in the Star Chamber against the Earl of Lincoln to the sum of £759, but at the same time it was appointed that the Earl and his counsel learned should attend at the Court to-day to show (if they could) sufficient matter for answer on their behalf; but seeing that neither he nor his counsel did attend, it is now ordered that the sum of money and other damages proved on the plaintiff's behalf shall stand good and be executed.

16th June. A WEDDING AT BLACKFRIARS.

This day the Lord Herbert, that is son to the Earl of Worcester, was married to Mistress Anne Russell, one of her Majesty's Maids of Honour. The Queen herself came to Blackfriars to grace the marriage. The bride met her Majesty at the waterside, where my Lord Cobham had provided a *lectica*, made like half a litter, wherein she was carried to my Lady Russell's by six knights. Her Majesty dined there and went afterwards to the Lord Cobham's, where she supped. After supper the masque came in, being of eight ladies; each was attired with a skirt of cloth of silver, a rich waistcoat wrought with gold and silver, a mantle of carnation taffeta cast under the arm, and their hair loose about their shoulders, curiously knotted and interlaced. These eight danced to the music brought by Apollo and there was a fine speech making mention of a ninth, much to her honour and praise.

Mistress Fitton led, and after they had done all their own ceremonies, these eight lady masquers chose eight ladies more to dance the measures. Mistress Fitton went to the Queen and wooed her to dance. Her Majesty asked her what she was. 'Affection,' she said. 'Affection!' said the Queen, 'Affection's false.' Yet her Majesty rose and danced; so did the Lady Marquess of Winchester.

18th June. A RIOT IN SOMERSET.

Of late the deputies of certain merchants of London, appointed by virtue of a licence from her Majesty to buy wheat for the forces in Ireland, were set upon by divers persons of the town of Shepton Mallett, who took from them their wheat by force and offered other violences to them. Hereof notice shall be taken at the next Assizes and diligent enquiry made that the chief authors and actors may be duly punished to the example of others.

A GREAT HAILSTORM.

Two days ago at the town of Ryffe in Norfolk and other towns adjoining there was a great tempest of hail, most of the stones as great as walnuts, and still to be taken up by handfuls, though wasted to the bigness of hazel nuts; many of the stones the length of a man's finger, bent and rugged. The force of the fall of them was so great that they brake the glass windows of houses, beat down the leaves of trees, and shore down the wheat and hemp to a great quantity.

22nd June. THE EARL OF LINCOLN TO BE IMPRISONED.

Seeing that the Earl of Lincoln refuseth to pay the sum of money that was awarded to the plaintiff in the late suit in the Star Chamber, the Warden of the Fleet is commanded to repair to the Earl and to require him in the name of the Council either to make present payment of that sum of £759, or else to yield himself into custody in the prison of the Fleet.

THE QUEEN AND THE IRISH KNIGHTS.

There was expectation in Court to-day that order would be taken for my Lord of Essex to be given the liberty of his house, but nothing is effected, for the Queen will hear of no motion upon this matter till some order be taken about the degrading of all the knights made since August last. Mr. Bacon is thought to be the man that moves her Majesty unto it, affirming that by the law the Earl had no authority to make them, being by her Majesty's own letter, of her own hand writing, commanded the contrary.

PLAYHOUSES AND PLAYERS TO BE RESTRAINED.

Complaints having been made to the Council generally of the disorders occasioned by stage plays, and especially against the building of the new house in Golding Lane by Edward Alleyn, sundry restrictions are now laid upon them. The Council consider that the exercise of plays (not being evil in itself) may with a good order and moderation be suffered in a well-governed State; and besides the Queen at some time taking recreation in the seeing of them, some order should be taken for the allowance of those meetest to yield her delight, and consequently houses allowed for public playing to keep the players in exercise. Nevertheless, because of the many particular abuses and disorders that do ensue, it is now ordered that two houses, and no more, shall be allowed, the Globe upon the Bankside for the use of the Lord Chamberlain's servants, and this new house for my Lord Admiral's men, but lest it add to the number of playhouses the Curtain shall be plucked down or put to some other use. Moreover these two companies shall play twice a week only and no oftener, and especially they shall refrain to play on the Sabbath day, and shall forbear altogether in time of Lent. Further the Lord Mayor and the justices of the peace of Middlesex and Surrey are charged with the execution of these orders.

23rd June. THE TREATY AT BOULOGNE.

Sir Thomas Edmonds is come over to Court to seek her Majesty's resolution in certain points which are like to occur at the first entrance into the treaty. As yet there is no meeting, the commissioners for the King of Spain still refusing any accommodation nor assenting to a course of equality in general. They now seek direction from the Archduke at Brussels.

24th June. AN ASSAULT PUNISHED.

To-day at the Sessions one Richard Drury, a brewer of East Smithfield, was fined 20s. and required to give security for his good behaviour for assaulting one Mrs. Bridget Stringer, knocking her down and throwing her into a cellar.

25th June. MR. BODLEY'S LIBRARY.

Now that the mechanical works appertaining to the Library at Oxford are brought to some good pass, Mr. Thomas Bodley the more zealously busieth himself and his friends about gathering in books of such as will be benefactors ; and to the end that there may be conserved a perpetual remembrance of every giver and his gift there is provided a register book. Mr. Bodley requesteth also that at the Convocation the names of the benefactors shall be published together with the quality of their bounty and benevolence ; and moreover that special request shall be made to those who are present, as they shall find opportunity to meet with any of those contributors, so they be careful to show them with what cheerfulness and comfort their gifts are embraced by the whole University.

29th June. THE IRISH KNIGHTS.

The proclamation for the annulling of the knighthoods conferred since last August was drawn and signed four days since, but not yet published. It is said that the Council are all of purpose to represent the inconveniences of that course and to be suitors to her Majesty, both for stay of the proclamation and my Lord's liberty. Upon the bruit of this proclamation Sir John Harington complaineth to Master Secretary that knighthood is like unto baptism and cannot be annulled, and to annul them now would be a dangerous example. Besides, such a proclamation will be accompanied with the secret and most bitter curses of divers and some very fair ladies, who are not yet so good philosophers as to neglect honour and embrace patience. If the annulling must go forward, at least let there be a proviso that the ladies may still hold their places.

Her Majesty had ordered the Lord Keeper to remove my Lord of Essex's keeper from him ; but a while after, being somewhat troubled with the remembrance of his making so many knights, made a stay of her former order, and sent unto the Earl for her own letter, which she writ unto him to make none. But with a very submissive letter he returned answer that he had lost it, or mislaid it, for he could not find it; which somewhat displeases her Majesty.

THE EARL OF LINCOLN'S CONTEMPT.

When the Warden of the Fleet required the Earl of Lincoln to pay the money judged against him or yield himself prisoner, according to the order of the Council last week, he contemptuously refused to do either. Now one of the sergeants-at-arms is despatched to charge him straightly, in the Queen's name, to yield himself prisoner, as he will answer the contrary to his peril.

30th June. NEW PLAYS.

Since Christmas the Lord Admiral's players have played these new plays at the Rose: *Owen Tudor* (by Drayton, Hathway, Munday and Wilson); *Truth's Supplication to Candlelight* (by Dekker); *The Spanish Moor's Tragedy* (by Day, Dekker and Haughton); *Damon and Pythias* (by Chettle); *The Seven Wise Masters* (by Chettle, Day, Dekker and Haughton); *Ferrex and Porrex* (by Haughton); *The Golden Ass and Cupid and Psyche* (by Chettle, Day and Dekker); *Strange News out of Poland* (by Haughton and Pett); *The Blind Beggar of Bethnal Green* (by Chettle and Day); *Fair Constance of Rome* (by Dekker, Drayton, Hathway and Munday).

1st July. A GREAT VICTORY IN FLANDERS.

From Flanders cometh news of a great victory of the Count Maurice of Nassau over the Archduke Albert, which battle was fought on Sunday the 22nd of last month. It was the intention of the Count Maurice to lay siege to Newport and to this end to hold Oudenburgh, Brendike and Suaskirke, and the Sconce Albertus that is upon the dunes before Ostend; but the second day of the siege he had intelligence that the enemy was come to Oudenburgh and that the Archduke was there himself in person. The Count therefore lest the enemy might cut off the passage between Newport and Ostend sent the regiment of the Scots and the regiment of the Almains to hinder their passage by a bridge which our men had made in a drowned land between Oudenburgh and the Sconce Albertus. But the enemy had passed the bridge before the Scots could come to make good the place, and so they fell under the execution of the vanguard of the enemy, being all Spaniards and the choicest men of the army, and were chased to the walls of Ostend.

Meantime his Excellency not knowing of the execution made upon the Scots caused the English and Freezes to be drawn up at a low water from the other side of the haven of Newport, where they were quartered before the town, and so brought all his forces to a head, at what time it was disputed whether they should send forth the troops as they passed over the water to second the Scots, or keep themselves together till further advertisement, which was the safer course and happily resolved upon.

Straitway upon this resolution part of the enemy's horse, being in number about 700, began to be discovered upon the sands as they came marching forward, with their foot troops following after. Then the Count Lodowick, General of the Horse, at his Excellency's command gave over the whole direction to Sir Francis Vere, who first commanded the six pieces of artillery which were planted upon the enemy to be discharged on the enemy's horse, and then charged himself with three troops of horse and beat them into the Dunes, the infantry of the enemy making a stand upon the sands.

The enemy's horse being thus driven into the Dunes, the commanders entered into dispute, whether it were best to advance forward and charge upon their foot troops as they stood upon the sands, or to keep in the Dunes where they stood embattled and there to attend the enemy; wherein Sir Francis Vere opposed himself to the whole council of war, saying that it was not safe to leave a place of advantage to go seek an enemy upon equal terms, considering that the enemy would be forced to seek battle; for it was impossible in that hasty march that they had come provided with necessaries to continue there. This resolution was agreed upon, and so it fell out according to that which Sir Francis had delivered; for after three hours expectation the enemy came on to charge the English which had the vanguard of the army.

Battle being joined the English after a short time forced the enemy to retreat, who flying to the tops of the Dunes now had the like advantage over our men as ours had before over them. In this way with varying fortunes the fight continued the space of three hours and a half, in which time the English dealt with the vanguard, the battle and rearward of the enemy, but were at length beaten back to their artillery where Sir Francis again brought them to a stand, and being himself hurt gave orders for the charge the second time, and commanded the following thereof to his brother Sir Horatio Vere ; who carried it so well that much of the fortune of the day is attributed to his valour ; for when our troops, seconded with two troops of horses, charged the enemy with a shout, after the battle was well joined, the enemy disrouted and never made head again.

In this battle there are slain of ours 6 captains, 7 lieutenants, 4 ancients, together with 16 gentlemen of my Lord's company ; of the soldiers 560 are slain and missing, and 250 hurt, together with 9 captains. The slain of the enemy number about 5,000, 110 ensigns are taken, and among the prisoners of note be Don Francisco de Mendoza, Admiral of Aragon ; the Count of Salins, the Count de la Fiere, Don Lewis de Valasco, Don Charles de Sapina.

6th July. The Earl of Lincoln's Contempt

When the Sergeant-at-arms went to arrest the Earl of Lincoln, the Earl refused to obey the orders of the Council, but withdrew and hid himself within his house and hath kept his doors shut against the Sergeant, so that he cannot execute the warrant without forcible entry. The Sergeant is now empowered to require the aid of the Queen's public officers and to force an entry.

A Riot at the Mermaid Tavern.

This day in the Star Chamber Sir Edward Baynham and three gentlemen for riots and misdemeanours were fined £200 each and imprisonment. They had gone to supper in Bread Street at the 'Mermaid,' and there they supped and there they stayed until 2 o'clock in disorder and excess of drink ; and then they departed with rapiers drawn, and menaced, wounded and beat the watch in Friday Street and Paul's Churchyard, uttering seditious words. The Lord Chief Justice, the Lord Treasurer and the Lord Keeper were for fining Williamson, the taverner, £40, but because he was known an honest man and of good government, and would not suffer music or illegal games in house, and sent for the Constable to keep good order, he was acquitted. And it was then delivered that no taverner nor alekeeper ought to suffer or receive company after 9 o'clock, and furthermore because drunkenness is now so common, general and odious, it is delivered as law that a common drunkard may be bound for his good behaviour.

9th July. THE TREATY AT BOULOGNE.

There is still no beginning of the treaty, for the audiencer that was sent to Brussels is not yet returned; wherefore Sir Thomas Edmonds, who is now returned to Boulogne, hath imparted unto the President Richardot that her Majesty hath great reason to renew her former distrusts and jealousies, not only by reason of these delays but upon advertisements which she hath received both of supplies of munitions and presents sent unto the rebels in Ireland, of negotiations begun with them and pledges received thereupon, and of promise of succour of men to be sent there in August next.

REINFORCEMENTS FOR IRELAND AND THE LOW COUNTRIES.

From twenty-seven counties and the City of London new troops are commanded for Ireland to the number of 100 horse and 2,000 foot, to be ready at Chester for embarkation on the 27th of the month. From the home counties also are required volunteers to serve in the Low Countries, which are being sent at the urgent request of the States of the United Provinces, from whom also they shall draw their pay.

11th July. DR. HAYWARD EXAMINED.

Dr. Hayward was examined this day concerning his book of Henry the Fourth before the Lord Keeper, the Lord Admiral, Mr. Secretary and the Chancellor of the Exchequer. He admitted that the stories mentioned in the Archbishop's oration, tending to prove that deposers of kings and princes have had good success, were not taken out of any chronicle but inserted by himself. Mr. Attorney would have it that Dr. Hayward intended the application of his book to this present time, the plot being that of a King who is taxed for misgovernment, and his Council for corrupt and covetous dealings for private ends: the King is censured for conferring benefits on hated favourites, the nobles become discontented, and the commons groan under continual taxation, whereupon the King is deposed and in the end murdered.

13th July. Dr. Hayward Committed to the Tower.

Dr. John Hayward is now committed to the custody of Sir John Peyton, the Lieutenant of the Tower.

The Examination of Wolfe.

To-day before the Attorney-General John Wolfe the stationer was examined concerning the printing of Dr. Hayward's book of King Henry IV last year. He declareth that the book had no epistle dedicatory or to the reader when first brought to him, but after some conversation between them it was dedicated to the Earl of Essex, he being a martial man. About 500 or 600 copies were sold before the order was received to cut out the epistle dedicated to the Earl of Essex, as no book ever sold better. The people calling for it exceedingly, about Easter a new edition was obtained from the Doctor, wherein many things were altered from the former, and an epistle apologetical added. Since that the last edition was suppressed, many have been to his shop for it ; but he himself had no recompense for printing either edition, save a few copies of the work. Moreover he was committed for fourteen days for the printing of the last edition and lost all the books.

15th July. The Victory at Newport.

There is a new ballad of the late victory at Newport, to the tune of 'Lusty Gallant,' beginning :

You that be desirous
  and therein take delight,
To hear of bloody battles
  and worthy warlike fight,
To Flanders bend your ears a while
  and you shall truly know
How valiantly our noble friends
  their foes did overthrow.

The Archduke of Austria,
  that bloody Spanish Lord,

Like Judas hath converted
his book into a sword;
To plant by cursed popery
in Flanders now again;
To bring the Queen of England's friends
in servitude to Spain.

19th July. THE TREATY AT BOULOGNE.

The Queen being exasperated by these long delays, for the audiencer is not yet returned from Brussels, hath straightly charged her commissioners that if the audiencer do not return by the end of this next week with such direction as may reconcile that point of precedency, so as they may proceed to treaty without any note of dishonour to her, then shall they return back immediately.

20th July. DR. HAYWARD'S BOOK.

Mr. Harsnett, my Lord Bishop of London's chaplain, is now in question by reason that he saw and allowed Dr. Hayward's book of Henry IV for the press. He would excuse himself, saying that the book was not delivered to him by the author, but by a gentleman in my Lord of London's house who, saying that it was but a cantel of our English chronicles, phrased and flourished over only to show the author's pretty wit, begged approbation for it, which Mr. Harsnett gave without reading the book; and besides at that time it was without epistle, preface or dedication.

26th July. THE BISHOP OF LONDON RETURNS.

My Lord Bishop of London is returned from Emden, bringing with him a vat of Rhenish wine containing six score gallons, which he sendeth to Sir Robert Cecil, having so surfeited at Emden in quaffing healths that he can now be well content to part with it.

27th July. THE SEMINARY PRIESTS IN LONDON PRISONS.

The seminary priests taken of late and committed to Newgate and other prisons about London not only have great resort unto them, but show a most obstinate and perverse carriage; for though they are known to be seminary priests, yet they stand upon new terms of instructions given to them neither to confess nor deny their priesthood, but refer themselves to such proofs as may be brought against them. The Bishop of London now sendeth for divers about London (that have lately come from the seminaries by reason of the dissensions among them and to whom the priests are well known) to examine them concerning the men; and if they shall be unwilling to confess and testify that these men are priests they may be committed to prison.

30th July. THE TREATY AT BOULOGNE.

The treaty at Boulogne is broken off and our commissioners are returning. A few days since, the audiencer at length returned from Brussels when it was delivered to our commissioners that the King of Spain could not proceed in the matter without receiving right in the honour of precedency which belongeth unto him; if it were delivered to his commissioners then they would straightway enter into treaty. Nor would they assent to any other way of treaty whereby the point of precedency might not be brought in question, though divers were proposed.

1st August. THE EARL OF SOUTHAMPTON.

Of late the Lord Deputy petitioned her Majesty that my Lord of Southampton should be made Governor of Connaught, but the Queen hath such ill conceit of him that she will none of it. The Earl being still very desirous to regain her Majesty's good opinion, now purposeth to go from Ireland to the Low Countries, and to live the rest of the summer in the States' army.

3rd August. THE EARL OF SOUTHAMPTON AND LORD GREY.

The Queen learning the Earl of Southampton hath withdrawn himself from Ireland into the Low Countries, where the Lord Grey of Wilton is at present, hath expressly commanded them on their allegiance in no sort to offer, accept or hearken to any challenge or meeting with each other, seeing that they are noblemen of valour, who are fit to reserve themselves for her Majesty's services and not to hazard them upon private quarrels. And because the Council would not have either of them pretend any note of disgrace in this command, the like letter is sent to each of them.

4th August. 'ENGLAND'S HELICON.'

Mr. John Bodenham hath now made a collection of the pastoral songs of our English poets, entitled *England's Helicon.* Herein is to be noted his care in the collecting that nothing was placed under any man's name, either at large or in letters, but was delivered by some especial copy coming to his hands. Moreover, if any stationer shall find fault that his copies are robbed by anything in this collection, why more in this than in any divine or human author, from whence a man (writing of that argument) shall gather any saying, sentence, simile or example, his name put to it who is the author of the same ? Further, if any man, in prizing his own birth or fortune, shall take in scorn that a far meaner man in the eye of the world is placed by him, then let him understand that that man's wit is set by his, not the man by him.

5th August. LEVIES FROM THE CITY.

From the City are now required 350 men for the Irish service, which shall nevertheless be set out at her Majesty's charges. They shall be taken from the masterlesss men of able bodies, and of such as cannot give good account of the means how they live, but not sickly, diseased rogues or weak persons. There are required also among them 15 carpenters, 10 rough masons or bricklayers, and bakers, coopers and 6 smiths.

Of the last levy made in the City of 200 men, 44 ran away. The Lord Mayor is further required to take especial care that those who are levied do not run away. He shall make known to them that this offence is felony ; and although her Majesty hath hitherto deferred to take away a man's life for such heinous crimes, yet now perceiving how common the offence is become, hath lately suffered some few to be executed for example's sake, that it may appear that as her toleration heretofore hath been out of her clemency so her proceeding now is agreeable to the ancient laws of this realm provided in like cases.

9th August. DESERTERS TO BE EXECUTED.

At the late Assizes in Essex six soldiers that were levied for the service in Ireland and did run away were condemned. Although the least offender deserveth to suffer death, and her Majesty desireth rather the reformation of the abuse than the severe punishment of the delinquents, nevertheless that some example may be made it is thought meet that the sheriff shall take two of the most lewd disposition of these six whose offence is most notorious and least show repentance, whereof one shall forthwith be executed in some principal town in the county, and the other sent unto Stratford the Bow, to be executed near unto the bridge, but in the county of Essex, on some market day in such sort as it may be publicly known also in those parts for what offence he doth suffer.

11*th August.* 'BEL-VEDÉRE.'

Mr. John Bodenham hath yet another book called *Bel-vedére or The Garden of the Muses*, gathering from the works of our English poets, some dead but for the most part still living, many learned, grave and witty sentences, each line being a several sentence, and none exceeding two lines at the uttermost. All which are subjected under apt and proper heads, to each being added an argument, similes and examples. These heads are sixty-seven in number and treat of God, of conscience, of virtue, of Kings, of friendship, of women, of fate and so forth.

13*th August.* THE MUTINOUS SOLDIERS AT CHESTER.

On receipt of the Council's late letter, the Mayor of Chester made known to the whole of the soldiers there what would be the reward of their running away, which proclamation struck such a terror into their hearts as has prevented the running away of whole hundreds. Yet some few steal away, and very few are returned by the county, so cunning are they in passing by all towns, bridges and highways. Some that were taken near the city, but without certain proof, were brought unto the place of execution in show to be hanged; where, standing upon the ladder with the ropes about their necks, upon their humble submission and the earnest entreaty of their captains and fellow-soldiers received pardon, conditional that if any man of their companies either mutiny for apparel or run away, both they and these offenders shall receive the extreme rigour of the law. By these means much quiet is wrought in the city.

14*th August.* SIR WALTER RALEGH AND THE EARL OF ESSEX.

Now that there is talk of admitting the Earl of Essex to his liberty, Sir Walter Ralegh privily urgeth Master Secretary not to relent. For, saith he, his malice is fixed and will not evaporate by any mild courses, for he will ascribe the alteration to her Majesty's pusillanimity and not to Sir Robert's good nature. The less he is made the less harm can he do, and if the Queen's favour fail him, he will again decline to a private person. Let the Queen hold this Bothwell while she hath him, for he will ever be the canker of her estate and safety. Princes are lost by security and preserved by prevention: if he have his liberty then we have seen the last of her good days and all ours.

15th August. AMBASSADORS FROM BARBARY.

There are newly come to London Muly Hamet Xarife, secretary and principal ambassador from the King of Barbary, and with him in commission two merchants, bearing letters for her Majesty. They were met at Dover by Sir Thomas Gerrard, the Knight Marshal, and divers gentlemen, and are now lodged at the house of Alderman Ratcliffe, near to the Royal Exchange. They speak by a Spanish interpreter. They are tawny Moors, very strangely attired and behavioured.

16th August. THE GOWRY CONSPIRACY.

News is come from Scotland that the King of Scots had lately like to have been murthered.

On 5th August the King having his residence at Falkland and being daily at the buck hunting, rode out to the Park between 6 and 7 of the clock in the morning, the weather wonderful pleasant and seasonable. But before he could leap on horseback, all the huntsmen with the hounds attending upon the green, Mr. Alexander Ruthven, second brother to the Earl of Gowry, hasted down to meet his Majesty, and after a very low courtesy, drew the King apart. Then he begins to discourse unto him how that he chanced the evening before to be walking abroad in the fields taking the air solitary alone, when he encountered a base fellow with a cloak cast about his mouth, of whom he enquired his name and errand in so solitary a place. Whereat the fellow became so faltered in his speech that he began to examine him the more closely, and perceiving something to be hid under his cloak, he cast up the laps of it and so found a great wide pot all full of coined gold in great pieces. Upon the sight whereof he took the fellow back to St. Johnstone and, without knowledge of any man, took the fellow, bound him and locked him in a little chamber, and leaving him there with his pot of gold had hasted to make his Majesty advertised thereof. After further discourse the King began to suspect that it was some foreign coin brought in by practising Papists and that the fellow was a Scots priest or a seminary so disguised.

Whereupon the King resolved to send back a servant of his own with Mr. Ruthven, with a warrant to the Provost and bailiffs of St. Johnstone to receive both the fellow and his money and to retain them till his further pleasure was known. At this Mr. Alexander stirred marvellously, protesting that if either the Lord his brother or the bailiffs of the town knew of it his Majesty would get a very bad count made to him of that treasure, and earnestly begged the King to ride thither at once to see for himself.

The King was stricken in great admiration both at the uncouthness of the tale and the strange behaviour of the relator; but the Court being already horsed and the game found, he was forced to break off, saying that he would consider of the matter and at the end of his chase give a resolute answer; and so hasted towards the place where the game was. Mr. Alexander, parting from the King very miscontent at his Majesty's long delay and slowness of resolution, then sent one of the men that were with him to ride in haste to the Earl to advertise him that he hoped to move his Majesty to come to St. Johnstone, and that he should not expect him for the space of three hours.

Meantime the King could not stay from musing and wondering upon the news, and sent to bring Mr. Alexander to him again, to whom he said that he was now resolved to ride with him on that errand in his own person, so soon as the chase was done.

The chase lasted from about 7 of the clock until 11, all which time Mr. Alexander was ever at the King's back, earnestly requesting him to hasten the end of the hunting so that he might the sooner ride to St. Johnstone. The buck being killed, the King by his importunities was persuaded to ride at once with him, and such was their haste that very few accompanied the King when he reached St. Johnstone.

When they were within a mile of St. Johnstone, Mr. Alexander rode forward to advertise the Earl, his brother, of the King's coming, who was at that time sitting in the midst of his dinner. Immediately therefore he rose from the board and warned all his servants and friends to accompany him to meet his Majesty, being in number three or four score, but the King's train did not exceed fifteen persons, without any kind of armour except swords.

After coming to the Earl's lodging the King stayed an hour before his dinner came in, the longsomeness of preparing and the badness of the cheer being excused upon the sudden coming of his Majesty unlooked for there. During this time the King enquired of Mr. Alexander when it was time to go to that private house; who answered all was sure enough and that there was no haste until his Majesty had dined at leisure. Moreover he prayed the King not to be seen to round with him before his brother, who might suspect what the matter should mean. The King therefore addressed himself to the Earl of Gowry and discoursed with him upon sundry matters, but could get no direct answers out of him, save half words and imperfect sentences.

Then the King sat down to his dinner, and when he had almost dined, the Earl after the customed use conveyed the noblemen and gentlemen of the Court forth to their dinner, yet he sat not down with them himself, but came back and stood silent at the end of the King's table; which his Majesty perceiving began to entertain him in a homely manner, wondering he had not remained to dine with his guests and entertain them there.

At length the King being ready to rise from dinner, Mr. Alexander standing behind his back pulled quietly upon him, rounding in his ear that it was time to go, but that he would fain be quit of the Earl his brother. Wherefore the King called for drink, and in a merry and homely manner said to the Earl that since he had forgotten to drink to his Majesty or sit with his guests and entertain them, he would drink to him his own welcome, desiring him to take it forth and drink to the rest of the company. Whereupon as he went forth, the King rose from the table and accompanied Mr. Alexander, passing through the end of the hall where the noblemen and his servants were sitting at their dinner. They passed up a turnpike and through three or four chambers, Mr. Alexander ever locking behind him every door as he passed, and so into a little study where he saw standing, with a very abased countenance, not a bondman but a freeman with a dagger at his girdle. Mr. Alexander locked the study door behind him, and at that instant changing his countenance, putting his hat on his head and drawing the dagger from the man's girdle, he held the point of it at the King's breast, avowing now that the King behoved to be in his will and used as he list, swearing many bloody oaths that if the King cried out one word or opened a window to look out, the dagger should straitway go to his heart, affirming also he was sure that now the King's conscience was burthened for murdering his father.

In this pass the King began then to dilate to Mr. Alexander how horrible a thing it was for him to meddle with the King's innocent blood, assuring him it would not be left unrevenged. Affirming also that he had no burthen in his father's execution, being at that time a minor of age and guided by a faction which overruled both him and the rest of the country. The King also promised, on the word of a Prince, that if he would spare his life and suffer him to go out again, he would never reveal to any flesh living, what was betwixt them at that time, nor never suffer him to incur any harm or punishment for the same.

At the King's persuasive language, Mr. Alexander appeared to be somewhat amazed, and uncovering his head again swore and protested that the King's life should be safe, if he would behave himself quietly. He said, moreover, that he would bring in the Earl, his brother; but to what purpose he would not discover. With that he bade the other man guard the King till his return and passed forth, locking the door after him. The King then demanded of the man whether he was appointed to be his murderer; who answered with a trembling and astonished voice and behaviour that as the Lord should judge him he was never made acquainted with that purpose; and moreover all the time that Mr. Alexander was menacing his Majesty, he was ever trembling, requesting him for God's sake not to meddle with the King or do him any harm. Thereupon, because before his going out Mr. Alexander had made the King swear that he should not cry nor open any window, the King commanded the fellow to open the window on his right hand; which he readily did.

While the King was in this dangerous state, none of his train knowing where he was, one of the Earl of Gowry's servants comes hastily in, assuring his master that the King was horsed and away, which the Earl reporting, the noblemen and the rest of his Majesty's train rushed all together to the gate in great haste, and some of them enquiring when his Majesty went forth, the Porter affirmed that the King was not yet gone forth. Whereupon the Earl looked very angrily upon him and said he was but a liar, and leaving the noblemen in confusion, he ran back through the close and up the stairs. The noblemen meanwhile all calling for their horses passed under the window of that study wherein the King was. By this Mr. Alexander had speedily returned to the King, and in desperate manner said he could not mend it, his Majesty behoved to die, and with that would have bound his hands with a garter. But the King suddenly wresting his hands away closed with him, and so wrestling with him, with Mr. Alexander's hand about his throat and some of his fingers in his mouth to have prevented him from crying out, drew him to the open window and cried out that he was being murdered, when his voice was instantly heard and known by the Duke of Lennox and the Earl of Mar, who even at this moment were beneath the window. They therefore all rushed in to the gate together.

In the meantime the King with struggling and wrestling had brought Mr. Alexander perforce through the open door of the study, having by now Mr. Alexander's head under his arm and himself on his knees.

Sir John Ramsay, not knowing what way first to enter after he had heard the King's cry, by chance had found the turnpike door open and following it up entered into the chamber where the King and Mr. Alexander were still struggling together. He struck Mr. Alexander twice or thrice with his dagger, and took him by the shoulders and shot him down the stair, where he was met by Sir Thomas Erskine and Sir Hugh Herries and another, who there upon the stair ended him. Then they entered the chamber where the King was, but before they could get the door shut the Earl of Gowry was upon them with seven of his servants. The King, being weaponless, fought for Mr. Alexander's sword that had fallen from his hand, but his servants thrust him back and shut him again in the little study, and thus having the King in safety reencountered the Earl of Gowry and his servants; yet though they were but four and the Earl and his men eight, after many strokes on both sides they gained the victory, the Earl of Gowry being stricken dead with a stroke through the heart, which Sir John Ramsay gave him, and the rest of the servants dung over the stairs with many hurts, as in like manner the King's servants were all three very sore wounded and hurt.

All the time of this fight, the Duke of Lennox, the Earl of Mar and the rest of the King's servants, were striking with great hammers upon the outer door, which Mr. Alexander had locked at his first going forth with the King; but by reason of the strength of the door it did bide them the space of half an hour and more before they could get it broken and have entrance, and found beyond expectation his Majesty alive and the Earl of Gowry lying dead at his feet. Immediately thereafter the King, kneeling down on his knees in the midst of his servants, with his own mouth gave thanks to God of that miraculous deliverance.

In the meanwhile there was a great tumult in the town, which continued for the space of two or three hours, until the King by oft speaking to them at the windows and causing the bailiffs and other honest men of the town to be brought into the chamber, he declared the whole form of that strange accident and delivered the bodies to their keeping.

It was eight o'clock in the evening before the King could depart out of the town for Falkland, but before he had ridden four miles the whole way was clad with all sort of people, both horse and foot, meeting him with great joy and acclamation.

17th August. THE EARL OF LINCOLN'S CONTEMPT.

When the Earl of Lincoln did at length yield himself to the Sergeant-at-arms and suffer himself to be imprisoned in the Fleet, he then refused to pay the Sergeant's fees; whereupon complaint was made to the Council and my Lord was commanded to make payment. To which he answered that he knew not what the amount of those fees was. Wherefore the Council, referring the matter to Mr. Garter King of the Heralds, are informed that the fee for the arrest of the person of an Earl is £5, and for the arrest of a Baron the fee is 5 marks, and 4 nobles the day for attendance, and when he doth ride 4 marks. The Council think his Lordship can allow no less unto the Sergeant-at-arms than the fee of a Baron, being 5 marks for the arrest, 4 nobles the day for his attendance 13 days, besides 2 days' riding which is 4 marks the day.

IRISH NEWS.

The Lord Deputy hath wrought great spoil upon the rebels in Offally, having taken 200 cows, more than 600 garrons, 500 sheep and great store of other small cattle. In numerous small encounters he hath everywhere had the better, killing the rebels and driving them from their fastnesses. Great quantities of corn have been destroyed, the most part of the wheat being cut down with their swords, unto which painful labour the soldiers could hardly be won until the captains and gentlemen gave the example and continued the work with them. Sir Oliver Lambert and Sir Arthur Savage likewise have taken great prize.

20th August. THE BARBARY AMBASSADOR.

This day the Ambassador of Barbary had audience at Nonsuch, where there was regal preparation in the manner of his receiving; rich hangings and furnitures sent for from Hampton Court; the guards very strong, in their rich coats; the pensioners with their axes; the Lords of the Order with their collars; a full court of Lords and Ladies. He passed through a guard of halberds to the Council Chamber where he rested; thence he was brought to the Presence, so to the Privy Chamber, and so to the Gallery, where her Majesty sat at the further end in very great state and gave them audience. It is given out that they come for her Majesty's letters to the Turk, to whom a brother of the King of the Barbaries is fled, to complain against him.

21st August. SEMINARIES EXECUTED AT YORK.

Two seminary priests were lately executed at York. The one named Robert Nutter departed out of England twenty two years ago and returning into England was apprehended and banished. After that he was taken in a French ship and brought into England, where he remained in Wisbeach and other prisons ; but last spring he escaped out of Wisbeach. He confessed that he was professed a friar of the order of St. Dominic during the time he was prisoner in Wisbeach. At his execution being required to pray for her Majesty he would not answer, nor would he declare whether he did take her Highness to be our lawful Queen. The other was named Edward Thwinge (known also as Hylton and Nysaunce). It appeared that he was a scholar of some understanding and much esteemed by the Papists : and yet he did defend amongst many other gross opinions that without offence he might equivocate (as he termed it) before a magistrate, which equivocation is plain lying, for being blamed because he had affirmed upon his first examination that he was born in Northumberland, whereas it did appear that he was born in the city of York, he said he did equivocate. Much good may come of this severity as well to terrify the priests from these parts as for the satisfaction of the people, for there was never any seminary priest executed in that county before, which toleration has made them overbold.

23rd August. 'MUCH ADO ABOUT NOTHING.'

That comedy of *Much Ado About Nothing*, written by Mr. Shakespeare, which at sundry times hath been acted by the Lord Chamberlain's men, is now printing. Herein is shown how one Claudio, having wooed the Lady Hero, was by the practices of a villain persuaded that she was false to him and at the time of their wedding shamed her before the congregation, but the practice being revealed, Claudio taketh her again to wife ; also the perverse humours of Benedick and Beatrice who are persuaded by a plot that each loves the other and so brought to a match. In this play there is a foolish constable, named Dogberry, that was played by Will Kemp.

25th August. DESERTERS FROM IRELAND.

Some of the soldiers that desert from the forces in the North of Ireland pass through the country of the traitors, who give them free passage into Scotland, by that means to procure the diminishing of her Majesty's forces. Through Scotland they convey themselves into the realm by Berwick and the north parts. The Wardens on the Border are bidden to take special heed for the apprehension of such.

26th August. THE EARL OF ESSEX RELEASED.

This day in the afternoon the Earl of Essex was sent for to York House, where the Lord Keeper, Lord Treasurer and Mr. Secretary signified her Majesty's pleasure unto him for liberty; only he is restrained from coming to Court without leave. The Earl told their honours that his purpose was to lead a retired life at Gray's in Oxfordshire, in his uncle Mr. Controller's house; but before he went he besought their Lordships to be his mean to her Majesty he might once come to her presence and kiss her hands, that with some contentment he might betake himself to his solitary life. But it is thought he shall not in haste receive that desired favour and grace.

27th August. A HEALING WELL IN CHESHIRE.

From Cheshire comes news of a well or spring in the Forest of Delamere called the New Found Well, the waters whereof are reported to have wrought many notable cures. The discovery was made by a certain countryman, one John Greenway, who being sick with the fits (as the vulgar people in those parts call the ague) was recommended by his physician to find out some good spring water, to drink of it, and to bathe and wash himself with it. This Greenway being well acquainted with the springs and other commodities of the forest had found out this pretty purling fountain, and was soon cured by drinking of it. Some while afterwards his sons being likewise taken with the fits were each of them severally eased by the use of the well. Hereupon the neighbours began to resort to the well, and people generally in very great numbers to ease not only the agues but all manner of outward grievances and sores; and the more trials were put in execution, the more credit and account it hath ever since gotten. Many notable cures are reported. Ralph Hichenson, a poor labourer fallen of late years very blind, as was well known to the worshipful gentlemen of the county who caused relief and provision for him according to the statute, hath recovered sight again, which serveth him well to go without leading, which before he could not do. One

Anthony Biggs, a soldier late in the regiment of Sir Samuel Bagnal, came forth of Ireland very lame, sick and feeble, not able to move farther than he was supported by crutches, on 24th July began to use this water and the 29th had recovered strength and went lustily homewards toward Somersetshire with only a walking staff in his hand. John Olton of Wottenhall, an honest credible man, having a rupture many years, and not able to go without the help of a steel girdle which he wore continually, hath hereby gotten remedy and goeth now lustily without his girdle.

These and very many cures are reported of this new found well.

30th August. ENGRAVED PORTRAITS FORBIDDEN.

There is of late times a use brought up to engrave in brass the picture of noblemen and other persons and then to sell them in paper, set forth oftentimes with verses and other circumstances not fit to be used. Because this custom doth grow common, and it is indeed not meet such public setting forth of any pictures but of her Majesty should be permitted (if the same be well done), the Council have given direction that hereafter no personage of any nobleman or other person shall be ingraven and put to sale publicly, and those prints already made shall be called in, unless the Archbishop of Canterbury shall think fit to allow them.

2nd September. THE PRIVATE HOUSE IN THE BLACKFRIARS.

Burbage hath leased the private playhouse in the Blackfriars, that his father built four years since but was inhibited from occupying, to Henry Evans; and here Evans and Master Nathaniel Giles that is Master of the boys of her Majesty's Chapel, will set up a company of boys for playing.

6th September. THE EARL OF ESSEX'S LETTER TO THE QUEEN.

My Lord of Essex hath pitifully again written to the Queen in these terms: 'Haste paper to that happy presence, whence only unhappy I am banished! Kiss that fair correcting hand which now lays plaisters to my lighter hurts, but to my greatest wound applieth nothing. Say thou camest from shaming, languishing, despairing Essex.'

10th September. SIR THOMAS POSTHUMUS HOBY'S COMPLAINT.

Little Sir Thomas Posthumus Hoby (that married Mistress Sidney who was formerly wife to Mr. Walter Devereux, my Lord of Essex's brother) maketh great complaint of a misdemeanour offered in his house by Mr. William Eure, son of the Lord Eure, Sir William Eure and others. About a fortnight since, Sir Thomas was standing in his Hall at Hackness in Yorkshire when there came in Sir William Eure's footboy and said that his master and sundry other gentlemen would come that night. Sir Thomas answered that he was sorry, his wife was ill, and he not so well provided for them as he wished, and desired the footboy to tell as much to his master, who answered that his master was hunting and he knew not where to find him. About two hours after, Mr. William Eure, Sir William, three gentlemen and the Lord Eure's yeoman faulconer came to Hackness with sundry other servants and boys, and Sir Thomas hearing they were come into his dining room went to them and told them they were welcome. Presently after this Sir William Eure's footboy took forth cards and laid them on the table, wherewith some of the gentlemen were exercised till supper. Sir Thomas stayed with them all the time at supper, which was spent by the gentlemen partly in discoursing of horses and dogs (sports whereunto Sir Thomas protesteth he never applied himself), partly with lascivious tales where every sentence was begun or ended with a great oath, and partly in inordinate drinking unto healths (abuses never practised by Sir Thomas). After supper Sir Thomas willed to have their chambers made ready and came himself to bring them to their lodgings; but they being at dice told him they would play awhile. So he did leave them, and went down and set his household to prayers as they were accustomed. When Sir Thomas and his family had begun to sing a psalm, the company above made an extraordinary noise with their feet, and some of them stood upon the stairs at a window opening into the hall and laughed all the time of prayers.

The next morning they went to breakfast in the dining room, and Sir Thomas hearing them call for more wine, sent for the key of the cellar, and told them they should come by no more wine from him. Then Sir Thomas sent to Mr. Eure to know how he would bestow that day, and told him if he would leave disquieting him with carding, dicing and excessive drinking, and fall to other sports he should be very welcome. After this message Mr. Eure sent to Lady Hoby that he would see her and begone, who prayed him to depart the house in quietness. As he went he called a servant of Sir Thomas and said 'Tell thy master he hath sent a scurvy message, and the next time I meet him I will tell him so, if he be upon the bench, and will pull him by the beard.' Whereat they all departed, and as they went threw stones at the windows and broke four quarrels of glass.

12th September. ONIE MCRORY SLAIN.

The Lord Deputy hath now made a progress in Leix, where he hath cut off that archtraitor Onie McRory O'More and one Callogh McWalter, a second person to Onie, and more bloody and dangerous than all the rest. Most of the rebel's corn is burnt and some of their cattle taken. These traitors were slain in skirmish with Sir Oliver Lambert's men. McWalter's head was brought in to the Lord Deputy that night, but McRory who did not die till the evening willed that his head should be cut off straightway upon his death and buried. This McRory it was who besides the killing of Captain Boswell and Sir Henry Dockwra's lieutenant last year and divers famous murders in those parts took prisoner the Earl of Ormond last April.

17th September. THE EARL OF LINCOLN RELEASED.

The Earl of Lincoln is now to be released from the Fleet upon bond in the sum of £1,000 to yield himself prisoner at or before the 15th of October; having first taken some order for payment of the fees due to the Sergeant-at-arms.

20th September. ABUSES IN DEVON.

Because of the common disorders in his diocese the Bishop of Exeter would have an Ecclesiastical Commission. He complaineth that about the coasts and country there is a dangerous increase of papists; of profane atheists also, so that it is a matter very common to dispute whether there be a God or not. In one place there was a ridiculous and profane marriage of a goose and a gander; a cat having an apron and a partlet was brought to Church to be baptised; a dead horse was brought to the communion table and his feet spread upon it as being prepared to receive the Sacrament. Ministers also are abused.

Libels are made upon every sermon almost in every town. Lately a gentleman asked an ancient preacher whether it was more needful to hang up all the preachers in England or all the dogs, declaring that if the dogs be hanged much sport would be lost, but the Bishop of every diocese might make priests again. Every day complaints are made by ministers who are railed on and shrewdly beaten by lewd persons; in one place a minister was made to kiss the bare hinder parts of a man. Jewism also aboundeth, twenty factions in one city; many conventicles held in gardens and fields and sermons preached at midnight; few or none come to church, but they will follow rattle headed preachers from town to town. There be many times certain persons who draw people into errors by feigned visions and revelations.

23rd September. THE EARL OF ESSEX'S LETTERS TO THE QUEEN.

My Lord of Essex is reported still to be sending submissive letters to her Majesty and again yesterday saying 'If conscience did not tell me that without imploring your Majesty's goodness at this time, most dear and most admired Sovereign, I should not only lose the present support of my poor estate but the hope of any ability to do your Majesty future service, and not that alone but the means of satisfying a great number of hungry and annoying creditors which suffer me in my retired life to have no rest, I would appear still before your Majesty as a mute person. But since this day sennight the lease which I hold by your Majesty's benevolence expireth, and that farm is both my chiefest maintenance and mine only means of compounding with the merchants to whom I am indebted, give me leave, I humbly beseech your Majesty to suit that canon to yourself that I received from yourself, your Majesty's courses tend *ad correctionem non ad ruinam.*'

25th September. A SAYING OF THE QUEEN.

Of late the Queen, Mr. Bacon being in her company, said that my Lord of Essex had written unto her some very dutiful letters, and that she had been moved by them; and when she took it to be the abundance of his heart, she found it to be but a preparation to a suit for the renewing of his farm of sweet wines. Whereunto Mr. Bacon replied, 'O Madam, how doth your Majesty construe these things, as if these two could not stand well together, which indeed Nature hath planted in all creatures. For there are but two sympathies, the one towards perfection, the other towards preservation; that to perfection, as the iron tendeth towards the loadstone; that to preservation, as the vine will creep towards a stake or prop that stands by it; not for any care to the stake but to uphold itself. And therefore, Madam, you must not extinguish my Lord's desire to do you service, it is as to his perfection, that which he thinks himself born for; whereas his desire to obtain this thing of you is but for a sustentation.'

The Collecting of Rags and Bones.

Many abuses are committed by idle and ill disposed persons that wander about the City under colour of collecting old cuttings of cloth, paper, rope, rags, cards, bones, etc., and having access to citizens' houses persuade their servants and apprentices to leave their masters or to rob from them things which, if discovered upon them, they pretend to have found in the streets. It is therefore enacted by the Common Council of the City of London that after the 1st November next only 40 persons shall be allowed to go about in such matter, all of whom shall be 40 years of age at least, and shall wear a known badge upon their breast delivered to them by the Treasurer and Governor of Bridewell Hospital, who shall buy all the things that they collect at a reasonable price, that the poor may be the better relieved and set on work thereby.

30th September. Fresh Complaints against the Earl of Lincoln.

A fresh complaint hath been made against my Lord of Lincoln by one Robert Saior for land sold him unto him, for which divers sums still remain due, £100 due by one Morrison my Lord's servant that is now a fugitive, and another £100 in my Lord's own bond which is unpaid and denied.

1st October. Sir Thomas Hoby's Complaint.

Sir Thomas Hoby having made his complaint to the Council of the North concerning the misdemeanour committed in his house, he was himself charged with wronging certain gentlemen by charging them to the Council with bearing murdering minds, with committing atheistical contempts, and to have exceeded in drink. Hereat a pacification was made, the gentlemen protesting themselves innocent of the matter charged and that they never meant anything in disgrace of Sir Thomas's wife. During the proceeding Sir Thomas said that he would complain to Sir Robert Cecil; to which the Lord Eure answered that Mr. Secretary would make the matter a jest to sport at; for when Sir Thomas had formerly complained of Mr. William Eure, Sir Robert Cecil did cause Mr. Eure to imitate Sir Thomas's preacher, using such gestures as he useth in his evening exercises; whereat Sir Robert laughed very heartily.

2nd October. 'ENGLAND'S PARNASSUS.'

Master Robert Allot hath now compiled a book called *England's Parnassus* or the choicest flowers of our modern poets, with their poetical comparisons, being descriptions of beauties, personages, castles, palaces, mountains, groves, seas, springs, rivers, together with many qualities and attributes, and containing in all more than two thousand pieces, and a table of the special matters contained in the book; which book he dedicateth to Sir Thomas Monson.

3rd October. COURT NEWS.

Great suit is made at Court that my Lord of Essex may continue the farm of the sweet wines; as yet it is not granted, but his officers continue in their places. The Earl came yesternight to Essex House where he lives private, his gate shut day and night. The Earl of Southampton and Lord Grey are both in London, but there is now little speech of their quarrel. From Scotland the news is that the King hath knighted all his servants that assisted him out of that peril of Gowry, but he conceives some displeasure against the ministers for that they would not in the pulpit preach against the horribleness of the fact. It is said that the Queen would have very great care taken that her Coronation day be with gallant solemnities at tilt and tourney, observed to the end the ambassador of Russia may hold it in admiration.

8th October. 'A MIDSUMMER NIGHT'S DREAM.'

Shakespeare's play of *A Midsummer Night's Dream* is to be printed.

13th October. Mr. Fulbecke's 'Historical Collection.'

Mr. William Fulbecke hath compiled *An Historical Collection* of the continual factions, tumults and massacres of the Romans and Italians, beginning where the history of Titus Livius doth end, and ending where Cornelius Tacitus doth begin, the whole reduced into three books entitled Clotho, Lachesis and Atropos. He declareth the use of this history to be threefold: first, the revealing of the great mischiefs of discord and civil dissension: secondly, the cause thereof, which is nothing else but ambition, for out of this seed groweth a whole harvest of evils: thirdly, the declaring of the remedy, which is by humble estimation of ourselves: by living well not by lutting well; by conversing in the light of the commonwealth with equals, not by complotting in dark conventicles against superiors; by hoping without aspiring, and by suffering without conspiring.

Noteth of Brutus that he deserveth not praise but dispraise for the slaying of Caesar, for will any man speak of the wisdom of Brutus when he thinketh upon the field of Philippi wherein Brutus was like to the comet who feeding upon vapours and vain opinions at length consumed and confounded himself? By bloodshed to seek for peace is by oil to quench fire. When any innovation or alteration is to be hatched, the state of things must be quiet and secure that the wheel may be easily turned about without hearing any noise. For to commit the murder of a sovereign Magistrate and to defend thyself by arms, is as if a man should cover himself from a shower of rain. No commonwealth can be without men of aspiring humours, and when such a murder is wrought they find present occasion to tumultuate, knowing that Anarchy breedeth confusion, and that it is best fishing in a troubled stream.

The Good News from Ireland.

The Lord Deputy on the 15th of last month took a journey into the North, being greatly hampered for many days by reason of the continual rain that fell. On the 2nd October there was a very great fight upon a sudden and unexpected. The day being somewhat fair, some of their horsemen coming near to our scouts about dinner time asked when the churls would have dined and come to the trenches. Immediately after dinner the Lord Deputy caused all the companies to be in arms with intent to muster them, but the rebels seeing our men in arms drew towards the camp. Hereupon our men by commandment presently fell out upon them with direction at first only to beat them into their trenches and so to make their retreat. But finding the enemy ready to entertain skirmish contrary to their wont, our men were commanded to give home to their trenches and to force them, which they did, and possessed them a good while, maintaining the fight with the rogues in their greatest strength almost four hours together, at what time our men being commanded off made a good and orderly retreat. Of our men were slain about 20, of the rogues between 300 and 400, and themselves do call this day's work their great overthrow. At Court there is great praise ascribed to the discretion and good directions of the Lord Deputy; that his army is fair and well disciplined; that our soldiers are now grown so bold and resolute that even upon terms they beat the rebels from their bogs and paces.

14th October. THE RUSSIAN AMBASSADOR.

The Russian ambassador had his first audience this day. He read the great titles of his master, delivered her Majesty his letter of audience, and presented unto her in open sort a timber of sables, and one single pair of excellent goodness. At this time there pass only many compliments. When he had done with her Majesty, he was brought to a great banquet and had his belly full of carouses. Sir Jerome Bowes brought him to the Court, my Lord Grey met him at the gate; my Lord of Cumberland at the Great Chamber; my Lord Chamberlain at the Presence; and so was brought back again.

16th October. A NEW BOOK OF SATIRES.

There is one S.R. hath written a book of Epigrams and Satires called *The letting of Humours' blood in the head-vein.*

OF MASTER HUMOURS.

Ask Humours why a feather he doth wear?
'It is his humour, by the Lord,' he'll swear.
Or what he doth with such a horsetail lock?
Or why upon a whore he spends his stock?

'He hath a humour doth determine so.'
Why in that stop-throat fashion doth he go
With scarf about his neck? Hat without band?
'It is his humour, sweet sir, understand.'
What cause his purse is so extreme distressed
That often times 'tis scarcely penny blest?
'Only a humour.' If you question why,
His tongue is ne'er unfurnish'd with a lie:
'It is his humour too'; he doth protest.
Or why with sergeants he is so oppressed
That like to ghosts they haunt him every day?
A rascal humour doth not love to pay.
Object, why boots and spurs are still in season?
His humour answers; 'humour is his reason.'
If you perceive his wits in wetting shrunk,
It cometh of a humour to be drunk.
When you behold his looks pale, thin and poor,
Th'occasion is his humour; and a whore.
And everything that he doth undertake,
It is a vein, for senseless humour's sake.

20th October. A Petition for Licence to Trade in the East Indies.

Seeing that the Dutch have made several very profitable voyages to the East Indies, which is denied to our merchants for want of free liberty of transportation, divers merchants of the City have petitioned the Queen for certain privileges and tolerations whereby they doubt not to furnish this realm and make a staple in London of all those spices and foreign commodities of the East Indies, which heretofore have been supplied at the hands of Portugals, Spaniards and other strangers. They petition that her Majesty would incorporate the first adventurers with a privilege in succession, for that a trade so far remote cannot be managed but by a joint or united stock; that the shipping and preparation for the East Indies, being not above six ships and six pinnaces yearly, be not stayed by pretence or occasion of service, for that the season of the preparation of the voyage being stayed or interrupted but one month the opportunity of the whole year's voyage is lost; that it may be lawful to transport foreign coin into those parts which is brought into the realm by English merchants, and for this first voyage, because of the shortness of the time, there may be coined in her Majesty's mint so much foreign coin as they shall want in the voyage; and also forasmuch as the commodities to be carried outward cannot be known but by divers and sundry experiences how they will be vented in those islands, they petition that they may carry out their commodities for six voyages free of custom, all custom to be answered on goods, spices and merchandise brought from thence.

26th October. ENGROSSING OF GRAIN.

Notwithstanding that this last harvest did not yield any cause of dearth, and also the great care taken to stay foreign transportations except for the service in Ireland, yet the prices of grain are generally risen to a great rate because of the evil practice of engrossing, and that not least by the justices of the peace in the counties. They are now commanded that offenders shall be bound to appear before the Council that they may be made more feelingly to know what chastisement their offences deserve; and if the justices shall continue negligent then will her Majesty be forced to appoint commissioners in the matter.

28th October. SHAKESPEARE'S 'MERCHANT OF VENICE.'

Shakespeare's play of *The Merchant of Venice*, wherein was shown the extreme cruelty of Shylock the Jew towards the merchant in cutting a just pound of his flesh and the obtaining of Portia by the choice of three caskets, is to be printed.

30th October. THE EARL OF ESSEX'S HOPES DASHED.

My Lord of Essex hath lost the farm of the sweet wines, for her Majesty keeps it in her own hands. He sues now only for grace, and that he may come to her presence, of which small hope as yet appeareth.

2nd November. THE DEATH OF MASTER HOOKER.

This day Master Richard Hooker rendered up his soul to God. He was born in Devonshire, a county fruitful of noble wits, and brought up at Oxford in Corpus Christi College, a divine for his modesty, temperance, meekness and other virtues, worthy of imitation, and famous for his accomplishment in several kinds of learning, which his books of *Ecclesiastical Polity*, set forth in English, and very well deserving to be turned into Latin, do abundantly testify to the world.

4th November. FOREIGN SHIPS NOT TO ENTER PORTSMOUTH.

It is reported that divers ships from France and other foreign nations do daily repair to the port and harbour of Portsmouth, a place of great importance and not of ordinary traffic of merchandise. The Council, seeing the doubtfulness of these times and especially at this season when certain of her Majesty's ships are appointed to lie there, have ordered that no foreign ships of any nation shall repair thither.

6th November. THE BARBARY AMBASSADORS.

The Barbary ambassadors are departed. Notwithstanding the kindness showed them here, together with their diet and all other provisions wholly at the Queen's charges, such was their inveterate hate unto our Christian religion and state as they could not endure to give any manner of alms or charity, either in money or broken meat unto any English poor, but reserved their fragments and sold the same unto such poor as would give most to them ; and whereas the chief pretence of their embassy was to require continuance of her Majesty's special favour towards their King, yet the English merchants hold it otherwise, by reason that during their half year's abode in London they have used all subtlety and diligence to know the prices, weights and measures, and all kinds of differences of such commodities as either their country sendeth hither or England transporteth thither. They carry away with them all sorts of English weights, measures and samples of commodities. They seem rather to have been espials than honourable ambassadors, for they omitted nothing that might damnify the English merchants.

9th November. THE QUEEN'S RETURN TO WHITEHALL.

It is commanded that when the Queen shall come to Whitehall lights shall be provided in every house in cressets to be held before the houses alongst the streets from Charing Cross to

Whitehall. The constables and housekeepers are warned to provide good store of cressets to be placed very thick all the way where the Queen is to pass.

12th November. ALLEYN'S NEW PLAYHOUSE.

The Lord Admiral's men now play at Mr. Alleyn's new playhouse, called the Fortune, where they have a new play by Dekker called *Fortune's Tennis.* This house is built square, being without 80 feet on all sides ; and within there are three galleries, 32 feet in height in all. The stage is like that of the Globe, 43 feet in width ; and in breadth coming forward to the midst of the yard, which is 55 feet square.

13th November. SIR WILLIAM CORNWALLIS'S 'ESSAYS.'

Mr. Henry Olney the printer hath put forth a little book of Essays written by Sir William Cornwallis the younger lest some mercenary hand coming upon a copy foully corrupted by often transcription should publish them unpolished to the world.

HIS ESSAY 'OF SLEEP'

My custom is about this time of day to sleep ; to avoid which now I choose to write : so, if this be a drowsy style, and sleepily done, I go not backward, for it serves in sleep's room. This sleep is to me in the nature that dung is to ground, it makes the soil of my apprehension more solid and tough, it makes it not so light and pleasant, and I am glad of it, for I find myself too much subject to a verbal quickness : thus I think it good for me that am of a dry barren mould ; but for others it may hap to make them too waterish : the cause of this is common as the effect, yet as some bodies are more subject to it than others, so meats of one kind provoke it more than another. This makes me often play the epicure, making my stomach a coward, to fight with partridge, pheasant and such fowl, whose airy parts are more fine, and poison not the brain with thick vapours. These four footed beasts are dull and gross, and so is what proceeds from them. Well, for my part I will put away this sleepy humour, for it is an extreme spender. When I come at the end of a week to reckon how I have bestowed it, in that seven days I find nothing but 'Item, in sleep': 'Item, in sleep'; and in the end, *summa totalis*, seven nights, seven afternoons, beside half hours and quarters at unaccustomed times; there is no proportion in this, especially to bestow it on so much winking. I cannot blame Alexander though he misliked it, and held that, and lust, the arguments of mortality: if he had used eight of clock-hours, the Persian Empire might yet have stood. Not so much but good husbands hate it; and *pedantes* have made it a main supporter of their instructions. I would liken it to death but that it is more terrible, for it is idleness; yet thus it is death for it kills eternity. Fame never yet knew a perpetual bed-presser. Is it not a pitiful thing to see a fellow bestow half his patrimony in hobby-horses? Then pity all them who having but a little time dedicate half that to sleep. But this is the effect of our bodies, who, in despite of our soul's divinity, will follow their natural inclinations to lie along and be senseless like their earthly original.

THE QUEEN ROYALLY RECEIVED.

This evening the Queen, being most honourably attended on by the prelates, nobles and judges of the Realm, was received near unto Chelsea by the Lord Mayor of London, with his brethren the aldermen all in scarlet, besides citizens in coats of velvet and chains of gold to the number of 500 on horseback, every one of them having two staff torches to attend on them; and they all waited on her to the royal palace at Westminster.

15th November. COURT RUMOURS.

There is a constant report that he which hath been so long a prisoner at Venice is now discovered to be the true Sebastian by many secret tokens upon his body, confirmed out of Portugal by those which knew him both child and man.

Out of Scotland it is said that there is no good agreement between the King and his wife; and many are of opinion that the discovery of some affection between her and the Earl of Gowry's brother (who was killed with him) was the true cause and motive of all that tragedy.

20th November. THE CATHOLIC DISSENSIONS.

The disputes between the archpriest and the secular priests still continue very hot, insomuch that about a month since the archpriest suspended two of them, by name Mush and Colleton, from their functions as priests, forbidding also all Catholics to receive the Sacraments from them, because that they have continued to make complaints against him. Thirty of the English priests that are imprisoned in Wisbeach have now signed an appeal to the See Apostolic at Rome, and demand of Blackwell his dismissory letters.

SIR ANTHONY SHIRLEY'S VOYAGE.

News is come that Sir Anthony Shirley, acting as ambassador for the Sophy was received with great ceremonies at Prague, where 'tis said, he will conclude an alliance with the Emperor against the Turk. Last month Blore and Jaggard the stationers were fined 6s. 8d. for printing contrary to order a book of Sir Anthony's voyage, all copies whereof are taken and burnt.

22nd November. THE NEW ART OF SETTING OF CORN.

There is a new book by Mr. Hugh Platt, *The new and admirable art of setting of corn*, wherein he condemneth the sowing of corn after ploughing, but would have each corn sown in little holes made in the earth of the depth of three or four inches; and hereby, saith he, cometh great increase in the crop. For whereas he that reapeth 4 quarters of wheat out of an acre doth hold himself well contented (which is a return of 8 for 1), yet some that have tried this new method have reaped many times as great. A gentleman in Surrey hath reaped 16 bushels out of one pint of wheat which he set, whereof some corns brought forth 40 and some 48 ears having 66, 68 and 72 corns in each ear, and other like examples.

28th November. NEWS FROM IRELAND.

The Lord Deputy hath now constructed a large and strong fort midway between Newry and Armagh wherein are placed 400 men with their victuals for two months. When this work was being begun Tyrone sent some of his men upon ours, having armed them so heavily with drink that some of them were unable to retire, and one of his best trusted servants, by name McCale O'Quin, was taken; but upon his taking there was no examination of him, drink having made him so senseless and speechless. In their return to Dublin the rebels would have impeached their progress in a narrow way, but in spite of their shot our men forced their way, having about 60 hurt and 10 killed, of whom my Lord's secretary, Master George Cranmer, was the only man of note: of the enemy 80 are reported slain. The army are now back in Dublin, where on the 17th the Lord Deputy knighted three English and one Irish, among them Captain Berry, who was one of the first that turned the fortune of the wars by a notorious valiant part he played, wherein he received five wounds, with so great admiration to the rebels themselves that they would not believe but that he was a devil.

1st December. My Lord of Essex's Passions.

Now that her Majesty hath deprived the Earl of Essex of all hope of the farm of sweet wines, it is confidently said that my Lord is vexed at heart and all on fire with indignation, insomuch that he hearkeneth to his friends who insinuate to him that now at length it plainly appeareth that the Queen, the Council and his adversaries are resolved to thrust him down into that extremity of poverty that he shall be forced to live upon the alms-basket; and being once become a poor man and neglected by the Queen, he will soon be neglected and slighted by all men, forsaken by his friends and scorned, insulted and triumphed over by his enemies. One who hath been with him lately reporteth that he is shifted from sorrow and repentance to rage and rebellion so suddenly as well proveth him devoid of good reason or right mind, uttering strange words bordering on strange designs, and his speeches of the Queen such as becometh no man that hath his right wits. My Lord hath ill advisers, and especially Henry Cuffe his man. This Cuffe is a man of secret ambitious ends of his own and of proportionate counsels smothered under the habit of a scholar, and slubbered over with a certain rude clownish fashion that hath the semblance of integrity.

3rd December. The Queen's Letter to Lord Mountjoy.

Of late the Lord Deputy having complained that he is but slenderly supported at home and maligned by his enemies likened himself to a scullion, which coming to the Queen's ears she wrote with her own hands to this effect: 'Mistress Kitchen-maid, I had not thought that precedency had been ever in question but among the higher and greater sort; but now I find by good proof that some of more dignity and greater calling may by good desert and faithful care give the upper hand to one of your faculty, that with your frying pan and other kitchen stuff have brought to their last home more rebels, and passed greater breakneck places than those that promised more and did less. Comfort yourself therefore in this that neither your careful endeavour, nor dangerous travails, nor heedful regards to our service, without your own by-respects, could ever have been bestowed upon a Prince that more esteems them, considers and regards them, than she for whom chiefly, I know, all this hath been done, and who keeps this verdict ever in store for you; that no vain glory nor popular fawning can ever advance you forward, but true vow of duty and reverence of Prince, which two before your life I see you do prefer. And though you lodge near Papists, and doubt you not for their infection, yet I fear you may fall in an heresy which I hereby conjure you from; that you suppose you be backbited by some to make me think you faulty of many oversights and evil defaults in your government. I would have you know for certain that as there is no man can rule so great a charge without some errors, yet you may assure yourself I have never heard of any had fewer; and such is your good luck that I have not known them, though you were warned of them. And learn this of me, that you must make difference betwixt admonitions and charges, and like of faithful advices as your most necessariest weapons to save you from blows of Princes' mislike. And so I absolve you *a poena et culpa*, if this you observe. And so God bless and prosper you as if ourself was where you are. Your Sovereign that dearly regards you.'

7th December. SUPPLIES FOR IRELAND.

There are now required for the Irish service 13,900 quarters of corn, and 1,000 men, to serve as shot, which are to be taken from 39 counties or places. To these men public notice shall be given that if any of them run away he shall be followed with hue and cry as a felon, and suffer death according to the laws of the realm. If any soldier shall fall sick by the way, or grow lame or so weak that he cannot march any further, the conductor shall present him to the mayor of the next town or a justice of the peace and there leave him to return into his county where he shall be recovered; and he shall be given a passport subscribed both by the conductor and the mayor or justice, expressing the cause why he was not able to march further.

10th December. The Black Galley of Dort.

Of late the Lords of the United States caused a galley to be made, called the *Black Galley* of Dort, that they might hinder the galleys from the Sluce from committing spoil upon their merchant ships; whereat many did murmur saying that it would be labour lost for the country. But on the last day of November this ship, with three or four sloops that were with her, seized upon the Admiral's ship that lay before Antwerp and took it, likewise a ship of Brussels and a ship of Mechelen and five convoy ships, all which were brought to Flushing, there being in these ships 54 pieces of ordnance, besides certain stone pieces.

11th December. A Discourse of Universities.

Mr. Samuel Lewkenor hath written a discourse of those cities wherein do flourish at this day privileged Universities (being in number 74), a work not altogether unprofitable nor unpleasant for such as are desirous to know the situation and customs of foreign cities without travelling to see them. Of the antiquity of our two ancient Universities noteth from sundry authorities that Oxford was first consecrated unto the Muses in the time of the Britons, again restored to her ancient fame by Alfred, a holy and religious Saxon king, in the year 873, but afterwards, being cruelly ravaged by the Danes and Harold Lightfoot, was left decayed until the time of William the Norman, when in the year 1130 a goodly and famous priory was founded there by one Robert Polenius, and the city being again adorned with many fair and goodly edifices newly began to flourish, and great multitudes of students to repair there, insomuch that in the reign of King John three thousand students were numbered in the University. Concerning the antiquity of Cambridge there are two several and discrepant opinions. Dr. John Caius labouring to prove its foundation in the year 4317 after the world's first creation, which was 539 years before our Saviour's nativity; but sundry others (imagining this antiquity to be somewhat far fetched) affirm that the University was erected in the time of

Sigebert, King of England, 530 years after our Saviour's incarnation. But whensoever or by whomsoever first erected, most certainly true it is, for the antiquity and worthiness thereof the University of Cambridge may at this time worthily contend with the most ancient and flourishing cities of the world.

15*th December.* A Boy seized to be a Player.

Three years since Mr. Nathaniel Giles, that is master of the Children of the Chapel Royal was by her Majesty's letters patent authorised to take up children in cathedrals, churches and chapels for the Queen's better service, but since he hath confederated with Henry Evans and a certain James Robinson in maintaining the playhouse in the Blackfriars; they have taken divers children from schools and apprentices from their masters solely to be employed in their interludes, such as one Nathan Field, scholar of the grammar school in London, kept by Mr. Mulcaster, Salmon Pavy apprentice to one Peerce, and four others. Two days ago under colour of their commission Evans and Robinson laid hands upon a boy named Thomas Clifton, the son of Henry Clifton, Esquire, as he walking from his house near Great St. Bartholemews to the grammar school in Christchurch, and dragged him away to the playhouse. When the father heard of it he went to the playhouse and there finding Giles, Evans and Robinson, and his son in their violent custody, he makes request to have his son released, which they refused to do. Whereupon he said that if he should complain unto some of the Council they would hardly answer it; to which they answered that he might complain to whom he would, and they would answer it, adding further that if the Queen would not bear them forth in the action, she should get another to execute her commission for them. When further the father declared that it was not fit that a gentleman of his sort should have his only son and heir to be so basely used, they replied that they had authority sufficient to take any nobleman's son in this land; and further to despite the father they delivered a scroll of paper, containing the part of one of their plays to the boy and commanded him to learn the same by heart, and delivered him into the custody of Evans, saying further that if he did not obey he should be surely whipped. But after a day and a night he is now released by the warrant of Sir John Fortescue and set at liberty.

20th December. THE FRENCH KING'S MARRIAGE.

The Princess Mary de Medicis, who was espoused to the French King by proxy at Florence on the 28th September last, was married to him at Lyons on the 7th of this month before a great assembly of people. The King came to Lyons on the 30th November whilst the Queen was at supper, whom he did long behold unknown among many others that were there. At the taking up of the table he retired to his own chamber, where he stayed till she was gone to her own lodging, whither he went to her. She met him at the door and offered to kneel down, but he took her in his arms where he held her embraced a long time. After his supper he retired to his own lodging wishing her to go to bed whither he would come and find her ; which he did accordingly, though she prayed him after his wearisome journey rather to repose and refresh himself. The King doth profess to the world great contentment saying that she doth far surpass the relation which hath been made of her.

21st December. A PROCLAMATION CONCERNING FIREARMS.

A proclamation is published reaffirming those statutes that forbid the carrying and shooting in guns by common and ordinary persons, for notwithstanding the law and penalties imposed, great and manifold insolencies and robberies have grown and been committed by the common carrying of guns, and especially of pistols, birding pieces, and other like short pieces and small shot. This licentiousness hath grown so far as it is usual not only with common persons travelling by the highways to carry pistols, but that ruffians and other lewd and dissolute men of the worst and basest condition in highways and streets, even of London itself, do in secret manner go provided of such means to do mischief. Moreover by this common abuse of carrying and shooting in fowling pieces and birding pieces great waste and spoil is made of game, as of pheasants, partridges and such other sort of game as should serve for the delight of her Majesty, the nobility and other men of quality ; whereby is grown not only such undecent and disorderly confusion among all sorts and degrees of men (every mean and base person taking to himself that which belongeth to men of the best sort and condition) as is very unseemly and unmeet in a well governed State, but also an extreme scarcity of all such kind of provisions both for her Majesty's purveyance and for the use of principal persons.

22nd December. THE EARL OF ESSEX'S DANGEROUS COURSES.

The Earl of Essex is now returned to London and it is much noted how his doors are set open to all comers. Sir Gelly Merrick, his steward, entertaineth at his table many captains, men of broken fortunes, discontented persons, and such as saucily use their tongues in railing against all men. Sermons are preached there daily by zealous ministers to which the citizens flock in great numbers; and my Lady Rich (who is in great disfavour with her Majesty for her adulteries) resorteth there daily. And if any showeth a dislike of these things, he is forthwith censured as an envier of my Lord's honour and liberty. Moreover, now and then he letteth fall words which show his disdainful stomaching the power his adversaries have with the Queen; nor will he listen to the wiser counsels of his friends. These things are brought to the Queen's ears and alienate her affection from him more and more, and especially one speech inflameth her most of all, for he said that being now an old woman, she is no less crooked and distorted in mind than she is in body.

27th December. THE QUEEN'S PAINTING.

It was commonly observed this Christmas that her Majesty when she came to be seen was continuously painted, not only all over her face, but her very neck and breast also, and that the same was in some places near half an inch thick.

31st December. A PRIVILEGE FOR THE DISCOVERY OF TRADE TO THE EAST INDIES.

Her Majesty hath granted a privilege to the Earl of Cumberland and gentlemen and merchants, that they may at their own charges set forth voyages by way of traffic and merchandises to the East Indians and to as many islands, cities and places thereabouts where trade may by likelihood be established. These adventurers shall be known as the Governor and Company of Merchants of London trading into the East Indies, and the first Governor, Master Thomas Smith, alderman. They are granted authority to make reasonable laws by the greatest part of a general assembly, and to punish offenders either in body or purse so it be not contrary to the laws of the realm. Moreover, they may transport merchandise out of the realm free of custom or other duties, as also to carry out in the first and subsequent voyages foreign coin and bullion to the value of £30,000, so as £6,000 thereof be coined in the mint in the Tower of London. There shall further be permitted six ships and six pinnaces and 500 mariners notwithstanding any restraint, except the Navy Royal go forth; nor shall any other subjects not free of the company trade in those parts without the licence and assent of the Company. Her Majesty will not grant to any others to enter into these parts during the term of 15 years; but if this privilege be found unprofitable for the Realm, then within two years warning given under the Privy Seal it shall be void, but if found beneficial then to be renewed with additions.

OTHER BOOKS SET FORTH ANNO 1600

A Clown's Book.

Armin the clown hath written a book called *Quips upon Questions*, in this last restraint having little else to do. Herein upon a word or question maketh he a rhyme extemporal and concludeth with a quip, as of—

He Plays the Fool.

True it is, he plays the fool indeed ;
But in the play, he plays it as he must :
Yet when the play is ended, then his speed
Is better than the pleasure of thy trust :
  For he shall have what thou that time has spent,
  Playing the fool, thy folly to content.

He plays the wise man then, and not the fool
That wisely for his living can do so :
So doth the carpenter with his sharp tool,
Cut his own finger oft, yet lives by it too :
  He is a fool to cut his limb, say I,
  But not so with his tool to live thereby.

Then 'tis his case that makes him seem a fool,
It is indeed, for it is antic made
Thus men wax wise when they do go to school,
Then for our sport we thank the tailor's trade,
  And him within the case the most of all,
  That seems wise-foolish, who a fool you call.

Meet him abroad, and he is wise methinks,
In courtesy, behaviour, talk or going
Of garment : Eke when he with any drinks,
Then are men wise their money so bestowing
  To learn by him one time a fool to seem,
  And twenty times for once, in good esteem.

Say I should meet him and not know his name,
What should I say, 'Yonder goes such a fool ?'

Ay, fools will say so ; but the wise will aim
At better thoughts : whom reason still doth rule.
Yonder's the merry man, it joys me much,
To see him civil when his part is such.

A merry man is often thought unwise
Yet mirth in modesty 's loved of the wise :
Then say, should he for a fool go
Quip *When he's a more fool that accounts him so ?*
Many men descant on another's wit,
When they have less themselves in doing it.

BRETON'S 'MELANCHOLICK HUMOURS.'

Master Nicholas Breton's *Melancholick Humours*, in verses of divers natures, which he commendeth chiefly to spirits of his own nature, full of melancholy, and as near Bedlam as Moorgate ; with a sonnet to the author by Ben Jonson.

'PALESTINA.'

There is a book called *Palestina*, written by one Mr. R. C. P., a bachelor of divinity, and printed at Florence. Herein is set forth the story of the birth of Christ in the form of a fable, or romance.

DARRELL'S ANSWER TO MR. HARSNETT.

Darrell hath compiled a book entitled *A true narration* of the strange and grievous vexation by the devil of seven persons in Lancashire, and William Somers of Nottingham, and displaying the doctrine of possession and dispossession of demoniacs out of the Word of God.

He hath written also an answer to Mr. Harsnett's book called *A detection of that sinful, shameful, lying and ridiculous discourse of Samuel Harsnett*, answering the former book page by page and declaring that it is now manifestly and apparently showed in the eyes of the world not only the unlikelihood, but the flat impossibility of the counterfeiting of Somers and the rest. Concludeth with a prayer to God that if he be guilty of that which is laid to his charge, his act may be registered to his perpetual infamy, his name rased out of the Book of Life, and his portion given among the hypocrites.

A Discourse of the Lancashire Possessions.

Mr. George More that was Darrell's companion when he dispossessed those seven persons in one house in Lancashire hath penned a discourse of the same, to serve, as he saith, as part of an answer to the book called *A discovery of the fraudulent practises.*

'The Picture of a Perfect Commonwealth.'

The picture of a perfect Commonwealth, describing as well the offices of Princes and inferior magistrates over their subjects, as also the duties of subjects towards their governors, being gathered forth of sundry authors by Mr. Thomas Floyd of Jesus College in Oxford. Treateth in 46 chapters of a commonwealth and its sundry kinds, as aristocracy, democracy, monarchy, and of those virtues and qualities whereof a magistrate should partake.

'Vicissitudo Rerum.'

An elegical poem of the interchangeable courses and varieties of things in this world entitled *Vicissitudo rerum*, hath been composed by Mr. John Norden, showing how Time turneth all things out of date and will prevail till she herself have end and timeless time succeedeth.

We at the present see *Time's* changing state,
And *Nature's* fearful alterations,
As if *Time* now did preach the *Heavens'* debate,
And *Stars* to band in dismal factions.
  Strange *signs* are seen, divine probations,
  That some *effect* will follow of *admire*,
  Too late, when come, to say it will retire.

The *Sun* and *Moon* eclipsed ne'er so much,
Comets and strange impressions in the *air*;
The *tides* and swelling *floods* were never such:
The *earth* doth tremble, *Nature* doth impair,
  Hid'ous *monsters* now possess the chair,
  Where erst dame *Nature's* true begotten seed
  Sat truly graced in her proper weed.

Such changes never have been seen of yore,
In *Countries* and in *Kingdoms* as of late,
Manners, and *Laws*, and *Religion's* lore
Never were prized at so mean a rate :
Such are the changes of this *Earth's* estate,
It may be said, *Time's* wings begin to fry,
Now couching low, that erst did soar so high.

'THE TRANSFORMED METAMORPHOSIS.'

An obscure poem by one Cyril Turner called *The Transformed Metamorphosis*, lamenting the deformities of these times, which book the author dedicateth in these terms to Sir Christopher Heydon :

Thou, thou that art the Muses *Adony*
Their Pyramis, adorner of their mount,
Thou Chrystalizer of their *Castaly*,
Thou Lilian-rose, sprung from the horse-foot mount,
To thee, Art's Patron, Champion to the highest,
That givest the Sun a fairer radiance,
To thee *Musophilus*, that still appliest
Thy sacred soul, to be Truth's esperance.
To thee, this Epinyctall register,
Rased out by *Eos*' rays, I write to thee.
To thee, this hoary *Hiems*, kill'd by *Ver* :
To thee, this metamorphosed Tragedy ;
To thee, I write my Apotheosy :
Mœcenas, strengthen my Tyrociny.

1601

1st January. THE QUEEN AND MR. BACON.

These last months the Queen hath been utterly alienated from Mr. Bacon, turning away from him with express and purposelike discountenance wherever she seeth him. Insomuch that being admitted to her presence he spake to her very plainly, saying that many loved him not because they think he hath been against my Lord of Essex: 'and you love me not because you know I have been for him; yet will I never repent me that I have dealt in simplicity of heart towards you both, without respect of cautions to myself; and therefore *uiuus uidensque pereo*: if I do break my neck, I shall do it in a manner as Master Dorrington did it, which walked upon the battlements many days and took a view and survey where he should fall. And so, Madam,' said he, 'I am not so simple but that I take a prospect of mine overthrow, only I thought I would tell you so much that you may know it was faith and not folly that brought me unto it, and so I will pray for you.' Upon which speeches, uttered with some passion, the Queen was exceedingly moved, and spake kind and gracious words to him, and willed him to rest upon this, '*gratia mea sufficit.*'

2nd January. THE EARL OF ESSEX.

The Earl of Essex nowadays is observed to be very close with the Earl of Southampton, Sir Charles Danvers, Sir Ferdinando Gorges, Sir John Davies and divers others. The resort of the multitude to Essex House to hear sermons is more frequent than usual, and some of the words of the preachers much noted, as that the superior majestrates of the realm have power to restrain kings themselves.

3rd January. AN ITALIAN DUKE IN LONDON.

There is come to London Virginio Orsino, Duke of Bracchiano, being sent, as it is said, by the French Queen to give her Majesty thanks for a token which she formerly sent. The Duke was honourably received by the Italian merchants in the city, and straightway some noblemen were sent to invite him to the Court, where he hath divers times been sumptuously feasted and entertained. The Queen hath been pleased to have many discourses with him and to dance before him, and he as a well experienced courtier knew to make show of admiring of her as most excellent and all her actions as incomparable. She invited him to go with her to her closet over the chapel, having given orders that the Communion table should be adorned with basin and ewer of gold and tapers, and other ornaments (some say also with a crucifix), and that all the ministers should be in rich copes. The Duke accompanied her, and she was very pleasant thereat, saying she would write to the Pope not to chide him for that fact, with other like discourses.

THE CROSS IN CHEAPSIDE.

Some of the Council have written to the Lord Mayor commanding him in her Majesty's name with all speed to cause the Cross in Cheapside to be repaired, and the cross and figure set up as perfectly as it was before. The like order was given some years since but the Mayor and aldermen refused to obey, saying that it was superstitious and wishing to set up in place thereof the figure of Justice. Now all diligence is to be used that it may be finished before the Duke's departure, that he may make relation thereof in foreign parts.

6th January. IRISH NEWS.

The Lord Deputy now continueth to press upon the rebels in Leinster. Upon Christmas Eve he surprised the house of the rebel Phelim McFeagh at Ballinacorr, took his son, slew divers, and fell upon such provisions as he had made for Christmas, which was good store of beef, great store of strong drink both wine and *aqua vitae.*

9th January. THE LORD GREY AND THE EARL OF SOUTHAMPTON.

To-day my Lord Grey, upon some new conceived discontent, assaulted my Lord of Southampton on horseback in the street with drawn sword, for which contempt against her Majesty's commandment he is committed to the Fleet. My Lord of Essex is greatly offended thereat.

11th January. THE NEW EAST INDIES COMPANY.

Now that the new authorised company of merchants preparing to trade to the East Indies have advanced their preparations for the voyage to a full readiness, certain that had heretofore assured by their subscriptions to advance sums of money would retract their promises; but upon complaint made to the Council they are commanded to furnish their promised contributions by Saturday next lest they be committed to prison.

13th January. BANBURY CROSS DEFACED.

The inhabitants of Banbury, being far gone in Puritanism, in a furious zeal have tumultuously assailed the Cross that stood in their market place, and so defaced it that scarcely one stone is left upon another. The chief actors in these riotous proceedings are enjoined to re-edify the cross and to appear before the Lords in the Star Chamber to receive some condign punishment.

14th January. THE EARL OF ESSEX.

The Earl of Essex is now altogether in his house near Temple Bar in no favour as yet with her Majesty, but growing again to wonted popularity, being often visited by many of the nobility, as the Earls of Worcester, Southampton, Sussex, Rutland, Bedford and others, with many captains and cavaliers, and a whole pack of Puritans, insomuch as it is thought both the Queen and Mr. Secretary stand in awe of him, and would make him surer if they durst. Not many days since, the Lord Treasurer sent his eldest son to visit him, and withal to tell him that he had dealt effectively with her Majesty on his behalf, and was in hope to have brought it to good forwardness, had not his Lordship in three respects hindered him. The one in permitting base captains and rascals (as Captain Baynham by name) to have free access unto him, who being desperately bent upon all occasions, her Majesty might justly fear no good meaning. The second for that his house was open to all new comers, where he often feasted some of the nobility and many others, whereby he discovered himself to affect popularity. The third, by having so many chaplains and so many exercises or Puritan sermons, or rather conventicles, that he drew multitudes thither, that the Queen could not but take it ill.

To these he answered that he knew no rascals that resorted

unto him, and not being prohibited speech of any, he saw no reason to withdraw himself from such as in good will pretended to visit him. To the second, he said he could not but in civility invite such as came to him to such fare as he had, which was not feasting, and that otherwise he invited or sent for none. To the last, that these exercises were no conventicle but rather spiritual conferences which was his only consolation, and therefore hoped her Majesty would permit him to use freely that comfort ; and for plurality of chaplains, he said he had but two of his own, confessing withal that some others, coming either with their Lords or masters, or without, and offering to make him a sermon, he neither did nor could refuse it, considering the pleasure and profit he received thereby.

16th January. Debasing the Irish Coin.

There was great consultation to-day at the Council touching the debasement of the Irish coin in order that the expenses of the Queen in vanquishing the traitors may be maintained, wherein sundry things were agreed. The debasing of coin enhances the price of all merchandise, especially foreign ; and also of victuals and all other things ; the soldiers receiving their pay in this kind will be discontented, as also pensioners, officers, soldiers and all who live by certain rents will be greatly harmed ; but freeholders who have lands in demesne or where they can raise the rent will not suffer much harm because they can double and treble their rents. It seemed to be resolved by all that the penny and halfpenny shall be coins of base metal entirely, and threepences, sixpences and shillings shall be coined whereof there shall be one part pure silver and three parts alloy ; and that a new stamp shall be devised to coin 100,000 for the service of Ireland only ; and all other coins current there shall be decried and disannulled, so that all shall return to England.

18th January. Deserters Pardoned.

Of those five deserters condemned in Essex last August, two were executed ; the three remaining are now pardoned.

22nd January. Dr. Hayward again Examined.

Dr. Hayward was again examined in the Tower concerning the writing of his book of Henry the Fourth. As for the epistle, he declared it to be of his own inditing, wherein he spoke generally of histories and intended no particular application to present history. He had read in Fox's book of *Acts and Monuments* that King Henry II never demanded subsidy of his subjects and left in treasure £900,000, besides jewels and plate; he inserted the same in the *History of Henry the Fourth*, because he taketh it to be lawful for any historiographer to insert any history of former time into that history he writes, though no other historian has mentioned the same. Being asked where he found the description of the Earl of Derby as not negligent to uncover the head, bow the body, stretch forth the neck, arm, etc., he declared that he found it in Hall and others that he was of a popular behaviour: but for the particulars he took the liberty of the best writers. He began this history a dozen years before, although he acquainted no man therewith. He hath received nothing from the printer for printing of the book.

25th January. MASTER HOOKER'S LAST BOOKS.

At the time of Mr. Hooker's death it was known that three books of his *Ecclesiastical Polity* lay unprinted though finished by him, whereof the learned had great expectation. Wherefore the Archbishop about a month after his death sent to the widow to inquire of her for these books, but she could not or would not give any account of them. Of late she was sent for by the Council to be examined concerning them. In the meantime the Archbishop invited her to dinner and in friendly manner put certain questions to her, whereupon she confessed that one Chark (formerly for his doctrines expelled from the University) and another minister that dwelt near Canterbury, came to her desiring to go into her husband's study to look upon some of his writings; and that they two being there burnt and tore many of them, assuring her that they were not fit to be seen.

26th January. THE QUEEN AND DR. HAYWARD'S BOOK.

The Queen being mightily incensed against Dr. Hayward's book, thinking it a seditious prelude to put into the people's head boldness and faction, said that she had an opinion that there was treason in it, and demanded of Mr. Bacon if he could not find any places in it that might be drawn within case of treason; whereto he answered, 'For treason surely I find none, but for felony very many.' And when her Majesty hastily asked him wherein he said that the author had committed very apparent theft, for he had taken most of the sentences of Cornelius Tacitus, and translated them into English, and put them into his text. At another time, when the Queen would not be persuaded that it was his writing whose name was to it but that it had some more mischievous author, she said with great indignation that she would have him racked to produce his author. Mr. Bacon replied, 'Nay, Madam, he is a doctor, never rack his person rack his style; let him have pen, ink and paper, and help of books and be enjoined to continue the story where it breaketh off, and I will undertake by collating the styles to judge whether he were the author or no.'

28th January. SIX GALLEYS TO BE BUILT.

Six galleys are now to be built for the defence of the Thames, whereof four shall be at the charges of her Majesty, and the remaining two by the City; and the Lord Mayor shall confer with the Justices in the County of Middlesex, and the chief officers at Westminster and St. Katharine's concerning the levying of the contribution.

1st February. A WINDMILL SPLIT BY WIND.

To-day a great tempest of wind brake the windmill beyond St. Giles Field near to Tyburn. The miller was thrown one way, another man another way, towards north and south; and part of the mill roof and half the millstone in like manner thrown divers ways.

3rd February. STRANGE EXPERIMENTS.

Many strange new experiments are made these days. Last week one came hopping from Charing Cross into Paul's bound in a sack, and this morning another carried up a horse and rode him on the top of Paul's steeple, with divers other such wagers.

5th February. THE NEW EARL OF PEMBROKE AND MRS. FITTON.

The Earl of Pembroke died a fortnight since leaving his lady as base as he could, and bestowing all on the young Lord, even to her jewels. The familiarity of the new Earl with Mistress Fitton, the Maid of Honour, was much noted some months since, for she would put off her head tire and tuck up her clothes, and take a large white cloak and would march as though she had been a man to meet the Earl out of Court. But now misfortune is befallen her, for she is proved with child, and the Earl of Pembroke, being examined, confesseth a fact but utterly renounceth all marriage. 'Tis to be feared that both will dwell in the Tower awhile for the Queen hath vowed to send them thither.

7th February. 'RICHARD THE SECOND' PLAYED.

Yesterday Sir Charles Percy, Sir Joscelyn Percy, the Lord Mounteagle and some others of my Lord of Essex's followers, came to some of the Lord Chamberlain's players and would have them play that play of the deposing and killing of King Richard II, promising to give them 40s. more than their ordinary to play it. The players answered that the play of King Richard was so old and so long out of use that they should have little or no company at it. Nevertheless at their request, and in consideration of 40s., they played it this afternoon at the Globe, when many of my Lord of Essex's followers were present.

THE EARL OF ESSEX AND THE COUNCIL.

To-day upon rumours that my Lord of Essex hath a design to right himself by force of his pretended wrongs, the Council sat at the Lord Treasurer's house, he being sick. They have sent to the Earl to come to them, but he excuseth himself. So Secretary Herbert is then sent for him, but he refuseth still, alleging danger to his own person and pretending that he shall be murdered in his bed this night.

8th February. THE EARL OF ESSEX'S TREASON.

About 10 of the clock this morning (being Sunday), the Lord Keeper, the Earl of Worcester, Sir William Knollys and the Lord Chief Justice, on the Queen's command repaired to the Earl of Essex's house, and finding the gate shut against them, after a little stay were let in at the wicket, which was shut upon them and all their servants kept out. Within the court was full of men, assembled in tumultuous sort; and at their coming in the Earls of Essex, Rutland, Southampton, and the Lords Sandys and Mounteagle, Sir Christopher Blount, Sir Charles Danvers, and many other knights, gentlemen and other persons unknown flocked together about the Lord Keeper. Thereupon he told the Earl of Essex that they were sent from her Majesty to understand the cause of their present assemblage, and to let them know that if they had any particular cause of grief, it should be heard and they have justice.

Hereat the Earl of Essex loudly declared that his life was sought; that he should have been murdered in his bed: that he had been perfidiously dealt with; that his hand had been counterfeited and letters written in his name; and therefore they were assembled to defend their lives; with other such like speeches. The Lord Keeper again assured him that whatever private offence he had against any person, they would faithfully and honourably submit it to her Majesty, and required him, if he would not declare it openly, to impart it to them privately.

Upon this there was a great clamour raised among the multitude, crying 'Away my Lord,' 'They abuse you,' 'They betray you,' 'They undo you,' 'You lose time.' So the Lord Keeper put on his hat and said with a loud voice, 'My Lord, let us speak with you privately and understand your griefs': at the same time he commanded them all on their allegiance, to lay down their weapons and depart. At this they brake out into an exceeding loud shout of 'All, all, all.' Meanwhile the Earl of Essex and most part of the company put on their hats, and so the Earl went into the house, the Lord Keeper following him. As they were going in, some of the disordered company cried, 'Kill them'; others, 'Cast the Great Seal out of the Window'; and others, 'Let us shop them up.' The Earl of Essex brought the Lord Keeper and the rest into his book chamber and there gave order to have the further door of that chamber shut fast. Then at his going forth he said, 'My Lords, be patient a while and stay here, and I will go into London and take order with the Mayor and Sheriffs for the City and will be here again within half an hour'; and so departed from the Lord Keeper, leaving him and the rest and divers of the gentlemen pensioners in that room guarded by Sir John Davies, Francis Tresham and Owen Salisbury with musket shot.

This coming of the Councillors being all unexpected my Lord of Essex forgot his main design, and, committing the defence of his house to Sir Gelly Meyrick, went hastily out with a party of 200 men or thereabouts, all lusty young men and of stout courage, but noways provided of arms like soldiers, most of them having their cloaks wrapped about their arms and only swords by their sides. The Earl of Bedford, the Lord Cromwell and other noblemen joined themselves with them as they went along.

Being entered into London he began to cry out, 'For the Queen! For the Queen! A plot is laid for my life.' And so went forward in much haste through the chief streets of the city to Sheriff Smith's house near Fenchurch, for he had been given to understand that the Sheriff who hath command of a thousand of the trained bands would be assistant to him upon all occasions. The citizens running together without any arms to gaze, he besought them to arm themselves else they would be of no use to him; nevertheless in the City not so much as one man of the meanest quality would take arms for him. Having passed well nigh the whole length of the City he came to the Sheriff's house, much perplexed in mind and in such a sweat that he was fain to shift his shirt; but Master Sheriff straightway withdrew himself by a back door to the Lord Mayor.

In the meantime the Lord Thomas Burleigh with Mr. Dethick, Garter King at Arms, entered the City and proclaimed the Earl of Essex and his complices to be traitors, though some opposed them, offering violence. And in like manner the Earl of Cumberland and Sir Thomas Gerrard, the Knight Marshal, in other parts of the City. Which, as soon as the Earl of Essex understood, he hasted out of the Sheriff's house with a melancholic and downcast countenance crying that England is appointed to be assigned over to the Infanta of Spain and calling upon the citizens to arm; but all in vain. When he saw that not a man took arms and that his own company slunk away from him privately by degrees, and heard withal that the Lord Admiral was coming with a strong party of men, he began now to cast away all hope. He purposed therefore in his mind to return home in hopes to obtain favour with the Queen by means of the Lord Keeper and the rest of the Council that were shut up in his house. Sir Ferdinando Gorges therefore persuaded the Earl that he should be sent to release the Councillors and to go with them to the Queen to intercede for a pardon, for as yet no blood was spilt and the citizens' minds still uncertain. The Earl consented that the Lord Chief Justice Popham should be released, but none else.

And now the Earl thinking to return home found a chain drawn across the street near the west gate of Paul's; and both pikes and musketeers placed against him by the care of the Bishop of London, under the command of Sir John Leveson. Hereupon the Earl drew his sword and commanded Sir Christopher Blount to set upon them, which he resolutely performed, falling fiercely upon one Waite whom he slew, but being himself sore wounded and taken prisoner. Here is also slain by the shot young Mr. Henry Tracy and one or two citizens. Being thus repulsed, his hat shot through, and many more slipping away from him, the Earl turned aside with some few which would not leave him to Queenhithe, and there getting boats returned home to his own house.

On his return, he found that all the Councillors had been released. He therefore broke open a casket that was in the house and burnt divers papers and a book, observing that they should tell no tales to hurt his friends, and likewise a black bag that he wore about his neck.

The Earl now prepared himself for defence, and being reduced to his last hope of expecting aid from the Londoners he fortified his house on all sides. The Lord Admiral straightway besieged the house to landwards; he assigned the Earls of Cumberland and Lincoln, the Lord Thomas Howard, the Lord Grey, the Lord Burleigh, the Lord Compton, and others with forces of horse and foot, to every man his post. Then he himself with the Lord Effingham and the Lord Cobham, Sir John Stanhope, Sir Robert Sidney, and Sir Fulke Greville seized upon the garden by the Thames' side.

Being now ready to assault the house, Sir Robert Sidney was sent to summon them to yield. The Earl of Southampton asked to whom they should yield; to their adversaries? that were to run themselves headlong to ruin; or to the Queen? that were to confess themselves guilty. 'But yet,' said he, 'if the Lord Admiral will give us hostages for our security, we will appear before the Queen ; if not we are everyone of us fully resolved to lose our lives fighting.'

The Lord Admiral returned word that neither were conditions to be propounded by rebels nor hostages to be delivered to them, yet he signified to the Earl of Essex that for sparing the weaker sex, he would permit the Countess his wife and the Lady Rich and their waiting gentlewomen, who filled all places with their shrieks and womanish cries, to come forth. Which the Earl took as a favour, only he desired that an hour or two's time might be granted him to fortify the place by which they should go forth ; which also was granted.

Before the hour was expired, the Earl, holding all things now for desperate and lost, resolved to force his way out ; and the Lord Sandys, being more aged than the rest, earnestly urged him to it, saying that the resolutest counsels are the safest ; that it is more honourable to die fighting than by the hand of the executioner. But the Earl again wavering in his resolution began to think of yielding, and gave notice that upon certain conditions he would yield. The Lord Admiral would admit of no conditions ; so the Earl requested three things. First, that they might be civilly dealt withal ; which was promised. Secondly, that their cause might be justly and fully heard ; to which the Admiral answered that there was no reason to doubt thereof. And lastly, that Mr. Ashton, a minister of God's word, might be with him in prison for his soul's comfort. The Lord Admiral answered that for these things he would make intercession to the Queen. So at 10 of the clock at night, all the noblemen came forth, and falling upon their knees, delivered their swords up to the Lord Admiral.

The Earls of Essex and Southampton were conducted by the Lord Admiral to the Archbishop's house at Lambeth and not to the Tower, because the night was dark and the river not passable under the Bridge.

At Court the constancy of the Queen was much noted. Even when a false alarm was brought that the City had revolted with him, she never was more amazed than she would have been to hear of a fray in Fleet Street. The report of the tumult was brought to her when at dinner, and she seemed nothing moved therewith, but only said that He that had placed her in that seat would preserve her in it; and so she continued at her dinner, not showing any sign of fear or distraction of mind, nor omitting anything this day that she hath been accustomed to do at other times.

9th February. A PROCLAMATION CONCERNING THE EARL OF ESSEX.

To-day there was made proclamation concerning yesterday's tumults, declaring that the Earl of Essex, accompanied with the Earls of Rutland and Southampton and divers others their complices, gentlemen of birth and quality, knowing themselves to be discovered in divers treasonable actions, did not only imprison the Keeper of the Great Seal of England, the Chief Justice of England, and others both of the Nobility and Council that were sent in the Queen's name to persuade the Earl to lay open his petitions and complaints, but also (after strait order given by him to murder the Councillors and others whensoever they should offer to stir out of that place) did traitorously issue into the City of London with arms, with great numbers; and there breaking into open act of rebellion, devised and divulged base and foolish lies, that their lives were sought, spreading out strange seditious inventions to have drawn the people to their party, with purpose to attempt traitorous actions both against her Majesty's person and the State, and to expose (as it now appeareth) the City and people with their goods to the spoil of a number of greedy and desperate persons their adherents; continuing still in arms, and killing divers of our subjects, after many proclamations of rebellion made by the King of Heralds.

Wherefore, seeing how they have found themselves disappointed of their expectation through the constancy and loyalty of her subjects, the Queen declareth not only in how thankful part she doth accept the loyal persisting of her subjects in their duty, and doth promise on her part that whensoever she shall have cause to show it, they shall find her more careful over them than for herself. Hereby also the people are admonished that seeing this open act was so sudden, that it cannot yet be thoroughly looked into, but it is to be presumed by the common example of all rebels in their actions that it was not without ministers dispersed in divers places to provoke the minds of the people to like of their attempts with calumniating her government and principal ministers. Wherefore they should give diligent heed in all places to the conversation of persons not well known for their good behaviour, and to the speeches of any that shall give out slanderous and undutiful words or rumours against her Majesty and her government; and those that be in authority to lay hold on such spreaders of rumours, and such as be not in authority to give advertisement that by the apprehension of such dangerous instruments, both the drift and purpose of evil minded persons may be discovered, their designs prevented, and our people conserved in such peace and tranquillity as heretofore, by God's favour, her Majesty hath maintained and doth hope still to continue amongst us.

10th February. SIR THOMAS HOBY.

Sir Thomas Hoby, who now reneweth his complaints of Mr. William Eure before the Star Chamber, hearing that Mr. Richard Cholmley (one of the defendants in his suit) is apprehended as being in the Earl of Essex's company, hath written to Sir Robert Cecil. He declareth that, whereas Mr. Cholmley's friends would have it thought he is a man of no power, he is on the contrary able to raise 500 men, hath his estates in the most dangerous parts of Yorkshire for popery and the most part along the sea coast, very apt to entertain bad intelligenced strangers.

NEWS FROM IRELAND: THE PRAISE OF THE LORD DEPUTY.

The Lord Deputy hath again checked the rebels in Leinster, taking great prey and spoiling all the rebels' county; and in one place called Monasterevan when the rebels would resist them 60 odd were slain upon the ground, whilst the harm our men had was but 20 of ours hurt and slain.

It is much noted by those of great experience in the Irish wars that never any Lord Deputy took the like pains, for he gives his body no rest: and although he were a very sickly gentleman in England, yet he keepeth health there the best of any. Besides he is endued with notable virtues befitting a general in such a country, for he hath excellent temperance in all things to discern between man and man. He hath secrecy in so excellent a measure that his intent cannot be discovered before it be done. Also he hath affability to please all men of service, and severity to make the wicked live in fear of him. All things that he himself or any man by his direction taketh in hand prosper or go forward, insomuch that he hath cast the coward out of his army that sometime troubled it very much, and driven him among the rebels.

12th February. A TREASONABLE PRACTISE IN THE COURT.

Captain Thomas Lee, one of the Earl of Essex's Irish Captains, has been seized in the palace, and being examined confesseth that he had an intention to have taken the Queen at supper time when she was at supper, and there to have locked the doors, pinning her up till he had forced her to sign a warrant for the Earl's delivery out of the Tower. This vile purpose he had already broken to Sir Henry Neville and Sir Robert Cross who discovered it. Lee was taken this same night watching at the privy chamber door to discover how he might the next day have access.

13th February. PROCEEDINGS IN THE STAR CHAMBER.

To-day (being the last Star Chamber day of the term), the Lord Keeper spake of the strangeness of this late action of the Earl of Essex, and of Captain Lee's attempt last night. It was noted that though my Lord is usually ready of speech he was in great perturbation and obliged to break off, drowned in tears. The Lord Admiral followed, representing the Queen's magnanimity in this great danger, so that she could hardly be prevented going out against them, to see if ever a rebel of them all durst show their faces against her. Sir William Knollys also spoke, and Sir Robert Cecil, who declared that for six years the Earl hath designed to become King of England; he hath practised upon people of all sorts, with the common people and soldiers, pretending that none care for them but himself.

THE EAST INDIA VOYAGE.

The ships set forth by the merchants of London at a cost of £72,000 for the East Indies this day departed from Woolwich. Master James Lancaster is appointed General, bearing her Majesty's commission of martial law. The ships are the

Dragon (that was formerly the *Malice Scourge* of my Lord of Cumberland), which is admiral, of 600 tons with 202 men, the *Hector*, 300 tons with 108, the *Ascension*, 260 tons with 82 men, the *Susan* with 88 ; and besides the *Guest* as victualler.

15*th February*. A PROCLAMATION.

By reason of these troubles there is at this time dispersed within the City and suburbs and continually increaseth a great multitude of base and loose people, that lie privily in corners and bad houses, listening after news and stirs and spreading rumours and tales, being of likelihood ready to lay hold of any occasion to enter into tumult and disorder. Wherefore by the Queen's proclamation, all persons that have no certain abode within the City, nor sufficient cause of stay or lawful business, shall straightway avoid and get them down into the country upon pain of death by martial law.

DIRECTIONS FOR PREACHERS.

The preachers in the City to-day were instructed to preach of the conspiracy, showing forth all the treasons of the Earl of Essex, how that he would have taken into his own power both the Queen and Council ; whereby the government must have been in his hands until her Highness either must have been sick, or dealt with as some King of this land was used, that he might reign himself ; and how he hath carried himself after a very insolent and ambitious sort, especially for six or seven years past, seeking by popular conversation to allure the hearts of the simple. In matters of religion his dissimulation and hypocrisy are now disclosed ; for he behaved himself to be accounted the only nobleman that cared for religion ; how his manner was to censure all men, saying that some were cold professors, others neuters or atheists, and lately when he has been busy plotting his treasons, two sermons in a day could scarce content him, such was his burning zeal to the Gospel. Moreover he so carried himself to the papists that all of them were persuaded they had possession of him. If he had not been prevented there had never been a rebellion in England since Richard the Second more desperate or dangerous.

Such were the instructions of the preachers, but as is usual in such cases, from malice or desire to please they amplified it beyond all probability; on the one side they cried 'crucify,' and on the other it is rumoured that the preachers of London will rise and deliver him out of the Tower.

The preacher at Paul's Cross was Mr. Hayward who preached on II Samuel, xxi. 17: 'Then David's men swore unto him, saying, Thou shalt go no more out with us to battle, lest thou quench the light of Israel'; wherein he delivered the whole matter of the Earl of Essex, according to his instructions. The auditory was great (though the Lord Mayor and his brethren were absent), and the applause for her Majesty's deliverance from the mischiefs intended exceeding great, loud and joyous.

Certain Prayers set forth for This Time.

Certain prayers fit the time are now set forth by authority, whereof the second is this:

'O Eternal and Gracious God, Father of Peace and Protector of Government, who with a special eye of providence watchest over the heads of Princes, upon whose safety the lives of many thousands do depend; we Thy humble Servants do bow down the knees of our hearts, and pour forth our souls in thankfulness before Thee, for Thy so gracious and merciful deliverance of our dread Sovereign, Thy Handmaid, from the traitorous intents and desperate conspiracies of disloyal subjects, who have risen up against Thine Anointed, and like unnatural children have rebelled against the Mother of their own times, that took them up from their cradles, and cherished them in her own bosom, and loaded them with honours and preferments, to the great dishonour of Thy Name, to the slander of Thy Gospel, to the danger of confusion to their native country. But Thou, O Lord of Hosts our deliverer, diddest overthrow them in their own imaginations, and by Thy judgments hast declared them enemies to Thine own Majesty: Thou diddest put Thy obedience into the hearts of Thy faithful people, and without shedding of their innocent blood diddest miraculously beat down the Swords of all that rose up against Thine ordinance; for which Thy unspeakable goodness towards us, vouchsafe, we beseech Thee, to receive the freewill offerings of our hearts, and calves of our lips in praises to Thy glorious name; who notwithstanding our manifold sins and transgressions hast not yet forgotten to be Gracious, heapest mercy upon mercy, and causest blessing to follow and overtake blessing, as the waves of the sea. To Thee therefore our Saviour and Defender, our Watch-Tower and our Rock, we will sing the songs of thankfulness, and call upon Thy blessed Name for evermore ; beseeching Thee so to continue the favour of Thy countenance towards Thine own Anointed Magistrate, and us her faithful people ; that our Light may never go out, and our Song never cease in this land ; but that Thy glorious acts may sound in every congregation, ever praise and honour and glory to Thee, that sittest upon the Throne for ever and ever. Amen.'

Captain Lee Condemned.

This day Captain Thomas Lee was put on his trial at the Sessions house near Newgate, before the Lord Chief Justice. He was conveyed to Newgate by 7 in the morning in a close coach, with both his hands manacled, and discreetly attended, but without any show of halberts that might draw concourse of the people. The Attorney-General declared that this Lee in the late rebellion had offered his service to the Lord Admiral and Mr. Secretary, as he pretended, to kill the Earl of Essex ; but afterwards when this was refused he came to Sir Henry Neville, and then to Sir Robert Cross. Sir Robert swore that upon Thursday about 5 at night Captain Lee came to his lodging, and taking him aside began to speak of these matters of treason, and said that if half a dozen resolute men, such as might have access to the Presence, would step into the Queen and kneel before her, and never rise till she had signed a warrant, and then send it by the Lord Admiral and never stir till the Earls of Essex and Southampton were brought to the Queen's presence, they might do it. To which Captain Lee replied that he never meant to be an actor himself, and moreover spake these words with an '*if*' ; 'if' such a thing could be done.

Then were read the depositions of one William Paris that said Lee pressed towards the Presence door, and mistrusting the worst drew after him and had some talk with him.

Next Mr. Attorney showed that there was love between him and the Earl of Essex, and spoke also of Lee's familiarity with Tyrone.

Later Mr. Attorney bade them mark his word 'force' her Majesty. To the which Lee answered, 'Why I did say it with an "If"; and then I am not a fool, but I know they must have been of a resolution that should have undertaken such a thing, and such as would not fear to displease her Majesty for half an hour to please her all her life after; but I never meant to have been an actor myself.'

The jury found him guilty, and Mr. Recorder with a very grave admonition to him to make him see his fault and fly to God's mercy for pardon, pronounced judgment which he took patiently.

16th February. Egyptians Sentenced.

At the Sessions two women, by name Joan Morgan and Anne Simpson, were found guilty of being seen and found in the society of vagabonds commonly called Egyptians, and call themselves Egyptians. The former put herself guilty and pleaded her pregnancy, but being found not pregnant by a jury of matrons, she is condemned to be hung; the latter likewise pleading pregnancy was reprieved, it being found by the jury of matrons that she is pregnant.

18th February. A Prognostication Suppressed.

A foolish prognostication of one Woodhouse considers this tumult the result of an eclipse last year. He set down that its influence would begin on the 20th of January and continue slight till the 18th of November, when it would be most felt, and last till the 14th of September, 1602, and then gradually decrease till the 12th of July, 1603. This eclipse, saith he, shows the unfortunate estate of sundry great ones, great destruction of many mean ones, and threatens death to ecclesiastical persons, lawyers and rulers; the middle-aged and lusty being especially threatened. This book is called in, though it be but a toy.

19th February. The Trial of the Two Earls.

This day were the Earls of Essex and Southampton arraigned in Westminster Hall, where a spacious court was made in the form of a square. Upon the sides of the square were made seats for the Peers, on the lower end a seat for the Judges, and at the upper end of the square a chair and a footstool under a canopy of state where the Lord Treasurer Buckhurst sat as Lord High Steward, who came into the Hall with seven sergeants-at-arms bearing maces before.

Then the Lord Thomas Howard, Constable of the Tower, Sir John Peyton, the Lieutenant, and the Gentleman Porter carrying the axe entered, the prisoners following them and came to the bar; and being within the two Earls kissed hands and embraced each other. So proclamation was made that the Peers summoned to the trial should answer their names, being six and twenty in number; and when the Lord Grey was called the Earl of Essex laughed upon the Earl of Southampton and jogged him by the sleeve. The Earl of Essex now desired to know whether the privilege permitted to every private person upon his trial might be granted to them, *viz.*, to make challenge of any of the Peers against whom they might have just cause of exception. To which the Lord Chief Justice Popham answered that verily the law did allow no challenge of any of the Peers, for such was the credit and estimation of the Peers of England that they are neither compelled to an oath on arraignment nor are subject to any exception. So the prisoners were called to hold up their right hands; which they did, the Earl of Essex saying that he had, before that time, done it often at her Majesty's command for a better purpose.

The case against them was opened first by Sergeant Yelverton. Next the Attorney spake of the laws concerning treason, and how the offence of the Earls was high treason, and how that they had consulted with their friends, conferring whether it were more advisable to take the Tower or to surprise the Court, or to try their friends in London. Then was read the deposition of Mr. Henry Widdrington that was present when the Councillors were shut up in Essex House. And then the Lord Chief Justice was sworn, and gave his evidence *viva voce* of that which had passed, and after him my Lord of Worcester; whereupon followed some disputing between Master Attorney and the Earl of Essex.

Sir Walter Ralegh was then called and his oath given him, at which the Earl of Essex said, 'What booteth it to swear the fox?' Sir Walter spake of his words with Sir Ferdinando Gorges on the Thames, upon the Sunday morning of the rising. Next were read the confessions of Sir Ferdinando, declaring that he was a great dissuader of the Earl from his attempts, and of his consultations with the two Earls. So the Earl of Essex desired to have Sir Ferdinando face to face and endeavoured to invalidate the credit of his evidence by the paleness and discomposure of his looks.

Divers other examinations also were read, as of Sir Charles Danvers, Sir John Davies, Sir Christopher Blount, the Earl of Rutland, the Lord Cromwell, the Lord Sandys, the Lord Mounteagle. When all had been read Mr. Attorney declared how all these depositions agreed and jumped together in each particular point, notwithstanding they were all severally examined, and without rack or torture. To which the Earl of Essex answered that all were moved by the self same fear and the self same examiner ; adding thereto that his intention was to have come with eight or nine honourable persons who had cause of discontentment unto her Majesty, and prostrating themselves at her feet to have put themselves at her mercy, desiring her to sever from her Majesty some that abused her ears with false informations, namely my Lord Cobham and Sir Walter Ralegh.

When some further wrangling words had passed, Mr. Francis Bacon arose and spake, saying that my Lord of Essex was like Pisistratus, that had a purpose to procure the subversion of a kingdom, and wanting aid for the accomplishing of his humour entered the city, and cut his body overthwart to the end they might conjecture he had been in danger. Further, said he, all that my Lord could answer to the charges were but shadows, and therefore it were best to confess and not to justify. Whilst Mr. Bacon was speaking my Lord interrupted him, saying that Mr. Bacon had written a letter on his behalf to the Queen ; which Mr. Bacon justified saying, 'I loved my Lord as long as he continued a dutiful subject, and spent more hours in making him a good servant than ever I did about my own business.'

'I acknowledge all your gifts,' replied the Earl. Then went he on to charge Sir Robert Cecil that he had declared to some of his fellow Councillors that the Infanta of Spain had better title to the Crown than some others of their competitors, and more to the like effect.

Scarce had he spoken these words when Sir Robert, who stood and heard all being hidden in a close room, came forth into the Court, and falling down on his knee besought the Lord Steward that he might answer so false and foul a report. Which being granted, he very vehemently challenged my Lord to name openly the Councillor to whom he spake these words. The Earl refused. Sir Robert therefore replied that it was to be held for an invented fiction; which the Earl denied, saying that my Lord of Southampton was present when it was told him. Then Sir Robert turned to the Earl of Southampton and adjured him to name the man. My Lord of Southampton therefore referred it to the bench, and to Mr. Secretary himself, whether in honour and reason he should name him. And when they all thought it reasonable, he declared that it was Sir William Knollys.

Then Sir Robert kneeling down again besought that Sir William Knollys might be sent for that he might have either a purgation or a condemnation. So Mr. Neville, one of the Privy Chamber, was sent, to whom Mr. Secretary said, 'I charge you, as you shall answer it at the dreadful Day of Judgment, that you tell her Majesty from me, that if any care of me or love to Sir William Knollys or any other respect shall move her to keep him back, and that he be not sent hither to satisfy the Court, I will live her Majesty's vassal and subject, but I will never serve her again as a Councillor.'

Further words passed between Mr. Secretary and the Earl; but by this time Sir William was come, of whom Sir Robert demanded if ever he heard him say that the Infanta of Spain had a better title than some other. Whereunto Sir William answered that he remembered Mr. Secretary talking of a book wherein the titles to the throne were set down he might perhaps say that the Infanta of Spain had a better title than some of them. To which my Lord of Essex said, 'But these words were reported to me in another sense.' Then said Sir Robert, 'Your malice whereby you seek to work me into hatred amongst all men hath flowed from no other cause than from my affection to peace for the good of my country and your own inflamed heart for war, for the benefit of military men which may be at your beck. Hence was set forth your Apology against the peace, hence was conceived a general hatred against those which were affected to the peace. For my part I am so far from inclining to the Infanta of Spain that even my mind is astonied to think thereof.'

Then Mr. Bacon spake again declaring that he had never seen such favour, so many digressions, such delivering of evidence by fractions, and so silly a defence of such great and notorious treasons. Further, to prepare matter and give fire at once was one of Machiavel's precepts; to remove a Councillor by force was rebellion. Hereupon the Judges were required to deliver their opinions, and all agreed that if subject do seek to serve himself by force, or to have access to the Prince against her will, it is treason.

Then were further depositions read and both Earls again spake in their own defence, though Mr. Attorney oftentimes interrupted them. At length the Lord High Steward directed the Peers to go together and ordered the Lieutenant of the Tower to withdraw his prisoners from the bar. So the Lords, who during this time had been refreshing themselves with beer and confections and taking their tobacco, went together into a private place provided for them, fairly hung with tapestry, behind the chair of Estate. After half an hour the Peers all came out again, and each man took his place. Then the Sergeant-at-arms began to call them by name, beginning at the junior Lord, who was Lord Thomas Howard, who stood up bareheaded.

Then said the Lord High Steward, 'My Lord Thomas Howard, whether is Robert Earl of Essex guilty of this treason whereupon he hath been indicted, as you take it upon your honour, or no?' To which the Lord Thomas Howard made answer, bending his body and laying his left hand upon his right side, saying, 'Guilty, my Lord, of high treason upon my honour.' And after the same manner said all the Peers in turn. Being called over anew, they found Henry Earl of Southampton guilty also of high treason.

So the prisoners were brought back to the bar and demanded what they could say, why they should not have judgment of death. To which the Earl of Essex answered that he was willing to die, but entreated their Lordships to interpose for her Majesty's pardon for the Earl of Southampton. He said, moreover, that he was not one who despised clemency, but he would not be found to make any cringing submission.

The Earl of Southampton spake somewhat more earnestly for pardon, and with such sweet favour and winning expressions, and such ingenuous modesty that he moved the hearts of all the standers-by to pity. So the Lord High Steward spake again to them and pronounced sentence of death upon them, that they should be hanged, bowelled and quartered. Then the Earl of Essex made certain requests, that he might have the same preacher to comfort him that had been with him since his troubles began and that the Lord Thomas Howard and the Lieutenant of the Tower might be partakers with him in receiving the Sacrament. He desired also pardon of the Lords Delaware and Morley for leading their sons into trouble, and of the Earl of Worcester and the Chief Justice for keeping them prisoners. So the Lord High Steward's staff being broken the Court dissolved, having sat from 9 in the morning until 6.

The news of this day's business was suddenly divulged throughout London, whereupon many forsook their suppers and ran hastily into the streets to see the Earl of Essex as he was led back to the Tower. He passed with a swift pace, bending his face towards the earth, and would not look upon any of them, though some spake directly to him.

20th February. THE EARL OF ESSEX.

This morning the Earl of Essex was visited by Dr. Dove, the Dean of Norwich, sent by the Lords of the Council to press him to acknowledge his offences. But to Dr. Dove's persuasions he answered in a passion, 'If you knew how many motions have been made to me to do my best to remove such evils as the commonwealth is burdened with, you would greatly wonder.' A while after there came to my Lord his chaplain, Master Abdy Ashton, who found him cheerful and prepared with great content for his end. But the Earl found no comforter in Mr. Ashton, who bitterly upbraided his Lord, saying that the Earl had manifested to all the world that his show of religion was mere hypocrisy, and his followers men of no means, but either base persons that he had raised or such as had lewdly consumed their own patrimony. 'Besides,' quoth he, 'howsoever you would colour it with other pretences, your end was an ambitious seeking of the crown, the hope whereof for your own raising made these men to follow, animate and applaud you; so that if by a true confession and unfeigned repentance you do not unburthen yourself of these sins, you shall carry out of the world a guilty soul before God, and leave upon your memorial an infamous name to posterity.'

These speeches of his chaplain, and many more besides, have so wrought upon the Earl that he hath sent to Lord Thomas Howard, Constable of the Tower, to move her Majesty to send to him the Lord Keeper, the Lord Treasurer, the Lord Admiral and Secretary Cecil, that he may now discharge his conscience.

21st February. ESSEX'S CONFESSIONS.

To-day the Queen acceded to the Earl of Essex's request that the four Lords of the Council should go to him, and before them he declared that Mr. Ashton had ploughed up his heart, and brought him down, and humbled him. Hereupon with great penitency he confessed his sorrow for his obstinate denials at the bar, desiring he might have liberty to set down in writing his whole project of coming to the Court. He confesseth how to divers of his followers directions were given to seize the Court; which being accomplished, he with the Earls of Southampton and Rutland and other noblemen should have gone into the Queen; and then having her in their possession, to have used the shadow of her authority for the changing of the Government, and called a parliament, and condemned all those whom they charged to have misgoverned the State.

He also earnestly desired that he might speak with Cuffe, his secretary, against whom he complained as having been a principal instigator to the violent courses which he had undertaken. He protested that he chiefly desired to show that he was not the only persuader of the great offences which they had committed but that Blount, Cuffe, Temple and those others who were at the private conspiracy at Drury House, had more dangerous and malicious ends for the disturbance of the State than could have been prevented if his project had gone forward, as appears by the confusion they drew him to, even in his own house, the morning that he went into the City.

This request being granted, and Cuffe brought, he vehemently charged him and said, 'Henry Cuffe, call to God for mercy and to the Queen, and deserve it by declaring truth, for I that must now prepare for another world, have resolved to deal clearly with God and the world and must needs say this to you, that none hath been a greater instigator of me than yourself to all these my disloyal courses into which I have fallen.'

23rd February. THE EARL OF ESSEX AND THE GARTER.

Mr. Richard Conningsby, Usher of the Black Rod for the Order of the Garter, is instructed according to his office to proceed to the Tower and there to disgrace and deprise the Earl of Essex of that honourable Order in pulling off of the George and the Garter.

24th February. AN AMBASSADOR FROM SCOTLAND.

The Earl of Mar is on his way to London in embassage from the Scottish King, and hath sent before him a gentleman to request that some spacious house may be taken for the convenient lodging of himself and his train.

THE PLAYERS AT COURT.

Last Sunday (22nd) the Children of the Chapel played at Court and to-night the Lord Chamberlain's players.

25th February, Ash Wednesday. THE EXECUTION OF THE EARL OF ESSEX.

Very late last night the Earl of Essex, being informed by the Lieutenant of the Tower that he was to die in the morning, opened his window and said to the guard, 'My good friends, pray for me, and to-morrow you shall see in me a strong God in a weak man; I have nothing to give you, for I have nothing left, but that which I must pay to the Queen to-morrow in the morning.'

This morning, between 7 and 8 of the clock, he was brought by the Lieutenant from his lodging, attended on by three divines: and all the way from his chamber to the scaffold, he called to God to give him strength and patience to the end, and he often intreated those that went with him to pray for him. He was apparelled in a gown of wrought velvet, a satin suit and felt hat, all black.

Those present to see him die were the Earls of Cumberland and Hertford; the Lords Bindon, Darcy, Compton; Lord Thomas Howard, Constable of the Tower; Sir John Peyton, the Lieutenant, with 15 or 16 partizans of the Guard; the three divines, Doctor Mountford, Barlow and Ashton; together with about a hundred others, knights, gentlemen and aldermen. Sir Walter Ralegh also was present, as he said to make answer if anything should be objected against him by the Earl; but others, believing that he came to feed his eyes with a sight of the Earl's blood, admonished him not to press upon the Earl at his death. He therefore withdrew himself, and looked on from out the Armoury.

Being come to the scaffold, which was three yards square and railed round in the high court above Caesar's Tower, he first turned himself to the divines and said, 'O God be merciful unto me the most wretched creature on the earth.' Then turning himself towards the noblemen that sat on a form placed before the scaffold, he vailed his hat and, making reverence to the Lords, laid it aside. Then he said:

'My Lords, and you my Christian brethren, who are to be witnesses of this my just punishment, I confess to the glory of God that I am a most wretched sinner, and that my sins are more in number than the hairs of my head; that I have bestowed my youth in pride, lust, uncleanness, vain glory, and divers other sins according to the fashion of this world, wherein I have offended most grievously my God; and notwithstanding divers good motions inspired unto me from the Spirit of God, the good which I would I have not done, and the evil which I would not I have done; for all which I humbly beseech our Saviour Christ to be the Mediator unto the Eternal Majesty for my pardon; especially for this my last sin, this great, this bloody, this crying, and this infectious sin, whereby so many for love of me have ventured their lives and souls, and have been drawn to offend God, to offend their sovereign, and to offend the world, which is so great a grief unto me as may be.'

He went on to pray for forgiveness, and for God's blessing upon the Queen, and the nobles and ministers of the Church and State, beseeching them and the world to have a charitable opinion of him for his intention towards her Majesty, whose death, he protested upon his salvation, he never meant, nor violence to her person: yet he confessed that he had received an honourable trial and was justly condemned. For his religion, he declared that he was never atheist nor papist, but hoped, as a true Christian, for his salvation from God only, by the mercy and merits of our Saviour Jesus Christ, crucified for our sins.

Then he put off his gown and ruff, and went up before the block. He called for the executioner, who on his knees asked him pardon, to whom he said, 'Thou art welcome to me; I forgive thee; thou art the minister of justice.' Then he kneeled down on the straw, and, with his eyes fixed to heaven and with long and passionate pauses in his speeches, he prayed unpremeditatedly, craving strength to rely to his last gasp on the promises of Christ and to have no worldly thought but only God before him. He then repeated the Lord's prayer, in which all present joined with floods of tears and lamentation. One of the divines put him in mind to say over his Belief, which he did, the doctor saying it softly before him. He was likewise remembered to forgive and pray for his enemies. Whereupon he beseeched God to forgive them as freely as he did, 'because,' said he, 'they bear the image of God as well as myself.'

Then his doublet being taken off, he stood up in a scarlet waistcoat, and bowing himself before the block, he said, 'O God give me true humility and patience to endure to the end, and I pray you all to pray with me and for me, and when you shall see me stretch out my arms and my neck on the block, and the stroke ready to be given, it would please the Everlasting God to send down His angels to carry my soul before His Mercy Seat.' Lying flat along one of the boards, his hands stretched out, he said, 'Lord have mercy upon me, Thy prostrate servant'; and therewithal fitting his head to the block he was willed by one of the doctors to say the beginning of the 51st Psalm, whereof when he had said two verses, the executioner being prepared, he uttered these words, 'Executioner, strike home. Come Lord Jesus, come Lord Jesus, and receive my soul: O Lord into thy hands I commend my spirit.' In the midst of which sentence the executioner struck. He had to strike three times, but neither arms, body nor head stirred ; then he lifted up the head saying, 'God save the Queen.'

The hangman as he returned from the Tower was beaten by the people, so that the sheriffs of London were called to assist and rescue him else he had been murdered.

THE CHARACTER OF THE LATE EARL OF ESSEX.

At the time of his death the Earl of Essex was in the 34th year of his age. In his young years he was brought up at Cambridge in studies of learning and true religion. He was recommended to the Queen by his step-father, the late Earl of Leicester, and at first had much ado to win her favour ; but when he had obtained it she chose him into the Order of St. George and made him of the Privy Council when he was scarce 23 years old, continually heaping honours and favours upon him. When he had now got not only an appearance but a real interest in the Queen's favour, he made it his business to go beyond both his equals and superiors ; to disparage all that were not at his devotion and frown upon those who had any grace with the Queen ; by his courteous behaviour and liberality to hunt after popular favour and applause, and reputation with the soldiery. He began also to use some contumacious carriage towards the Queen, especially after she had more than once restored him to her lost favour, whereby, together with an obstinate kind of extorting (as it were) favours from her, his proud neglect of dutifulness and respect towards her little by little changed and at length quite alienated the Queen's affection from him.

In these later days as he grew more attentive to business and matters, so he was less and less careful of his clothing ; for of a morning his chamber being commonly frequented with friends or suitors of one kind or another, when he was up, he gave his legs, arms and breast to his ordinary servants to button and dress him with little heed, his head and face to his barber, his eyes to his letters, and ears to petitioners, and many times all at once. Then a gentleman of his robes throwing a cloak over his shoulders, he would make a step into his closet, and after a short prayer he was gone.

And indeed he seemed not a man made for the Court, being

not easily induced to any unhandsome action; of an easy nature to take offence but harder to remit it; and one that could not conceal himself but carried his love and his hatred always in his brow and could not hide it. The main cause of his misfortune is threefold; affectation of popularity; desire of revenge; endeavouring to get more office of command into his private possession than the State could permit in any one subject. In a word, no man was more ambitious of glory, nor more careless of all things else.

27th February. CATHOLICS EXECUTED.

This day one Barkworth, a priest, was executed at Tyburn. Coming up into the cart in his black habit, his hood being taken off (his head being shaven but for a round circle on the nether part of his head), and his other garment taken off also, he stood in his shirt and a pair of hose. Here most joyfully and smilingly looking up into the heavens he blessed himself with the sign of the Cross, saying '*In nomine Patris, Filii et Spiritus Sancti, Amen.*' Then he turned himself towards the gallows tree, made the sign of the cross thereon and kissed it, and the rope also, which being put about his neck he turned himself and with a cheerful countenance and pleasant voice sang '*Haec est dies Domini; gaudeamus, gaudeamus, gaudeamus in ea.*' He confessed also that he was of the order of St. Benedict. The minister called on him to be penitent for his sins, and he said, 'Hold thy peace, thou art a simple fellow.' Then the minister wished him to remember that Christ died for him; and he elevating his eyes to heaven and holding the rope in his hands, answered 'And so do I for Him, and I would I had a thousand thousand lives to bestow upon him in this cause, *et maiorem charitatem nemo habet.*' He prayed also for the Queen and the Recorder. When the cart was drawn away he was immediately cut down and he stood upon his feet, and struggled with the executioners so that he was holden down by force upon the hurdle for the dismembering.

There was also one Arthur or Naylor executed, a Jesuit. Also a certain Mistress Line condemned for the escape of a supposed priest. Her weakness was such that she was carried to the Sessions where she was condemned betwixt two in a chair. At her execution, being urged amongst other things to confess that she had been a common receiver of many priests, she answered, 'Where I have received one I would to God I had been able to receive a thousand.' She behaved herself most meekly. She kissed the gallows and when the cart was drawn away she made the sign of the cross upon her and after that never moved.

1st March. THE SERMON AT PAUL'S CROSS.

This Sunday was the sermon at Paul's Cross preached by Dr. Barlow out of Matthew xxi. 22, 'Give unto Caesar the things of Caesar,' wherein he spoke of the confessions of my Lord of Essex made to him, and his words concerning the people of London; and concluding that had he been remitted and lived, there could have been neither safety to the Queen's person, nor peace to the land, nor hope of the Gospel's continuance.

A COMPLAINT AGAINST THE SHERIFF OF NORFOLK.

Complaint is made that the Sheriff of Norfolk, who was directed in the late action to seize upon the goods of Sir Christopher Heydon, not only set sixteen persons in the house but allowed his under officers to convey away a great part of the goods, notwithstanding that Sir Christopher's wife is with child. Moreover, there is a great library in one of his houses and from this many books are purloined.

3rd March. A TREATISE UPON TRADE.

Master Gerard de Malynes, merchant, hath written *A treatise of the Canker of England's Commonwealth*, in three parts; the first part whereof declareth the disease, which is an overbalancing of foreign commodities with home commodities; also our abuse in the course of exchange, so that of late years it has become a trade in rising and falling prices and not in commodities. The second part treateth of the cause of this disease of the body politic, which is that when more is given for our money in specie than by bills of exchange can be had, then our moneys are transported and a scarcity is made thereof at home, which abateth the price of our home commodities and advanceth the price of the foreign commodities beyond the seas. 'What shall we say,' quoth the author, 'to these bankers which commonly are in league with the financiers of the Low Countries and others, that are as it were belonging to their exchequers and mints, and have all the dealings for coins, with whose advice they can hoard up moneys when by public authority the coin are advanced by proclamation: and on the contrary to pay our moneys when money is proclaimed down: and then also the price of exchange is made accordingly, whereby the realm still loseth, and every man in particular, not knowing the weight and fineness of the money, but following the course of exchange as being carried away by the stream.' In the third part treateth of the remedy, which is that our merchants should have ability given them to import money: then would they bring the lesser quantity of foreign commodities, and the merchant stranger would bring more. And on the contrary the more ready money either *in specie* or by exchange that our merchants should make their return by, the more employment would they make upon our commodities, advancing the price thereof, which would augment the quantity by setting more people on work, and would also increase her Majesty's customs outward.

5th March. AN EMBASSY FROM SCOTLAND.

The Earl of Mar is newly come to London as ambassador from the King of Scotland. His errands as are generally supposed to be to congratulate the Queen of her safe delivery from the late conspiracy and to deal for Border causes.

THE CONSPIRATORS CONDEMNED.

To-day Sir Christopher Blount, Sir Charles Danvers, Sir John Davies, Sir Gelly Merrick and Henry Cuffe were arraigned at Westminster for high treason before the commissioners, being the Lord Admiral, the Lord Hunsdon, Mr. Secretary, Sir John Popham the Lord Chief Justice, Sir John Fortescue, Mr. Secretary Herbert and divers of the judges. They pleaded not guilty to the indictment as a whole, and a substantial jury was impanelled which consisted of aldermen of London and other gentlemen of good credit. They confessed indeed that it was their design to come to the Queen with so strong a force that they might not be resisted, and to require of her divers conditions and alterations of government; nevertheless they intended no personal harm to the Queen herself. To this the Lord Chief Justice answered that wherever the subject rebelleth or riseth in a forcible manner to overrule the royal will and power of the King, the laws make it a construction of his action that he intendeth to deprive the King both of crown and of life. The learned counsel further declared that this construction was no mystery or quiddity of the law, but an infallible conclusion warranted by reason and experience ; for the crown is not a garland or mere outward ornament but consists of pre-eminence and power ; and therefore when the subject will take upon him to give law to the King, he layeth hold of the crown and taketh the sword out of the King's hand. The crown is so fastened upon the King's head that it cannot be pulled off but head and life will follow, as all examples both at home and abroad do manifest. Then Mr. Attorney and other Queen's learned Counsel produced their evidence to the jury, which consisted principally of several confessions and the rest of the evidence used at the trial of the two Earls. Against Henry Cuffe was given in evidence Sir Charles Danvers' confession, who charged him that when there was a debating of the several enterprises which they should undertake, he did ever bind firmly and resolutely for attempting the Court. Against Sir Gelly Merrick the evidence was that he was commander over the house, which he fortified and barricaded against the Queen's forces brought against it by her Majesty's lieutenant.

Amongst other evidence was read the last confession of the Earl of Essex written in his own hand, wherein he had said that he thanked God that he was prevented, for otherwise he knew not what misery might have befallen this land, confessing that he intended to surprise the Court with a power of men ; and afterwards the Tower, to have countermined his actions and been a bridle to the City ; and then to have called a parliament. He had moreover called himself a burden unto the Commonwealth to be spewed out, and desiring his life to be shortened for that he knew the Queen could not be safe as long as he lived.

When all the evidence was done, the jury went out to agree upon their verdict, which after half an hour's time and more they brought in and found every man of the five prisoners severally guilty of high treason. Then the Queen's Sergeant prayed judgment and the Lord Chief Justice demanded of the prisoners what they could say for themselves why judgment should not be given against them. They all confessed their guilt, and the Lord Chief Justice, before passing judgment, used these words:

'I am sorry to see any so ill affected to this State as to become plotters and practisers against the State, and that so strongly as you and others in this action have done. And my grief is the more in this, men of worth, service and learning are the actors in this conspiracy! Shall it be said in the world abroad that we Englishmen, now after forty three years' peace under so gracious and renowned a Prince, are become weary of the government of such a Queen whom all the world else admires for her government? Consider it well, whosoever had best hopes in this attempt of change, what would have followed upon it. Let me tell you of the smallest hurt—the blood of children, families and friends; for none of yourselves can otherwise think but this action would have cost much blood. And I am sorry to think that Englishmen should seem to excuse themselves by ignorance of the law, which all subjects are bound to know and are born to have the benefit of. Some of you now at the Bar are Christians: where, I pray you, did you ever read or hear that it was lawful for the subject to command or constrain his sovereign? It is a thing against the law of God and all nations. God forbid that by actions men should be allowed to expound intents. Now your actions tending to a sovereignty cannot but by yourselves be expounded treason. But your intents, if they were otherwise, as you pretend, yet are they not to expound the law. For know this that the law which tends principally to the preserving of the Prince's person is more tender and precise than in any other point.' And so concluded, remembering them all to have a care of their souls.

11*th March*. Seditious Books.

It is reported that there are printed of late in Middleburgh, by means of some Englishmen of factious humour, a great number of books touching the succession to the Crown, under the name of Peter Wentworth (that died in the Tower in '97), which are matters not fit to be handled in that sort and published in her Majesty's time. These are intended to be sent over here and dispersed amongst such as are curious of novelties. Mr.

Gilpin, her Majesty's agent, dealeth with the States that the printer may be found out and the books seized upon.

THE EARL OF RUTLAND.

The Earl of Rutland was yesterday brought before the Lord Admiral and Mr. Secretary, who told him that the Queen meant to deal graciously and mercifully with him, and would spare his life's blood and dignity, and only punish him by a fine. Withal Mr. Secretary most kindly and like a father told him of the headiness and rashness of this his great fault.

Yesternight the great scaffold and clothes of estate were taken down and so are all the scaffolds about the King's Bench. Whereof it is now said that there shall be no more arraignments neither of Lord nor other, but all mercy coming.

PLAYS TO BE SUPPRESSED IN LENT.

The Lord Mayor is strictly charged to take order that all plays within the City and Liberties, especially at Paul's and in the Blackfriars, be suppressed during this time of Lent.

13th March. THE PRISONERS IN THE TOWER.

The Lady Cromwell having made humble suit to the Council on the behalf of her Lord that is a prisoner in the Tower, in regard that he is corpulent and sickly he may sometimes take the air upon the leads, it is now permitted that he, the Earl of Rutland, the Lord Sandys and Sir Henry Parker only for preservation of their health, may from time to time take the air, but only in the company of the Lieutenant and his deputy, and severally so that at no time they sight or conference with each other.

MERRICK AND CUFFE EXECUTED.

To-day Merrick and Cuffe were drawn to Tyburn and there executed. At the gallows Cuffe declared that he hoped for salvation in the atonement of his Saviour's blood. As for the rebellion, quoth he, 'I do here call God, his angels and my conscience to witness that I was not in the least concerned therein, but was shut up that whole day within the house, where I spent the time in very melancholy reflections.'

Here he was interrupted and advised not to disguise the truth by distinctions nor palliate his crime by specious pretences. He would again have spoken in excuse of certain of his speeches, but was again interrupted, and so began to apply himself to his devotions which he managed with a deal of fervour ; and then making a solemn profession of his creed, and asking pardon of God and the Queen, he was despatched by the executioner.

After him Sir Gilly Merrick suffered in the same way, and with a most undaunted resolution ; for, as if he were weary of living longer, he once or twice interrupted Cuffe and advised him to spare a discourse, which however rational was not very seasonable when he was taking leave of the world. He cleared the Lord Mountjoy from having any acquaintance with the design, and intreated those noblemen who stood by to intercede with the Queen that there might not be any further proceedings against such as had unwarily espoused this unhappy cause.

16th March. THE CITY WATCHES DISMISSED.

The Council have sent a letter of thanks to the Lord Mayor very graciously accepting of the great pains taken by the citizens in performing in these tumultuous times the extraordinary watches and wards that have been kept. The extraordinary watches at the gates are now dismissed.

MR. BACON TO WRITE AN ACCOUNT OF THE LATE TROUBLES.

Mr. Francis Bacon is instructed to draw up a particular account of the late troubles and to this end the Attorney hath sent him the confessions and examinations of the accused.

18th March. THE EXECUTION OF SIR CHARLES DANVERS AND SIR CHRISTOPHER BLOUNT.

Sir Charles Danvers being brought from the Tower unto the new built scaffold upon Tower hill, ascended the place wondrous cheerfully, saluting many of his friends. And learning that the Lord Grey was there on horseback near the scaffold he spake to him, saying that the enmity which he had borne him came not of any injury but by reason of his love for the Earl of Southampton, and now very heartily and humbly he besought the Lord Grey to forgive him. Then the Lord Grey said, 'I do forgive you with all my heart and intreat you that it may not trouble you at this time but to proceed in what else you have to say.' Then Sir Charles spoke of his condemnation, saying that he was clear of any intent of violence to be offered to her Majesty's person or his country, which he ever held most dear. Then he paused a while as not knowing what to say next, which he did divers times, and then began again to speak of his salvation in Jesus Christ. When he had so spoken for some time the Sheriff commanded him to be short, having used the like words divers times before, and the time was far spent. So he took leave of his friends, and having put off his gown and doublet in most cheerful manner, rather like a bridegroom than a prisoner appointed for death, prayed very devoutly kneeling before the block. His prayer ended, upon the sudden, as if he had flown, he threw his neck upon the block and, whilst he there held it, seemed to smile. His head was cut off with one stroke saving a little which an officer cut off with his knife.

His head and body being drawn aside and covered over with straw and all signs of any execution clean removed, Sir Christopher Blount ascended the scaffold, who above an hour past had been brought from the Gate house in Westminster and was privately kept in a house near the Tower hill until Sir Charles was executed; but he knew not so much. And understanding that Lord Grey and Sir Walter Ralegh were near, he made a speech unto them saying that when the Earl of Essex was in Ireland he had the consent of his friends to return to England with 3,000 of his best soldiers and chief leaders, and by them to have made his way to the Queen to have redressed all his wrongs. From which, said Sir Christopher, he only dissuaded him as a course too bloody and wished him to go peaceably and speedily only with two or three of his friends and kneel before the Queen. When he had asked forgiveness of God and the Queen, and of the Lord Grey and Sir Walter Ralegh, and of all others, he desired the world to witness he died a Catholic. Then he prayed kneeling; which done he fitted his neck to the block and received the stroke of death.

20th March. The Earl of Essex's Son.

The son of the late Earl of Essex that was by commandment committed to the charge of the Dean of Windsor is now again to be sent back to the College of Eton.

24th March. STRANGE RUMOURS.

Strange rumours are noised about of three rainbows seen in the Tower, and of a spectre appearing in the place where the Earl of Essex was beheaded. Others tell of a bloody block, seen by the guards, falling from heaven to earth upon that spot.

25th March. IRELAND.

The news from Ireland continueth good. Since his arrival in that country the Lord Deputy hath now made seven journeys against the rebels; and this summer coming he would go about to plant garrisons, confidently believing by the winter to end the war utterly.

27th March. A LEWD LIBEL.

There is a lewd libel abroad of the late troubles of such verses as these:

Chamberlain, Chamberlain,
He's of her Grace's kin;
Fool hath he ever been
With his Joan Silverpin.
She makes his cockscomb thin
And quake in every limb.
Quicksilver is in his head
But his wit's dull as lead;
Lord, for Thy pity.
Little Cecil trips up and down
He rules both Court and Crown,
With his brother Burleigh clown
In his great fox-furred gown.
With the long proclamation,
He swore he sav'd the town,
Is it not likely?

Ralegh doth time bestride;
He sits 'twixt wind and tide
Yet up hill he cannot ride,
For all his bloody pride.
He seeks taxes in the tin,
He polls the poor to the skin,
Yet he swears 'tis no sin.
Lord for Thy pity.

30th March. THE AMBASSADOR AND THE FRENCH KING.

Of late Mr. Winwood (that is now in the ambassador's room since Sir Henry Neville by his implication in the late rising is deprived of his employment) had audience with the French King and spoke of the confessions of the Earl of Essex, and how that he had petitioned that he might suffer privately from the view and presence of the world. Hereupon the King stayed him and said, 'Nay rather the clean contrary, for he desired nothing more than to die in public.' Thus far the ambassador had a pleasing audience, but when he spake of reimbursement for her Majesty's debt, to which the ambassador added the Queen's long forbearance, the necessity of her present affairs, the many promises made both by writing and by word of mouth, the King rose, saying that he would advise of it.

A BOOK OF DON SEBASTIAN.

There is a book called *The strangest adventure that ever happened, either in ages past or present*, being a discourse of Don Sebastian from the time of his voyage into Affric, when he was lost in the battle against the infidels in the year 1578 unto the 6th of January last past; a discourse full of divers curious histories, some ancient prophecies, and other matters to show that he whom the Signiory of Venice hath held as prisoner for more than two years is the true Don Sebastian.

5th April. A PROCLAMATION CONCERNING LIBELS.

It is proclaimed that whosoever shall in any sort either openly or secretly discover to any of the Lords of the Council or to the Lord Mayor the name of the authors, writers or dispersers of the traitorous and slanderous libels that are being spread abroad, whereby the offenders may be known and taken, shall have for his pains therein the sum of one hundred pounds of current money, paid and delivered unto him by the Lord Mayor.

9th April. LORD HENRY SEYMOUR'S COMPLAINT.

The Lord Henry Seymour is greatly annoyed in his dwelling house within the Blackfriars by reason that a common laystall or wharf for receipt of soil is erected within the liberties of Bridewell so near and directly under the windows of his principal lodgings, which besides the loathsome prospect thereof by reason of its very unwholesome savour is like to breed infection amongst his family and make his house altogether unfit to inhabit.

10th April. 'THE PLAIN MAN'S PATHWAY.'

Mr. Arthur Dent, preacher of South Shoebury in Essex, hath set forth a godly book called *The plain man's pathway to Heaven*, wherein every man may clearly see whether he shall be saved or damned, set forth dialogue wise, for the better understanding of the simple; which book, saith the author, 'meddleth not at all with any controversies in the Church, or anything in the State ecclesiastical, but only entereth into a controversy with Satan and Sin.'

12th April. A PETITION OF THE LORD MAYOR.

By reason of the many lewd rogues about the City that hope for spoil and in any sudden tumult would be ready to join themselves in any practise for the attaining their lewd desires, and more emboldened to commit disorder and to utter in word such seditious and lewd conceits they intend and conceive in heart, as by the example of them of late may appear, the Lord Mayor hath petitioned the Lords of the Council to authorize that some good and competent number of discreet persons, being freemen of the City, may be trained and instructed how to use themselves and their weapons in warlike manner that thereby they may be enabled and made apt for such service, and more able to lead the rest for the defence of her Majesty's person and of the City.

16th April. THE EARL OF NORTHUMBERLAND'S BROTHER RELEASED.

At the humble suit of the Earl of Northumberland his two brethren, Sir Charles Percy and Sir Jocelyn Percy, that are still in the Fleet prison for their part in the late rebellion, are to be committed to his Lordship's charge, he giving bonds for them of £500 in each.

17th April. THE COMPLAINT OF THE AMBASSADOR IN FRANCE.

Mr. Winwood complaineth that he is continually put off by the French who refuse to come to a resolution in the unpleasing matter which he negotiateth, for nothing sounds so ill in the ears of that Court as the repayment of their debts and the return of those good offices which they have received from their allies and neighbour Princes.

21st April. A DECLARATION OF THE TREASONS OF THE LATE EARL OF ESSEX.

There is set forth *A declaration of the practices and treasons attempted and committed by Robert, late Earl of Essex, and his complices*, containing the proceedings at the arraignments and the very confessions and other parts of the evidences, word for word taken out of the originals. Herein is shown first the ambitious nature of the late Earl to make himself the first person in the Kingdom, his conversing with the rebel Tyrone, his plotting since his disobedient return to England, his gathering of a faction, his plan for surprising the Court and obtaining possession of the Queen and the State and for possessing the City; his attempt to raise the City, and the defeat of that dangerous conspiracy. There is shown the effect of the evidence given at the trial; and lastly are printed the confessions and other evidence taken word for word out of the original.

This book is the work of Mr. Bacon at her Majesty's command, but with particular and express directions in every point; insomuch that when he had made a first draft of it, it was propounded to certain principal Lords of the Council and by them perused, weighed, censured, altered and made almost a new writing. And after it had passed their allowance it was again exactly perused by the Queen herself and some alterations made again by her appointment; and even after it was set to print the Queen, noting that Mr. Bacon could not forget his ancient respect to the Earl of Essex but termed him ever 'My Lord of Essex, my Lord of Essex' in almost every page of the book; which she thought not fit, but would have it 'Essex' or 'the late Earl of Essex.' Whereupon of force it was printed *de novo* and the first copies suppressed by her express command.

22nd April. THE EAST INDIA SHIPS.

Such has been the contrariety of the winds that the ships set forth to the East Indies have been so delayed in their departure that only two days since they departed from Tor Bay.

26th April. THE LORD PEMBROKE.

The Earl of Pembroke is taken with an ague in the Fleet prison by reason of his restraint. He is now allowed to depart to his house of Baynard's Castle, there to remain till her Majesty's further pleasure is known.

27th April. NEWS FROM THE FRENCH COURT.

It is said that Monsieur de Boissise, the French ambassador in London, who was present at the trial of the two Earls, sent back a letter very slanderously taxing both the proceeding and the justice of their condemnation, many copies whereof are spread abroad in the French Court. Nevertheless Mr. Winwood reporteth that the King with the body of his Court are possessed with a magnanimity of her Majesty's resolution and wish that their last King had had but part of her spirit to have quelled the insolencies of the Duke of Guise in his attempt of the barriers; and the King himself saith many times in the presence of his nobles that she only is a King, and she only knows how to rule; and that all are persuaded of the honour of her proceeding that reason of state, the dignity of her crown, the repose and weal of her subjects did require that course which had been taken and admitted no mean.

28th April. MORE SOLDIERS FOR IRELAND.

The Lords Lieutenant and Commissioners for Musters are commanded to provide a further supply of 40 horse (each man to be armed with a petronel) and 1,000 foot for the Irish service. The selected bands in each county are also to be viewed and mustered, which hath been forborne of late years, and the forces both of horse and foot trained according to former instructions, to the end that apt men may be chosen in place of those deceased or departed, deficiency in the armour, arms and other furniture replaced, likewise of horses and horsemen; and all be trained and disciplined to be made perfect in the use of their weapon and to know their marches.

29th April. A QUARREL BETWEEN THE ATTORNEY AND MR. BACON.

On the first day of term high words passed between Mr. Attorney Coke and Mr. Bacon in the Exchequer Court. Mr. Bacon was moving for a reseizure of the lands of a certain lapsed recusant and showed cause, whereat Mr. Attorney kindled at it and said, 'Master Bacon, if you have any tooth against me, pluck it out; for it will do you more hurt than all the teeth in your head will do you good.' Mr. Bacon answered coldly, 'Master Attorney, I respect you; I fear you not: and the less you speak of your own greatness the more I will think of it.' The Attorney replied, 'I think scorn to stand upon terms of greatness to you who are less than little; less than the least,' and gave other strange terms. Herewith stirred Mr. Bacon said, 'Mr. Attorney, do not depress me so far: for I have been your better, and may be again, when it please the Queen.' With this the other spake in choler and in the end bade him not meddle with the Queen's business but with his own; and that he was unsworn, and other speeches. Mr. Bacon answered that sworn or unsworn was all one to an honest man, and that he ever set his own service first and himself second; and wished to God that Mr. Attorney would do the like. Other disgraceful words Mr. Attorney gave, but Mr. Bacon made no reply.

9th May. COURT NEWS.

M. de Boissise hath had audience of the Queen to whom she declared in very good moderation that she did acquit him of the authorship of that offensive letter, only she insisted somewhat upon his son; for satisfaction whereof the young gentleman made many formal protestations and did promise that he would challenge all the world that could prove any such thing against him. This matter troubleth most of the noblemen, for copies have been sent to the Palsgrave and to divers other parts of the world, much to the scandal of all the peers in the kingdom.

The ambassadors of Scotland are well used of the Queen and are to depart this next week. It has been said by many that they meant to handle the matter of the succession and to demand peremptorily those lands in England which are in question between the Scottish King and the Lady Arabella with some other lofty propositions, but Mr. Secretary declareth that the principal scope of their journey is for congratulation of her Majesty's escape and to clear those imputations which have been thrown upon the King for dealing with the Pope and the King of Spain, and especially for suffering some subjects of

Scotland to carry provisions to the rebels in Ireland. They have made a request that the Queen will add a greater sum to that portion which her Majesty hath long since allowed him by way of gratuity ; which the Queen is resolved to grant, with promise to continue it as long as he shall make it appear unto the world that he is willing to deserve her extraordinary care and kindness unto him.

10th May. A Play Forbidden.

Great complaint is made that the players at the Curtain represent the persons of some gentlemen of good desert and quality that are yet alive under obscure manner, but in such a sort as the hearers may take note of the matter and the persons. The Justices of Middlesex are therefore bidden to examine them who made the play, and if the same shall appear unfit to be publicly showed to forbid it, and to take bonds of the chiefest of them if the subject be so odious and inconvenient as is informed.

The Sermon at Paul's Cross.

The sermon at Paul's Cross was preached by Dr. John Dove upon Matthew xix. verse 9, concerning adultery, wherein he declared that marriage is indissoluble and that not even after divorce may man nor woman, nocent nor innocent, marry again. Wherefore husbands should forgive their wives for their faults. Husbands must dwell with their wives as men of knowledge. The man is the woman's head ; the woman is but the image of the man, as the man is the image of God. But there must needs be more perfection in the head wherein are all the senses, vegetation and understanding than in the body, which hath but negation and one only sense, that is feeling. Wherefore a discreet man will of himself consider that by how much he exceedeth his wife in knowledge, understanding and all manner of perfection, so he ought to conceal many infirmities in the woman : to devour, as it were to swallow up, many indignities which do arise of her weakness.

11th May. Spanish Ships.

From Plymouth it is reported that there are come upon the coast two Spanish ships and a pinnace, which have taken divers fisher boats, some of which they discharged when they had examined the company. They examined them upon these points: how the rebellion of the Earl of Essex had proceeded, and to what head it had grown, and what noblemen were interested in that business and how many of them had lost their lives with him; what soldiers were to go for Ireland; what presses of men there were by land or sea; what fleets of either English or Dutch were preparing for sea; and whether there were not a Dutch fleet gone for the East Indies out of the harbour at Dartmouth.

12th May. THE IRISH COINAGE.

From Ireland it is said that the rebels rejoice that the Queen will send copper money into Ireland, making it an argument that her coffers are empty; and indeed it is to be feared that when the rebels make payment in silver and her Majesty in brass, it will strengthen the enemy and draw over not only the natural Irish that serve us but many of our natural English as well.

17th May. EXPORT OF PROVISION TO FRANCE FORBIDDEN.

There are divers jowtars, badgers, brokers and carriers and such like that ingross corn, butter, and cheese in the markets and buy up at the farmer's houses and great dairies the butter and cheese so fast as it is made, which they carry to the seaside, and from thence it is transported into France; by which abuse the corn and other provision for the service in Ireland cannot be furnished in the country at any reasonable rates. This abuse is now to cease.

18th May. FINES FOR THE LATE ACTION.

There is a commission to certain of the Council to fine and ransom the Lords and gentlemen who were in the late action. They have already rated the Earl of Rutland at £30,000, the Earl of Bedford at £10,000, Lord Sandys at £5,000, Lord Cromwell at £3,000, Sir Christopher Heydon at £2,000, and the rest at other sums.

20th May. CATHOLIC BOOKS.

In spite of the prohibitions of Blackwell the archpriest, the secular priests have written and caused to be printed divers books setting forth their cause; whereof one is in Latin, entitled *Declaratio motuum ac turbationum*, being dedicated to the Pope, and another in English, *The copies of certain discourses, which were extorted from diverse as their friends desired them, or their adversaries drove them to purge themselves of the most grievous crimes of schism, sedition and rebellion, faction and such like, most unjustly laid against them for not subscribing to the late authority at the first sending thereof into England.*

24th May. 'SAINT GEORGE FOR ENGLAND.'

Master de Malynes hath written an allegory entitled *Saint George for England, allegorically described*, wherein the Dragon is a monster compounded of covetousness and ambition, bringing inequality in a commonwealth by the means of his tail wherein lieth his greatest strength, making the expenses thereof far surmount the revenues.

25th May. A COMMISSION CONCERNING THE PRESERVATION OF THE WEALTH OF THE REALM.

The commissioners that were appointed to inquire concerning the preservation and augmentation of the wealth of the Realm and to consider of remedies, conclude that there be six causes chiefly of the decline of wealth, viz.: the overheaviness of our pound weight troy, being heavier by 3 dwts. than that of other countries; the overrichness of the monies of this realm, and the undervaluation in comparison to other countries; the disproportion of the value of our gold to our silver in respect of other countries adjoining to us; the overbalancing of foreign commodities vented out; the abuse of the exchange between us and other nations; the not making of a number of foreign commodities within this realm having opportunities for so doing. As for remedies, some hold that the exchange for all places should be kept at a certainty according to the value of coin and established with due consideration to prevent inconvenience. For redress of the excessive import of foreign commodities, the due execution of the statute of employments for strangers, together with some good laws for restraint thereof, should be put in execution, and good examples in forbearing the excessive use of foreign commodities would be a ready means thereto. Lastly some means might be devised to set to work our own people to make some of these foreign commodities whereby not only the over abundant imports will abate, but a great number of people that live either idle or by begging, will be set to work.

30th May. THE PROCLAMATION FOR THE IRISH MONEYS.

The proclamation for the new moneys in Ireland was set forth at Dublin on the 20th May, showing the reasons and appointing places of exchange at Dublin, Cork, Galway and Carigfergus in Ireland, and in England at London, Bristol and Chester.

7th June. IRISH NEWS.

By Lough Neagh Sir Arthur Chichester hath done good service against Tyrone, burning and destroying all along the Lough, and slaying men, women, child, horse, beast and whatsoever was found. Of late they fell suddenly upon one Patrick O'Quin, one of the chief men in Tyrone, slew him, his wife, sons, daughters, servants and followers, being many, and burnt all to the ground.

10th June. TRINITY COLLEGE IN DUBLIN.

The Provost and Fellows of Trinity College by Dublin have petitioned Sir Robert Cecil to become their Chancellor, which office was first held by the late Lord Treasurer, his father. Moreover, say they, their University College being as a graft of the famous University of Cambridge, they have good hope that as that orchard and paradise of learning receives this favour and comfort from him, so the same would not be denied to their little branch, yet indeed small, young and tender, but yet by the blessing of God it may in time bring forth some store of good fruit that may cause the hearts of many in the land to rejoice.

12th June. 'THE PASSIONS OF THE MIND.'

There is printing a book entitled *The passions of the mind*, by Master Thomas Wright, treating of the nature and effects of the passions upon our minds, bodies and behaviours. Noteth in the preface to the reader that amongst Italians and Spaniards we be accounted a simple and unwary nation, which, saith he, cometh of a natural inclination to honesty, a defect of conversation amongst strangers, and a certain natural complexion and constitution of body.

16th June. THE YOUNG LORD BURGH.

The Lord Burgh that was Deputy in Ireland and died there having left behind him a young son, of special hope and towardness, the Queen hath expressly signified her wish that he shall be brought up in the household of the Bishop of Winchester, considering that the best education of such children hath always been reputed to be in the houses of the most reverend and grave persons, where living under the eye and discipline of experience and good government they may in their tenderness be thoroughly seasoned with a true sense of religion and virtue, and be inured to a fashion of life fit for the nobility of their birth. The boy, being left with a weak estate and small means of living, but of quick and extraordinary spirit, is now commended to his Lordship's keeping, as one of special good gifts, a well governed family and plentiful housekeeping according to his place.

17th June. THE CASE OF JOHN DANIEL.

This day John Daniel, formerly servant to the late Earl of Essex, was condemned in the Star Chamber for his great and heinous misdemeanours. About September 1599, shortly after the Earl had been committed to the custody of the Lord Keeper, the Countess of Essex, then being in childbed, took a casket of letters written to her from the Earl and delivered them for safe keeping to her gentlewoman one Jane Rehora, whom Daniel afterward married. Daniel, finding the casket placed under his bed, very secretly and cunningly opened it, and thereout took some of the letters knowing them to be the Earl's, and minding by indirect means to gain to himself some great benefit. These letters he took one to Peter Bales, a scrivener, procuring him to counterfeit them as near as he could to the Earl of Essex's proper handwriting, and to observe the same length and distance of the lines, the scantling of the margent, and the proportion of the paper, so that the original and the copies might not be discerned one from another. And the better to provoke Bales, Daniel falsely said that the Countess had sent him. Further, Daniel read and dictated some of the letters whilst Bales writ them, wherein he not only found fault with Bales for not imitating the hand of the Earl so near as he wished, but also corrupted the copies by forging more matters in his reading than were contained in the original letters. Having obtained these copies Daniel said he meant to gull somebody.

About the beginning of the January following, the Countess sent for Mistress Daniel desiring to receive back her casket, whereunto Mrs. Daniel answered that it was very safe and had been seen by no creature living since she had them ; but when she had received the casket and privately opened it, she found many of her letters missing. Whereupon she went herself to Daniel's house to know how those letters were embezzled. To which after some talk had passed between them, Daniel replied that he could not imagine what way they were gone, unless a maid that his wife had newly put away had stolen them, but he would do his uttermost endeavour for finding of the letters again.

Nevertheless about the 1st of March following, Daniel wrote a letter to the Countess exknowledging that he had the letters, and that they might greatly concern her Lord ; and that he was become very much impoverished of late and decayed in his estate, above £3,000, during his service with the Earl ; yet upon some honourable consideration of his necessity he would safely restore the letters to her Ladyship again. The Countess therefore sent one of her servants divers times to Daniel, assuring him that she would relieve his wants to the best of her ability ; but Daniel not satisfied insisted upon the demand of £3,000, for, said he, he doubted not but if he should carry those letters to some persons of great quality and degree, they would give him so much for the same. The Countess not being able to provide so great a sum, yet being fearful and loath to hazard her husband's unkindness, resolved rather to sell her jewels than to leave such letters in the hands of so unhonest a man, and having made thereof the sum of £1,720 she gave it to Daniel, who delivered the forged letters, protesting withal voluntarily upon the Bible that he then delivered back all the letters, that none had read them, and that he had no copies of them.

All these things having been plainly manifested to the Court by the examination of Daniel in writing under his own hand and by his confession at the bar, he was utterly unable to make any defence or to yield any excuse or colour for his offences.

Hereupon Mr. Attorney, observing the great treachery of Daniel committed against so honourable a lady in the time of her childbed and amidst the sorrows and afflications for the great offence of her husband, which did highly aggravate the offence, prayed that he might receive some extraordinary and exemplary punishment.

Therefore the Court order that Daniel shall be committed to the Fleet, there to remain all the days of his life, and to pay £3,000 for a fine to her Majesty. Moreover that his offence may be notified to the public view he shall be set upon the pillory with his ears thereunto nailed, and a paper on his head inscribed with these words—'For forgery, corrupt cosenages, and other lewd practises.'

19th June. TWO BRETHREN PUNISHED.

This day two brothers, by name John and Thomas Tiffany, were punished for their outrages on two women. These two, by the device of one Nicholas Whittingham, came into the house in Fleet Street where Mistress Whittingham, his mother, dwelled, and there one of them took the maid and gagged her and bound her arms. The other goes up and pretends to view the same to take a lodging for a Western gentleman, and assails Mrs. Whittingham by the throat and would have forced her with his dagger in his mouth to have gagged her, but she striving and making great noise, he took a rug from the bed and wrapped her in it and almost smothered her with lying and sitting upon her. Then the other brought up the maid and laid her in the same chamber. Hereupon by reason of the great noise the neighbours came and knocked at the door. Then these two ungagged the maid and prayed her to be good to them and to let them out at a back door; but before they could get away the company came in and took them. For these causes they were sentenced to imprisonment during the Queen's pleasure, to be fined £500, and a pillory to be set up in Fleet Street over against the house where they used this violence; and there first to be whipped, then to be set upon the pillory and to be gagged with the same gags that they used to Mistress Whittingham and her maid, and then to lose their ears.

22nd June. 'DISCOURSES UPON SENECA THE TRAGEDIAN.'

Sir William Cornwallis hath now written sundry *Discourses upon Seneca the Tragedian*, wherefrom choosing certain moral sentences he enlargeth upon them; as from the *Thebais* that speech of Jocasta:

Gladius et spes et metus,
Sors caeca versat: praemium incertum petit
Certum scelus,

on which is appended a discourse of war, which, quoth he, 'is the remedy for a State surfeited with peace; it is a medicine for commonwealths sick of too much ease and tranquility, but carrieth a reforming nature and is a part of justice.' Concludeth that war's best use is the same that nurses make of Robin Goodfellow, to terrify; and the example much more safe and wholesome that is taken from the sight of our neighbours than from our own experience.

25th June. A BOOK AGAINST TABACCO.

There is a book printed describing the pernicious use of tabacco, entitled *Work for Chimney Sweepers*, wherein the author allegeth eight reasons in particular, as that it withereth and drieth up the natural moisture of our bodies, thereby causing sterility, in which respect it seemeth an enemy to the continuance and propagation of the human race; it dissipateth the natural heat and thereby is cause of crudities, rheums and infinite maladies. Moreover that the herb is in nature venemous, as may be gathered by the symptoms and accidents immediately following the immoderate drinking thereof, as violent vomits, many stools, great gnawings and torments in the guts and inward parts, coldness in external members, cramps, convulsions, cold sweats, ill colour, wanness of skin, defect of feeling, sense and understanding, loss of sight, giddiness of the head and brain, and to some hasty and untimely death. It is moreover a cause of melancholy, so that all melancholy persons and especially students and scholars ought to be very well advised in the use of so pernicious and dangerous a thing, lest that natural melancholy be converted into unnatural, and this also either into a corrosive and adust humour apt to inflame the brain, or else into a matter so hard and dry as that it be altogether hurtful and offensive to the unctuous and radical moisture of the life of man, and thereby occasion a hasty and untimely death.

29th June. THREE NEW COUNCILLORS.

This day were sworn of the Privy Council the Earls of Shrewsbury and Worcester and Sir John Stanhope.

There be now thirteen Lords of the Privy Council, *videlicet*, Dr. John Whitgift, Lord Archbishop of Canterbury; Sir Thomas Egerton, Lord Keeper of the Great Seal; Sir Thomas Sackville, Lord Buckhurst, Lord High Treasurer; Charles, Earl of Nottingham, Lord High Admiral; Gilbert, Earl of Shrewsbury; Edward, Earl of Worcester, Master of the Horse; Sir George Carey, Lord Hunsdon, Lord Chamberlain; Sir William Knollys, Controller of her Majesty's Household; Sir John Stanhope, Vice-Chamberlain; Sir Robert Cecil, Principal Secretary to her Majesty and Master of the Wards; Sir John Fortescue, Chancellor and Under-Secretary of the Exchequer; Sir John Popham, Lord Chief Justuce; Mr. John Herbert, one of her Majesty's secretaries.

30th June. THE QUEEN'S PRINTER.

The Queen's Printer, Mr. Robert Barker, complaineth that Bonham and John Norton, stationers of London, have of late not only procured one Andrew Hart a Scot to draw over the seas sundry English printers to the town of Dort for the imprinting of an English Bible and other privileged books there, but also they themselves at their own charge have imprinted the Psalms in metre in a volume to serve as an annex to the Bible. Hereby not only is the Queen's Printer abused and great hindrance received by many of her Majesty's subjects that have been set on works by him, but it is not unlikely that those printers at Dort, being persons of the most disordered sort, may also attempt to publish lewd and seditious books.

NEW PLAYS.

The Lord Admiral's men have played these new plays since Christmas last: *Robin Hood's Pen'orths* (by Haughton); *Hannibal and Scipio* (by Hathway and Rankins); *Scogan and Skelton* (by Hathway and Rankins); *The Conquest of Spain by John of*

Gaunt (by Hathway and Rankins); *All is not Gold that Glisters* (by Chettle); *The Conquest of the West Indies* (by Day, Haughton and Smith); *King Sebastian of Portingal* (by Chettle and Dekker); *The Six Yeomen of the West* (by Day and Haughton).

3rd July. A PROCLAMATION AGAINST TRANSPORTING MONEYS INTO IRELAND.

By reason of the extraordinary sums of money sent into Ireland of recent years infinite discommodities do occur to this Realm, for the same cometh either into the hands of the rebels, whereby they are enabled to provide for themselves arms and munitions from foreign parts, or else are transported into other countries by merchants for lack of commodities whereon to employ them; wherefore all subjects are put in mind of the former statutes against the transportation of coins of England into Ireland and severe penalties threatened against such as offend.

4th July. THE BLACKWATER PASSED.

The Lord Deputy hath now passed the Blackwater though the rebels fortified and entrenched themselves very strongly all along the river. Thus he hath gained a goodly county, stored with abundance of all sorts of grain, which shall be spoiled lest the enemy gather the corn into their own hands. Then they set to work to make a fort. Two days later there was a very hot skirmish with the rebels, Tyrone with all his horse and foot coming in. In this fight many men were hurt and killed on both sides, though but one Englishman, who was my Lord's chaplain standing by his side; which we may hold for a very good piece of policy to make the Irish cut one another's throats, without which this kingdom will never be quiet.

There are now constant rumours of the coming of the Spaniards to Ireland.

7th July. A THOUSAND MEN FOR OSTEND.

There is demanded of the City of London a levy of 1,000 men for service in the Low Countries, and towards the cost of their arms and apparel £3 10s. a man; and because there are many masterless men and other idle vagabonds in the suburbs, the justices of Middlesex and Surrey shall confer with the Lord

Mayor that at one time perfect search may be made in all houses and inns, and standing watches kept in all the ways and ends of the streets towards the fields.

8th July. OSTEND BESIEGED.

News is come that the enemy have laid siege to Ostend, having come before the town about noon on the 28th June, with eight regiments of foot men, which were 8,000 men strong besides the horsemen. There were then in the town in garrison one and twenty ancients of sundry regiments and one company of burghers, or townsmen, all under the direction of Captain Van der Noote. These presently prepared themselves for the defence, making harmless and displacing some of the enemies' artillery and labouring hard to make a new way between the heads that the passage of boats and shipping might be freed from the ordnance of the enemy. On the 1st of July, after they had sent away the most part of their wives and children, they received into the town from Zealand 28 companies of soldiers with great abundance of victual and other provision of war; and on the next day Sir Francis Vere with eight companies of Englishmen entered into the town also, who straightway issued out with his people, entrenching himself on the dry plots of ground next unto the walls on the west side from whence the enemy might have endamaged the town and battered the walls. On the 3rd Sir Francis with great force and resolution sallied upon the enemy with 800 men on the west side of the town, in which sally the enemy lost above 800 and among them one cornet of horsemen.

11th July. IRISH NEWS.

The Lord Deputy again maketh a journey against the rebels and hath planted a garrison in Lecale, and taken in all the castles, and there hath left Sir Richard Morrison to command both the county and 500 foot. He hath likewise at Armagh planted a garrison of 500 and 100 horse under command of Sir Henry Danvers. He now hath a mind to build a fort at the Blackwater when a proportion of the victuals shall come from England.

12th July. PUBLIC BURDENS EVADED.

The Lord Mayor is bidden by the Council to take diligent inquiry throughout the City and suburbs what Knights and gentlemen and others of good possessions and ability of living in the country, and being free of the City, do continue their habitation in London. By this abuse many whose habitations should be abroad, divers of them being Justices of the Peace, neglect and avoid the performance of any service to her Majesty and their country. They shift themselves from the burden of such taxes and impositions as are due upon any occasion of public service, pretending while they are in the City they are charged in the country, and endeavouring to free themselves in both places. They increase the dearth and scarcity of all things in the City by overcharging it with multitude and leave their poor neighbours in the country uncherished with any kind of hospitality.

20th July. MORE SOLDIERS FOR OSTEND.

For the relief of Ostend are now required 800 soldiers from the City and suburbs to be ready to be embarked four days hence, which shall be levied of those idle persons that live by shifting and bad means; the charges whereof are not to be borne by the City, but by certain of the counties, at the rate of £3 10s. a man.

21st July. SOLDIERS FROM THE COUNTIES.

In addition to the 800 men from the City, there are speedily required from the counties of Norfolk, Suffolk, Essex and Kent the number of 1,200 men for Ostend.

23rd July. 5,000 MEN FOR MUNSTER.

By reason of the news that the Spaniards will succour the rebels in Munster, 5,000 men are required from the counties to be embarked early next month.

25th July. NEWS FROM OSTEND.

There hath been hot fighting about Ostend this sennight past. On the 15th of July Sir Francis Vere again issued out of the town with 1,500 and began to entrench between the forts Isabella and Groostendorst on a high ground which in times past was an old churchyard, and is a very fit and apt place to separate these two forts from each other's help. To this place of burial the enemy came on the next day with 3,000 men, and after he had been thrice repulsed and put to the worst, took the place, but was with great force and dexterity driven from it again. This same day ten companies of soldiers arrived from London, so that now the town was furnished with 67 companies, which made up near the number of 7,000 men. These ten companies were straightway employed against the enemy and showed themselves very valorous, doing both then and since passing good service although men were of opinion that they would prove unfit for any service by reason they were raw and untrained.

Again on the 16th there was a great skirmish with the enemy, which was long maintained with great fury, valour and resolution on both sides, wherein the enemy would have lost more than he did, had our men been furnished with horsemen. It is written from Calais that after this fight there were carried out of the enemy's camp to Bruges 70 waggons laden with wounded men, and in every waggon 10 men at least: but when they were brought to Bruges they of the town would not receive them, saying that they had their hospitals already full and therefore required that they might be conveyed to some other towns. It was also reported that the enemy lost 450 men, besides those that are wounded; neither was this attempt accomplished without loss on our side.

Such as come from Ostend report for certain that within the town there wanteth not anything fit for the defence thereof, and that all victuals are very plentiful. English beer is sold for 2 stivers the can, great measure, for which there is no excise paid. On the south side the enemy hath raised a mount from whence he beateth the houses, but especially the Church and steeple which is wholly defaced, otherwise he doeth small annoyance to the town. They of the town have untiled and taken down many houses and also unpaved the streets that the enemy's shot may the less annoy them. The Governor and Sir Francis continually employ all their labour and industry, both within the town and without to raise mounts, and to finish other like works, and to that end such soldiers as will work and employ their time that way either by day or night have 12d. the day and 12d. the night.

Since the besieging of the town the five gallies of Sluys have destroyed a ship of war of Dort and without mercy slew 76 of her men, saving ten only, which for the most part are shorn and made slaves. Nevertheless one man was very miraculously saved who committed himself to the mercy of God and the merciless seas upon a piece of a mast rather than he would fall into the hands of his bloody enemies. After he had so floated upon the waves of the sea an hour or two he was taken up by another ship which had spied the man thus driving on the water.

2nd August. INVASION THREATENED.

Certain advertisement is come of the discovery of a fleet of Spanish ships upon the Western coast. The Captain of Portsmouth is bidden take present order for the safe keeping of that place, and to see provision made of victuals and other things necessary against any attempt that may be made; and likewise that the forces appointed to repair for defence may be in a readiness, that the beacons be watched, and the rest of the forces in such order as is meet they should be in these times of doubt. From divers ports and creeks in Hampshire, Sussex and Dorsetshire all mariners, pilots and seafaring men from the age of 16 to 60 are to be impressed and charged upon their allegiance to make present repair, upon warning given, unto Chatham. Shipping likewise to be stayed in these ports.

3rd August. A DISCOURSE OF SPIRITS.

Two preachers, John Deacon and John Walker, have written a learned work called *Dialogical Discourses of spirits and devils*, in eleven dialogues declaring their proper essence, natures, dispositions and operations, their possessions and dispossessions, very conducent and pertinent to the timely procuring of some Christian conformity in judgment for the peaceable compounding of the late sprung controversies; which book is published for many weighty reasons and especially lest the pestiferous opinions of Darrell lately broached abroad in pamphlets and printed apologies should pass underhand in the public view of tag and rag without the timely controlment of any.

4th August. THE QUEEN AND MR. LAMBARDE.

Mr. William Lambarde, that in January last was charged with the care of the records that be reposed in the Tower of London, to-day presented her Majesty with his *pandecta* or digest thereof. He had intended to present the book by the hands of the Countess of Warwick, but the Queen would not, 'for,' quoth she, 'if any subject of mine do me a service, I will thankfully accept it from his own hands.' Then opening the book she said, 'You shall see that I can read,' and so with an audible voice read over the epistle and the title. She demanded of him the meaning of certain terms. He severally expounded the meanings, whereat the Queen, seeming well satisfied, said that she would be a scholar in her age and thought it no scorn to learn during her life, being of the mind of that philosopher who in his last years began with the Greek alphabet. At length she fell upon the reign of King Richard the Second, saying 'I am Richard the Second, know ye not that?' To which Mr. Lambarde answered, 'Such a wicked imagination was determined and attempted by a most unkind gentleman, the most adorned creature that ever your Majesty made.' The Queen answered, 'He that will forget God will also forget his benefactors; this tragedy was played forty times in open streets and houses.' She asked him whether he had seen any true picture or lively representation of the countenance of King Richard. To which Mr. Lambarde answered that he had seen none but such as be in common hands. The Queen replied, 'The Lord Lumley, a lover of antiquities, discovered it fastened upon the backside of a door of a base room, which he presented unto me, praying, with my good leave, that I might put it in order with the rest of the ancestors and successors. I will command Thomas Knyvett, keeper of my house and gallery at Westminster, to show it unto thee.' Then she proceeded to the Rolls. At length she commended the work, not only for the pains thereof but also for that she had not received since her first coming to the crown any one thing that brought therewith so great delectation unto her; and so being called away to prayer, she put the book in her bosom, having from first to last forbidden Mr. Lambarde to fall upon his knee before her, concluding, 'Farewell, good and honest Lambarde.'

News of Ostend.

From Calais the news is that the enemy begin to wax cold and hopeless in his attempts before Ostend, and that a sennight ago the wind blowing a great gale from the north west brought such quantity of water upon the Flemish coast that the enemy stood above their knees in water in some of their trenches, and that the sea washing and undermining the foundation of the last mount made by the enemy on the south west side of the town, the same sunk and is wholly defaced, at what time they of Ostend issued out, and making great slaughter of their enemies brought one piece of ordnance into the town.

5th August. PRISONERS TO BE RELEASED FROM THE TOWER.

Her Majesty is now pleased to give order that the Earl of Rutland, the Lord Sandys, the Lord Cromwell, and Sir William Parker shall be released from the Tower upon payment of their charges, and be confined in the houses of private persons.

A BOOK ABOUT THE HORSE.

A certain L. W. C. hath written a book entitled *A very perfect discourse and order how to know the age of a horse*; also the diseases that breed in him, with the remedies to cure the same; as also the description of every vein and how and when to let him blood, according to the diversity of the disease. To know the age of a horse, note that the horse hath 40 teeth; the 30th month after his foaling he loseth two above and two beneath; in the 4th year he loseth two above and two beneath; when he is five he casteth all the rest both above and beneath. Those that come first above are hollow; when he is six his hollow teeth are filled up, and in the 7th year all the rest are filled up; then you can no longer judge of his age by his teeth.

6th August. MORE SOLDIERS FOR OSTEND.

Captain Crofts hath a direction to take up 200 voluntary soldiers for the service at Ostend, whereof the Council recommend to the Lord Mayor that he shall take up such vagrant and masterless men as haunt the City and convey them to Bridewell. The men thus taken, the Lord Mayor may intend a course against them according to his statute to see them whipped and corrected as they ought to be; and if any of them are willing to serve in the wars they may be delivered to Captain Crofts.

REWARDS FOR SERVICE.

Of the fine of Mr. Francis Tresham for the late troubles her Majesty is pleased to allot to the Lieutenant of the Tower £1,500; and of the fine of Mr. Catesby to Mr. Francis Bacon and to Sir Arthur Gorges £1,200 each, and to Captain Carpenter at Ostend the rest.

10th August. OSTEND.

The 1,200 men pressed out of Kent, Essex and other places are now in Ostend together with 3,000 old soldiers, all Walloons and Scots, so that there lieth within the town and in the trenches without some 8,000 men besides 3,000 more, which lie in ships of war before the town ready to be landed upon any occasion. These soldiers lack neither for victual nor money, and if any fall sick or are hurt they are sent out of the town to Flushing, Middleburgh and other places of Zealand where they are placed in hospitals and are so diligently attended as themselves can wish or desire wanting neither meat, drink, wine, physic nor surgery nor whatsoever else is requisite, but are cherished as if they were in their fathers' houses: surely a most godly and Christian deed of the people of these countries, which is a worthy mirror to us and to all other Christians teaching us to esteem of the poor and especially to have a fatherly care of the soldier, who (while we sleep quietly in our beds and go without fear about our worldly affairs at home) must watch and ward day and night in all weathers, and as often as he shall be by his Captain commanded venture his life against the enemy and us for the defence of our lives, wives, children, goods and country.

Upon Tuesday the 31st of July there was a long and fierce skirmish, wherein the enemy lost 400 men besides many that were hurt, and but 10 soldiers from the town slain. And again upon the 2nd of August, when in all men's judgment there were slain 300 and more of the enemy and of our men 32 and some few hurt. There was a mariner of Zealand that had his leg stricken off with a great shot who was taken up to be carried to the ship, but before he could be brought to the boat he was with another shot struck through the body that he straightway died, and so was rid of his pain. The like happened at another time to a soldier that was likewise slain, and being carried on four men's shoulders to the grave the coffin and corpse were shot through with another bullet, so that the men set the coffin on the ground and ran as fast as they could, striving who should get there first.

From Calais it is reported that upon Saturday the 5th the enemy attempting some works nearer to the town than heretofore had many pioners and soldiers to guard them, whereupon they sallied out of Sir Francis Vere's trenches and began a hot fight that was with great fury maintained on both sides, but in the end the enemy were forced by means of the artillery of the town to give back, whereupon our men followed with such fury that they forced the enemy even to his trenches and seized 7 pieces of ordnance. But while our soldiers were earnestly busied to nail and choke the pieces, a barrel of gunpowder standing near suddenly took fire whereby some 150 of our soldiers were blown up and scorched, yet not so sore hurt thereby but that some of them will again recover. Hereupon the enemy came afresh on our soldiers who being amazed with this sudden mishap were forced to retire. In this fight there were slain of the enemy 2,000 men, whereof 300 and more were horsemen besides 300 pioners; neither was the victory gotten without loss on our side, for there were slain of our men about 400 and near 300 hurt and scorched.

12th August. A Wife Beaten.

To-day one Reynold Holdaway, a smith of Whitechapel, was bound in the sum of £20 at the sessions to appear, having been charged to have beaten his own wife, of which beating she died.

14th August. Sir Francis Vere Hurt.

From Ostend comes news that Sir Francis Vere is hurt. He was standing upon the ramparts when a cannon shot from the enemy fell upon one of our cannons, the splinters whereof have hurt him in the head and back. The enemy hath raised a new battery on the sands to the east to cut off our victualling; another be to the east-south-east to shoot directly into our trenches.

19*th August*. IRISH NEWS.

The Lord Deputy is now busied with forming garrisons for the winter and destroying the rebels' corn, for without corn they have no other means to keep their bonnaghts, which are their hired men. He now importuneth fresh supplies, for at least half the force is Irish who cannot be trusted if the Spaniards come, and the force with my Lord, which should be nigh on 3,000, is but 1,800 able to take the field.

22*nd August*. A GRIEVOUS FIRE.

Two days since the town of Walton in Leicestershire was by a sudden fire in great part in a short space consumed with corn, household stuff and all other things whereby 200 persons are driven to great distress.

23*rd August*. A BOOK OF ASTRONOMY.

Master Thomas Blundeville hath written a book entitled *The theoriques of the seven planets*, showing all their divers motions and all other accidents, called passions, thereunto belonging; which is set forth with demonstrative figures that every man having skill in arithmetic may easily understand the same; a book most necessary for all gentlemen that are desirous to be skilful in astronomy, and for all pilots and seamen, or any others that love to serve the Prince on the sea, or by the sea to travel into foreign countries. To which are added tables to calculate the divers motions of the seven planets.

24*th August*. TRAITOROUS SOLDIERS.

Certain traitorous soldiers serving with the Archduke have sent into Ostend a letter persuading those within to leave their captains, which letter is to this effect: 'Gentlemen and loving countrymen.—The love we bear you binds us not to suffer you to be deceived by your commanders, who persuade you that such as render themselves are either hanged or extremely dealt withal; which is false as God is true, as by experience we can assure you. For we coming naked are clothed, and for our maintenance his Highness allows us 12d. sterling every day, which is good where things are plenty. Again, if we list to serve, we may under an English captain and with our own countrymen, our pay being equal with the Spaniards and as often paid. If you think it wrongful that the King of Spain doth aid the Irish, how can you assist those rebellious Hollanders against their lawful King.'

28th August. THE MARSHAL BIRON.

The Marshal Biron is very shortly coming to London from the French King with divers noblemen to attend him and see him honourably conducted. The Earl of Cumberland departeth with the Lord Zouch to meet him at Gravesend, whither he shall be conducted from Dover by Sir Edward Wotton, Sir Thomas Walsingham, Sir Moyle Finch and Sir John Leveson. There are also summoned to the Court, which is now on progress in Hampshire, the Earls of Sussex, Hertford, and Derby with the Countesses, the Lord Viscount Bindon, and other noblemen. In London Alderman Spencer's house, Crosby Place, is being made ready.

30th August. MORE CATHOLIC BOOKS.

The secular priests put forth two more books against Blackwell, whereof one is entitled *Relatio compendiosa turbarum* and dedicated to the Inquisition, and the other *The Hope of Peace.*

2nd September. KEMP RETURNED.

Will Kemp is now come back from his morris over the Alps, having traversed Germany and Italy with but poor return of fortune. Reporteth much of Sir Anthony Shirley whom he met at Rome serving as ambassador to the Sophy.

5th September. THE MARSHAL BIRON.

The Duke of Biron, Marshal of France, with divers noblemen of France and their following to the number of three hundred persons are arrived in London. The chief of them were conveyed in coaches from Tower wharf through the City into Bishopsgate street and there they are lodged in Crosby Place. The Court is still on progress in Hampshire, whither the Marshal proceedeth.

7th September. THE DUKE OF BIRON.

It is much noted that the Duke of Biron is not well attended, not one nobleman or gentleman being at hand to accompany him or entertain them, save Sir Arthur Savage and Sir Arthur

Gorges, till that Sir Walter Ralegh came. He hath carried them to Westminster to see the monuments, and to-day they were entertained at the Bear Garden, which they had great pleasure to see.

9th September. A PARLIAMENT TO BE SUMMONED.

A Parliament is to be summoned to meet at Westminster on the 27th of next month.

10th September. TWO PRIESTS GRANTED PASSPORTS.

Two priests, by name John Mush and Francis Barnaby, have been granted passports at the motion of the Lord Bishop of London to go out of the realm and pass over the seas without let or molestation. They go to lay the complaints of the seculars before the Pope at Rome.

THE MARSHAL BIRON.

This day the Marshal Biron accompanied with twenty of the nobility of France and attended on with 400 Frenchmen went on their way towards the Court, being met by my Lord of Cumberland. This night they lodged at the Vine, a house of my Lord Sandys, which hath been furnished with hangings and plate from the Tower and Hampton Court, and with seven score beds which the people of Hampshire have brought in upon two days' warning had to lend the Queen.

11th September. BRETON'S DIVINE POEMS.

There are two books of poems by Breton, the one called *A Divine Poem*, divided into two parts, 'The Ravished Soul,' and 'The Blessed Weeper'; the other *An excellent poem upon the longing of a blessed heart which loathing the world doth long to be with Christ*, with an addition upon the definition of love:

> If then henceforth you ask what thing is Love,
> In light, in life, in grace, in God, go look it:
> And if in these you do not truly prove,
> How in your hearts you may for ever book it;
> Unhappy think yourselves you have mistook it.
> For why the life that death hath over-trod
> Is but the Love of Grace, and that is God.

All kind of love but this is but mistaken ;
And all conceit but this is misconceived ;
All kind of love but this must be forsaken ;
All trust but in this truth may be deceived ;
All in this love all truth may be perceived :
All heart's belief and all soul's seal unto it,
All what is good this love doth only do it.

14th September. THE DUKE OF BIRON.

At the Court it is much noted that the French wear all black and no kind of bravery at all, wherefore Sir Walter Ralegh rode by night to London to provide himself with a plain black taffeta suit and a black saddle.

15th September. JONSON'S 'POETASTER.'

These fifteen weeks Ben Jonson hath meditated upon the arraignment of those that writ against him, and now his play of *Poetaster, his arraignment*, cometh forth upon the Blackfriars stage. The argument is of the court of Roman Augustus, and the disgracing of poet Ovid for his wantonness with the Emperor's daughter Julia. Bringeth also Horace upon the stage, plagued and tormented by one Crispinus, an inferior poet and writer of plays, and Demetrius, a needy botcher of plays. These two having wrongfully accused Horace before the Emperor are brought to trial, whereat Crispinus is given a pill and made to vomit up his tumourous words, as 'retrograde,' 'glibbery,' 'lubrical,' 'oblatrant,' 'furibund,' 'obstupefact'; and the two dismissed under oath that they will not malign the person or writings of Horace nor suffer the itch of their writing to overrun their performance in libel.

THE QUEEN AND THE DUKE OF BIRON.

The Queen hath very nobly entertained the Duke of Biron these last days both at the Vine and at Basing where the Court abide. On one of these days the Duke attended her Majesty at Basing park on hunting, where he stayed her coming and there saw her in such royalty and so attended by the nobility, so costly furnished and mounted as the like hath seldom been seen. But as the Queen came to the place where the Duke awaited her coming, the sheriff (as the manner is being bare headed and riding next before her) stayed his horse, thinking the Queen would have saluted the Duke; whereat she being much offended commanded the sheriff to go on. The Duke, bowing low towards his horse's mane with his cap off, following her very humbly about twenty yards, the Queen on a sudden took off her mask, looked back upon him and most graciously and courteously saluted him; for she held it not beseeming so mighty a Prince as herself and who so well knoweth all kingly majesty to make her stay directly against a subject before he had showed his obedience in following after her.

In her discourses with the Duke the Queen spake of the Earl of Essex, sharply accusing him of ingratitude, rash counsel and obstinately refusing to ask pardon, and wished that the French King would rather use a mild severity than an unwise and destructive clemency by cutting off the heads of treacherous and disloyal persons in time who sought nothing but innovations and the disturbance of the public quiet and tranquillity. Some also report that she showed the skull of the Earl to the Duke and the Frenchmen in her closet, or fastened upon a pole; which is a ridiculous vain story, for that was buried together with his body.

On his departure two hundred horses are commanded to be ready for his retinue at Gravesend and the like number at Sittingbourne, where Sir Thomas Vane and Sir Thomas Wilford with a convenient number conduct him to Dover. Moreover the Duke is allowed to carry out of the realm any horses or provisions for his use upon any note of his hand, such honour is the Queen disposed to do him.

16th September. A KIND FRIENDLY SNIPPING.

One hath written an exhortation to those wits who would write satires and epigrams, and the humorists who make collection of loathed behaviours to play their parts upon a stage, entitling it *No Whipping, nor tripping—but a kind friendly snipping*, whereby the author urgeth them to avoid such ill following of idle wits and rather to sing of heavenly matters and leave to brawl.

21st September. DIFFICULTIES OVER THE IRISH COINAGE.

The new money in Ireland hath reasonable good acceptance both with the army and the country, but her Majesty's main drift to withdraw the old sterling out of the realm is frustrated by the merchants who underhand seek to engross it by giving 2s. in the £ or more, when the Queen by her proclamation prescribeth but 12d. This fraud being but newly discovered there is as yet no remedy provided for it, but it cometh on in an underhand course as though the merchant might buy and sell the Queen's bullion as he doth his other shop wares, which in time will rob the exchange and reimburse to himself all the old silver in the realm.

23rd September. THE SUMMONS TO PARLIAMENT.

Albeit that the Earl of Rutland, the Earl of Bedford, and the Lords Sandys and Cromwell receive their writs of summons to this Parliament, yet it is thought fit by her Majesty that they shall forbear coming least by their appearance before her they renew a very displeasant remembrance of their late offence; yet are they suffered to name as their proxies whom they wish.

25th September. 'THE SPANISH TRAGEDY.'

Ben Jonson now writeth additions to *The Spanish Tragedy* for the Lord Admiral's men to play at the Fortune.

30th September. THE SPANIARDS LAND IN IRELAND.

News is come that the Spaniards landed on St. Matthew's day in Kinsale in Ireland which is yielded to them. There are reported to be 28 sail; they have landed 27 pieces of ordnance at Kinsale and are fortifying two or three places thereabout. There are not above 3,000 of whom 1,000 are Italians; they have many women and children with them.

FRESH TROOPS FOR IRELAND.

Upon this coming of the Spaniards to Ireland a further supply of 2,100 men is to be levied in the counties. Their arms shall be sorted in each hundred, 24 corslets with pikes, 40 calivers, 12 muskets with rests, and 12 corselets with bills with long stems, and all to be furnished with good Turkey swords with the best basket hilts.

5th October. FOUR HUNDRED MEN FROM THE CITY.

The City is now required to furnish 400 men for Ireland.

6th October. THE SOLDIERS FOR IRELAND TO BE INCREASED.

Letters now go forth to the Lords Lieutenant and other officers in the counties that the reinforcement lately ordered for Ireland shall be increased from 2,100 to 5,000 men to be ready to sail on the 20th of this month.

8th October. A MIRACULOUS POWDER.

One Mr. Thomas Russel with great labour and cost in the experimental performance hath come by a powder which he termeth *diacatholicon aureum*, or a general powder of gold, purging all offensive humours in man's body and good in general for all diseases where there needeth any purgation. It cureth five and fifty diseases and may be taken of all manner of people of what age so ever in the quantity of 2, 3 or 4 grains. The powder may be had at the Sign of the Hand and Pistol, near unto Ivy Bridge, for 2s. 6d. the grain.

9th October. THE QUEEN.

Sir John Harington was of late again at Court and had a short audience of her Majesty, but she sent him word by the Lord Buckhurst saying 'Go tell that witty fellow, my godson, to get home; it is no season now to fool it here'; which the knight liked as little as the Queen his Irish knighthood, and so took to his boots and returned to his plough in the bad weather, wishing that he had never received that honour of my Lord of Essex. The Queen in these days is quite disfavoured and unattired, and these troubles waste her much. She disregardeth every costly dish that cometh to the table, and taketh little but manchet and succory pottage. Every new message from the City doth disturb her, and she frowns on all the ladies. She walks much in her privy chamber, and stamps with her feet at ill news, and thrusts her rusty sword at times into the arras in great rage. My Lord Buckhurst is much with her, and few else since the City business; but the dangers are over, and yet she always keeps a sword by her table.

13th October. THE SOLDIERS FOR IRELAND.

The soldiers that embark at Rochester shall be furnished with a cassock of broad cloth, a pair of venetians, a doublet of canvas, a hat cap, two shirts of linen cloth, 2 bands of holland cloth, 3 pairs of kersey stockings and 3 pairs of shoes.

From the gentlemen in the county and the clergy are required 208 horsemen, each light horseman to be provided with a morocco saddle of buff or other good leather, and good furniture to it, a cuirass and casque, a northern staff, a long pistol, a sword and dagger, and a horseman's coat; the carabines to have a petronel in place of the staff and pistol.

20th October.. THE SPANISH LANDING.

Upon this landing of the Spaniards in Ireland Sir Richard Leveson is to be sent forth with seven of the Queen's ships, the *Wastspite*, the *Garland*, the *Defiance*, the *Nonpareil*, the *Swiftsure*, the *Crane* and the *Merlin*, with certain merchant ships of London. He is given full power and authority to employ them against the Spaniards and their ships, and to destroy them to the uttermost of his power; and to pursue them, if cause be given, and to invade the countries of the enemy. And should Sir Richard miscarry, Sir Amyas Preston, the vice-admiral, shall take charge of the fleet.

22nd October. INSUFFICIENT LEVIES.

The levies from Suffolk for the Irish wars were delivered 37 short of the 200 appointed to be at Rochester, and of the rest many unable for service; wherefore the captain petitioned the Lord Admiral for warrant to impress in Kent so many as shall be needed to make up their companies of tapsters, ostlers, chamberlains and other idle persons that pass to and fro in Gravesend barge.

27th October. THE PARLIAMENT ASSEMBLES.

This day was the first of the present Parliament. About three of the clock this afternoon the Queen went by land to Westminster riding in a chariot, all made open, only like a canopy at the top, being of cloth of silver or tissue, with divers Lords and others in their degree, being marshalled by the heralds; where having heard a sermon, she went into the Upper House. The knights, citizens and burgesses of the House of Commons having notice that her Majesty with divers Lords spiritual and temporal were set in the Upper House hasted thither; but before they came the door of the House was shut, and notwithstanding any means made by them was still kept shut until the Lord Keeper had ended his speech. Wherefore they returned back again to their own House much discontented.

The Lord Keeper declared that it was her Majesty's desire that this Parliament should be dissolved before Christmas and his advice was that laws in force might be revised and explained but no new laws made. Our enemies, saith he, are enemies to God, the Queen and the peace of this Kingdom, conspired to overthrow Religion, to reduce us to a tyrannical servitude, which enemies he named to be the Bishop of Rome and the King of Spain. Our state being thus, he summoned them to be provident, by reason we deal with a provident enemy; and confident because God hath ever, and he hoped will ever, bless the Queen with successful fortune.

Then he fell to persuade, because new occasions were offered of consultations, to be provident in provision of means for our defence and safety, seeing the King of Spain means to make England miserable by beginning with Ireland, neither doth he begin with the rebels, but with the territory of the Queen herself. Then showed he that treasure must be the means, for treasure is the sinews of war.

The speech being ended certain of those that had got into the Upper House returned to the Lower, among them Sir William Knollys, the Controller. When they had been set Mr. Lieffe stood up and showed the great wrong done unto the greatest of the members of the House in their not being suffered to come into the Upper House to hear her Majesty's pleasure, and humbly desired that the effect thereof might be imparted unto some of the members of this House for their better satisfaction; which Mr. Controller did think very reasonable and meet to be done at convenient time, so did he impute the fault wholly to the Gentleman usher of the Upper house.

After some further pause Mr. Controller stood up and declaring that his place was to break the silence of the House for that time, and putting the House in mind to make choice of a Speaker according to her Majesty's pleasure, showed that in his opinion he thought Mr. John Croke, Recorder of London, to be a very fit, able and sufficient man to supply the whole charge of the office of Speaker, being a gentleman very religious, very judicious, of a good conscience and well furnished with all other good parts; yet nevertheless he left the further consideration thereof to the House; and so did sit again.

Which done and no contrary voice at all being delivered, Mr. Croke, after some large pause first taken, stood up and very learnedly and eloquently endeavoured to disable himself at large for the burden of that charge, alleging his great defects both of nature and art fit to supply that place, and showing all full complements for the same to abound in many other learned and grave members of the House; in the end prayed most humbly that they would accept of his due excuse and be pleased to proceed to a new election; and then sat down again. Hereupon Mr. Controller stood up and said that hearing no negative voice he took it for a due election, and demanding the further opinion of the House therein, they all answered 'Yea.' Whereupon Mr. Controller and Sir John Stanhope, the Vice-Chamberlain, immediately went to Mr. Croke and did set him in the Chair. Which done Mr. Croke, after some little pause, stood up and yielding to the House his most humble thanks for their great good opinion of him and loving favour towards him; and praying them to accept of his willing mind and readiness, and to bear with his unableness and wants in the service of the House referred himself to their good favours.

It is said by some who were present that the Queen in all her robes would have fallen if some gentlemen had not suddenly cast themselves under that side that tottered and supported her.

29th October. Sir Thomas Hoby's Complaints.

To his former complaints of the outrage committed in his house, Sir Thomas Hoby now addeth that the gentlemen used very despiteful words of him, as that they would set horns at his gate, and keep his house by force; that they called him 'scurvy urchin' and 'spindle-shanked ape.'

30th October. The Speaker Presented.

About one of the clock this afternoon the Queen came by water to the Upper House, and being apparelled in her royal robes and placed in her chair of state, the knights and burgesses of the House of Commons, who had waited at the door of the Upper House the full space of half an hour with the Speaker, were at last as many as conveniently could let in. The Speaker was led up to the bar by Sir William Knollys and Sir John Fortescue, and presented to her Majesty, to whom he made three low reverences, and was approved and allowed by her, notwithstanding his excuse of weakness and inability made according to the usual form.

Then Mr. Speaker craved leave of her Majesty to show the dutiful thoughts and earnest affections of her loyal subjects; and so made a vehement invective against the tyranny of the King of Spain, the Pope's ambitions, the rebels of Ireland, which, he said, were like a snake cut in pieces which did crawl and creep to join themselves together again. And lastly with prayers to continue the prosperous estate and peace of this Kingdom which had been defended, as he said, by the mighty arm of our dread and sacred Queen.

To which the Queen answered openly herself, 'No, but by the mighty hand of God, Mr. Speaker.'

Then he proceeded to the last part to beseech for freedom of speech for every particular member of the House and their servants. And lastly, if any mistaking of any message delivered unto him from the Commons should happen, that her Majesty would attribute it to his weakness in delivery or understanding and not to the House.

Then the Queen called the Lord Keeper to her to whom she spake something in secret; and after the Lord Keeper spake in commendation of Mr. Speaker's grave speech, well divided, well contrived; the first proceeding from a sound invention, and the other from a settled judgment and experience. 'Touching your other request for freedom of speech,' said he, 'her Majesty willingly consenteth thereto, with this caution that the time be not spent in idle and vain matter, pointing the same out with froth and volubility of words, whereby the speakers may seem to gain some reputed credit by imbolding themselves to contradiction, and by troubling the House of purpose with long and vain orations to hinder the proceeding in matters of greater and more weighty importance.'

For liberties to themselves and persons, her Majesty commanded him to say that she ever intendeth to preserve the liberties of the House; 'but,' quoth he, 'you should not maintain and keep with you notorious persons either for life or behaviour, and desperate debtors who never come abroad but at these times ; pettifoggers and vipers of the Commonwealth ; prolling and common solicitors that set dissension between man and man, and men of the like condition to these. These her Majesty earnestly wisheth a law may be made against ; as also that no member of this Parliament would entertain or bolster up any men of the like humour or quality, on pain of her Majesty's displeasure.'

For his excuse of the House and himself, Mr. Speaker's sufficiency had so oftentimes been approved before her, that she doubted not of his sufficient discharge of the place he should serve in. 'Wherein,' quoth he, 'she willeth you to have a special regard not to make new and idle laws, and trouble the House with them, but rather look to the abridging and repealing of divers obsolete and superfluous statutes ; as also first to take in hand matters of greatest moment and consequence. In doing thus, Mr. Speaker, you shall fulfil her Majesty's commandment, do your country good, and satisfy her Highness's expectation.' Which being said, the Speaker made three reverences to her Majesty.

After which room being made the Queen passing through the Commons to go to the great chamber graciously offered her hand to the Speaker to kiss it ; but not one word she spake unto him. And as she went through the Commons, very few said 'God save your Majesty,' as they are wont in all great assemblies. And so she returned back again to Whitehall by water.

Then the Speaker with the rest of the Commons returned back to their own House, the Sergeant of the House carrying the mace before him. Here, after some good pause, Mr. Speaker did signify unto the members of the House that her Majesty's pleasure was that this Parliament should be a short Parliament ; and therefore she willed that members of the House should not spend the time in frivolous, vain and unnecessary motions and arguments ; and further showed that her Highness did purpose that the members of the House should have convenient scope to repair home before Christmas for her Majesty's better service in their countries.

2nd November. THE PARLIAMENT.

This day in the Parliament Sir Edward Hoby made a speech for the abridging of penal laws, which, said he, were like thorn that prick but yield no fruit; and that they not being looked to, it bred in us an alteration in manners; and therefore the proverb must needs be fulfilled *Morum mutatio mutationem legum requirit.* Times are not as they have been, and therefore the necessity of time makes a necessity of alteration of laws, and with many other circumstances touching the shortness of statutes he concluded by desiring a committee; to which the House agree.

Also monition was this day given by Mr. Speaker unto the members that they would forbear to come into the House with their spurs on, in regard it is very offensive to many. Others also moved to have boots and rapiers taken away.

3rd November. THE PARLIAMENT.

Motion was made on behalf of Mr. Fulke Onslow, Clerk of the House, for that it had pleased God to visit him with an ague, that it would please the House to vouchsafe their allowance unto Cadwallader Tydder his servant to execute his place as his deputy until he should be restored to health; which being willingly assented unto by the whole House the said Tydder took the Oath of Supremacy.

After certain bills had been considered, Mr. Secretary Cecil, being put in mind to relate the speech of the Lord Keeper on the first day of the Parliament, repeated that speech and afterwards spake on his own account of the danger of the King of Spain; of his putting an army into Ireland of 4,000 men under the conduct of a valiant, expert and hardy Captain; and of the enterprise at Ostend, and how dangerous to this Realm would be the loss of that town. He reminded them also that what they did was *pro aris et focis*; 'yea,' saith he, 'we do it for a Prince that desireth not to draw anything extraordinary out of the coffers of her subjects. She selleth her land to defend us, she supporteth all the neighbouring princes to gain their amity and establish our long peace, not these five or seven or ten years, but forty-three years for all our prosperities.'

6th November. A Wife Murderer.

One Robert Budden or Harmondsworth this day assaulted his wife and murdered her by seizing her neck with his hands and wringing and breaking it.

7th November. The Subsidy.

This afternoon the Committee of the House sat concerning the subsidy; and first Sir Walter Ralegh spoke, saying that in the last Parliament only three subsidies were granted upon fear that the Spaniards were coming; but now they are come even in the Queen's territories already and therefore the more to be respected and regarded. He urged therefore that less might not be done than before, and that bountiful contribution should be made by all according to their estates. When some few had given their opinion, Sir Robert Cecil spoke. The Queen, said he, hath occasion to use £300,000 before Easter; how this shall be raised and gathered, that is the question; for without this proportion of charge neither the Spaniards in Ireland can be repelled and the wars there maintained, neither her Majesty's other affairs be set on foot, nor provision sufficient made for foreign invasion. Then he yielded a particular account of the State itself. First, the whole last subsidy after the rate of four poundlands and eight groats goods came not to above £80,000; the subsidy of the clergy £20,000; the double fifteenths £60,000. Since my Lord of Essex's going into Ireland she hath spent £300,000: so the Queen is behind £140,000. He concluded, 'We would only show you the present state of the Queen and her affairs, wishing no man to look that we should give advice what is to be done, as though you yourselves, who are the wisdom of the land, could neither direct yourselves nor upon these reasons alleged judge of the necessity of the State.'

Mr. Controller, Sir John Fortescue, and Mr. Secretary Herbert spake to the like effect; only Sir John bade them remember that the Great Turk when he conquered Constantinople found therein three hundred millions of gold; if they, quoth he, had bestowed three millions in defence of their city, he could never have gotten it. From which blindness he prayed God defend us that we may not be backward to give four subsidies to her Majesty, for want whereof in time we may happen to lose that which will not be recovered or defended with a hundred.

So after other conferences and speeches, about 6 of the clock, it being dark night, the House rose confusedly and would sit no longer.

9th November. THE PARLIAMENT AND THE SUBSIDY.

This day Mr. Heyward Townsend presented a bill in Parliament against the multitude of common solicitors, disabling all persons to solicit any cause other than their own; excepting only four several sorts, *viz.*, lawyers and attornies in their own courts; where they be sworn servants in livery; and kinsmen within the fourth degree of consanguinity.

Then Mr. Secretary spake concerning the subsidy, showing what had been deliberated upon by the committee appointed by the House. One contention, said he, bred difference and difference cause of argument, both how to ease the State and make this subsidy less burdensome. Some were of opinion that the three pound men should be spared, because they had but small portions; others that the four pound men should give double, and the rest upwards should be higher sessed. Again, it was moved whether this subsidy should go in the name of a benevolence or contribution or of a fourth subsidy; but at length most voices resolved it should have the old name of subsidy, because *subsidium* and *auxilium* are one. And in respect of expedition, the time to be by the 1st of February.

Then after consultations had of the great occasions it was put to the question whether the double tenths and fifteenths should be paid by the 1st of February, *viz.*, for this fourth subsidy before the third began; and that the first payment of the first three subsidies should be brought in by the 10th of June, *viz.*, half a subsidy. And all said 'Yea' and not one 'No.'

Then they fell to discussing of means of collecting the subsidy, Mr. Francis Moore moving that the subsidy might be gathered by commission and not by the old roll, for peradventure some were dead, others fallen to poverty, others richer and so deserved to be enhanced, etc. Sir Arthur Gorge moved that order might be taken that justices of the peace might be sessed according to the statute, *viz.*, at twenty poundlands, whereas there be few justices that be above eight or ten pound by Mr. Secretary noted in his table book.

Then Sergeant Heyle stood up and made a motion, saying, 'Mr. Speaker I marvel much that the House will stand upon granting of a subsidy or the time of payment, when all we have is her Majesty's. Yea, she hath as much right to all our lands and goods as to any revenue of her Crown.'

At which all the House hemmed and laughed and talked.

'Well,' quoth Sergeant Heyle, 'all your hemming shall not put me out of countenance.'

So Mr. Speaker stood up and said, 'It is a great disorder that this should be used; for it is the ancient use of every man to be silent when one speaketh; and he that is speaking should be suffered to deliver his mind without interruption.'

So the Sergeant proceeded and when he had spoken a little while, declaring that he could prove his former position by precedent in the times of Henry the Third, King John, King Stephen, etc.; whereat the House hemmed again. And so he sat down.

Mr. Montague of the Inner Temple answered that there were no such precedents; and if all the preambles of subsidies were looked upon, he should find it were of free gift. And although her Majesty requireth this at our hands, yet it is in us to give not in her to exact of duty.

11*th November*. THE QUEEN'S SUSPICIONS.

Some days since the Duke of Lennox arrived in London from the King of Scots, and to-day he was received in audience. His coming at the very jump of a parliament was at first much suspected by her Majesty. Her suspicion is somewhat qualified though not wholly abated by the Duke's forbearing to speak anything from the King to disquiet her; but she is still infinitely offended with the rumour both in England and advertised from foreign parts that such a mystery was looked for; and that the people speak as freely by this occasion as if the title had been argued and establishment agreed upon.

SIR ANTHONY SHIRLEY'S TRAVELS.

Mr. William Parry, one of the gentlemen that set out with Sir Anthony Shirley in '98, is now returned with letters and an account of his travels which is being set forth in print.

Having reached Venice in May 1599, they compounded with an Italian ship to take them to Aleppo. On this ship some jars fell out between certain Italians, being some three score persons, and Sir Anthony's company, being but twenty-four, for it happened that certain villainous and opprobrious speeches towards her Majesty were made by one of these Italians, which being carried to Sir Anthony, he caused one of his company so to beat the man with a billet that it was impossible he should ever recover it. In the performance whereof he made a great outcry, whereupon all the Italians were in arms. The captain of the ship therefore demanded of Sir Anthony how any durst intermeddle in that kind under his command; whereunto Sir Anthony replied that it was an injury tending to the reproach and indignity of his Sovereign which he neither would nor could endure; and therewith all told him that if he should subborn or abet him therein, the one side should welter in their gore. Sir Anthony's brother also gave the captain a sound box, which was very hardly digested, and much mischief was likely to have fallen thereon had not certain merchants in the ship fearful of their goods pacified, with much ado, both parties. Thereafter the captain put them ashore on the island of Zant.

Thence with much danger they passed to Candia, and so to Cyprus, where they watered at an island the most pleasant place that eye ever beheld. Having at length reached Antioch they passed in the company of certain merchants bound to Aleppo, where they were right well entertained by the English consul and the rest of the English merchants.

As for the people of the country, besides that they are damned infidels and sodomitical Mahomets, they are beyond all measure most insolent, superbous and insulting, ever pressed to offer outrage to any Christian if he be not well guarded with janissaries. They sit at their meat as tailors sit upon their stalls cross-legged; for the most part passing the day in banqueting and carousing until they surfeit, drinking a certain liquor which they call 'coffe,' which is made of a seed much like mustard seed, which will soon intoxicate the brain, like our metheglin. They will not permit any Christian to come within their churches. They have no use of bells, but some priest three times a day mounts the top of their churches and there with an exalted voice cries out and invocates Mahomet to come in post, for they have long expected him. They have wives in number according to their wealth, two, three, four or upwards as they are able to maintain them. Also they have one thing most usual among them, yet it exceedeth the credit of our homebred countrymen, and this is that when they desire to hear news, they have pigeons that are so taught and brought to hand that they will fly with letters, fastened with string about their bodies, from places which are distant a quarter of a year's passage.

From Aleppo the company set forwards in the midst of August, and having come to the river Euphrates they passed down the same for three and twenty days, until at length they came to Babylon where they stayed for some time. That old tower of Babel is three days' journey from this place and by common report of the inhabitants about the height of Paul's. It is not hollow but solid throughout and consists of bricks baked in the sun of great breadth and thickness, interlined with canes plaited like mats which remain much less perished than the bricks.

Thence they joined themselves to a 'caravan' of Persians (which is a great many of camels laden and men in a company, not much unlike our carriers, many in a company here in England), with whom they journeyed in much hazard through the Courds country, the people whereof are altogether addicted to thieving, not much unlike the wild Irish, so that every night they did encamp they slily stole more or less from them, watched they never so warily. This people live altogether in tents, keeping of cattle. Then they entered into the King of Persia's country and after came nine days to Casbin, where they were right royally intreated. Here they were sent for to appear before the King, who welcomed Sir Anthony right heartily and would many times confer with him.

Of the customs of these Persians noteth that their merchandise and commodities are silks, both raw and otherwise, of all suits and colours, spice, drugs, pearls and other precious gems, together with carpets of divers kinds. They write from the right side of the paper to the left like the Turks, contrary to our manner; but they have not many books, much less libraries, amongst their best clerks. They are ignorant in all kinds of liberal and learned sciences, except it be in certain things pertaining to horses' furniture and some kinds of carpeting and silk works wherein they excel. Their buildings are for the most part made of brick, hardened in the sand, wherein they have very little furniture other than carpets spread upon their floors.

Near unto a town called Backo in Persia there issueth out of the earth in the manner of a water-spring a certain kind of oil in great abundance, which they from all parts of the Persian dominions do fetch upon camels, kine and asses to burn in their lamps.

From Persia Sir Anthony entered the dominions of the Emperor of Russia, having sailed for two months on the Caspian Sea; and after many weeks came at last to Musco, where they were sent for to come before the Emperor.

By this time there was with their company a Portingal friar that had accompanied them from Persia, a lewd whoremongering knave; which friar though he had been treated with great kindness alleged Sir Anthony to be but a man of mean parentage, that was come as a spy through the country for purposes of his own good and not of Persia and Christendom as he pretended. Whereupon Sir Anthony and his companions were for a space put in prison. But being at last brought before the commissioners to be examined, the friar in terms tried to thwart Sir Anthony, whose blood already boiled with the excess of his choler's heat, and unable to suppress it, he gave the fat friar such a sound box on the face that down he falls as if he had been struck with a thunderbolt. After which event Sir Anthony was better used, but constrained to stay for six months in that place before he was given leave to depart.

Thence they passed towards St. Nicholas to take shipping in mid May and being come to the seaside they there stayed for provision for their journey. In which time they were divers times invited aboard English ships where they were royally banqueted at the Agent's charges and the merchants'. From hence they took ship to Stade, and here Mr. Parry parted from Sir Anthony and landed at Dover in the midst of September last.

JONSON UNTRUSSED.

Dekker hath answered Jonson in a play called *Satiro-mastix or the untrussing of the humourous poet*, which the Lord Chamberlain's men play at the Globe and the Children at Paul's, wherein they try Horace before King William Rufus and crown him with nettles, causing him to swear an oath that hereafter he shall not swear to hang himself if he think any man, woman or child can write better plays and rhymes than himself ; nor sit in a gallery when his comedies have entered their actions and there make vile and bad faces at every line to make gentlemen have an eye to him ; nor, when the play is ended, to exchange courtesies and compliments with the gallants in the Lord's rooms to make all the house rise up in arms and cry 'that's Horace, that's he that pens and purges humours,' nor when he sups in a tavern amongst his betters shall he dip his manners in too much sauce, nor at table fling epigrams, emblems or play speeches about him to keep out of the danger of the shot.

13th November. SEVENTEEN POOR PEOPLE CRUSHED TO DEATH.

This day the Lady Mary Ramsay, widow to Sir John Ramsay, sometime Lord Mayor of London, was buried in the parish church of Christchurch by Newgate Market. A charitable dole was given for her on the same day in the afternoon at Leadenhall where seventeen poor and weak people were among the sturdy beggars crushed and trodden to death.

15th November. CATHOLIC BOOKS.

Yet more books are put forth this autumn by the secular priests, as *A true relation of the faction begun at Wisbeach ;* and *Important considerations ;* also *A sparing discourse of our English Jesuits ;* also *A dialogue betwixt a secular priest and a lay gentleman.*

This book entitled *Important considerations* is written to move all true and sound Catholics who are not wholly jesuited to acknowledge without equivocations, ambiguities or shiftings, that the proceedings of her Majesty and of the State with them since the beginning of her Highness' reign have been both mild and merciful ; and is dedicated to all dearly affected of both sexes, of all three ages, in every degree, state, and condition of life, as well for the gifts of graces given them as Catholics, 'as also for the gifts of nature given you as you are *English*, which to your Prince and country makes you loyal, serviceable and faithful, and of both mindful.' Inveigheth very bitterly against Parsons and the Jesuits as the cause of all the conspiracies of late years directed against the Queen, and also by their acts and slanderous writings of the calamities and trouble that have happened to them; which are far less, saith the writer, 'than any Prince living in her Majesty's case and so provoked would have inflicted upon us. Why, my masters, what would you have her to do? being resolved as she is in matters of Religion, except she should willingly cast off the care, not only of her State and Kingdom, but of her life also and princely estimation?'

As for the *Sparing Discourse of our English Jesuits* (which also speaketh very bitterly against Parsons), note herein that of late years the Jesuits no longer live according to their first institution of their order, for of late years they take such a course as if religion were nothing else but a mere political device, conceived, framed and upheld only by human wisdom and sleights of wit, and they were the men that by Machiavel's rules are raised up to maintain it by equivocations, detractions, dissimulation, ambition, contention for superiority, stirring up strife, setting kingdoms against kingdoms, raising of rebellions, murthering of Princes, and by we know not how many stratagems of Satan, coming out of hell, and tending to confusion. There are few King's Courts in Europe where some of their masterships do not reside, of purpose to receive and give intelligence unto their General at Rome of all the occurrents in these parts of the world, which they despatch to and fro by secret ciphers, having either a Jesuit or someone altogether Jesuited who *propter bonum societatis* must without scruple deliver to them the secrets of their Sovereigns to their uttermost knowledge.

Another thing also is much misliked by the secular priests, for it breedeth hatred to Catholics and danger, and that is their equivocating, which you may term in plain English lying and cogging. For this amongst others is one of their rules: that a man framing to himself a true proposition, when he is asked a question, he may conceal thereof as much as he thinketh good. For example: One demanding of you whether, if the Pope should come in warlike manner to invade this land by force of arms, you would take his part or the Queen's; you framing this answer in your mind, 'we will take the Queen's part, if the Pope will command us so to do,' may by their doctrine give this answer lawfully, *viz.* 'we will take the Queen's part'—and conceal the rest; whereby he that asked the question is plainly deluded.

A Merry Jest concerning Parsons.

In the year 1597 Parsons went out of Spain to Rome. At his coming thither he was visited in his lodgings by two Cardinals which gave present speeches in the City that out of doubt Fr. Parsons should be made a Cardinal. At which time Parsons being counselled by the physicians to keep his stomach warm, sent to his brother for scarlet to make him a stomacher; who, as soon as he heard the name of scarlet, was so possessed with an opinion of his brother's advancement that he procured two merchants to carry in a wagon divers pieces of scarlet to his brother's lodging for the making of his cardinal's robes. Parsons, finding his brother's error, was in a great chafe, and thereupon in all haste dismissed the merchants with their scarlet at a back door as secretly as he could. Howbeit the thing was so notorious that it could not be concealed, and caused indeed very many to jest and laugh at him. One (a man little favoured by this good Father) went in merriment to his lodging to congratulate his new advancement. But when the Father knew the purpose of his coming: 'Yes,' quoth he, 'doth he know it? It will be then in England within this fortnight.'

16th November. The Parliament.

To-day Mr. Henry Doyley, a barrister of Lincoln's Inn, made a motion saying, 'Mr. Speaker, I think myself bound in conscience to certify you of an infamous libel that is newly printed and spread abroad since the beginning of this Parliament. Saving your presence, Mr. Speaker, it is called *An assembly of Fools.*' The House wondered much at this motion and there was great murmuring. At last the Speaker asked him where the book was and where he saw it. He answered in the hands of one Mr. Henry Davies his clerk, but the clerk's name he knew not.

So, after consultation, the Sergeant was sent for Mr. Davies and his man into the Hall. After a while they came up, and notice being given the man only was sent for into the House; and, after some questions put, the Sergeant was commanded to take him forth, and to command one of his men to go with him to Lincoln's Inn to fetch the book. The book being brought was well scanned by the Privy Councillors and found to be a mere toy, an old book entitled *The Second Part of Jack of Dover*, a thing both stale and foolish; for which Mr. Doyley is well laughed at and his credit much impeached in the opinion of the House.

There was discussion also on pluralities of benefices in a bill for redressing certain inconveniences in the statute of 21 Henry VIII, which was variously disputed. Dr. Crompton amongst many other speeches wished that pluralities of offices might be taken from the laity, and then pluralities of benefices from the spirituality. In former ages impropriations were given to the spirituality and no pluralities allowed; also spiritual men were bound by ecclesiastical canons of marriage, so that they might live with far less charge than now they do; but having taken from them first the impropriations, they cannot keep that hospitality which is required. And next marriage being tolerated, they living at great charge both of wife and children, one benefice of small cure sufficeth not.

Dr. James said, 'It hath been said that pluralities are the cause of bringing corruption into the Church; but that, under favour, I think the contrary, because corruption is commonly where poverty is; but if competent living be given the minister, I see no reason why just men should judge there to be corruption. Secondly, it was said that it would be a means of preaching the word; for that I answer that if hope of competent living be taken away, it will be a means to make the best wits refuse the study of divinity. And therefore an historian saith well that *sublatis praemiis corrumpunt artes*. Consider besides that in England there are above eight thousand eight hundred and odd parishes, six hundred of which do but afford competent living for a minister; what then shall become of the multitude of our learned men? They have no other preferments unless it be some deanery, prebendary or such like, which is no easy matter to do, they being so few, especially in this catching age.

To give the best scholar but as great a proportion as the meanest artisan, or to give all alike, there is no equality ; for *inaequalibus aequalia dare absurdum.* And this will breed poverty in the greatest learned, which is the mother of contempt, a thing both dangerous and odious unto divinity. This must needs enforce preachers to preach *placentia*, which is a thing abhorred even of God himself. A preacher, who is no ordinary person, ought to have an extraordinary reward.'

After other speeches an old doctor of the Civil Law spake, but because he was too long and spake too low, the House hawked and spat and kept up a great coil to cause him make an end. Whereupon Sir Francis Hastings stood up and said, ' My masters, I utter mislike this strange kind of course in the House. It is an ancient use that every man here should speak his conscience, and that both freely and with attention. Yea though he speak never so absurdly. I beseech you therefore that this may be amended, and this troubling of any man in his speech no more used.' Then he addressed himself to the bill ; which in the end by the more voices is ordered to be committed.

20th November. A Book against Astrology.

Mr. John Chamber, one of the Prebendaries of the Chapel of Windsor and Fellow of Eton College hath written a learned treatise against judicial astrology. Noteth it as a gross and heathenish superstition, condemned by the Church in all ages. ' Witchcraft,' quoth he, ' because it toucheth our hogs and cattle sometime, findeth now and then some hard entertainment, as it well deserveth ; but this damnable superstition, which dishonoureth God, polluteth heaven, deceiveth and seduceth men, goeth without touch or check ; the astrologer 'scaping while the witch is punished.' Moreover of late some even of the practizers have gone about to reform it, setting out reformed almanacks wherein they have not meddled at all with wind, weather, dismal days, purges and such like, but only with changes of the moon, festival days, and such like.

A Bill concerning Monopolies.

There was great debate in the Parliament to-day concerning monopolies, and the best course of remedying these abuses, seeing that they touch upon her Majesty's prerogative. Whereupon Mr. Francis Bacon saith, 'For the prerogative royal of the Prince, for my own part I ever allowed of it, and it is such as I hope shall never be discussed. The Queen as she is our Sovereign hath both an enlarging and restraining power; for by her prerogative she may first set at liberty things restrained by statute law or otherwise, and secondly by her prerogative she may restrain things which be at liberty. For the first, she may grant *non obstante* contrary to the penal laws, which truly to my conscience'—and here he struck himself on the breast—'are as hateful to the subject as monopolies. For the second if any man out of his own wit, industry or endeavour finds out anything beneficial for the commonwealth, or bring in any new invention which every subject may use; yet in regard of his pains and travail therein, her Majesty is pleased to grant him a privilege to use the same only by himself or his deputies for a certain time. This is one kind of monopoly. Sometimes there is a glut of things when they be in excessive quantity, as perhaps of corn, and her Majesty gives licence of transportation to one man; this is another kind of monopoly.' Then he went on to say that this complaint was no stranger to the House; all could not be done at once, nor was it possible since the last Parliament to repeal all. 'If her Majesty,' saith he, 'make a patent, or as we term it a monopoly, unto any of her servants, that must go, and we cry out of it; but if she grant it to a number of burgesses or a corporation, that must stand, and that forsooth is no monopoly. I say, and I say again, that we ought not to deal, to judge or meddle with her Majesty's prerogative.' He would therefore have every man careful in this business.

Next Dr. Bennet spake of the great grievance of the monopoly of salts. Fire and water are not more necessary. But for other monopolies, of cards—at which word Sir Walter Ralegh blushed—dice, starch and the like, they are hurtful because monopolies, but there is a great difference in them.

When certain others had spoken, Mr. Francis Moore asked to what purpose is it to do anything by Act of Parliament, when the Queen will undo the same by her prerogative. There is no act of hers that hath been or is more derogatory to her own Majesty, more odious to the subject, more dangerous to the Commonwealth than the granting these monopolies.

Mr. Martin asked if these bloodsuckers be still let alone to suck up the best and principallest commodities which the earth hath given us, what shall become of us from what the fruits of our own soil and the commodities of our own labour which with the sweat of our brows, even up to the knees in mire and dirt we have laboured for, shall be taken by warrant of supreme authority which the poor subject dare not gainsay.

Sir Walter Ralegh spake up for his own monopoly of tin, declaring that before his patent whether tin were of 17s. or 50s. a hundred, yet the poor workmen never had above 2s. a week, finding themselves. But since his patent, whoever will may work; and buy tin at what price soever, they have 4s. a week truly paid. Notwithstanding, if all others were repealed, he would give his consent freely to the cancelling of this. After which speech there was a great silence.

When others had given their opinion, the bill is ordered to be considered by a committee to-morrow at 2 of the clock in the afternoon.

A Too Curious Gentleman.

There is one Mr. William March, a gentleman, that in the time of the Earl of Essex's rebellious action came out in the sudden tumult to see what was meant. Thereby he was taken and put in prison. Upon examination he is now found not to be directly charged and therefore shall be released.

21st November. The Committee for Monopolies.

This afternoon the committee for monopolies or patents of privilege sat. First Sir Edward Hoby informed the House of the great abuse of his patentee for salt in his county, that between Michaelmas and St. Andrew's tide, where salt (before the patent) was sold for 16d. a bushel, it is now sold for 14s. or 15s. a bushel. But after the Lord President had understanding thereof he committed the patentee and caused it to be sold for 16d. as before. In Lyme there is brought every year above 3,000 wey of salt, and every wey of salt is since the patent enhanced to 20s.; and where the bushel was wont to be 8d. it is now 16d. Mr. Francis Bacon thought the bill very unfit and would have them proceed by petition. Then Mr. Solicitor

Fleming said that the Queen had charged Mr. Attorney and himself that speedy and special order might be taken for these patents. That was in the beginning of Hillary term last; and they all knew the danger of that time and what great affairs of importance happened to prevent these businesses; and since that time nothing could be done for want of leisure. To which Sir Robert Wroth answered, 'I would but note, Mr. Solicitor, that you were charged to take order in Hillary term last; why not before? There was time enough ever since the last Parliament. I speak it, and I speak it boldly, these patentees are worse than they ever were.' There had been divers patents granted since the last Parliament. These are now in being, *viz.*, the patents for currants, iron, powder, cards, ox-shin bones, train oil, transportation of leather, lists of cloth, ashes, aniseeds, vinegar, sea coals, steel, *aqua vitae*, brushes, pots, saltpetre, lead, accidences, oil, calamint stone, oil of blubber, fumathoes or dried pilchers in the smoke and divers others. Whereat Mr. Hackwell of Lincoln's Inn stood up and asked, 'Is not bread there?' 'Bread?' quoth one. 'Bread?' quoth another. 'This voice seems strange,' quoth another. 'No,' quoth Mr. Hackwell, 'if order be not taken for these, bread will be there before the next Parliament.' The further consideration of this matter is appointed for Monday next.

News from Ireland.

The Lord Deputy with the Lord President and the army began the besieging of Kinsale on the 16th of last month. There has been much fighting on both sides. A Castle called Rincurran, very necessary to the defence of the town, has been taken by our men, with 86 Spaniards. Tyrone is now reported to be coming with a great force to join with the Spaniards, and the Lord President is gone with two regiments of foot and 325 horse to hinder his passage. Hereby the remainder of the army without Kinsale is less in numbers than the Spaniards within until fresh reinforcement shall come from England; so that the siege is at a stand, for it must be no small army that can force the place in winter time when the very trenches are continually filled with water and the decay of our men very great.

23rd November. MONOPOLIES.

There was further discussion to-day on the reading of the Bill of Monopolies, and because there was no common agreement on the manner of proceeding in a matter touching the Queen's Prerogative it was referred to a committee of the House in the afternoon. But nothing is further concluded save that there shall be a fresh meeting to-morrow.

24th November. THE MONOPOLIES.

To-day there was some loud confusion in the House touching some private murmuring of monopolies, whereupon Mr. Secretary Cecil spake, saying, 'The duty I owe and the zeal to extinguish monopolies makes me to speak now, and to satisfy their opinions that think there shall be no redress of these monopolies. Order is attended with these two handmaids, Gravity and Zeal ; but Zeal with Discretion. I have been, though unworthy, a member of this House in six or seven Parliaments, yet never did I see the House in so great confusion. I believe there never was in any Parliament a more tender point handled than the liberty of the subject, that when any is discussing this point he should be cried or coughed down. This is more fit for a grammar school than a Court of Parliament. I have been a Councillor of State this twelve years, yet did I never know it subject to construction of levity and disorder. Much more ought we to be regardful in so great and grave an Assembly. Why, we have had speeches upon speeches without either order or discretion. One would have had us proceed by Bill and see if the Queen would have denied it. Another that the patents should be brought here before us and cancelled ; and this were bravely done ! Others would have us to proceed by way of petition, which course doubtless is best. But for the first, and especially the second, it is so ridiculous that I think we should have had as bad success as the Devil himself would have wished in so good a cause.' He would therefore have every man rest satisfied till the Committee had brought in their resolution.

'WHAT YOU WILL.'

The Children of Paul's have a play by Marston called *What You Will*, whereof the argument is that a merchant Albano being reported drowned at sea, many suitors come about Celia his wife who would choose a French knight by name Laverdure. One Francisco, a perfumer, is disguised as Albano. Albano himself returneth and Celia refuseth him, supposing him to be a fiddler, but at length Albano taking his wife aside, persuadeth her of the truth. Note in this play the character of Lampatho Doria, one that hath spent much time in study and hath learned nothing but uncertainty: Saith he,

> 'I was a scholar; seven useful springs
> Did I deflower in quotations
> Of cross'd opinions 'bout the soul of man.
> The more I learnt the more I learnt to doubt:
> Knowledge and wit, faith's foes, turn faith about.'

Before the music sounds for the first Act, there come upon the stage three who sit talking before the candles are lighted and then fall to discoursing of the author: 'Shall his bosom faint,' saith one:

> 'If drunken Censure belch out sour breath
> From Hatred's surfeit on his labour's front?
> Nay, say some half a dozen rancorous breasts
> Should plant themselves on purpose to discharge
> Imposthum'd malice on his latest scene,
> Shall his resolve be struck through with the blirt
> Of a goose-breath?'

25th November. THE QUEEN SENDS FOR MR. SPEAKER.

This afternoon in the Parliament, after silence was made and everyone marvelling why Mr. Speaker stood up, he declared that it had pleased her Majesty to command him to attend her yesterday in the afternoon, from whom he had received a message to deliver to the House. After yielding them hearty thanks for their care in those things that concern her state, kingdom and consequently themselves, and for their speedy resolution in making of so hasty and so free a subsidy, she said that partly by information of her Council, partly by divers petitions that had been delivered unto her both going to the chapel and also to walk abroad, she understood that certain patents which she had granted were grievous to her subjects; and that the substitutes of the patentees had used great oppressions. Hereat she expressed great indignation, and declared that order should be taken forthwith, and not *in futuro* ; and that some should be instantly repealed, some suspended, and none put into execution but such as should first have a trial according to the law for the good of the people. Against the abuses her wrath was so incensed that she said that she neither could nor would suffer such to escape with impunity. And this was the message he had been commanded to deliver.

After a little pause and silent talking one with another, Mr. Secretary Cecil stood and spoke to the same effect, declaring that there are no patents now of force which shall not be revoked ; 'for what patent soever is granted, there shall be left to the overthrow of the patent a liberty agreeable to the law. There is no patent if it be *malum in se*, but the Queen was ill advised in her grant. But all to the generality be unacceptable. I take it there is no patent whereof the execution hath not been injurious. Would that they had never been granted. I hope there shall never be more.'

To which all the House said, 'Amen.'

Then went he on to declare, 'The notice of this is now public and you will perhaps judge this to be a tale to serve the time. But I would have all men know this much, that it is no jesting with a Court of Parliament, neither dares any man (for my part I dare not) so mock and abuse all the states of this Kingdom in a matter of this consequence and importance. I say therefore there shall be a Proclamation general throughout the Realm to notify her Majesty's resolution in this behalf. And because you may eat your meat more savourly than you have done, every man shall have salt as good cheap as he can either buy it or make it, freely without danger of that patent.' And so on of the rest.

'Then,' said he, 'must I needs give you this for a future caution, that whatsoever is subject to public expectation cannot be good, while the Parliament matters are ordinary talk in the street. I have heard myself, being in my coach, these words spoken aloud, "God prosper those that further the overthrow of the monopolies, God send the prerogative touch not our liberties." I will not wrong any so much as to imagine he was of this assembly. Yet let me give you this note, that the time was never more apt to disorder and to make ill interpretation of good meaning. I think those persons would be glad that all sovereignty was converted in popularity. We being here are but the popular branch, and our liberty the liberty of the subject; and the world is apt to slander most especially the ministers of government.'

Then Mr. Francis Moore moved two considerations, the first that Mr. Speaker should go unto the Queen to yield her most humble and hearty thanks, and withal to show the joy of her subjects at this deliverance; the other, that where divers speeches had been made extravagantly in the House Mr. Speaker should not only satisfy her Majesty by way of apology therein, but also humbly crave pardon.

Mr. Wingfield said that he agreed with all his heart to the first part of this motion, but utterly misliked the other; for, quoth he, 'for us to accuse ourselves by excusing a fault with which we are not charged were a thing in my opinion inconvenient and unfitting the wisdom of this House.'

To the like effect also spake Mr. George Moore and Mr. Francis Bacon.

So it was put to the question and concluded that thanks should be returned by the Speaker, and some twelve to go with him, and intreaty made to the Privy Council to obtain liberty to be admitted.

26th November. THE QUEEN'S MESSAGE TO THE HOUSE.

In the Parliament Mr. Secretary declared that he had received from the Queen a short answer in these words, 'You can give me no more thanks for that which I have promised than I can and will give you thanks for that which you have already performed,' meaning the subsidies and fifteenths. Adding that she would not receive their thanks till by a more affected consummation she had completed that work, at which time she will be well pleased to receive their thanks and to return her best favours.

27th November. SIR FERDINANDO GORGES TO BE RELEASED.

Sir Ferdinando Gorges that was committed to the Gatehouse at the time of the rebellion is now to be enlarged out of prison and committed to the charge of his brother, Mr. Edward Gorges, who is required to enter into bond in the sum £1,000 for his forthcoming.

THE PARLIAMENT.

There was much debate in the Parliament concerning a matter of privilege, for that several of the servants of the members have been arrested contrary to the privilege of the House. Two that offended in this manner were to-day brought to the bar; the first whereof was one Mr. Christopher Kennell that served a *subpoena* on Sir Edmund Morgan. Mr. Kennell said in his defence that he was, though poor, a gentleman born and well known to the House; nor would he wilfully commit such an offence, having himself been sometime a member of the House. Further, he protested that if there be either honesty or Christianity in him, he knew not that Sir Edmund Morgan was a member of the House; for as soon as he heard it he went to Sir Edmund's house to make an atonement with him, and while he was so doing the Sergeant came in and there arrested him, which arrest he most willingly obeyed. Wherefore he asked the House to have consideration of his eighteen years service of her Majesty. The other, one William Mackerells, being a poor simple fellow, could say nothing for himself, but only that he knew not Mr. Pemerton (upon whom he had served a *subpoena*) to be a member of this House, no not for his life. So the Sergeant was commanded to remove them forth.

Then Sir Edmund Morgan said that the gentleman was of good desert, sort and carriage, and did not, so he thought, know him to be of this House. Wherefore, in regard of his person and good service done to her Majesty, he prayed that the offence might be as freely remitted by the House as by himself. Which speech was marvellous well liked by the House.

Mr. Pemerton, being asked what he could say whether Mackerells knew him, answered ay, and that his man had told him. Further that Mackerells was a very knave, and therefore he would not entreat favour, but let him have the justice of the House. Which speech was generally misliked as churlish.

So Mr. Kennell and Mackerells were brought again to the bar, and after their offences laid open by the Speaker, he said it pleased the House to have so favourable consideration of their offences that they should only have three days imprisonment in the custody of the Sergeant and pay him their fees.

Then Mr. Downald moved that her Majesty's gracious message might be written in the books of Records of the House; and secondly that the House would move her Majesty and be an earnest means of speed lest that which is now meant indeed may by protraction of time be altered or perhaps not so happily effected. To which Mr. Secretary answered that it is no matter of toy for a Prince to notify in public a matter of this weight. But yesterday the Queen gave order for a draft of a proclamation; what needed this new zeal?

Later Mr. Secretary declared that the Queen had been informed of the desire of the House that Mr. Speaker with some selected company should render the most humble and dutiful thanks of the whole House, and her gracious answer was that she did vouchsafe that Mr. Speaker with forty, fifty or a hundred of the House, such as should be appointed, should have access unto her on Monday next in the afternoon at the Court.

28th November. A PROCLAMATION CONCERNING PRIVILEGES.

There is a proclamation published declaring that upon inquiry it hath been found that many of the privileges and grants made by her Majesty have been notoriously abused, and that upon false suggestions there have been obtained of the Lords of the Privy Council divers letters of assistance for the execution of these grants. Her Majesty is now pleased of her mere grace favour to all her loving subjects and by her regal power and authority to publish and declare all grants, and every clause, article and sentence in the Letters Patent thereof to be void that concern salt, salt upon salt, vinegar, *aqua vitae* or *aqua composita* or any liquor containing the same, salting and packing of fish, train oil, blubbers or livers of fish, poldavies and mildernixé, pots, brushes, bottles and starch.

As for the other privileges, namely, new drapery, Irish yarn, calves' skins, pelts, cards, glasses, searching and sealing of leather, and steel and such like, in which also there hath been hurt and prejudice to her subjects, her Majesty doth likewise declare that if any hereafter shall find themselves aggrieved by any of the grants, he may take his ordinary remedy by the laws of the Realm. Moreover no letters of assistance shall hereafter be written nor put into execution for the assistance of these grants. Herein also as her Majesty doth greatly commend the duty and obedience that her loving subjects have yielded in conforming themselves to the said grants, so she doth notify by these presents that if any of her subjects shall seditiously or contemptuously presume to call in question the power or validity of her prerogative Royal annexed to her Imperial Crown in such cases, all such persons so offending shall receive severe punishment according to their demerits.

Further, the restraint that was put upon the sowing of woad is lifted, provided that by reason of its noisome savour no woad shall be sown within three miles of the City of London or near any of her Majesty's houses of access, nor so near to any other great city or town corporate.

30th November. The Queen receives the Members of the House.

At the rising of the House this forenoon the Speaker asked the House what it was their pleasures that he should deliver unto her Majesty ; and Sir Edward Hoby stood up and said it was best he should devise that himself, the whole House would refer it to him ; and all said, 'Ay, ay, ay.'

This afternoon about 3 of the clock some seven score of the House met at the Great Chamber before the Council Chamber in Whitehall. At length the Queen came into the Council Chamber, where sitting under the Cloth of State at the upper end, the Speaker with all the company came in, and after three low reverences made he spake to this effect.

'Most sacred and most gracious Sovereign, we your faithful, loyal and obedient subjects and Commons here present, vouchsafed of your especial goodness (to our unspeakable comfort) access to your sacred presence, do in all duty and humbleness come to present that which no words can express, most humble and thankful acknowledgment of your most gracious message, and most bounden and humble thanks for your Majesty's most abundant goodness extended and performed to us. We cannot say, most gracious Sovereign, we have called and been heard, we have complained and have been helped ; though in all duty and thankfulness we acknowledge your sacred ears are ever open and ever bowed down to hear us, and your blessed hands ever stretched out to relieve us. We acknowledge, sacred Sovereign, in all duty and thankfulness we acknowledge, that before we call, your preventing Grace and all deserving goodness doth watch over us for our good, more ready to give than we can desire, much less deserve.'

When he had spoken further and concluded his speech, after three low reverences made, he with the rest kneeled down, and the Queen began to answer herself:

'Mr. Speaker, We have heard your declaration and perceive your care of our State, by falling into the consideration of a grateful acknowledgment of such benefits as you have received; and that your coming is to present thanks unto us, which I accept with no less joy than your loves can have desire to offer such a present. I do assure you that there is no Prince that loveth his subjects better, or whose love can countervail our love. There is no jewel, be it of never so rich a prize, which I prefer before this jewel, I mean your love; for I do more esteem it than any treasure or riches, for that we know how to prize, but love and thanks I count inestimable. And though God hath raised me high, yet this I count the glory of my Crown, that I have reigned with your loves. This makes me that I do not so much rejoice that God hath made me to be a Queen, as to be Queen over so thankful a people. Therefore I have cause to wish nothing more than to content the subject, and that is a duty which I owe. Neither do I desire to live longer days than I may see your prosperity; and that's my only desire. And as I am that person that, yet under God, hath delivered you, so I trust, by the Almighty power of God, that I still shall be His instrument to preserve you from envy, peril, dishonour, shame, tyranny and oppression, partly by means of your intended help, which we take very acceptably, because it manifesteth the largeness of your loves and loyalties unto your Sovereign. Of myself I must say this: I never was any greedy, scraping grasper, nor a strait fast-holding Prince, nor yet a waster. My heart was never set on worldly goods, but only for my subjects' good. What you do bestow on me I will not hoard it up, but receive it to bestow on you again. Yea mine own properties I count yours to be expended for your good. Therefore render unto them from me I beseech you, Mr. Speaker, such thanks as you imagine my heart yieldeth, but my tongue cannot express.'

Now all this while they were kneeling. So her Majesty said, 'Mr. Speaker, I would wish you and the rest to stand up, for I shall yet trouble you with longer speech.' So they all stood up, and she continued with her speech. Then she went on to speak of her indignation at the oppressions that had been wrought under colour of these patents. She hoped that God would not lay them to her charge, for that Kings also are to yield an account of their actions before the great Judge.

Then said she, 'To be a King and wear a crown is more glorious to them that see it than it is pleasure to them that bear it. For myself, I was never so much enticed with the glorious name of a King, or royal authority of a Queen, as delighted that God hath made me this instrument to maintain His truth and glory, and to defend this Kingdom from peril, dishonour, tyranny and oppression. There will never Queen sit in my seat with more zeal to my country, care to my subjects, and that will sooner with willingness yield and venture her life for your good and safety than myself. And though you have had and may have many Princes more mighty and wise sitting in this seat, yet you never had or shall have any that will be more careful and loving. Should I ascribe anything to myself and my sexly weakness, I were not worthy to live then, and of all most unworthy of the mercies I have had from God, Who hath ever yet given me a heart which never yet feared foreign or home enemies. I speak it to give God the praise as a testimony before you, and not to attribute anything to myself. For I, O Lord, what am I, whom practices and perils past should not fear! O what can I do'—and these words she spake with great emphasis—'that I should speak for any glory! God forbid.

'This, Mr. Speaker, I pray you deliver unto the House, to whom heartily recommend me. And so I commit you all to your best fortunes and further counsels.'

Then turning to the Controller and the Secretary and the rest of the Council she said, 'I pray you that before these gentlemen depart into their countries, you bring them all to kiss my hand.'

1st December. A Bill against Swearing.

On the discussion of certain amendments in a Bill against usual and common swearing, one Mr. Glasscock said that swearing was a thing moral and touching the soul and therefore fitted to be spoken of in a pulpit than in a Parliament; and if a man regard not the denunciation of God upon swearers, a pain of 10s. as is set down in the Bill would not make him refrain. Besides the penalty is to be taken upon condition before a Justice of peace. A justice of peace, saith he, is a living creature, yet for half a dozen of chickens will dispense with a whole dozen of penal statutes. There be 'basket Justices' and 'idol Justices' and unless sacrifice be offered them they know you not. 'If a warrant come from the Lords of the Council,' quoth he, 'to levy a hundred men, he will levy two hundred, and what with chopping and choosing, he'll gain a hundred pounds by the bargain. Nay, if he be to send out a warrant upon a man's request to have any fetched in upon suspicion of felony or the like, he will write the warrant himself, and you must put 2s. in his pocket as his clerk's fee (when God knows he keeps but two or three hinds) for his maintenance. Why we have passed here Bills of swearing, going to church, good ale and drunkenness; this is as good to them as if you had given them a subsidy and two fifteenths.'

Jonson's Apology.

Jonson hath written an apologetical dialogue to his *Poetaster*, censuring the world that would prefer his enemies to himself:

> But that these base and beggarly conceipts
> Should carry it, by the multitude of voices,
> Against the most abstracted work, oppos'd
> To the stuff'd nostrils of the drunken rout!
> O this would make a learn'd and liberal soul
> To rive his stained quill up to the back,
> And damn his long-watch'd labours to the fire,—
> Things that were born when none but the still night
> And his dumb candle saw his pinching throes,—
> Were not his own free merits a more crown
> Unto his travails than their reeling claps.

Declareth also that since the comic muse hath proved so

ominous he will try if tragedy have a more kind aspect. This dialogue, after the first pronouncing upon the stage, is now forbidden by authority.

2nd December. THE PARLIAMENT.

To-day the Bill for the more diligent resort to Church was read the second time, unto which divers spoke in the House, among them Mr. Carew Ralegh, who said that the Sabbath was ordained for four causes: to meditate upon the omnipotency of God, to assemble us to give thanks, that we might be the better enabled to follow our own affairs, and that we might hallow the day and sanctify the same. Then spake he of divers examples, notably of the year 1583, when the house of Paris Garden by God's judgment fell down as they were at the bear-baiting the 23rd of January on a Sunday, and four hundred persons were sorely crushed, yet by God's mercy only eight slain outright. He would that this brutish exercise should be used on some other day and not upon the Sunday, and doubted not but that great reformation will come if this Bill pass. Sir George Moore said that without going to church, doing Christian duties, we cannot be religious, and by religion we learn both our duty to God and to the Queen; wherefore the Bill being agreeable with the law of God and the rule of policy should be committed. Mr. Bond declared that he wished the Sabbath sanctified according to the precise rules of God's commandment, but with St. Augustine, *non iubendo sed docendo, magis monendo quam minando*. He liked not that power should be given to the justices of peace, for who almost are not grieved at the luxuriant authority of justices of peace. By this statute there is a constraint to come to divine service, and for neglect all must pay. He left to the House whether it stand with policy, when four subsidies and eight fifteenths be now granted, to bring the poorer sort into greater fear by these and such like laws.

Mr. Controller said that he was sorry after forty-three years under her Majesty's happy government they should now dispute this Bill; the old statute gave the penalty, this only the means of enforcing it. He much marvelled that men would dare accuse justices of peace, ministers to her Majesty without whom the commonwealth cannot be. If this boldness go on, they will accuse judges, and lastly the seat of justice itself. That all justices should be thus generally taxed, this is mere barbarism indeed; when her Majesty shall have understanding thereof, it will be no content unto her, and a scandal to them all.

Hereupon Mr. Glasscock declared that he spake only of the inferior sort of justices commonly called 'basket justices.'

Sir Robert Wroth said, 'I think the office of justice of peace is too good a calling for him that exclaims against it, and I think he'll ne'er have the honour to have it. It were good that they were named and that he told who they were; otherwise honest men will be loath to serve the Queen, when they shall be slandered without proof. Therefore I would he might answer it at the Bar.'

And all said, 'No, no.'

4th December. THE EARL OF NORTHUMBERLAND.

It is observed in Court that the Lord Cobham, Sir Walter Ralegh and my Lord of Northumberland (whose enemies call them the Diabolical Triplicity) meet every day at Durham House about some consultation; which moveth the best wits of the town to watch what shall ensue thence. The Earl of Northumberland now professeth to be of that party which is against the King of Scots' title to the Crown, insomuch that he told his wife that he had rather the King of Scots were buried than crowned, and that both he and all his friends would end their lives before her brother's great god should reign in his element. The Lady replied that rather than any other than King James should ever reign in this place she would rather eat their hearts in salt though she were brought to the gallows instantly. My Lord replied that Mr. Secretary had too much wit ever to live under a man that had foreign stock, having been so fortunate under a woman that was tractable and to be counselled. The Lady told him that he need not long triumph upon her poor brother's mishap, for if he kept in this mind she could expect no better end of him than the same or a worse destiny. Thus being newly reconciled, even to bedding together, which hath not been these two years, they parted again in passion. But after ten days he came again, not in affection, but desiring only an heir-male to prevent the brothers that are next, whom he hates damnably, and protesteth to some of his friends that next to his wife he abhorreth them above any.

After this he complained to Mr. Secretary of his wife's Scottish heart, and was desirous that the Queen should hear as much, but Sir Robert wished him to forbear because the world would abhor him for it; for, said Mr. Secretary, the case was as if a man could not hurt his enemy without hurting himself a great deal more, and therefore advised him to be circumspect in his own passion. The Earl replied that he had much ado to love his own daughters because they were of that generation. Mr. Secretary answered that they might prove like their father.

My Lord's enemies say also that this reconcilement with his wife was to fish out the secrets of the Essex faction, and to see which way they incline; whereupon he reporteth to the Lord Cobham and Sir Walter that all Essexians be Scottish.

6th December. THE DUKE OF BIRON'S VISIT.

Certain of the upholsterers and saddlers, that from whom the Lord Mayor took up saddles and stuff for the use of Duke of Biron when he was here, complain that they can get no satisfaction for their loss. They petitioned the Lords of the Council, who recommended them to the Lord Mayor, but remaining unsatisfied therein the Council again command them to the Lord Mayor, for it is not in reason that they should sustain this damage and loss.

9th December. THE PARLIAMENT.

This day it was disputed whether the Statute of Tillage should be continued; upon which Mr. Francis Bacon said that it stands not with the policy of the State that the wealth of the Kingdom should be ingrossed into a few graziers' hands. Sir Walter Ralegh was for its repeal; for he said that so many poor men are not able to find seed to sow so much as they are bound to plough, which they must do or incur the penalty of the law. Besides all nations now abound with corn; France offered the Queen to serve Ireland with corn for 16s. a quarter, which is but 2s. the bushel; if we should sell it so here the ploughman would be beggared. Wherefore he thought it best to set it at liberty, and leave every man free, which is the desire of a true Englishman. Mr. Secretary Cecil said, 'I do not dwell in the country, I am not acquainted with the plough: but I think that whosoever doth not maintain the plough destroys this Kingdom.' When warrants go from the Council for levying of men in the counties, and the certificates be returned, the greatest part of them are ploughmen. And excepting Sir Thomas More's *Utopia* or some such feigned commonwealth, you shall never find but that the ploughman is chiefly provided for. When it was put to the question, most said, 'Ay, ay, ay.'

10th December. WATSON'S QUODLIBET.

Watson, the secular priest, hath written a long book against the Jesuits entitled *A decacordon of ten Quodlibetical Questions concerning religion and the State*, wherein the author framing himself a Quidlibet to every Quodlibet decides a hundred cross interrogatory doubts about the general contentions betwixt the seminary priests and Jesuits at this present. Setteth down general and particular articles with the answer thereto, containing much matter and scandal concerning the Jesuits and their sundry practices.

12th December. DISORDERS IN THE HOUSE.

This afternoon the Bill for the more diligent coming to church on Sunday was read the third time; whereupon great discussion followed. After divers arguments it was put to the question whether the Bill be ingrossed, and the greater number could not be discerned. Whereupon Sir Robert Wroth showed that he had a proviso ready, which was that if any man came eight times a year to his Church and said the usual Divine Service twice every Sunday and holy day in his house with his whole family, that should be sufficient dispensation. This was utterly misliked; yet divers which were desirous to overthrow the Bill went forth with the proviso because they would have it joined to overthrow it. Whereupon the House was divided, and upon division, the 'ay, ay, ay' were 126, the 'no's' were 85. So the proviso passed.

Then, after a speech of Sir Walter Ralegh against it, the Bill was put to the question thrice together, and because the truth could not be discerned, the House was again divided; and the 'ay, ay, ay' went forth and were 105 and the 'no's' within

106. So they got it by one voice. Sir Edward Hoby, who was of the 'ay, ay, ay,' said that the Speaker was a member and therefore he hath a voice; but Sir Walter Ralegh answered, and was confirmed by the Speaker himself, that he was foreclosed of his voice by taking that place which they had pleased to impose upon him, and that he was to be indifferent to both parties, and withal showed that by order of the House the Bill was lost.

Then Mr. Bowyer declared that there had been foul and great abuse offered in this matter. A gentleman that would willingly go forth according to his conscience was pulled back; and he named him, Mr. Dale of the Middle Temple. Whereat Sir Walter Ralegh said, 'Why, if it please you, it is a small matter to pull one by the sleeve, for so I have done myself oftentimes.' And great loud speech and stir there was in the House.

When silence had been made Mr. Controller declared that it was a most intolerable disorder, for every man should go according to his conscience and not by compulsion; as for Sir Walter Ralegh he might be ashamed of it. And he was for having Mr. Dale to answer it at the bar.

Mr. Secretary Cecil said that the offence was great and punishable, 'and this I wish may be inflicted on him, that he whose voice may be drawn either forwards or backwards by the sleeve like a dog on a string may be no more of this House'; but he would not have him called to the bar. For the matter itself, the 'no's' were 106, and the 'ay, ay, ay' 105, the Speaker had no voice; and though he was sorry to say it, yet must he needs confess, lost it was, and farewell it.

There was another gentleman, a 'no' pulled out by two as well as the other kept in, and therefore it had happened even howsoever.

16th December. A FUNERAL SERMON PUBLISHED.

Some six months ago, about Whitsuntide, there died a certain Mistress Katharine Bettergh, the wife of a gentleman of Lancaster, one noted for her piety and godliness in the midst of papists by whose acts her husband suffered much damage, for they would slay his horses and cattle. A short while before she died, her sickness being in the manner of a hot burning ague which made her according to the nature of such diseases to talk somewhat wildly, she began to feel great weakness of faith; whereupon the papists of those parts spread it abroad as a sign that this was God's judgment upon the wicked. Nevertheless before her end, by the assistance of certain godly preachers, she was restored to her faith and died very peaceful. There is printing the two sermons delivered at her death and burial, entitled *Death's advantage little regarded* and *The soul's solace against sorrow*, together with a short account of her godly life.

19th December. THE PARLIAMENT DISSOLVED.

This afternoon was the Parliament dissolved, the Queen herself being present, with divers of the Lords spiritual and temporal in their parliament robes. The Speaker, with the members of the Lower House, being placed at the bar at the lower end of the Upper House, after the accustomed manner, spake to her Majesty in the name of the Commons, returning thanks for her pardon and with a prayer that she would accept the testimonies of their loves freely offered her, four entire subsidies and eight fifteenths and tenths; in speaking thereof he mistook and said 'four entire fifteenths and eight subsidies,' but he was remembered by some of the Council that stood near about him.

To which the Lord Keeper, in the name of the Queen, made answer. Touching their proceedings in the matter of her prerogative, she is persuaded subjects never did more dutifully, and that she understood they did but *obiter* touch her prerogative and not otherwise but by humble petition; and therefore that thanks a Prince may give to her subjects she willingly yielded; but she now well perceived that private respects are masqued under public pretence. Then he declared her thanks for their subsidy, speedily and freely given. He concluded with an admonition to justices of the peace that they would not deserve the epithets of prolling justices, justices of quarrels, who counted champetrie good chevesance, sinning justices who do such and consume the wealth and good of the Commonwealth; and also against those who lie, if not all the year, yet at least three-quarters in this City of London.

After these speeches were ended, the titles of all the Acts

were read in their due order, and her Majesty gave her royal assent to nineteen public Acts and ten private. Then was the Parliament dissolved by the Lord Keeper in these words: *Dominus Custos magni Sigilli ex mandato Dominae Reginae dissoluit praesens Parliamentum.*

The parliament being thus dissolved and each one ready to depart without any further expectation, the Queen raised herself out of her royal seat and made a short pithy speech. First she thanked God for her miraculous preservation from the many traitorous practices of miscreant subjects who designed thereto by foreign enemies have sought to take away her life. Next, quoth she, 'you shall understand that touching our civil government sithence the beginning of our reign, in all causes we have undertaken to hear and determine, our heart hath been as a plain table ready to receive any impression; so most willing to hear the allegations of each party, yet ever more inclining our sentence to the sincerity of proof and soundness of reason.'

Then spake she of the many petitions of the Low Countries and the actions of the late King of Spain therein, as also the young King, who will begin war upon us without cause nor drawn upon us by any provocation of ours, but a rash enterprise proceeding of malice or vainglory; whereby, she said, 'as we nothing fear, so let no man doubt but that the justice and omnipotence of God is such that in every war He giveth victory to the innocent and fighteth evermore for those that sincerely serve Him; upon which confidence we may repose ourselves in courage and alacrity, whatsoever be practized against us.

'Concerning our affection to our people, it is our happiest felicity and most inward joy that no Prince ever governed a more faithful, valiant, and loving people; whose peace and prosperity we evermore prefer before all temporal blessings; and be you well assured whether we make peace or war the good of our people shall be evermore preferred therein. We never attempted anything to damage or dishonour our people, and though we may not attribute merits to our own wit in choosing out the safe harbour for us all to anchor at, yet the finger of God, directing the action of all Princes that sincerely serve Him, and our long lived experience, though in a mean wit, shall make us to discern and embrace that which shall tend to the prosperity of our people; to whom I wish that they that wish them best may never wish in vain.'

20th December. A NOTE OF THE CHIEF STATUTES ENACTED IN THE LATE PARLIAMENT.

An Act for the relief of the poor similar to that which was enacted in the last Parliament.

An Act for the necessary relief of soldiers and mariners, similar to that which was enacted in the last Parliament, and in the Parliament of 1593.

An Act to redress the misemployment of lands, goods and stocks of money heretofore given to charitable uses.

An Act to prevent perjury and subornation of perjury and unnecessary expenses in suits of law, because that in many places where actions, plaints and suits are to be tried the defendants are wont, when the suits come to be tried, to sue to remove the cause to one of her Majesty's courts at Westminster, which is done for no other purpose but to put the parties plaintiff to great charges and expenses, and to give the defendants longer time to furnish themselves with some false witness to impugn the proofs openly made by the plaintiff; which is a great cause of perjury and of great expenses to plaintiffs.

An Act to avoid trifling and frivolous suits in law in her Majesty's Courts at Westminster, because of the infinite number of small and trifling suits commenced or prosecuted at Westminster which ought to be determined in inferior courts in the county.

An Act to avoid and prevent divers misdemeanours in idle and lewd persons because that the cutting and taking away of growing corn, robbing of orchards and gardens, digging up of fruit trees, breaking of hedges, pales and fences, cutting and spoiling of woods and underwoods and such like offences are now more commonly committed by lewd and mean persons than in former times; which offences are great causes of the maintaining of idleness, and besides the offenders are not able for the most part to make recompense or satisfaction.

An Act against fraudulent administration of intestate goods, to prevent that abuse whereby such persons as have the administration of the goods of others dying intestate procure the administration to be granted to some stranger of mean estate and not of kin to the intestate from whom they obtain deeds of gift by letters of attorney, whereby they obtain the state of the intestate into their own hands, and yet stand not subject to pay any debts owing by the intestate, and the creditors cannot obtain satisfaction for his lack of ability to satisfy of his own goods.

An Act for the true making and working of woollen cloths, against such abuses as straining, stretching, want of weight, flocks, sollace, chalk, flour, deceitful things, subtle sleights and untruths, so as the same cloths being put in water are found to shrink, rewey, pursy, squally, cockling, vandy, light and notably faulty, to the great dislike of foreign Princes and to the hindrance and loss of the buyer and wearer.

An Act for the recovering of many hundred thousand acres of marshes and other grounds within the Isle of Ely, and the counties of Cambridge, Huntingdon, Northampton, Lincoln, Norfolk, Suffolk, Sussex, Essex, Kent and the County Palatine of Durham.

An Act concerning matters of assurance used among merchants. It hath been an usage time out of mind amongst merchants when they make any great adventure (especially into remote parts) to give some consideration of money to other persons, which are commonly of no small number, to have from them an assurance of their goods, merchandises, ships and things adventured at such rates as both parties can agree upon, which dealing is commonly called a 'policy of assurance'; whereby it cometh to pass upon the loss or perishing of any ship there followeth not the undoing of any one man but the loss lighteth rather easily upon many than heavily upon few, and rather upon them that do not adventure than those that do adventure, whereby all merchants, specially the younger sort, are allured to venture more willingly. Heretofore such assurances have used to stand so justly and precisely upon their credits as few or no controversies have arisen, and these speedily decided by certain grave and discreet merchants appointed by the Lord Mayor of London. But of late divers persons have withdrawn themselves from that course, have sought to draw the parties assured to seek their monies of every several assurer by suits commenced in her Majesty's Courts to their great charges and delays. There is by this Act now appointed a standing Commission for such suits.

An Act for the more peaceable government of the parts of Cumberland, Northumberland, Westmoreland and the Bishopric of Durham, because that of late years there hath been in these counties many incursions, roads, robberies and burning and spoiling of towns, villages and houses, that divers subjects have been enforced to pay a certain rate of money, corn or cattle or other consideration, commonly there called by the name of 'black mail,' to sundry, being men of name, who are commonly great robbers and spoil takers, to be by them protected from the danger of such as do usually rob and steal in those parts, to the great impoverishing of the Queen's subjects, and her service and revenues great diminished. It is enacted that those who levy or pay 'black mail' shall be reputed felons and suffer pain of death without any benefit of clergy, sanctuary or objuration.

21st December. THE GREAT DANGER AT OSTEND.

The garrison of Ostend is now in great extremities. Of the 7,000 men that have been sent there not about 800 or 900 are able and fit to defend the works, so greatly are they consumed by their continual service and the assaults of the enemy. Moreover in this cold and tempestuous weather no succour of men or materials hath reached them for several weeks past. Of workmen there is even greater need, and the Archduke, who is present in person before the town, now hasteneth preparations for the assault.

JONSON'S 'POETASTER.'

Jonson hath published that comical satire of *Poetaster*, adding thereto the apologetical dialogue that was only once spoken upon the stage, wherein he defends himself against those who say that he taxed the law and lawyers, captains, and the players by their names, declaring that he chose Augustus Caesar's times, when wit and art were at their height in Rome, to show that Virgil, Horace, and the rest of those master spirits did not want detractors nor practisers against them.

22nd December. NO NEWS FROM IRELAND.

The Council are much troubled at the long silence from Ireland both in respect of the public proceedings and of the Lord Deputy himself, lest any disaster may have ensued, for no direct knowledge of any thing hath been received from the Lord Deputy since the coming over of Sir Thomas Savage, and that was by way of Dublin and five weeks past.

23rd December. A FURTHER SUPPLY FOR IRELAND.

A further supply of 2,000 men is now required for Ireland, to be armed and apparelled as those sent out this last autumn.

OSTEND.

From Ostend it is reported that the Spaniards have made an assault upon the palisadoes in the works outside the town and set them on fire, insomuch that for three days they have burnt continually. There are now too few men to man the outward defences.

24th December. AN EARTHQUAKE.

There hath been thunder and lightning oftentimes of late, and at noon to-day an earthquake in London.

THE FLEET RECALLED FROM IRELAND.

Sir Richard Leveson and the greater part of the Queen's ships serving in Ireland are to be recalled speedily to Plymouth for some special service, which, 'tis said, shall be to the coast of Spain to prevent any new supply thence for Ireland.

26th December. SPANISH PROVISIONS DESTROYED.

From Ireland comes news that Sir Richard Leveson hath wrought great destruction upon the Spanish ships in Castlehaven, sinking the admiral and three others and driving the vice-admiral ashore, where she lies bulged and half sunk. In these ships there was much provision of bread, wheat, wine, beef, poor Johns, sardines, pease, pork and vinegar, and not above five tons saved to the enemy. It is reported also that the rebel O'Donnell, being 6 miles from Holy Cross in Tipperary and intending to go to the aid of Tyrone, was prevented from making a passage by Cashel because of the Lord President's forces; the only other way lay over the mountains of Slewphelim, which in summer is easy to pass, but now by reason of the great rains impassable for horse or baggage. But there suddenly happened a great frost, the like whereof in that realm hath seldom been seen. The enemy, perceiving so good an opportunity offered to pass the mountains, took advantage of the time and rising in the night passed over the same; and marching by night and day without rest they went no less than 32 Irish miles, which is the greatest march that hath ever been heard of at this time of the year. O'Donnell is now joined with Tyrone before Kinsale.

29th December. SIR FRANCIS COSENETH THE ARCHDUKE.

New succours of men and munition and material are now entered into Ostend, and that danger for the time overpast by means of a stratagem wrought by the Lord General upon the Archduke. Upon the 20th of this month, Sir Francis sent Captain Ogle and Captain Fairfax over to the enemy, with faith given for their safe return, who were received by the Archduke, a truce and general cessation of all hostility on both sides being promised during the time of their treaty for land matters, but no further; whereby the abandoned works remained neutral but not lawfully to be possessed by them. The Archduke received them and demanded whether they had instruction to treat, and whether any fraud was intended. They replied that they were ignorant of any and were come as hostages, so that his Highness might be pleased to send to his Lordship about the proposed business. Accordingly there were sent Matthew Serano, Governor of Sluys, and one Don Augustiors, who came into the town. Hereupon Sir Francis, projecting still the means to gain time, when he perceived the Spaniards to have been attended over the water with about 60 horse, caused an alarm to be taken and charged them with breach of promise in the manner of their arming, and would neither speak with them nor see them, but gave peremptory command that they should be sent back to the place where they came over. By this time the sea being grown denied them passage. Thereupon back again into the town they came, when Sir Francis gave order that they should be sent away by the East. Don Serano being somewhat wearied desired to stay in the town all night, but that would not be granted ; and so through the town they were convoyed, up to the knees in dirt and mire, so that when they reached the quarter of the Count de Bucquoy they were thoroughly bedirtied, having made a compass of near 12 miles around the drowned lands and unable to reach the Archduke's quarter before next day at noon.

Next day they were commanded to try his Lordship once more and this time were admitted to come. The Serjeant Major of the town demanded which way he should bring them in, and Sir Francis willed him to guide them where they might come soft enough, for fear of embossing their feet on the hard stones, saying that besides their dirty walk they should come to as cold a bargain as ever they met withal in their lives. So they came to Sir Francis and said that now they hoped his Lordship and they should agree. He answers, 'The agreement is easily made if his Highness will raise his siege, and suffer us, as his poor neighbours, to live by him in peace.' Then to cut off further progression in this discourse, he tells them after their wearisome journey it is more fitting to entertain them with mean refreshing than with serious expostulation, and thereupon entreats them to supper, where they were entertained to fish, eggs and such junkets besides as a town so long besieged could afford, taking out in claret wine what they lacked in meat ; Serano drinking for his share above fifty-two glasses of wine, besides beer, answering every man in the cup, and yet gave no manner of appearance of yielding any way to distemper. During their sitting at supper many jests were bandied with good dexterity on both sides. Amongst others, Sir Francis saying that his Highness desired all and the States would willingly part with nothing, the Spaniard replied that Archduke demanded but his own. To that his Lordship told him that he had never studied the laws to judge of men's titles, but that in England we do commonly hold possession 11 points of the 12.

After supper the Spaniards, wearied with their late miry journeys, were by his Lordship conducted to their lodging where they rested till morning. But whilst they slept three ships of war laden with 6 companies of Zealand soldiers arrived in the road before the town. Hereupon betimes in the morning the Spaniards sent in post for Sir Francis's resolution, which was to this effect: that it was time that some wants through the long contrariety of the wind and other accidents had overtaken him, and thereby he enforced to make use of his wit, but now since the States had been mindful of him and his necessity supplied, he could not in honour proceed to traffic with them any further; with other words to the like effect.

The Spaniard, having the fair hopes of his fruitful harvest thus quite blasted with this nipping answer, suppressed his almost choking discontent in the most temperate manner he could, and with this cold breakfast (instead of his Christmas pie) he forthwith departed, leaving his companion behind him till our Captains should be returned home.

All the while of the parley the works in the old town were advanced with all diligence and secrecy possible, and made defensible; between noon and 2 of the clock the new forces were landed.

30th December. THE CHRISTMAS PLAY AT CAMBRIDGE.

The third part of the Play of *Parnassus* was played at St. John's College in Cambridge this Christmas, and the further misfortunes of the poor scholars shown. In one scene Master Danter the printer is shown, and in another Burbage and Kemp brought upon the stage to give them a lesson in playing, so that they have cause to lament that in this age scholars are prized so low and players so high:

> But is't not strange these mimic apes should prize
> Unhappy scholars at a hireling rate?
> Vile world that lifts them up to high degree,
> And treads us down in grovelling misery.
> England affords these glorious vagabonds,
> That carried erst their fardels on their backs,
> Coursers to ride on through the gazing streets,
> Sooping it in their glaring satin suits,
> And pages to attend their masterships:
> With mouthing words that better wits have fram'd
> They purchase lands, and now esquires are nam'd.

31*st December*. MORE MEN NEEDED.

A further supply of 2,000 men is now to be levied, making 4,000 in all, whereof 2,000 are to be ready to embark by the 10th January, and the remainder by the 20th.

THE ABUSE OF PLAYHOUSES.

Of late the Lord Mayor and aldermen complained again to the Council of the great abuse and disorder by reason of the multitude of playhouses, and the inordinate resort of idle people daily unto public stage plays. To which their Lordships reply that it is vain for them to take knowledge of great abuses and disorders, and to give order for redress if their directions find no better execution and observation, the fault whereof is to be imputed to the Lord Mayor and the Justices of Middlesex and Surrey, utterly neglecting that order which was made about a year and a half since.

NEW PLAYS.

The Lord Admiral's men have played these new plays following since Midsummer last: *Cardinal Wolsey* (by Chettle); *The Honourable Life of the humourous Earl of Gloucester with his Conquest of Portugal*; *Friar Rush and the Proud Woman of Antwerp* (by Day and Haughton); *Tom Dough* (by Day and Haughton); *The Six Clothiers* (by Hathway, Haughton and Smith).

'Love's Martyr.'

Love's Martyr or Rosaline's Complaint, by Robert Chester, allegorically shadowing the truth of love in the constant fate of the Phoenix and Turtle, with sundry other poems, dedicated to Sir John Salusbury. To these are added divers poetical exercises upon the phoenix and turtle by Shakespeare, Marston, Jonson, and others not named.

An Answer to Darrell.

Darrell's book called *The Doctrine of the possession and dispossession of demoniacs out of the word of God*, is now answered by Mr. Deacon and Mr. Walker in three new dialogues entitled *A Summary answer to all the material points in Mr. Darrell his books.*

'Affaniae.'

A little book of epigrams in Latin by Mr. Charles Fitzgeffrey called *Affaniae*, of which a number be written to poets of our days; together with *Cenotaphia*, being commemoration of the dead.

A Book of Essays.

A book by Mr. Robert Johnson entitled *Essays, or rather imperfect offers*, upon fifteen heads, being Greatness of mind, Wit, Education, Exercise, Learning, Experience, Histories, the Art Military, Travel, Affability, Jests, Discretion, Speech, Wisdom, Reputation, Liberality. Of Histories it is noted: 'History is the mixture of profit and delight, the seasoning of more serious studies, the reporter of cases adjudged by event, the interlude of our haps, the image of our present fortune, the compendiary director of our affairs, by which valour is quickened, judgment ripened, and resolution entertained. Here are the reasons why some estates live quietly, others turmoiled in continual disturbances, some flourish by the delights of peace, others by continuing war, some spend lavishly without profit, others sparingly with honour. Here we may see ruins without fear, dangerous wars without peril, the customs of all nations without expense.

'By this observation of noting causes and effects, counsels and successes, likeness between nature and nature, action and action, fortune and fortune, is obtained that wisdom, which teacheth us to deliberate with ripeness of judgment, to persevere in things deliberated, to execute with readiness, to temporise with inconveniences, to abide adversity, to moderate prosperity, to know the Scriptures, but in such sort that neither superstition make us vainly fearful, nor neglect cause us to be contemptuously presuming. And by opening to us the plots which gave life to all actions, it teacheth more than twenty men living successively can learn by practice, as the General by seeing the counsels which govern the event must necessarily profit more than the soldier, who not able to search into the causes, perceiveth only the naked events.'

'THE TRAVELLER'S BREVIAT.'

The Traveller's breviat, being an historical description of the most famous kingdoms in the world, relating their situations, manners, customs, civil government, and other memorable matters, translated into English by Mr. Robert Johnson.

MR. WEEVER'S 'MIRROR OF MARTYRS.'

Mr. John Weever hath now printed a poem of Sir John Oldcastle that was made ready for the print two years ago concerning the true Oldcastle, entitled *The Mirror of Martyrs, or the life and death of that thrice valiant Captain and most godly martyr, Sir John Oldcastle, Knight, Lord Cobham*, wherein the martyr speaketh in his own person. Endeth :

For Becket's sake erected was a tomb,
Like our Egyptian high pyramides,
Millions of barefoot pilgrims yearly come
With tapers burning to his holiness,
  Till Henry th'Eight by Cromwell's good procurement,
  Cast down this mock-ape toy, this vain allurement.

The glorious beauty of this brightest shrine,
The treasury of ever-springing gold :

Becket is set : now doth Oldcastle shine :
Him for a Saint within your Kalends hold.
  Thus fools admire what wisest men despiseth
  Thus fond affects do fall, when virtue riseth.

Wit, spend thy vigour, poets, wits' quintessence,
Hermes make great the world's eyes with tears ;
Actors make sighs a burden for each sentence,
That he may sob which reads, he swound which hears.
  Meantime, till life in death you do renew,
  Wits, poets, Hermes, actors, all adieu.

1602

1st January. A SAYING OF MARSTON.

Mr. John Marston these holidays danced with Alderman More's wife's daughter, a Spaniard born, when he fell into a strange commendation of her wit and beauty. When he had done, she thought to pay him home, and told him she thought he was a poet. ''Tis true,' said he, 'for poets fain and lie, and so did I when I commended your beauty, for you are exceeding foul.'

2nd January. THE GREAT LOSSES AT KINSALE.

News from Ireland showeth that the Irish rebels were within two miles of the Lord Deputy's army and have cut him off from Cork, keeping them away from their victuals and the vivandiers that follow the army. The state of the army is very weak. The 6,000 men lately come from England are consumed, so that 10 or 12 able men in a company is the ordinary proportion, and 30 or 40 sick, unable to do any duty is seen in every company; and of these few recover. The Spaniards on their parts endure infinite miseries, grown weak and faint with their spare diet, being no other than water and rusk; dogs, cats and garrons is a feast when they can get it.

3rd January. A DESPERATE ATTEMPT ON OSTEND.

The Archduke being deluded by the late parley and very angry with the chiefs of his council of war that diverted him from giving the assault upon that day when the parley was called for, took resolution to revenge himself on 28th December. Till that day the enemy had shot upon the town 163,200 cannon shot, scarce leaving a whole house standing, but now upon 28th December very early in the morning he began with 18 pieces of cannon and half cannon carrying bullets of 40 and 48 lbs. apiece, and that day shot above 2,200 cannot shot. During this furious battery the enemy all the day made great preparations to assault during the night, bringing down scaling ladders, great store of ammunition, hand-grenados and other material of war.

Towards evening he drew down his army and ordered that the Count Farneze, an Italian, should first give on with 2,000 Italian and Spaniards upon the sandhills, the breach and the curtain of the old town, the Governor of Dixmude with 2,000 upon the Porkespy and Helmont; with 500 upon the west ravelin, and with other in all 8,000 men to assault the west side, and the Count of Bucquoy to assault the east side, the east ravelin and the new haven.

Sir Francis Vere knowing the enemies' attempt that he would assault at low water slept not, but was exceeding careful and vigilant, and because there were no spare parts, beams and palisadoes in the magazine, caused divers houses that were shot to be pulled down and caused the carpenters to make palisadoes and stockadoes of them, and at high water he caused to be shut the west sluices and engrossed as much water as he could into the old and new town. Then he disposed his weak forces as best he could for the defence, for in all he could not muster above 1,200 to resist an army of 10,000 men. The ordnance he planted upon the bulwark called Helmont and upon the casement of the west bulwark, and here he made choice of the best cannoneers in the town, amongst the rest an Englishman called Francis the Gurmer, an excellent cannoneer; and because they should be sure to take their mark right upon their cog, before it grew dark he commanded them to let fly two or three cannon bullets upon the strand and towards the new haven to see for a trial where those bullets fell, that they might find their ground better in the night. Moreover upon the top of the breach and along the curtain of the old tower were set firkins of ashes, with *frize rutters* or quadrant tanters nails, three sticking in the ground and one upright, and many heaps of stones and brickbats, ropes of pitch, hoops bound with squibs, hand grenadoes and clubs (which they called Hercules clubs), with heavy heads of wood and nails driven into the squares of them; all these the Lord General prepared for the entertainment and welcome of the enemy.

When it began to grow darkish, a little before low water, Sir Francis Vere called for an old soldier, a gentleman of his company, to go out sentinel *perdu*, and creeping out to the strand between the two gabions gave him express command, if he saw an enemy, he should come into him silently without giving any alarum at all. He crept upon his belly as far as he could and at last discovered the Count Farneze with his 2,000 Italians, who were to fall on first. So he came in silently to Sir Francis, who asked him, 'What news?' 'My lord,' said he, 'I smell good store of gold chains, buff jerkins, Spanish cassocks and Spanish blades.' 'Ha!' says Sir Francis Vere, 'say'st thou so? I hope thou shalt have some of them anon,' and giving him a piece of gold he went up again to the top of the sandhill, where he gave express order to Serjeant Major Carpenter to go to Helmont and every man to his charge, and not to take any alarum or shoot off either cannon or musket shot till he himself gave the signal, and then to give fire as fast as they could charge and discharge.

When at length Sir Francis had got them under the scope of his cannon and small shot, he poured such a volley of cannon and musket shot upon, raking through their battalions and making such lanes amongst them upon the bare strand, which did so amaze and startle them that they were at a nonplus whether to fall on or retreat again, yet at last taking courage and tumbling over the dead bodies they rallied themselves and came under the sandhills and along the foot of the curtain to the very piles that were stuck under the wall, where they began to make ready to send a volley. Sir Francis Vere, seeing that they were presenting and ready to send a volley, commanded all the soldiers to lie down, while the enemies' shot flew like a shower of hail over their heads. This done, our men rising saw the enemy hasting to come up to the breach; and mounting up the wall of the old town Sir Francis flourishing his little sword called to them in Spanish and Italian 'Vienneza, vienneza,' causing the soldiers as they climbed to tumble down among them the ashes and other things that were provided for them.

The alarum being given it was admirable to see with what courage and resolution our men fought, even the sick soldiers came running from their huts up to the walls to fight their shares, and the women with their laps full of powder to supply them when they had shot away all their ammunition. Twice or thrice when the enemy strived to enter they were beaten off and could get no advantage. The fight upon the breach and the old town continued hotter and hotter for the space of above an hour, the enemy falling on at the same instant upon the Porkespy, Helmont, the west ravelin and quarries were all so bravely repulsed that they could not enter a man. At length having their bellies full, those on the west side beat a doleful retreat.

And now the General perceiving the enemy to fall off commanded his page to run as fast as ever he could to Serjeant Major Carpenter and the Auditor Fleming, who were upon Helmont, that they should straightway open the West Sluice, out of which there ran such a torrent through the channel of the west haven that upon their retreat it carried away many of their sound and hurt men into the sea. Then our men fell down our walls after them, slew a great many as they retreated and took some prisoners and stripped a great many of their men, and brought back chains, Spanish pistols, buff jerkins, cassocks, blades, swords and targets, and one wherein was enamelled in gold the Seven Worthies, worth 700 or 800 gilders. Among the rest that soldier which Sir Francis Vere had sent out to discover returned with as much booty as ever he could lug, saying that now Sir Francis Vere was as good as his word. All along the defences lay whole heaps of dead carcases, 40 or 50 upon an heap stark naked, goodly young men, Spaniards and Italians, and some dead horses with baskets of hand-grenadoes. They left also behind them their scaling ladders, great store of spades and shovels, bills, hatchets and axes and other material.

In this general assault the Archduke hath lost above 2,000 men, besides those that were carried into the sea, and a great number of noblemen, amongst them the Count D'Infero, an Italian who offered as much gold as he did weigh for his ransom and yet was slain by a private soldier, Don Durango, Maestro del Campo, Don Alvarez Suarez, Knight of the Order of St. Jaques, and Simon Anthonio the Serjeant Major General who had been hostage in Ostend a few days before. Upon our side are slain between 30 and 40 soldiers and about 100 hurt; and of men of command Captain Haughton, Captain Nicholas van den Lier, two English lieutenants, an ancient, two serjeants, and Mr. Tedcastle, gentleman of the General's horse, who was slain by his side with two musket balls chained together.

4th January. 'A DEFENCE OF TABACCO.'

One hath written *A Defence of Tabacco* in answer to that book called *Work for Chimney Sweepers*, replying to the eight reasons therein alleged to prove tabacco obnoxious. As for the objection that tabacco stinketh, appealeth to the multitude of indifferent voices; nor, if it doth, is it therefore to be thought utterly unprofitable in physic. As to his saying that tabacco leaveth in the brain a black, swart, sootish tincture, because it doth all to be-black the pipe, for proof let him not stand upon school syllogisms, but rather look but into the throats and nostrils of all the great tabacco takers and you shall find them as fair nosed gentlemen and as clean mouthed and throated as any man alive.

6th January. A GREAT VICTORY IN IRELAND.

From Ireland is come news of a great victory over Tyrone on the 24th December.

On 23rd December news was brought to the Lord Deputy that Don John d'Aquila by reason of his own necessities had earnestly importuned Tyrone to give an attempt upon the English camp. The Lord Deputy therefore had his whole army in readiness upon every sudden warning and at the same time strengthened the defences against the town of Kinsale. Very late that night he strengthened the ordinary guards, and commanded that the regiment volant (which was a squadron of eight companies selected out of all the old bands and appointed always to be in readiness and therefore exempted from all other duties) should draw out beyond the west of the camp and stand in arms.

A little before break of day the scouts discovered the rebels' matches in great numbers, whereupon the Lord Deputy caused the army to arm, so that when day broke Tyrone, who had intended to put all the Spaniards with 800 of the best Irish under Tyrrell within the town, found our army embattled upon a hill and well protected by a boggish glyn in front. Anon thinking it to be no day for him he retired the troops that he had advanced again to the body of his army beyond a ford, which was done in some disorder. Hereupon the Lord Deputy followed after and pressed him hard, so that the enemy was forced to stand firm in three bodies upon a ford of a bog. At length our horse making their way across charged the Irish horse and put them to flight, at the sight whereof the main battle dismaying, our men charged again upon them and utterly brake them. Tyrrell and the Spaniards for a time stood firm, but the Irish quitting the Spaniards, the Spaniards were in short time broken by the Lord Deputy's horse, of whom the chief commander was taken prisoner with 3 captains, 6 alferrez and 40 soldiers. Tyrone, O'Donnell and the rest of the Irish threw away their arms and fled.

There were found dead of the Irish rebels alone about 1,200 bodies and about 800 hurt, of whom many died that night. The chase continued for two miles, until our men were tired with killing. The enemy lost 2,000 arms brought to reckoning beside great numbers embezzled, all their powder and drums, and 9 ensigns. Those of the Irish that were taken prisoners being brought to the camp, though they offered ransoms, were all hanged. On our side only one man was slain and not above 8 hurt in all. Thus are the rebels utterly overthrown who but the very night before were so brave and confident of their own good success that they were in contention whose prisoner the Lord Deputy should be, whose the Lord President, and so of the rest.

7th January. NEWS FROM OSTEND.

Four days after the great assault made upon Ostend a drum was sent from the enemy to know what prisoners of quality were taken, also to have surcease of arms for two or three hours for to fetch and bury their dead, but it was not granted. The next day again they sent a drum to enquire after some great personages, prisoners of quality; whereunto it was answered that he should make specification of the names he sought. It was declared by the enemy that they had lost 1,200 slain and 1,000 hurt, besides those which were carried away in waggons and which were drowned in the sea. Those which assaulted in the old town had pouches or mails with them, wherein they had provided themselves of victuals for two or three days; they had also shovels, pickaxes, hatchets, spades and ladders, and other instruments which they all left behind.

8th January. 'THE UNMASKING OF THE POLITIC ATHEIST.'

One J. H. hath written a book called *The unmasking of the politic atheist* wherein he declareth that the principal cause of the evil nature of these times must needs be the corrupt nature of man bending too much unto papistry, and concludeth that papism is masked atheism seeing it makes religion an art of subtle policy.

12th January. A SAYING CONCERNING OSTEND.

Touching the antiparle at Ostend, Sir Francis Vere said that the banns must be asked thrice, and if at the last time any lawful cause can be shown, the marriage may be hindered. The Archduke answered he knew that was true, yet, he said, it was but a whore that offered herself.

16th January. OSTEND.

It is advised from Holland that some of the States were much displeased that Ostend was not then yielded, for now they think themselves bound in honour to defend it. The States soldiers go not to Ostend but by compulsion, calling it their slaughter-house, insomuch that some have been hanged for murmuring and refusing to go.

Certain English priests have lately been with the Pope's nuncios in Paris and Flanders but found no entertainment suitable to their desires. Bagshaw was most vehement, whereupon the Flemish nuncio persuaded the rest to leave him and his company.

18th January. 'THE MERRY WIVES OF WINDSOR.'

Some months since the players presented Sir John Falstaff before the Queen, who was so pleased therewith that she commanded Master Shakespeare to write another play showing Falstaff in love, which he is said to have finished in fourteen days, to her Majesty's no small delight. This play is now printing, entitled *A most pleasant and excellent conceited comedy of Sir John Falstaff and the merry wives of Windsor, intermixed with sundry variable and pleasing humours of Sir Hugh, the Welsh Knight, Justice Shallow and his wise cousin, Mr. Slender ; with the swaggering vein of Ancient Pistol and Corporal Nym.*

A GARDENER'S MISCHANCE.

Five days since one John Pemmer, a gardener at Harlington, administered in potion a quantity of powdered helebore to the wife of one Robert Fisher, she being sick and ignorant of the effect of so great a quantity of helebore, whereof the woman is now dead ; but the gardener not thought guilty of murder.

19*th January*. OSTEND.

Since the furious assault of the Archduke Sir Francis Vere hath busied himself in fortifying and repairing the defences in Ostend, doubting lest the enemy should renew his attempt. From Flanders it is reported that the Archduke had appointed to give a new assault upon the town with all his forces, and provided 2,000 armours of proof, but his soldiers have denied their service so that a mutiny is grown in his camp ; 200 and odd already apprehended and some of the ringleaders executed.

20*th January*. THE SPANISH SURRENDER AT KINSALE.

This night are there *feux de joye* for the good news come from Ireland. Following upon the great victory over Tyrone on 24th December, the Lord Deputy began to press on with the approaches to Kinsale, but after some days' labour Don John D'Aquila, the captain of the Spanish forces within, offered a parley, which being granted, Sir William Godolphin was employed in the negotiation. Hereupon Don John told Sir William that he found the Lord Deputy, although a sharp and powerful, yet an honourable enemy, and the Irish not only weak and barbarous, but as he feared perfidious friends. He was therefore so far in his affections reconciled to the one and distasted with the other, and did invite the Lord Deputy to make an overture of such composition so as they might depart on honourable terms, fitting such men of war as were not by necessity enforced but willingly induced to disengage themselves and to relinquish a people by whom their King and master had been so notoriously abused, if not betrayed.

Upon relation of these offers, after several conferences had been held, it was thought good by the Lord Deputy and his Council to proceed roundly to an agreement, seeing how needful it was to embrace this accord considering the state of our army almost utterly tired ; how full of danger and difficulty it was to attempt a breach defended by so many hands ; how the Queen's ships by want of victuals should shortly have been forced to depart ; together with the lack of munition and artillery ; and the great hazard to the whole country if the enterprise should fail. On the 2nd of this month therefore a treaty is concluded between the Lord Deputy and Don John whereby the Spaniard shall quit all those places that he holds in Ireland, departing with all that he hath. Shipping and victuals at just and reasonable rates shall be provided for them, and they undertake not to bear arms against her Majesty till they be unshipped in the ports of Spain.

At the meeting of Don John D'Aquila and the Lord Deputy, the Spaniard bemoaned his King's misfortune to be so abused as to trust such a nation that had no constancy nor resolution. The Lord Deputy asked him what he thought of the nature of the country. Don John replied that he remembered that part of Scripture, when the Devil carried Christ to the top of the pinnacle to show him all the world ; wherein, said he, ' I verily believe the Devil did hide Ireland from Him because it was fit for none but himself.'

26th January. THE CASE OF SIR THOMAS POSTHUMUS HOBY.

Sir Thomas Posthumus Hoby's complaints against the Lord Eure's kinsmen are to be heard in the Star Chamber to-morrow.

28th January. THE SIEGE OF OSTEND.

From Ostend, since the parley and the last assault, we have heard nothing, for the passage out of that town is not so easy as ships are willing to adventure but in cases of necessity, it being incredible to imagine what means the Archduke useth to stop up the new haven by raising such *gabionados* and cavaliers for his artillery, whereby to command all entering, as the like hath not been seen in any siege. Yet though the charge lieth heavily upon the States and her Majesty we must not desist ; for if we can still engage and waste that army which is the garland of Spain before that place, he will be at little ease to think of other enterprises. It can easily be discerned at what rate he values that port, for he continually maintained 5,000 men in forts to block it before it was besieged, and how fitly it stands to annoy England.

30th January. IRELAND.

Tyrone is now reported back in his own country, having lost more than 1,100 of his men in the late defeat. It is said that more were drowned in their retreat than killed, for those who would kiss them at their going forward did both strip and shoot bullets at them in their return; and for their arms they did drown them and tread them down in every bog and soft place under their feet.

2nd February. MR. JOHN DONNE'S MARRIAGE.

Three weeks before Christmas Mr. John Donne, that is secretary to my Lord Keeper, in secret married the daughter of Sir George More and now confesseth it to the lady's father through my Lord of Northumberland, excusing himself because he knew his present estate less than fit for her, and knowing that as he stood not right in the opinion of Sir George to have given an intimation would impossibilitate the whole matter. And the more to mitigate Sir George's passion he would have him remember that it is irremediably done and that if his Lord is incensed against him so both shall be destroyed.

'TWELFTH NIGHT.'

At the Middle Temple Feast this night they had a play called *Twelfth Night or What you Will*, much like the *Comedy of Errors*, or *Menechmi* in Plautus, but most like and near to that in Italian called *Inganni*. A good practice in it to make the Steward believe his lady widow was in love with him by counterfeiting a letter as from his lady in general terms, telling him what she liked best in him, and prescribing his gesture in smiling, his apparel, etc.; and then when he came to practise making him believe they took him to be mad.

8th February. CAREW'S 'SURVEY OF CORNWALL.'

That *Survey of Cornwall* made long since by Mr. Richard Carew is now by the importunity of his friends to be put in print.

11th February. MR. DONNE'S MARRIAGE.

Sir George More is so passionately enraged at his daughter's marriage that he hath procured Mr. Donne's dismissal from his place as secretary to my Lord Keeper. Now both Mr. Donne, the bridegroom, and Mr. Samuel Brooke that married them and Mr. Christopher Brooke that gave away the bride are all committed to several prisons.

12th February. THE SCOTTISH KING.

All our greatest men nowadays make great show of affection to the Scottish King, the most part it is thought rather of fear than love. London undoubtedly is much addicted that way and a great part of the northern counties. An agent of the Scottish King of late said that his master doubted nothing more than that he should obtain what he desired so greatly and without resistance, so that he should neither have fit occasion to advance his friends and followers, nor to pull down our English pride and insolence.

A NEW DISEASE.

After our earthquake we have now a new disease which very few escape, viz., a great pain of the head, aching in the bones, burning and distemper in all parts. A gentle sweat at the beginning is a present cure, otherwise it continueth four or five days, and so ceaseth. Few or none have died thereof, unless by their own unruly disorder.

13th February. THE OLD DEAN OF ST. PAUL'S DEAD.

Dr. Alexander Nowell, the old Dean of St. Paul's is dead, being nigh upon ninety years old, albeit his sight was not decayed. In the days of Queen Mary he lived an exile for the truth of the Gospel, but returned with the accession of her Majesty and was made Dean of Paul's *anno* 1560. For his meek spirit, deep learning, prudence and piety he was chosen to make the catechism for public use, such a one as should stand as a rule for faith and manners to posterity. He was a generous benefactor to Brazen Nose College in Oxford, wherein in his young years he studied for thirteen years, endowing its revenues with £200 a year for the maintenance of thirteen scholars. He delighted much in the exercise of fishing insomuch that his picture kept in Brazen Nose College is drawn with his lines, hooks and other tackling lying in a round on one hand, and his angles of several sorts on the other. Be it noted also that he was the first inventor of bottled ale, for leaving a bottle of ale (when fishing) in the grass he found it some days after no bottle but a gun, such was the sound at the opening thereof.

16th February. INSTRUCTIONS FOR THE FLEET.

Sir Richard Leveson shortly puts out to sea with a fleet of nine ships, being the *Repulse*, *Garland*, wherein Sir William Monson goeth as Vice-Admiral, *Defiance*, *Mary Rose*, *Wastpite*, *Nonpareil*, *Dreadnought*, *Adventure*, and a carvel. He is instructed to intercept and attack the Spanish fleet intended for Ireland, but if he fail to meet them then to repair to the Spanish coast to discover what preparations are making and to intercept such provisions as are sent thither, but not to molest the French since the French King has given his word that the enemy shall not be supplied from his country. Then he shall endeavour to obtain some profit towards the maintenance of her Majesty's great charges by taking either the outward or the homeward Indian fleet. He is victualled for five months.

20th February. PARSONS' ANSWER TO THE SECULARS.

Parsons hath written a book entitled *A brief apology, or defence of the Catholic Ecclesiastical hierarchy and subordination in England*, which is set forth 'for the true information and stay of all good Catholics by priests united in due subordination to the Right Reverend Archpriest, and other their Superiors.' Herein he showeth how greatly the Catholics are injured by these contentions, and how pleasing and profitable to heretics: discourseth at large upon the stirs at Wisbeach and Rome; and answereth the particular calumniations of the former books written by the secular priests.

Defendeth also equivocation, saying that doubtful speech or amphibology (as the doctors call it) is handled largely by all divines, and not only allowed but judged necessary in divers cases for avoiding lying and other inconveniences; which amphibology, or hiding the truth by prudent dissimulation, is held lawful in four general matters, viz., in covering the secrecy of confession; in divers cases of examinations both of witnesses and divers accused before judges; when it may concern the hurt of God's service or danger of our neighbours; about the external confession of faith and obligation therein. But, saith he, such as shall read the books of the secular priests and see the infinite number of untruths, lies, slanders and open falsehoods uttered therein without scruple of conscience, will little think needful the use of equivocations to these men, seeing that equivocations and prudent diversions of speech are allowed principally to men of scrupulous conscience for avoiding of lying.

21st February. A Petition for Association.

Mr. Thomas Digges hath set forth a pamphlet called *Humble Motives for association to maintain religion established*, published as an antidote against the pestilent treatises of secular priests, holding that the earnestness of the papists against the former Bill for 12d. to be had of such as are absent from divine service on Sundays, and their publishing of books pretending a controversy between secular priests and Jesuits, to be nothing else but to make way for a toleration of popery which they hoped to obtain by this Parliament. He declareth that, now the late Lord Treasurer is dead and the Earl of Essex through his fatal error taken away, the cry is 'priests be tolerable men, but puritans may not be abidden.' Petitioneth the Archbishops and Bishops to take heed how they hearten the papists and discourage the puritan, nay every sound protestant, by tolerating points of popery to be broached in pulpit or print and yet silence puritan preachers only for preaching without licence.

25th February. The King of Scots' Title.

Now that the Earl of Essex is dead men speak freely of the King of Scots' title to the throne when it shall please God to take away her Majesty, nor is any man's ambition discovered stirring to work for power to oppose his right, either by strengthening themselves with popularity, with arms, with followers, or by making themselves masters of the strength of the country. Nevertheless there is some fear among the better sort that those that the King should elect as his Council and instruments should be Scots, for the name of Scots is harsh in the ears of the vulgar; yet the Kings of Scotland have small reason to be enamoured of the faith of their subjects, and besides the King being half English is like to think the honour of being reputed a King of England greater than to be a King of Scots.

Some fear that the King, finding the time of expectation overlong, may hasten to obtain his right by force, by reason that his people will ever use persuasions to be stirring him ; that his friends and assistants are many, what by his allies in Denmark, his ancient league with France, and the Irish out of hope of more freedom in religion ; that her Majesty is now in her declining age and men look rather for the sun rising than the sun setting ; and besides that the forces of our country are diverted, some looking after Ireland, others assisting the Low Countries, and some few employing themselves towards Spain at sea.

1st March. THE YOUNG LORD BURGH DEAD.

The young Lord Burgh is dead in the Lord Bishop of Winchester's house. About three weeks since he complained of a crick in the neck, and thereupon kept his chamber but without any apparent fever. The physicians doubted the new disease in him. After a week he went to bed in reasonable plight and slept more heavily than he was wont, and the physicians now considered that he was failing with a kind of lethargy, which indeed continued to oppress him for over a week. Nor could it be conjectured how this disease should grow so strangely, only it was noted that he desired to feed much on fat meats, insomuch that the Bishop had many small combats with him to bring him from that diet, so that he would often go hungry from the table in sullen humour. When the body was opened the physicians found the vital parts very sound and fair, but the left side of the lung somewhat black and perished with a flux from his head. The outward tunicles of the brain they found clear and free from any corrupted phlegm, only in the inward cells of the brain they found four or five spoonfuls of water, and in the cell of the common sense, which lieth before, the signs of corruption which brake from him at the time of his death.

2nd March. THE LORD KEEPER'S CHARGE.

The Lord Keeper in his oration the last Star Chamber day of this last term gave special charge to the Judges of assize, Justices and other officers to be very vigilant over three sorts of persons, viz., Jesuits, priests and precisians, all which labour the subversion of the State, which cannot stand unless they be supplanted. Of three evils he said that the Jesuits were the worst ;

that there was never any notorious treason but they were the principal actors. And so took occasion to speak of the books written by the priests against them, which albeit some might have suspected heretofore to have been published but in their names, yet not as he said by the archtraitor Parsons his *Apology*, it was manifest they were the true authors, and that those their contentious humours were bred and nourished amongst themselves by pride and ambition. He spoke also much against the liberty that some priests enjoy, affirming also such as receive or relieve them to be within the compass of the law, and willed the Justices to have regard thereunto.

3rd March. COURT NEWS.

The Court hath been at Richmond these twelve days, but the Queen in many humours to have removed to Greenwich by reason of an ache in one of her arms, expecting more ease by change of air. A cunning bone setter or surgeon had lately a sight thereof; he said it was a wind with a cold rheumatic humour settled there, and to be removed by rubbing and applying first oils and ointments. Her Majesty told him he was mistaken, for that her blood and constitution was of its nature very hot. He replied that neither flesh nor blood in that part made any show thereof, but much more the contrary, whereat she was exceedingly displeased, commanding him from her presence, she being most impatient to hear of any decay in herself, and thereupon will admit no help of physic or surgery, fretting and storming when she feeleth any little pain, sometimes retiring herself from all access for three or four hours together.

Mr. Secretary, about Shrovetide, got a wrench in his ankle and by that means went not to Court the Sunday last, and the next day returned again to his house. Hereupon there is an imagination that some jars have happened between her Majesty and him, but of this no certainty. All the nobility seem weary of her passionate humours and withdraw themselves from Court by all devices possible.

The Lord Keeper and Lord Chief Justice do much mislike that by the favour of the Bishop of London the appellant priests have such liberty, and now it is expected that they and all others imprisoned in London shall be sent to the Tower.

The Bishop hath caused fifty copies of Parsons' *Apology* to be newly printed in London by the Queen's printer, some say *verbatim*, some say with marginal notes. He causeth them to be bound with clean paper between every leaf and so meaneth to present the Council and his friends therewithal.

10th March. WILL KEMP.

Will Kemp now plays at the Rose with my Lord of Worcester's men.

13th March. A MERRY JEST CONCERNING SHAKESPEARE.

Upon a time when Burbage played Richard the Third, there was a citizen grown so far in liking with him that before she went from the play she appointed him to come that night unto her by the name of 'Richard the Third.' Shakespeare overhearing their conclusion went before, was entertained and at his game ere Burbage came. Then message being brought that Richard the Third was at the door, Shakespeare caused return to be made that William the Conqueror was before Richard the Third. Shakespeare's name is William.

15th March. A PURITAN BOOK.

There is a book set forth secretly to favour the puritans, called *The Plea of the innocent*, published by one Jonas Nichols, wherein he declareth that this word puritan is fitter to be applied to papists, because they indeed arrogate unto themselves purity and holiness and despise all others, than to the preachers. Nevertheless the preachers were termed puritans for four reasons, *viz.*, scruple in the use of certain ceremonies, scruple in subscribing beyond the Statute, seeking for reformation of some ceremonies and some part of ecclesiastical discipline, and also because the people do hear sermons, talk of the Scriptures, and sing psalms together in private houses ; and because about the time of the beginning of the reign the preachers did somewhat refrain profane and unprofitable customs, the greater sort of the people, addicted partly to popery and partly to licentiousness, would scoff at them, calling them holy brethren and holy sistern, and saying, 'He is one of the pure and unspotted sheep.' This author goeth about to prove that the ministers seeking reformation are in no sort to be compared to papists in evil, much less to be equalified with traitors, seminaries or Jesuits. Moreover it is declared that it would be most profitable to the present state and government to hear the petitions of the ministers seeking reformation; but to hearken to papists and to tolerate them is most exceeding dangerous and pernicious. Concludeth that some things may be especially looked into which may and ought to induce both parties unto peace and to join lovingly in the building of God's house.

17th March. Court News.

The Bishop of London continues to patronise the priests and he is again backed by some principal men. The puritans have begun to oppose themselves to that course. Notwithstanding it is said that the Queen herself hath commanded the priests' faction to be still nourished, upon conceit that thereby the College of Cardinals will be divided in opinion and therewithal the Pope be distracted from determining the controversy or soliciting the King of Spain or any other to endanger our State; besides, that it will be a bridle to the Spanish to attempt anything, understanding of the disunion of such as he would most rely on, and so not trust to a broken staff. Howsoever Mr. Secretary disavoweth all good conceit of any priest whatsoever, setting it down for a ground that they cannot but wish and, as much as in them lieth, labour the alteration of the present Government and advancement of their own designs.

The coming of the Duke of Nevers is daily expected, and the Earl of Northumberland is appointed to meet, receive and conduct him. Many of the most rich hangings are fetched out of the Tower to adorn the Court and great preparation made for his honourable entertainment. The general opinion is that he cometh of curiosity to see the Court and country but some say that he desireth secretly a sight of Lady Arabella. A house is being prepared here privately in London where the lady, with those with whom she liveth, are expected soon after Easter.

The ache of the Queen's arm is fallen into her side, but she is still, thanks be to God, frolicly and merry, only her face showeth some decay, which to conceal when she cometh in public she putteth many fine cloths into her mouth to bear out her cheeks, and sometimes as she is walking she will put off her petticoat, as seeming too hot when others shake with cold. Mr. Secretary's ankle is now well, and he a courtier in as good grace and with as absolute a command as ever had any subject.

18th March. SIR FRANCIS VERE LEAVETH OSTEND.

On the 7th of this month did Sir Francis Vere resign up his government of Ostend unto others appointed by the States to succeed him, having valiantly defended it for above eight months against all the Archduke's power, and leaving it much better able to defend itself than it was at his first coming thither. So the same night he and his brother, Sir Horatio Vere, embarked themselves, having sent away their horses and baggage before them; and both carrying with them and leaving behind them the marks of their honour and renown, for the stoutest and bravest soldiers of the Low Countries, Spain, England, France, Scotland and Italy, whilst they eagerly contend for a barren plot of sand have found here as it were one common sepulchre, though an eternal monument of their valour.

20th March. A PROCLAMATION TO REPRESS PIRACIES.

Manifold and daily complaints being made of continual depredations and piracies committed on the seas by certain lewd and ill disposed persons pretending to make wars against the enemies of the Queen, certain articles are now set forth for the prevention of such practices. No man of war shall be furnished or set out to sea without licence under the Great Seal of the Admiralty given to the Judge of the High Court of the Admiralty, for the good behaviour of themselves and company. Any person whatsoever that shall take any ship that belongeth to her Majesty's friends and allies, or to any of their subjects, and shall take from them any goods, except it be goods bound for Spain or Portugal, shall suffer death, with confiscation of goods. No ship or vessel furnished in warlike manner shall pass into the Straits or Mediterranean Sea upon pain of confiscation of goods. Lastly it is straitly prohibited, upon pain of death, to all English men of war to sell, alienate or dispose of any goods taken at sea either in Argier, Tunis, Zant, Petrasse or any other place in Barbary, Greece, Italy or elsewhere, but in the Kingdom of England only: neither shall any of her Majesty's subjects residing for the time in Barbary or places adjoining or any other place out of England dare to buy such goods taken at sea upon pain of confiscation of their own goods, chattels and lands here in England.

25th March. MR. DONNE'S MARRIAGE.

Sir George More hath now yielded forgiveness to Master Donne for his marriage and together they petition the Lord Keeper that he will again take Mr. Donne to his Secretary ; but he refuseth, saying though he is unfeignedly sorry for what is done, it sorteth not with his place and credit to discharge and readmit servants at the request of passionate petitioners.

27th March. THE QUEEN'S SHIPS.

Sir Richard Leveson, being Admiral, sailed eight days since with five of the Queen's ships, and yesterday Sir William Monson with four to attend the coming of Hollander's ships.

28th March. THE SPANIARDS IN IRELAND.

Don John and all the rest of the Spaniards are now reported to have left Ireland.

9th April. VALUABLE SPANISH PRIZES.

From Plymouth it is reported that the *Refusal* of Sir John Gilbert's together with the *Diamond* of London and the *Wat* of Plymouth have arrived with two prizes that they took coming out of Lisbon, the one a ship of about 400 tons laden with sugar, pepper, cinnamon, and ginger and other goods, the other a fly boat of 140 tons with munition, gum, lacquer, china dishes with other goods esteemed by the Spaniards to be worth 20,000 ducats. They have also brought 4,500 ducats in plate and money, and a bag of small seed pearls weighing 25½ lbs. The whole value is said to be worth £100,000.

10th April. 'SWORD AND BUCKLER.'

One William Basse hath written a poem called *Sword and Buckler*, defending the profession of serving man against the censures of these days. Quoth he :

> But see how hateful is but lately grown
> This fatal title of a serving man,
> That every dunghill clown and every drone,

Nor wise in nature nor condition.
  Spares not to vilify our name and place
  In dunsical reproach and blockish phrase.

A morkin-gnoss that in his chimney nook
Sits carping how to advance his shapeless brood,
And in their several properties doth look
To see what's best to bring them all to good:
  One points he out a smith, and one a baker,
  A third a piper, fourth a collar maker;

If one more native gentle than the rest,
To be a serving man doth now demand,
Up starts his sire as bedlam or possess'd
And asks his son an if he will be hang'd,
  'Shalt be a hangman, villain, first,' quoth he.
  'Amen,' say I, so he be none for me.

The pearking citizen and mincing dame
Of any paltry beggared market town,
Through rotten teeth will giggle out the same,
Though not in so harsh manner as the clown:
  'I have but two sons, but if I had ten
  The worst of them should be no serving men.'

18th April. A Printer Hanged.

Peter Bullock a stationer and one named Ducket were hanged at Tyburn for printing offensive books.

The Queen and Dr. Barlow.

Of late Dr. Barlow, that is now one of her Majesty's chaplains, received a check at her Majesty's hands because he presumed to come in her presence when she had given special charge to the contrary, because she would not have the memory of the late Earl of Essex renewed by him who had preached against him at Paul's.

24th April. The Spanish Prizes.

There is much dispute at Plymouth concerning the sharing of the Spanish prizes taken by Sir John Gilbert's ship. Sir John himself is very discontented by the Lord Treasurer's command that he should be paid in specie, and declared that he would help himself since he was so little regarded. There come daily more and more claimers which pretend interest in the taking of the prizes, which were much pillaged both of pearl and pepper in Cornwall. The goods are not yet all landed because of the rain and foul weather. The value is now found to be less than was first reported.

27th April. SHIPS FROM THE STATES.

There are come into Dover road 7 ships of war of the Hollanders that are to join with the Queen's fleet bound for the southward.

28th April. A MASS SURPRISED.

There is an extraordinary accident in the Clink. Upon Low Sunday, upon information given, the Lord Chief Justice's men, with pursuivants and other officers, rushing in suddenly with drawn swords found altars and massing stuff prepared, and three priests by name Barnaby, Clark and Watson, with well over forty Catholics (most women and poor folk of the City) all assembled in the same chamber and some others adjoining, all amazed at this sudden accident. The officers took the names of all, committed Barnaby and Clark to close prison, convented the fact before Justice Dale dwelling in Southwark, who committed the most part to divers prisons. Watson with some others was sent close prisoner to the King's Bench.

Next day Watson was sent for to the Archbishop of Canterbury, where the Bishop of London also met him, where they entered into secret conference and after many kindnesses the Bishop of London conveyed him home with him and dismissed him, so he walketh free as before and practises still his function. Barnaby and Clark also had the liberty of the house and leave to go abroad as before. Thereupon, going to my Lord of London and complaining that promises were not kept and that the injury was so violent, he told them that the Chief Justice was of the Privy Council and therefore he could not hinder it, but that he would entreat on their behalf that no more such usage might be offered them.

3rd May. A NEGLIGENT PLEADER.

This day Sergeant Harris in a certain cause was retained for the plaintiff, and argued for the defendant; being become so negligent that he knows not for whom he speaks.

5th May. TROUBLES OF LANCASHIRE MINISTERS.

Certain ministers of Lancashire have petitioned Mr. Secretary to write a letter on their behalf to the Bishop of Chester, who would compel them to wear the cope, surplice and tippet, or put them out of their livings and forbid them to preach any more. These men take great pains in converting of papists to the true religion and have profited greatly these four years; and although they know that religion is not tied to any apparel, yet they hold that if they should wear such apparel, as they have much spoken against it, would be a great stumbling block to the converted, insomuch that some of them declare that they would sooner leave liberty and life too.

7th May. HARSH MEASURES BY THE LORD MAYOR.

Of late one Captain Allen, undertaking to raise a company of 200 men, brought out of the country many gallant men and some of good ability, and the rest were taken up in London, all being ranged under Allen's colour waiting transport. Meantime the Lord Mayor, having warrant for his pressing of men, took many of Captain Allen's soldiers out of their lodgings and beds and sent them away, and refused either to deliver them or supply them by others.

8th May. THE EARL OF NORTHUMBERLAND AND SIR F. VERE.

There hath been great quarrelling between my Lord of Northumberland and Sir Francis Vere; insomuch that my Lord sent Captain Whitlocke with a letter to Sir Francis that, if all were true he had heard, he had wronged him in such and such points, and therefore desired to be satisfied, wishing him to take his horse and bring one with him, as he of his honour would do the like, and meet him where he should appoint, willing him to send his determination, yea or no, by word of mouth and not by writing. Sir Francis wrote an answer and sent it by Captain Ogle, which the Earl refused to receive. The contents were that though he assured himself he could satisfy my Lord, yet he would not go about to satisfy any man that had his sword in his hand; but if they might meet in peaceable manner before any persons of state whom his Lorship would choose, he would give him reasonable satisfaction, otherwise let him take what course he would.

In this interim M. Charon understanding thereof went and informed the Queen, who sent express charge to the Earl upon his allegiance not to molest Sir Francis any way for that she had a special service to employ him in. The Earl obeyed, but sent her Majesty word she should find Sir Francis a knave, a coward, and a buffon; which coming to Sir Francis' ear, he gives out that the Earl is a liar and a base-minded man.

MR. CLARKE'S 'TRUMPET OF APOLLO.'

One Mr. John Clarke hath sent forth a book of the cures wrought by his medicines, and entitled *The Trumpet of Apollo*. The first is of a defensative cake against the plague (which is like to break out again this year by reason of the unnatural and intemperate season of the spring). Of this cake giveth the names of more than ninety persons that have taken the same, but withholdeth the receipt. Likewise setteth forth his cures of the ague and other diseases; and noteth sundry drinks and waters of rare use and virtue that can be had of the author at reasonable prices at his dwelling in the midst of Sheerlane hard by Temple Bar leading into Lincoln's Inn Fields.

10*th May*. THE FRENCH KING'S TROUBLES.

The French King is now at Blois, suffering from the gout in his right foot. As he passed down the river he visited his mistress at Bugancy, who followed him to Blois and was lodged in the Castle; which the Queen took with so much impatience that during her abode there she kept herself retired in her chamber, either spending the whole day in bed in tears and lamentations, or if she did rise yet would not be persuaded to put on other robes than those of her chamber. She refused to open the door to the King when he knocked; and being invited by the King to the comedy whither he did conduct the Marquise, she refused to go herself; and when the King sent for her she made this answer, that it was not decent that the Maids should go whither the Mistress would not go.

There is much discontent amongst some of the nobility and the meaner sort of the people, and it is openly bruited that certain of the nobility are in league against the King, notably the Marshal Biron, who is most feared and who hath most means to do harm both because of his former valour and of his present situation, being Governor of Burgoyne. The King hath sent for him by three several messengers.

12th May. CITY NEWS.

There hath been great pressing of late in London and strange as ever was known in England, committed by my Lord Mayor and the rest contrary to their instructions from the Lords of the Council, insomuch that this last Sunday (the 9th) letters were directed to Sir John Peyton and Sir Jerome Bowes to examine these indiscreet proceedings, and all such as had cause to complain should be heard and their causes redressed. So that upon the Tuesday following there was a proclamation in London that no gentleman or serving man should any more be impressed, for the week before they did not only press gentlemen and serving men, but lawyers, clerks, countrymen that had law causes, aye the Queen's men, knights, and as it was credibly reported one Earl, quite contrary to what the Council and especially my Lord Chief Justice had intended. For their meaning was that they should take out of all ordinaries all cheating companions as such as had no ability to live in such places, all such as they could find in bawdy houses and bowling alleys; which they never went to any but only to the bowling alleys. All the playhouses were beset in one day and very many pressed from thence, so that in all are pressed 4,000, besides 500 voluntaries, and all for Flanders.

Of late there have been several killed with knives. One Mr. Bowton was killed with a knife by a little boy, my Lord of Canterbury's page, being Sir Thomas Wyllford's son, and in the same week Boughton that is Mistress Fowler's brother. Captain Haynes that was in the Fleet about her horrible bawdry and beastly villainies, he killed another prisoner, for which he was hanged in Smithfield.

There is an Italian at Court that doth wonderful strange tricks upon the cards, as telling of any card that is thought, or changing one card from another though it be held by any man never so hard under his hand. The Queen gave him 200 crowns for showing his tricks, and divers gentlemen make meetings for him where he getteth sometimes 20, sometimes 40 crowns, and yet they say he spends it so strangely as he cannot keep a penny in his purse.

15th May. The Earl of Northumberland.

It is said that my Lord of Northumberland, together with Lord Cobham and Sir Walter Ralegh, are now come round to the party of King James. The Earl is unhappy, for both Court and town exclaim against his indiscretion for challenging a great commander of the state at such a time.

17th May. The Marshal Biron.

From France the news is that the Marshal Biron hath sent excuses to the King's summons, but his good meaning is suspected, though it is believed that the King's purpose is, if he will present himself, with courteous treatment and kind entertainment to regain him, and with the greatest favours to assure him to his service.

22nd May. News of Sir R. Leveson.

One Captain King hath brought letters from Sir Richard Leveson's fleet wherein he reporteth that on 31st March last he descried the West Indian fleet, 38 sail in all. He essayed to take one ship, but the night being exceeding dark and the sea suddenly growing high he was neither able to make her fast nor his people to enter her. Four several times his ship fell off and four times he boarded her again. Next morning the English Captains were called to council, and discerning the inequality of the match, they delivered their opinions that they might give blows and take blows, but without hope of profit, hazard their men and endanger their masts, and so be disabled to do what they went for. Hereupon they parted with much discontent as man can imagine to see so much wealth without power to take it. Yet they followed the fleet into the shore that day and the next in hope of a straggler, but the weather growing to be very fair would not yield such a benefit. Reporteth also that at Lisbon and the Groin there is no appearance of preparation and that most of the soldiers of Don Juan that came out of Ireland are dead.

24th May. A DEBATE IN THE COUNCIL CONCERNING PEACE.

There is great debate in the Council concerning the waste of treasure in these last seven years' wars, and the charge for Ireland being £400,000 *per annum*, and the treasure and men of England being wasted beyond endurance; for pots and pewter are selling amongst the poor for this present subsidy. The Lords are, it seems, all agreed that it is the Irish wars which have impoverished England, and not the wars of Spain or the Low Countries. They agree also that the Low Countries will never become subjects to Spain or France or any other but will maintain a continual war; nor may we with safety suffer Spain or the Archduke to be absolute in the Low Countries.

But they are disagreed touching peace to be moved by us with Spain. The Lord Treasurer saith that the war in the Low Countries is a lingering war to waste us and them, and that it is fittest to have peace with Spain before we be far spent; for the Spanish King hath a spring that yieldeth continual supply, his Indies; whilst we are like a standing water which war will exhaust and make dry. The Lord Admiral, Mr. Controller and Mr. Secretary think otherwise, that peace first moved by us were to her Majesty's dishonour, yet they would be content a treaty might be moved by them, for some good might arise by gaining time.

27th May. A SAYING OF SIR JOHN FORTESCUE.

Sir John Fortescue, speaking with a dear friend of the weakness of the time, said that his comfort was that he was as old and weak as the time itself, being born in the same year as the Queen; but yet he would advise his son to take a right course when the hour came, without taking knowledge in the meantime of any person or pretension; for he had found by experience that they that met Queen Mary at London were as well accepted, standing free from former combination, as they that went to Framlingham; and that they that came into the vineyard *hora undecima* had *denarium* as well as they that had sweat before all their fellows. The practice of opponents, as he thought, would cause the labours of all men to be holden and accounted meritorious that had so much discretion as in the meantime to be silent and indifferent.

31st May. Sir Anthony Shirley.

Sir Anthony Shirley abideth still at Venice, in the utmost extremity, protesting that he is persecuted by those from whom he should have expected comfort. The merchants there are forbidden to speak to him or his, and when he sent to the French King for letters to the French consul at Cairo about his return to Persia, Mr. Wotton told the King that letters had been sent against him by the Queen and the Council. He would have his actions considered apart from the Earl of Essex (by whom he was set out) and to be judged by their merits; if it be otherwise then may he be compelled by desperation to leap into precipitate courses with the Spaniards.

1st June. The Soldiers at Bristol.

The commissioners that were sent to view the 800 men sent out of 12 shires to Bristol declare that intolerable hindrances are offered to the service; there was never man beheld such strange creatures brought to any muster. They were most of them either old, lame, diseased, boys or common rogues. Few of them had any clothes; small, weak, starved bodies taken up in fairs, markets and highways to supply the places of better men at home; and if there were any better than the rest, they are found to have been set forth by malice.

On the 26th of May there was committed by the Gloucestershire men a great mutiny, which was overruled by the commissioners. Their course was to take one of the troop and commit him, commanding all the rest to their quarters. Then the whole company, set on by one lewd fellow, protested they would die but they would have their fellow again; but they took him also and both were carried to prison. The rest made show of going to their quarters, but waited their opportunity and set upon the officers that were guarding the prisoners; but they were beaten back and another of their chiefs taken. All that night they were strongly guarded, and a preacher was sent to the prisoners to prepare themselves to die in the morning. When the time was come, they were brought to the place of execution with halters about their necks and caused to go up the ladders, all the troops standing by. After they had said their prayers and expected no life, the commissioners caused them to be untied ; which example hath wrought much good, for now they are very quiet. The occasion of this meeting was because they might not have money to pay for their mashing and the mending of their shoes when they list.

2nd June. 'THE METAMORPHOSIS OF TABACCO.'

There is a new poem called *The Metamorphosis of tabacco*, in form of a feigned fable of the history of this herb ; beginneth :

> I sing the loves of the superior powers
> With the fair mother of all fragrant flowers,
> From which first love a glorious simple springs,
> Belov'd of heavenly Gods and earthly Kings.
> Let others in their wanton verses chaunt
> A beauteous face that doth their senses daunt,
> And on their Muse's wings lift to the sky
> The radiant beams of an enchanting eye.
> Me let the sound of great *Tabacco's* praise
> A pitch above base lovesick poets raise :
> Let me adore with my thrice-happy pen
> The sweet and sole delight of mortal men,
> The *cornucopia* of all earthly pleasure
> Where bankrupt Nature hath consum'd her treasure,
> A worthy plant, springing from Flora's hand,
> The blessed offspring of an uncouth land.
> Breath giving herb, none other I invoke
> To help me paint the praise of sugar'd smoke.

6th June. THE SERMON AT PAUL'S CROSS.

Mr. Barker preaching this day at Paul's Cross took as his text Luke ix, the last verse, and spake of the Archbishop of Canterbury as the sun amongst the ministers, and compared the old Dean of Paul's to the moon, and Dr. John Overall (that was made Dean last week) to the new moon, and the ministers to stars.

7th June. A SAYING CONCERNING SIR W. RALEGH.

A lewd fellow, coming before Sir Walter Ralegh to be examined concerning some wreck which he had gotten into his hands, and being demanded whether he would swear to such articles as they would propound, answered that he would swear to anything they would ask him. And then being admonished he should not be so rash in so serious a matter as concerned his soul so nearly, 'Faith,' said he, 'I had rather trust God with my soul than you with my goods.'

10th June. THE EARL OF NORTHUMBERLAND.

It is very secretly rumoured that my Lord of Northumberland hath sent to the Scottish King a gentleman of his house, Mr. Thomas Percy, who is now returned. This man is beloved of none and trusted by no one nobleman or gentleman of quality within the land beside his own faction; and is moreover very injudicious in his speech.

14th June. THE MARSHAL BIRON ARRESTED.

From France comes news that the Marshal Biron is a prisoner. He came to Fontainbleau slenderly accompanied and not with his ordinary train. The King received him with great appearance of love and kindness and entertained him with discourse the greatest part of that day. Next day the King gave order to the colonel of the light horse to draw his companies to the town and to keep them all night in arms and ready saddled. In the evening the guards were doubled and the gentlemen of the chamber commanded not to stray abroad. About 11 of the clock at night the King did send for the Marshal, who came and found him set upon his privy stool. After some speech held with him, being dismissed, as soon as he was out of the King's chamber, M. de Vitry, one of the captains of the Guards, seized him prisoner, saying that he was sorry but it was the King's commandment, and so willed him to surrender his weapon. The Marshal made some small resistance asking if he should render his weapon who had five and thirty wounds in his body, all received for the service of the King. The Count of Auvergne was likewise seized upon, together with the Lieutenant of the Marshal's company and his secretary.

This proceeding is termed a *coup d'estat*, and as it is presumed will strongly establish the sovereign authority.

15th June. A JESUIT BOOK AGAINST THE PRIESTS.

Parsons the Jesuit hath put forth another book against the secular priests entitled *A manifestation of the great folly and bad spirit of certain in England calling themselves secular priests*, written, as it is declared, 'by priests living in obedience.'

18th June. THE FLEET RETURNING.

The ships of Sir Richard Leveson's fleet are coming in to Plymouth, and already many sick men have been landed. There are many strong reports that they have taken a carrack.

19th June. THE IRISH MONIES.

The proclamation for the exchange of the old money for the new in Ireland is so ill observed that a new proclamation was set forth at Dublin on the 9th of the month commanding that no one hereafter shall traffic or trade with the decried moneys or use them for payment of fees, wages or debts upon pain of imprisonment and fine.

22nd June. A PROCLAMATION CONCERNING NEW BUILDINGS IN LONDON.

Proclamation is made that the Lord Mayor and other officers shall cause to be executed certain orders concerning new buildings and inmates in and about the City of London. No new buildings shall be erected about the City of London except upon the foundation of old ; and if any such shall be begun, the same shall forthwith be pulled down and the timber sold for benefit of the poor. No house or tenement shall be divided into several dwellings. All houses, tenements and buildings erected within these seven years past and not let out or being void of a tenant, the same not to be let to any unless the owner be content that the churchwardens and the minister, by allowance of two or more of the Justices, shall dispose of them for some of the poor, or for the good and behalf of the poor of the parish that are destitute of houses and at such rents as they shall allow. All sheds and shops that have been builded within seven years to be plucked down.

These and the like orders are again set forth because of the continual increasing of people in the City which could hardly be provided of victual and food and other like necessaries upon reasonable prices ; and especially for that great multitudes of people being brought to inhabit small rooms, whereof a great part being very poor and such as must live by begging or worse means, and being heaped together and in a sort smothered with many families of children and servants in one house or small tenement, it must needs follow that if any plague or universal sickness should by God's permission enter among those multitudes, it would spread itself not only in the confines of the City but throughout the whole realm.

26th June. A Rich Carrack Taken.

On 1st June news came to Sir Richard Leveson and Sir William Monson, then being near the Rock, that there was a carrack and eleven galleys in Cezimbra Road ; and on the next day all the captains resorted on board the Admiral to council, which took up most part of the day. At first there was an opposition by some who alleged the danger and impossibility of taking the carrack, being defended by the castle and eleven galleys, but Sir William Monson so prevailed that they all consented to go upon her the next day.

Early in the morning therefore, every man commanding and committing himself to God's tention and protection expected when to begin. A gale of wind happening about ten of the clock the Admiral weighed anchor, shot off a warning piece and put forth his flag in the main top. The Vice-Admiral did the like in his fore-top according to the custom of the sea. Every captain encouraged his men, so that they which were grown weak and feeble before now revived and bestirred themselves as if a new spirit had been infused into them. The Admiral was the first that gave the charge ; after him followed the rest of the ships with no less resolution in the commanders, showing great valour and gaining great honour. The last of all was the Vice-Admiral who, entering into the fight, still strove to luff up as near the shore as he could, where at length he came to anchor in such a place that he was continually fighting with the town, the fort, the galleys, and carrack all in one instant ; for he brought himself betwixt them all that he might play both his broadsides upon them. There might be seen the oars of the galleys swimming on the one side, and the slaves forsaking them on the other with offer to swim to us, everything being in confusion amongst them. And thus they fought till five of the clock in the afternoon.

Late in the afternoon the Admiral and the Vice-Admiral consulted in the *Dreadnought* how to preserve the carrack and enjoy her, and resolved to offer her parley and commanded all the ships to leave shooting till the return of the messenger. The man employed was one Captain Sewell, who had been four years prisoner in those galleys, and had escaped and swam to our ships, as did many Turks and Christians. He was to intimate as from himself that the galleys, whose strength they presumed upon, were beaten, some burnt, the rest fled; that our ships had possession of the road, the castle not being able to abide our ordnance, much less the carrack, and if they refused this offer of mercy they were to expect all the cruelty and rigour that a conqueror could show his enemy. After some conference to this effect, the captain of the carrack sent some gentlemen of rank who came aboard the *Dreadnought*. But after the delivery of their message, it seemed that there was an uproar in the carrack, some being of an opinion to entertain a parley, others to save themselves and set her on fire; which Sir William Monson hearing, without further conference with Sir Richard, he leaped suddenly into his boat and was rowed to the carrack. When he drew near to her he was known by divers gentlemen on board (for he hath in former times been a prisoner among them). Then he wished the captain to proceed to his propositions, which were that they should be safely set on shore that same night; that they should enjoy their ship and ordnance, as appertaining to the King, but our men their wealth; and lastly that the flag and ancient should not be taken down but worn while the carrack was unlading. Sir William replied that he knew it was the use of some men to demand great things when less would serve them, but for a conclusion he desired that what they intended might be quickly determined, for night growing on might advantage them; for his resolution, he was willing to yield that they should be put ashore with their arms that night, except eight or ten of the principal gentlemen whom he would detain three days; as for the other propositions he utterly refused them.

There was long expostulation upon these points, and Sir William seeing the obstinacy of the captain offered in a great rage to leap into his boat, resolving to leave off the treaty, which the rest of the gentlemen perceiving, and that he had propounded nothing but what might very well stand with their reputation, they entreated him once more to ascend into the carrack and they would enter into new capitulations. Hereupon it was agreed that a messenger should be sent to the Admiral to have his confirmation of the points concluded on, and that in the meantime the flag and ancient should be taken down; and if the Admiral should not consent they to have leisure to put forth their flag and ancient before the fight should begin; that the company should straightway be put on shore, but the captain with eight others of the principal gentlemen three days after; that the ship with her goods should be surrendered without any practise or treason; that they should use their endeavours that the castle should forbear shooting whilst our ships rode in the road. All of which was agreed.

Though three days were limited for setting the captain on shore yet it was held discretion not to detain them any longer than till the carrack was brought off safely to our ships, and therefore Sir William carried the captain and the rest of the gentlemen aboard his own ship where they supped and spent the night in music and other sports with great pleasure and delight. The morning following he accompanied them ashore.

In this fight the galleys were so miserably beaten and their slaves so pitifully slain that our men took two and burnt them, and there wanted nothing but boats to possess them all. The number of the enemy slain is unknown but must have been many; in all our ships there were but six slain and as many hurt. The ships that took part in this action were the *Wastpite*, the *Garland*, the *Nonpareil*, the *Dreadnought*, and the *Adventure*.

27th June. BIRON'S CONSPIRACY.

Some days since the French King called for Mr. Winwood to whom he used this speech. 'I have,' said he, 'discovered a dangerous practice which by the space of three years and more the Marshal Biron hath complotted with the King of Spain and Duke of Savoy against my person and my state. It is four months since I have had perfect knowledge of this confederacy, and could have been content to have concealed it, and would now have pardoned and remitted if by courtesy and fair means he would have been induced to confess and acknowledge his error; but now God have mercy on his soul. I cannot say, as the last King said at the death of the Duke of Guise, "now I am King," but I say I am sorry, and that with my heart, for this man's fall. Some say I am a hunter, others that I make love, but I wake when they sleep.'

The first discovery of these practices was in February last; and it is much to be marvelled that the Marshal Biron (but that God had blinded his understanding by the presumption of his own worth and valour, and by the bare conceit he had of the King's weakness and timorous nature) being in place of surety within his own government, should have come to render himself to the discretion of the King's mercy. No man did think that the King would put on this resolution, and if he did, that he would have maintained it. At Orleans he would not adventure it for fear the town should have risen and procured the Marshal's liberty; and if Monsieur de Rhosny had not violently persecuted this course, threatening otherwise never to see the King nor Court (for he found no safety in his own state but in the other's ruin), the King would have been content to have passed it over.

The prisoners after their arrest were sent to the Bastille, and two days later the King gave power to the Parliament to make the Marshal's process. He has confessed all the particularities that were demanded, only he doth deny that he ever practised against the King's life. At his first coming into the Bastille he was impatient, dogged and sullen, refusing to eat, or to name the King, much less with duty and respect; nor would he be induced to ask for grace and pardon; but cursed and damned at his folly which brought him into that place. He is now more moderate, yet not so mortified but that he would willingly live.

30th June. AN ATTEMPT ON THE SCOTTISH KING.

From Scotland comes advertisement of some treason intended against the King's person by an Englishman, but the sequel shows it rather to have been some frantic passion of the man than any sinister intent against the King. The man's name is Dethick; he had been an apprentice in London with one Mr. Hickes. After, became factor for him and others in

Florence, and there also did service for the State in being the means for conveyance of much intelligence by letter from Italy. Thence he came to Paris and so to Edinburgh where he saw the King, and as some say, had conference with him, but showing some distemper of head was not permitted that free access there which is usual. Being lodged at a banker's house near the Court he suddenly came down with his rapier drawn and killed one Great James in the shop. Thereupon apprehended and examined what he meant by killing James, he said he had not killed the right James. There are divers rumours about it, some that stand ill affected to Mr. Secretary make much of it, for that the brother of Mr. Hickes is most inward with Mr. Secretary, and this Dethick directs all letters to him. The Scottish King dissembleth as though it were nothing and hath now sent Ashton his agent to receive his pension. The Queen telleth him she marvelleth that Dethick is not hanged.

1st July. GREAT HAIL.

Yesterday in the afternoon there was great lightning and thunder, with hailstones in many places of nine inches compass, which at Sandwich in Kent lay a foot deep on the ground, brake the glass windows of churches and tiles of houses. Some barns also were fired by the lightning.

3rd July. A SUCCESS IN MUNSTER.

In Munster Sir George Carew, the Lord President, hath taken Tyrell's castle of Dunboy after several hours battery, when the assault was given and very desperately maintained some two hours by the enemy, being 143 in number, the best choice of all their forces; but then despair bred such confusion that they of the weakest resolution hopelessly leapt into the sea where boats attended such expected accident and there cut them in pieces. Others with firm constancy died in defending the breach with pikes and swords. The best knowing men retired into an inner cellar, whence they hoped to make composition for life which was refused by the Lord President unless they would yield to mercy, which they obstinately refused. That night they so continued, but in the morning they submitted and the Lord President caused 58 of them to be hanged. Some 50 more were killed on the breach and in the sea, and in an island near by others were killed and 29 taken who also were hanged. There were taken also 3 pieces of ordnance without and 10 pieces within the castle, together with about 20 barrels of powder.

The Lord President rescued alive 14, to see if he could draw them to do some more acceptable service that their lives were worth. The next day word was sent by Tyrell that he would do some acceptable service to redeem the lives of his men, and a stratagem was propounded in the effecting whereof he should obtain pardon and liberty for himself and his dependents. But having learnt in the meantime that a Spanish ship was come to Ardea he gave answer that he would ransom the prisoners but would never be false to the King of Spain, his master. The men were therefore executed, and on the 22nd June the Castle was blown up with powder. There is great fear that more Spaniards will shortly come to Ireland.

10th July. New Erected Buildings.

Although the Lord Mayor and the Justices of the peace in Middlesex go about to put into execution the late orders concerning the erecting of buildings and tenements, there are divers new frames being erected in those places within the City that pretend to be privileged. This abuse is greater in that the offenders do commit this disobedience against the proclamation at the very instant when they see strict order taken in other places. The Lord Mayor is now required to commit them to prison and not to release them until they have themselves taken order to pluck down these frames or to enter bond to answer the same in the Star Chamber.

14th July. The War in the Low Countries.

About a month since His Excellency Count Maurice, having drawn together his army at Skinkesconce hath made a journey into the enemy's country and some miles from St. Troyes and presented battle unto the enemy's camp with the greatest part of all his horse and foot but could not prevail with them to offer fight. Now hath he drawn back his forces and setteth down before Grave where they are busily engaged in digging trenches to prevent the enemy from attacking them in their quarters or from relieving the town. His force at the beginning of the march was 16,000 foot and 5,000 horse, 3,000 wagons which carried all sorts of provisions and would also have served for a fortification if the enemy would have fought; and besides 12 demicannon and 4 smaller pieces, 20 boats on carriages and provision enough to make a bridge to pass a river of 80 paces; also 24 mills which in 34 hours would grind corn sufficient to serve a greater army.

17th July. THE MARSHAL BIRON.

At his first examination the Marshal Biron being asked to reveal his complices refused, whereto he was willed to consider that he was in the hands of justice who wanted not means to draw the truth from him. He answered that he knew it well, and withal unbraced his doublet and showed his breast, covered with scars; and asked what part of his body they could put to torment which had not already sufficiently been torn for their safety and the service of his country.

Of late certain Italian comedians in Paris did set up that they would play *The English history* (*contre la Roine d'Angleterre*). Hereupon Mr. Winwood caused one of their bills to be taken down and brought before the Council, complaining greatly of this insolent indignity against the honour of her Majesty's estate. The play was inhibited and the chief of the company committed to prison where yet they remain. It was objected by some of the standers-by that the death of the Duke of Guise had been played at London, which Mr. Winwood answered was never done in the life of the last King; and, since by others, that the Massacre of St. Bartholomew hath been publicly acted and this King represented on the stage.

20th July. THE IRISH WAR.

The Lord Deputy hath now entered into Tyrone's country where he hath caused to be built a bridge across the Blackwater with a fort adjoining, and other forts are building able to hold soldiers enough to resist any force that the rebels can bring against them.

25th July. THE PLAGUE AT AMSTERDAM.

It is reported that the plague reigns very greatly at Amsterdam, wherefore many of the inhabitants are retiring themselves into this realm, and already are come with purpose to disperse themselves in the port towns and in London. The Lord Cobham and the Lord Mayor are charged to have diligent watch to prevent their landing. If any be already come into the towns they must be made to retire themselves into some quarters abroad in the fields the better to air themselves, and to remain until they have cleared themselves by the trial of 40 days.

26th July. THE PLAY OF 'HAMLET.'

Roberts the printer hath entered for the printing that play of my Lord Chamberlain's Men called *The Revenge of Hamlet, Prince of Denmark*, which they played of late, written by Shakespeare, a play that hath in it much to please the wiser sort.

28th July. COURT RUMOURS.

All our great persons now seek by all means to have the Scottish King well conceited of them, and he on the other side laboureth by many agents to entertain affections here, dissembling if he have any dislike. It is said that he hath in every part of the realm certain principal persons appointed immediately upon notice of the death of her Majesty to proclaim him, and to make what party they can for him. Yet others are said to have an intention to marry the Earl of Hertford's younger son with the Lady Arabella and to carry it that way.

A TREATY WITH THE KING OF DENMARK.

Now that a treaty is proposed between her Majesty and the King of Denmark and some Princes of the Empire, the Lord Eure is chosen to be the principal commissioner, which his Lordship would put from him, declaring that by long discontinuance from the Court he is disfurnished of such courtly respects as fitteth a messenger to so worthy a Princess. Further, the affairs of the country and delights have withdrawn him from the practice and exercise of languages and have long deprived him of the society of men of that quality, so that he can neither deliver message or entertain discourse with foreigners in any language save English; nor will his estate afford him means in so short a time except her Majesty furnish him with more than her ordinary allowance to men of her rank. To all of which answer is returned that the Queen cannot allow of my Lord's declining from this intended meeting; and from his lack of language and pretending to be unprovided of compliments, she answereth that it need no better answer than this, that a nobleman of England that hath seen France and Italy need never doubt to meet the best Dane or German in any place of Europe.

GREAT RAINS.

There have been great rains, lightning, tempest and hail of admirable bigness, five miles and more about, which brake many of the windows of the colleges at Oxford, but wrought much more hurt to the fields by beating down the corn.

29th July. THE EXECUTION OF THE DUKE OF BIRON.

The Duke of Biron was condemned by the Court of Parliament of France for his treasons on the 19th of this month to be publicly executed upon a scaffold in the Greve, but by order of the King he received the grace to die in the Bastille. Whereupon the Chancellor and Chief President of the Court of Parliament went directly to the Bastille, where as soon as the Duke perceived them, he said to those about him, 'Yonder cometh my death.'

The Chancellor having willed him to deliver up the order, meaning the collar of knighthood, he answered, 'Take it, I would I had never seen it.' And as the President would have pronounced the sentence decreed that morning for his private execution, he would in no wise hear him, but interrupting him at every word received it with very great impatiency. And as certain churchmen did admonish him to prepare himself to death, he said unto them, 'Make an end. Do you not see that villain staying for me?'—meaning the executioner. As he went up to the scaffold he remembered one of his sisters that was with child, enquiring whether she were delivered or no: then taking a diamond from his finger he desired that it might be given to her. He told of good store of money which he had here and there, but impeached nobody. And being upon the scaffold, as the executioner came near to make him ready, he commanded him not to touch him lest he put him in a fury, 'for,' said he, 'I will strangle you all.' His countenance was very furious, and oftentimes he looked about to see if he could surprise the executioner's sword. He covered his face and discovered it twice or thrice ; and at the second time he prayed one of his ghostly fathers to comfort him, for he himself could do no more ; and as he went about to uncover his face again, the executioner struck off his head.

His death generally is lamented, yet his best friends do acknowledge that from his infancy he hath been a great blasphemer and that he was of a disposition so savage that he has with his own hand murdered five hundred persons in cold blood.

30th July. SPEECHES OF THE EARL OF LINCOLN.

The Earl of Lincoln is called in question for a speech alleged to have been made shortly after the arraignment of the late Earl of Essex. Quoth he, 'I cannot be persuaded that the Queen will consent to the death of one with whom she has been so familiar. I myself have seen her kiss him twenty times.' Being taxed with this speech the Earl denied it very vehemently, declaring that the report is a practice put upon him by his enemies.

2nd August. THE QUEEN AT THE LORD KEEPER'S.

The Queen and the Court on their progress being entertained at the Lord Keeper's house at Harefield there came into the Presence a mariner with a box under his arm containing sundry things supposed to have come from the carrack. At his entry he sang a song of Cynthia, Queen of seas and lands, which being ended he made a short speech. He gave lots to the ladies for the things in his box, whereof twenty-nine were for gifts and five were blank, but in all a posy written. A while after the Countess of Derby (my Lord Keeper's wife), finding the Queen in her merriest moved that it would please her to accept of the Lady Strange and her sister to wait on her in her privy chamber, and to bestow them in marriage where she thought fit, or at least to give her leave to bestow them ; at which motion the Queen was exceedingly passionate and commanded silence in that behalf. The Queen hunteth every second or third day, for the most part on horseback, and showeth little decay in ability. A country woman viewing her in the progress told her neighbours standing near that the Queen looked very old and ill ; one of the guard, overhearing her, said she should be hanged for these words, and frighted the poor woman exceedingly.

3rd August. THE QUEEN AT HAREFIELD.

At the Queen's departing from Harefield one attired in black, as personating the place, made her speech of farewell, praying that the Queen would pardon her close imprisonment ever since her coming, praying that she would impute it to St. Swithin, who, quoth the speaker, 'of late hath raised so many storms as I was fain to provide this anchor for you'—whereat she presented the Queen with an anchor jewel—'when I understood you would put into this creek; but now since I perceive the harbour is too little for you and that you will hoist sail and be gone, I beseech you take this anchor with you; and I pray to Him that made both Time and Place, that in all places wherever you shall arrive, you may anchor as safely as you do, and ever shall do, in the hearts of my owners.' Further progress is now forborne by reason of the unseasonableness of the weather.

5th August. THE SIEGE OF THE GRAVE.

The army of the Count Maurice still lies before the Grave, where our English captains complain that the General will never make war but by sieges, except he have such great advantages of our army as he shall never have but by the absolute decay of the Spanish power. The ends and ambitions of the chiefs and captains are infinite, neglecting for their private ends the public business; the disagreement of the divers nations great; but the especial dulling of all active spirits is that everybody knows they serve a state from whom no gallant action can ever expect a brave reward.

12th August. A CONJUROR TAKEN.

Upon information given that mass had been said by one Simon Forman in a chamber of a house in Plymouth taken for Sir William Monson, the Mayor sent to search the house. In Forman's chamber were taken a chest and a portmantey wherein, being opened, were found certain wicked books of conjuration and some calculations what shall become of her Majesty's ships in this present service. The Mayor has bound Forman to appear before the judges at Exeter, but Sir William much favours him. The matter is by many in that town thought very dangerous.

17th August. THE SIEGE OF THE GRAVE.

Some days since they of the town of the Grave made a sally upon our English approaches, but were at length beat in again, where Sir Edward Cecil, with his whole troop of horse charging them close to the counterscarp, had his horse shot under him and 9 more of his troop hurt or slain. Our men lost besides 20 horse, 10 footmen and a captain, 2 lieutenants and 2 serjeants. The approaches are now advanced close to the counterscarp of the town and they doubt not within thirty days to carry it. Sir Francis Vere, being in the trenches, was shot with a musket from the town into the cheek bone of his face, which is all broken ; the bullet has gone back towards his neck, nevertheless the chirurgion says there is no danger of his life.

18th August. THE CONJUROR AT PLYMOUTH.

Sir William Monson being warned by a letter from Mr. Secretary that he should entertain a man suspected to be conjuror now declareth that the whole matter was an accident wherein he was like to have been abused by the folly of the Mayor. Sir William had of late a youth that served him that through the extremity of a calenture fell so extreme mad as he was forced continually to be watched and kept in a dark chamber. One day observing when all the servants were abroad he broke out of his chamber window and ran to one of his acquaintances in the town and told him that the day before he came into a house at 5 o'clock in the afternoon and saw this supposed conjuror, with six more, all disguised saying Mass, and going into a chamber above he found Sir William all alone. When Sir William heard of it and how that the Mayor had searched the house and the suspected man's house, he went to the Mayor and showed him how unlike it was any such thing could be, for that the time of day was against the use of Mass so to be said, and for himself he had never been in the house in his life, and on that day all the men in the fleet could witness he was aboard from 1 o'clock until 8 at night. Whereupon, after further consideration, the youth was kept that night with a watch to observe his humour, who report next day that he is found to be mad ; and all to proceed out of an idle brain.

20th August. The Lord Treasurer's Son.

The Lord Treasurer hath a young son, of all his children the finest and comeliest, with such a rare curled head as the Queen pleased to have very special liking of him, but such was his misfortune that in a very great sickness he fell into a lethargy from which time he hath fallen into a distraction of all his senses. This boy for his cure by practise of physic and otherwise in England and abroad hath cost my Lord above £2,000, and for the last two years hath been in Germany where he is reported rather worse than better. My Lord would now send him to Padua, to be committed to a council of physicians, for if the boy may be cured by skill of physic, that place above all the world doth yield the most rare and excellent physicians to perform it.

25th August. Tyrone a Fugitive.

The Lord Mountjoy still presseth upon Tyrone who is now beaten out of his country and lives in a part of O'Canes, a place of incredible fastness, where, though it be impossible to do him any hurt, yet by lying about him he shall soon be brought to great extremity, and if not taken then forced to fly the Kingdom. The Lord Deputy hath spent some days about Tullough Oge where the O'Neales are of old custom created, and there he hath spoiled the corn of all the country, and Tyrone's own corn. He hath moreover broken down the chair wherein the O'Neales are wonted to be created, being of stone, standing in a field. There are confident reports that the Spaniard will come again with a strong army of 15,000 and 2,000 horse.

3rd September. A Book of Conny-Catching.

One S. R. hath compiled a book called *Greene's Ghost haunting Conny-catchers*, adding to those things formerly written by Greene certain new shifts, together with the conceits of Dr. Pinchback a notable makeshift. This shifting companion with his boy having by a sleight persuaded mine host of a tavern at York that he was some wise doctor there lay without charge; and his fame being spread about the country, there came thither a gentleman who, desirous to make trial of his cunning, craved to know of him (his wife being then big with child) whether it was a male child or a woman child. He answered that he could say little thereto unless he saw her naked, hoping thereby to have shifted the gentleman off by this extraordinary imposition. Nevertheless the gentleman, persisting in his demand, caused his wife to show herself and twice she walked up and down the chamber naked in presence of Mr. Doctor, who being demanded again the former question, quoth he, 'from me-ward it is a boy and to me-ward it is a girl.' Wherefore the gentleman was greatly offended, calling him 'ass, dolt, patch, cockscomb, knave' and all other names he could devise. About four days after the gentlewoman fell in labour and was delivered of a boy and a girl; whereat the gentleman remembering the blunt answer of the Doctor and finding it to be true, was greatly astonished, supposing he had wronged the Doctor; and thereupon in recompense of amends granted him his house at commandment.

4th September. SIR E. DYMOCK AND THE EARL OF LINCOLN.

Upon the last Sunday in August, Sir Edward Dymock with certain of his friends and neighbours having conceived an injury of the Earl of Lincoln hath offered my Lord very gross abuse at Horncastle, by acting a play on the green hard by the maypole called *The Lord of Kyme*, to which the people and divers neighbours were invited. Herein by name one counterfeited the person of the Earl of Lincoln with his features and speeches, being fetched away by the Devil; and another played the vice who bequeathed his wooden sword to the Earl, and his cockscomb and bauble to the people that did not go to Horncastle with Sir Edward Dymock when he made a riot there about a month since. There was also a *dirige nos Domine* sung by most of the known whores of London, Lincoln and Boston, with *ora pro nobis* to the end of every verse. Also at the end of the play one having a minister's gown and corner cap, standing in a pulpit made for that purpose, uttered a profane prayer and preached a sermon out of the book of Mab.

7th September. THE DEATH OF MR. GEORGE GILPIN.

Three days since died Mr. George Gilpin at the Hague who hath served there as her Majesty's agent, in whom her Majesty hath long a very sufficient servant, in whose place another will not easily be found, for he that shall be sent had need speak the Low Dutch and be acquainted with that manner of government which differeth from all others.

10*th September*. COMPLAINTS AGAINST THE EARL OF LINCOLN.

Sir Edward Dymock greatly complaineth against my Lord of Lincoln. Sometime since, Sir Edward, having a lease of the manor of Horncastle, won a verdict against the Earl, who pretended a former lease and is now in possession and dwelleth there. Notwithstanding the Earl hath in many ways violated Sir Edward. He caused a little shed or watch house to be built upon an outpost of the grounds of purpose to keep divers loose fellows to disturb and drive off Sir Edward's cattle. When Sir Edward caused this shed to be destroyed the Earl called a privy sessions, pretending a force to be committed, and then compelled the undersheriff to make out warrants unto his own servants for the apprehending of Sir Edward and seven of his men. Sir Edward having tendered bail to the undersheriff and coming to the sessions to prosecute a bill of force against the base fellows that were lodged in the shed, the Earl, with his son Lord Clinton, sat upon the Bench, outfacing and appalling the jury, and gave Sir Edward the lie thrice and told him he was in a mad fit, with other most foul and opprobrious words. The jury then being charged with the indictments of force and conferring thereupon in the church, where they were appointed for that purpose, his Lordship's attorney, with divers others of his men, walked before the porch offering to confer them and outcountenancing some other of the jury. Whereupon Sir Edward, without his rapier, went to the inn where the other justices and the Earl were, to intreat them to take some indifferent cause, but the Earl at his first coming pulled the beard of a gentleman who accompanied him, and his son Mr. Edward Clinton jostled him, and Lord Clinton pulled out Sir Edward's dagger and stabbed at him. It is reported in those parts that the Earl meaneth to come to Sir Edward's house in Horncastle and bring fourscore men to pull him out thereof by the ears, and that he was advised by his attorney to pull the house down and stand to a fine in the court of Star Chamber rather than suffer Sir Edward to hold possession thereof.

15th September. THE GRAVE TAKEN.

The Grave is surrendered to the States, and on the 8th of this month the Count Maurice's guard marched into the town and the enemy came forth with their arms, flying colours, bag and baggage. They were almost 800 able soldiers and 20 horse. They left in the town about 20 pieces of artillery and 3,000 weight of powder. There have been lost before this town 11 captains and 400 soldiers, and the army at this instant is scant 10,000 foot and 3,500 horse; of our English there are not 4,000 able marching men.

A PROCLAMATION CONCERNING GAME.

Because of the neglect of former orders straight proclamation is now made that none shall take with nets, setting dogs or any other instruments or engines, any pheasants, partridges or fowl of the river within six miles of her Majesty's usual houses, viz., Windsor Castle, Whitehall, Hampton Court, Richmond, Greenwich, Oatlands or Nonesuch.

THE JESUITS.

It is said that there is a proclamation penned and ready for press against the Jesuits and all sorts of priests, that they should be charged by a certain day to depart the realm. The Bishop of London is very busy with three chaplains and as many scribes in composing some new book against Jesuits that it may be extant against the term.

''TIS MERRY WHEN GOSSIPS MEET.'

There is a new book called *'Tis Merry when Gossips Meet*, by S. R., being a poetical dialogue between a widow, a wife and a maid of their several states as they sit drinking in a tavern.

16th September. A NOBLE VISITOR.

There is present in London the Duke Philip Julius, Duke of Stettin Pomerania, a young man of 18 years that travelleth for his education with sixteen gentlemen and servants. They came to London four days ago and to-day were taken to see the Tower, where they were shown the armour, as much as it seemed was necessary for one hundred thousand men; also the 80 large pieces mostly taken from the Spaniard, and besides 200 cast pieces large and small, and the arrows prepared with pitch for firing at ships, the bows, arrows, lances and other weapons there stored. They saw also the place where the Earl of Essex was beheaded, but by reason that the Queen is not in London they were unable to see the royal jewels, the crown and the sceptre, nor the gown lined with the skin of a unicorn. In the afternoon they saw the bears baited, and the bulls, to their no small contentment.

18*th September*. THE DUKE OF STETTIN.

This day the Duke visited the museum of Mr. Robert Cotton where he saw many strange things, as arms from the East Indies, crowns from America, two teeth of sea horse, the horn of a rhinoceros also the tail with very coarse hairs, many strange birds and fishes; that famous fish called *remora* that hath scales almost square; also a mummy, together with many books written in India.

Thence they went to see the Children of the Chapel play, being informed that the children are required to act a play once a week to the end that they may acquire courteous manners, being furnished with the theatre and an abundance of costly garments. Those who would see a play must give as much as 8s., but there are always a number present, of whom many be reputable women, because useful precepts and good doctrine—so they were told—is pronounced there. All their plays they act by the light of candles, and for an hour before the play begins there is a concert of music on organs, lutes, pandoras, mandolins, violins and flutes. They noted that the singing of one boy was so tuneful that they had not heard the like of it, save for the nuns in Milan.

19*th September*. THE QUEEN AND SIR R. CECIL.

In Court there is much dancing, especially in the Privy Chamber, of country dances before the Queen, who is exceedingly pleased therewith. Of late the young Countess of Derby wearing about her neck in her bosom a picture which was in a dainty tablet, the Queen espying it asked what fine jewel it was. The Lady Derby was curious to excuse the showing of it, but the Queen would have it, and opening it and finding it to be Mr. Secretary's, snatched it away and tied it upon her shoe, walking long with it there. Then she pinned it upon her elbow and wore it some time there also; which Mr. Secretary being told of, he made certain verses and had Hales to sing them in his chamber. It was told her Majesty that Master Secretary had rare music and songs. She would needs hear them, and so this ditty was sung in her presence, wherein some of the verses argue that he repines not though her Majesty please to grace others, and contents himself with the favour he hath.

20th September. MR. THOMAS BODLEY.

Upon the death of Mr. Gilpin the Queen is resolved to send Mr. Thomas Bodley back once more to the Low Countries, but he protesteth that he is now so unfit and unable to wield that service that he petitioneth Mr. Secretary to be a means that her Majesty will be pleased not to cast the charge upon him.

THE BOOTY OF THE CARRACK.

The inventory now taken of the goods the carrack *St. Valentine* showeth: of calico 27,442 books besides many thousand bundles of wrought and coloured; of quilts 205; of Persian carpets 44; of Turkey carpets 10; of leather carpets 37; of raw silks 160 bundles; of sleaved silks 1589 papers; of stuff of silk 36 rolls; of canopies and testers of wrought silk 6; of seed pearls 14 bags; of pepper 1,095 hogsheads, besides many chests and hogsheads of cinnamon, ginger, green ginger and other conserves (whereof 41 barrels), cloves, maces, rice, cusco, with many medicinable drugs; and of ebony 1,260 pieces.

23rd September. COURT NEWS.

At Court it is noted that the Queen's health and disposition of body is excellent, she not being in every way better disposed these many years.

27th September. THE DUKE OF STETTIN AT COURT.

Yesterday the young German Duke came to the Court, which is now at Oatlands, where the Queen gave orders that he should be conducted to the garden close to the palace; and here she passed by him several times, walking very brisk, ever taking off her mask and bowing deeply towards the Duke, who, however, was unwilling to make himself known and stood almost behind his servants. The Queen sent also that he might kiss her hand, which he declined. At last she ordered some of her Lords and Councillors to approach, and they were obliged to remain on their knees all the while that she spake to them.

'The Christian Navy.'

Mr. Anthony Nixon hath a poem called *The Christian Navy*, wherein is plainly described the perfect course to sail to the haven of eternal happiness, which he dedicateth to the Archbishop of Canterbury. Herein is described, in manner of an allegory of a sea-voyage, the journey of the soul to the heavenly landing place.

The Careful Captain

He that amidst the raging ocean seas,
With sailing bark doth seek the happy port,
No leisure hath to give himself to ease,
No respite for due-season-losing sport ;
Each time-delaying calm doth him displease,
In nothing joys, in nothing pleasure finds,
Save in the blasts of prosperous happy winds.

His careful brain is busied evermore
In viewing well his compass and his card,
And minding still what dangers lie before,
What swelling sands, what rocks, what havens bar'd ;
With skilful head he seeks the safest shore,
Bringing his bark, through storms and tempests great,
To happy port and long desired seat.

Don Sebastian.

There are two new books of Don Sebastian printing, whereof one showeth how after his departure from Venice two years since he came to Naples and was there cast into prison, and afterwards sent to the galleys and is now at St. Lucar in Spain ; and of all that befell him as a prisoner ; and how that his coming very strangely fulfilled certain ancient prophecies. In the second are printed sundry letters written by an ancient man, called Dr. Teixeira, a Portugal, to a Bishop, the father's very good friend, with sundry other discourses of the unfortunate accidents this disastrous King hath sustained.

2nd October. SPANISH GALLEYS SUNK.

On the 23rd of last month Sir Robert Mansell in the *Hope* with the *Advantage* which Captain Jones commanded and two other Dutch men of war encountered six Spanish galleys in the Channel and so battered them that four are sunk and wrecked, the fifth past doing the enemy service, and the sixth the enemy are forced to newbuild at Dunkirk. Nevertheless though Sir Robert bore the greater part of this action, yet to his great indignation the Dutchmen put it abroad that the whole glory of that service is theirs.

5th October. A TALL GALLANT.

Lately one Mr. Ouseley of the Middle Temple, a young gallant but of a short cut, overtaking a tall stately stalking cavalier in the streets, made no more ado but slipped into an ironmonger's shop, threw off his cloak and rapier, fitted himself with bells, and straightway came skipping, whistling and dancing the morrice about that long swaggerer, who staringly demanded what he meant. 'I cry you mercy,' said the gentleman, 'I took you for a maypole.'

9th October. BIRON'S CONSPIRACY.

The Count d'Auvergne who was imprisoned in the Bastille for his privity in the Marshal Biron's late conspiracy hath now been released; and before the King at dinner he presented himself on his knees. The King asked him in the presence of the nobility what he demanded. He answered, pardon and grace. The King, after some pause, said, 'I grant you both; and say to you as Christ said to the woman in the Gospel, *allez vous en et ne pechez plus.*' And so raised him up and embraced him; which the nobility present afterward did, every one in his rank. The King then took him with him in his coach to the Louvre and the next day a-hunting, and so he remains in Court as before.

11th October. A CASE OF PLAGUE.

There is plague in two houses at Wapping which took in goods that came from Dantzic, not a person in either house escaping but all are dead. The goods had not been in their houses above three days. If extraordinary care be not taken the plague will break forth general in England.

12th October. THE EARL OF SUSSEX'S BASE WRONGS.

The Earl of Sussex keeps one Mistress Sylvester Morgan (sometime his lady's gentlewoman) as his mistress, calls her his Countess, hires Captain Whitlocke with money and cast suits to brave his Countess with telling her how he buys his wench a waistcoat of £10 and puts her in her velvet gown; and not content to abuse her by keeping a common wench, he strives to invent means of more grief to his Lady, who is of a very goodly and comely personage, of an excellent presence and a rare wit. She hath brought the Earl to allow her £1,700 a year for the maintenance of herself and her children while she lives apart.

16th October. A PLAY OF MARSHAL BIRON.

My Lord of Worcester's men at the Rose have a new play of the life and execution of the Marshal Biron.

21st October. TYRONE'S SUBMISSION.

Tyrone is now very desirous to submit himself to the Queen's mercy, and the Lord Deputy is reported willing to receive him seeing the danger of fresh Spanish succours; but the Queen herself remaineth determined not to give him grace in any kind who hath been the only cause of so much effusion of blood and the most ungrateful viper to her that raised him.

28th October. THE CHARGE TO THE NEW LORD MAYOR.

This day the new Lord Mayor was presented in the Exchequer by Mr. Croke, the Recorder. The Lord Chief Baron Periam in his speech recommended her Majesty's singular benefits to the thankful considerations of the City and admonished that there might be some monthly strict search made in the City for idle persons and masterless men, whereof, saith he, there are at this time 30,000 in London; these ought to be found out and well punished for they are the very scum of England and sink of iniquity.

The Lord Treasurer spake sharply and earnestly that of his certain knowledge there were two things her Majesty is desirous should be amended; both matters of importance, and if they be not better looked unto the shame will be unsupportable and their answer inexcusable. The first is now in time of plenty to make provision of corn to fill the magazines of the City as well for sudden occasions as for provision of the poor in time of dearth. The other is the erecting and furnishing of hospitals. These are things must be better regarded than they have been; otherwise howsoever he honour the City in his private person, yet it is his duty in regard of his place to call them to account for it.

31st October. THE SERMON AT PAUL'S CROSS.

To-day Dr. Dove preached at Paul's Cross against the excessive pride and vanity of women in apparel, which vice he said was in their husbands' power to correct. He reprehended two preachers that their auditory, being most of women, abounded in that superfluous vanity of apparel.

5th November. A PROCLAMATION FOR PROCEEDING AGAINST JESUITS AND SECULAR PRIESTS.

There is a proclamation setting forth the malice and insolency of the Jesuits and secular priests notwithstanding the forbearance of late years shown towards them. Yet by the books lately published it is manifest how wickedly they combine themselves together in the Realm for the advancement of our enemies, the persecuting of subjects, and the subversion of the State, being grown to such an height of impiety as they freely in their late treatises profess that the subjects are bound to fight against her Majesty and to join forces with any enemy that the Pope shall send under pretence of restoring the Roman religion. Such is become their pride and presumption that they thrust themselves into all affairs of State, adventuring in their writings and speeches to dispose of the Kingdom and Crown at their pleasures; and if any of a milder nature doth seem to acknowledge the lenity of her Highness' proceedings, it is a sufficient cause of their hatred and revenge to pursue him as an enemy: and besides their transporting the youth of the Realm into foreign seminaries thereby to corrupt the best families.

Of late much contention and controversy hath arisen between the Jesuits and the secular priests; the former seeking and practising continual plots for the invasion and conquest of the Kingdom, but the secular priests not only protesting against the same as a thing most wicked, detestable and damnable but also offering themselves to be the first to discover such traitorous practices and to be foremost by arms to suppress it. It is evident that the treason that is lodged within the hearts of the Jesuits and their adherents is fraughted with much more violent malice, peril and poison than the disobedience which is found in the secular priests that are opposite them ; nevertheless they concur notwithstanding in apparent disobedience and disloyalty, masking themselves under the vizard of pretended conscience, a suggestion of all others most perilous.

Moreover they insinuate almost daily into the minds of all sorts of people that there is some purpose to grant toleration of two religions within the Realm, which is indeed far from the imagination of her Majesty, being a course that would not only disturb the peace of the Church but bring this her State into confusion. Furthermore, this conceipt of a toleration is accompanied with great liberty in that they dare adventure to walk in the streets at noondays, to resort to prisons publicly, and execute their functions in contempt of the law, never ceasing to waken her Justice which hath lien in a slumber, insomuch that other natures (apt to innovation and affected much to their own opinions) have broken forth into factious invectives in print, presuming to censure her government for remissness as if no care were had by any but themselves.

Now therefore all Jesuits and the secular priests combined together with them that are at liberty are charged forthwith to depart out of the land ; and the secular priests also that are of the other party shall depart betwixt this and the 1st of January next, except such of them as shall present themselves to some of the Lords of the Privy Council, the Presidents of Wales and York, or the Bishops, and submit themselves to the Queen's mercy. And to the end that they may be the sooner avoided from hence all officers are charged to search places suspected and to apprehend all Jesuits and secular priests together with their receivers, relievers and maintainers.

6th November. THE EARL OF NORTHUMBERLAND.

It is said that the Earl of Northumberland lives apart again from his lady now she hath brought him an heir, which he said was the solder of their reconcilement. He lives at Sion House with the child and plays with it, being otherwise of a very melancholy spirit.

9th November. A DISCOURSE AGAINST MACHIAVELLI.

There is to be printed that translation into English made by Mr. Simon Paterick in 1577 of M. Gentillet's book against Machiavelli, with the title *A discourse upon the means of well governing and maintaining in good peace a Kingdom or other principality*; divided into three parts, namely, the council, the religion, and the policy which a Prince ought to hold and follow.

12th November. A COSENING PRANK.

This day there was a cosening prank played by one Venner, that gave out bills of a famous play at the Swan theatre on the Bankside to be acted only by certain gentlemen and gentlewomen of account. The price at coming in was 2s. or 18d. at least; and when he had gotten most part of the money into his hands he would have showed them a fair pair of heels, but he was not so nimble to get upon horseback but that he was fain to forsake that course and betake himself to the water where he was pursued and taken, and brought before the Lord Chief Justice, who would make nothing of it but a jest and a merriment and bound him over in £5 to appear at the Sessions. In the meantime the common people when they saw themselves deluded, revenged themselves upon the hangings, curtains, chairs, stools and walls, and whatsoever came in their way very outrageously and made great spoil. There was great store of good company and many noblemen.

17th November. THE QUEEN.

The Queen came to Whitehall from Richmond on Monday last, but whereas she ought to have come in great pomp, she was taken with some sudden distemper by the way and so went in her close barge, whereby the Lord Mayor and the citizens that rode out to meet her lost their labour.

The new proclamation against the priests is read in all parish churches of England.

20th November. VENNER'S PRANK.

Venner, that gentleman of Lincoln's Inn who lately played a conny catching trick over a play, coming to Court since in a black suit, boots and golden spurs, without a rapier, one told him he was not well suited, for golden spurs and a brazen face were ill sorted. Whereat another said, 'It seems he hath some mettle in him.'

21st November. THE TILTING.

Mr. Egerton, my Lord Keeper's son, brake a staff gallantly this tilting. There came a page skipping, 'Ha, well done i'faith,' said he, 'your grandfather never ran such a course.'

22nd November. THE TREATY IN DENMARK.

The Commissioners at Bremen complain that though the Danes at their first meeting entertained them with fair speeches and protested their desire for amity with her Majesty, yet such vehement debates, contradictions and deceptions have fallen out between them that little good is to be expected. The commissioners for the King of Denmark utterly refuse a perfect league and amity between the two Kingdoms. After three weeks had been vainly consumed they sent our commissioners two papers, one claiming the dominion of the Great Ocean and inhibiting our nation to fish or use any trade without license, the other a declaration against our nation for spoils committed on the seas and want of justice in England, preferring the justice of the Dunkirkers before ours.

28th November. THE SERMON AT PAUL'S CROSS.

This day Mr. Tolson of Queens' College in Cambridge preached at Paul's Cross, his text in Ephesians v. 25. He spake much against the Papists, who, quoth he, have a trick of appropriating the name of the Church to themselves only. As they read the Church it is their's dead sure; but this is but the fashion of Creislaus of Athens, a frantic fellow that would board all ships that arrived, search and take account of all things as they were his own, when poor fellow he was scarce worth the clothes on his back. The Papists call their Mass a bloodless sacrifice, but if we look back but to the late times before her Majesty's happy entrance, we may see tokens and witness enough that it is the most bloody that ever was invented. All were hot and zealous against the Papist at the beginning of her Majesty's reign; all cold, as it were asleep, nay dead in these times. Some slander the Court as though they were neuters;

some the Universities as inclining to Popery; many looking for a toleration; but whither shall we go? Here is the Word of Life.

6th December. THE QUEEN ENTERTAINED.

To-day the Queen dined at Sir Robert Cecil's new house in the Strand. She was very royally entertained, richly presented and marvellous well contented, but at her departure she strained her foot. His hall is well furnished with choice weapons which her Majesty took special notice of. There were sundry devices presented. At her entrance three women, a maid, a widow and a wife each commending their own states, but the virgin preferred. Another was one attired in habit of a Turk desirous to see her Majesty, but as a stranger without hope of that grace. Answer was made how gracious her Majesty is in admitting to presence, and how able to discourse in any language; which the Turk admired, and being admitted presents her with a rich mantle.

10th December. A REPLY TO PARSONS.

The secular priests have answered that book of Parsons entitled the *Manifestation*, calling it *A reply unto a certain libel, lately set forth by Father Parsons*; with an addition of a table of such uncharitable words and phrases as by him are uttered in that treatise.

22nd December. 'WONDERS WORTH THE HEARING.'

There is a new book by Breton, called *Wonders worth the hearing*, which being read or heard in a winter's evening by a good fire or a summer's morning in the green fields, may serve both to purge melancholy from the mind and gross humours from the body; written in form of a dialogue between Francisco and Lorillo, describing certain wonders of this age as a constable or a decayed soldier or an usurer.

SIR EDWARD WOTTON PROMOTED.

This day Sir William Knollys was promoted by her Majesty from the office of Controller to be Treasurer of the Household, and Sir Edward Wotton made Controller, and sworn of her Majesty's Privy Council.

24th December. THE LADY EFFINGHAM.

It is said that the Lady Effingham (wife of the Lord William Howard), as she was playing at shuttlecock, upon a sudden felt herself somewhat, and thereupon retiring herself into a chamber was brought to bed of a child without a midwife, she never suspecting that she had been with child. This play at shuttlecock is become so much in request at Court that the making of shuttlecocks is almost grown a trade in London.

25th December. MR. RICHARD HAWKINS' RETURN.

Mr. Richard Hawkins, son to the late Sir John, is now returned to England, having been a prisoner with the Spaniards these nine years and treated with most cruel usage.

27th December. THE QUEEN'S HEALTH.

The Queen doth now bear show of human infirmity too fast for that evil which we shall get by her death, and too slow for that good which she shall get by her releasement from pains and misery. Of late Sir John Harington was in the presence. Her Majesty enquired of some matters which he had written, and as she was pleased to note his fanciful brain he was not unheedful to feed her humour and read some verses; whereat she smiled once and said, 'When thou dost feel creeping Time at thy gate, these fooleries will please thee less; I am past my relish for such matters. Thou seest my bodily meat doth not suit me well; I have eaten but one ill tasted cake since yesternight.' She rated most grievously at some who minded not to bring up certain matters of account. Several men have been sent to, and when ready at hand her Highness hath dismissed them in anger; for who shall say, 'Your Highness hath forgotten?'

31st December. NEW PLAYS.

This past year the Lord Admiral's men have played these new plays: *Too Good to be True* (by Chettle, Hathway and Smith); *The Spanish Fig*; *Malcolm, King of Scots*; *Love parts Friendship* (by Chettle and Smith); *The Bristol Tragedy*; *Tobias* (by Chettle); *Caesar's Fall* (by Drayton, Dekker, Middleton, Munday and Webster); *Richard Crookback* (by Jonson); *The Danish Tragedy* (by Chettle); *The Widow's Charm* (by

Munday); *A Medicine for a Curst Wife* (by Dekker); *Samson; William Cartwright* (by Haughton); *Felmelanco*; *Mortimer*; *The Earl of Hertford*; *Joshua* (by Rowley); *Randal, Earl of Chester* (by Middleton); *Merry as Maybe* (by Day, Hathway and Smith); *The Set at Tennis* (by Munday).

OTHER BOOKS SET FORTH ANNO 1602

MR. DARRELL'S ANSWER TO THE PREACHERS.

Mr. Darrell hath now invectively answered the dialogues of the preachers, Deacon and Walker, in a pamphlet called *A Survey of certain dialogical discourses*, wherein, quoth he, 'how can I after so great vexation by the Bishop of London, so long imprisonment, such public producement into open courts, and lastly my pains to clear the truth from Mr. Harsnett's slanders, but like a tired and weather beaten bird, wish some quiet corner to rest myself in, and to dry my feathers in the warm sun. But it is not my lot, I think, to breath me, no, not a little.' As for their upbraiding him with printing books without privilege, he answereth that everyone is bound to observe the meaning of the law, which is to suppress falsehood and wickedness. But when such officers shall come in place to be set over this charge, which instead of suppressing error and sin will according to their own deceived humours suppress truth and virtue, here the meaning of the law is to be looked into and practised, and the letter is not precisely to be stood upon, which is abused by unworthy persons to a wrong purpose.

OBSERVATIONS IN THE ART OF ENGLISH POETRY.

A book by Master Thomas Campion, entitled *Observations in the art of English Poetry*, wherein he declareth the unaptness of rime in poesy, alleging it to be a vulgar and unartificial custom, contending that the English tongue will receive eight several kinds of numbers proper to itself which he exemplifieth; and as for the heroical verse that is distinguished by the dactile, it hath been oftentimes attempted in our English tongue, but with passing pitiful success; 'and no wonder, seeing it is an attempt altogether against the nature of our language. For both the concourse of our monosyllables make our verses unapt to slide, and also if we examine our polysyllables, we shall find few of them by reason of their heaviness willing to serve in place of a dactile.'

JOSEPHUS' WORKS ENGLISHED.

Dr. Thomas Lodge hath translated *The famous and memorable works of Josephus*, a man of much honour and learning among the Jews, being a history in twenty books, wherein the Antiquity of the Jews is discovered ; seven books of the wars of the Jews ; two books against Apion the Grammarian in justification of the former work ; a book touching the memorable martyrdom of the Machabees ; and Josephus' Life, written by himself. Note that warning of the author against those who will read history idly, seeing that many men, because they have read many excellent works will be capricious and pretend wisdom, resembling those tragedians who after they have discharged themselves of their parts and apparel, wherein they counterfeited the Emperor, yet retain his royal and princely manners ; and how that some trivial and light-witted, that make an eclipse of a shadow, make more of the emblem than the work, the habit than the Doctor ; so admirable effects worketh history in men's minds.

1603

8th January. MR. RICHARD HAWKINS.

Master Hawkins, being demanded on her Majesty's behalf why he went to the Court of Spain when he was first set at liberty, protested that he was moved by divers reasons, partly to see that Court and learn the parts of the King and his Council which are diversely reported, but more to do her Majesty service by discovering their secret practices and preparations, and also to work among the better sort a better opinion of her inclination to peace contrary to the persuasions of Jesuits and other traitors. He declareth that he was greatly importuned with large offers to enter the King of Spain's service, but he refused all.

10th January. A DEFENCE OF ASTROLOGY.

Two years since Mr. John Chamber published a treatise against astrology and now Sir Christopher Heydon has laboriously compiled *A Defence of Judicial Astrology*, wherein he goeth about to confute Mr. Chamber in 551 pages; addeth thereto sundry tables as of the places of Scripture, Councils, Fathers, Schoolmen and Divines in defence of Astrology; and a chronological list of historiographers, poets, philosophers, and physicians; together with a list of astronomers from the beginning of the world, of whom Adam and Seth were first.

30th January. THE TOLERATION OF THE LORD MOUNTJOY.

In Dublin the Lord Chancellor and Council have imprisoned divers for religion, and amongst them some Aldermen, during the absence of the Lord Deputy. But he mistakes of the matter for, saith he, a violent course herein will do little good to win men's consciences; and howsoever it is too soon to begin it, for it is most sure to breed a new war. The bringing in of the Inquisition did lose the King of Spain the Low Countries, and when the States were almost possessed of all the provinces they almost had lost all with too much violence in prosecuting the contrary religion. My Lord is of opinion that all religions do grow under persecution; it is truly good doctrine and example that must prevail.

31st January. A DECLARATION OF THE SECULAR PRIESTS.

Certain of the secular priests have drawn up a declaration giving an assurance of their fidelity to the Queen and her crown. They acknowledge the Queen's full sovereignty over them and all her subjects and protest their willingness to obey her as far as ever Christian priests do, as to pay tribute, pray for her life, prosperous reign and final happiness, considering that they have no warrant to disobey her in any civil or temporal matter. They protest that they would defend her and the realm against all conspiracies, and would reveal and to their uttermost power resist them. If the Pope should excommunicate her and her adherents, they and all lay Catholics would defend her notwithstanding and obey her, though some will misconstrue them; they would therefore make known publicly that while yielding Caesar's due unto her, they depart not from their duty to their supreme pastor; but confess him to have St. Peter's authority, given by our Saviour's commission, and will obey him as bound by the laws of God, which will stand with performance of their duty to their temporal Prince. They would spend their lives in defence of her Majesty, but lose their lives rather than infringe the authority of the Catholic Church.

1st February. ELEVEN SERGEANTS CALLED.

There were eleven Sergeants-at-law called this day. The Queen was at first unwilling to choose as many but for the urgency of the Lord Keeper and the Lord Justice, whose reasons are the age and infirmities of three of the learnedest judges, namely the two Chief Justices and Justice Walmsley, who has gout and palsy; the Chief Baron, Baron Clerk and Justice Clench are to be put on pension, and Justice Fenner will never run mad with learning. There remains only Justices Gawdy, Kingsmill and Yelverton, the youngest of whom is 60 years old. All these places are to be supplied with the serjeants who will be Judges hereafter. When the Queen was moved to have called another to have made up twelve she refused, saying she feared if there were twelve there would be one false brother among them. Of these eleven one is Mr. Barker of the Inner Temple ; for whose preferment the world finds no other reason but that he is Mr. Attorney's brother-in-law. 'Nay,' answered Mr. Bacon, 'if he be Mr. Attorney's brother-in-*law* he may well be a sergeant.' Whereat another said that it is well there should be one Barker among so many biters.

6th February. TYRONE TO BE RECEIVED.

The Queen hath now hardly consented that the Lord Deputy shall send for Tyrone with promise of security for his life only, and upon his arrival without further assurance to make stay of him.

7th February. A FENCER SLAIN.

Turner and Dun, two famous fencers, played their prizes this day at the Bankside, but Turner at last ran Dun so far in the brain at the eye, that he fell down straightway stone dead ; a goodly sport in a Christian state to see one man kill another !

9th February. THE VENETIAN AMBASSADOR GIVEN AUDIENCE.

This day Signior Scaramelli, who is come from Venice to make complaint for the piracies committed by our sailors upon the ships of Venice, was given audience at Richmond by her Majesty, there being present also all the Lords of the Council, and the ladies and gentlemen of the Court. The ambassador having been received with the customary compliments and having presented his letters of credit entered into his commission, and declared that whereas the Queen's subjects had been very excellently treated, there had been very grave excesses committed by English pirates, and that they of Venice trusted that the booty should speedily be restored.

Her Majesty, having read the letter which the ambassador brought, then rose to her feet and said that she was surprised that the Republic of Venice during the forty-four years of her reign had never made itself heard by her save to ask for something, nor had they given sign of holding her or her kingdom in that esteem which other princes had not refused. 'But,' quoth she, 'I would not be discourteous, though I would have you know that this kingdom is not so short of men that some lewd ruffians may not be found among them. Forasmuch as this question toucheth my subjects I will appoint commissioners who shall confer with you and make report to me, and I will do all that in me lies to give satisfaction to the Republic' ; which promise the Queen renewed at the departure of the ambassador, saying, 'But I know not if I have spoken the Italian well ; yet I think so, for I learnt it when a child and I believe that I have not forgotten it.'

So the ambassador is given leave to depart. There are appointed to treat with him the Lord Admiral, Mr. Secretary and Sir Edward Wotton.

12th February. BEN JONSON.

Ben Jonson the poet now lives upon one Townsend and scorns the world.

14th February. A PURITAN CONDEMNED.

This day Darling, out of whom Darrell formerly cast a devil and who is now a scholar of Oxford, being sent up with certain others, was convicted in the Star Chamber for some bold speeches uttered against some of the Lords of the Council. He wrote a letter to a friend wherein he taxed the Lord Treasurer and the Secretary of Papistry, as also Sir John Fortescue, my Lord of Canterbury, and my Lord of London, saying that one of them made way for Papistry ; that good laws were enacted against them but none executed, and a good proclamation lately set forth against priests, but it proved ridiculous, for that by my Lord of London especially, and others, they were still countenanced. Besides, he said, my Lady Buckhurst nursed Papistry in her lap, and that she heard Mass with my Lord Montacute in Salisbury Court. All which speeches he avowed with like boldness and impudency before all the Lords of the Council that they were not a little amazed to hear him. He is censured to stand upon the pillory and to have one ear cut off in Cheapside and the other in Oxford. The Lord Chief Justice told him he had done amongst others great injury to my Lord of London, affirming of his own knowledge that not any man hath done greater service to the State than the Bishop, for, saith he, he hath put a disunion between the priests themselves ; he hath caused them to write one against another, and to subscribe their names, which all the world thought impossible ever to come to pass.

Moreover the Bishop of London himself declared that Jesuits and secular priests confessed on examination that perjury was lawful for Catholics in England, because they say that Pope Pius V has excommunicated Queen Elizabeth; wherefore all her magistrates and their authority are of none effect. Moreover their text is: *iuramentum coram iudice non competente non obligat*, an oath taken before a judge that no competence bindeth not. And so, saith he, they hold it lawful for Catholics to cozen all Protestants in bargains and debts.

It is now manifest that the Bishop, on the advice of the Council and especially Mr. Secretary, has travailed to bring about discord between the Jesuits and the secular priests, whereby they have written divers railing quodlibets and pamphlets one against the other, so that the treacherous purpose of the Jesuits to depose the Queen as unlawful has appeared also from their very writings. Also in their appeal to Rome against each other they left the Pope in discontent; the Jesuits, who have the countenance of Spain in all things, because the plea of the secular priests was not rejected, the seculars because they are not more countenanced. Nevertheless with one consent they are against the Protestants, howsoever their writings would give colour to the contrary, as the Bishop and the Secretary say and believe.

15th February. MOORDITCH TO BE CLEANSED.

The commissioners met to-day at the Earl of Shrewsbury's house and ordered that a time should be appointed by certain magistrates of Middlesex and the City of London for cleansing Moorditch, the expense to be shared according to the proportions of the work in Middlesex and the City. Also that a contribution shall be made from the City for houses of correction to be erected in Middlesex and Surrey.

27th February. A PRIEST CONDEMNED.

Yesterday evening William Richardson, a priest of the College at Seville, was called before the Lord Chief Justice, having been arrested but that day, and indicted for high treason for being a priest and coming to England contrary to the Statute. He pleaded not guilty and refused trial for a while, because he said that the jury was ignorant and the Chief Justice made the law, wherefore on him would lie the guilt of his blood. The Lord Chief Justice asked him who was head of the Church. He answered, the Pope. 'Thou art a Jesuit!' quoth he. 'No,' said the prisoner. 'What dost thou think of Jesuits?' 'That they are good and religious men,' he answered. 'Thou art a traitor,' cried the Lord Chief Justice. 'As good a subject as your Lordship or any assistant on the bench,' he replied. At last he consented to trial and was condemned. He answered stoutly yet with great modesty and discretion, moving many to compassionate him. He desired the little time he had to live to be amongst his fellow Catholics, complaining of unchristian restraint, but the keeper was commanded to use him as before. This morning he was executed at Tyburn. He prayed for the Queen and showed great courage, yet with mildness and discretion; many pitying him and inveighing against the cruelty of the Lord Chief Justice, for he had not a day's liberty to provide for his death, as even common thieves have.

1st March. NEW PLAYS AT THE ROSE.

My Lord of Worcester's men have four new plays called *Christmas Comes but Once a Year* (by Chettle, Dekker, Heywood and Webster); *The Black Dog of Newgate* (by Day, Hathway and Smith); *The Blind Eats Many a Fly* (by Heywood), and *The Unfortunate General* (by Day, Hathway and Smith).

5th March. THE MISERABLE STATE OF THE IRISH REBELS.

Because of the constant destruction of their corn the rebels in divers parts of Ireland are reduced to most miserable estate. In many places carcases be scattered, all dead of the famine. The captains report that they discovered the most horrible spectacle of three children (whereof the eldest was not above ten years old) all eating and knawing with their teeth the entrails of their dead mother. In Newry some old women of those parts used to make a fire in the fields, and divers little children driving out the cattle in the cold mornings and coming thither to warm themselves were by them surprised and eaten. In ditches of towns and especially in the wasted counties no spectacle is more frequent than to see multitudes of poor people dead with their mouths all coloured green by eating nettles, docks, and all things they could rend above ground.

9th March. FEARS AT COURT.

From Court the news is the Queen much lamenteth the late death of the Countess of Nottingham, remaining ever since in a deep melancholy that she must die herself, and complaineth much of many infirmities wherewith she seemeth suddenly to be overtaken, as imposthumation in her head, aches in her bones and continual cold in her legs, besides a notable decay of judgment, insomuch as she cannot abide discourses of government and state, but delighteth to hear old Canterbury Tales to which she is very attentive. At other times she is impatient and testy, so as none of the Council but the Secretary dare come in her presence. The Lord Treasurer and Sir John Fortescue have written that her coffers are empty, and they want moneys for Ireland. She rages thereat greatly, so that neither of them dares come to Court, and it is thought to augment her infirmities. All are in a dump at Court; some fear present danger, others doubt she will not continue past the month of May; but generally all are of opinion that she cannot overpass another winter.

The rumours also of the Lady Arabella much afflict her; she rests ill at nights, forbears to use the air in the day and abstains more than usual from her meat, resisting physic. She is, moreover, suspicious of some about her as ill affected. Everyone's head is full of proclamations as to what shall become of us.

The succession is much talked of; the greater part of the realm are for the King of Scots, but many would oppose him had they any more potent competitor. There is continual posting between London and Scotland. The Queen gave the King of Scots £2,000 at Christmas, and has since augmented his pension by £2,000 a year; he is diligent to have all in readiness and has reviewed his forces. Meantime the Lord Burleigh is sent to the North to withstand the Scots; but so subtle is Master Secretary that hardly can it be judged which way he will take, and he as yet ruleth all. It is held for certain that his mind is averted that way, and it is as certain that he is altogether opposite the Spaniards, and hath a jealous conceit that the French King is tampering for the establishing of the crown upon himself or some of his.

The Lady Arabella is under guard and some say married; some say that she is mad. She is sent for to Woodstock where she is to be kept. Meanwhile the Secretary has often secret meetings with the Earl and Countess of Shrewsbury, after which they despatch messengers and packets of letters.

It is said that the Council will have 30,000 quarters of wheat laid up in London storehouses; the ditches cleansed and enlarged 2 feet, and a ditch and trench made to defend the suburbs on the north, from the Tower to Westminster, to be done in 14 days.

In Ireland Tyrone and the rebels make head with 3,000 followers and have cut off one or two garrison companies. The country is so discontent with base money and other miseries that the Deputy advises Tyrone's pardon upon submission. The Secretary obtained this but with great difficulty, the Queen pretending it most dishonourable to pardon a rebel that had made seven years' war with her, whereas she would not be permitted to spare Essex for one day's delict; and upon this when she reflects she falleth into great passion, and this also is thought one cause of her sickness. The Secretary has written to the Deputy to pardon Tyrone on any condition, as there must be surcease of arms in Ireland, or peace with Spain, which he cannot endure, and he is thought engaged by the States of the Low Countries to continue hostility with Spain.

THE QUEEN.

For the last nine days the Queen hath been much deprived of sleep, which was ever wont to moisten her body, and when she lacked it she was apt to be impatient. This continuance decays her appetite somewhat, and drieth her body much, wherein though she be free from sickness in stomach or head and in the day catcheth sleep, yet if it should continue many months it promiseth no other than a falling into some great weakness or consumption which would hardly be recovered in old age.

12th March. 'A WOMAN KILLED WITH KINDNESS.'

There is a new play at the Rose by Thomas Heywood played by my Lord of Worcester's men. Herein one Master Frankford, having taken into his household one Master Wendall as his familiar friend, is by him made cuckold; whereupon Mr. Frankford being informed thereof by his man and finding his wife and Wendall bedded together, takes no further revenge than to send his wife away to one of his manors, and all her goods with her lest anything remain in his house to remind him of that wrong. By which kindness Mrs. Frankford is so overcome that she quickly dieth of a broken heart. Showeth also the misfortunes of one Sir Charles Mountford that quarrelled with his neighbours at a hawking and slew two of his men.

13th March. AN OFFENSIVE SERMON.

Mr. Richard Stock in his sermon at Paul's Cross uttered these words: 'I have lived these some few years, and every year I have heard an exceeding outcry of the poor that they are much oppressed of the rich of this city, in plain terms, of the Common Council. All or most charges are raised by your fifteenths, wherein the burden is more heavy upon a mechanical and handicraft poor man than upon an alderman, proportion for proportion.' Further he said, 'You are magistrates for the good of them that are under you, not to oppress them for your own ease. I would speak to him which is the chief of the City for this year. What is past cannot be remedied, but for the future, as far as lies in your power, prevent these things.' These words are very offensively taken by the Lord Mayor and Aldermen of the City.

15th March. THE QUEEN'S SICKNESS.

The Queen has been so ill that her recovery was doubted, but now she begins to improve; for whereas she was ten or twelve days without being able to sleep, for the last three or four nights she has slept four or five hours, and also she begins to eat and drink something. She will not hear a word about medicine, nor has done during her illness. Four days ago she had a defluxion in the throat: some of the doctors thought it was a little aposthume which opened into her mouth and flowed down her throat and might choke her, for she was half an hour before she was able to speak, and was like a dead person; but thanks be to God, they found means to dry it up well. She has been better since and begins to recover.

16th March. 'A Declaration of Popish Impostures.'

Master Harsnett hath written a book called *A declaration of egregious popish impostures*, setting forth those devices practised by Edmunds (or Weston) a Jesuit, under pretence of casting out devils, some twenty years since that of late have been called into question by examination of the parties possessed. Noteth that these jugglers would act their dispossessions in some nobleman's void house in London, which houses in regard of their owner's callings being above reach of authority are commonly nowaday the sanctuaries for Popish treason, not that the noblemen themselves are privy to such meetings, but their corrupt housekeepers much in fault for entertaining such guests.

The dispossession was after this manner. First out comes the holy chair, and the possessed being a young woman is placed very demurely in it, with a cloth upon her head and a cross upon it. Then in comes the priest attired in an alb or a cope with a candle in his hand (or else he is *anathema* by the Council of Trent), and after the performance of a whole anticsuit of crosses he approaches very reverently to the chair. Then he first charms her in Latin, then he puts salt in her mouth, spittle upon her ears and eyes, and anoints her lips and her nose with oil, and so God and St. Francis save the young child.

The devils that possessed these women were of sundry natures and names as Pippin, Philpot, Maho, Modu, Hilco, Smolkin, Hillio, Hiaclito, Lusty Huffcap, Soforce, Frateretto, Fliberdigibbet, Hoberdidance, Tocabatto and many others.

He would have all those gloomy spirits to come from melancholy, and that the popish priests out of strange fables and fantastical dispositions so wrought upon children, old women and maids that they were afraid to cross a churchyard or a threeway leet, or to go for spoons into the kitchen without a candle; and no marvel, for the Devil was ever at hand (or a lewd friar) with ugly horns on his head, fire in his mouth, a cow's tail in his breech, eyes like a basin, fangs like a dog, claws like a bear, a skin like a negro and a voice roaring like a lion.

Then ‘boh’ or ‘oh’ in the dark was enough to make their hair stand upright.

Of such is shaped the true *Idea* of a witch, an old weather beaten crone having her chin and her knees meeting for age, hollow eyed, untoothed, going mumbling in the streets, one that hath forgotten her *paternoster*, yet hath a shrewd tongue in her head to call ‘a drab, a drab.’ If she have learned of an old wife in a chimney's end ‘pax, max, fax’ for a spell, or can say Sir John of Grantham's curse for the miller's eels that were stolen :

> ‘All you that have stolen the miller's eels,
> *Laudate Dominum de cœlis ;*
> And all they that have consented thereto,
> *Benedicamus Domino,*’—

why then, beware, look about you my neighbours, if any of you have a knavish boy of the school, or an idle girl of the wheel or a young drab of the sullens ; and she have a little help of the mother, epilepsy or cramp, to teach her roll her eyes, wry her mouth, gnash her teeth, startle with her body, hold her arms and hands stiff, make antic faces, grin, mow and mop like an ape, and can mutter out two or three words of gibridge as ‘olus, bolus’ ; and then withal old Mother Nobs hath by chance called her idle young housewife or bid the Devil scratch her ; then no doubt but Mother Nobs is a witch and the young girl star-blasted and possessed. Then it goes hard but you shall have some idle, addle, giddy, lymphatical, illuminate dottrell who being out of credit, learning, sobriety, honesty and wit, will take this holy advantage to raise the ruins of his desperate decayed name, and for his better glory will bepray the juggling drab and cast out Mop the Devil.

17th March. STIRRINGS AT COURT.

In this present sickness of her Majesty the Council have called to them of the nobility as are in Court, being the Earl of Northumberland, the Lord Thomas Howard and the Lord Cobham, both to give advice for the good of the state and the suppressing of such as would move insurrections, if the Queen should die.

Order is now given to press all such rogues as might be apt

to stir and send them to the Low Countries. The City of London is commanded to keep strong watch lest discontented persons may make head there; and likewise the Lord President in the North and the Lord President of Wales, and withal to have an eye to the papists. Some recusants of greatest note are committed and commanded, but without any manner of rigour. Commanders also of strong places are warned against surprises. Few stir at this time save that Sir Edward Baynham, a wild and free speaking young man, has braved it and protested that he will lose his life and so will forty thousand Catholics more ere the King of Scots shall come in. He is committed to prison. It is generally concluded that the Council are for the King of Scots.

19*th March*. THE QUEEN'S INDISPOSITION.

This night Sir Robert Carey, Warden of the Marches, came to Court, and the Queen hearing of his arrival sent for him. He found her in one of her withdrawing chambers, sitting low upon her cushions. She called Sir Robert to her and he kissed her hand, saying that it was his chiefest happiness to see her in safety and in health, which he wished might long continue. She took him by the hand and wrung it hard, saying, 'No, Robin, I am not well'; and discoursed of her indisposition and that her heart had been sad and heavy for ten or twelve days, and in her discourse fetching not so few as forty or fifty great sighs. Nor could Sir Robert move her from this melancholy humour which is too deeply rooted in her heart and hardly to be removed.

As to the cause of this melancholy there are divers opinions in the Court, as that it is through the violence of her sickness or for want of the Earl of Essex (which his friends would believe); or that after so great expenses in the Irish war she is prevailed with to pardon Tyrone; or because she hath heard whisperings that many of the nobility by underhand letters and messengers seek to curry favour with the King of Scots, as in truth they do so openly that they quarrel one with another about it. Hence is she come to look upon herself as a miserable forlorn woman, and in her grief and indignation is come to utter such speeches as these: 'They have yoked my neck: I have none whom I can trust: my condition is strangely turned upside down.' Moreover, which increaseth her grief and dissatisfaction, she is made to believe that her authority among the people is sensibly decayed.

STAGE PLAYS FORBIDDEN.

The Lord Mayor and the Justices of Middlesex and Surrey are commanded at this time to restrain stage plays till other directions be given.

22nd March. THE QUEEN'S SPEECH OF HER SUCCESSOR.

The Queen groweth worse and worse; but is now by persuasion of the Lord Admiral gotten to bed, having lain these last days upon her cushions. There is now no hope of her recovery because she refuseth all remedies. To-day the Lord Admiral being upon the right side of her bed, the Lord Keeper on the left, and Mr. Secretary at the bed's feet, all standing, the Lord Admiral put her in mind of a speech she made at Whitehall concerning the succession, and said that they in the name of all the rest of her Council came unto her to know her pleasure, who should succeed. Whereunto she replied, 'I told you my seat hath been the seat of Kings, and I will have no rascal to succeed me; and who should succeed me but a King?' The Lords not understanding this dark speech and looking one at another, at length Mr. Secretary boldly asked her what she meant by these words 'that no rascal should succeed her.' She replied that her meaning was a King should succeed her; 'and who,' quoth she, 'should that be but our cousin of Scotland.' They asked her whether that were her absolute resolution. Whereunto she answered, 'I pray you trouble me no more: I'll have none but him.'

23rd March. THE QUEEN'S SICKNESS.

This morning Dr. Parry, one of her Majesty's chaplains, preached at the Court at Richmond, and his prayer both in the beginning and conclusion of his sermon was so fervent and effectual for her Majesty that he left few eyes dry. Her Majesty hath been by fits troubled with melancholy some three or four months, but for this fortnight extreme oppressed with it, insomuch that she refused to eat anything, to receive any physic or admit any rest in bed till within these two or three days. She hath been in a manner speechless for two days, very pensive and silent; since Shrovetide sitting sometimes with her eye fixed upon one object many hours together, yet she always had her perfect senses and memory, and yesterday signified by the lifting up of her hand and eyes to heaven, a sign which Dr. Parry entreated of her, that she believed that faith which she hath caused to be professed, and looked faithfully to be saved by Christ's merits and mercy only, and no other means. She took great delight in hearing prayers, would often at the name of Jesus lift up her hands and eyes to Heaven. She would not hear the Archbishop speak of hope of her longer life, but when he prayed or spake of Heaven and those joys, she would hug his hand. It seems she might have lived if she would have used means; but she would not be persuaded, and princes must not be forced. Her physicians say she hath a body of a firm and perfect constitution, likely to have lived many years.

THE GREAT ANXIETIES OF THIS TIME.

The minds of all men at this time are in great perturbation at what may befall at her Majesty's death, lest the masterless men and malcontents may rise. In the palace the guards have been doubled and the pensioners are armed. The Queen's jewelry and silver have been sent to the Tower to be guarded with the Crown jewels; and many private persons likewise conceal their jewels, and some even themselves. Stirrings and alarms are in every house. Many of the ministers are hated of the people. In the City there is great fear of the Catholics, for there are forty thousand of them and they openly oppose themselves to the King of Scots. Moreover those Catholic Lords that have been summoned to Court have not yet obeyed. Yet the Catholics have no leaders and are at variance amongst themselves. The Lady Arabella is now closely guarded. There are many rumours concerning her. A few weeks since her chaplain, one Starkie, hanged himself, and it was said that she had contracted herself in marriage to the Earl of Hertford's son, and that he had disappeared and was no where to be found. Letters also have been taken, but it is given out that the truth of the matter is that she, being now thirty years old, and wishing to be free from the guardianship of the Countess of Shrewsbury, wrote to the Earl of

Hertford, asking him to free her, and promising to marry his son. But the Earl sent the letters to the Council.

THIS NIGHT'S NEWS FROM COURT.

From Court it is reported that the Queen is now grown speechless. This afternoon about four of the clock, after the Archbishop and the divines had been with her, the Lord Admiral, the Lord Keeper and Mr. Secretary came again to ask her resolution concerning her successor, and as she was now not able to speak, Mr. Secretary said, 'We beseech your Majesty, if you remain in your former resolution, and that you would have the King of Scots to succeed you in your kingdom, show some sign unto us.' Whereat suddenly heaving herself upwards in her bed and pulling her arms out of the bed, she held both her arms jointly together over her head in manner of a crown.

About six at night she made signs for the Archbishop and her chaplains to come to her. She lay upon her back with one hand in the bed and the other without. The Archbishop kneeled down by her and examined her first of her Faith, and she so punctually answered all his several questions by lifting up her eyes and holding up her hand as it was a comfort to all the beholders. Then he told her plainly what she was and what she was to come to; and though she had long been a great Queen here upon earth, yet shortly she was to yield an account of her stewardship to the King of Kings. After this he began to pray, and all that were by did answer him. After he had continued long in prayer till the old man's knees were weary, he blessed her and meant to rise and leave her. The Queen made a sign with her hand, which one of her ladies, knowing her meaning, told the Archbishop the Queen desired he would pray still. He did so for a long half-hour after and then thought to leave. The second time she made sign to have him continue in prayer. He did so for half an hour more, with earnest cries to God for her soul's health, which he uttered with that fervency of spirit as the Queen to the sight of all who were present much rejoiced thereat, and gave testimony to all of her Christian and comfortable end. By this time it was grown late and everyone departed, all but her women that attended her.

24th March. THE DEATH OF THE QUEEN.

Upon this day about 2 of the clock in the morning died Queen Elizabeth, surrendering this mortal kingdom for an immortal, being aged three score and ten years and having reigned 44 years 5 months and odd days.

THE END OF THE ELIZABETHAN JOURNAL

ABBREVIATIONS

The following additional abbreviations for titles frequently cited have been used in this volume :

CORRESPONDENCE OF KING JAMES VI. *Correspondence of King James VI of Scotland with Sir Robert Cecil and others in England during the reign of Queen Elizabeth.* Edited by J. Bruce. Camden Society, 1861.

II ELIZ. JOURNAL. *A Second Elizabethan Journal: being a record of those things most talked of during the years* 1595-1598. By G. B. Harrison, 1931.

FOLEY. *Records of the English Province of the Society of Jesus.* By Henry Foley, S.J., 1877, etc.

GAWDY LETTERS. *Letters of Philip Gawdy,* edited by I. H. Jeayes, 1906.

LAW. *The Archpriest Controversy.* By T. G. Law, 1896.

SECRET CORRESPONDENCE. *The Secret Correspondence of Sir Robert Cecil with James VI, King of Scotland.* Edited by David Dalrymple, 1766.

SMITH. Ricardi Smith Abendoniensis, *Rerum vulgatorum nota,* a manuscript in the British Museum (*Sloan,* 414, ff. 50-61).

WILBRAHAM'S JOURNAL. *The Journal of Sir Roger Wilbraham* . . . Edited by H. S. Scott. Camden Miscellany, vol. x. 1902.

NOTES

1599

3rd January. Court News. Chamberlain's *Letters*, p. 36.

4th January. Opinions concerning the Irish Expedition. *Nugae Antiquae*, i. 240. Bacon's *Apology*. Essex himself wrote a very frank summary of the disadvantages of his proposed journey in a letter to Lord Willoughby (*Salisbury Papers*, ix. 10).

5th January. English Prisoners Released. *Salisbury Papers*, ix. 7.

6th January. Backwardness in the City. *A.P.C.*, xxix. 432.

7th January. Soldiers from the Low Countries in Ireland. *A.P.C.*, xxix. 439-441.

9th January. Hindrances to Trade with France. *Salisbury Papers*, ix. 4.

10th January. Horse for Ireland. *A.P.C.*, xxix. 447.

11th January. Nashe's 'Lenten Stuff.' *A.R.*, iii. 134; *S.T.C.*, 18370; m.e. in R. B. McKerrow's edition of Nashe's *Works*, vol. iii. Nashe apparently died shortly afterwards. For *The Isle of Dogs* see *II Eliz. Journal*, p. 202.

17th January. Court News. Chamberlain's *Letters*, p. 38. Compare the story of Othello's adventures (I. iii. 129).

20th January. The Death of Edmund Spenser. Chamberlain's *Letters*, p. 41; Camden's *Elizabeth*.

21st January. Deserters at Bristol. *A.P.C.*, xxix. 485.

26th January. 'A Woman's Worth.' *A.R.*, iii. 136; *S.T.C.*, 11831. The author notes 75 authors from whom he drew this little collection of scraps and examples.

28th January. Irish News. *S.P. Ireland*, 203: 14.

29th January. Sir Richard Bingham Dead. *S.P. Ireland*, 203: 18. See also *II Eliz. Journal*, 302, 307, 323.

30th January. Silver's 'Paradoxes of Defence.' *A.R.*, iii. 137; *S.T.C.*, 22534. There is a sequel to this lively little book still extant in m.s. in the British Museum; both the *Paradoxes* and its sequel were printed by C. G. R. Matthey in 1898; and *Paradoxes* has been reissued in *The Shakespeare Association Facsimiles*, vol. 6, edited by J. Dover Wilson.

31st January. Sir Francis Vere rebuked. *A.P.C.*, xxix. 512.

9th February. 'A New Book of Good Husbandry.' *A.R.*, iii. 135; *S.T.C.*, 7268. Entered 15 January, dated 9th February on the title-page: it has some good fishermen's yarns, as of the frog that tore out a pike's eyes.

10th February. Scandals concerning Lady Coke. *S.P. Dom.*, 270: 102. See p. 31.

15th February. COURT RUMOURS. Chamberlain's *Letters*, p. 44; Smith, f. 50.

18th February. MORE MEN FOR IRELAND. *A.P.C.*, xxix. 573.

19th February. A STRANGE AND MIRACULOUS ACCIDENT. *A.R.*, iii. 139; *S.T.C.*, 20511.

21st February. A HISTORY OF HENRY THE FOURTH. *A.R.*, iii. 134; *S.T.C.*, 12995-97a. This book was entered on 9th January and was very widely circulated; it is still not uncommon in booksellers' catalogues. According to Wolfe's statement (p. 99), only one edition was sold, from which the offending epistle was excised after 5-600 copies had been sold. Actually, however, two editions printed by Alde exist, and two further editions (assigned to the seventeenth century) were printed; all bear the date 1599, and all have the offending epistle. See also pp. 98-9.

1st March. GENERAL NEWS. Chamberlain's *Letters*, p. 46.

6th March. A DISCOURSE OF MARRIAGE AND WIVING. *A.R.*, iii. 140; *S.T.C.*, 23690. The book was afterwards condemned; see 4th June.

8th March. A SPANISH SHIP BURNT. *Salisbury Papers*, ix. 90.

13th March. A PETITION OF THE MERCHANTS TRADING IN ITALY. *Salisbury Papers*, ix. 102.

15th March. GENERAL NEWS. Chamberlain's *Letters*, p. 48.

18th March. THE PRISONERS IN THE TOWER. *A.P.C.*, xxix. 659. The original volume of *A.P.C.* covering the period from 22nd April to 21st January, 1600, has been lost.

20th March. THE SCOTTISH PLEDGES' DESPERATION. *Salisbury Papers*, ix. 104.

25th March. SPANISH PREPARATIONS. *Salisbury Papers*, ix. 110.

27th March. THE EARL OF ESSEX'S INSTRUCTIONS. *Carew Papers*, 296, 297. The licence to return was later revoked; see p. 29.

THE DEPARTURE OF THE EARL OF ESSEX FOR IRELAND. Stow's *Annals*.

28th March. A PRAYER FOR MY LORD OF ESSEX'S GOOD SUCCESS. *S.T.C.*, 18632.

CHURCHYARD'S 'FORTUNATE FAREWELL.' *S.T.C.*, 5234; not entered. The spelling of the original is peculiar, as in most instances the letter 'e' is printed before the consonants which it usually follows, *e.g.* 'maeks,' 'haest,' 'taeks,' 'reproetch,' 'liek,' 'haets,' etc.

31st March. A PROCLAMATION CONCERNING THE ARMY IN IRELAND. *Proclamations*, 361.

2nd April. 'THE FOUNTAINS OF ANCIENT FICTION.' *A.R.*, iii. 142; *S.T.C.*, 4691. It is sometimes forgotten by scholars that Shakespeare and his contemporaries were well supplied with short cuts to classical learning. See also p. 61.

3rd April. MR. BODLEY'S LIBRARY. *S.P. Dom.*, 270 : 71.

5th April. A SKIRMISH IN IRELAND. *S.P. Ireland*, 203 : 101.

8th April. HILL'S 'SCHOOL OF SKILL.' *S.T.C.*, 13502; dated in the Epistle to the Reader, written by W. Jaggard the printer. A sane, interesting, and clear account of the Elizabethan idea of the Universe, written by a man who was no fool.

14th April. "NOSCE TEIPSUM.' *A.R.*, iii. 142 ; *S.T.C.*, 6355 ; m.e. in *The Complete Poems of Sir John Davies*, edited by A. B. Grosart, 1876, vol. i. This long and interesting poem is another example of that yearning for finite knowledge which was one of the several causes of the melancholic humour so prevalent amongst the younger intellectuals of the post-Armada generation. Davies, however, being fundamentally religious could resolve his difficulties in adoration of the Divine. The poem is of considerable importance to the student of Elizabethan ideas ; it was reissued in 1602, 1608, 1612, 1619. When first entered there was some suspicion of the book, for in the Stationers' Register occurs the note : 'This is authorised vnder the hand of the L. Bysshop of London provyded that yt must not be printed without his L. hand to yt agayne'—a reasonable precaution after the Hayward affair, when the offending Epistle had been slipped in after the book was passed for press ; see p. 100.

15th April. NEWS FROM SPAIN. *Salisbury Papers*, ix. 132.

20th April. A PLAY OF KING HENRY THE FIFTH. *S.T.C.*, 22289. The approximate date of the first performance of *Henry the Fifth* is fixed by the obvious reference to Essex's departure for Ireland (Act V, Chorus, l. 29). A pirated version was issued some time during 1600. The play was of considerable topical significance, and the speech of Henry V on the loneliness and responsibility of kingship (IV. i. 250) was particularly apt at this time.

26th April. THE EARL OF ESSEX IN DUBLIN. *S.P. Ireland*, 205 : 28.

30th April. THE SPANIARDS OUTSIDE PLYMOUTH. *S.P. Dom.*, 270 : 96, 97.

1st May. AN APOLOGY FOR DARRELL. *S.T.C.*, 6282. For Darrell's successes as an exorcist, see *II Eliz. Journal*, pp. 116, 117, 176-7, 241-2, 267-8, 292-3. He seems genuinely to have believed in his own powers, and his Puritan brethren supported him zealously ; but he was treated harshly by the ecclesiastical authorities who regarded him as an impostor. As a result the small pamphlet war which followed was concerned with the larger issue of Non-conformity and Establishment. Bancroft used the controversy (as he also used the Catholic Controversy) to discredit the Puritans. See also Index, 'Darrell, John.'

12th May. THE DUNKIRK PIRATES. *S.P. Dom.*, 270 : 109.

16th May. THE NEW LORD TREASURER. Smith, f. 51.

19th May. CATHOLIC TROUBLES. *A true relation of the Faction begun at Wisbeach*, c. 1601 ; m.e. in T. G. Law's *Jesuits and Seculars*. The controversy between the secular priests and the Jesuits, which occupied so much attention during the years 1599-1603, is exceedingly complex ; there are some forty contemporary pamphlets, and a mass of manuscript material. By separating the entries in the *Journal* (see Index under 'Catholic Controversy') the reader will be able to gather an outline of the dispute. For further guidance, see T. G. Law's *A historical sketch of the conflicts between Jesuits and Seculars in the reign of Queen Elizabeth*, 1889, and *The Archpriest Controversy*, 1896 ['Law No.V,' etc., in my notes refers to the Bibliographical Notes in this work, pp. cxxviii-cl] ; also *The Institution of the Archpriest Blackwell*, 1916, by J. H. Pollen, S.J. ; Foley, vol. i.; Camden's *Elizabeth*; Fuller's *Church History*; and State Papers, *passim*.

25th May. THE FRENCH KING AND HIS QUEEN. Winwood's *Memorials*, i. 27.

26th May. THE TRIAL OF MR. DARRELL. *S.T.C.*, 6287.

28th May. SPANISH PREPARATIONS. *S.P. Dom.*, 270 : 119. Many similar warnings were received at this time by the Council.

31st May. SIR WALTER RALEGH MADE WARDEN OF THE STANNARIES. *S.P. Dom.*, 270 : 123.

4th June. CERTAIN BOOKS BURNT. *A.R.*, iii. 677-8. As is shown by the ban now laid on English histories, the burning of the satirical books was the direct sequel to the affair of Hayward's *Henry the Fourth*. The Council were becoming alarmed, and acutely sensitive to the undercurrent of cynical criticism of those in authority which was so prevalent in these months. Of these eleven works, four were indecent, seven satirised recognisable individuals under feigned names.

7th June. A DEFEAT IN IRELAND. *S.P. Ireland*, 205 : 75, 108.

10th June. THE EARL OF SOUTHAMPTON. *S.P. Ireland*, 205 : 79. The offence was Southampton's marriage (see *II Eliz. Journal*, p. 305). The Queen's command was sent in a letter from the Council to Essex which concluded, 'This being Her Majesty's direction and commandment unto us, we do deliver it by these our letters as from herself, wherein having discharged our duties, we are sorry for the occasion.'

21st June. AN ASSAULT UPON SIR CHARLES CAVENDISH. Chamberlain's *Letters*, p. 54.

25th June. CATHOLIC TROUBLES. As for 19th May.

28th June. GENERAL NEWS. Chamberlain's *Letters*, p. 51.

30th June. RUMOURS. *S.P. Dom.*, 271 : 33 and 35.

PLAYS AT THE ROSE. *Hens. Diary*, i. 100-9; ii. 199-202.

5th July. DISSENSIONS AMONG OUR ENGLISH PAPISTS. Winwood's *Memorials*, i. 51. For Parson's books, see *I Eliz. Journal*, p. 340; *II Eliz. Journal*, 33, 57.

7th July. A POPISH TRICK. Winwood's *Memorials*, i. 55.

10th July. 'AS YOU LIKE IT.' This date is a guess; but in the reference (obviously topical) that 'Since the little wit that fools have was silenced, the little foolery that wise men have makes a great show,' there is probably an allusion to the bonfire of the Satires. Moreover, the discussion between Jacques and the Duke on the fool's privileges is an echo of the Satirists' claims. Marston, for instance, in *The Scourge of Villainy*, like Jacques, claims that he glances not upon 'privateness'; and indeed Jacques' Speech (II. vii. 69) reads like a comment on current literary politics.

THE ARCHBISHOP'S CHARITABLE FOUNDATION. Strype's *Whitgift*, p. 532.

14th July. A WITCH HANGED. Account appended to *The Trial of Maist. Darrell* (*S.T.C.*, 6287)

21st July. COURT RUMOURS. *S.P. Dom.*, 271 : 106.

26th July. A Stern Punishment in Ireland. *Carew MSS.*, 306.

30th July. The Queen's Offence with the Earl of Essex. *S.P. Ireland*, 205 : 121.

1st August. A Great Alarm and Irish News. Chamberlain's *Letters*, p. 55.

3rd August. Instructions for the Lord Burleigh. *S.P. Dom.*, 272 : 7.

The Spanish Alarm. *S.P. Dom.*, 271 : 140, 272 : 5.

4th August. Master Edward Coke's Lady. Chamberlain's *Letters*, p. 63.

5th August. The Forces mustering. Chamberlain's *Letters*, pp. 58-60.

7th August. Fresh Alarms. Chamberlain's *Letters*, p. 59 ; *Salisbury Papers*, ix. 282.

8th August. The Preparations in the City. Chamberlain's *Letters*, p. 60 ; *Salisbury Papers*, ix. 281, 280.

10th August. 'The Shoemaker's Holiday.' *S.T.C.*, 6523 ; *Hens. Diary*, i. 110 ; ii. 203. Approximate date of production. The 'book' was bought on 15th July and published without entry in 1600 ; see also 7th January, 1600.

12th August. The Defence Force. Chamberlain's *Letters*, p. 62 ; *Salisbury Papers*. ix. 428, 302.

18th August. A Lamentable Defeat in Ireland. *Sidney Papers*, ii. 117 ; *Penshurst Papers*, ii. 384.

22nd August. The Musters. *Salisbury Papers*, ix. 317 ; Stow's *Annals*.

An Order concerning Prices. *Proclamations*, 363.

23rd August. The Forces dispersing and Irish News. Chamberlain's *Letters*, pp. 61, 63. For Essex's previous generosity with knighthoods see *I Eliz. Journal*, pp. 62, 69, and *II Eliz. Journal*, p. 124. Cecil's considered opinion on the invasion scare is given in a letter to John Manners (*Rutland MSS.*, i. 356 : Hist. MSS. Com. XII Rep. Ap. iv) : 'though the brutes that have been brought from sea are more violent then are possible to be true, yett we knowe this for certayne that they have prepared in Spayne myghtely to resist the fleete of the Lowe Contreyes, which having now left the coast and being gone for the Canaries, the Spaniards that care not for that place in respect of other desecggs (*sic*) to better purpose, wilbe apt enough to convert the forces prepared for the defensive, to offend us whome they presume to fynde without any shippes at sea and without any store of commanders, things that will quicken the appetite of malitious enemyes.'

25th August. The Forces to be mustered again. *Salisbury Papers*, ix. 322. Stow's *Annals*.

26th August. The Musters. Stow's *Annals*.

27th August. The Musters. Stow's *Annals*.

30th August. The Scottish Ambassador. *Sidney Papers*, ii. 119.

31st August. Abuses of the Muster. *Salisbury Papers*, ix. 336, 337, 338, 326.

1st September. General News. *Sidney Papers*, ii. 119.

2nd September. The Advice of the Captains in Ireland. *S.P. Ireland*, 205 : 145, 157.

4th September. Training ceased. Stow's *Annals*.

12th September. Court News. *Sidney Papers*, ii. 122 ; *Penshurst Papers*, ii. 389.

The State of the North. *S.P. Dom.*, 272 : 112.

15th September. Mr. Bacon's Saying concerning the Earl of Essex. Bacon's *Apology*.

17th September. Irish News. *Sidney Papers*, ii. 125.

21st September. A Play of 'Julius Caesar.' The evidence for the approximate date of the production of *Julius Caesar* is unusually full ; see Chambers' *Shakespeare : Facts and Problems*, i. 396.

25th September. The Hollanders' Voyage to the West Indies. *S.T.C.*, 4556.

28th September. The Earl of Essex returns. *Sidney Papers*, ii. 127 ; *Penshurst Papers*, ii. 396-7. Essex and the Queen never met again.

29th September. My Lord of Essex. *Sidney Papers*, ii. 129, 130, 131 ; *Penshurst Papers*, ii. 397.

1st October. The Sabbatarian Doctrine. Strype's *Whitgift*, p. 530.

5th October. My Lord of Essex. *Sidney Papers*, ii. 131.

A Book for Ladies. *A.R.*, iii. 148 ; *S.T.C.*, 19993. Platt complains in a verse epistle, 'I writ to all but scarcely one believes' ; for other works see *I Eliz. Journal*, p. 311, and *II Eliz. Journal*, pp. 51, 132.

7th October. Foreign Rumours. *S.P. Dom.*, 273 : 1.

10th October. Tyrone's Treacheries. *S.P. Ireland*, 205 : 211, 214.

12th October. The French King's Divorce. Winwood's *Memorials*, i. 115, 116.

13th October. My Lord of Essex. *Sidney Papers*, ii. 132, 133.

18th October. Lord Mountjoy for Ireland. *Penshurst Papers*, ii. 404.

21st October. My Lord of Essex. *Sidney Papers*, ii. 135.

24th October. A New Play. *Sidney Papers*, ii. 136 ; *Penshurst Papers*, ii. 406. The play was presented again on 27th October. As there is no trace of this play in *Hens. Diary*, it was probably produced by the Chamberlain's Men. The real Vere was in London at this time. The battle was fought in January 1597 (see *II Eliz. Journal*, 162-4).

26th October. Court News. *Penshurst Papers*, ii. 406. For Sir Melchior's reputation see *II Eliz. Journal*, p. 286.

28th October. A Rash Captain. *Sidney Papers*, ii. 137.

1st November. A Play of Sir John Oldcastle. *Hens. Diary*, i. 113 ; *S.T.C.*, 18795 ; m.e. in *M.S.R.*, 1908. The prologue, self-righteously proclaiming that the play is 'no forged invention,' was intended as a cut at Shakespeare's original misuse of the name of Oldcastle for the fat knight of 1 *Henry IV*. Now that the Chamberlain's men were established at the new Globe—only a very short distance from the Rose—the rivalry between the companies became acute.

4th November. THE EARL OF ESSEX. *Sidney Papers*, ii. 139 ; *Penshurst Papers*, ii. 410.

7th November. A DICTIONARY OF THE SPANISH. *A.R.*, iii. 145 ; *S.T.C.*, 19620, entered 28th June, published about this date (*Penshurst Papers*, ii. 405, 413). The book is a finely printed folio, and the dialogues give useful pictures of contemporary habits of dress, food and manners.

10th November. TYRONE DENOUNCETH THE CESSATION. *S.P. Ireland*, 205 : 231.

12th November. THE DEATH OF MISTRESS RATCLIFFE. *Gawdy Letters*, p. 103.

13th November. THE QUEEN ROYALLY RECEIVED. Stow's *Annals*.

THE CHILDREN OF PAUL'S. *Penshurst Papers*, ii. 415 ; *Histriomastix* is reprinted in R. Simpson's *The School of Shakespeare*, vol. ii. 1878. See also *Eliz. Stage*, iv. 17.

14th November. SIR CALISTHENES BROOKE HURT. *Gawdy Letters*, p. 103.

15th November. SIR JOHN HARINGTON AT COURT. *Nugae Antiquae*, i. 309, 341, 355-6.

A DISCOVERY OF DARRELL'S PRACTICES. *A.R.*, iii. 150 ; *S.T.C.*, 12883 ; entered 15th May.

17th November. THE SERMON AT PAUL'S. *S.T.C.*, 13597.

'HYMNS TO ASTRÆA.' *A.R.*, iii. 151 ; *S.T.C.*, 6351 ; m.e. in *The Complete Poems of Sir John Davies*, by A. B. Grosart, 1876, vol. i.

A WARNING FOR FAIR WOMEN. *A.R.* iii. 151 ; *S.T.C.*, 25089. A crude piece.

20th November. AN ENGLISH NUNNERY IN BRUSSELS. *S.P. Dom.*, 273 : 27.

21st November. THE AMBASSADOR'S TART ANSWER. Winwood's *Memorials*, i. 128.

22nd November. 'GODFREY OF BULLOIGNE' TRANSLATED. *A.R.*, iii. 151 ; *S.T.C.*, 23697.

23rd November. COURT NEWS. *Sidney Papers*, ii. 142.

24th November. TYRONE'S DEMANDS. *S.P. Ireland*, 206 : 55.

25th November. THE PLAY OF ANTONIO'S REVENGE. *A.R.*, iii. 193 ; *S.T.C.*, 17473-4 ; m.e. in *M.S.R.*, 1922, and *The Works of John Marston*, edited by A. H. Bullen, vol. i. 1887. The description of late autumn in the Prologue to part ii. fixes the season of the first production ; the date of part i. is given in the Painter Scene, l. 1590.

27th November. THE EARL OF ESSEX. *Sidney Papers*, ii. 144.

28th November. PROCEEDINGS IN THE STAR CHAMBER. *Sidney Papers*, i. 146.

1st December. COURT NEWS. *Penshurst Papers*, ii. 421.

4th December. A WITCH EXECUTED. Account appended to *The Trial of Maist. Darrell* (*S.T.C.*, 6287).

10th December. A TRUCE WITH TYRONE. *S.P. Ireland*, 206 : 57.

13th December. THE EARL OF ESSEX'S SICKNESS. *Sidney Papers*, ii. 150.

14th December. THE STATE OF IRELAND. *S.P. Ireland*, 206 : 63.

15th December. THE EARL OF ESSEX'S ILLNESS. *Sidney Papers*, ii. 151.

16th December. A NEW PLAY. *S.T.C.*, 6517 ; m.e. in the Mermaid Series ; approximate date. *Hens. Diary*, i. 114-6 ; ii. 179.

24th December. BOISTEROUS WINDS. Stow's *Annals*.

28th December. COURT NEWS. *Sidney Papers*, ii. 154 ; *Penshurst Papers*, ii. 424.

29th December. A CAMBRIDGE CHRISTMAS PLAY. *The Pilgrimage to Parnassus*, edited from the manuscript by W. D. Macray, 1886.

30th December. A DEFENCE OF DARRELL. *S.T.C.*, 6287, dated 30th September in the first epistle, but not published till after the appearance of Harsnett's book.

31st December. NEW PLAYS AT THE ROSE. *Hens. Diary*, i. 110-7 ; ii. 203-8.

THESE BOOKS ALSO SET FORTH ANNO 1599

'WIT'S THEATRE OF THE LITTLE WORLD.' *S.T.C.*, 381. This is the third of a series of anthologies, of which the first two were Bodenham's *Politeuphuia* and Meres' *Palladis Tamia* (see *II Eliz. Journal*, pp. 213, 305), and, being a collection of brief anecdotes, is the most interesting. Much of the 'learning' so impressive in writers of the seventeenth century was fetched from such convenient epitomes.

'DIET'S DRY DINNER.' *S.T.C.*, 4207.

'THE MANSION OF MAGNANIMITY.' *S.T.C.*, 6054.

'A BOOK AGAINST PLAYS.' *S.T.C.*, 20616. A dull, bookish work.

'THE PASSIONATE PILGRIM.' *S.T.C.*, 22342 ; facsimile in 1905 by S. Lee, who added a long introduction.

WEEVER'S 'EPIGRAMS.' *S.T.C.*, 25224 ; m.e. by R. B. McKerrow, 1911.

1600

2nd January. NEW YEAR'S GIFTS. Nichols' *Progresses*, vol. iii. The gifts given to the Queen by her courtiers are often mentioned with amusement, whilst her gifts to her courtiers and servants are forgotten; the master cooks, for instance, presented marchpanes and were each rewarded with 7 ozs. of silver plate.

5th January. COURT NEWS. *Sidney Papers*, ii. 156.

7th January. THE PLAYERS AT COURT. As for 15th December, 1599.

11th January. A FENCER HANGED. Stow's *Annals*.

12th January. ALLEYN'S NEW PLAYHOUSE. *Hens. Papers*, pp. 4, 49; *Eliz. Stage*, iv. 326. The agreement with the builder is dated 8th January.

'THE PRESERVATION OF KING HENRY THE SEVENTH.' *A.R.*, iii. 154; *S.T.C.*, 13076. The book, though entered on this day, is dated 1599. This seems to be the last attempt in the reign to inflict the hexameter on English verse; the author's hope of encouragement for a second book was apparently not fulfilled.

COURT NEWS. *Sidney Papers*, ii. 133, 138. The Ladies of Essex's family remained conspicuously faithful to him during his troubles. They were the Countess of Leicester, his mother; Lady Walsingham, his mother-in-law; Lady Rich (who was formerly Sir Philip Sidney's 'Stella'), and the Countess of Northumberland, his sisters.

14th January. TWO PROCLAMATIONS MADE. *Proclamations*, 365, 366.

16th January. CONTRIBUTIONS FROM THE LAWYERS. *A.P.C.*, xxx. 27-31, which gives the names of those from whom the charge was levied—a useful catalogue of the leading barristers of the day.

19th January. RECUSANTS IN LONDON. Stow's *Annals*.

20th January. THE AMBASSADOR'S COMPLAINT FROM PARIS. *S.P. Dom.*, 274 : 12.

22nd January. A BOOK CONCERNING FISH AND FRUIT. *A.R.*, iii. 154; *S.T.C.*, 23708; entered 10th January, dated 22nd January, 1600 (not 1599) in the Epistle; a most intelligent and shrewd little work.

24th January. COURT NEWS. *Sidney Papers*, ii. 164.

2nd February. THE CROSS IN CHEAPSIDE. *A.P.C.*, xxx. 27.

THE EARL'S PICTURE. *Penshurst Papers*, ii. 435; see p. 113.

4th February. DELAYS IN THE COURT OF ADMIRALTY. *A.P.C.*, xxx. 43.

DESERTERS FROM IRELAND. *A.P.C.*, xxx. 55.

10th February. WILL KEMP'S WAGER. Kemp's dance, which caused a great sensation, is amusingly recounted in his *Nine Days' Wonder*; *S.T.C.*, 14923; m.e. by A. Dyce, Camden Society, 1840, and *Bodley Head Quartos*, vol. iv.

The Lord Mountjoy. *S.P. Ireland*, 207 : 96.

14th February. The Earl of Essex. *Sidney Papers*, ii. 166.

Kemp's Dance. See above.

17th February. The Archduke's Secretary. *A.P.C.*, xxx. 71.

21st February. The Earl of Essex. *Sidney Papers*, ii. 168.

23rd February. Kemp's Dance. As for 10th February.

25th February. A Preaching Friar. *S.P. Dom.*, 274 : 50.

The Earl of Essex. *Sidney Papers*, ii. 171.

26th February. A Saying concerning the Queen. *S.P. Dom.*, 274 : 49.

3rd March. An Ambassador from the Archduke. *Penshurst Papers*, ii. 441, 443, 444.

Kemp's Dance. As for 10th February.

8th March. Sir Thomas Wingfield's Complaints. *Salisbury Papers*, x. 57.

9th March. The New Playhouse prohibited. *A.P.C.*, xxx. 146.

The Lord Mountjoy at Dublin. *S.P. Ireland*, 207 : 130, 132, 133.

Court News. *Sidney Papers*, ii. 175, 176, 177. The play of *Oldcastle* was perhaps Shakespeare's *I. Henry IV.*, wherein the fat knight first appeared as Oldcastle.

Kemp reacheth Norwich. As for 10th February.

10th March. Disorderly Soldiers from Wales. *A.P.C.*, xxx. 152.

12th March. Defiant Seamen. *S.P. Dom.*, 274 : 76.

15th March. Court News. *Sidney Papers*, ii. 179.

A Proclamation concerning Gold and Silver. *Proclamations*, 371.

20th March. A History of the Turks. *A.R.*, iii. 161 ; *S.T.C.*, 17997. Dated 20th March in Epistle Dedicatory ; entered 27th May. Another example of the keen interest in history at this time, stimulated by the desire to find ' counsayle & forewarning mischiefs in the examples and harmes of others.'

21st March. The Earl of Essex. *Sidney Papers*, ii. 181.

22nd March. A Petition for the New Playhouse. *Hens. Papers*, p. 50 ; *Eliz. Stage*, iv. 327. Approximate date.

23rd March. Snow. Stow's *Annals*.

25th March. An Outrage in the City. *A.P.C.*, xxx. 203. See also p. 97.

28th March. A Proclamation against Woad. *Proclamations*, 373 ; see 28th November, 1601.

1st April. A Playhouse prevented. *Mid. Sessions Rolls*, i. 260.

3rd April. Court News. *Sidney Papers*, ii. 185.

4th April. The Bishop of London. *Penshurst Papers*, ii. 453, 454.

MORE SNOW. Stow's *Annals*.

8*th April*. LEVIES FROM THE CITY. *A.P.C.*, xxx. 235.

ALLEYN'S PLAYHOUSE. *Hens. Papers*, p. 51.

10*th April*. THE SELLING OF GAME. *A.P.C.*, xxx. 238. A hay is a rabbit net ; it is worth noting that the common rabbit needed protecting, presumably because its natural enemies were not destroyed by gamekeepers.

11*th April*. A SUICIDE. *Sidney Papers*, ii. 187.

12*th April*. COURT NEWS. *Sidney Papers*, ii. 187.

15*th April*. THE STRANGE FORTUNES OF TWO EXCELLENT PRINCES. *A.R.*, iii. 160 ; *S.T.C.*, 3702 ; m.e. in A. B. Grosart's edition of *The Works of Nicholas Breton*, vol. ii.

17*th April*. NEWS FROM IRELAND. *S.P. Ireland*, ii. 207 ; 74, 63. The immediate change of tone in letters and despatches from Ireland after Mountjoy's arrival is most noticeable. There is a competence and lack of fuss about his measures which contrast strongly with the continual indecision and querulousness of Essex.

19*th April*. THE EARL OF ORMOND TREACHEROUSLY TAKEN. *S.P. Ireland*, 207, ii. : 115, 101 ; *Penshurst Papers*, ii. 456.

22*nd April*. KEMP'S DANCE. *A.R.*, iii. 160 ; *S.T.C.*, 14923.

23*rd April*. THE GARTER FEAST. *Sidney Papers*, ii. 190 ; *Salisbury Papers*, x. 116.

A TOWN BURNT. *A.P.C.*, xxx. 340

A BOOK OF STRANGE MIRACLES. *A.R.*, iii. 157 ; *S.T.C.* 24135. Entered 4th March, dated 23rd April in the Epistle Dedicatory to Lord Buckhurst. This book has a new device for preserving the gentleman translator from the charge of vulgarly printing his own works. In the Epistle Dedicatory, signed Ferdinando Walker, the translation is said to be 'the first labour of a worthi Gentleman of your Lordships Countrey of Sussex' ; Walker follows with an Epistle to Lewis Lewkinor, humbly apologising for saving 'this poor Treatise, having so many long yeeres bien obscured among your wast papers.'

24*th April*. A MISHAP AT HAMPTON. *Mid. Sessions Rolls*, i. 261.

30*th April*. GENERAL NEWS. *S.P. Dom.*, 274 : 120.

2*nd May*. THE FRENCH KING'S MISTRESS. Winwood's *Memorials*, i. 176.

4*th May*. A SKIRMISH IN IRELAND. *S.P. Ireland*, 207, ii. : 132, 139.

5*th May*. A FEAST FOR M. LE CHATRE. *Sidney Papers*, ii. 193.

7*th May*. BETTER NEWS OF IRELAND. *S.P. Ireland*, 207, ii. : 104.

9*th May*. IRISH NEWS. *S.P. Ireland*, 207, iii. : 9.

10*th May*. THE EARL OF ESSEX'S 'APOLOGY' PRINTED. *Salisbury Papers*, x. 142 ; *Sidney Papers*, ii. 193. For a summary see *II Eliz. Journal*, p. 281.

MR. HERBERT OF THE PRIVY COUNCIL. *A.P.C.*, xxx. 314 ; Chamberlain's *Letters*, p. 75.

11th May. The Catholic Quarrels and the University of Paris. *A True Relation* (19th May, 1599), p. 80.

12th May. The Earl of Essex's Letter to the Queen. *S.P. Dom.*, 274 : 138 ; *Sidney Papers*, ii. 196. Essex's complaint that 'shortly they will play me upon the stage' was something more than a rhetorical flourish, for players in these years held the mirror close up to Nature. For examples of plays dealing directly with current topics and recent events, note the restrictions on printing plays (p. 21) ; the staging of the battle of Turnholt (p. 47) ; the seditious performance of *Richard II* (p. 144) ; the trouble at the Curtain (p. 180) ; the play on Sebastian (p. 189) ; the *Parnassus* plays (pp. 60, 248) ; Dymock's *Lord of Kyme* (p. 296) ; the play of the life and execution of Biron, acted with some realism (p. 302 and note) ; the shutting of the playhouses when the Queen's illness became acute (p. 325) ; in addition, the plays of the Stage War, wherein Jonson and his enemies attacked each other. Moreover it must be remembered that apart from the evidence of Henslowe's *Diary* (which is concerned only with the players connected with Henslowe and Alleyn) very little is known of the repertory of the Elizabethan playhouses.

16th May. A French Tumbler. *A.P.C.*, xxx. 327 ; *Penshurst Papers*, ii. 462.

18th May. Mr. Richard Hakluyt. *A.P.C.*, xxx. 330.

22nd May. The Treaty for Peace. Camden's *Elizabeth*. The transactions and correspondence of this abortive treaty are to be found in Winwood's *Memorials*, vol. i. book iii.

25th May. A Collection for Gamlingay. *A.P.C.*, xxx. 340.

27th May. Blackwell's Censure. *True Relation*, p. 82.

29th May. Breton's Poems of Pasquil. *A.R.*, iii. 158, 161 ; *S.T.C.*, 3675, 3677, 3679. Entered respectively on 20th March, 10th May and 29th May. They are expressions of the prevalent mood of melancholy, of the same catalogue nature as Hamlet's 'To be or not to be.'

31st May. Unseasonable Weather. Stow's *Annals*.

1st June. Court News. *Sidney Papers*, ii. 198.

2nd June. A Proclamation against those spreading Rumours. *Proclamations*, 374.

4th June. The Treaty of Boulogne. As for 22nd May.

6th June. The Earl of Essex before the Council. *Sidney Papers*, ii. 199, 200 ; *Salisbury Papers*, x. 178 ; Moryson's *Itinerary*, ii 311.

7th June. The Almsmen's Complaint. *A.P.C.*, xxx. 359.

10th June. 'A Treasury of Similes.' *A.R.* iii. 162 ; *S.T.C.*, 4382. The book has 860 pages ; the only source acknowledged is the Bible ; the rest of the similes may well be of the author's own devising.

12th June. A Foul Case of Bawdry. *Gawdy Letters*, p. 99 ; *Egerton MSS.*, 2804, f. 136. The case caused much excitement ; see also p. 276.

13th June. News from Ireland. *S.P. Ireland*, 207, iii. : 73, 63, 51.

15th June. The Council and the Earl of Lincoln. *A.P.C.*, xxx. 374.

16th June. A WEDDING AT BLACKFRIARS. *Sidney Papers*, ii. 203 For Mrs Fitton's subsequent troubles, see p. 143.

18th June. A RIOT IN SOMERSET. *A.P.C.*, xxx. 386.

A GREAT HAILSTORM. Stow's *Annals*.

22nd June. THE EARL OF LINCOLN TO BE IMPRISONED. *A.P.C.*, xxx. 402.

THE QUEEN AND THE IRISH KNIGHTS. *Salisbury Papers*, x. 208 ; *Sidney Papers*, ii. 204.

PLAYHOUSES AND PLAYS TO BE RESTRAINED. *A.P.C.*, xxx. 395.

23rd June. THE TREATY AT BOULOGNE. As for 22nd May.

24th June. AN ASSAULT PUNISHED. *Mid. Sessions Rolls*, i. 262.

25th June. MR. BODLEY'S LIBRARY. *Letters of Sir Thomas Bodley to the University of Oxford*, edited by G. W. Wheeler, 1927, p. 7. For the first proposal to found the Library see *II Eliz. Journal*, p. 259. The progress of the Library can be traced in the interesting *Letters of Sir Thomas Bodley to Thomas James*, also edited by G. W. Wheeler, 1926.

29th June. THE IRISH KNIGHTS. *Salisbury Papers*, x. 199, 208 ; *Sidney Papers*, ii. 204.

THE EARL OF LINCOLN'S CONTEMPT. *A.P.C.*, xxx. 430.

30th June. NEW PLAYS. *Hens. Diary*, i. 117-122 ; ii. 209-215.

1st July. A GREAT VICTORY IN FLANDERS. *A.R.*, iii. 165 ; *S.T.C.*, 17671, 17679.

6th July. THE EARL OF LINCOLN'S CONTEMPT. *A.P.C.*, xxx. 468.

A RIOT IN THE MERMAID TAVERN. Hawarde, p. 114 ; see p. 76.

9th July. THE TREATY AT BOULOGNE. As for 22nd May.

REINFORCEMENTS FOR IRELAND AND THE LOW COUNTRIES. *A.P.C.* xxx. 434, 444.

11th July. DR. HAYWARD EXAMINED. *S.P. Dom.*, 275 : 25. See pp. 9, 10.

13th July. DR. HAYWARD COMMITTED TO THE TOWER. *A.P.C.*, xxx. 499.

THE EXAMINATION OF WOLFE. *S.P. Dom.*, 275 : 28.

15th July. THE VICTORY AT NEWPORT. *S.T.C.*, 11029. *News from Flanders : a new ballad of the Great Overthrow.* There are 23 verses in in this lively ballad.

19th July. THE TREATY AT BOULOGNE. As for 22nd May.

20th July. DR. HAYWARD'S BOOK. *S.P. Dom.*, 275 : 31.

26th July. THE BISHOP OF LONDON RETURNS. *Salisbury Papers*, x. 245.

27th July. THE SEMINARY PRIESTS IN LONDON PRISONS. *A.P.C.*, xxx. 539. At this point Dr. Bancroft began to take an active part in fomenting the Catholic dissensions.

30th July. THE TREATY AT BOULOGNE. As for 22nd May.

1st August. THE EARL OF SOUTHAMPTON. *S.P. Ireland*, 207, iv. : 42.

3rd August. The Earl of Southampton and Lord Grey. *Salisbury Papers*, x. 262 ; *A.P.C.*, xxx. 551.

4th August. 'England's Helicon.' *A.R.*, iii. 168 ; *S.T.C.*, 3191. The apology for lifting other men's poems without permission suggests that authors and printers were beginning to object to such thefts of literary property, as they well might in the spate of anthologies of all kinds that were appearing at this time.

5th August. Levies from the City. *A.P.C.*, xxx. 561.

9th August. Deserters to be executed. *A.P.C.*, xxx. 589.

11th August. 'Bel-Vedére.' *A.R.*, iii. 168 ; *S.T.C.*, 3189 ; m.e. by the Spenser Society, 1875. Another example of the habit of making epitomes of 'sentences' in prose and verse ; compare 10th June 1599. The list of poets from whom Bodenham drew tribute contains forty names ; it does credit to his taste.

13th August. The Mutinous Soldiers at Chester. *Salisbury Papers*, x. 268.

14th August. Sir Walter Ralegh and the Earl of Essex. From a letter written by Ralegh to Cecil, *Salisbury Papers*, x. 439, also Edward's *Ralegh*, ii. 222. The date and actual occasion are uncertain, but the letter belongs to the period of Essex's eclipse.

15th August. Ambassadors from Barbary. Stow's *Annals* ; *Salisbury Papers*, x. 278 ; *Sidney Papers*, ii. 211 ; *Penshurst Papers*, ii. 478.

16th August. The Gowry Conspiracy. *Sidney Papers*, ii. 211 ; *A.R.*, iii. 173 ; *S.T.C.*, 21466; m.e. in *The Harleian Miscellany*. The account here given is from the official pamphlets. The sensational affair caused an enormous controversy which has persisted until modern times, some holding that James was not the lucky victim but treacherous murderer who skilfully stagemanaged a bogus plot.

17th August. The Earl of Lincoln's Contempt. *A.P.C.*, xxx. 598.

Irish News. *S.P. Ireland*, 207, iii. : 59.

20th August. The Barbary Ambassador. *Sidney Papers*, ii. 212.

21st August. Seminaries executed at York. *Salisbury Papers*, x. 283.

23rd August. 'Much Ado About Nothing.' *A.R.*, iii. 170 ; *S.T.C.*, 22304.

25th August. Deserters from Ireland. *A.P.C.*, xxx. 612.

26th August. The Earl of Essex released. *Sidney Papers*, ii. 213.

27th August. A Healing Well in Cheshire. *S.T.C.*, 24904. *Newes out of Cheshire of the new found well*, by W. G. The Epistle is dated 13th August, 1600.

30th August. Engraved Portraits forbidden. *A.P.C.*, xxx. 619 ; see p. 67.

2nd September. The Private House in the Blackfriars. From Chancery proceedings of 1612, printed in F. G. Fleay's *Chronicle History of the English Stage*.

6th September. The Earl of Essex's Letter to the Queen. *S.P. Dom.*, 275 : 61.

10th September. Sir Thomas Posthumus Hoby's Complaint. *Salisbury Papers*, x. 303. For an amusing account of Sir Thomas's wooing of the lady, see *Society Women of Shakespeare's Time* by Violet A. Wilson; also *The Diary of Lady Margaret Hoby*, edited by Dorothy M. Meads.

12th September. Onie McRory slain. *S.P. Ireland*, 207, pt. iv. : 109.

17th September. The Earl of Lincoln released. *A.P.C.*, xxx. 649, 652.

20th September. Abuses in Devon. *Salisbury Papers*, x. 450. Approximate date only.

23rd September. The Earl of Essex's Letters to the Queen. Devereux, ii. 125.

25th September. A Saying of the Queen. Bacon's *Apology*.

The Collecting of Rags and Bones. *S.P. Dom.*, 275 : 71.

30th September. Fresh Complaints against the Earl of Lincoln. *A.P.C.*, xxx. 669.

1st October. Sir Thomas Hoby's Complaint. *Salisbury Papers*, x. 325.

2nd October. 'England's Parnassus.' *A.R.*, iii. 173; *S.T.C.*, 378; m.e. by Charles Crawford, 1913.

3rd October. Court News. *Sidney Papers*, ii. 217; *Penshurst Papers*, ii. 486.

8th October. 'A Midsummer Night's Dream.' *A.R.*, iii. 174; *S.T.C.*, 22302.

13th October. Mr. Fulbecke's 'Historical Collection.' *A.R.*, iii. 174; *S.T.C.*, 11412. Entered 10th October, dated 13th in the preface. This book is an important instance of the Elizabethan habit of seeing modern examples in ancient history.

Good News from Ireland. *S.P. Ireland*, 207, v. : 122; *Penshurst Papers*, ii. 487.

14th October. The Russian Ambassador. *Sidney Papers*, ii. 318.

16th October. A New Book of Satires. *A.R.*, iii. 174; *S.T.C.*, 21393. The book was shortly afterwards called in and burnt, but a second edition was issued, and for defying the order twenty-eight printers were fined 2s. 6d. on 4th March 1601. The caricatures in this collection are lively, but S[amuel] R[owlands] is not above filching from his fellows; Epigram 35, for instance, is lifted almost without changes from the passage on Arrogancy in Lodge's *Wits' Misery*, quoted in *II Eliz. Journal*, pp. 149-50.

20th October. A Petition for Licence to trade in the East Indies. *Salisbury Papers*, x. 445.

26th October. Engrossing of Grain. *A.P.C.*, xxx. 733.

28th October. Shakespeare's 'Merchant of Venice.' *A.R.*, iii. 175; *S.T.C.*, 22296.

30th October. The Earl of Essex's Hopes dashed. *Sidney Papers*, ii. 220.

2nd November. The Death of Master Hooker. Camden's *Elizabeth*.

4th November. Foreign Ships not to enter Portsmouth. *A.P.C.*, xxx. 748.

6th November. The Barbary Ambassadors. Stow's *Annals* ; *Salisbury Papers*, x. 371.

9th November. The Queen's Return to Whitehall. *A.P.C.*, xxx. 762. The torchlight entry to Whitehall in anticipation of the festivities on Accession Day had come to be an annual ceremony. In present anxieties it was especially desirable that such popular demonstrations of loyalty should be encouraged.

12th November. Alleyn's New Playhouse. *Hens. Papers*, p. 4 ; *Hens. Diary*, i. 124 ; ii. 215. The Fortune was built by the same builders as the Globe ; and in the contract it is stipulated that the stage and 'all other Contrivitions Conveyances fashions thinge and thinges' shall be after the same fashion, except that 'carved proporcons called Satiers' shall be set on the principal and main posts of the frame. It is sometimes forgotten that even in the public playhouses though the stage was large the auditorium was small, thus allowing an intimacy between actor and spectator which is lost in modern production.

13th November. Sir William Cornwallis's 'Essays.' *A.R.*, iii. 176 ; *S.T.C.*, 5775. It is curious that this remarkable collection should have been overlooked by historians of Elizabethan literature.

The Queen Loyally received. Stow's *Annals.*

15th November. Court Rumours. Winwood's *Memorials*, i. 274.

20th November. The Catholic Dissensions. See John Colleton's *A Just Defence of the Slandered Priests*, 1602, pp. 202, 225. Blackwell's decree of suspension was dated 17th October, the petition 17th November.

Sir Anthony Shirley's Voyage. *Fugger Letters*, p. 230 ; *A.R.*, ii. 831 ; *S.T.C.*, 22425.

28th November. News from Ireland. *S.P. Ireland*, 207, iv. : 19, 25, 39. Mountjoy's private letters this autumn are full of complaints that in spite of his successes he is being ill-supported at home.

1st December. My Lord of Essex's Passions. Camden's *Elizabeth* ; *Nugae Antiquae*, i. 179 ; *Reliquae Wottonianae*, 1685, p. 180 ; approximate date.

3rd December. The Queen's Letter to Lord Mountjoy. Printed in R. Bagwell's *Ireland under the Tudors*, iii. 386. The kitchenmaid joke was kept up in several subsequent letters.

7th December. Supplies for Ireland. *A.P.C.*, xxx. 794, 798.

10th December. The Black Galley of Dort. *A.R.*, iii. 178 ; *S.T.C.*, 7064.

11th December. A Discourse of Universities. *S.T.C.*, 15566.

15th December. A Boy seized to be a Player. The father's complaint from Star Chamber Proceedings is printed in F. G. Fleay's *A Chronicle History of the London Stage*, p. 127. Evans was afterwards censured in the Star Chamber.

20th December. The French King's Marriage. Winwood's *Memorials*, i. 279, 283.

21st December. A Proclamation concerning Firearms. *Proclamations*, 376.

22nd December. THE EARL OF ESSEX'S DANGEROUS COURSES. Camden's *Elizabeth.*

27th December. THE QUEEN'S PAINTING. Foley, i. 8.

31st December. A PRIVILEGE FOR THE DISCOVERY OF TRADE TO THE EAST INDIES. Printed in *Purchas His Pilgrims*, MacLehose edition, 1905, ii. 366.

OTHER BOOKS SET FORTH ANNO 1600

A CLOWN'S BOOK. *S.T.C.*, 22573. This book is attributed to Singer in *S.T.C.* and the British Museum Catalogue, because in the only known copy there is a note that 'it professes to have been written by Clunnyco de Curtanio Snuffe, *i.e.* Snuff the Clown of the Curtain Theatre, John Singer, whose name in an old hand of the time is written underneath these words.' It is, however, the work of Robert Armin, who had joined the Chamberlain's Men after the departure of Will Kemp. (See E. Nungezer, *A Dictionary of Actors*, 1929, p. 18). Apparently Shakespeare afterwards remodelled this effort of the Company's Clown in Viola's speech on the Clown (*Twelfth Night*, III. i. 68).

BRETON'S 'MELANCHOLICK HUMOURS.' *S.T.C.*, 3666; m.e. in *The Works of Nicholas Breton*, 1879, vol. i., edited by A. B. Grosart; and by G. B. Harrison in 1930 with an essay on Elizabethan Melancholy.

'PALESTINA.' *S.T.C.* 4954. The author of this interesting curiosity, was Robert Chambers, priest.

DARRELL'S ANSWER TO MR. HARSNETT. *S.T.C.*, 6288, 6283; both books came from the same foreign press, the second is abusive.

A DISCOURSE OF THE LANCASHIRE POSSESSIONS. *S.T.C.*, 18070. The story is detailed in *II Eliz. Journal* (pp. 173-4, 176-8). The book was apparently printed by the same printer as *The Trial of Maist. Darrell* and Darrell's *Brief Apology* and is dated 1600 on the title-page, where it is stated that More has been a prisoner in the Clink 'almost for the space of two years.' At the conclusion it is stated, 'This discourse good Reader was dispatched in December last. The difficulties of printing hath hindered the publishing of it thus longe.'

THE PICTURE OF A PERFECT COMMONWEALTH. *S.T.C.*, 11119. Though of no great importance, the book is one of several symptoms that political theory was occupying many minds at this time.

VICISSITUDO RERUM. *S.T.C.*, 18642. An important work, being a survey, as it were, of the Elizabethan idea of the theory and movement of the Universe with special reference to present disturbances. The theme of the whole is the same as that of Ulysses' Speech on degree and discord (*Troilus and Cressida*, I. iii. 75). Norden expresses the prevailing feeling that this Universe is rotten, for 'Time by turns, turns all things out of date'; m.e. by D. C. Collins, *Shakespeare Association Facsimiles*, No. 4, 1932.

THE TRANSFORMED METAMORPHOSIS. *S.T.C.*, 24152; m.e. in *The Works of Cyril Tourneur*, edited by Allardyce Nicoll, 1930. The chief interest of this curious poem lies in its obscurity; I have been unable to discover what the poem is about though occasionally the stanzas echo some of the general grievances of the time. The style is a slabby compound of Marston at his worst, Spenser, with some smacks of Donne.

1601

1st January. The Queen and Mr. Bacon. Bacon's *Apology.*

2nd January. The Earl of Essex. Camden's *Elizabeth.*

3rd January. An Italian Duke in London and The Cross in Cheapside. Foley, i. 5.

6th January. Irish News. *S.P. Ireland,* 207, iv. : 103.

9th January. The Lord Grey and the Earl of Southampton. Camden's *Elizabeth* ; Winwood's *Memorials,* i. 292. Southampton had returned to London in September from the Lowlands campaign.

11th January. The New East Indies Company. *A.P.C.,* xxxi. 93.

13th January. Banbury Cross defaced. Foley, i. 8.

14th January. The Earl of Essex. Foley, i. 7.

16th January. Debasing the Irish Coin. Wilbraham's *Journal,* p. 37.

18th January. Deserters pardoned. *A.P.C.,* xxxi. 100.

22nd January. Dr. Hayward again examined. *S. P. Dom.,* 278 : 17.

25th January. Master Hooker's Lost Books. Walton's *Life of Hooker* is the authority for this well-known story. Professor Sisson, however, tells me that it is a fiction, or, rather, that it was one of several contradictory tales told by the disputing parties in a case which he has discovered in the Record Office.

The Queen and Dr. Hayward's Book. Bacon's *Apology.*

28th January. Six Galleys to be built. *A.P.C.,* xxxi. 119.

1st February. A Windmill split by Wind. Stow's *Annals.*

3rd February. Strange Experiments. Chamberlain's *Letters,* p. 102.

5th February. The New Earl of Pembroke and Mrs. Fitton. *Letters of Cecil to Carew,* p. 65.

7th February. 'Richard the Second' played. *S.P. Dom.,* 278 : 78, 85. Seeing the trouble that had been caused by Hayward's unhappy book, the action of Essex's followers was most significant. The players, however, were exonerated ; and indeed it is unlikely that the servants of the Lord Chamberlain would intentionally have made a demonstration in favour of one in disgrace at Court.

The Earl of Essex and the Council. *S.P. Dom.,* 278 : 49.

8th February. The Earl of Essex's Treason. Camden's *Elizabeth* ; Stow's *Annals* ; *S.P. Dom.,* 278 : 74, 75 ; *Sloan MSS.,* 718.

9th February. A Proclamation concerning the Earl of Essex. *Proclamations,* 382.

10th February. Sir Thomas Hoby. *Salisbury Papers,* xi. 39. Cholmley was afterwards fined £200 for his share in the rebellion.

News from Ireland: the Praise of the Lord Deputy. *S.P. Ireland*, 208, i.: 25.

12th February. A Treasonable Practice in the Court. *Letters of Cecil to Carew*, pp. 72-3.

13th February. Proceedings in the Star Chamber. *S.P. Dom.*, 278: 94.

The East India Voyage. *Purchas his Pilgrims*, ii. 392-3.

15th February. A Proclamation. *Proclamations*, 383.

Directions for Preachers. *S.P. Dom.* 278: 63, 94; *Salisbury Papers*, xi. 55.

Certain Prayers set forth for this Time. *S.T.C.*, 16531.

Captain Lee condemned. Cobbett's *State Trials*, 1809, i. 1403. Cecil writing to Sir George Carew says that Essex's death 'was the more hastened by that bloody practise of Thomas Lee' (*Letters to Carew*, p. 72), which gives a summary of Essex's confessions.

16th February. Egyptians sentenced. *Mid. Sess. Rolls*, i. 266.

18th February. A Prognostication suppressed. *S.P. Dom.*, 278: 94.

19th February. The Trial of the Two Earls. There are many accounts of this famous trial, notably in D. Jardine's *Criminal Trials*, Howell's *State Trials*, Camden's *Elizabeth*, Winwood's *Memorials*, *S.P. Dom.*, etc. For a detailed analysis of the course of the day's events, see Spedding's *Bacon*, vol. ix. chapter ix.

20th February. The Earl of Essex. Birch's *Memoirs*, ii. 475.

21st February. Essex's Confessions. *S.P. Dom.*, 278: 104; Birch's *Memoirs*, ii. 478.

23rd February. The Earl of Essex and the Garter. *A.P.C.*, xxxi. 180.

24th February. An Ambassador from Scotland. *A.P.C.*, xxxi. 180.

The Players at Court. *Elizabethan Stage*, iv. 113, 166.

25th February. The Execution of the Earl of Essex. *S.P. Dom.*, 278: 112, 114; Camden's *Elizabeth*. The Council were not a little anxious lest Essex might say too much at his execution, and very particular instructions were sent to Howard, Peyton and the divines that the Earl should confine himself to 'the confession of his great treasons and of his sins towards God; his hearty repentance and earnest and incessant prayers to God for pardon.' He was on no account to enter into particulars of his treason or to justify himself.

The Character of the Late Earl of Essex. Camden's *Elizabeth*; *Reliquiae Wottonianae*, 1685, p. 172; Stow's *Annals*. It is usual for historians to take sides with or against Essex and to twist the evidence accordingly. Truth, as usual, probably lies midway. The charm of his personality as a young man was such that he was given employments that he was not competent to carry out; and he listened readily to those about him who fed his vanity for their own ends. There is very little evidence that Cecil consistently intrigued for his destruction; on the contrary he was notably generous and forbearing in spite of great provocation. The whole affair, however, caused a vast turmoil of emotions which are clearly reflected in contemporary literature. So long as Essex was alive, there was perpetual danger of anarchy.

27th February. CATHOLICS EXECUTED. *Rutland MSS.*, i. 369.

1st March. THE SERMON AT PAUL'S CROSS. *S.T.C.*, 1454; *A.R.*, iii. 181; entered 18th March. The official account of the execution is appended.

A COMPLAINT AGAINST THE SHERIFF OF NORFOLK. *A.P.C.*, xxxi. 194.

3rd March. A TREATISE UPON TRADE. *A.R.*, iii. 181; *S.T.C.*, 17227. A most interesting discussion of the principles of trade, exchange, the gold and silver standard, inflation and deflation, and similar financial and economic problems.

5th March. AN EMBASSY FROM SCOTLAND. Winwood's *Memorials*, i. 301.

THE CONSPIRATORS CONDEMNED. Cobbett's *State Trials*, i. 1410-1451.

11th March. SEDITIOUS BOOKS. *A.P.C.*, xxxi. 216. See *II Eliz. Journal*, p. 333.

THE EARL OF RUTLAND. *Rutland MSS.*, i. 373.

PLAYS TO BE SUPPRESSED IN LENT. *A.P.C.*, xxxi. 218.

13th March. THE PRISONERS IN THE TOWER. *A.P.C.*, xxxi. 222.

MERRICK AND CUFFE EXECUTED. Cobbett's *State Trials*, i. 1411.

16th March. THE CITY WATCHES DISMISSED. *A.P.C.*, xxxi. 229.

MR. BACON TO WRITE AN ACCOUNT OF THE LATE TROUBLES. *S.P. Dom.*, 279 : 28; Spedding's *Bacon*, ix. 240.

18th March. THE EXECUTION OF SIR CHARLES DANVERS AND SIR CHRISTOPHER BLOUNT. Stow's *Annals*.

20th March. THE EARL OF ESSEX'S SON. *A.P.C.*, xxxi. 229.

24th March. STRANGE RUMOURS. Smith's *Diary*, f. 55v.

25th March. IRELAND. *S.P. Ireland*, 208, i. : 122.

27th March. A LEWD LIBEL. *S.P. Dom.*, 278 : 23; printed in Mrs. C. C. Stopes' *Life of Henry, Third Earl of Southampton*, p. 234. Three of seven stanzas are here quoted. The libel was apparently popular, as at least three contemporary copies survive.

30th March. THE AMBASSADOR AND THE FRENCH KING. Winwood's *Memorials*, i. 309.

A BOOK OF DON SEBASTIAN. *A.R.*, iii. 182; *S.T.C.*, 23864. See p. 4.

5th April. A PROCLAMATION CONCERNING LIBELS. *Proclamations*, 386.

9th April. LORD HENRY SEYMOUR'S COMPLAINT. *A.P.C.*, xxxi. 268. Elizabethan sanitary arrangements in the City were crude. The practice apparently was for the ordure from private houses to be collected in the jakes cart which dumped its contents on waste ground or in barges for disposal elsewhere.

10th April. 'THE PLAIN MAN'S PATHWAY.' *A.R.*, iii. 181 ; *S.T.C.*, 6626-37 ; entered 7th March, dated 10th April in the Epistle. This book was one of the principal instruments in the conversion of John Bunyan (see *Grace Abounding*, § 15) ; it was very popular ; the twenty-fifth edition came out in 1631, and it was still being reprinted in 1682.

12th April. A PETITION OF THE LORD MAYOR. *Remembrancia*, ii. 173. Misdated 1600.

16th April. THE EARL OF NORTHUMBERLAND'S BROTHER RELEASED. *A.P.C.*, xxxi. 283.

17th April. THE COMPLAINT OF THE AMBASSADOR IN FRANCE. Winwood's *Memorials*, i. 314.

21st April. A DECLARATION OF THE TREASONS OF THE LATE EARL OF ESSEX. *S.T.C.*, 1133 ; m.e. in Spedding's *Bacon*, ix. 245 ; see also x. 159, and Bacon's *Apology*. The m.s. was sent to the Queen's Printer on the 14th with command from the Council that he should use all expedition therein. The evidences given in this publication are not unduly falsified ; it shows from the confessions of Essex's followers that armed rebellion was discussed whilst he was still in Ireland and that an attempt on the Court had been carefully planned. The forestalling of the conspiracy by the summons to Essex to appear was accidental. It is easy enough to condemn Bacon for this part in the tragedy, but until Essex's cause became hopeless he had consistently done his best to save his former patron. Spedding's defence of Bacon (in his *Letters and Life of Francis Bacon*) should be read alongside the many attacks.

22nd April. THE EAST INDIA SHIPS. Purchas, ii. 393. They returned to England 11th September, 1603.

26th April. THE LORD PEMBROKE. *A.P.C.*, xxxi. 299. All the prisoners in the Tower continually complain to the Council of sickness. See p. 143.

27th April. NEWS FROM THE FRENCH COURT. Winwood's *Memorials*, i. 316 ; the offensive letter is given on p. 296.

28th April. MORE SOLDIERS FOR IRELAND. *A.P.C.*, xxxi. 315, 318. This demand was prefaced by a note that the speedy conclusion of the rebellion is expected and that the soldiers are now well victualled and accommodated.

29th April. A QUARREL BETWEEN THE ATTORNEY AND MR. BACON. Spedding's *Bacon*, x. 3.

9th May. COURT NEWS. Winwood's *Memorials*, i. 329.

10th May. A PLAY FORBIDDEN. *A.P.C.*, xxxi. 346.

THE SERMON AT PAUL'S CROSS. *A.R.*, iii. 185 ; *S.T.C.*, 7083.

11th May. SPANISH SHIPS. *Salisbury Papers*, xi. 192.

12th May. THE IRISH COINAGE. *Carew Papers*, 1601-3, 61.

17th *May.* EXPORT OF PROVISION TO FRANCE FORBIDDEN. *A.P.C.*, xxxi, 359.

18th May. FINES FOR THE LATE ACTION. Chamberlain's *Letters*, p. 108 ; *Salisbury Papers*, xi. 214, where the full list is given.

20th May. CATHOLIC BOOKS. Law, Nos. II, III.

24th May. 'Saint George for England.' *A.R.*, iii. 185; *S.T.C.*, 17226a.

25th May. A Commission concerning the Preservation of the Wealth of the Realm. *S.P. Dom.*, 279: 97; approximate date.

30th May. The Proclamation for the Irish Moneys. *Carew MSS.* 67.

7th June. Irish News. *S.P. Ireland*, 208, ii.: 68, 91.

10th June. Trinity College in Dublin. *Salisbury Papers*, xi. 257.

12th June. 'The Passions of the Mind.' *A.R.*, iii. 185; *S.T.C.*, 26039. The book is of some interest as a study in psychology. It was reissued in 1604 with a preface to the Earl of Southampton, and *A succinct philosophical declaration of the nature of the climacterical years occasioned by the death of Queen Elizabeth*; other editions exist dated 1620, 1621, 1630.

16th June. The Young Lord Burgh. *A.P.C.*, xxxi. 431.

17th June. The Case of John Daniel. *Egerton Papers*, p. 321.

19th *June.* Two Brethren punished. Hawarde, p. 124.

22nd June. 'Discourses upon Seneca the Tragedian.' *A.R.*, iii. 186; *S.T.C.*, 5774.

25th June. A Book against Tabacco. *A.R.*, iii. 186; *S.T.C.*, 12571. See also 4th January, 1602.

29th June. Three New Councillors. *A.P.C.*, xxxii. 487; xxxi. 467.

30th June. The Queen's Printer. *A.P.C.*, xxxii. 14.

New Plays. *Hens. Diary*, i. 125, 134-8; ii. 215-8.

3rd July. A Proclamation against transporting Moneys into Ireland. *Proclamations*, 387.

4th July. The Blackwater passed. *S.P. Ireland*, 208, iii.: 70, 83.

7th July. A Thousand Men for Ostend. *A.P.C.*, xxxii. 22, 26.

8th July. Ostend besieged. *S.T.C.*, 18893.

11th July. Irish News. *S.P. Ireland*, 208, iii.: 52.

12th July. Public Burdens evaded. *A.P.C.*, xxxii. 47.

20th July. More Soldiers for Ostend. *A.P.C.*, xxxii. 73, 75.

21st July. Soldiers from the Counties. *A.P.C.*, xxxii. 77.

23rd July. 5000 Men for Munster. *A.P.C.*, xxxii. 79.

25th July. News from Ostend. *S.T.C.*, 18893.

2nd August. Invasion threatened. *A.P.C.*, xxxii. 135.

3rd August. A Discourse of Spirits. *A.R.*, iii. 189; *S.T.C.*, 6439.

4th August. The Queen and Mr. Lambarde. Nichols' *Progresses*, vol. ii.; the original account is *MSS. Addit.* 15664, f. 226. Lambarde died on 19th August.

News of Ostend. As for 25th July.

5th August. Prisoners to be released from the Tower. *A.P.C.* xxxii. 143.

A BOOK ABOUT THE HORSE. *A.R.*, iii. 190 ; *S.T.C.*, 4287 ; a popular book, editions surviving of 1610 and 1631.

6th August. MORE SOLDIERS FOR OSTEND. *A.P.C.*, xxxii. 145.

REWARDS FOR SERVICE. *A.P.C.*, xxxii. 148.

10th August. OSTEND. *S.T.C.*, 18894.

12th August. A WIFE BEATEN. *Mid. Sess. Rolls*, i. 274.

14th August. SIR FRANCIS VERE HURT. *Salisbury Papers*, x. 264 (misdated 1600) ; xi. 322.

19th August. IRISH NEWS. *S.P. Ireland*, 209 : 10, 10a.

22nd August. A GRIEVOUS FIRE. *A.P.C.*, xxxii. 179.

23rd August. A BOOK OF ASTRONOMY. *A.R.*, iii. 191 ; *S.T.C.*, 3160.

24th August. TRAITOROUS SOLDIERS. *Salisbury Papers*, xi. 322.

28th August. THE MARSHAL BIRON. *A.P.C.*, xxxii. 190.

30th August. MORE CATHOLIC BOOKS. *S.T.C.*, 3106, 1884; Law, Nos. V and IV.

2nd September. KEMP RETURNED. Smith's *Diary*, f. 56.

5th September. THE MARSHAL BIRON. Stow's *Annals*.

7th September. THE DUKE OF BIRON. Edwards' *Ralegh*, ii. 233 ; *Salisbury Papers*, xi. 382.

9th September. A PARLIAMENT TO BE SUMMONED. *Egerton Papers*, p. 328.

10th September. TWO PRIESTS GRANTED PASSPORTS. *A.P.C.*, xxxii. 205.

THE MARSHAL BIRON. Stow's *Annals*.

11th September. BRETON'S DIVINE POEMS. *A.R.*, iii. 191 ; *S.T.C.*, 3648. Breton was a poet of many moods but one of the few who at this time could take refuge in mystical ecstacy from the disgust felt at the rottenness of the world. Most of the others, finding no emotional consolation in religious devotion, settled into a profound melancholy, or vented their feelings in snarling satires. Later some of these also (notably Donne, Hall and Marston) found their consolation in the priesthood.

14th September. THE DUKE OF BIRON. Edwards' *Ralegh*, ii. 234.

15th September. JONSON'S 'POETASTER.' *A.R.*, iii. 198 ; *S.T.C.*, 14781 ; m.e. (with *Satiromastix*) by J. H. Penniman ; entered 21st December. See also pp. 217, 234, 244. Approximate date.

THE QUEEN AND THE DUKE OF BIRON. Stow's *Annals* ; Camden's *Elizabeth* ; *A.P.C.*, xxxii. 213.

16th September. A KIND FRIENDLY SNIPPING. *A.R.*, iii. 192 ; *S.T.C.*, 3672.

21st September. DIFFICULTIES OVER THE IRISH COINAGE. *S.P. Ireland*, 209 : 68.

23rd September. THE SUMMONS TO PARLIAMENT. *A.P.C.*, xxxii. 218.

25th September. 'THE SPANISH TRAGEDY.' *Hens. Diary*, i. 149.

30th September. THE SPANIARDS LAND IN IRELAND. *S.P. Ireland*, 209 : 90, 91, 93, 107.

Fresh Troops for Ireland. *A.P.C.*, xxxii. 223.

5th October. Four Hundred Men from the City. *A.P.C.*, xxxii. 235.

6th October. The Soldiers for Ireland to be increased. *A.P.C.*, xxxii. 239.

8th October. A Miraculous Powder. *A.R.*, iii. 197; *S.T.C.*, 21455.

9th October. The Queen. *Nugae Antiquae*, i. 317.

13th October. The Soldiers for Ireland. *A.P.C.*, xxxii. 275, 277-286.

20th October. The Spanish Landing. *Egerton Papers*, p. 332.

22nd October. Insufficient Levies. *Salisbury Papers*, xi. 441.

27th October. The Parliament assembles. D'Ewes' *Journals*, pp. 598, 620; *Secret Correspondence*, p. 26.

29th October. Sir Thomas Hoby's Complaints. *Salisbury Papers*, xi. 546.

30th October. The Speaker presented. D'Ewes' *Journals*, pp. 600, 621.

2nd November. The Parliament. D'Ewes' *Journals*, p. 622.

3rd November. The Parliament. D'Ewes' *Journals*, p. 624.

6th November. A Wife Murderer. *Mid. Sess. Rolls*, i. 275.

7th November. The Subsidy. D'Ewes' *Journals*, p. 629.

9th November. The Parliament and the Subsidy. D'Ewes' *Journals*, p. 631.

11th November. The Queen's Suspicions. *Secret Correspondence*, p. 16; Chamberlain's *Letters*, p. 122.

Sir Anthony Shirley's Travels. *A.R.*, iii. 195; *S.T.C.*, 19343.

Jonson Untrussed. *A.R.*, iii. 195; *S.T.C.*, 6521. Approximate date. The play was entered on 11th November, which was probably the earliest possible date, as the entry was made 'vppon condicon that yt be lycensed to be printed.'

13th November. Seventeen Poor People Crushed to Death. Stow's *Annals*.

15th November. Catholic Books. Law, Nos. VIII, IX, X, XI.

16th November. The Parliament. D'Ewes' *Journals*, p. 639.

20th November. A Book against Astrology. *A.R.*, iii. 196; *S.T.C.*, 4941.

A Bill concerning Monopolies. D'Ewes' *Journals*, p. 644.

A too Curious Gentleman. *A.P.C.*, xxxii. 375.

21st November. The Committee for Monopolies. D'Ewes' *Journals*, p. 647.

News from Ireland. Fynes Moryson's *Itinerary*. MacLehose edition, iii. 1-29.

23rd November. Monopolies. D'Ewes' *Journals*, p. 648.

24th November. The Monopolies. D'Ewes' *Journals*, p. 651.

'WHAT YOU WILL.' *S.T.C.*, 17487; m.e. in *The Works of John Marston*, edited by A. H. Bullen, 1887, vol. ii. This play is important for an understanding of the prevailing spirit of disillusion, especially amongst intellectual young men of the post-Armada generation. Marston, through the person of Lampatho, has expressed much of his own feeling of the futility of academic study. In the Induction he replied generally to Jonson's attacks, but in contrast to Jonson's arrogant self-praise, he affected an excess of modesty. The play was not published till 1607. Approximate date.

25th November. THE QUEEN SENDS FOR MR. SPEAKER. D'Ewes' *Journals*, p. 651.

26th November. THE QUEEN'S MESSAGE TO THE HOUSE. D'Ewes' *Journals*, p. 654.

27th November. SIR FERDINANDO GORGES TO BE RELEASED. *A.P.C.*, xxxii. 387.

THE PARLIAMENT. D'Ewes' *Journals*, p. 655. There were several other cases of abuse of privilege in this Parliament.

28th November. A PROCLAMATION CONCERNING PRIVILEGES. *Proclamations*, 388; see 28th March, 1600.

30th November. THE QUEEN RECEIVES THE MEMBERS OF THE HOUSE. D'Ewes' *Journals*, p. 658.

1st December. THE PARLIAMENT. D'Ewes' *Journals*, p. 660. Another example of the general discontent, expressed, for instance, in Hamlet's disgust at the whips and scorns of time.

JONSON'S APOLOGY. As for 15th September. Approximate date.

2nd December. THE PARLIAMENT. D'Ewes' *Journals*. Master Carew Ralegh's proper sentiments are the more commendable since he had the reputation in 1594 of being a loose-tongued atheist; see *I Eliz. Journal*, p. 295.

4th December. THE EARL OF NORTHUMBERLAND. *Secret Correspondence*, p. 29.

6th December. THE DUKE OF BIRON'S VISIT. *A.P.C.*, xxxii. 415.

9th December. THE PARLIAMENT. D'Ewes' *Journals*, p. 674.

10th December. WATSON'S QUODLIBET. *S.T.C.*, 25123. Although dated 1602 the book was in circulation before Christmas (see Foley, i. 8); it is a storehouse of anti-Jesuit scandal and anecdote.

12th December. DISORDERS IN THE HOUSE. D'Ewes' *Journals*, p. 682.

16th December. A FUNERAL SERMON PUBLISHED. *A.R.*, iii. 197; *S.T.C.*, 12866. The book was very popular, and went into five editions.

19th December. THE PARLIAMENT DISSOLVED. D'Ewes' *Journals*, pp. 618, 689; Wilbraham's *Journal*, p. 44. D'Ewes entirely omits the speech.

20th December. A NOTE OF THE CHIEF STATUTES ENACTED IN THE LATE PARLIAMENT. *S.T.C.*, 9493, etc.

21st December. THE GREAT DANGER AT OSTEND. *A.R.*, iii. 199; *S.T.C.*, 24651. Also *A true and historical relation of the bloody battle of Nieuport . . . together with a brief relation of Sir Francis Vere . . . his parley at Ostend*, etc., by Henry Hexham; much of this account is included in Vere's *Commentaries* (m.e. in Arber's *Garner*, vol. i.). Hexham was Vere's page during the siege.

JONSON'S 'POETASTER.' *A.R.*, iii. 198.

22nd December. NO NEWS FROM IRELAND. *A.P.C.*, xxxii. 437. From the Council's letter to Lord Mountjoy, tactfully pointing out that 'very frequent advertisements of the state of all things there' is desirable 'because small mutations in those actions do make oftentymes a great inclination one waie or other.'

23rd December. A FURTHER SUPPLY FOR IRELAND. *A.P.C.*, xxxii. 440.

OSTEND. As for 20th December.

24th December. AN EARTHQUAKE. Stow's *Annals*.

THE FLEET RECALLED FROM IRELAND. *A.P.C.*, xxxii. 451, 455.

26th December. SPANISH PROVISIONS DESTROYED. *S.P. Ireland*, 209: 225, 232b.

28th December. SIR FRANCIS COSENETH THE ARCHDUKE. As for 20th December.

30th December. THE CHRISTMAS PLAY AT CAMBRIDGE. *A.R.*, iii. 304; *S.T.C.*, 19309. This third part was published in 1606; m.e. by W. D. Macray, 1886; see p. 60.

31st December. MORE MEN NEEDED. *A.P.C.*, xxxii. 477. This volume of *A.P.C.* ends on 2nd January, 1602; the volumes for the rest of the reign are lost.

THE ABUSE OF PLAYHOUSES. *A.P.C.*, xxxii. 466; see 22nd June, 1600.

NEW PLAYS. *Hens. Diary*, i. 138, 143-152; ii. 218-20.

OTHER BOOKS SET FORTH ANNO 1601

'LOVE'S MARTYR.' *S.T.C.*, 5119; m.e. by A. B. Grosart, 1878. For biographical details see *Poems by Sir John Salisbury and Robert Chester*, edited by Carleton Brown, 1913. The chief merit of this book is that Shakespeare was persuaded to add 'The Phoenix and Turtle.'

AN ANSWER TO DARRELL. *S.T.C.*, 6440; see also pp. 193, 311.

The energy of these two preachers was prodigious; both books came out in 1601, the former containing 356 closely printed pages, the latter 240.

'AFFANIAE.' *S.T.C.*, 10934. The collection is of no great merit, but interesting because of the epigrams to writers, amongst them Campion, Richard Carew, Chapman, Daniel, Jonson, Hall, Marston, Meres, Overbury; Nashe and Spenser are addressed in the *Cenotaphia*.

A BOOK OF ESSAYS. *S.T.C.*, 14695. Another example of the process of self-analysis.

'THE TRAVELLER'S BREVIAT.' *S.T.C.*, 3398.

MR. WEEVER'S 'MIRROR OF MARTYRS.' *S.T.C.*, 25226. This poem has a twofold minor interest. It contains a well-known reference to Shakespeare's *Julius Caesar*, which can therefore be dated in 1599, and it shows that the Oldcastle-Falstaff scandal caused considerable comment.

1602

1st January. A SAYING OF MARSTON. Manningham's *Diary*, p. 36.

2nd January. THE GREAT LOSSES AT KINSALE. *S.P. Ireland*, 209 : 249.

3rd January. A DESPERATE ATTEMPT AT OSTEND. As for 20th December; this account is taken mostly from Hexham. Ostend was desperately held in the Spanish War (as Ypres in the Great War) rather as a symbol of the diehard spirit than for its military value.

4th January. 'A DEFENCE OF TABACCO.' *A.R.*, iii. 199; *S.T.C.*, 6468.

6th January. A GREAT VICTORY IN IRELAND. *A.R.*, iii. 202; *S.T.C.*, 7434.

NEWS FROM OSTEND. *A.R.*, iii. 200; *S.T.C.*, 18891.

8th January. 'THE UNMASKING OF THE POLITIC ATHEIST.' *A.R.*, iv. 199; *S.T.C.*, 13934.

12th January. A SAYING CONCERNING OSTEND. Manningham's *Diary*, p. 15.

16th January. OSTEND. *Salisbury Papers*, xii. 607.

18th January. 'THE MERRY WIVES OF WINDSOR.' *A.R.*, iii. 199; for a discussion of the tradition that the play was written to order of the Queen, see the edition in the *New Shakespeare*, edited by A. T. Quiller-Couch and J. Dover Wilson, 1921, p. viii.

A GARDENER'S MISCHANCE. *Mid. Sess. Rolls*, i. 276.

19th January. OSTEND. As for 20th December.

20th January. THE SPANIARDS SURRENDER AT KINSALE. As for 4th January; Winwood's *Memorials*, i. 378.

26th January. THE CASE OF SIR THOMAS POSTHUMUS HOBY. See 10th September, 1600; *Society Women of Shakespeare's Times*, by Violet A. Wilson, p. 255.

28th January. THE SIEGE OF OSTEND. *Salisbury Papers*, xii. 33. From a letter of Sir R. Cecil to G. Nicholson, who adds, 'I send you a pamphlet written by a principal captain of Ostend wherein you shall see a true relation of all the proceedings. The style is but coarse, neither should it have passed in all things as it doth if I had seen it, but such is the greediness of printers as they will never refuse anything that is brought to the press.'

30th January. IRELAND. *S.P. Ireland*, 210 : 22.

2nd February. MR. JOHN DONNE'S MARRIAGE. *The Loseley Manuscripts*, edited by A. J. Kempe, 1836, pp. 326-343, and *The Life and Letters of John Donne*, by Edmund Gosse, 1899, chapter iv.

'TWELFTH NIGHT.' Manningham's *Diary*, p. 18. Shakespeare drew more than usual from current events in constructing this play. The Darrell case was still sufficiently recent for the 'possession' and 'dispossession' of the Puritan Malvolio to have topical flavour. For a notable instance of the love of sister for brother see pp. 34, 50. The rowdiness of Sir Toby and his fellow tipplers has already been noted as similar to the Hoby affair (see pp. 114-5, etc.) References are made to a pension from the Sophy (see p. 215), the new map of the Indies, and the chat between Viola and Feste (III. i. 1-30) would have reminded this audience of the notorious Fowler case (pp. 89-90), and the great controversy concerning equivocation (pp. 218-9). Moreover, if Shakespeare had read *News from Ostend*, he might well have drawn inspiration thence for Sebastian's escape from drowning (p. 193).

8th February. CAREW'S 'SURVEY OF CORNWALL.' *A.R.*, iii. 201; *S.T.C.*, 4615. This famous county history of Cornwall has been justly commended by Camden.

11th February. MR. DONNE'S MARRIAGE. As for 2nd February.

12th February. THE SCOTTISH KING and A NEW DISEASE. Foley, i. 9, 10.

13th February. THE OLD DEAN OF ST. PAUL'S DEAD. Camden's *Elizabeth*; Fuller's *Worthies* (Lancashire).

16th February. INSTRUCTIONS FOR THE FLEET. *S.P. Dom.*, 283 : 28; Monson's *Tracts*, ii. 151. The fleet sailed on 19th and 21st March.

20th February. PARSONS' ANSWER TO THE SECULARS. *S.T.C.*, 19392; Law, VI; see p. 268.

21st February. A PETITION FOR ASSOCIATION. *S.T.C.*, 6873. Approximate date of publication.

25th February. THE KING OF SCOTS' TITLE. *Correspondence of King James VI*, p. 55. From a letter written by the Earl of Northumberland to the King.

1st March. THE YOUNG LORD BURGH DEAD. *Salisbury Papers*, xii. 59, 66. The last symptoms and drastic remedies applied are described in detail in these two letters from the Bishop to Cecil.

2nd March. THE LORD KEEPER'S CHARGE. Foley, i. 20.

3rd March. COURT NEWS. Foley, i. 21-2. Parsons in his *Apology* gave Bancroft what he had been wanting—an open acknowledgment that equivocation was officially recognised and encouraged by the Jesuits.

10th March. WILL KEMP. *Hens. Diary*, i. 179.

13th March. A MERRY JEST CONCERNING SHAKESPEARE. Manningham's *Diary*, p. 39.

15th March. A PURITAN BOOK. *S.T.C.*, 18541. Though secretly issued, the book went into three editions. For the times the book is a sane and dignified appeal for toleration and unity.

17th March. COURT NEWS. Foley, i. 23, 24.

18th March. SIR FRANCIS VERE LEAVETH OSTEND. Hexham (see note on 20th December); the comment is from Camden's *Elizabeth*. For a possible echo of the general feeling see *Hamlet*, IV. iv. 16-64.

20th March. A PROCLAMATION TO REPRESS PIRACIES. *Proclamations*, 392.

25th March. MR. DONNE'S MARRIAGE. Gosse, i. 114; Walton's *Life*; see 2nd and 11th February.

27th March. The Queen's Ships. *Monson Tracts*, ii. 151.

28th March. The Spaniards in Ireland. *S.P. Ireland*, 210 : 65.

9th April. Valuable Spanish Prizes. *Salisbury Papers*, xii. 98, 100.

10th April. 'Sword and Buckler.' *A.R.*, iii. 203 ; *S.T.C.*, 1555. Compare the similar complaint of J. M. in *The Servingman's Comfort* (*II Eliz. Journal*, p. 278).

18th April. A Printer hanged. Stow's *Annals*.

The Queen and Dr. Barlow. Manningham's *Diary*, p. 51.

24th April. The Spanish Prizes. *Salisbury Papers*, xii. 105, 116, 117.

27th April. Ships from the States. *Salisbury Papers*, xii. 126.

28th April. A Mass surprised. Foley, i. 28.

3rd May. A Negligent Pleader. Manningham's *Diary*, p. 41.

5th May. Troubles of Lancashire Ministers. *Salisbury Papers*, xii. 142.

7th May. Harsh Measures by the Lord Mayor. *Salisbury Papers*, xii. 144.

8th May. The Earl of Northumberland and Sir F. Vere. Chamberlain's *Letters*, pp. 131-2, 140.

Mr. Clarke's 'Trumpet of Apollo.' *A.R.*, iii. 206 ; *S.T.C.*, 5353. A naive advertisement for a quack medicine.

10th May. The French King's Troubles. Winwood's *Memorials*, i. 406.

12th May. City News. *Gawdy Letters*, pp. 120, 121, 122. For the Fowler case, see 12th June, 1600.

15th May. The Earl of Northumberland. *Secret Correspondence*, pp. 66, 69.

17th May. The Marshal Biron. Winwood's *Memorials*, i. 408.

22nd May. News of Sir R. Leveson. *Salisbury Papers*, xii. 133. The letter is dated 30th April, and was delivered at Plymouth on 20th May.

24th May. A Debate in the Council concerning Peace. Wilbraham's *Journal*, p. 44.

27th May. A Saying of Sir John Fortescue. *Secret Correspondence*, p. 128.

31st May. Sir Anthony Shirley. *S.P. Dom.*, 284 : 78, 79 ; approximate date. Shirley had been so violent a partisan of Essex that his fate was bound up with his patron's.

1st June. The Soldiers at Bristol. *Salisbury Papers*, xii. 169.

2nd June. 'The Metamorphosis of Tabacco.' *A.R.*, iii. 202 ; *S.T.C.*, 1695 ; written by Sir John Beaumont. The easy 'Augustan' flow of the verse in this mock heroic poem is in great contrast to the crabbed harshness of most of the satirists who used this metre.

6th June. The Sermon at Paul's Cross. Manningham's *Diary*, p. 34.

7th June. A Saying concerning Sir W. Ralegh. Manningham's *Diary*, p. 34.

10th June. THE EARL OF NORTHUMBERLAND. *Secret Correspondence*, p. 105. This Percy was afterwards one of the principal conspirators in the Powder Plot. It is likely that on this occasion he brought back some kind of verbal promise of toleration for Catholics. Approximate date.

14th June. THE MARSHAL BIRON ARRESTED. Winwood's *Memorials*, i. 414.

15th June. A JESUIT BOOK AGAINST THE PRIESTS. *S.T.C.*, 19411; Law, XIV.

18th June. THE FLEET RETURNING. *Salisbury Papers*, xii. 196.

19th June. THE IRISH MONIES. *S.P. Ireland*, 211 : 50.

22nd June. A PROCLAMATION CONCERNING NEW BUILDINGS IN LONDON. *Proclamations*, 394. Less than a year later the plague did break out with the effect prognosticated.

26th June. A RICH CARRACK TAKEN. *Monson's Tracts*, ii. 151-176. The carrack, called the *St. Valentine*, 1700 tons, reached Plymouth on 23rd June. It was sunk in the following March.

27th June. BIRON'S CONSPIRACY. Winwood's *Memorials*, i. 417. The original letter, dated 17th June, gives an outline of the conspiracy, which, coming so soon after the Marshal's visit, caused a great sensation in England.

30th June. AN ATTEMPT ON THE SCOTTISH KING. Foley, i. 40.

1st July. GREAT HAIL. Stow's *Annals*.

3rd July. A SUCCESS IN MUNSTER. *S.P. Ireland*, 208, iii. : 26; 211 : 70; *Pacata Hibernia*, bk. iii., chapters viii, ix.

10th July. NEW ERECTED BUILDINGS. *Remembrancia*, ii. 190.

14th July. THE WAR IN THE LOW COUNTRIES. *Salisbury Papers*, xii. 267.

17th July. THE MARSHAL BIRON. Winwood's *Memorials*, i. 423.

20th July. THE IRISH WAR. *Moryson*, iii. 166 *et seq.*

25th July. THE PLAGUE AT AMSTERDAM. *Salisbury Papers*, xii. 247.

26th July. THE PLAY OF 'HAMLET.' *A.R.*, iii. 212; *S.T.C.*, 22275-6. The comment is Gabriel Harvey's.

28th July. COURT RUMOURS. Foley, i. 43.

A TREATY WITH THE KING OF DENMARK. *Salisbury Papers*, xii. 249, 274.

GREAT RAINS. Foley, i, 45.

29th July. THE EXECUTION OF THE DUKE OF BIRON. *A.R.*, iii. 213; *S.T.C.*, 12002; entered 5th August. Also Winwood's *Memorials*, i. 427.

30th July. SPEECHES OF THE EARL OF LINCOLN. *S.P. Dom.*, 284 : 80, 91.

2nd August. THE QUEEN AT THE LORD KEEPER'S. Nichols' *Progresses*, vol. iii.; Foley, i. 46. Nichols assigns this letter to a visit of 1601, but the mention of the carrack establishes the date.

3rd August. The Queen at Harefield. Nichols' *Progresses*, vol. iii. See *Egerton Papers* for a list of the gifts to help the entertainment; also E. Lodge's *Illustrations of British History, etc.*, 1838, iii. 135.

5th August. The Siege of the Grave. *Salisbury Papers*, xii. 259.

12th August. A Conjuror taken. *Salisbury Papers*, xii. 290.

17th August. The Siege of the Grave. *Salisbury Papers*, xii. 295.

18th August. The Conjuror at Plymouth. *Salisbury Papers*, xii. 552.

20th August. The Lord Treasurer's Son. *Salisbury Papers*, xii. 309.

25th August. Tyrone a Fugitive. Moryson, iii. 183 *et seq.*, 205.

3rd September. A Book of Conny-catching. *A.R.*, iii. 216; *S.T.C.*, 12243. S. R[owlands] has some new tales to offer but makes free use of Greene's conny-catching pamphlets.

4th September. Sir E. Dymock and the Earl of Lincoln. *Star Chamber Proceedings: Eliz.*, 5 L. 1-29. According to a paper in the Northumberland MSS. (Hist. MSS. Com., 3rd Rep., p. 57) the case was decided on 4th May 1610 (*sic*), when the three chief actors were ordered to be set in the pillory, whipped, and fined £300 each; Dymock was to be fined £1000 and imprisoned during the king's pleasure.

7th September. The Death of Mr. George Gilpin. *Salisbury Papers*, xii. 346, 384.

10th September. Complaints against the Earl of Lincoln. *Salisbury Papers*, xii. 410.

15th September. The Grave taken. *Salisbury Papers*, xii. 369.

A Proclamation concerning Game. *Proclamations*, 396.

The Jesuits. Foley, i. 47.

'Tis Merry when Gossips meet.' *A.R.*, iii. 216; *S.T.C.*, 21409. This poem by Rowlands gives a tolerable picture of a tavern scene, and in the preliminary pages, a 'Conference between an old fashioned reader and the bookseller's prentice'; m.e. for the Hunterian Club, 1880.

16th September. A Noble Visitor. *Diary of Duke of Stettin's Journey*, p. 13. The journal of the journey, which is one of the more interesting relations of England during the period, is reprinted in the *Transactions of the Royal Historical Society*, new series, vol. vi. 1892.

18th September. The Duke of Stettin. *Duke of Stettin's Journey*, p. 25. 'Robert Cotton' is my conjecture for 'Kopf' in the original.

19th September. The Queen and Sir R. Cecil. Letters from William Brown and the Earl of Worcester to the Earl of Shrewsbury, printed in Lodge's *Illustrations*, ii. 572, 575.

20th September. Mr. Thomas Bodley. *Salisbury Papers*, xii. 387.

The Booty of the Carrack. *Monson's Tracts*, ii. 346, where the list is given in full from *S.P. Dom.*, 285 : 12. The goods of the carrack were ultimately disposed of in 1604 and yielded £26,127 : 11s : 7d (including £736 : 8s : od from the prizes taken by Mansfield and Preston in 1601), of which the pepper fetched £9,386 : 7s : 8d.

23rd September. Court News. Lodge's *Illustrations*, ii. 582.

27th September. THE DUKE OF STETTIN AT COURT. *Duke of Stettin's Journey*, p. 51.

'THE CHRISTIAN NAVY.' *A.R.*, iii. 218; *S.T.C.*, 18583.

DON SEBASTIAN. *A.R.*, iii., 217; *S.T.C.*, 23865-6. Both books were entered together though the second is dated 1603.

2nd October. SPANISH GALLEYS SUNK. *A.R.*, iii. 219; *S.T.C.*, 17259.

5th October. A TALL GALLANT. Manningham's *Diary*, p. 53.

9th October. BIRON'S CONSPIRACY. Winwood's *Memorials*, i. 438.

11th October. A CASE OF PLAGUE. *Salisbury Papers*, xii. 438.

12th October. THE EARL OF SUSSEX'S BASE WRONGS. Manningham's *Diary*, p. 60.

16th October. A PLAY OF MARSHAL BIRON. *Hens. Diary*, i. 181-2; ii. 231; approximate date of performance. Henslowe records payment for a suit of black satin (see p. 201) and carpenter's wages 'to macke a scafowlde and barr.' So far as plays of contemporary history were concerned the Elizabethan actor had nice views on verisimilitude of presentation (see also p. 47). For other plays during the months covered by *III Eliz. Journal* which dealt with recent or topical events, see note on 12th May 1600.

21st October. TYRONE'S SUBMISSION. Moryson, iii. 232.

28th October. THE CHARGE TO THE NEW LORD MAYOR. Manningham's *Diary*, p. 72.

31st October. THE SERMON AT PAUL'S CROSS. Manningham's *Diary*, p. 74. Dr. Dove's previous, and not less sensational, sermon at Paul's Cross is noted on p. 180.

5th November. A PROCLAMATION FOR PROCEEDING AGAINST JESUITS AND SECULAR PRIESTS. *Proclamations*, 397. So long as the theory of the State was still based upon the interpretation of Christian doctrine, toleration of differences in religion was impossible. The strict Catholic was divided in his allegiance between the Pope and the Queen; and as the Queen was an excommunicated heretic, he was bound to support her enemies if commanded by the Pope. Extreme Puritans, rejecting both Church and State as anti-Christian, propounded revolutionary and democratic theories. All parties, however, agreed that a plurality of religions was against the policy of all States. See *I Eliz. Journal*, p. 208; *II Eliz. Journal*, pp. 159, 281-2; *III Eliz. Journal*, p. 314. For the 'factious invectives,' see pp. 265, 268.

6th November. THE EARL OF NORTHUMBERLAND. Manningham's *Diary*, p. 79.

9th November. A DISCOURSE AGAINST MACHIAVELLI. *A.R.*, iii. 221; *S.T.C.*, 11743. Gentillet's book seems to have been far better known in England than Machiavelli's *Il Principe*. Gentillet's method is to quote a passage from *Il Principe* and then to comment on it at length; his book appeared originally in 1576; the English translation is dated in the Epistle Dedicatory *Kalendo Augusti, Anno* 1577. It had not previously been printed.

12th November. A COSENING PRANK. Chamberlain's *Letters*, p. 163. For a long note on this affair see Chambers' *Eliz. Stage*, iii. 500. One of

Venner's original playbills still survives and is reproduced in facsimile in W. W. Greg's *Dramatic Documents from the Elizabethan Playhouses.* The play was called *England's Joy*.

17th November. THE QUEEN. Foley, i. 52.

20th November. VENNER'S PRANK. Manningham's *Diary*, pp. 82, 93.

21st November. THE TILTING. Manningham's *Diary*, p. 87.

22nd November. THE TREATY IN DENMARK. *Salisbury Papers,* xii. 471, 472.

28th November. THE SERMON AT PAUL'S CROSS. Manningham's *Diary*, p. 93.

6th December. THE QUEEN ENTERTAINED. Manningham's *Diary,* p. 99.

10th December. A REPLY TO PARSONS. Law, XIX.

22nd December. 'WONDERS WORTH THE HEARING.' *A.R.*, iii. 222; *S.T.C.*, 3714; entered 20th November, Epistle dated 22nd December. The book is somewhat after the style of Greene's *Quip for an Upstart Courtier.*

SIR EDWARD WOTTON PROMOTED. *A.P.C.*, xxxii. 490.

24th December. THE LADY EFFINGHAM. Manningham's *Diary*, p. 132.

25th December. MR. RICHARD HAWKINS' RETURN. *Salisbury Papers,* xii. 526.

27th December. THE QUEEN'S HEALTH. *Nugae Antiquae*, i. 320.

31st December. NEW FLAGS. *Hens. Diary*, i. 152-3, 165-72; ii. 220-6.

OTHER BOOKS SET FORTH ANNO 1602

MR. DARRELL'S ANSWER TO THE PREACHERS. *S.T.C.*, 6285.

OBSERVATIONS IN THE ART OF ENGLISH POETRY. *S.T.C.*, 4543; m.e. in the *Bodley Head Quartos*, vol. xiv.

JOSEPHUS' WORKS ENGLISHED. *S.T.C.*, 14809.

1603

8th January. Mr. Richard Hawkins. *Salisbury Papers*, xii. 590. The numerous letters of information which Hawkins wrote at great risk during his captivity are ample proof of his loyalty.

10th January. A Defence of Astrology. *S.T.C.*, 13266. Approximate date; published at Cambridge.

30th January. The Toleration of the Lord Mountjoy. *S.P. Ireland*, 212 : 118.

31st January. A Declaration of the Secular Priests. *S.P. Dom.*, 287 : 14.

1st February. Eleven Sergeants called. Manningham's *Diary*, p. 117; Spedding's *Bacon*, x. 5; *S.P. Dom.*, 287 : 12.

6th February. Tyrone to be received. Moryson, iii. 290.

7th February. A Fencer slain. Manningham's *Diary*, p. 130.

9th February. The Venetian Ambassador given Audience. *Cal. S.P. Venetian*, 1135.

12th February. Ben Jonson. Manningham's *Diary*, p. 130.

14th February. A Puritan condemned. Foley, i. 18 (misdated 1602); Chamberlain's *Letters*, p. 179; Wilbraham's *Journal*, p. 52. Bishop Bancroft's efforts to cause friction amongst Catholics were masterly but are hardly creditable to his holy office.

15th February. Moorditch to be cleansed. *S.P. Dom.* 287 : 31.

27th February. A Priest condemned. *S.P. Dom.*, 287 : 50, 51, 52.

1st March. New Plays at the Rose. *Hens. Diary*, i. 185-9; ii. 233-4.

5th March. The Miserable State of the Irish Rebels. Moryson, iii. 281.

9th March. Fears at Court. *S.P. Dom.*, 287 : 50, 52. The Countess of Nottingham died on 7th March.

The Queen. *Salisbury Papers*, xii. 668. From a letter of Cecil writing to Herbert at Embden.

12th March. 'A Woman killed with Kindness.' *Hens. Diary*, i. 189, 190; ii. 234; *S.T.C.*, 13371; m.e. in the Mermaid Series. For a recent account of Heywood see *Thomas Heywood, Poet and Miscellanist*, by A. M. Clark, 1931.

13th March. An Offensive Sermon. *Salisbury Papers*, xii. 672.

15th March. The Queen's Sickness. *S.P. Dom.*, 287 : 54.

16th March. 'A Declaration of Popish Impostures.' *A.R.*, iii. 229; *S.T.C.*, 12880. Harsnett thus follows his attack on the Puritan exorcists (see p. 51) by discrediting the Jesuit exorcists. The book is part of the subtle propaganda instigated by Bancroft. It is, however, lively and uproarious, owing a good deal to R. Scot's *Discovery of Witchcraft*. Students know of its existence because Shakespeare took hence the names of Edgar's devils; but it is worth reading for its own sake.

17th March. Stirrings at Court. *Correspondence of King James VI*, p. 73. The fifth letter of the Earl of Northumberland to the king.

19th March. The Queen's Indisposition. Camden's *Elizabeth*; *Memoirs of Robert Carey, Earl of Monmouth.*

Stage Plays forbidden. *A.P.C.*, xxxii. 492.

22nd March. The Queen's Speech of her Successor. Carey's *Memoirs*; *Cotton MSS.*, Titus, c. vii. f. 46 printed in Nichols' *Progresses*, vol. ii.

23rd March. The Queen's Sickness. Manningham's *Diary*, p. 145. This account written up at the time by one who had no special inside knowledge is a valuable indication of what was generally known.

The Great Anxieties of this Time. *Cal. State Papers, Venetian*, 1154, 1159, 1162, 1166, 1168. There is ample evidence of the general belief that the death of the Queen would be immediately followed by revolution or civil war. 'The report of her death (like a thunder-clap) was able to kill thousands, it took away the hearts from millions; for having brought up (even under her wing) a nation that was almost begotten and born under her; that never shouted any other *Ave* than for her name, never saw the face of any Prince but herself, never understood what that strange outlandish word *Change* signified: how was it possible but that her sickness should throw abroad an universal fear, and her death an astonishment' (Dekker, *The Wonderful Year*, 1603).

This Night's News from Court. As for 22nd March.

24th March. The Death of the Queen. Stow's *Annals*.

INDEX

(i) An Elizabethan Journal, 1591–1594
(ii) A Second Elizabethan Journal, 1595–1598
(iii) A Last Elizabethan Journal, 1599–1603

INDEX

INDEX

INDEX

INDEX

E

G

INDEX

INDEX

M

N

T

W